P9-CLZ-925

England

2005

by Darwin Porter & Danforth Prince

Here's what the critics say about Frommer's:

"Amazingly easy to use. Very portable, very complete."

—Booklist

"Detailed, accurate, and easy-to-read information for all price ranges."
—Glamour Magazine

"Hotel information is close to encyclopedic."

—Des Moines Sunday Register

"Frommer's Guides have a way of giving you a real feel for a place."
—Knight Ridder Newspapers

Wiley Publishing, Inc.

About the Authors

As a team of veteran travel writers, **Darwin Porter** and **Danforth Prince** have produced numerous titles for Frommer's, including best-selling guides to Italy, France, the Caribbean, and Germany. Porter, a former bureau chief of *The Miami Herald,* is also a Hollywood biographer, his most recent releases entitled *The Secret Life of Humphrey Bogart* and *Katharine the Great,* the latter a close-up of the private life of the late Katharine Hepburn. Prince was formerly employed by the Paris bureau of the *New York Times,* and is today the president of Blood Moon Productions and other media-related firms.

Published by:

Wiley Publishing, Inc.

111 River St.
Hoboken, NJ 07030-5774

ISBN 0-7645-6896-5

Editor: Michael Kelly
Production Editor: Ian Skinnari
Cartographer: Nicholas Trotter
Photo Editor: Richard Fox
Production by Wiley Indianapolis Composition Services

For information on our other products and services or to obtain technical support, please contact our Customer Care Department within the U.S. at 800/762-2974, outside the U.S. at 317/572-3993 or fax 317/572-4002.

Wiley also publishes its books in a variety of electronic formats. Some content that appears in print may not be available in electronic formats.

Manufactured in the United States of America

5 4 3 2 1

Contents

13   Shakespeare Country & the Heart of England   483

14   Cambridge & East Anglia   533

15   The East Midlands   570

16   The Northwest   596

List of Maps

An Invitation to the Reader

In researching this book, we discovered many wonderful places—hotels, restaurants, shops, and more. We're sure you'll find others. Please tell us about them, so we can share the information with your fellow travelers in upcoming editions. If you were disappointed with a recommendation, we'd love to know that, too. Please write to:

Frommer's England 2005
Wiley Publishing, Inc. • 111 River St. • Hoboken, NJ 07030-5774

An Additional Note

Please be advised that travel information is subject to change at any time—and this is especially true of prices. We therefore suggest that you write or call ahead for confirmation when making your travel plans. The authors, editors, and publisher cannot be held responsible for the experiences of readers while traveling. Your safety is important to us, however, so we encourage you to stay alert and be aware of your surroundings. Keep a close eye on cameras, purses, and wallets, all favorite targets of thieves and pickpockets.

Other Great Guides for Your Trip:

Frommer's England from $75 a Day
Frommer's London
Frommer's London from $90 a Day
Frommer's Irreverent Guide to London
Frommer's Scotland
England For Dummies
Road Atlas Britain

Frommer's Star Ratings, Icons & Abbreviations

Every hotel, restaurant, and attraction listing in this guide has been ranked for quality, value, service, amenities, and special features using a **star-rating system.** In country, state, and regional guides, we also rate towns and regions to help you narrow down your choices and budget your time accordingly. Hotels and restaurants are rated on a scale of zero (recommended) to three stars (exceptional). Attractions, shopping, nightlife, towns, and regions are rated according to the following scale: zero stars (recommended), one star (highly recommended), two stars (very highly recommended), and three stars (must-see).

In addition to the star-rating system, we also use **seven feature icons** that point you to the great deals, in-the-know advice, and unique experiences that separate travelers from tourists. Throughout the book, look for:

Finds	Special finds—those places only insiders know about
Fun Fact	Fun facts—details that make travelers more informed and their trips more fun
Kids	Best bets for kids and advice for the whole family
Moments	Special moments—those experiences that memories are made of
Overrated	Places or experiences not worth your time or money
Tips	Insider tips—great ways to save time and money
Value	Great values—where to get the best deals

The following **abbreviations** are used for credit cards:

AE	American Express	DISC	Discover	V	Visa
DC	Diners Club	MC	MasterCard		

Frommers.com

Now that you have the guidebook to a great trip, visit our website at **www.frommers.com** for travel information on more than 3,000 destinations. With features updated regularly, we give you instant access to the most current trip-planning information available. At Frommers.com, you'll also find the best prices on airfares, accommodations, and car rentals—and you can even book travel online through our travel booking partners. At Frommers.com, you'll also find the following:

- Online updates to our most popular guidebooks
- Vacation sweepstakes and contest giveaways
- Newsletter highlighting the hottest travel trends
- Online travel message boards with featured travel discussions

What's New in England & Wales

There will always be an England, or so the saying goes, and that may be true, but it won't always be the same country. The landscape is constantly shifting and being redefined at all times. For example, in 2003, Britain distanced itself from Europe in two significant ways: It joined the U.S. in ousting Saddam Hussein in Iraq, and it reportedly has decided against adopting the euro, retaining the British pound sterling as its mode of currency. Here are some more of the latest developments:

SETTLING INTO LONDON In chic Knightsbridge, Britain's wonder chef Marco Pierre White has taken over the once famous **Drones,** 1 Pont St., SW1 (✆ **020/7259-6166**). The place had gone stale, but no longer. The Continental cuisine is light, sophisticated, and delicately prepared. A trendy crowd, often including celebrities, is showing up at the doorstep.

EXPLORING LONDON The **Tate Britain** (Milbank, SW1; ✆ **020/7887-8000**) and **Tate Modern** (Bankside, SE1; ✆ **020/7887-8008**), located on opposite sides of the River Thames, are now linked by a "Tate to Tate boat" (✆ **020/7887-8888**), taking art lovers from one stellar museum to the other.

Long the residence of the late Queen Mother, **Clarence House,** Stable Yard Gate, SW1 (✆ **020/7766-7303**), has opened its doors to the public. The restored John Nash–designed mansion is now the official residence of the Prince of Wales.

THE THAMES VALLEY One of the best restaurants around the university city of Oxford actually floats. It's **Rosamund the Fair,** Tooley's, Banbury Museum, Spiceball Park Road, in Banbury (outside Oxford; ✆ **01295/ 278690**). A purpose-built narrow boat restaurant, this floating dining room serves a superb Continental and British cuisine as it cruises along the Oxford Canal. The cruise and dinner take about 2½ hours, a bit of an enchantment on a summer night with the swans gliding by.

HAMPSHIRE & DORSET In the village of Chawton, an Elizabethan manor has been converted into the **Chawton House Library** (✆ **01420/ 541010**). The manor, once owned by the brother of Jane Austen, is a center of study for early English (1600–1830) women's writing. The collection contains some 6,000 volumes and manuscripts.

WILTSHIRE & SOMERSET More and more visitors are renting a bike to explore the spa city of Bath. The best place to go for rentals is **The Bath & Dundas Canal Company,** Brass Knocker Basin at Monkton Combe (✆ **01225/722292**).

Bath is fabled for having a bevy of the finest restaurants in the West Country. The most excitement today generates around **Pimpernel's,** 15–16 Royal Crescent (✆ **01225/823333**), in one of the city's most deluxe hotels. Chef Steven Blake dazzles palates with his innovative British cuisine.

In the city of Bristol, the popular hotel, **Jarvis International Bristol,** has changed stripes and become the **Ramada Plaza Bristol,** Redcliffe Way (© **01179/260041**). The establishment still has the Jarvis's amenities and an unbeatable location in the town center.

DEVON The grandest address in this shire is **Bovey Castle,** North Bovey (© **01647/445016**), an elegant 1906 estate within a national park. It's been converted into one of the most luxurious accommodations in the southwest. For those seeking the ultimate retreat, where comfort and taste reign supreme, this is the way to go—providing you can afford the steep tariffs.

THE COTSWOLDS Among the most charming places to stay in all the Cotswolds is **Barnsley House,** in the village of Barnsley, outside Cirencester (© **01285/740000**). A hotel was installed in a 17th-century manor house in the midst of some of England's most spectacular private gardens, the creation of a world expert on gardens, the late writer Rosemary Verey.

SHAKESPEARE COUNTRY In Stratford-upon-Avon, the newly reorganized **Callands,** 13–14 Meer St. (© **01789/269304**), has become the restaurant of choice for most discerning visitors to the Bard's hometown. In the heart of town, near the Shakespeare Centre, Callands serves an eclectic and international cuisine with market-fresh ingredients.

In England's second city of Birmingham, the opening of the grand department store, **Selfridges,** Bullring Centre (© **0870/837-7377**), has been heralded as part of the new Renaissance of this once tarnished industrial wasteland. This new fashion emporium is dramatic in concept, its architecture inspired by a dress.

CAMBRIDGE & EAST ANGLIA A hotel of charm and grace has opened in Norfolk, the **Victoria,** Park Road (© **01328/711008**), in the little town of Holkham, 39km (24 miles) northwest of Norwich. On the grounds of the coast-bordering Holkham Estate, the motif of the restored property has been characterized as a "manor house meets the Raj" decor, with furniture and accessories from the state of Rajasthan in north India.

THE NORTHWEST In the city of Liverpool, **Mendips,** 251 Menlove Ave. (© **01517/427-7231**), the childhood home of John Lennon, has been restored and opened to tours for the general public. Yoko Ono purchased the late 1950s property and turned it over to the National Trust. Lennon composed many of his early songs on the front porch of this modest abode.

YORKSHIRE & NORTHUMBRIA In the far northern city of Leeds, **Quebecs,** 9 Quebec St. (© **0113/244-8989**), is part of the neo-Renaissance of this once industrially blighted city. An 1891 red-brick Victorian shell has been gutted with certain architectural features preserved and turned into a hotel of real charm and grace. Right in the center of the city, the hotel pays homage to the past while preserving much of the style of the Victorian era.

SOUTH WALES In Cardiff, the **Hanover International Hotel & Club,** Schooner Way, Atlantic Wharf, Cardiff Bay (© **029/2047-5000**), has emerged as a solid runner-up hotel to the city's stalwart, the St. David's Hotel & Spa. In the heart of Cardiff's waterfront development, the restored, part-Victorian warehouse has already become something of a landmark, with its modern, cruise-liner-style architecture and dramatic maritime theme.

The Best of England

Planning a trip to England presents a bewildering array of choices. We've scoured the country in search of the best places and experiences; in this chapter, we share our very personal and opinionated choices. We hope they give you some ideas to help you get started.

1 The Best Travel Experiences

- **A Night at the Theater:** The torch passed from Shakespeare still burns brightly. London's theater scene is acknowledged as the finest in the world, with two major subsidized companies: the Royal Shakespeare Company, performing at Stratford-upon-Avon and at the Barbican in London; and the National Theatre on the South Bank in London. Fringe Theater offers surprisingly good and often innovative productions staged in venues ranging from church cellars to the upstairs rooms of pubs.

- **Pub Crawling:** The pursuit of the pint takes on cultural significance in England. Ornate taps fill tankards and mugs in pubs that serve as the social heart of every village and town. Quaint signs for such names as the Red Lion, the White Swan, and the Royal Oak dot the landscape and beckon you in, not only for the pint but also for the conviviality—and perhaps even the entertainment or the food.

- **Motoring through the Cotswolds:** If *driving* involves a determined trip from one place to another, *motoring* is wandering at random. And there's no better place for it than the Cotswolds, less than 161km (100 miles) west

of London, its rolling hills and pasturelands peppered with ivy-covered inns and honey-colored stone cottages. See chapter 12.

- **Punting on the Cam:** This is Cantabrigian English for gliding along in a flat-bottom boat with a long pole pushed into the River Cam's shallow bed. You bypass the weeping willows along the banks, watch the strolling students along the graveled walkways, and take in the picture-postcard vistas of green lawns along the water's edge. See "Cambridge: Town & Gown" in chapter 14.

- **Touring Stately Homes:** England has hundreds of mansions open to visitors, some centuries old, and we tell you about dozens of them. The homes are often surrounded by beautiful gardens; when the owners got fanciful, they added splashing fountains and miniature pagodas or temples.

- **Shopping for Antiques:** Whatever treasure you're looking for, you can find it somewhere in England. We're talking Steiff teddy bears, a blunderbuss, an 1890 tin-plate toy train, an egg cup allegedly used by Queen Victoria, a first-edition English print from 1700, or the definitive Henry Harper grandfather clock. No one polishes up their antiques and curios quite as brightly as English dealers. From auction houses to quaint shops, from flea markets to country fairs, England, particularly Victorian England, is for sale.

- **Cruising on Lake Windermere:** Inspired by the lyric poetry of Wordsworth, you can board a boat at Windermere or Bowness and sail England's most famous lake. You'll see the Lake District's scenery, with its tilled valleys lying in the shadow of forbidding peaks, as it was meant to be viewed—from the water. A great jaunt is the round-trip from Bowness to Ambleside, at the head of the lake, and back around to the village of Lakeside, at the southern tip. See "Windermere & Bowness" in chapter 17.

2 The Best of Literary England

- **Samuel Johnson's House** (London; © 020/7353-3745): The backwater at No. 17 Gough Square, situated on the north side of Fleet Street, was Johnson's home from 1748 to 1759. Here he worked on his Rambler essays and his Dictionary, and here his beloved wife, "Tetty," died in 1752. See p. 186.

- **Keats House** (London; © 020/7435-2062): Most of the poet's brief life was spent in London, where he was born in 1795 in a livery stable run by his father. He moved to Hampstead in 1817 and met his fiancée, Fanny Brawne, there. In this house, he coughed blood into his handkerchief. "That drop of blood is my death warrant," he said. "I must die." He left for Rome in 1820 and died there a year later. See p. 191.

- **Jane Austen Country:** The author of *Pride and Prejudice* and *Sense and Sensibility* wrote of rural delights and a civilized society— set mainly in her beloved Hampshire. In 1809, she moved with her mother to Chawton, 80km (50 miles) south of Bath, where she lived until 1817. Her house is now a museum. Her novels *Persuasion* and *Northanger Abbey* are associated with the city of Bath, where she visited frequently in her youth and lived from 1801 to 1806. In her final year, she moved to 8 College St. in Winchester. She is buried in Winchester Cathedral. See chapters 8 and 9.

- **Stratford-upon-Avon** (Warwickshire): Although the bard remains a mysterious figure, the folks who live in touristy Stratford gleefully peddle his literary legacy, including Shakespeare's Birthplace, where the son of a glover was born on April 23, 1564. He died in Stratford on the same day, 52 years later. Anne Hathaway's Cottage, in the hamlet of Shottery, is also popular; Shakespeare married Hathaway when he was only 18 years old. See "Stratford-upon-Avon" in chapter 13.

- **Sherwood Forest** (East Midlands): You won't find Errol Flynn in Technicolor green tights gallivanting through a forest of mighty oaks with his band of merry men. Although most of the forest has been open grassland since the 14th century, it lives on in legend, literature, and lore as the most famous woodland in the world. At the Sherwood Forest Visitor Centre at Edwinstowe, the world of Friar Tuck and Little John live on. See "Nottinghamshire: Robin Hood Country" in chapter 15.

- **Grasmere** (The Lake District): William Wordsworth lived here with his sister, Dorothy, who commented on the "domestic slip of mountain" behind their home, Dove Cottage. The cottage itself is now part of the Wordsworth Museum, displaying manuscripts and memorabilia. The poet also lived for a time at nearby Rydal Mount, just north of Ambleside (one of his descendants still owns the property), where you can see gardens landscaped by the poet. Throughout the region, you'll find the landscapes that inspired this giant of English romanticism, including the shores of Ullswater, where Wordsworth saw his famous "host of golden daffodils." See "Grasmere" in chapter 17.

- **Haworth** (West Yorkshire): Second only to Stratford-upon-Avon as a major literary pilgrimage site is the home of the Brontë Parsonage Museum. Here, the famous Brontë sisters lived and spun their web of romance. Emily wrote *Wuthering Heights,* Charlotte wrote *Jane Eyre* and *Villette,* and even Anne wrote two novels, *The Tenant of Wildfell Hall* and *Agnes Grey,* though neither measures up to her sisters' work. See "Haworth: Home of the Brontës" in chapter 18.

- **Dylan Thomas Boathouse** (Laugharne, Wales): Sixteen kilometers (10 miles) east of Tenby in Wales, Swansea-born Dylan Thomas lived and worked. Later, of course, he was to be acclaimed as one of the great poets of the 20th century, but this "untidy wretch of a man" turned out his masterpieces in a modest little shack here. It's one of the most evocative literary shrines in Britain. See p. 727.

3 The Best of Legendary England

- **Stonehenge** (near Salisbury, Wiltshire): The most celebrated prehistoric monument in Europe, Stonehenge is some 5,000 years old. Despite "definitive" books on the subject, its original purpose remains a mystery. The romantic theory that Stonehenge was "constructed by the Druids" is nonsense; it was completed before the Druids reached Britain in the 3rd century B.C., but the legend persists. See p. 362.

- **Glastonbury Abbey** (Somerset): One of the great abbeys of England and once a center of culture and learning, Glastonbury quickly fell into ruins following the Dissolution of the Monasteries. One story about the abbey says that Jesus came here as a child with Joseph of Arimathea. According to another legend, King Arthur was buried at Glastonbury, the site of the fabled Avalon. See p. 387.

- **Tintagel** (Cornwall): On the windswept Cornish coast, the castle of Tintagel is said to be the birthplace of King Arthur. The castle was actually built much later than the Arthurian legend, around 1150. But who wants to stand in the way of a good story? No one in Cornwall, that's for sure. Tintagel merrily touts the King Arthur legend—in town, you can order an Excaliburger! See "Tintagel Castle: King Arthur's Legendary Lair" in chapter 11.

4 The Best of Ancient & Roman England

- **Roman Painted House** (Dover, Kent): Called Britain's "buried Pompeii," this 1,800-year-old structure has exceptionally well-preserved walls and an under-floor heating system used by the Romans. It's best known for its unique bacchic murals. See p. 278.

- **Avebury** (west of Marlborough, Wiltshire; east of Bath, Avon):

Although not as famous as Stone-henge, this is one of Europe's leading prehistoric monuments. Its circle of more than 100 stones—some of them weighing in at 50 tons—is arrayed on an 11-hectare (28-acre) site. See p. 363.

- **Roman Baths** (Bath, Avon): Dedicated to the goddess Sulis Minerva, these baths were founded by the Romans in A.D. 75. Among the finest Roman remains in the country, they're still fed by Britain's most famous hot-water spring. The site of the Temple of Sulis Minerva is excavated and open for viewing. See p. 368.

- **Corinium Museum** (Cirencester, in the Cotswolds): This museum contains one of the best collections of archaeological remains from the Roman occupation of Britain. You'll see Roman mosaics that have remained in Britain, along with provincial sculpture, such as figures of Minerva and Mercury. See p. 455.

- **Hadrian's Wall** (near Hexham, Northumberland): A World Heritage Site, this wall—now in ruins—was ordered built by Hadrian, the Roman emperor, in A.D. 122 to hold back barbarian invasions from the north. Marking the far northern border of the Roman Empire, the wall stretched 118km (73 miles) from Wallsend, or Wall's End, north of Newcastle upon Tyne in the east to Bowness-on-Solway beyond Carlisle in the west. A *milecastle* (small fort) was added at every mile along the wall. A highlight is Vindolanda, the last of eight successive Roman forts built on a site adjacent to the wall. See "Hexham, Hadrian's Wall & the Pennine Way" in chapter 18.

5 The Best of Norman & Medieval England

- **Battle Abbey** (East Sussex): At this site of the famous Battle of Hastings (fought on Oct. 14, 1066), the Normans defeated King Harold's English army. William the Conqueror built a great commemorative abbey here; the high altar of its church was erected over the spot where Harold fell in battle. The abbey was destroyed during the Dissolution of the Monasteries (1538–39). Some ruins and buildings remain, about which Tennyson wrote, "O Garden, blossoming out of English blood." See p. 284.

- **Hastings Castle** (Hastings, East Sussex): Now in ruins, this was the first of the Norman castles erected in England (ca. 1067). The fortress was defortified in 1216. An audiovisual presentation of the castle's history includes the famous battle of 1066. See p. 285.

- **Rye** (East Sussex): Near the English Channel, this port—one of England's best preserved towns—was a smuggling center for centuries. Writer Louis Jennings once wrote, "Nothing more recent than a Cavalier's Cloak, Hat and Ruffles should be seen on the streets of Rye." See "The Ancient Seaport of Rye" in chapter 7.

- **Dunster Castle** (Somerset): This castle was built on the site of a Norman castle granted to William de Mohun of Normandy by William the Conqueror shortly after his conquest of England. A 13th-century gateway remains from the original fortress. The Luttrell family held possession of the castle and its lands from 1376 until the National Trust took it over in 1976. See p. 391.

- **Warwick Castle** (Warwickshire): One of the major sights in the Midlands, little remains of William the Conqueror's motte-and-bailey castle of 1068, but much of its external structure remains unchanged since the mid-1300s. Today, Warwick Castle is the finest medieval castle in England, lying on a cliff overlooking the Avon River. Its most powerful commander in the 1400s was the earl of Warwick, who, during the War of the Roses, was called the "Kingmaker." One of the best collections of medieval armor and weapons in Europe is behind its walls. See p. 497.

- **Fountains Abbey & Studley Royal** (southwest of Ripon, in North Yorkshire): These ruins evoke monastic life in medieval England. In 1132, Cistercian monks constructed "a place remote from all the earth." Explore the ruins as well as the Studley Royal, whose lavish 18th-century landscaping is one of the few surviving examples of a Georgian green garden. See p. 680.
- **Conwy Castle** (North Wales): Edward I ordered this masterpiece of medieval architecture constructed after he'd subdued the last native prince of Wales. Visitors today can tour the royal apartment where Edward brought his queen, Eleanor. The castle's eight towers command the estuary of the River Conwy. See p. 753.

6 The Best of Tudor & Georgian England

- **Hampton Court Palace** (outside London): The most magnificent of the grand residences and royal palaces lining the River Thames west of Central London, Hampton Court was built in grand style for Cardinal Wolsey—until Henry VIII snatched it away. Henry added the great hall in 1532, forcing laborers to toil 24 hours a day in shifts. The sheer size of the palace is amazing, and on its grounds is the world's first indoor tennis court. See p. 191.
- **Bath** (Avon): Much magnificent 18th-century architecture remains exactly as Jane Austen saw it, despite repeated World War II bombings. At one time, Bath was the most fashionable spa in Britain. Architect John Wood (1704–54), among others, helped create a city of harmony and beauty, with landscaped terraces, famous crescents such as the Royal Crescent, and Palladian villas. See "Bath: Britain's Most Historic Spa Town" in chapter 9.
- **Kenilworth Castle** (Warwickshire): This castle was the setting for Sir Walter Scott's romantic novel, *Kenilworth,* first published in 1862, which recounts the supposed murder of Amy Robsart, wife of Robert Dudley, earl of Leicester. Elizabeth I had presented Kenilworth Castle to her favorite earl in 1563. The castle was destroyed after the civil war and is now in ruins. See p. 500.

7 The Best of Victorian England

- **Albert Memorial** (Kensington Palace, London): If any statue symbolizes an era, this flamboyant tribute to Victoria's consort, her beloved Albert (1819–61), does; it is the epitome of Victorian excess. The statue depicts Albert holding a catalog of the Great Exhibition. He overlooks the South Kensington Culture Centre, his last legacy. The 4m (14-ft.) high statue, with the blessing of the queen, went into place in 1876 and was instantly described as an "outsize reliquary casket." See p. 168.
- **Houses of Parliament** (London): No government building in England symbolizes the Victorian age

like the Palace of Westminster, housing Parliament. Replacing a palace destroyed by fire in 1834, it cost £2 million to build, a princely sum at the time. The building was completed in 1860 and turned out to be a Gothic fantasy, its facade decorated with monarchs ranging from William the Conqueror to Queen Victoria. See p. 162.

- **Osborne House** (southeast of East Cowes on the Isle of Wight): This was Queen Victoria and Prince Albert's most cherished residence. Constructed at Queen Victoria's own expense, it is imbued with her spirit. The rooms are a perfect period piece of Victoriana, with all their artifacts and stuffy chairs—a cozy clutter best evoked by her sitting room. Grief-stricken at the death of Albert in 1861, the Queen requested that the house be kept as it was upon the death of her husband. See p. 339.

- **Manchester** (Lancashire): A major inland port since 1894, Manchester long had a reputation as a blackened, foggy, and forbidding city, grim and dowdy, the worst of the Midlands. But it has been cleaned up, and today its center is filled with masterpieces of sturdy, solid Victorian architecture, including homes built for the great industrial barons of the 19th century. See "Manchester: Gateway to the North" in chapter 16.

- **National Railway Museum** (York): The first national museum to be built away from London is devoted to the locomotive that changed the face of Victorian England. Set in an original steam locomotive depot, the museum is filled with railway memorabilia left by the Victorians. More than 40 full-size locomotives are on display, plus the century-old Royal Saloon, in which Queen Victoria rode until her death (it's like a small hotel!). See p. 661.

8 The Best Museums

- **The British Museum** (London): When Sir Hans Sloane died in 1753, he bequeathed to England his vast collection of art and antiquities for only £20,000, forming the nucleus of a collection that would one day embrace everything from the Rosetta stone to the hotly contested Elgin marbles (Greece wants them back). It's all here—and much, much more—in one of the world's great museums. See p. 163.

- **The National Gallery** (London): One of the world's greatest collections of Western art dazzles the eye. Artists ranging from da Vinci to Rembrandt to Picasso is represented here. The gallery is especially rich in works by Renaissance artists. See p. 167.

- **Tate Britain** (London): Two great national collections—some 10,000 works—call this gallery home. Sir Henry Tate, a sugar producer, started the collection with only 70 or so paintings. But the Tate has grown and grown and was considerably enlarged when J. M. W. Turner bequeathed some 300 paintings and 19,000 watercolors to England upon his death. The Tate Modern, a repository of avant-garde modern art, is directly across the river. See p. 165.

- **The American Museum** (Claverton, 3km/2 miles east of Bath, Avon): Housed in a neoclassical country house, this collection presents 2 centuries of American life and styles—including George Washington's mother's recipe for gingerbread. See p. 367.

- **The Fitzwilliam Museum** (Cambridge, East Anglia): Although London dominates this list, some outstanding regional museums exist, including this gem near King's College. Exhibits range from paintings by Titian and Renoir to Chinese, Egyptian, and Greek antiquities. See p. 540.
- **Walker Art Gallery** (Liverpool, Lancashire): One of the finest collections of European and British paintings in Britain, this gallery deserves to be better known. A nearly complete study of British paintings is displayed here, from Tudor days to the present. The gallery also owns an outstanding collection of pre-Raphaelites. See p. 615.
- **National Museum of Wales** (Cardiff): This museum, Wales's finest, presents the panorama of the history of this little country from prehistoric times until the present. And its collection of 18th-century porcelain is one of the finest in the world. See p. 704.

9 The Best Cathedrals

- **Westminster Abbey** (London): One of the world's greatest Anglo-French Gothic buildings has witnessed a parade of English history—from the crowning of William the Conqueror on Christmas Day 1066 to the funeral of Princess Diana in 1997. With few exceptions, the kings and queens of England have all been crowned here, and many are buried here as well. See p. 161.
- **Canterbury Cathedral** (Canterbury, Kent): The object of countless pilgrimages, as described in Chaucer's *Canterbury Tales,* this cathedral replaced one that was destroyed by fire in 1067. A new cathedral was also destroyed by fire in 1174, when the present structure was built. Thomas à Becket, the archbishop of Canterbury, was murdered here, and his shrine was an important site for pilgrims until the Reformation. See p. 270.
- **Winchester Cathedral** (Winchester, Hampshire): Construction of the cathedral that dominates this ancient city and capital of old Wessex began in 1079. In time, Winchester Cathedral became England's longest medieval cathedral, noted for its 12-bay nave. Many famous people are buried here, including Jane Austen. See p. 320.
- **Salisbury Cathedral** (Salisbury, Wiltshire): The most stylistically unified of England's cathedrals, this edifice was built in the mid-13th century. Its landmark spire—its most striking feature—was completed in 1325. The cathedral epitomizes the Early English style of architecture. See p. 357.
- **Durham Cathedral** (Durham, Yorkshire): Completed between 1095 and 1133, this cathedral exemplifies Norman architecture on a broad scale. Its nave, a structure of almost majestic power, is its most notable feature. See p. 692.
- **York Minster** (York, Yorkshire): The largest Gothic cathedral north of the Alps is also among the grandest, with incredible stained-glass windows. Its unusual octagonal Chapter House has a late-15th-century choir screen by William Hyndeley. See p. 662.
- **Llandaff Cathedral** (Llandaff, Wales): Begun under the Normans, this cathedral outside Cardiff makes a dramatic impression. Its west front is one of the best works of medieval art in Wales. That didn't prevent Cromwell's armies from using the edifice as a beer hall. See p. 704.

10 The Best Castles, Palaces & Historic Homes

- **Woburn Abbey** (Woburn, Bedfordshire): A Cistercian abbey for 4 centuries, Woburn Abbey has been visited by everyone from Queen Victoria to Marilyn Monroe. You'll see Queen Victoria's bedroom, and the Canaletto room, with its 21 perspectives of Venice. The grounds, more popular than the house, include the Wild Animal Kingdom, the best zoological collection in England after the London Zoo. See p. 265.
- **Hatfield House** (Hertfordshire): Hatfield was the childhood home of Elizabeth I, who was under an oak tree there when she learned she had become queen of England. Hatfield remains one of England's largest and finest country houses, with antiques, tapestries, paintings, and even the red silk stockings Elizabeth I wore. See p. 264.
- **Windsor Castle** (Windsor, Berkshire): The largest inhabited stronghold in the world and England's largest castle, Windsor Castle has been a royal abode since William the Conqueror constructed a motte and bailey on the site 4 years after conquering England. Severely damaged by fire in 1992, the castle has been mainly restored. Its major attraction is the great Perpendicular Chapel of St. George's, begun by Edward IV. The chancel is known for its three-tiered stalls, with its misericords (ledges used for support) and ornate carvings. See p. 224.
- **Blenheim Palace** (Woodstock, near Oxford, Oxfordshire): England's answer to Versailles, this extravagant baroque palace was the home of the 11th duke of Marlborough, and the birthplace of Sir Winston Churchill. The structure was designed by Sir John Vanbrugh, of Castle Howard fame. Sarah, the duchess of Marlborough, battled the architects and builders from the beginning, wanting "a clean sweet house and garden be it ever so small." That she didn't get—the structure measures 255m (850 ft.) from end to end. Capability Brown designed the gardens. See p. 257.
- **Knole** (near Tonbridge, Kent): Begun in 1456 by the archbishop of Canterbury, Knole is celebrated for its 365 rooms (one for each day of the year), its 52 staircases (for each week of the year), and its 7 courts (for each day of the week). Knole, one of England's largest private houses set in a 404-hectare (1,000-acre) deer park, is a splendid example of Tudor architecture. See p. 289.
- **Penshurst Place** (near Tonbridge, Kent): One of England's most outstanding country homes, this mansion was the former residence of Elizabethan poet Sir Philip Sidney (1554–86). In its day, the house attracted literati, including Ben Jonson. The original 1346 hall has seen the subsequent addition of Tudor, Jacobean, and neo-Gothic wings. See p. 292.
- **Hever Castle & Gardens** (Edenbridge, Kent): This was the childhood home of Anne Boleyn, second wife of Henry VIII and mother of Queen Elizabeth I. In 1903, William Waldorf Astor, an American multimillionaire and Anglophile, bought the castle, restored it, and landscaped the grounds. From the outside, it still looks as it did in Tudor times, with a moat and drawbridge protecting the castle. See p. 292.
- **Beaulieu Abbey–Palace House** (Beaulieu, in New Forest): Home of the first Lord Montagu, Palace House blends monastic Gothic architecture from the Middle Ages

with Victorian trappings. Yet many visitors consider the National Motor Museum, also on the premises and with a collection of more than 250 antique automobiles, more fascinating than the house. See p. 334.

- **Harewood House & Bird Garden** (Harewood Village, West Yorkshire): Edwin Lascelles began constructing this house in 1759, and his "pile" has been called an essay in Palladian architecture. The grand design involved some major talents of the day, including Robert Adam, Thomas Chippendale, and Capability Brown, who developed the grounds. A 1.8-hectare (4½-acre) bird garden features exotic species from all over the world. See p. 680.

- **Castle Howard** (Malton, North Yorkshire): Sir John Vanbrugh's grand masterpiece, and also the first building he ever designed, it served as the principal location for *Brideshead Revisited.* A gilt-and-painted dome tops the striking entrance, and the park around Castle Howard is one of the most grandiose in Europe. See p. 679.

- **Caernarfon Castle** (North Wales): This is as close as Wales comes to having a royal palace. It was here that the investiture of Charles as Prince of Wales took place in 1969. Construction started in 1283 and proceeded rapidly, as 11 great towers and massive curtain walls were built to protect the castle's interior. See "Caernarfon" in chapter 20.

11 The Best Gardens

- **Royal Botanic Gardens, Kew** (near London): A delight in any season, everything blooms in profusion in this 121-hectare (300-acre) garden, from delicate exotics to commonplace flowers and shrubs. It's all part of a vast lab dedicated to identifying plants from all parts of the globe and also growing some for commercial purposes. An easy trip from London, Kew Gardens, as it's known, possesses the largest herbarium on earth. Fabled landscape architect Capability Brown helped lay out part of the grounds. See p. 193.

- **Sissinghurst Castle Garden** (near Maidstone, Kent): A notorious literary couple, Vita Sackville-West and Harold Nicolson, created this garden. Its flamboyant parentage, unusual landscaping (the grounds were laid between the surviving parts of an Elizabethan mansion), and location just 34km (21 miles) northeast of Cranbrook make it the most intriguing garden on London's doorstep. Overrun by

tourists in summer, it's lovely in autumn, when the colors are at their dramatic best. See p. 293.

- **Wisley Garden** (Wisley, Kent): Wisley Garden sprawls across 101 hectares (250 acres), filled with an abundance of flowers and shrubs. Maintained by the Royal Horticultural Society, it ranges from alpinelike meadows to summer carpets of flowers. In early summer, the gardens are brilliant with flowering rhododendrons. The landscaped orchid house alone is worth the trip here. See p. 294.

- **Stourhead** (near Shaftesbury, Dorset): Outside of the Greater London area is the most famous garden in England. The birthplace of English landscape gardening, Stourhead is still the best-executed example of the taste for natural landscaping that swept England in the 1700s. The grounds have been likened to a 3-D painting of an old master such as Constable. The gardens are a wealth of flowering shrubs, trees, and beds upon beds of multihued blooms. Grottoes, bridges, and temples also add to the allure. See p. 390.

- **Hidcote Manor Garden** (near Chipping Campden, in the Cotswolds): Just outside one of the Cotswolds' most charming towns, this stunning garden is laid out around a stone-built manor

house. The largest garden in the Cotswolds, and one of the most intriguing in all of Britain, it was created in 1907 by Major Lawrence Johnstone, an American horticulturist who traveled the world and brought back specimens to plant. See "Chipping Campden" in chapter 12.

12 The Best Luxury Hotels

- **Brown's Hotel** (London; ✆ 020/7493-6020): All Chippendale and chintz, Brown's was launched by the former manservant to Lord Byron in 1837, and it has been going strong ever since. Today, it occupies 14 historic houses just off Berkeley Square and coddles its well-heeled guests in luxury. See p. 111.

- **The Dorchester** (London; ✆ 800/727-9820 or 020/7629-8888): Acclaimed for decades as one of the world's great hotels, this citadel of luxury is owned by one of the richest men on earth, the sultan of Brunei. With such an owner, the hotel naturally drips with opulence. After a multimillion-pound restoration, "The Dorch" is more splendid than ever. The rooftop suites are dazzling, and the Promenade, the Grill Room, the Dorchester Bar, and the Oriental Room—London's most exclusive Chinese restaurant—all deserve their acclaim. See p. 110.

- **Chewton Glen Hotel** (New Milton, Hampshire; ✆ 01425/275341): On the fringe of New Forest between Lymington and Bournemouth, this hotel/health-and-country club is the best place to stay in southwest England. Service, taste, and quality are its hallmarks. The health club has a stunning design, with a centerpiece swimming pool and 28 hectares (70 acres) of manicured grounds. Guest rooms feature

period furniture. And the meals served in the Marryat Room Restaurant are prepared with first-rate ingredients. See p. 335.

- **StonEaston Park** (near Bath, Avon; ✆ 01761/241631): This splendid 1740 Palladian house has been massively and magnificently restored. Its gardens are reason enough to stay, but the bedrooms, with Chippendale or Hepplewhite four-poster beds, are equally worthy. Check in here for a taste of 18th-century luxury. See p. 373.

- **Thornbury Castle** (Thornbury, near Bristol, Somerset; ✆ 01454/281182): Henry VIII seized this castle for a royal abode, and Mary Tudor lived here for a while. Eventually it was returned to the progeny of its original owner, the duke of Buckingham. This luxurious choice has all the elements associated with English castle living—and even a garden for croquet. See p. 382.

- **Gidleigh Park Hotel** (Chagford, Devon; ✆ 01647/432367): Sixteen hectares (40 acres) of grounds in the Teign Valley surround a country-house hotel that is the epitome of gracious living. Every detail suggests the best of rural life: premier antiques, big English sofas, and floral arrangements from the hotel's gardens. All that and a reputation for fine food unequaled in the area. See p. 405.

- **The Lygon Arms** (Broadway, Cotswolds; ✆ 01386/852255):

Dating from 1532, this fabled inn in the Cotswolds has hosted many famous guests—Charles I used to drop in, and even Oliver Cromwell spent a night here, on the eve of the Battle of Worcester. Some of the inn's antiques are listed in *The Dictionary of English Furniture.* Request a room in the Tudor Wing with its tilted oak floors and wooden beams. Number 20, with its massive canopied bed, is our favorite. See p. 479.

- **Ettington Park Hotel** (Alderminster, south of Stratford-upon-Avon, Warwickshire; © **01789/450123**): From the plant-filled conservatory entrance to the spacious, antique-filled bedrooms, you know something special is here. The house is refurbished every year, and guests can soak up old England country-house living in the tasteful Victorian drawing room or the richly paneled library bar. See p. 493.

- **Sharrow Bay Country House Hotel** (Lake Ullswater, the Lake District; © **01768/486301**): This gem is known as much for its cuisine as for its accommodations. The location alone would justify checking in: a 4.8-hectare (12-acre) site, with several gardens, in a national park on bucolic Lake Ullswater, beneath Barton Fell. The lakeside dining room offers panoramic views of the water, and whether it is grilled scallops from the Kyle of Lochalsh or noisettes of English lamb, you can always find something delectable on the menu. See p. 654.

- **Bodysgallen Hall** (Llandudno, North Wales; © **800/260-8338** in the U.S., or 01492/584466): One of Wales's greatest country-house hotels, this 17th-century mansion lies on 81 hectares (200 acres) of gardens and parkland. Even though an antique, it oozes with modern comforts while retaining its charms in elegantly furnished suites. See p. 755.

13 The Best Moderately Priced Hotels

- **The Sanctuary House Hotel** (London; © **020/7799-4044**): In a historic building close to Westminster Abbey, a brewery has converted an old building into a traditional English inn with pub downstairs. It's like something you might find in the countryside of England, but instead it's in the historic heart of London. The place is a bit nostalgic, like the food served—all the old favorites such as roast beef, Welsh lamb, and Dover sole. See p. 123.

- **Fielding Hotel** (London; © **020/7836-8305**): Named after the novelist Henry Fielding of *Tom Jones* fame, this hotel is one of the most eccentric in London. You'll either love it or hate it. Most guests love its cramped, quirky, quaint aura, and its location at Covent Garden is unbeatable. Everything is old-fashioned and traditional, but if you complain that the bedrooms are too small, Smokey, the African Gray parrot, will tell you off! See p. 120.

- **Jenkins Hotel** (London; © **020/7387-2067**): Hailed by one London publication as one of the 10 best hotel values in town, the Jenkins was featured on the PBS *Mystery!* series, *Poirot.* Those seeking decent accommodations in Bloomsbury, at an affordable price, have made their way to this address in Cartwright Gardens ever since Maggie Jenkins opened the place in the 1920s. Rooms are small but well furnished, and some of the original Georgian charm remains. See p. 119.

- **Howfield Manor** (west of Canterbury, Kent; © **01227/738294**): This former manor house outside the cathedral city retains architectural treasures from its days as part of the Priory of St. Gregory. Bedrooms are divided between the original house and a new one. The manor is filled with character and has lots of details such as solid oak pieces and exposed beams. See p. 275.

- **Mermaid Inn** (Rye, Sussex; © **01797/223065**): England's most famous smugglers' inn, the Mermaid sheltered Elizabeth I on her visit to Rye in 1573. At the time of the queen's visit, the inn had already been operating for 150 years. Still going strong, it leans heavily on English romance—old-world furnishings, some four-poster beds, and even a secret staircase. From its doorstep, the cobblestone streets of ancient Rye await exploration. See p. 282.

- **Powder Mills Hotel** (Battle, Surrey; © **01424/775511**): Near the famous battlefield at Battle Abbey, this Georgian house stands on 61 hectares (150 acres). A historic property that once catered to luminaries such as the Duke of Wellington has been successfully converted to receive paying guests, housing them in style and comfort—all at an affordable price. See p. 285.

- **Apsley House Hotel** (Bath, Avon; © **01225/336966**): Away from the city center, this 1830 house was supposedly constructed for the duke of Wellington. Its owners have restored it and created a period house of character with an ambience of subdued elegance. See p. 371.

- **Chideock House Hotel** (Chideock, Dorset; © **01297/489242**): A former 15th-century thatched house, once used by the Roundheads in 1645, is now a hotel of charm and grace with fireplaces and individually decorated bedrooms. See p. 350.

- **Bickleigh Cottage Country Hotel** (Bickleigh, Devon; © **01884/855230**): This small, thatched, 17th-century cottage is a cliché of Devonshire country charm. A riverside garden leads down to the much-photographed Bickleigh Bridge, where swans and ducks glide by. The cottage rooms are cozy with oak beams and old fireplaces. See p. 401.

- **Ravenwood Hall** (Bury St. Edmunds, Suffolk; © **01359/270345**): Deep in the heart of East Anglia, this discovery was once called Tudor Hall. Today, it stands in a 2.7-hectare (7-acre) park and gardens with an outdoor pool and tennis courts. Sleep in a four-poster bed and immerse yourself in old England after having had a good dinner and a toasty "warm-up" at the fireplace. See p. 554.

- **Henllys Hotel** (The Old Courthouse, Betws-y-Coed, North Wales; © **01690/710534**): This luxurious B&B has the amenities of a small inn. It was converted from a Victorian magistrates court and is set in lovely gardens along the river. See p. 740.

14 The Best Restaurants

- **Gordon Ramsay at Claridge's** (London; © **020/7499-0099**): Gourmet—and famous Broadway musical producer—Andrew Lloyd Webber has proclaimed this hot chef the finest in London. Maybe that's going a bit far, but Ramsay is dazzling *tout* London with his pots and pans. Everything he does bears an innovative twist, and though he has learned from the past, he's hardly anchored there.

Try anything, but make sure you sample his "cappuccino" of white beans with grated truffles. You'll want to adopt him and take him home. See p. 132.

- **Le Gavroche** (London; © 020/ 7408-0881): Long known for its top-rate French cuisine, this stellar restaurant has risen to the top again following a bit of a slump in the 1990s. Go here for that grand meal and skip the trip to Paris (we don't really mean that). The menu options are a delight, with such tantalizing dishes as a cassoulet of snails with herb-seasoned frogs' legs. Naturally, the wine cellar is among London's finest. See p. 132.

- **The Square** (London; © 020/ 7495-7100): One of the great London restaurants to have emerged in the 21st century, this gourmet citadel is the domain of master chef Philip Howard, whose continental cuisine has dazzled the food critics of London. Howard is justifiably praised for his "magic" in the kitchen and for his use of "stunningly fresh" ingredients, which he deftly concocts into his masterpieces. See p. 133.

- **Le Manoir aux Quat' Saisons** (Great Milton, southeast of Oxford, Oxfordshire; © 01844/ 278881, or 800/845-4274 in the U.S.): The country-house hotel and restaurant of self-taught chef Raymond Blanc have brought him a TV series, as well as cookbooks and a school of cuisine. A new lightness, inspired mainly by Japan and the Mediterranean, is more evident in the celebrated chef's creations, and more meatless dishes appear on the seasonal menu. But the intensely French loyalties remain: sweetbread-stuffed pigs' trotters, kidneys, and foie gras, even veal tongue. See p. 252.

- **The Carved Angel** (Dartmouth, Devon; © 01803/832465): The elegant and airy Devon quay-side setting is ideal for the inspired cuisine of Joyce Molyneux, doyenne of British chefs. Her imaginative and inventive technique is based on strong British tradition, but increasingly, flavors and aromas of Provence, Italy, and even Asia are appearing on the menus. See p. 415.

- **Le Champignon Sauvage** (Cheltenham, the Cotswolds; © 01242/ 573449): David Everitt-Matthias has awakened the sleepy taste buds of Cheltenham. Thoroughly imbued in the French classics, he also adds more modern and lighter touches to his table d'hôte menus, the finest at this old spa. Some dishes reach into the old English repertoire, including stuffed leg of wild rabbit served with black pudding and turnip sauerkraut. His desserts are acclaimed as the most luscious in England. See p. 462.

- **The Moody Goose** (Bath, Somerset; © 01225/466688): The spa city of Bath offers some of the finest dining in the West Country, and in Bath itself this English restaurant is the market leader. A most refined cuisine is served here in an elegant Georgian setting. The kitchen is known for its passion for fresh ingredients, and everything is cooked to order and to perfection. See p. 374.

- **Le Talbooth** (Dedham, Essex; © 01206/323150): In Constable country, this restaurant dispenses its wares in a half-timbered Tudor building on the banks of the River Stour. In fair weather, you can dine alfresco under canvas parasols. The English/French a la carte menu changes six times a year, and special dishes change daily, reflecting the best produce available at the market. See p. 560.

- **Miller Howe Hotel** (Windermere, in the Lake District; © 01539/

442536): At John Tovey's Edwardian country house above Lake Windermere, the chef is renowned for his English cuisine. What makes his cooking unusual are the unexpected combinations: mashed rutabagas with cider, glazed carrots flavored with Pernod, and most definitely, the cardamom ice cream. See p. 637.

- **Walnut Tree Inn** (Abergavenny, South Wales; ℂ **01873/852797**). Dedicated foodies often drive all the way across South Wales to dine here, enjoying an unusual combination of kitchens—Welsh and Italian. One of the owners brought an 18th-century recipe for lasagna to Wales. The best of native Welsh produce is also featured. See p. 716.

15 The Best Pubs

- **Salisbury** (London; ℂ **020/7836-5863**): Glittering cut-glass mirrors, old-fashioned banquettes, and lighting fixtures of veiled bronze girls in flowing togas re-create the Victorian gin-parlor atmosphere in the heart of the West End. Theatergoers drop in for homemade meat pie or salad buffet before curtain. See p. 221.
- **Grenadier** (London; ℂ **020/7235-3074**): Arguably London's most famous pub, and reputedly haunted, the Grenadier was once frequented by the duke of Wellington's officers on leave from fighting Napoleon. It pours the best Bloody Marys in town, and filet of beef Wellington is always a specialty. See p. 219.
- **The Ship Inn** (Exeter, Devon; ℂ **01392/272040**): Frequented by Sir Francis Drake and Sir Walter Raleigh, this pub near Exeter Cathedral is the most celebrated in Devon. It still provides tankards of real ale, the same drink swilled by the likes of Sir John Hawkins. You can also eat here; portions are large, as in Elizabethan times. See p. 402.
- **The Cott Inn** (Dartington, near Totnes, Devon; ℂ **01803/863777**): Constructed in 1320, and believed to be the second-oldest inn in England, it's a low, rambling, two-story building of stone, cob, and plaster under a thatched roof. A gathering place for the locals of Dartington, it's a good place for a drink on a windy night, as log fires keep the lounge and bar snug. See p. 413.
- **The Punch Bowl Inn** (Lanreath, near Looe, Cornwall; ℂ **01503/220218**): Licensed since 1620 as a pub, this was a former rendezvous for smugglers. High-backed settees and old fireplaces evoke the atmosphere of old England. Sample drinks in one of the kitchens—among the few "kitchens" in England licensed in Britain as bars. See p. 428.
- **The Turk's Head** (Penzance, Cornwall; ℂ **01736/363093**): Dating from 1233, this durable local favorite is filled with artifacts and timeworn beams. Drinkers take their lagers into a summer garden or retreat inside to the snug chambers when the wind blows cold. See p. 434.
- **The Lamb Inn** (Burford, the Cotswolds; ℂ **01993/823155**): This is our favorite place for a lager in all the Cotswolds. In a mellow old house from 1430 with thick stones and mullioned and leaded windows, it's a good place to spend the night, have a traditional English meal, or quaff a beer. Snacks are served in the timeworn bars and lounges or in a garden in summer. See p. 467.
- **The Black Swan** (Stratford-upon-Avon, Warwickshire; ℂ **01789/297312**): A popular hangout for Stratford players since the 18th

century, over the years we've spotted everybody from Peter O'Toole to Lord Laurence Olivier having a drink. Locals affectionately call it "The Dirty Duck." In cool weather, an open fireplace blazes; stick around and order the chef's specialty: honey-roasted duck. See p. 495.

- **Griffin Inn** (Llyswen, South Wales; ✆ **01874/754241**): A cider house in the 15th century, this inn is frequented by fishermen casting into the River Wye. It was once voted Britain's "Pub of the Year," and it's just as good or better than ever. See p. 719.

16 The Best Websites for England

- **Britannia** (www.britannia.com): This site is more than a travel guide; it's chock-full of lively features, history, and regional profiles, including sections on Wales and King Arthur.
- **Automobile Association—UK** (www.theaa.com): An outstanding guide, this site lists hundreds of places to stay, ranked by price and quality with apparently objective reviews. Many lodgings accept online bookings. Dining information includes ratings based on food, service, atmosphere, and price. Most, but not all, restaurants list typical meal prices and which credit cards are accepted.
- **Londontown.com: The Official Internet Site for London** (www.londontown.com): This fab site from the city's tourist board will get you panting to start your trip. It lists accommodations, pubs, events, attractions, and places to live it up after dark. Daily special features include discount offers. You can download mini–area maps by Tube stop, attraction, theater, or street.
- **This Is London** (www.thisislondon.com): The *Evening Standard* operates this well-rounded site, which includes a frank guide to dining, drinking, and clubbing. You can search for city attractions and events. And the Hot Tickets section offers independent insider advice on theater, music, and comedy.
- **The 24 Hour Museum** (www.24hourmuseum.org.uk): It aims to promote Britain's thousands of museums, galleries, and heritage attractions—and, boy, does this excellent website do a good job. It is entertaining and downloads fast. You can search geographically or gear your holiday around one of its themed "trails" and tour Museums and the Macabre, Art Treasures of the North East, and so on.
- **Cathedrals of Britain** (www.cathedrals.org.uk): This well-designed site features dozens of cathedrals, organized by region. Each listing includes a couple of photos, advice for getting there, and history. You could surf here to plan an entire touring vacation.
- **English Heritage** (www.english-heritage.org.uk): This site has photographs and details of the hundreds of glorious historic castles, country houses, Roman sites, churches, abbeys, and ancient monuments cared for by this organization. It's a must-visit for pretrip planning.
- **Wales Cymru** (www.visitwales.com): The Welsh tourist bureau's website is loaded with information on accommodations, dining, special events, activities, and planning tips. The site also allows visitors to request brochures on outdoor activities, including golf, hiking, fishing, and cycling.

2

A Traveler's Guide to England's Art & Architecture

by Reid Bramblett

No one artist, period, or museum defines England's art and architecture. You can see the country's art in medieval illuminated manuscripts, Thomas Gainsborough portraits, and Damien Hirst's pickled cows. Its architecture ranges from Roman walls and Norman castles to baroque St. Paul's Cathedral and towering postmodern skyscrapers. This chapter will help you make sense of it all.

1 Art 101

CELTIC & MEDIEVAL (CA. 800 B.C.–16TH CENTURY)

The Celts, mixed with plenty of Scandinavian and Dutch tribes of varying origins, ruled England until the Romans established rule there in A.D. 43. **Celtic art** survived the Roman conquest and medieval Christianity mainly as carved swirls and decorations on the "Celtic Crosses" peppering cemeteries. During the medieval period, colorful Celtic images and illustrations decorated the margins of Bibles and Gospels, giving the books their moniker **"illuminated manuscripts."**

Important examples and artists of this period include:

- **Wilton Diptych, National Gallery, London.** The first truly important, truly British painting, this diptych (a painting on two hinged panels) was crafted in the late 1390s for Richard II by an unknown artist who mixed Italian and Northern European influences.
- **Lindisfarne Gospels, British Library, London.** One of Europe's greatest illuminated manuscripts from the 7th century, this work is particularly well crafted and well preserved.
- **Matthew Paris (d. 1259).** A Benedictine monk who illuminated his own writings, Paris put his significant artistic gifts to good use as the official St. Albans Abbey chronicler. Examples of his work are now in London's **British Library** and Cambridge's **Corpus Christi College.**

RENAISSANCE & BAROQUE (16TH–18TH CENTURIES)

The **Renaissance** hit England late, but its museums contain many important old-master paintings from Italy and Germany. Renaissance means "rebirth," in this case, the renewed use of Classical styles and forms originating in ancient Greece and Rome. Artists strove for greater naturalism, using newly developed techniques such as linear perspective. A few foreign Renaissance masters did come to work at the English courts and had an influence on some local artists, but significant Brits didn't emerge until the baroque.

The **baroque,** a more decorative version of the Renaissance approach, mixes compositional complexity and explosions of dynamic fury, movement, color, and figures with an exaggeration of light and dark, called *chiaroscuro,* and a kind of super-realism based on using peasants as models. The **rococo** period is baroque art gone awry, frothy, and chaotic.

Significant artists of this period include:

- **Pietro Torrigiano (1472–1528).** An Italian Renaissance sculptor, Torrigiano had to flee Florence after breaking the nose of classmate Michelangelo. He ended up in London crafting elaborate tombs for the Tudors in **Westminster Abbey,** including Lady Margaret Beaufort, and Henry VII and Elizabeth of York. London's **Victoria and Albert Museum** preserves Torrigiano's terra-cotta bust of Henry VII.

- **Hans Holbein the Younger (1497–1543).** A German Renaissance master of penetrating portraits, Holbein the Younger cataloged many significant figures in 16th-century Europe: Sir Thomas More's family (**Nostel Priory** outside Wakefield in West Yorkshire; this may be a copy); Henry VIII and the Duke of Norfolk (**Castle Howard** outside York); and Erasmus (whom Holbein knew; **Longford Castle,** Wiltshire). More portraits are in London's **National Gallery** and **National Portrait Gallery** and in **Windsor Castle.**

- **Anton Van Dyck (1599–1641).** This Belgian artist painted passels of portraits in the baroque style for the Stuart court, setting the tone for British portraiture for the next few centuries. You'll find his works in London's **National Portrait Gallery, National Gallery, Wallace Collection,** and **Wilton House,** with more in Oxford's **Ashmolean Museum** and Liverpool's **Walker Art Gallery.**

- **Joshua Reynolds (1723–92).** A fussy baroque painter and first president of the Royal Academy of Arts, Reynolds was a firm believer in a painter's duty to celebrate history. Reynolds spent much of his career casting his noble patrons as ancient gods in portrait compositions cribbed from Old Masters. Many of his works are in London's **National Gallery, Tate Britain, Wallace Collection,** and **Dulwich Picture Gallery;** Oxford's **Cathedral Hall;** Liverpool's **Walker Art Gallery;** and Birmingham's **Museum and Art Gallery** and **Barber Institute of Fine Arts.**

- **Thomas Gainsborough (1727–88).** Although he was a classical/baroque portraitist like his rival Reynolds, at least Gainsborough could be original. Too bad his tastes ran to rococo pastels, frothy feathered brushwork, and busy compositions. When not immortalizing noble patrons such as Jonathan Buttell (better known as "Blue Boy"), he painted a collection of landscapes just for himself. His works grace the **Victoria Art Gallery** in Bath (where he first came to fame), London's **National Gallery** and **National Portrait Gallery,** Cambridge's **Fitzwilliam Museum,** Oxford's **Cathedral Hall** and **Ashmolean Museum,** Liverpool's **Walker Art Gallery,** and Birmingham's **Museum and Art Gallery** and **Barber Institute of Fine Arts.**

THE ROMANTICS (LATE 18TH–19TH CENTURIES)

The romantics felt the classically minded Renaissance and baroque artists had gotten it wrong; the Gothic Middle Ages was the place to be. They idealized the romantic tales of chivalry; had a deep respect for nature, human rights, and the nobility of peasantry; and were suspicious of progress. Their paintings tended to be heroic, historic, dramatic, and beautiful. They were inspired by critic and art theorist **John Ruskin** (1819–1900), who traveled throughout Northern Italy and was among the first to sing the praises of pre-Renaissance painting and Gothic architecture.

Significant artists of this period include:

- **William Blake (1757–1827).** Romantic archetype, Blake snubbed the stuffy Royal Academy of Arts to do his own engraving, prints, illustrations, poetry, and painting. His works were filled with melodrama, muscular figures, and sweeping lines; modern, angst-ridden, "Goth" teens really dig his stuff. Judge for yourself at London's **Tate Britain** and Manchester's **Whitworth Art Gallery.**
- **John Constable (1776–1837).** Constable was a great British landscapist, whose scenes (especially those of happy, agricultural peasants) got more idealized with each passing year—while his compositions and brushwork became freer. You'll find his best stuff in London's **National Gallery** and **Victoria and Albert Museum,** and Liverpool's **Walker Art Gallery.**
- **J. M. W. Turner (1775–1851).** Turner, called by some "The First Impressionist," was a prolific and multitalented artist whose mood-laden, freely brushed, watercolor landscapes influenced Monet. The River Thames and London, where he lived and died, were frequent subjects. He bequeathed his collection of some 19,000 watercolors and 300 paintings to the people of Britain with the request that they be kept in one place. London's **Tate Britain** displays the largest number of Turner's works, while others grace London's **National Gallery,** Cambridge's **Fitzwilliam Museum,** Liverpool's **Walker Art Gallery,** Birmingham's **Museum and Art Gallery** and **Barber Institute of Fine Arts,** and Manchester's **Whitworth Art Gallery.**
- **Pre-Raphaelites (1848–1870s).** This "brotherhood" of painters declared that art had gone all wrong with Italian Renaissance painter Raphael (1483–1520) and set about to emulate the Italian painters who preceded him—though they were not actually looking at specific examples. Their symbolically imbued, sweetly idealized, hyper-realistic work depicts scenes from romantic poetry and Shakespeare as much as from the Bible. There were seven founders and many followers, but the most important were Dante Rossetti, William Hunt, and John Millais; you can see work by all three at London's **Tate Britain,** Oxford's **Ashmolean Museum,** Liverpool's **Walker Art Gallery,** and Manchester's **City Art Gallery.**

THE 20TH CENTURY

The only artistic movement or era the Brits can claim a major stake in is contemporary art, with many young British artists bursting onto the international gallery scene just before and after World War II. Art of the last century often followed international schools or styles—no major ones truly originated in Britain—and artists tended to move in and out of styles over their careers. If anything, the greatest artists of this period strove for unique and individual expression rather than adherence to a particular school.

In the examples below, a city name refers to the major modern art gallery in that location; "London" stands for the **Tate Modern,** "Birmingham" for the **Museum and Art Gallery,** and "Liverpool" for the **Walker Art Gallery.** Important British artists of the 20th century include:

- **Henry Moore (1898–1986).** A sculptor, Moore saw himself as a sort of reincarnation of Michelangelo. He mined his marbles from the same quarries as the Renaissance master and let the stone itself dictate the flowing, abstract, surrealistic figures carved from it. The **Henry Moore Institute** in Leeds, where he studied, preserves his drawings and sculpture. You'll also find his work in London, Liverpool, Birmingham, and Cambridge's **Fitzwilliam Museum** and **Clare College.**

- **Francis Bacon (1909–92).** A dark and brooding expressionist (a style that expresses an artist's inner thoughts and feelings), Bacon presented man's foibles in formats, such as the triptych (a set of three panels, often hinged and used as an altarpiece), that were usually reserved for religious subjects. Find his works in London, Birmingham, and Manchester's **Whitworth Art Gallery.**
- **Lucien Freud (b. 1922).** Freud's portraits and marvelous nudes live in a depressing world of thick paint, fluid lines, and harsh light. The grandson of psychiatrist Sigmund Freud, this artist has pieces in London, Liverpool, and Manchester's **Whitworth Art Gallery.**
- **David Hockney (b. 1937).** The closest thing to a British Andy Warhol, Hockney employs a less pop-arty style than the famous American—though Hockney does reference modern technologies and culture—and is much more playful with artistic traditions. His work resides in London and Liverpool.
- **Damien Hirst (b. 1965).** The guy who pickles cows, Hirst is a celebrity/artist whose work sets out to shock. He's a winner of Britain's Turner Prize, and his work is prominent in the collection of Charles Saatchi, whose Saatchi Gallery in London displays his holdings.

2 Architecture 101

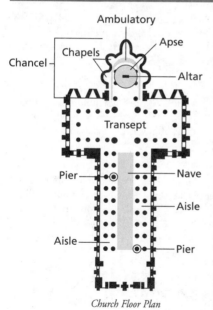

Church Floor Plan

While each architectural era has its distinctive features, there are some elements, floor plans, and terms common to many. This is particularly true of churches, large numbers of which were built in Europe from the Middle Ages through the 18th century.

From the Norman period on, most **churches** consist either of a single, wide **aisle,** or a wide central **nave** flanked by two narrower aisles. The aisles are separated from the nave by a row of **columns,** or square stacks of masonry called **piers,** connected by **arches.** Sometimes—especially in the medieval Norman and Gothic eras—there is a second level to the nave, above these arches (and hence above the low roof over the aisles) punctuated by windows called a **clerestory.**

This main nave/aisle assemblage is usually crossed by a perpendicular corridor called a **transept** near the far, east end of the church so that the floor plan looks like a **Latin Cross** (shaped like a crucifix). The shorter, east arm of the nave is called the **chancel;** it often houses the **altar** and stalls of the **choir.** Some churches use a **rood screen** (so called because it supports a *rood,* the Saxon word for *crucifixion*) to separate the nave from the chancel. If the far end of the chancel is rounded off, we call it an **apse.** An **ambulatory** is a curving corridor outside the altar and choir area, separating it from the ring of smaller chapels radiating off the chancel and apse.

Some churches, especially after the Renaissance when mathematical proportion became important, were built on a **Greek Cross** plan, with each axis the same length like a giant plus sign ("**+**").

It's worth pointing out that very few buildings (especially churches) were built in only one particular style. Massive, expensive structures often took centuries to complete, during which time tastes would change and plans would be altered.

NORMAN (1066–1200)

Aside from a smattering of ancient sights—**pre-classical** stone circles as at Stonehenge and Avebury and **Roman** ruins such as the Bath spa and Hadrian's Wall—the oldest surviving architectural style in England dates to when the 1066 Norman conquest brought the Romanesque era to Britain, where it flourished as the **Norman** style.

Churches in this style were large, with a wide nave and aisles to accommodate the masses who came to hear Mass and worship at the altars of various saints. But to support the weight of all that masonry, the walls had to be thick and solid (meaning they could be pierced only by few and small windows) resting on huge piers, giving Norman churches a dark, somber, mysterious, and often oppressive feeling.

IDENTIFIABLE FEATURES

- **Rounded arches.** These load-bearing architectural devices allowed the architects to open up wide naves and spaces, channeling all the weight of the stone walls and ceiling across the curve of the arch and down into the ground via the columns or pilasters.
- **Thick walls.**
- **Infrequent and small windows.**
- **Huge piers.** These load-bearing, vertical features resemble square stacks of masonry.
- **Chevrons.** These zigzagging decorations often surround a doorway or wrap around a column.

BEST EXAMPLES

- **White Tower, London (1078).** William the Conqueror's first building in Britain, White Tower is the central keep of the Tower of London. The fortress-thick walls and rounded archways are textbook Norman.

White Tower, London

- **Durham Cathedral (1093–1488).** The layout is Norman, save for the proto-Gothic, pointy rib vaulting along the nave. The massive piers are incised with chevrons.
- **Ely Cathedral (1083–1189).** The nave and south transept are perfectly Norman, though much of the rest of the interior is as Gothic as the exterior.

GOTHIC (1150–1550)

The French Gothic style invaded England in the late 12th century, trading rounded arches for pointy ones—an engineering discovery that freed church architecture from the heavy, thick walls of Norman structures and allowed ceilings to soar, walls to thin, and windows to proliferate.

Instead of dark, somber, relatively unadorned Norman interiors that forced the eyes of the faithful toward the altar where the priest stood droning on in unintelligible Latin, the Gothic interior enticed the churchgoers' gaze upward to high ceilings filled with light. While the priests conducted Mass in Latin, the peasants could "read" the Gothic comic books of stained-glass windows.

The squat, brooding exteriors of the Norman fortresses of God were replaced by graceful buttresses and soaring spires, which rose from town centers like beacons of religion.

The Gothic proper in Britain can be divided into three overlapping periods or styles: **Early English** (1150–1300), **Decorated** (1250–1370), and **Perpendicular** (1350–1550). While they all share some identifiable features (see the next section), others are characteristic of the individual periods.

Gothic style proved hard to kill in Britain. It would make comebacks in the 17th century as **Laudian Gothic** in some Oxford and Cambridge buildings, in the late 18th century as **rococo** or **Strawberry Hill Gotick** at Lacock Abbey, and in the 19th-century **Victorian Gothic Revival,** discussed later.

IDENTIFIABLE FEATURES

- **Pointed arches (all periods).** The most significant development of the Gothic era was the discovery that pointed arches could carry far more weight than rounded ones.

Cross Vault

  - **Cross vaults (all periods).** Instead of being flat, the square patch of ceiling between four columns arches up to a point in the center, creating four sail shapes, sort of like the underside of a pyramid. The "X" separating these four sails is often reinforced with ridges called **ribbing.** As the Gothic progressed, four-sided cross vaults became **fan vaults** (see below), and the spaces between the structural ribbing spanned with decorative **tracery** (see below).
  - **Flying buttresses (all periods).** These free-standing exterior pillars connected by graceful, thin arms of stone help channel the weight of the building and its roof out and down into the ground. Not every Gothic church has evident buttresses.
- **Dogtooth molding (Early English).** Bands of a repeated decoration of four triangle-shaped petals placed around a raised center.
- **Lancet windows (Early English).** Tall, thin pointy windows, often in pairs or multiples, all set into a larger, elliptical pointy arch.

- **Tracery (Decorated and Perpendicular).**
These delicate, lacy spider webs of carved
stone grace the pointy end of windows
and the acute lower intersections of **cross
vaults** (see above).
- **Fan vaults (Perpendicular).** Lots of
side-by-side, cone-shaped, concave vaults
springing from the same point, fan vaults
are usually covered in **tracery** (see above).

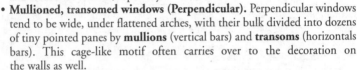

Fan Vault

- **An emphasis on horizontal and vertical lines
(Perpendicular).** What defines the Perpendicular is its broad
and rectilinear fashion, especially in the windows.
- **Mullioned, transomed windows (Perpendicular).** Perpendicular windows
tend to be wide, under flattened arches, with their bulk divided into dozens
of tiny pointed panes by **mullions** (vertical bars) and **transoms** (horizontals
bars). This cage-like motif often carries over to the decoration on
the walls as well.
- **Stained glass (all periods but more common later).** The multitude and
size of Gothic windows allowed them to be filled with Bible stories and
symbolism writ in the colorful patterns of stained glass. The use of stained
glass was more common in the later Gothic periods.
- **Rose windows (all periods).** These huge circular windows, often appearing as the centerpieces
of facades, are filled with elegant **tracery** (see
above) and "petals" of stained glass.
- **Spires (all periods).** These pinnacles of
masonry seem to defy gravity and reach toward
heaven itself.
- **Gargoyles (all periods).** Disguised as wide-
mouthed creatures or human heads, gargoyles
are actually drain spouts.
- **Choir screen (all periods).** Serving as the
inner wall of the ambulatory and outer wall of
the choir section, the choir screen is often
decorated with carvings or tombs.

BEST EXAMPLES

- **Early English: Salisbury Cathedral**
(1220–65) is unique in Europe for the
speed with which it was built
and the uniformity of its
architecture (even if the
spire was added 100 years
later, they kept it Early
English). The first to use
pointy arches was **Wells
Cathedral** (1180–1321),
which has 300 statues
on its original facade
and some early stained
glass.

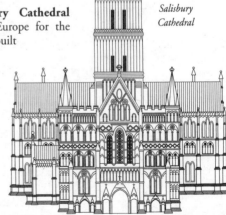

*Salisbury
Cathedral*

- **Decorated:** The facade, nave, and chapter house of **York Minster** (1220–1480), which preserves the most medieval stained glass in Britain, are Decorated, though the chancel is Perpendicular and the transepts are Early English. **Exeter Cathedral** (1112–1206) has an elaborate Decorated facade and fantastic nave vaulting.
- **Perpendicular: King's College Chapel at Cambridge** (1446–1515) has England's most magnificent fan vaulting, along with some fine stained glass. **Henry VII's Chapel** (1503–19) in London's Westminster Abbey is textbook Perpendicular.

RENAISSANCE (1550–1650)

While the Continent was experimenting with the Renaissance ideals of proportion, order, classical inspiration, and mathematical precision to create unified and balanced structures, England was still trundling along with the late **Tudor Gothic** Perpendicular style (the Tudor use of redbrick became a major feature of later Gothic revivals) in places such as Hampton Court Palace and Bath Abbey (great fan vaulting).

It wasn't until the Elizabethan era that the Brits turned to the **Renaissance** style sweeping the Continent. England's greatest Renaissance architect, **Inigo Jones** (1573–1652), brought back from his Italian travels a fevered imagination full of the exactingly Classical theories of **Palladianism**, a style derived from the buildings and publications of **Andrea Palladio** (1508–80). However, most English architects at this time tempered the Renaissance style with a heavy dose of Gothic-like elements.

IDENTIFIABLE FEATURES
- **Sense of proportion.**
- **Reliance on symmetry.**
- **Use of classical orders.** This specifies three different column capitals: Corinthian, Ionic, and Doric.

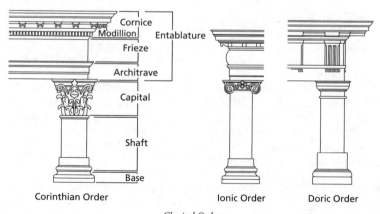

Corinthian Order   Ionic Order   Doric Order

Classical Orders

BEST EXAMPLES
- **Robert Smythson** (1535–1614). This early Elizabethan architect was responsible for two of the greatest mansions of the period: **Hardwick Hall**

(1590–97) in Derbyshire, virtually abandoned and therefore wonderfully preserved (if a bit dilapidated) in its 16th-century condition; and **Longleat House** (1559–80), an elegant Wiltshire manse with a park designed by Renaissance landscape architect and garden designer **Capability Brown.**

- **Inigo Jones (1573–1652).** Jones applied his theories of Palladianism to such edifices as **Queen's House** (1616–18 and 1629–35) in Greenwich; the **Queen's Chapel** (1623–25) in St. James's Palace and the **Banqueting House** (1619–22) in Whitehall, both in London; and the staterooms of Wiltshire's **Wilton House** (1603), where Shakespeare performed and D-Day was planned. Recently, London's **Shakespeare's Globe Theatre** dusted off one of his never-realized plans and used it to construct their new indoor theater annex.

BAROQUE (1650–1750)

England's greatest architect was **Christopher Wren** (1632–1723), a scientist and member of Parliament who got the job of rebuilding London after the Great Fire of 1666. He designed 53 replacement churches alone, plus the new St. Paul's Cathedral and numerous other projects. Other proponents of baroque architecture were **John Vanbrugh** (1664–1726) and his mentor and oft collaborator, **Nicholas Hawksmoor** (1661–1736), who sometimes worked in a more Palladian idiom.

IDENTIFIABLE FEATURES

- **Classical architecture rewritten with curves.** The baroque is similar to the Renaissance, but many of the right angles and ruler-straight lines are exchanged for curves of complex geometry and an interplay of concave and convex surfaces. The overall effect is to lighten the appearance of structures and to add some movement of line.
- **Complex decoration.** Unlike the sometimes severe designs of the Renaissance and other classically inspired styles, the baroque was often playful and apt to festoon structures with decorations intended to liven things up.

BEST EXAMPLES

- **St. Paul's Cathedral, London (1676–1710).** This cathedral is the crowning achievement of both English baroque and of Christopher Wren himself. London's other main Wren attraction is the **Royal Naval College,** Greenwich (1696).
- **Queen's College, Sheldonian Theatre, and Radcliffe Camera, Oxford.** **Queen's College** is the only campus of Oxford constructed entirely in one style, and it includes a library by Hawksmoor. The **Sheldonian Theatre** (1664–69), an almost classically subdued rotunda showing little of later baroque exuberance, was Wren's first crack at architecture. Compare this to the more baroque **Radcliffe Camera** (1737–49), designed by James Gibbs (1662–1754) who influenced Thomas Jefferson.
- **Blenheim Palace, Woodstock (early 1700s).** John Vanbrugh's crowning achievement, Blenheim Palace is a British Versailles surrounded by perhaps the best of Capability Brown's gardens.
- **Castle Howard, Yorkshire (1699–1726).** Another masterpiece by the team of Nicholas Hawksmoor and then-neophyte John Vanbrugh, Castle Howard became famous as a backdrop to *Brideshead Revisited.*

NEOCLASSICAL AND GREEK REVIVAL (1714–1837)

Many 18th-century architects cared little for the baroque period, and during the Georgian era (1714–1830) a restrained, simple **neoclassicism** reigned. It was balanced between a resurgence of the precepts of Palladianism (see "Renaissance" above) and an even more distilled vision of classical theory called **Greek revival.** This latter style was practiced by architects such as **James "Athenian" Stuart** (1713–88), who wrote a book on antiquities after a trip to Greece, and the somewhat less strict **John Soane** (1773–1837).

IDENTIFIABLE FEATURES
- **Mathematical proportion, symmetry, classical orders.** These classical ideals first rediscovered during the Renaissance are the hallmark of every classically styled era.
- **Crescents and Circuses.** The Georgians were famous for these seamless curving rows of identical stone town houses with tall windows, each one simple yet elegant inside.
- **Open double-arm staircases.** This feature was a favorite of the neo-Palladians.

BEST EXAMPLES
- **Bath (1727–75).** Much of the city of Bath was made over in the 18th century, most famously by the father and son team of **John Woods, Sr. and Jr.** (1704–54 and 1728–81, respectively). They were responsible, among others, for the **Royal Crescent** (1767–75), where you can visit one house's interior and even lodge in another.

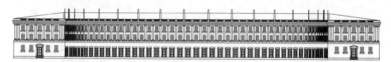

Royal Crescent, Bath

- **John Soane's London sights.** The best Greek revival building by Soane in London is his own idiosyncratic house (1812–13), now **Sir John Soane's Museum.** Of his most famous commission, the **Bank of England** (1732–34) in Bartholomew Lane, only the facade survived a 20th-century restructuring.
- **British Museum, London (1823).** Not the most important example of Greek revival, the British Museum, by Robert & Sidney Smirke, is one that just about every visitor to England is bound to see.

VICTORIAN GOTHIC REVIVAL (1750–1900)

While neoclassicists were sticking to their guns in Bath, the early romantic movement swept up others with rosy visions of the past. This imaginary and fairy-tale version of the Middle Ages led to such creative developments as the pre-Raphaelite painters (see "The Romantics" above) and Gothic revival architects, who really got a head of steam under their movement during the eclectic Victorian era.

Gothic "revival" is a bit misleading, as its practitioners usually applied their favorite Gothic features at random rather than faithfully recreating a whole structure. Aside from this eclecticism, you can separate the revivals from the originals by age (Victorian buildings are several hundred years younger and tend to be in considerably better shape) and size (the revivals are often much larger).

IDENTIFIABLE FEATURES

- **Mishmash of Gothic features.** Look at the features described under Gothic earlier in this chapter, and then imagine going on a shopping spree through them at random.
- **Eclecticism.** Few Victorians bothered with correctly rendering all the formal details of a particular Gothic era. They just wanted the overall effect to be pointy, busy with decorations, and terribly medieval.
- **Grand scale.** These buildings tend to be very, very large. This was usually accomplished by using Gothic only on the surface, with newfangled industrial-age engineering underneath.

BEST EXAMPLES

- **Palace of Westminster (Houses of Parliament), London (1835–52).** Charles Barry (1795–1860) designed the wonderful British seat of government in a Gothic idiom that, more than most, sticks pretty faithfully to the old Perpendicular period's style. His clock tower, usually called "Big Ben" after its biggest bell, has become an icon of London itself.

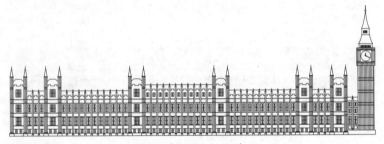

Palace of Westminster, London

- **Albert Memorial, London (1863–72).** In 1861 Queen Victoria commissioned George Gilbert Scott (1811–78) to build this massive Gothic canopy to memorialize her beloved husband.
- **Natural History Museum, London (1873–81).** The Natural History Museum is a delightful marriage of imposing neo-Gothic clothing hiding an industrial-age steel-and-iron framework, courtesy of architect Alfred Waterhouse (1830–1905).

THE 20TH CENTURY

For the first half of the 20th century, England was too busy expanding into suburbs (in an architecturally uninteresting way) and fighting World Wars to pay much attention to architecture. After the World War II Blitz, much of central London had to be rebuilt. Most of the new commercial buildings in the city held to a functional school of architecture aptly named Brutalism. It wasn't until the boom of the late 1970s and 1980s that **postmodern** architecture gave British architects a bold, new direction.

IDENTIFIABLE FEATURES
- **Skyscraper motif.** Glass and steel as high as you can stack it.
- **Reliance on historical details.** Like the Victorians, postmodernists also recycled elements from architectural history, from classical to exotic.

BEST EXAMPLES
- **Lloyd's Building, London (1978–86).** Lloyd's is *the* British postmodern masterpiece by Richard Rogers (b. 1933), who had a hand in Paris's funky Centre Pompidou.
- **Canary Wharf Tower, London (1986).** Britain's tallest building, by César Pelli (b. 1926), is the postmodern centerpiece of the Canary Wharf office complex and commercial development.
- **Charing Cross, London (1991).** Whimsical designer Terry Farrell (b. 1938) capped the famous old train station with an enormous postmodern office-and-shopping complex in glass and pale stone.

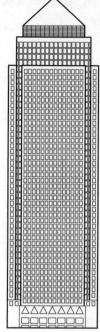

Canary Wharf Tower, London

3

Planning Your Trip to England & Wales

In the pages that follow, we outline the various regions of England and Wales, and explain their individual appeal to visitors. You'll find everything you need to know about the practicalities of planning your trip in advance: finding the best airfare, deciding when to go, figuring out British currency, and more.

1 The Regions in Brief

England is a part of the United Kingdom, which is made up of England, Wales, Scotland, and Northern Ireland. Only 130,347 sq. km (50,327 sq. miles)—about the same size as New York State—England has an amazing amount of rural land and natural wilderness and an astonishing regional, physical, and cultural diversity.

ENGLAND

London Some seven million Londoners live in this mammoth metropolis, a parcel of land that's more than 1,577 sq. km (609 sq. miles) in size. The City of London proper is merely 2.5 sq. km (1 sq. mile), but the rest of the city is made up of separate villages, boroughs, and corporations. London's neighborhoods and outlying areas are described in chapter 4.

The Thames Valley England's most famous river runs westward from Kew to its source in the Cotswolds. A land of meadows, woodlands, attractive villages, small market towns, and rolling hillsides, this is one of England's most scenic areas. Highlights include **Windsor Castle** (Elizabeth II's favorite residence) and nearby **Eton College,** founded by a young Henry VI in 1440. **Henley,** site of the Royal Regatta, remains our favorite Thames-side

town; and at the university city of **Oxford,** you can tour the colleges.

The Southeast (Kent, Surrey, & Sussex) This is the land of Charles Lamb, Virginia Woolf, Sir Winston Churchill, and Henry James. In this region are some of the nation's biggest attractions: **Brighton, Canterbury, Dover,** and dozens of country homes and castles—not only **Hever** and **Leeds castles,** but also **Chartwell,** the more modest abode where Churchill lived. In small villages, such as Rye and Winchelsea in Sussex, you discover the charm of the southeast. Almost all of the Sussex shoreline is built up, and seaside towns, such as Eastbourne and Hastings, are often tacky. In fact, though the area's major attraction is **Canterbury Cathedral,** the **Royal Pavilion at Brighton** rates as an outstanding, extravagant folly. Tea shops, antiques shops, pubs, and small inns abound in the area. Surrey is essentially a commuter suburb of London and is easily reached for day trips.

Hampshire & Wiltshire Southwest of London, these counties possess two of England's greatest **cathedrals,** Winchester and Salisbury, and one of Europe's most significant prehistoric

England & Wales: The Regions in Brief

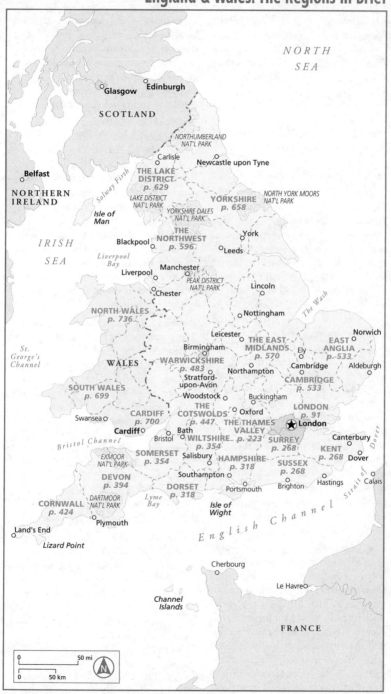

monuments, **Stonehenge.** Hampshire is bordered on its western side by the woodlands and heaths of **New Forest. Portsmouth** and **Southampton** loom large in naval heritage. You may also want to take a ferry over to the **Isle of Wight,** once Queen Victoria's preferred vacation retreat. In Wiltshire, you encounter the beginning of the **West Country,** with its scenic beauty and monuments. Here you'll find Wilton House, the 17th-century home of the earls of Pembroke, and Old Sarum, the remains of what is believed to have been an Iron Age fortification.

The Southwest (Dorset, Somerset, Devon, & Cornwall) These four counties are the great vacation centers and retirement havens of England. Dorset, associated with Thomas Hardy, is a land of rolling downs, rocky headlands, well-kept villages, and rich farmlands. Somerset—the Somerset of King Arthur and Camelot—offers such magical towns as **Glastonbury.** Devon has both **Exmoor** and **Dartmoor,** and its northern and southern coastlines are peppered with famous resorts such as Lyme Regis and villages such as Clovelly. In Cornwall, you're never more than 32km (20 miles) from the rugged coastline, which ends at **Land's End.** Among the cities worth visiting in these counties are **Bath,** with its impressive Roman baths and Georgian architecture; **Plymouth,** the departure point of the Mayflower; and **Wells,** the site of a great cathedral.

The Cotswolds A wonderful region to tour, this is a pastoral land of honey-colored limestone villages where rural England unfolds before you like a storybook. In the Middle Ages, wool made the Cotswolders prosperous, but now they put out the welcome mat for visitors, with famously lovely inns and pubs. Start at Burford, the traditional gateway to the region, continue on to Bourton-on-the-Water, Lower and Upper Slaughter, Stow-on-the-Wold,

Moreton-in-Marsh, and Chipping Campden, and finish at Broadway. **Cirencester** is the uncrowned capital of the south Cotswolds, and **Cheltenham** is still an elegant Regency spa. Our two favorite villages are **Painswick,** with its minute cottages, and **Bibury,** with Arlington Row, its cluster of former weavers' cottages.

Stratford & Warwick This region encompasses both Shakespeare country and the Midlands. The Midlands was the birthplace of the Industrial Revolution, which made Britain the first industrialized country in the world. Its foremost tourist town is **Stratford-upon-Avon,** but also drawing visitors are **Warwick Castle,** one of England's great castles, and the ruins of **Kenilworth Castle. Coventry,** heavily bombed in World War II, is visited mainly for its outstanding modern cathedral.

Birmingham & the West Midlands The area known as the West Midlands embraces the so-called "Black Country." **Birmingham,** nicknamed "Brum," is Britain's largest city after London. This sprawling metropolis is still characterized by its overpass jungles and tacky suburbs, as well as its great piles of Victorian architecture. Urban renewal is underway. The English marshes cut through the old counties of **Shropshire** and **Herefordshire. Ironbridge Gorge** was at the heart of the Industrial Revolution, and the famous **Potteries** are in Staffordshire.

East Anglia (Essex, Cambridgeshire, Norfolk, & Suffolk) East Anglia, a semicircular geographic bulge northeast of London, is the name applied to these four very flat counties. The land of John Constable is still filled with the landscapes he painted. **The Fens**—that broad expanse of fertile, black soil lying north of Cambridge—remains our favorite district. Go there to see **Ely Cathedral. Cambridge,** with its colleges and river, is the chief attraction. The most important museum is the **Fitzwilliam** in Cambridge, but visitors also flock to East Anglia for the scenery and its solitary beauty—fens, salt marshes, and villages of thatched cottages.

The East Midlands (Derbyshire, Leicestershire, Lincolnshire, Northamptonshire, & Nottinghamshire) This area encompasses some of the worst of industrial England, yet there is still great natural beauty to be found, as well as stately homes. These include **Chatsworth** in Derbyshire, the seat of the dukes of Devonshire; **Sulgrave Manor** in Northamptonshire, the ancestral home of George Washington; and **Althorp House,** also in Northamptonshire, the childhood home of Diana, Princess of Wales. **Lincoln** has one of England's great cathedrals, rebuilt in the 13th and 14th centuries. Bostonians like to visit their namesake, the old seaport town of **Boston. Nottingham** recalls Robin Hood, though the deforested Sherwood Forest is obviously not what it was in the outlaw's heyday.

The Northwest Stretching from Liverpool to the Scottish border, northwest England can be a rustic delight if you steer clear of its industrial pockets. Most people come here to follow in the footsteps of such romantic poets as Wordsworth, who wrote of the beauty of the Lake District (see below). But **Chester, Manchester,** and **Liverpool** merit stopovers along the way. The resort of **Blackpool** is big, brash, and a bit tawdry, drawing the working class of the Midlands for Coney Island–style fun by the sea. In contrast, the Roman city of Chester is a well-preserved medieval town, known for its encircling wall. And Liverpool is culturally alive and always intriguing, if only to see where the Beatles came from, but it also has a branch of London's Tate Gallery.

The Lake District The literary Lakeland evokes memories of the Wordsworths, Samuel Taylor Coleridge, John Ruskin, and Beatrix Potter, among others. **Windermere** is the best location for touring the area, but there are many other charming towns as well, including **Grasmere** and **Ambleside.** The Lake District contains some of England's most dramatic scenery.

Yorkshire & Northumbria Yorkshire will be familiar to fans of the Brontës and James Herriot. **York,** with its immense cathedral and medieval streets, is the city to visit, though more and more visitors are calling on the cities of **Leeds** and **Bradford.** Northumbria comprises **Northumberland, Cleveland, Durham,** and **Tyne and Wear** (the area around **Newcastle**). The whole area echoes the ancient border battles between the Scots and English. **Hadrian's Wall,** built by the Romans, is a highlight. The great cathedral at Durham is one of Britain's finest examples of Norman church architecture, and **Fountains Abbey** is among the country's greatest ecclesiastical ruins. Country homes abound; here you find **Harewood House** and **Castle Howard.**

WALES

Cardiff & South Wales The capital of Wales, **Cardiff** is a large seaport on the tidal estuary of the River Taff. As the center of the small land mass that is Wales, Cardiff admittedly can't be compared very well with London or Edinburgh, but it's a charmer in its own right. Newly restored, the capital invites with such attractions as that treasure trove, the **National Museum of Wales,** and **Cardiff Castle,** with all its rich architectural detail. If time remains, dip into **South Wales,** which isn't all remnants of the Industrial Revolution but is filled with beauty spots, such as the **Brecon Beacons National Park.** West of Cardiff is the city of

Swansea, opening onto Swansea Bay. This is Dylan Thomas country.

North Wales Even more rewarding in scenery than South Wales, North Wales is a land of mountain peaks, spectacular estuaries, and rugged cliffs brooding over secluded coves, little rivers, valleys, and lakes. Its great towns and villages include **Betws-y-Coed, Llandudno,** and **Conwy,** along with such historic castles as **Harlech, Caernarfon,** and especially **Conwy Castle,** ordered built by Edward I and a masterpiece of medieval architecture. In this region, **Snowdonia National Park** covers 2,176 sq. km (840 sq. miles) of North Wales coastal areas and rugged hills.

2 Visitor Information

Before you go, you can obtain general information from **Visit Britain** (www. visitbritain.com):

- In the United States: 551 Fifth Ave., 7th Floor, New York, NY 10176-0799 (✆ **800/462-2748** or 212/986-2266; fax 212/986-1188).
- In Canada: Suite 120, 5915 Airport Rd., Mississauga, ON L4V 1T1 (✆ **888/847-4885;** fax 905/405-1835).
- In Australia: Level 16, Gateway, 1 Macquarie Place, Sydney NSW 2000 (✆ **02/9377-4400;** fax 02/9377-4499).
- In New Zealand: Fay Richwite Blvd., 17th Floor, 151 Queen St., Aukland 1 (✆ **09/303-1446;** fax 09/377-6965).

For a full information package on London, write to **Visit London,** Glen House, Victoria, Stag Place, London SW1E 5LT (✆ **020/7932-2000**).

You can usually pick up a copy of *Time Out,* the most up-to-date source for what's happening in London, at any international newsstand. You can also check it out online at **www. timeout.co.uk**.

To book accommodations with a credit card (MasterCard or Visa), call the **Visit London Booking Office** at ✆ **020/7604-2890.** The office is open Monday through Friday from 9am to 6pm (London time). There is a £5 ($9.25) fee for booking.

Wales, like England, has a number of regional tourist offices, but the **Visit Wales Centre** is at Brunel House, 2 Fitzalan Rd., Cardiff CF24 0UY (✆ **08701/211-251;** www.visit wales.com). Detailed information is also available in London from the Wales Desk at the **Visit Britain Visitors Centre,** 1 Regent St., London SW1Y 4XT (✆ **020/7808-3838**).

WHAT'S ON THE WEB? The most useful site was created by a very knowledgeable source, the British Tourist Authority itself, with U.S. visitors targeted. A wealth of information is tapped at **www.visitbritain.org**, which lets you order brochures online, provides trip-planning hints, and even allows e-mail questions for prompt answers. All of Great Britain is covered.

Go to **www.baa.com** for a guide and terminal maps for Heathrow, Gatwick, Stansted, and several other airports in the U.K., including flight arrival times, duty-free shops, airport restaurants, and info on getting from the London airports to downtown London. Getting around London can be confusing, so you may want to visit **www.londontransport.co.uk** for up-to-the-minute info. For the latest on London's theater scene, consult **www.officiallondontheatre.co.uk**. At **www.multimap.com**, you can access detailed street maps for the whole United Kingdom—just key in the location or even just its postal code and a map of the area with the location circled appears. For directions to specific places in London, consult **www.streetmap.co.uk**.

You may also wish to check out one of the following websites. **AOL members** can type in the keyword **"Britain"** and find a vibrant guide to the U.K. that gives you the skinny on arts, dining, nightlife, and more. To access the AOL London guide, type in the keyword "London." **A2B Travel** (**www.a2btravel.com**) focuses on helping travelers plan and book their trips. It has lots of nifty tools such as bus, rail, and ferry guides; a point-to-point mileage calculator; and a guide to more than two dozen U.K. airports. At **www.britannia.com**, you'll find much more than a travel guide—it's chock-full of lively features, history, and regional profiles, including sections on Wales and King Arthur. **UK for Visitors,** from About.com (**http://gouk.about.com/travel/gouk**), is a useful gateway that links to local information sites all over the country. You may want to steer clear of its limited guide to hotels and restaurants, however.

3 Entry Requirements & Customs

ENTRY REQUIREMENTS

All U.S. citizens, Canadians, Australians, New Zealanders, and South Africans must have a passport with at least 2 months validity remaining. No visa is required. The immigration officer will also want proof of your intention to return to your point of origin (usually a round-trip ticket) and visible means of support while you're in Britain. If you're planning to fly from the United States or Canada to the United Kingdom and then on to a country that requires a visa (India, for example), you should secure that visa before you arrive in Britain.

Your valid driver's license and at least 1 year of driving experience is required to drive personal or rented cars.

For information on how to get a passport, go to the Fast Facts section of this chapter—the websites listed provide downloadable passport applications as well as the current fees for processing passport applications. For an up-to-date country-by-country listing of passport requirements around the world, go the "Foreign Entry Requirement" Web page of the U.S. State Department at **http://travel.state.gov**.

CUSTOMS
WHAT YOU CAN BRING INTO BRITAIN
Non-EU Nationals age 18 and older can bring in, duty-free, 200 cigarettes, 100 cigarillos, 50 cigars, or 250 grams of smoking tobacco. This amount is doubled if you live outside Europe. You can also bring in 2 liters of wine and either 1 liter of alcohol over 22 proof or 2 liters of wine under 22 proof. In addition, you can bring in 60cc (2 oz.) of perfume, a quarter liter (250ml) of eau de toilette, 500 grams (1 lb.) of coffee, and 200 grams (½ lb.) of tea. Visitors 15 and over may also bring in other goods totaling £145

Tips Plan Ahead for Passports

Allow plenty of time before your trip to apply for a passport; processing normally takes 3 weeks but can take longer during busy periods (especially spring). And keep in mind that if you need a passport in a hurry, you'll pay a higher processing fee. When traveling, safeguard your passport in an inconspicuous, inaccessible place such as a money belt and keep a copy of the critical pages with your passport number in a separate place. If you lose your passport, visit the nearest consulate of your native country as soon as possible for a replacement.

($268); the allowance for those 14 and under is £73 ($134). (Customs officials tend to be lenient about general merchandise, realizing the limits are unrealistically low.)

You can't bring your pet to Britain. Six months' quarantine is required before it is allowed in. An illegally imported animal may be destroyed.

Citizens of the U.K. who are **returning from a European Union (EU) country** will go through a separate Customs Exit (called the "Blue Exit") especially for EU travelers. In essence, there is no limit on what you can bring back from an EU country, as long as the items are for personal use (this includes gifts), and you have already paid the necessary duty and tax. However, customs law sets out guidance levels. If you bring in more than these levels, you may be asked to prove that the goods are for your own use. Guidance levels on goods bought in the EU for your own use are 3,200 cigarettes, 200 cigars, 3 kilograms of smoking tobacco, 10 liters of spirits, 90 liters of wine (of this not more than 60 liters can be sparkling wine), and 110 liters of beer.

U.K. citizens returning from **a non-EU country** have a customs allowance of: 200 cigarettes; 50 cigars; 250 grams of smoking tobacco; 2 liters of still table wine; 1 liter of spirits or strong liqueurs (over 22% volume); 2 liters of fortified wine, sparkling wine or other liqueurs; 60cc (ml) perfume; 250cc (ml) of toilet water; and £145 ($268) worth of all other goods, including gifts and souvenirs. For more information, contact HM Customs & Excise National Advice Service at ⓒ **0845/ 010-9000** (from outside the U.K., 020/8929-0152), or consult their website at **www.hmce.gov.uk.**

WHAT YOU CAN TAKE HOME FROM BRITAIN

Returning **U.S. citizens** who have been away for at least 48 hours are allowed to bring back, once every 30 days, $800

worth of merchandise duty-free. You'll be charged a flat rate of 4% duty on the next $1,000 worth of purchases. Be sure to have your receipts handy. On mailed gifts, the duty-free limit is $200 or less. With some exceptions, you cannot bring fresh fruits and vegetables into the United States. For specifics on what you can bring back, download the invaluable free pamphlet *Know Before You Go* online from the "Travel" sub-menu at **www.customs.gov.** Or contact **U.S. Customs & Border Protection,** 1300 Pennsylvania Ave. NW, Washington, DC 20229 (ⓒ **202/354-1000**), and request the pamphlet.

For a clear summary of **Canadian** rules, get the booklet *I Declare,* issued by the **Canada Border Services Agency** (ⓒ **800/461-9999** in Canada, or 204/983-3500; www.cbsa.gc.ca) and available online. Canada allows its citizens a C$750 exemption, and you're allowed to bring back duty-free 1 carton of cigarettes, 1 can of tobacco, 40 imperial ounces of liquor, and 50 cigars. In addition, you're allowed to mail gifts to Canada valued at less than C$60 a day, provided they're unsolicited and don't contain alcohol or tobacco (write on the package "Unsolicited gift, under C$60 value"). All valuables should be declared on the Y-38 form before departure from Canada, including serial numbers of valuables you already own, such as expensive foreign cameras. *Note:* The C$750 exemption can only be used once a year and only after an absence of 7 days.

The duty-free allowance in **Australia** is A$400 or, for those under 18, A$200. Citizens can bring in 250 cigarettes or 250 grams of loose tobacco, and 1,125 milliliters of alcohol. If you're returning with valuables you already own, such as foreign-made cameras, you should file form B263. A helpful brochure available from Australian consulates or Customs offices is *Know Before You Go.* For more information, call the **Australian**

Customs Service at © **02/6275-6666** in Australia; **202/797-3189** in the U.S., or log on to www.customs.gov.au.

The duty-free allowance for **New Zealand** is NZ$700. Citizens over 17 can bring in 200 cigarettes, 50 cigars, or 250 grams of tobacco (or a mixture of all three if their combined weight doesn't exceed 250g); plus 4.5 liters of wine and beer, or 1.125 liters of liquor. New Zealand currency does not carry import or export restrictions. Fill out a certificate of export, listing the valuables you are taking out of the country; that way, you can bring them back without paying duty. Most questions are answered in a free pamphlet available at New Zealand consulates and Customs offices: *New Zealand Customs Guide for Travellers, Notice no. 4.* For more information, contact **New Zealand Customs,** The Customhouse, 17–21 Whitmore St., Box 2218, Wellington (© **04/473-6099;** www.customs.govt.nz).

4 Money

It's a good idea to exchange at least some money—just enough to cover airport incidentals and transportation to your hotel—before you leave home so that you can avoid lines at airport ATMs (automated teller machines). You can exchange money at your local American Express or Thomas Cook office or your bank. If you're far away from a bank with currency-exchange services, American Express offers traveler's checks and foreign currency, though with a $15 order fee and additional shipping costs, at www.americanexpress.com or **800/807-6233.**

POUNDS & PENCE

Britain's decimal monetary system is based on the pound (£), which is made up of 100 pence (written as "p"). Pounds are also called **quid** by Britons. There are £1 and £2 coins, as well as coins of 50p, 20p, 10p, 5p, 2p, and 1p. Banknotes come in denominations of £5, £10, £20, and £50.

As a general guideline, the price conversions in this book have been computed at the rate of £1 = $1.85 (U.S.). Bear in mind, however, that exchange rates fluctuate daily.

ATMS

The easiest and best way to get cash away from home is from an ATM (automated teller machine). The **Cirrus** (© **800/424-7787;** www.mastercard.com) and **PLUS** (© **800/843-7587;** www.visa.com) networks span the globe; look at the back of your bank card to find out which network you're on, then call or check online for ATM locations at your destination. Be sure you know your personal identification number (PIN) before you leave home and be sure to find out your daily withdrawal limit before you depart. Also keep in mind that many banks impose a fee every time a card is used at a different bank's ATM, and that fee can be higher for international transactions (up to $5 or more) than for domestic ones (where they're rarely more than $1.50). On top of this, the bank from which you withdraw cash may charge its own

Tips Small Change

When you change money, ask for some small bills or loose change. Petty cash will come in handy for tipping and public transportation. Consider keeping the change separate from your larger bills so that it's readily accessible and you'll be less of a target for theft.

What Things Cost in London	British Pounds	U.S. Dollars
Taxi from Heathrow to Central London	£40.00	$74.00
Underground from Heathrow to Central London	£5.40	$10.00
Local telephone call	£0.20	$0.35
Double room at the Dorchester (very expensive)	£385.00	$712.00
Double room at the Hallam Hotel (moderate)	£100.00	$185.00
Double room at Boston Court (inexpensive)	£69.00	$128.00
Lunch for one at the Ivy (expensive)	£25.00	$46.00
Lunch for one at Ye Olde Cheshire Cheese (moderate)	£20.00	$37.00
Dinner for one, without wine, at Bibendum, The Oyster Bar (expensive)	£38.00	$70.00
Dinner for one, without wine, at Porter's English Restaurant (moderate)	£22.00	$41.00
Dinner for one, without wine, at Cork & Bottle Wine Bar (inexpensive)	£14.00	$26.00
Pint of beer	£2.50	$4.65
Coca-Cola	£1.80	$3.35
Cup of coffee	£1.60	$2.95
Roll of ASA 100 color film, 36 exposures	£7.50	$14.00
Admission to British Museum	Free	Free
Movie ticket	£6.00–£10.00	$11.00–$19.00
Theater ticket	£18.00–£70.00	$33.00–$130.00

fee. To compare banks' ATM fees within the U.S., use **www.bankrate. com**. For international withdrawal fees, ask your bank.

You can also get cash advances on your credit card at an ATM. Keep in mind that credit card companies try to protect themselves from theft by limiting the funds someone can withdraw outside their home country, so call your credit card company before you leave home.

TRAVELER'S CHECKS

Traveler's checks are something of an anachronism from the days before the ATM made cash accessible at any time. Traveler's checks used to be the only sound alternative to traveling with dangerously large amounts of cash. They were as reliable as currency, but, unlike cash, could be replaced if lost or stolen.

These days, traveler's checks are less necessary because most cities have

24-hour ATMs that allow you to withdraw small amounts of cash as needed. However, keep in mind that you will likely be charged an ATM withdrawal fee if the bank is not your own, so if you're withdrawing money every day, you may be better off with traveler's checks—provided that you don't mind showing identification every time you want to cash one.

You can get traveler's checks at almost any bank. **American Express** offers denominations of $20, $50, $100, $500, and (for cardholders only) $1,000. You'll pay a service charge ranging from 1% to 4%. You can also get American Express traveler's checks over the phone by calling © **800/221-7282;** Amex gold and platinum cardholders who use this number are exempt from the 1% fee.

Visa offers traveler's checks at Citibank locations nationwide, as well as at several other banks. The service charge ranges between 1.5% and 2%; checks come in denominations of $20, $50, $100, $500, and $1,000. Call © **800/732-1322** for information. AAA members can obtain Visa checks without a fee at most AAA offices or by calling © **866/339-3378. MasterCard** also offers traveler's checks. Call © **800/223-9920** for a location near you.

Foreign currency traveler's checks are useful if you're traveling to one country, or to the Euro zone; they're accepted at locations such as bed-and-breakfasts where dollar checks may not be, and they minimize the amount of math you have to do at your destination. **American Express, Visa,** and **MasterCard** offer checks in British pounds.

If you choose to carry traveler's checks, be sure to keep a record of their serial numbers separate from your checks in the event that they are stolen or lost. You'll get a refund faster if you know the numbers.

CREDIT CARDS

Credit cards are a safe way to carry money, they provide a convenient record of all your expenses, and they generally offer good exchange rates. You can also withdraw cash advances from your credit cards at banks or ATMs, provided you know your PIN. If you've forgotten yours, or didn't even know you had one, call the number on the back of your credit card and ask the bank to send it to you. It usually takes 5 to 7 business days, though some banks will provide the number over the phone if you tell them your mother's maiden name or some other personal information. Your credit card company will likely charge a commission (1% or 2%) on every foreign purchase you make, but don't sweat this small stuff; for most purchases, you'll still get the best deal with credit cards when you factor in

---

(*Tips* **Dear Visa: I'm off to Old Sodbury!**

Some credit card companies recommend that you notify them of any impending trip abroad so that they don't become suspicious and block your charges when the card is used numerous times in a foreign destination. Even if you don't call your credit card company in advance, you can always call your card's toll-free emergency number if a charge is refused— a good reason to carry the phone number with you. But perhaps the most important lesson here is to carry more than one card with you on your trip; a card might not work for any number of reasons, so having a backup is the smart way to go.

things such as ATM fees and higher traveler's check exchange rates.

Places in Britain that accept credit cards take MasterCard and Visa and to a much lesser extent, American Express. Diners Club trails in a poor fourth position.

5 When to Go

THE WEATHER

Yes, it rains, but you'll rarely get a true downpour—it's heaviest in November (2½ in. on average). British temperatures can range from 30°F to 110°F (–1°C–43°C), but they rarely drop below 35°F (2°C) or go above 78°F (26°C). Evenings are cool, even in summer. Note that the British, who consider chilliness to be wholesome, like to keep the thermostats about 10° below the American comfort level. Hotels have central heating systems, which are usually kept just above the goose bump (in Britspeak, "goose pimple") margin.

London's Average Daytime Temperatures & Rainfall

	Jan	Feb	Mar	Apr	May	June	July	Aug	Sept	Oct	Nov	Dec
Temp. (°F)	40	40	44	49	55	61	64	64	59	52	46	42
Temp. (°C)	4	4	7	9	13	16	16	18	15	11	8	6
Rainfall (in.)	2.1	1.6	1.5	1.5	1.8	1.8	2.2	2.3	1.9	2.2	2.5	1.9
Rainfall (mm)	53	41	38	38	46	46	56	58	48	56	64	48

Cardiff's Average Daytime Temperatures & Rainfall

	Jan	Feb	Mar	Apr	May	June	July	Aug	Sept	Oct	Nov	Dec
Temp. (°F)	40	40	43	46	52	57	61	61	57	52	44	42
Temp. (°C)	4	4	6	8	11	14	16	16	14	11	7	6
Rainfall (in.)	4.2	3.0	2.9	2.5	2.7	2.6	3.1	4.0	3.8	4.6	4.3	4.6
Rainfall (mm)	107	76	74	64	69	66	79	102	97	117	109	117

WHEN YOU'LL FIND BARGAINS

In short, spring offers the countryside at its greenest; autumn brings the bright colors of the northern moorlands; and summer's warmer weather gives rise to the many outdoor music and theater festivals. But winter offers savings across the board and a chance to see Britons going about their everyday lives largely unhindered by tourist invasions.

The cheapest time to travel to Britain is during the off season: from November 1 to December 12 and from December 25 to March 14. In the last few years, the airlines have offered irresistible fares during these periods. Remember that weekday flights are cheaper than weekend fares (often by 10% or more).

Rates generally increase between March 14 and June 5, then hit their peak in high travel seasons between June 6 and September 30 and December 13 and 24. July and August are also when most Britons take their holidays, so besides higher prices, you'll have to deal with crowds and limited availability of accommodations.

You can avoid crowds by planning trips for November or January through March. Sure, it may be rainy and cold—but England doesn't shut down when the tourists leave! In fact, the winter season includes some of London's best theater, opera, ballet, and classical music offerings, and gives visitors a more honest view of English life. Additionally, many hotel prices drop by 20%, and cheaper accommodations offer weekly rates (unheard of during peak travel times). By arriving after the winter holidays, you can also take advantage of post-Christmas sales to buy your fill of woolens, china, crystal, silver, fashion clothing, handicrafts, and curios.

HOLIDAYS

Britain observes New Year's Day, Good Friday, Easter Monday, May Day (first Mon in May), spring and summer bank holidays (the last Mon in May and Aug, respectively), Christmas Day, and Boxing Day (Dec 26).

ENGLAND & WALES CALENDAR OF EVENTS

January

Schroders London Boat Show, ExCel, Docklands (© **01784/ 223627;** www.londonboatshow. net). This is the largest boat show in Europe. Early January.

Charles I Commemoration, London. To mark the anniversary of the execution of King Charles I "in the name of freedom and democracy," hundreds of cavaliers march through central London in 17th-century dress, and prayers are said at Whitehall's Banqueting House. Call © **0207/930-4179** for details. Last Sunday in January.

Chinese New Year, London. The famous Lion Dancers in Soho perform free on the nearest Sunday to Chinese New Year. Either in late January or early February (based on the lunar calendar).

February

Jorvik Festival, York. This 2-week festival celebrates this historic cathedral city's role as a Viking outpost. For more information, call © **01904/621756;** www.jorvik-viking-centre.co.uk. Mid-February.

March

Crufts Dog Show, Birmingham. The English, they say, love their pets more than their offspring. Crufts offers an opportunity to observe the nation's pet lovers doting on 22,000 dogs, representing 180 breeds. It's held at the National Exhibition Centre, Birmingham, West Midlands. Tickets can be purchased at the door. For more information, call © **0121/780-4141;** www.crufts.org.uk. Early March.

April

Martell Grand National Meeting, outside Liverpool. England's premier steeplechase event takes place over a 6.5km (4-mile) course at **Aintree Racecourse,** Aintree (© **01515/ 232600;** www.aintree.co.uk). Early April.

Flora London Marathon. More than 30,000 competitors run from Greenwich Park to Buckingham Palace; call © **020/7902-0189** (www.London-marathon.co.uk) for information. If you'd like to take the challenge, call during May and June for an application. Mid-April.

Easter Parade, London. A memorable parade of brightly colored floats and marching bands occurs around Battersea Park. Easter Monday.

The Shakespeare Season, Stratford-upon-Avon. The Royal Shakespeare Company begins its annual season, presenting works by the Bard in his hometown, at the **Royal Shakespeare Theatre,** Waterside (© **0870/ 609-1110;** www.rsc.org.uk). Tickets are available at the box office, or through such agents as **Keith Prowse Global Tickets** (© **800/ 669-8687;** www.keithprowse.com). April through October.

May

Brighton Festival. England's largest arts festival features some 400 different cultural events. For information, contact the **Brighton Tourist Information Centre,**

10 Bartholomew Sq., Brighton BN1 1JS (℡ **0906/711-2255;** calls cost 50p [95¢] per minute; www. visitbrighton.com). Most of May.

Royal Windsor Horse Show. The country's major show-jumping presentation, held at the Home Park in Windsor, Berkshire, is attended by the queen herself. Call ℡ **0870/121-5370;** or see **www. royal-windsor-horse-show.co.uk** for more information. Mid-May.

Glyndebourne Festival. One of England's major cultural events, this festival is centered at the 1,200-seat Glyndebourne Opera House in Sussex, some 87km (54 miles) south of London. Tickets, which cost anywhere from £13 to £50 ($24–$93), are available from **Glyndebourne Festival Opera Box Office,** Lewes, East Sussex BN8 5UU (℡ **01273/ 812321;** www.glyndebourne.com). Mid-April to late August.

Bath International Music Festival. One of Europe's most prestigious international festivals of music and the arts features as many as 1,000 performers at various venues in Bath. For information, contact the **Bath Festivals Trust,** 5 Broad St., Bath, Somerset BA1 5LJ (℡ **01225/ 462231;** www.bathfestivals.org.uk). Late May to early June.

Chelsea Flower Show, London. The best of British gardening, with plants and flowers of the season, is displayed at the Chelsea Royal Hospital. Contact the local British Tourist Authority Office to find out which overseas reservations agency is handling ticket sales, or contact the **Chelsea Show Ticket Office,** Shows Department, Royal Horticultural Society, 80 Vincent Square, London SW1P 2PE (℡ **020/7828-4125;** www.rhs.org.uk). Late May.

Royal Academy's Summer Exhibition, London. This institution, founded in 1768, has for some 2 centuries held Summer Exhibitions of living painters at Burlington House, Piccadilly Circus. Call ℡ **020/7300-8000;** www.royal academy.org.uk for more information. Early June to mid-August.

Chichester Festival Theatre. Some great classic and modern plays are presented at this West Sussex theater. For tickets and information, contact the **Festival Theatre,** Oaklands Park, West Sussex PO19 4AP (℡ **01243/781312;** www.cft. org.uk). The season runs May through October.

June

Vodafone Derby Stakes. This famous horseracing event (the "Darby," as it's called here) is held at Epsom Downs, Epsom, Surrey. Men wear top hats; women, including the queen, put on silly millinery creations. For more details, call ℡ **01372/470047** or check out **www.epsomderby.co.uk.** First week of June.

Trooping the Colour. This is the queen's official birthday parade, a quintessential British event, with exquisite pageantry and pomp as she inspects her regiments and takes their salute as they parade their colors before her at the Horse Guards Parade, Whitehall. Tickets for the parade and two reviews, held on preceding Saturdays, are allocated by ballot. Applicants must write between January 1 and the end of February, enclosing a self-addressed stamped envelope or International Reply Coupon to the Ticket Office, HQ Household Division, Horse Guards, Whitehall, London SW1X 6AA. Tickets are free. The ballot is held in mid-March, and only successful applicants are informed in April. Call ℡ **020/7414-2479** for more details. Held on a day designated in June (not necessarily the queen's actual birthday).

Grosvenor House Art and Antique Fair, London. This very prestigious antiques fair is held at Le Méridien Grosvenor House, Park Lane. For information, contact **Grosvenor House Art and Antiques Fair,** Grosvenor House, 86–90 Park Lane, London W1A 3AA (℗ **020/ 74958743;** www.grosvenor-antiques fair.co.uk). Second week of June.

Aldeburgh Festival of Music and the Arts. The composer Benjamin Britten launched this 2-week festival in 1948. For more details on the events and for the year-round program, write to **Aldeburgh Foundation,** High Street, Aldeburgh, Suffolk IP17 1SP (℗ **01728/ 687110;** www.aldeburgh.co.uk). Mid- to late June.

Royal Ascot Week. Though Ascot Racecourse is open year-round for guided tours, events, exhibitions, and conferences, there are 25 race days throughout the year, with the feature races being the Royal. For information, contact **Ascot Racecourse,** Ascot, Berkshire SL5 7JX (℗ **01344/622211;** www.ascot.co. uk). Meeting in June, Diamond Day in late July, and the Festival at Ascot in late September.

The Exeter Festival. The town of Exeter hosts more than 150 events celebrating classical music, ranging from concerts and opera to lectures. Festival dates and offerings vary from year to year; more information is available by contacting the **Exeter Festival Office** at ℗ **01392/ 265205** (www.exeter.gov.uk). Late June to mid-July.

Lawn Tennis Championships, Wimbledon, London. Ever since players took to the grass courts at Wimbledon in 1877, this tournament has attracted quite a crowd, and there's still an excited hush and a certain thrill at Centre Court.

Savor the strawberries and cream that are part of the experience. Early bookings for the world's most famous tennis tournament are strongly advised. Acquiring tickets and overnight lodgings during the annual tennis competitions at Wimbledon can be difficult to arrange independently. Two outfits that book both hotel accommodations and tickets to the event include **Steve Furgal's International Tennis Tours,** 11305 Rancho Bernardo Rd., Suite 108, San Diego, CA 92127 (℗ **800/258-3664** or 858/675-3555; www.tours 4tennis.com); and **Championship Tennis Tours,** 15221 N. Clubgate Dr., Suite 1058, Scottsdale, AZ 85254 (℗ **800/468-3664** or 480/ 429-7700; www.tennistours.com). Tickets for Centre and Number One courts are obtainable through a lottery. Write in from August to December to **All England Lawn Tennis Club,** P.O. Box 98, Church Road, Wimbledon, London SW19 5AE (℗ **020/8944-1066;** www. wimbledon.org). Outside court tickets are available daily, but be prepared to wait in line. Late June to early July.

City of London Festival. This annual art festival is held in venues throughout the city. Call ℗ **020/ 7377-0540;** www.colf.org for information. Mid-June to mid-July.

Shakespeare Under the Stars, London. The Bard's works are performed at the **Open Air Theatre,** Inner Circle, Regent's Park, NW1 4NU, in London. Take the Tube to Baker Street. Performances are Monday through Saturday at 8pm; Wednesday, Thursday, and Saturday also at 2:30pm. Call ℗ **020/ 7935-5756;** www.openairtheatre. org for more information. Previews begin in June and last throughout the summer.

Ludlow Festival. This is one of England's major arts festivals, complete with an open-air Shakespeare performance within the Inner Bailey of Ludlow Castle. Concerts, lectures, readings, exhibitions, and workshops round out the offerings. From March onward, a schedule can be obtained from the box office. Write to **Ludlow Festival Box Office,** Castle Square, Ludlow, Shropshire SY8 1AY, enclosing a self-addressed stamped envelope (*C* **01584/ 872150;** www.ludlowfestival.co.uk). Late June to early July.

July

Henley Royal Regatta. This international rowing competition in Oxfordshire is the premier event on the English social calendar. For more information, call *C* **01491/572153;** www.hrr.co.uk. Early July.

Kenwood Lakeside Concerts, London. These annual concerts on the north side of Hampstead Heath have continued a British tradition of outdoor performances for nearly 50 years. Fireworks displays and laser shows enliven the premier musical performances. The audience catches the music as it drifts across the lake from the performance shell. For more information call *C* **020/8348-1286.** Every Saturday from early July to late August.

Cardiff Festival. In venues across the Welsh capital, this 3-week festival features pop, jazz, theater, street performances, funfairs, opera, comedies, and children's events. Most events are free and take place in public and open-air places. For more information, contact the **Cardiff Festival,** Health Park, Cardiff CF4 4EP (*C* **029/2087- 2087;** www.cardiff-festival.com). Late June to early August.

Aberystwyth Musical Festival. This is a pageant of cultural and sporting events in Aberystwyth, the cultural center of the western section of middle Wales. For more information, contact **Aberystwyth Arts Centre,** Penglais, Aberystwyth SW23 3DE (*C* **01970/622889;** www.musicfest-aberystwyth.org). End of July.

The Proms, London. A night at "The Proms"—the annual Henry Wood promenade concerts at Royal Albert Hall—attracts music aficionados from around the world. Staged almost daily (except for a few Sun), these traditional concerts were launched in 1895 and are the principal summer engagements for the BBC Symphony Orchestra. Cheering and clapping, Union Jacks on parade, banners, and balloons—it's great summer fun. Call *C* **020/ 7589-8212** or check out **www. bbc.co.uk/proms** for more details. Mid-July to mid-September.

August

Skandia Cowes Week, off the Isle of Wight. For details about this yachting festival, call *C* **01983/ 295744;** www.cowesweek.co.uk. Early August.

Pontardawe International Music Festival. The little Welsh village of Pontardawe, lying 13km (8 miles) north of Swansea, attracts some of the world's leading folk and rock musicians for its annual summer concert series. For more information, call *C* **01792/830200** or see www.pontardawefestival.org.uk. Mid-August.

Notting Hill Carnival, Ladbroke Grove, London. Notting Hill is the setting for one of the largest annual street festivals in Europe, attracting more than half a million people. There's live reggae and soul music plus great Caribbean food. Call *C* **020/8964-0544** or see **www. portowebbo.co.uk** for information. Two days in late August.

International Beatles Week, Liverpool. Tens of thousands of fans gather in Liverpool to celebrate the music of the Fab Four. There's a whole series of concerts from international cover bands, plus tributes, auctions, and tours. **Cavern City Tours,** a local company, offers hotel and festival packages that include accommodations and tickets to tours and events, starting around £107 ($197) for 2 nights. For information, contact **Cavern City Tours** at ✆ **0151/236-9091;** www.cavern-liverpool.co.uk or the **Tourist Information Centre** in Liverpool at ✆ **0151/709-8111.** Late August.

September

Burghley Horse Trials, Lincolnshire. This annual event is staged on the grounds of the largest Elizabethan house in England, Burghley House, Stamford, Lincolnshire (✆ **01780/752131;** www.burghley-horse.co.uk). Early September.

Raising of the Thames Barrier, Unity Way, SE18. Once a year, usually in September, a full test is done on this miracle of modern engineering; all 10 massive steel gates are raised against the low and high tides. Call ✆ **020/8854-1373** for exact date and time.

Horse of the Year Show, Wembley Arena, Wembley. Riders fly from every continent to join in this festive display of horsemanship (much appreciated by the queen). The British press calls it an "equine extravaganza." It's held at **Wembley Arena,** outside London. For more information, call ✆ **020/8900-9282** or see **www.hoys.co.uk.** Late September to early October.

October

Cheltenham Festival of Literature. This Cotswold event features readings, book exhibitions, and theatrical performances—all in the famed spa town of Gloucestershire. Call ✆ **01242/263494;** www. cheltenhamfestivals.co.uk for more details. Early to mid-October.

Opening of Parliament, London. Ever since the 17th century, when the English beheaded Charles I, British monarchs have been denied the right to enter the House of Commons. Instead, the monarch opens Parliament in the House of Lords, reading an official speech that is in fact written by the government. Queen Elizabeth II rides from Buckingham Palace to Westminster in a royal coach accompanied by the Yeoman of the Guard and the Household Cavalry. The public galleries are open on a first-come, first-served basis. Call ✆ **0870/960-3773** or surf the Web to **www. parliament.uk.** Late October to mid-November.

Quit Rents Ceremony, London. The origins of this ceremony go back so far they have been forgotten. The City Solicitor pays the Queen's Rememberancer (medieval term for collector of the queen's rents) token rents for properties long ago leased—in many cases no longer standing. It's all for fun, show, and tradition. For example, the solicitor will pay the rememberancer two faggots of wood, a billhook, and a hatchet for land in Shropshire. Or else 61 nails and 6 horseshoes for a long-gone forge in the Strand. The ceremony is held at the Royal Courts of Justice. Call ✆ **020/7947-6000** for more information. Early October.

November

London-Brighton Veteran Car Run. This race begins in London's Hyde Park and ends in the seaside resort of Brighton, in East Sussex. Call ✆ **01753/765-000** or see **www. vccofgb.co.uk** for more details. First Sunday in November.

Guy Fawkes Night, throughout England. This British celebration commemorates the anniversary of the "Gunpowder Plot," an attempt to blow up King James I and Parliament. Huge organized bonfires are lit throughout London, and Guy Fawkes, the plot's most famous conspirator, is burned in effigy. Check *Time Out* for locations. Early November.

Lord Mayor's Procession and Show, The City, London. The queen has to ask permission to enter the square mile in London called The City—and the right of refusal has been jealously guarded by London merchants since the 17th century. Suffice it to say that the lord mayor is a powerful character, and the procession from the Guildhall to the Royal Courts is appropriately impressive. You can watch the procession from the street; the banquet is by invitation only. Call ✆ **020/7332-1757;** www.lordmayorsshow.org for details. Second Saturday in November.

6 Travel Insurance

Given the uncertainties of international travel—lost luggage, trip cancellation, a medical emergency—buying insurance for your trip to Britain may be a good idea.

Check your existing insurance policies and credit card coverage before you buy travel insurance. You may already be covered for lost luggage, canceled tickets, or medical expenses. The cost of travel insurance varies widely, depending on the cost and length of your trip, your health, and the type of trip you're taking.

TRIP-CANCELLATION INSURANCE Trip-cancellation insurance helps you get your money back if you have to back out of a trip, if you have to go home early, or if your travel supplier goes bankrupt. Allowed reasons for cancellation can range from sickness to natural disasters to the State Department declaring your destination unsafe for travel. In this unstable world, trip-cancellation insurance is a good buy if you're getting tickets well in advance—who knows what the state of the world, or of your airline, will be in 9 months? Insurance policy details vary, so read the fine print—and especially make sure that your airline is on the list of carriers covered in case of bankruptcy. For information, contact one of the following insurers: **Access America** (✆ 866/807-3982; www.accessamerica.com); **Travel Guard International** (✆ 800/826-4919; www.travelguard.com); **Travel Insured International** (✆ 800/243-3174; www.travelinsured.com); and **Travelex Insurance Services** (✆ 888/457-4602; www.travelex-insurance.com).

MEDICAL INSURANCE Most health insurance policies cover you if you get sick away from home—but check, particularly if you're insured by an HMO. With the exception of certain HMOs and Medicare/Medicaid, your medical insurance should cover medical treatment—even hospital care—overseas. However, most out-of-country hospitals make you pay your bills up front, and send you a refund after you've returned home and filed the necessary paperwork. And in a worst-case scenario, there's the high cost of emergency evacuation. If you require additional medical insurance, try **MEDEX International** (✆ 800/527-0218 or 410/453-6300; www.medexassist.com) or **Travel Assistance International** (✆ 800/821-2828; www.travelassistance.com; for general information on services, call the company's Worldwide Assistance Services, Inc., at ✆ **800/777-8710**).

LOST-LUGGAGE INSURANCE

On domestic flights, checked baggage is covered up to $2,500 per ticketed passenger. On international flights (including U.S. portions of international trips), baggage is limited to approximately $9.05 per pound, up to approximately $635 per checked bag. If you plan to check items more valuable than the standard liability, find out whether your valuables are covered by your homeowner's policy, get baggage insurance as part of your comprehensive travel-insurance package or buy Travel Guard's "BagTrak" product. Don't buy insurance at the airport, as it's usually overpriced. Be sure to take any valuables or irreplaceable items with you in your carry-on luggage, as many valuables (including books, money, and electronics) aren't covered by airline policies.

If your luggage is lost, immediately file a lost-luggage claim at the airport, detailing the luggage contents. For most airlines, you must report delayed, damaged, or lost baggage within 4 hours of arrival. The airlines are required to deliver luggage, once found, directly to your house or destination free of charge.

7 Health & Safety

STAYING HEALTHY

You'll encounter few health risks while traveling in Britain. The tap water is safe to drink, the milk is pasteurized, and health services are good. The crisis over mad cow disease appears to be over, as do the effects of the epidemic of foot-and-mouth disease, which began in the spring of 2001 (and which cannot be passed to humans). Other than that, traveling to England doesn't pose any health risk.

WHAT TO DO IF YOU GET SICK AWAY FROM HOME

If you need a doctor, your hotel can recommend one, or you can contact your embassy or consulate. Outside London, dial © **100** and ask the operator for the local police, who will give you the name, address, and telephone number of a doctor in your area. *Note:* U.S. visitors who become ill while they're in Britain are eligible only for free *emergency* care. For other treatment, including follow-up care, you'll be asked to pay.

In most cases, your existing health plan will provide the coverage you need. But double-check; you may want to buy **travel medical insurance** instead. (See the section on insurance, above.) Bring your insurance ID card with you when you travel.

If you suffer from a chronic illness, consult your doctor before your departure. For conditions such as epilepsy, diabetes, or heart problems, wear a **Medic Alert Identification Tag** (© **800/825-3785;** www.medicalert.org), which will immediately alert doctors to your condition and give them access to your records through Medic Alert's 24-hour hot line.

Pack **prescription medications** in your carry-on luggage, and carry prescription medications in their original containers, with pharmacy labels—otherwise they won't make it through airport security. Also bring along copies of your prescriptions in case you lose your pills or run out. Don't forget an extra pair of contact lenses or prescription glasses. Carry the generic name of prescription medicines, in case a local pharmacist is unfamiliar with the brand name.

Contact the **International Association for Medical Assistance to Travelers (IAMAT)** (© **716/754-4883,** or 416/652-0137 in Canada; www.iamat.org) for tips on travel and health concerns in Britain. The United States

Centers for Disease Control and Prevention (© 800/311-3435; www.cdc.gov) provides up-to-date information on necessary vaccines and health hazards by region or country. If you get sick, consider asking your hotel concierge to recommend a local doctor—even his or her own. You can also try the emergency room at a local hospital; many have walk-in clinics for emergency cases that are not life-threatening. You may not get immediate attention, but you won't pay the high price of an emergency room visit.

STAYING SAFE

Like all big cities, London has its share of crime, but in general it is one of the safer destinations of Europe. Pickpockets are a major concern, though violent crime is relatively rare, especially in the heart of London, which hasn't seen a Jack the Ripper in a long time. Even so, it is not wise to go walking in parks at night. King's Cross at night is a dangerous area, frequented by prostitutes and the johns who purchase their services. In London, take all the precautions a prudent traveler would in going anywhere, be it in Los Angeles, Paris, or New York. Conceal your wallet or else hold onto your purse, and don't flaunt your wealth, be it jewelry or cash. In other words, do as your mother told you.

The same precautions prevail in larger cities such as Birmingham, Leeds, and Manchester. However, in rural Britain you are relatively safe, though if you watch a lot of murder mysteries on TV or read about them in paperbacks, there seem to be a lot of murders going on. Nonetheless, Britain is one of the safer destinations of the world, but the sensible precautions one would heed anywhere prevail, of course. In these uncertain times, it is always prudent to check the U.S. State Department's travel advisories at **http://travel.state.gov**.

8 Specialized Travel Resources

TRAVELERS WITH DISABILITIES

Many London hotels, museums, restaurants, and sightseeing attractions have wheelchair ramps, less so in rural England. Persons with disabilities are often granted special discounts at attractions, called "concessions" in Britain, and, in some cases, nightclubs. Free information and advice is available from **Holiday Care Service,** Sunley House, 7th Floor, 4 Bedford Park, Croydon, Surrey CR0 2AP (© **0845/124-9971;** fax 0845/124-9972; www.holidaycare.org).

Many bookstores in London carry *Access in London* (£7.95/$15), a publication listing facilities for persons with disabilities, among other things.

The transport system, cinemas, and theaters are still pretty much off-limits, but **London Transport** publishes a leaflet called *Access to the Underground,* which gives details of elevators and ramps at individual Underground stations; call © **020/7941-4500.** And the **London black cab** is perfectly suited for those in wheelchairs; the roomy interiors have plenty of room for maneuvering.

London's most visible organization for information about access to theaters, cinemas, galleries, museums, and restaurants is **Artsline,** 54 Chalton St., London NW1 1HS (© **020/7388-2227;** fax 020/7383-2653; www.artsline.org.uk). It offers free information about wheelchair access, theaters with hearing aids, tourist attractions, and cinemas. Artsline mails information to North America, but it's more helpful to contact Artsline once you arrive in London; the line is staffed Monday through Friday from 9:30am to 5:30pm.

An organization that cooperates closely with Artsline is **Tripscope,** The Vassall Centre, Gill Ave., Bristol BS16 2QQ (© **08457/585641** or 0117/939-7782; www.tripscope.org.uk), which offers advice on travel in Britain and elsewhere for persons with disabilities.

Many travel agencies offer customized tours and itineraries for travelers with disabilities. **Flying Wheels Travel** (© **507/451-5005;** www.flyingwheelstravel.com) offers escorted tours and cruises that emphasize sports and private tours in minivans with lifts. **Accessible Journeys** (© **800/846-4537** or 610/521-0339; www.disabilitytravel.com) caters specifically to slow walkers and wheelchair travelers and their families and friends.

Organizations that offer assistance to travelers with disabilities include the **MossRehab** (www.mossresourcenet.org), which provides a library of accessible-travel resources online; the **Society for Accessible Travel and Hospitality** (© **212/447-7284;** www.sath.org; annual membership fees: $45 adults, $30 seniors and students), which offers a wealth of travel resources for all types of disabilities and informed recommendations on destinations, access guides, travel agents, tour operators, vehicle rentals, and companion services; and the **American Foundation for the Blind** (© **800/232-5463;** www.afb.org), which provides information on traveling with Seeing Eye dogs.

Information for travelers with disabilities going to Wales is available from **Disability Wales,** Caerbragdy Industrial Estate, Bedwas Road, Caerphilly, Mid Glamorgan CF8 3SL (© **029/2088-7325;** www.dwac.demon.co.uk). The staff can tell you about facilities suitable in touring, accommodations, restaurants, cafes, pubs, public restrooms, attractions, and other phases of hospitality to make a trip pleasurable.

For more information specifically targeted to travelers with disabilities, the community website **iCan (www.icanonline.net/channels/travel/index.cfm)** has destination guides and several regular columns on accessible travel. Also check out the quarterly magazine **Emerging Horizons** ($15 per year, $20 outside the U.S.; www.emerginghorizons.com), and *Open World Magazine,* published by the Society for Accessible Travel and Hospitality (see above; subscription: $18 per year, $35 outside the U.S.).

GAY & LESBIAN TRAVELERS

Britain has one of the most active gay and lesbian scenes in the world, centered mainly around London, much less so in Cardiff. Gay bars, restaurants, and centers are also found in all large English cities, notably Bath, Birmingham, Manchester, and especially Brighton.

Lesbian and Gay Switchboard (© **020/7837-7324**) is open 24 hours a day, providing information about gay-related activities in London or advice in general. The **Bisexual Helpline** (© **020/8569-7500**) offers useful information, but only on Tuesday and Wednesday from 7:30 to 9:30pm, and Saturday between 9:30am and noon. London's best gay-oriented bookstore is **Gay's the Word,** 66 Marchmont St., WC1 (© **020/7278-7654;** www.gaystheword.co.uk; Tube: Russell Square), the largest such store in Britain. The staff is friendly and helpful and will offer advice about the ever-changing scene in London. It's open Monday through Saturday from 10am to 6:30pm, and Sunday from 2 to 6pm. At Gay's the Word as well as other gay-friendly venues, you can find a number of publications, many free, including the popular *Boyz.* Another free publication is *Pink Paper* (with a good lesbian section), and check out *9X,* filled with data about new clubs and whatever else is hot on the scene.

The International Gay & Lesbian Travel Association (IGLTA) (© 800/448-8550 or 954/776-2626; www.iglta.org) is the trade association for the gay and lesbian travel industry, and offers an online directory of gay and lesbian-friendly travel businesses.

Many agencies offer tours and travel itineraries specifically for gay and lesbian travelers. **Above and Beyond Tours** (© 800/397-2681; www.abovebeyondtours.com) is the exclusive gay and lesbian tour operator for United Airlines. **Now, Voyager** (© 800/255-6951; www.nowvoyager.com) is a well-known San Francisco–based gay-owned and -operated travel service.

The following travel guides are available at most travel bookstores and gay and lesbian bookstores, or you can order them from **Giovanni's Room** bookstore, 1145 Pine St., Philadelphia, PA 19107 (© 215/923-2960; www.giovannisroom.com); *Frommer's Gay & Lesbian Europe,* an excellent travel resource; *Out and About* (© 800/929-2268 or 415-644-8044; www.outandabout.com), which offers guidebooks and a newsletter 10 times a year packed with solid information on the global gay and lesbian scene; *Spartacus International Gay Guide* and *Odysseus,* both good, annual English-language guidebooks focused on gay men; the *Damron* guides, with separate, annual books for gay men and lesbians; and *Gay Travel A to Z: The World of Gay & Lesbian Travel Options at Your Fingertips,* by Marianne Ferrari (Ferrari Publications; Box 35575, Phoenix, AZ 85069), a very good gay and lesbian guidebook series.

SENIOR TRAVEL

Many discounts are available to seniors. Be advised that in Britain you often have to be a member of an association to get discounts. Public-transportation reductions, for example, are available only to holders of British Pension books. However, many attractions do offer discounts for seniors (women 60 or over and men 65 or over). Even if discounts aren't posted, ask if they're available.

If you're over 60, you're eligible for special 10% discounts on **British Airways (BA)** through its Privileged Traveler program. You also qualify for reduced restrictions on APEX cancellations. Discounts are also granted for BA tours and for intra-Britain air tickets booked in North America. **BritRail** offers seniors discounted rates on first-class rail passes around Britain. See "By Train from Continental Europe" in the "Getting There" section, later in this chapter.

Don't be shy about asking for discounts, but carry some kind of identification that shows your date of birth. Also, mention you're a senior when you make your reservations. Many hotels offer seniors discounts. In most cities, people over the age of 60 qualify for reduced admission to theaters, museums, and other attractions, and discounted fares on public transportation.

Members of **AARP,** 601 E St. NW, Washington, DC 20049 (© 888/687-2277 or 202/434-2277; www.aarp.org), get discounts on hotels, airfares, and car rentals. AARP offers members a wide range of benefits, including *AARP: The Magazine* and a monthly newsletter. Anyone over 50 can join.

Many reliable agencies and organizations target the 50-plus market. **Elderhostel** (© 877/426-8056; www.elderhostel.org) arranges study programs for those ages 55 and over (and a spouse or companion of any age) in the U.S. and in more than 80 countries around the world. Most courses last 2 to 4 weeks abroad, and many include airfare, accommodations in university dormitories or modest inns, meals, and tuition.

Recommended publications offering travel resources and discounts for seniors include: the quarterly magazine *Travel 50 & Beyond* (www.travel50andbeyond.com); *Travel Unlimited: Uncommon Adventures for the Mature Traveler* (Avalon); *101 Tips for Mature Travelers,* available from Grand Circle Travel (℄ **800/221-2610** or 617/350-7500; www.gct.com); *The 50+ Traveler's Guidebook* (St. Martin's Press); and *Unbelievably Good Deals and Great Adventures That You Absolutely Can't Get Unless You're Over 50* (McGraw-Hill).

FAMILY TRAVEL

If you have enough trouble getting your kids out of the house in the morning, dragging them thousands of miles away may seem like an insurmountable challenge. But family travel can be immensely rewarding, giving you new ways of seeing the world through smaller pairs of eyes.

On airlines, you must request a special menu for children at least 24 hours in advance. If baby food is required, however, bring your own and ask a flight attendant to warm it to the right temperature.

Arrange ahead of time for such necessities as a crib, bottle warmer, and a car seat (in England, small children aren't allowed to ride in the front seat).

If you're staying with friends in London, you can rent baby equipment from **Chelsea Baby Hire,** 31 Osborne House, 414 Wimbledon Park Rd., SW19 6PW (℄ **020/8789-9673;** www.chelseababyhire.com). **London Black Cab** (℄ **0845/108-3000;** www.londonblackcab.com) is a lifesaver for families; the roomy interior allows a stroller to be lifted right into the cab without unstrapping baby.

A recommendable London babysitting service is **Childminders** (℄ **020/7935-3000;** www.babysitter.co.uk).

You can also find babysitting available at most hotels.

To find out what's on for kids while you're in London, pick up the leaflet *Where to Take Children,* published by the London Tourist Board. If you have specific questions, ring **Kidsline** (℄ **020/7487-5040;** www.kidsline.co.uk) Monday through Friday from 4 to 6pm and summer holidays from 9am to 4pm, or the **London Tourist Board's** special children's information lines (℄ **0891/505490**) for listings of special events and places to visit for children. The number is accessible in London at 50p (95¢) per minute.

In this book, look also for our "Kids" icon, indicating attractions, restaurants, or hotels and resorts that are especially family friendly.

Familyhostel (℄ **800/733-9753;** www.learn.unh.edu/familyhostel) takes the whole family, including kids ages 8 to 15, on moderately priced domestic and international learning vacations. Lectures, field trips, and sightseeing are guided by a team of academics.

You can find good family oriented vacation advice on the Internet from sites such as the **Family Travel Network** (www.familytravelnetwork.com); **Traveling Internationally with Your Kids** (www.travelwithyourkids.com), a comprehensive site offering sound advice for long-distance and international travel with children; and **Family Travel Files** (www.thefamilytravelfiles.com), which offers an online magazine and a directory of off-the-beaten-path tours and tour operators for families.

STUDENT TRAVEL

If you're planning to travel outside the U.S., you'd be wise to arm yourself with an **International Student Identity Card (ISIC),** which offers substantial savings on rail passes, plane tickets, and entrance fees. It also provides you with basic health and life insurance and a 24-hour help line. The card is available for $22 from **STA Travel,** 86 Old Brompton Rd., London SW7 3LQ (© **800/781-4040** or 020/7581-4132; www.statravel.com; Tube: South Kensington), the biggest student travel agency in the world. If you're no longer a student but are still under 26, you can get a **International Youth Travel Card (IYTC)** for the same price from the same people, which entitles you to some discounts (but not on museum admissions).

    Travel CUTS (© **800/667-2887,** 416/614-2887, or 020/7361-6090 in London; www.travelcuts.com) offers similar services for both Canadians and U.S. residents. Irish students should turn to **USIT** (© **01/602-1600;** www.usitnow.ie).

    The International Student House, 229 Great Portland St., W1W 5PN (© **020/7631-8310;** www.ish.org.uk), lies at the foot of Regent's Park across from the Tube stop for Great Portland Street. It's a beehive of activity, such as discos and film showings, and rents blandly furnished, institutional rooms for £34 ($62) single, £26 to £27 ($47–$50) per person double, £21 ($19) per person triple, and £19 ($34) per person in a dorm. Laundry facilities are available; a £10 ($19) key deposit is charged. Reserve way in advance.

    University of London Student Union, Malet St., WC1E 7HY (© **020/7664-2000;** www.ulucube.com; Tube: Goodge St. or Russell Sq.), is the best place to go to learn about student activities in the Greater London area. The Union has a swimming pool, fitness center, gymnasium, general store, sports shop, ticket agency, banks, bars, inexpensive restaurants, venues for live events, an office of STA Travel, and many other facilities. It's open Monday through Thursday from 8:30am to 11pm, Friday from 8:30am to 1pm, Saturday

from 9am to 2pm, and Sunday from 9:30am to 10:30pm. Bulletin boards provide a rundown on events; some you may be able to attend, others may be "closed door."

SINGLE TRAVELERS

Many people prefer traveling alone, and for independent travelers, solo journeys offer infinite opportunities to make friends and meet locals. Unfortunately, if you like resorts, tours, or cruises, you're likely to get hit with a "single supplement" to the base price. Single travelers can avoid these supplements, of course, by agreeing to room with other single travelers on the trip. An even better idea is to find a compatible roommate before you go from one of the many roommate locator agencies.

    Travel Companion Exchange (TCE) (© **631/454-0880;** www.travelcompanions.com) is one of the nation's oldest roommate finders for single travelers. Register with them and find a travel mate who will split the cost of the room with you and be around as little, or as often, as you like during the day. **Travel Buddies Singles Travel Club** (© **800/998-9099;** www.travelbuddiesworldwide.com), based in Canada, runs small, intimate, single-friendly group trips and will match you with a roommate free of charge and save you the cost of single supplements. **TravelChums** (© **212/787-2621;** www.travelchums.com) is an Internet-only travel-companion matching service with elements of an online personals-type site, hosted by the respected New York–based Shaw Guides travel service. **The Single Gourmet Club** (www.singlegourmet.com/chapters.html) is an international social, dining, and travel club for singles of all ages, with offices in 21 cities in the U.S. and Canada. Membership costs $375 for the first year; $175 to renew.

    Many reputable tour companies offer singles-only trips. **Singles Travel**

International (𝄞 877/765-6874; www.singlestravelintl.com) offers singles-only trips to London. **Backroads** (𝄞 800/462-2848; www.backroads.com) offers more than 160 active trips to 30 destinations worldwide, including Bali, Morocco, and Costa Rica.

For more information, check out Eleanor Berman's *Traveling Solo: Advice and Ideas for More Than 250*

Great Vacations (Globe Pequot), a guide with advice on traveling alone, whether on your own or on a group tour. Or turn to the **Travel Alone and Love It** website (www.travelalone andloveit.com), designed by former flight attendant Sharon Wingler, the author of the book of the same name. Her site is full of tips for single travelers.

9 Planning Your Trip Online

SURFING FOR AIRFARES

The "big three" online travel agencies, **Expedia.com, Travelocity.com,** and **Orbitz.com** sell most of the air tickets bought on the Internet. (Canadian travelers should try Expedia.ca and Travelocity.ca; U.K. residents can go to Expedia.co.uk and Opodo.co.uk.) Each has different business deals with the airlines and may offer different fares on the same flights, so it's wise to shop around. Expedia and Travelocity will also send you **e-mail notification** when a cheap fare becomes available to your favorite destination. Of the smaller travel agency websites, **Side-Step** (www.sidestep.com) has gotten the best reviews from Frommer's authors. It's a browser add-on that purports to "search 140 sites at once," but in reality only beats competitors' fares as often as other sites do.

Also remember to check **airline websites,** especially those for low-fare carriers whose fares are often misreported or simply missing from travel agency websites. Even with major airlines, you can often shave a few bucks from a fare by booking directly through the airline and avoiding a travel agency's transaction fee. But you'll get these discounts only by **booking online:** Most airlines now offer online-only fares that even their phone agents know nothing about. For the websites of airlines that fly to and from your destination, go to "Getting There," later in this chapter.

Great **last-minute deals** are available through free weekly e-mail services provided directly by the airlines. Most of these are announced on Tuesday or Wednesday and must be purchased online. Sign up for these alerts at airline websites or check megasites that compile comprehensive lists of last-minute specials, such as **Smarter Living** (smarterliving.com). For last-minute trips, **lastminute.com** in Europe often has better deals than the major-label sites.

If you're willing to give up some control over your flight details, use an **opaque fare service** such as **Priceline** (www.priceline.com; www.priceline.co.uk for Europeans) or **Hotwire** (www.hotwire.com). Both offer rock-bottom prices in exchange for travel on a "mystery airline" at a mysterious time of day, often with a mysterious change of planes en route. The mystery airlines are all major, well-known carriers. But your chances of getting a 6am or 11pm flight are pretty high. Hotwire tells you flight prices before you buy. Priceline usually has better deals than Hotwire, and you no longer have to play their "name your price" game. You also have the option to pick your flights, times, and airlines from a list of prices they offer. If you're new at this, the helpful folks at **BiddingForTravel** (www.biddingfortravel.com) do a good job of demystifying Priceline's prices. Priceline and Hotwire are great for flights between the U.S. and England.

Frommers.com: The Complete Travel Resource

For an excellent travel-planning resource, we highly recommend Frommers.com (www.frommers.com). We're a little biased, of course, but we guarantee that you'll find the travel tips, reviews, monthly vacation giveaways, and online-booking capabilities thoroughly indispensable. Among the special features are our popular **Message Boards,** where Frommer's readers post queries and share advice (sometimes even our authors show up to answer questions); **Frommers.com Newsletter,** for the latest travel bargains and insider travel secrets; and **Frommer's Destinations Section,** where you'll get expert travel tips, hotel and dining recommendations, and advice on the sights to see for more than 3,000 destinations around the globe. When your research is done, the **Online Reservations System** (www.frommers.com/book_a_trip) takes you to Frommer's preferred online partners for booking your vacation at affordable prices.

For much more about airfares and savvy air-travel tips and advice, pick up a copy of *Frommer's Fly Safe, Fly Smart* (Wiley Publishing, Inc.).

SURFING FOR HOTELS

Of the "big three" sites, **Expedia** may be the best choice for hotel bookings online, thanks to its long list of special deals. **Travelocity** runs a close second. Hotel specialist sites **hotels.com** and **hoteldiscounts.com** are also reliable. An excellent free program, **TravelAxe** (www.travelaxe.net), can help you search multiple hotel sites at once, even ones you may never have heard of.

Priceline and Hotwire are even better for hotels than for airfares; with both, you're allowed to pick the neighborhood and quality level of your hotel before offering up your money.

Priceline's hotel product covers a good selection of U.K. hotels, though it's much better at getting five-star lodging for three-star prices than at finding anything at the bottom of the scale. *Note:* Hotwire overrates its hotels by one star—what Hotwire calls a four-star is a three-star anywhere else.

SURFING FOR RENTAL CARS

For booking rental cars online, you can usually find the best deals at rental-car company websites, although all the major online travel agencies also offer rental-car reservations services. Priceline and Hotwire work well for rental cars, too; the only "mystery" is which major rental company you get, and for most travelers the difference between Hertz, Avis, and Budget is negligible.

10 The 21st-Century Traveler

INTERNET ACCESS AWAY FROM HOME

Travelers have any number of ways to check their e-mail and access the Internet on the road. Of course, using your own laptop—or even a PDA (personal digital assistant) or electronic organizer with a modem—gives you the most flexibility. But if you don't have a computer, you can still access your e-mail and even your office computer from cybercafes.

WITHOUT YOUR OWN COMPUTER

It's hard nowadays to find a city that *doesn't* have a few cybercafes. Although there's no definitive directory for cyber-cafes—these are independent businesses, after all—three places to start looking are at **www.cybercaptive.com**, **www.netcafeguide.com**, and **www.cybercafe.com**.

Aside from formal cybercafes, most **youth hostels** have at least one computer you can get to the Internet on. And most **public libraries** across the world offer Internet access free or for a small charge. Avoid **hotel business centers,** which often charge exorbitant rates.

Most major airports now have **Internet kiosks** scattered throughout their gates. These kiosks, which you'll also see in shopping malls, hotel lobbies, and tourist information offices around the world, give you basic Web access for a per-minute fee that's usually higher than cybercafe prices. The kiosks' clunkiness and high price means that they should be avoided whenever possible.

To retrieve your e-mail, ask your **Internet Service Provider (ISP)** if it has a web-based interface tied to your existing e-mail account. If your ISP doesn't have such an interface, you can use the free **mail2web** service (www.mail2web.com) to view (but not reply to) your home e-mail. For more flexibility, you may want to open a free, Web-based e-mail account with **Yahoo! Mail** (mail.yahoo.com). (Microsoft's Hotmail is another popular option, but Hotmail has severe spam problems.) Your home ISP may be able to forward your e-mail to the Web-based account automatically.

If you need to access files on your office computer, look into a service called **GoToMyPC** (www.gotomypc.com). The service provides a Web-based interface for you to access and manipulate a distant PC from anywhere—even a cybercafe—provided your "target" PC is on and has an always-on connection to the Internet (such as with Road Runner cable).

The service offers top-quality security, but if you're worried about hackers, use your own laptop rather than a cybercafe to access the GoToMyPC system.

WITH YOUR OWN COMPUTER

Major Internet service providers (ISPs) have **local access numbers** around the world, allowing you to go online by simply placing a local call. Check your ISP's website or call its toll-free number and ask how you can use your current account away from home, and how much it will cost.

If you're traveling outside the reach of your ISP, the **iPass** network has dial-up numbers in most of the world's countries. You'll have to sign up with an iPass provider, who will then tell you how to set up your computer for your destination(s). For a list of iPass providers, go to www.ipass.com and click on "Reseller Locator." Under "Select a Country," pick the country that you're coming from, and under "Who is this service for?" pick "Individual." One solid provider is **i2roam** (www.i2roam.com; © **866/811-6209** or 920/233-5863).

Wherever you go, bring a **connection kit** of the right power and phone adapters, a spare phone cord, and a spare Ethernet network cable.

Most business-class hotels throughout the world offer dataports for laptop modems, and a few thousand hotels in the U.S. and Europe now offer high-speed Internet access using an Ethernet network cable. You'll have to bring your own cables either way, so **call your hotel in advance** to find out what the options are.

USING A CELLPHONE IN BRITAIN

The three letters that define much of the world's **wireless capabilities** are GSM (Global System for Mobiles), a big, seamless network that makes for easy cross-border cellphone use throughout Europe and dozens of other countries worldwide. In the U.S., T-Mobile, AT&T Wireless, and Cingular use this quasi-universal system; in Canada, Microcell and some Rogers customers are GSM, and all Europeans and most Australians use GSM.

If your cellphone is on a GSM system, and you have a world-capable phone such as many (but not all) Sony Ericsson, Motorola, or Samsung models, you can make and receive calls across civilized areas on much of the globe, from Andorra to Uganda. Just call your wireless operator and ask for "international roaming" to be activated on your account. Unfortunately, per-minute charges can be high—usually $1 to $1.50 in western Europe and up to $5 in places such as Russia and Indonesia.

World-phone owners can bring down their per-minute charges with a bit of trickery. Call up your cellular operator and say you'll be going abroad for several months and want to "unlock" your phone to use it with a local provider. Usually they'll oblige. Then, in your destination country, pick up a cheap, prepaid phone chip at a mobile phone store and slip it into your phone. (Show your phone to the salesperson, as not all phones work on all networks.) You'll get a local phone number in your destination country—and much, much lower calling rates.

Otherwise, **renting** a phone is a good idea. While you can rent a phone from any number of overseas sites, including kiosks at airports and at car-rental agencies, we suggest renting the phone before you leave home. That way you can give loved ones your new number, make sure the phone works, and take the phone wherever you go—especially helpful when you rent overseas, where phone-rental agencies bill in local currency and may not let you take the phone to another country.

Phone rental isn't cheap. You'll usually pay $40 to $50 per week, plus airtime fees of at least a dollar a minute. If you're traveling to Europe, though, local rental companies often offer free incoming calls within their home country, which can save you big bucks. The bottom line: Shop around.

Two good wireless rental companies are **InTouch USA** (© **800/872-7626;** www.intouchglobal.com) and **Road-Post** (© **888/290-1616** or 905/272-5665; www.roadpost.com). Give them your itinerary, and they'll tell you what wireless products you need.

Online Traveler's Toolbox

Veteran travelers usually carry some essential items to make their trips easier. Following is a selection of online tools to bookmark and use:

- **Visa ATM Locator** (www.visa.com), for locations of PLUS ATMs worldwide, or **MasterCard ATM Locator** (www.mastercard.com), for locations of Cirrus ATMs worldwide.
- **Intellicast** (www.intellicast.com) and **Weather.com** (www.weather.com) for weather forecasts for cities around the world, including London.
- **Mapquest** (www.mapquest.com), the best of the mapping sites, lets you choose a specific address or destination, and in seconds, it will return a map and detailed directions.
- **Universal Currency Converter** (www.xe.com/ucc) to find out what your dollar or pound is worth in more than 100 other countries.

InTouch will also, for free, advise you on whether your existing phone will work overseas; simply call © **703/ 222-7161** between 9am and 4pm Eastern Standard Time, or go to **http:// intouchglobal.com/travel.htm**.

For trips of more than a few weeks spent in one country, **buying a phone** becomes economically attractive, as many nations have cheap, no-questions-asked prepaid phone systems. Stop by a local cellphone shop and get the cheapest package; you'll probably pay less than $100 for a phone and a starter calling card. Local calls may be as low as 10¢ per minute, and in many countries incoming calls are free.

11 Getting There

BY PLANE

British Airways (© **800/247-9297**; www.britishairways.com) offers flights from 19 U.S. cities to Heathrow and Gatwick airports, as well as many others to Manchester. Nearly every flight is nonstop. With more add-on options than any other airline, British Airways can make a visit to Britain cheaper than you may have expected. Ask about packages that include both airfare and discounted hotel accommodations in Britain.

Known for consistently offering excellent fares, **Virgin Atlantic Airways** (© **800/862-8621**; www.virginatlantic.com) flies daily to either Heathrow or Gatwick from Boston, Newark, New York's JFK, Los Angeles, San Francisco, Washington's Dulles, Miami, Orlando, and Las Vegas.

American Airlines (© **800/433-7300**; www.aa.com) offers daily flights to Heathrow from half a dozen U.S. gateways—New York's JFK, Chicago, Boston, Miami, Los Angeles, and Dallas.

Depending on the day and season, **Delta Air Lines** (© **800/241-4141**; www.delta.com) runs either one or two daily nonstop flights between Atlanta and Gatwick. Delta also offers nonstop daily service from Cincinnati.

Northwest Airlines (© **800/225-2525** or 800/447-4747; www.nwa.com) flies nonstop from Minneapolis and Detroit to Gatwick.

Continental Airlines (© **800/ 231-0856**; www.continental.com) has daily flights to London from Cleveland, Houston, Newark, Orlando, and San Francisco.

United Airlines (© **800/241-6522**; www.united.com) flies nonstop from New York's JFK and Chicago to Heathrow two or three times daily, depending on the season. United also offers nonstop service from Dulles Airport, near Washington, D.C.; Newark; Los Angeles; and San Francisco.

For travelers departing from Canada, **Air Canada** (© **888/247-2262** in the U.S., or 800/268-7240 in Canada; www.aircanada.com) flies daily to London's Heathrow nonstop from Vancouver, Montreal, and Toronto. There are also frequent direct flights from Calgary, Ottawa, and St. John's. **British Airways** (© **800/ 247-9297**) has direct flights from Toronto, Montreal, and Vancouver.

For travelers departing from Australia, **British Airways** (© **800/247-9297**) has flights to London from Sydney, Melbourne, Perth, and Brisbane. **Qantas** (© **612/131313**; www.qantas.com) offers flights from Australia to London's Heathrow. Direct flights depart from Sydney and Melbourne. Some have the bonus of free stopovers in Bangkok or Singapore.

Departing from New Zealand, **Air New Zealand** (© **800/262-1234**; www.airnz.co.nz) has direct flights to London from Auckland. These flights depart daily.

Short flights from Dublin to London are available through **British**

Airways (℃ 800/247-9297), with four flights daily into London's Gatwick airport, and **Aer Lingus** (℃ 800/IRISH-AIR; www.aerlingus. com), which flies into Heathrow. Short flights from Dublin to London are also available through **Ryan Air** (℃ 01/249-7851; www.ryanair.com) and **British Midland** (℃ 0870/ 6070555; www.flybmi.com).

GETTING THROUGH THE AIRPORT

With the federalization of airport security, security procedures at U.S. airports are more stable and consistent than ever. Generally, you'll be fine if you arrive at the airport **1 hour** before a domestic flight and **2 hours** before an international flight; if you show up late, tell an airline employee and he or she will probably whisk you to the front of the line.

Bring a **current, government-issued photo ID** such as a driver's license or passport, and if you've got an E-ticket, print out the **official confirmation page;** you'll need to show your confirmation at the security checkpoint, and your ID at the ticket counter or the gate. (Children under 18 do not need photo IDs for domestic flights, but the adults checking in with them need them.)

Federalization has stabilized **what you can carry on** and **what you can't.** The general rule is that sharp things are out, nail clippers are okay, and food and beverages must be passed through the X-ray machine—but that security screeners can't make you drink from your coffee cup. Bring food in your carry-on rather than checking it, as explosive-detection machines used on checked luggage have been known to mistake food (especially chocolate, for some reason) for bombs. Travelers in the U.S. are allowed one carry-on bag, plus a "personal item" such as a purse, briefcase, or laptop bag. Carry-on hoarders can stuff all sorts of things

into a laptop bag; as long as it has a laptop in it, it's still considered a personal item. The Transportation Security Administration (TSA) has issued a list of restricted items; check its website (**www.tsa.gov/public/index.jsp**) for details.

FLYING FOR LESS: TIPS FOR GETTING THE BEST AIRFARE

Passengers sharing the same airplane cabin rarely pay the same fare. Travelers who need to purchase tickets at the last minute, change their itinerary at a moment's notice, or fly one-way often get stuck paying the premium rate. Here are some ways to keep your airfare costs down:

- Passengers who can book their ticket **long in advance,** who can **stay over Saturday night,** or who **fly midweek** or **at less-trafficked hours** will pay a fraction of the full fare. If your schedule is flexible, say so, and ask if you can secure a cheaper fare by changing your flight plans.
- You can also save on airfares by keeping an eye out in local newspapers for **promotional specials** or **fare wars,** when airlines lower prices on their most popular routes. You rarely see fare wars offered for peak travel times, but if you can travel in the off-months, you may snag a bargain.
- Search **the Internet** for cheap fares (see "Planning Your Trip Online," earlier in this chapter).
- **Consolidators,** also known as bucket shops, are great sources for international tickets, although they usually can't beat the Internet on fares within North America. Start by looking in Sunday newspaper travel sections; U.S. travelers should focus on the *New York Times, Los Angeles Times,* and *Miami Herald.* For less-developed destinations, small travel agents

---

Tips **Don't Stow It—Ship It**

If ease of travel is your main concern and money is no object, you can ship your luggage with one of the growing number of luggage-service companies that pick up, track, and deliver your luggage (often through couriers such as Federal Express) with minimum hassle for you. Traveling luggage-free may be ultra-convenient, but it's not cheap: One-way overnight shipping can cost from $100 to $200, depending on what you're sending. Still, for some people, especially the elderly or the infirm, it's a sensible solution to lugging heavy baggage. Specialists in door-to-door luggage delivery are **Virtual Bellhop** (www.virtualbellhop.com), **SkyCap International** (wwww.skycapinternational.com), and **Luggage Express** (www.usxpluggageexpress.com).

---

who cater to immigrant communities in large cities often have the best deals. *Beware:* Bucket shop tickets are usually nonrefundable or rigged with stiff cancellation penalties, often as high as 50% to 75% of the ticket price, and some put you on charter airlines with questionable safety records. Several reliable consolidators are worldwide and available on the Net. **STA Travel** (© 800/781-4040; www.statravel.com) is now the world's leader in student travel, thanks to their purchase of Council Travel. It also offers good fares for travelers of all ages. **Flights.com** (© 201/541-3867; www.flights.com) has excellent fares worldwide, but particularly to Europe. It also has "local" web-sites in 12 countries. **FlyCheap** (© 800/FLY-CHEAP; www.1800 flycheap.com) is owned by package-holiday megalith MyTravel and so has especially good access to fares for sunny destinations. **Air Tickets Direct** (© 800/778-3447; www.airticketsdirect.com) is based in Montreal and leverages the Canadian dollar for lower fares.

• Join **frequent-flier clubs.** Accrue enough miles, and you'll be rewarded with free flights and elite

status. It's free, and you'll get the best choice of seats, faster response to phone inquiries, and prompter service if your luggage is stolen, your flight is canceled or delayed, or if you want to change your seat. You don't need to fly to build frequent-flier miles—**frequent-flier credit cards** can provide thousands of miles for doing your everyday shopping.

BY CAR FROM CONTINENTAL EUROPE

If you plan to transport a rented car between Britain and France, check in advance with the car-rental company about license and insurance requirements and additional drop-off charges before you begin.

The English Channel is crisscrossed with "drive-on, drive-off" car-ferry services, with many operating from Boulogne and Calais in France. From either of those ports, Sealink ferries will carry you, your luggage, and, if you like, your car. The most popular point of arrival along the English coast is Folkestone.

Taking a car beneath the Channel is more complicated and more expensive. Since the Channel Tunnel's opening, most passengers have opted to ride the train alone, without being accompanied by their car. The Eurostar trains, discussed below, carry passengers only; *Le Shuttle* trains carry freight cars, trucks, and passenger cars.

Count on at least £223 ($413) for a return ticket but know that the cost of moving a car on Le Shuttle varies according to the season and day of the week. Frankly, it's a lot cheaper to transport your car across by conventional ferryboat, but if you insist, here's what you'll need to know: You'll negotiate both British and French customs as part of one combined process, usually on the English side of the Channel. You can remain within your vehicle even after you drive it onto a flatbed railway car during the 35-minute crossing. (For 19 min. of this crossing, you'll actually be underwater; if you want, you can leave the confines of your car and ride within a brightly lit, air-conditioned passenger car.) When the trip is over, you simply drive off the flatbed railway car and toward your destination. Total travel time between the French and English highway system is about 1 hour. As a means of speeding the flow of perishable goods across the Channel, the car and truck service usually operates 24 hours a day, at intervals that vary from 15 minutes to once an hour, depending on the time of day. Neither BritRail nor any of the agencies dealing with reservations for passenger trains through the Chunnel will reserve space for your car in advance, and considering the frequency of the traffic on the Chunnel, they're usually not necessary. For information about Le Shuttle car-rail service after you reach England, call © **0870/535-3535** or go online to **www.euro tunnel.com**.

Duty-free stores, restaurants, and service stations are available to travelers on both sides of the Channel. A bilingual staff is on hand to assist travelers at both the British and French terminals.

BY TRAIN FROM CONTINENTAL EUROPE

Britain's isolation from the rest of Europe led to the development of an independent railway network with different rules and regulations from those observed on the Continent. That's all changing now, but one big difference that may affect you still remains: If you're traveling to Britain from the Continent, *your Eurailpass will not be valid when you get there.*

In 1994, Queen Elizabeth and President François Mitterand officially opened the Channel Tunnel, or Chunnel, and the *Eurostar* express passenger train began twice-daily service between London and both Paris and Brussels. In 2003, the completion of a new section of high-speed rail in England, the **Channel Tunnel Rail** Link, shaved 20 minutes off the trip between London and Paris, reducing it to just 2 hours and 35 minutes (or 2 hr., 20 min. to Brussels). This extension allows Eurostar trains to go at the rate of 482kmph (300 mph). The $15 billion tunnel, one of the great engineering feats of all time, is the first link between Britain and the Continent since the Ice Age.

So if you're coming to London from say, Rome, your Eurailpass will get you as far as the Chunnel. At that point, you can cross the English Channel aboard the *Eurostar,* and you'll receive a discount on your ticket. Once in England, you must use a separate BritRail pass or purchase a direct ticket to continue on to your destination.

Rail Europe (© **877/272-RAIL** in the U.S., or 800/361-RAIL in Canada; www.raileurope.com) sells direct-service tickets on the Eurostar between Paris or Brussels and London. A one-way non-discounted fare from Paris to London costs $345 in first class and $249 in second class. Various discounted fares are available.

In London, make reservations for **Eurostar** by calling ℂ **0870/530-0003;** in France, call ℂ **08-36-35-35-39;** and in the United States, it's ℂ **800/EUROSTAR** (www.eurostar. com). Eurostar trains arrive and depart from London's Waterloo Station, Paris's Gare du Nord, and Brussels's Central Station.

BY FERRY/HOVERCRAFT FROM CONTINENTAL EUROPE

P&O Ferries (ℂ **0870/520-2020;** www.poferries.com) operates car and passenger ferries between Dover and Calais, France (25 sailings a day; 75 min. each way).

By far the most popular route across the English Channel is between Calais and Dover. **HoverSpeed** (ℂ **0870/524-0241;** www.hoverspeed.com) operates at least 12 hovercraft crossings daily; the trip takes 35 minutes. They also run a SeaCat (a catamaran propelled by jet engines) that takes slightly longer to make the crossing between Boulogne and Folkestone. The SeaCats depart about four times a day on the 55-minute voyage.

Traveling by hovercraft or SeaCat cuts the time of your surface journey from the continent to the United Kingdom. A hovercraft trip is definitely a fun adventure because the vessel is technically "flying" over the water. A SeaCat crossing from Folkestone to Boulogne is longer in miles, but it is covered faster than conventional ferry-boats making the Calais–Dover crossing. For reservations and information, call HoverSpeed (see above). For foot passengers, a typical adult fare, with a 5-day return policy, is £26 ($48) or half fare for children.

BY BUS

If you're traveling to London from elsewhere in the United Kingdom, consider purchasing a **Britexpress Card,** which entitles you to a 30% discount on National Express (ℂ **0870/580-8080;** www.national express.com) buses in England and Wales. Contact a travel agent for details.

Bus connections to Britain from the continent are generally not very comfortable, though some lines are more convenient than others. One line with a relatively good reputation is **Euro-lines,** 52 Grosvenor Gardens, London SW1W 0AU (ℂ **020/7730-8235;** www.eurolines.com). They book passage on buses traveling twice a day between London and Paris (9 hr.); three times a day from Amsterdam (12 hr.); three times a week from Munich (24 hr.); and three times a week from Stockholm (44 hr.). On the longer routes, which employ two alternating drivers, the bus proceeds almost without interruption, taking occasional breaks for meals.

12 Packages for the Independent Traveler

Before you start your search for the lowest airfare, you may want to consider booking your flight as part of a travel package. Package tours are not the same thing as escorted tours. Package tours are simply a way to buy the airfare, accommodations, and other elements of your trip (such as car rentals, airport transfers, and sometimes even activities) at the same time and often at discounted prices—kind of like one-stop shopping. Packages are sold in bulk to tour operators—who resell them to the public at a cost that usually undercuts standard rates.

One good source of package deals is the airlines themselves. Most major airlines offer air/land packages, including **American Airlines Vacations** (ℂ 800/321-2121; www.aavacations.com), **Delta Vacations** (ℂ 800/221-6666;

www.deltavacations.com), **Continental Airlines Vacations** (© 800/301-3800; www.coolvacations.com), and **United Vacations** (© 888/854-3899; www.unitedvacations.com). Great deals—probably the best of all the airline packagers—can often be found by booking a package tour through **Virgin Atlantic Airways** (© 800/862-8621; www.virgin.com).

Far and away, the most options are with **British Airways Holidays** (© 877/428-2228; www.british airways.com). Its offerings within the British Isles are more comprehensive than those of its competitors and can be tailored to your specific interests and budget. Many tours, such as the 9-day, all-inclusive tour through the great houses and gardens of England, include the ongoing services of a guide and lecturer. But if you prefer to travel independently, without following an organized tour, a sales representative can tailor an itinerary specifically for you, with discounted rates in a wide assortment of big-city hotels. If you opt for this, you can rent a car or choose to take the train. For a free catalog and additional information, call British Airways before you book; some of the company's available options are contingent upon the purchase of a round-trip transatlantic air ticket.

Several big **online travel agencies**—Expedia, Travelocity, Orbitz, Site59, and Lastminute.com—also do a brisk business in packages. If you're unsure about the pedigree of a smaller packager, check with the Better Business Bureau in the city where the company is based, or go online at **www.bbb.org**. If a packager won't tell you where it's based, don't fly with them.

Liberty Travel (© 888/271-1584 to be connected with the agent closest to you; www.libertytravel.com), one of the biggest packagers in the Northeast, often runs a full-page ad in the Sunday papers. **American Express**

Vacations (© 800/941-2639; www.travelimpressions.com) is another option. Check out its **Last Minute Travel Bargains** site (www.last minute.com), offered in conjunction with **American Express,** with deeply discounted vacation packages and reduced airline fares that differ from the E-savers bargains that Continental e-mails weekly to subscribers. **Northwest Airlines** offers a similar service. Posted on Northwest's website (www.nwa.com) every Wednesday, its **Cyber Saver Bargain Alerts** offer special hotel rates, package deals, and discounted airline fares.

Travel packages are also listed in the travel section of your local Sunday newspaper. Or check ads in the national travel magazines such as *Arthur Frommer's Budget Travel Magazine, Travel & Leisure, National Geographic Traveler,* and *Condé Nast Traveler.*

Package tours can vary by leaps and bounds. Some offer a better class of hotels than others. Some offer the same hotels for lower prices. Some offer flights on scheduled airlines, while others book charters. Some limit your choice of accommodations and travel days. You are often required to make a large payment up front. On the plus side, packages can save you money, offering group prices but allowing for independent travel. Some even let you to add on a few guided excursions or escorted day trips (also at prices lower than if you booked them yourself) without booking an entirely escorted tour.

Before you invest in a package tour, get some answers. Ask about the **accommodation choices** and prices for each. Then look up the hotels' reviews in a Frommer's guidebook and check their rates for your specific dates of travel online. You'll also want to find out what **type of room** you get. If you need a certain type of room, ask for it; don't take whatever is thrown your way. Request a nonsmoking room, a quiet room, a room with a view, or whatever you fancy.

Finally, look for **hidden expenses.** Ask whether airport departure fees and taxes, for example, are included in the total cost.

13 Escorted General-Interest Tours

Escorted tours are structured group tours with a group leader. The price usually includes everything from airfare to hotels, meals, tours, admission costs, and local transportation.

Many people derive a certain ease and security from escorted trips. Escorted tours—whether by bus, motor coach, train, or boat—let travelers sit back and enjoy their trip without having to spend lots of time behind the wheel. All the little details are taken care of; you know your costs up front; and there are few surprises. Escorted tours can take you to the maximum number of sights in the minimum amount of time with the least amount of hassle—you don't have to sweat over the plotting and planning of a vacation schedule. Escorted tours are particularly convenient for people with limited mobility.

On the downside, an escorted tour often requires a big deposit up front, and lodging and dining choices are predetermined. As part of a cloud of tourists, you'll get little opportunity for serendipitous interactions with locals. The tours can be jam-packed with activities, leaving little room for individual sightseeing, whim, or adventure—plus they also often focus only on the heavily touristed sites, so you miss out on the lesser-known gems.

Before you invest in an escorted tour, ask about the **cancellation policy:** Is a deposit required? Can they cancel the trip if they don't get enough people? Do you get a refund if they cancel? If *you* cancel? How late can you cancel if you are unable to go? When do you pay in full? *Note:* If you choose an escorted tour, think strongly about purchasing trip-cancellation insurance, especially if the tour operator asks you to pay up front. See the section on "Travel Insurance," earlier in this chapter.

You'll also want to get a complete **schedule** of the trip to find out how much sightseeing is planned each day and whether enough time has been allotted for relaxing or wandering solo.

The **size** of the group is also important to know up front. Generally, the smaller the group, the more flexible the itinerary, and the less time you'll spend waiting for people to get on and off the bus. Find out the **demographics** of the group as well. What is the age range? What is the gender breakdown? Is this mostly a trip for couples or singles?

Discuss what is included in the **price.** You may have to pay for transportation to and from the airport. A box lunch may be included in an excursion, but drinks may cost extra. Tips may not be included. Find out if you will be charged if you decide to opt out of certain activities or meals.

Before you invest in a package tour, get some answers. Ask about the **accommodation choices** and prices for each. Then look up the hotels' reviews in a Frommer's guide and check their rates for your specific dates of travel online. You'll also want to find out what **type of room** you get. If you need a certain type of room, ask for it; don't take whatever is thrown your way. Request a nonsmoking room, a quiet room, a room with a view, or whatever you fancy.

Finally, if you plan to travel alone, you'll need to know if a **single supplement** will be charged and if the company can match you up with a roommate.

Abercrombie & Kent (© 800/ 323-7308; www.abercrombiekent. com) offers extremely upscale escorted tours that are loaded with luxury. Their most unusual conveyance is the *Royal Scotsman* train, which, for 1 night and 2 days, hauls participants along less frequently used railway spurs of Wiltshire, Somerset, and Devon within vintage railway cars that were fashionable around the turn of the 20th century. Prices begin at $890 per person, double occupancy, for lots of local color and spit-and-polish service. Tours emphasize visits to sites of historical interest, and sometimes involve rides on buses that pick up and redeposit passengers at local railway stations.

One of Abercrombie's top rivals is **Travcoa** (© 800/992-2003; www. travcoa.com), which offers upscale tours by deluxe motor coach through the countryside of England and Wales. Tours last from 11 to 21 days, include at least 3 nights in London, usually at such citadels of glamour as The Dorchester (p. 110), and come with meals and virtually every other aspect of a holiday included in the price. Don't expect cost savings here: Without airfare, rates range from $7,295 to $16,295 per person double occupancy.

Other contenders in the upscale package-tour business include **Maupintour** (© 800/255-4266; www.maupintour.com) and **Tauck**

World Discovery (© 800/468-2825; www.tauck.com).

But not all escorted tours are so pricey. Mostly older British folks make up a large portion of the clientele of one of the United Kingdom's largest tour operators, **Wallace Arnold Holidays** (© 020/8686-2378; www. wallacearnold.com). Most of the company's tours last between 5 and 10 days, include lodgings (at solid but not particularly extravagant hotels) and most meals, and are reasonably priced from £245 ($453), without airfare.

U.S.-based **Trafalgar Tours** (© 800/854-0103; www.trafalgar tours.com), offers affordable packages with lodgings in unpretentious but comfortable hotels. It's one of Europe's largest tour operators. There may not be a lot of frills, but you can find 8-day itineraries priced from $685 per person, double occupancy, without airfare, that include stopovers in Stratford-upon-Avon and Bath; they also offer 8-day packages at first-class hotels in London, with some money-saving coupons thrown in, for around $490 to $930 per person, double occupancy.

One of Trafalgar's leading competitors, known for roughly equivalent moderately priced tours through Britain, is **Globus & Cosmos Tours** (© 800/338-7092; www.globusand cosmos.com).

14 Special-Interest Trips

BIKE TRIPS

If you're planning a bike trip on your own, you can take your two wheels on passenger trains in Britain if you pay a £5 ($9.25) extra charge. Brits have rediscovered the bicycle; by 2005, a National Cycle Network will cover about 16,000km (10,000 miles) throughout the country. The network will run from Dover in southeast Eng-

land to Inverness in the Highlands. Nearly 13,000km (8,000 miles) are open as of 2004. Go to www.sustrans. org.uk for route maps.

Most routes cross old railway lines, canal towpaths, and riversides. Among the more popular routes are the Sea-to-Sea Cycle Route, a 225km (140-mile) path linking the Irish Sea with the North Sea across the Pennine Hills and into the north Lake District and the Durham Dales. The Essex Cycle Route covers 402km (250 miles) of countryside, going through some of England's most charming villages; the Devon Coast-to-Coast route runs for 145km (90 miles) in southwest England, skirting the edge of Dartmoor; the West Country Way for 399km (248 miles) links the Cornish coast to Bath and Bristol; and the Severn and Thames route for 161km (100 miles) links two of Britain's major rivers.

For a free copy of "Britain for Cyclists," with information on these routes, call the **British Tourist Authority** at ℭ **888/VISITUK** or contact the **Cyclists Touring Club,** Cotterell House, 69 Meadrow, Godalming, Surrey GU7 3HS (ℭ **0870/873-0060;** www.ctc.org. uk), which can suggest routes and provide information. Memberships cost £31 ($56) a year.

FISHING

Fly-fishing was born here, and it's an art form. An expert in leading programs for fly-fishermen eager to experience the cold, clear waters of Britain is **Rod & Reel Adventures,** 32617 Skyhawk Way, Eugene, OR 97405 (ℭ **800/356-6982** or 541/349-0777; www.rodreeladventures.com). Don't expect smooth salesmanship at this place, but if you persevere, someone at this company should be able to link you up with a local fishing guide who can lead you to English waters that are well stocked with trout, perch, grayling, sea bream, Atlantic salmon, and such lesser-known species as rudd and roach. Rod & Reel Adventures has contacts in the Lake District and the Norfolk Broads. Such streams as the Wear, the Derwent, the Copuquet, and the Till are especially prolific.

If you prefer to go it alone, contact the **British Salmon & Trout Association,** Fishmonger's Hall, London Bridge, London EC4R 9EL (ℭ **020/ 7283-5838**), for information about British fishing regulations.

GOLF

Though the sport originated in Scotland, golf has been around in Britain since Edward VII first began stamping over the greens of such courses as Royal Lytham & St. Annes, in England's northwest, or Royal St. Georges, near London.

The unyielding reality is that golf in Britain remains a clubby sport where some of the most prestigious courses are usually reserved exclusively for members. Rules at most British golf courses tend to be stricter in matters of dress code and protocol than their equivalents in the United States.

If, however, your heart is set on enjoying a round or two on the emerald-colored turf of Britain, **Golf International,** 14 E. 38 St., New York, NY 10016 (ℭ **800/833-1389** or 212/ 986-9176; www.golfinternational. com), can open doors for you. Golf packages are arranged for anywhere from 7 to 14 days and can include as much or as little golf, on as many different courses, as a participant wants. Weeklong vacations, with hotels, breakfasts, car rentals, and greens fees included, range from $1,965 to $3,500 per person, double occupancy, airfare not included.

Worthy competitors that operate on a less comprehensive scale than Golf International include **Adventures in Golf,** 22 Greeley St., Suite 7, Merrimack, NH 03054 (ℭ **603/ 424-7320;** www.adventures-in-golf. com); and **Jerry Quinlan's Celtic Golf,** 1129 Rte. 9, Cape May Courthouse, NJ 08210 (ℭ **800/535-6148;** www.jqcelticgolf.com). Each of their tours is customized, and usually includes lodging in anything from simple guesthouses to five-star deluxe manor houses.

HIKING, WALKING & RAMBLING

England and Wales alone have some 161,000km (100,000 miles) of trails and footpaths. The **Ramblers' Association,** Camelford House, 87–90 Albert Embankment, 2nd Floor, London SE1 7TW (© 020/7339-8500; www.ramblers.org.uk), publishes an annual yearbook that lists some 2,500 bed-and-breakfasts near the trails; it costs £12 ($22). Send a check in British pounds for the yearbook if you plan to order before your trip; otherwise the yearbook can be purchased in England for £6 ($11).

Wilderness Travel, Inc., 1102 Ninth St., Berkeley, CA 94710 (© 800/368-2794 or 510/558-2488; fax 501/558-2789; www.wilderness travel.com), also specializes in treks and inn-to-inn hiking tours, plus less strenuous walking tours of Cornwall and the Cotswolds that combine transportation with walking sessions of 3 hours or less.

English Lakeland Ramblers, 18 Stuyvesant Oval, Suite 1A, New York, NY 10009 (© 800/724-8801 outside New York City, or 212/505-1020 within New York City; www. ramblers.com), offers 7- or 8-day walking tours for the average active person. On its Lake District tour, you'll stay and have your meals in a charming 17th-century country inn near Ambleside and Windermere. A minibus takes hikers and sightseers daily to trails and sightseeing points. Experts tell you about the area's culture and history and highlight its natural wonders. There are also tours of the Cotswolds, as well as inn-to-inn tours and privately guided tours.

Other contenders include **Country Walkers,** P.O. Box 180, Waterbury, VT 05676 (© 800/464-9255 or 802/244-1387; www.countrywalkers. com). This company's "walking vacations" last 5 to 7 days and tend to focus on such scenic areas as the Lake District, Cornwall, and the Cotswolds. These packages include overnight accommodations at well-respected, but not excessively luxurious, three-star hotels or the occasional manor house; most meals; and a guide who's well versed in local paths, trails, and lore. About 6.5km to 19km (4–12 miles) are covered each day. Prices start at $2,198 per person, double occupancy, without airfare.

To explore the mountain activities of Wales' Snowdonia National Park, contact Bob Postings at **Pathfinder,** Clynnog Fawr, Tan-yr-allt, Caernarfon, Gwynedd LL54 5NS, in North Wales (© 01286/660202; www. pathfindersnowdonia.co.uk). Bob and his skilled team specialize in walking the summits, rock climbing, kayaking and rafting, among other activities.

HORSEBACK RIDING

You can learn to ride or brush up on your skills at **Eastern Equation,** a facility located on the Essex/Suffolk border. British Horse Society–certified instructors teach riders at a facility with a large indoor arena, a jumping course, and 30 horses and ponies of various sizes and abilities. Many trails go directly from the farm to the countryside. You can stay in a room with a private bath at the beautiful 16th-century farmhouse (subject to availability) or find accommodations in a comfortable nearby hotel. Contact **Cross Country International,** P.O. Box 1170, Millbrook, NY 12545 (© 800/828-8768; www.equestrian vacations.com).

A number of American companies offer horseback-riding package tours of Britain. **Equitour,** P.O. Box 807, Dubois, WY 82513 (© 800/545-0019 or 307/455-3363; www.riding tours.com), is one such firm, specializing in package tours for riding enthusiasts who want to experience the horsey traditions of the land of foxes and hounds. Two types of tours can be arranged: stationary tours, with instruction in jumping and dressage over a 7-day period at a stable beside the Bristol Channel or on the fields of Dartmoor; and "progressive" tours in Wales, with treks of 4 to 10 days. Most riders, eager to experience as wide a view of England as possible, opt for the latter, spending nights at different B&Bs or inns and lodging their mount at nearby stables. Accommodations are simple, and prices are kept deliberately low. A 6-day horseback excursion in Cumbria that includes use of a horse and its tack, guide services, overnight accommodations, and all meals costs around $1,840 per person, double occupancy.

UNIVERSITY STUDY PROGRAMS

You can study British literature at renowned universities such as Oxford and Cambridge during the week and then take weekend excursions to the countryside of Shakespeare, Austen, Dickens, and Hardy. While doing your coursework, you can live in dormitories with other students and dine in elaborate halls or the more intimate Fellows' clubs. Study programs in England are not limited to the liberal arts, or to high school or college students. Some programs are designed specifically for teachers and seniors (see "Senior Travel," earlier in this chapter). For more information, contact organizations listed below or in the section "Student Travel," earlier in this chapter.

Affiliated with Richmond College, in London, **American Institute For** **Foreign Study,** River Plaza, 9 W. Broad St., Stamford, CT 06902 (© **800/727-2437** or 203/399-5000; www.aifs.com), offers 4 weeks and up of traveling programs for high school students, and internships and academic programs for college students. There are also programs leading to the British equivalent of an MBA.

IIE (Institute of International Education), U.S. Student Programs Division, 809 United Nations Plaza, New York, NY 10017 (© **800/445-0443** or 212/883-8200; www.iie.org), administers a variety of academic, training, and grant programs for the U.S. Information Agency (USIA), including Fulbright grants. It is especially helpful in arranging enrollments for U.S. students in summer school programs.

University Vacations, 3660 Bougainvillea Rd., Coconut Grove, FL 33133 (© **800/792-0100;** www.universityvacations.com), offers upmarket liberal arts programs at Oxford and Cambridge universities. Courses usually last 7 to 12 days and combine lectures and excursions with dining in the intimate Fellows' Dining Rooms. Accommodations are in private rooms with available en-suite facilities in the medieval colleges. There are neither formal academic requirements nor pressure for examinations or written requirements. Its summer headquarters is Magdalen College, Oxford.

Worldwide Classrooms, P.O. Box 1166, Milwaukee, WI 53201 (www.worldwide.edu), produces an extensive listing of schools offering study abroad programs in England and offers a directory-like catalog for $9.95.

15 Getting Around England & Wales

BY CAR

The British car-rental market is among the most competitive in Europe. Nevertheless, car rentals are often relatively expensive, unless you avail yourself of one of the promotional deals that are frequently offered by British Airways and others.

Because cars in Britain travel on the left side of the road, steering wheels are positioned on the "wrong" side of the vehicle. Keep in mind that most rental cars are manual, so be prepared to shift with your left hand; you'll pay more for an automatic—and make sure to request one when you reserve.

Most car-rental companies will accept your U.S. driver's license, provided you're 23 years old (21 in rare instances) and have had the license for more than a year. Many rental companies will grant discounts to clients who reserve their cars in advance (usually 48 hr.) through the toll-free reservations offices in the renter's home country. Rentals of a week or more are almost always less expensive per day than day rentals.

When you reserve a car, make sure you know the total price, including the 17.5% value-added tax (VAT).

Rentals are available through **Avis** (© 800/331-1212; www.avis.com), **British Airways** (© 800/AIRWAYS; www.british-airways.com), **Budget** (© 800/472-3325; www.budget.com), and **Hertz** (© 800/654-3131; www.hertz.com). **Kemwel Holiday Auto** (© 800/678-0678; www.kemwel.com) is among the cheapest and most reliable of the rental agencies. **Auto-Europe** (© 800/223-5555 in the U.S., or 0800/899893 in London; www.autoeurope.com) acts as a wholesale company for rental agencies in Europe.

Car-rental rates vary even more than airline fares. The price you pay depends on the size of the car, where and when you pick it up and drop it off, length of the rental period, where and how far you drive it, whether you purchase insurance, and a host of other factors. A few key questions could save you hundreds of dollars:

- Are weekend rates lower than weekday rates? Ask if the rate is the same for pickup Friday morning, for instance, as it is for Thursday night.
- Is a weekly rate cheaper than the daily rate? If you need to keep the car for 4 days, it may be cheaper to keep it for 5, even if you don't need it for that long.
- Does the agency assess a drop-off charge if you do not return the car to the same location where you picked it up? Is it cheaper to pick up the car at the airport compared to a downtown location?
- Are special promotional rates available? If you see an advertised price in your local newspaper, be sure to ask for that specific rate; otherwise you may be charged the standard cost. The terms change constantly, and phone operators may not volunteer information.
- Are discounts available for members of AARP, AAA, frequent-flier programs, or trade unions? If you belong to any of these organizations, you are probably entitled to discounts of up to 30%.
- What is the cost of adding an additional driver's name to the contract?
- How many free miles are included in the price? Free mileage is often negotiable, depending on the length of your rental.
- How much does the rental company charge to refill your gas tank if you return with the tank less than full? Though most rental companies claim these prices are "competitive," fuel is almost always cheaper in town. Try to allow enough time to refuel the car yourself before returning it.

RENTAL INSURANCE Before you drive off in a rental car, be sure you're insured. Hasty assumptions about your personal auto insurance or a rental agency's additional coverage could end up costing you tens of thousands of dollars—even if you are involved in an accident that was clearly the fault of another driver.

U.S. drivers who already have their own car insurance are usually covered in the United States for loss of or damage to a rental car and liability in case of injury to any other party involved in an accident. But coverage probably doesn't extend outside the United States. Be sure to find out whether you are covered in England, whether your policy extends to all persons who will be driving the rental car, how much liability is covered in case an outside party is injured in an accident, and whether the type of vehicle you are renting is included under your contract. (Rental trucks, sport utility vehicles, and luxury vehicles such as the Jaguar may not be covered.)

Most **major credit cards** provide some degree of coverage as well—provided they are used to pay for the rental. Terms vary widely, however, so be sure to call your credit card company directly before you rent. But though they will cover damage to or theft of your rental, *credit cards will not cover liability* or the cost of injury to an outside party and/or damage to an outside party's vehicle. If you do not hold an insurance policy or if you are driving outside the United States, you may want to seriously consider purchasing additional liability insurance from your rental company. Be sure to check the terms, however: Some rental agencies only cover liability if the renter is not at fault.

Bear in mind that each credit card company has its own peculiarities. Most American Express Optima cards, for instance, do not provide any insurance. American Express does not cover vehicles valued at over $50,000 when new, such as luxury vehicles or vehicles built on a truck chassis. Master-Card does not provide coverage for loss, theft, or fire damage, and only covers collision if the rental period does not exceed 15 days. Call your own credit card company for details.

DRIVING RULES & REQUIREMENTS

In Britain, *you drive on the left* and pass on the right. Road signs are clear and the international symbols are unmistakable.

You must present your passport and driver's license when you rent a car in Britain. No special British license is needed. It's a good idea to get a copy of the *British Highway Code,* available from almost any gas station or newsstand (called a "news stall" in Britain).

Warning: Pedestrian crossings are marked by striped lines (zebra striping) on the road; flashing lights near the curb indicate that drivers must stop and yield the right of way if a pedestrian has stepped out into the zebra zone to cross the street.

ROAD MAPS

The best road map is *The Ordinance Survey Motor Atlas of Great Britain,* whether you're trying to find the fastest route to Manchester or locate some obscure village. Revised annually, it's published by Temple Press and is available at most bookstores, including **Foyles Bookshop,** 113 and 119 Charing Cross Rd., London WC2 H0EB (℗ **020/7440-3225;** www.foyles.co.uk).

BREAKDOWNS

If you are a member of AAA in the United States, you are automatically eligible for the same roadside services you receive at home. Be sure to bring your membership card with you on your trip. In an emergency, call the Automobile Association of Great Britain's emergency road service (℗ **0800/085-2721**). If you are not a member of AAA, you may want to join one of England's two major auto clubs—the Automobile Association (AA) and the Royal Automobile Club (RAC). Membership, which can be obtained through your

---

Value **Comparison Shop!**

Many packages include airfare, accommodations, and a rental car with unlimited mileage. Compare these prices with the cost of booking airline tickets and renting a car separately to find out whether these offers are good deals.

---

car-rental agent, entitles you to free legal and technical advice on motoring matters, as well as a whole range of discounts on automobile products and services.

The **AA** is located at Carr Ellison House, William Armstrong Drive, Newcastle-upon-Tyne NE4 7YA (℗ **0870/550-0600;** www.theaa.com). The **RAC** can be contacted at P.O. Box 700, Bristol, Somerset BS99 1RB (℗ **0800/828282;** www.rac.co.uk).

If your car breaks down on the highway, you can call for **24-hour breakdown service** from a roadside phone. The 24-hour number to call for **AA** is ℗ **0800/262050;** for **RAC** it is ℗ **0800/828282.** All superhighways (called motorways in Britain) have special emergency phones that are connected to police traffic units, and the police can contact either of the auto clubs on your behalf.

GASOLINE   Called "petrol," gasoline is sold by the liter (4.2 liters to a gal.). Prices are much higher than in the States, and you'll probably have to serve yourself. In some remote areas, stations are few and far between, many closed on Sunday.

BY PLANE

British Airways (℗ **800/AIRWAYS**) flies to more than 20 cities outside London, including Manchester.

For passengers planning on visiting widely scattered destinations within the United Kingdom, perhaps with a side trip to a city on Europe's mainland, British Airways' **Europe Airpass** allows discounted travel in a continuous loop to between 3 and 12 cities

anywhere on BA's European and domestic air routes. Passengers must end their journey at the same point they begin it and fly exclusively on BA flights. Such a ticket (for instance, from London to Paris, then to Manchester, and finally to London again) will cut the cost of each segment of the itinerary by about 40% to 50% over individually booked tickets. The pass is available for travel to about a dozen of the most visited cities and regions of Britain, with discounted add-ons available to most of BA's destinations in Europe as well. (This Airpass is a good bargain for round-trip travel between London and Rome, but not very practical for air travel from, say, Rome to Madrid. You'd be better off traveling between points on the Continent by full-fare airline ticket, or by train, bus, or car.)

BA's Europe Airpass must be booked and paid for at least 7 days before a passenger's departure from North America. All sectors of the itinerary, including transatlantic passage from North America, must be booked simultaneously. Some changes are permitted in flight dates (but not in destinations) after the ticket is issued. Check with British Airways for full details and restrictions.

BY TRAIN

A Eurailpass is not valid in Great Britain, but there are several special passes for train travel outside London. For railroad information, go to Rail Travel centers in the main London railway stations (Waterloo, King's Cross, Euston, and Paddington).

You can download faxable order forms or order online using a BritRail Pass Shopping Cart feature (**www. britainontrack.com**).

BRITRAIL TRAVEL PASSES

BritRail Passes allow unlimited travel in England, Scotland, and Wales on any British rail scheduled train over the whole of the network during the validity of the pass without restrictions. If you're traveling beyond London anywhere in the United Kingdom, and plan to hop on and off the train, consider purchasing a **BritRail Classic (aka Consecutive) Pass.** These passes allow you to travel for a consecutive number of days for a flat rate. In first class adults pay $279 for 4 days, $405 for 8 days, $599 for 15 days, $765 for 22 days, and $909 for 1 month. In second class, fares are $189 for 4 days, $269 for 8 days, $399 for 15 days, $509 for 22 days, and $605 for 1 month. Seniors (60 and over) qualify for discounts in first class travel and pay $237 for 4 days, $344 for 8 days, $509 for 15 days, $650 for 22 days, and $773 for 1 month of first class travel. Passengers under 26 quality for a **Youth Pass:** $142 for 4 days, $202 for 8 days, $299 for 15 days, $382 for 22 days, and $454 for 1 month. One child (5–15) can travel free with each adult or senior pass by requesting the **BritRail Family Pass** when buying the adult pass. Additional children pay half the regular adult fare.

A more versatile pass is the **BritRail FlexiPass** allowing you to travel when you want, during a two-month period of time. In first class, it costs $349 for 4 days, $515 for 8 days, and $775 for 15 days of travel. Second class costs $239 for 4 days, $345 for 8 days, and $519 for 15 days of travel.

A new BritRail Pass for travel in England only, the **BritRail England Pass** is sold at a price 20% lower than regular BritRail Passes which cover rail travel throughout the U.K. (Britain, Scotland, Wales, and Northern Ireland). Starting at $149 for four consecutive days of travel in standard class, the BritRail England Pass is also offered for 8, 15, or 22 consecutive days or one month or as a Flexipass (days may be consecutive or nonconsecutive) for 4, 8, 15 days within a 2-month period. It is also available in first class, starting at $279 and at discounted prices for seniors (60 and over) in first class and youth (under 26) in standard class. As with other BritRail Passes, one child 5 to 15 may travel free when accompanied by an adult or senior purchasing a BritRail England Pass and requesting the Family Pass.

A **Freedom of Wales FlexiPass** is also offered through BritRail in the U.S. This economy pass offers two options—in an 8-day period you can travel any 4 days by rail and every day by bus for $113; or else in a 15-day period you can travel 8 days by rail and every day by bus for $173.

The **BritRail Days Out from London Pass** is best suited for visitors wishing to make day trips in Southern England to Oxford, Cambridge, Brighton, or Canterbury. The cost for 2 days within an 8-day period is $89 for adults and $45 for children in first class or $59 for adults and $30 for children in second class.

For more information on train pass options and on rail vacation packages in England and the U.K., contact **BritRail** (© **866/BRITAIL** or 877/ 677-1066; www.britrail.net and www. BritainSecrets.com).

Travelers who arrive from France by boat and pick up a BritRail train at Dover, arrive at **Victoria Station,** in the center of London. Those journeying south by rail from Edinburgh arrive at **King's Cross Station.**

Train Routes in England

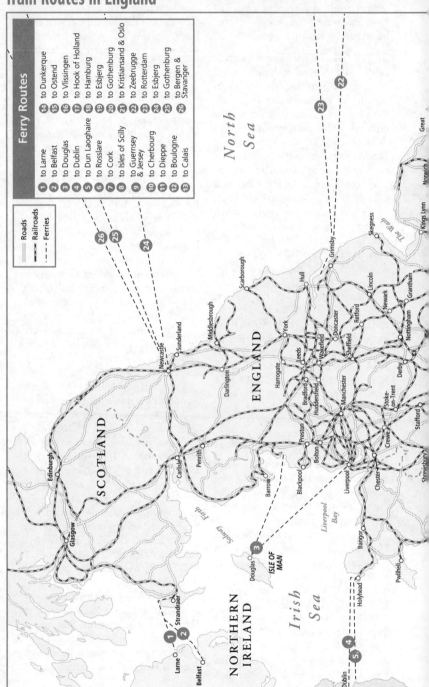

Ferry Routes

1. to Larne
2. to Belfast
3. to Douglas
4. to Dublin
5. to Dun Laoghaire
6. to Rosslare
7. to Cork
8. to Isles of Scilly
9. to Guernsey & Jersey
10. to Cherbourg
11. to Dieppe
12. to Boulogne
13. to Calais
14. to Dunkerque
15. to Ostend
16. to Vlissingen
17. to Hook of Holland
18. to Hamburg
19. to Esbjerg
20. to Gothenburg
21. to Kristiansand & Oslo
22. to Zeebrugge
23. to Rotterdam
24. to Esbjerg
25. to Gothenburg
26. to Bergen & Stavanger

Roads
Railroads
Ferries

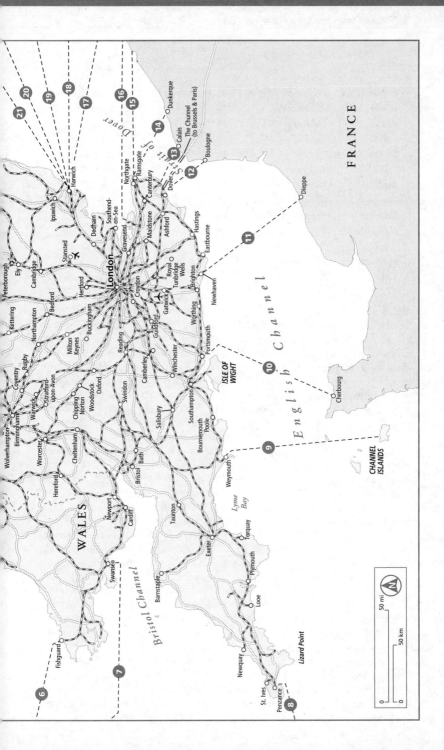

Train Travel from London to Principal Cities

To	Station	Typical No. of Trains Per Day	Miles	Travel Time
Bath	Paddington	25	107	1 hr. 11 min.
Birmingham	Euston/Paddington	35	113	1 hr. 37 min.
Bristol	Paddington	46	119	1 hr. 26 min.
Cardiff	Paddington	24	148	2 hr.
Carlisle	Euston	10	299	3 hr. 40 min.
Chester	Euston	16	179	2 hr. 36 min.
Exeter	Paddington	17	174	1 hr. 55 min.
Leeds	King's Cross	19	185	2 hr. 12 min.
Liverpool	Euston	14	193	2 hr. 34 min.
Manchester	Euston	16	180	2 hr. 27 min.
Newcastle	King's Cross	26	268	2 hr. 50 min.
Penzance	Paddington	9	305	5 hr.
Plymouth	Paddington	14	226	2 hr. 35 min.
York	King's Cross	27	188	1 hr. 57 min.

BY BUS

In Britain, a long-distance touring bus is called a "coach," and "buses" are taken for local transportation. An efficient and frequent express motorcoach network—run by National Express and other independent operators—links most of Britain's towns and cities. Destinations off the main route can be easily reached by transferring to a local bus at a stop on the route. Tickets are relatively cheap, often half the price of rail fare, and it's usually cheaper to purchase a round-trip (or "return") ticket than two one-way fares separately.

Victoria Coach Station, on Buckingham Palace Road (© **020/7730-3466**), is the departure point for most large coach operators. The coach station is located just 2 blocks from Victoria Station. For credit card sales (MasterCard and Visa only), call © **020/7730-3499** Monday through Saturday between 9am and 7pm. For cash purchases, get there at least 30 minutes before the coach departs.

National Express (© **0870/580-8080;** www.nationalexpress.com) runs long-distance coaches that are equipped with reclining seats, toilets, and non-smoking areas. You can obtain details about all coach services by calling the company between 8am and 10pm. The National Express ticket office at Victoria Station is open from 6am to 11pm.

You may want to consider National Express's **Tourist Trail Pass,** which offers unlimited travel on their network. (This company's service is most extensive in England and Wales.) A 2-day pass costs $109, a 5-day pass $169, an 8-day pass $259, and a 15-day pass $343 to $375.

For journeys within a 56km (35-mile) radius of London, try the **Green Line** coach service, 23–27 Endsleigh Rd., Merstham Redhill, Surrey RH1 3LX (© **0870/608-7261;** www.greenline.co.uk). With a 1-day **Diamond Rover Ticket,** costing £8 ($13) for adults and £5 ($8.25) for children, you can visit many of the attractions of Greater London and the surrounding region, including Windsor Castle and Hampton Court. The pass is valid for 1 day on almost all Green Line coaches and country buses Monday through Friday after 9am and all day on Saturday and Sunday.

Green Line has bus routes called Country Bus Lines that circle through the periphery of London. Though they do not usually go directly into the center of the capital, they do hook up with the routes of the Green Line coaches and red buses that do.

In Wales, 65 independent bus operators serve the little country. Public transport guides for local areas are available at tourist offices. One of the most important is **TrawsCambria** (© **0870/608-2608**), servicing the main north-south route through Wales. This bus will carry you from Cardiff to Holyhead and other points in the north of Wales, and BritRail and Freedom of Wales rail passes are valid on this run. The area around Cardiff is covered by **Cardiff Bus** (© **029/2066-6444;** www.cardiff bus.com). Most of North Wales is serviced by a regional bus company, **Arriva Cymru** (© **0870/120-1088**).

16 Tips on Accommodations

Reserve your accommodations as far in advance as possible, even in the so-called slow months from November to April. Tourist travel to London peaks from May to October, and during that period, it's hard to come by a moderate or inexpensive hotel room.

CLASSIFICATIONS
Unlike some countries, England has no rigid hotel classification system. The tourist board grades hotels by stars. Hotels are judged on standards, quality, and hospitality, and are rated "approved," "commended," "highly commended," and "deluxe." Five stars (deluxe) is the highest rating. A classification of "listed" refers to accommodations that are, for the most part, very modest.

All establishments from two stars upward are required to have 100% ensuite (private bathroom) facilities. In a one-star hotel, buildings are required to have hot and cold running water in all rooms, but in "listed" hotels, hot and cold running water in rooms is not mandatory. Star ratings are posted outside the buildings. However, the system is voluntary, and many hotels do not participate.

Many hotels, especially older ones, still lack private bathrooms for all rooms. However, most have hot and cold running water, and many have modern wings with all the amenities (and older sections that are less up to date). When making reservations, always ask what section of the hotel you'll be staying in.

All hotels once included in the room price a full English breakfast of bacon and eggs, but today that is true of only some hotels. A continental breakfast is commonly included, usually just tea or coffee and toast.

BED & BREAKFASTS
In towns, cities, and villages throughout Britain, homeowners take in paying guests. Watch for the familiar bed-and-breakfast (B&B) signs. Generally, these are modest family homes, but sometimes they may be built like small hotels, with as many as 15 rooms. If they're that big, they are more properly classified as guesthouses. B&Bs are the cheapest places you can stay in England and still be comfortable.

Hometours International (© **866/ 367-4668** or 865/690-8484; home tours@aol.com) will make bed-and-breakfast reservations in England, Scotland, and Wales. This is the only company to guarantee reservations for more than 400 locations in Britain. Accommodations are paid for in the United States in dollars, and prices start as low as $55 per person per night, though they can go as high as $105 per person in London. The company can also arrange for apartments in London or cottages in Great Britain that begin at $800 to $1,400 per week for a studio. In addition, it offers walking tours of Great Britain, with prices starting as low as $850 for 7 days, including meals, a guide, and accommodations.

Reservations for bed-and-breakfast accommodations in London can also be made by writing (not calling) the **British Visitor Centre,** 1 Regent St., London W1. Once in London, you can also visit their office (Tube: Piccadilly Circus).

In addition, Susan Opperman and Rosemary Lumb run **Bed and Breakfast Nationwide,** P.O. Box 2100, Clacton-on-Sea, Essex CO16 9BW, an agency specializing in privately owned bed-and-breakfasts all over Great Britain. Host homes range from small cottages to large manor houses, as well as working farms, and the prices vary accordingly. One thing you can be sure of is that owners have been specially selected for their wish to entertain visitors from overseas. Remember that these are private homes, so hotel-type services are not available. You will, however, be assured of a warm welcome, a comfortable bed, a hearty breakfast, and a glimpse of British life. Write for a free brochure. For bookings in accommodations outside London, call (© **01255/831235** or fax 01255/831437 daily between 9am and 6pm. Or check out their website at **www.bedandbreakfast nationwide.com**.

FARMHOUSES

In many parts of the country, farmhouses have one, two, even four rooms set aside for paying guests, who usually arrive in the summer months. Farmhouses don't have the facilities of most guesthouses, but they have a rustic appeal and charm, especially for motorists, as they tend to lie off the beaten path. Prices are generally lower than bed-and-breakfasts or guesthouses, and sometimes you're offered some good country home cooking

(at an extra charge) if you make arrangements in advance.

Farm Stay UK (© **024/7669-6909;** www.farmstayuk.co.uk) publishes an annual directory in early December that includes 1,000 farms and bed-and-breakfasts throughout the United Kingdom. The listings include quality ratings, the number of bedrooms, nearby attractions and activities, prices, and line drawings of each property. Also listed are any special details, such as rooms with four-poster beds or activities on the grounds (fishing, for example). Many farms are geared toward children, who can participate in light chores—gathering eggs or just tagging along—for an authentic farm experience. The prices range from £23 to £55 ($43–$102) a night and include an English breakfast and usually private facilities. (The higher prices are for stays at mansions and manor houses.)

Another option is self-catering accommodations, which are usually cottages or converted barns that cost from £175 to £522 ($324–$966) per week and include dishwashers and central heating. Each property is inspected annually not only by the Farm Holiday Bureau but also by the English Tourist Board. The majority of the properties, with the exception of those located in the mountains, are open year-round.

For a copy of the directory called *Stay on a Farm,* contact **Farm Stay UK,** National Agricultural Centre, Stoneleigh Park, Warwickshire CV8 2LZ (© **024/7669-6909;** www.farm stayuk.co.uk). It costs £3.95 ($7.30) for postage and may be purchased by credit card.

NATIONAL TRUST PROPERTIES

The National Trust of England, Wales, and Northern Ireland, 36 Queen Anne's Gate, London SW1H 9AS (© **0870/609-5380;** www.national trust.org.uk), is Britain's leading conservation organization. In addition to the many castles, forests, and gardens it maintains, the National Trust owns almost 310 houses and cottages in some of the most beautiful parts of England, Wales, and Northern Ireland. Some of these properties are in remote and rural locations; some have incomparable views of the coastline; and others stand in the heart of villages and ancient cities.

Most of these comfortable self-catering holiday accommodations are available for rental throughout the year. Examples include a simple former coast guard cottage in Northumbria, a gas-lit hideaway on the Isle of Wight, a gem of a country house above the Old Brewhouse at Chastleton, a 15th-century manor house in a hidden corner of the Cotswolds, and a superb choice of cottages in Devon and Cornwall. Houses can be booked for a week or more. Many can be booked for midweek or weekend breaks on short notice, particularly in autumn and winter. National Trust properties can sleep from 2 to 12 guests, and range in price from £179 ($331) per week for a small rental in winter to £1,906 ($3,526) per week for a larger property in peak season. Prices include value-added tax (VAT). Call © **0870/ 458-4422** for reservations.

Though anyone can book rentals in National Trust properties, it's worth mentioning the trust's U.S. affiliate, the **Royal Oak Foundation,** 26 Broadway, Suite 950, New York, NY 10004 (© **800/913-6565** or 212/ 480-2889; www.royal-oak.org), which publishes a full-color 350-page booklet that describes all National Trust holiday rental properties, their facilities, and prices. Copies cost $10 for nonmembers. Individual annual memberships are $50, and family memberships are $75. Benefits include free admission to all National Trust sites and properties open to the public, plus discounts on reservations at cottages and houses owned by them and discounted air and train travel.

HOLIDAY COTTAGES & VILLAGES

Throughout Britain, fully furnished studios, houses, cottages, "flats" (apartments), even trailers suitable for families or groups, can be rented by the month. From October to March, rents are sometimes reduced by 50%.

The British Tourist Authority and most tourist offices have lists available. The BTA's free *Apartments in London and Holiday Homes* lists rental agencies such as **At Home Abroad, Inc.,** 163 3 Ave., Box 319, New York, NY 10003 (© **212/421-9165;** www.athome abroadinc.com). Interested parties should write or fax a description of their needs; At Home Abroad will send listings at no charge.

British Travel International (© **800/327-6097** or 540/298-2232; www.britishtravel.com) represents between 8,000 and 10,000 rental properties in the United Kingdom, with rentals by the week (Sat–Sat), and requires a 50% payment at the time of booking. A catalog with pictures of their offerings is available for a $5 fee that is counted toward a deposit. They have everything from honey-colored, thatch-roofed cottages in the Cotswolds to apartments in a British university city. The company represents about 100 hotels in London whose rates are discounted by 5% to 50%, depending on the season and market conditions, and they have listings of some 4,000 bed-and-breakfast establishments.

Barclay International Group (BIG), 3 School St., Glen Cove, NY 11542 (© **800/845-6636** or 516/ 759-5100; www.barclayweb.com) specializes in short-term apartment (flat) rentals in London and cottages in the English countryside. These rentals can be appropriate for families, groups of friends, or businesspeople traveling together and are sometimes less expensive than equivalent stays in hotels. Apartments, available for stays as short as 1 night (though the company prefers that guests stay a minimum of 3 nights and charges a premium if your stay is shorter), are usually more luxurious than you'd imagine. Furnished with kitchens, they offer a low-cost alternative to restaurant meals. Apartments suitable for one or two occupants begin, during low season, at around $500 a week (including tax) and can go much higher for deluxe accommodations that offer many hotel-like features and amenities. For extended stays in the English countryside, BIG has country cottages in such areas as the Cotswolds, the Lake District, and Oxford, as well as farther afield in Scotland and Wales. The company can also arrange tickets for sightseeing attractions, BritRail passes, and various other "extras." A big catalog of their offerings costs $10.

At the cheaper end of the spectrum, there's **Hoseasons Holidays,** Lowestoft, NR32 2LW (© **01502/502588;** www.hoseasons.co.uk), a reservations agent based in Suffolk (East Anglia). They arrange stopovers in at least 400 vacation villages throughout Britain. Though many are isolated in bucolic regions far from any of the sites covered within this guide, others lie within an hour's drive of Stratford-upon-Avon. Don't expect luxury or convenience: Vacation villages in England usually consist of a motley assortment of trailers, uninsulated bungalows, and/or mobile homes perched on cement blocks. They're intended as frugal escapes for claustrophobic urbanites with children. Such a place may not meet your expectations for a vacation in the English countryside (and a minimum stay of 3 nights is usually required), but it's hard to beat the rate. A 3-day sojourn begins from £92 ($170) per person, double occupancy.

CHAIN HOTELS

Many American chains, such as Best Western, Hilton, and Sheraton are found throughout Britain. In addition, Britain has a number of leading chains with which North American travelers are generally not familiar. **Travelodge** (© **0870/085-0950;** www.travelodge.co.uk) is a good quality modern budget accommodations across the U.K. with a family restaurant on-site. **Swallow Hotels** (© **0845/600-4666;** www.swallowhotels.com) are modern government-rated four-crown hotels, most with leisure facilities. **Thistle Hotels** (© **0870/333-9292;** www.thistlehotels.com) is a well-regarded chain of upscale to moderate full-service hotels that caters to both business and leisure travelers. An exclusive chain of government-rated three-crown hotels is called **Malmaison** (© **01737/780200;** www.malmaison.com). There's not a bad hotel in their post. **Premier Lodge** (© **01604/824202;** www.premierlodge.co.uk) is a new chain of modern, moderately priced accommodations across the U.K., each one featuring a licensed restaurant.

HOUSE SWAPPING

The market leader in home exchanges is **HomeLink International,** P.O. Box 47747, Tampa, FL 33647 (© **800/638-3841** or 813/975-9825; www.homelink.org), which costs $70 to join. This is the oldest, largest, and best home exchange holiday organization in the world. The series is called a "home from home," and so it is. The only trouble is, you've got to turn your own home over to a stranger.

A competitor is **Intervac U.S. & International,** 30 Corte San Fernando, Tiburon, CA 94159 (© **800/756-HOME** or 415/435-3497; www.intervacus.com). To hook up with this outfitter, you pay $65 annually. Intervac is also adept at securing a list of home exchanges throughout Great Britain.

YOUTH HOSTELS

Youth Hostels Association (England and Wales) operates a network of 230 youth hostels in major cities, in the countryside, and along the coast. You can contact them at Customer Services Department, YHA, Trevelyan House, Dimple Road, Matlock, Derbyshire DE4 3YH (© **0870/ 870-8808;** www.yha.org.uk) for a free map with locations of each youth hostel and full details, including prices.

17 Tips on Shopping

When shopping for the best buys in England, note that British goods, even products from Wales, may offer sensational buys even when sold on home ground. You will also find Irish stores and Irish departments in some stores often selling merchandise at the same good value you'd find on a shopping trip to Ireland itself. Many French brands, it may come as a surprise, are less expensive in the United Kingdom than in France.

This section is an overview of Britain's shopping scene, including what's hot, where to get it, and how you can save money and secure value-added tax (VAT) refunds. If you're heading to London, check out chapter 5 for coverage of the capital's shopping and the famous sales.

THE BEST BUYS OF BRITAIN

When bargain hunting, focus on those goods that are manufactured in Britain and are liable to cost much more when exported. These include anything from The Body Shop and Filofax to Doc Martens; many woolens and some cashmeres; most English brands of bone china; and antiques, used silver, and rare books.

ANTIQUES   Whether you're looking for museum-quality antiques or simply fun junk, Britain has the stores, the resources, the stalls, and the markets. You can shop the fanciest of upmarket shops—mostly in London, Bath, and the Cotswolds—or browse through antiques shows, markets, fairs, buildings, centers, arcades, warehouses, jumble fairs, fetes, and car boot (trunk) sales throughout the country. (A car boot sale is the British version of a yard sale. Participants set up tables at an abandoned parking lot or airfield to sell their goods.)

Actually, prices are better once you get outside of London. Entire towns and areas in Britain are known to be treasure troves for those seeking anything from architectural salvage to a piece of the Holy Grail. Whereas the Cotswolds and Bath are known as charming places to shop for antiques, there are warehouses in Suffolk, Merseyside, and in the Greater Manchester (Yorkshire and Lancashire) area that aren't glamorous but offer dealers and those in the know the best buys. Serious shoppers can head directly to the Manchester area, get a car or van, and just start shopping. The best hunting grounds are Boughton (right outside Chester), Liverpool, Prestwich, and Stockport. Harrogate and nearby Knaresborough are known for antiques, but they offer a far more upscale scene with prices competitive to those in the Cotswolds.

AROMATHERAPY   The British must have invented aromatherapy—just about every store sells gels, creams, lotions, or potions made with the right herbs and essential oils to cure whatever ails you, including jet lag. Whether it works or not is secondary to the fact that most of the British brands are half the U.S. price when bought on home soil. **The Body Shop** becomes the best store in the world at prices like these. Check out drugstore brands as well. Shoppers like The Body Shop knockoffs that **Boots The Chemist** makes, as well as their own line (sold in another part of the store) of healing foot gels. Both of these are national brands available all over the United Kingdom. In addition, some small communities have homemade brands—check out **Woods of Windsor** (in the heart of downtown Windsor) for English flower soaps, lotions, and cures.

BASIC BRIT GEAR Don't assume any bargains on woolens, cashmeres, tweeds, and the like—often British quality is much higher than similar and less expensive goods available in the United States. If you want the best and expect it to last forever, you can't beat British-made, especially in gear that has been fine-tuned over the last century for the weather and outdoor lifestyle: from wax coats (**Barbour** is the leading status brand) to raincoats to guns (and English roses). While we can hardly put **Doc Martens** brand of shoes in the traditional Brit category, they do cost a lot less in Britain than in America. The other quintessential English accessory is the **Filofax,** sold in a variety of versions with inserts galore for 30% to 50% less than prices in the United States.

BEAUTY   PRODUCTS Dimestore brands of makeup cost less than they do in the United States. The French line **Bourjois** (made in the same factories that produce Chanel makeup) costs less in London than in Paris and isn't sold in the United States; Boots makes its own Chanel knockoff line, **Number 7.**

BONE CHINA Savings actually depend on the brand, but can be as much as 50% off U.S. prices. The trick is that shipping and U.S. duties may wipe out any savings; know what you're doing before you buy—and how you plan to get it back. Don't forget factory outlets that sell seconds.

DESIGNER THIS & THAT Designer clothing from any of the international makers may be less in London than in the United States or Paris, but know your prices. Often the only difference is the VAT refund, which at 15% to 17.5% is substantial. This game is also highly dependent on the value of the dollar.

While you won't get a VAT refund on used designer clothing, London has the best prices on used Chanel (and similar) clothing of any major shopping city.

HATS "Does anyone still wear a hat?" Elaine Stritch asked archly in the musical *Company.* In Britain, the answer is yes. Everyone wears a hat, including the queen. Hats are sold all over England in department stores and specialty stores. Resale shops are an excellent graveyard for m'lady's discards.

ROYAL SOUVENIRS Forget about investing in Diana memorabilia; word is that it won't appreciate significantly because there was so much of it. Still, royal collectibles can be cheap kitsch bought in street markets or serious pieces from coronations long past found in specialist's shops. If you're buying new for investment purposes, it must be kept in mint condition.

TAPESTRY & KNITTING For some reason, the British call needlepoint "tapestry." It's a passion, perhaps the seasonal flip side to gardening. Tapestry kits by the famous English designers, and Welsh queen of needles Elizabeth Bradley, cost a fraction of their U.S. prices when purchased anywhere in England or Wales.

Whereas Britain is famous for its sweaters (jumpers), what it should be famous for are the sweater kits: do-it-yourself jobs from the major designers that come with yarn, instructions, and a photo. English knitter-designers are cult heroes in Britain and do everything but knit autographs.

SHOPPING STRATEGIES

Most towns feature a main street, usually called the High Street. On this one road you'll find a branch of each of what is locally called "the High Street multiples," the chain stores that dominate the retail scene.

The leader among them is **Marks & Spencer,** a private label department store with high-quality goods at fair value prices. Others include **Boots The Chemist** (a drugstore); **Laura Ashley** (less expensive in the U.K.); **The Body Shop** (the most popular and politically correct bath and beauty statement of our times); **Monsoon** (a firm that sells hot fashion made from Far Eastern fabrics for moderate prices; they also have a dress-up division called **Twilight** and an accessories business called **Accessorize**); **Habitat** (sort of the English version of the Pottery Barn); and maybe (if you're lucky) **Past Times,** sort of a museum shop selling reproduction gifts and souvenirs. **Shelly's, Pied a Terre,** and **Hobbs** are all shoe stores selling everything from Doc Martens to expensive-looking cheap shoes. **Knickerbox** is usually found in train stations rather than on High streets, but it's interesting nonetheless—the store sells fashion underwear at what the British call moderate prices.

ANTIQUES GALORE Napoleon was wrong; Britain is not a nation of shopkeepers—it's a nation of antiques collectors. Weekends are devoted to fairs and markets; evenings can be spent reading the dozens of newsstand specialty magazines or the plethora of books geared toward collectors. Books in Britain are more expensive than in the U.S., but the selection of titles on design, home furnishings, do-it-yourself, and collecting is staggering.

A number of famous antiques fairs are held at certain times of the year, as well as several annual big-time events that attract several thousand dealers and thousands of shoppers. Among the best outside of London are those held at the **Newark and Nottinghamshire Showgrounds** (six times a year); **Sussex Midweek Fairs,** Ardingly (six

times a year); **Newmarket** (four times a year); **Shepton Mallet** (four times a year); **Cardiff International** (twice a year); and **Royal Welsh Showgrounds** (twice a year). For the exact dates of any of these events, contact **DMG Cooper Antiques Fairs** (© 01278/784912; fax 01278/79287; www.cooperantiques fairs.co.uk); or **DMG Antiques Fairs, Ltd.** (© 01636/702326; www.dmg antiquesfairs.co.uk.

For immediate information on antiques fairs and events, check the magazine section of the *Sunday Times* where you'll find the Antique Buyer's Guide, which lists fairs all over England, not just in London.

At continual **car boot sales,** as well as **house sales,** entire estates are cleaned out. There are only a few of these each year, and they become sort of voyeuristic social events; people drive for miles in order to attend. Advertisements are usually taken in magazines such as *Country Life*.

Just as house sales have boomed in recent years, the other big trend to come out of the recession is that **resale shops** are springing up all over. No one seems shy about admitting that her Chanel and Louis Feraud are secondhand. London has a lot of these shops, but many out-of-the-way towns and cities have enormous resale shops as well.

TAXES & SHIPPING Value-added tax (VAT) is the British version of sales tax, but it is a whopping 17.5% on most goods. This tax is added to the total so that the price on a sales tag already includes VAT. Non–European Union residents can get back all, or most, of this tax if they apply for a VAT refund (see the sidebar, "How to Get Your VAT Refund").

One of the first secrets of shopping in Britain is that the minimum expenditure needed to qualify for a refund on value-added tax (VAT) is a mere £50 ($93). Not every store honors this minimum—it's £100 ($185) at

How to Get Your VAT Refund

To receive back a portion of the tax paid on purchases made in Britain, first ask the store personnel if they do VAT refunds and what their minimum purchase is. Once you've achieved this minimum, ask for the paperwork; the retailer will have to fill out a portion themselves. Several readers have reported that merchants have told them that they can get refund forms at the airport on their way out of the country. *This is not true.* You must get a refund form from the retailer (don't leave the store without one), and it must be completed by the retailer on the spot.

Fill out your portion of the form and present it, along with the goods, at the Customs office in the airport. Allow a half-hour to stand in line. *Remember:* You're required to show the goods at your time of departure, so don't pack them in your luggage and check it; put them in your carry-on instead.

Once you have the paperwork stamped by the officials, you have two choices: You can mail the papers and receive your refund in either a British check (no!) or a credit card refund (yes!), or you can go directly to the Cash VAT Refund desk at the airport and get your refund in your hand, in cash. The bad news: If you accept cash other than sterling, you will lose money on the conversion rate. (If you plan on mailing your paperwork, try to remember to bring a stamp with you to the airport; if you forget, you can usually get stamps from stamp machines and/or the convenience stores in the terminal.)

Be advised that many stores charge a flat fee for processing your refund, so £3 to £5 ($5.55–$9.25) may be automatically deducted from the refund you receive. But because the VAT in Britain is 17.5%, if you get back 15%, you're doing fine.

Note: If traveling to other countries within the European Union, you don't go through any of this in Britain. At your final destination, before departure from the European Union, you file for all your VAT refunds at one time.

Harrods, £75 ($139) at Selfridges, £62 ($115) at Hermès, but it's far easier to qualify for a tax refund in Britain than almost any other country in the European Union.

Vendors at flea markets may not be equipped to provide the paperwork for a refund, so if you're contemplating a major purchase and really want that refund, ask before you fall in love. Be suspicious of any dealer who tells you there's no VAT on antiques. There didn't use to be, but there is now. The European Union has now made the British add VAT to antiques. Because dealers still have mixed stock, pricing should reflect this fact. So ask if it's included before you bargain on a price. Get to the price you're comfortable with, *then* ask for the VAT refund.

VAT is not charged on goods shipped out of the country, whether you spend £50 ($93) or not. Many London shops help you beat the VAT by shipping for you. But watch out: Shipping can double the cost of your purchase. Also, expect to pay U.S. duties when the goods reach home.

You may want to consider paying for excess baggage (rates vary with the airline) or have your packages shipped independently. Independent operators are generally less expensive than the airlines. Try **Excess Baggage** (© 020/8759-3344; www.excess-baggage.com), which can be found at Heathrow Airport in all four terminals.

DUTY-FREE AIRPORT SHOPPING Shopping at airports is big business, so big business has taken over the management of some of Britain's airports to ensure that passengers in transit are enticed to buy. All terminals at London Heathrow Airport are a virtual shopping mall.

Prices at the airport for items such as souvenirs and candy bars are higher than on the streets of London, but the duty-free prices on luxury goods are usually fair. There are often promotions and coupons that allow for pounds off at the time of the purchase.

Don't save all your shopping until you get to the airport, but do know prices on land and sea so that you know when to pounce.

18 Sightseeing Passes

Several passes can cut down considerably on entrance costs to the country's stately homes and gardens. If you plan to do extensive touring, you'll save a lot of pounds by using one of these passes instead of paying the relatively steep entrance fees on an attraction-by-attraction basis.

Listed below are three organizations that offer passes waiving admission charges to hundreds of historical properties located throughout the United Kingdom. Each is a good deal, as the money you'll save on visitation to just a few of the available sites will pay for the price of the pass.

BRITISH NATIONAL TRUST The National Trust offers members free entry to some 240 National Trust sites in Britain. Focusing on gardens, castles, historic parks, abbeys, and ruins, sites include Chartwell, St. Michael's Mount, and Beatrix Potter's House. The membership fee includes a listing of properties, maps, essential information for independent tours, and listings and reservations for holiday cottages located on the protected properties.

Individual memberships cost £34 ($63) annually, and family memberships, for up to seven people, run £63 ($116). Savings on admission charges, combined with discounts on holiday cottage reservations and British Air or BritRail travel, make this especially appealing. Visa and MasterCard are accepted.

Contact **The British National Trust,** 36 Queen Anne's Gate, London SW1H 9AS (© 0870/609-5380; www.nationaltrust.org.uk), or **The Royal Oak Foundation,** 26 Broadway, Suite 950, New York, NY 10004 (© 800/913-6565 or 212/480-2889; www.royal-oak.org).

ENGLISH HERITAGE This organization sells 7- and 14-day passes and annual memberships, offering free admission to more than 300 historical sites in England, and half-price admission to more than 100 additional sites in Scotland, Wales, and the Isle of Man. (Admission to these additional sites is free for anyone who renews his or her annual membership after the first year.) Sites include Hadrian's Wall, Stonehenge, and Kenilworth Castle.

Also included are: free or reduced admission to 450 historic reenactments and open-air summer concerts, a handbook detailing all properties, a map, and, with the purchase of an annual membership, events and concerts diaries, and *Heritage Today,* a quarterly magazine.

A 7-day Overseas Visitor Pass runs £15 ($28) for an adult or £32 ($59) for a family of six or less. A child accompanied by an adult goes free. A 14-day pass is £19 ($35) for an adult (free for a child) or £40 ($74) for a family. Annual memberships are also available with rates of £34 ($63) for an adult, £15 ($28) for those under 19. MasterCard and Visa are accepted.

For visitor passes and membership, contact **Customer Services, English Heritage,** 23 Savile Row, London W1S 2ET (© **020/7973-3000;** www. english-heritage.org.uk), or join directly at the site.

THE GREAT BRITISH HERITAGE PASS Available from **BritRail,** this pass allows entry to more than 500 public and privately owned historic properties, including Shakespeare's birthplace, Stonehenge, Windsor Castle, and Edinburgh Castle. Included in the price is *The Great British Heritage Gazetteer,* a brochure that lists the properties with maps and essential information.

A pass gains you entrance into private properties not otherwise approachable. A 4-day pass is $55, 7-day pass costs $85, a 15-day pass is available for $115, and a 1-month pass is $150. Passes are nonrefundable, and there is no discounted children's rate. A $10 handling fee is charged additionally for each ticket issued.

To order passes, contact **Visit Britain** at 551 Fifth Ave. (at 45th St.), New York, NY 10176 (© **800/462-2748** or 212/986-2266; www.visit britain.com). You can also order passes on the Web at www.britainontrack. com.

19 Recommended Reading

GENERAL & HISTORY

Anthony Sampson's *The Changing Anatomy of Britain* (Random House) still gives great insight into the idiosyncrasies of English society, Winston Churchill's *History of the English-Speaking Peoples* (Dodd Mead) is a tour de force in four volumes, while *The Gathering Storm* (Houghton-Mifflin) captures Europe on the brink of World War II.

My Love Affair with England (Ballantine), by Susan Allan Toth, tells of England's "many-layered past," and includes such tidbits as why English marmalade tastes good only when consumed as part of a real (make that greasy) English breakfast.

Britons: Forging the Nation (1707–1837) (Yale University Press), by Linda Colley, took more than a decade to finish. Ms. Colley takes the reader from the date of the Act of Union (formally joining Scotland and Wales to England) to the succession of the adolescent Victoria to the British throne. *Children of the Sun* (Basics Books), by Martin Green, portrays the "decadent" Twenties and the lives of such people as Randolph Churchill, Rupert Brooke, the Prince of Wales, and Christopher Isherwood.

In *A Writer's Britain* (Knopf), contemporary English author Margaret Drabble takes readers on a tour of the sacred and haunted literary landscapes of England, places that inspired Hardy, Woolf, Spenser, and Marvell.

Outsiders often paint more penetrating portraits than residents of any culture ever can. In England's case, many have expressed their views of the country at different periods. An early 18th-century portrait is provided by K. P. Moritz in *Journeys of a German in England in 1782* (Holt, Rinehart & Winston), about his travels from London to the Midlands. Nathaniel Hawthorne recorded his impressions in *Our Old Home* (1863), as did Ralph Waldo Emerson in *English Traits* (1856). For an ironic portrait of mid-19th-century Victorian British morals, manners, and society, seek out *Taine's Notes on England* (1872). Henry James comments on England at the turn of the 20th century in *English Hours*. In *A Passage to England* (St. Martins Press), Nirad Chaudhuri analyzes Britain and the British in a delightful, humorous book—a process continued today by such authors as Salman Rushdie, V. S. Naipaul, and Paul Theroux. Among the interesting portraits written by natives are Cobbet's *Rural Rides* (1830), depicting early-19th-century England; *In Search of England* (Methuen) by H. V. Morton; and *English Journey* (Harper) by J. B. Priestley. For what's really going on behind that serene Suffolk village scene, read Ronald Blythe's *Akenfield: Portrait of an English Village* (Random House).

ART & ARCHITECTURE

For general reference, there's the huge multivolume *Oxford History of English Art* (Oxford University Press), and also the *Encyclopedia of British Art* (Thames Hudson), by David Bindman. *Painting in Britain 1530–1790* (Penguin), by Ellis Waterhouse, covers British art from the Tudor miniaturists to Gainsborough, Reynolds, and Hogarth, while *English Art, 1870–1940* (Oxford University Press), by Dennis Farr, covers the modern period.

On architecture, for sheer amusing, opinionated entertainment try John Betjeman's *Ghastly Good Taste—the Rise and Fall of English Architecture* (St. Martin's Press). *A History of English Architecture* (Penguin), by Peter Kidson, Peter Murray, and Paul Thompson, covers the subject from Anglo-Saxon to modern times. Nikolaus Pevsner's *The Best Buildings of England: An Anthology* (Viking) and his *Outline of European Architecture* (Penguin) concentrate on the great periods of Tudor, Georgian, and Regency architecture. Mark Girouard has written several books on British architecture including *The Victorian Country House* (Country Life) and *Life in the English Country House* (Yale

University Press), a fascinating social/architectural history from the Middle Ages to the 20th century, with handsome illustrations.

ABOUT LONDON

London Perceived (Hogarth), by novelist and literary critic V. S. Pritchett, is a witty portrait of the city's history, art, literature, and life. Virginia Woolf's *The London Scene: Five Essays* (Random House) brilliantly depicts the London of the 1930s. *In Search of London* (Methuen), by H. V. Morton, is filled with anecdotal history and well worth reading, though written in the 1950s.

In *London: The Biography of a City* (Penguin), popular historian Christopher Hibbert paints a lively portrait. For some real 17th-century history, you can't beat the *Diary of Samuel Pepys* (written 1660–69), and for the flavor of the 18th century, try Daniel Defoe's *Tour Thro' London About the Year 1725* (Ayer).

Americans in London (William Morrow), by Brian N. Morton, is a street-by-street guide to clubs, homes, and favorite pubs of over 250 illustrious Americans who made London a temporary home. The *Guide to Literary London* (Batsford), by George Williams, charts literary tours through London from Chelsea to Bloomsbury.

The Architect's Guide to London (Reed International), by Renzo Salvadori, documents 100 landmark buildings with photographs and maps. *Nairn's London* (Penguin), by Ian Nairn, is a stimulating discourse on London's buildings. Donald Olsen's *The City as a Work of Art: London, Paris, and Vienna* (Yale University Press) is a well-illustrated text tracing the evolution of these great cities. *London One: The Cities of London and Westminster* and *London Two: South* (Penguin) are works of love by well-known architectural writers Bridget Cherry and Nikolaus Pevsner. David

Piper's *The Artist's London* (Oxford University Press) does what the title suggests—captures the city that artists have portrayed. In *Victorian and Edwardian London* (Batsford), John Betjeman expresses his great love of those eras and their great buildings. *Looking Up in London* by Jane Peyton (Wiley Academy) offers colorful photos of some of London's architectural features.

FICTION & BIOGRAPHY

Among English writers are found some of the greatest exponents of mystery and suspense novels from which a reader can get a good feel for English life both urban and rural. Agatha Christie, P. D. James, and Dorothy Sayers are a few of the familiar names, but the great London character is, of course, Sherlock Holmes, created by Arthur Conan Doyle. Any of these writers will give pleasure and insight into your London experience.

England's literary heritage is so vast, it's hard to select particular titles, but here are a few favorites. Master storyteller Charles Dickens re-creates Victorian London in such books as *Oliver Twist, David Copperfield,* and his earlier satirical *Sketches by Boz.*

Edwardian London and the '20s and '30s are captured wonderfully in any of Evelyn Waugh's social satires and comedies; any work from the Bloomsbury group will also prove enlightening, like Virginia Woolf's *Mrs. Dalloway,* which peers beneath the surface of the London scene. For a portrait of wartime London there's Elizabeth Bowen's *The Heat of the Day;* for an American slant on England and London there's Henry James's *The Awkward Age.*

Among 18th-century figures, there's a great biography of Samuel Johnson by his friend James Boswell, whose *Life of Samuel Johnson* (Modern Library College Editions) was first published in 1791. Antonia Fraser has written several biographies of English monarchs and political figures, including Charles II and Oliver Cromwell. Her most recent is *The Wives of Henry VIII* (Knopf), telling the sad story of the six women foolish enough to marry the Tudor monarch.

Another great Tudor monarch, Elizabeth I, emerges in a fully rounded portrait: *The Virgin Queen, Elizabeth I, Genius of the Golden Age* (Addison-Wesley), by Christopher Hibbert.

Another historian, Anne Somerset, wrote *Elizabeth I* (St. Martin's Press), which was hailed by some critics as the most "readable and reliable" portrait of England's most revered monarch to have emerged since 1934.

No woman—or man, for that matter—had greater influence on London than did Queen Victoria during her long reign (1837–1901). Sarah Ferguson, the duchess of York (Prince Andrew's former wife, "Fergie"), along with Benita Stoney, a professional researcher, captures the era in *Victoria and Albert: A Family Life at Osborne House* (Prentice Hall). One reviewer said that HRH writes about "England's 19th-century rulers not as historical figures but as a loving couple and caring parents."

Another point of view is projected in *Victoria: The Young Queen* (Blackwell), by Monica Charlot. This book has been praised for its "fresh information"; it traces the life of Victoria until the death of her husband, Prince Albert, in 1861. Queen Elizabeth II granted Charlot access to the Royal Archives.

In *Elizabeth II, Portrait of a Monarch* (St. Martin's Press), Douglas Keay drew on interviews with Prince Philip and Prince Charles.

Richard Ellman's *Oscar Wilde* (Knopf) also reveals such Victorian-era personalities as Lillie Langtry, Gilbert and Sullivan, and Henry James along the way. Quintessential English playwright Noel Coward and the London he inhabited, along with the likes of Nancy Mitford, Cecil Beaton, John Gielgud, Laurence Olivier, Vivien Leigh, Evelyn Waugh, and Rebecca West, are captured in Cole Lesley's *Remembered Laughter* (Knopf). *The Lives of John Lennon* (William Morrow), by Albert Goldman, traces the life of this most famous of all '60s musicians.

Dickens (Harper Perennial), by Peter Ackroyd, is a study of the painful life of the novelist. It's a massive volume, tracing everything from the reception of his first novel, *The Pickwick Papers*, to his scandalous desertion of his wife.

Other good reads include *Wild Spirit: The Story of Percy Bysshe Shelley* (Hodder & Stoughton), by Margaret Morley, a fictionalized biography of the poet. *Gertrude Jekyll* (Viking), by Sally Festing, paints a portrait of the woman called "the greatest artist in horticulture." *Anthony Trollope* (Knopf), by Victoria Glendinning, is a provocative portrait of the English novelist. *Lawrence and the Women: The Intimate Life of D. H. Lawrence* (HarperCollins), by Elaine Feinstein, examines involvements with female friends and lovers of this passionately sensitive novelist.

FAST FACTS: England & Wales

For information on London, refer to "Fast Facts: London," in chapter 4.

Area Codes The country code for England and Wales is **44**. The area code for London is **020**; Cardiff's area code is **029**.

Business Hours With many, many exceptions, business hours are Monday through Friday from 9am to 5pm. In general, stores are open Monday through Saturday from 9am to 5:30pm. In country towns, there is usually an early closing day (often on Wed or Thurs), when the shops close at 1pm.

Car Rentals See "Getting Around England & Wales," earlier in this chapter.

Climate See "When to Go," earlier in this chapter.

Currency See "Money," earlier in this chapter.

Customs See "Entry Requirements & Customs," earlier in this chapter.

Documents Required See "Entry Requirements & Customs," earlier in this chapter.

Drugstores In Britain, they're called "chemists." Every police station in the country has a list of emergency chemists. Dial "0" (zero) and ask the operator for the local police, who will give you the name of one nearest you.

Electricity British electricity is 240 volts AC (50 cycles), roughly twice the voltage in North America, which is 115 to 120 volts AC (60 cycles). American plugs don't fit British wall outlets. Always bring suitable transformers and/or adapters—if you plug an American appliance directly into a European electrical outlet without a transformer, you'll destroy your appliance and possibly start a fire. Tape recorders, VCRs, and other devices with motors intended to revolve at a fixed number of revolutions per minute probably won't work properly even with transformers.

Embassies & High Commissions See "Fast Facts: London," in chapter 4.

Emergencies Dial **999** for police, fire, or ambulance. Give your name, address, and telephone number and state the nature of the emergency.

Holidays See "When to Go," earlier in this chapter.

Information See "Visitor Information," earlier in this chapter, and the individual city/regional chapters that follow.

Legal Aid The American Services section of the U.S. Consulate (see "Embassies & High Commissions," under "Fast Facts: London," in chapter 4) will give you advice if you run into trouble abroad. They can advise you of your rights and will even provide a list of attorneys (for which you'll have to pay if services are used). But they cannot interfere on your behalf in the legal processes of Great Britain. For questions about American citizens who are arrested abroad, including ways of getting money to them, telephone the **Citizens Emergency Center** of the Office of Special Consulate Services in Washington, D.C. (✆ **202/647-5225**).

Liquor Laws The legal drinking age is 18. Children under 16 aren't allowed in pubs, except in certain rooms, and then only when accompanied by a parent or guardian. Don't drink and drive. Penalties are stiff.

In Britain, pubs can legally be open Monday through Saturday from 11am to 11pm, and on Sunday from noon to 10:30pm. Premises with a restaurant license can continue serving until midnight (11:30pm Sun), provided the sale of alcohol is ancillary to a table meal. Some businesses with a Supper Hours Certificate, and which provide live entertainment for diners, can apply to the licensing justices for an extended hours order, granting a further extension of drinking hours to 1am Monday through Saturday. In hotels, liquor may be served from 11am to 11pm to both residents and nonresidents; after 11pm, only residents, according to the law, may be served.

Mail Post offices and sub–post offices are open Monday through Friday from 9am to 5:30pm and Saturday from 9:30am to noon.

Sending an airmail letter to North America costs 42p (80¢) for 10 grams (.35 oz.), and postcards require a 34p (65¢) stamp. British mailboxes are painted red and carry a royal coat of arms. All post offices accept parcels for mailing, provided they are properly and securely wrapped.

Passports **For Residents of the United States:** Whether you're applying in person or by mail, you can download passport applications from the U.S. State Department website at **http://travel.state.gov/passport_services. html**. To find your regional passport office, either check the U.S. State Department website or call the toll-free number of the **National Passport Information Center** (✆ **877/487-2778**) for automated information.

For Residents of Canada: Passport applications are available at travel agencies throughout Canada or from the central **Passport Office,** Department of Foreign Affairs and International Trade, Ottawa, ON K1A 0G3 (✆ **800/567-6868;** www.ppt.gc.ca).

For Residents of the United Kingdom: To pick up an application for a standard 10-year passport (5-year passport for children under 16), visit your nearest passport office, major post office, or travel agency, or contact the **United Kingdom Passport Service** at ✆ **0870/521-0410** or search its website at **www.ukpa.gov.uk**.

For Residents of Ireland: You can apply for a 10-year passport at the **Passport Office,** Setanta Centre, Molesworth Street, Dublin 2 (© **01/ 671-1633;** www.irlgov.ie/iveagh). Those under age 18 and over 65 must apply for a 12€ 3-year passport. You can also apply at 1A South Mall, Cork (© **021/272-525**) or at most main post offices.

For Residents of Australia: You can pick up an application from your local post office or any branch of Passports Australia, but you must schedule an interview at the passport office to present your application materials. Call the **Australian Passport Information Service** at © **131-232,** or visit the government website at **www.passports.gov.au**.

For Residents of New Zealand: You can pick up a passport application at any New Zealand Passports Office or download it from their website. Contact the **Passports Office** at © **0800/225-050** in New Zealand or 04/474-8100, or log on to **www.passports.govt.nz**.

Police Dial **999** if the matter is serious. Losses, thefts, and other criminal matters should be reported to the police immediately.

Safety Stay in well-lit areas and out of questionable neighborhoods, especially at night. In Britain, most of the crime perpetrated against tourists is pickpocketing and mugging. These attacks usually occur in such cities as London, Birmingham, or Manchester. Most villages are safe.

Taxes To encourage energy conservation, the British government levies a 25% tax on gasoline (petrol). There is also a 17.5% national value-added tax (VAT) that is added to all hotel and restaurant bills and is included in the price of many items you purchase. This can be refunded if you shop at stores that participate in the Retail Export Scheme (signs are posted in the window). See the "How to Get Your VAT Refund" box in the "Tips on Shopping" section, earlier in this chapter.

In October 1994, Britain imposed a departure tax. Currently it is £40 ($74), but it is included in the price of your ticket.

Telephone To call England from North America, dial **011** (international code), **44** (Britain's country code), the local area codes (usually three or four digits and found in every phone number we've given in this book), and the seven-digit local phone number. The local area codes found throughout this book all begin with "0"; you drop the "0" if you're calling from outside Britain, but you need to dial it along with the area code if you're calling from another city or town within Britain. For calls within the same city or town, the local number is all you need.

For **directory assistance** in London, dial **142;** for the rest of Britain, **192**.
There are three types of public pay phones: those taking only coins, those accepting only phone cards (called Cardphones), and those taking both phone cards and credit cards. At coin-operated phones, insert your coins before dialing. The minimum charge is 10p (20¢).

Phone cards are available in four values—£2 ($3.70), £4 ($7.40), £10 ($19), and £20 ($37)—and are reusable until the total value has expired. Cards can be purchased from newsstands and post offices. Finally, the credit call pay phone operates on credit cards—Access (MasterCard), Visa, American Express, and Diners Club—and is most common at airports and large railway stations.

To make an international call from Britain, dial the international access code (**00**), then the country code, then the area code, and finally the local number. Or call through one of the following long-distance access codes: **AT&T USA Direct** (✆ 1800/CALLATT), **Canada Direct** (✆ 0800/890016), **Australia** (✆ 0800/890061), and **New Zealand** (✆ 0800/890064). Common country codes are: USA and Canada, **1**; Australia, **61**; New Zealand, **64**; and South Africa, **27**.

For calling **collect** or if you need an international operator, dial **155**.

Caller beware: Some hotels routinely add outrageous surcharges onto phone calls made from your room. Inquire before you call! It'll be a lot cheaper to use your own calling-card number or to find a pay phone.

Time Britain follows Greenwich mean time (5 hr. ahead of Eastern Standard Time), with British summertime lasting (roughly) from the end of March to the end of October. For most of the year, including summer, Britain is 5 hours ahead of the time observed in the eastern United States. Because of different daylight-savings-time practices in the two nations, there's a brief period (about a week) in autumn when Britain is only 4 hours ahead of New York, and a brief period in spring when it's 6 hours ahead of New York.

Tipping For cab drivers, add about 10% to 15% to the fare on the meter. However, if the driver loads or unloads your luggage, add something extra.

In hotels, porters receive 75p ($1.40) per bag, even if you have only one small suitcase. Hall porters are tipped only for special services. Maids receive £1 ($1.85) per day. In top-ranking hotels, the concierge will often submit a separate bill showing charges for newspapers and other items; if he or she has been particularly helpful, tip extra.

Hotels often add a service charge of 10% to 15% to most bills. In smaller bed-and-breakfasts, the tip is not likely to be included. Therefore, tip people for special services, such as the waiter who serves you breakfast. If several people have served you in a bed-and-breakfast, you may ask that 10% to 15% be added to the bill and divided among the staff.

In both restaurants and nightclubs, a 15% service charge is added to the bill, which is distributed among all the help. To that, add another 3% to 5%, depending on the service. Waiters in deluxe restaurants and nightclubs are accustomed to the extra 5%. Sommeliers (wine stewards) get about £1 ($1.85) per bottle of wine served. Tipping in pubs isn't common, but in wine bars, the server usually gets about 75p ($1.40) per round of drinks.

Barbers and hairdressers expect 10% to 15%. Tour guides expect £2 ($3.70), though it's not mandatory. Gas station attendants are rarely tipped, and theater ushers don't expect tips.

4

Settling into London

Europe's largest city is like a great wheel, with **Piccadilly Circus** at the hub and dozens of communities branching out from it. Because London is such a conglomeration of neighborhoods, each with its own personality, first-time visitors may be confused until they get the hang of it.

You'll probably spend most of your time in the **West End,** where many attractions are located, and in the historic part of London known as **The City,** which includes the Tower of London. This chapter will help you get your bearings.

1 Orientation

ARRIVING
BY PLANE

LONDON HEATHROW AIRPORT   West of London in Hounslow (✆ **0870/000-0123;** www.baa.co.uk), Heathrow is one of the world's busiest airports. It has four terminals, each relatively self-contained. Terminal 4, the most modern, handles the long haul and transatlantic operations of British Airways. Most transatlantic flights on U.S.-based airlines arrive at Terminal 3. Terminals 1 and 2 receive the intra-European flights of several European airlines.

Getting to Central London from Heathrow   It takes 35 to 40 minutes by the Underground (Tube) and costs £5.40 ($10) to make the 24km (15-mile) trip from Heathrow to the center of London. A taxi is likely to cost from £40 to £55 ($74–$102). For more information about Tube or bus connections, call ✆ **020/ 7222-1234.**

The British Airport Authority now operates **Heathrow Express** (✆ **0845/ 600-1515;** www.heathrowexpress.com), a 161kmph (100-mph) train service running every 15 minutes daily from 5:10am until 11:40pm between Heathrow and Paddington Station in the center of London. Trips cost £13 ($24) each way in economy class, rising to £21 ($39) in first class. Children under 15 go for free (when accompanied by an adult). You can save £1 ($1.85) by booking online or by phone. The trip takes 15 minutes each way between Paddington and Terminals 1, 2, and 3, 23 minutes from Terminal 4. The trains have special areas for wheelchairs. From Paddington, passengers can connect to other trains and the Underground, or they can hail a taxi. In addition to the online and phone options, you can buy tickets on the train, at self-service machines at Heathrow Airport, and from travel agents.

GATWICK AIRPORT   While Heathrow still dominates, more and more scheduled flights land at relatively remote **Gatwick** (✆ **0870/000-2468;** www. baa.co.uk), located some 40km (25 miles) south of London in West Sussex but only a 30-minute train ride away.

London at a Glance

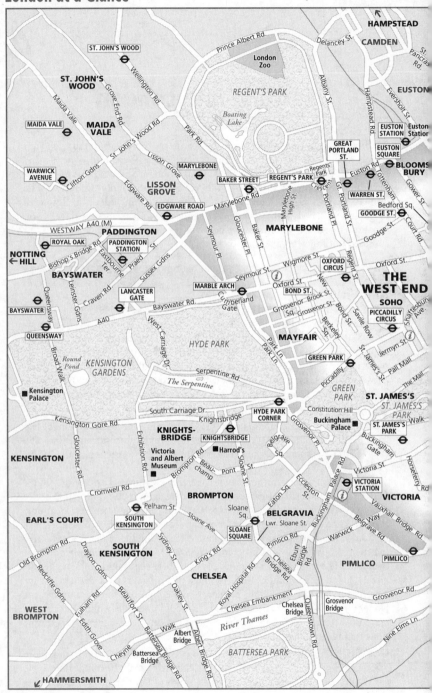

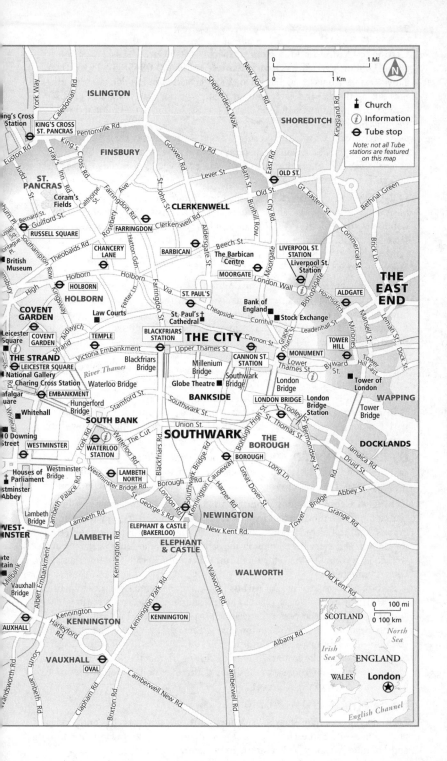

Getting to Central London from Gatwick   From Gatwick, the fastest way to get to London is via the **Gatwick Express trains** (© 0845/850-1530; www. gatwickexpress.co.uk), which leave for Victoria Station in London every 30 minutes during the day and every hour at night. The one-way charge is £11 ($20) express class for adults, £18 ($33) for first class, half price for children 5 to 15, free for children under 5.

A taxi from Gatwick to central London usually costs £50 to £105 ($93–$194). However, you must negotiate a fare with the driver before you enter the cab; the meter doesn't apply because Gatwick lies outside the Metropolitan Police District.

LONDON CITY AIRPORT   Located just 5km (3 miles) east of the bustling business community of Canary Wharf and 9.5km (6 miles) east of The City, London City Airport (© 020/7646-0088; www.londoncityairport.com) is served by 14 airlines (including Air France, Air Wales, British Airways, KLM, Lufthansa, and Swiss International Airlines) that fly from 18 cities in western Europe and Scandinavia.

Getting to Central London from London City Airport   A blue-and-white bus charges £6 ($11) each way to take you from the airport to the Liverpool Street Station, where you can connect with rail or Underground transportation to almost any destination. The bus runs daily every 10 minutes during the hours the airport is open (Mon–Fri 5:30am–9:30pm; Sat 5:30am–12:30pm; Sun 11am–9:30pm).

A shuttle bus can take you to Canary Wharf, where trains from the Dockland Line Railway make frequent 10-minute runs to The City. Here, passengers can catch the Underground from the Bank Tube station.

In addition, London Transport bus no. 473 goes from the City Airport to East London, where you can board any Underground at the Plaistow Tube station.

LONDON STANSTED AIRPORT   Located some 80km (50 miles) northeast of London's West End, **Stansted,** in Essex (© 0870/000-0303; www.baa.co.uk), handles mostly flights to and from the European continent.

Getting to Central London from Stansted   From Stansted, your best bet to central London is the **Stansted Express train** (© 0845/850-0150; www.stansted express.com) to Liverpool Street Station, which runs every 15 minutes from 8am to 4:30pm, and every 30 minutes in the early mornings, evening weekdays, and weekends. It costs £14 ($26) for a standard ticket and £20 ($37) for first class and takes 45 minutes.

By bus, you can take the **A6 Airbus** (www.nationalexpress.com), which runs regular departures 24 hours a day to both Victoria rail and coach stations, and costs £10 ($19). If you prefer the relative privacy of a taxi, you'll pay dearly for the privilege. For a ride to London's West End, they'll charge you from £50 ($93) for up to four passengers and from £110 ($204) for five or six passengers. Expect the ride to take around 75 minutes during normal traffic conditions, but beware of Friday afternoons when dense traffic may double your travel time. Our advice: Stick to the Express.

BY TRAIN
Each of London's train stations is connected to the city's vast bus and Underground network, and each has phones, restaurants, pubs, luggage storage areas, and London Transport Travel Information Centres.

Tips   London Fights Gridlock with Pounds

In a desperate move to ease traffic, gridlocked London has begun charging cars £5 ($9.25) to enter the most congested parts of central London. The charge is in effect from 7am to 6:30pm Monday through Friday. A network of some 700 video cameras record license plates of vehicles moving into the zone. Traffic fees, at least according to the mayor (who rides the Tube), are expected to cut car usage by 10% to 15%.

How to pay? Londoners can pay online, over the phone, or at specially installed machines at newspaper shops, petrol (gas) stations, and food stores. Before renting a car to drive into central London (not a good idea in the first place), check with your rental company about how the charges will apply to you.

If you're coming from France, the fastest way to get to London is by the **HoverSpeed** connection between Calais and Dover (see "By Ferry/Hovercraft from Continental Europe," under "Getting There," in chapter 3), where you can get a BritRail train into London. For one-stop travel, you can take the Chunnel train direct from Paris to Waterloo Station in London.

BY CAR

If you're taking a car ferry across the Channel, you can quickly connect with a motorway into London. *Remember to drive on the left.* London is encircled by a ring road, the M25. Determine which part of the city you wish to enter and follow the signs there.

Once you're in London, we don't recommend driving. Unfortunately, parking is scarce and expensive. Before you arrive in London, call your hotel and ask for advice on where to park your car.

VISITOR INFORMATION

The **Britain and London Visitors Centre,** 1 Regent St., Piccadilly Circus, London W1 (Tube: Piccadilly Circus), caters to walk-in visitors who need information about all parts of Britain. Telephone service has been suspended; you must show up in person and often wait in a lengthy line. On the premises, you'll find a BritRail ticket office, travel and theater ticket agencies, a hotel-booking service, a bookshop, and a souvenir shop. It's open Monday through Friday from 9:30am to 6:30pm and Saturday and Sunday from 10am to 4pm, with extended hours on Saturday from June to September.

The London Tourist Board's **Visit London,** 1 Warwick Row, London SW1E 5ER (© **020/7932-2000;** www.visitlondon.com; Tube: Victoria Station), can help you with almost anything. The phone center deals chiefly with accommodations in all price categories and can handle the whole spectrum of travelers' questions. It also arranges tour ticket sales, theater reservations, and offers a wide selection of books and souvenirs.

LONDON'S NEIGHBORHOODS IN BRIEF

The West End Neighborhoods

Mayfair Bounded by Piccadilly, Hyde Park, and Oxford and Regent streets, this is the most elegant, fashionable section of London, filled with luxury hotels, Georgian town houses, and swank shops. Grosvenor Square (pronounced

Grov-nor) is nicknamed "Little America," home to the American embassy and a statue of Franklin D. Roosevelt; Berkeley Square (*Bark*-ley) was made famous by the song "A Nightingale Sang in Berkeley Square." At least once you'll want to dip into this exclusive section. One curiosity of Mayfair is **Shepherd Market,** a tiny village of pubs, two-story inns, book and food stalls, and restaurants, sandwiched among Mayfair's greatness.

Marylebone First-timers to London head to Marylebone (*Mar*-le-bone) to explore Madame Tussauds or walk along Baker Street in the make-believe footsteps of Sherlock Holmes. The streets form a near-perfect grid, with major ones running north–south from Regent's Park toward Oxford Street. Marylebone Lane and High Street retain some of their former village atmosphere, but this is otherwise a now rather anonymous area. At Regent's Park, you can visit Queen Mary's Gardens or, in summer, see Shakespeare performed in an open-air theater.

St. James's Often called "Royal London," St. James's is home to Elizabeth II, who lives at the neighborhood's most famous address, Buckingham Palace. The neighborhood begins at Piccadilly Circus and moves southwest, incorporating Pall Mall, The Mall, St. James's Park, and Green Park; it's "frightfully convenient," as the English say, enclosing many of London's leading department stores. One must-see is Fortnum & Mason, at 181 Piccadilly, the world's most luxurious grocery store.

Piccadilly Circus & Leicester Square **Piccadilly Circus** is the very heart and soul of London—its gaudy living room. The circus isn't Times Square yet, but its traffic,

neon, and jostling crowds do nothing to make it fashionable. If you want a little more grandeur, retreat to the Regency promenade of exclusive shops, the Burlington Arcade, designed in 1819.

A bit more tawdry is **Leicester Square,** a center of theaters, restaurants, movie palaces, and nightlife. Once a chic address, it changed forever in the Victorian era when four towering entertainment halls were opened (even Queen Victoria saw a circus here). In time, the old palaces changed from stage to screen; three still show films.

Soho These densely packed streets in the heart of the West End are famous for a gloriously cosmopolitan mix of people and trades. A decade ago, much was heard about the decline of Soho, when the thriving sex industry threatened to engulf it. That destruction has now largely been halted. Respectable businesses have returned, and chic restaurants and shops prosper; it's now the heart of London's expanding gay colony. But Soho wouldn't be Soho without a few sex shops and porn theaters.

Soho starts at Piccadilly Circus and spreads out; basically bordered by Regent Street, Oxford Street, Charing Cross Road, and the theaters of Shaftesbury Avenue. Carnaby Street, a block from Regent Street, was the center of the universe in the Swinging '60s, and appears to be rising again. Across Shaftesbury Avenue, a busy street lined with theaters, is London's **Chinatown,** centered on Gerrard Street: small, authentic, and packed with excellent restaurants. But Soho's heart—with marvelous French and Italian delicatessens, fine butchers, fish stores, and wine merchants—is farther north, on Brewer, Old Compton, and Berwick streets; Berwick is also a wonderful open-air fresh-food market. To the north of Old Compton Street, Dean, Frith, and Greek streets have fine little restaurants, pubs, and clubs. The British movie industry is centered at Wardour Street.

Bloomsbury This district, a world in itself, lies northeast of Piccadilly Circus, beyond Soho. It is, among other things, the academic heart of London; you'll find the University of London, several other colleges, and many bookstores. Despite its student population, this neighborhood is fairly staid. Its reputation has been fanned by such writers as Virginia Woolf, who lived within its bounds and became one of the unofficial leaders of a group of artists and writers known as "the Bloomsbury Group."

The heart of Bloomsbury is **Russell Square,** and the streets jutting off from the square are lined with hotels and B&Bs. Most visitors come to the neighborhood to visit The British Museum, one of the world's greatest repositories of treasures. The British TeleCom Tower (1964) on Cleveland Street is a familiar landmark.

Nearby is **Fitzrovia,** bounded by Great Portland, Oxford, and Gower streets. Goodge Street, with its many shops and pubs, forms the heart of the "village." Once a major haunt of artists and writers—this was the stomping ground of Ezra Pound and George Orwell, among others—the bottom end of Fitzrovia is a virtual extension of Soho, with a cluster of Greek restaurants.

Holborn The old borough of Holborn, abutting The City to the west, takes in the heart of legal London— the city's barristers, solicitors, and law clerks call it home. A 14-year-old Dickens was once employed as a solicitor's clerk at Lincoln's Inn Fields. Old Bailey has stood for English justice through the years

(Fagin went to the gallows from this site in *Oliver Twist*). Everything here seems steeped in history. Even as you're quenching your thirst with a half pint of bitter at the Viaduct Tavern (126 Newgate St.; Tube: St. Paul's), you learn the pub was built over the notorious Newgate Prison (which specialized in death by pressing) and was named after the Holborn Viaduct, the world's first overpass.

Covent Garden & The Strand The flower, fruit, and "veg" market is long gone, but memories of Professor Higgins and Eliza Doolittle linger on. **Covent Garden** now contains the city's liveliest group of restaurants, pubs, and cafes outside of Soho, as well as some of the city's hippest shops—including the world's only Dr. Marten's Super Store. The restored marketplace, with its glass and iron roofs, has been called a "magnificent example of urban recycling." Covent Garden is traditionally London's theater area, and Inigo Jones's St. Paul's Covent Garden is known as the actors' church. The Theatre Royal Drury Lane was where Charles II's mistress Nell Gwynne made her debut in 1665.

Beginning at Trafalgar Square, **The Strand** runs east into Fleet Street and borders Covent Garden to the south. Flanked with theaters, shops, hotels, and restaurants, it runs parallel to the River Thames; to walk it is to follow the footsteps of Mark Twain, Henry Fielding, James Boswell, William Thackeray, and Sir Walter Raleigh. The Savoy Theatre helped make Gilbert and Sullivan a household name.

Westminster The seat of the British government since the days of Edward the Confessor, and dominated by the Houses of Parliament and Westminster Abbey, this area runs along the Thames to the east of

St. James's Park. **Trafalgar Square,** at the area's northern end and one of the city's major landmarks, remains a testament to England's victory over Napoleon in 1805, and the paintings in the **National Gallery** will restore your soul. Whitehall is the main thoroughfare, linking Trafalgar Square with Parliament Square. You can visit Churchill's Cabinet War Rooms; no. 10 Downing St., the world's most famous street address, home to Britain's prime minister; and **Westminster Abbey,** one of the world's great Gothic churches.

Westminster also encompasses **Victoria,** an area that takes its unofficial name from bustling Victoria Station, known as "the gateway to the Continent."

The City & Environs

The City When Londoners speak of "The City," they don't mean all of London; they mean the original square mile that's now the British version of Wall Street. The buildings of this district are known all over the world: the Bank of England, the London Stock Exchange, and Lloyd's of London. This was the origin of Londinium, as it was called by its Roman conquerors. Despite its age, The City doesn't easily reveal its past; much of it has been swept away by the Great Fire of 1666, the German bombs of 1940, the IRA bombs of the early 1990s, and the zeal of modern developers. Still, it retains its medieval character; one of its landmarks is **St. Paul's Cathedral,** the masterpiece of Sir Christopher Wren, which stood virtually alone amongst the rubble after the Blitz.

London's journalistic hub since William Caxton printed the first book in English, **Fleet Street** has been abandoned by most of the London tabloids for the Docklands development across the river.

The City of London still prefers to function on its own, separate from the rest of the city; in keeping with its independence, it maintains its own **Information Centre** at St. Paul's Churchyard, EC4 (✆ **020/ 7332-1456**). It's open Monday through Friday from 9:30am to 5pm and Saturday from 9:30am to 12:30pm.

Docklands In the last 2 decades, this area—bordered roughly by Tower Bridge to the west and London City Airport and the Royal Docks to the east—has witnessed an ambitious redevelopment. Thamesside warehouses have been converted to Manhattan-style lofts, and the neighborhood has attracted many businesses, including most of the Fleet Street newspapers, as well as museums, entertainment complexes, shops, and an ever-growing list of restaurants.

Canary Wharf, on the Isle of Dogs, is the heart of Docklands; a 240m (800-ft.) high tower designed by César Pelli, the tallest building in the United Kingdom, dominates this huge 29-hectare (71-acre) site. The Piazza is lined with shops and restaurants. On the south side of the river at Surrey Docks, the Victorian warehouses of **Butler's Wharf** have been converted by Sir Terence Conran into offices, workshops, houses, shops, and restaurants; Butler's Wharf is also home to the Design Museum.

To get to Docklands, take the Underground to Tower Hill and pick up the **Docklands Light Railway** (✆ **020/7222-1234**), which operates Monday through Saturday from 5:30am to 12:30am, and Sunday from 7:30am to 11:30pm.

The East End Traditionally one of London's poorest districts, it was nearly bombed out of existence by the Nazis. Hitler, in the words of one commentator at the time, created "instant urban renewal." The East End extends from the City Walls east encompassing Stepney, Bow, Poplar, West Ham, Canning Town, and other districts. The East End has always been filled with legend and lore. It's the home of the Cockney, London's most colorful character. To be a true Cockney, it's said that you must have been born "within the sound of Bow Bells," a reference to a church, St. Mary-le-Bow, rebuilt by Sir Christopher Wren in 1670. Many immigrants to London have found a home here.

South Bank Although not officially a district like Mayfair, South Bank is the setting today for the **South Bank Arts Centre,** now the largest arts center in Western Europe and still growing. Reached by Waterloo Bridge, it lies across the Thames from the Victoria Embankment. Culture buffs flock to its galleries and halls, including the National Theatre, Queen Elizabeth Hall, Royal Festival Hall, and the Hayward Gallery. It's also the setting of the National Film Theatre and the Museum of the Moving Image (MOMI). Neighborhoods nearby are Elephant & Castle and **Southwark,** home to the grand Southwark Cathedral. To get here, take the Tube to Waterloo Station.

Central London Beyond the West End

Knightsbridge One of London's most fashionable neighborhoods, Knightsbridge is a top residential and shopping district, just south of Hyde Park. **Harrods,** on Brompton Road, is its chief attraction. Right nearby, Beauchamp Place (*Beech*-am) is a Regency-era, boutique-lined little shopping street with a scattering of fashionable restaurants.

Belgravia South of Knightsbridge, this area has long been the aristocratic quarter of London, rivaling

Mayfair in grandness. Although it reached the pinnacle of its prestige during the reign of Queen Victoria, it's still a chic address; the duke and duchess of Westminster, one of England's richest families, still live at Eaton Square. Its centerpiece is Belgrave Square, built between 1825 and 1835. When the town houses were built, the aristocrats followed—the duke of Connaught, the earl of Essex, even Queen Victoria's mother, the duchess of Kent. Chopin, on holiday in 1837, was appropriately impressed: "And the English! And the houses! And the palaces! And the pomp, and the carriages! Everything from soap to the razors is extraordinary."

Chelsea This stylish Thames-side district lies south of Belgravia. It begins at Sloane Square, where flower sellers hustle their flamboyant blooms year-round. The area has been a favorite of writers and artists, including such names as Oscar Wilde (who was arrested here), George Eliot, James Whistler, J. M. W. Turner, Henry James, and Thomas Carlyle. Mick Jagger and Margaret Thatcher have been more recent residents, and the late Princess Diana and the "Sloane Rangers" of the 1980s gave it even more fame.

Its major boulevard is **King's Road,** where Mary Quant launched the miniskirt in the '60s and where the English punk look began. King's Road runs the entire length of Chelsea; it's at its liveliest on Saturday. The hip-hop of King's Road isn't typical of otherwise upmarket Chelsea, an elegant village filled with town houses and little mews dwellings that only successful stockbrokers and solicitors can afford to occupy.

On the Chelsea/Fulham border is **Chelsea Harbour,** a luxury development of apartments and restaurants with a private marina. You can spot its tall tower from far away; the golden ball on top moves up and down to indicate tide level.

Kensington This Royal Borough lies west of Kensington Gardens and Hyde Park and is traversed by two of London's major shopping streets, Kensington High Street and Kensington Church Street. Since 1689, when asthmatic William III fled Whitehall Palace for Nottingham House (where the air was fresher), the district has enjoyed royal associations. In time, Nottingham House became Kensington Palace, and the royals grabbed a chunk of Hyde Park to plant their roses. Queen Victoria was born here. "KP," as the royals say, was the home of Princess Diana and her two young princes for a time. Kensington Gardens is now open to the public.

Southeast of Kensington Gardens and Earl's Court, primarily residential **South Kensington** is often called "museumland" because it's dominated by a complex of museums and colleges—set upon land bought with the proceeds from Prince Albert's Great Exhibition, held in Hyde Park in 1851—that include the **Natural History Museum,** the **Victoria and Albert Museum,** and the **Science Museum;** nearby is **Royal Albert Hall.** South Kensington is also home to some fashionable restaurants and town-house hotels. One of the district's chief curiosities is the **Albert Memorial;** for sheer excess, the Victorian monument is unequaled in the world.

Earl's Court Earl's Court lies below Kensington, bordering the western half of Chelsea. For decades a staid residential district, Earl's Court now attracts a new and younger crowd (often gay), particularly at night, to

its pubs, wine bars, and coffee-houses. It's a popular base for budget travelers (particularly Australians), thanks to its wealth of B&Bs and budget hotels, and its convenient access to central London: A 15-minute Tube ride takes you into the heart of Piccadilly, via either the District or Piccadilly lines.

Once regarded as the boondocks, nearby **West Brompton** is seen today as an extension of central London. It lies directly south of Earl's Court (take the Tube to West Brompton) and directly southeast of West Kensington. It also has many good restaurants, pubs, and taverns, as well as some budget hotels.

Notting Hill Increasingly fashionable Notting Hill is bounded on the north by Bayswater Road and on the east by Kensington. Hemmed in on the north by West Way and on the west by the Shepherd's Bush ramp leading to the M40, it has many turn-of-the-20th-century mansions and small houses sitting on quiet, leafy streets, plus a growing number of hot restaurants and clubs. Gentrified in recent years, it's becoming an extension of central London.

On the north end, across Notting Hill, west of Bayswater, is the increasingly hip neighborhood known as **Notting Hill Gate;** its Portobello Road is home to one of London's most famous street markets. The area Tube stops are Notting Hill Gate, Holland Park, and Ladbroke Grove.

Nearby **Holland Park** is a stylish residential neighborhood visited chiefly by the chic guests of Halcyon Hotel, one of the grandest of London's small hotels.

Paddington & Bayswater Centering around Paddington Station, north of Kensington Gardens and Hyde Park, Paddington is one of the major centers in London, attracting budget travelers who fill up the B&Bs in Sussex Gardens and Norfolk Square. After the first railway was introduced in London in 1836, it was followed by a circle of sprawling railway termini, including Paddington Station, which spurred the growth of this middle-class area, now blighted in parts.

Just south of Paddington, north of Hyde Park, and abutting more fashionable Notting Hill to the west is **Bayswater,** a sort of unofficial area also filled with a large number of B&Bs attracting budget travelers. Inspired by Marylebone and elegant Mayfair, a relatively prosperous set of Victorian merchants built homes for their families in this area.

Farther Afield

Greenwich Some 6.5km (4 miles) from the city, Greenwich—ground zero for use in the reckoning of terrestrial longitudes—enjoyed its heyday under the Tudors. Henry VIII and both of his daughters, Mary I and Elizabeth I, were born here. Greenwich Palace, Henry's favorite, is long gone, though; today's visitors come to this lovely port village for nautical sights along the Thames, including the 1869 tea clipper *Cutty Sark.*

Hampstead This residential suburb of north London, beloved by Keats and Hogarth, is a favorite spot for weekending Londoners. Notables from Sigmund Freud to John Le Carré have lived here, and it remains one of the most desirable districts in the Greater London area to call home. Its centerpiece is **Hampstead Heath,** nearly 323 hectares (800 acres) of rolling meadows and woodlands with panoramic views; it maintains its rural atmosphere though engulfed by cityscapes on all sides. The hilltop village is filled with cafes, tearooms, and restaurants, as well as pubs galore, some with historic pedigrees.

Highgate With Hampstead, Highgate in north London is another choice residential area, particularly on or near Pond Square and along Hampstead High Street. Long a desirable place to live, Londoners used to flock to its taverns and pubs for "exercise and harmless merriment"; some still do. Today, most visitors come to see moody **Highgate Cemetery,** London's most famous cemetery, the final resting place of such famous figures as Karl Marx and George Eliot.

2 Getting Around

Remember that cars drive on the left, and vehicles have the right-of-way in London over pedestrians. Wherever you walk, always look both ways before stepping off a curb.

BY PUBLIC TRANSPORTATION

The London Underground and the city's buses operate on a common system of six fare zones. They radiate out in rings from the central zone 1, which is where most visitors spend the majority of their time. It covers an area from Aldgate East and Tower Gateway in the east to Notting Hill in the west, and from Waterloo in the south to Baker Street, Euston, and King's Cross in the north. To travel beyond these boundaries, you need at least a two-zone ticket. Note that all one-way, round-trip, and 1-day pass tickets are valid only on the day of purchase.

Tube and bus maps should be available at any Underground station. You can also download them before you travel from the excellent **London Transport (LT)** website at www.londontransport.co.uk. (You can also send away for a map by writing to **London Transport,** Travel Information Service, 42–50 Victoria St., London SW1H 0TL.) **London Transport Travel Information Centres** are at several major Tube stations: Euston, Liverpool Street Station, and Piccadilly Circus, as well as the BritRail stations at Euston and Victoria and each terminal at Heathrow Airport. Most are open daily (some close Sun) from at least 9am to 5pm. A **24-hour information service** is also available (© **020/7222-1234**).

DISCOUNT PASSES   If you plan to use public transportation a lot, investigate the range of fare discounts available. **Travelcards** offer unlimited use of buses, Underground, and BritRail services in Greater London for any period ranging from a day to a year. Travelcards are available from Underground ticket offices, Travel Information Centres, main post offices in the London area, and some newsstands. You need to bring a passport-size photo to purchase all but single-day and weekend Travelcards; you can take a photo at any of the instant photo booths in London's train stations. Children under age 5 generally travel free on the Tube and buses.

The **1-Day Travelcard** allows you to go anywhere throughout Greater London. For travel anywhere within zones 1 and 2, the cost is £5.30 ($9.80) for adults or £2.60 ($4.80) for children 5 to 15. The **Off-Peak 1-Day Travelcard,** which isn't valid until after 9:30am on weekdays (or on night buses), is even cheaper. For two zones, the cost is £4.30 ($7.95) for adults and £2 ($3.70) for children 5 to 15.

Weekend Travelcards are valid for 1 weekend, plus the Monday if it's a national holiday; they're not valid on night buses. Travel anywhere within zones 1 and 2 all weekend costs £6.40 ($12) for adults or £2 ($3.70) for kids 5 to 15.

1-Week Travelcards cost adults £17 ($31) and children £7 ($13) for travel in zones 1 and 2.

The 1-day **Family Travelcard** allows as many journeys as you want on the Tube, buses (excluding night buses) displaying the London Transport bus sign, and even the Docklands Light Railway or any rail service within the travel zones designated on your ticket. The family card is valid Monday through Friday after 9:30am and all day on weekends and public holidays. It's available for families as small as two (one adult and one child) to as large as six (two adults and four children). Cost is £2.80 ($5.20) per adult and 80p ($1.50) per child.

Tips **Don't Leave Home Without It**

For another option for public transportation in London, make sure you buy a **London Visitor Travelcard** before you leave home. This card, which allows unlimited transport within all six zones of Greater London's Underground (as far as Heathrow) and bus network, as well as some discounts on London attractions, isn't available in the U.K. You don't even need a passport picture. A pass good for 3 consecutive days of travel is $35 for adults, $16 for children 5 to 15; for 4 consecutive days of travel, it's $46 for adults, $19 for children; and for 7 consecutive days of travel, it's $69 for adults, $29 for children. Contact **BritRail Travel International,** 44 S. Broadway, White Plains, NY 10601 (© **800/677-8585,** or 800/555-2748 in Canada; www.raileurope.com). It will take up to 2 to 3 business days for the card to reach you at home.

You can also buy **Carnet** tickets, a booklet of 10 single Underground tickets valid for 12 months from the issue date. Carnet tickets are valid for travel only in zone 1 (central London) and cost £15 ($28) for adults and £5 ($9.25) for children (up to 15). A book of Carnet tickets saves you £5 ($9.25) over the cost of 10 separate single tickets.

BY UNDERGROUND

The Underground, or Tube, is the fastest and easiest way to get around. All Tube stations are clearly marked with a red circle and blue crossbar. Routes are conveniently color-coded.

If you have British coins, you can get your ticket at a vending machine. Otherwise, buy it at the ticket office. You can transfer as many times as you like as long as you stay in the Underground. The flat fare for one trip within the Central zone is £2 ($3.70). Trips from the Central zone to destinations in the suburbs range from £2.20 to £3.80 ($4.05–$7.05) in most cases. It's also possible to purchase weekly passes (see "Discount Passes," above), going for £17 ($31) for adults or £7 ($13) for children in the Central zone, £38 ($71) for adults or £17 ($31) for children for all six zones.

Slide your ticket into the slot at the gate, and pick it up as it comes through on the other side and hold on to it—it must be presented when you exit the station at your destination. If you're caught without a valid ticket, you'll be fined £10 ($19) on the spot. If you owe extra money, you'll be asked to pay the difference by the attendant at the exit. The Tube runs roughly from 5am to 11:30pm. After that you must take a taxi or night bus to your destination. For information on the London Tube system, call the **London Underground** at ✆ 020/7222-1234, but expect to stay on hold for a good while before a live person comes on the line. Information is also available on www.londontransport.co.uk.

BUSES

The first thing you learn about London buses is that nobody just boards them. You "queue up"—that is, form a single-file line at the bus stop.

The comparably priced bus system is almost as good as the Underground and gives you better views of the city. To find out about current routes, pick up a free bus map at one of London Transport's Travel Information Centres, listed above. The map is available in person only, not by mail. You can also obtain a map at **www.londontransport.co.uk/buses**.

As with the Underground, fares vary according to distance traveled. Generally, bus fares are £1 ($1.85), slightly less than Tube fares. If you want your stop called out, simply ask the conductor or driver. To speed up bus travel, passengers have to purchase tickets before boarding. Drivers no longer collect fares on board. Some 300 roadside ticket machines serve stops in central London. You'll need the exact fare, however, as ticket machines don't make change. It's still possible to pay on the double-decker red buses that continue to serve 20 of the 60 major bus routes in London, although in time these may be phased out.

Buses generally run 24 hours a day. A few night buses have special routes, running once an hour or so; most pass through Trafalgar Square. Keep in mind that night buses are often so crowded (especially on weekends) that they are unable to pick up passengers after a few stops. You may find yourself waiting a long time. Consider taking a taxi. Call the 24-hour **hot line** (✆ 020/7222-1234) for schedule and fare information.

BY TAXI

London cabs are among the most comfortable and best-designed in the world. You can pick one up either by heading for a cab rank or by hailing one in the street (the taxi is available if the yellow taxi sign on the roof is lighted); once it has stopped for you, a taxi is obliged to take you anywhere you want to go within 9.5km (6 miles) of the pickup point, provided it's within the metropolitan area. To **call a cab,** phone ℭ **020/7272-0272** or 020/7253-5000.

The meter starts at £3.80 ($7.05), with increments of £3.40 ($6.30) per mile thereafter, based on distance or time. Each additional passenger is charged 40p (75¢). Passengers pay 10p (20¢) for each piece of luggage in the driver's compartment and any other item more than .6m (2 ft.) long. Surcharges are imposed after 8pm and on weekends and public holidays. All these tariffs include VAT. Fares usually increase annually. It's recommended that you tip 10% to 15% of the fare.

If you call for a cab, the meter starts running when the taxi receives instructions from the dispatcher, so you could find that the meter already reads a few pounds more than the initial drop of £3.60 ($6.65) when you step inside.

Minicabs are also available, and they're often useful when regular taxis are scarce or when the Tube stops running. These cabs are meterless, so you must negotiate the fare in advance. Unlike regular cabs, minicabs are forbidden by law to cruise for fares. They operate from sidewalk kiosks, such as those around Leicester Square. If you need to call one, try **Brunswick Chauffeurs/Abbey Cars** (ℭ **020/8969-2555**) in west London; **London Cabs, Ltd.** (ℭ **020/8778-3000**) in east London; or **Newname Minicars** (ℭ **020/8472-1400**) in south London. You can find minicab kiosks near many Tube or BritRail stops, especially in outlying areas.

If you have a complaint about taxi service or if you leave something in a cab, contact the **Public Carriage Office,** 15 Penton St., N1 9PU (ℭ **020/7918-2000;** www.londontransport.co.uk/pco; Tube: Angel Station). If it's a complaint, you must have the cab number, which is displayed in the passenger compartment.

Cab sharing is permitted in London, as British law allows cabbies to carry two to five persons. Taxis accepting such riders display a notice on yellow plastic, with the words "Shared Taxi." Each of two riders sharing is charged 65% of the fare a lone passenger would be charged. Three persons pay 55%, four pay 45%, and five (the seating capacity of all new London cabs) pay 40% of the single-passenger fare.

BY CAR

Don't drive in congested London. It is easy to get around without a car, traffic and parking are nightmares, and—to top it all off—you'd have to drive from what you normally consider the passenger seat on the wrong side of the road. It all adds up to a big headache.

BY BICYCLE

One of the most popular bike-rental shops is **On Your Bike,** 52–54 Tooley St., London Bridge, SE1 (ℭ **020/7378-6669;** www.onyourbike.net; Tube: London Bridge), open Monday through Friday from 8am to 7pm, and Saturday from 10am to 6pm, Sunday noon to 5pm. The first-class mountain bikes, with high seats and low-slung handlebars, cost £15 ($28) per day, £30 ($56) per weekend, or £70 ($130) per week, and require a £200 ($370) deposit on a credit card.

FAST FACTS: London

American Express The main office is at 30–31 Haymarket, SW1 (✆ 020/ 7484-9600; Tube: Piccadilly Circus). Full services are available Monday through Saturday from 9am to 6pm. On Sunday from 10am to 5pm, only the foreign-exchange bureau is open.

Area Codes London now has only one area code: **020.** Within the city limits, you don't need to dial it; use only the eight-digit number. If you're calling London from home before your trip, the country code for England is **44.** It must precede the London area code. When you're calling London from outside Britain, drop the "0" in front of the local area code.

Babysitters If your hotel can't recommend a sitter, call **Childminders,** 6 Nottingham St. (✆ 020/7935-2049; www.babysitter.co.uk). The rates are £6.80 ($13) per hour during the day and £5.20 to £6.40 ($9.60–$12) per hour at night, with a 4-hour minimum. Hotel guests pay an £10 ($19) booking fee each time they use a sitter. You must also pay reasonable transportation costs.

Currency Exchange See "Money," in chapter 3.

Dentists For dental emergencies, call **Eastman Dental Hospital** (✆ 020/ 7915-1000; Tube: King's Cross).

Doctors In a medical emergency, call ✆ **999.** Some hotels also have doctors on call. **Medical Express,** 117A Harley St. (✆ 020/7499-1991; Tube: Regent's Park), is a private British clinic. If you need a prescription filled, stop by, but to fill the British equivalent of a U.S. prescription, you'll sometimes have to pay a surcharge of £20 ($37) in addition to the cost of the medication. The clinic is open Monday through Friday from 9:30am to 5:30pm.

Embassies & High Commissions

- The **U.S. Embassy** is at 24 Grosvenor Sq., W1 (✆ 020/7499-9000; www. usembassy.org.uk; Tube: Bond St.). However, for passport and visa information, go to the **U.S. Passport and Citizenship Unit,** 55–56 Upper Brook St., London, W1 (✆ 020/7499-9000, ext. 2563 or 2564; Tube: Marble Arch or Bond St.). Hours are Monday through Friday from 8:30am to 5:30pm. Passport and citizenship unit hours are Monday through Friday from 8:30 to 11:30am and Monday and Friday from 2 to 4pm.

- The **Canadian High Commission,** MacDonald House, 38 Grosvenor Sq., W1 (✆ 020/7258-6600; www.dfait-maeci.gc.ca/canadaeuropa/united_ kingdom; Tube: Bond St.), handles visas for Canada. Hours are Monday through Friday from 8am to 4pm; 8 to 11am for immigration services.

- The **Australian High Commission** is at Australia House, The Strand, WC2 (✆ 020/7379-4334; www.australia.org.uk; Tube: Charing Cross or Aldwych). Hours are Monday through Friday from 9am to 5:20pm; 9 to 11am for immigration services; passports 9:30am to 3:30pm.

- The **New Zealand High Commission** is at New Zealand House, 80 Haymarket at Pall Mall, SW1 (✆ 020/7930-8422; www.nzembassy.com; Tube: Charing Cross or Piccadilly Circus). Hours are Monday through Friday from 10am to 4pm.

- The **Irish Embassy** is at 17 Grosvenor Place, SW1 (✆ 020/7235-2171; http://ireland.embassyhomepage.com; Tube: Hyde Park Corner). Hours are Monday through Friday from 9:30am to 1pm and 2 to 5pm.

• The high commission of **South Africa,** South Africa House, Trafalgar Square, WC2N 5DP (℃ **020/7925-8900;** www.southafricahouse.com; Tube: Westminster), is open Monday through Friday from 9am to 5pm.

Emergencies In London, for police, fire, or an ambulance, dial ℃ **999.**

Hospitals The following offer emergency care in London, 24 hours a day, with the first treatment free under the National Health Service: **Royal Free Hospital,** Pond Street (℃ **020/7794-0500;** Tube: Belsize Park), and **University College Hospital,** Grafton Way, WC1E 3DB (℃ **020/7387-9300;** Tube: Warren St.). Many other London hospitals also have accident and emergency departments.

Hot Lines If you're in some sort of legal emergency, call **Release** (℃ **020/7729-9904**) 10am to 5:30pm. The **Rape Crisis Line** (℃ **0845/123-2324**) accepts calls after 6pm. **Samaritans,** 46 Marshall St. (℃ **020/7734-2800**), maintains a crisis hot line that helps with all kinds of trouble, even threatened suicides. From 9am to 9pm daily, a live attendant is on duty to handle emergencies; the rest of the time, a series of recorded messages tells callers other phone numbers and addresses where they can turn to for help. **Alcoholics Anonymous** (℃ **020/7833-0022**) answers its hot line daily from 10am to 10pm. The **AIDS** 24-hour hot line is ℃ **0800/567-123.**

Information See "Visitor Information," earlier in this chapter.

Internet Access You can send e-mails or check your messages at **Cyberia,** 39 Whitfield St. (℃ **020/7209-0984;** www.cyberiacafe.net).

Maps If you plan to explore London in any depth, you'll need a detailed street map with an index, not one of those superficial overviews given away at many hotels and tourist offices. The best ones are published by Falk, and they're available at most newsstands and nearly all bookstores. And no Londoner is without a *London A to Z,* the ultimate street-by-street reference, available at bookstores and newsstands everywhere.

Police In an emergency, dial ℃ **999** (no coins are needed).

Post Office The **Main Post Office,** 24–28 William IV St., WC2N 4DL (℃ **020/7484-9307;** Tube: Charing Cross), operates as three separate businesses: inland and international postal service and banking; philatelic postage stamp sales; and the post shop, selling greeting cards and stationery. All are open Monday through Friday from 8:30am to 6:30pm and Saturday 9am to 5:30pm.

Telephone For **directory assistance** for London, dial ℃ **118212** for full range of services; for the rest of Britain, dial ℃ **118118.** See also "Area Codes," above.

3 Where to Stay

Moving deeper into the 21st century, more than 10,000 hotel rooms have opened to the public from 2000 to 2004. That's good news for what had been an over-crowded situation. The downside is that most of these hotels are in districts far from the city center and are of the no-frills budget chain variety. In spite of these bandbox modern horrors sprouting up, some hoteliers wisely decided to adapt former public or institutional buildings rather than start from scratch.

Another trend noted is a shift away from the West End as the traditional hotel stomping ground. Of course, the fact that there is a dearth of old buildings to turn into hotels in the West End is the reason for the shift toward such salubrious sections of London as Greenwich, the Docklands, and even The City.

With all the vast improvements and upgrades made over the past few years, chances are you'll like your room. What you won't like is the price. Even if a hotel remains scruffy, London hoteliers have little embarrassment about jacking up prices. Hotels in all categories remain overpriced.

London boasts some of the most famous hotels in the world—temples of luxury such as Claridge's, The Dorchester, and The Ritz. The problem is that London has too many of these high-priced hotels (and many cheap budget options) and not enough moderately priced options.

Even at the luxury level, you may be surprised at what you don't get. Many of the stately Victorian and Edwardian gems are so steeped in tradition that they lack many modern conveniences that are standard in other luxury hotels around the world. Some have modernized with a vengeance, but others retain amenities from the Boer War era. London does have some cutting-edge, chintz-free hotels that seem to have been flown in straight from Los Angeles—complete with high-end sound systems and gadget-filled marble bathrooms. However, these cutting-edge hotels are not necessarily superior; though they're streamlined and convenient, they frequently lack the personal service and spaciousness that characterize the grand old hotels.

It's also harder to get a hotel room, particularly an inexpensive one, during July and August. Inexpensive hotels are also tight in June, September, and October. If you arrive without a reservation, begin looking for a room as early in the day as possible. Many West End hotels have vacancies, even in peak season, between 9 and 11am, but by noon they are often booked.

A NOTE ABOUT PRICES   Unless otherwise noted, published prices are rack rates for rooms with a private bathroom. Many include breakfast (usually continental) and a 10% to 15% service charge. The British government also imposes a VAT (value-added tax) that adds 17.5% to your bill. This is not included in the prices quoted in the guide. Always ask for a better rate, particularly at the first-class and deluxe hotels (B&Bs generally charge a fixed rate). Parking rates are per night.

RATE REGULATIONS   All hotels, motels, inns, and guesthouses in Britain with four bedrooms or more (including self-catering accommodations) must display notices listing minimum and maximum overnight charges in a prominent place in the reception area or at the entrance, and prices must include any service charge and may include VAT. It must be made clear whether these items are included; if VAT isn't included, then it must be shown separately. If meals are included, this must be stated. If prices aren't standard for all rooms, then only the lowest and highest prices need be given.

HOLBORN
EXPENSIVE

Renaissance London Chancery Court ★★★   The *London Times* may have gotten carried away with the hype, proclaiming this "one of the most exciting hotels in the world," but this landmark 1914 building in the financial district has been stunningly transformed into a government-rated five-star hotel, retaining the grandeur of the past but boasting all the comforts and conveniences of

London Accommodations

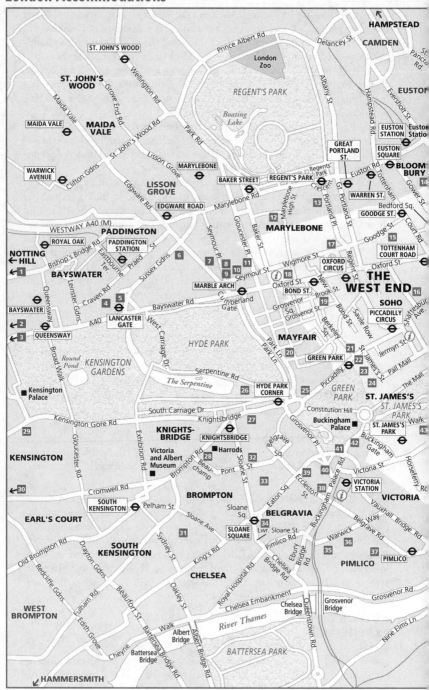

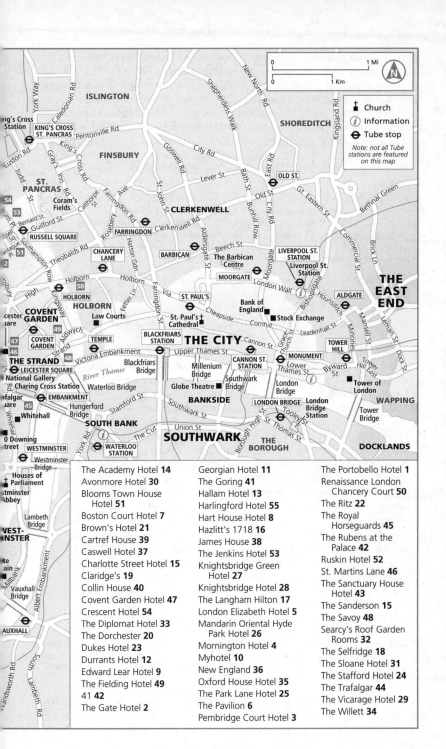

The Academy Hotel 14
Avonmore Hotel 30
Blooms Town House Hotel 51
Boston Court Hotel 7
Brown's Hotel 21
Cartref House 39
Caswell Hotel 37
Charlotte Street Hotel 15
Claridge's 19
Collin House 40
Covent Garden Hotel 47
Crescent Hotel 54
The Diplomat Hotel 33
The Dorchester 20
Dukes Hotel 23
Durrants Hotel 12
Edward Lear Hotel 9
The Fielding Hotel 49
41 42
The Gate Hotel 2

Georgian Hotel 11
The Goring 41
Hallam Hotel 13
Harlingford Hotel 55
Hart House Hotel 8
Hazlitt's 1718 16
James House 38
The Jenkins Hotel 53
Knightsbridge Green Hotel 27
Knightsbridge Hotel 28
The Langham Hilton 17
London Elizabeth Hotel 5
Mandarin Oriental Hyde Park Hotel 26
Mornington Hotel 4
Myhotel 10
New England 36
Oxford House Hotel 35
The Park Lane Hotel 25
The Pavilion 6
Pembridge Court Hotel 3

The Portobello Hotel 1
Renaissance London Chancery Court 50
The Ritz 22
The Royal Horseguards 45
The Rubens at the Palace 42
Ruskin Hotel 52
St. Martins Lane 46
The Sanctuary House Hotel 43
The Sanderson 15
The Savoy 48
Searcy's Roof Garden Rooms 32
The Selfridge 18
The Sloane Hotel 31
The Stafford Hotel 24
The Trafalgar 44
The Vicarage Hotel 29
The Willett 34

today. The surprise hit of 2003, this is a seven-floor Edwardian monument with a marble staircase. The building has been used as a backdrop for such films as *Howard's End* and *The Saint* because filmmakers were drawn to its soaring archways and classical central courtyard. The interior of the hotel encases you in womblike luxury. The glamorous and exceedingly comfortable rooms are all furnished with fine linens and decorated in different hues of cream, red, and blue. The bathrooms are about the most spacious in London, clad in Italian marble with lavish shower-and-tub combinations. The best accommodations are on the sixth floor, opening onto a cozy interior courtyard hidden from the busy world outside.

252 High Holborn, WC1V 7EN ✆ **800/468-3571** in the U.S. and Canada, or 020/7829-9888. Fax 020/ 7829-9889. www.renaissancehotels.com. 356 units. £180–£240 ($333–$444) double; £285–£465 ($527–$860) suite. AE, DC, MC, V. Valet parking £35 ($65). Tube: Holborn. **Amenities:** 2 restaurants; 2 bars; cocktail lounge; luxurious spa; business center; 24-hr. room service; massage; babysitting; sauna; laundry service; dry cleaning; nonsmoking rooms; rooms for those with limited mobility. *In room:* A/C, TV w/pay movies, dataport, coffeemaker, kitchenette, minibar, hair dryer, iron, safe.

MAYFAIR
VERY EXPENSIVE

Claridge's ★★★   That once-fading 1812 beauty has experienced a $75-million rebirth, and its staid image has changed. *Dynasty* diva Joan Collins may have staged her latest marriage here, but now Kate Moss is spotted in the hip bar, Elizabeth Hurley strolls through the lobby, and Gordon Ramsay—Britain's most talked about and controversial chef (and also the best)—is loud-mouthing it in the kitchen and swinging sharp knives for the benefit of the cameras. What would Queen Victoria have said about his foul tongue and fiery temper?

If you want to live in the total lap of luxury, at an even tonier address than The Dorchester, make it Claridge's. Though renovations have been extensive, much of the Art Deco style of the 1930s remains. You'll expect Fred Astaire and Ginger Rogers to emerge dancing at any minute. The hotel's strong sense of tradition and old-fashioned "Britishness" are also intact, in spite of the gloss and the hip clientele. Stand anywhere in any of the halls, and you'll find it easy to imagine the duke of Windsor striding through the halls, trailed by his two-timing wife. Afternoon tea at Claridge's remains a quintessentially English tradition. The accommodations here are the most diverse in London, ranging from the costly and stunning Brook Penthouse—complete with a personal butler—to the less-expensive so-called "superior queen" rooms with queen-size beds. You'll find sumptuous fabrics, exceedingly comfortable beds, elegant linens, chandeliers, and all sorts of modern amenities in the bedrooms. The bathrooms are the most elegant in Britain, with enormous tubs and showerheads the size of frying pans.

Brook St., London W1A 2JQ. ✆ **020/7629-8860.** Fax 020/7499-2210. www.the-savoy-group.com/claridges. 197 units. £370–£395 ($685–$731) double; from £515 ($953) suite. AE, DC, MC, V. Parking: £50 ($93). Tube: Bond St. **Amenities:** 3 restaurants; 2 bars; health club; salon; spa; 24-hr. room service; massage; business services; babysitting; laundry service; same-day dry cleaning; nonsmoking rooms; rooms for those with limited mobility. *In room:* A/C, TV/VCR (plus pay movies), fax, dataport, minibar, beverage maker, hair dryer, iron/ironing board, safe.

The Dorchester ★★★ *(Finds)*   One of London's best hotels, its elegance comes without an upper-crust attitude that can verge on snobbery. Few hotels have the time-honored experience of "The Dorch," which has maintained a tradition of fine comfort and cuisine since it opened in 1931.

Breaking from the neoclassical tradition, the most ambitious architects of the era designed a building of reinforced concrete clothed in terrazzo slabs. Within you'll find a 1930s take on Regency motifs: The monumental arrangements of flowers and the elegance of the gilded-cage promenade seem appropriate for a diplomatic reception, yet they convey a kind of comfort in which guests from all over the world feel at ease.

The Dorchester boasts guest rooms outfitted with Irish linen sheets on comfortable beds, plus all the electronic gadgetry you'd expect, and double- and triple-glazed windows to keep out noise, along with plump armchairs, cherry-wood furnishings, and, in many cases, four-poster beds piled high with pillows. The large bathrooms are equally stylish, with mottled Carrara marble and Lalique-style sconces, makeup mirrors and posh toiletries, and deep tubs. The best rooms offer views of Hyde Park.

53 Park Lane, London W1A 2HJ. (C) 800/727-9820 in the U.S., or 020/7629-8888. Fax 020/7409-0114. www.dorchesterhotel.com. 248 units. £330–£385 ($611–$712) double; from £500 ($925) suite. AE, DC, MC, V. Parking £33 ($61). Tube: Hyde Park Corner or Marble Arch. **Amenities:** 3 restaurants; bar; health club; spa; concierge; tour desk; car-rental desk; courtesy car; business services and center; small shopping arcade; 2 salons; 24-hr. room service; babysitting; laundry service; same-day dry cleaning; nonsmoking rooms; rooms for those with limited mobility. *In room:* A/C, TV/VCR, dataport, minibar, hair dryer, iron, safe.

EXPENSIVE

Brown's Hotel ★★★ Almost every year a hotel sprouts up trying to evoke an English country-house ambience with Chippendale and chintz; this quintessential town-house hotel watches these competitors come and go, and it always comes out on top. Brown's was founded by James Brown, a former manservant to Lord Byron, who knew the tastes of well-bred gentlemen and wanted to create a dignified, clublike place for them. He opened its doors in 1837, the same year Queen Victoria took the throne.

Brown's occupies 14 historic houses just off Berkeley Square and its guest rooms vary considerably in decor, but all show restrained taste in decoration and appointments; even the washbasins are antiques. Accommodations range in size from small to extra spacious; some suites have four-poster beds. Bathrooms come in a variety of sizes, but they are beautifully equipped with robes, luxurious cosmetics, tubs, and showers.

30 Albemarle St., London W1S 4BP. (C) 020/7493-6020. Fax 020/7493-9381. www.brownshotel.com. 118 units. £239–£345 ($442–$638) double; from £403 ($746) suite. AE, DC, MC, V. Off-site parking £40 ($74). Tube: Green Park. **Amenities:** Restaurant; bar; health club; concierge; business center; 24-hr. room service; laundry service; same-day dry cleaning; nonsmoking rooms. *In room:* A/C, TV/VCR (plus pay movies), dataport, minibar, hair dryer, safe.

The Park Lane Hotel ★★ Since 1924, this has been the most traditional of the Park Lane mansions, even more so than The Dorchester. Sheraton purchased the hotel in 1996, and continues to upgrade it, maintaining its quintessential British style. Its Silver Entrance remains an Art Deco marvel that has been used as a backdrop in many productions, including the classic BBC miniseries *Brideshead Revisited*.

Overlooking Green Park, the hotel offers luxurious accommodations that are a good deal—well, at least for pricey Park Lane, where anything under $500 a night is a bargain. Many suites have marble fireplaces and original marble bathrooms. The rooms have all benefited from impressive refurbishment. All have double-glazed windows to block out noise. The most tranquil rooms open onto a street in the rear. Rooms opening onto the court are dark. In the more deluxe rooms, you get trouser presses and better views. Bathrooms are generally spacious and well equipped with tub-and-shower combos; many also have robes.

Piccadilly, London W1J 7BX. ℂ **800/325-3535** in the U.S., or 020/7499-6321. Fax 020/7499-1965. www.sheraton.com. 307 units. £270–£310 ($500–$574) double; from £429 ($794) suite. AE, DC, MC, V. Parking £35 ($65). Tube: Hyde Park Corner or Green Park. **Amenities:** 2 restaurants; fabled 1920s palm court; bar; health club; concierge; business center; 24-hr. room service, laundry service; same-day dry cleaning; nonsmoking rooms; rooms for those with limited mobility. *In room:* A/C (in most rooms), TV w/pay movies, dataport, minibar, hair dryer, iron, safe.

The Selfridge The location, right next door to Selfridge's food hall off Oxford Street, is wonderful, especially for shoppers. In fact, the hotel's seven floors look as if they are part of Selfridge's itself. This mammoth hotel is a member of the Thistle hotel chain and caters to an even mix of business and leisure travelers. Ignore the drab entrance; the hotel brightens considerably in the second floor reception room, with its wingback chairs, antique art, pine-paneled walls, and a rustic bar whose half-timbered decor was brought and installed piece by piece from an English barn that stood in the Middle Ages. The rooms are hardly the finest in this part of town, but they are usually affordable, especially if you snag one of the promotional offerings (our editor once stayed here for £37/$68 a night—a steal!—thanks to an off-season special on Thistle's website). Accommodations are well maintained, nicely decorated, tranquil, and generally spacious, with small bathrooms. Double-glazing on the windows cuts back on noise. *Tip:* Try for a room facing Orchard Street, as these are larger. Also the best rooms are the premium units on floors 3 to 5.

Orchard St., London W1H 6JS. ℂ **800/847-4358** in the U.S., or 020/7408-2080. Fax 020/7409-2295. www.thistlehotels.com/selfridge. 294 units. £210–£236 ($389–$437) double; £379–£470 ($701–$870) suite. AE, DC, MC, V. Parking: £38 ($70). Tube: Bond St. **Amenities:** 2 restaurants; bar; 24-hr. room service; babysitting; laundry service; same-day dry cleaning; nonsmoking rooms; 1 room for those with limited mobility. *In room:* TV w/pay movies, dataport (in some), coffeemaker, hair dryer, safe (in some).

MARYLEBONE
VERY EXPENSIVE
The Langham Hilton ★★★ After it was bombed in World War II, this well-located hotel languished as dusty office space for the BBC until the early 1990s, when Hilton International took it over and painstakingly restored it. Today, it's Hilton's European flagship. The Langham's public rooms reflect the power and majesty of the British Empire at its apex. Guest rooms are somewhat less opulent but are still attractively furnished and comfortable, featuring French provincial furniture and red oak trim. Major refurbishment was carried out in 1999. All bathrooms are well kept and contain full tub-and-shower units. Ask for one of the rooms in the "52" series, as they are much grander and more spacious than the others. The hotel is within easy reach of Mayfair and Soho restaurants and theaters and Oxford and Regent Street shopping. Plus, Regent's Park is just blocks away.

1C Portland Place, London W1B 1JA. ℂ **800/774-1500** in the U.S., or 020/7636-1000. Fax 020/7323-2340. www.langham.hilton.com. 429 units. £199–£279 ($368–$516) double; £279 ($516) executive room; from £559 ($1,034) suite. AE, DC, MC, V. Parking: £35 ($65). Tube: Oxford Circus. **Amenities:** 2 restaurants; Edwardian-style palm court; bar; indoor pool; health club; spa; sauna; tour desk; courtesy car; business center; salon; 24-hr. room service; massage; babysitting; laundry service; same-day dry cleaning; nonsmoking rooms; rooms for those with limited mobility. *In room:* A/C, TV/VCR (plus pay movies), dataport, minibar, hair dryer, iron, safe.

EXPENSIVE
Durrants Hotel ★ This historic hotel off Manchester Square (established in 1789) with its Georgian-detailed facade is snug, cozy, and traditional—almost

like a poor man's Brown's (see above). We find it to be one of the most quintessentially English of all London hotels. You could invite the queen to Durrants for tea. Over the 100 years that they have owned the hotel, the Miller family has incorporated several neighboring houses into the original structure. A walk through the pine-and-mahogany-paneled public rooms is like stepping back in time: You'll even find an 18th-century letter-writing room. The rooms are bland but for elaborate cove moldings and comfortable furnishings, including good beds. Some are air-conditioned, and some are, alas, small. Bathrooms are also tiny, with shower-tub combinations but little room to maneuver.

26–32 George St., London W1H 6BJ. © 020/7935-8131. Fax 020/7487-3510. www.durrantshotel.co.uk. 92 units. £145–£165 ($268–$305) double; £180 ($333) family room for 3; from £285 ($527) suite. AE, MC, V. Tube: Bond St. or Baker St. **Amenities:** Restaurant; pub; concierge; 24-hr. room service; babysitting; laundry service; same-day dry cleaning; rooms for those with limited mobility. *In room:* A/C, TV, dataport, hair dryer, safe.

MODERATE

Hallam Hotel This heavily ornamented stone-and-brick Victorian—one of the few on the street to escape the Blitz—is just a 5-minute stroll from Oxford Circus. It's the property of brothers Grant and David Baker, who maintain it well. The hotel is warm and friendly, and the central location that you get for these prices can't be beat. The guest rooms, which were redone in 1991, are comfortably furnished with good beds. Some of the singles are so small they're called "cabinettes." Several of the twin-bedded rooms are quite spacious and have adequate closet space. Bathrooms, which have shower stalls, are a bit cramped.

12 Hallam St., Portland Place, London W1N 5LF. © 020/7580-1166. Fax 020/7323-4527. 25 units. £90 ($167) single; £100 ($185) double. Rates include English breakfast. AE, DC, MC, V. Tube: Oxford Circus. **Amenities:** Bar; nonsmoking rooms. *In room:* TV, coffeemaker, minibar, hair dryer.

Hart House Hotel ★ *Kids* Hart House is a long-enduring favorite with Frommer's readers. In the heart of the West End, this well-preserved historic building (one of a group of Georgian mansions occupied by exiled French nobles during the French Revolution) lies within easy walking distance of many theaters. The rooms—done in a combination of furnishings, ranging from Portobello antique to modern—are spick-and-span, each one with a different character. Favorites include no. 7, a triple with a big bathroom and shower. Ask for no. 11, on the top floor, if you'd like a brightly lit aerie. Housekeeping rates high marks here, and the bedrooms are comfortably appointed with chairs, an armoire, a desk, and a large chest of drawers. The shower-only bathrooms, although small, are efficiently organized. Hart House has long been known as a good, safe place for traveling families: Many of its rooms are triples, larger families can avail themselves of special family accommodations with connecting rooms, and all rooms are nonsmoking.

51 Gloucester Place, Portman Sq., London W1U 8JF. © 020/7935-2288. Fax 020/7935-8516. www.harthouse.co.uk. 15 units. £105 ($194) double; £130 ($241) triple; £150 ($278) quad. Rates include English breakfast. AE, MC, V. Tube: Marble Arch or Baker St. **Amenities:** Babysitting; laundry service; dry cleaning; rooms for those with limited mobility. *In room:* TV, dataport, coffeemaker, hair dryer.

INEXPENSIVE

Boston Court Hotel Upper Berkeley is a classic street of B&Bs; in days of yore, it was home to Elizabeth Montagu (1720–1800), "queen of the bluestockings," who defended Shakespeare against attacks by Voltaire. Today, it's a good, safe, respectable retreat at an affordable price. This unfrilly hotel offers accommodations in a centrally located Victorian-era building within walking distance of Oxford Street shopping and Hyde Park. The small, basic rooms have been refurbished and redecorated with a no-nonsense decor and have well-kept bathrooms with private showers.

26 Upper Berkeley St., Marble Arch, London W1H 7PF. © 020/7723-1445. Fax 020/7262-8823. www. bostoncourthotel.co.uk. 15 units, 7 with shower only. £69 ($128) double with shower only, £75–£79 ($139–$146) double with bathroom; £85–£89 ($157–$165) triple with bathroom. Rates include continental breakfast. MC, V. Tube: Marble Arch. **Amenities:** Laundry service; nonsmoking rooms. *In room:* TV w/pay movies, dataport, fridge, coffeemaker, hair dryer.

Edward Lear Hotel This popular hotel, situated a block from Marble Arch, is made all the more desirable by the bouquets of fresh flowers in its public rooms. It occupies a pair of brick town houses dating from 1780. The western house was the London home of 19th-century artist and poet Edward Lear, famous for his nonsense verse, and his illustrated limericks adorn the walls of one of the sitting rooms. Steep stairs lead up to cozy rooms which range from spacious to broom-closet size. Many bedrooms have been redecorated but still look a bit drab. Few can complain, as this is an area of £400 ($740) a-night mammoths. If you're looking for classiness, know that the bacon on your plate came from the same butcher used by the queen. One major drawback to the hotel: This is a very noisy part of town; rear rooms are quieter. Bathrooms are well maintained, most with a shower and tub.

28–30 Seymour St., London W1H 7JB. © 020/7402-5401. Fax 020/7706-3766. www.edlear.com. 31 units, 12 with bathroom. £67 ($124) double without bathroom, £74 ($137) double with bathroom; £79 ($146) suite. Rates include English breakfast. MC, V. Tube: Marble Arch. *In room:* TV w/pay movies, dataport, coffeemaker.

Georgian Hotel Central London, which is filled with luxury hotels, suffers an acute lack of small, personally run places, but Georgian House fills this gap. It lies near Sherlock Holmes's Baker Street and is within walking distance of Oxford Street and Regent's Park. Run by the same family since 1973, the Georgian House has a dedicated staff and management intent on improving the hotel. We especially like the top-quality English breakfast served here, and the way that original architectural features were retained even as modern comforts were added. Rooms have private bathrooms, and there's an elevator to all floors. Bedrooms are neutral in style and the ground-floor rooms are the least preferred. Don't expect views from some of the back rooms, which open onto a wall.

87 Gloucester Place (Baker St.), London W1H 3PG. © 020/7935-2211. Fax 020/7486-7535. www.london centralhotel.com. 19 units. £90 ($167) double; £100 ($185) triple; £130 ($241) family room. Rates include English breakfast. AE, MC, V. Tube: Baker St. *In room:* TV, coffeemaker.

ST. JAMES'S
VERY EXPENSIVE

The Ritz ✰✰✰ Built in French Renaissance style and opened by César Ritz in 1906, this hotel overlooking Green Park is synonymous with luxury. Gold-leafed molding, marble columns, and potted palms abound, and a gold-leafed statue, *La Source,* adorns the fountain of the oval-shaped Palm Court. After a major restoration, the hotel is better than ever: New carpeting and air-conditioning have been installed in the guest rooms, and an overall polishing has recaptured much of The Ritz's original splendor. Still, this Ritz lags far behind the much grander one in Paris (with which it is not affiliated). The Belle Epoque guest rooms, each with its own character, are spacious and comfortable. Many have marble fireplaces, elaborate gilded plasterwork, and a decor of soft pastel hues. A few rooms have their original brass beds and marble fireplaces. Bathrooms are elegantly appointed in either tile or marble and filled with deep tubs with showers, robes, phones, and deluxe toiletries. Corner rooms are grander and more spacious.

150 Piccadilly, London W1J 9BR. © 877/748-9536 in the U.S., or 020/7493-8181. Fax 020/7493-2687. www.theritzlondon.com. 133 units. £310–£405 ($574–$749) double; from £785 ($1,452) suite. Children under 12 stay free in parent's room. AE, DC, MC, V. Parking £54 ($100). Tube: Green Park. **Amenities:** 2 restaurants (including the Palm Court); bar; exercise room; concierge; business services; 2 salons; 24-hr. room service; massage; babysitting; laundry service; same-day dry cleaning; nonsmoking rooms; rooms for those with limited mobility. *In room:* A/C, TV/VCR (plus pay movies), fax, dataport, minibar, hair dryer, safe.

EXPENSIVE

Dukes Hotel ✫✫✫   Dukes provides elegance without ostentation in what was presumably someone's "Upstairs, Downstairs" town house. Along with its nearest competitors, the Stafford and 22 Jermyn Street, it caters to those looking for charm, style, and tradition in a hotel. It stands in a quiet courtyard off St. James's Street; turn-of-the-last-century gas lamps help put you into the proper mood before entering the front door. Each well-furnished guest room is decorated in the style of a particular English period, ranging from Regency to Edwardian. All rooms are equipped with marble bathrooms containing shower-tub combinations. Even though it's claustrophobically small—it was once described as England's smallest castle—Dukes offers full hotel services.

35 St. James's Place, London SW1A 1NY. © 800/381-4702 in the U.S., or 020/7491-4840. Fax 020/7493-1264. www.dukeshotel.co.uk. 89 units. £225–£260 ($416–$481) double; from £350 ($648) suite. AE, DC, MC, V. Parking £54 ($100). Tube: Green Park. **Amenities:** Restaurant; bar; health club; spa; concierge; tour desk; business services; 24-hr. room service; babysitting; laundry service; same-day dry cleaning; nonsmoking rooms; rooms for those with limited mobility. *In room:* A/C, TV, dataport, minibar, hair dryer, safe.

The Stafford Hotel ✫✫✫   Famous for its American Bar, its clubby St. James's address, and the warmth of its Edwardian decor, the Stafford is in a cul-de-sac off one of London's most centrally located and busiest neighborhoods. The recently refurbished late-19th-century hotel has retained a country-house atmosphere, with antique charm and modern amenities. The Stafford competes well with Dukes and 22 Jermyn Street for a tasteful, discerning clientele and seems to maintain a slight edge in attracting an upmarket clientele.

All the guest rooms are individually decorated, reflecting the hotel's origins as a private home. Many singles contain queen-size beds. Some of the deluxe units offer four-posters that will make you feel like Henry VIII. Nearly all the bathrooms are clad in marble with tubs and stall showers, toiletries, and chrome fixtures. A few of the hotel's more modern accommodations, boasting king-size beds, are located in the restored stable mews across the yard. Much has been done to preserve the original style of these rooms, including preservation of the original A-beams on the upper floors. You can bet that no 18th-century horse ever slept with the electronic safes, stereo systems, and quality furnishings (mostly antique reproductions) that these rooms feature. Units on the top floor are small. All rooms are nonsmoking.

16–18 St. James's Place, London SW1A 1NJ. © 800/525-4800 in the U.S., or 020/7493-0111. Fax 020/7493-7121. www.thestaffordhotel.co.uk. 81 units. £225–£250 ($416–$463) double; from £270 ($500) suite. AE, DC, MC, V. Tube: Green Park. **Amenities:** Restaurant; famous American bar; health club privileges nearby; concierge; business services; 24-hr. room service; babysitting; laundry service; same-day dry cleaning. *In room:* A/C, TV/VCR, fax, dataport, hair dryer, safe.

TRAFALGAR SQUARE
EXPENSIVE

The Royal Horseguards ✫   This hotel is owned by Thistle, a popular chain of hotels in Great Britain. This is their flagship hotel in London, close to

Parliament, Charing Cross, and Horse Guards, with rooms opening onto the River Thames near Trafalgar Square. This bustling area of London becomes relatively quiet at night. The hotel maintains some of the atmosphere it once knew during its role as a men's club. MPs still frequent the place, especially the bar, where a light signals them to finish their liquor fast and get back to Parliament to vote. Rooms have been refurbished, and for the most part they are comfortable, although we've found that many of them are too small, especially if you've arrived with a lot of luggage. Those accommodations with a river view are the best and the largest. The hotel is geared mainly to business travelers but could be ideal for sightseers as well. Most doubles are at the low end of the price scale.

2 Whitehall Court, London SW1A 2EJ. © **0870/3339-122.** Fax 0870/3339-222. www.thistlehotels.com/royalhorseguards. 280 units. £134–£329 ($248–$609) double; from £270 ($500) suite. AE, DC, MC, V. Tube: Embankment. Parking: £40 ($74). **Amenities:** Restaurant; bar; exercise room; business center; 24-hr. room service; laundry service; same-day dry cleaning; nonsmoking rooms. *In room:* A/C (in some), TV w/pay movies, dataport, minibar, coffeemaker, hair dryer, iron, safe.

The Trafalgar ★★   In the heart of landmark Trafalgar Square, this is Hilton's first boutique hotel in London. The facade of this 19th-century structure was preserved, while the guest rooms inside were refitted to modern standards. Because of the original architecture, many of the rooms are uniquely shaped and sometimes offer split-level layouts. Large windows open onto panoramic views of Trafalgar Square. The decor in the rooms is minimalist, and comfort is combined with simple luxury, including the deluxe tiled bathrooms with tub and shower combinations. The greatest view of London's cityscape is from the Hilton's rooftop garden.

Unusual for London, the bar, Rockwell, specializes in bourbon, with more than 100 brands. Jago is the hotel's organic-produce restaurant, serving comfort food.

2 Spring Gardens, Trafalgar Square, London SW1A 2TS. © **800/774-1500** in the U.S., or 020/7870-2900. Fax 020/7870-2911. www.trafalgar.hilton.com. 129 units. £159–£229 ($294–$424) double; from £289 ($535) suite. AE, DC, MC, V. Tube: Charing Cross. **Amenities:** Restaurant; bar; concierge; sauna; courtesy car; business services; 24-hr. room service; laundry service; same-day dry cleaning; nonsmoking rooms; rooms for those with limited mobility. *In room:* A/C, TV w/pay movies, dataport, minibar, beverage maker, hair dryer, safe.

SOHO
VERY EXPENSIVE
Charlotte Street Hotel ★★ *Finds*   In North Soho, a short walk from the heartbeat of Soho Square, this town house has been luxuriously converted into a high-end hotel that is London chic at its finest, possessing everything from a Los Angeles–style juice bar to a private screening room. The latter has made the hotel a hit with the movie, fashion, and media crowd, many of whom had never ventured to North Soho before. One local told us, "Charlotte Street is for those who'd like to imagine themselves in California." Midsize to spacious bedrooms have fresh, modern, English interiors and everything from two-line phones with voice mail to dataports and fax outlets. Bathrooms are state of the art, designed in solid granite and oak with twin basins, walk-in showers, and even color TVs. Guests can relax in the elegant drawing room and library with a log-burning fireplace. The decor evokes memories of the fabled Bloomsbury set of Virginia Woolf.

15–17 Charlotte St., London W1T 1RJ. © **800/553-6674** in the U.S., or 020/7806-2000. Fax 020/7806-2002. www.firmdale.com. 52 units. £220–£310 ($407–$574) double; from £340 ($629) suite. AE, MC, V. Tube: Tottenham Court. **Amenities:** Restaurant and long pewter bar; exercise room; 24-hr. room service; laundry service; same-day dry cleaning; nonsmoking rooms; rooms for those with limited mobility. *In room:* A/C, TV/DVD, fax, dataport, minibar, hair dryer, safe.

The Sanderson 🏵🏵🏵   Ian Schrager, the king of New York hip, has brought 10th Avenue in Manhattan to London. For his latest London hotel, Schrager secured the help of talented partners, Philippe Starck and Andra Andrei, to create an "ethereal, transparent urban spa," in which walls are replaced by glass and sheer layers of curtains. The hotel, located in a former corporate building near Oxford Street, north of Soho, comes with a lush bamboo-filled roof garden, a large courtyard, and spa. That's not all—its restaurant is directed by Alain Ducasse, arguably the world's greatest chef. The accommodations are cutting edge. Although the transformation of this building into a hotel has been remarkable, the dreary grid facade of aluminum squares and glass remains. Your bed is likely to be an Italian silver-leaf sleigh attended by spidery polished stainless-steel night tables and draped with a fringed pashmina shawl the color of dried lemon verbena.

50 Berners St., London W1T 3NG. ⓒ **020/7300-1400.** Fax 020/7300-1401. www.ianschragerhotels.com. 150 units. £205–£340 ($379–$629) double; from £400 ($740) suite. Ask about weekend specials. AE, DC, MC, V. Valet parking £44 ($81). Tube: Oxford Circus. **Amenities:** 2 Restaurant; 2 bars, health club; spa; concierge; business services; 24-hr. room service; in-room massage; babysitting; laundry service; same-day dry cleaning; nonsmoking rooms; rooms for those with limited mobility. *In room:* A/C, TV w/pay movies, dataport, minibar, beverage maker, hair dryer, safe.

EXPENSIVE

Hazlitt's 1718 🏵🏵 *Finds*   This gem, housed in three historic homes on Soho Square, is one of London's best small hotels. Built in 1718, the hotel is named for William Hazlitt, who founded the Unitarian church in Boston and wrote four volumes on the life of his hero, Napoleon.

Hazlitt's is a favorite with artists, actors, and models. It's eclectic and filled with odds and ends picked up around the country at estate auctions. Some find its Georgian decor a bit spartan, but the 2,000 original prints hanging on the walls brighten it considerably. Many bedrooms have four-poster beds, and some bathrooms have their original claw-foot tubs (only two units have a shower). Some of the floors dip and sway, and there's no elevator, but it's all part of the charm. It has just as much character as the Fielding Hotel (see below) but is a lot more comfortable. Some rooms are small, but most are spacious, all with state-of-the-art appointments. Most bathrooms have 19th-century styling but up-to-date plumbing, with oversize tubs and old brass fittings; the showers, however, are mostly hand-held. Accommodations in the back are quieter but perhaps too dark, and only those on the top floor have air-conditioning. Swinging Soho is at your doorstep; the young, hip staff will be happy to direct you to the local hot spots.

6 Frith St., London W1V 5TZ. ⓒ **020/7434-1771.** Fax 020/7439-1524. www.hazlittshotel.com. 23 units. £205–£255 ($379–$472) double; £300 ($555) suite. AE, DC, MC, V. Tube: Leicester Sq. or Tottenham Court Rd. **Amenities:** 24-hr. room service; babysitting; laundry service; same-day dry cleaning; nonsmoking rooms. *In room:* A/C (some rooms), TV/VCR, dataport, minibar, hair dryer, safe.

BLOOMSBURY
EXPENSIVE

The Academy Hotel 🏵   The Academy is in the heart of London's publishing district. If you look out your window, you see where Virginia Woolf and other literary members of the Bloomsbury Group passed by every day. Many original architectural details were preserved when these three 1776 Georgian row houses were joined. The hotel was substantially upgraded in the 1990s, with a bathroom added to every bedroom (whether there was space or not). Fourteen have a tub-shower combination; the rest have showers only. The beds, so they say, were built to "American specifications." True or not, they promise you a restful night's sleep. Grace notes include glass panels, colonnades, and intricate plaster-work on the facade. With overstuffed armchairs and half-canopied beds, rooms sometimes evoke English country-house living, but that of the poorer relations. Guests who have been here before always request rooms opening on the garden in back and not those in front with ducted fresh air, though the front units have double glazing to cut down on the noise. The theater district and Covent Garden are within walking distance. *Warning:* If you have a problem with stairs, know that no elevators rise to the four floors.

21 Gower St., London WC1E 6HG. ℂ 020/7631-4115. Fax 020/7636-3442. www.etontownhouse.com. 49 units. £163–£189 ($313–$350) double; £215 ($398) suite. AE, DC, MC, V. Tube: Tottenham Court Rd., Goodge St., or Russell Sq. **Amenities:** Bar; 24-hr. room service; laundry service; same-day dry cleaning; nonsmoking rooms. *In room:* A/C, TV, dataport, minibar, beverage maker, hair dryer, iron/ironing board, safe, trouser press.

Blooms Town House Hotel ✮   This restored 18th-century town house has a pedigree: It stands in what were formerly the grounds of Montague House (now The British Museum). It has had a distinguished, if eccentric, list of former occupants: everybody from Richard Penn (the Whig member of Parliament from Liverpool) to Dr. John Cumming, who firmly believed he'd witness the end of the world (on long winter nights, his ghostly presence has supposedly been spotted). Even though it's in the heart of London, the house has a coun-try-home atmosphere, complete with fireplace, period art, and copies of *Country Life* in the magazine rack. Guests take morning coffee in a walled garden over-looking The British Museum. In summer, light meals are served. The small- to medium-size bedrooms are individually designed with traditional elegance, in beautifully muted tones, and the shower/tub bathrooms are well maintained.

7 Montague St., London WC1B 5BP. ℂ **020/7323-1717.** Fax 020/7636-6498. www.bloomshotel.com. 26 units. £175–£192 ($324–$355) double. Extra person £40 ($74). AE, DC, MC, V. Tube: Russell Sq. **Amenities:** 24-hr. room service; courtesy car; laundry service; dry cleaning; nonsmoking rooms. *In room:* TV, minibar, coffeemaker, hair dryer, trouser press.

Myhotel ✮ *Finds*   Creating shock waves among staid Bloomsbury hoteliers, Myhotel is a London row house on the outside with an Asian moderne-style interior. It is designed according to feng shui principles—the ancient Chinese art of placement that analyzes the flow of energy in a space. The rooms have mirrors, but they're positioned so that you don't see yourself when you first wake up—feng shui rule no. 1 (probably a good rule, feng shui or no feng shui). Rooms are havens of comfort, taste, and tranquillity. Excellent sleep-inducing beds are found in all rooms, along with a small bathroom with a tub. Tipping is discouraged, and each guest is assigned a personal assistant responsible for that guest's happiness. Aimed at today's young, hip traveler, Myhotel lies within a short walk of Covent Garden and The British Museum.

11–13 Bayley St., Bedford Sq., London WC1B 3HD. ℂ 020/7667-6000. Fax 020/7667-6001. www.myhotels. co.uk. 78 units. £185–£250 ($342–$463) double; from £330 ($611) suite. AE, DC, MC, V. Tube: Tottenham Court Rd. **Amenities:** Restaurant; bar; exercise room; spa; car at discounted rate; 24-hr. room service; mas-sage; babysitting; laundry service; same-day dry cleaning; nonsmoking rooms. *In room:* A/C, TV w/pay movies, dataport, beverage maker, hair dryer, safe, trouser press (in some).

MODERATE

Harlingford Hotel *Value*   This hotel is comprised of three town houses built in the 1820s and joined together around 1900 with a bewildering array of stair-cases and meandering hallways. Set in the heart of Bloomsbury, it's run by a management that seems genuinely concerned about the welfare of its guests,

Travel Tip: He who finds the best hotel deal has more to spend on facials involving knobbly vegetables.

Hello, the Roaming Gnome here. I've been nabbed from the garden and taken round the world. The people who took me are so terribly clever. They find the best offerings on Travelocity. For very little cha-ching. And that means I get to be pampered and exfoliated till I'm pink as a bunny's doodah.

travelocity®

1-888-TRAVELOCITY / travelocity.com / America Online Keyword: Travel

unlike the management at many of the neighboring hotel rivals. (They even distribute little mincemeat pies to their guests during the Christmas holidays.) Double-glazed windows cut down on the street noise, and all the bedrooms are comfortable and inviting. Shower-only bathrooms are small, however, since the house wasn't originally designed for them. The most comfortable rooms are on the second and third levels, but expect to climb some steep English stairs (there's no elevator). Avoid the rooms on ground level, as they are darker and have less security. You'll have use of the tennis courts in Cartwright Gardens.

61–63 Cartwright Gardens, London WC1H 9EL. © 020/7387-1551. Fax 020/7387-4616. www.harlingford hotel.com. 44 units. £95 ($176) double; £105 ($194) triple; £110 ($204) quad. Rates include English breakfast. AE, DC, MC, V. Tube: Russell Sq., King's Cross, or Euston. **Amenities:** Use of tennis courts in Cartwright Gardens. *In room:* TV, coffeemaker, hair dryer.

INEXPENSIVE

Crescent Hotel   Although Ruskin and Shelley no longer pass by, the Crescent still stands in the heart of academic London. The private square is owned by the City Guild of Skinners (who are furriers, as you may have guessed), and you have access to their gardens and private tennis courts. Student residential halls of the University of London are across the street. The hotel owners view Crescent as an extension of their home and welcome you to its comfortably elegant Georgian surroundings, which date from 1810. Some guests have been returning for 4 decades. Bedrooms range from small singles with shared bathrooms to more spacious twin and double rooms with private showers. All have extras such as alarm clocks. Twins and doubles have private plumbing, with tiny bathrooms. Many rooms are singles, ranging in price from £46 to £83 ($85–$154), depending on the plumbing.

49–50 Cartwright Gardens, London WC1H 9EL. © 020/7387-1515. Fax 020/7383-2054. www.crescenthotel oflondon.com. 27 units, 18 with bathroom (some with shower only, some with tub and shower). £89 ($165) double with bathroom. Rates include English breakfast. MC, V. Tube: Russell Sq., King's Cross, or Euston. **Amenities:** Babysitting. *In room:* TV, coffeemaker, hair dryer.

The Jenkins Hotel ⭐ *Value*   Followers of the Agatha Christie TV series *Poirot* will recognize this Cartwright Gardens residence—it was featured in the series. The antiques are gone and the rooms are small, but some of the original charm of the Georgian house remains—enough so that the London *Mail on Sunday* proclaimed it one of the "ten best hotel values" in the city. The rooms are decorated in traditional Georgian style, many have been completely refurbished with new beds and upholstery, and all are nonsmoking. All but one room has a private bath; most have shower-only. The location is great, near The British Museum, theaters, and antiquarian bookshops. There are some drawbacks: no lift and no reception or sitting room. But this is a place where you can settle in and feel at home.

45 Cartwright Gardens, London WC1H 9EH. © 020/7387-2067. Fax 020/7383-3139. www.jenkinshotel. demon.co.uk. 13 units. £85 ($157) double; £105 ($194) triple. Rates include English breakfast. MC, V. Tube: Russell Sq., King's Cross, or Euston. **Amenities:** Use of washer/dryer. *In room:* TV, dataport, minibar, fridge, coffeemaker, hair dryer, iron, safe.

Ruskin Hotel   Although the hotel is named for author John Ruskin, the ghosts of other literary legends who lived nearby haunt you: Mary Shelley plotting her novel, *Frankenstein,* and James Barrie fantasizing about *Peter Pan.* This hotel has been managed for 2 decades by a hardworking family that enjoys a repeat clientele. Management keeps the place spick-and-span, though don't expect a decorator's flair. The furnishings, though well-polished, are a bit worn.

Double-glazing in the front blots out the noise, but we prefer the cozily old-fashioned chambers in the rear, as they open onto a park. Sorry, no elevator. The greenery in the cellar-level breakfast room provides a nice touch, and the breakfast is big enough to fortify you for a day at The British Museum next door. *Insider's tip:* Although the private bathrooms are ridiculously small, the shared bathrooms in the hall are generous and well maintained; all have shower units.

23–24 Montague St., London WC1B 5BH. © **020/7636-7388.** Fax 020/7323-1662. 32 units, 6 with bathroom. £67 ($124) double without bathroom; £84 ($155) double with bathroom. Rates include English breakfast. AE, DC, MC, V. Tube: Russell Sq. or Tottenham Court Rd. *In room:* Coffeemaker, hair dryer.

COVENT GARDEN
VERY EXPENSIVE

Covent Garden Hotel ★★★   This former hospital building lay neglected for years until it was reconfigured in 1996 by hot hoteliers Tim and Kit Kemp—whose flair for interior design is legendary—into one of London's most charming boutique hotels in one of the West End's hippest shopping neighborhoods. *Travel and Leisure* called this hotel one of the 25 hottest places to stay in the *world.* It remains so. Behind a bottle-green facade reminiscent of a 19th-century storefront, the hotel has a welcoming lobby outfitted with elaborate inlaid furniture and elegant draperies. Upstairs, accessible via a dramatic stone staircase, soundproof bedrooms are furnished in English style with Asian fabrics, many adorned with hand-embroidered designs. The hotel has a decorative trademark—each room has a clothier's mannequin, a female form draped in the fabric that decorates that particular room. Each room comes with luxurious amenities including full marble bathrooms with double vanities and deep soaking tubs. Some guests prefer the attic rooms with their sloping ceilings and small arched windows.

10 Monmouth St., London WC2H 9HB. © **800/553-6674** in the U.S., or 020/7806-1000. Fax 020/7806-1100. www.firmdale.com. 58 units. £245–£295 ($453–$546) double; £350–£795 ($648–$1,471) suite. AE, MC, V. Tube: Covent Garden or Leicester Sq. **Amenities:** Restaurant; bar; small exercise room; concierge; tour desk; business services; 24-hr. room service; massage; babysitting; laundry service; same-day dry cleaning; video library; nonsmoking rooms. *In room:* A/C, TV/VCR, dataport, minibar, hair dryer, safe.

St. Martins Lane ★★★   "Eccentric and irreverent, with a sense of humor," is how Ian Schrager describes his cutting-edge Covent Garden hotel, which he transformed from a 1960s office building into a chic enclave. This was the first hotel that Schrager designed outside the United States, after a string of successes from New York to West Hollywood. The mix of hip design and a sense of cool have been imported across the pond. Whimsical touches abound. For example, a string of daisies replaces DO NOT DISTURB signs. Rooms are all white, but you can use the full-spectrum lighting to make them any color. Floor-to-ceiling glass windows in every room offer a panoramic view of London, and down comforters and soft pillows ensure a good night's sleep. Some rooms are nonsmoking. Bathrooms are spacious and state-of-the-art, with deluxe toiletries.

45 St. Martins Lane, London WC2N 4HX. © **020/7300-5500.** Fax 020/7300-5501. www.ianschragerhotels. com. 204 units. £235–£325 ($435–$601) double; from £1,400 ($2,590) suite. AE, DC, MC, V. Tube: Covent Garden or Leicester Sq. **Amenities:** Restaurant; bar; state-of-the-art health club; spa services from nearby spa on request; courtesy car; business center; 24-hr. room service; babysitting; laundry service; same-day dry cleaning; rooms for those with limited mobility. *In room:* A/C, TV/VCR, dataport, minibar, hair dryer, safe.

MODERATE

The Fielding Hotel ★ *Finds*   One of London's more eccentric hotels, the Fielding is cramped, quirky, and quaint, and an enduring favorite. Luring media types, the hotel is named after novelist Henry Fielding of *Tom Jones* fame, who lived in Broad Court. It lies on a pedestrian street still lined with 19th-century gas lamps. The Royal Opera House is across the street, and the pubs, shops, and restaurants of lively Covent Garden are just beyond the front door. Rooms are small but charmingly old-fashioned and traditional. Some units are redecorated or at least "touched up" every year, though floors dip and sway, and the furnishings and fabrics, though clean, have known better times. The bathrooms, some with antiquated plumbing, are equipped with showers. But with a location like this, in the heart of London, the Fielding keeps guests coming back; in fact, many love the hotel's rickety charm. Children under 13 are not welcome.

4 Broad Ct., Bow St., London WC2B 5QZ. ℂ **020/7836-8305**. Fax 020/7497-0064. www.the-fielding-hotel.co.uk. 24 units. £100–£115 ($185–$213) double; £130 ($241) suite. AE, DC, MC, V. Tube: Covent Garden. **Amenities:** Bar; laundry service; nonsmoking rooms. *In room:* TV, dataport, coffeemaker.

ALONG THE STRAND
VERY EXPENSIVE

The Savoy ✩✩✩   Although not as swank as The Dorchester, this London landmark is the premier hotel in the Strand/Covent Garden area. Richard D'Oyly Carte built it in 1889 as an annex to his nearby Savoy Theatre, where many Gilbert and Sullivan operettas were staged. Each room is individually decorated with color-coordinated accessories, solid and comfortable furniture, large closets, and an eclectic blend of antiques, such as gilt mirrors, Queen Anne chairs, and Victorian sofas. Forty-eight units have their own sitting rooms. The handmade beds—real luxury models—have top-of-the-line crisp linen clothing and other lavish appointments. Some bathrooms have tubs, but most have a shower and tub. Bathrooms are spacious, with deluxe toiletries. The suites overlooking the river are the most sought after, and for good reason—the vistas are the best in London. *Tip:* Ask for one of the newer rooms, with a view of the river, in what was formerly a storage space. They are among the best in the hotel, with views of the Thames and Parliament.

The Strand, London WC2R 0EU. ℂ **800/63-SAVOY** in the U.S., or 020/7836-4343. Fax 020/7240-6040. www.the-savoy.co.uk. 263 units. £345–£425 ($638–$786) double; from £465 ($860) suite. AE, DC, MC, V. Parking £34 ($63). Tube: Charing Cross or Covent Garden. **Amenities:** 3 restaurants (including the celebrated Savoy Grill and the River Restaurant, which overlooks the Thames); 2 bars; city's best health club; spa; business center; sauna; 24-hr. room service; laundry service; dry cleaning; nonsmoking rooms; rooms for those with limited mobility. *In room:* A/C, TV/VCR, dataport, minibar, hair dryer, safe.

WESTMINSTER/VICTORIA
VERY EXPENSIVE

The Goring ✩✩✩   For tradition and location, the Goring is our first choice in Westminster. Just behind Buckingham Palace, it lies within easy reach of the royal parks, Victoria Station, Westminster Abbey, and the Houses of Parliament. It also offers the finest personal service of all its nearby competitors.

Built in 1910 by O. R. Goring, this was the first hotel in the world to have central heating and a private bathroom in every room. Today's guest rooms still offer all the comforts, including luxurious refurbished bathrooms with extralong tubs, red marble walls, dual pedestal basins, bidets, deluxe toiletries, and power showerheads. All bedrooms benefit from ongoing refurbishment, including frequent replacement of linens. The beds are among the most comfortable in London. Queen Anne and Chippendale are usually the decor styles, and the maintenance level is of the highest order. The rooms overlooking the garden are best. The charm of a traditional English country hotel is conjured up in the paneled drawing room, where fires crackle in ornate fireplaces on cool evenings.

15 Beeston Place, Grosvenor Gardens, London SW1W OJW. ✆ 020/7396-9000. Fax 020/7834-4393. www. goringhotel.co.uk. 74 units. £255–£340 ($472–$629) double; from £340 ($629) suite. AE, DC, MC, V. Parking £30 ($56). Tube: Victoria. **Amenities:** Grand afternoon tea in the drawing room (a London highlight); classic restaurant; bar; free use of nearby health club; 24-hr. room service; babysitting; laundry service; same-day dry cleaning; nonsmoking rooms; rooms for those with limited mobility. *In room:* A/C, TV w/pay movies, dataport, hair dryer, safe.

EXPENSIVE

41 ★★★ *Finds*   This relatively unknown but well-placed gem is a treasure worth seeking out, especially if you're looking for a touch of class. The property offers the intimate atmosphere of a private club combined with a level of personal service that's impossible to achieve at larger hotels. It's best suited to couples or those traveling alone—especially women, who will be made to feel comfortable. The cordial staff goes the extra mile to fulfill a guest's every wish. The surroundings match the stellar service. Public areas feature an abundance of mahogany, antiques, fresh flowers, and rich fabrics. Read, relax, or watch TV in the library-style lounge, where a complimentary continental breakfast, afternoon snacks, and evening canapés (all included in the room rate) are served each day.

Guest rooms are individually sized, but all feature elegant black-and-white color schemes, magnificent beds with Egyptian cotton linens, and "AV centers" that offer free Internet access and DVD/CD players. Most rooms have working fireplaces. The spotless marble bathrooms sport separate tubs and power showers (only one room has a tub/shower combo) and feature Penhaligon toiletries. The bi-level junior suites toss in a separate seating area (good for families looking for extra space) and Jacuzzi tubs.

41 Buckingham Palace Road, London SW1W OPS. ✆ 877/955-1515 in the U.S. and Canada, or 020/7300-0041. Fax 020/7300-0141. www.41hotel.com. 18 units. £200 ($370) double; £400–£500 ($740–$925) suite. Rates include continental breakfast, afternoon snacks, and evening canapés. Extra person £45 ($83). Special Internet packages and discounts available. AE, DC, MC, V. Tube: Victoria. **Amenities:** Lounge; bar; access to nearby health club; concierge; business center; 24-hr. room service; laundry service; dry cleaning; nonsmoking rooms; 1 room for those with limited mobility. *In room:* A/C, TV, minibar, tea/coffeemaker, hair dryer, iron/ironing board, safe.

The Rubens at the Palace ★★ *Value*   The very British Rubens is popular with Americans and Europeans seeking traditional English hospitality combined with the latest in creature comforts. And its location is one of the best in town—directly across the street from Buckingham Palace, only a 2-minute walk from Victoria Station. The public rooms are lavishly decorated with antiques, fabric wall coverings, and fresh flowers. A pianist plays in the military-style Cavalry Bar, the ideal place for a nightcap, on most evenings.

The size and decor of the guest rooms varies, but all feature grand comfort. Bathrooms vary in size, but almost all have deep tubs. Housed in a private wing, each of the eight "Royal Rooms" is named for an English monarch, and is decorated in the style of that ruler's period, but also features a host of modern luxuries. Some Royal Rooms aren't particularly big. If it's available and your budget allows, we suggest the Henry the Eighth room, a relatively large Tudor fantasy done up in red and gold, with a half-canopy bed fit for a king, and a spacious marble bathroom. *Note:* Always check the hotel's website for specials; the hotel often runs promotions that can make it an attractive value option.

39 Buckingham Palace, R.D. London SW1W OPS. ✆ 877/955-1515 in the U.S. and Canada, or 020/7834-6600. Fax 020/7828-5401. www.rubenshotel.com. 172 units. £210–£250 ($389–$463) double; £320–£480

($592–$888) Royal Room; £230–£260 ($426–$481) suite. AE, DC, MC, V. Tube: Victoria: **Amenities:** 2 restaurants; lounge; bar; access to nearby health club; concierge; tour desk; babysitting; 24-hr. room service; laundry service; same-day dry cleaning; nonsmoking rooms. *In room:* A/C, TV, dataport, minibar (in suites), coffeemaker, hair dryer, iron, safe.

MODERATE

New England   A family run business, going strong for nearly a quarter of a century, this hotel shut down at the millennium for a complete overhaul. Today, it's better than ever and charges an affordable price. Its elegant 19th-century exterior conceals a completely bright and modern interior. The hotel is justly proud of its clientele of "repeats." On a corner in the Pimlico area, which forms part of the City of Westminster, the hotel is neat and clean and one of the most welcoming in the area. It's also one of the few hotels in the area with an elevator. All the bathrooms have power showers.

20 Saint George's Dr., London SW1V 4BN. © 020/7834-1595. Fax 020/7834-9000. www.newenglandhotel. com. 25 units. £95–£99 ($176–$183) double; £119 ($220) triple; £139 ($257) quad. Rates include breakfast. AE, MC, V. Tube: Victoria. **Amenities:** Nonsmoking rooms; rooms for those with limited mobility. *In room:* TV, dataport, hair dryer.

The Sanctuary House Hotel   Only in the new London, where hotels are bursting into bloom like daffodils, would you find a hotel so close to Westminster Abbey. And a pub hotel, no less, with rooms on the upper floors above the tavern. The building was converted by Fuller Smith and Turner, a traditional brewery in Britain. Accommodations have a rustic feel, but they have first-rate beds, along with restored bathrooms with shower-tub combinations. Downstairs, a pub/restaurant, part of The Sanctuary, offers old-style British meals that have ignored changing culinary fashions. "We like tradition," one of the perky staff members told us. "Why must everything be trendy? Some people come to England nostalgic for the old. Let others be trendy." Actually, the food is excellent if you appreciate the roast beef, Welsh lamb, and Dover sole that pleased the palates of Churchill and his contemporaries. Naturally, there's always plenty of brew on tap.

33 Tothill St., London SW1H 9LA. © 020/7799-4044. Fax 020/7799-3657. www.fullershotels.com. 34 units. £85–£130 ($157–$241) double. AE, DC, MC, V. Parking £25 ($46). Tube: St. James's Park. **Amenities:** Restaurant; pub; limited room service; laundry service; dry cleaning; nonsmoking rooms; rooms for those with limited mobility. *In room:* A/C, TV, dataport, coffeemaker, hair dryer, trouser press.

INEXPENSIVE

Caswell Hotel   Thoughtfully run by Mr. and Mrs. Hare, Caswell is on a cul-de-sac, a calm oasis in a busy area. Mozart lived nearby while he completed his first symphony, as did that "notorious couple" of the literati, Harold Nicholson and Victoria Sackville-West. Beyond the chintz-filled lobby, the decor is understated, with four floors of well-furnished but not spectacular bedrooms. Both the private bathrooms (small units with shower stalls) and the corridor bathrooms are adequate and well maintained. How does the Caswell explain their success? One staff member said, "This year's guest is next year's business."

25 Gloucester St., London SW1V 2DB. © 020/7834-6345. www.hotellondon.co.uk. 19 units, 8 with bathroom. £55 ($102) double without bathroom; £75 ($139) double with bathroom. Rates include English breakfast. MC, V. Tube: Victoria. *In room:* TV, minibar, beverage maker, hair dryer, safe, no phone.

Collin House   This B&B emerges as a winner on a street lined with the finest Victoria Station–area B&Bs. William IV had just begun his reign when this house was constructed in 1830. Private, shower-only bathrooms have been discreetly installed, and everything works efficiently. For rooms without bathrooms, there are adequate hallway facilities, some of which are shared by only two rooms. Outside, traffic in this area of London is heavy, and the front windows are not soundproof, so be warned if you're a light sleeper. Year after year, the owners continually make improvements in the furnishings and carpets. All bedrooms, which vary in size, are comfortably furnished and well maintained. Two rooms are large enough for families. A generous breakfast awaits you each morning in the basement of this nonsmoking facility.

104 Ebury St., London SW1W 9QD. © and fax **020/7730-8031.** www.collinhouse.co.uk. 12 units, 8 with bathroom (shower only). £68 ($126) double without bathroom, £82 ($152) double with bathroom; £95 ($176) triple without bathroom. Rates include English breakfast. MC, V. Tube: Victoria. *In room:* TV, hair dryer available, safe, no phone.

James & Cartref House *(Kids* Hailed by many publications, including the *Los Angeles Times,* as one of the top 10 B&B choices in London, James House and Cartref House (across the street from each other) deserve their accolades. Each room is individually designed. Some of the large rooms have bunk beds that make them suitable for families. Clients in rooms with a private shower-only bathroom will find somewhat cramped quarters; corridor bathrooms are adequate and frequently refurbished. The English breakfast is so generous that you may end up skipping lunch. There's no elevator, but guests don't seem to mind. Both houses are nonsmoking. You're just a stone's throw from Buckingham Palace should the queen invite you over for tea. *Warning:* Whether or not you like this nonsmoking hotel will depend on your room assignment. Some accommodations are fine but several rooms (often when the other units are full) are hardly large enough to move around in. This is especially true of some third-floor units. Some "bathrooms" reminded us of those found on small ocean-going freighters. Ask before booking and request a larger room.

108 and 129 Ebury St., London SW1W 9QD. James House © **020/7730-7338;** Cartref House © **020/7730-6176.** Fax 020/7730-7338. www.jamesandcartref.co.uk. 19 units, 12 with bathroom. £70 ($130) double without bathroom, £85 ($157) double with bathroom; £135 ($250) quad with bathroom. Rates include English breakfast. AE, MC, V. Tube: Victoria. *In room:* TV, beverage maker, hair dryer, no phone.

Oxford House Hotel *(Value* Just a 10-minute walk from Victoria Station, Oxford House is known for value. Since many of its rooms sleep three to four guests, it's a family favorite as well. The owners operate this small hotel like the private family home that it is, and the atmosphere is informal. The biggest drawback is the lack of a private bathroom. However, only two bedrooms usually share one shower-only bathroom, so waiting time is minimal. Guests from all over the world converge in the TV lounge. Rooms are midsize and furnished with comfortable, well-chosen pieces. Although it's in a heavily congested area, Cambridge Street is not a major thoroughfare, and rooms tend to be tranquil.

92-94 Cambridge St., London SW1V 4QG. © **020/7834-6467.** Fax 020/7834-0225. 17 units, none with private bathroom. £45 ($83) double; £60 ($111) triple; £80 ($148) quad. Rates include English breakfast. AE, MC, V (5% surcharge). Tube: Victoria. *In room:* No phone.

IN & AROUND KNIGHTSBRIDGE
VERY EXPENSIVE

Mandarin Oriental Hyde Park Hotel ★★★ Set behind a stately looking late-19th-century brick facade whose style is defined by art historians as "Franco-Flemish," this is one of London's most appealing and historic hotels. It was built in 1889 as a private men's club, then converted into a hotel in 1902. In May of 2000, the hotel completed a £50-million restoration by its owners,

Mandarin Oriental. Today, the hotel occupies an enviable niche, wherein Edwardian grandeur and Asian postmodern chic manage to comfortably coexist. The restoration brought lavish amounts of brass, marble, mahogany, and stained glass back to its original turn-of-the-20th-century gloss, and added state-of-the-art infrastructures (many of them invisible) that will help carry this outstanding property deep into the 21st century. The lobby maintains a perpetually tasteful allegiance to pomp and circumstance, complete with a multi-million pound collection of paintings on long-term loan from the National Maritime Museum. Bedrooms are opulent, decorated with pale colors, countless yards of silk and satin, some of the meticulously restored antiques that have been in the hotel since its earliest years, and state-of-the-art tiled bathrooms with tubs big enough for several Sir Winstons at a time.

66 Knightsbridge, London SW1X 7LA. © **800/526-6566** for reservations in the U.S. and Canada, or 020/7235-2000. Fax 020/7235-2001. www.mandarinoriental.com. 200 units. £305–£545 ($564–$1,008) double; from £695 ($1,286) suite. AE, DC, MC, V. Tube: Knightsbridge. **Amenities:** 2 restaurants; bar; health club/exercise area; full-service spa with its own art collection and an emphasis on Asian healing and relaxation techniques; sauna; courtesy car; business center and services; 24-hr. room service; laundry service; same-day dry cleaning; nonsmoking rooms. *In room:* A/C, TV/DVD, dataport, minibar, hair dryer, safe.

EXPENSIVE

Knightsbridge Hotel ★★ (Value)   The Knightsbridge Hotel attracts visitors from all over the world seeking a small, comfortable hotel in a high-rent district. It's fabulously located, sandwiched between fashionable Beauchamp Place and Harrods, with many of the city's top theaters and museums close at hand. Built in the early 1800s as a private town house, this place sits on a tranquil, tree-lined square, free from traffic. Two of London's premier hoteliers, Kit and Tim Kemp, who have been celebrated for their upmarket boutique hotels, have gone more affordable with a revamp of this hotel in the heart of the shopping district. All the Kemp "cult classics" are found here including such luxe touches as granite-and-oak bathrooms, the Kemps' famed honor bar, and Frette linens. All the beautifully furnished rooms have shower-only private bathrooms clad in marble or tile. Most bedrooms are spacious and furnished with traditional English fabrics. The best rooms are nos. 311 and 312 at the rear, each with a pitched ceiling and a small sitting area. Bathrooms are clad in marble or tile.

10 Beaufort Gardens, London SW3 1PT. © **020/7584-6300.** Fax 020/7584-6355. www.firmdalehotels.com. 44 units. £155–£285 ($287–$527) double; from £335 ($620) suite. Rates include English or continental breakfast. AE, MC, V. Tube: Knightsbridge. **Amenities:** Bar; concierge; courtesy car; 24-hr. room service; babysitting; laundry service; same-day dry cleaning; nonsmoking rooms. *In room:* TV w/pay movies (DVD in most rooms), dataport, minibar, hair dryer, safe.

MODERATE

Knightsbridge Green Hotel ★   Repeat guests from around the world view this dignified 1890s structure as their home away from home. In 1966, when it was converted into a hotel, the developers kept its wide baseboards, cove moldings, high ceilings, and spacious proportions. Even without kitchens, the well-furnished suites come close to apartment-style living. The well-appointed marble bathrooms most with tubs and power showers. Most rooms are spacious, with adequate storage space. Bedrooms are decorated with custom-made colors and are often individualized—one has a romantic sleigh bed. This nonsmoking hotel is a solid choice for lodging, just around the corner from Harrods.

159 Knightsbridge, London SW1X 7PD. © **020/7584-6274.** Fax 020/7225-1635. www.theKGHotel.co.uk. 28 units. £145 ($268) double; from £170 ($315) suite. AE, DC, MC, V. Tube: Knightsbridge. **Amenities:** Limited room service; laundry service; same-day dry cleaning. *In room:* A/C, TV, dataport, beverage maker, hair dryer, safe.

Searcy's Roof Garden Rooms ★ (Finds) Searcy's, one of London's best catering firms, operates this recycled surprise: an old pumping station that has been turned into a hotel that's only a hop, skip, and a jump from Harrods and the boutiques of Sloane Street. At this Knightsbridge oasis, you press a buzzer and are admitted to a freight elevator that carries you to the third floor. Upstairs, you'll encounter handsomely furnished rooms with antiques, tasteful fabrics, comfortable beds (some with canopies), and often a sitting alcove. All bedrooms are nonsmoking. Some of the bathtubs are placed right in the room instead of in a separate unit. Opt, if possible, for room no. 7, 14, or 15. For an extra charge, the staff will bring you a continental breakfast. Check out the rooftop garden.

30 Pavilion Rd., London SW1X 0HJ. © 020/7584-4921. Fax 020/7823-8694. www.searcys.co.uk. 10 units. £140 ($259) double; £160–£190 ($296–$352) apt. Rates include continental breakfast. AE, DC, MC, V. Tube: Knightsbridge. **Amenities:** Communal kitchen; courtesy car; laundry service; dry cleaning; breakfast-only room service. *In room:* TV, hair dryer, iron/ironing board.

IN CHELSEA
EXPENSIVE

The Sloane Hotel ★★ This "toff" (dandy) address, a redbrick Victorian-era town house that has been tastefully renovated in recent years, is located in Chelsea near Sloane Square. It combines valuable 19th-century antiques with modern comforts. Our favorite spot here is the rooftop terrace; with views opening onto Chelsea, it's ideal for a relaxing breakfast or drink. Bedrooms come in varying sizes, ranging from small to spacious, but all are opulently furnished with flouncy draperies, tasteful fabrics, and sumptuous beds. Many rooms have draped four-poster or canopied beds and, of course, antiques. The deluxe bathrooms have combination tub and shower, with chrome power showers, wall-width mirrors (in most rooms), and luxurious toiletries.

29 Draycott Place, London SW3 2SH. © 800/324-9960 in the U.S., or 020/7581-5757. Fax 020/7584-1348. www.sloanehotel.com. 22 units. £215–£250 ($398–$463) double; from £250 ($463) suite. AE, DC, MC, V. Tube: Sloane Sq. **Amenities:** Airport transportation (with prior arrangement); business services; babysitting; 24-hr. room service; laundry service; same-day dry cleaning. *In room:* A/C, TV/VCR w/pay movies, dataport, hair dryer.

MODERATE

The Willett ★ (Value) On a tree-lined street leading off Sloane Square, this dignified Victorian town house lies in the heart of Chelsea. Named for the famous London architect William Willett, its stained glass and chandeliers reflect the opulence of the days when Prince Edward was on the throne. Under a mansard roof with bay windows, the hotel is a 5-minute walk from the shopping mecca of King's Road and close to such stores as Peter Jones, Harrods, and Harvey Nichols. Individually decorated bedrooms come in a wide range of sizes. All rooms have well-kept bathrooms, equipped with shower-tub combinations. Some rooms are first class, with swagged draperies, matching armchairs, and canopied beds. But a few of the twins are best left for Lilliputians.

32 Sloane Gardens, London SW1 8DJ. © 800-270-9206 in the U.S., or 020/7824-8415. Fax 020/7730-4830. www.willett-hotel.com. 19 units. £100–£170 ($185–$315) double. Rates include English breakfast. AE, DC, MC, V. Tube: Sloane Sq. **Amenities:** Concierge; limited room service; babysitting; laundry service; same-day dry cleaning; nonsmoking rooms. *In room:* A/C in most rooms, TV/VCR, dataport, fridge (in some), coffeemaker, hair dryer, iron, safe.

IN NEARBY BELGRAVIA
EXPENSIVE

The Diplomat Hotel ★ (Finds) Part of the Diplomat's charm is that it is a small and reasonably priced hotel located in an otherwise prohibitively expensive neighborhood. Only minutes from Harrods, it was built in 1882 as a private residence by noted architect Thomas Cubbitt. It's very well appointed and was completely overhauled in 2002 and 2003. The registration desk is framed by the sweep of a partially gilded circular staircase; above it, cherubs gaze down from a Regency-era chandelier. The staff is helpful, well mannered, and discreet. The high-ceilinged guest rooms are tastefully done in Victorian style. You get good—not grand—comfort here. Rooms are a bit small and usually furnished with twin beds. Bathroom, with shower stalls, are also small but well maintained.

2 Chesham St., London SW1X 8DT. © 020/7235-1544. Fax 020/7259-6153. www.btinternet.com/~diplomat. hotel. 26 units. £125–£170 ($231–$315) double. Rates include English buffet breakfast. AE, DC, MC, V. Tube: Sloane Sq. or Knightsbridge. **Amenities:** Snack bar; nearby health club; babysitting; business services; laundry service; same-day dry cleaning; rooms for those with limited mobility. *In room:* TV, dataport, coffeemaker, hair dryer, safe (in some), trouser press.

KENSINGTON
INEXPENSIVE

Avonmore Hotel *Finds*   The recently refurbished Avonmore is easily accessible to West End theaters and shops, yet it's located in a quiet neighborhood, only 2 minutes from the West Kensington Tube station. This privately owned place—a former National Award winner as the best private hotel in London—boasts wall-to-wall carpeting and radio alarms in each tastefully decorated room. All rooms have small shower-only bathrooms. The owner, Margaret McKenzie, provides lots of personal service. An English breakfast is served in a cheerful room and a wide range of drinks is available in the cozy bar.

66 Avonmore Rd., London W14 8RS. © 020/7603-4296. Fax 020/7603-4035. www.avonmorehotel.co.uk. 9 units. £90–£95 ($167–$176) double; £110–£115 ($204–$213) triple. Rates include English breakfast. AE, MC, V. Tube: West Kensington. **Amenities:** Breakfast room; bar; nonsmoking rooms. *In room:* TV, dataport, minibar, coffeemaker, hair dryer.

The Vicarage Hotel *Kids*   Owners Eileen and Martin Diviney enjoy a host of admirers on all continents. Their hotel is tops for old-fashioned English charm, affordable prices, and hospitality. Situated on a residential garden square close to Kensington High Street, not far from Portobello Road Market, this Victorian town house retains many original features. Individually furnished in country-house style, the bedrooms can accommodate up to four, making it a great place for families. If you want a little nest to hide away in, opt for the very private top-floor aerie (no. 19). Guests find the corridor shower-only bathrooms adequate and well maintained. Guests meet in a cozy sitting room for conversation and to watch the telly. As a thoughtful extra, hot drinks are available 24 hours a day. In the morning, a hearty English breakfast awaits.

10 Vicarage Gate, London W8 4AG. © 020/7229-4030. Fax 020/7792-5989. www.londonvicaragehotel.com. 17 units, 8 with bathroom. £102 ($189) double with bathroom, £78 ($144) double without bathroom; £95 ($176) triple without bathroom; £102 ($189) family room for 4 without bathroom. Rates include English breakfast. No credit cards. Tube: High St. Kensington or Notting Hill Gate. *In room:* TV, beverage maker, hair dryer, no phone.

NOTTING HILL
EXPENSIVE

Pembridge Court Hotel   This hotel, featuring an elegant cream-colored neoclassical facade, is located in the increasingly fashionable Notting Hill Gate residential neighborhood. Avid antiques hunters will like its proximity to Portobello Road. Most guest rooms contain at least one antique, as well as 19th-century engravings and plenty of warm-toned floral fabrics. Bathrooms are tiled in Italian marble and feature shower-tub combinations. Three air-conditioned deluxe rooms, all with VCRs, overlook Portobello Road: The Spencer and Churchill Rooms are decorated in blues and yellows, and the Windsor Room has a contrasting array of tartans.

34 Pembridge Gardens, London W2 4DX. ℂ 020/7229-9977. Fax 020/7727-4982. www.pemct.co.uk. 20 units. £160–£195 ($296–$361) double. Rates include English breakfast. AE, DC, MC, V. Tube: Notting Hill Gate. **Amenities:** Access to nearby health club with sauna and massage; business services; 24-hr. room service; babysitting; laundry service; same-day dry cleaning. *In room:* A/C, TV, dataport, fridge, hair dryer, safe, trouser press.

The Portobello Hotel On an elegant Victorian terrace near Portobello Road, two 1850s-era town houses have been combined to form a quirky property that has its devotees. We remember these rooms when they looked better, but they still have plenty of character. Who knows what will show up in what nook? Perhaps a Chippendale, a claw-foot tub, or a round bed tucked under a gauze canopy. Try for no. 16, with a full-tester bed facing the garden. Some of the cheaper rooms are so tiny that they're basically garrets, but others have been combined into large doubles. Most of the small bathrooms have showers but no tubs. An elevator goes to the third floor; after that, it's the stairs. Since windows are not double-glazed, request a room in the quiet rear. Some rooms are air-conditioned. Service is erratic at best, but this is still a good choice.

22 Stanley Gardens, London W11 2NG. ℂ **020/7727-2777.** Fax 020/7792-9641. www.portobello-hotel.co.uk. 24 units. £160–£180 ($296–$333) double; £200–£275 ($370–$509) suite. Rates include continental breakfast. AE, MC, V. Tube: Notting Hill Gate or Holland Park. **Amenities:** 24-hr. bar and restaurant in basement; business services; 24-hr. room service; laundry service; same-day dry cleaning; nearby gym. *In room:* A/C (some rooms), TV/VCR, dataport, minibar, beverage maker, hair dryer.

MODERATE

The Gate Hotel *(Finds* This antiques-hunters' favorite is the only hotel along the length of Portobello Road—and because of rigid zoning restrictions, it will probably remain the only one for years to come. It was built in the 1820s as housing for farmhands at the now-defunct Portobello Farms and has functioned as a hotel since 1932. It has two cramped but cozy bedrooms on each of its three floors. Be prepared for some *very* steep English stairs. Rooms are color-coordinated, with a bit of style, and have such extras as full-length mirrors and built-in wardrobes. Bathrooms are small, with tiled shower stalls (there is a shower-tub combo in one room). Housekeeping is excellent. Especially intriguing are the wall paintings that show what the Portobello Market used to look like: Every character looks like he is straight from a Dickens novel. The on-site manager can direct you to the attractions of Notting Hill Gate and nearby Kensington Gardens, both within a 5-minute walk.

6 Portobello Rd., London W11 3DG. ℂ 020/7221-0707. Fax 020/7221-9128. www.gatehotel.com. 7 units. £75–£99 ($139–$183) double. Rates include continental breakfast. AE, MC, V. Tube: Notting Hill Gate. **Amenities:** 24-hr. room service; laundry service; rooms for those with limited mobility. *In room:* TV, dataport, fridge, beverage maker, hair dryer, iron.

PADDINGTON & BAYSWATER
MODERATE

London Elizabeth Hotel This elegant Victorian town house is ideally situated, overlooking Hyde Park. Amid the buzz and excitement of central London, the hotel's atmosphere is an oasis of charm and refinement. Even before the hotel's recent £3-million restoration, it oozed character. Individually decorated rooms range from executive to deluxe and remind us of staying in an English country house. Deluxe rooms are fully air-conditioned, and some contain four-poster beds. Executive units usually contain one double or twin bed. Some rooms have special features such as Victorian antique fireplaces, and all contain first-rate bathrooms with showers and tubs. Suites are pictures of grand comfort and luxury—the Conservatory Suite boasts its own veranda, part of the house's original 1850 conservatory.

Lancaster Terrace, Hyde Park, London W2 3PF. (C) 020/7402-6641. Fax 020/7224-8900. www.london elizabethhotel.co.uk. 49 units. £115–£150 ($213–$278) double; £180–£250 ($333–$463) suite. Rates include buffet breakfast. AE, DC, MC, V. Parking £10 ($19). Tube: Lancaster Gate or Paddington. **Amenities:** Restaurant; bar; 24-hr. room service; laundry service; same-day dry cleaning; nonsmoking rooms. *In room:* A/C, TV, dataport, hair dryer, iron.

Mornington Hotel ⚘ Affiliated with Best Western, the Mornington brings a touch of northern European hospitality to the center of London. Just north of Hyde Park and Kensington Gardens, the hotel has a Victorian exterior and a Scandinavian-inspired decor. The area isn't London's most fashionable, but it's close to Hyde Park and convenient to Marble Arch, Oxford Street shopping, and the ethnic restaurants of Queensway. Recently renovated guest rooms are tasteful and comfortable, all with pay movies. Bathrooms are small but tidy, with showers and tubs. Every year we get our annual Christmas card from "the gang," as we refer to the hotel staff—and what a helpful crew they are.

12 Lancaster Gate, London W2 3LG. (C) 800/528-1234 in the U.S., or 020/7262-7361. Fax 020/7706-1028. www.mornington.com. 66 units. £135–£160 ($250–$296) double; £145 ($268) triple. Rates include Scandinavian and English cooked breakfast. AE, DC, MC, V. Tube: Lancaster Gate. **Amenities:** Bar; courtesy car; business center; laundry service; same-day dry cleaning. *In room:* TV w/pay movies, coffeemaker.

The Pavilion *Finds* Until the early 1990s, this was a rather ordinary-looking B&B. Then, a team of entrepreneurs with ties to the fashion industry took over and redecorated the rooms with sometimes-wacky themes, turning it into an idiosyncratic little hotel. The result is a theatrical and often outrageous decor that's appreciated by the many fashion models and music-industry folks who regularly make this their temporary home in London. Rooms are, regrettably, rather small, but each has a distinctive style. Examples include a kitschy 1970s room ("Honky-Tonk Afro"), an Oriental bordello–themed room ("Enter the Dragon"), and even rooms with 19th-century ancestral themes. One Edwardian-style room, a gem of emerald brocade and velvet, is called "Green with Envy." Each contains tea-making facilities and small bathrooms with excellent showers.

34–36 Sussex Gardens, London W2 1UL. (C) 020/7262-0905. Fax 020/7262-1324. www.pavilionhoteluk.com. 29 units. £100 ($185) double; £120 ($222) triple. Rates include continental breakfast. AE, DC, MC, V. Parking £5 ($9.25). Tube: Paddington Station. **Amenities:** Same-day dry cleaning; laundry service. *In room:* TV, dataport, beverage maker.

4 Where to Dine

London is one of the great food capitals of the world. Both its veteran and upstart chefs have fanned out around the globe for culinary inspiration and have returned with innovative dishes, flavors, and ideas that London diners have never seen before—or at least not at such unprecedented rates. These chefs are pioneering a new style of cooking called "Modern British," which is forever changing yet comfortingly familiar in many ways. They've committed to centering their dishes around local ingredients from field, stream, and air, and have become daringly innovative with traditional recipes—too much so in the view of some critics, who don't like fresh mango over their blood pudding.

Traditional British cooking has made a comeback, too. The dishes that British mums have been forever feeding their reluctant families are fashionable again.

Central London Dining

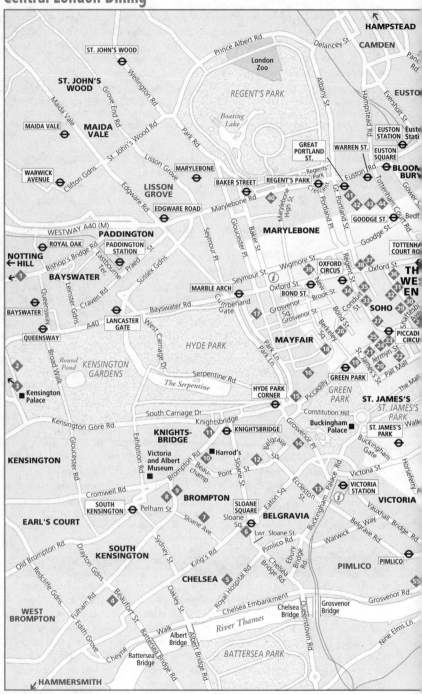

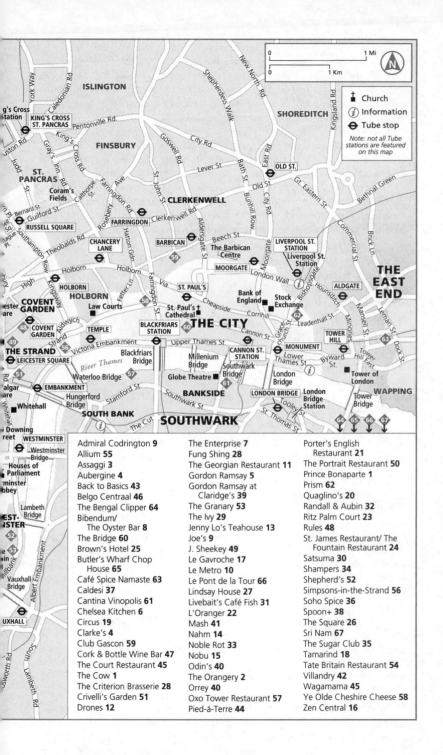

ISLINGTON

SHOREDITCH

✝ Church
ⓘ Information
Ⓔ Tube stop

Note: not all Tube stations are featured on this map

g's Cross Station
KING'S CROSS ST. PANCRAS
Pentonville Rd.

FINSBURY

ST. PANCRAS
Coram's Fields

OLD ST.

CLERKENWELL

FARRINGDON Clerkenwell Rd.

RUSSELL SQUARE

CHANCERY LANE

BARBICAN
The Barbican Centre

LIVERPOOL ST. STATION
Liverpool St. Station

MOORGATE
London Wall

THE EAST END

HOLBORN
Law Courts

ST. PAUL'S
St. Paul's † Cathedral

Bank of England
Stock Exchange

ALDGATE

COVENT GARDEN

TEMPLE

BLACKFRIARS STATION

THE CITY

MONUMENT
Lower Thames St.

TOWER HILL

THE STRAND
LEICESTER SQUARE

Blackfriars Bridge

CANNON ST. STATION

EMBANKMENT
Hungerford Bridge

Waterloo Bridge

Millenium Bridge
Globe Theatre ■

Southwark Bridge

London Bridge

Tower of London

WAPPING
Tower Bridge

Whitehall

SOUTH BANK

BANKSIDE

LONDON BRIDGE London Bridge Station

WESTMINSTER
Westminster Bridge

SOUTHWARK

64 65 66 67

Houses of Parliament
bbey

Lambeth Bridge

EST-ISTER

Vauxhall Bridge

UXHALL

Admiral Codrington **9**	The Enterprise **7**	Porter's English Restaurant **21**
Allium **55**	Fung Shing **28**	The Portrait Restaurant **50**
Assaggi **3**	The Georgian Restaurant **11**	Prince Bonaparte **1**
Aubergine **4**	Gordon Ramsay **5**	Prism **62**
Back to Basics **43**	Gordon Ramsay at Claridge's **39**	Quaglino's **20**
Belgo Centraal **46**	The Granary **53**	Randall & Aubin **32**
The Bengal Clipper **64**	The Ivy **29**	Ritz Palm Court **23**
Bibendum/ The Oyster Bar **8**	Jenny Lo's Teahouse **13**	Rules **48**
The Bridge **60**	Joe's **9**	St. James Restaurant/ The Fountain Restaurant **24**
Brown's Hotel **25**	J. Sheekey **49**	Satsuma **30**
Butler's Wharf Chop House **65**	Le Gavroche **17**	Shampers **34**
Café Spice Namaste **63**	Le Metro **10**	Shepherd's **52**
Caldesi **37**	Le Pont de la Tour **66**	Simpsons-in-the-Strand **56**
Cantina Vinopolis **61**	Lindsay House **27**	Soho Spice **36**
Chelsea Kitchen **6**	Livebait's Café Fish **31**	Spoon+ **38**
Circus **19**	L'Oranger **22**	The Square **26**
Clarke's **4**	Mash **41**	Sri Nam **67**
Club Gascon **59**	Nahm **14**	The Sugar Club **35**
Cork & Bottle Wine Bar **47**	Noble Rot **33**	Tamarind **18**
The Court Restaurant **45**	Nobu **15**	Tate Britain Restaurant **54**
The Cow **1**	Odin's **40**	Villandry **42**
The Criterion Brasserie **28**	The Orangery **2**	Wagamama **45**
Crivelli's Garden **51**	Orrey **40**	Ye Olde Cheshire Cheese **58**
Drones **12**	Oxo Tower Restaurant **57**	Zen Central **16**
	Pied-á-Terre **44**	

131

Yes, we're talking British soul food: bangers and mash, Norfolk dumplings, nursery puddings, cottage pie—the works. This may be a rebellion against the excessive minimalism of the nouvelle cuisine that ran rampant over London in the 1980s, but who knows? Maybe it's just plain old nostalgia. Pigs' nose with parsley-and-onion sauce may not be your idea of cutting-edge cuisine, but Simpson's-in-the-Strand is serving it for breakfast.

If you want a lavish meal, London is a good place to eat it. Some of the world's top restaurants call the city home. For those who don't want to break the bank, we include many affordable restaurants where you can dine well. You'll find that London's food revolution has infiltrated every level of the dining scene—even the lowly pub has entered London's culinary sweepstakes. Believe the unthinkable: At certain pubs, you can now dine better than in many restaurants. In some, standard pub grub has given way to Modern British and Mediterranean-style fare; in others, oyster bars have taken hold.

TAXES & TIPPING   All restaurants and cafes are required to display the prices of their food and drink in a place visible from outside. Charges for service, as well as any minimums or cover charges, must also be made clear. The prices shown must include 17.5% VAT. Most restaurants add a 10% to 15% service charge to your bill, but check to make sure. If nothing has been added, leave a 10% to 15% tip. It is not considered rude to tip, so feel free to leave something extra if service was good.

MAYFAIR
VERY EXPENSIVE

Gordon Ramsay at Claridge's ★★★ EUROPEAN   Gordon Ramsey is the hottest chef in London today, also going strong at his Chelsea restaurant, called Gordon Ramsay (p. 149). He now rules at the staid, traditional hotel of Claridge's, legendary since 1860 when Queen Victoria stopped by for tea with the Empress Eugenie. The famed Art Deco dining room still retains many of its original architectural features, but the cuisine is hardly the same. Most definitely Victoria wasn't served an *amuse-bouche* of pumpkin soup dribbled with truffle oil and studded with truffles. On a recent lunchtime visit, we were dazzled by a fixed-price menu (the only type served here) that wasn't outrageously priced.

Although the menu changes frequently, a memorable culinary highlight began with filets of baby red mullet on a juniper-flavored sauerkraut and went on to include a breast and confit leg of guinea fowl with vegetables and foie gras, finishing off with rum-baba with glazed oranges and crème fraîche. A three-course dinner was even more spectacular, featuring such delights as filet of sea bass rapped in fresh basil leaves and served with a caviar sauce, and roast Scottish baby lobster cooked slowly in lime butter and served with tomato couscous. The desserts are among our favorite in London, including the likes of a bread-and-butter brioche pudding with clotted-cream ice cream or a prune and Armagnac vanilla tart with *fromage blanc* in cream.

Brook St., W1. ℂ 020/7499-0099. Reservations required as far in advance as possible. Fixed-price lunch £30 ($56); a la carte menu £55 ($102); 6-course fixed-price dinner £65 ($120). Early bird fixed-price menu (5:45–6:30pm) £30 ($56). AE, DC, MC, V. Daily noon–3pm and Mon–Sat 5:45–11pm; Sun 5:45–10:30pm. Tube: Bond St.

Le Gavroche ★★★ CLASSICAL FRENCH   Although challengers come and go, this luxurious dining room remains the number-one choice in London for classical French cuisine. It may have fallen off briefly in the early 1990s, but it's fighting its way back to stellar ranks. There's always something special coming out of the kitchen of Burgundy-born Michel Roux; the service is faultless and the ambience formally chic without being stuffy. The menu changes constantly, depending on the fresh produce that's available and the current inspiration of the chef. But it always remains classically French, though not of the "essentially old-fashioned bourgeois repertoire" that some critics suggest. Signature dishes have been honed over years of unswerving practice, including the soufflé Suissesse, papillote of smoked salmon (salmon cooked in a greased paper wrapper), or whole Bresse chicken with truffles and a Madeira cream sauce. Game is often served, depending on availability. New menu options include cassoulet of snails with frog thighs, seasoned with herbs; mousseline of lobster in champagne sauce; and filet of red snapper with caviar and oyster-stuffed tortellini.

43 Upper Brook St., W1. © 020/7408-0881. Fax 020/7491-4387. Reservations required as far in advance as possible. Main courses £24–£45 ($44–$83); fixed-price lunch £42 ($78); menu exceptional £82 ($152) per person. AE, MC, V. Mon–Fri noon–2pm and 7–11pm; Sat 7–11pm. Tube: Marble Arch.

The Square ★★★ FRENCH   Hip, chic, casual, sleek, and modern, The Square still doesn't scare Le Gavroche as a competitor for first place on London's dining circuit, but it is certainly a restaurant to visit on a serious London gastronomic tour. Chef Philip Howard delivers the goods at this excellent restaurant. You get immaculate food in a cosseting atmosphere with abstract modern art on the walls. The chef has a magic touch with such concoctions as apple soup with grouse sausage. We urge you to savor the crusted saddle of lamb flavored with a shallot purée and fresh rosemary. Surprise dishes await in every corner of the menu—for example, loin of monkfish with pearl barley. Roast foie gras is a dazzling appetizer. Fish is stunningly fresh, and the Bresse pigeon is as good as it is in its hometown in France. If you're a vegetarian, stay clear of this place, as many dishes are aimed at the true carnivore. For dessert, try the lemon and lime soufflé with coconut ice cream.

6–10 Bruton St., W1. © 020/7495-7100. Reservations required. Fixed-price lunch £25–£30 ($46–$56); fixed-price dinner £55–£75 ($102–$139). AE, DC, MC, V. Mon–Fri noon–3pm; Mon–Sat 6:30–11pm; Sun 6:30–10pm. Tube: Bond St. and Green Park.

EXPENSIVE

Nahm ★★ THAI   The cookery here is extraordinary, and we like that the chef makes few, if any, concessions to Western palates. David Thompson even purchases rare books on Thai cookery and re-creates dishes that may have been lost for centuries. Take, for example, the salmon roe and fresh seafood mixed with spices and served in a fresh betel leaf, all of it garnished with watermelon. It sounds off-putting but is actually a taste sensation. The chef is against the "fusion fad," even though he's a Westerner himself (Australian) and is instead dedicated to the tenets of Thai cuisine. He's considered such an expert that even some of the citadels of haute Thai cuisine in Thailand seek his advice. Try the aromatic curry of beef with cucumber relish. For dessert, sample the addictive white sticky rice with mango topped with a coconut cream sauce.

In the Halkin Hotel, Halkin St., SW1. © 020/7333-1234. Reservations recommended. Main courses £13–£21 ($23–$39); fixed-price 4-course lunch £26 ($46); fixed-price 5-course dinner £47 ($87). AE, DC, MC, V. Mon–Fri noon–2:30pm and 7–11pm; Sat–Sun 7–11pm. Tube: Hyde Park Corner.

Nobu ★★ JAPANESE   London's innovative Japanese restaurant owes much to its founders, actor Robert de Niro and chef Nobu Matsuhisa. The kitchen staff is brilliant and as finely tuned as their New York counterparts. The sushi chefs create gastronomic pyrotechnics. Those on the see-and-be-seen circuit don't seem to mind the high prices that go with these incredibly fresh dishes. Elaborate preparations lead to perfectly balanced flavors. Where else can you find an excellent sea urchin tempura? Salmon tartare with caviar is a brilliant appetizer. Follow with a perfectly done filet of sea bass in a sour bean paste or soft-shell crab rolls. The squid pasta is sublime, as is sukiyaki; the latter dish is incredibly popular and with good reason. Cold sake arrives in a green bamboo pitcher.

In the Metropolitan Hotel, 19 Old Park Lane, W1. ℂ 020/7447-4747. Reservations required. Main courses £16–£35 ($30–$65); sushi and sashimi £4–£6 ($7.40–$11) per piece; fixed-price menu £70 ($130). AE, DC, MC, V. Mon–Fri noon–2:15pm; Mon–Thurs 6–10:15pm; Fri–Sat 6–11pm; Sun 6–9:30pm. Tube: Hyde Park Corner.

Tamarind ⚡ INDIAN   In favor with both critics and the lunchtime business crowd, Tamarind is the most popular Indian restaurant in Mayfair. The basement dining room has gold pillars and a tandoor window so that you can watch the chefs pull their flavorful dishes from the ovens. Chef Alfred Prasad leads a culinary brigade from Delhi that maintains the style of cooking they knew at home. The team selects the best, freshest ingredients in the markets each day. The kitchen prides itself on nouvelle dishes, but also excels at traditional Indian fare. The monkfish marinated in saffron and yogurt is delectable, and the mixed kabob platter, with all the kabobs cooked in a charcoal-fired tandoor, is extraordinary—these chefs are the kings of kabobs. Your best bet for a curry? The prawns in a five-spice mixture. Vegetarians will find refuge here, especially if they go for the *dal bukhari,* a black-lentil specialty of northwest India.

20 Queen St., W1. ℂ 020/7629-3561. Reservations required. Main courses £11–£28 ($19–$52); 3-course fixed-price dinner menu £34–£56 ($63–$104); fixed-price 3-course lunch £17 ($31). AE, DC, DISC, MC, V. Mon–Fri noon–2:45pm; Mon–Sat 6–11:15pm; Sun noon–2:15pm and 6–10:15pm. Tube: Green Park.

MODERATE

Noble Rot ⚡ CONTINENTAL   Danish-born Soren Jessen strikes again with this modern European venue. Ladies-who-lunch and shoppers drop in during the day, but at night the lighting is lowered and the atmosphere turns romantic. Some of the best regional specialties of the Continent are prepared in light variations here, with imaginative culinary twists. You may begin a meal with roast pumpkin soup and Pecorino cheese or else foie gras with a hazelnut dressing. Main dishes are concise, focused, and delicious, especially the supreme of guinea fowl on a bed of spinach purée and truffle *jus,* and especially the poached truffled chicken breast with fresh morels in a Riesling sauce.

3–5 Mill St., W1. ℂ 020/7629-8877. Reservations required. Main courses £17–£23 ($31–$42); fixed-price lunch £16–£20 ($30–$37). AE, MC, V. Mon–Fri noon–3pm and Mon–Sat 6–11pm. Tube: Oxford Circus.

Zen Central SZECHUAN/INDIAN/CANTONESE   Movie stars always seem to have an advance scouting party informing them of the best places to dine in a foreign city. So when we heard that Eddie Murphy and Tom Cruise were heading here, we followed. We didn't spot any stars, but we found a designer-chic Mayfair restaurant with a cool, dignified decor in black and white. Mirrors cover much of the interior (maybe that's why movie stars like it?).

Served by a competent staff, the cuisine is first-rate. Start with the soft-shelled crabs cooked in a crust of salt. The steamed sea bass is perfectly cooked and, for extra flavor, served with a black bean sauce. Pork chops with lemon grass have a Thai flavor, and the baked lobster with crushed roast garlic and slivers of tangerine peel is worth a trip from anywhere. Vegetarian meals are also available. The chef's braised fish cheeks, sharks' fins, and bird's nest soup serves up flavors enjoyed in China. There is little catering to conventional Western palates, so most dishes taste the same as they would in their homeland. Most dishes are at the lower end of the price scale.

20–22 Queen St., W1. © 020/7629-8103. Reservations recommended. Main courses £10–£35 ($19–$65). AE, DC, MC, V. Mon–Sat 12:15–2:45pm and 6:15–11:15pm; Sun 12:15–2:30pm and 6:15–11pm. Tube: Green Park.

INEXPENSIVE

The Granary *Value* TRADITIONAL BRITISH   This family operated country-style restaurant serves a simple flavor-filled array of home-cooked dishes that are listed daily on a blackboard. These may include lamb casserole with mint and lemon; pan-fried cod; or avocado stuffed with prawns, spinach, and cheese. Vegetarian meals include mushrooms stuffed with mixed vegetables, stuffed eggplant with curry sauce, and vegetarian lasagna. Tempting desserts are bread-and-butter pudding and apple brown Betty (both served hot). The large portions guarantee you won't go hungry. The cooking is standard, but quite good for the price.

39 Albemarle St., W1. © 020/7493-2978. Main courses £8.90–£9.90 ($16–$18). MC, V. Mon–Fri 11:30am–7pm; Sat 11:30am–3pm. Tube: Green Park.

ST. JAMES'S
EXPENSIVE

L'Oranger ⭐ FRENCH   This bistro-cum-brasserie occupies a high-ceilinged space in an affluent neighborhood near the bottom of St. James's Street. Amid paneling, burnt-orange and forest-green paint, patterned carpeting, immaculate linens, flowers, and a uniformed waitstaff, you'll appreciate the choreographed set fixed-price menus of executive chef Michel Laurent. The clientele, whom pundits frequently refer to as "people who have made it," have praised the chef's arrangement of flavors. Depending on the chef's inspiration, the set menu may include filet of beef with "condiments" that include mashed potatoes and a croustillant of bone marrow in the Provençal style; leek and potato cappuccino garnished with flaked, garden-poached codfish; a salad of winter vegetables with black truffles and caviar; Dover sole with curried seasonal fruits and *fumet* dressing and filet of wild sea bass with artichokes, pink radishes, and vanilla-flavored olive oil. Only fixed-price menus are served here.

5 St. James's St., SW1A. © 020/7839-3774. Reservations recommended. Fixed-price lunch £24–£28 ($44–$52); fixed-price dinner £12–£32 ($22–$59). AE, DC, MC, V. Mon–Fri noon–2pm; Mon–Sat 6:30–10:30pm. Tube: Green Park.

MODERATE

Circus *Value* BRITISH/INTERNATIONAL   This place buzzes during pre- and post-theater times with London foodies anxious to sample the wares of chef Richard Lee. A minimalist haven for power design and eating in the very heart of London, this restaurant took over the ground floor and basement of what used to be the Granada Television building at the corner of Golden Square and Beak Street. The place evokes a London version of a Left Bank Parisian brasserie. You may want to taste the divine skate wing with "crushed" new potatoes accompanied by a thick pesto-like medley of rocket blended with black olives. Or else try the tasty sautéed chili-flavored squid with bok choy, made even more heavenly with a tamarind dressing. The sorbets are a nice finish to a meal, especially the delectable mango and pink grapefruit version. Of course, if you're ravenous, there's always the velvety smooth amaretto cheesecake with a coffee sauce. Service is a delight.

1 Upper James St., W1. © 020/7534-4000. Reservations required. Main courses £13–£19 ($24–$34); fixed-price menus £13–£15 ($23–$28) 5:45–7:15pm and 10:30pm–midnight. AE, DC, MC, V. Daily noon–2:30pm; Mon–Sat 6pm–midnight. Bar menu daily noon–3am. Tube: Piccadilly Circus.

Quaglino's ✸ CONTINENTAL   Come here for fun, not culinary subtlety and finesse. In 1993, noted restaurateur and designer Sir Terence Conran brought this restaurant—first established in 1929 by Giovanni Quaglino—into the postmodern age with a vital new decor. Menu items have been criticized for their quick preparation and standard format; but considering that on some nights up to 800 people may show up, the marvel is that this place functions as well as it does. That's not to say there isn't an occasional delay. The menu changes often, but your choices may include goat cheese and caramelized onion tart; seared salmon with potato pancakes; crab tartlet with saffron; and roasted cod and ox cheek with chargrilled vegetables. The prawns and oysters are the most ordered items. *Note:* A mezzanine with bar features live jazz every Friday and Saturday night and live piano music the rest of the week.

16 Bury St., SW1. ✆ 020/7930-6767. Reservations recommended. Main courses £13–£20 ($23–$36); fixed-price menu (available only for lunch and pre-dinner theater between 5:30 and 6:30pm) 2 courses £17 ($31); 3 courses £19 ($34). AE, DC, MC, V. Daily noon–2:30pm; Mon–Thurs 5:30–11:30pm; Fri–Sat 5:30pm–12:30am; Sun 5:30–10:30pm. Tube: Green Park.

PICCADILLY CIRCUS & LEICESTER SQUARE
EXPENSIVE

Fung Shing ✸✸ CANTONESE   In a city where the competition is stiff, Fung Shing emerges as London's finest Cantonese restaurant. Firmly established as a culinary landmark, it dazzles with classic and nouvelle Cantonese dishes. Look for the seasonal specials. Some of the dishes may be a bit experimental, notably stir-fried fresh milk with scrambled egg white, but you'll feel right at home with the soft-shell crab sautéed in a light batter and served with tiny rings of red-hot chile and deep-fried garlic. Chinese gourmets come here for the fried intestines; you may prefer the hotpot of stewed duck with yam. The spicy sea bass and the stir-fried crispy chicken are worthy choices. There are more than 150 dishes from which to choose and most are moderate in price.

15 Lisle St., WC2. ✆ 020/7437-1539. Reservations required. Main courses £10–£26 ($19–$46); fixed-price menus £17–£34 ($31–$63). AE, DC, MC, V. Daily noon–11:30pm. Tube: Leicester Sq.

The Ivy ✸✸ MODERN BRITISH/INTERNATIONAL   Effervescent and sophisticated, The Ivy is the dining choice of visiting theatrical luminaries and has been intimately associated with the theater district ever since it opened in 1911. With its ersatz 1930s look and tiny bar near the entrance, this place is fun, and hums with the energy of London's glamour scene. The kitchen has a solid appreciation for fresh ingredients and a talent for preparation. Favorite dishes include white asparagus with sea kale and truffle butter; seared scallops with spinach, sorrel, and bacon; and salmon fish cakes. You'll also find such English desserts as sticky toffee (sponge cake soaked in a thick caramelized syrup) and caramelized bread-and-butter pudding. Meals are served quite late to accommodate the posttheater crowd.

1 West St., WC2. ✆ 020/7836-4751. Reservations required. Main courses £9–£35 ($17–$65); Sat–Sun fixed-price 3-course lunch £20 ($36). AE, DC, MC, V. Mon–Sat noon–3pm and daily 5:30pm–midnight (last order); Sun noon–3:30pm. Tube: Leicester Sq.

J. Sheekey ✸ SEAFOOD   British culinary tradition lives on at this fish joint, long a favorite of West End actors. The jellied eels that delighted Laurence Olivier and Vivien Leigh are still here, along with an array of fresh oysters from the coasts of Ireland and Brittany, plus that Victorian favorite, fried whitebait. Sheekey's fish pie is still on the menu, as is Dover sole. The old "mushy" peas still appear, but the chefs also offer the likes of steamed organic sea beet. Opt for the traditional dishes or specials based on the fresh catch of the day. The double chocolate pudding soufflé is a delight, and many favorite puddings remain.

28–32 St. Martin's Court, WC2. ✆ 020/7240-2565. Reservations recommended. Main courses £10–£31 ($19–$57). AE, DC, MC, V. Mon–Sat noon–3pm and 5:30pm–midnight; Sun noon–3:30pm and 6pm–-midnight. Tube: Leicester Square.

MODERATE

Livebait's Café Fish ✿ SEAFOOD   Don't you love the name? The catch of the day can be chargrilled or pan-fried as you desire. We know of no better place in London to sample seafood favorites enjoyed by Brits back in the days of Sir Winston Churchill—we're talking smoked haddock kedgeree (a mixture of fish, rice, and hard-boiled eggs), cockles, steamed mussels, smoky grilled sardines, and the like. We like to go when the Dover sole is brought in. This eclectic menu includes fish flown all the way from the U.S. Unlike some of the soggy chips (fries) at nearby dives, the ones here are crisp and fluffy. Our moist-fleshed sea bream, served with a crisp skin, made us want to "hasten ye back" to the restaurant the next night. From grandma's pantry comes Bailey's cheesecake or sticky toffee pudding to finish off the meal.

36–40 Rupert St., W1. ✆ 020/7287-8989. Reservations required. Main courses £10–£18 ($19–$33); fixed-price dinner £10 ($19). AE, MC, V. Mon–Sat noon–11pm and Sun noon–9pm. Tube: Piccadilly Circus.

INEXPENSIVE

Cork & Bottle Wine Bar ✿ *Value* INTERNATIONAL   Don Hewitson, a connoisseur of fine wines for more than 30 years, presides over this trove of blissful fermentation. The ever-changing wine list features an excellent selection of Beaujolais Crus from Alsace, 30 selections from Australia, 30 champagnes, and a good selection of California labels. If you want something to wash down, the most successful dish is a raised cheese-and-ham pie, with a cream cheese-like filling and crisp well-buttered pastry—not your typical quiche. There's also chicken and apple salad, black pudding, Mediterranean prawns with garlic and asparagus, lamb in ale, and tandoori chicken.

44–46 Cranbourn St., WC2. ✆ 020/7734-7807. Reservations not accepted after 6:30pm. Main courses £6.50–£12 ($12–$22); glass of wine from £3.50 ($6.50). AE, DC, MC, V. Mon–Sat 11am–11pm; Sun noon–11pm. Tube: Leicester Sq.

SOHO
EXPENSIVE

Spoon+ ✿ AMERICAN   In Ian Schrager's hot new Sanderson Hotel, this is a branch of the Spoon that master chef Alain Ducasse lures *tout Paris* to. Like its Paris namesake, this is Monsieur Ducasse's take on "American fusion" cuisine. This is the only place you can go in London to eat a Frenchman's take on that American favorite—macaroni and cheese. Although some menu items seemed designed more to shock, much of what is offered here is really good, especially the crab ceviche (crab marinated in lime juice) or the iced tomato soup (great choice) offered at the beginning. Spoon+ chefs allow you to compose your own meal or at least pair up ingredients—perhaps a beautiful sole with a crushed lemon confit, or do you prefer it with satay sauce? You make the choices. You choose from a trio of columns: main course, sauce, and accompanying side dish. On our last visit, we found the restaurant ridiculously overpriced but then reconsidered when the entertainment of the evening arrived. Our fellow diners turned out to be none other than Madonna and her husband, Guy Ritchie.

50 Berners St., W1. ✆ 020/7300-1400. Reservations imperative. Main courses £21–£30 ($39–$56). AE, DC, MC, V. Daily noon–3pm; Mon–Sat 6–11:30pm; Sun 6–10:30pm. Tube: Leicester Sq. or Covent Garden.

Lindsay House ★★ MODERN BRITISH   Irish-born chef Richard Corrigan is one of our all-time favorites in London. As in an old-fashioned speakeasy, you ring the doorbell for admittance to a Regency town house deep in Soho. Unfolding before you are gilded mirrors and bare wooden floors. The staircase delivers you to one of two floors. Corrigan is one of the most inventive chefs in London, with creative offerings changing daily based on market availability. What inspires Corrigan at the market is what will end up on your plate at night. You may start with a cured foie gras rolled in spicy gingerbread or else ravioli of rabbit in its own consommé. For your main, expect such delightful courses as pan-roasted filet of red mullet or squab served with fried cabbage and bacon. An excellent poached rump of veal may also rest on your plate. Desserts are a delight—always unexpected, always a delightful surprise such as marinated pumpkin with pistachio and chocolate sorbet.

21 Romilly St., W1. ⓒ 020/7439-0450. Reservations recommended. Main courses lunch only £20–£25 ($37–$46); fixed-price 3-course lunch £25 ($46); fixed-price 3-course dinner £48 ($89). AE, DC, MC, V. Mon–Fri noon–2:30pm and Mon–Sat 6–11pm. Tube: Leicester Sq.

MODERATE

The Criterion Brasserie ★ MODERN BRITISH/FRENCH   Designed by Thomas Verity in the 1870s, this palatial neo-Byzantine mirrored marble hall is a glamorous backdrop for a superb cuisine, served under a golden ceiling, with theatrical peacock-blue draperies. The menu is wide ranging, offering everything from Paris brasserie food to "nouvelle-classical," a combination of classic French cooking techniques with some of the lighter, more experimental leanings of modern French cuisine. The food is excellent but falls short of sublime. Still, roast skate wing with deep-fried snails is delectable, as is roast saddle of lamb stuffed with mushrooms and spinach.

224 Piccadilly, W1. ⓒ 020/7930-0488. Main courses £14–£23 ($26–$42); fixed-price 2-course lunch £15 ($28); fixed-price 3-course lunch £18 ($33). AE, MC, V. Daily noon–2:30pm and 5:30–11pm. Tube: Piccadilly Circus.

Randall & Aubin ★ *Finds* SEAFOOD   Past the sex boutiques of Soho you stumble upon this real discovery, whose consultant is TV chef Ed Baines, an ex-Armani model who turned this butcher shop into a cool, hip champagne-and-oyster bar. It's an ideal place to take a lover for a *Sex and the City*–type of meal and some champagne or a bottle of wine. You're never rushed here. The impressive shellfish display of the night's goodies is the "bait" used to lure you inside. Chances are you won't be disappointed. Loch Fyne oysters, lobster with chips, pan-fried fresh scallops—the parade of seafood we've sampled here has in each case been genuinely excellent. The *soupe de poisson* or fish soup is the best in Soho, or else you may want one of the hors d'oeuvres such as delightful Japanese style fish cakes or fresh Cornish crab. Yes, they still have Sevruga caviar for lotto winners. For the rare meat eater only, there is a limited array of dishes such as a perfectly roasted chicken on the spit that has been flavored with fresh herbs. The lemon tart with crème fraîche rounds off a perfect meal.

16 Brewer St., W1. ⓒ 020/7287-4447. Reservations not accepted. Main courses £11–£19 ($19–$34). AE, DC, MC, V. Mon–Sat noon–11pm; Sun 4–10:30pm. Tube: Piccadilly Circus.

The Sugar Club ★ PACIFIC RIM   This restaurant, with its adventurous menu, comes from the land Down Under, attracting homesick Aussies with a kangaroo salad. The elegant and spacious setting is inviting, with soft textures, pale cream colors, and wooden floors. The restaurant offers a bar waiting area for diners, and an open kitchen. Every area is nonsmoking except for the bar.

The flavors are often stunning—a good example is the amazingly fresh sashimi of Iki Jimi yellowtail with a black-bean-and-ginger salsa. Throughout the menu, flavors surprise the palate in the most exciting ways. You may dig into the duck leg braised in tamarind and star anise, with coconut rice, or try the pan-fried turbot with spinach, sweet potato, and red curry sauce. Many of the starters are vegetarian and can be upgraded to a main course. For dessert, the blood-orange curd sorbet is devastatingly delicious.

21 Warwick St., W1. ℭ **020/7437-7776.** Reservations recommended. Main courses £14–£23 ($26–$43). AE, DC, MC, V. Daily noon–3pm and Mon–Sat 5:30–11pm; Sun 6–10:30pm. Tube: Piccadilly Circus or Oxford Circus.

INEXPENSIVE

Satsuma JAPANESE   This funky Japanese canteen is all the rage in London. The clean lines, stark white walls, and long wooden tables may suggest an upmarket youth hostel. But patrons come for good food at reasonable prices. The restaurant is ideal for a pretheater visit. Your meal comes in a lacquered bento box on a matching tray. Try the chicken teriyaki or fresh chunks of tuna and salmon. The dumplings are excellent, as is the miso soup. A specialty is the large bowl of seafood ramen, with noodles swimming in a well-seasoned broth studded with mussels, scallops, and prawns. Tofu steaks are a delight, as are udon noodles with wok-fried chicken and fresh vegetables. You can finish with deep-fried tempura ice cream.

56 Wardour St., W1. ℭ **020/7437-8338.** Reservations not accepted. Main courses £6–£16 ($11–$30). AE, MC, V. Mon–Tues noon–11pm; Wed–Thurs noon–11:30pm; Fri–Sat noon–midnight; Sun noon–10:30pm. Tube: Piccadilly Circus.

Shampers CONTINENTAL   This is a favorite of West End wine bar aficionados. In addition to the street-level wine bar serving snacks, there's a more formal basement-level restaurant. In either venue, you can order such main dishes as grilled calves' liver with bacon, fries, and salad; pan-fried large prawns with ginger, garlic, and chile; and platters of cheeses. Salads are popular, including grilled eggplant salad with tomato, avocado, buffalo mozzarella, and pesto; and spicy chicken salad. The platter of Irish mussels cooked in a cream-and-tarragon sauce is everybody's favorite. The restaurant is closed in the evening, but the wine bar serves an extensive menu, offering such dishes as fresh squid, tuna steak, pan-fried tiger prawns, free-range chicken, and a variety of other tasty specialties. There is also a special daily menu.

4 Kingly St. (between Carnaby and Regent sts.), W1. ℭ **020/7437-1692.** Reservations recommended. Main courses £8.75–£15 ($16–$27). AE, DC, MC, V. Restaurant: Mon–Sat noon–3pm. Wine Bar: Mon–Sat noon–11pm. Closed Dec 24–Jan 2. Tube: Oxford Circus or Piccadilly Circus.

Soho Spice INDIAN   This is one of central London's most stylish Indian restaurants, combining a hip atmosphere with the flavors and scents of southern India. You may opt for a drink at the cellar bar before heading to the street-level dining room, decorated in saffron, cardamom, bay, and pepper hues. A staff member dressed in similarly vivid apparel will propose a wide array of choices, including slow-cooked Indian tandoori specials that feature lamb, chicken, fish, or vegetables with combinations of spices. The a la carte menu offers a variety of courses, including *jhinga hara pyaz,* spicy queen prawns with fresh spring onions, and *paneer pasanda,* cottage cheese slices stuffed with spinach and served with almond sauce. The cuisine will satisfy traditionalists but also has a modern flair.

124–126 Wardour St., W1. ℭ **020/7434-0808.** Reservations recommended. Main courses £9.95–£15 ($19–$28); fixed-price dinner £20 ($37). AE, V. Mon–Thurs 11:30am–12:30am; Fri–Sat 11:30am–3am; Sun 12:30–10:30pm. Tube: Tottenham Court Rd.

TRAFALGAR SQUARE
MODERATE
Crivelli's Garden ✿ ITALIAN/FRENCH   In The National Gallery, this hot new dining choice lies over the foyer of the Sainsbury Wing, providing a panoramic view of fabled Trafalgar Square. The view's a bonus—it's the cuisine that attracts visitors. The restaurant is named for a striking mural by Paulo Rego that is painted on one side of a wall. The chefs are at home with Italian dishes, offering such choices such as grilled skewered squid with eggplant and sun-dried tomato salad. The steamed salmon with leeks, cilantro, and ginger is an excellent dish, as is the red pepper ravioli in a chive sauce. There is a cafe offshoot of Crivelli's Garden in the basement of the main building, which is a good choice for sandwiches, pastas, soups, and pastries.

In The National Gallery, Trafalgar Square, WC2. ✆ 020/7747-2869. Reservations required. Fixed-price lunch and Wed dinner £16–£20 ($30–$37). AE, DC, MC, V. Daily 10am–5:30pm and Wed 6–8:30pm. Tube: Charing Cross.

The Portrait Restaurant ✿ MODERN BRITISH   This rooftop restaurant is a sought-after dining ticket on the fifth floor of the National Portrait Gallery's Ondaatje Wing. Along with the view (Nelson's Column, the London Eye, Big Ben, and the like), you get superb meals. Patrons usually go for lunch, not knowing that the chefs also cook on Thursday and Friday nights. In spring, there's nothing finer than the green English asparagus. All the main courses are filled with flavor. The high quality of the produce really shines through in such dishes as the whole plaice cooked in shrimp butter, and the roasted organic chicken. For your "pudding," nothing is finer than the chocolate and pecan tart with espresso ice cream. Chefs aren't afraid of simple preparations mainly because they are assured of the excellence of their products. The wine list features some organic choices.

In the National Portrait Gallery, Trafalgar Square, WC2. ✆ 020/7313-2490. Reservations recommended. Main courses £11–£19 ($20–$35). AE, MC, V. Sat–Wed 10am–5pm; Thurs–Fri 5:30–8:30pm. Tube: Leicester Sq. or Charing Cross.

BLOOMSBURY
VERY EXPENSIVE
Pied-à-Terre ✿ FRENCH   This foodie heaven understates its decor in favor of an intense focus on its subtle, sophisticated cuisine. You'll dine in a strictly minimalist room, where gray-and-pale pink walls complement metal furniture and focused lighting that reveals a collection of modern art. France is the inspiration for the impressive wine list and some of the cuisine. The menu changes with the seasons and may include halibut filets with queen scallops and caramelized endive; roasted partridge with pear; and the house specialty, a ballotine (stuffed and rolled into a bundle) of duck confit. If you're not dining with a vegetarian, braised pigs' head is another specialty. Our favorite is the sea bass with vichyssoise (a thick soup of potatoes, leeks and cream) and caviar sauce. The food is beautifully presented on hand-painted plates with lush patterns.

34 Charlotte St., W1. ✆ 020/7636-1178. Reservations recommended. Fixed-price 3-course lunch £21.50–£35 ($40–$65); fixed-price 3-course dinner £45–£60 ($83–$111); 8-course tasting menu £65 ($120). AE, MC, V. Tues–Fri noon–2:30pm (last order); Mon–Sat 7–11pm. Closed last week of Dec and first week of Jan. Tube: Goodge St.

MODERATE
Back to Basics ✿✿ SEAFOOD   Ursula Higgs's bistro draws discerning palates seeking some of the freshest seafood in London. When the weather's fair, you can dine outside. Otherwise, retreat inside to a vaguely Parisian setting with

a blackboard menu and checked tablecloths. The fish is served in large portions, and you can safely forgo an appetizer unless you're ravenous. More than a dozen seafood dishes are offered; the fish can be broiled, grilled, baked, or poached, but frying is not permitted. In other words, this is no fish and chippie. Start with a bowl of tasty, plump mussels or sea bass flavored with fresh basil and chile oil. Brill appears with green peppercorn butter, and plaice is jazzed up with fresh ginger and soy sauce. For the meat eater, there is a T-bone steak or roast chicken. Also try the pastas and the vegetarian dishes. Freshly made salads accompany most meals, and an excellent fish soup is offered daily. For dessert, try the bread pudding or the freshly made apple pie.

21A Foley St., W1. ℂ 020/7436-2181. Reservations recommended. Main courses £9.25–£16 ($17–$29). AE, DC, MC, V. Daily noon–3pm and 6–10pm. Tube: Oxford Circus or Goodge St.

INEXPENSIVE

The Court Restaurant ⭐ *Value* CONTINENTAL   Nothing in London brings culture and cuisine together quite as much as this gem of a restaurant on the sixth floor of The British Museum with views opening onto Norman Fester's millennium development, the Great Court. The restaurant overlooks the famous round Reading Room and nestles close to the spectacular glass-and-steel roof. For museum buffs, it's the perfect venue for morning coffee, hot or cold lunches, afternoon tea, or a dinner.

The chef, Mandula Sachdev, turns out a succulent menu of familiar favorites such as *coq au vin* (chicken casserole in red wine), sesame-seed coated Scottish salmon, or savory lamb and mint sausages with a "mash" of parsnips. You can watch the cooks as they prepare the market-fresh dishes for the day. The most blissful ending to a meal here is the chocolate truffle cake, which is really pure cocoa. The museum even serves its own beer, and it can compete with the product of any brewery.

The British Museum, Great Russell St., WC1. ℂ 020/7323-8978. Reservations required. Main courses £9.50–£13 ($18–$24). Two-course fixed-price menu £11–£12 ($19–$21). AE, MC, V. Mon–Wed 11am–5pm; Thurs–Sat 11am–9pm; Sun 11am–5pm. Tube: Holborn, Tottenham Court Rd., Russel Square.

Wagamama JAPANESE   This noodle joint, in a basement just off New Oxford Street, is noisy and overcrowded, and you'll have to wait in line for a table. It calls itself a "nondestination food station" and caters to some 1,200 customers a day. Many dishes are built around ramen noodles with your choice of chicken, beef, or salmon. Try the tasty *gyoza,* light dumplings filled with vegetables or chicken. Vegetarian dishes are available, but skip the so-called "Korean-style" dishes.

4 Streatham St., WC1. ℂ 020/7323-9223. Reservations not accepted. Main courses £5.50–£11 ($10–$20). AE, MC, V. Mon–Sat noon–11pm; Sun 12:30–10pm. Tube: Tottenham Court Rd.

COVENT GARDEN & THE STRAND
EXPENSIVE

Rules ⭐ TRADITIONAL BRITISH   If you're looking for London's most quintessentially British restaurant, eat here. London's oldest restaurant was established in 1798 as an oyster bar; today, the antler-filled Edwardian dining rooms exude nostalgia. You can order such classic dishes as Irish or Scottish oysters, jugged hare, and mussels. Game dishes are offered from mid-August to February or March, including wild Scottish salmon; wild sea trout; wild Highland red deer; and game birds such as grouse, snipe, partridge, pheasant, and woodcock. As a finale, the "great puddings" continue to impress.

35 Maiden Lane, WC2. ℂ 020/7836-5314. Reservations recommended. Main courses £15–£21 ($28–$39). AE, DC, MC, V. Daily noon–11:30pm. Tube: Covent Garden.

Simpson's-in-the-Strand ★★ *Kids* TRADITIONAL AND MODERN BRITISH   Simpson's is more of an institution than a restaurant. Long a family favorite with lots of large tables, it has been in business since 1828, and as a result of a recent £2-million renovation, it's now better than ever with its Adam paneling, crystal, and an army of grandly formal waiters (to whom nouvelle cuisine means anything after Henry VIII) serving traditional British fare.

Most diners agree that Simpson's serves the best roasts in London, an array that includes roast sirloin of beef, roast saddle of mutton with red-currant jelly, roast Aylesbury duckling, and steak, kidney, and mushroom pie. (Remember to tip the tailcoated carver.) For a pudding, you may order the treacle roll and custard or Stilton with vintage port. Simpson's also serves traditional breakfasts. The most popular one, is "The Ten Deadly Sins": a plate of sausage; fried egg; streaky and back bacon; black pudding; lambs' kidneys; bubble-and-squeak; baked beans; lambs' liver; and fried bread, mushrooms, and tomatoes. That will certainly fortify you for the day.

100 The Strand (next to the Savoy Hotel), WC2. ✆ 020/7836-9112. Reservations required. Main courses £15–£25 ($28–$46); fixed-price pretheater dinner £17–£21 ($30–$39); breakfast from £16 ($30). AE, DC, MC, V. Mon–Fri 7:15–10:30am; Mon–Sat 12:15–2:30pm and 5:30–10:45pm; Sun 6–8:30pm. Tube: Charing Cross or Embankment.

MODERATE

Belgo Centraal BELGIAN   Chaos reigns supreme in this cavernous basement, where mussels mariniéres with frites, plus 100 Belgian beers, are the raison d'être. Take a freight elevator past the busy kitchen and into a converted cellar, divided into two large eating areas. One section is a beer hall seating about 250; the menu here is the same as in the restaurant, but you don't need reservations. The restaurant side has three nightly seatings: 5:30, 7:30, and 10pm; at the first two you can choose one of three fixed-price menus. Although heaps of fresh mussels are the big attraction, you can opt for fresh Scottish salmon, roast chicken, a perfectly done steak, or one of the vegetarian specialties. Gargantuan plates of wild boar sausages arrive with *stoemp,* Belgian mashed spuds and cabbage. Belgian stews, called *waterzooï,* are also served. With waiters in maroon monk's habits and black aprons barking orders into headset microphones, it's all a bit bizarre.

50 Earlham St., WC2. ✆ 020/7813-2233. Reservations required for the restaurant. Main courses £9–£12 ($17–$22); fixed-price menus £21–£26 ($38–$47). AE, DC, MC, V. Mon–Thurs noon–11pm; Fri–Sat noon–11:30pm; Sun noon–10:30pm. Closed Christmas. Tube: Covent Garden.

Porter's English Restaurant ★★ *Kids* TRADITIONAL BRITISH   The seventh earl of Bradford serves "real English food at affordable prices." He succeeds notably—and not just because Lady Bradford turned over her carefully guarded recipe for banana-and-ginger steamed pudding. This comfortable, two-storied restaurant is family friendly, informal, and lively. Porter's specializes in classic English pies, including Old English fish pie; lamb and apricot; and, of course, bangers and mash. Main courses are so generous— and accompanied by vegetables and side dishes—that you hardly need appetizers. They have also added grilled English fare to the menu, with sirloin and lamb steaks and marinated chicken. The puddings, including bread-and-butter pudding or steamed syrup sponge, are served hot or cold, with whipped cream or custard. The bar does quite a few exotic cocktails, as well as beers, wine, or English mead. A traditional English tea is also served from 2:30 to

5:30pm for £4.75 ($8.80) per person. Who knows? You may even bump into His Lordship.

17 Henrietta St., WC2. ℂ **020/7836-6466.** Reservations recommended. Main courses £8.95–£13 ($17–$24); fixed-price menu £20 ($37). AE, DC, MC, V. Mon–Sat noon–11:30pm; Sun noon–10:30pm. Tube: Covent Garden or Leicester Sq.

WESTMINSTER/VICTORIA
EXPENSIVE

Allium ✦ *Finds* MODERN BRITISH/EUROPEAN Located in the Dolphin Square Hotel in this discreet residential district, chef Anton Edelmann is winning the discerning palates of the area with his take on fine dining. In the dining room's sophisticated Art Deco setting, you can partake of the chef's excellent blend of flavors and his passion for new combinations. For starters, the ravioli here is not only stuffed with butternut squash but also served with a pumpkin purée and a foie gras velouté. Rosemary-scented figs come baked with goat cheese. Well-prepared main dishes based on quality ingredients include a rump of lamb with black olives and rosemary jus or roasted partridge with glazed chestnuts. The steamed filet of sea bass is our favorite, served with caviar, baby spinach, and a red wine jus. For dessert, you've arrived in heaven if you order the apricot and chocolate soufflé in its own sorbet.

Dolphin Sq., Chichester St., SW1. ℂ **020/7798-6767.** Reservations required. Main courses £10–£24 ($19–$44); fixed-price 2-course lunch £18 ($32), 3-course lunch £22 ($40); fixed-price 3-course dinner £33 ($60). AE, DC, MC, V. Tues–Fri noon–2:30pm; Tues–Sat 6–10:30, Sun noon–2:30pm. Tube: Pimlico.

Shepherd's TRADITIONAL BRITISH Some observers claim that many of the inner workings of the British government operate from this conservative, likable restaurant. Set in the shadow of Big Ben, it enjoys a regular clientele of barristers, MPs, and their constituents from far-flung districts. Don't imagine that the intrigue occurs only at lunchtime; evenings seem just as ripe an hour for negotiations, particularly over the restaurant's roast rib of Scottish beef served with (what else?) Yorkshire pudding. So synchronized is this place to the goings-on at Parliament that a Division Bell rings in the dining room, calling MPs back to the House of Commons when it's time to vote. Even the decor is designed to make them feel at home, with leather banquettes, sober 19th-century accessories, and a worthy collection of European portraits and landscapes.

The menu reflects years of British culinary tradition, and dishes are prepared intelligently with fresh ingredients. In addition to the classic roast, dishes include a cream-based mussel stew; hot salmon and potato salad with dill dressing; salmon and prawn fishcakes in spinach sauce; roast leg of lamb with mint sauce; wild rabbit; marinated venison with braised red cabbage in juniper sauce; and the English version of crème brûlée, known as "burnt Cambridge cream."

Marsham Court, Marsham St., at the corner of Page St., SW1. ℂ **020/7834-9552.** Reservations recommended. Fixed-price meals £26 ($48) for 2 courses, £29 ($54) for 3 courses. AE, DC, MC, V. Mon–Fri 12:30pm–3pm and 6:30–11pm (last order at 11pm). Tube: Pimlico or St. James.

MODERATE

Tate Britain Restaurant ✦✦ *Value* MODERN BRITISH This restaurant is particularly attractive to wine fanciers. It offers what may be the best bargains for superior wines anywhere in Britain. Bordeaux and burgundies are in abundance, and the management keeps the markup between 40% and 65%, rather than the 100% to 200% added in most restaurants. In fact, the prices here are lower than they are in most wine shops. Wine begins at £15 ($28) per bottle, or

£3.95 ($7.30) per glass. Oenophiles frequently come for lunch. The restaurant offers an English menu that changes about every month. Dishes may include pheasant casserole, pan-fried skate with black butter and capers, and a selection of vegetarian dishes. One critic found the staff and diners as traditional "as a Gainsborough landscape." Access to the restaurant is through the museum's main entrance on Millbank.

Millbank, SW1. ℰ 020/7887-8825. Reservations recommended. Main courses £11–£18 ($19–$33); fixed-price 2-course lunch £18 ($32); fixed-price 3-course lunch £21 ($38). AE, DC, MC, V. Mon–Sat noon–3pm; Sun noon–4pm. Tube: Pimlico. Bus: 77 or 88.

INEXPENSIVE

Jenny Lo's Teahouse CANTONESE/SZECHUAN   London's noodle dives don't get much better than this. Before its decline, Ken Lo's Memories of China offered the best Chinese dining in London. The late Ken Lo, whose grandfather was the Chinese ambassador to the Court of St. James, made his reputation as a cookbook author. Jenny Lo is Ken's daughter, and her father taught her many of his culinary secrets. Belgravia matrons and young professionals come here for perfectly prepared, reasonably priced fare. Ken Lo cookbooks contribute to the dining room decor of black refectory tables set with paper napkins and chopsticks. Opt for such fare as a vermicelli rice noodle dish (a large plate of noodles topped with grilled chicken breast and Chinese mushrooms) or white noodles with minced pork. Rounding out the menu are stuffed Peking dumplings, chile-garnished spicy prawns, and wonton soup with slithery dumplings. The black-bean-seafood noodle dish is a delight, as is the chile beef soup.

14 Eccleston St., SW1 9LT. ℰ 020/7259-0399. Reservations not accepted. Main courses £5.75–£8 ($11–$15). No credit cards. Mon–Fri 11:30am–3pm; Sat noon–3pm; Mon–Sat 6–10pm. Tube: Victoria Station.

THE CITY

For locations of the restaurants below, refer to the map "Central London Dining," earlier in this chapter.

EXPENSIVE

Prism ★★ MODERN ENGLISH/CONTINENTAL   In the financial district, called The City, this restaurant attracts London's movers and shakers, at least those with demanding palates. In the former Bank of New York, Harvey Nichols—known for his chic department store in Knightsbridge—took this 1920s neo-Grecian hall and installed Mies van der Rohe chairs in chrome and lipstick-red leather. In this setting, traditional English dishes from the north are given a light touch—try the tempura of Whitby cod or cream of Jerusalem artichoke soup with roasted scallops and truffle oil. For first course, you may opt for a small, seared calves' liver with a mushroom risotto or try a salad composed of flecks of Parmesan cheese seasoning a savoy cabbage salad and Parma ham. The menu reveals the chef has traveled a bit—note such dishes as Moroccan spiced chicken livers, lemon and parsley couscous, and a zesty chile sauce.

147 Leadenhall St., EC3. ℰ 020/7256-3888. Reservations required. Main courses £16–£25 ($30–$46). AE, DC, DISC, MC, V. Mon–Fri noon–3pm and 6–10pm. Tube: Bank or Monument.

MODERATE

The Bridge ★★ INTERNATIONAL/MODERN BRITISH   As far as restaurants go, the most panoramic view of the new riverside architecture is from the terrace of this glass-walled restaurant next to the Millennium Bridge. It looks out across the Thames to Shakespeare's Globe Theatre and the Tate Modern. Peter Gladwin, the executive chef, roams the world for inspiration—perhaps a velvety smooth gazpacho from Spain. For appetizers, try such delights as the tiger prawns with red grapefruit, avocado and ginger, the smoked trout, or the delectable French onion soup. For something really English, opt for the thinly sliced and quick-seared calves' liver, served with smoky bacon and mashed potatoes laced with sage. If you want to drop in for drinks and a look at that view, you can order dim sum at the bar. The house wine, Nutbourne Sussex Reserve from Gladwin's own Sussex vineyard, has won several awards. Desserts feature the chef's own homemade ice cream and iced lemon vodka parfait.

1 Paul's Walk, EC4. © 020/7236-0000. Reservations required. Main courses £12–£14 ($22–$26). AE, MC, V. Mon–Fri 11am–10pm. Tube: St. Paul's.

Café Spice Namaste ⭐⭐ INDIAN   This is our favorite Indian restaurant in London, where the competition is stiff. It's cheerfully housed in a landmark Victorian hall near Tower Bridge, just east of the Tower of London. The Parsi chef, Cyrus Todiwala, is a former resident of Goa (a Portuguese territory absorbed by India long ago), where he learned many of his culinary secrets. He concentrates on southern and northern Indian dishes with a strong Portuguese influence. Chicken and lamb are prepared a number of ways, from mild to spicy-hot. As a novelty, Todiwala occasionally even offers a menu of emu dishes; when marinated, the meat is rich and spicy and evocative of lamb. Emu is not the only dining oddity here. Ever have ostrich gizzard kabob, alligator tikka, or minced moose, bison, and blue boar? Many patrons journey here just for the complex chicken curry known as *xacutti*. Lambs' livers and kidneys are also cooked in the tandoor. A weekly specialty menu complements the long list of regional dishes. The homemade chutneys alone are worth the trip; our favorite is made with kiwi. All dishes come with fresh vegetables and Indian bread. With its exotic ingredients, often time-consuming preparation, impeccable service, warm hospitality, and spicy but subtle flavors, this is no Indian dive.

16 Prescot St., E1. © 020/7488-9242. Reservations required. Main courses £12–£16 ($22–$30). AE, DC, MC, V. Mon–Fri noon–3pm and 6:15–10:30pm; Sat 6:30–10:15pm. Tube: Tower Hill.

Club Gascon ⭐⭐ *(Finds)* FRENCH   This slice of southwestern France serves such tasty treats as foie gras, Armagnac, and duck confit. Chef Pascal Aussignac is all the rage in London, ever since he opened his bistro next to the meat market in Smithfield. He dedicates his bistro to his favorite ingredient: foie gras. Foie gras appears in at least nine different incarnations on the menu, and most of the first-class ingredients are imported from France. His menu is uniquely divided into these categories—"The Salt Route," "Ocean," and "Kitchen Garden." The best way to dine here is to arrive in a party of four or five and share the small dishes, each harmoniously balanced and full of flavor. Each dish is accompanied by a carefully selected glass of wine. After a foie gras pig-out, proceed to such main courses as a heavenly quail served with pear and rosemary honey. A cassoulet of morels and truffles transforms a plain but perfectly cooked steak. To finish an absolutely elegant repast—dare we call it too rich—there is a selection of "puds," as the British say, ranging from strawberries with basil sorbet to a confit of rhubarb and sherry vinegar. If those don't interest you, opt for a moist almond tart with a biting shot of Granny Smith–apple juice.

57 West Smithfield, EC1. © 020/7796-0600. Reservations required. Fixed-price 5-course menu £38 ($70). Main courses £7–£16 ($13–$30). AE, MC, V. Mon–Fri noon–2pm; Mon–Thurs 7–10pm; Sat 7–10:30pm. Tube: Barbican.

INEXPENSIVE

Ye Olde Cheshire Cheese *(Kids)* BRITISH   The foundation of this carefully preserved building was laid in the 13th century, and it holds the most famous of the old City chophouses and pubs. Established in 1667, it claims to be the spot where Dr. Samuel Johnson (who lived nearby) entertained admirers with his acerbic wit. Charles Dickens and other literary lions also patronized the place. Later, many of the ink-stained journalists and scandalmongers of 19th- and early-20th-century Fleet Street made it their watering hole. You'll find five bars and two dining rooms here. The house specialties include "Ye Famous Pudding" (steak, kidney, mushrooms, and game) and Scottish roast beef with Yorkshire pudding and horseradish sauce. Sandwiches, salads, and standby favorites such as steak and kidney pie are also available, as are dishes such as Dover sole. The Cheshire is the best and safest venue to introduce your children to a British pub.

Wine Office Court, 145 Fleet St., EC4. ✆ 020/7353-6170. Main courses £7.50–£10 ($14–$19). AE, DC, MC, V. Meals: Mon–Fri noon–9:30pm; Sat noon–2:30pm and 6–9:30pm; Sun noon–2:30pm. Drinks and bar snacks: Mon–Fri 11:30am–11pm. Tube: St. Paul's or Blackfriars.

DOCKLANDS
EXPENSIVE

Butler's Wharf Chop House ✿ TRADITIONAL BRITISH   Of the four restaurants housed in Butler's Wharf, this one is the closest to Tower Bridge. It maintains its commitment to moderate prices. The Chop House was modeled after a large boathouse, with banquettes, lots of exposed wood, flowers, candles, and windows overlooking Tower Bridge and the Thames. Lunchtime crowds include workers from the city's financial district; evening crowds are made up of friends dining together leisurely.

Dishes are largely adaptations of British recipes: fish and chips with mushy peas; steak-and-kidney-pudding with oysters; roast rump of lamb with garlic mash and rosemary; and grilled pork filet with apples, chestnuts, and cider sauce. After, there may be a chocolate and caramel tart. The bar offers such choices as Theakston's best bitter, several English wines, and a half-dozen French clarets by the jug.

36E Shad Thames, SE1. ✆ 020/7403-3403. Reservations recommended. Main courses dinner £13–£25 ($23–$46); fixed-price 2-course lunch £20 ($37); fixed-price 3-course lunch £24 ($44). AE, DC, MC, V. Mon–Sun noon–3pm; Mon–Sat 6–11pm. Tube: Tower Hill or London Bridge.

Le Pont de la Tour ✿ INTERNATIONAL   At the edge of the Thames near Tower Bridge, the Butler's Wharf complex holds condos, rental apartments, offices, and an assortment of food and wine shops collectively known as the Gastrodome. Built in the mid–19th century as a warehouse, it's now another Terence Conran playland. From its windows, diners and shoppers enjoy sweeping views of some of the densest river traffic in Europe.

The **Bar and Grill's** live piano music (on evenings and weekends) and wide choice of wines and cocktails creates one of the most convivial atmospheres in the area. Although such dishes as ham and foie gras terrine, and langoustines mayonnaise are featured, the culinary star is a heaping platter of fresh shellfish— perfect when shared with a friend, accompanied by a bottle of wine.

In bold contrast is the large, more formal room known simply as **The Restaurant.** Filled with burr oak furniture and decorated with framed lithographs of early-20th-century Parisian cafe society, it offers excellent food and a polite but undeniable English reserve. The menu may list such temptations as roast rabbit wrapped in herbs with pancetta and a mustard vinaigrette or whole roast-buttered lobster with herbs. One especially winning selection is best end of lamb, with a black olive and herb crust in a red-pepper sauce. All the fish is excellent, but none better than the Dover sole, which can be ordered grilled or meunière.

36D Shad Thames, Butler's Wharf, SE1. ✆ **020/7403-8403**. Reservations highly recommended in the Bar and Grill; recommended in The Restaurant. Bar and Grill main courses £14–£20 ($26–$37); The Restaurant main courses £42–£45 ($78–$83). AE, DC, MC, V. The Restaurant: Daily noon–3pm; Mon–Sat 6–11pm. Bar and Grill: Daily noon–3pm and 6–11pm. Tube: Tower Hill or London Bridge.

MODERATE

The Bengal Clipper ✪ INDIAN   This former spice warehouse by the Thames serves what it calls "India's most remarkable dishes." The likable and often animated restaurant is outfitted with cream-colored walls, tall columns, and modern artwork inspired by the Moghul Dynasty's depictions of royal figures, soaring trees, and well-trained elephants. Seven windows afford sweeping views over the industrialized Thames-side neighborhood, and live piano music plays in the background. The cuisine includes many vegetarian choices derived from the former Portuguese colony of Goa and the once-English colony of Bengal. There is a zestiness and spice to the cuisine, but it's never overpowering. The chefs keep the menu fairly short so that all ingredients can be purchased fresh every day.

A tasty specialty is stuffed *murgh masala,* a tender breast of chicken with potatoes, onions, apricots, and almonds, cooked with yogurt and served with a delectable curry sauce. The perfectly cooked duckling (off the bone) comes in a tangy sauce with a citrus bite. One of the finest dishes we tasted in North India is served here and has lost nothing in the transfer: marinated lamb simmered in cream with cashew nuts, seasoned with fresh ginger. One of the best offerings from the Goan repertoire is the *karkra chop,* a spicy patty of minced crab blended with mashed potatoes and peppered with Goan spices.

Shad Thames, Butler's Wharf, SE1. ✆ **020/7357-9001**. Reservations recommended. Main courses £10–£25 ($19–$46); fixed-price menu from £10 ($19); Sun buffet £7.75 ($14). AE, DC, MC, V. Daily noon–2:30pm and 6–11:30pm. Tube: Tower Hill.

CANARY WHARF
MODERATE

Sri Nam ✪ *Finds* THAI   Celebrity chef Ken Hom is the chief exponent of Thai cookery in London, and even the Thai community agrees that he's the best. Some of his culinary secrets are revealed in his book, *Foolproof Thai Cookery.* At Canary Wharf, Sri Nam brings an authentic and very spicy (read: hot) cuisine to foodies who like to dine on the Thames. There's a buzz-filled cafe-bar on the ground floor and a more formal restaurant upstairs. The Thai cuisine served here is a fusion of modern with traditional, the latter in theory the type served to the "King of Siam." The Asian bar on the ground floor serves drinks from the Far East, plus beers and wines. The ground-floor bar also caters to those seeking speedy lunches or an early supper.

Climb the sweeping staircase for more serious dishes served against a backdrop of rich, dark woods, lush silks, and bright lanterns. The classic star of the menu is *pad thai,* a delightful stir-fry of noodles with eggs, vegetables, and bean sprouts, garnished with ground peanuts and fresh coriander. Served here (and rarely seen on other London menus) is lamb masaman, a curry from south Thailand, featuring lamb flavored with peanuts and potatoes. The signature dish—and is it ever good—is Bangkok's hot green curry with chiles, coconut milk, bamboo shoots, baby eggplant, and lime leaves.

N. Colonnade, 10 Cabot Sq., Canary Wharf, E14. ✆ **020/7715-9515**. Reservations required. Main courses £8–£18 ($15–$33). AE, DC, MC, V. Mon–Sat 11:30am–3pm and 6–10pm, Sat noon–9pm. Tube: Canary Wharf.

SOUTH BANK
EXPENSIVE

Cantina Vinopolis ⭐ *Finds* CONTINENTAL   Not far from the re-created Globe Theatre of Shakespeare's heyday, this place has been called a "Walk-Through Wine Atlas." In the revitalized Bankside area, south of the Thames near Southwark Cathedral, this bricked, walled, and high-vaulted brasserie was converted from long-abandoned Victorian railway arches. Inside you can visit both the Vinopolis Wine Gallery and the Cantina Restaurant. Although many come here just to drink the wine, the food is prepared with quality ingredients (very fresh), and the menu is sensibly priced. Start with a bit of heaven like the pea and ham soup. Dishes are full of flavor and never overcooked. Pan-fried snapper, with crushed new potatoes and salsa verde won us over. A rump of lamb was tender and perfectly flavored and served with a polenta cake. Many of the dishes have the good country taste of a trattoria you'd find in the countryside of southern Italy. Naturally, the wine list is the biggest in the U.K.

1 Bank End, London Bridge, SE1. 𝒞 020/7940-8333. Reservations required. Main courses £14–£16 ($26–$30). AE, DC, MC, V. Mon–Sat noon–3pm and 6–10:45pm; Sun noon–3:45pm. Tube: London Bridge.

Oxo Tower Restaurant ⭐ INTERNATIONAL/ASIAN   In the South Bank complex, on the eighth floor of the Art Deco Oxo Tower Wharf, you'll find this dining sensation. It's operated by the department store Harvey Nichols. Down the street from the newly rebuilt Globe Theater, this 140-seat restaurant could be visited for its view alone, but the cuisine is also stellar. You'll enjoy a sweeping view of St. Paul's Cathedral and The City, all the way to the House of Parliament. The decor is chic 1930s style.

The cuisine, under Chef David Sharland, is rich and prepared with finesse. Menu items change based on the season and the market. Count on a modern interpretation of British cookery, as well as the English classics. The fish is incredibly fresh here. The whole sea bass for two is delectable, as is the roast rump of lamb with split pea, mint purée and balsamic vinegar sauce. Recently, we were impressed with the roast filet of Plaice with olive oil, and truffle cabbage cream, and the roast squab with buttered cabbage and a foie gras sauce.

Barge House St., South Bank, SE1. 𝒞 020/7803-3888. Main courses £10–£18 ($19–$33); fixed-price lunch £20 ($36). AE, DC, MC, V. Mon–Fri noon–3pm; Mon–Sat 6–11:30pm; Sat–Sun noon–2:30pm; Sun 6–10:30pm. Tube: Blackfriars or Waterloo.

KNIGHTSBRIDGE
MODERATE

Drones ⭐ CONTINENTAL   Britain's wonder chef Marco Pierre White took this once-famous but stale restaurant and has once again turned it into a chic dining venue, decorated with black-and-white photographs of the famous people lining the wall. Redesigned by David Collins, it is now called "the Ivy of Belgravia." The food and Art Deco ambience is delightful, as is the staff. Food is fresh and delicately prepared, including such favorites as cauliflower cream soup with truffles and sea scallops or smoked haddock and rice pudding. All the delectable meat and fish dishes are prepared with consummate care and served with a certain finesse. Always expect some unusual flavor combination, such as oxtail *en daube* with a rutabaga purée and a bourguignon garnish. For dessert, a summer specialty is *gelée* of red fruits with a raspberry syrup drizzled on.

1 Pont St., SW1 X9EJ. 𝒞 020/7259-6166. Reservations required. Main courses £9.50–£22 ($18–$41). Mon–Fri noon–2:30pm and 6–11pm; Sat 6–11pm; Sun noon–3:30pm. Tube: Knightsbridge.

INEXPENSIVE

Le Metro INTERNATIONAL   Located just around the corner from Harrods, Le Metro draws a fashionable crowd to its basement precincts. The place serves good, solid, reliable food prepared with flair. The menu changes frequently, but try the chargrilled salmon with pesto, or the chicken and asparagus pie. You can order special wines by the glass.

28 Basil St., SW3. ✆ 020/7589-6286. Main courses £7–£11 ($13–$20). AE, DC, MC, V. Mon–Sat 7:30am–11pm. Tube: Knightsbridge.

CHELSEA
VERY EXPENSIVE

Aubergine ✿✿ FRENCH   "Eggplant" is luring savvy diners down to the lower reaches of Chelsea where new chef Williams Drabble takes over from where the renowned Gordon Ramsay left off. Drabble, who earned his first Michelin star in 1998, has remained true to the style and ambience of this famous establishment. Although popular with celebrities, the restaurant remains unpretentious and refuses to pander to the whims of the rich and famous. (Madonna was once refused a late-night booking!)

Every dish is satisfyingly flavorsome, from warm salad of truffled vegetables with asparagus purée to roasted monkfish served with crushed new potatoes, roasted leeks, and red-wine sauce. Starters continue to charm and delight palates, ranging from ravioli of crab with mussels, chili, ginger, and coriander nage, to terrine of foie gras with confit of duck and pears poached in port. Also resting on your Villeroy & Boch aubergine plate may be mallard with a celeriac fondant or assiette of lamb with a thyme-scented jus. Another stunning main course is a tranche of sea bass with bouillabaisse potatoes. A new dish likely to catch your eye is roasted veal sweetbreads with caramelized onion purée and a casserole of cèpe mushrooms. There are only 14 tables, so bookings are imperative.

11 Park Walk, SW10. ✆ 020/7352-3449. Reservations required and accepted up to 4 weeks in advance. 3-course lunch £32 ($59); fixed-price 3-course dinner £50 ($93); menu gourmand £72 ($133). AE, DC, MC, V. Mon–Fri noon–2:30pm; Mon–Sat 7–10:30pm. Tube: South Kensington.

Gordon Ramsay ✿✿✿ *Finds* FRENCH   One of the city's most innovative and talented chefs is Gordon Ramsay. All of London is rushing to sample Mr. Ramsay's wares, and he has had to turn away some big names. The queen hasn't been denied a table yet, but that's only because she hasn't called.

Every dish from this kitchen is gratifying, reflecting subtlety and delicacy without any sacrifice to the food's natural essence. Try, for example, Ramsay's celebrated cappuccino of white beans with grated truffles. His appetizers are likely to dazzle: salad of crispy pigs' trotters with calves' sweetbreads, fried quail eggs and a cream vinaigrette, or foie gras three ways: sautéed with quince, *mi-cuit* with an Earl Grey consommé, or pressed with truffle peelings. From here, you can grandly proceed to filet of brill poached in red wine, grilled filet of red mullet on a bed of caramelized endives, or else caramelized Challandaise duck cooked with dates. Desserts are equally stunning, especially the pistachio soufflé with chocolate sorbet or the passion fruit and chocolate parfait.

68 Royal Hospital Rd., SW3. ✆ 020/7352-4441. Reservations essential (1 month in advance). Fixed-price lunch £35 ($65) for 3 courses; fixed-price dinner £65 ($120) for 3 courses or £80 ($148) for 7 courses. AE, DC, MC, V. Mon–Fri noon–2:30pm and 6:30–10:30pm. Tube: Sloane Sq.

INEXPENSIVE

Chelsea Kitchen INTERNATIONAL   This simple restaurant feeds large numbers of Chelsea residents in a setting that's changed little since 1961. The food and the clientele move fast, almost guaranteeing that the entire inventory of ingredients is sold out at the end of each day. Menu items usually include leek-and-potato soup, chicken Kiev, chicken parmigiana, steaks, sandwiches, and burgers. The clientele includes a broad cross-section of Londoners—all having a good and cost-conscious time.

98 King's Rd., SW3. ⓒ **020/7589-1330.** Reservations recommended. Main courses £4–£6 ($7.40–$11); fixed-price menu £6.40 ($12). MC, V. Daily 7am–11:45pm. Tube: Sloane Sq.

KENSINGTON & SOUTH KENSINGTON
EXPENSIVE

Bibendum/The Oyster Bar ⭐ FRENCH/MEDITERRANEAN   In trendy Brompton Cross, this still-fashionable restaurant occupies two floors of a garage that's now an Art Deco masterpiece. Though its heyday came in the early 1990s, the white-tiled room, with stained-glass windows, lots of sunlight, and a chic clientele, is still an extremely pleasant place. The eclectic cuisine, known for its freshness and simplicity, is based on what's available seasonally. Dishes may include roast pigeon with celeriac purée and apple sauté, rabbit with artichoke and parsley sauce, or grilled lamb cutlets with a delicate sauce. Some of the best dishes are for splitting between two people, including Bresse chicken flavored with fresh tarragon, and grilled veal chops with truffle butter.

Simpler meals and cocktails are available in the **Oyster Bar** on the building's street level. The bar-style menu stresses fresh shellfish presented in the traditional French style, on ice-covered platters adorned with strands of seaweed. It's a crustacean-lover's dream.

81 Fulham Rd., SW3. ⓒ **020/7581-5817.** Reservations required in Bibendum; not accepted in Oyster Bar. Main courses £16–£24 ($30–$44); fixed-price 3-course lunch £29 ($53); cold seafood platter in Oyster Bar £48 ($89) for 2. AE, DC, MC, V. Bibendum: Mon–Fri noon–2:30pm and 7–11pm; Sat–Sun 12:30–3pm and 7–11pm. Oyster Bar: Mon–Sat noon–10:30pm; Sun noon–3pm and 7–10:30pm. Tube: South Kensington.

Clarke's ⭐ MODERN BRITISH   Sally Clarke is one of the finest chefs in London, and this is one of the hottest restaurants around. *Still.* She opened it in the Thatcher era, and it's still going strong. In this excellent restaurant, everything is bright and modern, with wood floors, discreet lighting, and additional space in the basement where tables are more spacious and private. Some people are put off by the fact that there is only a fixed-price menu, but the food is so well prepared that diners rarely object to what ends up in front of them. The menu, which changes daily, emphasizes chargrilled foods with herbs and seasonal veggies. You may begin with an appetizer salad of blood orange with red onions, watercress, and black olive–anchovy toast, then follow with roasted breast of chicken with black truffle, crisp polenta, and arugula. Desserts are likely to include a warm pear-and-raisin puff pastry with maple syrup ice cream. Just put yourself in Clarke's hands—you'll be glad you did.

124 Kensington Church St., W8. ⓒ **020/7221-9225.** Reservations recommended. Fixed-price lunches £15–£17 ($27–$31); fixed-price 4-course dinner £50 ($92); Sat brunch £7.50–£11 ($14–$20). AE, DC, MC, V. Mon 12:30–2pm; Tues–Fri 12:30–2pm and 7–10pm; Sat brunch 11am–2pm and dinner 7–10pm. Tube: High St. Kensington and Notting Hill Gate.

MODERATE

Admiral Codrington ⭐ *Finds* ENGLISH/CONTINENTAL   Once a lowly pub, this stylish bar and restaurant is now all the rage. The exterior has been maintained, but the old "Cod," as it is affectionately known, has emerged to offer plush dining with a revitalized decor by Nina Campbell and a glass roof that rolls back on sunny days. The bartenders still offer a traditional pint, but the sophisticated menu features such delectable fare as grilled calves liver and crispy bacon or pan-fried rib-eye with a truffled horseradish cream. Opt for the charbroiled tuna with eggplant caviar and a red pepper vinaigrette.

17 Mossop St., SW3. © 020/7581-0005. Reservations recommended. Main courses £10–£15 ($19–$28). AE, MC, V. Mon–Sat 11:30am–midnight; Sun noon–10:30pm. Tube: South Kensington.

The Enterprise TRADITIONAL BRITISH/EUROPEAN The Enterprise's proximity to Harrods attracts both regulars and out-of-town shoppers. Although the joint swarms with singles at night, during the day it attracts the ladies who lunch. With banquettes, white linen, and fresh flowers, you won't mistake it for a lowly boozer. The kitchen serves respectable traditional English fare as well as European favorites, all prepared with fresh ingredients. Featured dishes include fried salmon cakes with butter spinach, golden calamari, and grilled steak with fries and salad. The juicy, properly aged, flavorful, and thin entrecôte slice of beef is about the best you can find in London.

35 Walton St., SW3. © 020/7584-3148. Reservations accepted only for lunch Mon–Fri. Main courses £8–£13 ($15–$24). AE, MC, V. Daily 12:30–2:30pm; Sat–Sun 12:30–3:30pm; daily 6–10pm (the bar is open all day). Tube: South Kensington and Knightsbridge.

Joe's ⭐ *(Finds* MODERN BRITISH One of three London restaurants established by fashion designer Joseph Ettedgui, it's often filled at breakfast and lunch with well-known names from the British fashion, music, and entertainment industries, thanks to its sense of glamour and fun. You can enjoy such dishes as spiced venison strips and vegetables, fresh fish of the day or pasta of the day. Also very popular is Joe's Burger, the chargrilled vegetables, or the grilled chicken on a bed of steamed vegetables. It's all safe, but a bit unexciting. No one will mind if your meal is composed exclusively of appetizers. There's a bar near the entrance, a cluster of tables for quick meals near the door, and more leisurely (and gossipy) dining available in an area a few steps up. The atmosphere remains laid back and unstuffy, just like trendsetters in South Ken prefer it. With a name like Joe's, what else could it be?

126 Draycott Ave., SW3. © 020/7225-2217. Reservations required on weekdays, not accepted on weekends. Main courses £10–£15 ($19–$28). AE, MC, V. Daily 9:30am–6pm. Tube: South Kensington.

MARYLEBONE
EXPENSIVE

Odin's ⭐ INTERNATIONAL This elegant restaurant is one of at least four in London owned by chef Richard Shepherd and actor Michael Caine. Set adjacent to its slightly less expensive twin, Langan's Bistro, it features ample space between tables and an eclectic decor that includes evocative paintings and Art Deco accessories. As other restaurants nearby have come and gone, the cookery here remains solid and reliable. The standard of fresh ingredients and well-prepared dishes is always maintained. The menu changes with the seasons: Typical fare may include forest mushrooms in brioche, braised leeks glazed with mustard and tomato sauce, roast duck with applesauce and sage and onion stuffing, or roast filet of sea bass with a juniper cream sauce.

27 Devonshire St., W1. © 020/7935-7296. Reservations required. Fixed-price 2-course lunch or dinner £26 ($48); fixed-price 3-course lunch or dinner £29 ($54). AE, DC, MC, V. Mon–Fri 12:30–2:30pm and 6:30–11pm. Tube: Regent's Park.

Orrey ⭐⭐ INTERNATIONAL/MODERN FRENCH With ingredients imported from France, this is one of London's classic French restaurants. Sea bass from the shores of Montpellier, olive oil from Maussane-les-Alpilles, mushrooms from the fields of Calais, and poultry from Bresse—they all turn up on a highly refined menu, the creation of chef Andre Garret. On the second floor of The Conran Shop in Marylebone, Orrey changes its menu seasonally to take advantage of the best produce. Garret is a purist in terms of ingredients. Our favorites among his first-rate dishes are Bresse pigeon with savoy cabbage and mushroom ravioli or duckling with an endive tatin and cèpe (flap mushrooms) sauce. Everything has a brilliant often-whimsical touch as evoked by the sautéed leeks in pumpkin oil. Skipping the blueberry soufflé, we ended with a cheese plate featuring a Banton goat cheese from Provence so fresh that it oozed onto the plate. Enjoy lazy summer evenings on a fourth-floor terrace while drinking and ordering light fare from the bar menu.

55 Marylebone High St., W1. © 020/7616-8000. Reservations required. Main courses £17–£30 ($31–$56); fixed-price 3-course lunch menu £24 ($43); 6-course fixed-price menu £55 ($102). AE, DC, MC, V. Daily noon–3pm; Mon–Sat 7–11pm; Sun 7–10:30pm. Tube: Baker St.

MODERATE

Assaggi ★★ *Finds* ITALIAN   Some of London's finest Italian cuisine is served in this room above a pub. This place is a real discovery, and completely unpretentious. The relatively simple menu highlights the creative, outstanding cookery. All the ingredients are fresh and deftly handled by a skilled kitchen staff. Simplicity and flavor reign throughout. The appetizers, such as smoked swordfish salad or beef carpaccio, are so truly sublime that you'll want to make a meal entirely of them. At least three freshly made pastas are featured nightly. The tortellini (pocket-shaped noodles filled with cheese) with pork and a zesty tomato sauce is especially delicious. For a main course, opt for such delights as the thick, juicy, tender grilled veal, flavored with fresh rosemary; or the grilled sea bass with braised fennel. Another savory choice is a plate of lamb cutlets (without any fat) with eggplant and a raisin salad. The flourless chocolate cake is the finest you'll find this side of northern Italy.

39 Chepstow Place, W2. © 020/7792-5501. Reservations required (as far in advance as possible). Main courses £16–£20 ($30–$37). DC, MC, V. Mon–Fri 12:30–2:30pm and 7:30–11pm; Sat 1–2:30pm and 7:30–11pm. Closed 2 weeks at Christmas. Tube: Notting Hill Gate.

Caldesi ITALIAN   Good food, reasonable prices, fresh ingredients, and authentic Tuscan family recipes attract a never-ending stream of patrons to this eatery founded by owner and head chef Giancarlo Caldesi. The extensive menu includes a wide array of pasta, fish, and meat dishes. Start with the excellent *insalata Caldesi,* made with tomatoes slow-roasted in garlic and rosemary oil, and served with mozzarella flown in from Tuscany. Pasta dishes include an especially flavor-filled homemade tortellini stuffed with salmon. Monkfish and prawns are flavored with wild fennel and fresh basil, or you may sample the tender duck breast à l'orange, steeped in white wine, honey, thyme, and rosemary.

15–17 Marylebone Lane, W1. © 020/7935-9226. Reservations required. Main courses £9–£20 ($17–$37). AE, MC, V. Mon–Fri noon–2:30pm; Mon–Sat 6–11pm. Tube: Bond St.

Mash ★ *Finds* CONTINENTAL   What is it, you ask? A bar? A deli? A microbrewery? Actually, it's all of the above, plus a restaurant. Breakfast and weekend brunch are the highlights, but don't ignore dinner. The owners of the hot Atlantic Bar & Grill have opened this "sunken chill-out zone" created by leading designer John Currin. The atmosphere is trendy, hip, breezy, and arty. The novelty decor includes curvy sci-fi lines that may remind you of a *Star Trek* set, and lizard-eye lighting fixtures, but ultimately the food is the attraction.

Suckling pig with spring cannellini stew made us forget all about the trendy mirrored bathrooms. So did the terrific pizzas emerging from the wood-fired oven. On another occasion, we returned for sea bass freshly grilled over wood and presented enticingly with grilled artichoke. Also try the chargrilled tuna with sautéed new potatoes, wilted spinach, and puttanesca dressing.

19–21 Great Portland St., W1. © 020/7637-5555. Reservations required. Main courses £9–£15 ($17–$28); fixed-price 2-course lunch £12 ($22); 3-course lunch £15 ($28). AE, DC, MC, V. Mon–Sat 7–11am, noon–3pm, and 6–11pm. Tube: Oxford Circus.

Villandry ★ INTERNATIONAL/CONTINENTAL   Food lovers and gourmands flock to this food store, delicatessen, and restaurant, where racks of the finest meats, cheese, and produce in the world are displayed and changed virtually every hour. The best of the merchandise is whimsically transformed into the restaurant's menu choices. The setting is an oversize Edwardian-style storefront north of Oxford Circus. The inside is a kind of minimalist temple dedicated to the glories of fresh produce and esoteric foodstuffs. Ingredients here change so frequently that the menu is rewritten twice a day—during our latest visit, it proposed such perfectly crafted dishes as breast of duck with fresh spinach and a gratin of baby onions; and pan-fried turbot with deep-fried celery, artichoke hearts, and hollandaise sauce.

170 Great Portland St., W1. © 020/7631-3131. Reservations recommended. Main courses £16–£21 ($30–$39). AE, DC, MC, V. Restaurant: Mon–Sat noon–3pm and 6–10:30pm. Food store: Mon–Sat 8am–10pm; Sun 11am–4pm. Tube: Great Portland St.

NOTTING HILL GATE
MODERATE

The Cow ★ *Finds* MODERN BRITISH   You don't have to be a young fashion victim to enjoy the superb cuisine served here (although many of the diners are). Tom Conran (son of entrepreneur Sir Terence Conran) holds forth in this increasingly hip Notting Hill watering hole. It looks like an Irish pub, but the accents you'll hear are trustafarian rather than street-smart Dublin. With a pint of Fuller's or London Pride, you can linger over the modern European menu, which changes daily but is likely to include ox tongue poached in milk; mussels in curry and cream; or a mixed grill of lamb chops, calves' liver, and sweetbreads. The seafood selections are delectable. "The Cow Special"—a half-dozen Irish rock oysters with a pint of Guinness or a glass of wine for £7 ($12)—is the star of the show. A raw bar downstairs serves other fresh seafood choices. To finish, skip the filtered coffee served upstairs (it's wretched), and opt for an espresso downstairs.

89 Westbourne Park Rd., W2. © 020/7221-0021. Reservations required. Main courses £14–£20 ($26–$37). MC, V. Mon–Sat 6–11pm; Sun 12:30–4pm (brunch) and 6:30–10pm; bar daily noon–4pm and 6pm–midnight. Tube: Westbourne Grove.

INEXPENSIVE

Prince Bonaparte INTERNATIONAL   This offbeat restaurant serves great pub grub in what used to be a grungy boozer before Notting Hill Gate became fashionable. Now pretty young things show up, spilling onto the sidewalk when the evenings are warm. The pub is filled with mismatched furniture from schools and churches; and CDs of jazz and lazy blues fill the air, competing with the babble. It may seem at first that the staff doesn't have its act together, but once the food arrives, you won't care—the dishes served here are very good. The menu roams the world for inspiration: Moroccan chicken with couscous is as good or better than any you'll find in Marrakech, and the seafood risotto is delicious. Roast lamb, tender and juicy, appears on the traditional Sunday menu. We recommend the London Pride or Grolsch to wash it all down.

80 Chepstow Rd., W2. ✆ **020/7313-9491**. Reservations required. Main courses £9.50–£15 ($18–$28). AE, MC, V. Mon–Sat noon–11pm; Sun noon–10:30pm. Tube: Notting Hill Gate or Westbourne Park.

5 Afternoon Tea

Everyone should indulge in a formal afternoon tea at least once while in London. This relaxing, drawn-out, civilized affair usually consists of three courses, all elegantly served on delicate china: first, dainty finger sandwiches (with the crusts cut off, of course); then fresh-baked scones served with jam and deliciously decadent clotted cream (also known as Devonshire cream); and lastly, an array of bite-size sweets. All the while, an indulgent server keeps the pot of your choice fresh at hand. Sometimes ports or aperitif are on offer for your final course. A quintessential British experience; here are a few of our favorite places to indulge.

COVENT GARDEN & THE STRAND
MAYFAIR

Brown's Hotel 🌟 Along with the Ritz, Brown's ranks as one of the most chic venues for tea in London. Tea is served in the drawing room, which is decorated with English antiques, oil paintings, and floral chintz—much like the drawing room of a country estate. Give your name to the concierge upon arrival; he'll seat you at one of the sofas and settees or at a low table. There's a choice of 12 teas, plus sandwiches, scones, and pastries (all made in the hotel kitchens) rolled around on a trolley for your selection.

29–34 Albemarle St., W1. ✆ **020/7518-4108**. Reservations recommended. Afternoon tea £25 ($46). AE, DC, MC, V. Daily 2–5:30pm. Tube: Green Park.

Ritz Palm Court 🌟🌟🌟 This is the most fashionable place in London to order afternoon tea—and the hardest to get into without reserving way in advance. The spectacular setting is straight out of *The Great Gatsby*, complete with marble steps and columns, and a baroque fountain. You can choose from a long list of teas served with delectable sandwiches and luscious pastries.

In The Ritz Hotel, Piccadilly, W1. ✆ **020/7493-8181**. Reservations required at least 8 weeks in advance. Jeans and sneakers not accepted. Jacket and tie required for men. Afternoon tea £32 ($59). AE, DC, MC, V. 3 seatings daily at 1:30pm, 3:30, and 5:30pm. Tube: Green Park.

St. James Restaurant & The Fountain Restaurant This pair of tea salons functions as a culinary showplace for London's most prestigious grocery store, Fortnum & Mason. The more formal of the two, the St. James, on the store's fourth floor, is a pale green and beige homage to formal Edwardian taste. More rapid and less formal is The Fountain Restaurant, on the street level, where a sense of tradition and manners is very much a part of the dining experience, but in a less opulent setting. There is no longer an "official" afternoon tea at The Fountain, but you can order pots of tea plus food from an a la carte menu that includes sandwiches, scones, and the like.

In Fortnum & Mason, 181 Piccadilly, W1. ✆ **020/7734-8040**. St. James afternoon tea £19 ($34); high tea £21 ($38). The Fountain: a la carte menu £4.50–£12 ($8.35–$22). AE, DC, MC, V. St. James: Mon–Sat 3–5:30pm. The Fountain: Mon–Sat 3–6pm. Tube: Piccadilly Circus.

KNIGHTSBRIDGE

The Georgian Restaurant For as long as anyone can remember, tea at Harrods has been a distinctive feature of Europe's most famous department store. A flood of visitors is gracefully herded into a high-volume but elegant room. Many come here for the ritual of the tea service, as staff members haul silver pots and trolleys laden with pastries and sandwiches through the cavernous dining hall. Most exotic is Betigala tea, a rare blend from China, similar to Lapsang Souchong.

On the 4th floor of Harrods, 87–135 Brompton Rd., SW1. © 020/7225-6800. High tea £19 ($34) or £26 ($47) with Harrods champagne per person. AE, DC, MC, V. Mon–Sat 3:15–5:30pm (last order). Tube: Knightsbridge.

KENSINGTON

The Orangery ★ *Finds*   In its way, the Orangery is the most amazing place for afternoon tea in the world. Set 45m (150 ft.) north of Kensington Palace, it occupies a long narrow garden pavilion built in 1704 by Queen Anne. In homage to her original intentions, rows of potted orange trees bask in sunlight from soaring windows, and tea is served amid Corinthian columns, ruddy-colored bricks, and a pair of Grinling Gibbons woodcarvings. There are even some urns and statuary that the royal family imported from Windsor Castle. The menu includes soups and sandwiches, with a salad and a portion of upscale potato chips known as kettle chips. The array of different teas is served with high style, accompanied by fresh scones with clotted cream and jam, and Belgian chocolate cake.

In the gardens of Kensington Palace, W8. © 020/7376-0239. Reservations not accepted. Pot of tea only £1.75–£1.95 ($3.25–$3.60); summer cakes and puddings £2.95–£3.95 ($5.45–$7.30); sandwiches £5.95–£8.95 ($11–$17). MC, V. Daily 10am–6pm. Tea 3–5pm. Tube: High St. Kensington or Queensway.

5

Exploring London

London is more eclectic and electric than it's been in years. Some even think it has surpassed New York for sheer energy, outrageous fashion, trendy restaurants, and a nightlife that's second to none.

But we don't want to mislead. London is more open and dynamic than it has been since 1969, but it's not one giant house party. Problems exist here, as elsewhere, that all the trendy restaurants and pricey boutiques in the world can't obliterate. The gulf between rich and poor continues to widen, and violent crime, once relatively rare, is on the rise.

And though the cool youth culture is grabbing headlines, it's not all there is to London today. What makes the city so fascinating is its cultural diversity. It seems that half the world is flocking there, not just from the far-flung former colonies of the once great British Empire, but also from Algeria, Argentina, China, and Senegal. With their talent and new ideas, these recent transplants are transforming a city once maligned as a drab, stuffy metropolis. In London today, where everything's changing, only the queen appears the same. (After she's gone, even the House of Windsor may be in for a shake-up.)

In this chapter, we can explore only a fraction of what's exciting in London. We went in search of what's causing the hottest buzz in shopping and nightlife, but we also provide plenty of detail about London's time-tested treasures: ancient monuments, literary shrines, walking tours, Parliament debates, royal castles, waxworks, palaces, cathedrals, and royal parks.

SUGGESTED ITINERARIES
For the first-time visitor, the question is never what to do, but what to do first.

If You Have 1 Day
No first-time visitor should leave London without a visit to **Westminster Abbey,** with Poets' Corner and its royal tombs. Also see the **Changing of the Guard** at Buckingham Palace if it's on, and walk over to **10 Downing Street,** home of the prime minister. After lunch, walk to **Big Ben** and the **Houses of Parliament.** Dine at a little restaurant in **Covent Garden,** such as Porter's, owned by the earl of Bradford. Try one of their classic English pies (maybe lamb and apricot). For a pretheater drink, head to the ultimate Victorian pub, the Red Lion in Mayfair, the kind of place Oscar Wilde might have chosen for a brandy. If you're so inclined, see a play—musical or drama—in the West End. London has the best English-language theater in the world; the offerings are even greater than in New York.

If You Have 2 Days
Day 1 Spend Day 1 as above.

Day 2 Devote a good part of the second day exploring **The British Museum,** one of the best museums in the world. In the afternoon, visit the **Tower of London** and see the **Crown Jewels** (expect slow-moving lines). Later, go to a local place for dinner, such as Shepherd's in Westminster, where you may dine alongside MPs from the House of Commons. Perhaps you'll catch another play that evening or head for one of London's zillion-and-one nightclubs to dance the night away.

If You Have 3 Days

Days 1–2   Spend Days 1 and 2 as above.

Day 3   In the morning, visit the masterworks in **The National Gallery.** For an afternoon change of pace, head to **Madame Tussauds** if you have kids in tow. Take a walking tour of **St. James's.** In the evening, attend a **West End** play or a performance at the National Theatre or Queen Elizabeth Hall at South Bank Centre.

If You Have 4 or 5 Days

Days 1–3   Spend Days 1, 2, and 3 as above.

Day 4   In the morning, head for **The City,** London's financial district. Your major sightseeing goal here will be **St. Paul's Cathedral,** designed by Sir Christopher Wren. Take a walking tour of The City. In the afternoon, head for **King's Road** in Chelsea for some boutique hopping and to dine at one of **Chelsea's** many restaurants. Later that evening, take in a show at a **Soho** nightclub, such as Ronnie Scott's, which hosts some of the city's best jazz.

Day 5   Explore the **Victoria and Albert Museum** in the morning, then go to the **Tate Britain Gallery** for a look at some of its many masterpieces; have lunch at its restaurant, which offers some of the best values on wine in Britain. For a historic glimpse of the dark days of World War II, visit the **Cabinet War Rooms** at Clive Steps, where Churchill directed British operations. Spend the evening at the theater.

1 The Top Attractions

As a rule, and unless otherwise stated in the listings below, children's prices at London attractions apply to those aged 16 and under. You must be 60 years of age or older to obtain available senior discounts at some attractions. For students to get available discounted admissions, they must have a valid student ID card.

Tower of London ⭐⭐⭐   This ancient fortress continues to pack in the crowds, largely because of its macabre association with the legendary figures who were imprisoned and/or executed here, with more spooks to the square foot than in any other building in the whole of haunted Britain. Even today, centuries after the last head rolled on Tower Hill, a shivery atmosphere of impending doom lingers over the mighty walls. Plan on spending a lot of time here.

The Tower is actually an intricately patterned compound of structures built throughout the ages for varying purposes, mostly as expressions of royal power. The oldest is the **White Tower,** begun by William the Conqueror in 1078 to keep London's native Saxon population in check. Later rulers added other towers, more walls, and fortified gates, until the building became something like a small town within a city. Until the reign of James I, the Tower was also one of the royal residences. But above all, it was a prison for distinguished captives.

Every stone of the Tower tells a story—usually a gory one. In the **Bloody Tower,** according to Shakespeare, the two little princes (the sons of Edward IV) were murdered by henchmen of Richard III. Attempts have been made by some

London Attractions

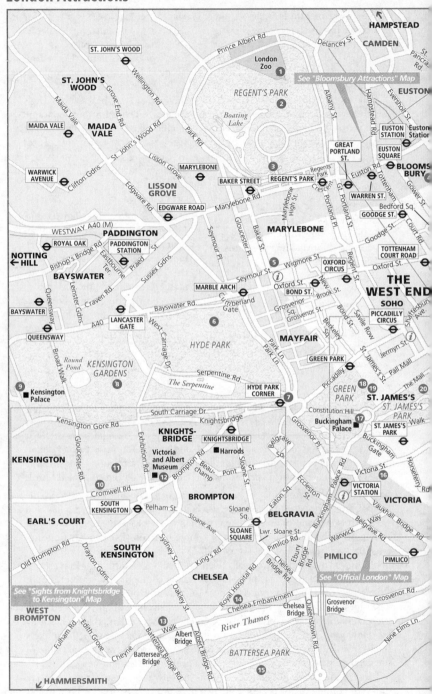

See "Bloomsbury Attractions" Map

See "Official London" Map

See "Sights from Knightsbridge to Kensington" Map

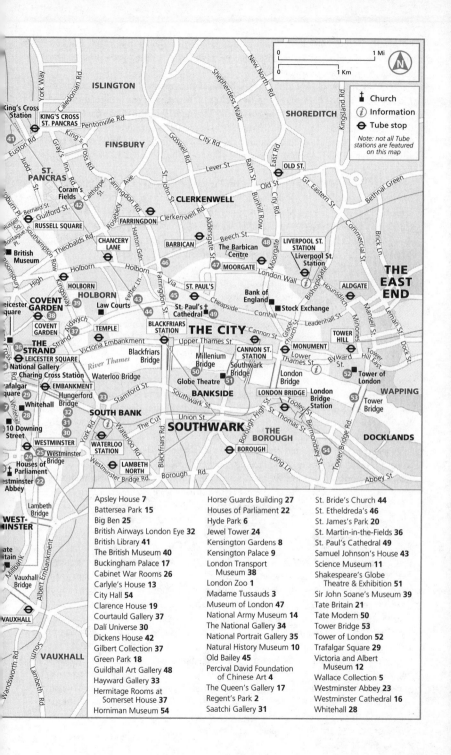

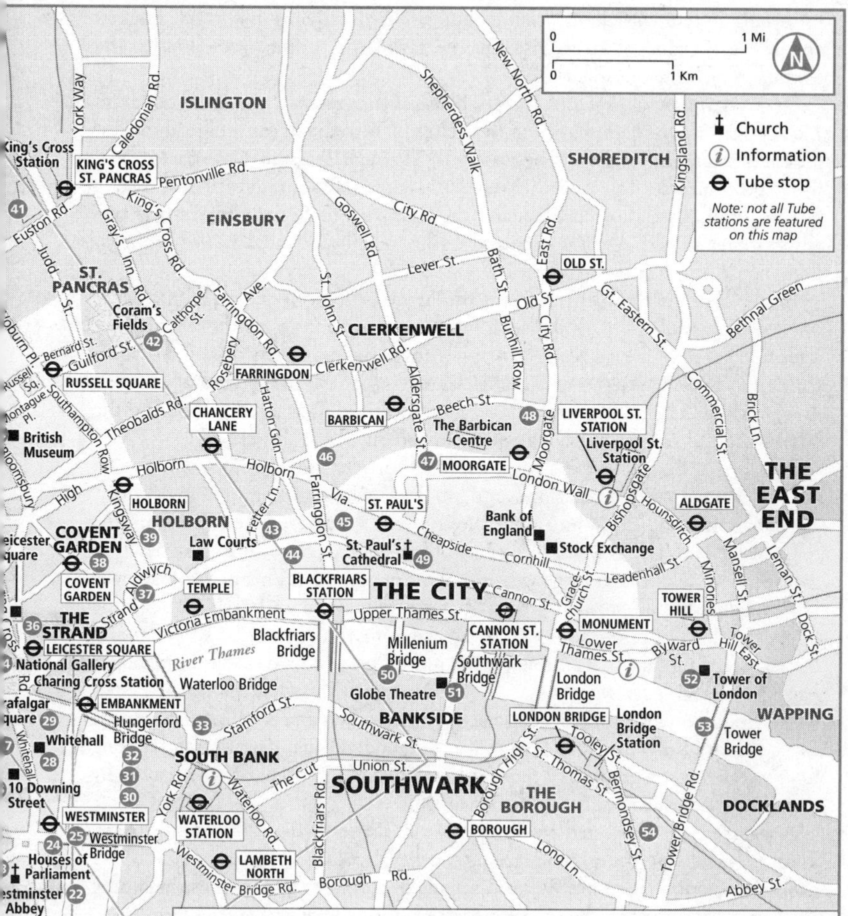
0
1 Mi
0
1 Km
N
Church
Information
Tube stop
Note: not all Tube stations are featured on this map
ISLINGTON
SHOREDITCH
FINSBURY
CLERKENWELL
ST. PANCRAS
KING'S CROSS ST. PANCRAS
King's Cross Station
OLD ST.
LIVERPOOL ST. STATION
Liverpool St. Station
FARRINGDON
RUSSELL SQUARE
CHANCERY LANE
BARBICAN
The Barbican Centre
MOORGATE
British Museum
HOLBORN
ST. PAUL'S
ALDGATE
THE EAST END
COVENT GARDEN
Law Courts
Bank of England
Stock Exchange
St. Paul's Cathedral
THE CITY
BLACKFRIARS STATION
TEMPLE
TOWER HILL
MONUMENT
CANNON ST. STATION
THE STRAND
LEICESTER SQUARE
National Gallery
Charing Cross Station
River Thames
Blackfriars Bridge
Millenium Bridge
Southwark Bridge
London Bridge
Tower of London
Waterloo Bridge
Globe Theatre
BANKSIDE
LONDON BRIDGE
London Bridge Station
WAPPING
EMBANKMENT
Hungerford Bridge
Tower Bridge
Whitehall
SOUTH BANK
10 Downing Street
SOUTHWARK
THE BOROUGH
DOCKLANDS
WESTMINSTER
WATERLOO STATION
BOROUGH
Westminster Bridge
Houses of Parliament
LAMBETH NORTH
Westminster Abbey
Lambeth Bridge
WEST-MINSTER
Vauxhall Bridge
VAUXHALL
Pentonville Rd.
Caledonian Rd.
York Way
Euston Rd.
Gray's Inn Rd.
King's Cross Rd.
Goswell Rd.
City Rd.
New North Rd.
Shepherdess Walk
Kingsland Rd.
East Rd.
Old St.
Gt. Eastern St.
Bethnal Green
Commercial St.
Brick Ln.
Lever St.
Bath St.
Bunhill Row
City Rd.
St. John St.
Farringdon Rd.
Clerkenwell Rd.
Aldersgate St.
Beech St.
Moorgate
London Wall
Bishopsgate
Houndsditch
Theobalds Rd.
Southampton Row
Guilford St.
Holborn
High Holborn
Kingsway
Fetter Ln.
Hatton Gdn.
Farringdon St.
Cheapside
Cornhill
Leadenhall St.
Minories
Mansell St.
Leman St.
Dock St.
Aldwych
Strand
Victoria Embankment
Cannon St.
Upper Thames St.
Lower Thames St.
Gracechurch St.
Byward St.
Tower Hill East
Stamford St.
Southwark St.
Union St.
The Cut
Waterloo Rd.
York Rd.
Borough High St.
Tooley St.
St. Thomas St.
Bermondsey St.
Tower Bridge Rd.
Long Ln.
Abbey St.
Blackfriars Rd.
Borough Rd.
Westminster Bridge Rd.
Whitehall
Millbank
Albert Embankment
South Lambeth Rd.
Wandsworth Rd.

Apsley House **7**
Battersea Park **15**
Big Ben **25**
British Airways London Eye **32**
British Library **41**
The British Museum **40**
Buckingham Palace **17**
Cabinet War Rooms **26**
Carlyle's House **13**
City Hall **54**
Clarence House **19**
Courtauld Gallery **37**
Dalí Universe **30**
Dickens House **42**
Gilbert Collection **37**
Green Park **18**
Guildhall Art Gallery **48**
Hayward Gallery **33**
Hermitage Rooms at Somerset House **37**
Horniman Museum **54**
Horse Guards Building **27**
Houses of Parliament **22**
Hyde Park **6**
Jewel Tower **24**
Kensington Gardens **8**
Kensington Palace **9**
London Transport Museum **38**
London Zoo **1**
Madame Tussauds **3**
Museum of London **47**
National Army Museum **14**
The National Gallery **34**
National Portrait Gallery **35**
Natural History Museum **10**
Old Bailey **45**
Percival David Foundation of Chinese Art **4**
The Queen's Gallery **17**
Regent's Park **2**
Saatchi Gallery **31**
St. Bride's Church **44**
St. Etheldreda's **46**
St. James's Park **20**
St. Martin-in-the-Fields **36**
St. Paul's Cathedral **49**
Samuel Johnson's House **43**
Science Museum **11**
Shakespeare's Globe Theatre & Exhibition **51**
Sir John Soane's Museum **39**
Tate Britain **21**
Tate Modern **50**
Tower Bridge **53**
Tower of London **52**
Trafalgar Square **29**
Victoria and Albert Museum **12**
Wallace Collection **5**
Westminster Abbey **23**
Westminster Cathedral **16**
Whitehall **28**

historians to clear Richard's name, but Richard remains the chief suspect, and his deed caused him to lose the "hearts of the people" according to the *Chronicles of London* at the time.

Sir Walter Raleigh spent 13 years before his date with the executioner in Bloody Tower. On the walls of the **Beauchamp Tower,** you can still read the last messages scratched by despairing prisoners. Through **Traitors' Gate** passed such ill-fated, romantic figures as Robert Devereux, the second earl of Essex, a favorite of Elizabeth I. A plaque marks the eerie place at **Tower Green** where two wives of Henry VIII, Anne Boleyn and Catherine Howard, and the 9-day queen, Lady Jane Grey, lost their lives.

In the latest development here, the presumed prison cell of Sir Thomas More opened to the public in 2000. More left this cell in 1535 to face his executioner after he'd fallen out with King Henry VIII over the monarch's desire to divorce Catherine of Aragon, the first of his six wives. In the lower part of the Bell Tower, More is believed to have lived here in this whitewashed cell during the last 14 months of his life, though some historians doubt this claim.

The Tower, besides being a royal palace, a fortress, and a prison, was also an armory, a treasury, a menagerie, and, in 1675, an astronomical observatory. Reopened in 1999, the White Tower holds the **Armouries,** which date from the reign of Henry VIII, as well as a display of instruments of torture and execution that recall some of the most ghastly moments in the Tower's history. In the Jewel House, you'll find the tower's greatest attraction, the **Crown Jewels.** Here, some of the world's most precious stones are set into robes, swords, scepters, and crowns. The Imperial State Crown is the most famous crown on earth; made for Victoria in 1837, it's worn today by Queen Elizabeth when she opens Parliament. Studded with some 3,000 jewels (principally diamonds), it includes the Black Prince's Ruby, worn by Henry V at Agincourt. You'll have to stand in long lines to catch just a glimpse of the jewels as you and hundreds of others scroll by on moving sidewalks, but the wait is worth it.

A **palace** once inhabited by King Edward I in the late 1200s stands above Traitors' Gate. It's the only surviving medieval palace in Britain. Guides are dressed in period costumes. Reproductions of furniture and fittings, including Edward's throne, evoke the era, along with burning incense and candles.

Oh, yes—don't forget to look for the ravens. Six of them (plus two spares) are all registered as official Tower residents. According to a legend, the Tower of London will stand as long as those black, ominous birds remain, so to be on the safe side, one of the wings of each raven is clipped.

One-hour guided tours of the entire compound are given by the Yeoman Warders (also known as "Beefeaters") every half hour, starting at 9:30am from the Middle Tower near the main entrance. The last guided walk starts about 3:30pm in summer, 2:30pm in winter, weather permitting, of course.

You can attend the nightly **Ceremony of the Keys,** the ceremonial locking-up of the Tower by the Yeoman Warders. For free tickets, write to the Ceremony of the Keys, Waterloo Block, Tower of London, London EC3N 4AB, and request a specific date, but also list alternate dates. At least 6 weeks' notice is required. All requests must be accompanied by a stamped, self-addressed envelope (British stamps only) or two International Reply Coupons. With ticket in hand, you'll be admitted by a Yeoman Warder at 9:35pm. Frankly, we think it's not worth the trouble you go through to see this rather cheesy ceremony, but we know some diehard Anglophiles who disagree with us.

Insider's tip: The secret of avoiding the Tower's notoriously long lines is to buy your ticket in a kiosk inside the Tube station before emerging above ground and to go early in the morning. Avoid Sundays between noon and 2pm if you can—crowds are at their worst then.

Tower Hill, EC3. (C) **0870/756-6060.** www.tower-of-london.org.uk. Admission £14 ($25) adults, £11 ($19) students and seniors, £9 ($17) children, free for children under 5, £38 ($69) family ticket for 5 (but no more than 2 adults). Mar–Oct Mon–Sat 9am–6pm, Sun 10am–6pm; Nov–Feb Tues–Sat 9am–5pm, Sun and Mon 10am–5pm. Tube: Tower Hill.

Westminster Abbey ★★★   With its square twin towers and superb archways, this Early English Gothic abbey is one of the greatest examples of ecclesiastical architecture on earth. But it's far more than that: It's the shrine of a nation, the symbol of everything Britain has stood for and stands for, the place in which most of its rulers were crowned and where many lie buried.

Nearly every figure in English history has left his or her mark on Westminster Abbey. Edward the Confessor founded the Benedictine abbey in 1065 on this spot, overlooking Parliament Square. The first English king crowned in the abbey was Harold in 1066. The man who defeated him at the Battle of Hastings that year, William the Conqueror, was also crowned here. The coronation tradition has continued to the present day, broken only twice (by Edward V and Edward VIII). The essentially Early English Gothic structure existing today owes more to Henry III's plans than to those of any other sovereign, although many architects, including Christopher Wren, have contributed to the abbey.

Built in the early 16th century, the **Henry VII Chapel** is one of the loveliest in Europe, with its fan vaulting, Knights of Bath banners, and Torrigiani-designed tomb of the king himself, over which hangs a 15th-century Vivarini painting, *Madonna and Child.* Also here, ironically buried in the same tomb, are Catholic Mary I and Protestant Elizabeth I (whose archrival, Mary Queen of Scots, is entombed on the other side of the Henry VII Chapel). In one end of the chapel, you can stand on Cromwell's memorial stone and view the **Royal Air Force chapel** and its Battle of Britain memorial window, unveiled in 1947 to honor the RAF.

You can also visit the most hallowed spot in the abbey, the **shrine of Edward the Confessor** (canonized in the 12th c.). In the chapel is the Coronation Chair, made at the command of Edward I in 1300 to display the Stone of Scone. Scottish kings were once crowned on it (it has since been returned to Scotland).

When you enter the transept on the south side of the nave and see a statue of the Bard with one arm resting on a stack of books, you've arrived at **Poets' Corner.** Shakespeare himself is buried at Stratford-upon-Avon, but resting here are Chaucer, Ben Jonson, Milton, Shelley, and many others, including an American, Henry Wadsworth Longfellow. You'll also find monuments to just about everybody: Chaucer, Shakespeare, "O Rare Ben Johnson" (his name misspelled), Samuel Johnson, George Eliot, Dickens, and others. The most stylized monument is Sir Jacob Epstein's sculptured bust of William Blake. More recent tablets commemorate Dylan Thomas and Lord Laurence Olivier.

Statesmen and men of science—such as Disraeli, Newton, and Darwin—are also interred in the abbey or honored by monuments. Near the west door is the 1965 memorial to Sir Winston Churchill. In the vicinity of this memorial is the tomb of the **Unknown Soldier,** commemorating the British dead of World War I.

Although most of the Abbey's statuary commemorates notable figures of the past, 10 new statues were unveiled in July 1998. Placed in the Gothic niches above the West Front door, these statues honor 10 modern-day martyrs drawn from every continent and religious denomination. The sculptures include Elizabeth of Russia, Janani Luwum, and Martin Luther King, Jr.; they represent all those who have sacrificed their lives for their convictions.

Off the Cloisters, the **College Garden** is the oldest garden in England, under cultivation for more than 900 years. Established in the 11th century as the abbey's first infirmary garden, this was once a magnificent source of fruits, vegetables, and medicinal herbs. Five trees in the garden were planted in 1850 and continue to thrive today. Surrounded by high walls, flowering trees dot the lawns, and park benches provide comfort where you can hardly hear the roar of passing traffic. It's open only on Tuesday through Thursday, April through September from 10am to 6pm, and October through March from 10am to 4pm.

Insider's tip: Far removed from the pomp and glory is the **Abbey Treasure Museum,** with a bag of oddities. They're displayed in the undercroft or crypt, part of the monastic buildings erected between 1066 and 1100. Here are royal effigies that were used instead of the real corpses for lying-in-state ceremonies because they smelled better. You'll see the almost lifelike effigy of Admiral Nelson (his mistress arranged his hair) and even that of Edward III, his lip warped by the stroke that felled him. Other oddities include a Middle English lease to Chaucer, the much-used sword of Henry VI, and the Essex Ring Elizabeth I gave to one of her favorites (the earl of Essex) when she was feeling good about him.

On Sunday, the Royal Chapels are closed, but the rest of the church is open unless a service is being conducted. For times of services, phone the **Chapter Office** (*©* 020/7654-4832).

Broad Sanctuary, SW1. *©* 020/7654-4900. www.westminster-abbey.org. Admission £7.50 ($14) adults; £5 ($9.25) for students, seniors, and children 11–16; free for children under 11; family ticket £15 ($28). Mon–Tues and Thurs–Fri 9:30am–3:45pm; Wed 9:30am–7pm; Sat 9am–1:45pm. Tube: Westminster or St. James's Park.

Houses of Parliament *ﬁﬁ*

The Houses of Parliament, along with their trademark clock tower, are the ultimate symbol of London. They're the stronghold of Britain's democracy, the assemblies that effectively trimmed the sails of royal power. Both the House of Commons and the House of Lords are in the former royal Palace of Westminster, the king's residence until Henry VIII moved to Whitehall. The current Gothic Revival buildings date from 1840 and were designed by Charles Barry. (The earlier buildings were destroyed by fire in 1834.) Assisting Barry was Augustus Welby Pugin, who designed the paneled ceilings, tiled floors, stained glass, clocks, fireplaces, umbrella stands, and even the inkwells. There are more than 1,000 rooms and 3km (2 miles) of corridors.

The clock tower at the eastern end houses the world's most famous timepiece. **Big Ben** refers not to the clock tower itself, but to the largest bell in the chime, which weighs close to 14 tons and is named for the first commissioner of works.

You may observe parliamentary debates from the **Stranger's Galleries** in both houses. Sessions usually begin in mid-October and run through July, with recesses at Christmas and Easter. The debates in the House of Commons are often lively and controversial (seats are at a premium during crises). The chances of getting into the House of Lords when it's in session are generally better than for the more popular House of Commons, where even the queen isn't allowed.

For years, London tabloids have portrayed members of the House of Lords as a bunch of "Monty Pythonesque upper-class twits," with one foreign secretary calling the House of Lords "medieval lumber." Today, under Tony Blair's Labour government, the House of Lords is being shaken up as peers lose their hereditary posts. Panels are studying what to do with this largely useless house, its members often descendants of royal mistresses and ancient landowners.

Those who'd like to book a tour can do so, but it takes a bit of work. Both houses are open to the general public for guided tours only for a limited season in July and August. The palace is open Monday, Tuesday, Friday, Saturday from 9:15am to 4:30pm during those times. All tour tickets cost £7 ($13) adults, £5 ($9.25) for seniors, students, and children under 16. Under 4 years old is free. For advance tickets, call © **0870/906-3773.**

If you arrive just to attend a session, these are free. You line up at Stephen's Gate, heading to your left for the entrance into the Commons or to the right for the Lords. The London daily newspapers announce sessions of Parliament.

Insider's tip: The hottest ticket and most exciting time to visit is during Prime Minister's Question Time, Monday to Wednesday from 2:30 to 3:10pm, Thursday 3 to 3:30pm, which must seem like hours to Tony Blair, who is virtually on the hot seat. Blair holds his own admirably against any and all who try to embarrass him and his government.

Across the street is the **Jewel Tower** ⚐, Abingdon St. (© **020/7222-2219**), a hidden gem and one of only two surviving buildings from the medieval palace of Westminster. It was constructed in 1365 as a place where Edward III could stash his treasure trove. The tower hosts an exhibition on the history of that governing body and makes for a great introduction to the inner workings of the British government. The video presentation on the top floor is especially informative. A touch-screen computer allows visitors to take a virtual tour of both houses of Parliament. The tower is open daily: from 10am to 6pm April through September, 10am to 5pm in October, and 9:30am to 4pm November to March. Admission is £2.20 ($4.05) for adults, £1.70 ($3.15) for students and seniors, and £1.10 ($2.05) for children.

Westminster Palace, Old Palace Yard, SW1. House of Commons © 020/7219-4272. House of Lords © 020/ 7219-3107. www.parliament.uk. Free admission. House of Lords open mid-Oct to Aug Mon–Wed from 2:30pm, Thurs from 11am, and sometimes Fri (check by phone). House of Commons open mid-Oct to Aug Mon 2:30–10:30pm; Tues–Wed 11:30am–7:30pm; Thurs 11:30am–6pm; Fri call ahead—not always open. Both houses are open for tours (see above). Join line at St. Stephen's entrance. Tube: Westminster.

The British Museum ⚐⚐⚐ Set in scholarly Bloomsbury, this immense museum grew out of a private collection of manuscripts purchased in 1753 with the proceeds of a lottery. It grew and grew, fed by legacies, discoveries, and purchases, until it became one of the most comprehensive collections of art and artifacts in the world. It's utterly impossible to take in this museum in a day.

The overall storehouse splits basically into national collections of antiquities; prints and drawings; coins, medals, and bank notes; and ethnography. Even on a cursory first visit, be sure to see the Asian collections (the finest assembly of Islamic pottery outside the Islamic world), the Chinese porcelain, the Indian sculpture, and the Prehistoric and Romano-British collections. Special treasures you also may want to see include the **Rosetta Stone** in the Egyptian Room, whose discovery led to the deciphering of hieroglyphs; the **Elgin Marbles** in the Duveen Gallery, a priceless series of pediments, metopes, and friezes from the Parthenon in Athens; and the legendary **Black Obelisk** in the Nimrud Gallery, dating from around 860 B.C. Other treasures include the contents of Egyptian royal tombs (including mummies); fabulous arrays of 2,000-year-old jewelry, cosmetics, weapons, furniture, and tools; Babylonian astronomical instruments; and winged lions (in the Assyrian Transept) that once guarded Ashurnasirpal's

---

Tips Timesaver

With 4km (2½ miles) of galleries, The British Museum is overwhelming. To get a handle on it, we recommend taking a 1½-hour overview tour for £8 ($15), £5 ($9.25) for seniors, students, and children under 16. Daily at 10:30am, 1pm, or 3pm. Afterward, you can return to the galleries that most interest you. If you have a limited time to spend on the museum, concentrate on the Greek and Roman rooms (nos. 1–15), which hold the golden hoard of booty both bought and stolen from the Empire's once far-flung colonies. For information on the British Library, see p. 176.

---

palace at Numrud. The exhibits change throughout the year, so if your heart is set on seeing a specific treasure, call ahead to make sure it's on display.

Insider's tip: If you're a first-time visitor, you will, of course, want to concentrate on some of the fabled treasures previewed above. But what we do is duck into The British Museum several times on our visits to London, even if we have only an hour or two, to see the less heralded but equally fascinating exhibits. These include wandering room nos. 33, 34, and 91 to 94 to take in the glory of the Orient, covering Taoism, Confucianism, and Buddhism. The Chinese collection is particularly strong. Sculpture from India is as fine as anything at the Victoria and Albert. The ethnography collection is increasingly being beefed up, especially the Mexican Gallery in room no. 33C, which traces that country's art from the 2nd millennium B.C. to the 16th century A.D. A gallery nearby for the North American collection is also open. One section is devoted to the **Sainsbury African Galleries** ⊛, one of the finest collections of African art and artifacts in the world, featuring changing displays selected from more than 200,000 objects. Finally, and as an amusing sideline, the museum has opened a new money gallery in room no. 68, tracing the story of money.

The Great Court, completed in 2000, is an inner courtyard that is canopied by a lightweight, transparent roof transforming the area into a covered square, housing a Centre for Education, exhibition space, bookshops, and restaurants. The center of the Great Court features the Round Reading Room restored to its original decorative scheme.

Great Russell St., WC1. ⓒ 020/7323-8299. www.thebritishmuseum.ac.uk. Free admission. Sat–Wed 10am–5:30pm; Thurs–Fri 10am–8:30pm. Tube: Holborn, Tottenham Court Rd., Goodge St., or Russell Sq.

Buckingham Palace ⊛⊛   This massive, graceful building is the official residence of the queen. The redbrick palace was built as a country house for the notoriously rakish duke of Buckingham. In 1762, it was bought by King George III, who needed room for his 15 children. It didn't become the official royal residence, though, until Queen Victoria took the throne; she preferred it to St. James's Palace. From George III's time, the building was continuously expanded and remodeled, faced with Portland stone, and twice bombed (during the Blitz). Located in a 16-hectare (40-acre) garden, it's 108m (360 ft.) long and contains 600 rooms. You can tell whether the queen is at home by the Royal Standard flying at the masthead.

Since 1993, much of the palace has been open for tours during an 8-week period in August and September, when the royal family is usually vacationing outside London. Visitors can tour the State Room, the Grand Staircase, the Throne Room, and other areas designed by John Nash for George IV, as well as the huge Picture Gallery, which displays masterpieces by Van Dyck, Rembrandt, Rubens, and others. You can't actually visit the Queen's bedroom, and the tour doesn't encompass the actual living quarters of the royals—only the state rooms where they carry out their royal duties. Even so and in spite of the huge admission price, most visitors are excited at the idea of even going inside Buckingham Palace. Admission charges help pay for repairs to Windsor Castle, badly damaged by fire in 1992. You have to buy a timed-entrance ticket on the same day you tour the palace. Tickets go on sale at 9am, but rather than lining up outside the gate at sunrise with other tourists—it's one of London's most popular attractions—book with credit card by phone and save yourself a dreary morning.

Visitors are also allowed to stroll through the royal family's garden, along a 446m (1,485-ft.) walk on the south side of the grounds, with views of a lake and the usually off-limits west side of the palace. The garden is home to 30 types of birds, including the great crested grebe, plus 350 types of wildflowers.

Buckingham Palace's most famous spectacle is the vastly overrated **Changing of the Guard** (daily Apr–July and every other day the rest of the year). The new guard, marching behind a band, comes from either the Wellington or Chelsea Barracks and takes over from the old guard in the forecourt of the palace. The ceremony begins at 11:30am, though it's frequently canceled for bad weather, major state events, and other harder-to-fathom reasons—always check before you go. We like the changing of the guards at Horse Guards better (p. 174) where you can actually see the men marching and don't have to battle such tourist hordes. However, few first-time visitors can resist the Buckingham Palace changing of the guard. If you're one of them, arrive as early as 10:30am and claim territorial rights to a space directly in front of the palace. If you're not firmly anchored here, you'll miss much of the ceremony. Call ahead for times.

Insider's tip: You can avoid the long queues at Buckingham Palace by purchasing tickets before you go through **Keith Prowse,** 234 West 44th St., Suite 1000, New York, NY 10034 (© **800/223-6108** or 212/398-1054; www. keithprowse.com). You'll have to pick the exact date on which you'd like to go. Visitors with disabilities can reserve tickets directly through the palace by calling © **020/7930-5526.**

At end of The Mall (on the road running from Trafalgar Sq.). © 020/7170-4299 or 020/7321-2233. www. royal.gov.uk. Palace tours £13 ($24) adults, £11 ($20) seniors, £6.50 ($12) children under 17. Changing of the Guard free. Palace open for tours Aug 1–Sept 26 daily 9:30am–4:15pm. Changing of the guard daily Apr–July at 11:30am, and every other day for the rest of the year at 11am. Tube: St. James's Park, Green Park, or Victoria.

Tate Britain 🛇🛇🛇 Fronting the Thames near Vauxhall Bridge in Pimlico, the Tate looks like a smaller and more graceful relation of The British Museum. The most prestigious gallery in Britain, it houses the national collections covering British art from the 16th century to the present day, as well as an array of

---

(**Tips Warning**

The schedule for the Changing of the Guard ceremony is variable at best. In theory at least, the guard is changed daily from some time in April to mid-July, at which time it goes on its "winter" schedule—that is, every other day. Always check locally with the tourist office to find out whether it's likely to be staged at the time of your visit. The ceremony has often been cut at the last minute, leaving thousands of tourists feeling they have missed out on a London must-see.

international artists. In the spring of 2000, the Tate moved its collection of 20th- and 21st-century art to the **Tate Modern** (see below). This split opened more space at the Tate Britain, but the collection here is still much too large to be displayed at once, so the works on view change from time to time.

The older works include some of the best of Gainsborough, Reynolds, Stubbs, Blake, and Constable. William Hogarth is well represented, particularly by his satirical *O the Roast Beef of Old England* (known as *The Gate of Calais*). The illustrations of William Blake, the incomparable mystical poet known for such works as *The Book of Job, The Divine Comedy,* and *Paradise Lost,* are here. The **collection of works by J. M. W. Turner** 🟆🟆🟆 is its largest collection of works by a single artist; Turner willed most of the paintings and watercolors here to the nation.

Also on display are the works of many major 19th- and 20th-century painters, including Paul Nash. In the modern collections are works by Matisse, Dalí, Modigliani, Munch, Bonnard, and Picasso. Truly remarkable are the several enormous abstract canvases by Mark Rothko, the group of paintings and sculptures by Giacometti, and the paintings of one of England's best-known modern artists, the late Francis Bacon. Sculptures by Henry Moore and Barbara Hepworth are also occasionally displayed.

Insider's tip: After you've seen all the grand art, don't hasten away so quickly. Drop in to the Tate Gallery Shop for some of the best art books and the most high-quality printed postcards in London. As a whimsical touch, the gallery sells T-shirts with art masterpieces printed on them. Those ubiquitous Tate Gallery canvas bags seen all over London are also sold here, as are the town's best art posters. Invite your friends for tea at the Coffee Shop with its excellent cakes and pastries or lunch at the Tate Britain Restaurant (p. 143). You get to enjoy good food, Rex Whistler art, and the best and most reasonably priced wine list in London.

Millbank, SW1. © 020/7887-8000. www.tate.org.uk. Free admission; special exhibitions sometimes incur a charge varying from £3–£8.50 ($5.55–$16). Daily 10am–5:50pm. Tube: Pimlico.

Tate Modern 🟆🟆🟆 In a transformed Bankside Power Station in Southwark, this museum, which opened in 2000, draws some two million visitors a year to see the greatest collection of international 20th-century art in Britain. How would we rate the collection? At the same level of the Pompidou in Paris with a slight edge over New York's Guggenheim. Of course, New York's Museum of Modern Art remains in a class of its own. Tate Modern is also viewer friendly with eye-level hangings. All the big painting stars are here, a whole galaxy ranging from Dalí to Duchamp, from Giacometti to Matisse and Mondrian, from Picasso and Pollock to Rothko and Warhol. The Modern is also a gallery of 21st-century art, displaying new and exciting art recently created.

You can cross the Millennium Bridge, a pedestrian-only walk from the steps of St. Paul's, over the Thames to the new gallery. Or else you can take the **Tate to Tate** boat (© **020/7887-8888**), which takes art lovers on a 18-minute journey across the Thames from the Tate Britain to the Tate Modern, with a stop at the London Eye and the Saatchi Gallery. A day pass costs £5 ($9.25) for adults and £2.50 ($4.65) for children. Leaving from Millbank Pier, this catamaran is decorated by the trademark colorful dots of that *enfant terrible* artist Damien Hirst.

The Tate Modern makes extensive use of glass for both its exterior and interior, offering panoramic views. Galleries are arranged over three levels and provide different kinds of space for display. Instead of exhibiting art chronologically and by school, the Tate Modern, in a radical break from tradition, takes a thematic approach. This allows displays to cut across movements.

Bankside, SE1. © 020/7887-8008. www.tate.org.uk. Free admission. Sun–Thurs 10am–6pm; Fri–Sat 10am–10pm. Tube: Southwark.

The National Gallery ★★★   This stately neoclassical building contains an unrivaled collection of Western art that spans 7 centuries—from the late 13th to the early 20th—and covers every great European school. For sheer skill of display and arrangement, it surpasses its counterparts in Paris, New York, Madrid, and Amsterdam.

The largest part of the collection is devoted to the Italians, including the Sienese, Venetian, and Florentine masters. On display are such works as Leonardo's *Virgin of the Rocks;* Titian's *Bacchus and Ariadne;* Giorgione's *Adoration of the Magi;* and unforgettable canvases by Bellini, Veronese, Botticelli, and Tintoretto. Botticelli's *Venus and Mars* is eternally enchanting.

Of the early-Gothic works, the Wilton Diptych (French or English school, late 14th c.) is the rarest treasure; it depicts Richard II being introduced to the Madonna and Child by John the Baptist and the Saxon kings, Edmund and Edward the Confessor.

And don't forget the Spanish giants: El Greco's *Agony in the Garden* and portraits by Goya and Velázquez. The Flemish-Dutch school is represented by Brueghel, Jan van Eyck, Vermeer, Rubens, and de Hooch; the Rembrandts include two of his immortal self-portraits. None of van Eyck's art creates quite the stir that the *Arnolfini Portrait* does. You probably studied this painting from 1434 in Art History 101. The stunning work depicts Giovanni di Nicolao Arnolfini and his wife, who is not pregnant as is often thought. She is merely holding up her full-skirted dress in the contemporary fashion. An immense French Impressionist and post-Impressionist collection includes works by Manet, Monet, Degas, Renoir, and Cézanne. Particularly charming is the peep-show cabinet by Hoogstraten in one of the Dutch rooms: It's like spying through a keyhole.

The National Gallery does have some fine 18th-century British masterpieces, including works by Hogarth, Gainsborough, Reynolds, Constable, and Turner, but the Tate Britain remains the museum to visit if you're looking for British art.

Guided tours of The National Gallery are offered daily at 11:30am and 2:30pm with an extra tour at 6:30pm on Wednesday. To enhance your experience, a Gallery Guide Soundtrack is available. A portable CD player provides audio information on paintings of your choice with the push of a button. Although this service is free, voluntary contributions are appreciated.

Insider's tip: The National Gallery has a computer information center where you can design a personal tour map. The computer room, located in the Micro Gallery, includes a dozen hands-on workstations. The online system lists 2,200 paintings and has background notes for each artwork. The program includes four indexes that are cross-referenced for your convenience. Using a touch-screen computer, you design your own personalized tour by selecting a maximum of 10 paintings you would like to view. Once you have made your choices, you print a personal tour map with your selections; this mapping service is free.

North side of Trafalgar Sq., WC2. © 020/7747-2885. www.nationalgallery.org.uk. Free admission. Thurs–Tues 10am–6pm; Wed 10am–9pm. Tube: Charing Cross, Embankment, or Leicester Sq.

Kensington Palace ★   Once the residence of British monarchs, Kensington Palace hasn't been the official home of reigning kings since George II. It was acquired in 1689 by joint monarchs William III and Mary II as an escape from the damp royal rooms along the Thames. Since the end of the 18th century, the palace has been home to various members of the royal family, and the State Apartments are open for tours.

It was here, in 1837, that a young Victoria was roused from her sleep with the news that her uncle, William IV, had died and that she was now queen of England. You can view a nostalgic collection of Victoriana, including some of her memorabilia. In the apartments of Queen Mary II is a striking 17th-century writing cabinet inlaid with tortoiseshell. Paintings from the Royal Collection line the walls of the apartments. A rare 1750 lady's court dress and splendid examples of male court dress from the 18th century are on display in rooms adjacent to the State Apartments. The former apartment of the late Princess Margaret has opened to the public as an education center and an exhibition space for royal ceremonial dress. The palace was once also the home of Diana, princess of Wales, and her two sons (Harry and William now live with their father at St. James's Palace), and is probably best known for the millions of flowers placed in front of it during the days following Diana's death.

Be warned in advance: You don't get to see the apartments where Princess Di lived or where both Di and Charles lived until they separated.

Kensington Gardens are open daily to the public for leisurely strolls through the manicured grounds and around the Round Pond. One of the most famous sights is the controversial **Albert Memorial** 𝕬𝕬, a lasting tribute not only to Victoria's consort but also to the questionable artistic taste of the Victorian era. A wonderful afternoon tea is offered in The Orangery (p. 155).

The Broad Walk, Kensington Gardens, W8. ℂ 087/0751-5170. www.kensington-palace.org.uk. Admission £11 ($19) adults, £7 ($13) students and seniors, £6.50 ($12) children, free under 5, £31 ($57) family. Mar–Oct daily 10am–7pm; Nov–Feb daily 10am–6pm. Tube: Queensway or Notting Hill Gate; High St. Kensington on south side.

St. Paul's Cathedral 𝕬𝕬𝕬 That St. Paul's survived World War II at all is a miracle, because it was badly hit twice during the early years of the bombardment of London. But St. Paul's is accustomed to calamity, having been burned down three times and destroyed once by invading Norsemen. It was during the Great Fire of 1666 that the old St. Paul's was razed, making way for a new structure designed by Sir Christopher Wren and built between 1675 and 1710. It's the architectural genius's ultimate masterpiece.

The classical dome of St. Paul's dominates The City's square mile. The golden cross atop it is 110m (365 ft.) above the ground; the golden ball on which the cross rests measures 2m (6 ft.) in diameter yet looks like a marble from below. Surrounding the interior of the dome is the Whispering Gallery, an acoustic marvel in which the faintest whisper can be heard clearly on the opposite side—so be careful of what you say. You can climb to the top of the dome for a spectacular 360-degree view of London.

Although the interior looks almost bare, it houses a vast number of monuments. The duke of Wellington (of Waterloo fame) is entombed here, as are Lord Nelson and Sir Christopher Wren himself. At the east end of the cathedral is the American Memorial Chapel, honoring the 28,000 U.S. service personnel who lost their lives while stationed in Britain in World War II.

Guided tours last 1½ hours and include parts of the cathedral not open to the general public. Tours run Monday through Saturday at 11, 11:30am, 1:30, and 2pm. Recorded tours lasting 45 minutes are available throughout the day.

St. Paul's is an Anglican cathedral with daily services at the following times: matins at 7:30am Monday to Saturday; Holy Communion Monday through

---

Moments **Roses Are Red**

One of the most enjoyable aspects of a spring visit to London is saunter-ing through the free gardens of St. Paul's when the roses are in bloom.

Saturday at 8am and 12:30pm; and evensong Monday through Saturday at 5pm. On Sunday, Holy Communion is at 8 and 11:30am, matins at 10:15am, and evensong at 3:15pm. Admission charges don't apply if you're attending a service.

St. Paul's Churchyard, EC4. ℂ 020/7236-4128. www.stpauls.co.uk. Cathedral and galleries £7 ($13) adults, £6 ($11) seniors and students, £3 ($5.55) children 6–16. Guided tours £2.50 ($4.65) adults, £2 ($3.70) students and seniors, £1 ($1.85) children; recorded tours £3.50 ($6.50). Free for children 5 and under. Sight-seeing Mon–Sat 8:30am–4pm. No sightseeing Sun (services only). Tube: St. Paul's.

Clarence House 🌟🌟   From 1953 until her death in 2002, the Queen Mother lived at Clarence House in a wing of St. James's Palace. The John Nash–designed residence was constructed between 1825 and 1927. Today, it is the official resi-dence of the Prince of Wales, and is open to the public only during a specified period of the year (see below). The present Queen Elizabeth and the Duke of Edinburgh lived here following their marriage in 1947.

After the death of the Queen Mother, the house was refurbished and redeco-rated, with antiques and art added from the royal collection. You can take a guided tour of five of the elegant staterooms, where much of the queen's collec-tion of works of art and furniture are on display, along with pieces added by Prince Charles. The queen had an impressive collection of 20th-century British art, including works by John Piper, Augustus John, and Graham Sutherland. She also was known for her superb collection of Fabergé and English porcelain and silver, especially pieces from her family collection (the Bowes-Lyon family).

Stable Yard Gate, SW1. ℂ 020/7766-7303. www.royal.gov.uk. Admission £5.50 ($10) adults, £3 ($5.55) ages 5–17, free 4 and under. Aug 4–Oct 17 (dates subject to change—call first) daily 9:30am–6pm (last admission at 5pm). Tube: Greek Park or St. James's Park.

Victoria and Albert Museum 🌟🌟🌟   The Victoria and Albert (V&A) is the greatest museum in the world devoted to the decorative arts. It's also one of the liveliest and most imaginative museums in London—where else would you find the quintessential "little black dress" in the permanent collection?

The medieval holdings include such treasures as the Early English Gloucester Candlestick; the Byzantine Veroli Casket, with its ivory panels based on Greek plays; and the Syon Cope, a highly valued embroidery made in England in the early 14th century. An area devoted to Islamic art houses the Ardabil Carpet from 16th-century Persia.

The V&A houses the largest collection of Renaissance sculpture outside Italy. A highlight of the 16th-century collection is the marble group *Neptune with Triton* by Bernini. The cartoons by Raphael, which were conceived as designs for tapestries for the Sistine Chapel, are owned by the queen and are on display here. A most unusual, huge, and impressive exhibit is the Cast Courts, life-size plaster models of ancient and medieval statuary and architecture.

The museum has the greatest collection of Indian art outside India, plus Chinese and Japanese galleries as well. In complete contrast are suites of English furniture, metalwork, and ceramics, and a superb collection of portrait miniatures, including the one Hans Holbein the Younger made of Anne of Cleves for the ben-efit of Henry VIII, who was again casting around for a suitable wife.

The Dress Collection includes corsetry through the ages that's sure to make you wince. There's also a remarkable collection of musical instruments.

Fifteen galleries—called **The British Galleries** ★★★—present the story of British design from 1500 to 1900. From Chippendale to Morris, all of the top British designers are featured in some 3,000 exhibits displayed. Star exhibits range from the 5m (17-ft.) high Melville Bed (1697) with its luxurious wild silk damask and red silk velvet hangings, to 19th-century classics such as furniture by Charles Rennie Mackintosh. One of the most prized possessions is the "Great Bed of Ware," mentioned in Shakespeare's *Twelfth Night,* and the wedding suite of James II.

Insider's tip: In the winter of 2004, V&A opened a suite of five renovated painting galleries that were originally built in 1850. A trio of these galleries focus on British landscapes as seen through the eyes of Turner, Constable, and others. Constable's oil sketches were donated by his daughter, Isabel, in 1888. Another gallery showcases the bequest of Constantine Ionides, a Victorian collector, with its cold masters such as Botticelli, Delacroix, Degas, Tintoretto, and Ingres. There's even a piano here designed by the famous Edward Burne-Jones, which once belonged to Ionides's brother.

The V&A is home to the best museum shop in London, selling cards, books, and the usual items, along with reproductions from the museum archives.

Cromwell Rd., SW7. ℂ 020/7942-2000. www.vam.ac.uk. Free admission. Daily 10am–5:45pm (Wed until 10pm). Tube: South Kensington.

Trafalgar Square One of the landmark squares of London, Trafalgar Square honors one of England's great military heroes, Horatio Viscount Nelson (1758–1805), who died at the Battle of Trafalgar. Although he suffered from sea-sickness all his life, he went to sea at the age of 12 and was an admiral at the age of 39. Lord Nelson was a hero of the Battle of Calvi in 1794 where he lost an eye, the Battle of Santa Cruz in 1797 where he lost an arm, and the Battle of Trafalgar in 1805 where he lost his life.

The square today is dominated by a 44m (145-ft.) granite column, the work of E. H. Baily in 1843. The column looks down Whitehall toward the Old Admiralty, where Lord Nelson's body lay in state. The figure of the naval hero towers 5m (17 ft.) high, not bad for a man who stood 1.5m (5 ft. 4 in.) in real life. The capital is of bronze cast from cannons recovered from the wreck of the *Royal George.* Queen Victoria's favorite animal painter, Sir Edward Landseer, added the four lions at the base of the column in 1868. The pools and fountains were not added until 1939, the last work of Sir Edwin Lutyens.

Political demonstrations still take place at the square and around the column, which has the most aggressive pigeons in London. These birds will even land on your head or perform less desirable stunts. Actually, the birds are part of a long feathery tradition, for this site was once used by Edward I (1239–1307) to keep his birds of prey. Called "Longshanks," he came here often before he died of dysentery in 1307. Richard II, who ruled from 1377 to 1399, kept goshawks and falcons here, too. By the time of Henry VII, who ruled from 1485 to 1509, the square was used as the site of the royal stables. Sir Charles Barry, who designed the Houses of Parliament, created the present square in the 1830s.

The good news is that Trafalgar Square has become more user friendly. A grand staircase has replaced the street between the square and the National Gallery. That's not all: Pedestrian crossings on the other streets enveloping the square make approaching it on foot less risky. Before, you were likely to get run

Frommer's Favorite London Experiences

Cruising London's Waterways. Tube: Charing Cross. In addition to the Thames, London is riddled with an antique canal system, complete with towpath walks, bridges, and wharves. Replaced by the railroad, the system was forgotten until recently rediscovered by a new generation. An urban renewal effort has restored the system, with bridges painted and repaired, and towpaths cleaned up. See "Organized Tours," later in this chapter.

Viewing the Turners at the Tate. Upon his death in 1851, J. M. W. Turner bequeathed his personal collection of 19,000 watercolors and some 300 paintings to the people of Britain. He wanted his finished works, some 100 paintings, displayed under one roof. Today at the Tate, you get not only Turner but also glimpses of the Thames through the museum's windows. How appropriate—the artist lived and died on its banks in Chelsea and painted the river in its many changing moods.

Enjoying a Traditional Afternoon Tea. Nothing is more typically British, and it's a great way to spend an afternoon. We suggest our favorite places for tea in chapter 4.

Rowing on the Serpentine. When the weather is right, we like to head to this 17-hectare (41-acre) artificial lake, dating from 1730 and located in Hyde Park. A stream was dammed to create the artificial lake, whose name derives from its winding, snakelike shape. At the Boathouse, you can rent a boat by the hour. With the right companion, it's one of the most idyllic ways to spend a sunny London afternoon.

Wandering through Covent Garden. George Bernard Shaw got his inspiration for *Pygmalion* here, where the character of Eliza Doolittle sold violets to wealthy opera goers and became a household name around the world. The old fruit and vegetable market, with its Cockney cauliflower peddlers and butchers in blood-soaked aprons, is long gone. But what's left is just as interesting: Covent Garden today is London's best example of urban renewal. An antiques market is in the piazza on Monday, a crafts market Tuesday through Saturday.

Watching the Sunset at Waterloo Bridge. Waterloo Bridge is the best place in London to watch the sun set over Westminster. From here, you can also see the last rays of sunlight bounce off the city spires in the East End.

Spending a Night at the West End Theater. London is the theatrical capital of the world. The live stage offers a unique combination of variety, accessibility, and economy—and a look at next year's Broadway hit.

Crawling the London Pubs. With some 5,000 pubs within the city limits, you would be crawling indeed if you tried to have a drink in each of them. Enough traditional ones remain, especially in central London, to make it worthwhile to go on a crawl, perhaps fortifying yourself with a ploughman's lunch or a plate of shepherd's pie.

over by a speeding vehicle. Of course, the summer fun of concerts, street entertainment, and open-air cafe-sitting will continue.

To the southeast of the square, at 36 Craven St., stands a house once occupied by Benjamin Franklin when he was a general of the Philadelphia Academy
(1757–74). On the north side of the square rises The National Gallery, constructed in the 1830s. In front of the building is a copy of a statue of George
Washington by J. A. Houdon.

National Portrait Gallery ★★   In a gallery of remarkable and unremarkable
pictures (they're collected here for their notable subjects rather than their artistic quality), a few paintings tower over the rest, including Sir Joshua Reynolds's
first portrait of Samuel Johnson ("a man of most dreadful appearance"). Among
the best are Nicholas Hilliard's miniature of a handsome Sir Walter Raleigh and
a full-length Elizabeth I, along with the Holbein cartoon of Henry VIII. A portrait of William Shakespeare (with a gold earring, no less) by an unknown artist
bears the claim of being the "most authentic contemporary likeness" of its subject. One of the most famous pictures in the gallery is the group portrait of the
Brontë sisters (Charlotte, Emily, and Anne) painted by their brother, Bramwell.
An idealized portrait of Lord Byron by Thomas Phillips is also on display.

The galleries of Victorian and early-20th-century portraits were radically
redesigned recently. Occupying the whole first floor, they display portraits from
1837 (when Victoria took the throne) to present day; later 20th-century portraiture includes major works by such artists as Warhol and Hambling. Some of
the more flamboyant personalities of the past 2 centuries are on show: T. S.
Eliot, Disraeli, Macmillan, Sir Richard Burton, Elizabeth Taylor, Baroness
Thatcher, and our two favorites: G. F. Watts's famous portrait of his great actress
wife, Ellen Terry, and Vanessa Bell's portrait of her sister, Virginia Woolf. The
late Princess Diana is on the Royal Landing; this portrait seems to attract the
most viewers.

In 2000, Queen Elizabeth opened the Ondaatje Wing of the gallery, granting
the gallery more than 50% more exhibition space. The most intriguing of the
new space is the splendid Tudor Gallery, opening with portraits of Richard III
and Henry II, his conqueror in the Battle of Bosworth in 1485, as well as a portrait of Shakespeare that the gallery first acquired in 1856. Rooms lead through
centuries of English monarchs, with some literary and artistic figures thrown in.
A Balcony Gallery displays more recent figures whose fame has lasted longer
than Warhol's predicted 15 minutes. This new wing certainly taps into the cult
of the celebrity.

St. Martin's Place, WC2. ✆ 020/7306-0055. www.npg.org.uk. Free admission; fee charged for certain temporary exhibitions. Mon–Wed 10am–6pm; Thurs–Fri 10am–9pm; Sat–Sun 10am–6pm. Tube: Charing Cross or
Leicester Sq.

Tower Bridge ★★   This is one of the world's most celebrated landmarks and
possibly the most photographed and painted bridge on earth. In spite of its
medieval appearance, Tower Bridge was actually built in 1894.

In 1993, an exhibition opened inside the bridge to commemorate its century-
old history; it takes you up the north tower to high-level walkways between the
two towers with spectacular views of St. Paul's, the Tower of London, and the
Houses of Parliament—a photographer's dream. You're then led down the south
tower and on to the bridge's original engine room, with its Victorian boilers and
steam-pumping engines that used to raise and lower the bridge for ships to pass.
Exhibits in the bridge's towers use advanced technology, including animatronic
characters, video, and computers to illustrate the history of the bridge. Admission

Finds **Drake's Long Voyage**

As you're strolling along the riverside, you come upon the old dock of St. Mary Overie, SE1. Here to your delight is an exact replica of the *Golden Hinde,* in which Sir Francis Drake circumnavigated the globe. It's amazingly tiny for such an around-the-world voyage. But this actual ship has sailed around the world some two dozen times, exploring both oceans and the American coast. Visits are daily from 10am to 5pm, Guided tours cost £3.50 ($6.50) for adults, £3 ($5.55) for students and seniors, and £2.50 ($4.65) for children. For information, call ℂ **020/7403-0123** or visit www.goldenhinde.co.uk.

to the **Tower Bridge Exhibition** is £5.50 ($10) for adults, £4.25 ($7.85) for seniors and students, and £3 ($5.55) for children 5 to 15; family discounts available; it's free for children 5 and under. Open daily from 10am to 6pm (last entrance 5:30pm). Closed Christmas Eve and Christmas Day.

At Tower Bridge, SE1. ℂ **020/7403-3761.** www.towerbridge.org.uk. Tube: Tower Hill or London Bridge.

2 More Attractions

OFFICIAL LONDON

Whitehall ✸, the seat of the British government, grew up on the grounds of Whitehall Palace and was turned into a royal residence by Henry VIII, who snatched it from its former occupant, Cardinal Wolsey. Whitehall extends south from Trafalgar Square to Parliament Square. Along it you'll find the Home Office, the Old Admiralty Building, and the Ministry of Defence.

Visitors today can see the **Cabinet War Rooms** ✸, the bombproof bunker suite of rooms, just as they were when abandoned by Winston Churchill and the British government at the end of World War II. You can see the Map Room with its huge wall maps, the Atlantic map a mass of pinholes (each hole represents at least one convoy). Next door is Churchill's bedroom-cum-office, which has a bed and a desk with two BBC microphones on it for his famous speech broadcasts that stirred the nation. In 2003, nine more underground Cabinet War Rooms were restored and open to the public, including the Chiefs of Staff map room, Churchill's kitchen and dining room, Sir Winston's private detectives' room, and Mrs. Churchill's bedroom. There's everything here from a pencil cartoon of Hitler to a mousetrap in the kitchen to the original chamber pots under the beds (they had no flush toilets).

The **Transatlantic Telephone Room,** its full title, is little more than a broom closet, but it housed the Bell Telephone Company's special scrambler phone, called *Sigsaly,* and it was where Churchill conferred with Roosevelt. Visitors are provided with a step-by-step personal sound guide, providing a detailed account of each room's function and history.

The entrance to the War Rooms is by Clive Steps at the end of King Charles Street, SW1 (ℂ **020/7930-6961;** www.iwm.org.uk/cabinet; Tube: Westminster or St. James's), off Whitehall near Big Ben. Admission is £7.50 ($14) for adults, £6 ($11) for students and seniors, and free for children under 16. The rooms are open April through September daily from 9:30am to 6pm, and October through March daily from 10am to 6pm (last admission is 5:15pm year-round); closed during Christmas holidays. Tube: Westminster or St. James's.

At the Cenotaph (honoring both world wars' dead), turn down unpretentious **Downing Street** to the modest little town house at no. 10, flanked by two bobbies. Walpole was the first prime minister to live here; Churchill was the most famous. But Margaret Thatcher was around longer than any of them.

Nearby, north of Downing Street, is the **Horse Guards Building** ⚡, Whitehall (no phone; Tube: Westminster), now the headquarters of the horse guards of the Household Division and London District. There has been a guard change here since 1649, when the site was the entrance to the old Palace of Whitehall. You can watch the Queen's Life Guards ceremony at 11am Monday through Saturday (10:10am Sun). You can also see the hourly smaller **change of the guard,** when mounted troopers are changed. And at 4pm, you can watch the evening inspection, when 10 unmounted troopers and two mounted troopers assemble in the courtyard.

Across the street is Inigo Jones's **Banqueting House,** Palace of Whitehall, Horse Guards Avenue (© **020/7515-5178;** Tube: Westminster), site of the execution of Charles I. William and Mary accepted the crown of England here, but they preferred to live at Kensington Palace. The **Banqueting House** was part of Whitehall Palace, which burned to the ground in 1698, but the ceremonial hall escaped razing. Its most notable feature today is an allegorical ceiling painted by Peter Paul Rubens. Admission to the Banqueting House is £4 ($7.40) for adults, £3 ($5.55) for seniors and students, £2.60 ($4.80) for children under 16, and free for children under 5. It's open Monday through Saturday from 10am to 5pm (last admission 4:30pm). Tube: Westminster or Embankment.

LEGAL LONDON

The smallest borough in London, bustling Holborn (pronounced *Ho*-burn) is often referred to as Legal London, home of the city's barristers, solicitors, and law clerks. It also embraces the university district of Bloomsbury. Holborn, which houses the ancient **Inns of Courts**—Gray's Inn, Lincoln's Inn, Middle Temple, and Inner Temple—was severely damaged during World War II bombing raids. The razed buildings were replaced with modern offices, but the borough still retains pockets of its former days.

At the 60 or more **Law Courts** presently in use on The Strand, all civil and some criminal cases are heard. Designed by G. E. Street, the neo-Gothic buildings (1874–82) have more than 1,000 rooms and 5.5km (3½ miles) of corridors. Sculptures of Christ, King Solomon, and King Alfred grace the front door; Moses is depicted at the back. Admission is free, and courts are open during sessions Monday through Friday from 10am to 4:30pm. No cameras, tape recorders, video cameras, or cellphones are allowed during sessions. Tube: Holborn or Temple.

The court known as the **Old Bailey,** on Newgate Street, EC4 (© **020/ 7248-3277**), replaced the infamous Newgate Prison, once the scene of public hangings and other forms of "public entertainment." It's fascinating to watch the bewigged barristers presenting their cases to the high court judges. Entry is strictly on a first-arrival basis, and guests line up outside. Courts 1 to 4, 17, and 18 are entered from Newgate Street, and the balance from Old Bailey (the street). To get here, take the Tube to Temple, Chancery Lane, or St. Paul's. Travel east on Fleet Street, which along the way becomes Ludgate Hill. Cross Ludgate Circus and turn left to the Old Bailey, a domed structure with the figure of Justice standing atop it. Admission is free; children under 14 are not admitted, and ages 14 to 16 must be accompanied by adult. No cameras, tape recorders, or

Official London: Westminster & Whitehall

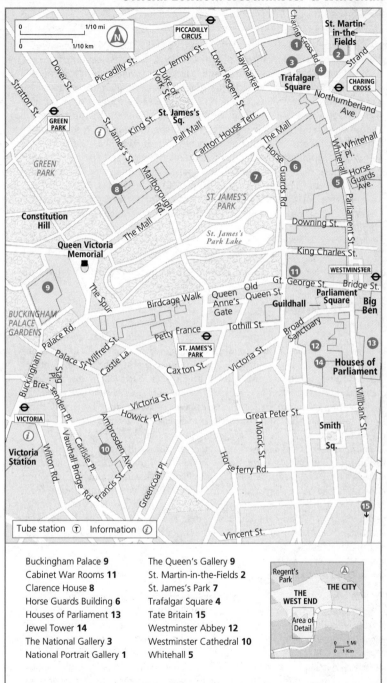

Buckingham Palace **9**
Cabinet War Rooms **11**
Clarence House **8**
Horse Guards Building **6**
Houses of Parliament **13**
Jewel Tower **14**
The National Gallery **3**
National Portrait Gallery **1**

The Queen's Gallery **9**
St. Martin-in-the-Fields **2**
St. James's Park **7**
Trafalgar Square **4**
Tate Britain **15**
Westminster Abbey **12**
Westminster Cathedral **10**
Whitehall **5**

Finds   **A City of Wine**

At **Vinopolis**, 1 Bank End, Park Street, SE1 (℃ **0870/241-4040;** www.vinopolis.co.uk), you can partake of London's largest selection of wine sold by the glass. On the South Bank, this "city of wine" lies in cavernous railway arches created in Victoria's era. The bacchanalian attraction was created at the cost of £23 million, in a multimedia format, so it seems as though you are journeying through some of the earth's most prestigious wine regions. You can even drive a Vespa through the Tuscan countryside or take a "flight" over the vineyards of Australia. The price of entrance includes free tastings of five premium wines, and an on-site shop sells almost any item related to the grape. The site also boasts a good restaurant (see Cantina Vinopolis on p. 148). Admission is £13 ($23) for adults, free for ages 5 to 15, and £12 ($21) for seniors. Open Monday, Friday, and Saturday noon to 9pm, and Tuesday, Thursday, and Sunday noon to 6pm.

cellphones are allowed. Hours are Monday through Friday from 9:30am to 1pm and 2 to 4pm. The best time to line up is 9am.

MORE MUSEUMS

Apsley House 🍴   The former town house of the Iron Duke, the British general (1769–1852) who defeated Napoleon at the Battle of Waterloo and later became prime minister, this building was designed by Robert Adam and constructed in the late 18th century. Wellington once retreated behind the walls of Apsley House, fearing an attack from Englishmen outraged by his autocratic opposition to reform. In the vestibule is a colossal marble statue of Napoleon by Canova—ironic, to say the least; it was presented to the duke by King George IV. In addition to the famous *Waterseller of Seville* by Velázquez, the Wellington collection includes works by Correggio, Jan Steen, and Pieter de Hooch.

Insider's tip: Apsley House has some of the finest silver and porcelain pieces in Europe. Grateful to Wellington for saving their thrones, European monarchs endowed him with treasures. Head for the Plate and China Room on the ground floor first. The Sèvres Egyptian service was intended as a divorce present from Napoleon to Josephine, but she refused it. Eventually, Louis XVIII of France presented it to Wellington. The Portuguese Silver Service in the dining room was created between 1812 and 1816: It has been hailed as the single greatest artifact of Portuguese neoclassical silver.

Hyde Park Corner, W1. ℃ 020/7499-5676. Admission £4.50 ($8.35) adults, £3 ($5.55) students, free for children under 18 and seniors over 60. Tues–Sun 11am–5pm. Tube: Hyde Park Corner.

British Library 🍴🍴   This is one of the world's greatest libraries, with a collection of some 12 million books, manuscripts, and other items, moved from The British Museum to its own home here in St. Pancras. In the new building, you get modernistic beauty rather than the fading glamour and the ghosts of Karl Marx, Thackeray, and Virginia Woolf of the famous old library at The British Museum. Academics, students, writers, and bookworms visit from all over the world. On a recent visit, we sat next to a student researching the history of pubs.

The bright, roomy interior is far more inviting than the rather dull redbrick exterior suggests. The most spectacular room is the Humanities Reading Room, constructed on three levels and with daylight filtered through the ceiling.

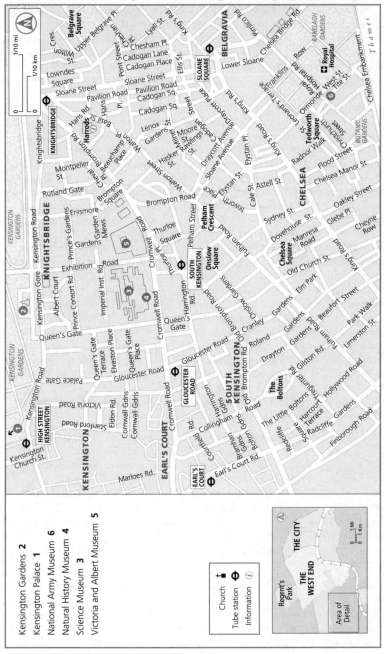

Kensington Gardens **2**
Kensington Palace **1**
National Army Museum **6**
Natural History Museum **4**
Science Museum **3**
Victoria and Albert Museum **5**

Church
Tube station
Information

Regent's
Park

THE CITY

THE
WEST END

Area of
Detail

0   1 Mi
0   1 Km

The fascinating collection includes such items of historical and literary interest as two of the four surviving copies of the Magna Carta (1215), a Gutenberg Bible, Nelson's last letter to Lady Hamilton, and the journals of Captain Cook. Almost every major author—Dickens, Jane Austen, Charlotte Brontë, Keats, and hundreds of others—is represented in the section devoted to English literature. Beneath Roubiliac's 1758 statue of Shakespeare stands a case of documents relating to the Bard, including a mortgage bearing his signature and a copy of the First Folio of 1623. There's also an unrivaled collection of philatelic items.

Visitors can also view the Diamond Sutra, dating from 868, said to be the oldest surviving printed book. Using headphones set up around the room, you can also hear thrilling audio snippets such as James Joyce reading a passage from *Finnegans Wake*. Curiosities include the earliest known tape of a birdcall, dating from 1889. Particularly intriguing is an exhibition called "Turning the Pages." You can, for example, electronically read a complete Leonardo da Vinci notebook, putting your hands on a special computer screen that flips from one page to another. There is a copy of *The Canterbury Tales* from 1410, and even manuscripts from *Beowulf* (ca. 1000). Illuminated texts from some of the oldest known Biblical displays include the *Codex Sinaitticus* and *Codex Alexandrius*, 3rd-century Greek gospels. In the Historical Documents section are epistles by everybody from Henry VIII to Napoleon, from Elizabeth I to Churchill. In the music displays, you can seek out works by Beethoven, Handel, Stravinsky, and Lennon and McCartney. An entire day spent here will only scratch the surface.

Walking tours of the library cost £6 ($11) for adults or £4.50 ($8.65) for seniors, students, and children. They are conducted Monday, Wednesday, and Friday at 3pm. A tour with a visit to one of the reading rooms is conducted Saturday 10:30am and 3pm and Sunday at 11:30am and 3pm. The cost of these tours are £7 ($13) for adults, £5.50 ($10) for students and seniors, and reservations are advised 3 weeks in advance.

96 Euston Rd., NW1. 📞 020/7412-7000. www.bl.uk. Free admission. Mon and Wed–Fri 9:30am–6pm; Tues 9:30am–8pm; Sat 9:30am–5pm. Tube: King's Cross/St. Pancras or Euston.

City Hall　On the South Bank of the Thames adjacent to Tower Bridge, the mayor of London and the London Assembly got a new home in 2002. A gleaming, egg-shaped building, a 10-story steel-and-glass structure, was dedicated by Her Majesty. The new home for city government has become London's latest—some say, most controversial—landmark. Half of City Hall is open to the public who'd like to come in and look around. The views from its rooftop gallery are worth the trek over to the South Bank. An exhibition space highlights changing cultural exhibits, and there is also a cafe on-site.

The Queen's Walk, SE1. 📞 020/7983-4100. www.london.gov.uk. Free admission. Visitors Centre daily 8am–8pm; cafe daily 9:30am–5pm. Tube: London Bridge.

Courtauld Gallery　The nucleus of this collection was acquired by Samuel Courtauld who died in 1947 leaving his collection to the University of London. Today it houses the biggest collection of Impressionist and post-Impressionist paintings in Britain, with masterpieces by Monet, Manet, Degas, Renoir, Cézanne, van Gogh, and Gauguin. The gallery also has a superb collection of old-master paintings and drawings, including works by Rubens and Michelangelo; early-Italian paintings, ivories, and majolica; the Lee collection of old masters; and early-20th-century English, French, and British paintings.

The new galleries on the second floor display a series of paintings and sculptures, some 100 pieces of art from the late 19th and 20th centuries, including

Value **Museum Discounts**

A tourist ticket provides admission to more than 50 attractions in and around London, plus a pocket guidebook (free travel on public transport is available at an additional cost). **The London Pass** costs £23 ($43) for 1 day, £44 ($81) for 3 days, or £61 ($113) for 6 days (children pay £15/$28, £29/$54, or £41/$76), and includes free admission to St. Paul's Cathedral, HMS *Belfast,* the Jewish Museum, the Tower of London, and many more. Go to **www.londonpass.com** for more information.

an outstanding grouping of Fauve paintings along with art by everybody from Matisse to Dufy, along with a remarkable series of paintings and drawings by Kandinsky. We come here at least once every season to revisit one work in particular: Manet's exquisite *A Bar at the Folies-Bergère* ✰. Many of the paintings are displayed without glass, giving the gallery a more intimate feeling than most. This gallery is but one of three major attractions at Somerset House. For information about the other attractions, such as the Gilbert Collection and the Heritage Rooms, see below.

Somerset House, The Strand, WC2. © 020/7848-2777. www.courtauld.ac.uk. Admission £5 ($9.25) adults, £4 ($7.40) seniors and students, free for children under 18. Free admission Mon 10am–2pm. Daily 10am–6pm; last admission 5:15pm. Tube: Temple or Covent Garden, Charing Cross, Holborn.

Dalí Universe ✰ *(Finds)*   Next to the "London Eye," this exhibition is devoted to the remarkable Spanish artist, Salvador Dalí (1904–89), and is one of London's newest attractions. Featuring more than 500 works of art, including the Mae West Lips sofa, the exhibitions are divided into a trio of themed areas: Sensuality and Femininity, Religion and Mythology, and Dreams and Fantasy. Showcased are important Dalí sculptures, rare graphics, watercolors, and even furnishings and jewelry. You can feast on such surreal works as Dalí's monumental oil painting for the Hitchcock movie, *Spellbound,* or view a series of original watercolors and collages including the mystical Tarot Cards, and see the world's largest collection of rare Dalí graphics, illustrating themes from literature.

County Hall, Riverside Building, South Bank, SE1. © 020/7620-2720. www.daliuniverse.com. Admission £8.50 ($16) adults, £7 ($13) students and seniors, £5.50 ($10) ages 8–16, £3.50 ($6.50) ages 4–7, and £23 ($43) family ticket. Daily 10am–5:30pm. Tube: Waterloo.

Gilbert Collection ✰✰✰ *(Finds)*   In 2000, Somerset House became the permanent home for the Gilbert Collection of decorative arts, one of the most important bequests ever made to England. Sir Arthur Gilbert made his gift of gold, silver, mosaics, and gold snuffboxes to the nation in 1996, at which time the value was estimated at £75 million. The collection of some 800 objects in three fields (gold and silver, mosaics, and gold snuffboxes) is among the most distinguished in the world. The silver collection here is arguably better than the one at the V&A. The array of mosaics is among the most comprehensive ever gathered, with Roman and Florentine examples dating from the 16th to the 19th centuries. The gold and silver collection has exceptional breadth, ranging from the 15th to the 19th centuries, spanning India to South America. It is strong in masterpieces of great 18th-century silversmiths, such as Paul de Lamerie. Such exhibits as the Maharajah pieces, the "Gold Crown," and Catherine the Great's Royal Gates are fabulous. The gallery also displays one of the most representative collections of gold snuffboxes in the world, with some 200 examples. Some of the snuffboxes were owned by Louis XV,

Frederick the Great, and Napoleon. The Gilbert Collection is only one of three major museums and galleries at Somerset House. For recommendations of the other two, see the Courtauld Gallery (above) or the Hermitage Rooms below.

Somerset House, The Strand WC2. (© 020/7240-9400. www.gilbert-collection.org.uk. Admission £5 ($9.25) adults, full-time students and under 18 free. Daily 10am–6pm. Tube: Temple, Covent Garden, Charing Cross, or Embankment.

Guildhall Art Gallery ⭐   In 1999, Queen Elizabeth opened this £70-million gallery in The City, a continuation of the original gallery, launched in 1886, that was burned down in a severe air raid in May 1941. Many famous and much-loved pictures, which for years were known only through temporary exhibitions and reproductions, are once again available for the public to see in a permanent setting. The gallery can display only 250 of the 4,000 treasures it owns at a time. A curiosity is the huge double-height wall built to accommodate Britain's largest independent oil painting, John Singleton Copley's *The Defeat of the Floating Batteries at Gibraltar, September 1782.* The Corporation of London in The City owns these works and has been collecting them since the 17th century. The most popular art is in the Victorian collection, including such well-known favorites as Millais's *My First Sermon* and *My Second Sermon,* and Landseer's *The First Leap.* There is also a large landscape of Salisbury Cathedral by John Constable. Since World War II, all paintings acquired by the gallery have concentrated on London subjects.

Guildhall Yard, E.C. 2P2EJ. (© 020/7332-3700. www.guildhall-art-gallery.org.uk. Admission £2.50 ($4.65) adults, £1 ($1.85) students and seniors, children under 16 free. Fri and after 3:30pm on every other day free. Mon–Sat 10am–5pm; Sun noon–4pm. Tube: Bank, St. Paul's, Mansion House, or Moorgate.

Hayward Gallery   Opened by Elizabeth II in 1968, this gallery presents a changing program of major contemporary and historical exhibits. It's managed by the South Bank Board, which also includes Royal Festival Hall, Queen Elizabeth Hall, and the Purcell Room. Every exhibition is accompanied by a variety of educational activities, including tours, workshops, lectures, and publications. The gallery closes between exhibitions, so call before crossing the Thames.

Belvedere Rd., South Bank, SE1. (© 020/7960-5226. www.hayward.org.uk. Admission varies but usually £8 ($15) adults, £5.50 ($10) students and seniors, free for children under 12. Hours subject to change, depending on the exhibit: Thurs, Sat–Mon 11am–7pm; Fri 11am–9pm; Tues–Wed 11am–8pm. Tube: Waterloo.

Hermitage Rooms at Somerset House ⭐⭐⭐   This is a virtual branch of St. Petersburg's State Hermitage Museum, which owns a great deal of the treasure trove left over from the czars, including possessions of art-collecting Catherine the Great. Now you don't have to go to Russia to see some of Europe's great treasures.

The rotating exhibitions will change, but you'll get to see such Czarist treasures as medals, jewelry, portraits, porcelain, clocks, and furniture. A rotating "visiting masterpiece" overshadows all the other collections. Some items that amused us on our first visit (and you are likely to see similar novelties) were a wig made entirely out of silver thread for Catherine the Great; a Wedgwood "Green Frog" table service; and two very rare Chinese silver filigree toilet sets. The rooms themselves have been designed in the style of the Winter Palace at St. Petersburg. *Note:* Because this exhibit attracts so much interest, tickets should be purchased in advance. Tickets are available from Ticketmaster at (© **020/7413-3398** (24 hr.). You can book online at **www.ticketmaster.co.uk**. The other two museums at Somerset House, the Courtauld Galleries and the Gilbert Collection, were previewed above.

Somerset House, The Strand, WC2. ℂ **020/7845-4600**. www.hermitagerooms.com. Admission £5 ($9.25) adults, £4 ($7.40) students under 16 free and seniors. Daily 10am–6pm. Tube: Temple, Covent Garden, Charing Cross, or Holborn.

London Transport Museum 👉 *Kids* This splendidly restored Victorian building once housed the flower market. Now it's home to horse buses, motor buses, trams, trolley buses, railway vehicles, models, maps, posters, photographs, and audiovisual displays that trace 200 years of London transport history. The story is enlivened by several interactive video exhibits—you can put yourself in the driver's seat of a bus or Tube train. The fabulous gift shop sells a variety of London Transport souvenirs. Much to the glee of parents, the museum has added "kidzones"—interactive programs for children so that parents can enjoy the museum without having to entertain the kids.

Covent Garden Piazza, WC2. ℂ **020/7379-6344**, or 020/7565-7299 for recorded info. www.ltmuseum. co.uk. Admission £5.95 ($11) adults, £4.50 ($8.35) students and seniors, free for children under 16 accompanied by an adult. Sat–Thurs 10am–6pm; Fri 11am–6pm (last entrance at 5:15pm). Tube: Covent Garden, Leicester Sq., Holborn, or Charing Cross.

Madame Tussauds *Overrated* *Kids* Madame Tussauds is not so much a wax museum as an enclosed amusement park. A weird, moving, sometimes terrifying (to children) collage of exhibitions, panoramas, and stage settings, it manages to be most things to most people, most of the time.

Madame Tussaud attended the court of Versailles and learned her craft in France. She personally took the death masks from the guillotined heads of Louis XVI and Marie Antoinette (which you'll find among the exhibits). She moved her original museum from Paris to England in 1802. Her exhibition has been imitated in every part of the world, but never with the realism and imagination on hand here. Madame herself molded the features of Benjamin Franklin, whom she met in Paris. All the rest—from George Washington to John F. Kennedy, Mary Queen of Scots to Sylvester Stallone—have been subjects for the same painstaking (and often breathtaking) replication.

In the well-known Chamber of Horrors—a kind of underground dungeon—are all kinds of instruments of death, along with figures of their victims. The shadowy presence of Jack the Ripper lurks in the gloom as you walk through a Victorian London street. Present-day criminals are portrayed within the confines of prison. The latest attraction to open here is "The Spirit of London," a musical ride that depicts 400 years of London's history, using special effects that include audio-animatronic figures that move and speak. Visitors take "time-taxis" that allow them to see and hear "Shakespeare" as he writes and speaks lines, be received by Queen Elizabeth I, and feel and smell the Great Fire of 1666 that destroyed London.

We've seen these changing exhibitions so many times over the years that we feel they're a bit cheesy, but we still remember the first time we were taken here as a kid. We thought it fascinating back then.

Insider's tip: To avoid the long lines, sometimes more than an hour in summer, call in advance and reserve a ticket for fast pickup at the entrance. If you don't want to bother with that, be aggressive and form a group of nine people waiting in the queue. A group of nine or more can go in almost at once through the "group door." Otherwise, go when the gallery first opens or late in the afternoon when crowds have thinned.

Marylebone Rd., NW1. ℂ **0870/400-3000**. www.madame-tussauds.co.uk. Admission £18 ($33) adults, £15 ($28) seniors, £14 ($26) children under 16. Warning: Admission prices can go higher at certain peak periods Sat–Sun. Mon–Fri 9:30am–5:30pm; Sat–Sun 9am–6pm. Tube: Baker St.

Museum of London ⭐⭐   In the Barbican district near St. Paul's Cathedral, the Museum of London allows visitors to trace the city's history from prehistoric times to the postmodern era through relics, costumes, household effects, maps, and models. Anglo-Saxons, Vikings, Normans—they're all here, displayed on two floors around a central courtyard. The exhibits are arranged so that visitors can begin and end their chronological stroll through 250,000 years at the museum's main entrance, and exhibits have quick labels for museum sprinters, more extensive ones for those who want to study, and still more detail for scholars. It's an enriching experience for everybody—allow at least an hour for a full (but still quick) visit.

You'll see the death mask of Oliver Cromwell; the Great Fire of London in living color and sound; reconstructed Roman dining rooms with kitchen and utensils; cell doors from Newgate Prison, made famous by Charles Dickens; and an amazing shop counter with pre–World War II prices on the items. But the pièce de résistance is the lord mayor's coach, built in 1757 and weighing 3 tons. Still used each November in the Lord Mayor's Procession, this gilt-and-red horse-drawn vehicle is like a fairy-tale coach. Early in 2002 the museum unveiled its latest permanent gallery, occupying an entire floor. Called the World City Gallery, it examines through its exhibits life in London between 1789 and 1914, the beginning of World War I. Some 2,000 objects are on view.

Free lectures on London's history are often given during lunch hours; ask at the entrance hall if one will be given the day you're here. You can reach the museum, which overlooks London's Roman and medieval walls, by going up to the elevated pedestrian precinct at the corner of London Wall and Aldersgate, 5 minutes from St. Paul's.

150 London Wall, EC2. ✆ 020/7600-3699. www.museumoflondon.org.uk. Free admission (except for certain exhibitions). Mon–Sat 10am–5:50pm; Sun noon–5:50pm. Tube: St. Paul's or Barbican.

National Army Museum ⭐   Located in Chelsea, this museum traces the history of the British land forces, the Indian army, and colonial land forces. The collection starts with 1485, the date that the Yeomen of the Guard was formed. The saga of the forces of the East India Company is also traced, from its beginning in 1602 to Indian independence in 1947. The gory and glory are all here—everything from Florence Nightingale's lamp to the cloak wrapped around the dying General James Wolfe at Québec in 1759. There are also "cases of the heroes," mementos of such outstanding men as the duke of Marlborough and the duke of Wellington. But the field soldier isn't neglected either: The Nation in Arms Gallery tells the soldier's story in two world wars, including an exhibit of the British Army in the Far East from 1941 to 1945.

Royal Hospital Rd., SW3. ✆ 020/7730-0717. www.national-army-museum.ac.uk. Free admission. Daily 10am–5:30pm. Closed Good Friday, 1st Mon in May, Dec 24–26, and Jan 1. Tube: Sloane Sq.

Natural History Museum ⭐⭐ *Kids*   This is the home of the national collections of living and fossil plants, animals, and minerals, with many magnificent specimens on display. The zoological displays are quite wonderful; though not up to the level of the Smithsonian in Washington, D.C., they're definitely worthwhile and exciting exhibits designed to encourage people of all ages to learn about natural history. The Mineral Gallery displays marvelous examples of crystals and gemstones. Visit the Meteorite Pavilion, which exhibits fragments of rock that have crashed into the earth, some from the farthest reaches of the galaxy. What attracts the most attention is the dinosaur exhibit, displaying 14 complete skeletons. The center of the show depicts a trio of full-size robotic

Deinonychus enjoying a freshly killed Tenontosaurus. In the exhibition "Earth Today and Tomorrow," visitors are invited to explore the planet's dramatic history from the big bang to its inevitable death.

The latest development here is the new Darwin Centre, with final completion scheduled for 2008, though there is already much on view. Dedicated to the great naturalist Charles Darwin, the center reveals the museum's scientific work with specimens, research, and outreach activities. You're given an insider look that answers such questions as how specimens are collected today (ethical considerations as well). These are not just specimens in a bottle. You learn, for example, how mosquito DNA helps scientists track down the spread of malaria, or about the alien habitat of the deep sea and the strange animals, which inhabit these murky depths. Fourteen behind-the-scenes free tours (ages 10 and up only) are given of the museum daily; you should book immediately upon entering the museum if you're interested.

Cromwell Rd., SW7. ℂ 020/7942-5000. www.nhm.ac.uk. Free admission. Mon–Sat 10am–5:50pm; Sun 11am–5:50pm (last admission at 5:30pm). Tube: South Kensington.

Percival David Foundation of Chinese Art ★

This foundation displays the greatest collection of Chinese ceramics outside China. Approximately 1,700 ceramic objects reflect Chinese court taste from the 10th to 18th centuries and include many pieces of exceptional beauty. An extraordinary collection of stoneware from the Song (960–1279) and Yuan (1279–1368) dynasties includes examples of rare Ru and Guan wares. Among the justifiably famous blue and white porcelains are two unique temple vases, dated by inscription to A.D. 1351. A wide variety of polychrome wares is also represented; they include examples of the delicate doucai wares from the Chenghua period (1465–87) as well as a remarkable group of 18th-century porcelains.

53 Gordon Sq., WC1. ℂ 020/7387-3909. www.pdfmuseum.org.uk. Free admission; donations encouraged. £4 ($6.60) per person for a guided tour of 10–20 people. Admission to the library must be arranged with the curator ahead of time. There is a charge for use of the library. Mon–Fri 10:30am–5pm. Tube: Russell Sq. or Euston Sq.

The Queen's Gallery ★★

The refurbished gallery at Buckingham Palace reopened to the public in 2002 in time for the Golden Jubilee celebration of Queen Elizabeth II. Visitors going through the Doric portico entrance will find three times as much space as before. A chapel for Queen Victoria in 1843, the 1831 building by John Nash was destroyed in an air raid in 1940. The gallery is dedicated to changing exhibitions of the wide-ranging treasure trove that forms the Royal Collection. Anticipate special exhibitions of paintings, prints, drawings, watercolors, furniture, porcelain, miniatures, enamels, jewelry, and other works of art. At any given time, expect to see such artistic peaks as Van Dyck's equestrian portrait of Charles I; the world-famous *Lady at the Virginal* by Vermeer; a dazzling array of gold snuff boxes, paintings by Monet from the collection of the late Queen Mother, personal jewelry, studies by Leonardo da Vinci; and even the recent and very controversial portrait of the present queen by Lucian Freud.

Buckingham Palace, SW1. ℂ 020/7321-2233. www.royal.gov.uk. Admission £7.50 ($14) adults, £6 ($11) students and seniors, £4 ($7.40) children 5–16, ages 4 and under free. Daily 10am–5:30pm. Tube: Hyde Park Corner, Green Park, or Victoria.

Saatchi Gallery ★★★

Art lovers define the controversial collector, Charles Saatchi, as the vision of the 21st century—or else they demand he be jailed at once and the key thrown away. If you're not among the faint-of-heart, you can make your way to this river-bordering Edwardian pile on the South Bank, a one-time seat of city government until Margaret Thatcher did away with the local council. Saatchi's taste for cocksure spectacle and his outrageous showcases defined modern British art in the 1990s. This former ad man has been called everything from a "modern day Medici" to "a Machiavellian mogul." He could even outrage part of New York City with his Chris Ofili's glittery Madonna with elephant dung that went on show in Brooklyn (it now rests peacefully in this gallery).

It's all here, ranging from Sarah Lucas's photograph of herself with cash stuffed between her legs or fried eggs on her breasts, to Damien Hirst's pickled shark. Hirst's sliced-up cow appears butchered in separate glass containers that evoke Donald Judd boxes. Take delight—or horror—at Richard Wilson's famous *20:50*, a surrealistic chest-high lake of smelly sump oil. And, of course, you can't leave the gallery without checking out Marc Quinn's frozen "head," cast from nine pints of blood plasma extracted from the artist over a period of several months, or Marcus Harvey's *Myra*, a portrait of the child murderer Myra Hindley.

County Hall, Southbank, SE1. © 020/7823-2363. www.saatchi-gallery.co.uk. Admission £8.75 ($16) adults, £6.75 ($12) students and seniors, £26 ($48) family ticket. Sun–Thurs 10am–8pm; Fri–Sat 10am–10pm. Tube: Waterloo.

Science Museum ★★★ *(Kids* This museum traces the development of science and industry and their influence on everyday life. These scientific collections are among the largest, most comprehensive, and most significant anywhere. On display is Stephenson's original rocket and the tiny prototype railroad engine; you can also see Whittle's original jet engine and the Apollo 10 space module. The King George III Collection of scientific instruments is the highlight of a gallery on science in the 18th century. Health Matters is a permanent gallery on modern medicine. The museum has two hands-on galleries, as well as working models and video displays.

Insider's tip: A large addition to this museum explores such topics as genetics, digital technology, and artificial intelligence. Four floors of a new Welcome Wing shelter half a dozen exhibition areas and a 450-seat IMAX theater. One exhibition explores everything from drug use in sports to how engineers observe sea life

Treasure Trove of Modern Art Goes Up in Flames

On May 26, 2004, a fire swept through a warehouse in East London, destroying millions of pounds worth of work done by some of the leading British contemporary artists of today. Art collector Charles Saatchi suffered the greatest loss, as many of the painters he has championed since the early 1990s lost art that went up in flames.

Ironically, one of the works destroyed was *Hell*, by the Chapman brothers, a series of nine miniature landscapes in glass tanks depicting scenes of disaster and destruction not unlike the fire itself. Saatchi himself commissioned *Hell* for a retrospective at his gallery for half a million pounds.

Even though the works lost are considered irreplaceable by leading British art critics, the loss will not affect visitors to the Saatchi Gallery in 2005. Visitors will be treated to a vast array of some of Saatchi's greatest treasures. The warehouse held artworks that were going to be displayed at his gallery on a rotational basis or lent to other leading galleries in Britain and abroad.

with robotic submarines. On an upper floor, visitors can learn how DNA was used to identify living relatives of the Bleadon Man, a 2,000-year-old Iron Age Man. On the third floor is the computer that Tim Berners-Lee used to design the World Wide Web outside Geneva, writing the first software for it in 1990.

Note also the marvelous interactive consoles placed strategically in locations throughout the museum. These display special itineraries, including directions for getting to the various galleries for families, teens, adults, and those with special interests.

Exhibition Rd., SW7. © 0870/870-4868. www.sciencemuseum.org.uk. Free admission. Daily 10am–6pm. Closed Dec 24–26. Tube: South Kensington.

Sir John Soane's Museum ☆   This is the former home of Sir John Soane (1753–1837), an architect who rebuilt the Bank of England (not the present structure). With his multiple levels, fool-the-eye mirrors, flying arches, and domes, Soane was a master of perspective and a genius of interior space (his picture gallery, for example, is filled with three times the number of paintings a room of similar dimensions would be likely to hold). William Hogarth's satirical series, *The Rake's Progress,* includes his much-reproduced *Orgy* and *The Election,* a satire on mid-18th-century politics. Soane also filled his house with paintings and classical sculpture. On display is the sarcophagus of Pharaoh Seti I, found in a burial chamber in the Valley of the Kings. Also exhibited are architectural drawings from the collection of 30,000 in the Soane Gallery.

13 Lincoln's Inn Fields, WC2. © 020/7405-2107. www.soane.org. Free admission (donations invited). Tues–Sat 10am–5pm; 1st Tues of each month 6–9pm. Tours given Sat at 2:30pm; £3 ($5.55) tickets distributed at 2pm, first-come, first-served (group tours by appointment only). Tube: Holborn.

Wallace Collection ☆☆ (*Finds*)   Located in a palatial setting (the modestly described "town house" of the late Lady Wallace), this collection is a contrasting array of art and armaments. The collection is evocative of the Frick Museum in New York and the Musée d'Jacque André in Paris. The art collection (mostly French) includes works by Watteau, Boucher, Fragonard, and Greuze, as well as such classics as Frans Hals's *Laughing Cavalier* and Rembrandt's portrait of his son Titus. The paintings of the Dutch, English, Spanish, and Italian schools are outstanding. The collection also contains important 18th-century French decorative art, including furniture from a number of royal palaces, Sèvres porcelain, and gold boxes. The European and Asian armaments, on the ground floor, are works of art in their own right: superb inlaid suits of armor, some obviously for parade rather than battle, with more businesslike swords, halberds, and magnificent Persian scimitars.

Manchester Sq., W1. © 020/7563-9500. www.the-wallace-collection.org.uk. Free admission. Mon–Sat 10am–5pm; Sun noon–5pm. Tube: Bond St. or Baker St.

LITERARY LANDMARKS

See the discussion of Hampstead Village in section 4, "Sights on the Outskirts," for details on Keats House. See section 1, "The Top Attractions," for details on Poets' Corner in Westminster Abbey.

Born in London in 1882, the author Virginia Woolf lived and worked in **Bloomsbury,** and she wrote many of her works in London. Virginia spent her formative years at 22 Hyde Park Gate, off Kensington High Street, west of Royal Albert Hall. After the death of her father, the family left Kensington for Bloomsbury and settled in the area around The British Museum (upper-class Victorians at that time, however, didn't view Bloomsbury as "respectable"). From 1905, they lived first at 46 Gordon Sq., east of Gower Street and University College. It was here that the nucleus of the soon-to-be celebrated Bloomsbury Group was created, which would in time embrace Clive Bell (husband of Vanessa) and Leonard Woolf, who was to become Virginia's husband. Later, Virginia lived at 29 Fitzroy Sq., west of Tottenham Court Road, in a house once occupied by George Bernard Shaw. During the next 2 decades, Virginia resided at several more addresses in Bloomsbury, including on Brunswick Square, Tavistock Square, and Mecklenburg Square; these homes have either disappeared or been altered beyond recognition. During this time, the Bloomsbury Group reached out to include artists Roger Fry and Duncan Grant, and Virginia became friends with economist Maynard Keynes and author E. M. Forster. At Tavistock Square (1924–39) and at Mecklenburg Square (1939–40), she operated Hogarth Press with Leonard. She published her own early work here, as well as T. S. Eliot's *The Waste Land*. To escape from urban life, Leonard and Virginia purchased Monk's House in the village of Rodmell between Lewes and Newhaven in Sussex. Here, they lived until 1941 when Virginia drowned herself in the nearby Ouse. Her ashes were buried in the garden at Monk's House.

Carlyle's House   From 1834 to 1881, Thomas Carlyle, author of *The French Revolution,* and Jane Baillie Welsh Carlyle, his noted letter-writing wife, resided in this modest 1708 terraced house. Furnished essentially as it was in Carlyle's day, the house is located about ¾ block from the Thames, near the Chelsea Embankment along King's Road. The most interesting room is the not-so-soundproof "soundproof" study in the sky-lit attic. It's filled with Carlyle memorabilia—his books, a letter from Disraeli, personal effects, a writing chair, even his death mask.

24 Cheyne Row, SW3. ✆ 020/7352-7087. Admission £3.80 ($7.05) adults, £1.80 ($3.35) children 5–16, free for children 4 and under. Wed–Fri 2–5pm; Sat–Sun, Mon (bank holidays) 11am–5pm. Closed Nov–Mar. Tube: Sloane Sq.

Dickens House   In Bloomsbury stands the simple abode in which Charles Dickens wrote *Oliver Twist* and finished *The Pickwick Papers* (his American readers actually waited at the dock for the ship that brought in each new installment). The place is almost a shrine for a Dickens fan; it contains his study, manuscripts, and personal relics, as well as reconstructed interiors.

48 Doughty St., WC1. ✆ 020/7405-2127. www.dickensmuseum.com. Admission £5 ($9.25) adults, £4 ($7.40) students and seniors, £3 ($5.55) children, £14 ($26) families. Mon–Sat 10am–5pm; Sun 11am–5pm (last admission at 4:30pm). Tube: Russell Sq. or Holborn.

Samuel Johnson's House ★★   Dr. Johnson and his copyists compiled a famous dictionary in this Queen Anne house, where the lexicographer, poet, essayist, and fiction writer lived from 1748 to 1759. Although Johnson also lived at Staple Inn in Holborn and at a number of other places, the Gough Square house is the only one of his residences remaining in London. The 17th-century building has been painstakingly restored, and it's well worth a visit.

17 Gough Sq., EC4. ✆ 020/7353-3745. www.drjh.dircon.co.uk. Admission £4 ($7.40) adults, £3 ($5.55) students and seniors, £1 ($1.85) children. May–Sept Mon–Sat 11am–5:30pm; Oct–Apr Mon–Sat 11am–5pm. Tube: Blackfriars or Chancery Lane. Walk up New Bridge St. and turn left onto Fleet; Gough Sq. is tiny and hidden, north of Fleet St.

Shakespeare's Globe Theatre & Exhibition ★   A re-creation of what was probably the most important public theater ever built, it's on the exact site where many of Shakespeare's plays opened. The late American filmmaker, Sam Wanamaker, worked for some 20 years to raise funds to re-create the theater as it existed in Elizabethan times, thatched roof and all. A fascinating exhibit tells

Bloomsbury Attractions

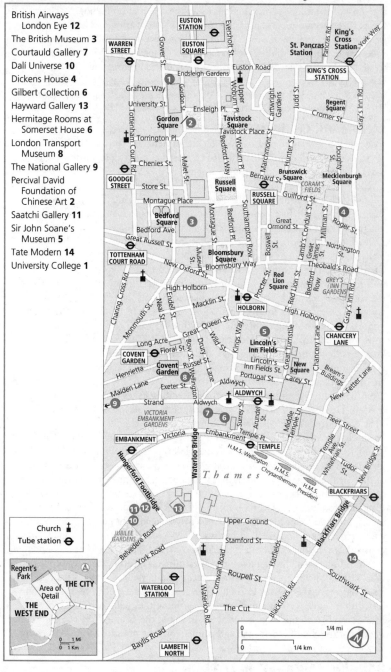

the story of the Globe's construction, using the material (including goat hair in the plaster), techniques, and craftsmanship of 400 years ago. The new Globe isn't an exact replica: It seats 1,500 patrons, not the 3,000 who regularly squeezed in during the early 1600s, and this thatched roof has been specially treated with a fire retardant. Guided tours are offered throughout the day.

21 New Globe Walk, Southwark, SE1. (©) 020/7902-1400. www.shakespeares-globe.org. Admission £8 ($15) adults, £6.50 ($12) students and seniors, £5.50 ($10) children 15 and under. Oct–Apr daily 10am–5pm; May–Sept daily 9am–noon and 12:30–5pm. Tube: Mansion House or London Bridge.

LANDMARK CHURCHES

Many of the churches listed below offer free **lunchtime concerts**—it's customary to leave a small donation. A full list of churches offering lunchtime concerts is available from the London Tourist Board.

St. Martin-in-the-Fields ⭐, overlooking Trafalgar Square, WC2 (© 020/ 7766-1100; www.stmartin-in-the-fields.org; Tube: Charing Cross), is the Royal Parish Church. The first known church on the site dates from the 13th century, but the present classically inspired church, with its famous steeple, dates from 1726. From St. Martin's vantage position in the theater district, it has drawn many actors to its door—none more notable than Nell Gwyn, the mistress of Charles II. On her death in 1687, she was buried in the crypt. Throughout the war, many Londoners rode out uneasy nights in the crypt, while Blitz bombs rained down overhead. One, in 1940, blasted out all the windows. Today, the crypt has a pleasant restaurant, a bookshop, and a gallery. It is home to London's original **Brass Rubbing Centre** (© 020/7930-9306).

St. Bride's Church ⭐, on Fleet Street (© 020/7427-0133; Tube: Blackfriars), known as the church of the press, is a remarkable landmark: The current church is the eighth one that has stood here. Its spire has four octagonal tiers capped by an obelisk that's topped off with a ball and vane. This soaring confection (70m/234 ft. tall) reportedly inspired the wedding cakes of a pastry cook who lived on Fleet Street in the late 17th century. The crypts are now a museum.

St. Etheldreda's, Britain's oldest Roman Catholic church, lies on Ely Place, Holborn Circus, EC1 (© 020/7405-1061; Tube: Farringdon or Chancery Lane), leading off Charterhouse Street at Holborn Circus. Built in 1251, it was mentioned by the Bard in both *Richard II* and *Richard III*. One of the survivors of the Great Fire of 1666, the church was built by, and property of, the diocese of Ely. Until this century, the landlord of Ye Olde Mitre public house near Ely Place had to obtain his license from the Justices of Cambridgeshire rather than in London, and today Ely Place remains a private road with impressive iron gates and a gatekeeper's lodge, all administered by six elected commissioners. The church has a distinguished musical tradition, with 11am Latin Mass on Sunday.

The spectacular brick-and-stone **Westminster Cathedral,** Ashley Place (© 020/7798-9055; www.westminstercathedral.org.uk; Tube: Victoria), is headquarters of the Roman Catholic church in Britain. Done in high Byzantine style, it's massive; 100 different marbles compose the richly decorated interior. Mosaics emblazon the chapels and the vaulting of the sanctuary. If you climb to the top of the 82m (273-ft.) tall campanile, you'll be rewarded with a sweeping view over Victoria and Westminster.

HANGING "AROUND" IN LONDON

The world's largest observation wheel, the **British Airways London Eye** ⭐⭐, Millennium Jubilee Gardens (© 0870/500-0600; www.londoneye.com), opened in February 2000. The fourth-tallest structure in London, it offers panoramic views that extend for some 40km (25 miles) if the weather's clear. Passengers are carried in 32 "pods" that make a complete revolution every half-hour. Along the way you see some of London's landmarks from a bird's-eye point of view.

Built of steel by a European consortium, this eye was conceived and designed by London architects Julia Barfield and David Marks, who claimed inspiration from both the Statue of Liberty in New York and the Eiffel Tower in Paris. Some two million visitors are expected to ride the eye every year.

The eye lies close to Westminster Bridge (you can hardly miss it). Tickets for the ride are £12 ($21) for adults, £9 ($17) for seniors and students; £5.75 ($11) for children 5 to 15. In May and September hours are Monday to Thursday 9:30am to 8pm, Friday to Sunday 9:30am to 10pm; June Monday to Thursday 9:30am to 9pm; Friday and Sunday 9:30am to 10pm; July and August daily 9:30am to 10pm; October to April daily 9:30am to 8pm. Tube: Westminster or Waterloo.

3 London's Parks & Gardens

London has the greatest system of parklands of any large city on the globe. Not as rigidly laid out as the parks of Paris, London's are maintained with a loving care and lavish artistry that puts their American equivalents to shame.

The largest—and one of the world's biggest—is **Hyde Park** ⟨★⟩, W2. With the adjoining Kensington Gardens, it covers 636 acres (252h) of central London with velvety lawn interspersed with ponds, flower beds, and trees. Hyde Park was once a favorite deer-hunting ground of Henry VIII. Running through the width is a 41-acre lake known as the Serpentine. Rotten Row, a 2.5km (1½-mile) sand track, is reserved for horseback riding, and on Sunday attracts some skilled equestrians.

At the northeastern corner of Hyde Park, near Marble Arch, is **Speaker's Corner** (www.speakerscorner.net), where anyone can speak. The only rules: You can't blaspheme, be obscene, or incite a riot. The corpse of Oliver Cromwell was hung up here in a cage for the public to gape at or throw rotten eggs at. The king wanted to warn others against what might happen to them if they wished to abolish the monarchy. The tradition actually began in 1855—before the legal right to assembly was guaranteed in 1872—when a mob of 150,000 gathered to attack a proposed Sunday Trading Bill. Orators from all over Britain have been taking advantage of this spot ever since.

Lovely **Kensington Gardens,** W2, blending with Hyde Park, border on the grounds of Kensington Palace. These gardens are home to the celebrated statue of Peter Pan, with the bronze rabbits that toddlers are always trying to kidnap. The Albert Memorial is also here, and you'll recall the sea of flowers and tributes left here after the death of Diana, Princess of Wales.

East of Hyde Park, across Piccadilly, stretch **Green Park** ⟨★⟩ and **St. James's Park** ⟨★⟩, W1, forming an almost-unbroken chain of landscaped beauty. This is an ideal area for picnics, and one that you'll find hard to believe was once a festering piece of swamp near a leper hospital. There is a romantic lake, stocked with a variety of ducks and pelicans, descendants of the pair that the Russian ambassador presented to Charles II in 1662.

Regent's Park ⟨★★★⟩, NW1, covers most of the district by that name, north of Baker Street and Marylebone Road. Designed by 18th-century genius John Nash to surround a palace of the prince regent that never materialized, this is the most classically beautiful of London's parks. The core is a rose garden planted around a small lake alive with waterfowl and spanned by humped Japanese bridges. The open-air theater and London Zoo are here, and, as in all local parks, hundreds of deck chairs are on the lawns for sunbathers. The deck-chair attendants, who collect a small fee, are mostly college students on vacation.

The **London Zoo** ⚝ (© 020/7722-3333; www.londonzoo.co.uk) is more than 150 years old. Run by the Zoological Society of London, the 15-hectare (36-acre) garden houses some 8,000 animals, including some of the rarest species on earth. It has waned in popularity the last few years, but a recent campaign won the zoo corporate sponsorship that is funding a modernization program. Zoo admission is £13 ($24) for adults, £11 ($20) for students and seniors, £9.75 ($18) for children 4 to 14, and free for children under 3. The zoo is open daily from 10am to 5:30pm (closes at 4pm Nov–Feb). Take the Tube to Camden Town or bus no. 274 or Z2 in summer only.

Battersea Park, SW11 (© 020/8871-7530), is a vast patch of woodland, lakes, and lawns on the south bank of the Thames, opposite Chelsea Embankment between Albert Bridge and Chelsea Bridge. Formerly known as Battersea Fields, the present park was laid out between 1852 and 1858 on an old dueling ground. The park, which measures 1km (¾ mile) on each of its four sides, has a lake for boating, a fenced-in deer park with wild birds, and fields for tennis and football (soccer). There's even a children's zoo. The park's architectural highlight is the Peace Pagoda, built of stone and wood. The park, open May through September daily from dawn until dusk, is not well serviced by public transportation. The nearest Tube is in Chelsea on the right bank (Sloane Sq.); from here it's a brisk 15-minute walk. If you prefer the bus, take no. 137 from the Sloane Square station, exiting at the first stop after the bus crosses the Thames.

4 Sights on the Outskirts

HAMPSTEAD HEATH & VILLAGE ⚝

Located about 6.5km (4 miles) north of the center of London, **Hampstead Heath,** a 32-hectare (800-acre) expanse of high heath surrounded entirely by London, is a chain of continuous park, wood, and grassland. On a clear day you can see St. Paul's Cathedral and even the hills of Kent south of the Thames. For years, Londoners have come here to fly kites, sun worship, fish the ponds, swim, picnic, or jog. In good weather, it's also the site of big 1-day fairs. At the shore of Kenwood Lake, in the northern section, is a concert platform devoted to symphony performances on summer evenings. In the northeast corner, in Waterlow Park, ballets, operas, and comedies are staged at the Grass Theatre in June and July.

When the Underground came to **Hampstead Village** (Tube: Hampstead) in 1907, its attraction as a place to live became widely known, and writers, artists, architects, musicians, and scientists—some from The City—came to join earlier residents. D. H. Lawrence, Rabindranath Tagore, Percy Bysshe Shelley, Robert Louis Stevenson, and Kingsley Amis once lived here; John Le Carré still does.

The Regency and Georgian houses in this village are just 20 minutes by Tube from Piccadilly Circus. Along Flask Walk, a pedestrian mall, is a palatable mix of historic pubs, toyshops, and chic boutiques. The original village, on the side of a hill, still has old roads, alleys, steps, courts, and groves to be strolled through.

Fenton House This National Trust property is on the west side of Hampstead Grove, just north of Hampstead Village. You pass through beautiful wrought-iron gates to reach the redbrick house in a walled garden. Built in 1693, it's one of the earliest, largest, and finest houses in the Hampstead section, and contains the outstanding Benton-Fletcher collection of early keyboard musical instruments, dating from 1540 to 1805. Occasional concerts are given.

Windmill Hill, NW3. © **020/7435-3471**. Admission £4.60 ($8.50) adults, £2.30 ($4.25) children, £12 ($21) family ticket. Mar Sat–Sun 2–5pm; Apr–Oct Sat–Sun 11am–5pm, Wed–Fri 2–5pm. Closed Nov–Feb. Tube: Northern Line to Hampstead.

Freud Museum   After he and his family left Nazi-occupied Vienna as refugees, Sigmund Freud lived, worked, and died in this spacious three-story house in northern London. In view are rooms with original furniture, letters, photographs, paintings, and the personal effects of Freud and his daughter, Anna. In the study and library, you can see the famous couch and Freud's large collection of Egyptian, Roman, and Asian antiquities.

20 Maresfield Gardens, NW3. © **020/7435-2002**. www.freud.org.uk. Admission £5 ($9.25) adults, £2 ($3.70) full-time students, free for children under 12. Wed–Sun noon–5pm. Tube: Jubilee Line to Finchley Rd.

Highgate Cemetery   A stone's throw east of Hampstead Heath, Highgate Village has a number of 16th- and 17th-century mansions and small cottages, lining three sides of the now-pondless Pond Square. Its most outstanding feature, however, is this beautiful cemetery, laid out around a huge, 300-year-old cedar tree and laced with serpentine pathways. The cemetery was so popular and fashionable in the Victorian era that it was extended on the other side of Swain's Lane in 1857. The most famous grave is that of Karl Marx, who died in Hampstead in 1883; his grave, marked by a gargantuan bust, is in the eastern cemetery. In the old western cemetery—accessible only by guided tour, given hourly in summer— are scientist Michael Faraday and poet Christina Rossetti.

Swain's Lane, N6. © **020/8340-1834**. www.highgate-cemetery.org. Western Cemetery guided tour £3 ($5.55). Eastern Cemetery £2 ($3.70) admission, £1 ($1.85) camera pass charge (no video cameras; hand-held still cameras only). Western Cemetery Mar–Oct guided tours only Mon–Fri at 2 and 4pm, and Sat–Sun hourly 11am–4pm; Nov–Feb tours Sat–Sun hourly 11am–3pm; Eastern Cemetery Apr–Oct Mon–Fri 10am–4:30pm, Sat–Sun 11am–4:30pm, Nov–Mar Mon–Fri 10am–3:30pm, Sat–Sun 11am–3:30pm. Both cemeteries closed at Christmas and during funerals. Tube: Northern Line to Archway, then walk or take bus no. 143, 210, 271.

Keats House ★★   The poet lived here for only 2 years, but that was approximately two-fifths of his creative life; he died of tuberculosis in Rome at the age of 25 (in 1821). In Hampstead, Keats wrote some of his most celebrated odes, including "Ode on a Grecian Urn" and "Ode to a Nightingale." His Regency house possesses the manuscripts of his last sonnet ("Bright star, would I were steadfast as thou art") and a portrait of him on his deathbed in a house on the Spanish Steps in Rome.

Wentworth Place, Keats Grove, NW3. © **020/7435-2062**. www.cityoflondon.gov.uk/keats. Admission £3 ($5.55) adults, £1.50 ($2.80) students and seniors, free for children under 16. Apr–Oct Tues–Sun noon–5pm; Nov–Mar call for hours. Tube: Northern Line to Hampstead or Belize Park.

Kenwood House ★★   Kenwood House was built as a gentleman's country home and was later enlarged and decorated by the famous Scottish architect Robert Adam, starting in 1764. The house contains period furniture and paintings by Turner, Frans Hals, Gainsborough, Reynolds, and more.

Hampstead Lane, NW3. © **020/8348-1286**. Free admission. Apr–Oct daily 10am–5pm; Nov–Mar daily 10am–4pm. Tube: Northern Line to Golders Green, then bus no. 210.

HAMPTON COURT
Hampton Court Palace ★★★   The 16th-century palace of Cardinal Wolsey can teach us a lesson: Don't try to outdo your boss, particularly if he happens to be Henry VIII. The rich cardinal did just that, and he eventually lost his fortune,

power, prestige, and ended up giving his lavish palace to the Tudor monarch. Henry took over, even outdoing the Wolsey embellishments. The Tudor additions included the Anne Boleyn gateway, with its 16th-century astronomical clock that even tells the high-water mark at London Bridge. From Clock Court, you can see one of Henry's major contributions, the aptly named Great Hall, with its hammer-beam ceiling. Also added by Henry were the tiltyard (where jousting competitions were held), a tennis court, and a kitchen.

To judge from the movie *A Man for All Seasons,* Hampton Court had quite a retinue to feed. Cooking was done in the Great Kitchen. Henry cavorted through the various apartments with his wife of the moment—from Anne Boleyn to Catherine Parr (the latter reversed things and lived to bury her erstwhile spouse). Charles I was imprisoned here at one time and managed to temporarily escape his jailers.

Although the palace enjoyed prestige and pomp in Elizabethan days, it owes much of its present look to William and Mary—or rather to Sir Christopher Wren, who designed and had built the Northern or Lion Gates, intended to be the main entrance to the new parts of the palace. The fine wrought-iron screen at the south end of the south gardens was made by Jean Tijou around 1694 for William and Mary. You can parade through the apartments today, filled as they were with porcelain, furniture, paintings, and tapestries. The King's Dressing Room is graced with some of the best art, mainly paintings by old masters on loan from Queen Elizabeth II. Finally, be sure to inspect the royal chapel (Wolsey wouldn't recognize it). To confound yourself totally, you may want to get lost in the serpentine shrubbery maze in the garden, also the work of Wren. More and more attention is focusing on improving and upgrading the famous gardens here—the formal gardens are among the last surviving examples of garden methods and designs from several important periods of history.

The 24-hectare (60-acre) gardens—including the Great Vine, King's Privy Garden, Great Fountain Gardens, Tudor and Elizabethan Knot Gardens, Board Walk, Tiltyard, and Wilderness—are open daily year-round from 7am until dusk (but not later than 9pm) and can be visited free except for the Privy Garden. A garden cafe and restaurant is in the Tiltyard Gardens.

Hampton Court, on the north side of the Thames and 21km (13 miles) west of London, is easily accessible. Frequent trains run from Waterloo Station (Network Southeast) to Hampton Court Station (© **0845/748-4950** or 01603/ 764776). Victoria Station (© **020/7730-3466**) buses numbered 216, 411, 451, 461, 513, 726, and R68 make the trip from Victoria Coach Station on Buckingham Palace Road (just southwest of Victoria Station). If you're driving from London, take the A308 to the junction with the A309 on the north side of Kingston Bridge over the Thames.

© **0870/752-7777.** www.hrp.org.uk. Admission £11.80 ($22) adults, £8.70 ($16) students and seniors, £7.70 ($14) children 5–15, free for children under 5, family ticket £35 ($65). Gardens open year-round daily 7am–dusk (no later than 9pm); free admission to all except Privy Garden (admission £4/$7.40 adults, £3/$5.55 students and seniors, £2/$3.70 child, £12/$22 family) without palace ticket during summer months. Cloisters, courtyards, state apartments, great kitchen, cellars, and Hampton Court exhibition open Mar 28–Oct 25 Mon 10:15am–6pm, Tues–Sun 9:30am–6pm, last entry 5:15pm; Oct 26–Mar 27 Mon 10:15am–4:30pm, Tues–Sun 9:30am–4:30pm, last entry 3:45pm.

KEW ★★★

About 15km (9 miles) southwest of central London, Kew is home to one of the best-known botanical gardens in Europe. It's also the site of **Kew Palace** ★★, former residence of George III and Queen Charlotte. A dark redbrick structure,

---

Finds Live Like a King

The **Landmark Trust,** Shootesbrooke, Maidenhead, Berkshire SL6 3SW (℅ 01628/825925; www.landmarktrust.co.uk), an architectural preservation charity, oversees two palace buildings that offer modest rental facilities on the grounds of Hampton Palace. The first, Fish Court, sleeps six and originally housed the palace pastry chefs. Four-day bookings cost £585 to £873 ($1,082–$1,615), with weekly bookings costing £1,056 to £1,850 ($1,954–$3,423). Sleeping eight guests, the Georgian House is a former palace kitchen, with private garden. It accepts 4-night bookings for £666 to £1,044 ($1,232–$1,931) or weekly bookings for £1,176 to £2,269 ($2,176–$4,198). You're not in the palace proper but on its grounds; you have the run of the place at night and can explore the gardens.

---

it is characterized by its Dutch gables. The house was constructed in 1631, and at its rear is the Queen's Garden in a very formal design and filled with plants thought to have grown here in the 17th century. The interior is very much an elegant country house of the time, fit for a king, but not as regal as Buckingham Palace. You get the feeling that someone could have actually lived here as you wander through the dining room, the breakfast room, and go upstairs to the queen's drawing room where musical evenings were staged. The rooms are wall-papered with designs actually used at the time. Perhaps the most intriguing exhibits are little possessions once owned by royal occupants here—everything from snuffboxes to Prince Frederick's gambling debts. The most convenient way to get to Kew is to take the **District Line** Tube to the Kew Gardens stop, on the south bank of the Thames. Allow about 30 minutes.

Royal Botanic Gardens, Kew ✦✦✦ These world-famous gardens offer thousands of varieties of plants. But Kew Gardens, as its known, is no mere pleasure garden—it's essentially a vast scientific research center that happens to be beautiful. The gardens, on a 121-hectare (300-acre) site, encompass lakes, greenhouses, walks, pavilions, and museums, along with fine examples of the architecture of Sir William Chambers. Among the 50,000 plant species are notable collections of ferns, orchids, aquatic plants, cacti, mountain plants, palms, and tropical water lilies.

No matter what season you visit, Kew always has something to see, from the first spring flowers through to winter. Gigantic hothouses grow species of shrubs, blooms, and trees from every part of the globe, from the Arctic Circle to tropical rainforests. Attractions include a newly restored Japanese gateway in traditional landscaping, as well as exhibitions that vary with the season. The newest greenhouse, the Princess of Wales Conservatory (beyond the rock garden), encompasses 10 climatic zones, from arid to tropical; it has London's most thrilling collection of miniature orchids. The Marianne North Gallery (1882) is an absolute gem, paneled with 246 different types of wood that the intrepid Victorian artist collected on her world journeys; she also collected 832 paintings of exotic and tropical flora, all displayed on the walls. The Visitor Centre at Victoria Gate houses an exhibit telling the story of Kew, as well as a bookshop.

Kew. ℅ 020/8940-1171. www.rbgkew.org.uk. Admission £8.50 ($16) adults, £6 ($11) students and seniors, free for children 16 and under. Feb 9–Mar 26 daily 9:30am–5:30pm; Mar 27–Sept 5 Mon–Fri 9:30am–6:30pm, Sat–Sun 9:30am–7:30pm; Sept 6–Oct 30 daily 9:30am–6pm; Oct 31–Feb 8 daily 9:30am–4:15pm. Tube: District Line to Kew Gardens.

GREENWICH ★★★

When London overwhelms you, and you'd like to escape for a beautiful, sunny afternoon on the city's outskirts, make it Greenwich.

Greenwich Mean Time is the basis of standard time throughout most of the world, and Greenwich has been the zero point used in the reckoning of terrestrial longitudes since 1884. But this lovely village—the center of British seafaring when Britain ruled the seas—is also home of the Royal Naval College, the National Maritime Museum, and the Old Royal Observatory. In dry dock at Greenwich Pier is the clipper ship *Cutty Sark* (see "The Last of the Great Clipper Ships," below).

ESSENTIALS

GETTING THERE   The fastest way to get to Greenwich is to take the tube in Central London to Waterloo Station, where you can take a fast train to Greenwich Station.

The Tube is for speed, taking only 15 minutes, but if you'd like to travel the 6.5km (4 miles) to Greenwich the way Henry VIII did, you still can. In fact, getting to Greenwich is still half the fun. The most appealing way involves boarding any of the frequent ferryboats that cruise along the Thames at intervals that vary from every half-hour (in summer) to every 45 minutes (in winter). Boats that leave from Charing Cross Pier (Tube: Embankment) and Tower Pier (Tube: Tower Hill) are run by **Catamaran Cruisers, Ltd.** (© **020/7987-1185;** www. catamarancruisers.co.uk). Depending on the tides and the carrier you select, travel time varies from 50 to 75 minutes each way. Passage is £6 to £10 ($11–$19) round-trip for adults, £4 to £6 ($7.40–$11) round-trip for children 5 to 12; it's free for those under 5.

VISITOR INFORMATION   The **Greenwich Tourist Information Centre** is at 2 Cutty Sark Gardens (© **0870/608-2000**); open daily from 10am to 5pm. The Tourist Information Centre conducts **walking tours** of Greenwich's major sights. Tours cost £4 ($6.60) for adults and £3 ($4.95) for students, seniors, and children, and depart daily at 12:15 and 2:15pm, and last 1½ to 2 hours. Advance reservations aren't required, but you may want to phone in advance to find out any last-minute schedule changes.

SEEING THE SIGHTS

The **National Maritime Museum,** the **Old Royal Observatory,** and **Queen's House** stand together in a beautiful royal park, high on a hill overlooking the Thames. All three attractions are free to get into and open daily from 10am to 5pm. For more information, call © **020/8312-6608** or visit **www.nmm.ac.uk**.

From the days of early seafarers to 20th-century sea power, the **National Maritime Museum** ★★ illustrates the glory that was Britain at sea. The cannon, relics, ship models, and paintings tell the story of a thousand naval battles and a thousand victories, as well as the price of those battles. Look for some oddities here—everything from the dreaded cat-o'-nine-tails used to flog sailors until 1879 to Nelson's Trafalgar coat, with the fatal bullet hole in the left shoulder clearly visible. In time for the millennium, the museum spent £20 million in a massive expansion that added 16 new galleries devoted to British maritime history and improved visitor facilities.

Old Royal Observatory ★ is the original home of Greenwich Mean Time. It has the largest refracting telescope in the United Kingdom and a collection of historic timekeepers and astronomical instruments. You can stand astride the meridian and set your watch precisely by the falling time-ball. Sir Christopher

Wren designed the Octagon Room. Here the first royal astronomer, Flamsteed, made his 30,000 observations that formed the basis of his *Historia Coelestis Britannica*. Edmond Halley, he of the eponymous Halley's Comet, succeeded him. In 1833, the ball on the tower was hung to enable shipmasters to set their chronometers accurately.

Designed by Inigo Jones, **Queen's House** ✹✹ (1616) is a fine example of this architect's innovative style. It's most famous for the cantilevered tulip staircase, the first of its kind. Carefully restored, the house contains a collection of royal and marine paintings and other objets d'art.

The Wernher Collection at Ranger's House ✹✹, Chesterfield Walk (✆ 020/8853-0035), is a real find and one of the finest and most unusual 19th-century mixed-art collections in the world. Acquired by a German diamond dealer, Sir Julius Wernher, the collection contains some 650 exhibits, some dating as far back as 3 B.C. It's an eclectic mix of everything, including jewelry, bronzes, ivory, antiques, tapestries, porcelain pieces, and classic paintings. Hanging on the walls of the gallery are rare works by such old masters as Hans Memling and Filippino Lippi, along with portraits by such English painters as Reynolds and Romney. One salon is devoted to the biggest collection of Renaissance jewelry in Britain. Look also for the carved medieval, Byzantine, and Renaissance ivories along with Limoges enamels and Sevrès porcelain. The most unusual items are enameled skulls and a miniature coffin complete with 3-D skeleton. Don't expect everything to be beautiful—Wernher's taste was often bizarre. Admission is £5 ($9.25) adults, £3.80 ($7.05) seniors and students, £2.50 ($4.65) children, free for children under 5. Open June through August Wednesday through Sunday 10am to 5pm, and September and October Saturday and Sundya only 10am to 5pm. Call for additional opening times. *Note:* The museum is closed from December 22 to March 2.

Nearby is the **Royal Naval College** ✹✹, King William Walk, off Romney Road (✆ 020/8269-4747; www.greenwichfoundation.org.uk). Designed by Sir

The Last of the Great Clipper Ships

Nearly 6.5km (4 miles) east of London, at Greenwich Pier, now in permanent dry dock, lies the last and ultimate word in sail power: the **Cutty Sark** ✹✹, King William Walk, Greenwich, SE10 (✆ 020/8858-3445; www.cuttysark.org.uk; bus no. 177, 180, 188, or 199). Named after the witch in Robert Burns's poem "Tam O'Shanter," it was the greatest of the clipper ships that carried tea from China and wool from Australia in the most exciting ocean races ever sailed. The *Cutty Sark*'s record stood at a then unsurpassed 584km (363 miles) in 24 hours. Launched in Scotland in 1869, the sleek black three-master represented the final fighting run of canvas against steam. Although the age of the clippers was brief, they outpaced the steamers as long as wind filled their billowing mountain of sails. On board the *Cutty Sark* is a museum devoted to clipper lore. Admission is £4.25 ($7.85) for adults and £2.95 ($5.45) for children over 5, £3.25 ($6) students, and seniors. A family ticket costs £11 ($19). It's open daily from 10am to 5pm, with last admission at 4:30pm.

Christopher Wren in 1696, it occupies 4 blocks named after King Charles, Queen Anne, King William, and Queen Mary. Formerly, Greenwich Palace stood here from 1422 to 1640. It's worth stopping in to see the magnificent Painted Hall by Thornhill, where the body of Nelson lay in state in 1805, and the Georgian chapel of St. Peter and St. Paul. Open daily from 10am to 5pm; admission is free.

5 Especially for Kids

In 2003, the London Tourist Board launched a new website—Kidslovelondon. com—providing both a fun and educational guide for planning time in the capital. The site boasts interactive quizzes, up-to-date information on what's hot, and children's reviews of London attractions, with tips on everything from walking with "dinosaurs" to cool places to eat.

London has fun places for kids of all ages. In addition to what's listed below, kids love **Madame Tussauds,** the **Science Museum,** the **London Transport Museum,** the **Natural History Museum,** the **Tower of London,** and the **National Maritime Museum** in Greenwich, all discussed earlier in this chapter.

Bethnal Green Museum of Childhood   This branch of the Victoria and Albert specializes in toys. The variety of dolls alone is staggering; some have such elaborate period costumes that you don't even want to think of the price tags they would carry today. With the dolls come dollhouses, from simple cottages to miniature mansions, complete with fireplaces, grand pianos, kitchen utensils, and carriages. You'll also find optical toys, marionettes, puppets, a considerable exhibit of soldiers and war toys from both World War eras, trains and aircraft, and a display of clothing and furniture relating to the social history of childhood.

Cambridge Heath Rd., E2. ℂ 020/8983-5200. www.museumofchildhood.org.uk. Free admission. Sat–Thurs 10am–5:50pm. Tube: Central Line to Bethnal Green.

Horniman Museum   This century-old museum set in 16 acres of landscaped gardens is quirky, funky, and fun. The collection was accumulated by Frederick Horniman, a Victorian tea trader. A full range of events and activities takes place here, including storytelling and art and crafts sessions for kids, along with workshops for adults. The museum owns some 350,000 objects ranging from a gigantic, overstuffed walrus to such oddities as oversize model insects. There are also displays of live insects and a small aquarium constructed in waterfall-like tiers. The torture chair thought to have been an original used at the Spanish Inquisition was proven to be a fake, but the instruments are genuine.

100 London Rd., Forest Hill, SE23. ℂ 020/8699-1872. www.horniman.ac.uk. Free admission except for temporary exhibitions. Daily 10:30am–5:30pm. Tube: Forest Hill.

The London Dungeon   This ghoulish place was designed to chill the blood while reproducing the conditions of the Middle Ages. Set under the arches of London Bridge Station, the dungeon is a series of tableaux more grisly than those at Madame Tussauds. The rumble of trains overhead adds to the atmosphere, and tolling bells bring a constant note of melancholy; dripping water and caged rats make for even more atmosphere. Naturally, it offers a burning at the stake as well as a torture chamber with racking, branding, and fingernail extraction, and a spine-chilling "Jack the Ripper Experience." The special effects were originally conceived for major film and TV productions. They've recently added a new show called "Judgment Day." You're sentenced to death (by actors, of course) and taken on a boat ride to meet your fate. If you survive, a Pizza Hut is on-site, and a souvenir shop sells certificates that testify you made it through the works.

28–34 Tooley St., SE1. © 020/7403-7221. www.thedungeons.com. Admission £13 ($24) adults, £11 ($21) students and seniors, £8.95 ($17) children under 15. Admission includes Judgment Day boat ride. Sept–July daily 10:30am–5pm; Aug daily 10am–7:30pm. Tube: London Bridge.

London Aquarium ⚐ One of the largest aquariums in Europe, this South Bank attraction boasts 350 species of fish, everything from British freshwater species to sharks that once patrolled the Pacific. Observe the bountiful riches of the coral reefs of the Indian Ocean, and what lurks in the murky depths of the Atlantic and Pacific Oceans, including an array of eels, sharks, piranhas, rays, jellyfish, and other denizens of the deep. You ford a freshwater stream into a mangrove swamp to reach a tropical rainforest. The seawater, incidentally, is just normal Thames water mixed with 8 tons of salt at a time.

County Hall, Westminister Bridge Rd., SE1. © 020/7967-8000. www.londonaquarium.co.uk. Admission £9.75 ($18) adults, £7.50 ($14) students and seniors, £6.25 ($12) ages 3–14, family ticket £29 ($54). Daily 10am–6pm. Tube: Waterloo.

6 Organized Tours

BUS TOURS

For the first-timer, the quickest and most economical way to bring the big city into focus is to take a bus tour. One of the most popular is **The Original London Sightseeing Tour,** which passes by all the major sights in just about 1½ hours. The tour, which uses a traditional double-decker bus with live commentary by a guide, costs £15 ($28) for adults, £10 ($19) for children under 16, free for those under 5. The tour allows you to hop on or off the bus at any point in the tour at no extra charge. The tour plus admission to Madame Tussauds is £28 ($52) for adults, £20 ($37) for children.

Departures are from convenient points within the city; you can choose your departure point when you buy your ticket. Tickets can be purchased on the bus or at a discount from any London Transport or London Tourist Board Information Centre. Most hotel concierges also sell tickets. For information or phone purchases, call © 020/8877-1722. It's also possible to book online at **www. theoriginaltour.com**.

Big Bus Company Ltd., Waterside Way, London SW17 (© **020/8944-7810** or 0800/169-1365; www.bigbus.co.uk), operates a 2-hour tour in summer, departing frequently between 8:30am and 4:30pm daily from Marble Arch by Speakers Corner, Green Park by the Ritz Hotel, and Victoria Station (Buckingham Palace Rd. by the Royal Westminster Hotel). Tours cover the highlights— 18 in all—ranging from the Houses of Parliament and Westminster Abbey to the Tower of London and Buckingham Palace (exterior looks only), accompanied by live commentary. The cost is £17 ($31) for adults, £8 ($15) for children. A 1-hour tour follows the same route but covers only 13 sights. Tickets are valid all day; you can hop on and off the bus as you wish.

WALKING TOURS

The Original London Walks, 87 Messina Ave., P.O. Box 1708, London NW6 4LW (© **020/7624-3978;** http://london.walks.com), the oldest established walking-tour company in London, is run by an Anglo-American journalist/actor couple, David and Mary Tucker. Their hallmarks are variety, reliability, reasonably sized groups, and—above all—superb guides. The renowned crime historian

Donald Rumbelow, the leading authority on Jack the Ripper and author of the classic guidebook *London Walks,* is a regular guide, as are several prominent actors (including classical actor Edward Petherbridge). Walks are regularly scheduled daily and cost £5 ($9.25) for adults, £4 ($7.40) for students and seniors; children under 15 go free. Call for schedule; no reservations needed.

Discovery Walks, 67 Chancery Lane, London WC2 (© **020/8530-8443;** www.Jack-the-Ripper-Walk.co.uk), are themed walks, led by Richard Jones, author of *Frommer's Memorable Walks in London.*

RIVER CRUISES

A trip up or down the river gives you an entirely different view of London from the one you get from land. You see how the city grew along and around the Thames and how many of its landmarks turn their faces toward the water. Several companies operate motor launches from the Westminster piers (Tube: Westminster), offering panoramic views of one of Europe's most historic waterways en route.

Thames River Services, Westminster Pier, Victoria Embankment, SW1 (© **020/7930-4097;** www.westminsterpier.co.uk), concerns itself only with downriver traffic from Westminster Pier to such destinations as Greenwich (see "Sights on the Outskirts," earlier in this chapter). The most popular excursion departs for Greenwich (a 50-min. ride) at half-hour intervals between 10am and 4pm from April, May, September, and October, and between 10:30am and 5pm from June to August; from November to March, boats depart from Westminster Pier at 40-minute intervals daily from 10:40am to 3:20pm. One-way fares are £6.60 ($12) for adults, £3.30 ($6.10) for children under 16, £5.40 ($10) for seniors. Round-trip fares are £8.20 ($15) for adults, £4.10 ($7.60) for children, £6.70 ($12) for seniors. A family ticket for two adults and up to three children under 15 costs £18 ($33) one-way, £22 ($41) round-trip.

Westminster Passenger Association (Upriver) Ltd., Westminster Pier, Victoria Embankment, SW1 (© **020/7930-2062** or 020/7930-4721; www. wpsa.co.uk), offers the only riverboat service upstream from Westminster Bridge to Kew, Richmond, and Hampton Court, with regular daily sailings from the Monday before Easter until the end of October on traditional riverboats, all with licensed bars. Trip time, one-way, can be as little as 1½ hours to Kew and from 2½ to 4 hours to Hampton Court, depending on the tide. Cruises from Westminster Pier to Hampton Court via Kew Gardens leave daily at 10:30, 11:15am, and noon. Round-trip tickets are £18 ($33) for adults, £12 ($22) for seniors, and £9 ($17) for children ages 4 to 14; one child under 4 accompanied by an adult goes free.

7 Shopping

THE TOP SHOPPING STREETS & NEIGHBORHOODS

Several key streets offer some of London's best retail stores—or simply one of everything—compactly located in a niche or neighborhood so that you can just stroll and shop.

THE WEST END The West End includes the Mayfair district and is home to the core of London's big-name shopping. Most of the department stores, designer shops, and multiples (chain stores) have their flagships in this area.

The key streets are **Oxford Street** for affordable shopping (start at Marble Arch Tube station if you're ambitious, or Bond St. station if you just want to see some of it) and **Regent Street,** which intersects Oxford Street at Oxford Circus (Tube: Oxford Circus).

While there are several branches of the private label department store **Marks & Spencer,** their Marble Arch store (on Oxford St.) is the flagship, and worth shopping for their high-quality goods. There's a grocery store in the basement and a home-furnishings department upstairs.

Regent Street has fancier shops—more upscale department stores (including the famed **Liberty of London**), multiples **(Laura Ashley),** and specialty dealers—and leads all the way to Piccadilly.

In between the two, parallel to Regent Street, is **Bond Street.** Divided into New and Old, Bond Street (Tube: Bond St.) also connects Piccadilly with Oxford Street and is synonymous with the luxury trade. Bond Street has had a recent revival and is the hot address for all the international designers; **Donna Karan** has not one, but two shops here. Many international hotshots have digs surrounding hers, from **Chanel** and **Ferragamo** to **Versace.**

Burlington Arcade (Tube: Piccadilly Circus), the famous glass-roofed, Regency-style passage leading off Piccadilly, looks like a period exhibition and is lined with intriguing shops and boutiques. The small, smart stores specialize in fashion, jewelry, Irish linen, cashmere, and more. If you linger in the arcade until 5:30pm, you can watch the beadles in their black-and-yellow livery and top hats ceremoniously put in place the iron grills that block off the arcade until 9am the next morning, at which time they just as ceremoniously remove them to mark the start of a new business day. Also at 5:30pm, a hand bell called the Burlington Bell is sounded, signaling the end of trading.

Just off Regent Street (actually tucked right behind it) is **Carnaby Street** (Tube: Oxford Circus), which is also having a comeback. While it no longer dominates the world of pacesetting fashion as it did in the 1960s, it's still fun to visit for teens who may need cheap souvenirs, a purple wig, or a little something in leather. A convenient branch of **Boots the Chemists** is also here.

For a total contrast, check out **Jermyn Street,** on the far side of Piccadilly, a tiny 2-block-long street devoted to high-end men's haberdashers and toiletries shops; many have been doing business for centuries. Several hold royal warrants, including **Turnball & Asser,** where HRH Prince Charles has his pj's made.

The West End leads to the theater district, and so two more shopping areas: the still-not-ready-for-prime-time **Soho,** where the sex shops are slowly being turned into cutting-edge designer shops; and **Covent Garden,** which is a masterpiece unto itself. The marketplace has eaten up the surrounding neighborhood so that even though the streets run a little higgledy-piggledy and you can easily get lost, it's fun to just wander and shop.

KNIGHTSBRIDGE & CHELSEA This is the second-most famous of London's retail districts and the home of **Harrods** (Tube: Knightsbridge). A small street nearby, **Sloane Street,** is chockablock with designer shops; **Cheval Place,** in the opposite direction, is also lined with designer resale shops.

Walk toward Museum Row, and you'll soon find **Beauchamp Place** (pronounced *Bee*-cham; Tube: Knightsbridge). The street is only a block long, but it features the kinds of shops where young British aristos buy their clothing.

Head out at the **Harvey Nichols** end of Knightsbridge, away from Harrods, and shop your way through the designer stores on Sloane Street (**Hermès, Armani, Prada,** and the like), then walk past Sloane Square and you're in an altogether different neighborhood: Chelsea.

> ⌒ *Tips* **Shipping It Home**
>
> You can ship purchases on your flight home by paying for excess baggage
> (rates vary with the airline), or you can have your package shipped inde-
> pendently. Independent operators are generally less expensive than the
> airlines. Try **Burns International Facilities,** at Heathrow Airport Terminal 1
> (© **020/8745-5301**) and Terminal 4 (© **020/8745-6460**). But remember, you
> can avoid the VAT up front only if you have the store ship directly to you.
> If you ship via Excess Baggage or London Baggage, you still have to pay
> the VAT up front and apply for a refund. See chapter 3 for more on claim-
> ing your VAT refund.

King's Road (Tube: Sloane Sq.), the main street of Chelsea, which starts at
Sloane Square, will forever remain a symbol of London in the Swinging Sixties.
Today, the street is still frequented by young people, but with fewer Mohican
haircuts, "Bovver boots," and Edwardian ball gowns than before. More and
more, King's Road is a lineup of markets and "multistores," large or small con-
glomerations of indoor stands, stalls, and booths in one building or enclosure.

Chelsea doesn't begin and end with King's Road. If you choose to walk the
other direction from Harrods, you connect to a part of Chelsea called **Brompton Cross,** another hip and hot area for designer shops made popular when
Michelin House was rehabbed by Sir Terence Conran for **The Conran Shop.**

Also seek out **Walton Street,** a tiny little snake of a street running from
Brompton Cross back toward the museums. About 2 blocks of this 3-block
street are devoted to fairy-tale shops for m'lady where you can buy aromatherapy from **Jo Malone,** needlepoint, costume jewelry, or meet with your interior
designer, who runs a small shop of objets d'art.

Finally, don't forget all those museums right there in the corner of the shopping streets. They all have great gift shops.

KENSINGTON & NOTTING HILL   **Kensington High Street** is the new
hangout of the classier breed of teen who has graduated from Carnaby Street and
is ready for street chic. While a few staples of basic British fashion are on this
strip, most of the stores feature items that stretch, are very, very short, or are
very, very tight. The Tube station here is High Street Kensington.

From Kensington High Street, you can walk up **Kensington Church Street,**
which, like Portobello Road, is one of the city's main shopping avenues for
antiques. Kensington Church Street dead-ends into the Notting Hill Gate Tube
station, which is where you would arrive for shopping on **Portobello Road.** The
dealers and the weekend market are 2 blocks beyond.

THE DEPARTMENT STORES

Contrary to popular belief, Harrods is not the only department store in London.
The British invented the department store, and they have lots of them—mostly
in Mayfair, and each with its own customer profile.

Fenwick of Bond Street   Fenwick (the "w" is silent), dating from 1891, is a
stylish fashion store that offers an excellent collection of designer women's wear,
ranging from moderately priced ready-to-wear items to more expensive designer
fashions. A wide range of lingerie in all price ranges is also sold. 63 New Bond St.,
W1. © 020/7629-9161. Tube: Bond St.

Fortnum & Mason   The world's most elegant grocery store is a British tradition dating from 1707. This store exemplifies the elegance and style you would expect from an establishment with three royal warrants. Enter and be transported to another world of deep-red carpets, crystal chandeliers, spiraling wooden staircases, and unobtrusive, tail-coated assistants.

The grocery department is renowned for its impressive selection of the finest foods from around the world—the best champagne, the most scrumptious Belgian chocolates, and succulent Scottish smoked salmon. Wander through the four floors and inspect the bone china and crystal cut glass, find the perfect gift in the leather or stationery departments, or reflect on the changing history of furniture and ornaments in the antiques department. Dining choices include **St. James Restaurant, The Fountain Restaurant,** and also **The Patio** (for details on taking afternoon tea here, see chapter 4). Fortnum & Mason offers exclusive and specialty ranges for the home, as well as beauty products and fashions for both women and men. 181 Piccadilly, W1. © 020/7734-8040. Tube: Piccadilly Circus.

Harrods   An institution as firmly entrenched in English life as Buckingham Palace and the Ascot Races, Harrods is an elaborate emporium, at times as fascinating as a museum. The sheer range, variety, and quality of merchandise are dazzling. If you visit only one store in all of England, make it Harrods, even if you're just looking.

The fifth floor is devoted to sports and leisure, with a wide range of equipment and attire. Toy Kingdom is on the fourth floor, along with children's wear. The Egyptian Hall, on the ground floor, sells crystal from Lalique and Baccarat, plus porcelain. You'll also find a men's grooming room, an enormous jewelry department, and a fashion-forward department for younger customers. In the basement, you'll find a bank, a theater-booking service, and a travel bureau. Harrods Shop for logo gifts is on the ground floor. When you're ready for a break, you have a choice of 22 restaurants and bars. Best of all are the Food Halls, stocked with a huge variety of foods and several cafes. Harrods began as a grocer in 1849, still the heart of the business. 87–135 Brompton Rd., Knightsbridge, SW1. © 020/7730-1234. Tube: Knightsbridge.

John Lewis   Trends come and go but this department store remains one of the most traditional outlets in London. Their motto is that they are never knowingly undersold, and they mean that. We've always found great bargains at this store, most recently in a clearance sale of fine earthenware by Royal Stafford. Whatever you're looking for, ranging from mauve Egyptian towels to clothing and jewelry, it's likely to be for sale here. 278–306 Oxford St., W1. © 020/7629-7711. Tube: Oxford Circus.

Liberty   This major British department store is celebrated for its Liberty Prints: top-echelon, carriage-trade fabrics, often in floral patterns, that are prized by decorators for the way they add a sense of English tradition to a room. The front part of the store on Regent Street isn't particularly distinctive, but don't be fooled: Some parts of the place have been restored to Tudor-style splendor that includes half-timbering and lots of interior paneling. Liberty houses six floors of fashion, china, and home furnishings, as well as the famous Liberty Print fashion fabrics, upholstery fabrics, scarves, ties, luggage, and gifts. 210–220 Regent St., W1. © 020/7734-1234. Tube: Oxford Circus.

SOME CLASSIC LONDON FAVORITES

ANTIQUES   See also "The Markets," below. Portobello Road is really the prime hunting ground.

At the **Antiquarius Antiques Centre,** 131–141 King's Rd., SW3 (© 020/ 7969-1500; Tube: Sloane Sq.), more than 120 dealers offer specialized merchandise, such as antique and period jewelry, silver, first-edition books, boxes, clocks, prints, and paintings, with an occasional piece of antique furniture. You'll find a lot of items from the 1950s. Closed Sunday.

Alfies Antique Market, 13–25 Church St., NW8 (© 020/7723-6066; Tube: Marylebone or Edgware Rd.), is the biggest and one of the best-stocked conglomerates of antiques dealers in London, all crammed into the premises of what was built before 1880 as a department store. It contains more than 370 stalls, showrooms, and workshops scattered over 3,251 sq. meters (35,000 sq. ft.) of floor space. Closed Sunday and Monday. A whole antiques district has grown up around Alfies along Church Street.

ARCHITECTURAL SALVAGE The market leader in architectural salvage in London, **LASSCO,** Mark St., off St. Paul St., EC2 (© 020/7749-9944; Tube: Old St.), comprises five companies specializing in a particular area of architectural salvage, mostly from 19th-century buildings before they were demolished in London and in England. Some of their architectural salvage comes from famous London buildings such as Harrods and, on occasion, St. Paul's Cathedral. Our favorite branch is the LASSCO Warehouse division, a rummager's dream of Victoriana. Another favorite is the House and Garden division, with affordable replicas of period features for indoors or outdoors. You can purchase a piece of English history here, finding a valuable souvenir to take home with you. We recently purchased a Victorian oval brass mortise set for £47 ($87).

ARTS & CRAFTS Gabriel's Wharf, 56 Upper Ground, SE1 (© 020/7401-2255; Tube: Blackfriars, Southwark) is a South Bank complex of shops, restaurants, and bars open Tuesday through Sunday from 11am to 6pm (dining and drinking establishments open later). Lying 2 minutes by foot from Oxo Tower Wharf, it is filled with some of the most skilled of London craftspeople, turning out original pieces of sculpture, jewelry, ceramics, art, and fashion. From food to fashion, from arts to crafts, it awaits you here. The place is a lot of fun at which to poke around.

BATH & BODY Branches of **The Body Shop** are seemingly everywhere. Check out the one at 375 Oxford St., W1 (© 020/7409-7868; Tube: Bond St.). Prices are much lower in the United Kingdom than in the United States.

Boots the Chemists has branches all over Britain. A convenient branch is at 490 Oxford St., W1C (© 020/7491-8546; Tube: Marble Arch). The house brands of beauty products are usually the best, be they Boots' products (try the cucumber facial scrub), Boots' versions of The Body Shop (two lines, Global and Naturalistic), or Boots' versions of Chanel makeup (called No. 7).

Stock up on essential oils, or perhaps dream pillows, candles, sachets of letters of the alphabet, and aromatherapy fans at **Culpeper the Herbalist,** 8 The Market, Covent Garden, WC2 (© 020/7379-6698).

Floris, 89 Jermyn St., SW1 (© 020/7930-2885; Tube: Greek Park), stocks a variety of toilet articles and fragrances in floor-to-ceiling mahogany cabinets, which are architectural curiosities in their own right, dating from the Great Exhibition of 1851.

Lush, 11 The Piazza, Covent Garden (© 020/7240-4570; Tube: Covent Garden), sells the most intriguing handmade cosmetics in London. This outlet is always launching something new, such as its latest soap, "Rock Star," looking very pink and smelling like a Creamy Candy Bubble Bar. Tam O'Santa is an allspice, sandalwood, and frankincense bubble bath; and the selection goes on and on, the products made of fresh fruit and vegetables, the finest essential oils, and safe synthetics—no animal ingredients.

The Victorian perfumery called **Penhaligon's,** 41 Wellington St., WC2 (℃ **020/7836-2150;** Tube: Covent Garden), offers a large selection of perfumes, after-shaves, soaps, and bath oils for women and men. Gifts include antique-silver scent bottles and leather traveling requisites.

FASHION, PART I: THE TRUE BRIT Every internationally known designer worth his or her weight in shantung has a boutique in London, but the best buys are on the sturdy English styles that last forever.

The name **Burberry,** 165 Regent St., SW1 (℃ **020/7930-3343;** Tube: Piccadilly Circus), has been synonymous with raincoats ever since Edward VII publicly ordered his valet to "bring my Burberry" when the skies threatened. An impeccably trained staff sells the famous raincoats, along with excellent men's shirts, sportswear, knitwear, and accessories. Raincoats are available in women's sizes and styles as well. Prices are high, but you get quality and prestige.

The finest name in men's shirts, **Hilditch & Key,** 37 and 73 Jermyn St., SW1 (℃ **020/7734-4707;** Tube: Piccadilly Circus or Green Park), has been in business since 1899. The two shops on this street both offer men's clothing (including a bespoke shirt service) and women's ready-made shirts. Hilditch also has an outstanding tie collection. Shirts go for half price during the twice-yearly sales. Men fly in from all over the world for them.

FASHION, PART II: THE CUTTING EDGE Currently the most cutting-edge shopping street in London is **Conduit Street,** W1 in Mayfair (Tube: Oxford Circus). Once known for its dowdy display of international airline offices, it is now London's smartest street for fashion. Trendy shops are opening between Regent Street and the "blue chip" boutiques of New Bond Street even as we speak. Current stars include **Vivienne Westwood,** 44 Conduit St., W1 (℃ **020/7439-1109**), who has overcome her punk origins to become the grande dame of English fashion. One of the most avant-garde, creative British designers, **Alexander McQueen,** 4–5 Old Bond St., W1 (℃ **020/7355-0088**), has moved in to give the neighborhood his blessing. No one pays more attention to fashion detail and craftsmanship than the celebrated McQueen.

Other famous designers with boutiques on Conduit Street include **Krizia,** 24 Conduit St., W1 (℃ **020/7491-4987**); **Yohji Yamamoto,** 14–15 Conduit St., W1 (℃ **020/7491-4129**); and **Issey Miyake,** 52 Conduit St., W1 (℃ **020/ 7349-3300**).

The Library, 268 Brompton Rd., SW3 (℃ **020/7589-6569;** Tube: South Kensington or Knightsbridge). In spite of its name, this is a showcase for some of the best of the young designers for men. It's very cutting edge without dipping into the extremities of male fashion. The Library is famous for having introduced Helmut Lang to London, but now features such designers as Fabrizio del Carlo, Kostas Murkudis, or even Alexander McQueen.

FASHION, PART III: VINTAGE & SECONDHAND CLOTHING A London institution since the 1940s, **Pandora,** 16–22 Cheval Place, SW7 (℃ **020/ 7589-5289;** Tube: Knightsbridge), stands in fashionable Knightsbridge, a stone's throw from Harrods. Several times a week, chauffeurs drive up with bundles packed anonymously by the gentry of England. One woman voted best-dressed at Ascot several years ago was wearing a secondhand dress acquired here. Prices are

The Comeback of Carnaby Street

What happened to Carnaby Street? A faded echo left over from the swinging sixties? That was true for a long time. You went there only when your purple wig looked a bit battered. However, Carnaby is rising again. A new influx of talented designers and offbeat shops are popping up not only on Carnaby but also along its offshoot streets— Newburgh, Foubert's Place, Kingly Street, Marlborough Court, and Lowndes Court. Innovative boutiques seem to open each week behind small Georgian shop fronts.

Among the zillions of shops here are such favorites as **Mikey,** 26 Carnaby St., W1 (© **020/7437-1101**), London's pioneering jewelry shop, which has chosen Carnaby Street for its flagship store. Search for street-bred and urban cool here (svelte is the current London word for cool). **Lambretta Clothing,** 29 Carnaby St., W1 (© **020/7437-7078**), retains the Mod lifestyle philosophy and has launched a complete range of casual wear for men and footwear for men and women. The look has a distinct retro feel, but uses the latest fibers and fabric finishes for the modern and active lifestyle of today. **All Saints,** 1 Great Titchfield St, W1 (© **020/7323-3883**), is the creation of noted designer Stuart Trevor, one of the most innovative designers under the British label noted for menswear brands.

To reach the stores above, take the tube to Oxford Circus.

generally one-third to one-half the retail value. Outfits are usually no more than two seasons old.

For the best in original street wear from the '50s, the '60s, and the '70s, **Pop Boutique,** 6 Monmouth St., WC2 (© **020/7497-5262;** Tube: Covent Garden), is tops. Right next to the chic Covent Garden Hotel, it has fabulous vintage wear at affordable prices—leather jackets for £48 ($79), for example, the equivalent selling for $300 in New York.

Note: There's no value-added tax (VAT) refund on used clothing.

FILOFAX All major department stores sell Filofax supplies, but the full range is carried in Filofax stores. Go to the main West End branch, **The Filofax Centre,** at 21 Conduit St., W1 (© **020/7499-0457;** Tube: Oxford Circus); it's larger and fancier than the Covent Garden branch at 69 Neal St. (© **020/ 7836-1977**), with the entire range of inserts and books and prices that will floor you: at least half off the U.S. going rate. They also have good sales; calendars for the next year go on sale very early in the previous year (about 10 months in advance).

FURNITURE **David Linley Furniture,** 60 Pimlico Rd., SW1 (© **020/ 7730-7300;** Tube: Sloane Sq.). This is a showcase for the remarkable furniture of the Viscount Linley, a designer who bears a resemblance to his mother, the late Princess Margaret. He designs pieces of furniture of a complex nature, both in terms of design and structure. For example, one of his designs is called the Apsley House Desk in French walnut with ebony and nickel-plated detailing, containing secret drawers. The desk is rimmed with a miniature of the neoclassical Apsley

House. The director at the Victoria and Albert Museum has predicted that Linley's furnishings and accessories will become the designs of the antiques of the future.

HOME DESIGN & HOUSEWARES At the **Conran Shop,** Michelin House, 81 Fulham Rd., SW3 (© **020/7589-7401;** Tube: South Kensington), you'll find high style at reasonable prices from the man who invented it all for Britain: Sir Terence Conran. It's great for gifts, home furnishings, and tabletop knickknacks—or just for gawking. **The Couverture Shop,** 310 King's Rd., SW3 (© **020/7795-1200;** Tube: Sloane Sq.), is an emporium of the unexpected, with original products for both adults and children as well as the home. It's strongest on what they call "bedroom must-haves," embracing bed linen, throws, cushions, and the like. Vintage finds along with designer pieces—often handmade—are also sold.

SHOES Dr. Marten makes a brand of shoe that has become so popular that now an entire department store sells accessories, gifts, and even clothes: **Dr. Martens Department Store,** 1 King St., WC2 (© **020/7497-1460;** Tube: Covent Garden). Teens come to worship here because ugly is beautiful and the prices are far better than they are in the United States or elsewhere in Europe.

Shoes for both men and women are stocked at **Natural Shoe Store,** 21 Neal St., WC2 (© **020/7836-5254;** Tube: Covent Garden), which also does repairs. The selection includes all comfort and quality footwear, from Birkenstock to the best of the British classics.

TOYS Hamleys, 188–196 Regent St., W1 (© **0870/333-2455;** Tube: Oxford Circus), is the finest toy shop in the world—more than 35,000 toys and games on seven floors of fun and magic. A huge selection is offered, including soft, cuddly stuffed animals, as well as dolls, radio-controlled cars, train sets, model kits, board games, outdoor toys, and computer games. A small branch is also at Covent Garden and another at Heathrow Airport.

TRAVEL SERVICES The retail flagship of British Airways, **British Airways Travel Shop,** in Selfridge's Lower Grand Floor, Oxford St., W1 (© **020/7491-4989;** Tube: Bond St.), housed on three floors, offers not only worldwide travel and ticketing but also a wide range of services and shops including a clinic for immunizations, a pharmacy, a bureau de change, a passport and visa service, and a theater-booking desk. The ground floor sells luggage, guidebooks, maps, and other goods.

THE MARKETS
THE WEST END Covent Garden Market (© **020/7836-9136;** Tube: Covent Garden), the most famous market in all of England—possibly all of Europe—offers several different markets daily from 9am to 6pm (we think it's most fun to come on Sun, though it will be packed). George Bernard Shaw got his inspiration for *Pygmalion* here, where the character of Eliza Doolittle sold violets to wealthy operagoers. It can be a little confusing until you dive in and explore it all. **Apple Market** is the fun, bustling market in the courtyard where traders sell, well, everything. Many of the items are what the English call collectible nostalgia, including a wide array of glassware and ceramics, leather goods, toys, clothes, hats, and jewelry. Some merchandise is truly unusual. Many items are handmade, with some craftspeople selling their own wares—except on Mondays, when antiques dealers take over. Out back is **Jubilee Market** (© **020/7836-2139**), also an antiques market on Mondays. Every other day, it's

sort of a fancy hippie-ish market with cheap clothes and books. Out front are a few tents of cheap stuff, except on Monday.

The market itself (in the superbly restored hall) is one of the best shopping opportunities in London. Specialty shops sell fashions and herbs, gifts and toys, books and personalized dollhouses, hand-rolled cigars, and much, much more. You'll find bookshops and branches of famous stores (**Hamley's, The Body Shop**), and prices are kept moderate.

St. Martin-in-the-Fields Market (Tube: Charing Cross) is good for teens and hipsters, who can make do with imports from India and South America, crafts, and some local football souvenirs. Located near Trafalgar Square and Covent Garden; hours are Monday through Saturday from 11am to 5pm, and Sunday from noon to 5pm.

Berwick Street Market (Tube: Oxford Circus or Tottenham Court Rd.) may be the only street market in the world that's flanked by two rows of strip clubs, porno stores, and adult-movie dens. Don't let that put you off, however. Six days a week in the scarlet heart of Soho, this array of stalls and booths sells probably the best and cheapest fruit and vegetables in town. It also hawks ancient records, tapes, books, and old magazines, any of which may turn out to be collectors' items one day. It's open Monday through Saturday from 8am to 5pm.

On Sunday mornings along **Bayswater Road,** artists hang pictures, collages, and crafts on the railings along the edge of Hyde Park and Kensington Gardens for more than a mile. If the weather's right, start at Marble Arch and walk. You'll see much of the same thing by walking along the railings of **Green Park** along Piccadilly on a Saturday afternoon.

NOTTING HILL   **Portobello Market** (Tube: Notting Hill Gate) is a magnet for collectors of virtually anything. It's mainly a Saturday happening, from 6am to 5pm. You needn't be here at the crack of dawn; 9am is fine. Once known mainly for fruit and vegetables (still sold here throughout the week), in the past 4 decades Portobello has become synonymous with antiques. But don't take the stallholder's word for it that the fiddle he's holding is a genuine Stradivarius left to him in the will of his Italian great-uncle; it might just as well have been "nicked" from an East End pawnshop.

The market is divided into three major sections. The most crowded is the antiques section, running between Colville Road and Chepstow Villas to the south. (*Warning:* There's a great concentration of pickpockets in this area.) The second section (and the oldest part) is the "fruit and veg" market, lying between Westway and Colville Road. In the third and final section is a flea market, where Londoners sell bric-a-brac and lots of secondhand goods they didn't really want in the first place. But looking around still makes for interesting fun.

Note: Some 90 antiques and art shops along Portobello Road are open during the week when the street market is closed. This is actually a better time for the serious collector to shop because you'll get more attention from dealers, and you won't be distracted by the organ grinder.

SOUTH BANK   Open on Fridays only, **New Caledonian Market** is commonly known as the **Bermondsey Market,** because of its location on the corner of Long Lane and Bermondsey Street (Tube: London Bridge, then bus no. 78, or walk down Bermondsey St.). The market is at the extreme east end, beginning at Tower Bridge Road. It's one of Europe's outstanding street markets for the number and quality of the antiques and other goods. The stalls are well known, and many dealers come into London from the country. Prices are generally lower here than at Portobello and the other markets. It gets under way at

5am—with the bargains gone by 9am—and closes at noon. Bring a "torch" (flashlight) if you go in the wee hours.

NORTH LONDON   If it's Wednesday, it's time for **Camden Passage** (℗ **020/7359-0190;** Tube: Northern Line to Angel) in Islington, where each Wednesday and Saturday there's a very upscale antiques market. It starts in Camden Passage and then sprawls into the streets behind. It's on Wednesdays from 7am to 2pm, and Saturdays from 8am to 5pm. A book market is held on Thursday 9am to 5pm.

Don't confuse Camden Passage with Camden Market (very, very downtown). **Camden Market** (Tube: Camden Town) is for teens and others into body piercing, blue hair (yes, still), and vintage clothing. Serious collectors of vintage may want to explore during the week, when the teen scene isn't quite so overwhelming. Market hours are from 9:30am to 5:30pm daily, with some parts opening at 10am.

8 · London After Dark

Weekly publications such as *Time Out* and *Where* carry full entertainment listings, including information on restaurants and nightclubs. You'll also find listings in daily newspapers, notably the *Times* and the *Telegraph*.

THE THEATER

In London, you'll have a chance to see the world-renowned **English theater** on its home ground. Matinees are on Wednesday (Thurs at some theaters) and Saturday. Theaters are closed on Sunday. It's impossible to describe all of London's theaters in this space, so below are listed just a few from the treasure trove.

GETTING TICKETS

To see specific shows, especially hits, purchase your tickets in advance. The best method is to buy your tickets from the theater's box office, which you can do over the phone using a credit card. You'll pay the theater price and pick up the tickets the day of the show. You can also go to a reliable ticket agent (the greatest cluster is in Covent Garden), but you'll pay a fee, which varies depending on the show. You can also make theater reservations through ticket agents. In the case of hit shows, only brokers may be able to get you a seat, but you'll pay for the privilege. For tickets and information before you go, try **Keith Prowse,** 234 West 44th St., Suite 1000, New York, NY 10036 (℗ **800/223-6108** or 212/398-1468; www.keithprowse.com). They also have offices in London at the **British Visitors Centre,** 1 Regents St., W1 V1PJ (℗ **020/7014-8550**), or at the **Harrods** ticket desk, 87–135 Brompton Rd. (℗ **020/7589-9109**), located on the lower-ground floor opposite the British Airways desk. They'll mail tickets to your home or fax you a confirmation and leave your tickets at the box office. Instant confirmations are available with special "overseas" rates for most shows. A booking and handling fee of up to 20% is added to the ticket price.

Another option is **Theatre Direct International (TDI;** ℗ **800/334-8457** in the U.S.; www.tdi-groups.com). TDI specializes in providing London fringe theater tickets, but they also have tickets to major productions, including those of the Royal National Theatre and Barbican. The service allows you to arrive in London with your tickets or to have them held for you at the box office.

London theater tickets are priced quite reasonably when compared with the United States. Prices vary greatly depending on the seat—from £18 to £70 ($33–$130). Sometimes gallery seats (the cheapest) are sold only on the day of the performance, so you'll have to head to the box office early in the day and

> **(Value** Ticket Bargains
>
> The **Society of London Theatre** (℗ 020/7557-6700; www.officiallondon theatre.co.uk/tkts) operates a **TKTS booth** in Leicester Square, where tickets for many shows are available at half price, plus a £2.50 ($4.65) service charge. The booth now sells additional tickets the day of performances at 25% off and at full price for any of 55 theaters, including the English National Opera and the Royal Opera House. All major credit and debit cards are accepted. The TKTS booth also offers a limited number of seats for shows that are usually sold out. Hours are Monday to Saturday 10am to 7pm, Sunday noon to 3pm.

return an hour before the performance to queue up, because they're not reserved seats.

Many of the major theaters offer reduced-price tickets to students on a standby basis but not to the general public. When available, these tickets are sold 30 minutes prior to curtain. Line up early for popular shows, as standby tickets go fast and furious. Of course, you must have a valid student ID.

Warning: Beware of scalpers who hang out in front of theaters with hit shows. Many report that scalpers sell forged tickets, and their prices are outrageous.

THE MAJOR COMPANIES & THEATERS

Barbican Theatre—Royal Shakespeare Company   The Barbican is the London home of the Royal Shakespeare Company, one of the world's finest theater companies. The core of its repertoire remains, of course, the plays of William Shakespeare. It also presents a wide-ranging program in its two theaters. Three productions are in repertory each week in the Barbican Theatre—a 2,000-seat main auditorium with excellent sight lines throughout, thanks to a raked orchestra. The Pit, a small studio space, is where the company's new writing is presented. The Royal Shakespeare Company performs both here and at Stratford-upon-Avon. It is in residence in London during the winter months; in the summer, it tours in England and abroad. For more information on the company and its current productions, check **www.rsc.org.uk**. The Barbican box office is open daily 9am to 8pm. In the Barbican Centre, Silk St., Barbican, EC2Y. ℗ 020/7638-8891. www.barbican.org.uk. Barbican Theatre £5–£40 ($9.25–$74). The Pit £7–£24 ($13–$44) matinees and evening performances. Tube: Barbican or Moorgate.

Open-Air Theatre   This outdoor theater is in Regent's Park; the setting is idyllic, and both seating and acoustics are excellent. Presentations are mainly of Shakespeare, usually in period costume. Its theater bar, the longest in London, serves both drink and food. In the case of a rained-out performance, tickets are offered for another date. The season runs from June to mid-September, Monday through Saturday at 8pm, plus Wednesday, Thursday, and Saturday matinees at 2:30pm. Inner Circle, Regent's Park, NW1. ℗ 0870/060-1811. http://openairtheatre.org. Tickets £8.50–£25 ($16–$46). Tube: Baker St.

Royal Court Theatre   This theater has always been a leader in producing provocative, cutting-edge, new drama. In the 1950s, it staged the plays of the angry young men, notably John Osborne's then-sensational *Look Back in Anger;* earlier it debuted the plays of George Bernard Shaw. A recent work was *The Beauty Queen of Leenane,* which won a Tony on Broadway. The theater is home to the English Stage Company, formed to promote serious stage writing. Box office hours are daily from 10am to 6pm. Sloane Sq., SW1. © 020/7565-5000. www.royalcourttheatre.com. Tickets £7.50–£28 ($14–$51); call for the latest information. Tube: Sloane Sq.

Royal National Theatre   Home to one of the world's greatest stage companies, the Royal National Theatre is not one but three theaters—the Olivier, reminiscent of a Greek amphitheater with its open stage; the more traditional Lyttelton; and the Cottesloe, with its flexible stage and seating. The National presents the finest in world theater, from classic drama to award-winning new plays, including comedies, musicals, and shows for young people. A choice of at least six plays is offered at any one time.

It's also a full-time theater center, with an amazing selection of bars, cafes, restaurants, free foyer music and exhibitions, short early-evening performances, bookshops, backstage tours, riverside walks, and terraces. You can have a three-course meal in Mezzanine, the National's restaurant; enjoy a light meal in the brasserie-style Terrace cafe; or have a snack in one of the coffee bars. South Bank, SE1. © 020/7452-3000. www.nt-online.org. Tickets £11–£40 ($20–$74); midweek matinees, Sat matinees, and previews cost less. Tube: Waterloo, Embankment, or Charing Cross.

Shakespeare's Globe Theatre   In May 1997, the new Globe Theatre—a replica of the Elizabethan original, thatched roof and all—staged its first slate of plays (*Henry V* and *A Winter's Tale*) yards away from the site of the 16th-century theater where the Bard originally staged his work.

Productions vary in style and setting; not all are performed in Elizabethan costume. In keeping with the historic setting, no lighting is focused just on the stage, but floodlighting is used during evening performances to replicate daylight in the theater—Elizabethan performances took place in the afternoon. Theatergoers sit on wooden benches of yore—in thatch-roofed galleries, no less—but these days you can rent a cushion to make yourself more comfortable. About 500 "groundlings" can stand in the uncovered yard around the stage, just as they did when the Bard was here. Mark Rylane, the artistic director of the Globe, wanted the theatergoing experience to be as authentic as possible—he told the press he'd be delighted if the audience threw fruit at the actors, as they did in Shakespeare's time.

From May to September, the company intends to hold performances Tuesday through Saturday at 2 and 7pm. There will be a limited winter schedule. In any season, the schedule may be affected by weather because this is an outdoor theater. Performances last 2½ to 4 hours, depending on the play.

For details on the exhibition that tells the story of the painstaking re-creation of the Globe, as well as guided tours of the theater, see p. 186. New Globe Walk, Bankside, SE1. © 020/7902-1400. Box office 020/7902-1401. www.shakespeare-globe.org. Tickets £5 ($9.25) for groundlings, £11–£29 ($20–$54) for gallery seats. Exhibition tickets £8 ($15) adults, £6.50 ($12) students and seniors, £5 ($9.25) ages 5–15. Tube: Mansion House or Blackfriars.

Theatre Royal Drury Lane   Drury Lane is one of London's oldest and most prestigious theaters, crammed with tradition—not all of it respectable. This, the fourth theater on this site, dates from 1812; the first was built in 1663. Nell Gwynne, the rough-tongued cockney lass who became Charles II's mistress, used to sell oranges under the long colonnade in front. Nearly every star of London theater has taken the stage here at some time. It has a wide-open repertoire but leans toward musicals, especially long-running hits. The box office is open Monday through Saturday from 10am to 8 pm. Guided tours of the backstage

area and the front of the house are given most days at 2:15pm and 4:45pm. Call
© **020/7494-5091** for more information. Catherine St., Covent Garden, WC2. © 020/
7494-5000. Tickets £9–£58 ($17–$107). Evening performances Mon–Sat 8pm; matinees Wed and
Sat 3pm. Tube: Covent Garden.

THE REST OF THE PERFORMING ARTS SCENE

Currently, London supports five major orchestras—the **London Symphony,**
the **Royal Philharmonic,** the **Philharmonia Orchestra,** the **BBC Symphony,**
and the **BBC Philharmonic**—several choirs, and many smaller chamber groups
and historic instrument ensembles. Look for the **London Sinfonietta,** the
English Chamber Orchestra, and of course, the **Academy of St. Martin-in-
the-Fields.** Performances are in the South Banks Arts Centre and the Barbican.
Smaller recitals are at Wigmore Hall and St. John's Smith Square.

Barbican Centre   The largest art and exhibition center in Western Europe,
the roomy and comfortable Barbican complex is a perfect setting for enjoying
music and theater. Barbican Hall is the permanent home address of the **London
Symphony Orchestra** as well as host to visiting orchestras and performers, from
classical to jazz, folk, and world music.

In addition to the hall and the two Royal Shakespeare Company theaters, the
Barbican Centre encompasses the Barbican Art Gallery, a showcase for visual
arts; the Concourse Gallery and foyer exhibition spaces; Cinemas One and Two,
which show recently released mainstream films and film series; the Barbican
Library, a general lending library that places a strong emphasis on the arts; the
Conservatory, one of London's largest plant houses; and restaurants, cafes, and
bars. The Barbican Centre's box office is open daily from 9am to 8pm. Silk St., The
City, EC2. © **020/7638-8891.** www.barbican.org.uk. Tickets £8–£42 ($15–$78). Tube: Barbican
or Moorgate.

English National Opera   Built in 1904 as a variety theater and converted
into an opera house in 1968, the London Coliseum is the city's largest theater.
One of two national opera companies, the English National Opera performs a
wide range of works from classics to Gilbert and Sullivan to new and experimental works, staged with flair and imagination. All performances are in
English. A repertory of 18 to 20 productions is presented 5 or 6 nights a week
for 11 months of the year (dark in July). Although balcony seats are cheaper,
many visitors seem to prefer the upper circle or dress circle. London Coliseum, St.
Martin's Lane, WC2. © **020/7632-8300.** www.eno.org. Tickets £5–£30 ($9.25–$56) balcony,
£20–£78 ($37–$144) upper or dress circle or stalls; about 100 discount balcony tickets sold on the
day of performance from 10am. Tube: Charing Cross or Leicester Sq.

Royal Albert Hall   Opened in 1871 and dedicated to the memory of Victoria's
consort, Prince Albert, the circular building holds one of the world's most famous
auditoriums. With a seating capacity of 5,200, it's a popular place to hear music
by stars such as Eric Clapton and Tracy Chapman. Occasional sporting events
(especially boxing) figure strongly here, too.

Since 1941, the hall has been the setting for the BBC Henry Wood Promenade
Concerts, known as **"The Proms,"** a concert series that lasts for 8 weeks between
mid-July and mid-September. The Proms have been a British tradition since
1895. Although most of the audience occupies reserved seats, true aficionados
usually opt for standing room in the orchestra pit, which affords close-up views
of the musicians performing on stage. Newly commissioned works are often pre-
miered here. The final evening of The Proms is the most traditional; the rousing
favorites "Jerusalem" or "Land of Hope and Glory" echo through the hall. For

tickets, call Ticketmaster (② **0870/534-4444**) directly, or the theater's box office is open daily from 9am to 9pm. Kensington Gore, SW7 2AP. ② **020/7589-8212**. www. royalalberthall.com. Tickets £18–£52 ($33–$96), depending on the event. Tube: South Kensington.

Royal Festival Hall   In the aftermath of World War II, the principal site of London's music scene shifted to the south bank of the Thames. Three of the most acoustically perfect concert halls in the world were erected between 1951 and 1964. They include Royal Festival Hall, the Queen Elizabeth Hall, and the Purcell Room. Together they hold more than 1,200 performances a year, including classical music, ballet, jazz, popular music, and contemporary dance. Also here is the internationally renowned **Hayward Gallery.**

Royal Festival Hall, which opens daily at 10am, offers an extensive array of things to see and do, including free exhibitions in the foyers and free lunchtime music at 12:30pm. On Friday, Commuter Jazz in the foyer from 5:15 to 6:45pm is free. For paying events, the box office is open daily from 9am to 8pm. The Poetry Library is open Tuesday to Sunday from 10am to 8pm, and shops display a wide selection of books, records, and crafts. The Festival Buffet has a wide variety of food at reasonable prices, and bars dot the foyers. The People's Palace offers lunch and dinner with a panoramic view of the River Thames. Reservations by calling ② **020/7928-9999** are recommended. On the South Bank, SE1. ② **0870/ 401-8181**. www.rfh.org.uk. Tickets £6–£55 ($11–$102). Tube: Waterloo or Embankment.

The Royal Opera House—The Royal Ballet & the Royal Opera   The Royal Ballet and the Royal Opera make their home in a magnificently restored theater presenting world-class performances of opera and dance. Reopened in 1999, opera and ballet aficionados of yesterday hardly recognize the place, with its spectacular public spaces, including the Vilar Floral Hall, a rooftop restaurant, and bars and shops. The entire northeast corner of one of London's most famous public squares has been transformed, finally realizing Inigo Jones's original vision for this colonnaded piazza. Regular backstage tours are possible daily at 10:30am, 12:30, and 2:30pm (not on Sun or matinee days).

Performances of the Royal Opera are usually sung in the original language, but supertitles are projected, translating the libretto for the audience. The Royal Ballet, which compares favorably with the Kirov and the Paris Opera Ballet, performs a repertory with a tilt toward the classics, including works by its earlier choreographer/directors Sir Frederick Ashton and Sir Kenneth MacMillan. Box office hours at the Royal Opera are daily from 10am to 8pm. Bow St., Covent Garden, WC2. ② **020/7304-4000**. www.royalopera.org. Tickets £15–£170 ($28–$315). Tube: Covent Garden.

Sadler's Wells Theatre   This premier venue for dance and opera occupies the site of a theater that was built in 1683, on the location of a well that was prized for the healing powers of its waters. In the early 1990s, the old-fashioned, turn-of-the-20th-century theater was demolished, and construction began on an innovative new design that was completed at the end of 1998. The original facade has been retained, but the interior has been completely revamped to create a stylish cutting-edge theater design. The new theater offers both traditional and experimental dance. Performances usually start at 8pm, and the box office is open from Monday to Saturday 10am to 8pm. Rosebery Ave., EC1. ② **020/7863- 8198**. www.sadlers-wells.com. Tickets £11–£50 ($19–$92). Tube: Angel.

Wigmore Hall   An intimate auditorium, Wigmore Hall offers an excellent regular series of song recitals, piano and chamber music, early and baroque music, and jazz. A free list of the month's programs is available from Wigmore.

A cafe-bar and restaurant are on the premises; a cold supper can be preordered if you are attending a concert. Wigmore Hall's box office is open Monday through Saturday from 10am to 7pm; call for Sunday hours. 36 Wigmore St., W1. © 020/7935-2141. www.wigmore-hall.org.uk. Tickets £10–£35 ($19–$65). Performances nightly, plus Sun Morning Coffee Concerts and Sun concerts at 11:30am or 4pm Nov to mid-Mar; mid-Mar to Oct 7pm. Tube: Bond St. or Oxford Circus.

OUTSIDE CENTRAL LONDON

Kenwood Lakeside Concerts These band and orchestral concerts on the north side of Hampstead Heath have been a British tradition for some 50 years. In recent years, laser shows and fireworks have added to a repertoire that includes everything from rousing versions of the *1812 Overture* to jazz and such operas as *Carmen.* The final concert of the season always features some of the Pomp and Circumstance marches of Sir Edward Elgar, everyone's favorite imperial composer. Music drifts across the lake to serenade wine-and-cheese parties on the grass. Kenwood, Hampstead Lane, Hampstead Heath, London NW3 7JR. © 020/7413-1443. Tickets for adults £11 ($20) for seats on the grass lawn, £13–£18 ($24–$33) for reserved deck chairs. Reductions of 12.5% for students and persons over 60. Every summer Sat at 7:30pm July to early Sept. Tube: Golders Green or Archway, then bus no. 210.

THE CLUB & MUSIC SCENE

COMEDY

The Comedy Store This is London's most visible showcase for established and rising comic talent. Inspired by comedy clubs in the United States, this club has given many comics their start. Today a number of them are established TV personalities. Even if their names are unfamiliar, you'll enjoy the spontaneity of live comedy performed before a British audience. Visitors must be 18 and older; dress is casual. Reserve through Ticketmaster (© 020/7344-4444); the club opens 2¼ hours before each show. Shows begin at 8pm Tuesday through Sunday; Fridays and Saturdays feature an additional show at midnight. *Insider's tip:* Go on Tuesday when the humor is more cutting edge and topical. 1A Oxendon St., off Piccadilly Circus, SW1. © 087/0060-2340. Cover £12–£15 ($22–$28). Tube: Leicester Sq. or Piccadilly Circus.

LIVE MUSIC

The Bull & Gate Outside central London, and smaller, cheaper, and often more animated and less touristy than many of its competitors, The Bull & Gate is the unofficial headquarters of London's pub rock scene. Indie and relatively unknown rock bands are often served up back to back by the half dozen in this somewhat-battered Victorian pub. If you like spilled beer, this is off-the-beaten-track London at its most authentic. The place operates pub hours, with music nightly from 8pm to midnight. 389 Kentish Town Rd., NW5. © 020/8806-8062. Cover £5 ($9.25). Tube: Kentish Town.

Shepherd's Bush Empire In an old BBC television theater, with great acoustics, this is a major venue in London for big-name pop and rock stars. Announcements appear in the local press. There's a capacity seating of 2,000. The box office is open Monday through Friday from noon to 5pm and Saturday from noon to 6pm. Shepherd's Bush Green, W12. © 020/8354-3300. Ticket prices vary according to show. Tube: Hammersmith.

Sound Right in the very heart of London, this 700-seat venue books the big acts, everybody from Sinead O'Connor to Puff Daddy or the Spice Girls. This is really a music restaurant, one of the best of its type in London. The program is forever changing; call to see what's happening at the time of your visit. Swiss Centre at 10 Wardour St., Leicester Sq., W1. ℂ 020/7287-1010. Tickets £8–£12 ($15–$22). Tube: Leicester Sq.

TRADITIONAL ENGLISH MUSIC
Cecil Sharpe House   CSH was the focal point of the folk revival in the 1960s, and it continues to treasure and nurture the style. Here you'll find a whole range of traditional English music and dance. Call to find out what's happening; the box office is open from Monday to Friday 9:30am to 5:30pm. 2 Regent's Park Rd., NW1. ℂ 020/7485-2206. Tickets £7–£10 ($13–$19). Tube: Camden Town.

JAZZ & BLUES
Ain't Nothing But Blues Bar   The club, which bills itself as the only true blues venue in town, features local acts and occasional touring American bands. On weekends, prepare to wait in line. From the Oxford Circus Tube stop, walk south on Regent Street, turn left on Great Marlborough Street, and then make a quick right on Kingly Street. Hours are Monday through Thursday 6pm to 1am, Friday and Saturday 6pm to 2:30am, and Sunday 7:30pm to midnight. 20 Kingly St., W1. ℂ 020/7287-0514. Cover Thurs £3 ($5.55); Fri–Sat £5 ($9.25); free before 8:30pm. Tube: Oxford Circus.

100 Club   Although less plush and expensive than some jazz clubs, 100 Club is a serious contender. Its cavalcade of bands includes the best British jazz musicians and some of their Yankee brethren. Rock, R&B, and blues are also on tap. The club is open Sunday through Wednesday 7:30 to 11:30pm, Thursday and Friday 8pm to 12:30am, and Saturday 7:30pm to 1am; also open from noon to 3pm on Thursday and Friday. 100 Oxford St., W1. ℂ 020/7636-0933. Cover £7–£12 ($13–$22); discounts available for club members. Tube: Tottenham Court Rd. or Oxford Circus.

Pizza Express   Don't let the name fool you: This restaurant-bar serves up some of the best jazz in London by mainstream artists. While enjoying a thin-crust Italian pizza, check out a local band or a visiting group, often from the United States. Although the club has been enlarged, it's important to reserve ahead of time. Open daily from 11:30am to midnight, jazz starts at 9pm. 10 Dean St., W1. ℂ 020/7437-9595. Cover £11–£20 ($20–$37). Tube: Tottenham Court Rd.

Ronnie Scott's Club   Inquire about jazz in London and people immediately think of Ronnie Scott's, long the European vanguard for modern jazz. Located in the heart of Soho, only the best English and American combos, often fronted by a top-notch vocalist, are booked here. The programs inevitably make for an entire evening of cool jazz. In the Main Room, you can watch the show from the bar or sit at a table, from which you can order dinner. The Downstairs Bar is more intimate; among the regulars at your elbow may be some of the world's most talented musicians. On weekends, the separate Upstairs Room has a disco called Club Latino. The club is open Monday through Saturday from 8:30pm to 3am. 47 Frith St., W1. ℂ 020/7439-0747. Cover nonmember Mon–Thurs £15 ($28), member £5 ($9.25), Fri–Sat nonmember £25 ($46), member £10 ($19). Tube: Leicester Sq. or Piccadilly Circus.

606 Club   Located in a discreet basement site in Chelsea, the 606 presents live music nightly. Predominantly a venue for modern jazz, style ranges from traditional to contemporary. Local musicians and some very big names play here, whether planned gigs or informal jam sessions after their shows elsewhere in town. This is actually a jazz supper club in the boondocks of Fulham; because of license requirements, patrons can only order alcohol with food. Open Monday through Wednesday 7:30pm to 1am, Thursday 8pm to 1:30am, Friday and Saturday 8pm to 1:30am, and Sunday 8pm to midnight. 90 Lots Rd., SW10. ℂ 020/7352-5953. Cover Mon–Thurs £7 ($13); Fri–Sat £9 ($17); Sun £6–£8 ($11–$15). Tube: Earl's Court.

DANCE, DISCO & ECLECTIC

Bar Rumba   Despite its location on Shaftesbury Avenue, this Latin bar and club could be featured in a book of Underground London. A hush-hush address, it leans toward radical jazz fusion on some nights, phat funk on other occasions. The club boasts two full bars and a different musical theme every night; Tuesday and Wednesday are the only nights you probably won't have to queue at the door. Monday's "That's How It Is" showcase features jazz, hip-hop, and drum and bass; Friday's provides R&B and swing; and Saturday's "Garage City" buzzes with house and garage. On weeknights you have to be 18 and up; the age limit is 21 on Saturday and Sunday. Widely varying hours are Monday 9pm to 3:30am; Tuesday, Thursday, and Friday 6pm to 3:30am; Wednesday and Sunday 8pm to 3:30am; and Saturday 7pm to 6am. 36 Shaftesbury Ave., W1. ℂ 020/ 7287-6933. Cover £3–£12 ($5.55–$22). Tube: Piccadilly Circus.

Cargo   Another watering hole in ultratrendy Hoxton draws a smart urban crowd from more expensive West End flats. Its habitués assure us it's the place to go for a "wicked time" and great live bands. If not bands, then great DJs dominate the night. The joint is jumping by 9:30 nightly because it has a limited license and must close at 1am. It's fun and funky, with two big arched rooms, fantastic acoustics, and a parade of videos. As to the patrons, the bartender characterized it just right: "We get the freaks and the normal people." Drinks are reasonably priced, as is the self-styled "street food." Open Monday through Thursday 6pm to 1am, Friday noon to 3am, Saturday 6pm to 3am, and Sunday 1pm to midnight. Kingsland Viaduct, 83 Rivington St., Shoreditch, EC2. ℂ 020/7739-3440. Cover (after 10pm) £5–£9 ($9.25–$17), depending on the entertainment. Tube: Old St.

The Cross   In the backwaters of Kings Cross, this club has stayed hot since 1993. London hipsters come here for private parties thrown by Rough Trade Records or Red Or Dead, or just to dance in the space's cozy brick-lined vaults. It's always party time here. Call to find out who's performing. Open Friday 11pm to 6am and Saturday and Sunday 10pm to 6am. The Arches, 27–31 York Way, N1. ℂ 020/7837-0828. Cover £8–£15 ($15–$28). Tube: Kings Cross.

The End   Better than ever after its recent enlargement, this club has a trio of large dance floors along with four bars and a chill-out area. Speaker walls blast you into orbit. The End is the best club in London for house and garage. It's real cutting edge, drawing both straight and gay London. "We can't tell the difference anymore," the club owner confessed, "and who cares anyway?" From its drinking fountain to its ritzy toilets, the club is alluring. Dress for glam and to be seen on the circuit. Some big names in London appear on weekends. The club's hours are Monday and Thursday 10pm to 3am, Friday 10pm to 6am, and Saturday 10pm to 7am. 18 West Central St., WC1. ℂ 020/7419-9199. Cover £4–£15 ($7.40–$28). Tube: Tottenham Court Rd.

Equinox   Built in 1992 on the site of the London Empire, a dance emporium that has witnessed the changing styles of social dancing since the 1700s, the Equinox has established itself as a perennial favorite and frequently hosts the U.K.'s hottest talent. It contains nine bars, the largest dance floor in London, and a restaurant modeled after a 1950s American diner. With the exception of rave, virtually every kind of dance music is featured here, including dance hall, pop, rock, and Latin. The setting is lavishly illuminated with one of Europe's largest lighting rigs, and the crowd is as varied as London itself. Summer visitors can enjoy their theme nights, which are geared to entertaining a worldwide audience, including a once-a-month "Ibiza" foam party—you'll actually boogie the night away on a foam-covered floor. Open Monday through Saturday 9pm to 3am (until 3:30am on Fridays and Saturdays). Leicester Sq., WC2. ✆ **020/7437-1446.** Cover £6–£12 ($11–$22), depending on the night of the week. Tube: Leicester Sq.

Fabric   Still going strong since its opening in 1999, when other competitors have come and gone since, Fabric's main allure is its license for 24-hour music and dancing from Thursday to Sunday night. Fabric is one of the most famous clubs in the increasingly trendy East London sector; it is said that when the owners power up the underfoot subwoofer, lights dim in London's East End. On some crazed nights, at least 2,500 members of young London, plus a medley of international visitors, crowd into this mammoth place. It has a trio of dance floors, bars wherever you look, unisex toilets, chill-out beds, and even a roof terrace. Live acts are presented every Friday, with DJs reigning on weekends. 77A Charterhouse St., EC1. ✆ **020/7336-8898.** Cover £12–£15 ($22–$28). Fri 9:30pm–5am; Sat 10pm–7am; Sun 10pm–5am. Tube: Farringdon.

Hippodrome   Located near Leicester Square, the popular Hippodrome is London's grand old daddy of discos, a cavernous place with a great sound system and lights to match. It was Princess Di's favorite scene in her barhopping days. Tacky and touristy, the 'Drome is packed on weekends. Corner of Cranbourn St. and Charing Cross Rd., WC2. ✆ **020/7437-4311.** Cover £8–£11 ($15–$20). Mon–Fri 9pm–3am; Sat 9pm–3:30am. Tube: Leicester Sq.

Limelight   Although opened in 1985, this large dance club—located inside a former Welsh chapel that dates from 1754—has only recently come into its own. The dance floors and bars share space with plenty of cool Gothic nooks and crannies. DJs spin the latest house music. 136 Shaftesbury Ave., WC1. ✆ **020/7434-0572.** Cover £2–£12 ($3.70–$22). Mon–Fri 10pm–3am; Sat 9pm–3:30am. Tube: Leicester Sq.

Ministry of Sound   Removed from the city center, this club-of-the-hour is still going strong after all these years. It remains hot, hot, hot. With a large bar and an even bigger sound system, it blasts garage and house music to energetic crowds that pack the two dance floors. If the stimulants in the rest of the club have gone to your head, you can chill in the cinema room. *Note:* The club's cover charge is stiff, and bouncers decide who is cool enough to enter, so leave the sneakers and denim at home and slip into your grooviest and most glamorous club wear. 103 Gaunt St., SE1. ✆ **020/7740-8600.** Cover £12–£15 ($22–$28). Fri 10:30pm–5am; Sat 11pm–7am. Tube: Elephant & Castle.

Notting Hill Art Club   One of the hippest nighttime venues in London, the club's action takes place in a no-frills basement in increasingly fashionable Notting Hill Gate. One habitué called it "the coolest night club on earth." Yes, that was Liam Gallagher you spotted dancing with Courtney Love. To justify the name of the club, art exhibitions are sometimes staged here. Most of the clients are under 35; other than that they come from the widest range of backgrounds—from Madonna wannabes to Bob Marley wannabes. The music is eclectic, varying from night to night—jazz improv, Latino salsa, hip-hop, indie, whatever. 21 Notting Hill Gate, W11. ✆ **020/7460-4459.** Cover £3–£6 ($5.55–$11). Wed 6pm–1am; Tues 8pm–1am; Fri–Sat 8pm–2am; Sun 4pm–1am. Tube: Notting Hill Gate.

Scala This area of London is risky at night. So much so the security staff at the club is happy to escort you to a taxi when you're leaving. In spite of its crime-ridden surroundings, this is a hot, happening venue for young London. A former movie theater has been converted into this successful club, where DJs spin the latest music and ramped balconies offer dancing on different tiers. The gigantic screen blows your mind with scintillating visuals. Some nights are theme oriented such as a long-running gay-mixed extravaganza called *Popstarz*. The music runs the range from garage to R&B to Latin salsa. Wear anything except on Saturday nights when caps and sportswear are forbidden. 275 Pentonville Rd., Kings Cross, N1. ℂ 020/7833-2022. Cover £9–£15 ($17–$28). Fri–Sat 10pm–5am; otherwise opening times vary. Tube: Kings Cross.

Trap This is one of the leading clubs of the West End lying in the vicinity of Oxford and Regent streets. It's a stylish rendezvous, drawing a crowd in their 20s and 30s to its plush precincts. The young Mick Jagger or aspirant Madonna of today may be seen lounging on one of the large white-covered sofas across from the sleek bar. Drinks are expensive, so be duly warned. Recorded music plays for dancing; Thursday and Friday nights are especially busy. A supper club adjoins the joint and is open for most of the night. 201 Wardour St., W1. ℂ 020/7434-3820. Cover £5–£15 ($9.25–$28). Tues–Wed 5pm–midnight; Thurs–Fri 5pm–3am; Sat 5–10pm. Tube: Tottenham Court Rd. or Oxford Circus.

Vibe Bar As more and more of hip London heads east, bypassing even Clerenwell for Hoxton, Vibe has been put on the map. *The Evening Standard* named it among the top five DJ bars in London. The paper compared it to an "expensively distressed pair of designer jeans." It's a nightspot operated by Truman Brewery. In summer the action overflows onto a courtyard. Patrons check their e-mail, lounge on comfortable couches, and listen to diverse music such as reggae, Latin, jazz, R&B, Northern Soul, African, or hip-hop. 91–95 Brick Lane, E1. ℂ 020/7428-0491. Cover: Free or £1–£2 ($1.85–$3.70) sometimes assessed after 6pm. Sun–Thurs 1:30–11pm; Fri–Sat 7:30pm–1am. Tube: Liverpool St.

Zoo Bar The owners spent millions of pounds outfitting this club in the slickest, flashiest, and most psychedelic decor in London. If you're looking for a true Euro nightlife experience replete with gorgeous au pairs and trendy Europeans, this is it. Zoo Bar upstairs is a menagerie of mosaic animals beneath a glassed-in ceiling dome. Downstairs, the music is intrusive enough to make conversation futile. Clients range from 18 to 35; androgyny is the look of choice. 13–18 Bear St., WC2. ℂ 020/7839-4188. Cover £3–£7 ($5.55–$13) after 10pm. Mon–Fri 4pm–3:30am; Sat 1pm–3:30am; Sun 4pm–12:30am. Tube: Leicester Sq.

THE GAY & LESBIAN SCENE

The most reliable source of information on gay clubs and activities is the **Lesbian and Gay Switchboard** (ℂ 020/7837-7324). The staff runs a 24-hour service for information on gay-friendly places and activities. *Time Out* also carries listings on such clubs. Also a good place for finding out what's hot and hip is **Prowler Soho,** 3–7 Brewer St., Soho, W1 (ℂ 020/7734-4031; Tube: Piccadilly Circus), the largest gay lifestyle store in London. (You can also buy anything from jewelry to CDs and books, fashion, and sex toys.) It's open until midnight on Friday and Saturday.

Admiral Duncan Gay men and their friends go here to drink and to have a good time but also to make a political statement. British tabloids shocked the world on April 30, 1999, when they revealed that this old pub had been bombed, with three people dying in the attack. Within 6 weeks, the pub defiantly reopened in the wake of such insane intolerance. We're happy to report it's back in business and better than ever; even nongays show up to show their support. 54 Old Compton St., W1. © 020/7437-5300. Mon–Sat noon–11pm; Sun noon–10:30pm. Tube: Piccadilly Circus.

The Box Adjacent to one of Covent Garden's best-known junctions, Seven Dials, this sophisticated Mediterranean-style bar attracts all types of men. In the afternoon, it is primarily a restaurant, serving meal-size salads, club sandwiches, and soups. Food service ends abruptly at 5:30pm, after which the place reveals its core: a cheerful, popular place of rendezvous for London's gay and countercultural crowds. The Box considers itself a "summer bar," throwing open doors and windows to a cluster of outdoor tables that attracts a crowd at the slightest hint of sunshine. 32–34 Monmouth St. (at Seven Dials), WC2. © 020/7240-5828. Mon–Sat 11am–11pm; Sun noon–10:30pm (cafe Mon–Sat 11am–5:30pm; Sun noon–6pm). Tube: Covent Garden.

Candy Bar The most popular lesbian bar in London at the moment, it has an extremely mixed clientele from butch to fem, from young to old. With a bar and a club downstairs, design is simple, with bright colors and lots of mirrors upstairs while darker and more flirtatious downstairs. Men are welcome as long as they are escorted by a woman. 4 Carlisle St., W1 © 020/7494-4041. Cover £5–£7 ($9.25–$13). Mon–Thurs 5–11pm; Fri–Sat 8pm–2am; Sun 7–11pm. Tube: Tottenham Court Rd.

The Edge Few bars in London can rival the tolerance, humor, and sexual sophistication found here. The first two floors are done up with accessories that, like an English garden, change with the seasons. Dance music can be found on the high-energy and crowded lower floors. One reader claims the bartenders water down the drinks. Three menus are featured: a funky daytime menu, a cafe menu, and a late-night menu. Dancers hit the floors starting around 7:30pm. Clientele ranges from the flamboyantly gay to hetero pub-crawlers out for a night of slumming. 11 Soho Sq., W1. © 020/7439-1313. Mon–Sat 11:30am–1am; Sun noon–10:30pm. Tube: Tottenham Court Rd.

First Out First Out prides itself on being London's first (est. 1986) all-gay coffee shop. Set in a 19th-century building whose wood panels have been painted the colors of the gay liberation rainbow, the bar offers an exclusively vegetarian menu. Cappuccino and whiskey are the preferred libations; curry dishes, potted pies in phyllo pastries, and salads are the foods of choice. Don't expect a raucous pickup scene—some clients come here with their grandmothers. Look for the bulletin board with leaflets and business cards of gay and gay-friendly entrepreneurs. 52 St. Giles High St., W1 © 020/7240-8042. Mon–Sat 10am–11pm; Sun 11am–10:30pm. Tube: Tottenham Court Rd.

G.A.Y. The name notwithstanding, the clientele here is mixed, and on a Saturday night this could well be the most rollicking club in London. A mammoth place, this club draws a young crowd to dance at this pop extravaganza with its mirrored disco balls. Overheard recently: One young man asked another his sexual orientation. The reply: "Total confusion!" London Astoria, 157 Charing Cross Rd., WC2. © 020/7434-9592. Admission £10–£13 ($19–$24). Mon–Fri 10:30pm–4am; Sat 10:30pm–4:30am. Tube: Tottenham Court Rd.

Heaven This club in the vaulted cellars of Charing Cross Railway Station is a London landmark. Owned by the same investors who brought the world Virgin Atlantic Airways, Heaven is one of the biggest and best-established gay venues in

Britain. Painted black and reminiscent of an air-raid shelter, the club is divided into at least four distinct areas, connected by a labyrinth of catwalk stairs and hallways. Each area has a different activity going on. Heaven also has theme nights, frequented at different times by gays, lesbians, or a mostly heterosexual crowd. Thursday in particular seems open to anything, but Saturday is gay only. The Arches, Villiers St., WC2. © 020/7930-2020. Cover £5–£12 ($9.25–$22). Mon and Wed 10:30pm–3am; Fri 10:30pm–6am; Sat 10:30pm–5am. Tube: Charing Cross or Embankment.

THE BAR & PUB SCENE
OUR FAVORITE BARS

American Bar   The bartender in this sophisticated gathering place is known for his special concoctions, "Savoy Affair" and "Prince of Wales," as well as what is reputedly the best martini in town. Monday through Saturday evenings, jazz piano is featured from 7 to 11pm. Near many West End theaters, the location is ideal for a pre- or post-theater drink. In The Savoy, The Strand, WC2. © 020/7836-4343. Smart casual: No jeans, sneakers, T-shirts. Tube: Charing Cross, Covent Garden, or Embankment.

Beach Blanket Babylon   Go here for a hot singles bar that attracts a crowd in their 20s and 30s. This Portobello joint—named after a kitschy musical revue in San Francisco—is close to the Portobello market and is a huge pickup spot. The decor is a bit wacky, no doubt designed by an aspiring Salvador Dalí who decided to make it a fairy-tale grotto (or did he mean a medieval dungeon?). Saturday and Sunday nights are the hot, crowded times to show up for bacchanalian revelry. 45 Ledbury Rd., W11. © 020/7229-2907. Tube: Notting Hill Gate.

Cantaloupe   This bustling pub and restaurant is hailed as the bar that jumpstarted the increasingly fashionable Shoreditch scene. Business people leaving their jobs in the City mix with East End trendies in the early evening at what has been called a "gastro pub/pre-club bar." Wooden tables and benches are found up front, although the Red Bar is more comfortable, as patrons lounge on Chesterfield chairs. The urban beat is courtesy of the house DJ. Its restaurant and tapas menus are first-rate. 35-42 Charlotte Rd., Shoreditch, EC2. © 020/7613-4411. Tube: Old St.

The Lobby Bar   This bar and the bar associated with the Axis restaurant are in one of London's trendiest five-star hotel. We advise that you check out the dramatic visuals of both before selecting your preferred nesting place for a drink or two. The Lobby Bar occupies what was built in 1907 as the very grand, very high-ceilinged reception area for one of London's premier newspapers. If that setting doesn't appeal to you, check out the travertine, hardwood, and leathersheathed bar in the Axis restaurant. The Lobby Bar is open daily from 10am to 10:45pm; the Axis bar is open at hours that correspond to those of the restaurant. In the Hotel One Aldwych, 1 Aldwych, WC2. © 020/7300-1000. Tube: Covent Garden.

The Mandarin Bar   No other bar in London showcases the art of the cocktail as artfully as this one. Designed by design-industry superstar Adam Tihany around a geometric theme of artfully backlit glass, it provides the kind of cool, hip, and confidently prosperous venue where men look attractive, women look fantastic, and cocktails are sublime. These are prepared without fuss behind frosted-glass panels, in a style akin to a holy rite at a pagan temple, then presented with tact and charm. There's live music every Monday through Saturday from 9pm till closing, and a leather-upholstered area off to the side, with a state-of-the-art air filtration system, for cigar smokers and their fans. In the Mandarin Oriental Hyde Park Hotel, 66 Knightsbridge, SW1. © 020/7235-2000. Tube: Knightsbridge.

Finds **Drinks à la Americana**

Everybody's heard of the Hard Rock Cafe, but the real news coming out of London is the sudden opening of so many American-theme bars. The best one is **Navajo Joe,** 34 King St., WC2 (✆ **020/7240-4008;** Tube: Covent Garden), which offers the largest tequila selection outside of Mexico and whose southwestern cuisine is already starting to win some restaurant awards.

Match EC1 An epicenter of the fashionable set in London has put the P in partying in the once-staid Clerkenwell district. High on the list for evening fun is Match, drawing a 20s-to-30s crowd. Drinkers sit on elegant sofas or retreat to one of the cozy booths for a late bitedown. The bar claims to be the home of the cocktail, Cosmopolitan, that swept across the speakeasies of New York. The bartenders make some of the best drinks in London but warn you that "there is no such thing as a chocolate martini." 45–47 Clerkenwell Rd., EC1. ✆ **020/7250-4002.** Tube: Farringdon.

The Phoenix Artist Club Want something so old it's new again? This is where Lord Laurence Olivier made his stage debut in 1930, although he couldn't stop giggling even though the play was drama. Live music is featured, but it's the hearty welcome, the good beer, and friendly patrons that make this "rediscovered" theater bar worth a detour. 1 Phoenix St., WC2. ✆ **020/7836-1077.** Tube: Tottencourt Court Rd.

THE WORLD'S GREATEST PUB CRAWL
BELGRAVIA
Grenadier *Finds* Tucked away in a mews, the Grenadier is one of London's reputedly haunted pubs. Aside from the poltergeist, the basement houses the original bar and skittles alley used by the duke of Wellington's officers on leave from fighting Napoleon. The scarlet front door of the one-time officers' mess is guarded by a scarlet sentry box and shaded by a vine. The bar is nearly always crowded. Lunch and dinner are offered daily—even Sunday, when it's a tradition to drink Bloody Marys here. In stalls along the side, you can order good-tasting fare based on seasonal ingredients. Well-prepared dishes include pork Grenadier and chicken and Stilton roulade. Snacks such as fish and chips are available at the bar. 18 Wilton Row, SW1. ✆ **020/7235-3074.** Tube: Hyde Park Corner.

BLOOMSBURY
Museum Tavern Across the street from The British Museum, this pub (ca. 1703) retains most of its antique trappings: velvet, oak paneling, and cut glass. It lies right in the center of the University of London area and is popular with writers, publishers, and researchers from the museum. (Supposedly, Karl Marx wrote while dining in the pub.) Traditional English food is served: shepherd's pie, sausages cooked in English cider, turkey-and-ham pie, ploughman's lunch, and salads. Several English ales, cold lagers, cider, Guinness, wines, and spirits are available. Food and coffee are served all day; the pub gets crowded at lunchtime. 49 Great Russell St., WC1. ✆ **020/7242-8987.** Tube: Holborn or Tottenham Court Rd.

THE CITY
Bow Wine Vaults Bow Wine Vaults has existed since long before the wine-bar craze began in the 1970s. One of the most famous wine bars of London, it attracts

cost-conscious diners and drinkers to its vaulted cellars for such traditional fare as deep-fried Camembert, lobster ravioli, and a mixed grill, along with fish. More elegant meals, served in the street-level dining room, include mussels in cider sauce, English wild mushrooms in puff pastry, beef Wellington, and steak with brown-butter sauce. Adjacent to the restaurant is a cocktail bar that's popular with City employees after work (open weekdays 11:30am–11pm). 10 Bow Churchyard, EC4. ☎ 020/7248-1121. Tube: Mansion House, Bank, or St. Paul's.

Jamaica Wine House   Jamaica Wine House was one of the first coffeehouses in England and, reputedly, the Western world. For years, merchants and daring sea captains came here to transact deals over rum and coffee. Nowadays, the two-level house dispenses beer, ale, lager, and fine wines, among them a variety of ports. The oak-paneled bar is on the street level, attracting a jacket-and-tie crowd of investment bankers. You can order standard but filling dishes such as a ploughman's lunch and toasted sandwiches. St. Michael's Alley off Cornhill, EC3. ☎ 020/7929-6972. Tube: Bank.

Ye Olde Cock Tavern   Dating from 1549, this tavern boasts a long line of literary patrons: Samuel Pepys mentioned the pub in his diaries, Dickens frequented it, and Tennyson referred to it in one of his poems (a copy of which is framed and proudly displayed near the front entrance). It's one of the few buildings in London to have survived the Great Fire of 1666. At street level, you can order a pint as well as bar food, steak-and-kidney pie, or a cold chicken-and-beef plate with salad. At the Carvery upstairs, a meal includes a choice of appetizers, followed by lamb, pork, beef, or turkey. 22 Fleet St., EC4. ☎ 020/7353-8570. Tube: Temple or Chancery Lane.

Ye Olde Watling   Ye Olde Watling was rebuilt after the Great Fire of 1666. On the ground level is a mellow pub; upstairs is an intimate restaurant where, under oak beams and at trestle tables, you can dine on simple English main dishes for lunch. The menu varies daily, with such choices and reliable standbys as fish and chips, lamb satay, lasagna, fishcakes, and usually a vegetarian dish. All are served with two vegetables or salad, plus rice or potatoes. 29 Watling St., EC4. ☎ 020/7653-9971. Tube: Mansion House.

COVENT GARDEN

Lamb & Flag   Dickens once hung out in this pub, and the room itself is little changed from the days when he prowled this neighborhood. The pub has an amazing and somewhat scandalous history. Dryden was almost killed by a band of thugs outside its doors in December 1679; the pub gained the nickname the "Bucket of Blood" during the Regency era (1811–20) because of the routine bare-knuckled prizefights that broke out here. Tap beers include Courage Best and Directors, Old Speckled Hen, John Smith's, and Wadworth 6X. 33 Rose St., off Garrick St., WC2. ☎ 020/7497-9504. Tube: Leicester Sq.

Nag's Head   The Nag's Head is one of London's most famous Edwardian pubs. In days of yore, patrons had to make their way through lorries of fruit and flowers to drink here. But when the market moved, 300 years of British tradition faded away. Today, the pub is patronized mainly by young people. The draft Guinness is very good. Lunch is typical pub grub: sandwiches, salads, pork cooked in cider, and garlic prawns. The sandwich platters mentioned above are served only during the lunch hour (noon–4pm); however, snacks are available in the afternoon. 10 James St., WC2. ☎ 020/7836-4678. Tube: Covent Garden.

EAST END (WAPPING)

Prospect of Whitby   One of London's most historic pubs, it was founded in the days of the Tudors, taking its name from a coal barge that made trips between Yorkshire and London. Come here for a tot, noggin, or whatever it is you drink and soak up its traditional pubby atmosphere. It has quite a pedigree. Dickens and Samuel Pepys used to drop in, and Turner came here for weeks at a time studying views of the Thames. In the 17th century, the notorious Hanging Judge Jeffreys used to get drunk here while overseeing hangings he'd ordered at the adjoining Execution Dock. Tables in the courtyard look out over river views. You can order a Moorlands Old Speckled Hen from a hand pump or a malt whiskey. 57 Wapping Wall, El. © 020/7481-1095. Mon–Fri 11:30am–3pm and 5:30–11pm; Sat 11:30am–11pm; Sun noon–10:30pm. Tube: Wapping.

HOLBORN

Cittie of Yorke   This pub boasts the longest bar in all of Britain, rafters ascending to the heavens, and a long row of immense wine vats, all of which give it the air of a great medieval hall—appropriate because a pub has existed at this location since 1430. Samuel Smith's is on tap. 22 High Holborn, WC1. © **020/7242-7670.** Tube: Holborn or Chancery Lane.

KNIGHTSBRIDGE

Nag's Head   This Nag's Head (not to be confused with the more renowned one at 10 James St.; see above) is snuggled on a back street a short walk from the Berkeley Hotel. Previously a jail dating from 1780, it's said to be the smallest pub in London, although others claim that distinction. In 1921, it was sold for £12 ($22) and 6p (10¢). Have a drink up front or wander to the tiny little bar in the rear. For food, you may enjoy "real ale sausage" (made with pork and ale), shepherd's pie, or even the quiche of the day. This warm and cozy pub, with a welcoming staff, is patronized by a cosmopolitan clientele—newspaper people, musicians, and curious tourists. This pub touts itself as an "independent," or able to serve any "real ale" they choose because of their lack of affiliation. 53 Kinnerton St., SW1. © 020/7235-1135. Tube: Hyde Park.

LEICESTER SQUARE

Salisbury *(finds)*   Salisbury's glittering cut-glass mirrors reflect the faces of English stage stars (and hopefuls) sitting around the curved buffet-style bar. A less prominent place to dine is the old-fashioned wall banquette with its copper-topped tables and Art Nouveau decor. The pub's specialty, home-cooked pies set out in a buffet cabinet with salads, is really quite good and inexpensive. 90 St. Martin's Lane, WC2. © **020/7836-5863.** Tube: Leicester Sq.

MAYFAIR

Shepherd's Tavern   This pub is one of the focal points of the all-pedestrian shopping zone of Shepherd's Market. It's set amid a warren of narrow, cobble-covered streets behind Park Lane, in an 18th-century town house very similar to many of its neighbors. The street-level bar is cramped but congenial. Many of the regulars recall this tavern's popularity with the pilots of the Battle of Britain. Bar snacks include simple plates of shepherd's pie and fish and chips. More formal dining is available upstairs in the cozy, cedar-lined Georgian-style restaurant; the classic British menu probably hasn't changed much since the 1950s. You can always get Oxford ham or roast beef with Yorkshire pudding. 50 Hertford St., W1. © **020/7499-3017.** Tube: Green Park.

NOTTING HILL GATE

Ladbroke Arms   Previously honored as London's "Dining Pub of the Year," Ladbroke Arms is that rare pub known for its food. A changing menu includes chicken breast stuffed with avocado and garlic steak in pink-peppercorn sauce. With background jazz and rotating art prints, the place strays a bit from a traditional pub environment, but it makes for a pleasant stop and a good meal. The excellent Eldridge Pope Royal is on tap, as well as John Smith's and Courage Directors, and several malt whiskies. 54 Ladbroke Rd., W11. ℭ 020/7727-6648. Tube: Notting Hill Gate.

ST. JAMES'S

Red Lion   This little Victorian pub, with its early-1900s decorations and mirrors that are 150 years old, has been compared in spirit to Manet's painting *A Bar at the Folies-Bergére* (on display at the Courtauld Gallery). You can order pre-made sandwiches, but once they're gone you're out of luck. On Saturday, homemade fish and chips are also served. Wash down your meal with Ind Coope's fine ales or the house's special beer, Burton's, an unusual brew made of spring water from the Midlands town of Burton-on-Trent. 2 Duke of York St. (off Jermyn St.), SW1. ℭ 020/7321-0782. Tube: Piccadilly Circus.

SOHO

Dog & Duck   This snug little joint, a Soho landmark, is the most intimate pub in London. One former patron was author George Orwell, who came here to celebrate his sales of *Animal Farm* in the United States. A wide mixture of patrons of all ages and persuasions flock here, chatting amiably while ordering the delights of Tetley's LA or Timothy Taylor Landlord. Perhaps in autumn customers will ask for Addlestones Cider. A lot of patrons head later for Ronnie Scott's Jazz Club, which is close by. If business warrants it, the cozy upstairs bar is opened. 18 Bateman St. (corner of Frith St.), W1. ℭ 020/7494-0697.

SOUTHWARK

George   Preserved by the National Trust, the existing structure here was built to replace the original pub, which was destroyed in the Great Fire. The pub's accolades date from 1598, when it was reviewed as a "faire inn for the receipt of travellers." No longer an inn, it's still a great place to enjoy Flowers Original, Boddington's, and London Pride Abbot on tap. Off 77 Borough High St., SE1. ℭ 020/7407-2056. Tube: Northern Line to London Bridge or Borough.

TRAFALGAR SQUARE

Sherlock Holmes   The Sherlock Holmes was the old gathering spot for the Baker Street Irregulars, a once-mighty clan of mystery lovers who met here to honor the genius of Sir Arthur Conan Doyle's most famous fictional character. Upstairs, you'll find a re-creation of the living room at 221B Baker Street and such "Holmesiana" as the serpent of *The Speckled Band* and the head of *The Hound of the Baskervilles*. In the upstairs dining room, you can order complete meals with wine. Try "Copper Beeches" (grilled butterfly chicken breasts with lemon and herbs). You select dessert from the trolley. Downstairs is mainly for drinking, but there's a good snack bar with cold meats, salads, cheeses, and wine and ales sold by the glass. 10 Northumberland St., WC1. ℭ 020/7930-2644. Tube: Charing Cross or Embankment.

6

The Thames Valley

The historic Thames Valley and Chiltern Hills lie so close to London that you can easily reach them by car, train, or Green Line coach. In fact, you can explore this area during the day and return to London in time to see a West End show.

The most visited historic site in England is **Windsor Castle,** 34km (21 miles) west of London. If you base yourself in Windsor, you can spend another day exploring some of the sights on its periphery, including **Eton** (which adjoins Windsor), **Runnymede,** and **Windsor Great Park.**

If your visit coincides with the spring social sporting season, you can head to Ascot or Henley-on-Thames for the famous social sporting events: Ascot and the Royal Regatta. Be sure to wear a hat!

Some great historic homes and gardens in the area include Woburn Abbey, Hatfield House, Hughenden Manor, Mapledurham House, and Wellington Ducal Estate. If your time is severely limited, the two most important country mansions to visit are

Woburn Abbey and **Hatfield House.** Woburn Abbey could consume an entire day, whereas you can visit Hatfield in a morning or afternoon.

It's not just the historic homes that make the Home Counties intriguing to visit; the land of river valleys and gentle hills makes for wonderful drives. The beech-clad Chilterns are at their most beautiful in spring and autumn. This 64km (40-mile) chalk ridge extends in an arc from the Thames Valley to the old Roman city of St. Albans in Hertfordshire. The whole region is popular for boating holidays on its 322km (200-mile) network of canals.

Oxfordshire is a land of great mansions, old churches of widely varying architectural styles, and rolling farmland. Certainly your main reason for visiting Oxfordshire is to explore the university city of **Oxford,** about an hour's ride from London by car or train. It's not a good day trip, though, as it has too much to see and do. Plan to spend the night; the next morning you can visit Blenheim Palace, England's answer to Versailles.

1 Windsor & Eton ✿

34km (21 miles) W of London

Were it not for the castle, Windsor might still be a charming Thames town to visit. But because it is the home of the best-known asset the royal family possesses, it is overrun in summer by tourists who all but obscure the town's charm.

The good news is that after the disastrous fire of 1992, Windsor Castle is restored, though some of the new designs for it have been called a "Gothic shocker" or "ghastly." Actually, in spite of some media criticism, a remarkable activity in restoration went on, as woodcarvers, gilders, and plasterers followed the same techniques as did their predecessors in the Middle Ages, when William the Conqueror built the castle. Queen Elizabeth opened the state apartments in November 1997 following a $62 million project that returned most of the ruined part of the castle to its original condition. Windsor Castle remains Britain's second-most-visited historic building, behind the Tower of London, attracting 1.2 million visitors a year.

ESSENTIALS

GETTING THERE   More than a dozen trains per day make the 30-minute trip from Waterloo or Paddington Station in London (you'll have to transfer at Slough to the Slough–Windsor shuttle train). The cost is £7.30 ($14) round-trip. Call ✆ **0845/748-4950** or visit www.railtrack.co.uk for more information.

Green Line coaches (✆ **0870/608-7261;** www.greenline.co.uk) nos. 700 and 702 from Hyde Park Corner in London take about 1½ hours, depending on the day of the week. A same-day round-trip costs £8 ($15). The bus drops you near the parish church, across the street from the castle. Buses also depart from Victoria station, Colonnades, stop 1.

If you're driving from London, take the M4 west.

VISITOR INFORMATION   A **Tourist Information Centre** is located across from Windsor Castle on High Street (✆ **01753/743900;** www.windsor.gov.uk). It is open Monday through Friday and Sunday from 10am to 4pm, Saturday from 10am to 5pm. It also books walking tours for the Oxford guild of guides.

CASTLE HILL SIGHTS

Queen Mary's Dolls' House   A palace in perfect miniature, the Dolls' House was given to Queen Mary in 1923 as a symbol of national goodwill. The house, designed by Sir Edwin Lutyens, was created on a scale of 1 to 12. It took 3 years to complete and involved the work of 1,500 tradesmen and artists. Every item is a miniature masterpiece; each room is exquisitely furnished and every item is made exactly to scale. Working elevators stop on every floor, and there is running water in all five bathrooms.

Castle Hill. ✆ **01753/831118** for recorded information. Admission is included in entrance to Windsor Castle. Mar–Oct daily 10am–4pm; Nov–Feb daily 10am–3pm. As with Windsor Castle, it's best to call ahead to confirm opening times.

St. George's Chapel ★★★   A gem of the Perpendicular style, this chapel shares the distinction with Westminster Abbey of being a pantheon of English monarchs (Victoria is a notable exception). The present St. George's was founded in the late 15th century by Edward IV on the site of the original Chapel of the Order of the Garter (Edward III, 1348). You first enter the nave, which contains the tomb of George V and Queen Mary, designed by Sir William Reid Dick. Off the nave in the Urswick Chapel, the Princess Charlotte memorial provides an ironic touch; if she had survived childbirth in 1817, she, and not her cousin Victoria, would have ruled the British Empire. In the aisle are tombs of George VI and Edward IV. The latest royal burial in this chapel was an urn containing the ashes of the late Princess Margaret. The Edward IV "Quire," with its imaginatively carved 15th-century choir stalls, evokes the pomp and pageantry of medieval days. In the center is a flat tomb, containing the vault of the beheaded Charles I, along with Henry VIII and his third wife, Jane Seymour. Finally, you may want to inspect the Prince Albert Memorial Chapel, reflecting the opulent tastes of the Victorian era.

Castle Hill. ✆ **01753/865538.** www.stgeorges-windsor.org. Admission is included in entrance to Windsor Castle. Mon–Sat 9:45am–4:15pm. Closed Sun and for a few days in June and Dec.

Windsor Castle ★★★   William the Conqueror first ordered a castle built on this location, and since his day it has been a fateful spot for English sovereigns:

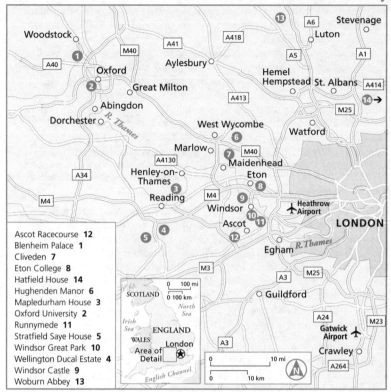

Woodstock

M40 • 1

A40 Oxford • 2 Aylesbury

A41 Great Milton

Abingdon

Dorchester R. Thames

West Wycombe • 6

Marlow • 7 **M40** Maidenhead

A4130 Henley-on-Thames Eton • 8

Reading **M4** Windsor • 9 • 10

A34 Ascot • 11 • 12

M4 • 5 • 4 Egham R. Thames

M3

13 **A6** Stevenage
Luton

A418 **A5** **A1**

Hemel Hempstead St. Albans **A414**

A413 • 14 →

Watford **M25**

Heathrow Airport **LONDON**

A3 **M25**

M3 Guildford

A3 **A24** **M23**
Gatwick Airport
Crawley
A264

SCOTLAND
0 100 mi
0 100 km
North Sea
Irish Sea
ENGLAND
WALES London
Area of Detail ★
English Channel

0 — 10 mi
0 — 10 km
N

Ascot Racecourse **12**
Blenheim Palace **1**
Cliveden **7**
Eton College **8**
Hatfield House **14**
Hughenden Manor **6**
Mapledurham House **3**
Oxford University **2**
Runnymede **11**
Stratfield Saye House **5**
Windsor Great Park **10**
Wellington Ducal Estate **4**
Windsor Castle **9**
Woburn Abbey **13**

King John cooled his heels at Windsor while waiting to put his signature on the Magna Carta at nearby Runnymede; Charles I was imprisoned here before losing his head; Queen Bess did some renovations; Victoria mourned her beloved Albert, who died at the castle in 1861; the royal family rode out much of World War II behind its sheltering walls; and when Queen Elizabeth II is in residence, the royal standard flies. With 1,000 rooms, Windsor is the world's largest inhabited castle.

The apartments display many works of art, armor, three Verrio ceilings, and several 17th-century Gibbons carvings. Several works by Rubens adorn the King's Drawing Room and in the relatively small King's Dressing Room is a Dürer, along with Rembrandt's portrait of his mother, and Van Dyck's triple portrait of Charles I. Of the apartments, the grand reception room, with its Gobelin tapestries, is the most spectacular.

George IV's elegant **Semi-State Chambers** ★★ is open only from the end of September until the end of March. They were created by the king in the 1820s as part of a series of Royal Apartments designed for his personal use. Seriously damaged in 1992, they have been returned to their former glory, with lovely antiques, paintings, and decorative objects. The Crimson Drawing room is evocative of the king's flamboyant taste with gilt, crimson silk damask hangings, and sumptuous art works.

In November 1992, a fire swept through part of the castle, severely damaging it. The castle has since reopened, and its public rooms are available for viewing.

It is recommended that you take a free guided tour of the castle grounds, including the Jubilee Gardens. Guides are very well informed and recapture the rich historical background of the castle.

In our opinion, the Windsor **changing of the guard** ✪ is a more exciting experience than the London exercises. The guard marches through the town whether the court is in residence or not, stopping the traffic as it wheels into the castle to the tunes of a full regimental band; when the queen is not here, a drum-and-pipe band is mustered. From April to July, the ceremony takes place Monday through Saturday at 11am. In winter, the guard is changed every 48 hours Monday through Saturday. It's best to call © **020/7321-2233** for a schedule.

Castle Hill. © 020/7321-2233. www.royalresidences.com. Admission £12 ($22) adults, £6 ($11) children 16 and under, £30 ($56) family of 4 (2 adults and 3 children under 17). Mar–Oct daily 9:45am–5:15pm; Nov–Feb daily 9:45am–4:15pm. Last admission 1 hr. before closing. Closed for periods in Apr, June, and Dec when the royal family is in residence.

Jubilee Gardens   To celebrate Queen Elizabeth's Jubilee, the .8-hectare (2-acre) Jubilee Gardens were created inside the castle's main entrance. Filled with trees, roses, and flowering shrubs, they were created by Tom Stuart-Smith, a Chelsea Flower show gold medalist. The gardens are the first established at Windsor Castle since the days of George IV in the 1820s. The gardens extend from the main gates of Windsor to St. George's Gate on Castle Hill. Color is provided by broad swaths of woodland perennials. White rambling roses clothing the old stone walls are particularly romantic.

Same hours and admission as for castle.

Windsor Farm Shop   Had any of the queen's jars of jam lately, maybe her homemade pork pie, or a bottle of her special brew? If not, head for this outlet, selling produce from her estates outside Windsor, including pheasants and partridges bagged at royal shoots. This retail outlet is found in converted Victorian potting sheds on the edge of the royal estate. Much of the produce bears the seal of the Royal Farms. The cream, yogurt, ice cream, and milk come from the two Royal Dairy farms. This latest make-a-pound scheme was devised by the brain of Prince Philip. The meat counter is especially awesome, with its cooked hams and massive ribs of beef. The steak-and-ale pies are especially tasty. You can stock up on the queen's vittles and head for a picnic in the area. You can also purchase 15-year-old whisky from Balmoral Castle in Scotland.

Datchet Rd., Old Windsor. © **01753/623800**. www.windsorfarmshop.co.uk. Free admission. Mon–Fri 9am–5pm; Sat 9am–5pm; Sun 10am–4pm.

NEARBY ETON COLLEGE ✪✪

Eton is home of what is arguably the most famous public school (Americans would call it a private school) in the world. From Windsor Castle's ramparts, you can look down on the river and onto the famous playing fields of Eton.

To get there, take a train from Paddington Station, go by car, or take the Green Line bus to Windsor. By car, take the M4 to Exit 5 to go straight to Eton.

Insider's tip: Parking is likely to be a problem, so we advise turning off the M4 at Exit 6 to Windsor; you can park here and take an easy stroll past Windsor Castle and across the Thames bridge. Follow Eton High Street to the college.

Eton College (© **01753/671000;** www.etoncollege.com) was founded by 18-year-old Henry VI in 1440. Some of England's greatest men, notably the duke of Wellington, have played on these fields. Twenty prime ministers were educated here, as well as such literary figures as George Orwell, Aldous Huxley, Ian Fleming, and Percy Bysshe Shelley, who, during his years at Eton (1804–10), was called "Mad Shelley" or "Shelley the Atheist" by his fellow pupils. Prince William, second in line to the throne, was recently a student here. If it's open, take a look at the Perpendicular chapel, with its 15th-century paintings and reconstructed fan vaulting.

The history of Eton College since its inception in 1440 is depicted in the **Museum of Eton Life,** Eton College (*©* **01753/671000**), located in vaulted wine cellars under College Hall, which were originally used as a storehouse by the college's masters. The displays, ranging from formal to extremely informal, include a turn-of-the-20th-century boy's room, schoolbooks, and canes used by senior boys to apply punishment they felt needful to their juniors.

Admission to the school and museum is £3.80 ($7.05) for adults and £3 ($5.55) for children under 15. You can also take guided tours for £4.90 ($9.05). Eton College is open from March 27 to April 20 and July 3 to September 7 daily 10:30am to 4:30pm and April 21 to July 2 and September 8 to October 3 daily from 2 to 4:30pm. Call in advance; Eton may close for special occasions. These dates vary every year depending on term and holiday dates. It's best to call.

MORE TO DO IN & AROUND WINDSOR

Windsor is largely Victorian, with lots of brick buildings and a few remnants of Georgian architecture. In and around the castle are two cobblestone streets, Church and Market, which have antiques shops, silversmiths, and pubs. After lunch or tea, you can stroll along the 5km (3-mile), aptly named **Long Walk.**

Savill Garden, Wick Lane, Englefield Green, Egham, and Surrey (*©* **01753/ 860222**) are all in **Windsor Great Park** ⍟, which is signposted from Windsor, Egham, and Ascot. Started in 1932, the 14-hectare (35-acre) garden is one of the finest of its type in the northern hemisphere. The display starts in spring with rhododendrons, camellias, and daffodils beneath the trees; then throughout the summer are spectacular displays of flowers and shrubs presented in a natural and wild state. It's open daily year-round (except at Christmas) from 10am to 6pm (to 4pm in winter). There is no admission charge, except for the Savill Garden. Admission prices for the Savill Garden vary throughout the year: from November to March, £3.50 ($6.50) for adults, £3 ($5.55) for seniors, £1.25 ($2.30) for children aged 6 to 16; in April and May, £5.50 ($10) adults, £5 ($9.25) for seniors, £2.50 ($4.65) children aged 6 to 16; and from June to October £4.50 ($8.35) adults, £4 ($7.40) for seniors, £1.50 ($2.80) children aged 6 to 16. Children 5 and under are admitted free. The location is 8km (5 miles) from Windsor along the A30; turn off at Wick Road and follow the signs to the gardens. The nearest rail station is at Egham; you'll need to take a taxi a distance of 5km (3 miles). A licensed, self-service restaurant and gift shop is on-site.

Adjoining Savill Garden are the **Valley Gardens,** full of shrubs and trees in a series of wooded natural valleys running to the water. Open daily year-round, entrance to the gardens is free, though parking is £3 ($5.55) per vehicle.

On the B3022 Bracknell/Ascot Road, outside Windsor, **Legoland** (*©* **0870/ 504-0404;** www.lego.com/legoland), a 61-hectare (150-acre) theme park, opened in 1996. Although a bit corny, it's fun for the entire family. Attractions, spread across five main activity centers, include Duplo Gardens, offering a boat ride, puppet theater, and water works, plus a Miniland, showing European cities or villages re-created in minute detail from millions of Lego bricks. Enchanted Forest has treasure trails, a castle, and animals created from Lego bricks. The latest attraction is Dragon Knight's Castle, taking you back to the days of knights and dragons and including a blazing dragon roller coaster. The park is open daily from 10am to 6pm from mid-March to October. Admission varies through the season, starting at £21 to £23 ($39–$43) for adults, £19 to £20 ($35–$37) for seniors, and for children 3 to 15 (free for children 2 and under).

Only 5km (3 miles) south of Windsor is **Runnymede,** the 75-hectare (188-acre) meadow on the south side of the Thames, in Surrey, where it's believed that King John put his seal on the Great Charter after intense pressure from his feudal barons and lords. Today, Runnymede is also the site of the John F. Kennedy Memorial, an acre of English ground given to the United States by the people of Britain. The memorial, a large block of white stone, is hard to see from the road, but is clearly signposted and reached after a short walk. The pagoda that shelters it was placed here by the American Bar Association to acknowledge the fact that American law stems from the English system. The historic site, to which there is free access all year, lies beside the Thames, 1km (½ mile) west of the hamlet of Old Windsor on the south side of the A308. If you're driving on the M25, exit at Junction 13. The nearest rail connection is at Egham, 1km (½ mile) away. Trains depart from London's Waterloo Station and take about 25 minutes.

BUS & BOAT TOURS, HORSE RIDES & GUIDED WALKS OF WINDSOR

The tourist office can put you in touch with a Blue Badge (official) guide to lead you on a **walking tour** of town. The cost depends upon the number of people and the length of the tour. Advance booking is essential.

Boat tours depart from Windsor's main embarkation point along Windsor Promenade, Barry Avenue, for a 35-minute round-trip to Boveney Lock. The cost is £4.40 ($8.15) for adults, half price for children. You can also take a 2-hour tour through the Boveney Lock and up past stately private riverside homes, the Bray Film Studios, Queens Eyot, and Monkey Island, for £6.80 ($13) for adults, half price for children. There's also a 45-minute tour from Runnymede on board the *Lucy Fisher,* a replica of a Victorian paddle steamer. You pass Magna Carta Island, among other sights. This tour costs £4.40 ($8.15) for adults, half price for children. In addition, longer tours between Maidenhead and Hampton Court are offered. The boats offer light refreshments and have a well-stocked bar, plus the decks are covered in case of an unexpected shower. Tours are operated by **French Brothers, Ltd.,** Clewer Boathouse, Clewer Court Road, Windsor (✆ **01753/851900;** www.boat-trips.co.uk).

SHOPPING

For a survey of the best antiques for sale in Windsor, walk along the shops of **High Street, King Edward Court,** and **Peascod Street.** You can tell the folks back home your purchase was a "discard" from the queen at Windsor Castle.

Finds **Where the Empress of India Rests**

Queen Victoria, who ruled an empire, including India, on which the sun never set, died on January 22, 1901, and was buried beside her beloved Prince Albert in a mausoleum at **Frogmore** (a private estate on the grounds of Windsor Castle), a mile from Windsor. The prince consort died in December 1861. The house, gardens, and mausoleum are open only a few days out of the year, usually in May and August, from around 10am to 5:30pm (last admission at 4pm). The cost for adults is £5.50 ($10); seniors pay £4.50 ($8.35). Call ✆ **020/7766-7305** for more details, or visit www.royalresidences.com.

> **Moments** **Windsor from a Victorian Carriage**
>
> You can take a 30-minute **carriage ride** up the sycamore-lined length of Windsor Castle's Long Walk. Horses with their carriages and drivers should be lined up beside the castle waiting for fares, charging from about £19 ($35) for up to four passengers for a 30-minute ride or £39 ($72) for one hour ride. Carriages run from 12.30 to 5.30pm, or later according to demand. Call, South Gates, Wick Lane, Englefield Green, Surrey ℂ **01784/ 435983** for further information.

Windsor Royal Station, the shopping center at the main railway station (ℂ **0800/923-0017**), has a concentration of shops, often with London connections such as Liberty's Department Store.

If you're not going to Scotland, head for the **Edinburgh Woollen Mill,** 10 Castle Hill (ℂ **01753/855151**), with the finest selection of Scottish knitwear and tartans in Windsor. Plenty of tweeds, of course, for both men and women.

A colorful traditional English perfumery, **Woods of Windsor,** Queen Charlotte Street (ℂ **01753/868125**), dates from 1770. It offers soaps, shampoos, scented drawer liners, and hand and body lotions, all prettily packaged in pastel-flower and bright old-fashioned wraps.

At **Billings & Edmonds,** 132 High St., Eton (ℂ **01753/861348**), you may think you've blundered into a time warp. This distinctive clothing store supplies school wear, suits made to order, and a complete line of cufflinks, shirts, ties, and accessories.

Asquith's Teddy Bear Shop, 33 High St., Eton (ℂ **01753/831200**), appeals to your inner child with every bear imaginable, including Winnie and Paddington. Bear clothes from dungarees to Eton College uniforms mix with more than 500 teddy bears in stock. The store also sells furniture for the bears.

WHERE TO STAY IN THE WINDSOR AREA

During the Ascot races and Windsor Horse Show, reservations are necessary far in advance.

The Castle Hotel ⭐ In the shadow of Windsor Castle, on the main street, is this solid choice with a dignified Georgian facade. It was originally built in the 15th century to shelter the workers laboring on the town's foundations and royal buildings. The grounds behind the hotel once served as the stable yard for Windsor Castle, but now they contain a modern wing, where the bedrooms are much more sterile than those in the main building. All rooms contain well-maintained bathrooms; some rooms have four-poster beds.

18 High St., Windsor, Berkshire SL4 1LJ. ℂ **01753/851011.** Fax 01753/830244. www.macdonaldhotels. co.uk. 111 units. £140–£178 ($259–$329) double; £200–£250 ($370–$463) suite. AE, DC, MC, V. Children 12 and under stay free in parent's room. **Amenities:** 2 restaurants; bar; 24-hr. room service; laundry service; non-smoking rooms. *In room:* TV, dataport, coffeemaker, hair dryer, safe, trouser press.

The Oakley Court Hotel ⭐⭐ Built beside the Thames (a 20-min. drive from Heathrow) by a Victorian industrialist, the Oakley Court is imbued with a sense of tradition. Today it's affiliated with the Queen's Moat House hotel chain. The building's jutting gables and bristling turrets have lent themselves to the filming of several horror movies, including *The Rocky Horror Picture Show* and *Dracula.* Last renovated in 1997, the hotel is a comfortable place to stay— far superior to choices in the heart of Windsor. Although the grandest public areas are in the main house, most rooms are in a trio of well-accessorized modern wings that ramble through the estate's 14 hectares (35 acres) of parks and gardens. Some rooms offer four-poster beds and views of the River Thames.

Windsor Rd., Water Oakley, Windsor, Berkshire SL4 5UR. ℂ 01753/609988. Fax 01628/637011. www.moat househotels.com. 118 units. £184 ($340) double (weekends with breakfast), £229 ($424) double (Mon–Fri with breakfast). AE, DC, MC, V. Take the river road, A308, 5km (3 miles) from Windsor toward Maidenhead. **Amenities:** Restaurant; bar; health club; indoor heated swimming pool; gym with sauna/steam room; Jacuzzi; boat rentals; 24-hr. room service; babysitting; laundry service; dry cleaning; nonsmoking rooms; rooms for those with limited mobility. *In room:* A/C, TV, dataport (in most rooms), minibar, hair dryer, safe, trouser press.

Royal Adelaide Hotel

This interesting Georgian building is opposite the famous Long Walk leading to Windsor Castle, 5 minutes away. Named for Queen Adelaide, who visited the premises during her reign, thereby dubbing it "royal," all its well-furnished rooms have recently been refurbished. Though small, bathrooms have sufficient shelf space and have shower-tub combinations.

46 King's Rd., Windsor, Berkshire SL4 2AG. ℂ 01753/863916. Fax 01753/830682. www.meridianleisure.com. 42 units. £100–£150 ($185–$278) double. Rates include English breakfast. AE, DC, MC, V. **Amenities:** Restaurant; bar; room service (only for breakfast and dinner); babysitting; nonsmoking rooms; 1 room for those with limited mobility. *In room:* TV, dataport, coffeemaker, hair dryer, iron/ironing board, safe, trouser press.

Runnymede Hotel & Spa 🏫🏫

Because of the dearth of any top-of-the-line hotel within Windsor itself, more and more guests who want to lodge in the area are seeking out this hotel and spa on the lovely banks of the Thames between Windsor and Staines. A privately owned hotel, the complex lies only 30 minutes by train from London just off the A30. The spa is one of the finest in the Greater London and Greater Windsor area, offering personalized exercise programs and health care treatments. Its focal point is a splendid neoclassical-style pool.

Bedrooms are fairly spacious and beautifully designed with classical prints on the walls. All accommodations come with a first-rate private bathroom with tub and shower. There is a light, airy quality to the modernized bedrooms, each with a range of color-coordinated schemes. The contemporary Left Bank restaurant is one of the finest in the area, opening onto the Thames and designed around an aquatic theme, with a trio of aquariums and an open seafood bar. The menu is Mediterranean inspired, or else you can enjoy tasty pub grub and real ales in Charlie Bell's. In summer there is a riverside terrace and gardens.

Windsor Rd., Egham, Surrey TW20 0AG. ℂ 01784/220980. Fax 01784/220976. www.runnymedehotel.com. 180 units. Mon–Thurs £210–£238 ($389–$440) double; Fri–Sun £140–£176 ($259–$326). AE, MC, V. Take route A308 out of Windsor, a 15-min. drive. **Amenities:** Restaurant; pub; bar; 24-hr. room service; spa; 3 tennis courts; babysitting; laundry service; dry cleaning; nonsmoking rooms; rooms for those with limited mobility. *In room:* A/C, TV, dataport, minibar, beverage maker, hair dryer, trouser press.

Sir Christopher Wren's House Hotel 🏫

Designed by Christopher Wren in 1676 as his home, this former town house occupies a prime position on the Thames, just a 3-minute walk from the castle. Wren's oak-paneled former study is equipped with his Empire desk, a fireplace, and shield-back Hepplewhite chairs. The bay-windowed main drawing room opens onto a garden and a riverside flagstone terrace for after-dinner coffee and drinks. Rooms come in a wide range of sizes and have well-kept bathrooms; some have fine old furniture and a full-canopied bed, others have a half-canopied bed. Several bedrooms overlook the river. Room no. 2, Wren's bedroom, is said to be haunted.

Thames St., Windsor, Berkshire SL4 1PX. ℂ 01753/861354. Fax 01753/860172. www.sirchristopherwren. co.uk. 92 units. Mon–Thurs £206 ($381) double; Fri–Sun £156–£170 ($289–$315) double; Mon–Thurs £283 ($524) suite; Fri–Sun £233 ($431) suite. Weekend rates include breakfast. AE, DC, MC, V. Parking £10 ($19). **Amenities:** Restaurant; bar; gym; spa; sauna; concierge; secretarial services; 24-hr. room service; babysitting;

laundry service; dry cleaning; nonsmoking rooms; 1 room for those with limited mobility. *In room:* TV, data-port, coffeemaker, hair dryer, trouser press.

Ye Harte & Garter Hotel   On Castle Hill opposite Windsor Castle is the old Garter Inn. Named for the Knights of the Garter and used as the setting for scenes in Shakespeare's *The Merry Wives of Windsor,* the Garter burned down in the 1800s and was rebuilt as part of one hostelry that included the Harte. From the front rooms, you can watch the guards marching up High Street every morning on their way to change the guard at the castle. The recently renovated rooms are comfortable and rather functionally furnished, though they vary greatly in size. More expensive are the Windsor rooms, which have front views and Jacuzzis. All rooms have small but well-maintained bathrooms with shower-tub combination.

31 High St., Windsor, Berkshire SL4 1PH. © **01753/863426.** Fax 01753/830527. www.harteandgarter.com. 39 units. Mon–Thurs £140 ($259) double; Fri–Sun £105 ($194) double; Mon–Thurs £165 ($303) suite; Fri–Sun £190 ($352) suite. Rates include breakfast. AE, DC, MC, V. **Amenities:** 2 restaurants; bar; laundry service; dry cleaning; nonsmoking rooms; rooms for those with limited mobility. *In room:* TV, coffeemaker, hair dryer, trouser press.

WHERE TO DINE IN WINDSOR & ETON

Many visitors prefer to dine in Eton; most of the restaurants and fast-food places along the main street of Windsor, in front of the castle, serve dreary food.

If you want only a light lunch, such as omelets or salads, head for **Nell Gwynne's House,** 6 Church St. (© **01753/850929**), once the home of the mistress of Charles II. It's only a short walk from the castle, so his majesty didn't have far to go at night. It's open daily 11:30am to 11pm.

Antico ★ ITALIAN   Eton's finest Italian restaurant, Antico serves Mediterranean food in a formal setting. People have been dining here for 200 years, though not from an Italian menu. On your way to the tiny bar, you pass a cold table, displaying hors d'oeuvres and cold meats. With many fish dishes, such as grilled fresh salmon, Dover sole, or sea bass, and a wide selection of pastas, the food is substantial and filling—a good value, but rarely exciting.

42 High St., Eton. © **01753/863977.** Reservations strongly recommended. Main courses £11–£20 ($20–$37); 3-course fixed price lunch menu £12.50 ($23). AE, MC, V. Mon–Fri 12:30–2:30pm; Mon–Sat 7–10:30pm. Closed bank holidays.

Crooked House Tea Rooms ★ *Finds* CONTINENTAL   Historically called Market Cross House, this is a charming old relic from 1687. It acquired its tilt after it was restructured in 1718. A mixture of original and unseasoned timber resulted in its much-photographed crooked look. A secret passage from its cellar leads directly to Windsor Castle, suggesting an unknown but intriguing connection. Next to the Crooked House is the shortest street in Britain, measuring 15.2m (51 ft., 10 in.). It's called Queen Charlotte Street. The Tea Rooms serves the best Cornish clotted cream tea in the area along with a "High Tea." It also offers a variety of light lunches and fresh homemade soups throughout the day.

51 High St. © **01753/857534.** Reservations not needed. Light lunches £5–£7.50 ($9.25–$14); High tea £8.25 ($15); Cornish clotted cream tea £6 ($11). MC, V. Daily 10am–6pm.

Gilbey's Bar and Restaurant MODERN BRITISH/CONTINENTAL   Just across the bridge from Windsor, this charming place is located on Eton's main street, among the antiques shops. Furnished with pinewood tables and simple chairs, a glassed-in conservatory is out back. A brigade of seven chefs turns out quite good modern British dishes. Begin with one of the well-prepared soups or a smoked-salmon-and-artichoke tart. Main dishes include pan-fried skate wing with a champagne or chile-and-caper risotto. For dessert, try the delicious white-and-dark mousse with amaretto cream.

82–83 High St., Eton. ✆ **01753/854921.** Reservations recommended. Main courses £10.50–£16.95 ($19–$31). AE, DC, MC, V. Mon–Fri noon–2:30pm; Sat–Sun noon–3pm; Mon–Thurs 6–9:30pm; Fri–Sat 6–10:30pm; Sun 6–9:30pm.

The Oak Leaf Restaurant at the Oakley Court Hotel ★★ INTERNATIONAL   In the mid-1990s, this chic London restaurant, known for its delectable food and sophisticated clientele, moved from central London to this new setting beside the Thames. Today, under the supervision of chef Damien Bradley, the reincarnated Oak Leaf serves a modern cuisine that may include a parfait of duck livers with a confit of red onions and mandarin oranges, or a pavé of Scottish salmon with creamed leeks served with broad beans and a red-wine shallot sauce.

Windsor Rd., Water Oakley, Windsor. ✆ **01753/609988.** Reservations recommended. Main courses £17–£25 ($31–$46); table d'hôte lunch and dinner £29.50 ($55). AE, DC, MC, V. Daily 7–10am, 12:30–2:30pm (no lunch on Sun), and 7–10pm.

Strok's MODERN BRITISH/CONTINENTAL   This restaurant, located near the castle, is Windsor's most elegant and charming, possessing garden terraces, a conservatory, and a dining room designed a bit like a greenhouse. Chef Philip Wild selects an individual garnish to complement each well-prepared dish. For starters, try the tower of smoked salmon and asparagus. For a main course, enjoy the rosettes of spring lamb with beans, artichokes and an herb Yorkshire pudding, or a seafood platter of lobster, king prawns, crab, mussels, and shrimps. A variety of vegetarian dishes is also offered. At dinner, a pianist entertains.

In Sir Christopher Wren's House Hotel, Thames St., Windsor. ✆ **01753/861354.** Main courses £15–£20 ($27–$37); fixed-price menu £29.50 ($55). AE, DC, MC, V. Daily 12:30–2:30pm and 6:30–10pm.

ON THE OUTSKIRTS

The Fat Duck ★★★ MODERN   In the post nouvelle cuisine era, the self-taught master chef Heston Blumenthal is pioneering a type of cuisine known as "molecular gastronomy." His results are hailed by many British food critics as the "hottest and most exciting restaurant in the country." Molecular cookery, in Blumenthal's vocabulary, means "understanding the science of cooking and experiencing its varied results." That may not mean a lot to you, but it leads to questioning techniques and theories of cooking known for centuries. Who said, for example, that an ice cream can't be made of crab or that mashed potatoes can't be mixed with lime jelly? The chef admits that sometimes confusion reigns in the brain when he serves sardines on toast sorbet. "Your palate expects a dessert and you therefore taste more sweetness than actually exists." The grain mustard ice cream and the red cabbage gazpacho were firsts for us—and a delight. Don't become unduly alarmed. Not all dishes are this experimental. Try, for example, the slow-cooked saddle of lamb with lamb tongue and onion purée or poached sea bass flavored with rosemary and vanilla. Snail porridge appears with Jabugo ham, a poached skate wing with cockles and braised celeriac.

1 High St., Bray. ✆ **01628/580333.** Reservations required. Fixed-price lunch £33 ($60). Fixed-price dinner £52 ($96) for 2 courses; £60 ($111) for 3 courses. AE, DC, DISC, MC, V. Tues–Sat noon–2pm and 7–9:30pm. Leave the motorway at Exit 4. On the roundabout, take the exit to Maidenhead (A404M/M4) and follow the dual Carriage Way to the roundabout at the M4. Take the first left exit to Maidenhead Central. At the second roundabout, take the exit to Bray and Windsor (A308). Continue for half a mile and turn left at the sign to Bray Village (B3028). After entering the village, continue past the bottleneck; The Fat Duck is on the right hand side adjacent to the Hinds Head Hotel.

WINDSOR AFTER DARK

Except for pub life, it's fairly quiet. The major cultural venue is **Theatre Royal,** Thames Street (© **01753/853888;** www.theatreroyalwindsor.co.uk), with a tradition of putting on plays that goes back 2 centuries. The theater is one of the finest regional theaters in England, often drawing first-rate actors or stars from London's West End. During the 6 weeks preceding Christmas, a series of pantomimes are presented. The box office is open Monday to Saturday 10am to 8pm (call the phone number above for bookings). Performances are Monday to Saturday at 8pm; Thursday matinee at 2:30pm; Saturday matinee at 4:45pm. Tickets cost between £15 to £90 ($27–$167).

SIDE TRIPS FROM WINDSOR

If you have time to spare, you can take any number of fascinating excursions. But if you can squeeze in only one, make it Hughenden Manor (see below).

HUGHENDEN MANOR: DISRAELI CALLED IT HOME

Hughenden Manor ★★ This country manor not only gives insight into the age of Victoria but also acquaints us with a remarkable man: Benjamin Disraeli, one of the most enigmatic figures of 19th-century England. At age 21, "Dizzy" anonymously published his five-volume novel, *Vivian Grey.* In 1839, he married an older widow for her money, though they apparently developed a most harmonious relationship. He entered politics in 1837 and continued writing novels, his later ones meeting with more acclaim.

In 1848, Disraeli acquired Hughenden Manor, a country house that befitted his fast-rising political and social position. He served briefly as prime minister in 1868, but his political fame rests on his stewardship as prime minister from 1874 to 1880. He became friends with Queen Victoria who, in 1877, paid him a rare honor by visiting him at Hughenden. In 1876, Disraeli became the earl of Beaconsfield; he died in 1881. Instead of being buried at Westminster Abbey, he preferred the simple little graveyard of Hughenden Church.

Today, Hughenden houses an odd assortment of memorabilia, including a lock of Disraeli's hair, letters from Victoria, and a portrait of Lord Byron.

High Wycombe. © **01494/755573.** Admission £4.50 ($8.35) adults, £2.25 ($4.15) children, £12 ($21) family ticket. Garden only £1.60 ($2.95) adults, 80p ($1.50) for children. Apr–Oct Wed–Sun 1–5pm; Mar Sat–Sun only 1–5pm. Closed Nov–Feb and Good Friday. From Windsor take M4 (toward Reading), then A404 to A40. Continue north of High Wycombe on A4128 for about 2.5km (1½ miles). From London (Heathrow Airport), catch coach A40 (operated by Carousel Buses) to High Wycombe, then board a Beeline bus (High Wycombe–Aylesbury no. 323 or 324).

WEST WYCOMBE ★

Snuggled in the Chiltern Hills 48km (30 miles) west of London and 24km (15 miles) northwest of Windsor, the village of West Wycombe still has an atmosphere of the early 18th century. The thatched roofs have been replaced by tiles, and some of the buildings have been replaced, but the village is still 2 centuries removed from the present day.

From Windsor, take the M4 (toward Reading), then the A404 to the A40. Signs to follow en route include Maidenhead, Marlow, and Oxford. If you previously visited Hughenden Manor, the village of West Wycombe lies immediately to the west.

A visit to West Wycombe wouldn't be complete without a tour of **West Wycombe Park,** seat of the Dashwood family. Now owned by the National Trust, it's of both historical and architectural interest. The house is one of the best examples of Palladian-style architecture in England. The interior is lavishly decorated with paintings and antiques from the 18th century.

In the mid–18th century, Sir Francis Dashwood began an ambitious building program at West Wycombe. His strong interest in architecture and design led Sir Frances to undertake a series of monuments and parks that are still among the finest in the country.

Sir Francis also commissioned the excavation of a cave on the estate. Its primary purpose was to serve as a meeting place for "The Knights of St. Francis of Wycombe," later known as the notorious Hellfire Club, which spent its time partying and drinking. It seems that some satanic rites also took place here—not so much to invoke Satan, as to inspire general debauchery. The cave is about 1km (½ mile) long, filled with stalactites and stalagmites, and dotted with statues of Sir Francis, his friend Lord Sandwich, and even Ben Franklin.

The house and grounds are open June through August, Sunday through Thursday from 2 to 6pm. Admission is £5 ($9.25) for adults, £2.50 ($4.65) for children, and £13 ($23) for a family ticket. If you wish to visit only the grounds (Apr–Aug), the cost is £6.20 ($11). The caves are open daily March through October from 11am to 5:30pm; off-season hours are only on Saturday and Sunday from 11am to 5:30pm. Admission is £3.75 ($6.95) for adults or £2.50 ($4.65) for seniors and children. The cave tour includes stops for talks about former Hellfire members; it lasts 30 minutes. For more information, call the West Wycombe Estate Office at West Wycombe (© **01494/524411**), or the caves at © **01494/533739.**

Other sights include the **Church of St. Lawrence,** perched on West Wycombe Hill and topped by a huge golden ball. Parts of the church date from the 13th century; its interior was copied from a 3rd-century Syrian sun temple. The view from the hill is worth the trek up. Near the church stands the **Dashwood Mausoleum,** built in a style derived from Constantine's Arch in Rome.

After your tour, head for **George & Dragon,** High Street (© **01494/464414;** www.george-and-dragon.co.uk), for a pint or a good, inexpensive lunch. In a building that dates back to 1720, this former coaching inn has a cheerful log fire, a comfortable-size bar (that nevertheless gets crowded on weekends), and an impressive oak staircase with its own ghost. A separate nonsmoking room is open to children, as well as a children's play area and a garden for dining outside. If you like West Wycombe and want to stay over, eight cozily furnished rooms with private bathroom, phone, hair dryer, coffeemaker and TV, cost £75 ($139) for a double; £80 ($148) for a four-poster room, including breakfast.

CLIVEDEN: FORMER HOME OF LADY ASTOR

Cliveden 🌟🌟   Now a National Trust property, Cliveden, former home of Lady Astor, stands on a constructed terrace of mature gardens high above the Thames. The estate's original mansion and sweeping lawns were created by William Winde in 1666 for the second duke of Buckingham. Later, the father of King George III reared his sons here. After a fire in 1795, Sir Charles Barry, the architect of the House of Parliament, converted the house into its present gracefully symmetrical form. A soaring clock tower was added to one side as a later Victorian folly. When the house was sold by the duke of Southerland to the Astors in 1893, Queen Victoria lamented the passage. The house remained part of the Astor legacy, a repository of a notable collection of paintings and antiques, until 1966.

The surrounding **gardens** have a distinguished variety of plantings, ranging from Renaissance-style topiary to meandering forest paths with vistas of statuary and flowering shrubs. Garden features are a glade garden, a magnificent parterre, and an amphitheater where "Rule Britannia" was played for the first time. There are 150 hectares (375 acres) of gardens and woodland to explore.

The manor also accepts paying guests, and it's a spectacular place to stay, as we've described below.

16km (10 miles) northwest of Windsor. ℂ **01628/605069.** Admission to grounds £6.50 ($12) for adults, £3.20 ($5.90) for children; family ticket £17 ($31). Admission to house £1 ($1.85) extra. Grounds open mid-Mar to Oct daily 11am–6pm, Nov–Dec 11am–4pm. House open Apr–Oct Thurs and Sun 3–5:30pm (3 rooms of the mansion are open to the public, as is the Octagon Temple, with its rich mosaic interior). From Windsor, follow M4 toward Reading to the junction at no. 7 (direction Slough West). At the roundabout, turn left onto A4, signposted Maidenhead. At the next roundabout, turn right, signposted Burnham. Follow the road for 4km (2½ miles) to a T junction with B476. The main gates to Cliveden are directly opposite.

WHERE TO STAY & DINE

Cliveden House ✩✩✩   Lady Astor's former estate is one of the most beautiful and luxurious hotels in England. Often acclaimed as "hotel of the year" by various rating services in England, this majestic property was home to a Prince of Wales and a scattering of dukes before the Astors moved in. It was also a setting for the infamous Profumo scandal of the 1960s that shook the Empire.

Rooms—named for famous guests who've stayed here, including T. E. Lawrence and Charlie Chaplin—are sumptuous, each furnished in impeccable taste. The bathrooms with deep marble tubs are among the finest we've seen in England. Less preferred are recently added rooms in the Clutton Wing. Nothing (except perhaps renting Lady Astor's bedroom itself) is more elegant here than walking down to the river and boarding a hotel boat for a champagne cruise before dinner. In the morning you can go horseback riding on the 150-hectare (376-acre) estate along the riverbank.

Cliveden, Taplow, Maidenhead, Berkshire SL6 0JF. ℂ **01628/668561.** Fax 01628/661837. www.cliveden house.co.uk. 39 units. £295–£395 ($546–$731) double; £855–£1,375 ($1,582–$2,545) cottage (2 nights minimum). Rates include English breakfast. AE, DC, MC, V. **Amenities:** 2 restaurants; bar; 2 heated pools (1 indoor, 1 outdoor); 3 tennis courts (1 indoor, 2 outdoor); squash court; health club; spa with steam rooms; 24-hr. room service; babysitting; laundry service; dry cleaning; nonsmoking rooms. *In room:* A/C (in some rooms), TV, dataport, minibar, hair dryer, safe.

THE COTTAGE WHERE MILTON WROTE PARADISE LOST

The modern residential town of **Gerrards Cross** is often called the Beverly Hills of England, as it attracts many wealthy Londoners, among others. To the north of it is **Chalfont St. Giles,** where poet John Milton lived during the Great Plague in 1665. To reach it, take the A355 north from Windsor, bypassing Beaconsfield until you come to the signposted cutoff for Chalfont St. Giles to the east.

Chalfont St. Giles today is a typical English village, though its history goes back to Roman times. The charm of the village is in its center, with shops, pubs, and cafes clustered around the green and the village pond.

The 16th-century **John Milton's Cottage,** Chalfont St. Giles (ℂ **01494/ 872313;** www.miltonscottage.org), is the site where the great poet completed *Paradise Lost* and started *Paradise Regained.* Its four rooms contain many relics and exhibits devoted to Milton. It is open March through October, Tuesday through Sunday from 10am to 1pm and 2 to 6pm, charging adults £3 ($5.55) and children under 15 £1 ($1.85).

2 Ascot

45km (28 miles) W of London

While following the royal buckhounds through Windsor Forest, Queen Anne decided to have a racecourse on Ascot Heath. The first race meeting at Ascot, which is directly south of Windsor at the southern end of Windsor Great Park, was held in 1711. Since then, the Ascot Racecourse has been a symbol of high society as pictures of the royal family, including the queen and Prince Philip, have been flashed around the world. Ladies: Be sure to wear a hat.

GETTING THERE

Trains travel between Waterloo in London and Ascot Station, which is about 10 minutes from the racecourse. The trip takes about 1 hour, and trains arrive roughly every 30 minutes during the day. For rail information, call ℂ **0845/ 748-4950** or visit www.railtrack.co.uk.

Buses frequently depart from London's Victoria Coach Station. Call ℂ **0870/ 580-8080** for more information or visit www.nationalexpress.com.

If you're driving from Windsor, take the A332 west.

ASCOT RACECOURSE ✸

Ascot Racecourse, High Street (ℂ **01344/622211;** www.ascot.co.uk), England's largest and most prestigious course, is open throughout the year. The facility hosts 27 days of racing yearly. The highlight of the Ascot social season is the above-mentioned **Royal Meeting** (or **Royal Week**), when many women wear fancy hats and white gloves. Excellent racing also takes place on De Beers Diamond Day (4th Sat in July) and during the Festival at Ascot (last Fri, Sat, and Sun in Sept), when the prize money usually exceeds £1 million per event.

You can buy tickets for one of three distinctly different observation areas, known locally as "enclosures." These include the Members' Enclosure, which, during the Royal Meeting (5 days in June), is known as the Royal Enclosure. Also available are Tattersall's Enclosure, largest of the three; and the Silver Ring, which does not enjoy direct access to the paddocks and has traditionally been the site of most of Ascot's budget seating. Except during the Royal Meeting, newcomers can usually secure viewing space in the Member's Enclosure, but only if they call ahead to confirm that space is available. Tickets cost £35 ($65) for seats in the Member's Enclosure, £52 ($96) in the Grandstand and Paddock, and £16 ($30) in the Silver Ring. Prices depend on the race and the season. Children 16 and under are admitted free if accompanied by an adult, and there is free supervised daycare for children under 8.

Beginning January 1 every year, you can arrange advance bookings for guaranteed seating in the most desirable areas during the most popular races. Write for tickets to the Secretary's Office, Ascot Racecourse, Ascot, Berkshire SL5 7JN. For admission to the Royal Enclosure, write to Her Majesty's Representative, Ascot Office, St. James's Palace, London SW1. First-timers usually have difficulty being admitted to the Royal Enclosure, because their application must be endorsed by someone who has been admitted to the Royal Enclosure at least eight times before. Credit cards are accepted at ℂ **01344/876456.** Car parking is free except on June 22, July 27, and during the Festival Meeting in September.

WHERE TO STAY & DINE

Berystede Country House Hotel ✸   This hotel just south of Ascot is a Victorian fantasy of medieval towers, steeply pitched roofs, and a landscaped garden. Drawing racegoers and businesspeople, it also caters to conferences (at which time it's best avoided). With their high ceilings and chintz, rooms evoke a private country house. Recently refurbished bedrooms are decorated in period styles, most often Victorian. The best rooms are in the main house and are more

Finds Golf, Goldfinger & Posh Decadence

One of Europe's greatest hotels lies only 30 minutes from London's West End and in close proximity to Ascot and Windsor. It's **Stoke Park Club,** Park Rd., Stoke Poges, Buckinghamshire SL2 4PG (© **01753/717171** in the U.S., or 01753/717171; www.stokeparkclub.com). Golfers from all over the world flock to the 27-hole golf course designed by celebrated architect Harry Shapland Colt. James Bond defeated Goldfinger on its 18th green in 1964. Each bedroom or suite is individually decorated with antiques, paintings, and original prints, and all bedrooms feature fireplaces. Bathrooms are in marble, and some bedrooms open onto balconies. Double rooms range from £275 to £335 ($509–$620) per night, with suites costing from £395 ($731). The hotel has three indoor tennis courts, six Wimbledon-standard grass tennis courts, and four all-weather tennis courts; a spa; indoor heated pool that incorporates two underwater massage areas with hydroseat Jacuzzis; a steam room; and a gym.

spacious and better decorated. Most of the other rooms are in a more modern annex with less character. Most rooms have a tub and shower; 26 bedrooms are designated nonsmoking. For optimum sunshine and more room, try to book room no. 360 or 369.

Bagshot Rd., Sunninghill Ascot, Berkshire SL5 9JH. © **01344/623311.** Fax 01344/872301. www.berystede. com. 90 units. £110–£201 ($204–$372) double; £180–£250 ($333–$463) suite. AE, DC, MC, V. Take A330 2.5km (1½ miles) south of Ascot. **Amenities:** Restaurant; bar; 24-hr. room service; babysitting; laundry service; dry cleaning; rooms for those with limited mobility. *In room:* TV, dataport, coffeemaker, hair dryer, iron/ironing board, safe, trouser press.

Brockenhurst *Value* A small, tastefully refurbished 1905 Edwardian hotel of charm and distinction, Brockenhurst is conveniently situated near shops and the train station. Bedrooms are generally spacious and have well-appointed bathrooms with shower-tub combinations. Clean and comfortable, the decor is mostly modern, though some rooms contain antiques. Classy and reasonably priced, this is a very good alternative to the pricey Royal Berkshire or Berystede.

Brockenhurst Rd., S. Ascot, Berkshire SL5 9HA. © **01344/621912.** Fax 01344/873252. www.brockenhurst. com. 20 units. £79–£100 ($146–$185) double. Rates include continental breakfast. AE, MC, V. **Amenities:** Restaurant, bar; babysitting; laundry service. *In room:* TV, dataport, coffeemaker, hair dryer, trouser press.

The Royal Berkshire ★★ This is a prestigious and elegant hotel with a rich history. Built in Queen Anne style in 1705, it housed the Churchill family for many years. The stylish rooms are divided between the main house and an annex. All rooms are spacious with thick carpeting, large comfortable beds, and well-kept bathrooms with shower-tub combinations. While the annex rooms are exceedingly comfortable and well furnished, each redecorated in 1996, they aren't equal to those in the main building. If you want the character of old England, opt for the main building.

London Rd., Sunninghill, Ascot, Berkshire SL5 OPP. © **01344/623322.** Fax 01344/627100. www.ramada jarvis.co.uk. 63 units. £215–£245 ($398–$453) double; £245–£335 ($453–$620) suite. AE, DC, MC, V. Take A322 3km (2 miles) northeast of Ascot. **Amenities:** Restaurant; bar; 2 outdoor tennis courts; indoor heated pool; health club; spa; sauna; 24-hr. room service; babysitting; laundry service; dry cleaning; nonsmoking rooms; rooms for those with limited mobility. *In room:* TV, fridge, coffeemaker, hair dryer, trouser press.

3 Henley-on-Thames & the Royal Regatta

56km (35 miles) W of London

At the eastern edge of Oxfordshire, Henley-on-Thames, a small town and resort on the river at the foothills of the Chilterns, is the headquarters of the **Royal Regatta,** held annually in late June and early July. Henley, which lies on a stretch of the Thames that's known for its calm waters, unobstructed bottom, and predictable currents, is a rower's mecca. The regatta, which dates from the first years of Victoria's reign, is the major competition among international oarsmen and oarswomen, who find it both challenging and entertaining.

The Elizabethan buildings, tearooms, and inns along the town's High Street will live up to your preconception of an English country town. Henley-on-Thames is an excellent (though pricey) stopover en route to Oxford; its fashionable inns are far from cheap.

ESSENTIALS

GETTING THERE   Trains depart from London's Paddington Station but require a change at the junction in Twyford. More than 20 trains make the journey daily; the trip takes about 40 minutes. For rail information, call ✆ **0845/748-4950** or visit www.railtrack.co.uk.

About 10 buses depart every day from London's Victoria Coach Station for Reading. From Reading, take local bus no. 421 to Henley. These buses depart every hour. Call **0870/580-8080** for more information or visit www.national express.com.

If you're driving from London, take the M4 toward Reading to Junction 819; then head northwest on the A4130.

VISITOR INFORMATION   The **Tourist Information Centre** is at King's Arms Barn, King's Road (✆ **01491/578034**). Winter hours are Monday through Saturday from 9:30am to 5pm, and Sunday from 11am to 4pm. Summer hours are Monday through Saturday from 9:30am to 6pm, and Sunday from 10am to 5pm.

THE HENLEY ROYAL REGATTA ★★

The Henley Royal Regatta, held the first week in July, is one of the country's premier racing events. For a close-up view from the Stewards' Enclosure, you'll need a guest badge, only obtainable through a member. In other words, you have to know someone to obtain special privileges, but admission to the Regatta Enclosure is open to all. Entry fees are £30 to £80 ($56–$148). Information is available from the Secretary, Henley Royal Regatta, Henley-on-Thames, Oxfordshire RG9 2LY (✆ **01491/572153;** www.hrr.co.uk).

During the annual 5-day event, up to 100 races are organized each day, with starts scheduled as frequently as every 5 minutes. This event is open only to all-male crews of up to nine at a time. In late June, rowing events for women are held at the 3-day Henley Women's Regatta.

If you want to float on the waters of the Thames yourself, stop by the town's largest and oldest outfitter, **Hobbs & Sons, Ltd.,** Station Road Boathouse (✆ **01491/572035**), established in 1870. Open daily from April to October from 8:30am to 5:30pm, their armada of watercraft includes rowboats that rent for between £8 to £10 ($15–$19) per hour. Motorboats can be rented for £20 to £50 ($37–$93) per hour. Prices include fuel. On the premises, a chandlery shop sells virtually anything a boat crew could need, as well as souvenir items such as straw boaters' hats and commemorative T-shirts.

MUSEUM CELEBRATING THE THAMES

River & Rowing Museum *Finds*   This museum celebrates the Thames and those oarsmen and oarswomen who row upon it. Opened by Queen Elizabeth in 1998, the museum, designed by English architect David Chipperfield, is the finest of its kind in Britain. A short walk south of Henley Bridge, it opens onto the banks of the Thames. The Rowing Gallery follows the saga of rowing from the days of the Greeks. It's all here: models of Arctic whaleboats in the 1700s, elaborate Venetian gondolas fit for a doge, and coastal lifeboats that pulled many a victim from the cold waters of the North Sea. In a more modern exhibit, you'll find the boat in which British oarsmen captured the gold medal in the Olympic games at Atlanta in 1996. The museum reaches out to embrace the saga of the Thames itself, as well as the history of the regatta in Henley.

Mill Meadows. ℂ **01491/415600.** www.rrm.co.uk. Admission £4.95 ($9.15) adults, £3.75 ($6.95) seniors and children, £14 ($26) family ticket for 4, £17 ($31) for 5, and £19 ($36) for 6. Daily 10am–5pm.

WHERE TO STAY & DINE IN THE AREA

It's impossible to find a room during the Royal Regatta, unless you've made reservations months in advance.

Red Lion Hotel *★*   This ivy-covered coaching inn (ca. 1531) near Henley offers a guest list that reads like a hall of fame: Johnson and Boswell, George IV (who, it is said, consumed 14 mutton chops 1 night), and Charles I. You can book the room in which Princess Grace stayed when her brother Jack was competing in the Royal Regatta in 1947. Most of the well-furnished rooms overlook the Thames. Bedrooms are midsize to spacious, each with a small but well-organized private bathroom with a shower and tub. The three most expensive rooms sport four-poster beds.

Hart St., Henley-on-Thames, Oxfordshire RG9 2AR. ℂ **01491/572161.** Fax 01491/410039. www.redlion henley.co.uk. 26 units. £145–£165 ($268–$305) double. AE, MC, V. **Amenities:** Restaurant; bar; limited room service; babysitting; laundry service; dry cleaning. *In room:* TV, dataport, coffeemaker, hair dryer.

Stonor Arms *★★*   For the area's finest dining and accommodations, head to the village of Stonor, 6.5km (4 miles) north of Henley. For those who wish to stay over, a wing of rooms in this establishment is handsomely furnished with English and French antiques. You get grand comfort here, from fine bed linen to the roomy and well-equipped bathrooms with shower-tub combinations. The decor is classy but not overdone, and some rooms (on the ground floor) open on to the beautiful gardens. Cots for children can be added to most rooms.

Stonor (by A4130 on B480 near Henley-on-Thames), Oxfordshire RG9 6HE. ℂ **01491/638866.** Fax 01491/638863. 11 units. Mon–Thurs £135 ($250) and Fri–Sun £155 ($287) double. Rates include English breakfast. AE, MC, V. **Amenities:** Restaurant; bar; limited room service; babysitting; laundry service; dry cleaning; non-smoking rooms. *In room:* TV, dataport, coffeemaker, hair dryer, trouser press.

SIDE TRIPS FROM HENLEY
A ROMANTIC BOAT TRIP TO A HISTORIC HOME

Mapledurham House *Finds*   The Blount family mansion lies beside the Thames in the unspoiled village of Mapledurham. In the house, you'll see the Elizabethan ceilings and the great oak staircase, as well as the portraits of the two beautiful sisters with whom the poet Alexander Pope, a frequent visitor here, fell in love. The family chapel, built in 1789, is a fine example of modern Gothic architecture. Cream teas with homemade cakes are available at the house. On the grounds, the last working water mill on the Thames still produces flour.

The most romantic way to reach this lovely old house is to take the boat that leaves the promenade next to Caversham Bridge at 2pm on Saturday, Sunday, and bank holidays from Easter to September. The journey upstream takes between 30 and 80 minutes, and the boat leaves Mapledurham again at 5pm for the return trip to Caversham, giving you plenty of time to walk through the house. The round-trip boat ride from Caversham costs £4.50 ($8.35) for adults and £3 ($5.55) for children. You can get further details about the boat from **Thames Rivercruise Ltd.,** Pipers Island, Bridge Street, Caversham Bridge, Reading (ⓒ **01189/481088;** www.thamesrivercruise.co.uk).

Mapledurham. ⓒ **01189/723350.** www.mapledurham.co.uk. Admission to house and mill £6 ($11) adults, £3 ($5.55) children 5–14, free for children 4 and under. Easter–Sept Sat–Sun and bank holidays 2–5pm. Closed Oct–Easter. From Henley-on-Thames, head south along A4155 toward Reading. At the junction with A329 head west. Mapledurham is signposted from this road. Or take the boat trip described above.

THE WELLINGTON DUCAL ESTATE

Stratfield Saye House ⭐   This combined house and country park provides tangible evidence of the fortune of the duke of Wellington and his descendants. The complex's centerpiece is the Stratfield Saye House, the home of the dukes of Wellington since 1817, when the 17th-century house was bought for the Iron Duke to celebrate his victory over Napoleon at the Battle of Waterloo. A grateful Parliament granted a large sum of money for its purchase. Many memories of the first duke remain in the house, including his billiard table, battle spoils, and pictures. The funeral carriage that once rested in St. Paul's Cathedral crypt is on display. In the gardens is the grave of Copenhagen, the charger ridden to battle at Waterloo by the first duke. There are also extensive landscaped grounds, together with a tearoom and gift shop.

Although extensive parks and gardens surround Stratfield Saye, all except those immediately adjacent to the house are closed to the public. If you're looking for greenery and lovely landscaping, you'll find it 5km (3 miles) away, on the opposite side of the A33 highway, at the **Wellington Country Park.**

1.5km (1 mile) west of Reading, beside A33 to Basingstoke. ⓒ **01256/882882.** www.stratfield-saye.co.uk. Admission £6 ($11) adults, £3 ($5.55) children 5–15, free for children under 5. July 6–Aug 1 daily 11:30am–5pm. From Henley, head south along A1455.

Wellington Country Park ⭐ *Finds*   Under the same administration as Stratfield Saye, this favorite place for locals to picnic and stroll has a nice lake and miles of well-maintained walking paths. But a handful of attractions is inside as well: The park contains a riding school, a miniature steam railway, a deer park, and the Thames Valley Time Trail, a walk-through series of exhibits related to the geology of the region and the dinosaurs that once inhabited it.

Riseley, Reading, Berkshire RG7 1SP. ⓒ **01189/326444.** www.wellington-country-park.co.uk. Admission £4.80 ($8.90) adults, £2.50 ($4.65) children 5–16, free for children under 5. Park and exhibits open mid-Mar 1 to early Nov daily 10am–5:30pm.

MARLOW: RETREAT OF THE *COMPLEAT ANGLER*

This Thames-side town, 56km (35 miles) northwest of London and 13km (8 miles) east of Henley-on-Thames, is a miniature version of the better-known Henley. To reach it from Henley, take route 4155 and just follow the signs. Many prefer its more pastoral look to the larger Henley.

The town stands on a great loop of the riverbank between Maidenhead and Oxford. Here, along this middle reach of the Thames, is some of the most beautiful rural scenery in England, a land of green fields and deep woods, of stately mansions and parks. It was in these surroundings that Izaak Walton wrote his immortal work on fishing, *The Compleat Angler,* which was published in 1655.

On the south bank of the river facing Marlow itself stood the inn in which he stayed. That inn still stands and is named after his work.

WHERE TO STAY & DINE

The Compleat Angler Hotel ★★   This hotel of charm and character blends architectural eras, including Queen Anne, Regency, Georgian, and Victorian. It occupies an emerald swath of lawns stretching down to the banks of the Thames. It's had a long and distinguished list of guests, including Percy Shelley and his wife, Mary, along with Dame Nellie Melba (for whom the peach dessert was named), J. M. Barrie (author of *Peter Pan*), and F. Scott Fitzgerald. The hotel is a well-organized and impeccably polite center of English chintz, predictably elegant bars, and very fine dining. Each room is outfitted much like those found in a private country home, with antiques or reproductions and plush, comfortable beds. The more expensive rooms look out on the Thames. The finest accommodations are in a modern wing with balconies overlooking the rushing weir. Modern bathrooms with separate showers are the order of the day.

Marlow Bridge, Bisham Rd., Marlow, Buckinghamshire SL7 1RG. © **01628/484444.** Fax 01628/486388. www.compleatangler-hotel.co.uk. 64 units. £248–£280 ($459–$518) double; £395–£495 ($731–$916) suite. AE, DC, MC, V. **Amenities:** 2 restaurants; bar; limited room service; babysitting; laundry service; dry cleaning. *In room:* A/C, TV, dataport, CD player, minibar, coffeemaker, hair dryer, iron/ironing board, safe, trouser press.

4 Oxford: The City of Dreaming Spires ★★

87km (54 miles) NW of London; 87km (54 miles) SE of Coventry

A walk down the long sweep of The High, one of the most striking streets in England; a mug of cider in one of the old student pubs; the sound of May Day dawn when choristers sing in Latin from Magdalen Tower; students in traditional gowns whizzing past on rickety bikes; towers and spires rising majestically; nude swimming at Parson's Pleasure; the roar of a cannon launching the bumping races; a tiny, dusty bookstall where you can pick up a valuable first edition— all that is Oxford, home of one of the greatest universities in the world.

Romantic Oxford is still here, but to get to it, you have to experience the bustling and crowded city that is also Oxford. You may be surprised by a never-ending stream of polluting buses and the fast-flowing pedestrian traffic—the city core feels more like London than once-sleepy Oxford. Surrounding the university are suburbs that keep growing, and not in a particularly attractive manner.

At any time of the year, you can enjoy a tour of the colleges, many of which represent a peak in England's architectural history, as well as a valley of Victorian contributions. The Oxford Tourist Information Centre (see below) offers guided walking tours daily throughout the year. Just don't mention the other place (Cambridge), and you shouldn't have any trouble. Comparisons between the two universities are inevitable: Oxford is better known for the arts, Cambridge more for the sciences.

The city predates the university—in fact, it was a Saxon town in the early part of the 10th century. By the 12th century, Oxford was growing in reputation as a seat of learning, at the expense of Paris, and the first colleges were founded in the 13th century. The story of Oxford is filled with conflicts too complex and detailed to elaborate upon here. Suffice it to say, the relationship between town and gown wasn't as peaceful as it is today. Riots often flared, and both sides were guilty of abuses. Nowadays, the young people of Oxford take out their aggressiveness in sporting competitions.

Ultimately, the test of a great university lies in the caliber of the people it turns out. Oxford can name-drop a mouthful: Roger Bacon, Sir Walter Raleigh, John Donne, Sir Christopher Wren, Samuel Johnson, William Penn, John Wesley, William Pitt, Matthew Arnold, Lewis Carroll, Harold Macmillan, Graham Greene, A. E. Housman, T. E. Lawrence, and many others. Women were not allowed until 1920, but since then many have graduated from Oxford and gone on to fame—Indira Gandhi and Margaret Thatcher both graduated from Somerville College.

ESSENTIALS

GETTING THERE   Trains from Paddington Station reach Oxford in 1½ hours. Five trains run every hour. A cheap, same-day round-trip ticket costs £17 ($31); a 5-day round trip ticket is £19 ($35). For more information, call © 0845/748-4950 or visit www.railtrack.co.uk.

The **Oxford Express (operated by The Oxford Bus Company)** provides coach service from London's Victoria Station (© 0870/580-8080; www.national express.com) to the Oxford Bus Station (bus no. X90). Coaches usually depart about every 30 minutes during the day; the trip takes approximately 1¾ hours. A same-day round-trip ticket costs £11 ($20) for adults, £5.50 ($10) for children 3 to 15.

If you're driving, take the M40 west from London and just follow the signs. Traffic and parking are a disaster in Oxford, and not just during rush hours. However, there are four large park-and-ride parking lots on the north, south, east, and west of the city's ring road, all well marked. Parking is 60p ($1) per car. From 9:30am on and all day Saturday, you pay £1.40 ($2.60) or £1.80 ($3.35) for a round-trip ticket for a bus ride into the city, which drops you off at St. Aldate's Cornmarket or Queen Street to see the city center. The buses run every 8 to 10 minutes in each direction. There is no service on Sunday. The parking lots are on the Woodstock road near the Peartree traffic circle, on the Botley road toward Farringdon, on the Abingdon road in the southeast, and on the A40 toward London.

VISITOR INFORMATION   The **Oxford Tourist Information Centre** is at 15 to 16 Broad Street (© 01865/726871; www.visitoxford.org). The center sells a comprehensive range of maps, brochures, and souvenir items, as well as the famous Oxford University T-shirt. It provides hotel-booking services for £3 ($5.55). Guided walking tours leave from the center daily (see below). Open Monday through Saturday from 9:30am to 5pm and Sunday and bank holidays in summer from 10am to 3:30pm.

GETTING AROUND   Competition thrives in Oxford transportation, and the public benefits with swift, clean service by two companies. The **Oxford Bus Company,** 395 Cowley Rd. (© 01865/785400; www.oxfordbus.co.uk), has green Park and Ride buses that leave from four parking lots in the city using the north-south or east-west routes. A round-trip ticket costs £1.80 ($3.35). Their Airline buses are blue and travel to Heathrow and Gatwick. A one-way ticket from Oxford to Heathrow costs £14 ($26) for adults, £7 ($13) for children aged 5 to 15. A one-way ticket from Oxford to Gatwick costs £21 ($39) for adults, £11 ($19) for children aged 5 to 15. The company's red local buses cover 15 routes in all suburbs, with a day pass allowing unlimited travel for £2.90 ($5.45). Weekly and monthly passes are available.

The competition, **Stagecoach,** Unit 4, Horsepath, Cowley (© 01865/ 772250; www.stagecoach-oxford.co.uk), uses blue-and-cream minibuses and

Oxford

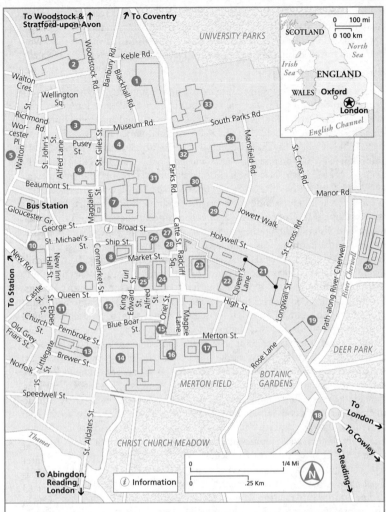

SCOTLAND

North
Sea

Irish
Sea

ENGLAND

WALES   Oxford

London

English Channel

0   100 mi
0   100 km

Keble Rd.

Walton
Cres.

Wellington
Sq.

Richmond
Wor-
cester
Pl.

Walton

Woodstock Rd.

Banbury Rd.

Blackhall Rd.

Museum Rd.

South Parks Rd.

Mansfield Rd.

St. Cross Rd.

Manor Rd.

St. John's St.

Alfred Lane

St. Giles St.

Pusey
St.

Beaumont St.

Bus Station

Gloucester Gr.

George St.

St. Michael's
St.

New Inn
Hall St.

Cornmarket St.

Magdalen
St.

Ship St.

Broad St.

Market St.

Turl
St.

King
Edward
St.

Alfred
St.

Oriel
St.

Queen St.

Castle
St.

St. Ebbes
St.

Church
St.

Old Grey
Friars St.

Pembroke St.

Littlegate
St.

Brewer St.

Norfolk
St.

Speedwell St.

Blue Boar
St.

Magpie
Lane

Oriel St.

Parks Rd.

Catte St.

Radcliff
Sq.

Holywell St.

Jowett Walk

Queen's
Lane

High St.

Longwall St.

St. Cross Rd.

Path along River Cherwell

River Cherwell

Merton St.

Rose Lane

MERTON FIELD

BOTANIC
GARDENS

DEER PARK

CHRIST CHURCH MEADOW

Thames

St. Aldates St.

New Rd.

To Station

Castle

To Abingdon,
Reading,
London ↓

To London →

To Cowley →

To Reading →

Information

0   1/4 Mi
0   .25 Km

N

red-blue-and-orange coaches. City buses leave from Queen Street in Oxford's city center. Explorer passes cost £5.50 ($10). This ticket allows unlimited travel for a day in all Oxfordshire on Stagecoach buses. There is also a 1 day ticket that allows unlimited travel within Oxford city (called Dayrider) and it costs £2.80 ($5.20).

EXPLORING THE CITY

The best way to get a running commentary on the important sights is to take a 2-hour **walking tour** through the city and the major colleges. The tours leave daily from the Oxford Tourist Information Centre at 11am and 2pm. Tours costs £6.50 ($12) for adults and £3 ($5.55) for children under 16; the tours do not include New College or Christ Church. There are two tours that leave the Oxford Information Centre on Saturdays at 11am and 2pm. These tours include admission to Christ Church. Cost £7.50 ($14) adults, £3.50 ($6.50) children under 16.

The **Oxford Story,** 6 Broad St. (✆ **01865/728822;** www.oxfordstory.co.uk), is a concise and entertaining audiovisual ride through the campus. It explains the structure of the colleges and highlights architectural and historical features. Visitors are also filled in on the general background of the colleges and the antics of some of the famous people who have passed through the University's portals. In July and August, the audiovisual presentation is daily from 9:30am to 5pm. From September to December, it runs Monday through Saturday from 10am to 4:30pm, Sunday 11am to 4:30pm; and from January to June Monday through Saturday from 10am to 4:30pm, Sunday 11am to 4:30pm. Admission is £7 ($13) for adults and £5.50 ($10) for seniors, students, and children. A family ticket for two adults and two children is £23 ($43).

For a good orientation, hour-long, open-top bus tours around Oxford are available from **Guide Friday,** whose office is at the railway station (tours also start from the railway station; other pick-up points are: Sheldonian Theatre, Gloucester Green Bus Station, and Pembroke College) (✆ **01865/790522**). Buses leave every 20 minutes daily; in summer, buses leave every 5 to 10 minutes. Tickets are good for the day. Tours run daily from 9:30am to 3:45pm November through January, daily from 9:30am to 4:45pm February and March, and daily 9:30am to 6:30pm April through October. The cost is £9 ($17) for adults, £7 ($13) for students and seniors, £3 ($5.55) for children 5 to 14 years old; a family ticket for two adults and two children is £19 ($35). Children under 5 get to ride free. Tickets can be purchased from the driver.

The **Tourist Information Centre,** 15–16 Broad St. (✆ **01865/726871;** www. visitoxford.org), offers a ghost tour, which explores Oxford's ghoulish and gory past. The office also has a number of walking tours, with the ghost tour available Friday and Saturday evenings June through September and on October 31 (Halloween) from 7:45pm, covering the dark alleyways around the ancient schools. The cost is £5.85 ($11) for adults and £3 ($5.55) for children; tickets are available at the office during the day. Day tours begin at 10am daily, including Christmas, even for one person.

⟮Moments⟯ A Nostalgic Walk

Our favorite pastime here is to take **Addison's Walk** through the water meadows. The stroll is named after a former Oxford alumnus, Joseph Addison, the 18th-century essayist and playwright noted for his contributions to *The Spectator* and *The Tatler*.

Moments **Punting the River Cherwell**

Punting on the River Cherwell remains the favorite outdoor pastime in Oxford. At Punt Station, **Cherwell Boathouse,** Bardwell Road (© **01865/ 515978;** www.cherwellboathouse.co.uk), you can rent a punt (flat-bottom boat maneuvered by a long pole and a small oar) for £10 to £12 ($19–$22) per hour, plus a £50 to £60 ($93–$111) deposit. Similar charges are made for punt rentals at Magdalen Bridge Boathouse. Punts are rented from mid-March to mid-October, daily from 10am until dusk. Hours of operation seem to be rather informal, however, and you're not always guaranteed that someone will be here to rent you a boat, even if the punt itself is available.

EXPLORING OXFORD UNIVERSITY

Many Americans arriving at Oxford ask, "Where's the campus?" If a local looks amused when answering, it's because Oxford University is, in fact, made up of 35 colleges sprinkled throughout the town. To tour all of these would be a formidable task. It's best to focus on just a handful of the better-known colleges.

A word of warning: The main business of a university is, of course, to educate—and this function at Oxford has been severely hampered by the number of visitors who disturb the academic work of the university. So visiting is restricted to certain hours and small groups of six or fewer. Furthermore, visitors are not allowed at all in certain areas, but the tourist office will be happy to advise you when and where you may take in the sights of this great institution.

AN OVERVIEW   For a bird's-eye view of the city and colleges, climb **Carfax Tower** ⚐, located in the center of the city. This structure is distinguished by its clock and figures that strike on the quarter-hour. Carfax Tower is all that remains from St. Martin's Church, where William Shakespeare once stood as godfather for William Davenant, who also became a successful playwright. A church stood on this site from 1032 until 1896. The tower used to be higher, but after 1340 it was lowered, following complaints from the university to Edward III that townspeople threw stones and fired arrows at students during town-and-gown disputes. Admission is £1.50 ($2.80) for adults, 60p ($1.10) for children. The tower is open year-round, except for from Christmas Eve to January 1. April through October, hours are from 10am to 5pm daily. Off-season hours are Monday through Saturday from 10am to 3:30pm. Children under 5 are not admitted. For information, call © **01865/792653.**

CHRIST CHURCH ⚐⚐   Begun by Cardinal Wolsey as Cardinal College in 1525, Christ Church (© **01865/276150;** www.chch.ox.ac.uk), known as the House, was founded by Henry VIII in 1546. Facing St. Aldate's Street, Christ Church has the largest quadrangle of any college in Oxford. Tom Tower houses Great Tom, an 18,000-pound bell. It rings at 9:05pm nightly, signaling the closing of the college gates. The 101 times it peals originally signified the number of students in residence at the time the college was founded. Although the student body has grown significantly, Oxford traditions live forever. There are some interesting portraits in the 16th-century Great Hall, including works by Gainsborough and Reynolds. There's also a separate portrait gallery.

The college chapel was constructed over a period of centuries, beginning in the 12th century. (Incidentally, it's not only the college chapel but also the

---

Finds **A Pokey Home for Old Masters**

Almost overlooked by the average visitor is an unheralded little gem known as **Christ Church Picture Gallery,** entered through the Canterbury Quad. Here you come across a stunning collection of old masters, mainly from the Dutch, Flemish, and Italian school, including works by Michelangelo and Leonardo da Vinci. Open April through September, Monday through Saturday from 10:30am to 1pm and 2 to 5:30pm (closes at 4:30pm Oct–Mar). Admission is £2 ($3.70) for adults or £1 ($1.85) for students and seniors.

---

cathedral of the diocese of Oxford.) The cathedral's most distinguishing features are its Norman pillars and the vaulting of the choir, dating from the 15th century. In the center of the great quadrangle is a statue of Mercury mounted in the center of a fishpond. You can visit the college and cathedral between 9am and 5:30pm, though times vary (1–5:30pm on Sunday). It's best to call before you visit. The entrance fee is £4 ($7.40) for adults and £3 ($5.55) for children.

MAGDALEN COLLEGE   Pronounced *Maud*-lin, Magdalen College, High Street (© **01865/276000;** www.magd.ox.ac.uk), was founded in 1458 by William of Waynflete, bishop of Winchester and later chancellor of England. Its alumni range from Wolsey to Wilde. Opposite the botanic garden, the oldest in England, is the bell tower, where the choristers sing in Latin at dawn on May Day. Charles I, his days numbered, watched the oncoming Roundheads from this tower. Visit the 15th-century chapel, in spite of many of its latter-day trappings. Ask when the hall and other places of special interest are open. The grounds of Magdalen are the most extensive of any Oxford college; there's even a deer park. You can visit all year round between 1pm and dusk daily. Admission is £3 ($5.55).

MERTON COLLEGE✶✶   Founded in 1264, Merton College, Merton Street (© **01865/276310;** www.merton.ox.ac.uk), is among the three oldest colleges at the university. It stands near Corpus Christi College on Merton Street, the sole survivor of Oxford's medieval cobbled streets. Merton College is noted for its library (which was closed at press time), built between 1371 and 1379 and said to be the oldest college library in England. Though a tradition once kept some of its most valuable books chained, now only one book is secured in that manner to illustrate that historical custom. One of the library's treasures is an astrolabe (an astronomical instrument used for measuring the altitude of the sun and stars) thought to have belonged to Chaucer. You pay £1 ($1.85) to visit the ancient library as well as the Max Beerbohm Room (the satirical English caricaturist who died in 1956). The library and college are open Monday through Friday from 2 to 4pm, and Saturday and Sunday from 10am to 4pm. It's closed for 1 week at Easter and Christmas and on weekends during the winter.

NEW COLLEGE   New College, Holywell St. (© **01865/279555;** www.new.ox.ac.uk), was founded in 1379 by William of Wykeham, bishop of Winchester and later lord chancellor of England. His college at Winchester supplied a constant stream of students. The first quadrangle, dating from before the end of the 14th century, was the initial quadrangle to be built in Oxford and formed the architectural design for the other colleges. In the antechapel is Sir Jacob Epstein's remarkable modern sculpture of Lazarus and a fine El Greco painting of

St. James. One of the treasures of the college is a crosier (pastoral staff of a bishop) belonging to the founding father. Don't miss the beautiful garden outside the college, where you can stroll among the remains of the old city wall and the mound. It's an evocative, romantic site. The college (entered at New College Lane) can be visited from Easter to October, daily between 11am and 5pm; and in the off season daily between 2 and 4pm. Admission is £1.50 to £2 ($2.80–$3.70), depending on what is open, from Easter to October and free off season.

THE OLD BODLEIAN LIBRARY ⭐⭐   This famed library on Catte Street (② 01865/277224; www.bodley.ox.ac.uk) was launched in 1602, initially funded by Sir Thomas Bodley. It is home to some 50,000 manuscripts and more than five million books. Over the years the library has expanded from the Old Library complex to other buildings, including the Radcliffe Camera next door. The easiest way to visit the library is by taking a guided tour, leaving from the Divinity School across the street from the main entrance. In summer there are four tours Monday through Friday, and two on Saturday; in winter, two tours leave per day. Call for specific times.

Ashmolean Museum ⭐   This is the oldest public museum in Britain. Founded in 1683 and under the control of the University of Oxford, it is devoted to art and archaeology, presented to the University of Oxford by Elias Ashmole (1617–92). Collections are divided into five different departments: Antiquities (from Paleolithic to Victorian times), Cast Gallery (strong on Roman and Greek sculpture), Eastern Art (from the Islamic world to Tibet and China), Heberden Coin Room (coins and medals from around the world), and Western Art (a wide range of drawings, paintings, prints, and sculpture). The highlights of the original collection, still at the museum, are drawings by Michelangelo, a collection of gems known as "the Alfred jewel," and a Chinese gallery of objets d'art.

Beaumont St. ② 01865/278000. www.ashmol.ox.ac.uk. Free admission; donations appreciated. Tues–Sat 10am–5pm; Sun 2–5pm. Museum stays open June–Aug until 7:30pm on Thurs.

SHOPPING

Golden Cross, an arcade of first-class shops and boutiques, lies between Cornmarket Street and the Covered Market (or between High and Market sts.). Parts of the colorful gallery date from the 12th century. Many buildings remain from the medieval era, along with some 15th- and 17th-century structures. The market also has a reputation as the Covent Garden of Oxford, with live entertainment on Saturday mornings in summer. In the arcade shops is a diverse selection of merchandise, including handmade Belgian chocolates, specialty gifts, clothing for both women and men, and luxury leather goods.

Tips **A Quiet Oasis**

Though ignored by the average visitor, the **Botanic Gardens** (② 01865/286690; www.botanic-garden.ox.ac.uk) opposite Magdalen were first planted in 1621 on the site of a Jewish graveyard from the early Middle Ages. Bounded by a curve of the Cherwell, they still stand today and are the best place in Oxford to escape the invading hordes. Open daily from 9am to 5pm March to October (until 6pm May–Sept); Monday through Friday 9am to 4:30pm November to February (last admission 45 min. before closing). Admission is £2 ($3.70).

In its way, **Alice's Shop,** 83 St. Aldate's (© **01865/723793**), played an important role in English literature. Set within a 15th-century building that has housed some kind of shop since 1820, it functioned as a general store (selling brooms, hardware, and the like) during the period that Lewis Carroll, at the time a professor of mathematics at Christ Church College, was composing *Alice in Wonderland.* It is believed to have been the model for important settings within the book. Today, the place is a favorite stopover of Lewis Carroll fans from as far away as Japan, who gobble up commemorative pencils, chess sets, party favors, bookmarks, and in rare cases, original editions of some of Carroll's works.

The **Bodleian Library Shop,** Old School's Quadrangle, Radcliffe Square, Broad Street (© **01865/277216**), specializes in Oxford souvenirs, from books and paperweights to Oxford banners and coffee mugs.

Castell & Son (The Varsity Shop), 13 Broad St. (© **01865/244000;** www. varsityshop.co.uk), is the best outlet in Oxford for clothing emblazoned with the Oxford logo or heraldic symbol. Choices include both whimsical and dead-on-serious neckties, hats, T-shirts, pens, beer and coffee mugs, and cuff links. It's commercialized Oxford, but it's still got a sense of relative dignity and style. A second location is at 109–114 High St. (© **01865/241848**).

Which College to Choose? Oxford or Cambridge?

Not everyone can go to both Oxford and Cambridge, so which should you choose if pressed for time and can spare only a day out of London? We'd opt for Cambridge over Oxford because Cambridge more closely lives up to the image of what an English university town is like.

Although the university dominates central Oxford, it is also an industrial city known for its motor industry. Its 120,000 permanent residents seem to keep to themselves and go about their lives trying to evade the thousands of tourists descending on their inner core. Of course, Oxford has some of England's greatest architecture, some excellent museums, and great student pubs. On an ideal itinerary, it should not be crossed off the list.

Then there is Cambridge. It's really an agricultural market town, a more tranquil and secluded place, set at the doorstep of the Fens, a vast area just north of the city that's a strange but fascinating terrain of reclaimed marshland and quaking bogs. In addition to its architecture and university, Cambridge allows you to preview the life of East Anglia, still one of the country's bucolic landscapes as painted by John Constable.

Unlike the city of Oxford, Cambridge is more compact and can be more easily walked and explored on a rushed day trip. You can go "punting" on the River Cam; explore "the Backs," that green swathe of land straddling the river; and walk the 1km (½-mile) parade of colleges from Magdalene to Peterhouse. Not bad for a day's outing. You may so fall in love with English university towns, you'll decide to stay in England for that extra day so you can take in Oxford after all.

WHERE TO STAY

Accommodations in Oxford are limited, though recently, motels have sprouted on the outskirts—good for those who want modern amenities. In addition, if you have a car, you may want to consider country houses or small B&Bs on the outskirts of town, the best choices in the area if you don't mind commuting.

Bedrooms, albeit expensive ones, are also provided at Le Manoir aux Quat' Saisons (reviewed under "Where to Dine," below).

The **Oxford Tourist Information Centre,** Gloucester Green, behind the bus bays (**℃ 01865/726871;** www.visitoxford.org), operates a year-round room-booking service for a £3 ($5.55) fee, plus a 10% refundable deposit. If you'd like to seek lodgings on your own, the center has a list of accommodations, maps, and guidebooks.

EXPENSIVE

Old Bank Hotel 🌟🌟   The first hotel created in the center of Oxford in 135 years, the Old Bank opened late in 1999, and immediately surpassed the traditional favorite, the Randolph, in style and amenities. Located on Oxford's main street and surrounded by some of its oldest colleges and sights, the building dates back to the 18th century and was indeed once a bank. The hotel currently features a collection of 20th-century British art handpicked by the owners. Bedrooms are comfortably and elegantly appointed, often opening onto views. A combination of velvet and shantung silk-trimmed linen bedcovers give the accommodations added style. Each unit includes a well-kept bathroom with terra-cotta or marble tiles.

92–94 High St., Oxford OX1 4BN. ℃ 01865/799599. Fax 01865/799598. www.oxford-hotels-restaurants. co.uk. 42 units. £160–£235 ($296–$435) double; £265–£320 ($490–$592) suite. AE, DC, MC, V. Bus: 7. **Amenities:** Restaurant; bar; concierge; 24-hr. room service; babysitting; laundry service; dry cleaning; 1 room for those with limited mobility; nonsmoking rooms. *In room:* A/C, TV, dataport, CD player, coffeemaker, hair dryer, safe.

Old Parsonage Hotel 🌟🌟   This extensively renovated hotel, near St. Giles Church and Keble College, is so old it looks like an extension of one of the ancient colleges. Originally a 13th-century hospital, it was restored in the early 17th century. In the 20th century, a modern wing was added, and in 1991 it was completely renovated and made into a first-rate hotel. This intimate old hotel is filled with hidden charms such as tiny gardens in its courtyard and on its roof terrace. In this tranquil area of Oxford, you feel like you're living at one of the colleges yourself. The rooms are all nonsmoking and individually designed but not large; all the units have marble bathrooms with shower-tub combinations and each of them opens onto the private gardens; 10 of them are on the ground floor.

1 Banbury Rd., Oxford OX2 6NN. ℃ 01865/310210. Fax 01865/311262. www.oxford-hotels-restaurants. co.uk. 30 units. £135–£170 ($250–$315) double; £195 ($361) suite. AE, DC, MC, V. Bus: 7. **Amenities:** Restaurant; bar; 24-hr. room service; car and limo service for hire; laundry service; dry-cleaning. *In room:* TV, dataport, hair dryer, safe, trouser press.

The Randolph 🌟   Since 1864, the Randolph has overlooked St. Giles, the Ashmolean Museum, and the Cornmarket. The hotel is an example of how historic surroundings can be combined with modern conveniences to make for elegant accommodations. The lounges, though modernized, are cavernous enough for dozens of separate and intimate conversational groupings. The furnishings are traditional. Some rooms are quite large; others are a bit cramped. All units come equipped with well-maintained bathrooms containing shower-tub combinations. The double-glazing on the windows appears inadequate to keep out the noise of midtown traffic. In this price range, we'd opt first for the more stylish and intimate Old Parsonage before checking in here.

Beaumont St., Oxford, Oxfordshire OX1 2LN. *©* **0870/400-8200.** Fax 01865/791678. www.macdonald hotels.co.uk. 114 units. £120–£195 ($222–$361) double; £355–£600 ($657–$1,110) suite. AE, DC, MC, V. Parking £22 ($41). Bus: 7. **Amenities:** Restaurant; 2 bars; concierge; 24-hr. room service; babysitting; laundry service; dry cleaning; nonsmoking rooms. *In room:* TV, dataport, coffeemaker, hair dryer, trouser press.

MODERATE

Eastgate Hotel 🖈   The Eastgate, built on the site of a 1600s structure, stands within walking distance of Oxford College and the city center. Recently refurbished, it offers modern facilities while somewhat retaining the atmosphere of an English country house. The bedrooms are well worn but still cozy and range in size from small to medium. The bathrooms have minimum space but are equipped with shower-tub combinations.

23 Merton St., The High St., Oxford, Oxfordshire, OX1 4BE. *©* **0870/400-8201.** Fax 01865/791681. www.macdonaldhotels.co.uk. 64 units. £160 ($296) double; £180 ($333) suite. AE, DC, MC, V. Bus: 3, 4, 7, or 52. **Amenities:** Restaurant; bar; limited room service; babysitting; laundry service; dry cleaning; nonsmoking rooms. *In room:* A/C, TV, dataport, coffeemaker, hair dryer, trouser press.

The Oxford Hotel   This is a good choice if you have a car; it's 3km (2 miles) north of the city center, and hidden from traffic at the junction of A40 and A34. It attracts a lot of business travelers, but also visitors, and is a good base for exploring not only Oxford but also the Cotswolds, which are within easy reach. The M40 motorway is just a 13km (8-mile) drive away. Rooms are motel-like, with modern, contemporary furnishings that are comfortable and spacious, but as of this writing, the hotel is undergoing extensive refurbishing and upgrading. Some bedrooms are set aside for nonsmokers. The shower-only bathrooms are nothing special but are well maintained.

Godstow Rd., Wolvercote Roundabout, Oxford, Oxfordshire OX2 8AL. *©* **01865/489988.** Fax 01865/310259. www.paramount-hotels.co.uk. 168 units. £159–£179 ($294–$331) double. AE, DC, MC, V. Bus: 6. **Amenities:** Restaurant; bar; pool; 2 squash courts; spa; limited room service; laundry service; dry cleaning; rooms for those with limited mobility. *In room:* A/C, TV, dataport, coffeemaker, hair dryer, safe, trouser press.

Weston Manor 🖈🖈   Ideal as a center for touring the district (Blenheim Palace is only 8km/5 miles away), this 5.2-hectare (13-acre) manor is owned and run by the Osborn family. It has existed since the 11th century; portions of the present building date from the 14th and 16th centuries. The estate is the ancestral home of the earls of Abingdon and Berkshire. It was also an abbey until Henry VIII abolished the abbeys and assumed ownership of the property. Of course, there are ghosts: Mad Maude, the naughty nun who was burned at the stake for her "indecent and immoral" behavior, returns to haunt the Oak rooms. Prince Rupert, during the English Civil War, hid from Cromwell's soldiers in one of the fireplaces, eventually escaping in drag as a "maiden of the milk bucket."

The reception lounge is dominated by a Tudor fireplace and a long refectory table. Most of the rooms are spacious and furnished with antiques (often four-poster beds), old dressing tables, and chests. Bedrooms are divided between the main house and a former coach that was skillfully converted into well-equipped guest rooms. Regardless of location, each bedroom is first rate with extremely comfortable beds and fine linen, plus modernized bathrooms with adequate shelf space and a shower-tub combination. Half of the bedrooms are set aside for nonsmokers.

Weston-on-the-Green, Oxfordshire OX25 3QL. ℂ **01869/350621**. Fax 01869/350901. www.westonmanor. co.uk. 35 units. £154 ($285) double; £215–£225 ($398–$416) suite. Rates include English breakfast. AE, DC, MC, V. Drive 9.5km (6 miles) north of Oxford on A34. **Amenities:** Restaurant; bar; outdoor heated pool; limited room service; laundry service; dry cleaning; rooms for those with limited mobility. *In room:* A/C, TV, dataport, coffeemaker, hair dryer, iron/ironing board.

INEXPENSIVE

Dial House *Value*   Three kilometers (2 miles) east of the heart of Oxford, beside the main highway leading to London, is this country-style house originally built between 1924 and 1927. Graced with mock Tudor half-timbering and a prominent blue-faced sundial (from which it derives its name), it has cozy and recently-renovated rooms. Bathrooms are small and most have showers only, but a few offer a combination tub and shower. The owners, the Morris family, serve only breakfast in their bright dining room. The entire property is nonsmoking.

25 London Rd., Headington, Oxford, Oxfordshire OX3 7RE. ℂ and fax **01865/760743**. www.oxfordcity.co. uk/accom/dialhouse. 8 units. £65–£70 ($120–$130) double; £85 ($157) family room. AE, MC, V. Bus: 2, 2A, 7, 7A, or 22. *In room:* TV, coffeemaker, hair dryer, safe, no phone.

Galaxie Private Hotel   When it was built about a century ago, this redbrick hotel served as a plush private mansion for a prosperous local family. This little nonsmoking hotel is better than ever following a recent refurbishment and upgrade, with a conservatory lounge added. Although most of its garden is now a parking lot, it still stands in a neighborhood of similar large houses in the suburb of Summertown. Each of the well-maintained bedrooms is equipped with reading lights, electric shaver outlets, hot and cold running water, and central heating. Furnishings are of a high standard. Most units come with tidily kept, shower-only bathrooms. Although no meals other than breakfast are served, the hotel is within a short walk of at least five restaurants and two pubs. A public leisure center, with two indoor pools, is located just behind the hotel. A public bus runs down Banbury Road to the center of Oxford.

180 Banbury Rd., Oxford, Oxfordshire OX2 7BT. ℂ **01865/515688**. Fax 01865/556824. www.galaxie.co.uk. 34 units, 30 with bathroom. £78 ($144) double without bathroom; £90 ($167) double with bathroom. Rates include English breakfast. MC, V. **Amenities:** Breakfast room; lounge; 1 room for those with limited mobility. *In room:* TV, hair dryer, coffeemaker, dataport.

Green Gables   This hotel was originally a large Edwardian private residence of a local toy manufacturer. Today's hosts, among the best in Oxford, continue to make improvements to this property. Many of the bedrooms in this non-smoking facility are quite large; all are in spic-and-span condition, each with a private shower-only bathroom. The breakfast room is bright and inviting. Trees screen the house from the main road, and parking for eight cars is available.

326 Abingdon Rd., Oxford, Oxfordshire OX1 4TE. ℂ **01865/725870**. Fax 01865/723115. www.greengables. uk.com. 11 units. £52–£70 ($96–$130) double. Rates include English breakfast. AE, MC, V. 1.6km (1 mile) south of Oxford on A4144. **Amenities:** Breakfast room, lounge; 1 room for those with limited mobility. *In room:* TV, coffeemaker, dataport.

Tilbury Lodge Private Hotel *Kids*   On a quiet country lane about 3km (2 miles) west of the center of Oxford, this small hotel is less than a mile from the railway station, where hotel staff will pick you up to save you the walk. Eddie and Eileen Trafford accommodate guests in their well-furnished and comfortable rooms. The most expensive room has a four-poster bed; there is a also a room suitable for families. Rooms vary in size, but most are cozy with adequate space. Bathrooms, although tiny, are well kept, usually with a shower. The guesthouse also has a Jacuzzi and welcomes children.

5 Tilbury Lane, Eynsham Rd., Botley, Oxford, Oxfordshire OX2 9NB. ☏ **01865/862138.** Fax 01865/863700. 9 units. £66–£75 ($122–$139) double. Rates include English breakfast. MC, V. Bus: 4A, 4B, or 100. **Amenities:** Jacuzzi. *In room:* TV, coffeemaker, hair dryer.

WHERE TO DINE
VERY EXPENSIVE

Le Manoir aux Quat' Saisons ⋆⋆⋆ FRENCH (MODERN)   Some 19km (12 miles) southeast of Oxford, Le Manoir aux Quat' Saisons offers the finest cuisine in the Midlands. The gray- and honey-colored stone manor house was originally built by a Norman nobleman in the early 1300s, and over the years has attracted many famous visitors. Today, the restaurant's connection with France has been masterfully revived by the Gallic owner and chef, Raymond Blanc. His reputation for comfort and cuisine attracts guests from as far away as London.

You can enjoy such creative treats as roasted squab and foie gras ravioli with wild mushrooms; roasted grouse in a blackberry-and-red-wine sauce; or a truly delectable roasted breast of Barbary hen duck with figs and fennel seeds and a pan-fried foie gras. Each dish is an exercise in studied perfection.

Accommodations are also available here. The gabled house was built in the 1500s and improved and enlarged in 1908. Each very pricey room—rates are £275 to £485 ($509–$897) for a double; £490 to £875 ($907–$1,619) for a suite—is decorated boudoir style with luxurious beds and linens, ruffled canopies, and high-quality antique reproductions, plus deluxe bathrooms with thick towels and a hair dryer.

Great Milton, Oxfordshire. ☏ **800/845-4274** in the U.S., or 01844/278881. Fax 01844/278847. www.manoir. com. Reservations required. Main courses £26–£38 ($48–$70); lunch menu du jour £45 ($83); lunch or dinner menu gourmand £95 ($176). AE, DC, MC, V. Daily noon–2:30pm and 7:15–9:45pm. Take Exit 7 off M40 and head along A329 toward Wallingford; look for signs for Great American Milton Manor about a mile after.

EXPENSIVE

Cherwell Boathouse Restaurant ⋆ FRENCH/MODERN ENGLISH An Oxford landmark on the River Cherwell, it's owned by Anthony Verdin, assisted by a young crew. With an intriguing fixed-price menu, the cooks change the fare every 2 weeks to take advantage of the availability of fresh vegetables, fish, and meat. There is a very reasonable, even exciting, wine list. The kitchen is often cited for its "sensible combinations" of ingredients The success of the main dishes is founded on savory treats such as grilled quail with a garlic and oregano dressing; pan-fried medallions of beef with a shallot and truffle sauce, and chargrilled loin of pork with a chorizo-laced butter. A special treat is the grilled gray mullet with ratatouille accompanied by a basil and chile sauce. For dessert, indulge on the lemon and almond roulade. The style is sophisticated yet understated, with a heavy reliance on quality ingredients that are cooked in such a way that natural flavors are always preserved.

Bardwell Rd. ☏ **01865/552746.** www.cherwellboathouse.co.uk. Reservations recommended. Fixed-price dinner from £23 ($42); Sun lunch £21.50 ($40); Mon–Fri lunch £20 ($36). AE, DC, MC, V. Mon–Sun 12:30pm–2pm and 6:30–9pm. Closed Dec 24–30. Bus: Banbury Rd.

Rosamund the Fair ⋆ *Finds* CONTINENTAL/BRITISH   This establishment accurately bills itself as Oxfordshire's cruising restaurant. A purpose-built narrow boat restaurant, this floating dining room cruises along the Oxford Canal in and around Banbury, as you dine but also say hello to the swans. The chefs might get by with the novelty of it all, but they also serve a sublime cuisine. The boat seats 20 people who for 2½ hours enjoy the dinner and the cruise. Between courses you can go on deck and admire the view. A recent menu delighted us with such starters as mango, avocado, and papaya salad with a lime and yogurt dressing, followed by sea bream with deep fried leeks and a lime butter sauce. Our dining partner selected ravioli with a salmon and chervil mousse with champagne sauce—a delightful choice—followed by a perfectly prepared best end of lamb with a mustard hollandaise glaze and rosemary jus. The dessert specialty is "swan profiteroles" with a rich chocolate sauce.

Tooley's, Banbury Museum, Spiceball Park Rd., Banbury. $\textcircled{C}$ **01295/278690**. Reservations required. Fixed-price menu £52 ($96) per person lunch or dinner. AE, MC, V. Lunch and dinner cruises Tues–Sun at 12:30pm and 7:30pm. Closed Jan.

MODERATE

Gee's Restaurant ✦ MEDITERRANEAN/INTERNATIONAL   This restaurant, in a spacious Victorian glass conservatory, was converted from what for 80 years was the leading florist of Oxford. Its original features were retained by the owners, the Old Parsonage Hotel (see above), who have turned it into one of the most nostalgic and delightful places to dine in the city. Open since 1984, it has come more into fashion under its talented chefs. From students to professors, clients are mixed, but all enjoy a well-chosen list of offerings. Based on fine ingredients and a skilled preparation, you are likely to enjoy such main courses as roast sea bass with chargrilled fennel and an herb dressing; roast breast of guinea fowl with shallots braised in red wine (served with field mushrooms), or homemade semolina gnocchi with baby spinach, goat's cheese, and pine nuts.

61 Banbury Rd. $\textcircled{C}$ **01865/553540**. Reservations recommended. Fixed-price lunch £13–£17 ($24–$31); main courses £11–£20 ($20–$37). AE, MC, V. Mon–Sat noon–2:30pm and 6–11pm; Sun noon–11pm.

Le Petit Blanc ✦ FRENCH/MEDITERRANEAN   The biggest culinary news in Oxford is the return of Raymond Blanc with another Le Petit Blanc. (A previous one proved disappointing.) Monsieur Blanc is a wiser restaurateur now, and this buzzing brasserie is doing just fine. A former piano shop has been converted into a stylish place offering a menu that promises something for every palate. Here you can get a taste of the famous chef's creations without the high prices of his famed Le Manoir aux Quat' Saisons. The menu is more straightforward here, with a large emphasis on fresh ingredients.

The food is wholesome and delicious, based on authentic provincial French cuisine, complemented by Mediterranean and Asian accents. We recently took delight in an appetizer, deep-fried goat's cheese with an olive tapenade, French beans, and tomato chutney, followed by a perfectly roasted John Dory with a coriander dressing. For other main courses, the braised rabbit with sweet onion tarte tatin and flap mushrooms, or the Oxford sausage with parsley mash, Madeira, and sweet onion sauce are superb. The desserts are first-rate, especially the raspberry soufflé.

71–72 Walton St. $\textcircled{C}$ **01865/510999**. Reservations recommended. Main courses £10–£15 ($19–$28); fixed-price lunch £16 ($30). AE, DC, MC, V. Mon–Sat noon–3:30pm and 6–11pm; Sun 12:30–3pm and 6:30–10:30pm.

INEXPENSIVE

Al-Salam ✦ *Value* LEBANESE   Some Oxford students think this place offers the best food value in the city, and because it's a bit less expensive (and a bit less formal) than its major competitor (the also-recommended Al-Shami, see below), we tend to agree. You'll dine within one of three sand-colored dining rooms, each separated from the other with antique (and very solid) wooden doors. Ironically, the newest of the three rooms, added in 2002, looks as if it's the oldest, thanks to stone-built arches and a commitment to the kinds of raw materials (wood and masonry) that would have been available in Lebanon a century ago. The menu depends on what's available in the marketplace and the chef's skill is reflected in such dishes as king prawns sautéed with a garlic and tomato sauce, or spicy lamb with a chile-and-onion sauce. Long lines can form at the door, especially on Fridays and Saturdays. The location is 2 minutes from both the bus and train stations.

6 Park End St. © 01865/245710. Reservations recommended. Main courses £7.50–£12 ($14–$22). MC, V. Daily noon–midnight.

Al-Shami LEBANESE   Bearing the archaic name for the city of Damascus, this Lebanese restaurant is a bit more formal than its also-recommended competitor, Al-Salam (see above). It contains two separate dining rooms: One with blessings from the Koran stenciled in calligraphic patterns under the coves; the other with pale beige walls and lots of wood paneling. Expect a clientele of local residents, with probably fewer students than you're likely to find at Al-Salam, and a formally dressed, Arabic- and English-speaking staff wearing black trousers, bow ties, and white vests. Many diners don't go beyond the appetizers because they comprise more than 35 delectable hot and cold selections—everything from falafel to a salad made with lamb's brains. Charcoal-grilled chopped lamb, chicken, or fish constitute most of the main-dish selections. In between, guests nibble on raw vegetables. Desserts are chosen from the cart, and vegetarian meals are also available.

25 Walton Crescent. © 01865/310066. Reservations recommended. Main courses £5.75–£12 ($11–$22); fixed-price menu £15 ($28). MC, V. Daily noon–midnight.

Browns *Value* ENGLISH/CONTINENTAL   Oxford's busiest and most bustling English brasserie suits all groups, from babies to undergraduates to grandmas. A 10-minute walk north of the town center, it occupies the premises of five Victorian shops whose walls were removed to create one large, echoing, and very popular space. A thriving bar trade (where lots of people seem to order Pimms) makes the place an evening destination in its own right.

A young and enthusiastic staff serves traditional English cuisine. Your meal may include meat pies, hot salads, burgers, pastas, steaks, or poultry. Afternoon tea here is a justly celebrated Oxford institution. Reservations are not accepted, so if you want to avoid a delay, arrive here during off-peak dining hours.

5–11 Woodstock Rd. © 01865/511995. Main courses £6–£15 ($11–$28). MC, V. Mon–Sat 11am–11:30pm; Sun 11:30am–11:30pm. Bus: 2 or 7.

OXFORD AFTER DARK
THE PERFORMING ARTS
Highly acclaimed orchestras playing in truly lovely settings mark the Music at Oxford series at the **Oxford Playhouse Theatre,** Beaumont Street (© **01865/ 305305;** www.oxfordplayhouse.com). The autumn season runs from mid-September to December, the winter season from January to April, the spring–summer season from May to early July. Tickets range from £9 to £24 ($17–$44). Classical music is performed by outstanding groups such as the European Union Chamber Orchestra, the Canterbury Musical Society, the Bournemouth Symphony, and the Guild Hall String Ensemble of London. All performances are held in the Sheldonian Theatre, a particularly attractive site, designed by Sir Christopher Wren, with paintings on the ceiling. The Playhouse Box Office is open Monday to Saturday 9.30am (Wed 10am) to 6.30pm (or half

---

Tips Outdoor Bargains

For some of the best productions in England, with some of the most talented actors, ask the tourist office about summer performances in the college gardens. Student productions have traditionally been held there, but increasingly, professional companies have been taking over the space. Two Shakespeare troupes perform here, as well as other groups. Ticket costs are significantly less than you'd find for a comparable experience elsewhere.

---

an hour after the start of an evening performance) and from at least 2 hours before a performance on Sundays.

New Theatre (formerly The Apollo) George Street (© **01865/320760** for administration, or call Ticketmaster © 0870/606-3500 for bookings), is Oxford's primary theater. Tickets are £6.50 to £49.50 ($12–$92). A continuous run of comedy, ballet, drama, opera, and even rock contributes to the variety. The Welsh National Opera often performs, and The Glyndebourne Touring Opera appears regularly. Advance booking is recommended, though some shows may have tickets the week of the performance. Don't try for tickets for popular shows on the same day. The box office is open Monday to Saturday 10am to 8pm (6pm if there is not evening performance).

THE CLUBS: BLUES, JAZZ & "CELTIC ROCK"

As a sign of the times, **Freud,** Walton Street (© **01865/311171**), has turned a 19th-century church, stained-glass windows and all, into a jazz and folk club with an expansive array of drink choices. The cover charge is £4.50 ($8.35) after 10pm on Friday and Saturday. Open Sunday to Tuesday 11am to midnight and Wed-Sat 11am-2am.

Old Fire Station, 40 George St. (© **01865/297190**), covers all the bases, including live entertainment, a bar, theater, art museum, and a new science museum called Curiosity, with a light show and other exhibits. The restaurant, open daily at noon, serves breakfast until 9pm, with free coffee, tea, and toast. Music cover charges begin at 9pm and are £6 to £8 ($11–$15) nightly. Offerings change nightly but include 1970s disco, blues, jazz, and local bands. Open noon to 2am.

Zodiac, 190 Crowley Rd. (© **01865/420042**), presents everything from easy listening to "Celtic Rock." The cover varies from £4 to £11 ($7.40–$20) depending on the group featured. It's usually open from about 7:30pm to 2am Monday through Friday, from 9pm to 2am Saturday and Sunday. Club ownership is shared by some major English bands, and local and big-name bands are featured along with DJs, so call ahead to be sure of what you're getting.

THE PUB SCENE

These places are all good choices for affordable meals, too.

The Head of the River, Abingdon Road at Folly Bridge, near the Westgate Centre Mall (© **01865/721600**), is operated the family brewery Fuller Smith and Turner. It's a lively place offering true traditional ales and lagers, along with good sturdy fare. In summer, guests sit by the river and can rent a punt or a boat with an engine. Twelve rooms, all with bathroom and overlooking the river, are available for £78 to £95 ($144–$176) in summer, including breakfast, newspaper, and parking.

Finds Pubs with a Pedigree

Every college town the world over has a fair number of bars, but few can boast local watering holes with such atmosphere and history as Oxford.

A short block from The High, overlooking the north side of Christ Church College, the **Bear Inn**, on 6 Alfred Street (② **01865/728164**), is an Oxford landmark, built in the 13th century and mentioned time and time again in English literature. The Bear brings together a wide variety of people in a relaxed way. You may talk with a raja from India, a university don, or a titled gentleman who's the latest in a line of owners that goes back more than 700 years. Some former owners developed an astonishing habit: clipping neckties. Around the lounge bar you'll see the remains of thousands of ties, which have been labeled with their owners' names.

Even older than the Bear is the **Turf Tavern,** 7 Bath Place (off Holywell St.; ② **01865/243235**), on a very narrow passageway near the Bodleian Library. The pub is reached via St. Helen's Passage, which stretches between Holywell Street and New College Lane. (You'll probably get lost, but any student worth his beer can direct you.) Thomas Hardy used the place as the setting for *Jude the Obscure*. It was "the local" of the future U.S. president Bill Clinton during his student days at Oxford. In warm weather, you can choose a table in any of the three separate gardens that radiate outward from the pub's central core. For wintertime warmth, braziers are lighted in the courtyard and in the gardens. A food counter set behind a glass case displays the day's fare—salads, soups, sandwiches, and so on. Local ales (including one named Headbanger, with a relatively high alcohol content) are served, as well as a range of wines.

Just outside of town, hidden away some 4km (2½ miles) north of Oxford, the **Trout Inn,** 195 Godstow Rd., Wolvercote (② **01865/302071**), is a private world where you can get ale and beer and standard fare. Have your drink in one of the historic rooms, with their settles (wooden benches), brass, and old prints, or go out in sunny weather to sit on a stone wall. On the grounds are peacocks, ducks, swans, and herons that live in and around the river and an adjacent weir pool; they'll join you if you're handing out crumbs. Take an arched stone bridge, architecture with wildly pitched roofs and gables, add the Thames River, and you have the Trout. The Smoking Room, the original 12th-century part, complements the inn's relatively "new" 16th-century bars. Daily specials are featured. Hot meals are served all day in the restaurant; salads are featured in summer, and there are grills in winter. On your way there and back, look for the view of Oxford from the bridge. Take bus no. 6A, 6B, or 6C to Wolvercote, then walk 1km (½ mile); it's also fun to bike here from Oxford. Opening hours are: Sunday noon to 10:30pm, Monday to Saturday 11am to 11pm.

At **The Eagle and Child,** 49 Saint Giles St. (② **01865/302925**), literary history suffuses the dim, paneled alcoves and promotes a sedate atmosphere. For at least a quarter of a century, it was frequented by the likes of C. S. Lewis and

J. R. R. Tolkien. In fact, *The Chronicles of Narnia* and *The Hobbit* were first read aloud at this pub. Known as the "Bird and Baby," this hallowed ground still welcomes the local dons, and the food is good. It's a settled, quiet place to read the newspapers and listen to classical music on CDs.

The King's Arms, 40 Holywell St. (© **01865/242369**), hosts a mix of students, gays, and professors. One of the best places in town to strike up a conversation, the pub, owned by Young's Brewery, features six of the company's ales along with visiting lagers and bitters that change periodically.

5 Woodstock & Blenheim Palace

100km (62 miles) NW of London; 13km (8 miles) NW of Oxford

The small country town of Woodstock, birthplace in 1330 of the Black Prince, ill-fated son of King Edward III, lies on the edge of the Cotswolds. Some of the stone houses here were constructed when Woodstock was the site of a royal palace. This palace had so suffered the ravages of time that its remains were demolished when Blenheim Palace was built. Woodstock was once the seat of a flourishing glove industry.

ESSENTIALS

GETTING THERE   Take the train to Oxford (see "Essentials," in section 4). The Gloucester Green bus (no. 20) leaves Oxford about every 12 minutes during the day. The trip takes just over a half-hour. Call **Stagecoach** (© **0870/608-2608;** www.stagecoachbus.com) for details. If you're driving, take the A44 from Oxford.

VISITOR INFORMATION   The **Tourist Information Centre** is at the Oxfordshire Museum, Park Street (© **01993/813276**), open Monday through Saturday from 10am to 5pm and Sunday from 1 to 5pm in winter; Monday through Saturday 9:30am to 5pm and Sunday 1 to 5pm in summer.

ONE OF ENGLAND'S MOST MAGNIFICENT PALACES

Blenheim Palace ✸✸✸ *Kids*   The extravagantly baroque Blenheim Palace is England's answer to Versailles. Blenheim is the home of the 11th duke of Marlborough, descendant of the first duke John Churchill, once an on-again, off-again favorite of Queen Anne's. In his day (1650–1722), the first duke became the supreme military figure in Europe. Fighting on the Danube near a village named Blenheim, Churchill defeated the forces of Louis XIV, and the lavish palace of Blenheim was built for the duke as a gift from the queen. It was designed by Sir John Vanbrugh, who was also the architect of Castle Howard; the landscaping was created by Capability Brown. The palace is loaded with riches: antiques, porcelain, oil paintings, tapestries, and chinoiserie. North Americans know Blenheim as the birthplace of Sir Winston Churchill. The room in which he was born is included in the palace tour, as is the Churchill exhibition: four rooms of letters, books, photographs, and other relics. Today, the former prime minister lies buried in Bladon Churchyard, near the palace.

Insider's tip: The **Marlborough Maze,** 540m (1,800 ft.) from the palace, is the largest symbolic hedge maze on earth, with an herb and lavender garden, a butterfly house, and inflatable castles for children. Also, be sure to look for the Castle's gift shops, tucked away in an old palace dairy. Here you can purchase a wide range of souvenirs, handicrafts, and even locally made preserves.

© **01993/811091.** www.blenheimpalace.com. Admission £11–£13 ($20–$23) adults, £8.50–£10 ($16–$19) students and seniors, £5.50–£7 ($10–$13) children 5–15, free for children under 5. Family ticket £28–£33 ($52–$61). Daily 10:30am–5:30pm. Last admission 4:45pm. Closed mid-Dec to mid-Feb.

WHERE TO STAY & DINE

The Bear Hotel ★★   The Bear Hotel is one of the six oldest coaching inns in England, dating from the 16th century. The half-stone structure is located in the center of Woodstock. Richard Burton and Elizabeth Taylor, at the height of their tempestuous romance in the 1960s, stayed in the Marlboro suite, an attractively decorated sitting room plus a bedroom and bathroom. According to legend, one of the chambers of the hotel is haunted. Rooms come in a variety of sizes and styles, but each offers grand comfort and a mix of modern luxuries with antiques; nine of the rooms contain four-poster beds. Bedrooms have recently been refurbished and contain well-kept bathrooms with shower-tub combinations. The hotel continues to maintain high standards of innkeeping. Blazing hearth fires are found throughout the hotel when the days and nights are cool.

Park St., Woodstock, Oxfordshire OX20 1SZ. © **0870/400-8202.** Fax 01993/813380. www.macdonaldhotels. co.uk. 54 units. £150–£198 ($278–$366) double; from £258 ($477) suite. AE, DC, MC, V. **Amenities:** Restaurant; bar; 24-hr. room service; babysitting; laundry service; dry cleaning; nonsmoking rooms. *In room:* A/C, TV, CD player, minibar, coffeemaker, hair dryer, iron/ironing board, safe, trouser press.

Feathers ★   Just a short walk from Blenheim Palace, Feathers dates from the 17th century and has been an inn since the 18th century. The bedrooms in this beautifully furnished hotel are individually decorated. Some units have draped awnings over the beds. The bathrooms are luxuriously clad in marble with shower-tub combinations and deluxe toiletries. The two lounges have wood fires. A multitude of stuffed birds (from which the house took its name) adorn the bar; from here you can go into the delightful garden in the courtyard.

Market St., Woodstock, Oxfordshire OX20 1SX. © **01993/812291.** Fax 01993/813158. www.feathers.co.uk. 20 units. £135–£155 ($250–$287) double; £200–£290 ($370–$537) suite. Rates include English breakfast. AE, DC, MC, V. **Amenities:** Restaurant; bar; limited room service; babysitting; laundry service. *In room:* TV, hair dryer.

TWO FAVORITE LOCAL PUBS

Star Inn, 22 Market Place (© **01993/811373**) has three locally brewed real ales from which to choose: Tetley's, Wadworth's 6X, and Marston's Pedigree. You can enjoy the requisite bar munchies as well as full dinners. The management boasts that its half-shoulder of lamb is the most tender around because of the slow cooking process. You can also pick and choose from a hot and cold buffet that features salads and sandwich fixings.

King's Head is tucked away at 11 Park Lane (© **01993/812164**) in Woodstock. Tourists seem to like the "potato pub," as the locals call it, though it's a bit hard to find. The name comes from the wide variety of stuffed potato skins that the pub serves. Enjoy these with a real ale; the owners are sure to have a different specialty ale every month. If you come for dinner, a three-course meal, which may include fish, ribs, or homemade lasagna, costing from £6 to £10 ($11–$19). Open Monday to Saturday 9am to 10:30pm and Sunday 10am to 10pm.

6 Aylesbury

74km (46 miles) NW of London; 35km (22 miles) E of Oxford

Aylesbury has retained much of its ancient charm and character, especially along the narrow Tudor alleyways and in the 17th-century architecture of the houses in the town center. Among the more interesting structures is St. Mary's Church, which dates from the 13th century and features an unusual spirelet.

The 15th-century King's Head Public House, a National Trust property, has seen many famous faces in its time, including Henry VIII, who was a frequent guest while he was courting Anne Boleyn.

The market, which has been an integral part of the town since the 13th century, is still a thriving force in Aylesbury life, with markets held on Wednesday, Friday, and Saturday, and a flea market on Tuesday. During the 18th and 19th centuries, ducks were the most famous commodity of the Aylesbury market. The pure white ducks were a delicacy for the rich and famous of London and were much desired for their dinner tables. The demand for the Aylesbury duck declined in the 20th century, though not before the breed became threatened with extinction. Today, however, most ducks found on restaurant menus are raised elsewhere, and the threat to the Aylesbury duck has subsided. The ivory fowl are now enjoyed more for their beauty than their flavor.

ESSENTIALS

GETTING THERE Aylesbury is 1 hour and 12 minutes by train from London's Marylebone Station, or 25 minutes off the M25 via the A41. For rail information, call (C) **0845/748-4950** or visit www.railtrack.co.uk.

VISITOR INFORMATION The **Aylesbury Tourist Information Centre,** 8 Bourbon St. ((C) **01296/330559**), is open April through October from 9:30am to 5pm Monday through Saturday. From November to March, hours are Monday through Saturday from 10am to 4:30pm.

SEEING THE SIGHTS

Aylesbury is blessed with an abundance of interesting architecture. If you aren't busy spending money at the market, you may want to stroll through the town to see the houses and buildings that line the streets. **Hickman's Almshouses** and the **Prebendal Houses** are structures that date from the 17th century; you can walk by after enjoying tea at St. Mary's Church, which is just down the road.

Buckinghamshire County Museum *Kids* This museum is located in two buildings, a house and a grammar school, both dating from the 18th century. The latest addition to the recently refurbished museum is the Roald Dahl Children's Gallery. Dahl's children's books, especially *Charlie and the Chocolate Factory* and *James and the Giant Peach,* come to life as visitors ride in the Great Glass Elevator or crawl inside the Giant Peach. Hands-on exhibits don't stop upon entering the main museum, however. Innovative displays focusing on the cultural heritage of Buckinghamshire are interactive and touchable. Advance arrangements are necessary for the Children's Gallery because of the large number of school groups that visit.

Church St. (C) **01296/331441**. www.buckscc.gov.uk/museum/index.stm. Admission to main museum is free. Children's Gallery £3.50 ($6.50) adults, £2.75 ($5.10) children. Mon–Sat 10am–5pm; Sun 2–5pm.

Oak Farms Rare Breeds Park While in the area, you'll of course want to see the famous Aylesbury ducks; this is the best place to catch sight of the once-threatened species. The traditional working farm is home to a variety of animals, from sheep to pigs, many of which are rare breeds. Guests can hand-feed special food to the animals, take a picnic of their own, and enjoy a nature trail.

Off A41 on the way to Broughton. (C) **01296/415709**. Admission £3 ($5.55) adults, £2 ($3.70) ages 16 and under. Daily 10am–5:30pm. Closed Nov to mid-Feb.

Waddesdon Manor *&* Built by Baron Ferdinand de Rothschild in the 1870s, the manor features French Renaissance architecture and a variety of

French furniture, carpets, and porcelain. Eighteenth-century artwork by several famous English and Dutch painters is exhibited, and, of course, you can view wine cellars. In the surrounding gardens, an aviary houses exotic birds. On the premises is a restaurant and gift shop, both featuring a vast assortment of Rothschild wines.

Bicester Rd. (*C*) **01296/653226**. www.waddesdon.org.uk. Admission to house and grounds £11 ($20) adults, £8 ($15) children aged 5–15; free under 5; grounds only £4 ($7.40) adults, £2 ($3.70) children aged 5–15; free under 5. House open Mar–Oct Wed–Sun and bank holidays 11am–4pm. Grounds and aviary Mar to late Dec Wed–Sun and bank holidays 10am–5pm. Audio guide can be hired at the entrance for £1 ($1.85). Bus: 16 or 17

WHERE TO STAY & DINE

Hartwell House ★★★ One of England's great showcase country estates and a member of Relais & Châteaux, Hartwell House lies just 3km (2 miles) southwest of Aylesbury (the nearest rail station) on the A418, and about 32km (20 miles) from Oxford or an hour's drive from Heathrow. It stands on 36 hectares (90 acres) of landscaped parkland. As you enter the house, you're transported back to another era and can enjoy a medley of architectural styles, ranging from the 16th through the 18th centuries. The home was built for the Hampden and Lee families, ancestors of the Confederacy's General Robert E. Lee. You can wander from the morning room to the oak-paneled bar, pausing in the library where a former tenant, the exiled Louis XVIII, signed the document returning him to the throne of France. This property stands on the Vale of Aylesbury.

Rooms are as regal as the prices. The stellar accommodations literally ooze with comfort, charm, and character, even those recently built in a converted stable block. Many of the rooms have garden fabrics, plus luxurious bathrooms with bathrobes and shower-tub combinations.

Oxford Rd., Aylesbury, Buckinghamshire HP17 8NL. (*C*) **01296/747444**. Fax 01296/747450. www.hartwell-house.com. 48 units. £240–£395 ($444–$731) double; £445–£700 ($823–$1,295) suite. AE, MC, V. **Amenities:** 2 restaurants; bar; 2 tennis courts; health club (includes indoor heated pool; whirlpool bath; sauna; steam room and gym); salon; 24-hr. room service; laundry service; dry-cleaning; nonsmoking rooms; rooms for those with limited mobility. *In room:* TV, dataport, hair dryer, safe, trouser press.

West Lodge Hotel Close to Aylesbury, this Victorian hotel on the A41 outdoes all others in the area with its facilities, the best of which must be its own hot-air balloon. The comfortable rooms are furnished with nice extras and private shower-only bathrooms. For dinner, Montgolfier is a French restaurant located across the street named after the brothers who made the first successful hot-air balloon flight in 1783.

45 London Rd., Aston Clinton, Aylesbury HP22 5HL. (*C*) **01296/630362**. Fax 01296/630151. www.westlodge. co.uk. 9 units. £78 ($144) double. Rates include breakfast. AE, DC, MC, V. **Amenities:** Breakfast room; bar; Jacuzzi; sauna; limited room service; nonsmoking rooms; rooms for those with limited mobility. *In room:* TV, dataport, coffeemaker, hair dryer.

AYLESBURY AFTER DARK

Hobgoblin, Kingsbury Square (*C* **01296/415100**), has been in service as a pub for only a couple of years, but this structure was built in 1742. Among on-tap offerings are house ales, Hobgoblin and Wychwood, as well as John Smith's, and there is also a full bar. Snack food is available, as are such distractions as pool tables, TVs, and video games. Sunday nights are karaoke. On weekends, the second floor opens as a dance club called **the Gate.** Hours are Friday and Saturday from 10pm to 3am, with a cover charge of £2 ($3.70) before midnight, £4 ($7.40) after midnight, and £3 ($5.55) after 1am.

7 St. Albans ⓧ

43km (27 miles) NW of London; 66km (41 miles) SW of Cambridge

Dating back 2,000 years, today's cathedral city of St. Albans was named after a Roman soldier who was the first Christian martyr in England. Medieval pilgrims made the trek to visit the shrine of St. Alban, and visitors today still find the ancient cathedral city and the surrounding countryside inspiring.

Peter Rabbit was created in this county by Beatrix Potter, and George Bernard Shaw found inspiration in the view from his countryside home near Ayot St. Lawrence. As you explore St. Albans and nearby attractions, you'll tread in the footsteps of Good Queen Bess and Henry VIII, who passed through before you.

Although today industry has crept in and Greater London keeps getting greater and greater, St. Albans is situated at the center of what was known as "the market basket of England." The 1,000-year-old tradition of the street market continues as merchants of every kind set up colorful stalls to display their goods. Held on Wednesday and Saturday, it's one of the largest in the southeast.

Tourism has also become important to the town, near the M25 and the M1 and on the way to many historic homes and attractions. St. Albans itself is home to several museums, well-preserved Roman ruins, and beautiful gardens.

ESSENTIALS

GETTING THERE   St. Albans is easily reached from London. Silverlink trains (formerly North London Railways) leave from London's Euston Station every 40 minutes (change train in Watford Junction and in St Albans Abbey). The rail connection, ThamesLink, takes you from London to St. Albans in just 20 minutes. From London, Green Line coach no. 724 also runs to St. Albans frequently (Green Line buses to St. Albans depart only from Heathrow airport). For rail information, call ⓒ **0845/748-4950** or visit www.railtrack.co.uk. For bus information, dial ⓒ **0870/608-2608** or visit www.stagecoachbus.com.

If you're driving, take the M25 Junction 21A or 22; M1 Junctions 6, 7, or 9; and A1 (M) Junction 3.

VISITOR INFORMATION   The **Tourist Information Centre** is at the Town Hall, Market Place (ⓒ **01727/864511**). From Easter to October, its hours are Monday through Saturday from 9:30am to 5:30pm; off-season hours are Monday through Saturday from 10am to 4pm. From the end of July until mid-September, the office is also open most Sundays from 10:30am to 4:30pm.

EXPLORING THE TOWN

The Association of Honorary Guides, a trained group of local volunteers, provides **guided walks.** These include a tour of the Roman Verulamium and the Medieval Town, a ghost walk, and a coaching-inn walking tour. In addition to pre-booked tours, free public guided walks are available on Sunday; the tour begins at 11:15am and 3pm at the tourist information center. Guides are also available on Sunday at the Verulamium Museum and Roman Theatre at 2:30pm to give short talks on a number of topics concerning the Romans and their time in the area. You can get full details from the Tourist Information Centre (see above).

Cathedral of St. Albans ⓧ, Holywell Hill and High Street (ⓒ **01727/860780;** www.stalbanscathedral.org.uk), is still known as "The Abbey" to locals, though Henry VIII dissolved it as such in 1539. Construction of the cathedral began in 1077, one of the early Norman churches of England. The bricks, especially visible in the tower, came from Verulamium, an old Roman city located at the foot of the hill. The nave and west front date from 1235.

The new chapter house, the first modern structure built beside a great medieval cathedral in the country, was opened by the queen in 1982. The building houses an information desk, gift shop, and restaurant. There is also a video detailing the history of the cathedral that you can view for free (donations appreciated).

The cathedral and chapter house are generally open daily from 8am to 5:30pm. In addition to church services, organ recitals are often open to the public. The church's choir can sometimes be heard rehearsing, if they're not on tour.

Verulamium Museum at St. Michael's ✦ (© **01727/751810;** www.stalbans museums.org.uk) stands on the site of the ancient Roman city of the same name. Here you'll view some of the finest Roman mosaics in Britain as well as re-created Roman rooms. Part of the Roman town hall, a hypocaust (an ancient design for heating rooms), and the outline of houses and shops are still visible in the park that surrounds the museum. Open year-round Monday through Saturday from 10am to 5:30pm and Sunday from 2 to 5:30pm, admission is £3.30 ($6.10) for adults, £2 ($3.70) for seniors and children, and £8 ($15) for a family ticket. By car, Verulamium is 15 to 20 minutes from Junction 21A on the M25; it is also accessible from Junctions 9 or 6 on the M1; follow the signs for St. Albans and the Roman Verulamium. A train to St. Albans City Station will put you within 3km (2 miles) of the museum.

Just a short distance from Verulamium is the **Roman Theatre** (© **01727/ 835035**). The structure is the only theater of the period that is open to visitors in Britain. You can tour the site daily between 10am and 5pm (4pm in winter). Admission is £1.60 ($2.95) for adults, £1.10 ($2.05) for students and seniors, and 50p (95¢) for children.

Museum of St. Albans, Hatfield Road (© **01727/819340;** www.stalbans museums.org.uk), details the history of St. Albans from the departure of the Romans to the present day. Open Monday through Saturday from 10am to 5pm and Sunday from 2 to 5pm, admission is free. Located in the city center, it's a 5-minute walk from St. Albans City Station.

Batchwood's 18-hole golf course is one of the finest public courses in the country. The Batchwood Indoor Tennis Centre, which has four indoor courts plus outdoor courts, has professional coaches available for all play levels. Both the golf and the tennis center are located on the grounds of the **Batchwood Hall Mansion** on Batchwood Drive (© **01727/844250**).

SHOPPING

The twice-weekly **street market,** held every Wednesday and Saturday on St. Peters Street, is defined by its frantic pace. In contrast, modern off-street precincts and small specialty shops in St. Albans combine to create a unique, laid-back atmosphere the rest of the week.

The Past Times Shop, 33 Market St. (© **01727/812817**), sells items that cover 12 historic eras. Here you'll find books on historic places, jewelry, clothes, and CDs featuring music from a variety of time periods.

For antiques, visit **By George,** 23 George St. (© **01727/853032**). St. Albans's largest antiques center, the building also houses a tearoom and crafts arcade. At **St. Albans Antique Centre,** 9 George St. (© **01727/844233**), up to 20 dealers gather to sell their goods. You can browse through the furniture and collectibles, then have a light snack in the tearoom or tour the gardens.

WHERE TO STAY

The Black Lion Inn   This is the nicest pub hotel in the area, and one of the best bargains. A former bakery built in 1837, it lies in the most colorful part of town, St. Michael's Village, where bustling coaches from London once arrived. Bedrooms are simple and plain and, although a bit cramped, are well maintained, each with a small bathroom with a shower or a tub-shower combination.

St. Michael's Village, Fishpool St., St. Albans, Hertfordshire AL3 4SB. ✆ **01727/851786.** Fax 01727/859243. www.theblacklioninn.com. 16 units, 14 with bathroom. £60 ($111) double without bathroom, £64 ($118) double with bathroom. AE, MC, V. **Amenities:** Restaurant; bar; babysitting; laundry service. *In room:* TV, coffeemaker, hair dryer, iron/ironing board, trouser press.

St. Michael's Manor ✸✸   Set on 2 hectares (5 acres) of beautifully maintained lakeside gardens, it dates from 1586 but was recently upgraded and refurbished. Constructed on medieval fortifications, the hotel stands in award-winning gardens with an abundance of wildlife. It's hard to imagine you're in a city. Rooms are individually decorated with fine antique pieces. Each has a certain charm with no bad choice among them. Rooms are stocked with everything from mineral water to a teddy bear to sleep with. Bathrooms are luxurious and come with robes, a pumice stone, and even plastic ducks for your bath. The Manor also has a superb restaurant, the Terrace Room, with an ornate Victorian conservatory overlooking the floodlit lawns, which offers wonderful regional English cooking.

St. Michael's Village, Fishpool St., St. Albans, Hertfordshire AL3 4RY. ✆ **01727/864444.** Fax 01727/848909. www.stmichaelsmanor.com. 22 units. £175–£240 ($324–$444) double; £300 ($555) suite. Special weekend rate from £140–£250 ($259–$463) double. Rates include English breakfast. AE, MC, V. **Amenities:** Restaurant; bar; 24-hr. room service; laundry; dry cleaning; nonsmoking rooms. *In room:* A/C, TV, dataport, coffeemaker, hair dryer.

Sopwell House ✸✸✸   This place is in a neck-to-neck competition with St. Michael's Manor (see above), though Sopwell has more facilities. A private mansion from the days of George III, it once belonged to Lord Louis Mountbatten and has seen its share of royal heads. Converted into a hotel of taste, charm, and character, it occupies nearly a dozen acres 3km (2 miles) southeast of the city center. Avoid it if it's hosting a conference, but at other times you can enjoy the grace of an English country house. From the drawing room to the library, public rooms are elegant and comfy. Some of the bedrooms are equipped with four-poster beds and have a traditional feel, whereas others are more contemporary. Regardless, the decor is tasteful, rather chic, and handsomely coordinated. All rooms are accompanied by amenity-filled marble bathrooms with "power showers" and scales.

Cottonmill Lane, St. Albans, Hertfordshire AL1 2HQ. ✆ **01727/864477.** Fax 01727/844741. www.sopwell house.co.uk. 108 units. Mon–Thurs £169 ($313) double; £189–£199 ($350–$368) suite. Reduced weekend rates from £158 ($292) double. Children extra. AE, DC, MC, V. **Amenities:** 2 restaurants; 2 bars; indoor heated pool; spa; salon; 24-hr. room service; babysitting; laundry service; rooms for those with limited mobility; nonsmoking rooms. *In room:* A/C in some rooms, TV, dataport (in some), coffeemaker, hair dryer, safe (in some), trouser press.

WHERE TO DINE

Magnolia Conservatory ✸ FRENCH/ENGLISH   Consistently serving the best food in the area, this restaurant lies beneath a glass roof that's pierced with a trio of magnolias whose leaves gracefully arch into the open air outside. The ambience is light, elegant, upscale, and inviting, partly because of its formal and well-trained staff, and partly because the food is more sophisticated and prepared with more flair than anywhere else in town. You may begin with an award-winning version of seared scallops with chile-and-lime salsa. Main courses change with new chef Ian Pennet's inspiration, but we enjoyed the roasted filet of lamb with cream sauce. Dessert anyone? With your significant other (it's served only for two), sample the Sopwell Symphony, a degustation of half a dozen of the chef's favorite desserts, arranged on the same platter.

Also on premises is a terrace bar that's open daily (only in summer) from 11am to 11pm. The food it serves is a lot more down-home and also a lot cheaper.

In the Sopwell House Hotel, Cottonmill Lane. ℂ **01727/864477.** Reservations highly recommended. Main courses £15–£20 ($28–$37); fixed-price lunch £16–£18 ($30–$33); fixed-price dinner £25 ($46). AE, DC, MC, V. Tues–Fri and Sun noon–2:30pm; Mon–Sat 7–10pm and Sun 7–9:30pm.

THEATER PERFORMANCES

St. Albans's nightlife centers around theater. The Company of Ten, with its base at the **Abbey Theatre,** Westminster Lodge, Holywill Hill (ℂ **01727/857861;** www.abbeytheatre.org.uk), is one of the leading amateur dramatic companies in Britain. The troupe presents 10 productions each season in either the well-equipped main auditorium or a smaller studio. Performances begin at 8pm; tickets cost from £6 to £8 ($11–$15). The box office is open Monday to Saturday 9:30am to noon and Monday to Friday 8 to 9pm.

The **Maltings Arts Theatre,** in the Maltings Shopping Centre (ℂ **01727/ 844222**), presents performances based on literature—from Shakespeare to modern novels. Plays are generally presented only once and begin at 8pm on Thursday, Friday, and Saturday (there is a children's show at 3pm). Tickets are £7.50 to £14 ($14–$25). The theatre box office is open Tuesday to Saturday from 11am to 5pm.

SIDE TRIPS FROM ST. ALBANS

Hatfield House ✮✮✮ Hatfield was a part of the lives of both Henry VIII and Elizabeth I. In the old palace, begun in 1497, Elizabeth romped and played as a child. Though Henry was married to her mother, Anne Boleyn, at the time of Elizabeth's birth, the marriage was later nullified (Anne lost her head, Elizabeth, her legitimacy). Henry would also stash away his oldest daughter, Mary Tudor, at Hatfield. But when Mary became Queen of England and set about earning the dubious distinction of "Bloody Mary," she found Elizabeth to be a problem and kept her for a while in the Tower of London, eventually letting her return to Hatfield. In 1558, Elizabeth learned of her succession to the throne of England while at Hatfield.

Only the banqueting hall of the original Tudor palace remains; the rest of the house is Jacobean. The brick and stone structure that exists today has much antique furniture and many tapestries and paintings, as well as three often-reproduced portraits, including the ermine and rainbow portraits of Elizabeth I. The Great Hall is suitably medieval, complete with a minstrel's gallery. One of the rarest exhibits is a pair of silk stockings, said to have been worn by Elizabeth herself, the first woman in England to don such apparel. The park and the gardens are also worth exploring. Luncheons and teas are available from 11am to 5pm in the converted coach house in the Old Palace yard.

Elizabethan banquets are staged with much gaiety and music in the banqueting hall of the Old Palace on Tuesday, Friday, and Saturday. Guests are invited to drink in an anteroom, then join the long tables for a feast of five courses with continuous entertainment from a group of Elizabethan players, minstrels, and jesters. Wine is included in the cost of the meal, but you're expected to pay for predinner drinks yourself. The menu isn't particularly medieval, and you're granted the (modern-day) luxury of knives and forks, but the entertainment is charming, and the event is consistently popular and often filled to capacity.

The cost of the banquet is £36 ($67) on Tuesday, £37 ($68) on Friday, and £41 ($75) on Saturday. For reservations and more information, call either the number listed below or 📞 **01707/262055,** or go online to **www.theoldpalace. co.uk.**

9.5km (6 miles) east of St. Albans on A414. 📞 **01707/262823** for information. www.hatfield-house.co.uk. Admission £7.50 ($14) adults, £4 ($7.40) for persons under 16. Easter Sat–Sept 30, house is open daily noon–4pm; park and gardens open daily 11am–5:30pm. From St. Albans, take A414 east and follow the brown signs that lead you directly to the estate. By bus, take the University bus from St. Albans City Station. Hatfield House is directly across from Hatfield Station.

Mosquito Aircraft Museum This is the oldest aircraft museum in Britain. The hall where the de Havilland Aircraft Company developed the "Mosquito," known as the most versatile aircraft of World War II, is no longer open to the public. However, the museum displays more than 20 types of aircraft, including modern military and civil jets, along with aircraft engines and other memorabilia. Several of the displays are hands-on exhibits.

On the grounds of Salisbury Hall, just off the main M25 London–St. Albans Rd. 📞 **01727/822051.** www. dehavillandmuseum.co.uk. Admission £5 ($9.25) adults; £3 ($5.55) children 5–16, seniors, and students with identification; free for children under 5; £13 ($24) family ticket. Mar–Oct Tues, Thurs, and Sat 2–5:30pm; Sun and bank holidays 10:30am–5:30pm. Take M25 Junction 22 at London Colney about 8km (5 miles) south of St. Albans. The museum is on B556.

Shaw's Corner *(Finds)* George Bernard Shaw lived here from 1906 to 1950. The utilitarian house, with its harsh brickwork and rather comfortless interior, is practically as he left it at his death. In the hall, for example, his hats are still hanging, as if ready for him to don one. Shaw wrote 6 to 8 hours a day, even when he'd reached his 90s. Evidence of his longtime relationship with the written word is obvious; one of his old typewriters is even still in position. Shaw, of course, was famous for his eccentricities, his vegetarianism, and his longevity. And, of course, for his vast literary output, the most famous of which remains *Pygmalion,* on which the musical *My Fair Lady* was based.

Off Hill Farm Lane, in the village of Ayot St. Lawrence. 📞 **01438/820307.** Admission £3.60 ($6.65) adults, £2 ($3.70) children. Apr–Oct Wed–Sun and bank holidays 1–5pm. From St. Albans, take B651 to Wheathampstead. Pass through the village, go right at the roundabout, and take the first left turn. A mile up on the left is Brides Hall Lane, which leads to the house.

8 Woburn Abbey: England's Great Georgian Manor *(★★★)*

71km (44 miles) N of London

Aside from Windsor Castle, the most visited attraction in the Home Counties is Woburn Abbey, which is so spectacular you should try to visit even if you have to miss all the other historic homes described in this chapter. The great 18th-century Georgian mansion has been the traditional seat of the dukes of Bedford for more than 3 centuries.

TOURING THE ESTATE

Woburn Abbey In the 1950s, the present duke of Bedford opened Woburn Abbey to the public to pay off his debt of millions of pounds in inheritance taxes. In 1974, he turned the estate over to his son and daughter-in-law, the marquess and marchioness of Tavistock, who reluctantly took on the business of running the 75-room mansion. And what a business it is, drawing hundreds of thousands of visitors a year and employing over 300 people to staff the shops and grounds.

Its state apartments are rich in furniture, porcelain, tapestries, silver, and a valuable art collection, including paintings by Van Dyck, Holbein, Rembrandt, Gainsborough, and Reynolds. Of all the paintings, one of the most notable is the Armada Portrait of Elizabeth I. Her hand rests on the globe, as Philip's invincible armada perishes in the background.

Queen Victoria and Prince Albert visited Woburn Abbey in 1841; Victoria's Dressing Room displays a fine collection of 17th-century paintings from the Netherlands. Among the oddities and treasures at Woburn Abbey are a Grotto of Shells, a Sèvres dinner service (gift of Louis XV), and a chamber devoted to memorabilia of "The Flying Duchess," the wife of the 11th duke of Bedford, a remarkable woman who disappeared on a solo flight in 1937 (coincidentally, the same year as Amelia Earhart). The duchess was 72 years old at the time.

Today, Woburn Abbey is surrounded by a 1,214-hectare (3,000-acre) deer park that includes the famous Père David deer herd, originally from China and saved from extinction at Woburn. The **Woburn Safari Park** has lions, tigers, giraffes, camels, monkeys, Przewalski's horses, bongos, and other animals.

1km (½ mile) from the village of Woburn, which is 21km (13 miles) southwest of Bedford. ⓒ 01525/290666. www.woburnabbey.co.uk. Admission £8.50 ($16) adults, £7.50 ($14) seniors, £4 ($7.40) children. House open late Mar to Oct Mon–Sat 11am–4pm, Sun 11am–5pm; Oct and Jan to late Mar Sat–Sun and bank holidays 11am–4pm. Park open late Mar to late Sept daily 10am–5pm. In summer, travel agents can book you on organized coach tours out of London. Otherwise, if driving, take M1 north to Junction 12 or 13, where directions are signposted.

NEARBY SHOPPING & AFTERNOON TEA

In a wonderful old building, **Town Hall Antiques,** Market Place (ⓒ 01525/290950), is a treasure trove of collectibles and antiques, including Early English porcelain and pieces from the 1940s. Some unusual commemorative items are also sold, such as an array of Victorian, Georgian, and Edwardian memorabilia. There's something here to suit a wide range of pocketbooks including clocks, Victorian jewelry, brass, copper, "kitchenalia," paintings (originals and reproductions), guns, and swords.

At teatime, head to **Copperfields,** 15 Market Place (ⓒ 01525/290464), inside a B&B with low-beamed ceilings that add to its intimacy and charm. A pot of tea with clotted cream and a cake is £4 ($7.40). Baked goods include scones, and chocolate, lemon, Victoria sponge, carrot, coffee, and fruitcakes, as well as daily specials. The tearoom is open Thursday through Tuesday, but it's a good idea to call on weekends between January and Easter as it may be closed if business is slow.

WHERE TO STAY

The Inn at Woburn ⭐   After visiting the abbey, head here for food and lodging at the gates of the estate. This Georgian coaching inn has a checkered history that blends the old and new. Tastefully modernized, it preserves a certain mellow charm. Guests are housed in one of several well-furnished and beautifully maintained rooms, which were last refurbished in 2002. A more recent block provides "executive bedrooms," which don't have the charm of the older units but are more up-to-date and comfortable. Each room has a small bathroom with a shower-tub combination and good maintenance.

1 George St., Woburn, Bedfordshire MK17 9PX. ⓒ 01525/290441. Fax 01525/290432. www.theinnat woburn.com. 58 units. £120–£148 ($222–$274) double; £180 ($333) suite. Children under 16 stay free in

parent's room. AE, DC, MC, V. **Amenities:** Restaurant; bar; limited room service; babysitting; laundry service; nonsmoking rooms; rooms for those with limited mobility. *In room:* TV, minibar, coffeemaker, hair dryer, safe, trouser press.

WHERE TO DINE

Paris House ★★ CONTINENTAL/FRENCH   This reconstructed timbered house stands in a park where you can see deer grazing. The black-and-white building originally stood in Paris where it was constructed for the Great Exhibition 1878, but it was torn down and transplanted, timber by timber, to Woburn. Since 1983, it has been the domain of Bedfordshire's finest chef, Peter Chandler, the first English apprentice of the legendary Roux brothers. Chandler has brought his own innovative touch to the dishes served here. He still regularly visits France for new ideas and is known for his use of the freshest of seasonal ingredients. Try his delectable marinated Cajun prawns, delicately spiced savory, or his duck confit in a black currant and orange sauce. The chef is rightly known for his *tulipe en fantaisie,* a sugar-fairy fantasy with fruit and ice cream.

Woburn Park (3.5km/2¼ miles southeast of Woburn on A4012). ℂ **01525/290692.** Reservations required. Fixed-price dinner £55 ($102); fixed-price lunch £30 ($56). AE, DC, MC, V. Tues–Sat noon–2pm and 7–10pm; Sun noon–2pm. Closed Feb.

7

Kent, Surrey & Sussex

South and southeast of London are the shires (counties) of Kent, Surrey, and Sussex—fascinating areas within easy commuting distance of the capital.

In **Kent, Canterbury** is the major highlight and makes the best base for exploring the area. Another convenient option is **Dover,** Britain's historic gateway to the Continent and famed for its white cliffs. Though Kent is on London's fringe, it's far removed in spirit and scenery. Since the days of the Tudors, cherry blossoms have enlivened the fertile landscape. Orchards and hop fields abound, earning Kent its title, "garden of England"—in England, that's tough competition. Kent suffered severe destruction during World War II, as it was the alley over which the Luftwaffe flew in its blitz of London. But despite much devastation, it's still filled with interesting old towns and castles.

In fact, Kent has some of Europe's grandest mansions. If time is limited, seek out the big four: **Knole,** one of the largest private houses of England, a great example of Tudor architecture; **Hever Castle,** dating from the end of the 13th century, a gift from Henry VIII to the "great Flanders mare," Anne of Cleves; **Penshurst Place,** a magnificent English Gothic mansion, and one of the outstanding country houses of Britain; and lovely **Leeds Castle,** near Maidstone, dating from A.D. 857. Although it doesn't compare with these grand castles, **Chartwell** also merits a visit because of the man who used to call it home: Sir Winston Churchill. For more advice on how to tour these homes, refer to "Kent's Country Houses, Castles & Gardens," later in this chapter.

With the continuing expansion of London's borders, it's a wonder that the tiny county of **Surrey** hasn't been gobbled up and turned into a sprawling suburb. Yet its countryside remains unspoiled, though many people commute from here to London (only about 45 min. to an hour away).

If King Harold hadn't loved **Sussex** so much, English history might have been changed forever. Had the brave Saxon waited longer in the north, he could have marshaled more adequate reinforcements before striking south to meet the Normans. But Duke William's soldiers were ravaging the countryside he knew so well, and Harold rushed down to counter them.

Harold's enthusiasm for Sussex is understandable. The landscape rises and falls like waves. The county is known for its woodlands, from which came the timbers to build England's mighty fleet in days gone by. The shires lie south of London and Surrey, bordering Kent in the east, Hampshire in the west, and opening directly onto the English Channel, where the coast is dotted with seaside towns.

Like other sections in the vulnerable south of England, Sussex was the setting of some of the most significant events in English history. Apart from the Norman landings at **Hastings,** the most life-changing transformation occurred in the 19th century, as middle-class Victorians flocked to the seashore, pumping new spirit into **Brighton** and even old Hastings.

The old towns and villages of Sussex, particularly **Rye** and **Winchelsea,** are far more intriguing than the seaside resorts. No Sussex village is lovelier than **Alfriston** (and the innkeepers know it, too); **Arundel** is noted for its castle; and the cathedral city of **Chichester** is a mecca for theater buffs. The old market town of **Battle** was the setting for the Battle of Hastings in 1066.

Where to base yourself in Sussex? The best option is Brighton, because it has a wide choice of hotels, restaurants, and nightclubs. There's more excitement here at "London by the Sea" than at Hastings. If you're seeking old-English charm and village life, head instead to Alfriston or Rye.

1 Canterbury ✸✸✸

90km (56 miles) SE of London

Under the arch of the ancient West Gate journeyed Chaucer's knight, solicitor, nun, squire, parson, merchant, miller, and others—spinning tales. They were bound for the shrine of Thomas à Becket, archbishop of Canterbury, who was slain by four knights of Henry II on December 29, 1170. (The king later walked barefoot from Harbledown to the tomb of his former friend, where he allowed himself to be flogged in penance.) The shrine was finally torn down in 1538 by Henry VIII, as part of his campaign to destroy the monasteries and graven images. But Canterbury, by then, had already become an attraction.

The medieval Kentish city on the River Stour is the ecclesiastical capital of England. Once completely walled, many traces of its old fortifications remain. Canterbury was inhabited centuries before the birth of Jesus Christ. Although its most famous incident was the murder of Becket, the medieval city witnessed other major events in English history, including Bloody Mary's order to burn nearly 40 victims at the stake. Richard the Lion-Hearted returned this way from crusading, and Charles II passed through on the way to claim his crown.

Canterbury pilgrims continue to arrive today, except now they're called day-trippers and they overrun the city and its monuments. It's amazing that the city's central core is as interesting and picture-perfect as it is, considering the enormous damage caused by the Nazi blitz of 1941. The city has an active university life—mainly students from Kent—and an enormous number of pubs. Its High Street is filled with shoppers in from the country. We suggest exploring Canterbury in the early morning or the early evening, after the busloads have departed.

ESSENTIALS

GETTING THERE   Frequent train service arrives from Victoria, Charing Cross, Waterloo, and London Bridge stations. The journey takes 1½ hours. For rail information, call ✆ **0845/748-4950** or visit www.railtrack.co.uk.

The bus from Victoria Coach Station takes 2 to 3 hours and leaves every hour. For schedules, call ✆ **0870/580-8080** or visit www.nationalexpress.com.

If you're driving from London, take the A2, then the M2. Canterbury is sign-posted all the way. The city center is closed to cars, but it's only a short walk from several parking areas to the cathedral.

VISITOR INFORMATION   A few doors from St. Margaret's Church, the **Canterbury Tourist Information Centre,** 34 St. Margaret's St., Canterbury CT1 2TG (✆ **01227/378100**), is open daily from 10am to 4pm April through October, and from 9am to 5pm November through March.

GETTING AROUND BY BIKE For a £50 ($93) deposit, you can also arrange rentals at **Downland Cycle Hire,** West Railway Station (© 01227/479643), which charges £11 ($20) per day.

SEEING THE SIGHTS

Canterbury Cathedral ★★★ The foundation of this splendid cathedral dates from A.D. 597, but the earliest part of the present building is the great Romanesque crypt built around A.D. 1100. The monastic quire erected on top of this at the same time was destroyed by fire in 1174, only 4 years after the murder of Thomas à Becket on a dark December evening in the northwest transept, which is still one of the most famous places of pilgrimage in Europe. The destroyed quire was immediately replaced by a magnificent early Gothic one, the first major expression of that architectural style in England.

The cathedral is noteworthy for its medieval tombs of royal personages, such as King Henry IV and Edward the Black Prince, as well as numerous archbishops. To the later Middle Ages belong the great 14th-century nave and the famous central "Bell Harry Tower." The cathedral stands on spacious precincts amid the remains of the buildings of the monastery—cloisters, chapter house, and Norman water tower—which have survived intact from Henry VIII's dissolution.

Becket's shrine was destroyed by the Tudor king, but the site of that tomb is in Trinity Chapel, near the high altar. The saint is said to have worked miracles, and the cathedral has some rare stained glass depicting those feats.

But the most miraculous event is that the windows escaped Henry VIII's agents of destruction as well as Hitler's bombs. The windows were removed as a precaution at the beginning of the war. During the war, a large area of Canterbury was flattened, but the main body of the church was unharmed. However, the cathedral library was damaged during a German air raid in 1942. The replacement windows of the cathedral were blown in, which proved the wisdom of having the medieval glass safely stored away.

11 The Precincts. © 01227/762862. www.canterbury-cathedral.org. Admission £4 ($7.40) adults, £3 ($5.55) students, seniors, and children. Guided tours, £3.50 ($6.50) adults, £2.50 ($4.65) students and seniors, £1.50 ($2.80) children. Easter–Sept 30 Mon–Sat 9am–6:30pm; Oct 1–Easter Mon–Sat 9am–4:30pm; year-round Sun 12:30–2:30pm and 4:30–5:30pm.

OTHER ATTRACTIONS

Canterbury Roman Museum This museum is located beneath street level and is constructed around actual archaeological excavations. Interactive computer shows and the actual handling of Roman artifacts bring the past to life for all ages. The Roman town of Durovernum Cantiacorum was established shortly after Emperor Claudius's invasion of the area in A.D. 43 and continued to flourish for nearly 400 years. Visitors can follow the archaeologists' detective work through an excavated Roman house site containing patterned mosaics that were discovered after the wartime bombing.

Butchery Lane. © 01227/785575. Admission £2.70 ($5) adults, £1.70 ($3.15) students, seniors, and children, £7 ($13) family ticket. Year-round Mon–Sat 10am–5pm; June–Oct Sun 1:30–5pm. Last entry time is 4pm. Closed Christmas week and Good Friday.

The Canterbury Tales One of the most visited museums in town re-creates the pilgrimages of Chaucerian England through a series of medieval tableaux. Visitors are handed headsets with earphones, which give oral recitations of five of Chaucer's *Canterbury Tales* and the murder of St. Thomas à Becket. Audiovisual

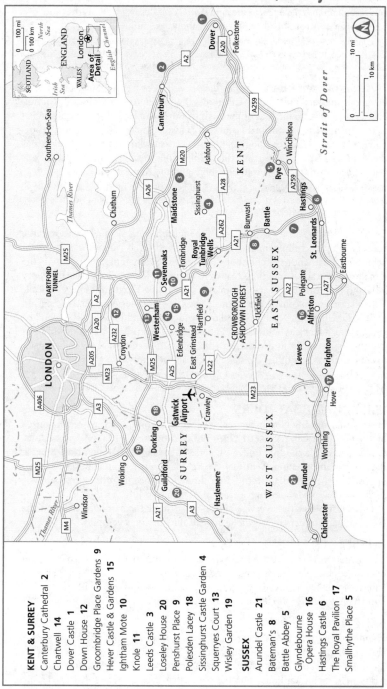

aids bring famous characters to life, and stories of jealousy, pride, avarice, and love are recounted. A tour of all exhibits takes about 45 minutes.

23 St. Margaret's St. (off High St., near the cathedral). ✆ **01227/454888**. Admission £6.95 ($13) adults, £5.95 ($11) students and seniors, £5.25 ($9.70) children 5–16, free for children 4 and under. Family ticket £23 ($42). Mar–Aug 10am–4:30pm daily; Sept–Oct 10am–5:30pm daily; Nov–Feb 10am–5pm daily.

Museum of Canterbury   Set in the ancient Poor Priests' Hospital with its medieval interiors and soaring oak roofs, the museum features award-winning displays to showcase the best of the city's treasures and lead visitors through crucial moments that have shaped Canterbury's history. State-of-the-art video, computer, and hologram technology transport visitors back in time to such events as the Viking raids and the wartime Blitz. Collections include a huge display of pilgrim badges from medieval souvenir shops and the Rupert Bear Gallery.

Stour St. ✆ **01227/452747**. Admission £3.10 ($5.75) adults, £2.10 ($3.90) students, seniors, and children, £8.20 ($15) family. Year-round Mon–Sat 10:30am–5pm; June–Sept Sun 1:30–5pm. Last entry time is 4pm. Closed Christmas week and Good Friday.

St. Augustine's Abbey 𝕽𝕽   One of the most historic religious centers in the country, only its ruins remain, mostly at ground level. Augustine was buried here, along with other archbishops and Anglo-Saxon kings. Adjacent to the remains are the abbey buildings that were converted into a royal palace by Henry VIII and used briefly by several monarchs, including Elizabeth I and Charles I.

In an attempt to convert the Saxons, Pope Gregory I sent Augustine to England in 597. Ethelbert, the Saxon King, allowed Augustine and his followers to build a church outside the city walls, and it endured until Henry VIII tore it down. In its day, the abbey church rivaled the cathedral in size, and enough of the ruins remain to conjure the whole of the cloister, church, and refectory.

Corner of Lower Chantry Lane and Longport Rd. ✆ **01227/767345**. Admission £3.50 ($6.50) adults, £2.60 ($4.80) students and seniors, £1.80 ($3.35) children. Apr–Sept 10am–6pm daily; Oct–Mar 10am–4pm daily.

WALKING & BOAT TOURS

From Easter to early November, daily guided tours of Canterbury are organized by the **Guild of Guides** (✆ **01227/459779**), costing £3.75 ($6.95) for adults, £2.75 ($5.10) for children under 14, and £10 ($19) for a family ticket. Meet at the Tourist Information Centre at 34 St. Margaret's St., in a pedestrian area opposite of the cathedral, from Easter through to the end of the October daily at 2pm and also Monday to Saturday at 11:30am in July and August.

From just below the Weavers House, boats leave for half-hour **trips on the river** with a commentary on the history of the buildings you pass.

HORSEBACK RIDING

The **Bursted Manor Riding Centre** in Pett Bottom (✆ **01227/830568**) is open Wednesday, Saturday and Sunday 8am to 6pm, Tuesday and Thursday 8am to 4pm. The last lesson is at 7pm on weekdays and 5pm on Saturday and Sunday. A 1-hour group lesson or hack ride is available for £24 ($44).

SHOPPING

Handmade pottery (vases, mugs, and teapots in earth colors of blues, greens, and browns) is sold at **Canterbury Pottery,** 38a Burgate, just before Mercury Lane (✆ **01227/452608;** www.canterburypottery.co.uk). It is sturdy fare that wears well, including house-number plates that take 2 weeks to complete, but can be mailed to your home.

Put on your tweed jacket and grab your pipe for a trip to a secondhand **Chaucer Bookshop,** 6 Beer Cart Lane (✆ **01227/453912;** www.chaucer-bookshop.co.uk),

Canterbury

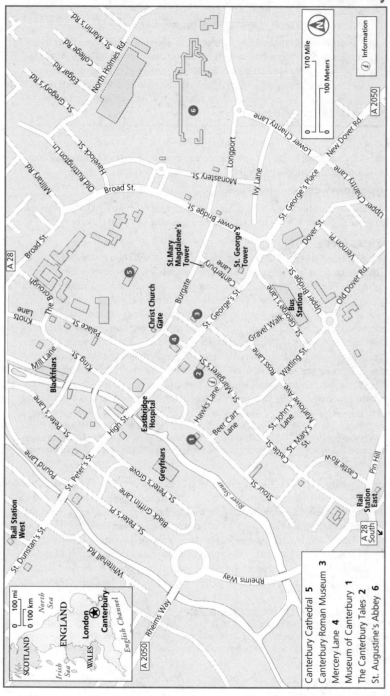

Canterbury Cathedral **5**
Canterbury Roman Museum **3**
Mercery Lane **4**
Museum of Canterbury **1**
The Canterbury Tales **2**
St. Augustine's Abbey **6**

273

Moments **A Stroll down "Medieval" Lane**

The most charming street in Canterbury is **Mercery Lane,** a bustling lane that evokes the charm of Canterbury as it existed in the Middle Ages. A walk along this street also gives you the best views of the western towers of Canterbury Cathedral and an equally good view of Christ Church Gate. Mercery Lane is an extension of St. Margaret's Street and runs between the High Street and Burgate.

---

with first editions (both old and modern), out-of-print books, special leather-bound editions, and a large selection of local history books.

WHERE TO STAY

In spite of all its fame as a tourist destination, Canterbury still lacks a really first-class hotel. What you get isn't bad, but it's not state of the art.

MODERATE

The Chaucer Hotel 🌟 Located on a historic street, the recently refurbished Chaucer Hotel is in a Georgian house that stands a few minutes' walk from the cathedral. Comfortably furnished rooms lie at the end of a labyrinth of stairs, narrow hallways, and doors. (The hotel staff carries your luggage and parks your car.) The best rooms, with views over Canterbury rooftops and the cathedral, are nos. 60, 61, and 65. All rooms, however, are named in a wonderfully quirky way that honors former archbishops as well as some of Chaucer's racier pilgrims. Units range from midsize to most spacious, each chamber evoking a country inn. The most elegant room is no. 16, the honeymoon chamber with a Henry VIII–style four-poster bed. If you'd like to share a room with a ghost, book no. 62. Bathrooms are fairly large with a shower-tub combination and heated rack.

63 Ivy Lane (off Lower Bridge St.), Canterbury, Kent CT1 1TU. ℭ **888/892-0038** in the U.S. and Canada, or 01227/464427. Fax 01227/450397. www.macdonaldhotels.co.uk. 42 units. £100–£150 ($185–$278) double. Rates include breakfast. AE, DC, MC, V. **Amenities:** 2 restaurants; bar; secretarial services; 24-hr. room service; babysitting; laundry service; dry cleaning; nonsmoking rooms. *In room:* A/C, TV, dataport, minibar, coffeemaker, hair dryer, safe, trouser press.

County Hotel 🌟 The leading hotel in Canterbury, it's been around since the closing years of Victoria's reign, with a recorded history going back to the end of the 12th century. The time-mellowed atmosphere is exemplified by the residents' lounge on the second floor, with its old timbers and carved antiques. The hotel is constantly refurbished. Its sumptuous suite is the best room in Canterbury. A dozen period rooms have either Georgian or Tudor four-poster beds; opt for these if available. Rooms have thoughtful extras, such as hospitality trays, fruit baskets, and mineral water. Beds are four-poster, half-tester, or carved oak. Bathrooms are tiled and well maintained, with shower and tub.

High St., Canterbury, Kent CT1 2RX. ℭ **01227/766266.** Fax 01227/451512. www.macdonaldhotels.co.uk. 74 units. £100–£139 ($185–$257) double; £170 ($315) suite. Rates include breakfast. AE, DC, MC, V. Parking £2.50 ($4.65). **Amenities:** Restaurant; bar; 24-hr. room service; babysitting; laundry service; rooms for those with limited mobility; nonsmoking rooms. *In room:* TV, dataport, coffeemaker, hair dryer, iron/ironing board, trouser press.

Ebury Hotel 🌟 *Value* One of the finest B&Bs in Canterbury, this gabled Victorian house stands on .8 hectares (2 acres) of gardens at the city's edge, easy walking distance from the city center. Built in 1850, it's composed of two separate houses that were joined several years ago; the management also rents flats on a weekly basis. The accommodations are roomy and pleasantly decorated. The rooms range from small to medium, each with traditional styling and a small bathroom, mainly with a tub-and-shower combination. Rooms are constantly being refurbished. ***Note:*** Rooms fill up quickly, so it's important to reserve in advance.

65–67 New Dover Rd., Canterbury, Kent CT1 3DX. ⓒ 01227/768433. Fax 01227/459187. www.ebury-hotel.co.uk. 15 units. £75–£95 ($139–$176) double; £95–£105 ($176–$194) triple; £105–£115 ($194–$213) quad. Rates include English breakfast. AE, MC, V. Closed mid-December to mid-January. Follow the signs to A2, Dover Rd., on left-hand side, south of the city. **Amenities:** Restaurant; bar; heated indoor pool; spa; limited room service; laundry service; dry cleaning; nonsmoking rooms. *In room:* TV, dataport, coffeemaker, hair dryer, iron/ironing board, trouser press.

Falstaff Hotel Just 360m (1,200 ft.) from the West Station, this classic Canterbury choice, complete with a flagstone-covered courtyard, retains its sense of history. Next to the Westgate Tower, it has a parking lot and easy access to the M2 and the M20. Many of the small, cozy rooms evoke old England with their polished oak tables, leaded glass windows, and original ceiling beams; most have solid modern furniture. Some units are large enough to accommodate small families, and most of the accommodations are designated nonsmoking. All rooms have neatly kept bathrooms mainly with shower-tub combinations. Public rooms are as cozy as the bedrooms, and you can relax in a comfortable lounge.

8–10 St. Dunstan's St., Canterbury, Kent CT2 8AF. ⓒ 01227/462138. Fax 01227/463525. www.corushotels.co.uk. 47 units. £110 ($204) double. Rate includes breakfast. AE, DC, MC, V. **Amenities:** Restaurant; bar; lounge; limited room service; laundry service; dry cleaning; rooms for those with limited mobility. *In room:* TV, dataport, coffeemaker, hair dryer, trouser press.

Howfield Manor 🄰🄰 *Finds* Once part of the estate of the Priory of St. Gregory, this is one of the most charming country manors near Canterbury. It's not plush, but it's a good and reliable choice, with enough beams and private nooks to please the traditionalist. Set on 2 hectares (5 acres) of rolling meadows, the house offers snug, attractive rooms with solid comfort. Rooms in the original house have more character (exposed beams), whereas rooms in the new wing are larger and furnished with solid oak pieces. All units offer comfortable beds. Bathrooms are small but well appointed, each with a shower stall. All rooms are nonsmoking.

Chartham Hatch (3km/2 miles from Canterbury along A28 Ashford Rd.), Canterbury, Kent CT4 7HQ. ⓒ 01227/738294. Fax 01227/731535. www.howfieldmanor.co.uk. 15 units. £100 ($185) double; £115 ($213) suite. Rates include English breakfast. AE, MC, V. Take A28 3.5km (2¼ miles) from Canterbury. **Amenities:** Restaurant; bar; 24-hr. room service; laundry service; dry cleaning. *In room:* TV, dataport, hair dryer, trouser press.

INEXPENSIVE

Cathedral Gate Hotel For those who want to stay close to the cathedral and perhaps have a view of it, this is the choice. Built in 1438, adjoining Christchurch Gate and overlooking the Buttermarket, this former hospice was one of the first fashionable teahouses in England in the early 1600s, and the interior reveals many little architectural details of that century. Rooms are modestly furnished, with sloping floors and massive oak beams. You'll sleep better than the former pilgrims who often stopped over here, sometimes crowding in as many as six to eight in a bed. Rooms with bathroom have a shower stall; otherwise corridor bathrooms are adequate and you rarely have to wait in line for your turn at them.

36 Burgate, Canterbury, Kent CT1 2HA. ⓒ 01227/464381. Fax 01227/462800. www.cathgate.co.uk. 26 units, 13 with bathroom (shower only). £48–£58 ($89–$107) double without bathroom, £88 ($163) double with bathroom. Rates include continental breakfast. AE, DC, MC, V. **Amenities:** Restaurant; bar; 24-hr. room service. *In room:* TV, dataport, coffeemaker, hair dryer, trouser press.

WHERE TO DINE

Duck Inn *(Finds* ENGLISH   Once called the Woodsmen Arms, this restaurant is known as the Duck Inn because of its low door. (As you entered, the clientele would shout "Duck!") Set in the Pett Bottom valley in a 16th-century structure, it offers traditional English fare. Diners can sit outdoors in the English country garden in the summer. The menu posted on chalkboards changes weekly, though a few standard English favorites remain on a permanent basis. For the main course, the menu may include game pies (in season), and some duck preparation is always on the menu. James Bond fans will appreciate the location; according to *You Only Live Twice,* 007 grew up next door to the Duck Inn.

Pett Bottom, near Bridge. *(C)* 01227/830354. Reservations recommended. Main courses £6.95–£12 ($13–$22). MC, V. Tues–Sat 11am–11pm; Sun noon–10:30pm. Drive 8km (5 miles) outside Canterbury near the village of Bridge on the road to Dover.

Old Well Restaurant CONTINENTAL   At this country manor (see How-field Manor, above), nonresidents and guests can enjoy a meal served in the chapel, dating from 1181. The old well can still be seen; monks drew their water here. Head chef James Wealinds and his brigade create a market-fresh cuisine that's prepared daily. The excellent food is backed up by a homey atmosphere, friendly service, and a well-chosen wine list. You may start with smoked haddock and parsley fish cake, and proceed to sirloin steak with red onion gravy. Arrive early to enjoy a drink in the Priory Bar, with its trompe l'oeil murals and a real "priesthole" (the bar staff will be delighted to explain what that means, just to get the conversation rolling).

At Howfield Manor, Chartham Hatch. *(C)* 01227/738294. Reservations recommended. Main courses £11–£18 ($20–$33); fixed-price menu £20 ($37). AE, MC, V. Daily noon–2pm and 7–9pm.

Sully's *(R)* ENGLISH/CONTINENTAL   This restaurant is located in the city's most distinguished hotel (see County Hotel, above). Although the place is without windows and the decor is a bit dated (ca. 1965), the seating and comfort level are first-rate. Considering the quality of the ingredients, the menu offers good value. You can always count on a selection of plain, traditional English dishes, but try one of the more imaginatively conceived platters instead. We recommend the grilled lemon sole or the roasted pheasant breast with kumquats served on lentils with caramelized apple and a mellow curry cream.

In the County Hotel, High St. *(C)* 01227/766266. Reservations recommended. Main courses £14–£18 ($26–$33); fixed-price lunch £9.95 ($19) for 2 courses; fixed-price dinner £24 ($44). AE, DC, MC, V. Daily 7–10am, 12:30–2pm, and 7–9pm.

Tuo e Mio ITALIAN   Tuo e Mio is a bastion of zesty Italian cookery. Signor R. P. M. Greggio, known locally as "Raphael," sets the style and plans the menu at his casual and long-standing bistro. Some dishes are standard, including the pastas, beef, and veal found on most Italian menus, but the daily specials have a certain flair, based on the freshest ingredients available on any given day. Try the fish dishes, including skate, which is regularly featured. A selection of reasonably priced Italian wines accompanies your meal.

16 The Borough. *(C)* 01227/761471. Reservations recommended, especially at lunch; call *(C)* 01227/472362. Main courses £7.50–£16 ($14–$30); fixed-price lunch £13 ($24). AE, DC, MC, V. Tues 7–10:45pm; Wed–Sat noon–2:30pm and 7–10:45pm; Sun noon–2:30pm and 7–10pm. Closed last 2 weeks in Aug.

CANTERBURY AFTER DARK

Gulbenkian Theatre, University of Kent, Giles Lane (*(C)* 01227/769075; www.kent.ac.uk/gulbenkian), is open from 11am to 5pm during school terms (except

Cricket Week, the first week in Aug) and offers a potpourri of jazz and classical productions, dance, drama, comedy, and a mix of new and student productions. Tickets cost £5 to £16 ($9.25–$30).

Marlowe, The Friars (© **01227/787787;** www.marlowetheatre.com), is Canterbury's only commercial playhouse. It's open year-round and offers drama, jazz and classical concerts, and contemporary and classical ballet. Tickets cost from £8.50 to £36 ($16–$67). The box office at Marlow Theatre is open Monday to Saturday 10am to 9pm and until 7:00pm on nonperformance nights. Most shows begin at 7:30pm.

A favorite local pub, **Alberry's Wine & Food Bar,** 39A St. Margaret's St. (© **01227/452378**), offers live music, mostly jazz, played by local and student groups. Cover charges range from £3 ($5.55). The menu offers affordable daily specials and light snacks at lunch and dinner.

A laid-back student hangout, **The Cherry Tree,** 10 White Horse Lane (© **01227/451266**), offers a wide selection of beers, including Bass Ale on draft, Cherry Tree ale, three traditional lagers, and four bitters. The atmosphere is clubby, filled with casual conversation. If you visit for lunch, you'll find a 32-item menu—the best pub menu in town—plus three types of ploughman's lunch. On Sundays, they offer a traditional English roast for £5 ($9.25).

Another good choice on your Canterbury pub-crawl is **The Flying Horse,** 1 Dover St. (© **01227/463803**), which attracts a garrulous mix of young and old. This 16th-century pub bridges generations from oldsters to the hip student crowd.

2 The White Cliffs of Dover

122km (76 miles) SE of London; 135km (84 miles) NE of Brighton

In Victoria's day, Dover was popular as a seaside resort; today it's known as a port for cross-Channel car and passenger traffic between England and France (notably Calais). One of England's most vulnerable and easy-to-hit targets during World War II, repeated bombings destroyed much of its harbor. The opening of the Channel Tunnel (Chunnel) in 1994 renewed Dover's importance.

Unless you're on your way to France or want to use Dover as a base for exploring the surrounding countryside, you can skip a visit here. Dover is rather dull except for those white cliffs. Even its hotels are second-rate; many people prefer to stay in Folkestone, about 16km (10 miles) to the southwest.

ESSENTIALS

GETTING THERE Frequent trains run from Victoria Station or Charing Cross Station in London, daily from 5am to 10pm. You arrive at Priory Station, off Folkestone Road. During the day, two trains per hour depart from Canterbury East Station heading for Dover. For rail information, call © **0845/748-4950** or visit www.railtrack.co.uk.

Frequent buses leave throughout the day—daily from 7am to 11:30pm—from London's Victoria Coach Station bound for Dover. Call © **0870/580-8080** for schedules or visit www.nationalexpress.com. The local bus station is on Pencester Road (© **01304/240024**). Stagecoach East Kent provides daily bus service between Canterbury and Dover.

If driving from London, head first to Canterbury (see "Essentials," in section 1), then continue along the A2 southeast until you reach Dover, on the coast.

VISITOR INFORMATION The **Tourist Information Centre** is on Old Town Gaol Street (© **01304/205108**). April, May, and September it's open

Monday through Friday from 9am to 5:30pm, Saturday and Sunday from 10am to 4pm; June, July and August daily from 9am to 5:30pm. From October to the end of March, Monday to Friday 9am to 5:30pm and Saturday 10am to 4pm.

EXPLORING DOVER

Your best view of the famous **white cliffs** is when arriving at Dover by ferry or hovercraft from Calais. Otherwise, walk out to the end of the town's Prince of Wales pier, the largest of the town's western docks. From there, the cliffs loom above you. Or drive 8km (5 miles) east to the pebble-covered beaches of the fishing hamlet of Deal. A local fisher may take you on an informal boat ride.

Deal Castle Deal Castle is .5km (¼ mile) south of the Deal town center, 8km (5 miles) from Dover. A defensive fort built around 1540, it's the most spectacular example of the low, squat forts constructed by Henry VIII. Its 119 gun positions made it the most powerful of his defense forts. Centered around a circular keep surrounded by two rings of semicircle bastions, the castle was protected by an outer moat. The entrance was approached by a drawbridge with an iron gate. The castle was damaged by bombs during World War II but has been restored to its earlier form. The admission price includes audio tours.

On the seafront. ℂ **01304/372762**. Admission £3.50 ($6.50) adults, £2.60 ($4.80) seniors, £1.80 ($3.35) children. Apr–Sept daily 10am–6pm; Oct–Mar Wed–Sun 10am–4pm. Closed Dec 24–26.

Dover Castle Rising nearly 120m (400 ft.) above the port is one of the oldest and best-known castles in England. Its keep was built at the command of Becket's fair-weather friend, Henry II, in the 12th century. The ancient castle was called back to active duty as late as World War II. The "Pharos" on the grounds is a lighthouse built by the Romans in the first half of the 1st century. The Romans first landed at nearby Deal in 54 B.C., but after 6 months they departed and didn't return until nearly 100 years later, in A.D. 43, when they stayed and occupied the country for 400 years. The castle houses a military museum and a film center, plus "Live and Let's Spy," an exhibition of World War II spying equipment. Audio tours are included in admission price.

Castle Hill. ℂ **01304/211067**. Admission £8.50 ($16) adults, £4.30 ($7.95) children under 15, £6.40 ($12) students and seniors, £21 ($39) family. Apr–Sept daily 10am–6pm (last tour at 5pm); Oct daily 10am–5pm (last tour at 4pm); Nov–Mar daily 10am–4pm (last tour at 3pm).

Roman Painted House This 1,800-year-old Roman structure, called Britain's "buried Pompeii," has exceptionally well-preserved walls and an underfloor heating system. It's famous for its unique bacchic murals and has won four national awards for presentation. Brass-rubbing is also offered. You'll find it in the town center near Market Square.

New St. ℂ **01304/203279**. Admission £2 ($3.70) adults, 80p ($1.50) seniors and children 16 and under. Apr–Sept Tues–Sun 10am–5pm.

Secret War Time Tunnels *(finds)* These secret tunnels, used during the evacuation of Dunkirk in 1940 and the Battle of Britain, can now be explored on a guided tour. The tunnels were originally excavated to house cannons to be used (if necessary) against an invasion by Napoleon. Some 60m (200 ft.) below ground, they were the headquarters of Operation Dynamo, when more than 300,000 troops from Dunkirk were evacuated. Once forbidden ground to all but those with the strongest security clearance, you can stand in the very room where Ramsey issued orders; experience the trauma of life in an underground operating theater; and look out over the English Channel from the hidden, clifftop balcony, just as Churchill did during the Battle of Britain.

Dover Castle, Castle Hill. © **01304/211067** or 01304/201628. Admission £8.50 ($16) adults, £6.40 ($12) seniors, £4.30 ($7.95) children. Apr–Sept daily 10am–6pm; Oct–Mar daily 10am–4pm. Last tour leaves 1 hr. before castle closing time.

WHERE TO STAY

The Churchill   Dover's most consistently reliable hotel is this interconnected row of town houses built to overlook the English Channel in the 1830s. After World War I, the premises were transformed into a hotel, and in 1994 it was completely refurbished. It offers a seafront balcony, a glass-enclosed front veranda, and tranquil rooms. Ranging from small to spacious, many rooms offer uninterrupted views of the coast of France. Eurotunnel travelers find the compact bathrooms with shower stalls comfortable. The hotel lies close to the eastern and western docks and the Hoverport for travel to and from France and Belgium.

Waterloo Crescent, Dover Waterfront, Dover, Kent CT17 9BP. © **01304/203633.** Fax 01304/216320. www. churchill-hotel.com. 66 units. £82 ($152) double; £92 ($170) triple; £97 ($179) quad. AE, DC, MC, V. **Amenities:** Restaurant; bar; health club with sauna; salon; 24-hr. room service; laundry service; dry cleaning; nonsmoking rooms. *In room:* TV w/pay movies, dataport, minibar (in some rooms), coffeemaker, hair dryer, trouser press.

The Dovercourt Hotel   Situated 5km (3 miles) north of Dover's Center, within a semi-industrial maze of superhighways and greenbelts, the court was originally custom-built as a motel in the 1970s. Bedrooms are carefully positioned so that most of them overlook lawns (and a view of the motorway), fields, and a children's playground next door. Each room is functional and comfortable, and all are nonsmoking; the tidy shower-only bathrooms are extremely compact.

Singledge Lane, Whitfield, near Dover CT16 3LF. © **01304/821230.** Fax 01304/825576. www.ramada international.com. 68 units. Mon–Thurs £79 ($146) double; Fri–Sun £69 ($128) double. AE, DC, MC, V. Lies adjacent to the Whitfield exit of the A2 motorway. **Amenities:** Restaurant; bar; 24-hr. room service; laundry service; dry cleaning; 1 room for those with limited mobility. *In room:* TV w/pay movies, dataport, coffeemaker, hair dryer, trouser press.

Wallett's Court ℛ *(Finds)*   Surrounded by fields and gardens in a tiny hamlet 2.5km (1½ miles) east of Dover, this is our preferred stopover in the area. Rebuilt in the Jacobean style in the 1400s, it rests on a foundation dated from the time of the Norman Conquest of England. In 1975, the property was in seriously dilapidated condition until members of the Oakley family bought and restored it. The setting, near cliff tops overlooking the English Channel, is savored by bird-watchers and hill climbers. Each carefully restored bedroom features a different decorative theme, with the more expensive ones containing four-poster beds. Some lie within a barn that was comfortably converted into living quarters. Richly accessorized, each has a vivid Edwardian country-house motif and lots of mementos. Bathrooms, though small, are neatly organized; half have shower-tub combinations, the rest showers only.

West Cliffe, St. Margaret's at Cliffe, Dover, Kent CT15 6EW. © **01304/852424.** Fax 01304/853430. www. wallettscourt.com. 16 units. £99–£159 ($183–$294) double. Rates include English breakfast. AE, DC, MC, V. Closed Dec 24–27. Follow A258 for 2.5km (1½ miles) east from the center of Dover (signposted Deal). Wallett's Court is signposted off A258. **Amenities:** Restaurant; bar; indoor heated pool; outdoor tennis court; health club; spa; limited room service; babysitting; laundry service; dry cleaning; nonsmoking rooms; rooms for those with limited mobility. *In room:* TV, dataport, minibar, coffeemaker, hair dryer.

WHERE TO DINE

Wallett's Court ℛ BRITISH/INTERNATIONAL   One of the most appealing restaurants in the area lies within a half-timbered Jacobean-era manor house, grandly restored over 15 years by Chris Oakley and his family. Within a dining room that's exemplary for its sense of history, you can enjoy dishes such as leek and potato soup; a Kentish huntsman's platter (terrine of game served with apple jelly); salmon with a champagne and shallot sauce; or Scottish Angus beef with a wine and tarragon sauce. The menu changes every month, but meals are always relatively formal, well prepared, and in most cases, very appealing.

West Cliffe, St. Margaret's at Cliffe (In Wallett's Court hotel, see review above). ✆ **01304/852424.** Reservations recommended. 3-course fixed-price dinner £35 ($65). AE, DC, MC, V. Sun–Fri noon–2pm; daily 7–9pm. Closed 1 week at Christmas.

3 The Ancient Seaport of Rye ★★

100km (62 miles) SE of London

"Nothing more recent than a Cavalier's Cloak, Hat and Ruffles should be seen on the streets of Rye," said Louis Jennings. This ancient town, formerly an island, flourished in the 13th century. In its early days, **Rye** was a smuggling center, its residents sneaking in contraband from the marshes to stash away in little nooks.

But the sea receded from Rye, leaving it perched like a giant whale out of water, 3km (2 miles) from the Channel. Attacked several times by French fleets, Rye was practically razed in 1377. But it rebuilt itself successfully, in full Elizabethan panoply. When Queen Elizabeth I visited in 1573, she was so impressed that she bestowed upon the town the distinction of Royal Rye. This has long been considered a special place and over the years has attracted famous people, such as novelist Henry James.

Its narrow cobblestone streets twist and turn like a labyrinth, and jumbled along them are buildings whose sagging roofs and crooked chimneys indicate the town's medieval origins. The town overflows with sites of architectural interest.

Neighboring Winchelsea has also witnessed the water's ebb. It traces its history from Edward I and has experienced many dramatic moments, such as sacking by the French. In the words of one 19th-century writer, Winchelsea is "a sunny dream of centuries ago." The finest sight of this dignified residential town is a badly damaged 14th-century church with a number of remarkable tombs.

ESSENTIALS

GETTING THERE   From London, the Southern Region Line offers trains south from Charing Cross or Cannon Street Station, with a change at Ashford, before continuing on to Rye. You can also go via Tunbridge Wells with a change in Hastings. Trains run every hour during the day, arriving at the Rye Train Station off Cinque Ports Street. The trip takes 1½ to 2 hours. Call ✆ **0845/748-4950** or visit www.railtrack.co.uk for schedules and information.

You'll need to take the train to get to Rye, but once there you'll find buses departing every hour on the hour for many destinations, including Hastings. Various bus schedules are posted on signs in the parking lot. For bus information on connections in the surrounding area, call ✆ **0870/608-2608.**

If driving from London, take the M25, M26, and M20 east to Maidstone, going southeast along the A20 to Ashford. At Ashford, continue south on the A2070.

VISITOR INFORMATION   The **Rye Tourist Office** is in the Heritage Centre on the Strand Quay (✆ **01797/226696**). It's open daily from March to the end of October from 9:30am to 5pm, and November through February from 10am to 4pm and Sunday from 10am to 2pm. The Heritage Centre houses a free exhibition and is also home to **Story of Rye,** a sound-and-light show depicting more than 700 years of Rye's history. Adults pay £2.50 ($4.65), students and seniors £1.50 ($2.80), and children £1 ($1.85).

EXPLORING THE AREA

In Rye, the old town's entrance is **Land Gate,** where a single lane of traffic passes between massive, 12m (40-ft.) high stone towers. The top of the gate has holes through which boiling oil used to be poured on unwelcome visitors, such as French raiding parties.

Rye has had potteries for centuries, and today is no exception, with a number of outlets in town. The best potteries include the **Rye Pottery,** Ferry Road (✆ **01797/223038**); **Rye Tiles,** Wishward Street (✆ **01797/223038**); **David Sharp Ceramics,** The Mint (✆ **01797/222620**); and the **Cinque Ports Pottery,** Conduit Hill (✆ **01797/222033**), where you can see the potters at work during the week. The town also abounds in antiques and collectibles shops and new and used bookstores.

Lamb House   Henry James lived at Lamb House from 1898 to 1916. Many James mementos are scattered throughout the house, which is set in a walled garden. Its previous owner joined the gold rush in North America but perished in the Klondike, and James was able to buy the freehold for a modest £2,000. Some of his well-known books were written here. In *English Hours,* James wrote: "There is not much room in the pavilion, but there is room for the hard-pressed table and tilted chair—there is room for a novelist and his friends."

West St. (at the top of Mermaid St.). ✆ **01892/890651**. Admission £2.75 ($5.10) adults; £1.30 ($2.40) children. Wed and Sat 2–6pm. Closed Nov–Mar.

Rye Castle Museum   This stone fortification was constructed around 1250 by King Henry III to defend the coast against attack by the French. For 300 years it was the town jail but has long since been converted into a museum. In 1996, the medieval Ypres Tower was restored.

Gungarden. ✆ **01797/226728**. Admission £2.90 ($5.35) adults, £2 ($3.70) students and seniors, £1.15 ($2.15) children, £5.95 ($11) family ticket. Apr–Oct Mon–Tues and Fri 10:30am–1pm and 2:30–5pm, Sat–Sun 10:30am–1pm and 2–5pm; Nov–Mar Sat–Sun 10:30am–3pm.

Smallhythe Place *(Finds*   On the outskirts of Winchelsea, this was for 30 years the country house of Dame Ellen Terry, the English actress acclaimed for her Shakespearean roles, and who had a long theatrical association with Sir Henry Irving; she died in the house in 1928. This timber-framed structure, known as a "continuous-jetty house," was built in the first half of the 16th century and is filled with Terry memorabilia—playbills, props, makeup, and a striking display of costumes. An Elizabethan barn, adapted as a theater in 1929, is open for viewing on most days.

Smallhythe (on B2082 near Tenterden, about 9.5km/6 miles north of Rye). ✆ **01580/762334**. Admission £3.75 ($6.95) adults, £1.80 ($3.35) children, £9.30 ($17) family ticket. Mid-Mar to mid-Nov Sat–Wed 11am–5pm. Take bus no. 312 from Tenterden or Rye.

St. Mary's Parish Church   One notable historical site is the mid-12th-century church with its 16th-century clock flanked by two gilded cherubs (known as Quarter Boys because of their striking of the bells on the quarter-hour). The church is often referred to as "the Cathedral of East Sussex" because of its expansive size and ornate beauty. If you're brave, you can climb a set of wooden stairs and ladders to the bell tower of the church for an impressive view.

Church Square. ✆ **01797/224935**. Admission to tower £2 ($3.70) adults, £1 ($1.85) children. Contributions appreciated to enter the church. June–Aug daily 10am–7pm; off season daily 10am–5:30pm.

WHERE TO STAY

Durrant House Hotel   This beautiful Georgian house, restored in 2003, is set on a quiet residential street at the end of Market Street. The charm and character of the nonsmoking facility are enhanced by a cozy lounge with an arched, brick fireplace. The renowned artist Paul Nash lived next door until his death in 1946; in fact, his celebrated view, as seen in his painting *View of the Rother,* can be enjoyed from the River Room, a four-poster bedroom suite. Bedrooms range from small to medium in size, some of them big enough for families, other having four-poster beds. All rooms come with tidy bathrooms and shower units. At one time, the house was used as a relay station for carrier pigeons; these birds brought news of the victory at Waterloo.

Market St. (off High St.), Rye, E. Sussex TN31 3LA. © **01797/223182.** Fax 01797/226940. www.durranthouse. com. 6 units. £68–£75 ($126–$139) double; £90 ($167) 4-poster room. Rates include English breakfast. MC, V. **Amenities:** Lounge; babysitting. *In room:* TV, coffeemaker, hair dryer.

The George 🏵   This coaching inn enjoys a long history dating from 1575. In the 18th century, it drew a diverse clientele: some traveling by horse-drawn carriage, others by boat between London and France. The half-timbered architecture charms a visitor like no other small inn in the region (except the Mermaid, which has even more of an antique atmosphere). Some of the timbers may be from the wreck of an English ship broken up in Rye Harbour after the defeat of the Spanish Armada. Bedrooms are snug, furnished in traditional English country-house style; each with a compact shower-only bathroom. Two accommodations are large enough for family use, though most units are a bit small. Five bedrooms are designated as nonsmoking.

High St., Rye, E. Sussex TN31 7JP. © **01797/222114.** Fax 01797/224065. £90 ($167) double; £110 ($204) suite. AE, DC, MC, V. **Amenities:** Restaurant; bar; breakfast-only room service; babysitting; laundry service; dry cleaning. *In room:* TV, dataport, minibar, coffeemaker, hair dryer, iron/ironing board, safe, trouser press.

Hope Anchor Hotel   At the end of a cobblestone street, on a hill dominating the town, stands this 17th-century hostelry, which enjoys panoramic views of the surrounding countryside and overlooks the Strand Quay, where impressive yachts can be seen at their moorings. Oak beams and open fires in winter make this a most inviting place to spend a few days. Bedrooms are comfortable, ranging from small to midsize; two feature four-poster beds and have recently been refurbished. All rooms are nonsmoking. Bathrooms are small, often with a tub-and-shower combination.

Watchbell St., Rye, E. Sussex TN31 7HA. © **01797/222216.** Fax 01797/223796. www.thehopeanchor.co.uk. 12 units, 11 with bathroom. £90–£100 ($167–$185) double with bathroom. Rates include English breakfast. MC, V. **Amenities:** Restaurant; bar; laundry service; dry cleaning; all nonsmoking rooms. *In room:* TV, coffeemaker, hair dryer.

Mermaid Inn 🏵🏵   The Mermaid Inn is one of the most famous of the old smugglers' inns of England, known to that band of cutthroats, the real-life Hawkhurst Gang, as well as to Russell Thorndike's fictional character, Dr. Syn. (One of the rooms, in fact, is called Dr. Syn's Bedchamber, and is connected to the bar by a secret staircase, stowed away in the thickness of the wall.) This place, with its Elizabethan associations and traditional touches, remains one of the most romantic old-world inns in Sussex. The most sought-after rooms are in the building overlooking the cobblestone street. Five units have four-poster beds. The accommodations vary considerably in shape and size, some quite large, others a bit cramped, as befits a building of this age. Comfort is the keynote, regardless of room assignment. Six units are spacious enough for a small family. Bathrooms are compact but have good maintenance, some with both tub and shower.

Mermaid St. (between West St. and The Strand), Rye, E. Sussex TN31 7EY. © **01797/223065.** Fax 01797/ 225069. www.mermaidinn.com. 31 units, 29 with bathroom. £80–£100 ($148–$185) per person double with breakfast, £110–£130 ($204–$241) per person double with breakfast and dinner. AE, DC, MC, V. **Amenities:** Restaurant; bar; 24-hr. room service; babysitting; laundry service; dry cleaning. *In room:* A/C, TV, hair dryer.

White Vine House 🕿 *(Finds)*   The winner of several awards for the beauty of its small front garden and the quality of its restoration, this charming house dates from 1568. Restored from an almost derelict shell in 1987, and recently refurbished by its owners, the creeper-clad inn carefully maintains the Georgian detailing of the formal public rooms and the Tudor-style wall and ceiling beams of the antique bedrooms. The soft beds with fine linens are most comfortable, and the tiny shower bathrooms are tidily maintained.

High St., Rye, E. Sussex TN31 7JF. © **01797/224748.** Fax 01797/223599. www.whitevinehouse.co.uk. 7 units. £90–£115 ($167–$213) double; £140 ($259) family room. Rates include English breakfast. AE, DC, MC, V. **Amenities:** Restaurant (breakfast only). *In room:* TV, coffeemaker, hair dryer.

WHERE TO DINE

Our preferred spot for teatime is the **Swan Cottage Tea Rooms,** 41 The Mint, High St. (© **01797/222423**), dating from 1420 and situated on the main street. This black-and-white half-timbered building is one of the most historic in town. We gravitate to the room in the rear because of its big brick fireplace. Delectable pastries and freshly made cakes await you along with a selection of teas, including Darjeeling, Earl Grey, Pure Assam, and others.

Flushing Inn 🕿 SEAFOOD/ENGLISH   The best restaurant in Rye, this 16th-century inn has preserved the finest of the past, including a wall-size fresco dating from 1544 that depicts a menagerie of birds and heraldic beasts. A rear dining room overlooks a flower garden. A special feature is the Sea Food Lounge Bar, where sandwiches and plates of seafood are available. You can begin with the justifiably praised hors d'oeuvres—a fine selection of smoked fish and shellfish. Main dishes range from locally caught Rye Bay plaice to an old-fashioned loin of English lamb prepared with honey and lavender.

4–5 Market St. © **01797/223292.** Reservations recommended. Fixed-price meal from £20 ($37) at lunch, £40 ($74) at dinner. AE, DC, MC, V. Wed–Mon noon–1:30pm; Wed–Sun 7–8:30pm. Closed 1st 2 weeks in Jan and 1st 2 weeks in June.

The Landgate Bistro MODERN BRITISH   People come from miles around to dine in this pair of interconnected Georgian shops whose exteriors are covered with "mathematical tiles" (18th-century simulated brick, applied over stucco facades to save money). Inside, Toni Ferguson-Lees and her partner, Nick Parkin, offer savory modern British cuisine. Skillfully prepared dishes may include braised squid with white wine, tomatoes, and garlic; Dover sole; and grilled English lamb with butter beans, bacon, and fresh basil.

5–6 Landgate. © **01797/222829.** Reservations required on weekends. Main courses £9.90–£13 ($19–$24); fixed-price menu Tues–Thurs £17 ($31). AE, DC, MC, V. Tues–Fri 7–9:30pm; Sat 7–10pm (closing time may vary).

4 1066 & All That: Hastings 🕿🕿🕿 & Battle 🕿🕿

Hastings: 72km (45 miles) SW of Dover; 101km (63 miles) SE of London. Battle: 55km (34 miles) NE of Brighton; 88km (55 miles) SE of London

The world has seen bigger skirmishes, but few are as well remembered as the Battle of Hastings in 1066. When William, duke of Normandy, landed on the Sussex coast and lured King Harold (already fighting Vikings in Yorkshire) south to defeat, the destiny of the English-speaking people was changed forever.

The actual battle occurred at what is now Battle Abbey (13km/8 miles away), but the Norman duke used Hastings as his base of operations. You can visit the abbey, and then have a cup of tea in Battle's main square, and then you can be off, as the rich countryside of Sussex is much more intriguing than this sleepy market town.

Present-day Hastings is a little seedy and run-down. If you're seeking an English seaside resort, head for Brighton instead.

ESSENTIALS

GETTING THERE   Daily trains run hourly from London's Victoria Station or Charing Cross to Hastings. The trip takes 1½ to 2 hours. The train station at Battle is a stop on the London-Hastings rail link. For rail information, call ✆ **0845/748-4950** or visit www.railtrack.co.uk.

Hastings is linked by bus to Maidstone, Folkestone, and Eastbourne, which has direct service with scheduled departures. **National Express** operates regular daily service from London's Victoria Coach Station. If you're in Rye or Hastings in summer, several frequent buses run to Battle. For information and schedules, call ✆ **0870/580-8080** or visit www.nationalexpress.com.

If you're driving from the M25 ring road around London, head southeast to the coast and Hastings on the A21. To get to Battle, cut south to Sevenoaks and continue along the A21 to Battle via the A2100.

VISITOR INFORMATION   In Hastings, the **Hastings Information Centre** is at Queen's Square, Priory Meadow (✆ **01424/781111;** www.hastings.gov.uk). It's open Monday to Friday from 8:30am to 6:15pm; Saturday 9am to 5pm; Sunday 10:30am to 4:30pm.

In Battle, the **Tourist Information Centre** at 88 High St. (✆ **01424/773721;** www.battle-tourism.co.uk) is open April through September daily from 9:30am to 5:30pm; off season Monday through Saturday from 10am to 4pm and Sunday from 11am to 3pm.

EXPLORING THE HISTORIC SITES

Battle Abbey 🏰 *Kids*   King Harold, last of the Saxon kings, fought bravely here, not only for his kingdom but also for his life. As legend has it, he was killed by an arrow through the eye, and his body was dismembered. To commemorate the victory, William the Conqueror founded Battle Abbey; some of the construction stone was shipped from his lands at Caen in northern France.

During the Dissolution of the Monasteries from 1538 to 1539 by King Henry VIII, the church of the abbey was largely destroyed. Some buildings and ruins, however, remain in what Tennyson called "O Garden, blossoming out of English blood." The principal building still standing is the Abbot's House, which is leased to a private school for boys and girls and is open to the general public only during summer holidays. Of architectural interest is the gatehouse, which has octagonal towers and stands at the top of Market Square. All of the north Precinct Mall is still standing, and one of the most interesting sights of the ruins is the ancient Dorter Range, where the monks once slept.

The town of Battle flourished around the abbey; even though it has remained a medieval market town, many of the old half-timbered buildings have regrettably lost much of their original character because of stucco plastering carried out by past generations.

This is a great place for the kids. A themed play area is here, and at the gate, a daily activity sheet is distributed. You can relax with a picnic or stroll in the parkland that once formed the monastery grounds.

At the south end of Battle High St. (a 5-min. walk from the train station). 🕾 **01424/773792.** Admission £5 ($9.25) adults, £2.50 ($4.65) children, £3.80 ($7.05) students and seniors, £13 ($23) family ticket. Apr–Sept daily 10am–6pm; Oct daily 10am–5pm; Nov–Mar daily 10am–4pm.

Hastings Castle 👁👁 In ruins now, the first of the Norman castles built in England sprouted on a western hill overlooking Hastings, around 1067. Precious little is left to remind us of the days when proud knights, imbued with a spirit of pomp and spectacle, wore bonnets and girdles. The fortress was defortified by King John in 1216 and was later used as a church. Owned by the Pelham dynasty from the latter 16th century to modern times, the ruins have been turned over to Hastings. There is now an audiovisual presentation of the castle's history, including the famous battle of 1066. From the mount, you'll have a good view of the coast and promenade.

Castle Hill Rd., West Hill. 🕾 **01424/781112.** Admission £3.40 ($6.30) adults, £2.75 ($4.65) students and seniors, £2.25 ($4.15) children, £10 ($19) family ticket. Easter–Sept daily 10am–5pm; Oct–Easter daily 11am–3pm. Take the West Hill Cliff Railway from George St. to the castle for £1 ($1.85), £50 ($95) for children.

WHERE TO STAY
IN HASTINGS

Beauport Park Hotel 👁 This hotel has a cozy country-house aura and is more intimate and hospitable than The Royal Victoria (reviewed below). Originally the private estate of General Murray, former governor of Quebec, the building was destroyed by fire in 1923 and rebuilt in the old style. It's surrounded by beautiful gardens; the Italian-style grounds in the rear feature statuary and flowering shrubbery. Rooms range from midsize to large, and some are fitted with elegant four-poster beds. Nine bedrooms are set aside for nonsmokers. The self-contained Pine Lodge is equipped with a double, twin, children's room, living area, sauna, and kitchen. All the bathrooms have shower-tub combinations.

Battle Rd. (A2100), Hastings, E. Sussex TN38 8EA. 🕾 **01424/851222.** Fax 01424/852465. www.beauport parkhotel.co.uk. 26 units. £130 ($241) double; £155 ($287) suite Pine Lodge. Rates include English breakfast. AE, DC, MC, V. Head 5.5km (3½ miles) northwest of Hastings, to the junction of A2100 and B2159. **Amenities:** 2 restaurants; bar; outdoor heated pool; tennis court; badminton court; croquet; limited room service; laundry service; dry cleaning. *In room:* TV, dataport, coffeemaker, hair dryer, trouser press.

The Royal Victoria This seafront hotel, constructed in 1828, offers the most impressive architecture in town and the best accommodations in Hastings or St. Leonards. It has welcomed many famous visitors, including its namesake, Queen Victoria herself. Many of the elegant and comfortably appointed rooms have separate lounge areas and views of the English Channel and Beachy Head. Many of the bedrooms are extremely large; all of them look as if Laura Ashley traipsed through, as evoked by dozens of half-tester beds in English chintz. Some of the accommodations are large enough for families, and a number of them are duplexes. Some of the units are wheelchair accessible. Bathrooms are roomy and well maintained, with a tub-and-shower combo.

Marina, St. Leonards, Hastings, E. Sussex TN38 0BD. 🕾 **01424/445544.** Fax 01424/721995. www.royal victoria-hotel.co.uk. 56 units. £130 ($241) double. Children 15 and under stay free in parent's room. Rates include English breakfast. AE, DC, MC, V. **Amenities:** Restaurant; 3 bars; 24-hr. room service; laundry service; dry cleaning; rooms for those with limited mobility. *In room:* TV, dataport, coffeemaker, hair dryer, iron/ironing board, safe, trouser press.

IN BATTLE

Powder Mills Hotel 👁 *Finds* Near Battle Abbey and adjacent to the fabled battlefield of 1066, this restored Georgian house sits on 60 hectares (150 acres). On-site was a thriving gunpowder industry, which operated for two centuries beginning in 1676. The name of the hotel honors that long-ago tradition. Privately owned by Douglas and Julie Cowpland, the property has attracted such distinguished guests as the duke of Wellington. It's also said to be haunted by a lady dressed in white. Bedrooms are spacious and tastefully furnished, mostly with antiques and various period pieces. Some rooms offer four-poster beds; all come with a well-maintained private bathroom with tub or shower. Grace notes include log fires on winter evenings, a drawing room, a music room, and the Orangery Restaurant with its colonial-style wicker seating.

Powder Mills Lane, Battle, E. Sussex TN33 0SP. ℂ **01424/775511.** Fax 01424/774540. www.powdermills hotel.com. 35 units. £115–£145 ($213–$268) double; £185 ($342) suite. Rates include English breakfast. AE, DC, MC, V. **Amenities:** Restaurant; bar; limited room service; outdoor pool; fishing; babysitting; laundry service; dry cleaning; nonsmoking rooms. *In room:* TV, dataport, beverage maker, hair dryer, trouser press.

WHERE TO DINE

Victoria's Tea Room (D-Day's)   Courthouse Street in Hasting's Old Town has attracted as many as 17 antiques stores in recent years, creating a kind of mecca for antiques buyers. Their hub and centerpiece, and site of endless cups of up to 20 varieties of tea, is this combination tearoom and antiques store. The owners, D-Day White (who was born on the day of the famous invasion in Normandy) and Beverly, have transformed their 18th-century premises into the coziest tearoom in town and filled its nether regions with an intriguing collection of period furniture and "collectible junk" that includes everything from Victorian sideboards to gas masks from World War I. The place is especially appealing when the wind and rain blow in from the Channel.

19 Courthouse St., Hastings Old Town. ℂ **01424/465205.** Cream teas £2.95 ($5.45); sandwiches £2.75–£3.95 ($5.10–$7.30). No credit cards. Mon–Thurs and Sat 10am–4:30 or 5pm; Sun noon–4:30pm.

5 Royal Tunbridge Wells

58km (36 miles) SE of London; 53km (33 miles) NE of Brighton

Dudley Lord North, courtier to James I, is credited with the accidental discovery in 1606 of the mineral spring that led to the creation of a fashionable resort, Royal Tunbridge Wells. Over the years, "Chalybeate Spring" became known for its curative properties, the answer for everything from too many days of wine and roses to failing sexual prowess. It's still possible to take the waters today.

The spa resort reached its peak in the mid–18th century under the foppish patronage of Beau Nash (1674–1761), a dandy and final arbiter on how to act, what to say, and even what to wear (for example, he got men to remove their boots in favor of stockings). Tunbridge Wells continued to enjoy a prime spa reputation up through the reign of Queen Victoria, who used to vacation here as a child, and in 1909, Tunbridge Wells received its Royal status.

Today, the spa is long past its zenith. But the town is a pleasant place to stay—it can be used as a base for exploring the many historic homes in Kent (see "Kent's Country Houses, Castles & Gardens," below); it's very easy, for example, to tour Sissinghurst and Chartwell from here.

The most remarkable feature of the town itself is **The Pantiles** ⦿, a colonnaded walkway for shoppers, tea drinkers, and diners, built near the wells. If you walk around town, you'll see many other interesting and charming spots. Entertainment is presented at the **Assembly Hall** and **Trinity Arts Centre.**

ESSENTIALS

GETTING THERE   Two to three trains per hour leave London's Charing Cross Station during the day bound for Hastings, going via the town center of

Royal Tunbridge Wells. The trip takes 50 minutes. For **rail information,** call
✆ **0845/748-4950** or visit www.railtrack.co.uk. No direct bus links with
Gatwick Airport or London; however, hourly service exists during the day
between Brighton and Royal Tunbridge Wells (call ✆ **0870/580-8080** for the
bus schedule or visit www.nationalexpress.com). You can purchase tickets
aboard the bus.

If you're driving, after reaching the ring road around London, continue east
along the M25, cutting southeast at the exit for the A21 to Hastings.

VISITOR INFORMATION The **Tourist Information Centre,** Old Fish
Market, The Pantiles (✆ **01892/515675**), provides a full accommodations list
and offers a reservations service. The office is open from 9am to 5pm Monday
through Saturday (10am–6pm July–Aug), and from 10am to 4pm on Sunday
(10am–5pm May to Aug).

WHERE TO STAY

The Spa Hotel *(Kids)* Standing on 6 hectares (15 acres), this building dates
from 1766. Once a private home, it was converted to a hotel in 1880 and
remains the town's leading hotel. The kind of old-fashioned place where guests
check in for long stays, bedrooms are of various sizes and shapes, as was typical
in the 19th century. Bedrooms are individually furnished, some with four-poster
beds, and many offer panoramic vistas. Thirteen units are available for nonsmokers. Bathrooms are tidy and compact with shower-tub combinations.
The hotel offers a few activity options for kids, including a special pony-riding
paddock.

Mt. Ephraim, Royal Tunbridge Wells, Kent TN4 8XJ. ✆ **800/528-1234** in the U.S., or 01892/520331. Fax 01892/
510575. www.spahotel.co.uk. 71 units. £127–£147 ($235–$272) double; £135–£180 ($250–$333) suite. Children 13 and under stay free in parent's room. AE, DC, MC, V. From The Pantiles, take Major Yorks Rd. **Amenities:**
Restaurant; bar; lounge; indoor heated pool; lighted tennis court; dance studio; health club; concierge; salon;
24-hr. room service; babysitting; laundry service; dry cleaning; nonsmoking rooms; rooms for those with limited
mobility. *In room:* TV, dataport, hair dryer, iron/ironing board (some rooms), safe, trouser press.

WHERE TO DINE

Gracelands Palace SZECHUAN/CANTONESE We don't know which we
like more here: the excellent Chinese food or the owner, Paul Chan, providing
an evening's cabaret entertainment of Elvis Presley's biggest hits, including
"Love Me Tender." Pictures and memorabilia of Elvis decorate the walls. But
instead of one of the dishes so beloved by Elvis, such as peanut butter and
banana sandwiches with lots of mayonnaise, you get such delights as tender
beef flavored with ginger and scallions or else crispy duck with pancakes and
cucumber. For an appetizer, the sesame prawn toast is a delight. Friday and
Saturday are the main karaoke nights, but Chan is likely to take to the mike any
night.

3 Cumberland Walk. ✆ **01892/540754.** Reservations recommended. 2-course fixed-price menu £16.50
($31); 3-course fixed-price menu £19 ($35). AE, MC, V. Mon 6pm–midnight; Tues–Sat noon–1:45pm and
6pm–midnight.

Thackeray's House ENGLISH/FRENCH You'll get a bit of history and the
finest food in town, as this 1660 house was once inhabited by novelist William
Makepeace Thackeray, who wrote *Tunbridge Toys* here. Owner-chef Bruce Wass
worked at one of our favorite restaurants in London, Odin's, before setting up this
place here. He has created an elegant atmosphere, backed by attentive service,
for his specialties. Care goes into all his dishes, and many have flair, including an

occasional salad of preserved duck with quail's eggs. He reaches perfection with roasted saddle of rabbit with grilled polenta and red cabbage, or best end of lamb with Dijon mustard and herb-crusted roast garlic.

85 London Rd. (at the corner of Mt. Ephraim Rd.). ℂ **01892/511921.** Reservations required. Main courses £15–£28 ($28–$52); 2-course lunch £13 ($23); 3-course lunch £14 ($25). MC, V. Tues–Sun noon–2:30pm; Tues–Sat 6:30–10pm.

6 Kent's Country Houses, Castles & Gardens

Many of England's finest country houses, castles, and gardens are in Kent, where you'll find the palace of Knole, a premier example of English Tudor-style architecture; Hever Castle, the childhood home of Anne Boleyn, and later the home of William Waldorf Astor; Leeds Castle, a spectacular castle with ties to America; and Penshurst Place, a stately home that was a literary salon of sorts during the first half of the 17th century. Kent also has a bevy of homes that once belonged to famous men but have since been turned into intriguing museums, such as Chartwell, where Sir Winston Churchill lived for many years, and Down House, where Charles Darwin wrote *On the Origin of Species.* Here you can amble down the same path the naturalist trod every evening.

It would take at least a week to see all of these historic properties—more time than most visitors have. When you make your choices, keep in mind that Knole, Hever, Penshurst, Leeds, and Chartwell are the most deserving of your attention.

We have found the guided tours to some of Kent's more popular stately homes too rushed and too expensive to recommend. Each attraction can be toured far more reasonably on your own. Because public transportation into and around Kent can be awkward, we advise driving from London, especially if you plan to visit more than one place in a day. Accordingly, this section is organized as you may drive it from London. However, if it's possible to get to an attraction via public transportation, we include that information in the individual listings below.

If you only have a day, you may want to confine your time to Chartwell, former home of Winston Churchill; and Knole, one of England's largest private estates with a vast complex of courtyards and buildings. You need an entire second day to visit Leeds Castle and Hever Castle. Leeds allows morning visits (most castles and country homes in Kent can only be visited in the afternoon), so you can see Leeds in the morning, then tour Hever Castle that afternoon.

If you have more time for castle-hopping, visit Canterbury Cathedral on the morning of your third day, then tour Penshurst Place in the afternoon. (See the "Canterbury" section earlier in this chapter for details on Canterbury.) Penshurst is one of the finest Elizabethan houses in England, and its Baron's Hall is one of the greatest interiors to have survived from the Middle Ages.

Chartwell ℛ Sir Winston Churchill's home from 1922 until his death, though not as grand as his birthplace (Blenheim Palace; p. 257), Chartwell has preserved its rooms as the Conservative politician left them—maps, documents, photographs, pictures, personal mementos, and all. Two rooms display gifts that the prime minister received from people all over the world. A selection of many of his well-known uniforms includes his famous "siren-suits" and hats. Many of Churchill's paintings are displayed in a garden studio. You can see the garden walls that the prime minister built with his own hands and the pond where he sat to feed the Golden Orfe. A restaurant on the grounds serves food from 11am to 5:30pm on days when the house is open.

Near the town of Edenbridge. ℂ **01732/868381.** Admission to house, garden, and studio £7 ($13) adults, £3.50 ($6.50) children, £18 ($32) family. Late Mar to June and Sept to early Nov Wed–Sun 11am–5pm;

July–Aug Tues–Sun 11am–5pm. If driving from London, head east on M25, taking the exit to Westerham. Drive 3km (2 miles) south of Westerham on B2026 and follow the signs.

Down House   Here stands the final residence of the famous naturalist Charles Darwin. In 1842, upon moving in, he wrote, "House ugly, looks neither old nor new." Nevertheless, he lived there "in happy contentment" until his death in 1882. The drawing room, dining room, billiard room, and old study have been restored to the way they were when Darwin was working on his famous, and still controversial, book *On the Origin of Species,* first published in 1859. The garden retains its original landscaping and a glass house, beyond which lies the Sand Walk or "Thinking Path," where Darwin took his daily solitary walk.

On Luxted Rd., in Downe. © **01689/859119.** Admission £6.30 ($12) adults, £4.70 ($8.70) students and seniors, £3.20 ($5.90) children. Apr–Sep Wed–Sun 10am–6pm; Oct Wed–Sun 10am–5pm; Nov to mid-Dec Wed–Sun 10am–4pm; Feb–Mar Wed–Sun 10am–4pm, closed mid-Dec to Feb. From Westerham, get on A233 and drive 9km (5½ miles) south of Bromley to the village of Downe. Down House is .5km (¼ mile) southeast of the village. From London's Victoria Station, take a train (available daily) to Bromley South, then go by bus no. 146 (Mon–Sat only) to Downe or to Orpington by bus no. R2.

Groombridge Place Gardens   These formal gardens, with a vineyard and woodland walks, date from the 17th century. Part of the complex includes an Enchanted Forest, an ancient woodland in which the artist Ivan Hicks designed a series of "interactive" gardens, using natural objects, native wild flowers, mirrors, and glass to create a mysterious, surreal ambience. The White Rose Garden is compared favorably to that at fabled Sissinghurst. The English Knot Garden is based on paneling in the drawing room of an English country house. In the Fern Valley, huge Jurassic plants are as old as time. At the center is Groombridge Place, built on the site of a 12th-century castle and one of the most beautiful moated manor houses in England. Sir Christopher Wren, or so it is believed, helped with the architecture. The palace was built in 1662 by one of the courtiers to King Charles II, Philip Packer. Sir Arthur Conan Doyle was a regular visitor to the house to take part in séances, and the manor was the setting for the Sherlock Holmes mystery, *The Valley of Fear.*

The gardens are often visited after an exploration of Knole near Sevenoaks. After leaving Sevenoaks, you can take route A21 southeast until you reach the junction of route A26 south. Follow this route until you see the signposted cut-off heading west to the little village of Groombridge and its gardens.

Groombridge. © **08192/861444.** www.groombridge.co.uk. Admission £8.50 ($16) adults, £7.50 ($14) seniors, £7 ($13) children 3–12, £29 ($47) family ticket. Apr–Oct daily 9:30am–6pm.

Knole ★★   Begun in the mid–15th century by Thomas Bourchier, archbishop of Canterbury, and set in a 404-hectare (1,000-acre) deer park, Knole is one of the largest private houses in England and is one of the finest examples of pure English Tudor–style architecture.

Henry VIII liberated the former archbishop's palace from the church in 1537. He spent considerable sums of money on Knole, but history records only once visit (in 1541) after extracting the place from the reluctant Archbishop Cranmer. It was a royal palace until Queen Elizabeth I granted it to Thomas Sackville, first earl of Dorset, whose descendants have lived here ever since. (Virginia Woolf, often a guest of the Sackvilles, used Knole as the setting for her novel *Orlando.*)

The house covers 2.8 hectares (7 acres) and has 365 rooms, 52 staircases, and 7 courts. The elaborate paneling and plasterwork provide a background for the 17th- and 18th-century tapestries and rugs, Elizabethan and Jacobean furniture,

---

Tips   **Teatime at Knole**

Although most people don't know this, you can take afternoon tea at Knole. From the early 17th century, the tearooms here were used as a brew house where beer and ale were brewed regularly. Today, you can enjoy a pot of tea with scones, jam, and cream, or else devour one of their gâteaux such as carrot-and-walnut sponge topped with a cream-cheese-and-lemon-juice icing.

---

and collection of family portraits. If you want to see a bed that's to die for, check out the state bed of James II in the King's Bedroom.

8km (5 miles) north of Tonbridge, at the Tonbridge end of the town of Sevenoaks. © 01732/462100. Admission to house £6 ($11) adults, £3 ($5.55) children, £15 ($28) family. Admission to gardens £2 ($3.70) adults, £1 ($1.85) children. House open late Mar to early Nov Wed–Sun 11am–4pm; Good Friday and bank holiday Mon 11am–4pm. Gardens open only 1st Wed of the month in May–Sept 11am–4pm; last admission at 3pm. Park is open daily to pedestrians and open to cars only when the house is. To reach Knole from Chartwell, drive north to Westerham, pick up A25, and head east for 13km (8 miles). Frequent train service is available from London (about every 30 min.) to Sevenoaks, and then you can take the connecting hourly bus service, a taxi, or walk the remaining 2.5km (1½ miles) to Knole.

Ightham Mote 🏰   Dating from 1340, Ightham Mote was extensively remodeled in the early 16th century, and remodeling is still going on. The chapel, with its painted ceiling, timbered outer wall, and ornate chimneys, reflects the Tudor period. You'll cross a stone bridge over a moat to its central courtyard. From the Great Hall, known for its magnificent windows, a Jacobean staircase leads to the old chapel on the first floor, where you go through the solarium, which has an oriel window, to the Tudor chapel.

Unlike many other ancient houses in England that have been occupied by the same family for centuries, Ightham Mote passed from owner to owner, with each family leaving its mark on the place. When the last private owner, an American who was responsible for a lot of the restoration, died, he bequeathed the house to the National Trust, which chose to keep the Robinson Library laid out as it was in a 1960 edition of *Homes & Gardens*.

© 01732/810378. Admission £6.50 ($12) adults, £3.25 ($6) children, £17 ($31) family. Sun–Mon and Wed–Fri 10am–5:30pm. Closed Nov–Mar. Drive 9.5km (6 miles) east of Sevenoaks on A25 to the small village of Ivy Hatch; the estate is 4km (2½ miles) south of Ightham; it's also signposted from A227.

Squerryes Court   Built in 1681, this manor house has been owned by the Warde family for the last 250 years. At one time, British General James Wolfe, who commanded forces in the bombardment of Quebec, lived here with his family. The house still contains pictures and relics of General Wolfe's family. The Warde family has restored the formal gardens, dotting banks surrounding the lake with spring bulbs, herbaceous borders, and old roses to retain its beauty year-round, and returned rooms to their original uses. You can enjoy the fine collection of old-master paintings from the Italian, 17th-century Dutch, and 18th-century English schools, along with antiques, porcelain, and tapestries, all acquired or commissioned by the family in the 18th century. General Wolfe received his commission on the grounds of the house—the spot is marked by a cenotaph.

1km (½ mile) west of the center of Westerham (10 min. from Exit 6 or Exit 5 on M25). © 01959/562345. www.squerryes.co.uk. Admission to house and garden £5 ($9.25) adults, £4.40 ($8.15) students and seniors, £2.70 ($5) children under 16, family ticket £13 ($23). Garden only £3 ($5.55) adults, £2.90 ($5.35) seniors, £1.70

($3.15) children under 16, family ticket £7.50 ($14). Apr 1–Sept 30, Wed, Thurs, Sun, and Bank Holiday Mondays, grounds are open noon–5:30pm, house 1:30–5:30pm. Take A25 just west of Westerham and follow the signs.

TOURING LEEDS CASTLE: "THE LOVELIEST IN THE WORLD" ✿✿✿

Once described by Lord Conway as the loveliest castle in the world, Leeds Castle (✆ **01622/765400;** www.leeds-castle.com) dates from A.D. 857. Originally constructed of wood, it was rebuilt in 1119 in its present stone structure on two small islands in the middle of the lake; it was an almost impregnable fortress before the importation of gunpowder. Henry VIII converted it to a royal palace.

The castle has strong ties to America through the sixth Lord Fairfax who, as well as owning the castle, owned 2,023,428 hectares (5 million acres) in Virginia and was a close friend and mentor of the young George Washington. The last private owner, the Hon. Lady Baillie, who restored the castle with a superb collection of fine art, furniture, and tapestries, bequeathed it to the Leeds Castle Foundation. Since then, the royal apartments, known as *Les Chambres de la Reine* (the queen's chambers), in the Gloriette, the oldest part of the castle, have been open to the public. The Gloriette, the last stronghold against attack, dates from Norman and Plantagenet times, with later additions by Henry VIII.

Within the surrounding parkland is a wildwood garden and duckery where rare swans, geese, and ducks abound. The redesigned aviaries contain a superb collection of birds, including parakeets and cockatoos. Dog lovers will enjoy the Dog Collar Museum at the gatehouse, with a unique collection of collars dating from the Middle Ages. A nine-hole golf course is open to the public. The Culpepper Garden is a delightful English country flower garden. Beyond are the castle greenhouses, with the maze centered on a beautiful underground grotto and the vineyard recorded in William the Conqueror's survey document, the *Domesday Book* (1085), once again producing Leeds Castle English white wine.

From March to October, the park is open daily from 10am to 5pm; the castle, daily from 11am to 5:30pm. From November to February, the park is open daily from 10am to 3pm; the castle, daily from 10:15am to 3:30pm. The castle and grounds are closed on the last Saturday in June and the first Saturday in July before open-air concerts. Admission to the castle and grounds is £13 ($23) for adults and £9 ($17) for children. Students and seniors pay £11 ($20). A family ticket costs £39 ($72). You can visit the Grounds only for £10 ($19) for adults, £6.50 ($12) for children, £33 ($61) family ticket. Car parking is free, with a free ride on a fully accessible minibus available for those who cannot manage the 1km (½-mile) or so walk from the parking area to the castle.

Trains run frequently from London's Victoria Station to Maidstone. Buses run weekdays from London's Victoria Coach Station to Maidstone, 58km (36 miles) to the southeast. If you're driving from London's ring road, continue east along the M26 and the M20. The castle is 6.5km (4 miles) east of Maidstone at the junction of the A20 and the M20 London-Folkestone roads.

Snacks, salads, cream teas, and hot meals are offered daily at a number of places on the estate, including Fairfax Hall, a restored 17th-century tithe barn, and the Terrace Restaurant, which provides a full range of hot and cold meals.

Kentish Evenings are presented in Fairfax Hall only for a few days in December, at Christmas time, starting at 7pm with a cocktail reception, then a private guided tour of the castle. Guests feast on a five-course banquet, starting with smoked salmon mousse, followed by broth and roast beef carved at the table, plus seasonal vegetables. A half bottle of wine is included in the overall price of £49

($91) per person. During the meal, musicians play appropriate music for the surroundings and the occasion. Advance reservations are required, made by calling the castle. Kentish Evenings finish at 12:30am, so it's best to stay overnight nearby.

Instead of driving back late at night, you can spend the night at **Grange Moor Hotel/Grange Park,** 4–8 St. Michael's Rd. (off Tonbridge Rd.), Maidstone, Kent ME16 8BS (**☎ 01622/677623;** fax 01622/678246; www.grangemoor.co.uk), which are two buildings facing each other across the street. Grange Moor is the main accommodation, with 51 well-furnished rooms, each with private bathroom, phone, coffeemaker, and TV. The cost is £55 ($102) for a double, Monday through Thursday, and £54 ($100) on other nights, including an English breakfast. Across the street, Grange Park has only 12 rooms but is similarly furnished, renting for £54 to £55 ($100–$102) a night, including an English breakfast. Both places are located in a tranquil residential area that's close to the center of Maidstone. A Tudor-style bar and restaurant offers a three-course meal for £18 ($33). Children are welcome in both the bar and restaurant area.

MORE KENT ATTRACTIONS

Hever Castle & Gardens ★★   Hever Castle dates from 1270, when the massive gatehouse, the outer walls, and the moat were first constructed. Some 200 years later, the Bullen (or Boleyn) family added a comfortable Tudor dwelling house inside the walls. Hever Castle was the childhood home of Anne Boleyn, the second wife of Henry VIII and mother of Queen Elizabeth I.

In 1903, William Waldorf Astor acquired the estate and invested time, money, and imagination in restoring the castle, building the Tudor Village, and creating the gardens and lakes. The Astor family's contribution to Hever's rich history can be appreciated through the castle's collections of furniture, paintings, and objets d'art, as well as the quality of its workmanship, particularly in the woodcarving and plasterwork.

The gardens are ablaze with color throughout most of the year. The spectacular Italian Garden contains statuary and sculpture dating from Roman to Renaissance times. The formal gardens include a walled Rose Garden, fine topiary work, and a maze. There's a 14-hectare (35-acre) lake and many streams, cascades, and fountains.

☎ 01732/865224. www.hevercastle.co.uk. Admission to castle and gardens £8.80 ($16) adults, £7.40 ($14) students and seniors, £4.80 ($8.90) children ages 5–14. Family ticket (2 adults, 2 children) £22 ($41). Garden only £7 ($13) adults, £6 ($11) students and seniors, £4.60 ($8.50) children ages 5–14. Family ticket £19 ($34). Free for children 4 and under. Gardens daily 11am–6pm; castle daily noon–6pm; closes at 4pm Mar and Nov. Closed Dec–Feb. Follow the signs northwest of Royal Tonbridge Wells; it's 5km (3 miles) southeast of Edenbridge, midway between Sevenoaks and East Grinstead, and 30 min. from Exit 6 of M25.

Penshurst Place ★★ *Kids*   Stately Penshurst Place is one of Britain's outstanding country houses, as well as one of England's greatest defended manor houses, standing in a peaceful rural setting that has changed little over the centuries. In 1338, Sir John de Pulteney, four times lord mayor of London, built the manor house whose Great Hall still forms the heart of Penshurst. The boy king, Edward VI, presented the house to Sir William Sidney, and it has remained in that family ever since. In the first half of the 17th century, Penshurst was known as a center of literature and attracted such personages as Ben Jonson, who was inspired by the estate to write one of his greatest poems.

The Nether Gallery, below the **Long Gallery** with its suite of ebony-and-ivory furniture from Goa, houses the Sidney family collection of armor. You can also see the splendid state dining room. In the Stable Wing is a toy museum, with playthings from past generations. On the grounds are nature and farm trails plus an adventure playground for children.

9.5km (6 miles) west of Tonbridge. ℂ 01892/870307. www.penshurstplace.com. Admission to house and grounds £7 ($13) adults, £6.50 ($12) students and seniors, £5 ($9.25) children 5–16, family ticket £20 ($37); grounds only £5.50 ($10) adults, £5 ($9.25) students and seniors, £4.50 ($8.35) children 5–16, family ticket £17 ($31). Free for children 4 and under. Mar–Oct daily, house noon–5:30pm, grounds 10:30am–6pm (Sat–Sun only in Mar). Closed Nov–Feb. From M25 Junction follow A21 to Tonbridge, leaving at the Tonbridge (North) exit; then follow the brown tourist signs. The nearest mainline station is Tonbridge.

Sissinghurst Castle Garden 🐾🐾   These spectacular gardens, which are situated between surviving parts of an Elizabethan mansion, were created by one of England's most famous and dedicated gardeners, Bloomsbury writer Vita Sackville-West, and her husband, Harold Nicolson. In spring, the garden is resplendent with flowering bulbs and daffodils in the orchard.

The white garden reaches its peak in June. The large herb garden, a skillful montage that reflects her profound plant knowledge, has something to show all summer long, and the cottage garden, with its flowering bulbs, is at its finest in the fall. Meals are available in the Granary Restaurant. The garden area is flat, so it is wheelchair accessible; however, only two wheelchairs are allowed at a time.

ℂ 01580/715330. Admission £7 ($13) adults, £3.50 ($6.50) children, family ticket £18 ($32). Apr–Oct Mon–Tues and Fri 11am–6:30pm, Sat–Sun 10am–6:30pm. The garden is 85km (53 miles) southeast of London and 24km (15 miles) south of Maidstone. It's most often approached from Leeds Castle, which is 6.5km (4 miles) east of Maidstone at the junction of A20 and M20 London-Folkestone roads. From this junction, head south on B2163 and A274 through Headcorn. Follow the signposts to Sissinghurst.

7 Historic Mansions & Gardens in Dorking & Guildford

Dorking, birthplace of Lord Laurence Olivier, lies on the Mole River at the foot of the North Downs. Within easy reach are some of the most scenic spots in the shire, including Silent Pool, Box Hill, and Leith Hill.

The guildhall in **Guildford,** a country town on the Wey River, has an ornamental projecting clock that dates from 1683. Charles Dickens claimed that High Street, which slopes to the river, was one of the most beautiful in England.

ESSENTIALS

GETTING THERE   Frequent daily train service to Dorking takes 35 minutes from London's Victoria Station. The train to Guildford departs London's Waterloo Station and takes 40 minutes. For information, call ℂ **0845/748-4950** or visit www.railtrack.co.uk.

National Express operates buses from London's Victoria Coach Station daily, with a stopover at Guildford on its runs from London to Portsmouth. For schedules, call ℂ **0870/580-8080** or visit www.nationalexpress.com. It's usually more convenient to take the train.

If you're driving to Dorking, take the A24 south from London. If you're driving to Guildford from London, head south along the A3.

VISITOR INFORMATION   The **Guildford Tourist Information Centre** is at 14 Tunsgate (ℂ **01483/444333**). It's open October through April, Monday through Saturday from 9:30am to 5pm, and May through September, Monday through Saturday from 9am to 5:30pm and Sunday from 10am to 4:30pm.

THE TOP SIGHTS

Loseley House 🐾   This beautiful and historic Elizabethan mansion visited by Queen Elizabeth I, James I, and Queen Mary has been featured on TV and in numerous films. Its works of art include paneling from Henry VIII's Nonsuch Palace, period furniture, a unique carved chalk chimney piece, magnificent ceilings, and cushions made by Queen Elizabeth I. Lunches and teas are served in the Courtyard Restaurant from 11am to 5pm.

Loseley Park (4km/2½ miles southwest of Guildford). ℂ 01483/304440. Admission £6 ($11) adults, £5 ($9.25) students and seniors, £3 ($5.55) children. May–Sept Wed–Sun 11am–5pm.

Polesden Lacey   Built in 1824, this former Regency villa houses the Greville collection of antiques, paintings, and tapestries. In the early part of the 20th century it was enlarged to become a comfortable Edwardian country house, home of celebrated hostess Mrs. Ronald Greville, who frequently entertained royalty from 1906 to 1939. The estate has 560 hectares (1,400 acres). Stroll the 18th-century garden, lined with herbaceous borders and featuring a rose garden and beech trees.

A few miles from Great Bookham, off A246 Leatherhead-Guildford rd. ℂ 01372/452048. Admission to grounds £5 ($9.25) adults, £2.50 ($4.65) children, £13 ($23) family; admission to house £8 ($15) adults, £4 ($7.40) children, £20 ($37) family. Grounds daily 11am–6pm. House Mar 22–Oct Wed–Sun and bank holidays 11am–5pm.

Wisley Garden 🕿🕿   Every season, this 101-hectare (250-acre) garden, one of the great gardens of England, has a profusion of flowers and shrubs, ranging from the alpine meadow carpeted with wild daffodils in spring, to Battleston Hill brilliant with rhododendrons in early summer, to the heather garden's colorful foliage in fall, and a riot of exotic plants in the greenhouses in winter. Recent developments include model gardens and a landscaped orchid house. This garden is the site of a laboratory where botanists, plant pathologists, and entomologists experiment and assist amateur gardeners. A large gift shop stocks a variety of gardening books.

Wisley (near Ripley, just off M25, Junction 10, on A3 London-Portsmouth rd.). ℂ 01483/224234. www.rhs.org.uk/gardens/wisley/index.asp. Admission £7 ($13) adults, £2 ($3.70) children 6–16, free for children under 6. Mar–Oct Mon–Fri 10am–6pm, Sat–Sun 9am–6pm; Nov–Feb Mon–Fri 10am–4:30pm, Sat–Sun 9am–4:30pm (last admission 1 hr. before closing).

WHERE TO STAY & DINE
IN DORKING

Burford Bridge Hotel 🕿   This inn is the best in Dorking, offering stylish living in a rural town. At the foot of beautiful Box Hill, the hotel has many historical associations. Keats completed "Endymion" here in 1817; Wordsworth and Robert Louis Stevenson also visited the hotel. You get the best of both the old and the new, including a tithe barn (ca. 1600). All the guest rooms were refurbished in early 2003. Bathrooms are compact with shower-tub combinations but little shelf space. The grounds include a flowered patio and fountain that are particularly enjoyable in summer.

Box Hill, Dorking, Surrey RH5 6BX. ℂ 01306/884561. Fax 01306/887821. www.macdonaldhotels.co.uk. 57 units. £140–£190 ($259–$352) double. Rates include breakfast. AE, DC, MC, V. Take A24 2.5km (1½ miles) north of Dorking. **Amenities:** Restaurant; bar; heated outdoor pool; 24-hr. room service; laundry service; dry cleaning; nonsmoking rooms. *In room:* TV, dataport, coffeemaker, hair dryer, trouser press.

White Horse Hotel   Just 16km (10 miles) from Gatwick Airport, this inn is supposed to have been the home of the "Marquis of Granby" in *The Pickwick Papers*. Dickens was known to have frequented the bar parlor. Several bedrooms have recently been refurbished, and all are comfortable and well maintained; a few have four-poster beds. Some units are in a rather sterile modern annex. Bathrooms are small, with minimal shelf space and shower-and-tub combinations. Called "the most interesting house in Dorking," the inn has a restaurant, as well as the Pickwick Bar that offers a moderately priced table d'hôte dinner. The hotel also has a rose garden and can arrange a temporary membership in a nearby sports club with its own swimming pool.

High St., Dorking, Surrey, RH4 1BE. ℂ 800/225-5843 in the U.S. and Canada, or 0870/400-8282. Fax 01306/880386. www.macdonaldhotels.co.uk. 78 units. £100–£160 ($185–$296) double. Rates include breakfast. AE, MC, V. **Amenities:** Restaurant, bar; 24-hr. room service; laundry service; dry cleaning; nonsmoking rooms. *In room:* TV, coffeemaker, hair dryer, iron, trouser press.

IN GUILDFORD

Holiday Inn   Though part of a chain, the feeling of heritage at this hotel is conveyed by its natural red-elm joinery, marble floors, and landscaped grounds. The bedrooms incorporate both living and sleeping areas. Both business travelers and visitors fill the attractively decorated bedrooms, which are generally mid-size. Four are set aside for nonsmokers. The latest addition to the hotel contains a series of modern rooms that are better appointed and more spacious than the older units. Bathrooms are compact but contain shower-tub combinations.

Egerton Rd., Guildford, Surrey GU2 5XZ. ℂ 0870/400-9036. Fax 01483/302960. www.holiday-inn.com. 167 units. £79–£220 ($146–$407) double; £25 ($46) to upgrade suite. AE, MC, V. Head about 3km (2 miles) southwest of the center of Guildford, just off A3. **Amenities:** Restaurant; bar; indoor heated pool; health club; 24-hr. room service; babysitting; laundry service; dry cleaning; nonsmoking rooms; rooms for those with limited mobility. *In room:* TV w/pay movies, dataport, minibar, coffeemaker, hair dryer, iron/ironing board, safe, trouser press.

Inn on the Lake   This haven of landscaped gardens with ducks drowsing on pools beside the lake is only 5km (3 miles) from Guildford. The rooms are decorated with pretty country prints and tasteful furniture. Thoughtful extras include magazines and sewing kits. Six accommodations have spa bathrooms and private balconies. All the compact bedrooms are well equipped with well-maintained bathrooms containing mostly shower-tub combinations. The house,

---

⌒Finds Shelley's House: A Bygone Era

One of the most exclusive hotels in England, **Alexander House,** Turners Hill, West Sussex RH10 4QD (ℂ 01342/714914; www.alexanderhouse. co.uk), evokes a bygone era but yet is imbued with modern comforts. Though secluded on its own grounds, it is hardly remote, lying just 15 minutes by car from Gatwick Airport. In the 17th century, the estate was owned by the family of poet Percy Bysshe Shelley. All 15 guest rooms and 6 luxurious suites are designed with utter poshness—one four-poster bed was a gift of Napoleon, for example. Set on 54 hectares (135 acres) of private gardens and parkland, the hotel also offers an award-winning restaurant known for its classic French and English cuisine. A double is £250 to £295 ($463–$546), suites from £370 ($685). Leave the M23 at junction 10 and follow signs for East Grinstead. At the second roundabout, follow signs for Turners Hill (B2028). In Turners Hill Village, turn left at the crossroads (B2110) to East Grinstead; Alexander House is on the left-hand side after about 2.5km (1½ miles).

listed in the *Domesday Book,* has Tudor, Georgian, and Victorian associations. A postwar addition blends more or less gracefully into the complex.

Ockford Rd., Godalming, Surrey GU7 1RH. ℭ **01483/419997.** Fax 01483/410852. 16 units. Mon–Fri £80 ($148) double; weekends £50 ($93) double. Rates include English breakfast. AE, MC, V. From Guildford, take A3100 south for 5km (3 miles). **Amenities:** Restaurant; bar. *In room:* TV, hair dryer, trouser press.

WHERE TO SHARE A PINT

Weyside, Millford (ℭ **01483/568024**), a riverside pub with a terraced garden and large conservatory on the River Wey, offers traditional pub food with home-made specials served daily at lunch and dinner; bar snacks are available all day. A variety of real ales are on tap. Children are welcome until 9pm.

The White House, 8 High St. (ℭ **01483/302006**), is another riverside pub, with a conservatory overlooking a lovely waterside garden. Pub grub is available at lunch and dinner; sandwiches are offered all day. They serve traditional London ales aged in barrels.

8 Chichester

50km (31 miles) W of Brighton; 111km (69 miles) SW of London

Chichester might have been just a market town if the Chichester Festival Theatre had not been born there. One of the oldest Roman cities in England, Chichester draws a crowd from all over for its theater. Though it lacks other attractions, the town is a good base for exploring a history-rich part of southern England.

ESSENTIALS

GETTING THERE   Trains depart for Chichester from London's Victoria Station once every hour during the day. The trip takes 1½ hours. However, if you visit Chichester to attend the theater, plan to stay over—the last train back to London is at 9pm. For rail information, call ℭ **0845/748-4950** or visit www.railtrack.co.uk.

Buses leave from London's Victoria Coach Station once a day. For schedules, call ℭ **0870/580-8080** or visit www.nationalexpress.com.

If you're driving from London's ring road, head south on the A3, turning onto the A286 for Chichester.

VISITOR INFORMATION   The **Tourist Information Centre,** 29A South St. (ℭ **01243/775888**), is open Monday through Saturday from 9:15am to 5:15pm, and from April to September, also Sunday from 10am to 4pm.

THE CHICHESTER FESTIVAL THEATRE ✯

Only a 5-minute walk from the Chichester Cathedral and the old Market Cross, the 1,400-seat theater, with its apron stage, stands on the edge of Oaklands Park. It opened in 1962, and its first director was none other than Lord Laurence Olivier. Its reputation has grown steadily, pumping new vigor and life into the former walled city, although originally many irate locals felt the city money could have been better spent on a swimming pool instead of a theater.

Chichester Festival Theatre, built in the 1960s, offers plays and musicals during the summer (May–Sept), and in the winter and spring months, orchestras, jazz, opera, theater, ballet, and a Christmas show for the entire family.

The **Minerva,** built in the late 1980s, is a multifunctional cultural center that includes a theater plus dining and drinking facilities. The Minerva Studio Theatre and the Chichester Festival Theatre are managed by the same board of governors but show different programs and different plays.

Finds **Bosham: A Hidden Surprise**

In addition to the sights listed in this section, you may want to stop in nearby **Bosham,** which is primarily a sailing resort and one of the most charming villages in West Sussex. It's 6.5km (4 miles) west of Chichester on the A259, and there's a good bus service between the two towns. Bosham was the site where Christianity was first established on the Sussex coast. The Danish king, Canute, made it one of the seats of his North Sea empire, and it was the home of a manor (now gone) of the last of England's Saxon kings. Harold sailed from here to France on a journey that finally culminated in the invasion of England by William the Conqueror in 1066.

Bosham's little **church** was depicted in the Bayeux Tapestry. Its graveyard overlooks the boats, and the church is filled with ship models and relics, showing the villagers' link to the sea. A daughter of King Canute is buried inside. Near the harbor, it is reached by a narrow lane.

Theater reservations made over the telephone will be held for a maximum of 4 days (call ☎ **01243/781312;** www.cft.org.uk). Season ticket prices range from £9 to £30 ($17–$56).

A RACE TRACK

One of the most famous sports-car-racing courses in the world, **Goodwood Motor Circuit** (☎ **01243/755060;** www.goodwood.co.uk), reopened in 1998 near Chichester, restored to its look of 50 years ago. The course became dangerous for faster cars and was retired as an active track in the 1960s, as the 4km (2½-mile) circuit was never modernized. Now, that is part of its charm, offering a chance to relive the days when courageous drivers raced Jaguars or Ferraris on tracks enveloped by cornfields and hay bales. The course is now used for special exhibition races featuring historic sports cars from the '50s and '60s. The track can be reached by taking the A3 to Milford and the A283 to Petwork, then the A285 to Halnaker, following the signposts from there. Call to see if any exhibitions are being staged during your visit to the area.

Roman Palace   This is what remains of the largest Roman residence yet discovered in Britain. Built around A.D. 75 in villa style, it has many mosaic-floored rooms and even an under-floor heating system. The gardens have been restored to their original 1st-century plan. The story of the site is told both by an audiovisual program and by text in the museum. Guided tours are offered twice a day. (See what an archaeological dig in July 1996 unearthed.)

North of A259, off Salthill Rd. (signposted from Fishbourne; 2.5km/1½ miles from Chichester). ☎ **01243/785859.** Admission £5.20 ($9.60) adults, £2.70 ($5) children, £13 ($25) family ticket. Mar–Oct daily 10am–5pm (to 6pm in Aug); Feb and Nov to mid-Dec daily 10am–4pm; closed mid-Dec to Jan. Buses stop regularly at the bottom of Salthill Rd., and the museum is within a 10-min. walk of British Rail's station at Fishbourne.

Weald & the Downland Open Air Museum   In the beautiful Sussex countryside, historic buildings, saved from destruction, are reconstructed on a 16-hectare (40-acre) downland site. The structures show the development of traditional building from medieval times to the 19th century, in the weald and downland area of southeast England. Exhibits include a Tudor market hall, a working water mill producing stone-ground flour, a blacksmith's forge, plumbers' and carpenters' workshops, a toll cottage, a charcoal burner's camp, and a 19th-century village school. A "new" reception area with shops and offices is set in Longport House, a 16th-century building rescued from the site of the Channel Tunnel.

At Singleton, 9.5km (6 miles) north of Chichester on A286 (the London Rd.). ℂ **01243/811363.** www. wealddown.co.uk. Admission £7 ($13) adults, £6.50 ($12) seniors, £4 ($7.40) students and children 5–15, family ticket £19 ($35). Mar–Oct daily 10:30am–6pm; Nov–Feb Sat–Sun 10:30am–4pm. Bus no. 60 from Chichester.

WHERE TO STAY IN THE AREA

Forge Hotel *(Finds)* This is a typical 17th-century brick and flint cottage set on well-landscaped grounds with the South Downs Way only a short distance to the north. The cottage has been meticulously restored, with beautiful interiors of tasteful decoration and homelike touches such as fresh flowers and mineral water. Each bedroom comes with a private bathroom with shower. You'll have to negotiate steep stairs to some of the rooms, but one ground-floor room is suitable for those with mobility impairments. The owner Neil Rusbridger is also a chef, preparing "house party" menus. Smoking is permitted only in the public areas, not in the bedrooms.

Chilgrove, Chicester, W. Sussex PO1B 9HX. ℂ **01243/535333.** Fax 01243/535363. www.forgehotel.com. 4 units. £69 ($128) double. Rate includes breakfast. AE, MC, V. **Amenities:** Restaurant; bar; limited room service. *In room:* TV, hair dryer.

Marriott Goodwood Park Hotel & Country Club This is the most upmarket hotel in the area. Goodwood House was the home to the dukes of Richmond for more than 300 years. The hotel now located on these grounds was built in the 1786 style of the original Goodwood House. Bedrooms have been refurbished and upgraded, and easily qualify as the best in the area. Some of the rooms open onto panoramic views, and 66 accommodations are set aside for nonsmokers. Each bathroom is equipped with an efficient shower bathroom.

Goodwood, Chichester PO18 0QB. ℂ **01243/775537.** Fax 01243/520120. www.marriott.com. 94 units. £75–£201 ($139–$372) double; £221 ($409) suite. Rates include breakfast. AE, DC, MC, V. **Amenities:** 2 restaurants; 3 bars; indoor heated pool; 18-hole golf course; 2 outdoor tennis courts; health club with sauna; Jacuzzi; concierge; 24-hr. room service; babysitting; laundry service; dry cleaning; rooms for those with limited mobility. *In room:* TV, dataport, minibar, coffeemaker, hair dryer, iron/ironing board, safe, trouser press.

Millstream Hotel Bosham Lane The Millstream, built in the 1700s to provide food and accommodation for travelers through Sussex from other parts of England, is 8km (5 miles) south of Chichester. The hotel is in the hamlet of Bosham, with its beautiful harbor. Behind a facade of weathered yellow bricks, the hotel exudes a sense of history. The rooms, modern in style, have recently been redecorated and upgraded. All bathrooms contain shower-tub combinations.

Bosham Line, Chichester, W. Sussex PO18 8HL. ℂ **01243/573234.** Fax 01243/573459. www.millstream-hotel.co.uk. 35 units. £129–£149 ($239–$276) double; £179–£199 ($331–$368) suite. Rates include English breakfast. Double room and half board available (2 nights stay minimum) £146 ($270) weekdays, £164 ($303) Sat–Sun. AE, DC, MC, V. Bus: Bosham bus from Chichester. Take the road to the village of Bosham and its harbor, off A27. **Amenities:** Restaurant; bar; 24-hr. room service; babysitting; laundry service; dry cleaning; nonsmoking rooms; rooms for those with limited mobility. *In room:* TV, dataport, minibar, coffeemaker, hair dryer, iron, safe, trouser press.

Ship Hotel A classic Georgian building, the Ship is only a few minutes' walk from Chichester Cathedral, Chichester Festival Theatre, and many fine antiques shops. Built as a private house in 1790 for Admiral Sir George Murray, it retains an air of elegance and comfort. A grand staircase leads from its main entrance to the bedrooms, which are named after historic ships. All of the rooms have bathrooms with shower-tub combinations and have recently been refurbished. Some rooms have four-poster beds; others are specially designated for families.

North St., Chichester, W. Sussex PO19 1NH. © 01243/778000. Fax 01243/788000. www.shiphotel.com. 38 units. £79–£99 ($146–$183) double. Rates include English breakfast. AE, DC, MC, V. **Amenities:** Restaurant; bar; lounge; limited room service; laundry service; dry cleaning; nonsmoking rooms. *In room:* TV, dataport, coffeemaker, hair dryer, iron, trouser press.

The Spread Eagle Hotel 🏰🏰 *(Finds)* This 1430 inn, and the market town of Midhurst, are so steeped in history that the room you sleep in and the pavement you walk on probably have a thousand tales to tell. The rooms here are medieval in character, with beams, small mullioned windows, and unexpected corners. The most elegant have four-poster antique beds, fireplaces, and 500-year-old wall paneling. Most rooms have a shower-and-tub combination; the four rooms in the Market House annex across from the main hotel have showers only. The eagle in the lounge is the actual one from the back of Hermann Göring's chair in the Reichstag. It was acquired for its apt illustration of the hotel's name.

South St., Midhurst, W. Sussex GU29 9NH. © 01730/816911. Fax 01730/815668. www.hshotels.co.uk. 39 units. £135–£225 ($250–$416) double; £225 ($416) suite. Rates include English breakfast. AE, DC, MC, V. Midhurst bus from Chichester. **Amenities:** Restaurant; bar; indoor heated pool; health spa with sauna and steam room; gym; salon; 24-hr. room service; laundry service; dry cleaning; nonsmoking rooms. *In room:* TV, dataport, coffeemaker, hair dryer.

WHERE TO DINE IN THE AREA

Comme ça 🏰 FRENCH This is the best French restaurant in town—in fact, the best restaurant, period. The unpretentious decor blends old Victorian and Edwardian prints with objets d'art. The theme continues in the new garden room leading through French doors to an enclosed patio and garden. In summer, you'll want to dine out here, although in winter, a log fire in the inglenook fireplace welcomes you to the bar. Try delights of the field or river, such as baked fresh Scottish salmon or seared Scottish scallops with prawns, fresh mussels cooked with cider, shallots and cream; and roasted boneless rack of lamb scented with rosemary. Only the finest-quality ingredients are used. All menus have vegetarian dishes, and special dietary requirements can also be catered to.

67 Broyle Rd. (a 10-min. walk from the town center). © 01243/788724. Reservations required. Main courses £13–£15 ($24–$28); fixed-price 2-course lunch £17 ($31); fixed-price 3-course lunch £20 ($37). MC, V. Tues–Sun 12:15–2pm; Tues–Sat 6–9:30pm.

White Horse ENGLISH/FRENCH The wine cellar at this informally elegant country restaurant is one of the most comprehensive in Britain, partly because of the careful attention the owners pay to the details of their 18th-century inn, whose patina has been burnished every day since it was built in 1765. The menu is heavy on local game in season, bought from people known by the owners. Menu choices include roast breast of pheasant on a bed of celeriac purée, and roast lamb in a reduced sauce.

1 High St., Chilgrove. © 01243/535219. Reservations required on weekends. Main courses £9.50–£25 ($18–$46). AE, MC, V. Tues–Sun noon–2pm and 7–10pm. Closed Dec 25–26. Head 10km (6½ miles) north of Chichester on B2141 to Petersfield.

9 Arundel Castle 🏰🏰

34km (21 miles) W of Brighton; 93km (58 miles) SW of London

The small town of Arundel in West Sussex nestles at the foot of one of England's most spectacular castles. Without the castle, it would be just another English market town. The town was once an Arun River port, and its residents enjoyed the prosperity of considerable trade and commerce. Today, however, the harbor traffic has been replaced with buses filled with tourists.

ESSENTIALS

GETTING THERE   Trains leave hourly during the day from London's Victoria Station. The trip takes 1¼ hours. For rail information, call © **0845/748-4950** or visit www.railtrack.co.uk.

Most bus connections are through Littlehampton, opening onto the English Channel west of Brighton. From Littlehampton, you can leave the coastal road by taking bus no. 702 (run by Stagecoach Coastline), which runs between Littlehampton and Arundel every 30 minutes (6:20am–7:45pm) during the day. If you're dependent on public transportation, the Tourist Information Centre (see below) keeps an update on the possibilities.

If you're driving from London, follow the signs to Gatwick Airport, and from there head south toward the coast along the A29.

VISITOR INFORMATION   The **Tourist Information Centre,** 61 High St. (© **01903/882268**), is open from April to October, daily from 9am to 6pm and on weekends from 10am to 5pm; off season daily from 10am to 4pm.

SEEING THE SIGHTS

Arundel Castle ⋒⋒   The ancestral home of the dukes of Norfolk, Arundel Castle is a much-restored mansion of considerable importance. Its legend is associated with some of the great families of England—the Fitzalans and the powerful Howards of Norfolk. This castle received worldwide exposure when it was chosen as the backdrop for *The Madness of King George* (it was "pretending" to be Windsor Castle in the film).

Arundel Castle has suffered destruction over the years, particularly during the civil war, when Cromwell's troops stormed its walls, perhaps in retaliation for the 14th earl of Arundel's (Thomas Howard) sizable contribution to Charles I. In the early 18th century, the castle had to be virtually rebuilt, and in late Victorian times it was remodeled and extensively restored again. Today it's filled with a valuable collection of antiques, along with an assortment of paintings by old masters, such as Van Dyck and Gainsborough.

Surrounding the castle, in the center off High Street, is a 445-hectare (1,100-acre) park whose scenic highlight is Swanbourne Lake.

On Mill Rd. © **01903/883136.** www.arundelcastle.org. Admission £9.50 ($18) adults, £7.50 ($14) students and seniors, £6 ($11) children 5–16, free for children 4 and under. Family ticket £25 ($45). Apr–Oct Sun–Fri noon–5pm. Last admission 4pm. Closed Nov–Mar.

Arundel Cathedral   A Roman Catholic cathedral, the Cathedral of Our Lady and St. Philip Howard stands at the highest point in town. A. J. Hansom, inventor of the Hansom taxi, built it for the 15th duke of Norfolk. However, it was not consecrated as a cathedral until 1965. The interior includes the shrine of St. Philip Howard, featuring Sussex wrought-iron work.

On the street level, adjacent to rooms housing the tourist information office, is the **Heritage of Arundel Museum.** It displays memorabilia, antique costumes, and historic documents relating to the history of Arundel and its famous castle.

London Rd. © **01903/882297.** www.arundelcathedral.org. Free admission, but donations appreciated. Daily 9:30am–dusk. From the town center, continue west from High St.

WHERE TO STAY IN THE AREA

Amberley Castle Hotel ⋒⋒ *Finds*   The best place for food and lodging is near the village of Amberley. Joy and Martin Cummings offer accommodations in a 14th-century castle with sections dating from the 12th century. Elizabeth I held the lease on this castle from 1588 to 1603, and Cromwell's forces attacked it during the civil war. Charles II visited the castle on two occasions. Each of the sumptuous rooms, all doubles, is named after a castle in Sussex; each has a generously sized private Jacuzzi bathroom with luxury toiletries and bathrobes. All rooms also have a video library. Bedrooms are the ultimate in English country-house luxury; you can choose from four-poster, twin four-poster, or brass double beds. *Note:* this hotel is a member of Relais & Châteaux.

Amberley, near Arundel, W. Sussex BN18 9ND. © 01798/831992. Fax 01798/831998. www.amberleycastle. co.uk. 19 units. £170 ($315) double, £295–£340 ($546–$629) suite. AE, DC, MC, V. Take B2139 north of Arundel; the hotel is 2.5km (1½ miles) southwest of Amberley. **Amenities:** 2 restaurants; bike rental; 24-hr. room service; concierge; 18-hole golf course; outdoor tennis court; massage; dry cleaning; nonsmoking rooms. *In room:* TV/VCR, dataport, minibar, coffeemaker, hair dryer, trouser press.

Hilton Avisford Park ⚑ This is not your usual Hilton. Set in 36 hectares (89 acres) of gardens and lovely parkland, it opens onto England's South Downs. Once it was the home of Baronet Montagu, admiral and friend of Lord Nelson. Now successfully converted into a hotel, it is completely modernized but still keeps some of the allure of its original construction. Bedrooms come in a range of styles, sizes, and designs, and are handsomely laid out each with a tiled bathroom with shower and tub. The hotel is also the best equipped in the area, especially if sports are part of your vacation. There is a first-class restaurant on-site.

Yapton Lane, Walberton, Arundel, W. Sussex BN18 9JJ. © 01243/551215. Fax 01243/552485. www.arundel. hilton.com. 139 units. Summer £210–£230 ($389–$426) double, £260 ($481) suite. Off season £108–£128 ($200–$237) double, £158 ($292) suite. Lies 4.8km (3 miles) west of Arundel on B2132 (off A27). **Amenities:** Restaurant; bar; indoor heated pool; golf course; tennis court; fitness room; business center; 24-hr. room service; babysitting; laundry/valet; nonsmoking rooms; 1 room for those with limited mobility. *In room:* TV w/pay movies, dataport, fridge, hair dryer, iron/ironing board.

Norfolk Arms A former coaching inn, the Norfolk Arms is on the main street just a short walk from the castle. It's the best place to stay if you want to be in the market town itself. The lounges and dining room are in the typically English country-inn style. The hotel has been restored with many modern amenities blending with the old architecture. The bedrooms are handsomely maintained and furnished, each with personal touches. Rooms vary considerably in size, from small to spacious. Some rooms lie in a separate modern wing overlooking the courtyard. Four bedrooms are large enough for small families. Each unit comes with a small bathroom equipped with a shower-tub combination.

22 High St., Arundel, W. Sussex BN18 9AD. © 01903/882101. Fax 01903/884275. www.norfolkarmshotel. com. 34 units. £120–£130 ($222–$241) double. Children under 14 stay free when sharing room with two paying adults. Rates include breakfast. AE, DC, MC, V. **Amenities:** Restaurant; 2 bars; limited room service; laundry service; dry cleaning; nonsmoking rooms. *In room:* TV, coffeemaker, hair dryer, trouser press.

Portreeves Acre This modern, two-story house built by a local architect lies within a stone's throw of the ancient castle and rail station. Today the glass-and-brick edifice is the property of Charles and Pat Rogers. Double guest rooms are on the ground floor and have views of the flowering acre in back. Each bedroom is well organized and includes a small bathroom with a shower stall. The property is bordered on one side by the River Arun.

2 Causeway, Arundel, W. Sussex BN18 9JJ. © 01903/883277. 3 units. £50 ($93) double. Rates include English breakfast. No credit cards. *In room:* TV, coffeemaker.

WHERE TO DINE
China Palace BEIJING/SZECHUAN The most prominent Chinese restaurant in the region, it has an elaborately carved 17th-century ceiling imported by a former owner from a palace in Italy. Interior decorations include the artfully

draped sails from a Chinese junk. It's located across the road from the crenellated fortifications surrounding Arundel's castle. The Beijing and Szechuan cuisine includes such classic dishes as Peking duck, king prawns Kung Pao, and lobster with fresh ginger and spring onions.

67 High St. ℂ **01903/883702.** Reservations recommended on weekends. Main courses £7–£8 ($13–$15); fixed-price 3-course dinner for two £37 ($68). AE, MC, V. Daily noon–2:15pm and 6pm–midnight.

Queens Room Restaurant ★★ ENGLISH/CONTINENTAL   No contest: The best cuisine around Arundel is served at the Amberley Castle Hotel (see above). The chef has raided England's culinary past for inspiration but gives his dishes modern interpretations. We especially admire his use of natural ingredients from the area—wild Southdown rabbit, lavender, lemon thyme, and nettles. The menu changes frequently, though the special menu of the day is always alluring. The gourmet Castle Cuisine menu is worth driving across Sussex to enjoy. One recent menu included poached halibut with smoky soy broth and roasted guinea fowl with sweet potato fondant. The intermediate course was a quince-and-gin water-rice. (Where else can you find that?) Desserts such as a warm gratin of orange and dark chocolate with Grand Marnier sabayon make a perfect finish. The staff is attentive and friendly, yet warmly informal, and there's a well-chosen wine list.

In the Amberley Castle Hotel, Amberley, near Arundel. ℂ **01798/831992.** Reservations required. 3-course fixed-price dinner £36–£45 ($67–$83); 2-course lunch £16 ($30). AE, DC, MC, V. Daily noon–2pm and 7–9:30pm.

10 Brighton: London by the Sea ★★

84km (52 miles) S of London

Brighton was one of the first of the great seaside resorts of Europe. The Prince of Wales (later George IV), the original swinger who was to shape so much of its destiny, arrived in 1783; his presence and patronage gave it immediate status.

Fashionable dandies from London, including Beau Brummell, turned up. The construction business boomed as Brighton blossomed with charming and attractive town houses and well-planned squares and crescents. From the Prince Regent's title came the voguish word *Regency,* which was to characterize an era, but more specifically refers to the period between 1811 and 1820. Under Victoria, and despite the fact that she cut off her presence, Brighton continued to flourish.

But earlier in this century, as the English began to discover more glamorous spots on the Continent, Brighton lost much of its old joie de vivre. People began to call it "tatty," and it began to feature the usual run of fun-fair-type English seaside amusements. However, that state of affairs changed long ago, owing largely to the huge number of Londoners who moved in (some of whom now commute); the invasion has made Brighton increasingly lighthearted and sophisticated today. It now attracts a fair number of gay vacationers, and a beach east of town has been set aside for nude bathers (Britain's first such venture).

ESSENTIALS
GETTING THERE   Fast trains (41 a day) leave from Victoria or London Bridge Station, making the trip in 55 minutes. For rail information, call ℂ **0845/748-4950** or visit www.railtrack.co.uk. Buses from London's Victoria Coach Station take about 2 hours.

If you're driving, the M23 (signposted from central London) leads to the A23, which takes you into Brighton.

VISITOR INFORMATION   At the **Tourist Information Centre,** 10 Bartholomews Sq. (ℂ **0906/711-2255;** www.visitbrighton.com) opposite the

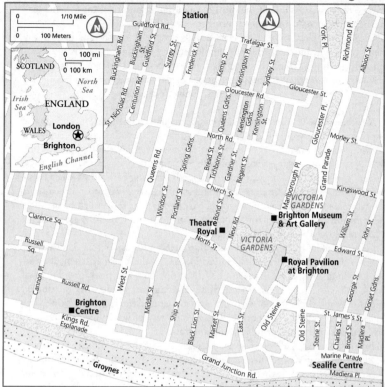

town hall, you can make hotel reservations, reserve tickets for National Express coaches, and pick up a list of current events. This phone number can be called only within the U.K. and costs 50p (80¢) per minute), It's open Monday through Friday from 9am to 5pm and Saturday from 10am to 4pm; from March to October also on Sundays from 10am to 4pm.

GETTING AROUND **Brighton & Hove Bus and Coach Company** serves both Brighton and Hove with frequent and efficient service. Local fares are only £1.20 ($2.20), and free maps of the company's routes are available at the Tourist Information Centre (see above). You can also call the company directly at **01273/886200** or visit www.buses.co.uk.

SPECIAL EVENTS If you're here in May, the international **Brighton Festival** (© **01273/709709;** www.brighton-festival.org.uk), the largest arts festival in England, features drama, literature, visual art, dance, and concerts ranging from classical to rock. A festival program is available annually in February for those who want to plan ahead.

THE ROYAL PAVILION

The Royal Pavilion at Brighton ★★★ Among royal residences in Europe, the Royal Pavilion at Brighton, a John Nash version of an Indian Moghul's palace, is unique. Ornate and exotic, it has been subjected over the years to the most devastating wit of English satirists and pundits, but today we can examine it more objectively as one of the most outstanding examples of the oriental tendencies of England's romantic movement.

Originally a farmhouse, a neoclassical villa was built on the site in 1787 by Henry Holland, but it no more resembled its present appearance than a caterpillar does a butterfly. By the time Nash had transformed it from a simple classical villa into an oriental fantasy, the prince regent had become King George IV, and the king and one of his mistresses, Lady Conyngham, lived in the palace until 1827.

A decade passed before Victoria, then queen, arrived in Brighton. Though she was to bring Albert and the children on a number of occasions, the monarch and Brighton just didn't mix. The very air of the resort seemed too flippant for her. By 1845, Victoria began packing, and the royal furniture was carted off. Its royal owners gone, the Pavilion was in serious peril of being torn down when, by a narrow vote, Brightonians agreed to purchase it. Gradually it was restored to its former splendor, enhanced in no small part by the return of much of its original furniture, including many items on loan from the Queen. A new exhibit tours the Royal Pavilion Gardens.

Of exceptional interest is the domed **Banqueting Room,** with a chandelier of bronze dragons supporting lilylike glass globes. In the Great Kitchen, with its old revolving spits, is a collection of Wellington's pots and pans from his town house at Hyde Park Corner. In the **State Apartments,** particularly the domed salon, dragons wink at you, serpents entwine, and lacquered doors shine. The Music Room, with its scalloped ceiling, is a fantasy of water lilies, flying dragons, reptilian paintings, bamboo, silk, and satin.

In the first-floor gallery, look for Nash's views of the Pavilion in its elegant heyday. Other attractions include **Queen Victoria's Apartments,** beautifully recreated, and the impressively restored **South Galleries,** breakfast rooms for George IV's guests. Refreshments are available in the Queen Adelaide Tea Room, which has a balcony overlooking the Royal Pavilion Gardens.

Ⓒ 01273/290900. www.royalpavilion.org.uk. Admission £5.80 ($11) adults, £4 ($7.40) students and seniors, £3.40 ($6.30) children ages 5–15, £15 ($28) family ticket, free for children 5 and under. Apr–Sept daily 9:30am–5:45pm; Oct–Mar daily 10am–5:15pm. Closed Dec 25–26.

OTHER ATTRACTIONS

Brighton Museum & Art Gallery ⚐   After a £10 million redevelopment, one of the great cultural attractions in the southeast of England has opened. In Victorian buildings opposite the Royal Pavilion, the museum is devoted to an eclectic collection of world art and artifacts, ranging from Salvador Dalí's "Mae West's Lips Sofa" to costumes worn at King George IV's coronation in 1821. Employing all the latest museum interpretative techniques, the museum is one of the most user-friendly outside London. The central gallery displays 20th-century decorative art, including furniture by Philippe Starck, works by Lalique and Bugatti, and a host of other luminaries. You'll see everything from Henry Willett's collection of 2,000 pieces of innovative porcelain to Shiro Kuramata's "How High the Moon Chair" from 1986 (it was inspired by the Duke Ellington jazz standard). The "Fashion & Style" Gallery draws upon Brighton's extensive collections of period costumes. In the museum's World Art Collection, you'll find some 15,000 objects collected from the Americas, Africa, Asia, and the Pacific, ranging from Vietnamese water puppets to a black basalt George Washington bust by Wedgwood.

Royal Pavilion Gardens. Ⓒ 01273/290900. www.brighton.virtualmuseum.info. Free admission. Tues 10am–7pm; Wed–Sat 10am–5pm; Sun 2–5pm.

SEASIDE AMUSEMENTS & ACTIVE PURSUITS

The beaches at Brighton aren't sandy; they're pebbly, and unfortunately, the waters are polluted. So instead of swimming, most visitors sunbathe, promenade along the boardwalk, play video arcade games, drink in local pubs and "caffs," and generally enjoy the sea air. Beachfront areas are more for the promenade crowd, which often consists of gay men and women.

Brighton is also the site of Britain's first officially designed clothing-optional beach, located a short walk west of the Brighton Marina. Local signs refer to it simply as "Nudist Beach." Telescombe Beach, mostly frequented by gay men and lesbians, lies 7km (4½ miles) to the east of the Palace Pier.

You can't miss the **Brighton Pier,** a Victorian iron structure jutting seaward toward France. Built between 1889 and 1899 and renovated during the early 1990s, it's lined with somewhat tacky concessions and a late-night crowd that's a bit more sinister than the one that frequents it during the day.

If you want to rent or charter a boat, stop by the Brighton Marina, at the intersection of the A259 and King's Cliff Parade (© **01483/417782**). There's good fishing at the marina as well, but the breakwaters near Hove may be better because there aren't as many boats or swimmers in that area.

One of the best and most challenging 18-hole golf courses around is the **East Brighton Golf Club,** Roedean Road (© **01273/604838**). A less challenging 18-hole course is the **Hollingbury Park Golf Club,** Ditchling Road (© **01273/552010**). Buses from the **Old Steine** are available to both courses.

An indoor pool, diving pool, learner's pool, solarium, and water slide are all available daily at the **Prince Regent Swimming Complex,** Church St. (© **01273/685692**).

If you enjoy wagering on the horses, the **Brighton Races** are held frequently between April and October at the **Brighton Racecourse,** Race Hill (© **01273/603580**). An admission fee of £11 to £16 ($20–$30) is charged.

SHOPPING

Mall rats head for **Churchill Square,** Brighton's spacious shopping center, which has major chain stores. The shopping center runs from Western Road to North Street (about 3km/2 miles long) and offers many inexpensive shops and stalls with great buys on everything from antiques to woolens. On Saturdays, there are many more antique exhibits and sidewalk stalls. Open Monday to Saturday 9am to 7pm and Sun 11am to 5pm.

Regent Arcade, which is located between East Street, Bartholomew Square, and Market Street, sells artwork, jewelry, and other gift items, as well as high-fashion clothing.

Everyone raves about the shopping on **The Lanes,** though you may find them too quaint. The Lanes are a close-knit section of alleyways off North Street in Brighton's Old Town; many of the present shops were formerly fishers' cottages. The shopping is mostly for tourists, and while you may fall for a few photo ops, you'll find that the nearby **North Laine**—between The Lanes and the train station—is the area for up-and-coming talent and for alternative retail. Just wander along a street called Kensington Gardens to get the whole effect. Innumerable shops are located in The Lanes that carry antique books and jewelry, and many boutiques are found in converted backyards on Duke Lane just off Ship Street. In the center of The Lanes is Brighton Square, which is ideal for relaxing or people-watching near the fountain on one of the benches or from a cafe-bar.

Brighton has a good **flea market** in the parking lot of the train station. It's open Monday to Saturday 10am to 5:30pm and Sunday 10:30am to 5pm. On the first Tuesday of each month, there's the **Brighton Racecourse Antiques and Collectors Fair** (9am–3pm) with about 300 stalls.

The **Brighton Marina** has many stores to visit. **Leave It to Jeeves** (© 01273/818585) has old photographs of the local area, illustrations, prints, and a complete framing service.

In addition to its malls and shopping complexes, Brighton also abounds in specialty shops. One of our favorites is the finest gift shop in Brighton, **The Pavilion Shop,** 4–5 Pavilion Guildings, Brighton (© 01273/292792), next to The Royal Pavilion. You can purchase gift and home-furnishing items in the style of design schools that created the look (from Regency to Victorian) at The Royal Pavilion. Books, jams, needlepoint kits, notebooks, pencils, stencil kits, and other souvenirs are also available. Latest British designers for women are showcased at a fashionable store, **Pussy,** 3A Kensington Gardens (© 01273/604861).

WHERE TO STAY

Gay travelers should refer to "Brighton's Gay Scene," later in this section, for a selection of gay-friendly accommodations.

VERY EXPENSIVE

The Grand ⭒⭒⭒   Brighton's premier hotel, the original Grand was constructed in 1864 and entertained some of the most eminent Victorians and Edwardians. This landmark was massively damaged in a 1984 terrorist attack directed at Margaret Thatcher and other key figures in the British government. Mrs. Thatcher narrowly escaped, though several of her colleagues were killed; entire sections of the hotel looked as if they had been hit by an air raid. The incident gave the present owners, De Vere Hotels, the challenge to create a new Grand, and frankly, the new one is better than the old. It's the most elegant Georgian re-creation in town.

You enter via a glassed-in conservatory and register in a grandiose public room, with soaring ceilings and elaborate moldings. The rooms, of a very high standard, are generally spacious with many extras, including hospitality trays and Sony PlayStations. The sea-view rooms have minibars, and new beds and furniture; the deluxe rooms offer separate sitting rooms and views of the English Channel. "Romantic rooms" offer double whirlpool baths, and some rooms are equipped with additional facilities for travelers with disabilities. All standard rooms have been refurbished with new bathrooms.

Kings Rd., Brighton, E. Sussex BN1 1FW. © 01273/224300. Fax 01273/224321. www.grandbrighton.co.uk. 200 units. £240–£345 ($444–$638) double; from £650 ($1,203) suite. Rates include English breakfast. AE, DC, MC, V. Parking £14 ($26). Bus: 1, 2, or 3. **Amenities:** Restaurant; bar; indoor heated pool and Jacuzzi; gym; spa with sauna; salon; 24-hr. room service; babysitting; laundry service; dry cleaning; nonsmoking rooms; rooms for those with limited mobility. *In room:* TV, dataport, minibar, coffeemaker, hair dryer, safe, trouser press.

EXPENSIVE

Hilton Brighton Metropole ⭒   Originally built in 1889, with a handful of its rooms housed in a postwar addition, the Brighton Metropole is the largest hotel in Brighton and one of the city's top three or four hotels (though not as grand as the Grand). This hotel, with a central seafront location, often hosts big conferences. The recently refurbished rooms are comfortable and generous in size with roomy sitting areas. The spacious bathrooms include faux marble vanities and tub-and-shower combos. Each room has a Sony PlayStation game console.

106 King's Rd., Brighton, E. Sussex BN1 2FU. © 01273/775432. Fax 01273/207764. www.hilton.co.uk/brightonmet. 334 units. £152–£232 ($281–$429) double. Rates include English breakfast. AE, DC, MC, V. Parking £7.50 ($14). Bus: 1, 2, or 3. **Amenities:** Restaurant; bar; indoor heated pool; spa; 24-hr. room service; gym; babysitting; laundry service; dry cleaning; nonsmoking rooms; rooms for those with limited mobility. *In room:* TV, dataport, minibar (in suites), coffeemaker, hair dryer, trouser press.

Thistle Brighton 🌟🌟   This relatively modern hotel is one of the finest in the south of England, topped in Brighton only by the Grand. Rising from the seafront, just minutes from the Royal Pavilion, it has been luxuriously designed for maximum comfort. Rooms tend to be large but are often blandly decorated in a sort of international modern style. Each is exceptionally comfortable, with small sitting areas and long desks. Tile bathrooms come with shower-tub combinations, deluxe toiletries, and even rubber ducks to play with in your bath.

King's Rd., Brighton, E. Sussex BN1 2GS. ℂ **01273/206700.** Fax 01273/820692. www.thistlehotels.com. 208 units. £125–£240 ($231–$444) double; £210–£314 ($389–$581) suite. Children under 17 stay free in parent's room. AE, DC, MC, V. Bus: 1, 2, or 3. **Amenities:** Restaurant; 2 bars; indoor heated pool; health club with spa; 24-hr. room service; babysitting; laundry service; dry cleaning; nonsmoking rooms; rooms for those with limited mobility. In room: A/C, TV, dataport, minibar, coffeemaker, hair dryer, iron/ironing board, safe, trouser press.

MODERATE

Blanch House 🌟 *Finds*   Is it a hotel or is it theater? This small hotel in a restored Georgian building is known for its very theatrical theme rooms, ranging from Moroccan to "Snowstorm" to our favorite "The Decadence Suite." For those who got off on the movie of the same name, there is always "Boogie Nights." Either queen- or king-size beds have been installed, and each accommodation comes with a well-maintained private bathroom with shower. The bar is one of the hippest in Brighton where the competition is severe, and the on-site restaurant is a gastronomic delight with such offerings as seared pigeon breast with grilled salsify and butternut squash and a fresh pea and mint risotto with honeyed parsnip "pearls."

17 Atlingworth St., Brighton, E. Sussex BN2 1PL. ℂ **01273/603504.** Fax 01273/689813. www.blanchhouse. co.uk. 12 units. £125–£150 ($231–$278) double; £250 ($463) suite. Rates include breakfast. MC, V. **Amenities:** Restaurant; bar. In room: TV, coffeemaker, hair dryer, iron/ironing board.

Nineteen 🌟 *Finds*   Only a few minutes' walk from the beach, this rather stunning urban hotel lies close to the Brighton Pier. It's located in Kemptown, a rapidly gentrified and up-and-coming section of Brighton. The hotel is an oasis of pure white, its bedrooms filled with works by contemporary local artists. This artwork is all that breaks the pure white, that and slatted silver blinds and glass beds illuminated by blue lighting. That same subtle blue lighting bathes the rooms in a lovely glow. Everything is as modern as tomorrow, including state-of-the-art bathrooms with tub and shower. Glass brick platforms support the comfortable beds. Guests are invited to make their own snacks in the cellar kitchen.

19 Broad St., Brighton, E. Sussex BN2 1TJ. ℂ **01273/675529.** Fax 01273/675531. www.hotelnineteen.co.uk. 8 units. £100–£180 ($185–$333) double. Rates include breakfast. Minimum of 2 nights required for weekend bookings. MC, V. **Amenities:** Breakfast room; bar; breakfast only room service; nonsmoking rooms. In room: TV, beverage maker, hair dryer.

Old Ship Hotel 🌟   First used as an inn in 1559, this hotel, a favorite among conference groups, is the largest and best of Brighton's middle-priced choices. The place is proud of its pedigree and was once the site of royal gatherings and society balls. Most of its structure dates from the 1880s; despite many subsequent modernizations, it retains a sense of its late Victorian origins. Nearly two-thirds of the rooms are nicely furnished, with modern bathrooms containing shower-tub combinations; the rest are still somewhat dowdy. The east wing has the most smartly furnished rooms. Brighton's oldest hotel, it has managed to stay abreast of the times in comfort. Prices drop if you stay for more than 1 night.

King's Rd., Brighton, E. Sussex BN1 1NR. ℂ **01273/329001.** Fax 01273/820718. www.paramount-hotels. co.uk. 152 units. £175 ($324) double; £300 ($555) suite. Children under 12 stay free in parent's rooms. Rates include English breakfast. AE, DC, MC, V. Parking £15 ($28). Bus: 1, 2, or 3. **Amenities:** Restaurant; bar;

24-hr. room service; babysitting; laundry service; dry cleaning; nonsmoking rooms. *In room:* TV, dataport, coffeemaker, hair dryer, iron/ironing board, safe, trouser press.

INEXPENSIVE

Paskins Hotel   This well-run ecofriendly hotel is a short walk from the Palace Pier and Royal Pavilion. Rates depend on plumbing and furnishings, the most expensive units fitted with four-poster beds. Bedrooms are individually decorated with contemporary styling. Bathrooms, compact but tidily maintained, have shower stalls. Recent upgrading has made this one of the more charming B&Bs in Brighton. A friendly, informal atmosphere prevails; the freshly cooked award-winning English breakfast (vegetarians are specially catered to), served in a cozy room, is one of the best in town.

19 Charlotte St., Brighton, E. Sussex BN2 1AG. © **01273/601203.** Fax 01273/621973. www.paskins.co.uk. 19 units, 16 with shower. £55–£80 ($102–$148) double without shower, £80–£100 ($148–$185) double with shower, £130 ($241) double with 4-poster bed. Children 10 and under sharing with 2 adults are charged £10 ($19). Rates include English breakfast. AE, DC, MC, V. Bus: 7 or 52. **Amenities:** Lounge; breakfast room; limited room service. *In room:* TV, dataport, coffeemaker, hair dryer, iron/ironing board, trouser press.

Regency Hotel   This typical 1820 Regency town house, once the home of Jane, dowager duchess of Marlborough, and great-grandmother of Sir Winston Churchill, is a skillfully converted family managed hotel with licensed bar and modern comforts. Many rooms enjoy window views across the square and out to the sea. Bedrooms are nonsmoking, though you can smoke in the lounge bar. Rooms come in a variety of shapes and sizes, but each is well furnished with such extras as bedside radios. Bathrooms are small but adequate, each with a shower stall. The Regency Suite has a half-tester bed (1840) and antique furniture, along with a huge bow window dressed with ceiling-to-floor swagged curtains and a balcony facing the sea and West Pier. The Regency is only a few minutes' walk from the Conference Center and an hour by train or car from Gatwick Airport.

28 Regency Sq., Brighton, E. Sussex BN1 2FH. © **01273/202690.** Fax 01273/220438. www.regencybrighton. co.uk. 14 units, all with shower. £85–£95 ($157–$176) double; £150 ($278) Regency suite. Rates include English breakfast. AE, DC, MC, V. Parking £12 ($22). Bus: 1, 2, 3, 5, or 6. **Amenities:** Bar; lounge; breakfast only room service; laundry service. *In room:* TV, dataport, coffeemaker, hair dryer, iron.

Topps Hotel   This cream-colored hotel enjoys a diagonal view of the sea from its position beside the sloping lawn of Regency Square. Each room is differently shaped and individually furnished. In 2000, the owners began a gradual refurbishment of all bedrooms. Except for the singles, most rooms have a fireplace. All units have well-kept bathrooms with shower-tub combinations. Try for a unit with four-poster bed and private balcony opening to a view of the sea.

17 Regency Sq., Brighton, E. Sussex BN1 2FG. © **01273/729334.** Fax 01273/203679. toppshotel@aol.com. 15 units. £75–£84 ($139–$155) double. Rates include English breakfast. AE, DC, MC, V. Parking £9.20–£11 ($17–$19). Bus: 1, 2, 3, 5, or 6. **Amenities:** Limited room service; laundry service; nonsmoking rooms. *In room:* TV, minibar, coffeemaker, hair dryer, iron/ironing board, safe, trouser press.

IN NEARBY HOVE

The Dudley   Near the seafront in Hove, the Dudley is just a few blocks from the resort's bronze statue of Queen Victoria. Going up marble steps, you register within view of 18th-century antiques and oil portraits of Edwardian-era debutantes. The large, high-ceilinged public rooms emphasize the deeply comfortable chairs and the chandeliers. The bedrooms offer tall windows and conservatively stylish furniture. Bedrooms are usually midsize with walnut furnishings and brass lamps. Bathrooms are well appointed with a bidet, baths with marble basins, and heated towel racks. The hotel is currently renovating and upgrading some of its bedrooms and public areas.

Lansdowns Place, Hove, Brighton, E. Sussex BN3 1HQ. © **01273/736266.** Fax 01273/729802. www.thedudley hotel.co.uk. 72 units. £115 ($213) double. AE, DC, MC, V. Bus: 2 or 5. **Amenities:** Restaurant; bar; 24-hr. room service; babysitting; laundry service; dry cleaning; nonsmoking rooms; rooms for those with limited mobility. *In room:* TV, coffeemaker, hair dryer, iron/ironing board, trouser press.

Sackville Hotel   Its lime- and cream-colored neobaroque facade was built across the road from the beach in 1902, but today, in a comfortably updated form, the Sackville welcomes visitors with high-ceilinged bedrooms featuring big windows, sea views, and Queen Anne furnishings. Bedrooms range from small to spacious, all with a compact and tidily maintained bathroom with a shower stall. Eight units sport terraces.

189 Kingsway, Hove, Brighton, E. Sussex BN3 4GU. © **01273/736292.** Fax 01273/731598. 45 units. £90–£110 ($167–$204) double. AE, DC, MC, V. Bus: 1, 2, or 5. **Amenities:** Bar; nonsmoking rooms. *In room:* TV, coffeemaker, hair dryer, iron, safe, trouser press.

WHERE TO DINE

The **Mock Turtle Tea Shop,** 4 Pool Valley (© **01273/327380**), is a small but busy tearoom that has many locals stopping by to gossip and take their tea. They offer a variety of cakes, flapjacks, tea breads, and light, fluffy scones with homemade preserves. Everything is made fresh daily. The most popular item is the scones with strawberry preserves or whipped cream. They also serve a wide variety of good teas.

EXPENSIVE

China Garden BEIJING/CANTONESE   The menu at the China Garden is large and satisfying. It may not be ready for London, and it's certainly pricey, but it's the brightest in town, with many classic dishes deftly handled by the kitchen staff. Dim sum (a popular luncheon choice) is offered only until 4pm. Try crispy sliced pork Szechuan style, or Peking roast duck with pancakes.

88 Preston St. (in the town center off Western Rd.). © **01273/325124.** Reservations recommended. Main courses £18–£35 ($33–$65); fixed-price menus £18–£35 ($33–$65). AE, DC, MC, V. Mon–Tues noon–11pm; Wed–Sun noon–11:30pm. Closed Dec 25–26.

One Paston Place ✿ FRENCH   Mark (the chef) and Nicole Emmerson offer a wisely limited menu based on the freshest of ingredients available at the market. You may begin with a delectable almond-coated quail and parsnip pancake, then move on to a savory anchovy-studded sea bass with grilled stuffed squid and a lemon and basil couscous. Vegetarian dishes are available on request. For dessert, try the sumptuous almond and amaretto soufflé with apricot coulis.

1 Paston Place (near the waterfront off King's Cliff). © **01273/606933.** www.onepastonplace.co.uk. Reservations required. Main courses £21–£23 ($39–$43); fixed-price 2-course lunch £17 ($31); fixed-price 3-course lunch £21–£23 ($39–$43). AE, DC, MC, V. Tues–Sat 12:30–1:45pm and 7:30–9:45pm. Closed 3 weeks in Dec and Jan and 2 weeks in Aug.

MODERATE

English's Oyster Bar and Seafood Restaurant SEAFOOD   This popular seafood restaurant occupies a trio of very old fishermen's cottages. Owned and operated by the same family since the end of World War II, it sits in the center of town, near Brighton's bus station. For years, diners have enjoyed native oysters on the half shell, a hot seafood platter with hollandaise sauce and garlic butter, fried Dover sole, and fresh, locally caught plaice. The upstairs dining area incorporates murals depicting Edwardian dinner and theater scenes. In summer, guests can dine alfresco on the terrace.

29–31 East St. ☎ **01273/327980.** www.englishs.co.uk. Reservations recommended. Main courses £11–£20 ($20–$37); fixed-price 2-course menu £7.95 ($15). AE, DC, MC, V. Mon–Sat noon–9:30pm; Sun 12:30–9:30pm.

Redz ENGLISH   A longtime favorite, the Old Ship Hotel Restaurant, in the center of town, enjoys an ideal location on the waterfront. When possible, locally caught fish is on the menu, from Dover sole to pan-fried red bream filet. Try such dishes as Magret duck breast, served sliced with shallot and orange confit and juniper and red currant jus. Vegetables that accompany the main dishes are always fresh and cooked "new style." Sometimes local dishes such as turkey from Sussex appear on the menu, but with a French sauce. The wine list is excellent. Stop in the adjoining pub for a before- or after-dinner drink.

In the Old Ship Hotel, King's Rd. ☎ **01273/329001.** Reservations recommended. Main courses £8–£13 ($15–$24). AE, DC, MC, V. Daily noon–2pm and 6–9pm. Bus: 1, 2, or 3.

INEXPENSIVE

Brighton Rock Beach House ★ *Finds*   Brighton grows hipper and hipper, the latest rage being a take on a Cape Cod beach bar, the type that JFK Jr. might have dropped in on in days of yore. This gay-friendly spot was inspired by the U.S. travels of its owner, Neil Woodcock. At this light, spacious, and airy bar, drinks are consumed at a glass-topped bar covering sand, driftwood, shells, and pebbles. The lunch also has a New England spin. Savor those old favorites such as a creamy clam chowder, a Boston meatloaf, a vegetable hot pot, and—get this—a savory lobster cheesecake. For dessert, the chef leaves Cape Cod heading south for a Key lime pie. The bar even has its own transport cafe: an old Jeep parked outside with a table in the back where patrons can sit and sip their drinks.

6 Rock Place. ☎ **01273/601139.** Reservations not needed. Main courses £6–£12 ($11–$22). Mon–Sat noon–11pm; Sun noon–10:30pm.

Terre à Terre ★★ *Finds* VEGETARIAN/VEGAN   The finest vegetarian restaurant on the south coast of England, this is a truly outstanding choice even if you're a carnivore. You dine in a trio of spacious rooms in vivid colors, and everything has a bustling brasserie aura. Cooks roam the world for inspiration in the preparation of their delectable dishes. Sushi, couscous, pizza—it's all here and does it ever taste good, especially the selection of tapas. To give you an idea of what to expect, select as an appetizer a perfectly textured baked Spanish custard with a deliciously crisp and caramelized topping, adorned with a well-ripened passion fruit. Breads are Italian, and the house wine is organic French. Children's meals are available.

71 East St. ☎ **01273/729051.** Reservations recommended. Main courses £11–£13 ($20–$23). AE, DC, MC, V. Tues 6:30–10:30pm; Wed–Fri noon–3pm and 6:30–10:30pm; Sat–Sun noon–11pm.

BRIGHTON AFTER DARK

Brighton offers lots of entertainment options. You can find out what's happening by picking up the local entertainment monthly, the *Punter,* and by looking for *What's On,* a single sheet of weekly events posted throughout the town.

Two theaters offer drama throughout the year: the **Theatre Royal,** New Road (☎ 01273/328488), with pre-London shows; and the **Gardner Arts Centre** (☎ 01273/685861; www.gardnerarts.co.uk), a modern theater-in-the-round, located on the campus of Sussex University, a few miles northeast of town in Falmer. Bigger concerts are held at **Brighton Centre,** Russell Road (☎ 0870/ 900-9100; www.brightoncentre.co.uk), a 5,000-seat facility featuring mainly pop-music shows.

Nightclubs also abound. Cover charges range from free admission (most often on early or midweek nights) to £10 ($19), so call the clubs to find out about admission fees and updates in their nightly schedules, which often vary from week to week or season to season.

The smartly dressed can find their groove at **Steamers,** King's Road (℡ **01273/775775**), located in the Hilton Metropole Hotel, which insists on stylish casual attire. **Creation,** West Street (℡ **01273/321628**), is a popular club that features Gay Night once a month. **The Escape Club,** 10 Marine Parade (℡ **01273/606906**), home to both gay and straight dancers, has two floors for dancing, and offers different music styles on different nights of the week.

One of the best hunting grounds for dance clubs is **Kingswest,** a King's Road complex that houses two clubs featuring a blend of techno, house, and disco. **Event II** (℡ **01273/732627**) sports more than $1 million worth of lighting and dance-floor gadgetry.

Gloucester, Gloucester Plaza (℡ **01273/699068**), has a variety of music through the week, from '70s and '80s music to alternative and groove. For a change of pace, visit **Casablanca,** Middle Street (℡ **01273/321817**), which features jazz with an international flavor.

Pubs are a good place to kick off an evening, especially the **Colonnade Bar,** New Road (℡ **01273/328728**), serving drinks for over 100 years. The pub gets a lot of theater business because of its proximity to the Theatre Royal. **Cricketers,** Black Lion Street (℡ **01273/329472**), is worth a stop because it's Brighton's oldest pub, parts of which date from 1549. Drinking lures them to **Fortune of War,** 157 King's Rd. (℡ **01273/205065**).

H. J. O'Neils, 27 Ship St. (℡ **01273/827621**), is an authentic Irish pub located at the top of The Lanes. A stop here will fortify you with traditional Irish pub grub, a creamy pint of Guinness, and a soundtrack of folk music. Of course, they make the best Irish stew in town.

BRIGHTON'S GAY SCENE

After London, Brighton has the most active gay scene in England. Aside from vacationers, it's home to gay retirees and executives who commute into central London by train. The town has always had a reputation for tolerance and humor, and according to the jaded owners of some of the town's 20 or so gay bars, more drag queens live within the local Regency town houses than virtually anywhere else in England.

But the gay scene here is a lot less glittery than in London. And don't assume that the south of England is as chic as the south of France. Its international reputation is growing, but despite that, gay Brighton remains thoroughly English, and at times, even a bit dowdy.

GAY-FRIENDLY PLACES TO STAY

Brighton Court Craven Hotel   This three-story hotel isn't particularly exciting and doesn't have many facilities, but it's the cheapest option we recommend, and it has an atmosphere of casual permissiveness. It's proud of a clientele that's almost 100% gay and mostly male. Breakfasts are served communally, with all the traditional English accompaniments. Bedrooms are rather bare bones: You stay here for the camaraderie—not grand comfort.

2 Atlingworth St., Brighton BN2 1PL. ℡ **01273/607710.** 12 units, all with shower. Mon–Thurs £50 ($93) double; Fri–Sun £55 ($102) double. Rates include breakfast. MC, V. **Amenities:** Bar. *In room:* TV, coffeemaker.

Cowards Guest House   Originally built in 1807, this five-story Regency-era house is extremely well maintained. Inside, Jerry and his partner, Cyril (a cousin

Finds   A Side Trip to Kipling's Hometown

"Heaven looked after it in the dissolute times of mid-Victorian restoration and caused the vicar to send his bailiff to live in it for 40 years, and he lived in peaceful filth and left everything as he found it," wrote Rudyard Kipling.

He was writing of **Bateman's** 👥 (℡ **01435/882302**), the 17th-century ironmaster's house in the village of Burwash, on the A265, the Lewes–Etchingham road, some 43km (27 miles) northeast of Brighton, close to the border with Kent. Born in Bombay, India, in 1865, Kipling loved the countryside of Sussex, and the book that best expressed his feelings for the shire is *Puck of Pook's Hill,* written in 1906. The following year he won the Nobel Prize for literature. He lived at Bateman from 1902 until his death in 1936. His widow died 3 years later, leaving the house to the National Trust.

Kipling is known mainly for his adventure stories, such as *The Jungle Book* (1894) and *Captains Courageous* (1897). He is also remembered for his tales concerning India, including *Kim* (1901). He lived in America after his marriage to Caroline Balestier in 1892. But by 1896, he had returned to the south of England, occupying a house at Rottingdean, a little village on the Sussex Downs, 6.5km (4 miles) east of Brighton. Here he wrote the famous line: "What should they know of England who only England know?" In a steam-driven motorcar, Kipling and Caroline set out to explore Sussex, of which they were especially fond. Though the population of Rottingdean was only that of a small village, they decided at some point that it had become too crowded. In their motorcar one day, they spotted Bateman's, their final home. "It is a good and peaceable place standing in terraced lawns nigh to a walled garden of old red brick, and two fat-headed oasthouses with redbrick stomachs, and an aged silver-grey dovecot on top," Kipling wrote.

The Burwash city fathers invited Kipling to unveil a memorial to the slain of World War I, and he agreed. It's in the center of town at the church. Kipling said that visitors should "remember the sacrifice." Both the church and an inn across the way appear in the section of *Puck of Pook's Hill* called "Hal o' the Draft." The famous writer and son of Anglo-Indian parents died in London and was given an impressive funeral before burial in Poets' Corner at Westminster Abbey.

The interior of Bateman's is filled with Asian rugs, antique bronzes, and other mementos the writer collected in India and elsewhere. Kipling's library is quite interesting. The house and gardens are open April through October, Saturday through Wednesday from 11am to 5pm. Admission is £5.50 ($10) for adults, £2.70 ($5) for children.

of the late playwright and bon vivant Noël Coward), welcome only gay men of all degrees of flamboyance. Don't expect any frills in the conservative, standard rooms, like those you may find in any modern hotel in Britain. It offers very few extras, though a number of gay bars and watering holes lie nearby.

12 Upper Rock Gardens, Brighton BN2 1QE. ℡ **01273/692677**. 8 units, 2 with shower. £60–£70 ($111–$130) double. Rates include full English breakfast. MC, V. *In room:* TV, coffeemaker.

New Europe   Hands-down, this is the largest, busiest, and most fun gay hotel in Brighton. First, it's a bona fide hotel, not a B&B as most of Brighton's other gay-friendly lodgings are. Unlike many of its competitors, it welcomes women, though very few of them tend to be comfortable. Because of the high jinks and raucousness that can float up from the bars below, rooms can be noisy, but are nonetheless comfortable, clean, and unfrilly. All units have well-kept bathrooms with shower units. The staff is happy to camp it up for you before your arrival (adding balloons, champagne, flowers, and streamers), for a fee.

31–32 Marine Parade, Brighton BN2 1TR. (C) **01273/624462.** Fax 01273/624575. www.legendsbar.co.uk. 30 units. £60–£70 ($111–$130) double. Rates include breakfast. AE, DC, MC, V. **Amenities:** 2 bars. *In room:* TV, coffeemaker.

GAY NIGHTLIFE

A complete, up-to-date roster of the local gay bars is available in any copy of *G-Scene* magazine ((C) **01273/749947**), distributed free in gay hotels and bars throughout the south of England. See also "Brighton After Dark," above, for a few popular dance clubs.

Doctor Brighton's Bar, 16 Kings Rd., The Seafront ((C) **01273/328765**), is the largest and most consistently reliable choice. The staff expends great energy on welcoming all members of the gay community. In their words, "We get everyone from 18-year-old designer queens to 50-year-old leather queens, and they, along with all their friends and relatives, are welcome." Originally built around 1750, with a checkered past that includes stints as a smuggler's haven and an abortion clinic, it also has more history and more of the feel of an old-time Victorian pub than any of its competitors. It's open Monday through Saturday from noon to 11pm, and Sunday from noon to 10:30pm. With no real lesbian bar in town, gay women tend to congregate at Doctor Brighton's.

Two of the town's busiest and most flamboyant gay bars lie within the New Europe hotel (see above). The one with the longer hours is **Legends,** a pubby, clubby bar with a view of the sea that's open to the public daily from noon to 11pm and to residents of the New Europe and their guests until 5am. Legends features cross-dressing cabarets three times a week (Tues and Thurs at 9pm, Sun afternoons at 2:30pm), when tweedy-looking English matrons and diaphanous Edwardian vamps are portrayed with loads of tongue-in-cheek satire and humor. **Schwarz** is a cellar-level denim and leather joint that does everything it can to encourage its patrons to wear some kind of uniform. Schwarz is open only Friday and Saturday from 10pm to 2am and charges a £4 to £6 ($7.40–$11) cover.

The Marlborough, 4 Princes St. ((C) **01273/570028**), has been a staple on the scene for years. Set across from the Royal Pavilion, this Victorian-style pub has a cabaret theater on its second floor. It remains popular with the gay and, to a lesser degree, straight communities. A changing roster of lesbian performance art and both gay and straight cabaret within the second-floor theater is presented.

11 Alfriston ✦✦ & Lewes ✦

97km (60 miles) S of London

Nestled on the Cuckmere River, Alfriston is one of the most beautiful villages of England. It lies northeast of Seaford on the English Channel, near the resort of Eastbourne and the modern port of Newhaven. During the day, Alfriston is overrun by coach tours (it's that lovely and that popular). The High Street, with its old market cross, looks just like what you would always imagine a traditional

English village to be. Some of the old houses still have hidden chambers where smugglers stored their loot (alas, the loot is gone). There are also several old inns.

About a dozen miles away along the A27 toward Brighton is the rather somber market town of Lewes. (Thomas Paine lived at Bull House on High Street in what is now a restaurant.) Because the home of the Glyndebourne Opera is only 8km (5 miles) to the east, it's hard to find a place to stay, even in Lewes, during the renowned annual opera festival.

ESSENTIALS

GETTING THERE　Trains leave from London's Victoria Station and London Bridge Station for Lewes. One train per hour makes the 1¼-hour trip daily. Trains are more frequent during rush hours. For rail information, call © **0845/748-4950** or visit www.railtrack.co.uk. Alfriston has no rail service.

Buses run daily to Lewes from London's Victoria Coach Station, though the 3-hour trip has so many stops that it's better to take the train. Call © **0870/580-8080** for schedules or visit www.nationalexpress.com.

A bus runs from Lewes to Alfriston every 30 minutes. It's operated by **RDH (bus no. 125)** © **01273/890477.** For bus information and schedules in the area, call © **0870/608-2608.** The bus station at Lewes is on East Gate Street in the center of town.

If you're driving, head east along the M25 (the London ring road), cutting south on the A26 via East Grinstead to Lewes. Once at Lewes, follow the A27 east to the signposted turnoff for the village of Alfriston.

VISITOR INFORMATION　The **Tourist Information Centre** is in Lewes at 187 High St. (© **01273/483448**). In season, from Easter until the end of October, hours are Monday through Friday from 9am to 5pm, Saturday from 10am to 5pm, and Sunday from 10am to 2pm. Off-season hours are Monday through Friday from 9am to 5pm and Saturday 10am to 2pm.

THE GLYNDEBOURNE OPERA FESTIVAL ☆

In 1934, a group of local opera enthusiasts established an opera company based in the hamlet of Glyndebourne, which is 2.5km (1½ miles) east of Lewes and 8km (5 miles) northwest of Alfriston. The festival has been running ever since and is now one of the best regional opera companies in Britain.

In 1994, the original auditorium was demolished, and a dramatic modern glass, brick, and steel structure, designed by noted English architect Michael Hopkins, was built adjacent to some remaining (mostly ornamental) vestiges of the original building. The new auditorium is known for its acoustics.

Operas are presented only between mid-May and late August, and productions tend to be of unusual works. For information, contact the **Glyndebourne Festival,** P.O. Box 2624, Glyndebourne (Lewes), E. Sussex BN8 5UW (© **01273/815000;** www.glyndebourne.co.uk). You can call the box office at © **01273/813813.** Tickets range from £10 to £150 ($19–$278). You can usually get last-minute tickets because of cancellations by season-ticket holders. But if you want to see a specific show, it's a good idea to buy a ticket several months in advance. Credit card orders (Visa and MasterCard) are accepted, and for an additional postage charge, you can have tickets delivered to you. And it's fun to pack your own champagne picnic to enjoy before the performance; you can stock up from shops in Lewes.

To get to the theater from Lewes, take the A26 to the B2192, following the signs to Glynde and Glyndebourne. From Alfriston, follow the hamlet's main street north of town in the direction of the A27, then turn left following signs first to Glynde, then to Glyndebourne.

EXPLORING THE TWO TOWNS

Anne of Cleves House   This half-timbered house was part of Anne of Cleves's divorce settlement from Henry VIII, but Anne never lived in the house and there's no proof that she ever visited Lewes. Today it's a museum of local history, cared for by the Sussex Archaeological Society. The museum has a furnished bedroom and kitchen and displays of furniture, local history of the Wealden iron industry, and other crafts.

52 Southover High St., Lewes. ⓒ **01273/474610.** Admission £2.90 ($5.35) adults, £2.60 ($4.80) students and seniors, £1.45 ($2.70) children. Apr–Nov Mon–Sat 10am–5:30pm, Sun noon–5pm; Dec–Mar Tues, Thurs, and Sat 10am–5:30pm. Bus: 123.

Drusilla's Park *Kids*   This fascinating but not-too-large park has a flamingo lake, Japanese garden, and unusual breeds of some domestic animals, among other attractions. The park is perfect for families with children. Check out the newly converted £85,000 bat house, where a family of 20 Rodrigues fruit bats have taken up residence. With a wingspan of about 1m (3 ft.) and rich golden brown fur, they are one of the most beautiful and rarest bat species in the world.

About 1.5km (1 mile) outside Alfriston, off A27. ⓒ **01323/874100.** www.drusillas.co.uk. Admission £10 ($19) adults, £9.50 ($18) children (2–12); free for children under 2. Daily 10am–5pm (until 4pm in winter). Closed Dec 24–26.

Museum of Sussex Archaeology   Lewes, of course, matured in the shadow of its Norman castle. Adjacent to the castle is this museum, where a 20-minute audiovisual show is available by advance request. Audio tours of the castle are also available.

169 High St., Lewes. ⓒ **01273/486290.** Joint admission ticket to both castle and museum £4.30 ($7.95) adults, £2.50 ($4.65) children, £3.80 ($7.05) students and seniors, family ticket £12 ($21). Both sites Tues–Sat 10am–5:30pm; Sun–Mon 11am–5:30pm. Closed Dec 25–26. Bus: 27, 28, 121, 122, 166, 728, or 729.

WHERE TO STAY
IN ALFRISTON

Dean's Place Hotel   For English country-house living, at a reasonable price, Dean's Place dates to the 1300s, though much improved and architecturally altered over the years. Set in beautifully landscaped gardens, it is a cliché of English country charm with creeper-covered walls. Bedrooms come in a variety of sizes, each comfortably appointed with firm beds and well-kept bathrooms with shower-tub combinations. The staff is polite and helpful. The location is convenient for trips to Lewes and Brighton, among other places.

Seaford Rd., Polgate, East Sussex BN26 5TW. ⓒ **01323/870248.** Fax 01323/870918. www.deansplacehotel. co.uk. 36 units. £105–£168 ($194–$311) double. Rates include breakfast. AE, MC, V. On the 2nd roundabout after Lewes, take the 3rd exit for Alfriston and Drusilla's Zoo. Pass through Alfriston to the south side. The hotel is on the left-hand side of the road. **Amenities:** Restaurant; bar; putting green; croquet; 24-hr. room service; laundry service; nonsmoking rooms. *In room:* TV, coffeemaker, hair dryer, iron/ironing board.

The Star Inn *⚘*   The Star Inn—the premier place to stay—occupies a building dating from 1450, though it was originally founded in the 1200s to house pilgrims en route to Chichester and the shrine of St. Richard. Located in the center of the village, its carved front remains unchanged. The lounges are on several levels, a forest of old timbers. We infinitely prefer the rooms in the main building, which have far more character even though they've been altered and renovated over the years (most recently in 2004). Out back is a more sterile motel wing, with studio rooms. Bedrooms vary in size and style, but each one in the main building is well maintained with an old-world aura. All bedrooms, including those in the motel wing, have a small bathroom with a shower-tub combination.

High St., Alfriston, E. Sussex BN26 5TA. (✆) **01323/870495.** Fax 01323/870922. 37 units. £68–£168 ($126–$311) double. Rates include breakfast. AE, DC, MC, V. **Amenities:** Restaurant; bar; 24-hr. room service; babysitting; laundry service; nonsmoking rooms. *In room:* TV, dataport, coffeemaker, hair dryer, iron/ironing board, trouser press.

White Lodge Country House Hotel   This converted private home is opulently furnished and situated amid 2 hectares (5 acres) of gardens. The public rooms are outfitted like French salons, with carved 18th- and 19th-century antiques, many of them gilded. Bronze statues inspired by classical Greek myths are placed about. Each of the beautifully furnished rooms has countryside views. There is an English provincial country-style aura to the rooms, which are usually midsize, individually decorated, and adorned with plenty of sofas and armchairs. The roomy bathrooms have deluxe toiletries and shower-tub combinations.

Sloe Lane (a 5-min. walk from the village center off A27), Alfriston, E. Sussex BN26 5UR. (✆) **01323/870265.** Fax 01323/870284. www.whitelodge-hotel.com. 19 units. £95–£125 ($176–$231) double; £125 ($231) suite. Rates include English breakfast. MC, V. Bus: Southdown no. 712. **Amenities:** Restaurant; bar; 24-hr. room service; laundry service; dry cleaning; nonsmoking rooms. *In room:* TV w/pay movies, coffeemaker, hair dryer, trouser press.

IN LEWES

Shelleys Hotel ♠   The earl of Dorset owned this 1526 manor house before it was sold to the Shelley family, wealthy Sussex landowners (and relatives of the poet Percy Bysshe Shelley). Radical changes were made to the architecture in the 18th century. A complete refurbishment in 1994 turned the hotel into a rather luxurious country house retreat. There are traditional details throughout, such as the family coat of arms in the central hall. The standards of the management are reflected in the fine antiques, bowls of flowers, paintings and prints, well-kept gardens, and most importantly, helpful staff. The bedrooms are personal, individually furnished, usually spacious, and most comfortable. Room no. 11 has a 16th-century frieze of bacchanalian figures and a design of entwining grapes and flowers. Each unit has a well-appointed bathroom with tub and shower.

High St., Lewes, E. Sussex BN7 1XS. (✆) **01273/472361.** Fax 01273/483152. www.shelleys-hotel.com. 19 units. £120–£145 ($222–$268) double; £180–£210 ($333–$389) suite. Children under 6 stay free in parent's room. AE, DC, MC, V. **Amenities:** Restaurant; bar; 24-hr. room service; babysitting; laundry service; dry cleaning; nonsmoking rooms. *In room:* TV, dataport, minibar, coffeemaker, hair dryer, trouser press.

WHERE TO DINE
IN ALFRISTON

Around teatime, head for **The Tudor House,** on Alfriston's High Street (✆ **01323/870891**). The well-lit interior has two tearooms that provide a calm setting for afternoon tea. Cheese, ham-and-cheese, and egg-salad sandwiches and muffins, Danish, scones, and cakes are served. Afternoon tea costs £3.75 to £4.50 ($6.95–$8.35), sandwiches £2.75 to £2.95 ($5.10–$5.45) and cakes and pastries from £1.50 ($2.80). Open daily from 10:30am to 5pm.

Moonrakers ♠ ENGLISH   The welcome is warm at this charming 16th-century restaurant with old beams, inglenook fireplace, and convenient location in the heart of town. The cuisine is well prepared, with market-fresh ingredients. Dishes may include salmon in puff pastry with prawn and creamy vermouth stuffing, English lamb with port and red currant sauce, and a dessert specialty of sticky toffee pudding. The restaurant has a comprehensive wine list and a polite staff. Logs burn brightly in the fireplace during winter, and in summer there's a flowering patio for outside dining. The two dining rooms are reserved, respectively, for smokers and nonsmokers.

High St. ℭ 01323/870472. Reservations essential on weekends. Main courses £12–£19 ($22–$35); fixed-price menus for Sun lunch only £14–£17 ($26–$31). AE, MC, V. Tues–Sat 7–10pm; Sun noon–3:30pm. Closed 1st 2 weeks in Jan.

IN LEWES

Pailin *(Kids)* THAI Spicy hot Thai food has come to Lewes, though some of the fiery hot dishes have been toned down for English taste buds. Begin perhaps with the lemon chicken soup with lemon grass, followed by a crab-and-prawn "hot pot." A special favorite with locals is the barbecued marinated chicken, which is served with a spicy but delectable sweet-and-sour plum sauce. Vegetarian meals are served, and children are welcome and given small portions at reduced prices.

20 Station St. ℭ 01273/473906. Reservations not needed. Main courses £6–£10 ($11–$19); fixed-price lunch or dinner £14–£16 ($26–$30). AE, DC, MC, V. Mon–Sat noon–3pm and 6–10:30pm. Closed Nov 5 and Dec 25–26.

A SIDE TRIP FROM LEWES: VIRGINIA WOOLF'S HOME ℱ & THE BLUEBELL RAILWAY

The small downland village of **Rodmell** lies midway between Lewes and the port of Newhaven on C7. It's known for **Monk's House,** a National Trust property that was bought by Virginia and Leonard Woolf in 1919, and was their home until his death in 1969. Much of the house was furnished and decorated by Virginia's sister, Vanessa Bell, and the artist Duncan Grant.

The house has limited visiting hours: from April to October, and then only on Wednesday and Saturday from 2 to 5:30pm. Admission is £2.60 ($4.80) adults, £1.30 ($2.40) children 5 and up, and free for children 4 and under. A family ticket costs £6.90 ($13). More information is available by calling the headquarters of the **National Trust** in East Sussex (ℭ 01892/890651).

Rodmell also has a 12th-century church, a working farm, and a tiny Victorian school still in use. Take Southdown bus no. 123 from the Lewes rail station.

The trail of Virginia Woolf also leads to **Charleston Farmhouse,** along the A27 at Charleston, near Firle, 9.5km (6 miles) outside Lewes (ℭ 01323/811265). This house is the former country residence of Virginia's sister, Vanessa Bell, and the artist Duncan Grant. They were the glittering faces of the artistically influential "Bloomsbury Group" early in the 20th century. Preserved much as they left it, the property is filled with mementos and is open to guided tours only. An abbreviated tour costs £6 ($11); a longer "connoisseur" tour is £7 ($13). The trust that runs the property also has changing exhibitions and sponsors an annual literary and arts festival. Dates vary, so call for information.

The all-steam **Bluebell Railway** starts at Sheffield Park Station near Uckfield in East Sussex (ℭ 01825/722370), on A275 between East Grinstead and Lewes. The name is taken from the spring flowers that grow alongside the track, running from Sheffield Park to Kingscote. It's a delight for railway buffs, with locomotives dating from the 1870s through the 1950s, when British Railways ended steam operations. You can visit locomotive sheds and a small museum, then later patronize the bookshop or have lunch in a large buffet, bar, and restaurant complex. The round-trip is 1½ hours as the train wanders through a typical English countryside. It costs £8.50 ($16) adults, £4.20 ($7.75) for children 3 to 15 years, with a family ticket going for £23 ($43). Trains run daily from May to September, and Saturday and Sunday the rest of the year.

Hampshire & Dorset: Austen & Hardy Country

This countryside is reminiscent of scenes from Burke's *Landed Gentry,* from fireplaces where stacks slowly deplete as logs burn, to wicker baskets of apples freshly picked from a nearby orchard. Old village houses, now hotels, are charming. Beyond the pear trees, on the crest of a hill, lie the ruins of a Roman camp. The hunt gathers at a village pub, with two rows of kegs filled with varieties of cider.

You're in **Hampshire** and **Dorset,** two shires jealously guarded as special rural treasures. Everybody knows of Southampton and Bournemouth, but less known is the hilly countryside farther inland. You can travel endless lanes and discover tiny villages and thatched cottages untouched by the industrial invasion.

Jane Austen wrote of Hampshire's firmly middle-class inhabitants, all doggedly convinced that Hampshire was the greatest place on earth. Her six novels, including *Pride and Prejudice* and *Sense and Sensibility,* earned her a permanent place among the pantheon of 19th-century writers, and unexpected popularity among 1990s film directors and producers. Her books provide an insight into the manners and mores of the English who soon established a powerful empire. You can visit her grave in **Winchester Cathedral** and the house where she lived, **Chawton Cottage.**

Hampshire encompasses the **South Downs, the Isle of Wight** (Victoria's favorite retreat), and the naval city of **Portsmouth.** More than 36,421

hectares (90,000 acres) of the **New Forest** were preserved by William the Conqueror as a private hunting ground; this vast woodland and heath remains ideal for walking and exploring. Although Hampshire is filled with many places of interest, we've concentrated on two major areas: **Southampton,** for convenience, and **Winchester,** for history.

Dorset is Thomas Hardy country. Some of its towns and villages, though altered considerably, are still recognizable from his descriptions. "The last of the great Victorians," as he was called, died in 1928 at age 88. His tomb occupies a position of honor in Westminster Abbey.

One of England's smallest shires, Dorset encompasses the old seaport of **Poole** in the east and **Lyme Regis** (known to Jane Austen) in the west. Dorset is a southwestern county and borders the English Channel. It's known for its cows, and Dorset butter is served at many an afternoon tea. This is mainly a land of farms and pastures, with plenty of sandy heaths and chalky downs.

The most prominent tourist center of Dorset is the Victorian seaside resort of **Bournemouth.** If you don't stay here, you can try a number of Dorset's other seaports, villages, and country towns; we mostly stick to the areas along the impressive coastline.

You'll find the most hotels, but not the greatest charm, at Bournemouth. (More intriguing is the smaller Lyme Regis, with its seaside promenade, the

Cobb, a favorite of Jane Austen and a setting for *The French Lieutenant's Woman*.) If you're interested in things maritime, opt for Portsmouth, the premier port of the south and home of HMS *Victory*, Nelson's flagship. For history buffs and Austen fans, Winchester, the ancient capital of England, with a cathedral built by William the Conqueror, makes a good base for exploring the countryside.

The best beaches are at Bournemouth, set among pines with sandy beaches and fine coastal views, and **Chesil Beach,** a 32km (20-mile) long bank of shingle running from Abbottsbury to the Isle of Portland—great for beachcombing. However, the most natural spectacle is New Forest itself, 375 sq. km (145 sq. miles) of heath and woodland, once the hunting ground of Norman kings.

1 Winchester ★★

116km (72 miles) SW of London; 19km (12 miles) N of Southampton

The most historic city in all of Hampshire, Winchester is big on legends, because it's associated with King Arthur and the Knights of the Round Table. In the Great Hall, which is all that remains of Winchester Castle, a round oak table, with space for King Arthur and his 24 knights, is attached to the wall—but all that spells is undocumented romance. What is known, however, is that when the Saxons ruled the ancient kingdom of Wessex, Winchester was the capital.

The city is also linked with King Alfred, who is believed to have been crowned here and is honored today by a statue. The Danish conqueror Canute came this way too, as did the king he ousted, Ethelred the Unready (Canute got his wife, Emma, in the bargain).

Of course, Winchester is a mecca for Jane Austen fans. You can visit her grave in Winchester Cathedral (Emma Thompson did, while working on her adapted screenplay of *Sense and Sensibility*), as well as Chawton Cottage, Jane Austen's house, which is 24km (15) miles east of Winchester.

Its past glory but a memory, Winchester is essentially a market town today, lying on the downs along the Itchen River. Although Winchester hypes its ancient past, the modern world has arrived, as evidenced by the fast food and cheap retail-clothing stores that mar its otherwise perfect High Street.

ESSENTIALS

GETTING THERE Frequent daily train service runs from London's Waterloo Station to Winchester. The trip takes 1½ hours. For rail information, call ℂ **0845/748-4950** or visit www.railtrack.co.uk. Arrivals are at Winchester Station, Station Hill, northwest of the city center. **National Express** buses leaving from London's Victoria Coach Station depart regularly for Winchester during the day. The trip takes 2 hours. Call ℂ **0870/580-8080** or visit www.national express.com for schedules and information.

If you're driving, from Southampton drive north on the A335; from London, take the M3 motorway southwest.

VISITOR INFORMATION The **Tourist Information Centre,** at the Winchester Guildhall, The Broadway (ℂ **01962/840500;** www.visitwinchester. co.uk), is open from October to May, Monday through Saturday from 10am to 5pm; from June to September, Monday through Saturday from 9:30am to 5:30pm, and Sunday from 11am to 4pm. From May to October, guided walking tours are conducted for £3 ($5.55) per person, departing from this tourist center. Departure times vary; check with the center once you're there.

EXPLORING THE AREA

Castle Great Hall ✯ This is the only part that remains of the castle first erected in Winchester by the Normans. Dating from the 1200s, it is one of the finest examples of a medieval hall in England, with its timber roof supported on columns of Purbeck marble. The first fortress here was erected by William the Conqueror after he'd subdued England. Henry III rebuilt a castle on its foundation. Once it was a royal seat, and the English Parliament met here for the first time in 1246. The castle played a part in English history, including the trial of Sir Walter Raleigh who was condemned to death here in 1603 for conspiring against King James I. It wasn't until 1618, however, that the gallant knight was beheaded. A mammoth statue of Queen Victoria dominates the main floor. The work of Sir Alfred Gilbert, more famous for the statue of *Eros* in London's Piccadilly Circus, was created to mark Victoria's golden Jubilee in 1887. The hall displays a table known in local legend as King Arthur's Round Table, with places for a dozen knights. The table was probably carved in the 13th century, despite the myth surrounding it. Henry VIII, hosting a visit of the Holy Roman Emperor Charles V, attempted to pass the table off as authentic, even painting a replica of Arthur on the table. The Emperor wasn't fooled, pointing out the remarkable resemblance of the painting of "Arthur" to Henry himself.

You can also see an exhibition on the history of the castle and walk through the tranquil Queen Eleanor's Medieval Garden.

Castle Hill. ✆ **01962/846476**. Free admission. Daily 10am–5pm.

The Hospital of St. Cross ✯✯ Founded in 1132, the hospital is the oldest charitable institution in England. It was established by Henri du Blois, the grandson of William the Conqueror, as a link for social care and to supply life's necessities to the local poor and famished travelers. It continues the tradition of providing refreshments to visitors. Simply stop at the Porter's Lodge for a Wayfarer's Dole, and you'll receive some bread and ale. St. Cross is set in the beautiful scenery that inspired Keats and Trollope and is still the home of 25 brothers, whose residence is on one side of the historic landmark.

Cross Rd. ✆ **01962/851375**. Admission £2 ($3.70). May–Sept daily 9:30am–5pm; off season daily 10:30am–3:30pm.

Winchester Cathedral ✯✯✯ For centuries, this has been one of the great churches of England. The present building, the longest medieval cathedral in Britain, dates from 1079, and its Norman heritage is still in evidence. When a Saxon church stood on this spot, St. Swithun, bishop of Winchester and tutor to young King Alfred, suggested modestly that he be buried outside. Following his subsequent indoor burial, it rained for 40 days. The legend lives on: Just ask a resident of Winchester what will happen if it rains on St. Swithun's Day, July 15, and you'll get a prediction of rain for 40 days.

In the present building, the nave, with its two aisles, is most impressive, as are the *chantries* (chapels), the *reredos* (late-15th-century ornamental screens), and the elaborately carved choir stalls. Jane Austen is buried here; her grave is marked with a commemorative plaque. Also, chests contain the bones of many Saxon kings and the remains of the Viking conqueror Canute and his wife, Emma, in the presbytery. The son of William the Conqueror, William Rufus (who reigned as William II), is also buried at the cathedral.

The library houses Bishop Morley's 17th-century book collection, and an exhibition room contains the 12th-century Winchester Bible. The Triforium

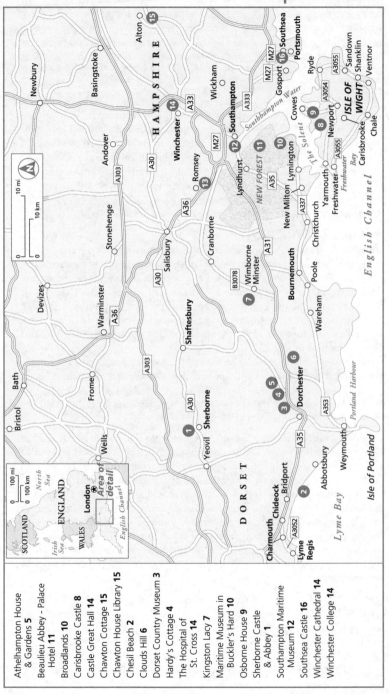

shows sculpture, woodwork, and metalwork from 11 centuries and affords magnificent views over the rest of the cathedral.

The Close. ℂ **01962/857200**. www.winchester-cathedral.org.uk. Free admission to the cathedral, but £3.50 ($6.50) donation requested. Admission to library and Triforium Gallery £1 ($1.85) adults, 50p (95¢) children. Free guided tours year-round 10am–3pm hourly. Crypt is often flooded during winter, but part may be seen from a viewing platform. Library and Triforium Gallery Wed and Sat 11am–3:30pm.

Winchester College ⭐ Winchester College was founded by William of Wykeham, bishop of Winchester and chancellor to Richard II, and was first occupied in 1394. Its buildings have been in continuous use for 600 years. The structures vary from Victorian Tudor Gothic to the more modern trimmings of the New Hall designed in 1961. The Chapel Hall, kitchens, and the Founder's Cloister date from the 14th century. In the 17th century, buildings were added on the south side, including a schoolroom constructed between 1683 and 1687.

73 Kings Gate. ℂ **01962/621209**. www.winchestercollege.org. Admission £3.50 ($6.50). Tues and Thurs 10:45am–noon; Mon, Wed, Fri–Sat 10:45am–noon and 2:15–3:30pm; Sun 2:15–3:30pm.

OUTSIDE OF WINCHESTER

Chawton Cottage ⭐ You can see where Jane Austen spent the last 7½ years of her life, her most productive period. In the unpretentious but pleasant cottage is the table on which she penned new versions of three of her books and wrote three more, including *Emma*. You can also see the rector's George III mahogany bookcase and a silhouette likeness of the Reverend Austen presenting his son to the Knights. In this cottage, Jane Austen became ill in 1816 with what would have been diagnosed by the middle of the 19th century as Addison's disease. She died in July 1817.

The grounds feature an attractive garden where you can picnic and an old bake house with Austen's donkey cart. A bookshop stocks new and secondhand books.

Chawton. ℂ **01420/83262**. Admission £4 ($7.40) adults, £3 ($5.55) students and seniors, 50p (95¢) children 8–18. Mar–Nov daily 11am–4:30pm; Dec–Feb Sat–Sun 11am–4pm. Closed Dec 25–26. 1.5km (1 mile) southwest of Alton off A31 and B3006, 24km (15 miles) east of Winchester.

Chawton House Library Set on 111 hectares (275 acres) the Elizabethan manor once owned by the brother of Jane Austen has been restored and turned into a center for the study of Early English women's writing from 1600 to 1830. In the former home of Edward Austen Knight, the collection contains some 6,000 volumes and manuscripts written by women as well as some 2,000 antique volumes. Much of the collection came from Sandy Lerner, an American and Austen fan. Of course, works by Austen are featured, but also rare manuscripts by such famous women writers as Mary Shelley and Fanny Burney. The grounds are being returned to the way they looked in the late 18th century.

Chawton. ℂ **01420/541010**. www.chawton.org. Admission £7.50 ($14) including tour. Tours Tues–Fri by appointment only.

SHOPPING Fill up those empty suitcases at **Cadogan,** 30–31 The Square (ℂ **01962/877399**), with an upscale and stylish selection of British clothing for both men and women. For a unique piece of jewelry by one of today's most acclaimed designers, stroll into **Carol Darby Jewellery,** 23 Little Minster St. (ℂ **01962/867671**). The oldest book dealer in town is **P&G Wells,** 11 College St. (ℂ **01962/852016**), with new releases and secondhand fiction and nonfiction.

WHERE TO STAY

Lainston House ⭐⭐⭐ The beauty of this fine, restored William-and-Mary redbrick manor house strikes visitors as they approach via a long, curving,

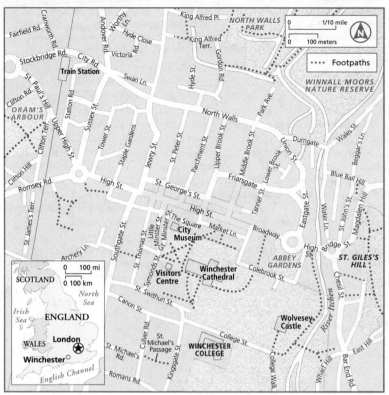

tree-lined drive. It's situated on 25 hectares (63 acres) of rolling land and linked with the name Lainston in the *Domesday Book*. Elegance is keynote inside the stately main house, where panoramically big suites are located. Other rooms, less spacious but also comfortable and harmoniously furnished, are in a nearby 1990 annex. Bathrooms are well equipped, with robes, and deluxe toiletries; some have two-person tubs and separate tubs and showers. The better units have large dressing areas and walk-in closets. The latest block of beautifully appointed rooms is a series of six converted stables.

Sparsholt, Winchester, Hampshire SO21 2LT. ✆ 01962/863588. Fax 01962/776672. www.exclusivehotels. co.uk. 50 units. £160–£340 ($296–$629) double; £360 ($666) suite. AE, DC, MC, V. Take B3420 2.5km (1½ miles) northwest of Winchester. **Amenities:** Restaurant; bar; 2 outdoor tennis courts; gym; concierge; limited room service; babysitting; laundry service; dry cleaning; rooms for those with limited mobility. *In room:* TV, dataport, hair dryer, safe.

The Winchester Royal This fine hotel is a comfortable choice. Built at the end of the 16th century as a private house, it was used by Belgian nuns as a convent for 50 years before being turned into a hotel, quickly becoming the center of the city's social life. Only a few minutes' walk from the cathedral, it still enjoys a secluded position. A modern extension overlooks gardens, and all rooms have traditional English styling. Bedrooms in the main house are more traditional than those in the modern wing, but each accommodation is well appointed. All rooms have well-kept bathrooms with shower-tub combinations.

St. Peter St., Winchester, Hampshire SO23 8BS. © **800/528-1234** in the U.S., or 01962/840840. Fax 01962/ 841582. www.marstonhotels.com. 75 units. £114–£148 ($211–$274) double; £139–£173 ($257–$320) suite. Rates include English breakfast. AE, DC, MC, V. **Amenities:** 2 restaurants; bar; 24-hr. room service; babysitting; laundry service; dry cleaning; nonsmoking rooms. *In room:* TV, dataport (in some), coffeemaker, hair dryer, trouser press.

Wykeham Arms ⊛ *Finds*   Our longtime favorite in Winchester, it lies behind a 200-year-old brick facade in the historic center of town, near the cathedral. Rooms are traditionally furnished with antiques or reproductions and such touches as fresh flowers and baskets of potpourri. Most bedrooms are a bit small but attractively appointed; all are nonsmoking. Six rooms were recently added in a 16th-century building that faces the original hotel. The annex has the most luxurious accommodations, the rooms more spacious. The large modern bathrooms are well equipped, each with tub and shower. A large suite with cozy fire-warmed sitting room and upstairs bedroom is also available. Overlooking the Winchester College Chapel, these rooms have the same amenities as the original rooms. *Note:* The hotel does not accept children under 14 as guests.

75 Kingsgate St., Winchester, Hampshire SO23 9PE. © **01962/853834.** Fax 01962/854411. 14 units. £90 ($167) double in original building, £98 ($181) double in extension; £120 ($222) suite. Rates include English breakfast. AE, DC, MC, V. **Amenities:** Restaurant; bar. *In room:* TV, dataport, minibar, coffeemaker, hair dryer.

WHERE TO DINE

Hotel du Vin & Bistro ⊛ *Value*   ENGLISH/CONTINENTAL   This inn offers both food and lodging, bringing a touch of chic to Winchester. It's a town-house hotel that dates from 1715 and has a walled garden. Gerard Basset and Robin Hutson learned their lessons well at exclusive Chewton Glen (p. 335) before embarking on their own enterprise. The chef, Eddie Gray, delivers some of the finest food in Winchester today. The bistro food is excellent and a good value. The menu always features regional ingredients: Try the Torbay sole filet served with spinach and potato galette, with a mushroom, white-wine, and cream sauce. Basset has collected the finest wine list in the county.

You can stay overnight in one of 23 rooms decorated with a wine theme. The comfortable rooms have good beds, antiques, TVs, and state-of-the-art bathrooms with shower-tub combination, costing from £109 to £225 ($202–$416).

14 Southgate St., Winchester, Hampshire SO23 9EF. © **01962/841414.** Fax 01962/842458. www.hotelduvin. com. Reservations recommended. Main courses £13–£16 ($23–$30). AE, DC, MC, V. Daily noon–2pm and 7–10pm.

Old Chesil Rectory ⊛⊛⊛   FRENCH   One of the finest restaurants in Hampshire, the 15th-century building, restored over the years, is aglow with half-timbered architecture and whitewashed panels. White candles, white flowers, and white table linen create a lovely mood for dining. The chef, Robert Quehan, turns out refined versions of classic French dishes, made lighter for more modern and discerning palates. The menu is adjusted seasonally to take advantage of regional

---

Moments **Rambling Around Winchester**

For a day of rambling through the countryside, stroll part of South Downs Way, a 159km (99-mile) trail from Winchester to Eastbourne; Clarendon Way, a 39km (24-mile) path from Winchester to Salisbury; or Itchen Way, a beautiful riverside trail from near Cheriton to Southampton. The Tourist Information Centre (see above) will provide complete details on the best spots.

Finds   A Lager at England's Oldest Bar

Royal Oak Pub, Royal Oak Passage (© **01962/842701**), is located in a passageway next to the God Begot House on the High Street. A busy pub with plenty of atmosphere, it reputedly has the oldest bar in England. The cellar of this establishment was originally built in 944 to dispense drink to Winchester's pilgrims; the present building was constructed in 1630 atop the much older foundation.

---

produce. For example, a perfectly flavored and delicately balanced wild mushroom risotto appears in autumn, and a fresh asparagus greets the spring. The chef believes in "weddings" in the kitchen—for example, veal loin is mated with liver or pork with classic black pudding. Roasted brill with wild mushrooms and onion compote is one of the most richly textured dishes we've enjoyed here. Desserts are made here, including such offerings as chocolate tart with coffee anglaise.

1 Chesil St. © **01962/851555.** Reservations required. Fixed-price lunch £35 ($65) for 2 courses, £38 ($70) for 3 courses; fixed-price dinner £35 ($65) for 2 courses, £42 ($78) for 3 courses. DC, MC, V. Tues–Sat noon–3pm and 7pm–midnight.

WINCHESTER AFTER DARK

The place to go is **The Porthouse,** Upper Brook Street (© **01962/869397**), a pub-cum-nightclub, sprawling across three floors. Different nights have different themes, from karaoke to retro music from the 1960s through the 1980s. On Friday, the 25-plus crowd takes over. The only cover, ranging from £3 to £5 ($5.55–$9.25), is charged on Friday, and Saturday nights after 9pm. A ground-floor pub offers lunch.

2 Portsmouth ⊀ & Southsea

121km (75 miles) SW of London; 31km (19 miles) SE of Southampton

Virginia, New Hampshire, and Ohio may have a Portsmouth, but the forerunner of them all is the old port and naval base on the Hampshire coast, seat of the British Navy for 500 years. German bombers in World War II leveled the city, hitting about nine-tenths of its buildings. But the seaport was rebuilt admirably and now aggressively promotes its military attractions. It draws visitors interested in the nautical history of England as well as World War II buffs.

Its maritime associations are known around the world. From Sally Port, the most interesting district in the Old Town, countless naval heroes have embarked to fight England's battles, including on June 6, 1944, when Allied troops set sail to invade occupied France.

Southsea, adjoining Portsmouth, is a popular seaside resort with fine sands, lush gardens, bright lights, and a host of vacation attractions. Many historic monuments are along the stretches of open space, where you can walk on the Clarence Esplanade, look out on the Solent Channel, and view the busy shipping activities of Portsmouth Harbour.

ESSENTIALS

GETTING THERE   Trains from London's Waterloo Station stop at Portsmouth and Southsea Station frequently throughout the day. The trip takes 2½ hours. Call © **0845/748-4950** or visit www.railtrack.co.uk.

National Express coaches out of London's Victoria Coach Station make the run to Portsmouth and Southsea every 2 hours during the day. The trip takes

2 hours and 45 minutes. Call ✆ **0870/580-8080** or visit www.nationalexpress.com for information and schedules.

If you're driving from London's ring road, drive south on the A3.

VISITOR INFORMATION The **Tourist Information Centre,** at The Hard in Portsmouth (✆ **023/9282-6722**), is open daily April through September from 9:30am to 5:45pm, and October through March from 9:30am to 4:30pm.

EXPLORING PORTSMOUTH & SOUTHSEA

You may want to begin your tour on the Southsea front, where you can see a number of **naval monuments,** including the big anchor from Nelson's ship, *Victory,* and a commemoration of officers and men of HMS *Shannon* for heroism in the Indian Mutiny. An obelisk with a naval crown honors the memory of the crew of HMS *Chesapeake,* and a massive column, the Royal Naval Memorial, honors those lost at sea in the two world wars. A shaft is also dedicated to men killed in the Crimean War. Commemorations also honor those who fell victim to yellow fever in Queen Victoria's service in Sierra Leone and Jamaica.

MARITIME ATTRACTIONS IN PORTSMOUTH

You can buy a ticket that admits you to four attractions: HMS *Victory,* the *Mary Rose,* the HMS *Warrior 1860,* and the Royal Naval Museum. It costs £15 ($27) for adults, £1.90 ($3.50) for seniors and for children ages 5 to 16; family ticket (two adults, three children) £48 ($88). Check at the Visitor Centre of the Portsmouth Historic Dockyard (✆ **023/9286-1512**) or you can buy them online at www.historicdockyard.co.uk.

HMS *Victory* ★★★ Of major interest is Lord Nelson's flagship, a 104-gun, first-rate ship that is the oldest commissioned warship in the world, launched May 7, 1765. It earned its fame on October 21, 1805, in the Battle of Trafalgar, when the English scored a victory over the combined Spanish and French fleets. It was in this battle that Lord Nelson lost his life. The flagship, after being taken to Gibraltar for repairs, returned to Portsmouth with Nelson's body on board (he was later buried at St. Paul's in London).

1–7 College Rd., in Portsmouth Naval Base. ✆ 023/9286-1533. www.historicdockyard.co.uk. See above for admission prices. Apr–Oct daily 10am–5:30pm; Nov–Mar daily 10am–5pm. Closed Dec 25. Use the entrance to the Portsmouth Naval Base through Victory Gate and follow the signs.

The Mary Rose Ship Hall and Exhibition ★ The *Mary Rose,* flagship of the fleet of King Henry VIII's wooden men-of-war, sank in the Solent Channel in 1545 in full view of the king. In 1982, Prince Charles watched the *Mary Rose* break the water's surface after more than 4 centuries on the ocean floor, not exactly in shipshape condition, but surprisingly well preserved nonetheless. Now the remains are on view, but the hull must be kept permanently wet.

The hull and more than 20,000 items brought up by divers constitute one of England's major archaeological discoveries. On display are the almost-complete equipment of the ship's barber-surgeon, with cabin saws, knives, ointments, and plaster all ready for use; long bows and arrows, some still in shooting order; carpenters' tools; leather jackets; and some fine lace and silk. Close to the Ship Hall is the *Mary Rose* Exhibition, where artifacts recovered from the ship are stored, featuring an audiovisual theater and spectacular two-deck reconstruction of a segment of the ship, including the original guns. A display with sound effects recalls the sinking of the vessel.

College Rd., Portsmouth Naval Base. ✆ 023/9275-0521. www.historicdockyard.co.uk. See above for admission prices. Apr–Oct daily 10am–5:30pm; Nov–Mar daily 10am–5pm. Closed Dec 25. Use the entrance to the Portsmouth Naval Base through Victory Gate and follow the signs.

Royal Naval Museum ⭐

The museum is next to Nelson's flagship, HMS *Victory,* and the *Mary Rose,* in the heart of Portsmouth's historic naval dockyard. The only museum in Britain devoted exclusively to the general history of the Royal Navy, it houses relics of Nelson and his associates, together with unique collections of ship models, naval ceramics, figureheads, medals, uniforms, weapons, and other memorabilia. Special displays feature "The Rise of the Royal Navy" and "HMS *Victory* and the Campaign of Trafalgar."

In the dockyard, Portsmouth Naval Base. ℂ **023/9272-7562.** www.historicdockyard.co.uk. See above for admission prices. Apr–Oct daily 10am–5:30pm; Nov–Mar daily 10am–5pm. Use the entrance to the Portsmouth Naval Base through Victory Gate and follow the signs.

Royal Navy Submarine Museum

Cross Portsmouth Harbour by one of the ferries that bustles back and forth all day to Gosport. Some departures go directly from the station pontoon to HMS *Alliance* for a visit to the submarine museum, which traces the history of underwater warfare and life from the earliest days to the present nuclear age. Within the refurbished historical and nuclear galleries, the principal exhibit is HMS *Alliance,* and after a brief audiovisual presentation, visitors are guided through the boat by ex-submariners. Outside the museum, you can see midget submarines, not all of them English, including an X-craft.

Haslar Jetty Rd., Gosport. ℂ **023/9252-9217.** www.rnsubmus.co.uk. Admission £4.50 ($8.35) adults, £3 ($5.55) children and seniors, £12 ($22) family. Apr–Oct daily 10am–5:30pm; Nov–Mar daily 10am–4:30pm. Last tour 1 hr. before closing. Closed Dec 25. Bus: 19. Ferry: from The Hard in Portsmouth to Gosport.

MORE ATTRACTIONS

Charles Dickens's Birthplace Museum The 1804 small terrace house, in which the famous novelist was born in 1812 and lived for a short time, has been restored and furnished to illustrate the middle-class taste of the southwestern counties of the early 19th century.

393 Old Commercial Rd. (near the center of Portsmouth, off Mile End Rd./M275 and off Kingston Rd.). © 023/9282-7261. www.charlesdickensbirthplace.co.uk. Admission £2.50 ($4.65) adults, £1.80 ($3.35) seniors, £1.50 ($2.80) students, free for children 12 and under. Apr–Oct daily 10am–5:30pm. Closed Nov–Mar.

D-Day Museum Next door to Southsea Castle, this museum, devoted to the Normandy landings, displays the Overlord Embroidery, which shows the complete story of Operation Overlord. The appliquéd embroidery, believed to be the largest of its kind (82m/272 ft. long and 1m/3 ft. high), was designed by Sandra Lawrence and took 20 women of the Royal School of Needlework 5 years to complete. A special audiovisual program includes displays such as reconstructions of various stages of the mission. You'll see a Sherman tank in working order, jeeps, field guns, and even a DUKW (popularly called a Duck), an incredibly useful amphibious truck that operates on land and sea.

Clarence Esplanade (on the seafront), Southsea. © 023/9282-7261. www.ddaymuseum.co.uk. Admission £5 ($9.25) adults, £3.75 ($6.95) seniors, £3 ($5.55) children and students, £13 ($24) family; free for children under 5. Apr–Sept 10am–5:30pm; Oct–Mar 10am–5pm. Closed Dec 24–26.

Portchester Castle On a spit of land on the northern side of Portsmouth Harbour are the remains of this castle, plus a Norman church. Built in the late 12th century by King Henry II, the castle is set inside the impressive walls of a 3rd-century Roman fort built as a defense against Saxon pirates when this was the northwestern frontier of the declining Roman Empire. By the end of the 14th century, Richard II had modernized the castle and had made it a secure small palace. Among the ruins are the hall, kitchen, and great chamber of this palace.

On the south side of Portchester off A27 (between Portsmouth and Southampton, near Fareham). © 023/ 9237-8291. Admission £3.50 ($6.50) adults, £2.60 ($4.80) seniors, £1.80 ($3.35) children 5–15, free for children 4 and under. Apr–Oct daily 10am–6pm; Nov–Mar daily 10am–4pm.

Southsea Castle A fortress built of stones from Beaulieu Abbey in 1545 as part of King Henry VIII's coastal defense plan, the castle is now a museum. Exhibits trace the development of Portsmouth as a military stronghold, as well as the naval history and the archaeology of the area. The castle is in the center of Southsea near the D-Day Museum.

Clarence Esplanade, Southsea. © 023/9282-7261. www.southseacastle.co.uk. Admission £2.50 ($4.65) adults, £1.80 ($3.35) seniors, £1.50 ($2.80) students and children ages 13–18, £6.50 ($12) family; free for children 12 and under. Apr–Sept daily 10am–5:30pm. Closed Oct–Mar.

WHERE TO STAY

The Royal Beach Hotel The balconied Victorian facade of this hotel, directly east of Southside Common, rises above the boulevard running beside the sea. Restored by its owners, the hotel's interior decor ranges from contemporary to full-curtained traditional, depending on the room. However, it doesn't stack up with the nearby Marriott. Each of the bedrooms has been renovated with built-in furniture. The bathrooms are small but well maintained, with tubs and showers.

South Parade, Southsea, Portsmouth, Hampshire PO4 ORN. © 023/9273-1281. Fax 023/9281-7572. www. royalbeachhotel.co.uk. 126 units. £85 ($157) double; £195 ($361) suite. Rates include English breakfast. Children under 6 stay free in parent's room. AE, DC, MC, V. **Amenities:** Restaurant; bar; 24-hr. room service; laundry service; dry cleaning; nonsmoking rooms; rooms for those with limited mobility. *In room:* TV, dataport, coffeemaker, hair dryer, safe, trouser press.

Westfield Hall ★ *Finds* In the resort of Southsea, two early-20th-century homes near the water have been turned into a hotel with a certain charm and character. One of the most inviting and most comfortable of the little family run hotels in the area, this highly commendable establishment offers a warm welcome and beautifully maintained and comfortably furnished bedrooms, each with a full bath with tub or shower or else private shower. Many accommodations are graced with large bay windows. Guests enjoy the use of three lounges.

65 Festing Rd., Southsea, Portsmouth, Hampshire PO4 0NQ. ℂ **023/9282-6971.** Fax 023/9287-0200. www. whhotel.info. 27 units. £70–£90 ($130–$167) double. AE, DC, MC, V. **Amenities:** Restaurant; nonsmoking rooms. *In room:* TV, dataport, coffeemaker, hair dryer.

IN NEARBY WICKHAM

The Old House Hotel ★ *Finds* A handsome early Georgian (1715) structure, the Old House is surrounded by low, medieval timber structures around the square. The hotel has undergone a classic refurbishment, giving it the look of a proud English country house. The paneled rooms on the ground and first floors of the hotel contrast with the beamed bedrooms on the upper floors, once the servants' quarters. All bedrooms have period furniture, many pieces original antiques, and warm, comfortable beds. They are also all nonsmoking. Bathrooms are big enough to have a shower stall as well as a tub.

The Square, Wickham, Fareham, Hampshire PO17 5JG. ℂ **01329/833049.** Fax 01329/833672. www.the oldhousehotelandrestaurant.co.uk. 12 units. £75–£120 ($139–$222) double. Rates include continental breakfast. AE, DC, MC, V. Bus no. 69 from Fareham. Head 14km (9 miles) west from Portsmouth on M27; exit at number 10. The village is 3km (2 miles) north of the junction of B2177 and A32. **Amenities:** Restaurant; bar; guest lounge. *In room:* TV, dataport, coffeemaker, hair dryer.

WHERE TO DINE

Bistro Montparnasse ★ BRITISH/FRENCH Serving the best food in the area, this bistro offers a welcoming atmosphere and background music to get you in the mood. Fresh produce is delicately prepared in the well-rounded selection of dishes here. The cooking is familiar fare but well executed. Although the menu changes, you may try the roast rack of lamb with a walnut and herb crust. Homemade breads and fresh fish, caught locally, are the specialties.

103 Palmerston Rd., Southsea. ℂ **023/9281-6754.** www.bistromontparnasse.co.uk. Reservations recommended. 2-course lunch £13 ($24); 3-course lunch £16 ($30); 2-course dinner £20 ($37); 3-course dinner £25 ($46). AE, MC, V. Tues–Sat 1:45–2pm and 7–9:30pm. Southsea bus. Follow the signs to the D-Day Museum, and at the museum turn left and go to the next intersection; the restaurant is on the right.

3 Southampton

140km (87 miles) SW of London; 259km (161 miles) E of Plymouth

For many North Americans, England's number-one passenger port, home base for the *QE2,* is the gateway to Britain. Southampton is a city of sterile wide boulevards, parks, and dreary shopping centers. During World War II, some

31.5 million men set out from here (in World War I, more than twice that number), and Southampton was repeatedly bombed, destroying its old character. Today, the rather shoddy downtown section represents what happens when a city's architectural focus is timeliness rather than grace, with more to see on the city's outskirts than in the city itself. If you're spending time in Southampton, you may want to explore some of the major sights of Hampshire nearby (New Forest, Winchester, the Isle of Wight, and Bournemouth, in neighboring Dorset).

Its supremacy as a port dates from Saxon times when the Danish conqueror Canute was proclaimed king here in 1017. Southampton was especially important to the Normans and helped them keep in touch with their homeland. Its denizens were responsible for bringing in the bubonic plague, which wiped out a quarter of the English population in the mid–14th century. On the Western Esplanade is a memorial tower to the Pilgrims, who set out on their voyage to the New World from Southampton on August 15, 1620. Both the *Mayflower* and the *Speedwell* sailed from here but were forced by storm damages to put in at Plymouth, where the *Speedwell* was abandoned.

In the spring of 1912, the "unsinkable" White Star liner, the 46,000-ton *Titanic,* sailed from Southampton on its maiden voyage. Shortly before midnight on April 14, while steaming at 22 knots, the great ship collided with an iceberg and sank to the bottom of the icy Atlantic. The sinking of the *Titanic,* subject of the Oscar-winning box office smash of 1997, is one of the greatest disasters in maritime history, as 1,513 people perished.

ESSENTIALS

GETTING THERE Trains depart from London's Waterloo Station several times daily. The trip takes just over an hour. Call ℭ **0845/748-4950** or visit www.railtrack.co.uk.

National Express operates hourly departures from London's Victoria Coach Station. The trip takes 2½ hours. Call ℭ **0870/580-8080** or visit www.national express.com for information and schedules.

If you're driving, take the M3 southwest from London.

VISITOR INFORMATION The **Tourist Information Centre,** 9 Civic Centre Rd. (ℭ **023/8022-1106**), is open Monday, Tuesday, Thursday, and Friday from 8:30am to 5:30pm, Wednesday from 10am to 5:30pm, Saturday 9:30am to 5pm; closed Good Friday and Easter Monday, Christmas, December 26, and New Year's Day.

EXPLORING SOUTHAMPTON

Ocean Village and the town quay on Southampton's waterfront are bustling with activity and are filled with shops, restaurants, and entertainment possibilities.

West Quay Retail Park, the first phase of Southampton's £250 million Esplanade development, has become a major hub for shoppers. The central shopping area is pedestrian-only, and tree- and shrub-filled planters provide a backdrop for summer flowers and hanging baskets. You can sit and listen to the *buskers* (street entertainers) or perhaps watch the world parade from one of the nearby restaurants or pavement cafes. For a vast array of shops, try the **Town Quay** (ℭ **023/8023-4397**), the **Canutes Pavilion** at Ocean Village (ℭ **023/8022-8353**), or **Southampton Market** (no phone).

The most intriguing shopping on the outskirts is at the **Whitchurch Silk Mill,** 28 Winchester St., Whitchurch (ℭ **01256/892065**). Admission is £3.50 ($6.50) for adults, £3 ($5.55) for seniors, £1.75 ($3.25) for children, and £8.75 ($16) for a family ticket. Visitors flock to this working mill, located in colorful

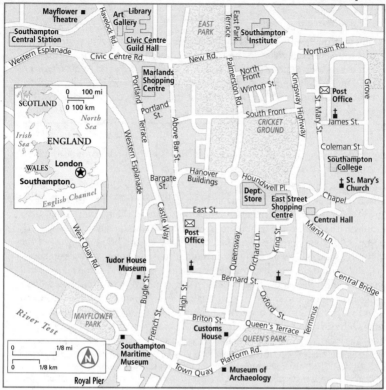

surroundings on the River Test. Historic looms weave silk here as in days of old, and you can observe water-wheel-powered machinery, warping, and winding. The gift shop sells silk on the roll, ties, scarves, handkerchiefs, jewelry, and souvenirs. Hours are Tuesday through Sunday from 10:30am to 5pm.

Southampton Maritime Museum This museum is housed in an impressive 14th-century stone warehouse with a magnificent timber ceiling. Its exhibits trace the history of Southampton, including a model of the docks as they looked at their peak in the 1930s. Also displayed are artifacts from some of the great ocean liners whose home port was Southampton.

The most famous of these liners was the fabled *Titanic,* which was partially built in Southampton and sailed from this port on its fateful, fatal voyage. James Cameron's box office smash has increased traffic to the relatively small *Titanic* exhibit at the museum. It features photographs of the crew (many of whom were from Southampton) and passengers, as well as letters from passengers, Capt. Edward Smith's sword, and a video with a dated interview with the fallen captain plus modern interviews with survivors.

The Wool House, Town Quay. ✆ **023/8022-3941.** Free admission. Apr–Sept Tues–Fri 10am–1pm and 2–5pm, Sat 10am–1pm and 2–4pm, Sun 2–5pm; Oct–Mar Tues–Fri 10am–4pm, Sat 10am–1pm and 2–4pm, Sun 1–4pm.

WHERE TO STAY

Finding a place to stay right in Southampton isn't as important as it used to be. Very few ships now arrive, and accommodations outside the city are generally

---

Value Those Shoes Are Made for Walking

City tour guides offer a wide range of **free guided walks** and regular **city bus tours.** Guided walks of the town are offered free of charge throughout the year on Sunday and Monday at 10:30am; in July and August, twice daily at 10:30am and 2:30pm. Tours start at Bargate. For details of various boat or bus trips that may be offered at the time of your visit, check with the tourist office.

---

better. For more choices in the area, refer to "Where to Stay Around the New Forest," in the next section.

De Vere Grand Harbour Hotel ★★   If you must stay in town and you can afford it, this is the most comfortable place to be. Completed in 1994, the five-story structure, sheathed in granite and possessing a dramatically tilted glass facade, is the most exciting hotel to open in Southampton since World War II. Some 30 of the brightly painted bedrooms have air-conditioning. Most of the bathrooms are filled with luxuries, including tubs, and separate walk-in showers, and granite vanities. Bathroom extras include both hand-held and overhead showers, and robes and rubber ducks in the executive rooms only. Bedrooms range from midsize to spacious, with a pair of armchairs and traditional polished wood surfaces, plus snug beds. About nine of the rooms are equipped for persons with disabilities. Some rooms offer balconies; some have waterfront views.

W. Quay Rd., Southampton, Hampshire S015 1AG. (℃ 023/8063-3033. Fax 023/8063-3066. www.deveregrand harbour.co.uk. 172 units. £190–£210 ($352–$389) double; £290–£390 ($537–$722) suite. Rates include English breakfast. AE, DC, MC, V. **Amenities:** 2 restaurants; 2 bars; indoor pool; gym; spa bath; steam room; sauna; 24-hr. room service; babysitting; laundry service; dry cleaning; nonsmoking rooms. *In room:* TV, dataport, minibar, coffeemaker, hair dryer, safe, trouser press.

Dolphin Hotel ★   If you want tradition, this is your best choice. This bow-windowed Georgian coaching house in the center of the city was Jane Austen's choice, and Thackeray's, too. Even Queen Victoria visited via her horse-drawn carriage. The rooms vary widely in size but are generally spacious and well equipped. Bedrooms are being refurbished as part of an ongoing restoration program. Three rooms are large enough for families. Each unit comes with a bathroom, which for the most part contain shower-tub combinations.

35 High St., Southampton, Hampshire S014 2HN. (℃ 023/8033-9955. Fax 023/8033-3650. www.dolphin hotel.co.uk. 73 units. £90–£130 ($167–$241) double; £120–£130 ($222–$241) suite. Children under 16 stay free in their parent's room. AE, DC, MC, V. Bus: 2, 6, or 8. **Amenities:** Restaurant; bar; 24-hr. room service; laundry service; dry cleaning; nonsmoking rooms. *In room:* TV, dataport, coffeemaker, hair dryer, trouser press.

Holiday Inn Southampton   This 10-floor high-rise across from Mayflower Park was built near the new docks to overlook the harbor and is only 5 minutes away from the city center. Rooms are standard but generally spacious, with built-in furniture and picture-window walls, and have recently been refurbished and upgraded to ensure a pleasant stay. Only one unit has facilities for persons with disabilities. Bathrooms are routine motel-style tiled affairs with shower-tub combinations. It's not big on extras, but what you get is adequate for the price.

Herbert Walker Ave., Southampton, Hampshire S015 1HJ. (℃ 800/225-5843 in the U.S. and Canada, or 0870/ 400-9073. Fax 023/8033-2510. www.holiday-inn.com. 132 units. £135–£155 ($250–$287) double. AE, DC, MC, V. **Amenities:** Restaurant; bar; health club; sauna; whirlpool; indoor pool; 24-hr. room service; laundry service; dry cleaning; rooms for those with limited mobility. *In room:* TV, dataport, coffeemaker, hair dryer, trouser press.

WHERE TO DINE

Langleys Bistro FRENCH/BRITISH   Since its establishment in 1994, this restaurant continues to grow in popularity. It deserves its local fame. In these tastefully decorated precincts, you get a relaxed bistro ambience with posters and mirrors of Southampton's heyday in the steamship era decorating the walls. The location is convenient, lying near Southampton's dockland. Under the whir of summer ceiling fans, you can peruse the menu. Dishes come in generous portions, and chefs show a certain skill. Roasted sea bass filets appear enticingly on a bed of green beans topped with prawns and toasted almonds. One of the best poultry dishes is a breast of chicken married to some intriguing flavors such as fresh tarragon, shallots, and West Country ham. The chefs also turn out premiere Scottish filet of beef with a Roquefort and bacon sauce or else with wild mushrooms and cognac. The staff has a small bar area for an aperitif, where you can also sample some of the finest cognacs, ports, and champagne.

10–11 Bedford Place. © 023/8022-4551. Reservations required. Main courses £12–£18 ($21–$33); 2-course fixed-price lunch £14 ($26), 3-course fixed-price lunch £17 ($31); 2-course fixed-price dinner £17 ($31), 3-course fixed-price dinner £21 ($39). AE, DC, MC, V. Mon–Fri noon–2pm; Mon–Sat 6:30–10:30pm.

The Red Lion ENGLISH   One of the few architectural jewels to have survived World War II, this pub traces its roots to the 13th century (as a Norman cellar), but its Henry V Court Room, with high ceilings and rafters, is from Tudor times. The room was the scene of the trial of the earl of Cambridge and his accomplices, Thomas Grey and Lord Scrope, who were condemned to death for plotting against the life of the king in 1415. Today, the Court Room is adorned with coats-of-arms of the noblemen who were peers of the condemned trio. The Red Lion is a fascinating place for a drink and a chat. Typical pub snacks are served in the bar, whereas in the somewhat more formal restaurant section, the well-seasoned specialties include an array of steaks (including sirloin), stews, roasts, and fish platters.

55 High St. © 023/8033-3595. Reservations not needed. Main courses £4.95–£13 ($9.15–$24); pub snacks £2.50–£3.95 ($4.65–$7.30). MC, V. Daily 11am–11pm. Pub: Daily 11am–11pm. Bus: 1, 2, 6, or 8.

A SIDE TRIP TO BROADLANDS: HOME OF THE LATE EARL OF MOUNTBATTEN

Broadlands   Broadlands was the home of the late Earl Mountbatten of Burma, who was assassinated in 1979. Earl Mountbatten, who has been called "the last war hero," lent the house to his nephew, Prince Philip, and Princess Elizabeth as a honeymoon haven in 1947, and in 1981, Prince Charles and Princess Diana spent the first nights of their honeymoon here.

Broadlands is now owned by Lord Romsey, Earl Mountbatten's eldest grandson, who has created a fine exhibition and audiovisual show that depicts the highlights of his grandfather's brilliant career as a sailor and statesman. The house, originally linked to Romsey Abbey, was transformed into an elegant Palladian mansion by Capability Brown and Henry Holland. Brown landscaped the parkland and grounds.

13km (8 miles) northwest of Southampton in Romsey, on A31. © 01794/505010. www.broadlands.net. Admission £7 ($13) adults, £6 ($11) students and seniors, £4 ($7.40) children 12–16, free for children under 12. June 10–Sept 1 daily 1–4:30pm.

4 The New Forest

153km (95 miles) SW of London; 16km (10 miles) W of Southampton

Encompassing 37,231 hectares (92,000 acres), the New Forest is a large tract created by William the Conqueror, who laid out the limits of this then-private hunting preserve. Successful poachers faced the executioner if they were caught, and those who hunted but missed had their hands severed. Henry VIII loved to hunt deer in the New Forest, but he also saw an opportunity to build up the British naval fleet by supplying oak and other hard timbers to the boatyards at Buckler's Hard on the Beaulieu River.

Today you can visit the old shipyards and the museum, with its fine models of men-of-war, pictures of the old yard, and dioramas showing the building of these ships, their construction, and their launching. It took 2,000 trees to construct one man-of-war. A motorway cuts through the area, and the once-thick forest has groves of oak trees separated by wide tracts of common land that's grazed by ponies and cows, hummocked with heather and gorse, and frequented by rabbits. But away from the main roads, where signs warn of wild ponies and deer, you'll find a private world of peace and quiet.

ESSENTIALS

GETTING THERE   By train, go to Southampton, where you can make rail connections to a few centers in the New Forest. Where the train leaves off, you can make bus connections to all towns and many villages. Southampton and Lymington have the best bus connections to New Forest's villages.

If you're driving, head west from Southampton on the A35.

VISITOR INFORMATION   The **New Forest Visitor Centre,** Main Car Park, Lyndhurst (© **023/8028-2269**), is open daily from 10am to 5pm.

SEEING THE SIGHTS

Beaulieu Abbey-Palace House ★★   The abbey and house, as well as the National Motor Museum, are on the property of Lord Montagu of Beaulieu (pronounced *Bew*-ley). A Cistercian abbey was founded on this spot in 1204, and you can explore its ruins. The Palace House, surrounded by gardens, was the gatehouse of the abbey before it was converted into a private residence in 1538.

National Motor Museum ★★, one of the best and most comprehensive automotive museums in the world, with more than 250 vehicles, is on the grounds and is open to the public. Famous autos include four land-speed record holders, among them Donald Campbell's Bluebird. The collection was built around Lord Montagu's family collection of vintage cars. A special feature is called "Wheels." In a darkened environment, visitors travel in specially designed "pods" that carry up to two adults and one child along a silent electric track. Moving at a predetermined but variable speed, each pod can rotate almost 360 degrees. Seated in these, you'll view displays (with sound and visual effects) spanning 100 years of motor development without the fatigue of standing in line. For further information, contact the visitor reception manager at the John Montagu Building (© **01590/612345**).

Beaulieu, on B3056 in the New Forest (8km/5 miles southeast of Lyndhurst and 23km/14 miles west of Southampton). © **01590/612345**. www.beaulieu.co.uk. Admission £13 ($24) adults, £12 ($22) seniors and students, £6.60 ($12) children 5–12, free for children under 5, £35 ($65) family (2 adults and up to 3 children). May–Sept daily 10am–6pm; Oct–Apr daily 10am–5pm. Closed Dec 25. Buses run from the Lymington bus station Mon–Sat; Sun you'll need a taxi or car.

Maritime Museum ★   Buckler's Hard, a historic 18th-century village 4km (2½ miles) from Beaulieu on the banks of the River Beaulieu, is where ships for Nelson's fleet were built, including the admiral's favorite, *Agamemnon,* as well as *Eurylus* and *Swiftsure.* The Maritime Museum highlights the village's shipbuilding history as well as Henry Adams, master shipbuilder; Nelson's favorite ship; Buckler's Hard and Trafalgar; and models of Sir Francis Chichester's yachts and items of his equipment. The cottage exhibits re-create 18th-century life in

Buckler's Hard—stroll through the New Inn of 1793 and a shipwright's cottage of the same period or look in on the family of a poor laborer.

The walk back to Beaulieu, 4km (2½ miles) on the riverbank, is well-marked through the woodlands. During the summer, you can take a 20-minute cruise on the River Beaulieu in the present *Swiftsure,* an all-weather catamaran cruiser.

Buckler's Hard. ℂ **01590/616203.** Admission to Buckler's Hard £5.25 ($9.70) adults, £4.75 ($8.80) seniors, £3.75 ($6.95) children 5-17, £16 ($30) family ticket (2 adults, 3 children); cruise fare £3 ($5.55) adults, £2.50 ($4.65) seniors, £2 ($3.70) children 5–17. Easter–Sept daily 10am–5:30pm; Oct–Easter daily 10am–4pm.

WHERE TO STAY AROUND THE NEW FOREST
VERY EXPENSIVE
Chewton Glen Hotel ★★★   A gracious country house on the fringe of the New Forest, Chewton Glen, within easy reach of Southampton and Bournemouth, is the finest place to stay in southwest England (with princely rates to match). In the old house, a magnificent staircase leads to well-furnished double rooms opening onto views of the spacious grounds. In the new wing, you find yourself on the ground level, with French doors opening onto your own private patio. Accommodations vary widely and come in different shapes, sizes, and periods, but each is equipped with a double or twin bed. Attic accommodations and some newly refurbished rooms contain air conditioners. The best accommodations are the Croquet Lawn Rooms, which open onto the greens and have big private balconies or terraces. The bathrooms in all rooms are luxurious, with deluxe toiletries, tubs, and separate power showers in large stalls. Some rooms can accommodate those with mobility impairments. Log fires burn and fresh flowers add fragrance; the garden sweeps down to a stream and then to rhododendron woods.

Christchurch Rd., New Milton, Hampshire BH25 6QS. ℂ **01425/275341.** Fax 01425/283045. www.chewton glen.com. 58 units. £270–£445 ($500–$823) double; £520–£780 ($962–$1,443) suite. AE, DC, MC, V. After leaving the village of Walkford, follow signs off A35 (New Milton–Christchurch Rd.), through parkland. **Amenities:** Restaurant; bar; 2 pools (1 indoor, 1 outdoor); 4 tennis courts (2 indoor, 2 outdoor); 9-hole golf course; spa; health club; Jacuzzi; sauna; 24-hr. room service; laundry service; dry cleaning; rooms for those with limited mobility. *In room:* A/C (some rooms), TV, hair dryer, safe, trouser press.

EXPENSIVE
Master Builders House Hotel ★★   This hotel is located about 4km (2½ miles) south of Beaulieu, in the historic maritime village of Buckler's Hard. This 17th-century redbrick building was once the home of master shipbuilder Henry Adams, who incorporated many of his shipbuilding techniques into the construction of this lovely old house. Views from some of the bedrooms overlook the grass-covered slipways that, centuries ago, were used to ease newly built ocean vessels into the calm waters of the nearby river.

Most of the hotel's comfortable and conservatively decorated accommodations are in a modern wing, built after World War II. If you like the creaky floorboards and charm of old-world England, opt for one of the six old-fashioned bedrooms in the main house. If you want a greater amount of luxuries and more space, select a room in the purpose-built annex; these are plainer but better equipped. Bedrooms vary in size and shape; most are equipped with king-size beds and contain such thoughtful touches as mineral water and bathrobes. Bathrooms are small but efficiently organized with luxury toiletries, tubs, and power showers.

Buckler's Hard, Beaulieu, Hampshire SO42 7XB. ℂ **01590/616253.** Fax 01590/616297. www.themaster builders.co.uk. 25 units. £170–£245 ($315–$453) double. Rates include English breakfast. Half board £210–£285 ($389–$527) double. AE, MC, V. **Amenities:** Restaurant; bar; limited room service; laundry service; dry cleaning; nonsmoking rooms; rooms for those with limited mobility. *In room:* TV, coffeemaker, hair dryer.

The Montagu Arms ⭐⭐   This hotel has an interesting history; it was built in the 1700s to supply food and drink to the laborers who hauled salt from the nearby marshes to other parts of England. The garden walls were constructed with stones salvaged from Beaulieu Abbey after it was demolished by Henry VIII. The hexagonal column supporting a fountain in the hotel's central courtyard is one of six salvaged, according to legend, from the ruined abbey's nave. Bedrooms are individually decorated in an English country house tradition, come in a range of shapes and sizes, and have extras including a trouser press and a writing desk. Many units contain a traditional four-poster bed. The small bathrooms are beautifully maintained, each with tub and shower.

Palace Lane, Beaulieu, New Forest, Hampshire, SO42 7ZL. ⓒ **01590/612324.** Fax 01590/612188. www. montaguarmshotel.co.uk. 23 units. £160–£170 ($296–$315) double; £210–£240 ($389–$444) suite. Rates include English breakfast. £25 ($46) per extra person in room. AE, DC, MC, V. **Amenities:** 2 restaurants; 2 bars; 24-hr. room service; nearby spa; laundry service; dry cleaning; all nonsmoking rooms. *In room:* TV, hair dryer, trouser press.

MODERATE

Balmer Lawn Hotel ⭐ *Kids*   This hotel lies about a 10-minute walk from Brockenhurst's center in a woodland location. Built as a private home during the 17th century, it was later enlarged into an imposing hunting lodge. During World War II, it was a military hospital. (In the past decade, many overnight guests have spotted the ghost of one of the white-coated doctors with his stethoscope, roaming the hotel's 1st floor.) The hotel has a pleasant and humorous staff (which refers to the ghost as "Dr. Eric"). A good range of bedrooms, in all shapes and sizes, all have an individual character; bathrooms are small, with tub-and-shower combinations. Request a room with a view of the forest. There are three family bedrooms, and children up to 16 stay free in their parent's room.

Lyndhurst Rd., Brockenhurst, Hampshire SO42 7ZB. ⓒ **01590/623116.** Fax 01590/623864. www.blh.co.uk. 55 units. £130–£160 ($241–$296) double. Rates include English breakfast. AE, DC, MC, V. Take A337 (Lyndhurst-Lymington Rd.) about 1km (½ mile) outside Brockenhurst. **Amenities:** Restaurant; bar; 2 pools (1 indoor, 1 outdoor); tennis court; gym; sauna; Jacuzzi; 2 squash courts; limited room service; laundry service; dry cleaning; nonsmoking rooms; rooms for those with limited mobility. *In room:* TV, dataport, coffeemaker, hair dryer, trouser press.

Carey's Manor ⭐⭐ *Finds*   This manor house dates from Charles II, who used to come here when it was a hunting lodge. Greatly expanded in 1888, the building became a country hotel in the 1930s. Much improved in recent years, the old house is still filled with character, possessing mellow, timeworn paneling and a carved oak staircase. Each bedroom, whether in the restored main building or in the garden wing, has a bathroom with a shower-tub combination and bathrobes. Most rooms have balconies. Six rooms contain an old-fashioned four-poster bed, but whether your room does or not, it will still have a firm bed offering cozy comfort. *Note:* Children under 10 are not accepted as guests.

Lyndhurst Rd., Brockenhurst, Hampshire SO42 7RH. ⓒ **01590/623551.** Fax 01590/622799. www.careys manor.co.uk. 79 units. £149–£179 ($276–$331) double; £199–£239 ($368–$442) suite. Rates include English breakfast. AE, DC, MC, V. From the town center, head toward Lyndhurst on A337. **Amenities:** 2 restaurants; bar; indoor pool; gym; sauna; solarium; salon; 24-hr. room service; spa; laundry service; dry cleaning; nonsmoking rooms. *In room:* TV, dataport, coffeemaker, hair dryer, trouser press.

The Crown Hotel   Though the present building is only 100 years old, a hostelry has been here on the main street of the New Forest village of Lyndhurst for centuries. For generations, it has been a favorite of visitors to the New Forest, who delight in its gardens, where afternoon tea is served, or its roaring fireplace in winter. Bedrooms are most inviting, each furnished in the classic tradition of an English country house, with features such as four-poster bed, in many cases. Some rooms are more modern, with padded headboards and fine furnishings. A few of the superior rooms can accommodate families. Small bathrooms are modern and well appointed, each with a tub and shower.

9 High St., Lyndhurst, Hampshire SO43 7NF. ⓒ **800/528-1234** in the U.S., or 023/8028-2922. Fax 023/8028-2751. www.crownhotel-lyndhurst.co.uk. 38 units. £135–£145 ($250–$268) double; £155–£195 ($287–$361) suite. Rates include English breakfast. Children under 16 stay for £15 ($28) in parent's room. AE, DC, MC, V. Bus: 56 or 56A. Exit M27 at Junction 1 and drive 5km (3 miles) due south. **Amenities:** Restaurant; bar; 24-hr. room service; babysitting (by arrangement); laundry service; dry cleaning service; nonsmoking rooms. *In room:* TV, dataport, coffeemaker, hair dryer, trouser press.

Lyndhurst Park Hotel   This large Georgian country house lies on 2 hectares (5 acres) of beautiful gardens. Located at the edge of town where Lyndhurst meets the New Forest, this hotel often attracts conferences. Much of the property remains characteristically rustic, though filled with modern comforts. Bedrooms are medium in size and extremely well kept, often with brass headboards crowning the fine English beds. Bathrooms are tiled and fully carpeted, each with tub and shower.

High St., Lyndhurst, Hampshire SO43 7NL. ⓒ 023/8028-3923. Fax 023/8028-3019. www.lyndhurstparkhotel. co.uk. 59 units. £105–£135 ($194–$250) double. Rates include English breakfast. Children under 14 stay free in parent's room. AE, DC, MC, V. Bus: 56. **Amenities:** Restaurant; bar; heated outdoor pool; tennis court; sauna; 24-hr. room service; laundry service; nonsmoking rooms. *In room:* TV, coffeemaker, hair dryer, trouser press.

New Park Manor Hotel ✦   This former royal hunting lodge, from the days of William the Conqueror and a favorite of Charles II, is the only hotel in the New Forest itself. Though now a modern country hotel, the original rooms have been preserved, with such features as beams and, in some rooms, open log fires. Since its purchase in 1998 by the Countess von Essen, the hotel has been much improved; each room is nonsmoking and has been individually furnished; several rooms and suites have four-poster beds. Most rooms have a view overlooking the forest. Bathrooms are small but well organized, each with a tub and shower.

Lyndhurst Rd., Brockenhurst, Hampshire SO42 7QH. ⓒ 01590/623467. Fax 01590/622268. www.new parkmanorhotel.co.uk. 24 units. £110–£190 ($204–$352) double. 1 child over age 4 can stay in parent's room for £30 ($56) extra per night. Rates include breakfast. AE, DC, MC, V. Head 3km (2 miles) north off A337 (Lyndhurst-Brockenhurst Rd.) toward the New Forest Show Ground. **Amenities:** Restaurant; bar; horseback riding; limited room service; babysitting; laundry service; dry cleaning. *In room:* TV, dataport, coffeemaker, hair dryer, trouser press.

WHERE TO DINE

Simply Poussin ✦ FRENCH/ENGLISH   Serving the best food in the area, this restaurant is located in what was originally a 19th-century stable and workshop. To reach it, pass beneath the arched alleyway (located midway between nos. 49 and 55 Brookley Rd.) and enter the stylishly simple premises directed by English-born chef Alexander Aitken and his wife, Caroline.

Amid a decor accented with framed 19th-century poems and illustrations celebrating poultry, the staff offers fish and game dishes, with ingredients usually fresh from the nearby New Forest. Try "Fruits of the New Forest," individually cooked portions of pigeon, wild rabbit, hare, and venison, encased in puff pastry and served with game sauce. Dessert choices change seasonally but usually include lemon tart with lime sorbet or passion fruit soufflé.

The Courtyard, at the rear of 49–55 Brookley Rd., Brockenhurst. ⓒ 01590/623063. Reservations recommended 1 month in advance on weekends. 2-course lunch £10 ($19); 3-course lunch £15 ($28); 2-course dinner £15 ($28); 3-course dinner £20 ($37). MC, V. Tues–Sat noon–2pm and 7–10pm.

5 The Isle of Wight ★ ★

146km (91 miles) SW of London; 6.5km (4 miles) S of Southampton

The Isle of Wight is known for its sandy beaches and its ports, long favored by the yachting set. The island has attracted such literary figures as Alfred Lord Tennyson and Charles Dickens. Tennyson wrote his beloved poem "Crossing the Bar" en route across the Solent from Lymington to Yarmouth. A vacation on the island sounds a bit dated, though many British families come to relax and enjoy the natural beauty. You may want to come just for the day. Some parts are rather tacky, especially Sandown and Shanklin, though other areas out on the island are still tranquil and quite beautiful.

The Isle of Wight is compact, measuring 37km (23 miles) from east to west, 21km (13 miles) north to south. **Ryde** is the railhead for the island's transportation system. **Yarmouth** is something else—a busy little harbor providing a mooring for yachts and also for one of the lifeboats in the Solent area.

Cowes is the premier port for yachting in Britain. Henry VIII ordered the castle built here, but it's now the headquarters of the Royal Yacht Squadron. The seafront, the Prince's Green, and the high cliff road are worth exploring. Hovercraft are built in the town, which is also the home and birthplace of the well-known maritime photographer Beken of Cowes. In winter, everyone wears oilskins and wellies, leaving a wet trail behind them.

Newport, a bustling market town in the heart of the island, is the capital and has long been a favorite of British royalty. Along the southeast coast are the twin resorts of **Sandown,** with its new pier complex and theater, and **Shanklin,** at the southern end of Sandown Bay, which has held the British annual sunshine record more times than any other resort. Keats once lived in Shanklin's Old Village. Farther along the coast, **Ventnor** is called the "Madeira of England" because it rises from the sea in a series of steep hills.

On the west coast are the many-colored sand cliffs of **Alum Bay.** The Needles, three giant chalk rocks, and the Needles Lighthouse, are the farther features of interest at this end of the island. If you want to stay at the western end of Wight, consider **Freshwater Bay.**

ESSENTIALS

GETTING THERE A direct train from London's Waterloo Station to Portsmouth deposits travelers directly at the pier for a ferry crossing to the Isle of Wight; ferries are timed to meet train arrivals. Travel time from London to the arrival point of Ryde on the Isle of Wight (including ferry-crossing time) is 2 hours. One train per hour departs during the day from London to Portsmouth. For rail information, call ☏ **0845/748-4950** or visit www.railtrack.co.uk.

Drive to Southampton and take the ferry, or leave Southampton and head west along the A35, cutting south on the A337 toward Lymington on the coast, where the ferry crossing to Yarmouth (Isle of Wight) is shorter than the trip from Southampton.

Red Funnel operates a vehicle ferry service from Terminal 1 in Southampton to West Cowes; the trip takes 55 minutes. An inclusive round-trip fare (valid for 5 days) costs from £51.50 to £71 ($95–$131) for four persons, depending on the season. More popular with train travelers from Waterloo Station in London is a Hi-Speed passenger-only catamaran operating from the Town Quay Terminal 2 in Southampton, going to West Cowes; the trip takes 22 minutes. A day return fare costs £13 ($23) for adults and £6.30 ($12) for children. For ferry departure times, call ☏ **0870/444-8898** or visit www.redfunnel.co.uk.

The **Wight Link ferry** (© 0870/582-7744; www.wightlink.co.uk), operates between Portsmouth and Ryde, taking 20 minutes and costing £13 ($25) for adults and £6.70 ($12) for children, round-trip standard return. Daytime departures are every 30 minutes in summer and every 60 minutes in winter. A final option involves a Hovercraft that travels from Southsea (Portsmouth's neighbor) to Ryde, charging £9.80 ($18) for adults and £4.50 ($8.35) for children for day return.

GETTING AROUND   Visitors can explore the Isle of Wight just for the day on the Island Explorer bus service. Tickets may be purchased on the bus, and you can board or leave the bus at any stop on the island. The price of a Day Rover is £7 ($13) for adults and £4 ($7.40) for children. It also entitles you to passage on the island's only railway, which runs from the dock at Ryde to the center of Shanklin, a distance of 13km (8 miles). For further information, call **Southern Vectis** at © 01983/532373 or visit www.svoc.co.uk.

VISITOR INFORMATION   The **information office** is at 67 High St., Shanklin (© **01983/862942**). It's open Monday through Saturday from March to mid-July and September through October from 9am to 5:30pm, from mid-July to August from 9am to 8:45pm, and November through March from 10am to 4:30pm. It's best to call first, as these hours are subject to change.

QUEEN VICTORIA'S FAVORITE RESIDENCE & A MEDIEVAL CASTLE

Carisbrooke Castle ★★   This fine medieval castle lies in the center of the Isle of Wight. In 1647, during one of the most turbulent periods of English history, Charles I was imprisoned here, far from his former seat of power in London, by Cromwell's Roundheads. On the castle premises is the 16th-century Well House, where, during periods of siege, donkeys took turns treading a large wooden wheel connected to a rope that hauled up buckets of water from a well. Accessible from the castle's courtyard is a museum (© **01983/523112**) with exhibits pertaining to the social history of the Isle of Wight and the history of Charles I's imprisonment.

Carisbrooke, 2km (1¼ miles) southwest of Newport. © **01983/522107**. Castle and museum £5 ($9.25) adults, £3.80 ($7.05) seniors and students, £2.50 ($4.65) children, £13 ($23) family ticket. Apr–Sept daily 10am–6pm; Oct–Mar daily 10am–4pm. Bus: 91A.

Osborne House ★★   Queen Victoria's most cherished residence was built at her own expense. Prince Albert, with his characteristic thoroughness, contributed to many aspects of the design of the Italian-inspired mansion, which stands amid lush gardens, right outside the village of Whippingham. The rooms remain as Victoria knew them, down to the French piano she used to play and all the cozy clutter of her sitting room. Grief-stricken at the death of Albert in 1861, she asked that Osborne House be kept as it was, and so it has been. Even the turquoise scent bottles he gave her, decorated with cupids and cherubs, are still in place. In her bedroom at Osborne House, the queen died on January 22, 1901.

1.5km (1 mile) southeast of East Cowes. © **01983/200022**. House and grounds £8.50 ($16) adults, £6.40 ($12) seniors, £4.30 ($7.95) children, £21 ($39) family ticket. Admission to grounds only £5 ($9.25) adults, £3.80 ($7.05) seniors, £2.50 ($4.65) children, £13 ($23) family ticket. Apr–Sept daily 10am–6pm (house closes at 5pm); Oct–Mar, Sun–Thurs 10am–2:30pm (guided tours only). Closed Dec 25–26, Jan 1. Bus: 4 or 5.

WHERE TO STAY

Bourne Hall Country Hotel   Many visitors prefer to base at Shanklin. At Bourne Hall, they receive a warm welcome from the owners, who have one of the area's best-equipped hotels. The hotel stands on nearly 1.2 hectares (3 acres), adjoining open farmland. Bedrooms are furnished in a delightful English country-house style. Some have recently been redecorated, and even those that haven't are still in fine shape. All are nonsmoking rooms. Each small bathroom is well maintained and all contain a shower.

Luccombe Rd., Shanklin, Isle of Wight PO37 6RR. © **01983/862820.** Fax 01983/865138. www.bournehall hotel.co.uk. 31 units. £80–£120 ($148–$222) bed-and-breakfast, £115–£139 ($213–$257) double. Rates include half board and transfers. AE, DC, MC, V. **Amenities:** Restaurant; bar; 2 pools (1 indoor, 1 outdoor); Jacuzzi; sauna. *In room:* TV, dataport, coffeemaker, hair dryer.

The George Hotel ⭐⭐   The best cuisine and most elegant lodgings are at this former governor's residence dating from the 17th century. Between the quay and the castle, overlooking the Solent, this is a tranquil oasis in this port so beloved by English yachties. The good-size bedrooms are individually decorated, each with style and an eye for comfort, with well-maintained private bathrooms with tub-and-shower combination. All rooms are nonsmoking. The professionalism of this place is to be applauded. It's leagues ahead of some of the dowdy properties on the island, many of them looking like leftovers from Victoria's era. Even if you aren't a guest, call for a reservation in one of The George's two dining options (see below).

Quay St. PO41 OPE Yarmouth, Isle of Wright. © **01983/760331.** Fax 01983/760425. www.thegeorge.co.uk. 17 units. £175–£245 ($324–$453) double. Rates include English breakfast. AE, DC, MC, V. **Amenities:** 2 restaurants; bar; limited room service; laundry service. *In room:* A/C, TV.

Hotel Ryde Castle *(Kids)*   This historic seafront castle looking onto the Solent makes a fine base for exploring the island. The castle, dating from the 16th century, has been added to over the centuries. Field Marshall Montgomery stayed here before D-Day landings. With its crenellated ivy-clad exterior and its well-kept public rooms, the hotel attracts families as well as single visitors. Bedrooms, small to medium in size, have an inviting aura with traditional British styling. Comfort is the keynote here, and some accommodations have a more romantic aura and a four-poster bed. Each room has a small private bathroom; most rooms offer sea views. All rooms are nonsmoking. Kids can hang around at the children's play area or look for the friendly ghost rumored to be a hotel resident.

The Esplanade, Ryde, Isle of Wight PO33 1JA. © **01983/563755.** Fax 01983/566906. www.oldenglish.co.uk. 21 units. £75–£100 ($139–$185) double. Rates include English breakfast. AE, DC, MC, V. **Amenities:** Restaurant; bar; limited room service. *In room:* TV, coffeemaker.

St. Catherine's Hotel   This hotel lies a few minutes' walk from Sandown's sandy beach, leisure center, and pier complex. With its sun lounges, theater, and Sandown railway station, St. Catherine's was built in 1860 of creamy Purbeck stone and white trim for the dean of Winchester College. A modern extension was added for streamlined and sunny bedrooms, which have duvets, white furniture, and built-in headboards. Bathrooms are small, each with a shower-tub combination. The brightly redecorated lounge has matching draperies at the wide bay windows, along with card tables and a small library of books.

1 Winchester Park Rd., Sandown, Isle of Wight PO36 8HJ. © and fax **01983/402392.** 19 units. £50–£100 ($93–$185) double. Rates include English breakfast. MC, V. **Amenities:** Restaurant; bar; 24-hr. room service; nonsmoking rooms; rooms for those with limited mobility. *In room:* TV, coffeemaker, hair dryer.

Wight Mouse Inn ⭐ *(Finds)* *(Kids)*   The Wight Mouse is a cheerful place to stay. This old coaching inn lies on the most southerly part of the island, where the vegetation is almost tropical. From here, you can see over the Channel to the mainland coast. Though a bit small, each bedroom is prettily decorated in an

English country-house style, and has a private bathroom (usually with a tub-and-shower combination). Children are warmly welcomed and can burn off energy in MouseWorld, an indoor play area, or at the outdoor playground.

Newport Rd. (B3399; 45m/150 ft. off Military Rd.), Chale, Isle of Wight PO38 2HA. ✆ and fax **01983/730431**. www.wightmouseinns.co.uk. 16 units. £50–£80 ($93–$148) double. Children ages up to 16 stay with parents for £20 ($37). Rates include English breakfast. MC, V. **Amenities:** Bar; nonsmoking rooms. *In room:* TV, coffeemaker, hair dryer.

WHERE TO DINE

The Cottage ENGLISH   In a 200-year-old stone-sided cottage, this restaurant is set among thatch-covered buildings in the center of Shanklin. Inside, two floors of pink and blue dining rooms are accented by lace tablecloths and heavy oak beams. For starters, try the delicious avocado Ritz. As a main course, you can enjoy such treats as braised guinea fowl smothered in a port and apricot sauce, or Dover sole pan-fried with lemon butter. For the more adventurous, try the ostrich, pan-fried and served with a green peppercorn sauce. Two lounges accommodate smokers. The garden and courtyard are open in summer for drinks.

8 Eastcliff Rd., Shanklin Old Village. ✆ **01983/862504**. Reservations recommended. Main courses £12–£17 ($22–$31). AE, DC, MC, V. Tues–Sun noon–2pm; Tues–Sat 7pm–midnight.

The Restaurant/The Brasserie ★★   The most refined cuisine on the island is at The George (see above). One kitchen services the formal restaurant and the relaxed brasserie. The restaurant is imbued with a rich aura of candlelight and painted panels, and the best view of the Solent is from the sunny brasserie. The restaurant is known for its quality ingredients, deftly handled and beautifully presented in showcase fixed-price dinners. Try such delights as trio of duck, with foie gras, duck ravioli, and rillettes, or halibut wedded to langoustine. For dessert, try another trio, a medley of chocolate sweets with raspberry sauce, or in summer, rhubarb mousse with blueberries poached in licorice.

In The George Hotel, Quay St. ✆ **01983/760331**. In the Restaurant: 4-course dinner £45 ($83). In the Brasserie: Main courses £14–£20 ($26–$37); fixed-price lunch £25 ($46). AE, MC, V. Restaurant: Tues–Sat 7–10pm. Brasserie: Daily noon–3pm and 7–10pm.

6 Bournemouth ⋆

167km (104 miles) SW of London; 24km (15 miles) W of the Isle of Wight

This south coast resort at the doorstep of the New Forest didn't just happen: It was carefully planned and executed—a true city in a garden. Flower-filled, park-dotted Bournemouth is filled with an abundance of architecture inherited from those arbiters of taste, Victoria and her son, Edward. (The resort was discovered back in Victoria's day, when sea bathing became an institution.) Bournemouth's most distinguished feature is its *chines* (narrow, shrub-filled, steep-sided ravines) along the coastline.

Bournemouth, along with neighboring Poole and Christchurch, forms the largest urban area in the south of England. It makes a good base for exploring a historically rich part of England; on its outskirts are the New Forest, Salisbury, Winchester, and the Isle of Wight.

ESSENTIALS

GETTING THERE   An express train from London's Waterloo Station to Bournemouth takes 2½ hours, with frequent service throughout the day. For schedules and information, call ✆ **0845/748-4950** or visit www.railtrack.co.uk. Arrivals are at the Bournemouth Rail Station, on Holden Surst Road.

Buses leave London's Waterloo Station every 2 hours during the day, heading for Bournemouth. The trip takes 2½ hours. Call ☏ **0870/580-8080** or visit www.nationalexpress.com for information and schedules.

If you're driving, take the M3 southwest from London to Winchester, then the A31 and the A338 south to Bournemouth.

VISITOR INFORMATION   The **information office** is at Westover Road (☏ **01202/451731**). From May to September, it's open Monday through Saturday from 9am to 7pm, Sunday from 10am to 5:30pm; from September to May, hours are Monday through Saturday from 9:30am to 5:30pm.

EXPLORING THE AREA

The resort's amusements are varied. At the **Pavilion Theatre,** you can see West End–type productions from London. The **Bournemouth Symphony Orchestra** is justly famous in Europe. And there's the usual run of golf courses, band concerts, variety shows, and dancing.

And of course, this seaside resort has a spectacular beach—11km (7 miles) of uninterrupted sand stretching from Hengistbury Head to Alum Chine. Most of it is known simply as **Bournemouth Beach,** although its western edge, when it crosses over into the municipality of Poole, is called **Sandbanks Beach.** Beach access is free, and a pair of blue flags will indicate where the water's fine for swimming. The flags also signify the highest standards of cleanliness, management, and facilities. A health-conscious, nonsmoking zone now exists at Durley Chine, East Beach, and Fisherman's Walk. Fourteen full-time lifeguards patrol the shore and the water; they are helped by three volunteer corps during the busiest summer months. The promenade is traffic-free during the summer. There are two piers, one at Boscombe and the other at Bournemouth.

Amenities at the beach include beach bungalows, freshwater showers, seafront bistros and cafes, boat trips, rowboats, pedalos, jet skis, and Windsurfers. Cruises run in the summer from Bournemouth Pier to the Isle of Wight.

The traffic-free town center, with its wide avenues, is elegant but by no means stuffy. Entertainers perform on the corners of streets that are lined with boutiques, cafes, street furniture, and plenty of meeting places. Specialized shopping is found mainly in the suburbs—Pokesdown for antiques and collectibles, Westbourne for individual designer fashion and home accessories. Victorian shopping arcades can be found in both Westbourne and Boscombe.

WHERE TO STAY
VERY EXPENSIVE

Langtry Manor Hotel ⋆ *Finds*   A much more atmospheric choice and run with a more personal touch than the Carlton and Norfolk Royale, the Red House, as this hotel was originally called, was built in 1877 for Lillie Langtry, a gift from Edward VII to his favorite mistress. The house has all sorts of reminders of its illustrious inhabitants, including initials scratched on a windowpane and carvings on

---

Moments **The "Green Lungs" of Bournemouth**

About a sixth of Bournemouth's nearly 4,856 hectares (12,000 acres) consists of green parks and flowerbeds such as the **Pavilion Rock Garden,** which is perfect for a stroll. The total effect, especially in spring, is striking and helps explain Bournemouth's continuing popularity with the garden-loving English.

a beam of the entrance hall. On the half-landing is the peephole through which the prince could scrutinize the assembled company before coming down to dine, and one fireplace bears his initials. The bedrooms, each a double, range from ordinary twins to the Lillie Langtry Suite, Lillie's own room, with a four-poster bed and a double heart-shaped bathtub; or you can rent the Edward VII Suite, furnished as it was when His Royal Highness lived in this spacious room with a working fireplace and a cast-iron bathtub in the Edwardian-style bathroom. All bathrooms are tiled and beautifully maintained; some have Jacuzzis.

26 Derby Rd. (north of Christchurch Rd., A35), E. Cliff, Bournemouth, Dorset BH1 3QB. © 01202/553887. Fax 01202/290115. www.langtrymanor.com. 27 units. £149–£228 ($276–$422) double; £189 ($350) suite for 2. Rates include English breakfast. AE, MC, V. **Amenities:** Restaurant; bar; limited room service; dry cleaning; 1 room for those with limited mobility. *In room:* TV/VCR, dataport, minibar, hair dryer.

Menzies Carlton Hotel ✿   More of a resort than an ordinary hotel, the Carlton sits atop a seaside cliff lined with private homes and other hotels. This Edwardian pile, with panoramic views, is one of the best places to stay in Bournemouth. It exudes a 1920s aura, with rather opulent public rooms. Extensively renovated, most bedrooms are spacious and open onto views of the sea. Many of the rooms have marbled wallpaper, mottled mirrors, and armchairs, and bathrooms are generous in size and have a combination tub and shower. On the downside, readers have complained that in some rooms the double glazing on the windows does little to cut down on the noise level.

Meyrick Rd., E. Overcliff, Bournemouth, Dorset BH1 3DN. © 01202/552011. Fax 01202/299573. www.book menzies.com. 73 units. £150–£200 ($278–$370) double; from £260 ($481) suite. AE, DC, MC, V. **Amenities:** Restaurant; bar; 24-hr. room service; 2 heated pools (1 outdoor, 1 indoor); health club and spa; sauna; Jacuzzi; solarium; laundry service; dry cleaning; nonsmoking rooms. *In room:* TV, dataport, coffeemaker, hair dryer, trouser press.

The Priory Hotel   This hotel lies 3km (2 miles) west of Bournemouth in Wareham, beside the River Frame and near the village church. It has a well-tended garden adorned by old trees. Inside, a paneled bar and a lounge filled with antiques open onto views of the lawn. Rooms are individually decorated (often with fine antiques) and offer much comfort, including such items as mineral water, fruit, and bathrobes; some feature four-poster beds. Some accommodations are in a well-crafted annex. Most of the small bathrooms contain a tub-and-shower combination; a few have Jacuzzis. *Note:* Children under 8 are not permitted as guests, and those over 8 are charged full price.

Church Green, Wareham, Dorset BH20 4ND. © 01929/551666. Fax 01929/554519. www.thepriory hotel.co.uk. 18 units. £165–£205 ($305–$379) double; £285 ($527) suite; B&B plus dinner £220–£260 ($407–$481) double; £345 ($638) suite. Rates include English breakfast. DC, MC, V. **Amenities:** 2 restaurants; bar; limited room service; laundry service; dry cleaning. *In room:* TV, dataport, minibar (some), hair dryer.

Royal Bath Hotel ⋆⋆⋆ This early Victorian version of a French château, with towers and bay windows looking out over the bay and Purbeck Hill, dates from June 28, 1838, the very day of Victoria's coronation. After the adolescent Prince of Wales (later Edward VII) stayed here, the hotel added "Royal" to its name. Over the years, it has attracted notables from Oscar Wilde to Rudolf Nureyev to the great prime minister, Disraeli. In luxury and style, it is in a neck-and-neck race with the Carlton. It's located in a 1.2-hectare (3-acre) garden where cliff-top panoramas open onto the sea. The mostly spacious bedrooms are furnished with a certain English style and grace, and the larger rooms have sitting areas. All rooms are nonsmoking. Most bedrooms have been recently refurbished, and the bathrooms are well maintained, luxurious, and come with Neutrogena bath products; superior rooms also offer bathrobes and slippers.

Bath Rd., Bournemouth, Dorset BH1 2EW. ℭ **01202/555555.** Fax 01202/554158. www.devereroyalbath.co.uk. 140 units. £175–£220 ($324–$407) double; £260 ($481) junior suite; £325 ($601) twin/double suite. Rates include English breakfast. AE, DC, MC, V. Parking £8.50 ($16). **Amenities:** 2 restaurants; bar; indoor pool; health spa; Jacuzzi; sauna; limited room service; laundry service; dry cleaning; 1 room for those with limited mobility. *In room:* TV w/pay movies, minibar, coffeemaker, hair dryer, iron/ironing board, trouser press.

EXPENSIVE

Bournemouth Highcliff Marriott ⋆⋆⋆ This 1888 cliff-side hotel is one of the best in Bournemouth, rivaled only by the Carlton and Royal Bath. The high-ceilinged interior has been tastefully renovated. A funicular elevator takes guests from the hotel to the seaside promenade. Many bedrooms have beautiful views of the sea. Each is traditionally furnished in elegant English style and is located in the main building or in coast-guard cottages built in 1912. Rooms are generally spacious, with midsize bathrooms with tub-and-shower combination.

105 St. Michael's Rd., W. Cliff, Bournemouth, Dorset BH2 5DU. ℭ **0870/4007211.** Fax 0870/4007311. www. marriotthotels.com/bohbm. 157 units. £115–£150 ($213–$278) double; from £160 ($296) suite. Rates include English breakfast. AE, DC, MC, V. **Amenities:** Restaurant; bar; 2 pools (1 indoor, 1 outdoor); sauna; solarium; tennis court; gym; whirlpool; 24-hr. room service; babysitting; laundry service; dry cleaning; nonsmoking rooms; rooms for those with limited mobility. *In room:* A/C, TV w/pay movies, dataport, minibar, coffeemaker, hair dryer, iron/ironing board, trouser press.

The Mansion House ⋆ (Finds) In nearby Poole, this 18th-century town house is for those seeking charm and atmosphere. The neoclassical detailing and fan-shaped windows are the pride and well-maintained joy of the owners. Graciously furnished bedrooms provide plenty of quiet, well-decorated corners for relaxation and offer homey touches such as mineral water. The building has been extended to provide roomy and inviting accommodations, each individually decorated according to various themes (Oriental, Georgian, French, for example) with comfortable furnishings. Two rooms have four-poster beds; two are suitable for families. Most bathrooms have a tub-and-shower combination.

7–11 Thames St., Poole (6.5km/4 miles west of Bournemouth), Dorset BH15 1JN. ℭ **01202/685666.** Fax 01202/665709. www.themansionhouse.co.uk. 32 units. £130–£140 ($241–$259) double; £145 ($268) suite. Rates include English breakfast. AE, DC, MC, V. **Amenities:** 2 restaurants; 2 bars; 24-hr. room service; babysitting; nonsmoking rooms. *In room:* TV, dataport, hair dryer.

Norfolk Royale Hotel ⋆⋆ One of the oldest and most prestigious hotels in town, a few blocks from the seafront and central shopping area, it recently underwent a major £5 million renovation program, restoring it to its former Edwardian elegance, with a two-tier, cast-iron veranda. Nevertheless, we think it still plays second fiddle to both the Carlton and the Royal Bath. It exudes the atmosphere of a country estate, with formal entrance, rear garden, and fountain shaded by trees. Rooms and suites have been luxuriously appointed with the styles of the period blending with modern comforts. Bathrooms are of good size and well equipped with both a tub and shower.

Richmond Hill, Bournemouth, Dorset BH2 6EN. ✆ **01202/551521.** Fax 01202/229729. www.englishrose hotels.co.uk. 96 units. £150 ($278) double; £255 ($472) suite. Rates include breakfast. Children 3–16 £7.50–£13 ($14–$23) per night. AE, DC, MC, V. **Amenities:** Restaurant; bar; indoor pool; Jacuzzi; sauna; limited room service; babysitting; laundry service; nonsmoking rooms; rooms for those with limited mobility. *In room:* TV, minibar, coffeemaker, hair dryer, trouser press.

INEXPENSIVE

The New Westcliff Hotel *Value*   This hotel is a 5-minute walk from the town center, near Durley Chine, and was once the luxurious south-coast home of the duke of Westminster, who had it built in 1876. Now run by the Blissert family, the hotel draws lots of repeat business. All rooms are comfortably furnished and well maintained; some have four-posters. As befits a former private home, bedrooms come in various shapes and sizes, but each is fitted with a good bed plus a small bathroom with adequate shelf space and a shower. There's a large garden and a parking area.

27 Chine Crescent, W. Cliff, Bournemouth, Dorset BH2 5LB. ✆ **01202/551062.** Fax 01202/315377. www. newwestcliffhotel.co.uk. 55 units. £72–£100 ($133–$185) double. Rates include English breakfast. Half board £41–£58 ($76–$107) per person. MC, V. **Amenities:** Restaurant; 2 bars; indoor heated pool; Jacuzzi; sauna; solarium; theater area with surround-sound cinema; nonsmoking rooms; rooms for those with limited mobility. *In room:* TV, coffeemaker, hair dryer, trouser press.

WHERE TO DINE

Oscars ⭐ FRENCH   Sporting Oscar Wilde mementos, Bournemouth's best restaurant is located cliff side, with panoramic sea views. The chef, John Wood, presents a la carte dishes as well as fixed-price menus. The excellent appetizers may include a terrine of salmon scallops and king prawns with a saffron and basil jelly. The imaginative main courses may include filet of steamed bass with sesame crust, cucumber noodles, mussels and lemon-grass jus; or Dorset lamb enhanced with zucchini duxelle bay-flavored jus, and dauphinoise of celeriac and potatoes.

In the Royal Bath Hotel, Bath Rd. ✆ **01202/555555.** Reservations required. Fixed-price lunch, £14–£19 ($25–$34), fixed-price dinner £25–£32 ($46–$59). AE, DC, MC, V. Daily 12:30–2pm and 7:30–10pm.

BOURNEMOUTH AFTER DARK

A choice of major art venues offers great performances year-round. **International Centre's Windsor Hall** hosts leading performers from London, the **Pavilion** puts on West End musicals as well as dancing with live music, and the **Winter Gardens,** the original home and favorite performance space of the world-famous Bournemouth Symphony Orchestra, offers regular concerts. Program and ticket information for all three venues is available by calling ✆ **0870/1113000.**

EN ROUTE TO DORCHESTER: A 17TH-CENTURY MANSION

Kingston Lacy   An imposing 17th-century mansion set on 101 hectares (250 acres) of wooded park, Kingston Lacy was the home of the Bankes family for more than 300 years. They entertained such distinguished guests as King Edward VII, Kaiser Wilhelm, Thomas Hardy, and George V. The house displays a magnificent collection of artwork by Rubens, Titian, and Van Dyck, as well as an important collection of Egyptian artifacts.

The present structure replaced Corfe Castle, the Bankes family home that was destroyed in the civil war. During her husband's absence while performing duties as chief justice to King Charles I, Lady Bankes led the defense of the castle, withstanding two sieges before being forced to surrender to Cromwell's forces in 1646 because of the actions of a treacherous follower. The keys to Corfe Castle hang in the library at Kingston Lacy.

At Wimborne Minster, on B3082 (Wimborne-Blandford Rd.), 2.5km (1½ miles) west of Wimborne. ℂ 01202/883402. Admission to the house, garden, and park £7.20 ($13) adults, £3.60 ($6.65) children, £19 ($35) family ticket. Garden only £3.60 ($6.65) adults, £1.80 ($3.35) children, £9.50 ($18) family ticket. House: mid-Mar to Oct Wed–Sun 11am–5pm. Garden and Park: mid-Mar to Oct daily 10:30am–6pm; Nov to mid-Dec Fri–Sun 10:30am–4pm; Feb to mid-Mar Sat–Sun 10:30am–4pm. Closed mid-Dec to Jan.

7 Dorchester: Hardy's Home ⭑

193km (120 miles) SW of London; 43km (27 miles) W of Bournemouth

In his 1886 novel *The Mayor of Casterbridge,* Thomas Hardy gave Dorchester literary fame. Actually, Dorchester was notable even in Roman times, when Maumbury Rings, the best Roman amphitheater in Britain, was filled with the sounds of 12,000 spectators screaming for the blood of the gladiators. Today, it's a sleepy market town that seems to go to bed right after dinner.

ESSENTIALS

GETTING THERE   Trains run from London's Waterloo Station each hour during the day. The trip takes 2½ hours. For rail information, call ℂ 0845/748-4950 or visit www.railtrack.co.uk. Dorchester has two train stations, the South Station at Station Approach and the West Station on Great Western Road. For information about both, call ℂ 0845/748-4950.

Several **National Express** coaches a day depart from London's Victoria Coach Station heading for Dorchester. The trip takes 3¾ hours. Call ℂ 0870/580-8080 or visit www.nationalexpress.com for information and schedules.

If driving from London, take the M3 southwest, but near the end take the A30 toward Salisbury to connect with the A354 for the final approach to Dorchester.

VISITOR INFORMATION   The **Tourist Information Centre** is at Unit 11, Antelope Walk (ℂ 01305/267992). It's open from April to October, Monday through Saturday from 9am to 5pm (also open Sun 10am–3pm from May–Sept); November to March, Monday through Saturday from 9am to 4pm.

SEEING THE SIGHTS

Athelhampton House & Gardens ⭑⭑   This is one of England's great medieval houses and the most beautiful and historic in the south, lying a mile east of Puddletown. Thomas Hardy mentioned it in some of his writings but called it Athelhall. It was begun during the reign of Edward IV on the legendary site of King Athelstan's palace. A family home for over 500 years, it's noted for its 15th-century Great Hall, Tudor great chamber, state bedroom, and King's Room.

In 1992, a dozen of the house's rooms were damaged by an accidental fire caused by faulty wiring in the attic. Skilled craftspeople, however, restored all the magnificent interiors.

Insider's tip: Though many visitors come to see the house, the gardens are even more inspiring. Dating from 1891, they are full of vistas, and their beauty is enhanced by the River Piddle flowing through and by fountains. These walled gardens, winners of the HHA/Christies garden of the year award, contain the famous topiary pyramids and two pavilions designed by Inigo Jones. You'll see fine collections of tulips and magnolias, roses, and lilies, and also a 15th-century dovecote. Yes, they were often visited by Thomas Hardy.

On A35, 8km (5 miles) east of Dorchester. ℂ 01305/848363. www.athelhampton.co.uk. Admission £7.75 ($14) adults, £7 ($13) seniors, £5.50 ($10) students. Mar–Oct Mon–Thurs 10am–5pm and Sun 10:30am–5pm; Nov–Feb Sun 10:30am–dusk. Take the Dorchester-Bournemouth Rd. (A35) east of Dorchester for 8km (5 miles).

Dorset County Museum 🎯   This museum has a gallery devoted to memorabilia of Thomas Hardy's life. In addition, you'll find an archaeological gallery with displays and finds from Maiden Castle, Britain's largest Iron Age hill fort, plus galleries on the geology, local history, and natural history of Dorset.

High West St. (next to St. Peter's Church). ℂ **01305/262735.** Admission £4.20 ($7.75) adults, £3.20 ($5.90) seniors and children 5–16, £9.20 ($17) family, free for under 5. July–Sept daily 10am–5pm; Oct–June Mon–Sat 10am–5pm. Closed Good Friday, Christmas Day.

Hardy's Cottage   Thomas Hardy was born in 1840 at Higher Bockhampton. His home, now a National Trust property, may be visited by appointment. Approach the cottage on foot—it's a 10-minute walk—after parking your vehicle in the space provided in the woods. Write in advance to Hardy's Cottage, Higher Bockhampton, Dorchester, Dorset DT2 8QJ, England, or call the number below.

Higher Bockhampton (5km/3 miles northeast of Dorchester and 1km/½ mile south of Blandford Road/A35). ℂ **01305/262366.** Admission £3 ($5.55). Apr–Oct Thurs–Mon 11am–5pm. Closed Nov–Mar.

WHERE TO STAY & DINE IN & AROUND DORCHESTER

Kings Arms Hotel   In business for more than 3 centuries, the Kings Arms offers great bow windows above the porch and a swinging sign hanging over the road, a legacy of its days as a coaching inn. It's still the best place to stay within Dorchester's center, though superior lodgings are on the outskirts. An archway leads to the courtyard and parking area at the back of the hotel. All rooms are nonsmoking and comfortably furnished; most are small to medium in size and have been modernized while retaining a traditional English aura. The shower-only bathrooms are tiled and rather cramped.

30 High East St., Dorchester, Dorset DT1 1HF. ℂ **01305/265353.** Fax 01305/260269. 25 units. £48 ($89) double. AE, MC, V. **Amenities:** Restaurant; bar. *In room:* TV, coffeemaker, hair dryer, trouser press.

Summer Lodge 🎯🎯   In this country-house hotel (a Relais & Châteaux property) 24km (15 miles) north of Dorchester, resident owners Nigel and Margaret Corbett provide care, courtesy, and comfort. Once home to heirs of the earls of Ilchester, the house, in the village of Evershot, stands on 1.6 hectares (4 acres) of secluded gardens. Evershot appears as Evershed in *Tess of the D'Urbervilles,* and author Thomas Hardy (that name again) designed a wing of the house. More recently, Summer Lodge hosted many stars of the locally filmed *Sense and Sensibility,* including Emma Thompson.

In this relaxed, informal atmosphere, bedrooms have views either of the garden or over village rooftops to fields beyond. The hotel is regularly redecorated

---

Finds In Search of Hardy's Heart

One mile (1.6km) east of Dorchester is **Stinsford Church,** where Hardy's heart is buried. Hardy was christened in this church, and his death wish was to be entombed here. However, because he was such a towering figure in English literature at the time of his death, his estate agreed to have him buried at Westminster Abbey. In partial deference to his wishes though, his heart was donated to Stinsford Church.

To get to the church, officially called the Church of St. Michael, follow the signs from Dorchester for the Kingston Maurward Agricultural College, then just before the entrance gates to the college, turn right, following the signs toward the Stinsford Church.

Finds Time Out for an Old-Fashioned Cuppa

The best place for tea in this bustling market town is the **Potters,** 19 Durngate St. (© **01305/260312**), with a blue-and-white interior and a small herb-and-flower garden out back with several tables. A proper sit-down tea is served for £3.50 ($6.50). You can also order freshly made sandwiches, cakes, scones, and pastries.

---

and recarpeted. Bedrooms are individually decorated and have many comforts, as reflected by such extras as hot-water bottles, fresh flowers, and racks of magazines. Most of the bathrooms have a tub-and-shower combination. Though centrally heated, the hotel offers log fires in winter. Guests can sit around the fire in a convivial atmosphere.

Summer Lane, Evershot, Dorset DT2 0JR. © **01935/83424.** Fax 01935/83005. www.relaischateaux.com. 24 units. £214–£360 ($396–$666) double. Rates include English breakfast, afternoon tea, and 3-course dinner and newspaper. AE, DC, MC, V. Head north from Dorchester on A37. **Amenities:** Restaurant; bar; outdoor pool; tennis court; croquet lawn; 24-hr. room service; laundry service. *In room:* TV, coffeemaker, hair dryer.

Yalbury Cottage Hotel and Restaurant ★ *Finds*   This thatch-roofed cottage with inglenooks and beamed ceilings is in a small country village within walking distance of Thomas Hardy's cottage and Stinsford Church. The cottage is some 300 years old and was once home to a local shepherd and the keeper of the water meadows. A mile to the north is Thorncombe Wood (home to badgers, deer, and many species of birds), offering a pleasant stroll and a chance to see Hardy's birthplace, which is tucked in under the edge of the woods. The bedrooms overlook the English country garden beyond, reflecting a mood of tranquillity, and have pinewood furniture in the English cottage style. Bedrooms received considerable refurbishing in 2002 and are now more comfortable than ever. All rooms are nonsmoking. Bathrooms are well appointed and clad in tiles, each with a tub and shower.

Lower Bockhampton, near Dorchester, Dorset DT2 8PZ. © **01305/262382.** Fax 01305/266412. www.smooth hound.co.uk/hotels/yalbury. 8 units. £90–£94 ($167–$174) double. Half board £138–£142 ($255–$263) double. Rates include breakfast. MC, V. Head 3km (2 miles) east of Dorchester (A35) and watch for signs to Lower Bockhampton. **Amenities:** Restaurant; limited room service; babysitting; laundry service; 1 room for those with limited mobility. *In room:* TV, coffeemaker, hair dryer.

8 Dorset's Coastal Towns: Chideock, Charmouth & Lyme Regis ★★

Chideock and Charmouth: 253km (157 miles) SW of London; 1.5km (1 mile) W of Bridport. Lyme Regis: 258km (160 miles) SW of London; 40km (25 miles) W of Dorchester

Chideock is a charming village hamlet of thatched houses with a dairy farm in the center. About a mile from the coast, it's a gem of a place for overnight stopovers, and even better for longer stays. You may be tempted to explore the countryside and the rolling hills.

On Lyme Bay, Charmouth, like Chideock, is another winner. A village of Georgian houses and thatched cottages, Charmouth provides some of the most dramatic coastal scenery in West Dorset. The village is west of Golden Cap, which, according to adventurers who measure such things, is the highest cliff along the coast of southern England.

Also on Lyme Bay, near the Devonshire border, the resort of Lyme Regis is one of the most attractive centers along the south coast. For those who shun big, commercial resorts, Lyme Regis is ideal—it's a true English coastal town with a mild climate. Seagulls fly overhead, the streets are steep and winding, and walks along Cobb Beach are brisk. The views, particularly of the craft in the harbor, are so photogenic that John Fowles, a longtime resident of the town, selected it as the site for the 1980 filming of his novel *The French Lieutenant's Woman*.

During its heyday, the town was a major seaport. Later, Lyme developed into a small spa, including among its visitors Jane Austen. She wrote her final novel, *Persuasion* (published posthumously and based partly on the town's life), after staying here in 1803 and 1804.

ESSENTIALS

GETTING THERE   The nearest train connection to Chideock and Charmouth is Dorchester (see "Essentials," in the Dorchester section, above). Buses run frequently through the day, west from both Dorchester and Bridport.

To get to Lyme Regis, take the London–Exeter train, getting off at Axminster and continuing the rest of the way by bus. For rail information, call © **0845/748-4950** or visit www.railtrack.co.uk. Bus no. 31 runs from Axminster to Lyme Regis (one bus per hour during the day). There's also **National Express** bus service. Call © **0870/580-8080** or visit www.nationalexpress.com for schedules and information.

If you're driving to Chideock and Charmouth from Bridport, continue west along the A35. To get to Lyme Regis from Bridport, continue west along the A35, cutting south to the coast at the junction with the A3070.

VISITOR INFORMATION   In Lyme Regis, the **Tourist Information Centre,** at Guildhall Cottage, Church Street (© **01297/442138**), is open November to March, Monday to Saturday 10am to 3pm; April daily 10am to 5pm; May to September, Monday to Friday from 10am to 4pm and Saturday and Sunday from 10am to 5pm; and October, daily from 10am to 5pm.

EXPLORING THE TOWNS

Chideock and Charmouth are the most beautiful villages in Dorset. It's fun to stroll though them to see the well-kept cottages, well-manicured gardens, and an occasional 18th- or 19th-century church. Charmouth, more than Chideock, boasts a small-scale collection of unusual antiques shops. Both villages are less than a mile from the western edge of **Chesil Beach,** one of the Hampshire coast's most famous (and longest) beaches. Although it's covered with shingle (sharp rocks), and hard on your feet if you go sunbathing, the beach nonetheless provides 8km (5 miles) of sweeping views toward France.

Another famous building is **The Guildhall,** Bridge Street (call the tourist office for information), whose Mary and John Wing (built in 1620) houses the completed sections of an enormous tapestry woven by local women. Depicting Britain's colonization of North America, it's composed of a series of 3.5m-by-1m (11 ft.–by–4 ft.) sections, each of which took a team of local women 2 years to weave. Admission is free, but to add a stitch to the final tapestry as a kind of charitable donation costs £1.50 ($2.80). It's open Monday through Friday from 10am to 4pm, but only if someone is working on the tapestry.

The surrounding area is a fascinating place for botanists and zoologists because of the predominance of blue Lias, a sedimentary rock well suited to the formation of fossils. In 1810, Mary Anning (at the age of 11) discovered one of

---

Moments Following the Town Crier

In Lyme Regis, one of the town's most visible characters is **Richard J. Fox,** three-time world champion Town Crier who, though retired, still does **guided walks.** Famed for his declamatory delivery of official (and sometimes irreverent) proclamations, he followed a 1,000-year-old tradition of newscasting. Dressed as Thomas Payne, a dragoon who died in Lyme Regis in 1644 during the civil war, Mr. Fox leads visitors on a 1½-hour walk around the town every Tuesday and Thursday at 2:30pm, beginning at The Guildhall (mentioned above). No reservations are necessary, and the price is £3 ($5.55) for adults and £2 ($3.70) for children. He can be reached on the premises of **Mister Fox,** 17 Haye Close St. (☎ **01297/443568** or 01297/445097). This shop sells such wares as woodcrafts and shells and is open daily 10am to 5pm.

---

the first articulated ichthyosaur skeletons. She went on to become one of the first professional fossilists in England. Books outlining walks in the area and the regions where fossils can be studied are available at the local information bureau.

WHERE TO STAY & DINE
IN CHIDEOCK & CHARMOUTH

Chideock House Hotel ✦✦ *(Finds*   In a village of winners, this 15th-century thatched house is the prettiest. The house was used by the Roundheads in 1645, and ghosts of the village martyrs still haunt it, because their trial was held here. Located near the road, behind a protective stone wall, the house has a garden in back; a driveway leads to a large parking area. The beamed lounge, recently face-lifted, has two fireplaces, one an Adam fireplace with a wood-burning blaze on cool days. Bedrooms are individually decorated and vary in size; superior rooms have dressing gowns and toiletries. Each has a little bathroom containing a shower-tub combination.

Main St., Chideock, Dorset DT6 6JN. ☎ **01297/489242.** Fax 01297/489184. www.chideockhousehotel.com. 8 units, all with bathroom. £75–£85 ($139–$157) double. Rates include English breakfast. £125–£135 ($231–$250) double with half board (minimum 2 days). AE, MC, V. Bus: 31 from Bridport. **Amenities:** Restaurant; bar; nonsmoking rooms. *In room:* TV, coffeemaker, hair dryer.

White House ✦   The White House is the best place to stay in Charmouth. This Regency home, with its period architecture and bow doors, is well preserved and tastefully furnished. Ian and Liz Simpson took this place, constructed in 1827, and made it comfortable, with touches such as electric kettles in their handsomely furnished bedrooms. Rooms range in size from small to medium and include such extras as complimentary decanters of sherry and homemade shortbread. All rooms are nonsmoking. Bathrooms are small but have a combination tub and shower.

2 Hillside, The Street, Charmouth, Dorset DT6 6PJ. ☎ **01297/560411.** Fax 01297/560702. www.whitehouse hotel.com. 8 units. £120–£180 ($222–$333) double. Rates include English breakfast and 5-course table d'hôte. MC, V. Closed Nov–Jan, but open for New Year's Day. Bus: 31 from Bridport. **Amenities:** Restaurant; bar; limited room service; laundry service; dry cleaning; rooms for those with limited mobility. *In room:* TV, coffeemaker, hair dryer.

IN LYME REGIS

Hotel Alexandra ✦   Built in 1735, this hotel is situated on a hill about 5 minutes from the center of Lyme Regis. Today, it has the best bedrooms and amenities of any inn in town, though it lacks the personal charm of Kersbrook Hotel (see below). In bedrooms once occupied by such "blue bloods" as Dowager Countess Poulett or Duc du Stacpoole, you sleep in grand comfort in the handsome beds. Most rooms command superb sea views over Lyme Regis and the Cobb. Expect such extras as thermostatic heating, along with small but beautifully maintained private bathrooms. It has been discreetly modernized around its original character.

Pound St., Lyme Regis, Dorset DT7 3HZ. *C* **01297/442010.** Fax 01297/443229. www.lymeregis.co.uk. 26 units. £94–£122 ($174–$226) double. Rates include English breakfast. DC, MC, V. **Amenities:** Restaurant; bar; limited room service; laundry service; dry cleaning; nonsmoking rooms; rooms for those with limited mobility. *In room:* TV, dataport, coffeemaker, hair dryer.

Kersbrook Hotel *(Finds)* Built of stone in 1790, and crowned by a thatch roof, the Kersbrook sits on a ledge above the village (which provides a panoramic view of the coast), on .6 hectare (1½ acres) of gardens landscaped according to the original 18th-century plans. The public rooms have been refurnished with antique furniture, re-creating old-world charm with modern facilities. All of the small to medium-size bedrooms have a certain 17th-century charm, with furnishings ranging from antique to contemporary. Rooms are comfortable, and bathrooms are tidily maintained with adequate shelf space and showers.

Pound Rd., Lyme Regis, Dorset DT7 3HX. *C*/fax **01297/442596.** www.lymeregis.com/kersbrook-hotel. 10 units. £70–£75 ($130–$139) double. Rates include breakfast. AE, MC, V. Closed Dec–Jan. **Amenities:** Bar; breakfast room. *In room:* TV, coffeemaker, hair dryer, iron/ironing board.

The Royal Lion Hotel *(Kids)* This former coaching inn dates from 1610, growing throughout the years to incorporate oak-paneled bars, lounges, and comfortably up-to-date bedrooms. Situated in the center of town on a hillside climbing up from the sea, the hotel features country-inspired furnishings and such venerable antiques as the half-tester bed regularly used by Edward VII when he was Prince of Wales. Bedrooms are divided between the main house, where the traditionally furnished rooms have more character and fireplaces, and a modern wing, where rooms have contemporary furnishings and the added advantage of a private terrace with sea view. Bathrooms are small but efficiently organized, each with a shower. Children are welcomed and some of the hotel's family rooms have bunk beds.

Broad St., Lyme Regis, Dorset DT7 3QF. *C* **01297/445622.** Fax 01297/445859. www.royallionhotel.com. 30 units. £80–£108 ($148–$200) double with breakfast, £102–£134 ($189–$248) double with breakfast and dinner. AE, DC, MC, V. **Amenities:** Restaurant; bar; lounge; indoor pool; Jacuzzi; sauna; game room; nonsmoking rooms. *In room:* TV, coffeemaker.

9 Sherborne *(★)*

206km (128 miles) SW of London; 31km (19 miles) NW of Dorchester

A little gem of a town with well-preserved medieval, Tudor, Stuart, and Georgian buildings still standing, Sherborne is in the heart of Dorset, surrounded by wooded hills, valleys, and chalk downs. It was here that Sir Walter Raleigh lived before his fall from fortune.

ESSENTIALS
GETTING THERE Frequent trains depart from London's Waterloo Station through the day. The trip takes 2 hours. For information, call *C* **0845/748-4950** or visit www.railtrack.co.uk.

One **National Express** coach departs daily from London's Victoria Coach Station. Call *C* **0870/580-8080** or visit www.nationalexpress.com for information and schedules.

If you're driving, take the M3 west from London, continuing southwest on the A303 and the B3145.

VISITOR INFORMATION   The **Tourist Information Centre,** on Digby Road (© **01935/815341**), is open April through October, Monday through Saturday from 9am to 5pm, and November through March, Monday through Saturday from 10am to 3pm.

EXPLORING SHERBORNE

In addition to the attractions listed below, you can go to **Cerne Abbas,** a village south of Sherborne, to see the Pitchmarket, where Thomas and Maria Washington, uncle and aunt of American president George Washington, lived.

Sherborne Abbey ★★   One of the great churches of England, this abbey was founded in A.D. 705 as the Cathedral of the Saxon Bishops of Wessex. In the late 10th century, it became a Benedictine monastery, and since the Reformation it has been a parish church. Famous for its fan-vaulted roof added by Abbot Ramsam at the end of the 15th century, it was the first of its kind erected in England. Inside are many fine monuments, including Purbeck marble effigies of medieval abbots as well as Elizabethan "four-poster" and canopied tombs. The baroque statue of the earl of Bristol stands between his two wives and dates from 1698. A public school occupies the abbey's surviving medieval monastic buildings and was the setting for the classic film *Goodbye, Mr. Chips.*

Abbey Close. © **01935/812452.** Free admission but donations for upkeep welcomed. Apr–Sept daily 8am–5pm; Oct–Mar daily 8:30am–4pm.

Sherborne Castle ★   Sir Walter Raleigh built this castle in 1594, when he decided that it would not be feasible to restore the old castle (see below) to suit his needs. This Elizabethan residence was a square mansion; later owners added four Jacobean wings to make it more palatial. After King James I had Raleigh imprisoned in the Tower of London, the monarch gave the castle to a favorite Scot, Robert Carr, banishing the Raleighs from their home. In 1617, it became the property of Sir John Digby, first earl of Bristol, and has been the Digby family home ever since. The mansion was enlarged by Sir John in 1625, and in the 18th century, the formal Elizabethan gardens and fountains of the Raleighs were altered by Capability Brown, who created a serpentine lake between the two castles. The 8 hectares (20 acres) of lawns and pleasure grounds around the 20-hectare (50-acre) lake are open to the public. In the house are fine furniture, china, and paintings by Gainsborough, Lely, Reynolds, Kneller, and Van Dyck, among others.

Cheap St. (off New Rd. 1.5km/1 mile east of the center). © **01935/813182.** www.sherbornecastle.com. Castle and grounds £7 ($13) adults, £6.50 ($12) seniors, free for ages 15 and under. Grounds only £3.50 ($6.50) adults, free for ages 15 and under. Apr 1–Oct 31 Tues–Thurs; Sat–Sun and bank holidays 11am–5pm. Last admission 4:30pm.

Sherborne Old Castle ★   The castle was built by the powerful Bishop Roger de Caen in the early 12th century, but it was seized by the crown at about the time of King Henry I's death in 1135 and Stephen's troubled accession to the throne. The castle was given to Sir Walter Raleigh by Queen Elizabeth I. The gallant knight built Sherborne Lodge in the deer park close by (now privately owned). The buildings were mostly destroyed in the civil war, but you can still see a gatehouse, some graceful arcades, and decorative windows.

Castleton, off A30, 1km (½ mile) east of Sherborne. © **01935/812730.** Admission £2 ($3.70) adults, £1.50 ($2.80) seniors and students, £1 ($1.85) children 5–16, free for children 4 and under. Apr–Sept daily 10am–6pm; Oct–Mar daily 10am–1pm and 2–5pm. Follow the signs 1.5km (1 mile) east from the town center.

WHERE TO STAY

Eastbury Hotel ⭐ This Georgian town-house hotel, Sherborne's best, is situated in its own walled garden near the 8th-century abbey and the two castles. Built in 1740 during the reign of George II, it has a traditional ambience, with its own library of antiquarian books. Beautifully restored, it retains its 18th-century character. Bedrooms are named after flowers and are handsomely maintained and decorated. Rooms are small to medium in size, bright and inviting, and furnished in a traditional way, often graced with fresh flowers; some have four-poster beds. All rooms are nonsmoking. The fully equipped bathrooms are tidily maintained and have bathrobes. After a restful night's sleep, you can sit outside and enjoy the well-kept garden.

Long St., Sherborne, Dorset DT9 3BY. ℂ **01935/813131**. Fax 01935/817296. www.theeastburyhotel.co.uk. 22 units. £96–£105 ($178–$194) double. Rates include English breakfast. AE, MC, V. **Amenities:** Restaurant; 2 bars; limited room service; laundry service; dry cleaning; 1 room for those with limited mobility. *In room:* TV, coffeemaker, hair dryer, trouser press.

The Sherborne Hotel Built of red brick in 1969, this two-story hotel lies near a school and a scattering of factories and houses. Though popular with business travelers, it's more elegant than a typical roadside hotel, with more amenities than may be expected and easy access to Sherborne's historic center. Attracting both business travelers and visitors, the hotel gets high marks for quality. Its bedrooms, small to medium in size, are too functional to be the most glamorous in the area. Eleven of the rooms are spacious enough for small families. The small bathrooms are tidily kept, each with shower-tub combination.

Horsecastles Lane (near A30 and about 1.5km/1 mile west of Sherborne's center), Sherborne, Dorset DT9 6BB. ℂ **01935/813191**. Fax 01935/816493. 58 units. Sun–Thurs £75 ($139) double; Fri–Sat £85 ($157) double. Rates include English breakfast. AE, DC, MC, V. **Amenities:** Restaurant; bar; limited room service; nonsmoking rooms. *In room:* TV, dataport (in some), coffeemaker, hair dryer, trouser press.

WHERE TO DINE

Eastbury Hotel Restaurant FRENCH/INTERNATIONAL In a tasteful setting in this previously recommended hotel, this restaurant tastefully presents a range of well-prepared dishes based on fresh ingredients. This cuisine is backed up by one of the finest wine lists in the area. There is an imaginative, intellectual use of flavors as in the roasted Barbary duck breast enhanced by the flavor of fresh ginger and honey. A whole Dover sole is grilled to perfection and served with baby greens along with coriander-laced butter. The tantalizing filet of English beef comes with Stilton cheese, fondant potatoes, and Savoy cabbage. The salads are made fresh daily, as are homemade soups and a selection of appetizers, along with some luscious desserts.

Long St. ℂ **01935/813131**. Reservations recommended. Lunch main courses £8.50–£10 ($16–$19); dinner main courses £14–£19 ($26–$35). AE, MC, V. Daily noon–2pm and 7–9:30pm.

9

Wiltshire & Somerset

For our look at the "West Countree," we move into Wiltshire and Somerset, two of the most historic shires of England. Once you reach this area of pastoral woodland, London seems far removed. For a total view of the West Country, you can also visit Devon and Cornwall (see chapters 10 and 11).

Most people agree that the West Country, a loose geographical term, begins at **Salisbury,** with its Early English cathedral. Nearby is **Stonehenge,** England's oldest prehistoric monument. (Both Stonehenge and Salisbury are in Wiltshire.) When you cross into Wiltshire, you enter a country of chalky, grassy uplands and rolling plains. Much of the shire is agricultural; a large part is pasture.

Somerset has some of the most beautiful scenery in England. The undulating limestone hills of **Mendip** and the irresistible **Quantocks** are especially lovely in spring and fall. Somerset opens onto the Bristol Channel, with **Minehead** serving as its chief resort. The shire is rich in legend and history, possessing particularly fanciful associations with King Arthur and Queen Guinevere, Camelot, and Alfred the Great. Its villages are noted for tall towers of its parish churches.

You may find yourself in a vine-covered pub, talking with the regulars and sampling Somerset's famous cider, or perhaps you'll stroll through a large estate in the woods surrounded by bridle paths and sheep walks (Somerset was once a great wool center). Or maybe you'll settle down in a 16th-century thatched stone farmhouse amidst orchards in a vale.

Somerset also encompasses the territory around the old port of **Bristol** and the old Roman city of **Bath,** known for its abbey and spa water, lying beside the river Avon.

The two best places to base yourself while you explore the area are Bath and Salisbury. From Salisbury, you can visit Stonehenge and **Old Sarum,** the two most fabled ancient monuments in the West Country. Yet some say visiting the stones at **Avebury** is a much more personal experience. And **Glastonbury,** with its once-great abbey that is now a ruined sanctuary, may be one of Britain's oldest inhabited sites. The greatest natural spectacle in the area is **Exmoor National Park,** once an English royal hunting preserve, stretching for 686 sq. km (265 sq. miles) on the north coast of Devon and Somerset. Many terrific country houses and palaces are also in this region, including **Wilton House,** the site of 17th-century state-rooms designed by Inigo Jones. The other two major attractions, **Longleat House** and the fabled gardens at **Stourhead,** can be visited in a busy day while you're based at Bath.

1 Salisbury ★★

145km (90 miles) SW of London; 85km (53 miles) SE of Bristol

Long before you enter Salisbury, the spire of its cathedral comes into view—just as John Constable captured it on canvas. The 121m (404-ft.) pinnacle of the Early English and Gothic cathedral is the tallest in England.

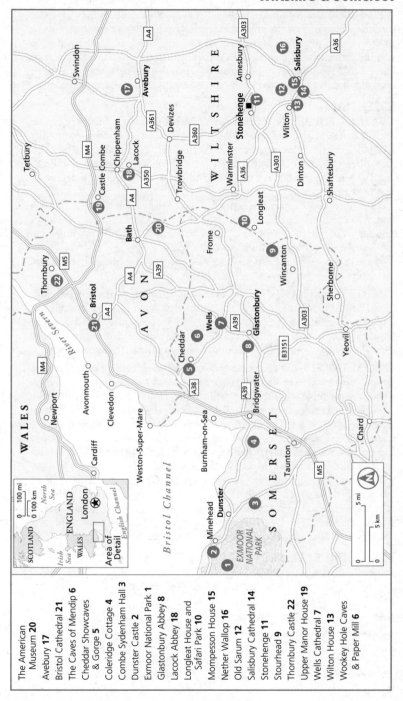

The American
Museum **20**
Avebury **17**
Bristol Cathedral **21**
The Caves of Mendip **6**
Cheddar Showcaves
& Gorge **5**
Coleridge Cottage **4**
Combe Sydenham Hall **3**
Dunster Castle **2**
Exmoor National Park **1**
Glastonbury Abbey **8**
Lacock Abbey **18**
Longleat House and
Safari Park **10**
Mompesson House **15**
Nether Wallop **16**
Old Sarum **12**
Salisbury Cathedral **14**
Stonehenge **11**
Stourhead **9**
Thornbury Castle **22**
Upper Manor House **19**
Wells Cathedral **7**
Wilton House **13**
Wookey Hole Caves
& Paper Mill **6**

Salisbury, or New Sarum, lies in the valley of the River Avon. Filled with Tudor inns and tearooms, it is the only true city in Wiltshire. It's an excellent base for visitors anxious to explore Stonehenge or Avebury, who, unfortunately, tend to visit the cathedral and then rush on their way. But the old market town is an interesting destination on its own, and if you choose to linger here for a day or two, you find that its pub-to-citizen ratio is perhaps the highest in the country.

ESSENTIALS

GETTING THERE   **Network Express trains** depart for Salisbury hourly from Waterloo Station in London; the trip takes 1½ hours. Sprinter trains offer fast, efficient service every hour from Portsmouth, Bristol, and South Wales. Also, direct rail service is available from Exeter, Plymouth, Brighton, and Reading. For rail information, call © **0845/748-4950** in the United Kingdom or visit www.railtrack.co.uk.

Three **National Express buses** per day run from London, Monday through Friday. On Saturday and Sunday, three buses depart Victoria Coach Station for Salisbury. The trip takes 2½ hours. Call © **0870/580-8080** for schedules and information or visit www.nationalexpress.com.

If you're driving from London, head west on the M3 to the end of the run, continuing the rest of the way on the A30.

VISITOR INFORMATION   The **Tourist Information Centre** is at Fish Row (© **01722/334956**) and is open October through April, Monday through Saturday from 9:30am to 5pm; May, Monday through Saturday from 9:30am to 5pm and Sunday from 10:30am to 4:30pm; June through September, Monday through Saturday from 9:30am to 6pm and Sunday from 10:30am to 4:30pm.

SPECIAL EVENTS   The Salisbury **St. George's Spring Festival** in April is a traditional medieval celebration of the city's patron saint. You can witness St. George slaying the dragon in the Wiltshire mummers play and see acrobats and fireworks.

With spring comes the annual **Salisbury Festival** (© **01722/332977;** www.salisburyfestival.co.uk). The city drapes itself in banners, and street theater—traditional and unexpected—is offered everywhere. There are also symphony and chamber music concerts in Salisbury Cathedral, children's events, and much more. It takes place from mid-May to the beginning of June.

At the end of July, you can see the **Salisbury Garden and Flower Show,** Hudson's Field (© **01189/478996**), a treat for gardening enthusiasts, with a floral marquee packed with Chelsea exhibits, as well as display gardens created especially for the event. Plenty more for the rest of the family includes specialty food tasting, crafts sales, and a vintage and classic car show.

EXPLORING SALISBURY

You can easily see Salisbury by foot, either on your own or by taking a guided daytime or evening walk sponsored by the Tourist Information Centre (see above). Tickets are £2.50 ($4.65) for adults and £1 ($1.85) for children.

Mompesson House ⊛   This is one of the most distinguished houses in the area. Built by Charles Mompesson in 1701, while he was a member of Parliament for Old Sarum, it is a beautiful example of the Queen Anne style and is well known for its fine plasterwork ceilings and paneling. It also houses a collection of 18th-century drinking glasses. Visitors can wander through a garden and order a snack in the garden tearoom.

Cathedral Close. © **01722/335659**. Admission £4 ($7.40) adults, £2 ($3.70) children under 18. Apr–Oct Sat–Wed 11am–5pm. Closed Nov–Mar.

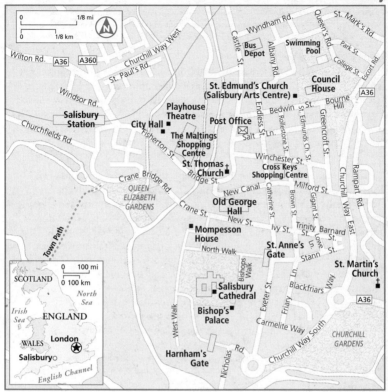

Salisbury Cathedral ★★★ You'll find no better example of the Early English pointed, architectural style than Salisbury Cathedral. Construction on this magnificent building began as early as 1220 and took only 45 years to complete. (Most of Europe's grandest cathedrals took 3 c. to build.) Salisbury Cathedral is one of the most homogenous of all the great European cathedrals.

The cathedral's 13th-century octagonal chapter house possesses one of the four surviving original texts of the Magna Carta, along with treasures from the diocese of Salisbury and manuscripts and artifacts belonging to the cathedral. The cloisters enhance the cathedral's beauty, along with an exceptionally large close. At least 75 buildings are in the compound, some from the early 18th century and others from much earlier.

Insider's tip: The 121m (404-ft.) spire was one of the tallest structures in the world when completed in 1315. In its day, this was far more advanced technology than the world's tallest skyscrapers. Amazingly, the spire was not part of the original design and was conceived and added some 30 years after the rest. The name of the master mason is lost to history. In 1668, Sir Christopher Wren expressed alarm at the tilt of the spire, but no further shift has since been measured. The whole ensemble is still standing; if you trust towering architecture from 700 years ago, you can explore the tower on guided visits Monday through Saturday from 9:30am to 4pm (extra tours in summer depending on demand). The cost of the tour is £3 ($5.55).

The Close, Salisbury. ☎ 01722/555120. www.salisburycathedral.org.uk. Suggested donation £3.80 ($7.05) adults, £3.30 ($6.10) students and seniors, £2 ($3.70) children, £8.50 ($16) family ticket. Jan–May and Sept–Dec Mon–Sat 7:15am–6:15pm; June–Aug Mon–Sat 7:15am–7:15pm. Sun year-round 7:15am–6:15pm.

SIGHTS NEARBY

Old Sarum ★   Believed to have been an Iron Age fortification, Old Sarum was used again by the Saxons and flourished as a walled town into the Middle Ages. The Normans built a cathedral and a castle here; parts of the old cathedral were taken down to build the city of New Sarum (Salisbury).

3km (2 miles) north of Salisbury off A345 on Castle Rd. ☎ 01722/335398. Admission £2.50 ($4.65) adults, £1.90 ($3.50) seniors, £1.30 ($2.40) children. Apr–Sept daily 10am–5pm; Oct daily 10am–5pm; Nov–Mar daily 11am–3pm. Bus nos. 3, 5, 6, 7, 8, and 9 run every 30 min. during the day from the Salisbury bus station.

Wilton House ★★   This home of the earls of Pembroke is in the town of Wilton. It dates from the 16th century but has undergone numerous alterations, most recently in Victoria's day, and is noted for its 17th-century staterooms, designed by celebrated architect Inigo Jones. Shakespeare's troupe is said to have entertained here, and Eisenhower and his advisers prepared here for the D-Day landings at Normandy, with only the Van Dyck paintings as silent witnesses.

The house is filled with beautifully maintained furnishings and world-class art, including paintings by Rubens, Brueghel, and Reynolds. You can visit a reconstructed Tudor kitchen and Victorian laundry.

On the 8.4-hectare (21-acre) estate are giant cedars of Lebanon trees, the oldest of which were planted in 1630, as well as rose and water gardens, riverside and woodland walks, and a huge adventure playground for children.

5km (3 miles) west of Salisbury on A36. ☎ 01722/746720. www.wiltonhouse.com. Admission £9.75 ($18) adults, £8 ($15) seniors, £5 ($9.25) children 5–15, £24 ($44) family ticket, free for children under 5. Price inclusive of grounds. Easter–Oct Tues–Sun 10:30am–5:30pm (last entrance at 4:30pm). Grounds open Mon.

SHOPPING

Many shops in Salisbury are set in beautiful medieval timber-framed buildings. As you wander through the colorful market or walk the ancient streets, you'll find everything from touristy gift shops to unique specialty stores.

Hard-core shoppers and locals gravitate to the **Old George Mall Shopping Centre,** 23B High St. (☎ **01722/333500**), a short walk from the cathedral. With over 40 individual shops and High Street stores, you can find the latest fashions as well as household appliances, CDs, toiletries, and greeting cards.

Another place of note, situated within a 14th-century building with hammered beams and some original windows, is **Watsons,** 8–9 Queen St. (☎ **01722/320311**). This elegant store carries bone china from Wedgwood, Royal Doulton, and Aynsley; Dartington glassware; and a fine line of paperweights.

We always stop in at **Rivermead Books,** 30 Catherine St. (☎ **01722/325818**), which sells an array of secondhand books, plus some rare first editions. We once purchased an autographed murder mystery by Agatha Christie here for a reasonable price.

WHERE TO STAY
EXPENSIVE

Grasmere House ★ *Kids*   Grasmere House stands near the confluence of the Nadder and Avon rivers on .6 hectares (1½ acres) of grounds. Constructed in 1896 for Salisbury merchants, the house still suggests a family home. The original architectural features were retained as much as possible, including a "calling box" for servants in the dining room. A conservatory restaurant and bar overlooks the cathedral, as do three luxurious rooms. Four rooms are in the original house, with the remainder in a new wing. Each room has a distinctive character and often opens onto a scenic view. Two rooms are suitable for guests with disabilities. Two accommodations are large enough for families and the hotel welcomes young children. Each bathroom is well-maintained and most have shower-and-tub combinations.

70 Harnham Rd., Salisbury, Wiltshire SP2 8JN. ✆ **01722/338388**. Fax 01722/333710. www.grasmere hotel.com. 20 units. £95–£155 ($176–$287) double. Rates include English breakfast. AE, DC, MC, V. Take A3094 2.5km (1½ miles) from town center. **Amenities:** Restaurant; bar; limited room service; babysitting; laundry service; nonsmoking rooms. *In room:* TV, dataport, coffeemaker, hair dryer, iron, trouser press.

Red Lion Hotel ★ *(Value)*   From the 1300s, the Red Lion continues to accommodate wayfarers from London on their way to the West Country. This Best Western–affiliated hotel no longer reigns supreme in town—we prefer the White Hart and The Rose and Crown—but it's a fine choice and somewhat more affordable than those two. Cross under its arch into a courtyard with a hanging, much-photographed creeper, a red lion, and a half-timbered facade, and you'll be transported back to an earlier era. This antique-filled hotel is noted for its unique clock collection, which includes a skeleton organ clock in the reception hall. Each small to medium-size bedroom is individually furnished and tastefully decorated. Two units are spacious enough for families, and the most expensive rooms have four-poster beds. All the well-kept bathrooms contain shower-tub combinations.

4 Milford St., Salisbury, Wiltshire SP1 2AN. ✆ **800/528-1234** in the U.S., or 01722/323334. Fax 01722/ 325756. www.the-redlion.co.uk. 51 units. £110–£122 ($204–$226) double; £142 ($263) suite. AE, DC, MC, V. **Amenities:** Restaurant; bar; limited room service; laundry service; dry cleaning; 1 room for those with limited mobility. *In room:* TV, coffeemaker, hair dryer.

The Rose and Crown ★★★   This half-timbered, 13th-century gem stands with its feet almost in the River Avon; beyond the water, you can see the tall spire of the cathedral. Because of its tranquil location, it's our top choice. From here, you can easily walk over the arched stone bridge to the center of Salisbury in 10 minutes. Old trees shade the lawns and gardens between the inn and the river, and chairs are set out so that you can enjoy the view and count the swans. The inn has both a new and an old wing. The new wing is modern, but the old wing is more appealing, with its sloping ceilings and antique fireplaces and furniture. Bedrooms in the main house range from small to medium in size, though those in the new wing are more spacious and better designed.

Harnham Rd., Salisbury, Wiltshire SP2 8JQ. ✆ **01722/399955**. Fax 01722/339816. www.corushotels.com. 28 units. £118 ($218) double. Rates include breakfast. AE, DC, MC, V. Take A3094 2.5km (1½ miles) from the center of town. **Amenities:** Restaurant; 2 bars; 24-hr. room service; rooms for those with limited mobility. *In room:* TV, hair dryer, iron/ironing board, trouser press.

White Hart ★   Combining the best of old and new, the White Hart is a Salisbury landmark from Georgian times. Its classic facade is intact, with tall columns crowning a life-size hart. The older accommodations are traditional, and a new section has been added in the rear, opening onto a large parking area. New-wing units are tastefully decorated; although rooms in the main building have more style and character, many are quite small. Bathrooms are a bit small in many cases, each with a shower-tub combination. You can enjoy a before-dinner drink, followed by a meal of modern English fare, in the White Hart Restaurant.

1 St. Johns St., Salisbury, Wiltshire SP1 2SD. ✆ **888/892-0038** in U.S., or 01722/327476. Fax 01722/412761. www.macdonaldhotels.co.uk. 68 units. £110–£160 ($204–$296) double. Rates include breakfast. AE, DC, MC, V. **Amenities:** Restaurant; bar; 24-hr. room service; nonsmoking rooms. *In room:* TV, coffeemaker, minibar, iron/ironing board, safe.

INEXPENSIVE

The Beadles ★★ *Finds* A traditional modern Georgian house with antique furnishings and a view of the cathedral, The Beadles offers unobstructed views of the beautiful Wiltshire countryside from its .4-hectare (1-acre) gardens. It's situated in a small, unspoiled English village, 11km (7 miles) from Salisbury, which offers excellent access to Stonehenge, Wilton House, the New Forest, and the rambling moors of Thomas Hardy country. Even the road to Winchester is an ancient Roman byway. Furnished tastefully, this nonsmoking household contains rooms with twins or doubles, each with a full private bathroom. Owners David and Anne-Marie Yuille-Baddeley delight in providing information on the area.

Middleton, Middle Winterslow, near Salisbury, Wiltshire SP5 1QS. ✆ **01980/862922.** Fax 01980/863565. www.guestaccom.co.uk/754.htm. 3 units. £60 ($111) double. Rates include English breakfast. MC, V. Turn off A30 at Pheasant Inn to Middle Winterslow. Enter the village, make the first right, turn right again, and it's the first right after "Trevano." **Amenities:** Dining room; tour services. *In room:* TV, coffeemaker, hair dryer, iron/ironing board.

Cricket Field House Hotel ★ *Finds* This snug B&B takes its name from the cricket field it overlooks. The original structure was a gamekeeper's cottage that has been handsomely converted. In its own large garden, the family run house is comfortably furnished and modernized, and completely nonsmoking. Rooms are in both the main house and an equally good pavilion annex. Each unit is decorated and furnished individually, and has a small but neatly kept shower-only bathroom.

Wilton Rd., Salisbury, Wiltshire SP2 9NS. ✆ **01722/322595.** www.cricketfieldhousehotel.co.uk. 14 units. £55–£85 ($102–$157) double. Rates include English breakfast. AE, MC, V. Lies on the A36, 3km (2 miles) west of Salisbury. **Amenities:** Restaurant for guests only; limited room service; laundry service; dry cleaning; rooms for those with limited mobility. *In room:* TV, coffeemaker, hair dryer, trouser press.

Wyndham Park Lodge From this appealing Victorian 1880 house, it's an easy walk to the heart of Salisbury and its cathedral, and about a 5-minute walk to a swimming pool and the bus station. The small to midsize rooms are comfortably furnished with Victorian and Edwardian antiques. They have either one double or two twin beds. Only one unit has a tub-and-shower combination; the rest have efficient showers. This establishment is completely nonsmoking.

51 Wyndham Rd., Salisbury, Wiltshire SP1 3AB. ✆ **01722/416517.** Fax 01722/328851. www.wyndhampark lodge.co.uk. 4 units. £45–£49 ($83–$91) double; £65–£69 ($120–$128) family room for 3. Rates include English breakfast. MC, V. **Amenities:** Breakfast room. *In room:* TV, coffeemaker, hair dryer, iron/ironing board.

A CHOICE IN NEARBY DINTON

Howard's House ★ *Finds* Housed in a 17th-century dower house that has been added to over the years and set in a medieval hamlet, this property is the most appealing small hotel and restaurant in the area. Much care is lavished on the decor, with fresh flowers in every public room and bedroom. Most bedrooms are spacious in size, and one room is large enough for a family. All units contain

---

Fun Fact Sleuthing After Miss Marple

Thirteen kilometers (8 miles) east of Salisbury is the little village of **Nether Wallop** (not to be confused with Over Wallop or Middle Wallop, also in the area). Agatha Christie fans should note that it's the fictitious town of St. Mary Mead, Miss Marple's home, in the PBS *Miss Marple* mysteries. It's 19km (12 miles) from Stonehenge and 16km (10 miles) from Winchester, on a country road between the A343 and the A30.

well-kept bathrooms with shower-tub combinations; some rooms have four-poster beds. The hotel has attractive gardens, and on chilly nights, log fires burn.

Teffont Evias, near Salisbury, Wiltshire SP3 5RJ. ℂ 01722/716392. Fax 01722/716820. www.howards househotel.com. 9 units. £145–£165 ($268–$305) double. Rates include English breakfast. AE, MC, V. Leave Salisbury on the A36 until you reach a roundabout. Take the first left leading to the A30. On the A30, continue for 5km (3 miles) coming to the turnoff (B3089) for Barford Saint-Martin. Continue for 6.5km (4 miles) on this secondary road to the town of Teffont Evias, where the hotel is signposted. **Amenities:** Restaurant; bar; laundry service. *In room:* TV, hair dryer, bathrobes.

WHERE TO DINE

See "Salisbury After Dark," below, for a selection of pubs with affordable fare.

Foodies should stop at **David Brown Food Hall & Tea Rooms,** 31 Catherine St. (ℂ **01722/329363**), carrying the finest fresh foods—meats, cheeses, breads, and other baked goods—making it a terrific place to put together a picnic.

Harper's Restaurant ENGLISH/INTERNATIONAL   The chef-owner of this place prides himself on specializing in homemade and wholesome "real food." The pleasantly decorated restaurant is on the second floor of a redbrick building at the back end of Salisbury's largest parking lot, in the center of town. In the same all-purpose dining room, you can order from two different menus, one with affordable bistro-style platters, including beefsteak casserole with "herbey dumplings." A longer menu, with items that take more time to prepare, includes all-vegetarian pasta diavolo, or spareribs with french fries and rice.

6–7 Ox Row, Market Sq. ℂ 01722/333118. Reservations recommended. Main courses £6.20–£13 ($11–$24); 2-course fixed-price meal £7.50–£8.50 ($14–$16) at lunch and dinner. AE, DC, MC, V. Mon–Sat noon–2pm; daily 6–9:30pm (10pm Sat). Closed Sun Oct–May.

Howard's House Hotel Restaurant ✪ INTERNATIONAL   If you'd like to dine in one of the loveliest places in the area, and enjoy a refined cuisine at the same time, leave Salisbury and head for this previously recommended hotel. It's a 14km (9-mile) drive to Teffort Evias but well worth the trip. The village itself is one of the most beautiful in Wiltshire.

The elegantly appointed restaurant showcases a finely honed cuisine prepared with first-class ingredients. The menu changes daily but is likely to feature such starters as a terrine of marinated venison, pheasant, and wild boar with pistachios or else pan-seared king scallops with a spicy rocket salad with a lemongrass couscous. Main courses are very appealing with well-balanced flavors, as exemplified by the oven-baked filet of monkfish with Parma ham in a mussel and saffron broth or the roast breast of mallard with a confit of duck leg along with pan-sautéed foie gras and game gravy.

Teffont Evias, near Salisbury. ℂ 01722/716392. Reservations required. Main courses £18–£23 ($33–$43); fixed-price menu £24 ($44). AE, MC, V. Daily 12:30–2pm, 7:30–9pm; Sun noon–2pm. For directions, see the Howard's House listing in the "Where to Stay" section above.

LXIX ✪ MODERN ENGLISH   Close to the Salisbury Cathedral, this is the finest dining room within the city itself. It's awakened the sleepy taste buds of Salisbury, which has suffered for decades without a really good first-class restaurant. In a stylish contemporary interior, a modern English but French-inspired cuisine is served. Ingredients are adjusted on the menu to take advantage of the changing seasons. Try, for example, roasted sea bass with a "mash" of spinach served in a velvety smooth and chive-laced white butter sauce. One excellent dish is Angus beef served with foie gras and very thick potatoes cooked like french fries. A more delicate offering, but one equally good is *mille feuille,* "a thousand leaves," in this case, puff pastry filled with wild mushrooms and toasted peanuts. Smoked river eel adds an exotic touch to the menu.

69 New St. ✆ 01722/340000. Reservations not required. Main courses £6.90–£14 ($13–$26). AE, DC, MC, V. Mon–Sat noon–3pm and 6–11pm. Closed Dec 24–Jan 2.

Salisbury Haunch of Venison ENGLISH   Right in the heart of Salisbury, this creaky-timbered chophouse (it dates from 1320) serves excellent dishes, especially English roasts and grills. Stick to its specialties and you'll rarely go wrong. Begin with a tasty warm salad of venison sausages with garlic croutons, and then follow with the time-honored roast haunch of venison with parsnips and juniper berries. Other classic English dishes are served as well, including grilled Barnsley lamb chops with bubble and squeak (cabbage and potatoes).

1 Minster St. ✆ 01722/322024. Main courses £8.25–£16 ($15–$30); bar platters for lunches, light suppers, and snacks £4–£8 ($7.40–$15). MC, V. Daily noon–2pm; Mon–Sat 6–9pm. Pub Mon–Sat 11am–11pm; Sun noon–3pm and 7–10:30pm. Closed Christmas and Easter.

SALISBURY AFTER DARK

The Salisbury Playhouse, Malthouse Lane (✆ **01722/320117** or 01722/ 320333 for the box office; www.salisburyplayhouse.com), produces some of the finest theater in the region. Food and drink are available from the bar and restaurant to complete your evening's entertainment.

The City Hall, Malthouse Lane (✆ **01722/334432** or 01722/327676 for the box office; www.cityhallsalisbury.co.uk), has a program of events to suit most tastes and ages in comfortable surroundings. A thriving entertainment center, it attracts many of the national touring shows in addition to local amateur events, exhibitions, and sales, thus providing good entertainment at a reasonable price.

The Salisbury Arts Center, Bedwin Street (✆ **01722/321744**), housed within the former St. Edmund's Church, offers a wide range of performing and visual arts. A typical program contains a broad mix of music, contemporary and classic theater, and dance performances, plus cabaret, comedy, and family shows. Regular workshops are available for all ages in arts, crafts, theater, and dance. The lively cafe-bar is a pleasant meeting place.

Many a Salisbury pub-crawl begins at the Haunch of Venison (see above). Another good pub is **The Pheasant** on Salt Lane, near the bus station (✆ **01722/320675**), which attracts locals as well as visitors on their way to Stonehenge. Snacks, ploughman's lunches, and hot pub grub, including meat pies, are served all day. It's all washed down with a goodly assortment of ales. The **Avon Brewery Inn,** 75 Castle St. (✆ **01722/327280**), is decorated like a Victorian saloon from the gay 1890s. Its idyllic garden setting overlooks the River Avon. It offers some of the tastiest and most affordable food in town.

2 Prehistoric Britain: Stonehenge ☆☆☆ & Avebury ☆☆

Stonehenge ☆☆☆   This huge circle of lintels and megalithic pillars, believed to be approximately 5,000 years old, is the most important prehistoric monument in Britain.

Some visitors are disappointed when they see that Stonehenge is nothing more than concentric circles of stones. But perhaps they don't understand that Stonehenge represents an amazing engineering feat, because many of the boulders, the bluestones in particular, were moved many miles (perhaps from southern Wales) to this site.

The widely held view of 18th- and 19th-century romantics that Stonehenge was the work of the druids is without foundation. The boulders, many weighing

---

Finds Biking to Stonehenge

If you'd like to bike out to Stonehenge, go to **Hayball's Cycle Shop,** 26–30 Winchester St. (© **01722/411378**), which rents mountain bikes for £10 ($19) per day. For an extra £2.50 ($4.65), you can keep the bike overnight. A £25 ($46) cash deposit is required. A 7-day rental is £65 ($120). Open daily from 9am to 5:30pm.

---

several tons, are believed to have predated the arrival in Britain of the Celtic culture. Recent excavations continue to bring new evidence to bear on the origin and purpose of Stonehenge. Controversy surrounds the prehistoric site, especially since the publication of _Stonehenge Decoded_ by Gerald S. Hawkins and John B. White, which maintains that Stonehenge was an astronomical observatory—that is, a Neolithic "computing machine" capable of predicting eclipses.

Your ticket permits you to go inside the fence surrounding the site that protects the stones from vandals and souvenir hunters. You can go all the way up to a short rope barrier, about 15m (50 ft.) from the stones.

A full circular tour around Stonehenge is possible. A modular walkway was introduced to cross the archaeologically important avenue, the area that runs between the Heel Stone and the main circle of stones. This enables visitors to complete a full circuit of the stones and to see one of the best views of a completed section of Stonehenge as they pass by, an excellent addition to the informative audio tour.

Wilts & Dorset (© **01722/336855;** www.wdbus.co.uk) runs several buses daily (depending on demand) from Salisbury to Stonehenge, as well as buses from the Salisbury train station to Stonehenge. The bus trip to Stonehenge takes 40 minutes, and a round-trip ticket costs £6 ($11) for adults and £3 ($5.55) for children ages 5 to 14 (4 and under ride free).

At the junction of A303 and A344/A360. © 01980/623108 for information. Admission £5 ($9.25) adults, £3.80 ($7.05) students and seniors, £2.50 ($4.65) children, £13 ($23) family ticket. June–Aug daily 9am–7pm; Mar 16–May and Sept–Oct 15 daily 9am–5pm; Oct 16–Mar 15 daily 9:30am–4pm. If you're driving, head north on Castle Rd. from the center of Salisbury. At the first roundabout (traffic circle), take the exit toward Amesbury (A345) and Old Sarum. Continue along this road for 13km (8 miles) and then turn left onto A303 in the direction of Exeter. You'll see signs for Stonehenge, leading you up A344 to the right. It's 3km (2 miles) west of Amesbury.

Avebury ★★   One of the largest prehistoric sites in Europe, Avebury lies on the Kennet River, 11km (7 miles) west of Marlborough and 32km (20 miles) north of Stonehenge. Some visitors say visiting Avebury, in contrast to Stonehenge, is a more organic experience—you can walk right up and around the stones, as no fence keeps you away. Also, the site isn't mobbed with tour buses.

Visitors can walk around the 11-hectare (28-acre) site at Avebury, winding in and out of the circle of more than 100 stones, some weighing up to 50 tons. The stones are made of _sarsen,_ a sandstone found in Wiltshire. Inside this large circle are two smaller ones, each with about 30 stones standing upright. Native Neolithic tribes are believed to have built these circles.

Wilts & Dorset (© **01722/336855;** www.wdbus.co.uk) has two buses (nos. 5 and 6) that run between the Salisbury bus station and Avebury five times a day Monday through Saturday and 3 times a day on Sunday. The one-way trip takes 1 hour and 40 minutes. Round-trip tickets are £6 ($11) for adults, £4.20 ($7.75) seniors, £12 ($21) family ticket, and £3 ($5.55) for children ages 5 to 14 (4 and under ride free).

Also here is the **Alexander Keiller Museum** (© **01672/539250**), which houses one of Britain's most important archaeological collections, including material from excavations at Windmill Hill and Avebury, and artifacts from other prehistoric digs at West Kennet, Long Barrow, Silbury Hill, West Kennet Avenue, and the Sanctuary. The museum is open April through October daily from 10am to 6pm, November through March daily from 10am to 4pm. Admission is £4.20 ($7.75) for adults, £2.10 ($3.90) for children, and £10 ($19) family ticket.

On A361 between Swindon and Devizes (1.5km/1 mile from the A4 London-Bath Rd.). The closest rail station is at Swindon, 19km (12 miles) away, which is served by the main rail line from London to Bath. For rail information, call © **0845/748-4950** or visit www.railtrack.co.uk. A limited bus service (no. 49) runs from Swindon to Devizes through Avebury.

3 Bath: Britain's Most Historic Spa Town ⭐⭐⭐

185km (115 miles) W of London; 21km (13 miles) SE of Bristol

In 1702, Queen Anne made the trek from London to the mineral springs of **Bath,** launching a fad that was to make the city the most celebrated spa in England.

The most famous name connected with Bath was the 18th-century dandy Beau Nash, who cut a striking figure as he made his way across the city, with all the plumage of a bird of paradise. This polished arbiter of taste and manners made dueling déclassé. While dispensing (at a price) trinkets to the courtiers and aspirant gentlemen of his day, Beau was carted around in a sedan chair.

The 18th-century architects John Wood the Elder and his son provided a proper backdrop for Nash's considerable social talents. These architects designed a city of stone from the nearby hills, a feat so substantial and lasting that Bath today is the most harmoniously laid-out city in England. During Georgian and Victorian times, this city, on a bend of the River Avon, attracted leading political and literary figures, such as Dickens, Thackeray, Nelson, and Pitt. Canadians may already know that General Wolfe lived on Trim Street, and Australians may want to visit the house at 19 Bennett St., where their founding father, Admiral Phillip, lived. Even Henry Fielding came this way, observing in *Tom Jones* that the ladies of Bath "endeavour to appear as ugly as possible in the morning, in order to set off that beauty which they intend to show you in the evening."

Even before its Queen Anne, Georgian, and Victorian popularity, Bath was known to the Romans as Aquae Sulis. The foreign legions founded the baths here (which you can visit today) to ease rheumatism in their curative mineral springs.

Remarkable restoration and careful planning have ensured that Bath retains its handsome look today. The city suffered devastating destruction from the infamous Baedeker air raids of 1942, when Luftwaffe pilots seemed more intent on bombing historical buildings than on hitting any military targets.

After undergoing major restoration in the postwar era, Bath today has somewhat of a museum look, with the attendant gift shops. Its parks, museums, and architecture continue to draw hordes of visitors, and because of this massive tourist invasion, prices remain high. It's one of the high points of the West Country and a good base for exploring Avebury.

ESSENTIALS

GETTING THERE   Trains leave London's Paddington Station bound for Bath once every half-hour during the day. The trip takes about 1½ hours. For rail information, call © **0845/748-4950** or visit www.railtrack.co.uk.

Bath

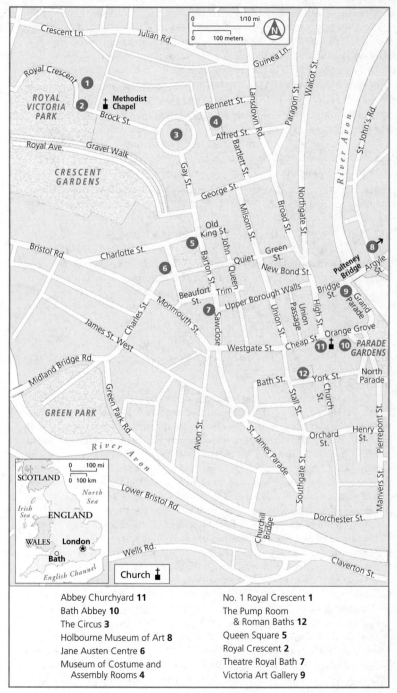

Crescent Ln.
Julian Rd.
Guinea Ln.
Walcot St.
Royal Crescent
1
Paragon St.
ROYAL VICTORIA PARK
2
Methodist Chapel
Bennett St.
Lansdown Rd.
River Avon
St. John's Rd.
Brock St.
3
4
Alfred St.
Royal Ave.
Gravel Walk
Bartlett St.
CRESCENT GARDENS
George St.
Gay St.
Northgate St.
Broad St.
Old King St.
Milsom St.
Bristol Rd.
Charlotte St.
5
John St.
Quiet
Green St.
8
Pulteney Bridge
Argyle St.
6
Barton St.
Queen
New Bond St.
Beaufort St.
Trim
Upper Borough Walls
Bridge St.
9
Grand Parade
Charles St.
Monmouth St.
7
Sawclose
Union Passage
High St.
Orange Grove
PARADE GARDENS
James St. West
Union St.
Westgate St.
Cheap St.
11
10
Midland Bridge Rd.
Bath St.
12
York St.
North Parade
GREEN PARK
Green Park Rd.
Avon St.
Stall St.
Church St.
Henry St.
Pierrepont St.
River Avon
St. James Parade
Orchard St.
Manvers St.
Lower Bristol Rd.
Southgate St.
Dorchester St.
Churchill Bridge
Wells Rd.
Claverton St.

SCOTLAND
North Sea
Irish Sea
ENGLAND
WALES
London
Bath
English Channel

Church ✝

Abbey Churchyard **11**

Bath Abbey **10**

The Circus **3**

Holbourne Museum of Art **8**

Jane Austen Centre **6**

Museum of Costume and Assembly Rooms **4**

No. 1 Royal Crescent **1**

The Pump Room & Roman Baths **12**

Queen Square **5**

Royal Crescent **2**

Theatre Royal Bath **7**

Victoria Art Gallery **9**

A **National Express** coach leaves London's Victoria Coach Station every 90 minutes during the day. The trip takes 3½ hours. Coaches also leave Bristol bound for Bath and make the trip in 40 minutes. For schedules and information, call ℂ **0870/580-8080** or visit www.nationalexpress.com.

Drive west on the M4 to the junction with the A4, then continue west to Bath.

VISITOR INFORMATION   The **Bath Tourist Information Centre** is at Abbey Chambers, Abbey Church Yard (ℂ **01225/477101;** www.visitbath.co.uk), next to Bath Abbey. It's open June through September, Monday through Saturday from 9:30am to 6pm, Sunday from 10am to 4pm; off season, Monday through Saturday from 9:30am to 5pm and Sunday from 10am to 4pm. It is closed Christmas Day and New Year's Day.

GETTING AROUND   One of the best ways to explore Bath is by bike. Rentals are available at **The Bath & Dundas Canal Company,** Brass Knocker Basin at Monkton Combe (ℂ **01225/722292;** www.bathcanal.com). Daily rentals go for £14 ($26).

SPECIAL EVENTS   Bath's graceful Georgian architecture provides the setting for one of Europe's most prestigious international festivals of music and the arts, the **Bath International Music Festival.** For 17 days in late May and early June each year, the city is filled with more than 1,000 performers. The festival focuses on classical music, jazz, new music, and the contemporary visual arts, with orchestras, soloists, and artists from all over the world. In addition to the main music and art program, the festival offers walks, tours, and talks, plus free street entertainment, a free Festival Club, and opening night celebrations with fireworks. For information, contact the **Bath Festivals Box Office,** 2 Church St., Abbey Green, Bath BA1 1NL (ℂ **01225/463362;** www.bathmusicfest.org.uk).

SEEING THE SIGHTS

Stroll around to see some of the buildings, crescents, and squares in town. The **North Parade** (where Goldsmith lived) and the **South Parade** (where English novelist and diarist Frances Burney once resided) represent harmony, as well as the work of John Wood the Elder, who also designed beautiful **Queen Square,** where both Jane Austen and Wordsworth once lived. Also of interest is **The Circus** ★★★, built in 1754, as well as the shop-lined **Pulteney Bridge,** designed by Robert Adam and often compared to the Ponte Vecchio of Florence.

The younger John Wood designed the **Royal Crescent** ★★★, an elegant half-moon row of town houses (copied by Astor architects for their colonnade in New York City in the 1830s). At **No. 1 Royal Crescent** (ℂ **01225/428126**), the interior has been redecorated and furnished by the Bath Preservation Trust to look as it might have toward the end of the 18th century. The house lies at one end of Bath's most magnificent crescents, west of the Circus. Admission is £4 ($7.40) for adults and £3.50 ($6.50) for children, seniors, and students; a family ticket is £12 ($22). Open from mid-February to October, Tuesday through Sunday from 10:30am to 5pm, and November, Tuesday through Sunday from 10:30am to 4pm (last admission 30 min. before closing); closed Good Friday.

Free 1¾-hour walking tours are conducted throughout the year by the **Mayor's Honorary Society** (ℂ **01225/477786**). Tours depart from outside the Roman Baths Sunday through Friday at 10:30am and 2pm, Saturday at 10:30am; May through September, another tour is added on Tuesday, Friday, and Saturday at 7pm.

The **Jane Austen Centre,** 40 Gay St. (ℂ **01225/443000;** www.janeausten. co.uk), is located in a Georgian town house on an elegant street where Miss

Austen once lived. Exhibits and a video convey a sense of what life was like in Bath during the Regency period. The center is open Monday to Saturday from 10am to 5:30pm and Sunday from 10:30am to 5:30pm. Admission is £4.65 ($8.60) for adults, £3.95 ($7.30) students, £13 ($23) family ticket, and £2.50 ($4.65) children.

The American Museum ✦✦   Some 4km (2½ miles) outside Bath, get an idea of what life was like in America prior to the mid-1800s. The first American museum established outside the U.S., it sits proudly on extensive grounds high above the Somerset Valley. Among the authentic exhibits shipped over from the States are a New Mexico room, a Conestoga wagon, the dining room of a New York town house of the early 19th century, and (on the grounds) a copy of Washington's flower garden at Mount Vernon. Throughout the summer, the museum hosts various special events, from displays of Native American dancing to very realistic reenactments of the Civil War.

Claverton Manor, Bathwick Hill. ✆ 01225/460503. www.americanmuseum.org. Admission £6.50 ($12) adults, £5.50 ($10) students and seniors, £18 ($32) family ticket, £3.50 ($6.50) children 5–16, free for 4 and under. Late Mar to Nov Tues–Sun noon–5pm for the museum, Tues–Fri 1–6pm and Sat–Sun noon–6pm for the garden. Nov to late Mar by appointment only. Bus: 18.

Bath Abbey ✦   Built on the site of a much larger Norman cathedral, the present-day abbey is a fine example of the late Perpendicular style. When Queen Elizabeth I came to Bath in 1574, she ordered a national fund to be set up to restore the abbey. The west front is the sculptural embodiment of a Jacob's Ladder dream of a 15th-century bishop. When you go inside and see its many windows, you'll understand why the abbey is called the "Lantern of the West." Note the superb fan vaulting with its scalloped effect. Beau Nash was buried in the nave and is honored by a simple monument totally out of keeping with his flamboyant character. The Bath Abbey Heritage Vaults opened in 1994 on the south side of the abbey. This subterranean exhibition traces the history of Christianity at the abbey site since Saxon times.

Orange Grove. ✆ 01225/422462. www.bathabbey.org. £2.50 ($4.65) donation requested. Admission to the Heritage Vaults £2.50 ($4.65) adults, £1.50 ($2.80) students, children, and seniors. Abbey Apr–Oct Mon–Sat 9am–6pm; Nov–Mar Mon–Sat 9am–4:30pm; year-round Sun 1–2:30pm and 4:30–5:30pm. The Heritage Vaults Mon–Sat 10am–3:30pm (last entrance).

Holbourne Museum of Art ✦ *Finds*   This has been called, quite accurately, "one of the most perfect small museums of Europe." It was constructed in 1796 as a building in which to entertain guests to Sydney Gardens, the luminaries including Jane Austen. It was converted into a museum at the turn of the 20th century to display a collection of Sir William Holburne's treasures, such as a bronze nude favored by Louis XIV, along with some of the finest Renaissance majolica in England. Also on display are works illuminating the glittering society of 18th-century Bath at its pinnacle, including masterpieces by Thomas Gainsborough, such as *The Byam Family* on indefinite loan. Other choice tidbits from this treasure trove include the lovely portrait of *The Reverend Carter Thelwall and His Family* by Stubbs, and such surprising exhibits as a Steinway piano used by Rachmaninoff for rehearsals of his music. The museum is also the temporary venue of traveling exhibits.

Great Pulteney St. ✆ 01225/466669. www.bath.ac.uk/Holburne. Admission £3.50 ($6.50). Mid-Feb to mid-Dec Tues–Sat 10am–5pm, Sun 2:30–5:30pm. Closed mid-Dec to mid-Feb.

Museum of Costume and Assembly Rooms ✦✦   Operated by the National Trust and housed in an 18th-century building, the grand **Assembly**

Rooms played host to dances, recitals, and tea parties. Damaged in World War II, the elegant rooms have been gloriously restored and look much as they did when Jane Austen and Thomas Gainsborough attended society events here.

Housed in the same building, the **Museum of Costume** sports one of the best collections of fashion and costume in Europe. A fascinating audio tour escorts visitors through the history of fashion—including accessories, lingerie, and shoes—from the 16th century to the present day. Highlights include a 17th-century "silver tissue" dress; an ultra-restricting whalebone corset; an original suit, once owned by Dame Margot Fonteyn, from Christian Dior's legendary "New Look" collection; and the ultrasheer Versace dress made famous—or infamous—by actress Jennifer Lopez. The museum is also famous for its "Dress of the Year" collection, which highlights notable ideas in contemporary style. Some selections have been notably prescient; its choice for the 1987 dress of the year was by then-unknown designer John Galliano. Only 2,000 of the museum's 30,000 items are on display at any one time, but exhibits change frequently and special themed collections are often presented.

Bennett St. ⓒ **01225/477789.** www.museumofcostume.co.uk. Admission £6 ($11) adult, £5 ($9.25) students and seniors, £4 ($7.40) children age 6 and over, £17 ($31) family ticket. Admission includes free audio tour. Nov–Feb daily 11am–5pm; Mar–Oct 11am–6pm; last admission 1hr. before closing. Closed Dec 25–26.

The Pump Room ⭐ **& Roman Baths** ⭐⭐   Founded in A.D. 75 by the Romans, the baths were dedicated to the goddess Sulis Minerva; in their day, they were an engineering feat. Even today, they're among the finest Roman remains in the country, and they are still fed by Britain's most famous hot-spring water. After centuries of decay, the original baths were rediscovered during Queen Victoria's reign. The site of the Temple of Sulis Minerva has been excavated and is now open to view. The museum displays many interesting objects from Victorian and recent digs (look for the head of Minerva).

Coffee, lunch, and tea, usually with music from the Pump Room Trio, can be enjoyed in the 18th-century pump room, overlooking the hot springs. You can also find a drinking fountain with hot mineral water that tastes horrible.

In the Bath Abbey churchyard, Stall St. ⓒ **01225/477785.** www.romanbaths.co.uk. Admission £9 ($17) adults, £5 ($9.25) children, £24 ($44) family ticket. Apr–Sept daily 9am–6pm; Oct–Mar Mon–Sat 9am–5pm.

Theatre Royal Bath   Theatre Royal, located next to the new Seven Dials development, was restored in 1982 and refurbished with plush seats, red carpets, and a painted proscenium arch and ceiling; it is now the most beautiful theater in Britain. It has 880 seats, with a small pit and grand tiers rising to the upper circle. Despite all the work, Theatre Royal has no company, depending upon touring shows to fill the house during the 8-week theater season each summer. Beneath the theater, reached from the back of the stalls or by a side door, are the theater vaults, where you will find a bar in one with stonewalls. The next vault has a restaurant, serving an array of dishes from soup to light a la carte meals.

A studio theater at the rear of the main building opened in 1996. The theater publishes a list of forthcoming events; its repertoire includes West End shows, among other offerings.

Sawclose. ⓒ **01225/448844.** www.theatreroyal.org.uk. Tickets £10–£30 ($19–$56). Box office Mon–Sat 10am–8pm; Sun noon–8pm. Shows Mon–Wed at 7:30pm; Thurs–Sat at 8pm; Wed and Sat matinees at 2:30pm.

Victoria Art Gallery   This relatively unknown gallery showcases the area's best collection of British and European art from the 15th century to the present. Most of the works are on display in the sumptuous Victorian Upper Gallery.

The collection includes paintings by artists who have lived and worked in the Bath area, including Gainsborough. Singled out for special attention is the art of Walter Richard Sickert (1860–1942) now that he has been "outed" as the real Jack the Ripper in Patricia Cornwell's bestseller, *Portrait of a Killer: Jack the Ripper—Case Closed.* In the two large modern galleries downstairs, special exhibitions are shown. These exhibitions change every 6 to 8 weeks and are likely to feature displays ranging from cartoons to boat sculpture.

Bridge St. © **01225/477233.** www.victoriagal.org.uk. Free admission. Tues–Fri 10am–5:30pm; Sat 10am–5pm; Sun 2–5pm.

SHOPPING

Bath is loaded with markets and fairs, antiques centers, and small shops, with literally hundreds of opportunities to buy (and ship) anything you want (including the famous spa waters, for sale by the bottle). Prices are traditionally less than in London but more than in the British boonies.

The whole city is basically one long, slightly uphill shopping area. It's not defined by one high street, as are so many British towns—if you arrive by train, don't be put off by the lack of scenery. Within 2 blocks are several shopping streets. The single best day to visit, if you are a serious shopper intent on hitting the flea markets, is Wednesday.

The Bartlett Street Antiques Centre, Bartlett Street (© **01225/466689**), encompasses 20 dealers and 50 showcases displaying furniture, silver, antique jewelry, paintings, toys, military items, and collectibles.

Walcot Reclamation, 108 Walcot St. (© **01225/444404**), is Bath's salvage yard. This sprawling and appealingly dusty storeroom of 19th-century architectural remnants is set .5km (¼ mile) northeast of the town center. Its 1,858-sq. m (20,000-sq.-ft.) warehouse offers pieces from demolished homes, schools, hospitals, and factories throughout south England. Mantelpieces, panels, columns, and architectural ornaments are departmentalized into historical eras. Items range from a complete, dismantled 1937 Georgian library crafted from Honduran mahogany to objects costing around £10 ($19) each. Anything can be shipped by a battery of artisans who are trained in adapting antique fittings for modern homes.

The largest purveyor of antique coins and stamps in Bath, **The Bath Stamp & Coin Shop,** 12–13 Pulteney Bridge (© **01225/463073**), offers hundreds of odd and unusual numismatics. Part of the inventory is devoted to Roman coins, some of which were unearthed in archaeological excavations at Roman sites near Bath.

Near Bath Abbey, the **Beaux Arts Gallery,** 13 York St. (© **01225/464850**), is the largest and most important gallery of contemporary art in Bath, specializing in well-known British artists including Ray Richardson, John Bellany, and Nicola Bealing. Closely linked to the London art scene, the gallery occupies a pair of interconnected, stone-fronted Georgian houses. Its half-dozen showrooms exhibit objects beginning at £30 ($56).

The very upscale **Rossiter's,** 38–41 Broad St. (© **01225/462227**), sells very traditional English tableware and home decor items. They'll ship anywhere in the world. Look especially for the display of Moorcraft ginger jars, vases, and clocks, as well as the Floris perfumes.

Whittard of Chelsea, 14 Union Passage (© **01225/483529**), is the most charming and unusual tea emporium in Bath. Inside, you'll find strainers, tea cozies and teas from all parts of what used to be the Empire. Looking for a fabulously exotic tea to wow your friends back home? How about monkey-picked oolong—a Chinese tea made from plants so inaccessible their leaves can only be gathered by trained monkeys.

WHERE TO STAY
VERY EXPENSIVE

Bath Priory ★★★   Converted from one of Bath's Georgian houses in 1969, the Priory is situated on .8 hectares (2 acres) of formal and award-winning gardens with manicured lawns and flowerbeds. The rooms are furnished with antiques; our personal favorite is Clivia (all rooms are named after flowers or shrubs), a nicely appointed duplex in a circular turret. Rooms range from medium in size to spacious deluxe units, the latter with views, large sitting areas, and generous dressing areas. Each has a lovely old English bed, often a half-tester; bathrooms are beautifully kept and come with a set of deluxe toiletries.

Weston Rd., Bath, Somerset BA1 2XT. © **01225/331922.** Fax 01225/448276. www.thebathpriory.co.uk. 28 units. £245 ($453) standard double; £360 ($666) deluxe room. Rates include English breakfast. AE, DC, MC, V. **Amenities:** Restaurant; bar; 2 pools (1 indoor, 1 outdoor); health club; Jacuzzi; sauna; concierge; 24-hr. room service; babysitting; laundry service; dry cleaning; croquet lawn; nonsmoking rooms; rooms for those with limited mobility. *In room:* A/C, TV, hair dryer.

Bath Spa Hotel ★★★   This stunning restored 19th-century mansion is a 10-minute walk from the center of Bath. Behind a facade of Bath stone, it lies at the end of a tree-lined drive on 2.8 hectares (7 acres) of landscaped grounds, with a Victorian grotto and a Grecian temple. In its long history, it served many purposes (once as a hostel for nurses) before being returned to its original grandeur. The hotel uses log fireplaces, elaborate moldings, and oak paneling to create country house charm. The rooms are handsomely furnished, and most of them are spacious. Most beds are doubles, and some even offer an old-fashioned four-poster. The marble bathrooms are among the city's finest, each with long tubs, hand-held showers, and deluxe toiletries.

Sydney Rd. (east of the city, off A36), Bath, Somerset BA2 6JF. © **01225/444424.** Fax 01225/444006. www. macdonaldhotels.co.uk. 102 units. Sun–Thurs £225–£290 ($416–$537) double; Fri–Sat £300–£340 ($555–$629) double; weeklong £315–£425 ($583–$786) suite. Rates include breakfast. AE, DC, MC, V. **Amenities:** 2 restaurants; bar; indoor pool; outdoor tennis court; health spa; 24-hr. room service; salon; laundry service; valet; nonsmoking rooms. *In room:* TV, minibar, coffeemaker, hair dryer, safe, trouser press, bathrobes.

The Royal Crescent ★★★   This special place stands proudly in the center of the famed Royal Crescent. Long regarded as Bath's premier hotel (before the arrival of the even better Bath Spa), it has attracted the rich and famous. The bedrooms, including the Jane Austen Suite, are lavishly furnished with such amenities as four-poster beds and marble tubs. Each room is individually designed and offers such comforts as bottled mineral water, fruit plates, and other special touches. Bedrooms, generally quite spacious, are elaborately decked out with thick wool carpeting, silk wall coverings, and antiques, each with a superb and rather sumptuous bed. Bathrooms are equally luxurious with deluxe toiletries and robes.

15–16 Royal Crescent, Bath, Somerset BA1 2LS. © **888/295-4710** in the U.S., or 01225/823333. Fax 01225/339401. www.royalcrescent.co.uk. 45 units. £207–£377 ($383–$697) double; from £382 ($707) suite. AE, DC, MC, V. **Amenities:** Restaurant; bar; health club; indoor pool; steam room; 24-hr. room service; babysitting; laundry service; dry cleaning. *In room:* TV, dataport, minibar, beverage maker, hair dryer, safe, bathrobes.

EXPENSIVE

The Francis ★   An integral part of Queen Square, the Francis is an example of 18th-century taste and style, but we find it too commercial and touristy. Originally consisting of six private residences dating from 1729, the Francis was opened as a private hotel by Emily Francis in 1884 and has offered guests first-class service for more than 100 years. Many of the well-furnished and traditionally styled bedrooms overlook Queen Square, named in honor of George II's consort, Caroline. Rooms range in size from rather small to medium, with either twin or double beds. Accommodations in the older building have more charm, especially the upper floor. Bathrooms are small but equipped with heated towel racks, plus a combination tub and shower.

Queen Sq., Bath, Somerset BA1 2HH. ☎ **888/892-0038** in the U.S. and Canada, or 0870/400-8223. Fax 01225/319715. www.macdonaldhotels.co.uk. 95 units. £108–£168 ($200–$311) double; £210 ($389) suite. Rates include breakfast. AE, DC, MC, V. Parking £5 ($9.25). **Amenities:** Restaurant; bar; 24-hr. room service; babysitting; laundry service; dry cleaning; nonsmoking rooms; rooms for those with limited mobility. *In room:* TV, dataport, fridge, hair dryer, iron/board, trouser press.

Pratt's Hotel ⭐   Once the home of Sir Walter Scott, Pratt's dates from the heady days of Beau Nash. Functioning as a hotel since 1791, it has become part of the legend and lore of Bath. Several elegant terraced Georgian town houses were joined together to form this complex with a very traditional British atmosphere. Rooms are individually designed, and as is typical of a converted private home, bedrooms range from small to spacious (the larger ones are on the lower floors). Regardless of their dimensions, the rooms are furnished in a comfortable though utilitarian style, with small but efficiently organized shower-only bathrooms.

S. Parade, Bath, Somerset BA2 4AB. ☎ **01225/460441.** Fax 01225/448807. www.prattshotel.com. 46 units. £130–£160 ($241–$296) double. Children under 14 sharing a room with 2 adults stay free. Rates include English breakfast. AE, DC, MC, V. Parking £10 ($19). **Amenities:** Restaurant; bar; 24-hr. room service; laundry service; dry cleaning; iron/ironing board. *In room:* TV, coffeemaker, hair dryer, trouser press.

The Queensberry Hotel ⭐   A gem of a hotel, this early Georgian-era town house has been beautifully restored by Stephen and Penny Ross. In our view, it is now among the finest places to stay in a city where the competition for restored town-house hotels is fierce. The marquis of Queensberry commissioned John Wood the Younger to build this house in 1772. Rooms—often spacious but usually medium in size—are delightful, each tastefully decorated with antique furniture and such thoughtful extras as fresh flowers. Bathrooms are well kept and equipped with good showers and tubs.

Russell St., Bath, Somerset BA1 2QF. ☎ **01225/447928.** Fax 01225/446065. www.thequeensberry.co.uk. 29 units. £100–£195 ($185–$361) double; £285 ($527) suite. Rates include continental breakfast. AE, MC, V. **Amenities:** Restaurant; bar; 24-hr. room service; babysitting; laundry service; dry cleaning. *In room:* TV, hair dryer, iron/ironing board.

MODERATE

Apsley House Hotel ⭐⭐ *Finds*   This charming and stately building, just 1.5km (1 mile) west of the center of Bath, dates from 1830, during the reign of William IV. In 1994, new owners refurbished the hotel, filling it with country-house chintzes and a collection of antiques borrowed from the showrooms of an antiques store they own. (Some furniture in the hotel is for sale.) Style and comfort are the keynote here, and all the relatively spacious bedrooms are inviting, appointed with plush beds and tidy shower-tub combination.

141 Newbridge Hill, Bath, Somerset BA1 3PT. ☎ **01225/336966.** Fax 01225/425462. www.apsley-house.co.uk. 9 units. £70–£140 ($130–$259) double; £100–£160 ($185–$296) suite. Rates include English breakfast. AE, MC, V. Take A4 to Upper Bristol Rd., fork right at the traffic signals into Newbridge Hill, and turn left at Apsley Rd. **Amenities:** Bar; limited room service; babysitting; laundry service; dry cleaning; nonsmoking rooms. *In room:* TV, dataport, coffeemaker, hair dryer, iron.

Duke's Hotel   A short walk from the heart of Bath, this 1780 building is fresher than ever following a complete restoration in 2001. Many of the original Georgian features, including cornices and moldings, have been retained.

Rooms, ranging from small to medium, are exceedingly comfortable. All of the bathrooms are small but efficiently arranged and sport shower-tub combinations or just showers. Guests can relax in a refined drawing room or patronize the cozy bar overlooking a garden. The entire setting has been called a "perfect *Masterpiece Theatre* take on Britain," with a fire burning in the grate.

53–54 Great Pulteney St., Bath, Somerset BA2 4DN. ☎ 01225/787960. Fax 01225/787961. www.dukes bath.co.uk. 18 units. £85–£155 ($157–$287) double; £115 ($213) family room. Rates include English breakfast. MC, V. Bus: 18. **Amenities:** Restaurant; bar; limited room service; business services; babysitting; laundry service; dry cleaning; rooms for those with limited mobility. *In room:* TV, hair dryer, bathrobes.

Sydney Gardens Hotel   This spot is reminiscent of the letters of Jane Austen, who wrote to friends about long walks she enjoyed in Sydney Gardens, a public park just outside the city center, a 15- to 20-minute walk away. In 1852, this Italianate Victorian villa was constructed of gray stone on a lot immediately adjacent to the gardens. Three rooms have twin beds, two have large double beds and the family room has 1 large bed and 2 singles. Each accommodation is individually decorated with an English country-house charm, each with a bathroom with a small, shower-tub combination. A footpath runs beside a canal for leisurely strolls. The entire property is nonsmoking.

Sydney Rd., Bath, Somerset BA2 6NT. ☎ **01225/464818.** Fax 01225/484347. www.sydneygardens.co.uk. 6 units. £80–£115 ($148–$213) double. Rates include English breakfast. MC, V. **Amenities:** Breakfast room. *In room:* TV, coffeemaker, hair dryer, iron/ironing board.

Tasburgh House Hotel   Set about 1.5km (1 mile) east of Bath center, amid 2.8 hectares (7 acres) of parks and gardens, this spacious Victorian country house dates from 1890. The redbrick structure contains a large glassed-in conservatory, stained-glass windows, and antiques. Bedrooms are tastefully decorated, often with half-tester beds, and most have sweeping panoramic views. Two rooms have four-poster beds. All the bathrooms are excellent, and five of them are equipped with a tub-and-shower combination, the rest with shower only. The entire facility is nonsmoking. As there is no air-conditioning, windows have to be opened on hot summer nights, which will subject you to a lot of traffic noise. The Avon and Kennet Canal runs along the rear of the property, and guests enjoy summer walks along the adjacent towpath.

Warminster Rd., Bath, Somerset BA2 6SH. ☎ **01225/425096.** www.bathtasburgh.co.uk. 12 units. £110–£135 ($204–$250) double; £130 ($241) triple; £160 ($296) quad. Rates include English breakfast. DC, MC, V. Bus: 4. **Amenities:** Bar; laundry service; dry cleaning. *In room:* TV, dataport, coffeemaker, hair dryer.

INEXPENSIVE

Badminton Villa   Located about a kilometer (½ mile) south of the city center, this house dates from 1883. Constructed of honey-colored blocks of Bath stone, it lies on a hillside with sweeping views over the world-famous architecture of Bath. In 1992, John and Sue Barton transformed it from a villa in disrepair to one of the most charming small hotels in Bath. Furnishings are an eclectic but unpretentious mix of objects gathered by the Burtons during their travels. The small to medium-size bedrooms feature double-glazed windows, and bathrooms have a tub or an upgraded shower. There's also a three-tiered garden with patio. This establishment is entirely nonsmoking.

10 Upper Oldfield Park, Bath, Somerset BA2 3JZ. ☎ 01225/426347. Fax 01225/420393. www.s-h-systems.co. uk/hotels/badminton.html. 5 units. £72 ($133) double; £75–£85 ($139–$157) triple. Rates include English breakfast. MC, V. Bus: 14. **Amenities:** Breakfast room; guest lounge. *In room:* TV, coffeemaker, hair dryer, iron.

Laura Place Hotel   Built in 1789, this hotel hides behind a stone facade, and it lies within a 2-minute walk of the Roman Baths and Bath Abbey. This very formal hotel has been skillfully decorated with antique furniture and fabrics evocative of the 18th century. The bedrooms here are exceedingly cozy in the best tradition of an English B&B. Baths are small, usually with a shower stall instead of a tub, but have adequate shelf space. *Note:* The hotel closes in the winter months (times vary according to the year).

3 Laura Place, Great Pulteney St., Bath, Somerset BA2 4BH. ℭ **01225/463815.** Fax 01225/310222. 8 units. £75–£95 ($139–$176) double; £120 ($222) family suite. Rates include English breakfast. AE, MC, V. Bus: 18 or 19. **Amenities:** Breakfast room. *In room:* TV, coffeemaker, hair dryer, safe.

Number Ninety Three   This small, well-run guesthouse is a traditional, British-style B&B. The small to midsize bedrooms have soft, cozy beds, and the owners undertake a continuing program of maintenance and redecoration in the slower or winter months. Bathrooms are small with a shower stall. The elegant Victorian house serves a traditional English breakfast, and it is within easy walking distance from the city center and the rail and national bus stations. Its owner is a mine of local information. The entire property is nonsmoking.

93 Wells Rd., Bath, Somerset BA2 3AN. ℭ **01225/317977.** 4 units. £45–£65 ($83–$120) double; £60–£81 ($111–$150) triple. Rates include English breakfast. No credit cards. Bus: 3, 13, 14, 17, or 23; ask for Lower Wells Rd. stop. **Amenities:** Breakfast room. *In room:* TV, coffeemaker, hair dryer.

IN NEARBY HINTON CHARTERHOUSE

Homewood Park ★★   This small, family-run hotel, set on 4 hectares (10 acres) of grounds, dates from the 18th century. Overlooking the Limpley Stoke Valley, it's a large Victorian house with grounds adjoining the 13th-century ruin of Hinton Priory. You can play croquet in the garden. Riding and golfing are available nearby, and beautiful walks in the Limpley Stoke Valley lure guests. Each of the small to midsize rooms is luxuriously decorated and most overlook the award-winning gardens and grounds or offer views of the valley. Each unit has a well-managed bathroom with a shower-tub combination or just shower.

Hinton Charterhouse, Bath, Somerset BA2 7TB. ℭ **01225/723731.** Fax 01225/723820. www.homewood park.com. 19 units. £145–£220 ($268–$407) double; £265 ($490) suite. Rates include English breakfast. AE, DC, MC, V. Take A36 (Bath-Warminster Rd.) 9.5km (6 miles) south of Bath. **Amenities:** Restaurant; bar; pool; limited room service; babysitting; laundry service; dry cleaning. *In room:* TV, dataport, hair dryer.

IN NEARBY STON EASTON

Ston Easton Park ★★★ *Finds*   This is one of the great country hotels of England. From the moment you pass a group of stone outbuildings and century-old beeches set on a 12-hectare (30-acre) park, you know you've come to a very special place. The mansion was created in the mid-1700s from the shell of an Elizabethan house; in 1793, Sir Humphry Repton designed the landscape. In 1977, after many years of neglect, Peter and Christine Smedley acquired the property and poured money, love, and labor into its restoration.

The tasteful rooms are filled with flowers and antiques, and feature spacious, sumptuous beds. A gardener's cottage was artfully upgraded from a utilitarian building to contain a pair of intensely decorated and very glamorous suites. In addition to the cottage suite, plus the "standard and deluxe" rooms of the main house, you'll find half a dozen "state rooms," four of which have four-poster beds, and all of which contain lavish but genteel decor. Bathrooms are equally luxurious with deluxe toiletries and shower-tub combinations.

Ston Easton, Somerset BA3 4DF. ℭ **01761/241631.** Fax 01761/241377. www.stoneaston.co.uk. 24 units, 1 cottage suite, 7 state rooms. £150–£335 ($278–$620) double; from £605 ($1,119) 3-room cottage suite; £335 ($620) state room. AE, DC, MC, V. Lies 19km (12 miles) south of Bath; follow A39 south to the sign-posted turnoff to the hamlet of Ston Easton. **Amenities:** Restaurant; tennis court; croquet; billiard room; limited room service; babysitting; laundry service. *In room:* TV, dataport, hair dryer, iron/ironing board, safe.

IN NEARBY HUNSTRETE

Hunstrete House ★★   This fine Georgian house is situated on 37 hectares (92 acres) of private parkland. Six units in the Courtyard House are attached to the main structure and overlook a paved courtyard. Swallow Cottage, which adjoins the main house, has its own private sitting room, double bedroom, and bathroom. Units in the main house are decorated with antiques; all have sitting areas with armchairs and sofas. Awaiting you are little extras such as a selection of magazines and a decanter of sherry. The one shower-only bathroom is also luxurious.

Hunstrete, Chelwood, near Bristol, Somerset BS38 4NS. ℭ **01761/490490.** Fax 01761/490732. www.hunstrete house.co.uk. 25 units. £170–£205 ($315–$379) double; £195–£205 ($361–$379) superior double; £235–£275 ($435–$509) suite. Half board £350 ($648) double; £400 ($740) suite for 2. Rates include English breakfast. AE, DC, MC, V. Take A4 about 5.5km (3½ miles) west of Bath, then A368 another 5.5km (3½ miles) toward Weston-super-Mare. **Amenities:** Restaurant; bar; heated outdoor pool; limited room service; babysitting; laundry service; nonsmoking rooms. *In room:* TV, hair dryer, iron/ironing board, trouser press.

WHERE TO DINE

The best place for afternoon tea is **The Pump Room & Roman Baths** (see "Seeing the Sights," earlier in this chapter). Another choice, just a 1-minute walk from the Abbey Church and Roman Baths, is **Sally Lunn's House,** 4 North Parade Passage (ℭ **01225/461634**), where visitors have been eating for more than 1,700 years. For £5 ($9.25), you can get the Fantastic Sally Lunn Cream Tea, which includes toasted and buttered scones served with strawberry jam and clotted cream, along with your choice of tea or coffee.

Café Retro, York Street (ℭ **01225/339347**), serves a variety of teas and coffees. You can order a pot of tea for £1.20 ($2.20) or a large cappuccino for £1.70 ($3.15) and add a tea cake for £1.30 ($2.40).

EXPENSIVE

The Moody Goose ★★★ ENGLISH   In a highly competitive city, this "bird" serves the finest and most refined cuisine. In an elegant, landmarked Georgian terrace in the center of the city, the restaurant has two cozy dining rooms and a little bar. The kitchen has an absolute passion for fresh ingredients and food cooked to order, and the chefs believe in using produce grown as near home as possible, though the Angus beef comes in from Scotland, and the fresh fish from the coasts of Cornwall and Devon. Natural flavors are appreciated here and not smothered in sauces. Even the breads, ice creams, and petits fours are homemade. The kitchen team is expert at chargrilling.

Launch your repast with such temptations as pan-fried veal sweetbreads with a salad of pink grapefruit and walnuts or a brown trout confit in puff pastry. For a main dish, be dazzled with whole roasted quail with braised chicory and roasted apple, roasted rump of lamb, or poached filet of halibut with fresh clams. We're especially fond of the desserts, particularly a fresh rhubarb cheesecake.

7A Kingsmead Sq. ℭ **01225/466688.** Reservations required. Main courses £18–£20 ($33–$36); fixed-price lunch £18 ($32); fixed-price dinner £25 ($46). AE, DC, MC, V. Mon–Sat noon–1:30pm and 6–9:30pm.

The Olive Tree MODERN ENGLISH/MEDITERRANEAN   Stephen and Penny Ross operate one of the most sophisticated little restaurants in Bath. Stephen uses the best local produce, with an emphasis on freshness. The menu is changed to reflect the season, with game and fish being the specialties. You may begin with grilled scallops with noodles and pine nuts, or Provençal fish soup with rouille and croutons. Then you could proceed to grilled Aberdeen Angus rump filet, creamed onions, and rosemary in a red-wine-and-peppercorn jus. Stephen is also known for his desserts, which are likely to include such treats as a hot chocolate soufflé or an apricot and almond tart.

In the Queensberry Hotel, Russel St. ℂ **01225/447928.** Reservations highly recommended. Main courses £17–£18 ($31–$33); 3-course fixed-price lunch £16 ($30); 3-course fixed-price dinner £26 ($48). AE, MC, V. Tues–Sat noon–2pm and 7–10pm; Sun 7–9:30pm.

Pimpernel's 🕭🕭 BRITISH   The Royal Crescent contains this city's most stunning collection of Georgian architecture. In a discreet hotel, the unmarked door of the Royal Crescent Hotel leads to this on-site restaurant, Pimpernel's, now hailed as one of the West Country's finest dining choices. With his garden and cozy inside dining room, Chef Steven Blake dazzles the discerning palates of Bath with a series of perfectly prepared and innovative dishes. His contemporary British menu roams the world for inspiration. The setting is romantic, with hand-painted wall coverings and distinctive pottery from Dartington. Through elegant French windows, tables overlook the private gardens. Sterling craftsmanship marks a menu that includes roasted sea bass with a funnel purée, corn-fed chicken poached in a coriander and ginger butter sauce, or roe venison with potatoes dauphinoise, baby spinach, and wild mushrooms. To finish, opt for the delightful cherry soufflé with vanilla bean ice cream.

15-16 Royal Crescent. ℂ **01225/823333.** Reservations required. Fixed-price lunch £19–£25 ($34–$46); 3-course fixed-price dinner £49 ($91). AE, DC, MC, V. Daily noon–2pm and 7–9:30pm (10:30pm Sat).

Popjoy's Restaurant MODERN BRITISH/CONTINENTAL   Two sprawling dining rooms on separate floors are in this Georgian home (ca. 1720) where Beau Nash and his mistress, Julianna Popjoy, once entertained friends and set the fashions of the day. Inventiveness and solid technique go into many of the dishes. The food is unpretentious and generally quite satisfying. The starters are always imaginative and good tasting, as exemplified by the guinea fowl and wood pigeon terrine with cranberry jam and brandy-soaked prunes. Equally excellent is the smoked-fish plate with oak-smoked salmon, tuna, trout, and egg with fresh horseradish served with a glass of iced Smirnoff Black label. A certain exoticism appears in the oven-roasted Barbary duck breast with a wild bramble and cherry marmalade, or the stir-fried shiitake mushrooms, bok choy, zucchini, and roasted almonds on sun-dried tomatoes.

Sawclose. ℂ **01225/460494.** www.popjoys.co.uk. Reservations recommended. Main courses £18–£22 ($33–$41); 3-course fixed-price lunch £16 ($30). AE, DC, MC, V. Mon–Sat noon–2pm and 6–11pm.

MODERATE

The Hole in the Wall 🕭 MODERN ENGLISH/FRENCH   This much-renovated Georgian town house is owned by Gunna and Christopher Chown, whose successful restaurant in Wales has received critical acclaim. Menu choices change frequently, according to the inspiration of the chef and the availability of ingredients. Begin with such delights as a foie gras and duck-liver terrine with pistachio and red-onion marmalade. Proceed to a tasty breast of free-range chicken with wild mushrooms and leeks; or pan-fried filets of red mullet with a yellow pepper sauce. Desserts are often a surprise—say, rhubarb parfait with a confit of ginger.

16 George St. ℂ **01225/425242.** Reservations recommended for weekdays and required Sat. Main courses £9.50–£17 ($18–$31); 2-course lunch £11 ($20); 3-course dinner £24 ($43). AE, MC, V. Daily 11am–11pm.

The Moon and Sixpence INTERNATIONAL   One of the leading restaurants and wine bars of Bath, The Moon and Sixpence occupies a stone structure east of Queen Square. The food may not be as good as that served at more acclaimed choices, including The Hole in the Wall, but the value is unbeatable. At lunch, a large cold buffet with a selection of hot dishes is featured in the wine bar section. In the upstairs restaurant overlooking the bar, full service is offered. Main courses may include filet of lamb with caramelized garlic or roast breast of duck with Chinese vegetables. Look for the daily specials on the Continental menu.

6A Broad St. (℃ **01225/460962**. Reservations recommended. Main courses £13–£15 ($23–$28); fixed-price lunch £7.95 ($15). AE, MC, V. Daily noon–2:30pm; Mon–Thurs 5:30–10:30pm; Fri–Sat 5:30–10:30pm; Sun 6–10:30pm.

Woods *Value* MODERN ENGLISH/FRENCH/ASIAN   Named after John Wood the Younger, architect of Bath's famous Assembly Room, which lies across the street, this restaurant is run by horseracing enthusiast David Price and his French-born wife, Claude. A fixed-price menu is printed on paper, whereas the seasonal array of a la carte items is chalked onto a frequently changing blackboard. Good bets include the pear and parsnip soup or chicken cooked with mushrooms, red wine, and tarragon.

9–13 Alfred St. (℃ **01225/314812**. Reservations recommended. Main courses £9.50–£18 ($18–$33); fixed-price lunch £9.50 ($18); fixed-price dinner £13–£25 ($24–$46). MC, V. Mon–Sat noon–2:30pm and 6–10:30pm; Sun noon–2pm.

BATH AFTER DARK

To gain a very different perspective of Bath, you may want to take the **Bizarre Bath Walking Tour** (℃ **01225/335124**), a 1½-hour improvisational tour of the streets during which the tour guides pull pranks, tell jokes, and behave in a humorously annoying manner toward tour-goers and unsuspecting residents. Running nightly at 8pm from Easter to October, no reservations are necessary; just show up, ready for anything, at the Huntsman Inn at North Parade Passage. Cost is £5 ($9.25) for adults, £4.50 ($8.35) for students and children.

After your walk, you may need a drink, or may want to check out the local club and music scene. At **The Bell,** 103 Walcot St. (℃ **01225/460426**), music ranges from jazz and country to reggae and blues on Monday and Wednesday nights and Sunday at lunch. On music nights, the band performs in the center of the long, narrow 400-year-old room.

The two-story **Hat and Feather,** 14 London St. (℃ **01225/425672**), has live musicians or DJs playing funk, reggae, or dance music Tuesday to Saturday.

SIDE TRIPS FROM BATH
LACOCK: AN 18TH-CENTURY VILLAGE ✿

From Bath, take the A4 about 19km (12 miles) to the A350, then head south to Lacock, a National Trust village showcasing English architecture from the 13th through the 18th centuries.

Unlike many villages that disappeared or were absorbed into bigger communities, Lacock remained largely unchanged because of a single family, the Talbots, who owned most of it and preferred to keep their traditional village traditional. Turned over to the National Trust in 1944, it's now one of the best-preserved villages in all of England with many 16th-century homes, gardens, and churches. Notable is **St. Cyriac Church,** Church Street, a Perpendicular-style church built by wealthy wool merchants between the 14th and 17th centuries.

Lacock Abbey, High Street (℃ **01249/730227**), founded in 1232 for Augustinian canonesses, was updated and turned into a private home in the 16th century. It fell victim to Henry VIII's Dissolution, when, upon establishing the Church of England, he seized existing church properties to bolster his own wealth. Admission for all church properties is £7 ($13) for adults and £3.50

($6.50) for children; a family ticket costs £18 ($33). Open from March to October, daily from 1 to 5:30pm. It is closed Tuesday and Good Friday.

While on the grounds, stop by the medieval barn, home to the **Fox Talbot Museum** (✆ **01249/730459**). Here, William Henry Fox Talbot carried out his early experiments with photography, making the first known photographic prints in 1833. In his honor, the barn is now a photography museum featuring some of those early prints. Open daily, March through October from 11am to 5:30pm. Admission is included in the Lacock Abbey admission (listed above).

Where to Stay

At the Sign of the Angel ⚐ The rooms at this inn, built in the 14th century, are quiet and split between the main building and a 17th-century garden cottage. Each guest room is distinctly decorated with a host of antiques. One room has a magnificently carved Spanish bed that is said to have belonged to Isambard Kingdom Brunel, the famous railway and canal builder. Some rooms are standard and rather small, others are more spacious—no. 12, for example, has a four-poster bed, and no. 3 is a generously sized superior room with a very large bed. Bathrooms have adequate shelf space and a tub or shower.

Church St., Lacock, Chippenham, Wiltshire SN15 2LB. ✆ **01249/730230.** Fax 01249/730527. www.lacock. co.uk. 10 units. £99–£150 ($183–$278) double. Rates include English breakfast. AE, MC, V. **Amenities:** Restaurant; limited room service. *In room:* TV, coffeemaker, hair dryer, iron/ironing board.

Where to Dine

The George Inn (Kids) ENGLISH Housed in a building that has been used as a pub since 1361, The George Inn has been modernized since then and is run today by John Glass. It still maintains many of its vestiges from the past—uneven floors, a large open fireplace with a dog-wheel once used for spit roasting—and has an extensive garden used as a dining area in the summer, as well as a children's playground. About 30 daily specials are chalked onto a blackboard in addition to a regular menu of fish, meat, and vegetarian dishes. Two of the most popular desserts are bread-and-butter pudding and sticky toffee pudding.

The grounds are made up of 40 hectares (100 acres) of gardens, with plenty of walks, and even a lake. It all adds up to a peaceful and serene setting. No credit cards are accepted at the farm, but rates include taxi service to The George Inn, from which guests can walk to all the attractions in this National Trust village.

4 West St., Lacock, Wiltshire SN15 2LH. ✆ **01249/730263.** Main courses £7.95–£14 ($15–$26). MC, V. Mon–Fri 10am–2:30pm and 5–11pm; Sat–Sun noon–9pm.

CASTLE COMBE ⚐⚐

Once voted England's prettiest village, the financially disastrous *Dr. Doolittle* was filmed here, and the 15th-century **Upper Manor House,** used as Rex Harrison's residence in the movie, is its most famous site. Consisting of one street lined with cottages (known simply as "The Street"), it is the quintessential sleepy village, easily explored in its entirety during a morning or afternoon, before moving on to your next destination. Located 16km (10 miles) northeast of Bath, take the A46 north 9.5km (6 miles) to the A420, then head east to Ford, following the signs north to Castle Combe. From Lacock, take the A350 north to Chippenham, then get on the A420 west and follow the signs.

Where to Stay & Dine

Manor House Hotel & Golf Club ⚐ The house and accompanying estate date from the 14th century and once served as the baronial seat in Castle Combe. The main building and its accompanying cottages sit regally on 19 hectares (47 acres) of gardens with wooded trails and a lake. The trout-stocked

River Bybrook flows south of the manor, and fishing is permitted. Bedrooms come in a variety of sizes, and some have four-poster beds. You can stay either in the main house or in a row of original stone cottages on the grounds. The latter have recently been upgraded to meet the standards of the main house. Eight rooms are large enough for families. Bathrooms are superbly kept, each with a tub and shower or just a shower.

Castle Combe, Wiltshire SN14 7HR. © 01249/782206. Fax 01249/782159. www.exclusivehotels.co.uk. 48 units. £105–£450 ($194–$833) double. AE, DC, MC, V. **Amenities:** Restaurant; bar; pool; 18-hole golf course; 2 tennis courts; croquet lawn; gym; sauna; limited room service; babysitting; laundry service; dry cleaning; rooms for those with limited mobility. *In room:* TV, dataport, coffeemaker, hair dryer, iron.

4 Bristol ★★

193km (120 miles) W of London; 21km (13 miles) NW of Bath

Bristol, the largest city in the West Country, is just across the Bristol Channel from Wales and is a good place to base yourself for touring western Britain. This historic inland port is linked to the sea by 11km (7 miles) of the navigable River Avon. Bristol has long been rich in seafaring traditions and has many links with the early colonization of America. In fact, some claim that the new continent was named after a Bristol town clerk, Richard Ameryke. In 1497, John Cabot sailed from Bristol and pioneered the discovery of the northern half of the New World.

Although Bath is much more famous as a tourist mecca, Bristol does have some attractions, such as a colorful harbor life, that makes it at least a good overnight stop in your exploration of the West Country.

ESSENTIALS

GETTING THERE   Bristol Airport (© 0870/121-2747) is conveniently situated beside the main A38 road, just over 11km (7 miles) from the city center.

Rail services to and from the area are among the fastest and most efficient in Britain. **First Great Western** runs very frequent services from London's Paddington Station to each of Bristol's two main stations: Temple Meads in the center of Bristol and Parkway on the city's northern outskirts. The trip takes 1¼ hours. For rail information, call © 0845/748-4950 or visit www.firstgreatwestern.co.uk.

National Express buses depart every hour during the day from London's Victoria Coach Station, making the trip in 2½ hours. For more information and schedules, call © 0870/580-8080 or visit www.nationalexpress.com.

If you're driving, head west from London on the M4.

VISITOR INFORMATION   The **Tourist Information Centre** is at Anchor Rd., Bristol (© 0870/444-0654; www.visitbristol.co.uk). In winter, it's open Monday to Saturday from 10am to 5pm and Sunday from 11am to 4pm; from 9:30am to 6:30pm daily in summer.

EXPLORING THE TOWN

Guided **walking tours** are conducted in summer and last about 1½ hours. They depart from Neptune's Statue on Saturday at 2:30pm and on Thursday at 7pm. Guided tours are also conducted through Clifton, a suburb of Bristol, which has more Georgian houses than Bath. Consult the Tourist Information Centre (see above) for more information.

Clifton Suspension Bridge, spanning the beautiful Avon Gorge, has become the symbol of the city of Bristol. Originally conceived in 1754, it was completed more than 100 years later, in 1864. The architect, Isambard Kingdom Brunel, died 5 years before its completion. His fellow engineers completed the bridge as a memorial to him.

At-Bristol 🎔🎔 This museum brings science, nature, and art to life at this unique West Country attraction at Bristol's harborside. The physicist, Paul Davies, has hailed the "awesome extravaganza for setting new standards for making science and technology both accessible and fun." The area's only giant-screen **IMAX Theatre** takes you on a 3-D journey to an International Space Station, its screen rising to a height of four floors with "digital surround sound." It's called "the next best thing to being there." Also at the IMAX Theatre you can take an incredible journey through the workings of the human body or be transported from snow-capped peaks to the kaleidoscopic reefs of color and life in the ocean off the Baja California peninsula. The West Country's first true 21st-century science center, **Explore** features a "hands-on, minds-on" experience of science. At this world-of-tomorrow attraction, you can do everything from enter the eye of a tornado to be the star of your own TV sitcom. At **Wildwalk** you can journey from the origins of life itself to the ends of the earth, coming face to face with scorpions and walk through a tropical forest with free-flying birds and butterflies. The Open Spaces between the exhibits are full of shops and cafes, with sculptures and beautiful landscaping. It's also a venue for live performances.

Anchor Rd., Harbourside. ℭ **01179/092000.** www.at-bristol.org.uk. Single attraction tickets: £7.50 ($14) adults, £4.95 ($9.15) children to Explore; £6.50 ($12) adults, £4.50 ($8.35) children to Wildwalk; £6.50 ($12) adults, £4.50 ($8.35) children to IMAX. 2 attractions on same day: £12 ($22) adults, £8.20 ($15) children for Explore and Wildwalk; £12 ($22) adults, £8.20 ($15) children for Explore and IMAX; and £11 ($20) adults, £7.75 ($14) children for Wildwalk and IMAX. Daily 10am–6pm.

Bristol Cathedral 🎔 Construction of the cathedral, once an Augustinian abbey, began in the 12th century; the central tower was added in 1466. The chapter house and gatehouse are good examples of late Norman architecture. The cathedral's interior was singled out for praise by Sir John Betjeman, the late poet laureate.

In 1539, the abbey was closed, and the incomplete nave was demolished. The building was turned into the Cathedral Church of the Holy and Undivided Trinity in 1542. In 1868, plans were drawn up to complete the nave to its medieval design. The architect, G. E. Street, found the original pillar bases, so the cathedral is much as it would have been when it was still the abbey church. J. L. Pearson added the two towers at the west end and further reordered the interior.

The eastern end of the cathedral, especially the choir, gives the structure a unique place in the development of British and European architecture. The nave, choir, and aisles are all of the same height, making a large hall. Bristol Cathedral is the major example of a "hall church" in Great Britain and one of the finest anywhere in the world.

College Green. ℭ **01179/264879.** www.bristol-cathedral.co.uk. Free admission; £2.50 ($4.65) donation requested. Daily 8am–6pm. Bus: 8 or 9.

SS *Great Britain* In Bristol, the world's first iron steamship and luxury liner has been partially restored to its 1843 appearance, though it's still a long way from earning its old title of a "floating palace." This vessel, which weighs 3,443 tons, was designed by Isambard Brunel, a Victorian engineer. Incidentally, in 1831 (at the age of 25), Brunel began the Bristol landmark Clifton Suspension Bridge over the 76m (250-ft.) deep Somerset Gorge at Clifton (see above).

City Docks, Great Western Dock. ℭ **01179/260680.** www.ss-great-britain.com. Admission £6.25 ($12) adults, £5.25 ($9.70) seniors, £3.75 ($6.95) children, £16.50 ($31) family. Apr–Oct daily 10am–5:30pm; Nov–Mar daily 10am–4:30pm. Bus no. 511 from city center, a long haul.

St. Mary Redcliffe Church 🌟🌟   The parish church of St. Mary Redcliffe is one of the finest examples of Gothic architecture in England. Queen Elizabeth I, on her visit in 1574, is said to have described it as "the fairest, goodliest and most famous parish church in England." Thomas Chatterton, the boy poet, called it "the pride of Bristol and the western land." The American Chapel (St. John's Chapel) houses the tomb and armor of Admiral Sir William Penn, father of Pennsylvania's founder.

12 Colston Parade. ℂ **01179/291487**. Free admission. Donations are welcome. Daily 9am–5pm.

Theatre Royal   Built in 1766, this is now the oldest working playhouse in the United Kingdom. It is the home of the Bristol Old Vic. Backstage tours leave from the foyer. Tours are run Friday and Saturday at 11:30pm and cost £3 ($5.55) for adults and £2 ($3.70) for children and students under 19. Call the box office for the current schedule.

King St. ℂ **01179/493993**. Box office ℂ 01179/877877. www.bristol-old-vic.co.uk. Tickets £8.50–£20 ($16–$37). Any City Centre bus.

SHOPPING

The biggest shopping complex is **Broadmead,** mainly pedestrianized with branches of all High Street stores, plus cafes and restaurants. Many specialty shops are found at **Clifton Village,** in a Georgian setting where houses are interspaced with parks and gardens. Here you'll find a wide array of shops selling antiques, arts and crafts, and designer clothing. Opened in 1991, the **Galleries** is a totally enclosed mall, providing three levels of shopping and restaurants. The **St. Nicholas Markets** opened in 1745, still going strong, selling antiques, memorabilia, handcrafted gifts, jewelry, and haberdashery. The **West End** is another major shopping area, taking in Park Street, Queen's Road, and Whiteladies Road. These streets are known for clothing outlets, bookstores, and unusual gift items from around the world, as well as wine bars and restaurants.

The best antiques markets are **The Bristol Antique Centre,** at Brunel Rooms, Broad Plain, **Clifton Antiques Market** and **New Antiques Centre,** at the Mall in Clifton, and **Clifton Arcade,** at Boyces Avenue, also in Clifton. Both Clifton outlets are closed on Monday, but The Bristol Antique Centre is open daily, including Sunday.

WHERE TO STAY
EXPENSIVE

Bristol Marriott City Centre 🌟   In the heart of town at the edge of Castle Park, this modern 11-story hotel is one of Bristol's tallest buildings, far superior to other chains in amenities, style, and comfort. Many improvements have been undertaken since it was a rather ordinary Holiday Inn, and it attracts business travelers as well as foreign tourists. The comfortable rooms are conservatively modern. Bathrooms have tubs and power showers, plus adequate shelf space. A hotel renovation, including refurbishment of all guest rooms, was scheduled for completion in November 2004.

2 Lower Castle St., Bristol BS1 3AD. ℂ **800/228-9290** in the U.S. and Canada, or 01179/294281. Fax 01179/225838. www.marriott.com. 294 units. Mon–Thurs £129–£159 ($239–$294) double; Fri–Sun from £63 ($117) double. AE, DC, MC, V. Bus: 9. **Amenities:** 2 restaurants; bar; pool; spa; sauna; 24-hr. room service; babysitting; laundry service; dry cleaning; gym; nonsmoking rooms; rooms for those with limited mobility. *In room:* A/C, TV, dataport, minibar, coffeemaker, hair dryer, iron/ironing board, trouser press.

Hotel du Vin 🌟 *Finds*   This stylish Anglo-French run hotel is one of Bristol's best examples of recycling. Six 18th-century sugar-refining warehouses, lying in the vicinity of the docklands, were taken over and sensitively restored into this inviting small hotel. Today, you'll find a series of "loft-style" bedrooms with superb beds covered in soft Egyptian linen. Each accommodation comes with a well-maintained and state-of-the-art bathroom with what management prefers to call "serious" showers (read: large). The special bathroom toiletries are made exclusively for the hotel by Arran Aromatics on the Scottish Isle of Arran; if you fall in love with these products, you can buy gift boxes of them to take home with you. As much as possible, the original industrial features of the warehouses have been retained for dramatic effect. Even if you're not a guest, you may want to visit for a drink in The Sugar Bar or a first-class meal in the contemporary French restaurant. For such a small hotel, the wine cellar here is most impressive, and specially staged wine tastings and dinners are a frequent event throughout the year.

Narrow Lewin Mead, Bristol, Somerset BS1 2NU. (C) **01179/255577**. Fax 01179/251199. www.hotelduvin.com. 40 units. £125–£140 ($231–$259) double; £175–£295 ($324–$546) suite. AE, DC, MC, V. **Amenities:** Restaurant; 2 bars; breakfast-only room service; laundry service; dry cleaning; library; billiard room. *In room:* A/C, TV, dataport, minibar, coffeemaker, hair dryer, safe, trouser press.

Ramada Plaza Bristol   Situated conveniently amid the commercial bustle of the town center, this modern six-story hotel offers a good, safe haven for the night (though some readers have commented that the pealing bells of St. Mary Redcliffe next door have awakened them early in the morning). With six stories designed in a rather bland international style, two floors of the bedrooms are designated as nonsmoking. Bedrooms range from small to medium and include mostly double beds. Bathrooms are clad in marble and contain tubs and showers.

Redcliffe Way, Bristol, Somerset BS1 6NJ. (C) **01179/260041**. Fax 01179/230089. www.ramadainternational. com. 201 units. £145 ($268) double; £195 ($361) suite. AE, DC, MC, V. **Amenities:** Restaurant; bar; indoor pool; health club; steam room; sauna; 24-hr. room service; babysitting; laundry service; dry cleaning; rooms for those with limited mobility. *In room:* TV, dataport, coffeemaker, hair dryer, iron, trouser press.

INEXPENSIVE

Downlands House   This well-appointed Victorian home is on a tree-lined road on the periphery of the Durdham Downs. About 3km (2 miles) from the center of Bristol, it lies on a bus route in a residential suburb. The recently redecorated bedrooms have private, shower-only bathrooms or adequate hallway facilities. It's basic, but inviting.

33 Henleaze Gardens, Henleaze, Bristol, Somerset BS9 4HH. (C)/fax **01179/621639**. www.downlandshouse. com. 10 units, 7 with bathroom. £50 ($93) double without bathroom, £65 ($120) double with bathroom. Rates include English breakfast. AE, MC, V. Bus: 1, 2, 3, or 501. **Amenities:** Breakfast room; nonsmoking rooms; 1 room for those with limited mobility. *In room:* TV, coffeemaker, hair dryer.

Oakfield Hotel   Instead of finding lodging in the center of Bristol, many visitors head for the leafy Georgian suburb of Clifton, 1.5km (1 mile) north, near the famous Suspension Bridge. This impressive 1840s guesthouse is on a quiet street, and everything is kept spick-and-span. Each room has hot and cold running water and central heating, though the furnishings are modest. The mattresses are a bit thin but are still comfortable. Bathrooms, though small, are adequate for the job, each with a shower.

52–54 Oakfield Rd., Clifton, Bristol BS8 2BG. (C) **01179/733643**. Fax 01179/744141. 27 units, none with bathroom. £45 ($83) double. Rates include English breakfast. No credit cards. Bus: 8 or 9. **Amenities:** Restaurant; limited room service. *In room:* TV, coffeemaker.

Tyndall's Park Hotel   This elegant early Victorian house retains many of its original features, including a marble fireplace and ornate plasterwork. Note the fine staircase in the imposing entrance hall. The hotel still observes the old

Finds   Spending the Night in a Tudor Castle

Nineteen kilometers (12 miles) north of Bristol, Thornbury is a genuine Tudor castle, now a hotel. Many of the crenellations and towers were built in 1511. The last defensive castle constructed in England, its owner was beheaded by Henry VIII for certain words spoken in haste. Henry confiscated the lands and, to celebrate, stayed here for 10 days with Anne Boleyn in 1535. Later, Mary Tudor spent 3 years of her adolescence here.

Today, you can stay at **Thornbury Castle** ★★ (© **01454/281182;** fax 01454/416188; www.thornburycastle.co.uk) and step back into history. The castle, built by Edward Stafford (3rd duke of Buckingham) in 1510, is surrounded by thick stone walls, trees, vineyards, and gardens. After you check in, you reach the 25 bedrooms and 3 suites by way of stone and spiral staircases. Every room is filled with character and is superbly fitted with fine furniture and many amenities, including televisions and telephones; eight have four-poster beds. Each has a deluxe mattress and a sumptuous bathroom. At night, the baronial public rooms are lit by candle.

Rates, which include continental breakfast, are £130 to £370 ($241–$685) for a double; £295 to £370 ($546–$685) for the suites. American Express, Diners Club, MasterCard, and Visa are accepted. To get there from Bristol, take the B4061; continue downhill to the monumental water pump, bear left, and continue for 270m (900 ft.).

We also recommend Thornbury for its cuisine. French and English dishes highlight the menus at the hotel's three dining rooms. Chef Nick Evans changes the menu daily and uses only the best and freshest ingredients to prepare his innovative meals. Dishes may include boned wood pigeon with mangold, a dark green-leaf vegetable of the mangel-wurzel plant that many consider superior to spinach. He also takes care to create some very English desserts, such as treacle tart with Cornish clotted cream. The good wine list is especially strong on Bordeaux and Burgundy. You can even sample Thornbury Castle's own wine, made from the Muller-Thurgau grapes in the castle's vineyards.

Even if you're not staying at the hotel, you can call for reservations in the dining room. The three-course main menu costs £22 ($41). Dinner goes for £43 ($79) per person and is served from 7 to 9:30pm daily.

traditions of personal service. There is a Victorian aura in the bedrooms, which range from small to medium, and each is clean and comfortable. Bathrooms are small but adequate, each with a shower-tub combination.

4 Tyndall's Park Rd., Clifton, Bristol BS8 1PG. © **01179/735407.** Fax 01179/237965. www.tyndallspark hotel.co.uk. 15 units. £58 ($107) double. Rates include English breakfast. MC, V. Bus: 8 or 9. **Amenities:** Rooms for those with limited mobility. *In room:* TV, dataport, coffeemaker, hair dryer, iron/ironing board.

WHERE TO DINE

Bell's Diner ★ *Finds* MEDITERRANEAN   This little hideaway serves savory cuisine from the sunny Mediterranean, and does so exceedingly well. The daily offerings change frequently, based on the day's shopping for market-fresh ingredients, but what you get is usually well prepared, fresh, and flavorful. In what used to be "the little shop on the corner," this bistro has been installed with tables sitting on hardwood floors, the walls adorned with cityscapes. Most of the recipes are imaginative, and sometimes surprising, as in the case of the slow braised pork belly served with foie gras. The perfectly roasted breast of chicken comes with a delightful accompaniment of black truffle potatoes, and the grilled tuna is still moist—never dried out—and served with fresh rocket leaves and a tangy tomato confit.

1 York Rd., Montpelier. © 01179/240357. Reservations required. Main courses £14–£18 ($26–$33); 8-course fixed-price menu £45 ($83). AE, MC, V. Tues–Fri noon–2pm; Mon–Sat 7–11pm. Closed 1 week in Dec. To find the restaurant, follow A38 north (signposted Stokes Croft), turning right on Ashley Rd. and taking the next left at Picton St. Picton leads into York Rd.

Byzantium ★★ BRITISH/FRENCH   The buzz in Bristol is about this restaurant. The decor alone is stunning, with stone, crystal, wood, marble, and glass combined to create an unusual, even offbeat, restaurant with rich colors, informal corners, and subtle lighting, plus the sweep of a marble staircase. The cuisine almost could be called fusion though it's basically French, evoking both the near and far east. The venue is on two floors, with a cavernous bar/lounge downstairs with padded seats where entertainment is provided—from tango and belly dancing to magicians. The restaurant's "Food Lantern" is unique in Bristol, consisting of a selection of elaborate nibbles served on a two-tier iron slate. For a main course, we recently were delighted with Challans duck prepared two ways—a duck leg marinated in red wine and braised, and the breast pink roasted and garnished with streaky bacon. An elaborate John Dory appeared roasted with seared scallops and a crispy king prawn mousse garnished with chile, ginger, garlic, and coriander linguini with a coconut-cream sauce. For dessert, a second Food Lantern is brought out, laden with a selection of "little puddings."

2 Portwall Lane. © 01179/221883. Reservations required. Main courses £14–£20 ($26–$37). AE, MC, V. Mon–Sat 6:30pm–2am.

Lords Restaurant FRENCH   In the center of Bristol, this classic French restaurant has been installed in the cellar of what used to be a bank vault. Some of the old safety deposit chamber atmosphere remains, including the iron grille doors and the checkerboard marble floors. Paintings by local artists decorate the walls, and the service is friendly and efficient. The cuisine is excellent, using fresh, regional produce when available. The combination of ingredients and flavors is skillful, as exemplified by the wild sea bass, which is flavored with saffron and fresh basil. The roast loin of venison is cooked to perfection and served in a medley of beet roots and sour cream. Well-balanced flavors are repeated again in a sauté of guinea fowl with a shallots and a wild mushroom confit. The fish soup is the best in town.

43 Corn St. © 01179/262658. Reservations recommended. Main courses £16–£20 ($30–$37). AE, MC, V. Mon–Fri noon–2pm; Mon–Sat 6–9:30pm. Closed 1 week in Apr and in Dec and 2 weeks in Aug.

BRISTOL AFTER DARK

On a cultural note, **Bristol Old Vic,** King St. (© **01179/877877;** www.bristol-old-vic.co.uk), is the oldest working theater in the country, known for its performances (often Shakespeare) that were first launched in 1766. The theatrical grouping uses a trio of theaters for its shows, mainly the Theatre Royal, although some performances are staged at other venues such as the new Vic Studio and the Basement Theatre. Music lovers gravitate to the performances at **St. George's,** Great George St., off Park Street (© **01179/230359;** www.stgeorgesbristol.co.uk), a converted church from the 1700s. Today, instead of gospel you will hear everything from jazz concerts to classical musical performances. At lunch, concerts are a regular feature.

Bath may be more stiff and formal, but Bristol clubs and pubs are more laid-back, drawing more working-class Brits than yuppies. Some of the best pubs are along King Street, especially **Llandoger Trow,** 5 King St. (© **01179/260783**), with its mellow West Country ambience. A favorite watering hole of students is **Baroque,** 2 Byron Place (© **01179/299322**).

Acid jazz and other types of music rain down in **Thelka** (© **01179/293301**), a converted freight steamer moored on the Grove. The other leading venue for jazz is the **Bebop Club** at The Bear, Hotwell Road (© **01179/877796**). The leading comedy club is **Jester's,** 142 Cheltenham Rd. (© **01179/096655**). Covers range from £3 to £13 ($5.55–$24) but can vary depending on the entertainment offered.

5 Wells ★★ & the Caves of Mendip ★
198km (123 miles) SW of London; 34km (21 miles) SW of Bath

To the south of the Mendip Hills, the cathedral town of Wells is a medieval gem. Wells was a vital link in the Saxon kingdom of Wessex—important long before the arrival of William the Conqueror. Once the seat of a bishopric, it was eventually toppled from its ecclesiastical hegemony by the rival city of Bath. But the subsequent loss of prestige has paid off handsomely for Wells today: After experiencing the pinnacle of prestige, it fell into a slumber—and much of its old look was preserved.

Many visitors come only for the afternoon or morning, look at the cathedral, then press on to Bath for the evening. But though it's rather sleepy, Wells's old inns make a tranquil stopover.

ESSENTIALS
GETTING THERE   Wells has good bus connections with surrounding towns and cities. Take the train to Bath (see "Essentials," under "Bath," earlier in this chapter) and continue the rest of the way by First Bristol bus no. 173. Departures are every hour Monday through Saturday and every 2 hours on Sunday. Both no. 376 and 377 buses run between Bristol and Glastonbury every hour daily, with a stop at Wells each way. Call © **01179/553231** or 0870/6082608 for schedules and information.

If you're driving, take the M4 west from London, cutting south on the A4 toward Bath and continuing along the A39 into Wells.

VISITOR INFORMATION   The **Tourist Information Centre** is at the Town Hall, Market Place (© **01749/672552**), and is open daily November to March from 10am to 4pm and April to October from 9:30am to 5:30pm.

SEEING THE SIGHTS
After a visit to the cathedral, walk along its cloisters to the moat-surrounded **Bishop's Palace.** The Great Hall, built in the 13th century, is in ruins. Finally, the street known as the **Vicars' Close** is one of the most beautifully preserved streets in Europe.

Easily reached by heading west out of Wells, the Caves of Mendip are two exciting natural attractions: the great caves of Cheddar and Wookey Hole (see below).

Cheddar Showcaves & Gorge ★★   A short distance from Bath, Bristol, and Wells is the village of Cheddar, home of cheddar cheese. It lies at the foot of Cheddar Gorge, within which lie the Cheddar Caves, underground caverns with impressive formations. The caves are more than a million years old, including Gough's Cave, with its cathedral-like caverns, and Cox's Cave, with its calcite sculptures and brilliant colors. The Crystal Quest is a dark walk "fantasy adventure" taking you deep underground, and in the Cheddar Gorge Heritage Centre, you'll find a 9,000-year-old skeleton. You can also climb Jacob's Ladder for clifftop walks and Pavey's Lookout Tower for views over Somerset—on a clear day you may even see Wales.

Adults and children over 12 years of age can book an Adventure Caving expedition for £14 ($26), which includes overalls, helmets, and lamps. Other attractions include local craftspeople at work, ranging from the glass blower to the sweets maker, plus the Cheddar Cheese & Cider Depot.

Cheddar, Somerset. ✆ 01934/742343. www.cheddarcaves.co.uk. Admission £9.50 ($18) adults, £6.50 ($12) children 5–15, £26 ($48) family ticket, free for 5 and under. Easter–Sept daily 10am–5pm; Oct–Easter daily 10:30am–4:30pm. Closed Dec 24–25. From A38 or M5, cut onto A371 to Cheddar.

Wells Cathedral ☆☆☆   Begun in the 12th century, this is a well-preserved example of Early English architecture. The medieval sculpture (six tiers of statues recently restored) of its west front is without equal. The western facade was completed in the mid–13th century. The landmark central tower was erected in the 14th century, with the fan vaulting attached later. The inverted arches were added to strengthen the top-heavy structure.

Much of the stained glass dates from the 14th century. The fan-vaulted Lady Chapel, also from the 14th century, is in the Decorated style. To the north is the vaulted chapter house, built in the 13th century and recently restored. Look also for a medieval astronomical clock in the north transept.

In the center of town, Chain Gate. ✆ 01749/674483. www.wellscathedral.org.uk. Free admission but donations appreciated: £4.50 ($8.35) adults, £3 ($5.55) seniors, £1.50 ($2.80) students and children. Apr–Sept daily 7am–7pm; Oct–Mar daily 7am–6pm.

Wookey Hole Caves & Paper Mill ☆   Just 3km (2 miles) from Wells, you'll first come upon the source of the Axe River. In the first chamber of the caves, as legend has it, is the Witch of Wookey turned to stone. These caves are believed to have been inhabited by prehistoric people at least 60,000 years ago. A tunnel, opened in 1975, leads to the chambers unknown in early times, and previously accessible only to divers.

Leaving the caves, follow a canal path to the mill, where paper has been made by hand since the 17th century. Here, the best-quality handmade paper is made by skilled workers according to the tradition of their ancient craft. Also in the mill are "hands-on vats," where visitors can try their hand at making a sheet of paper, and an Edwardian Penny Pier Arcade where you can exchange new pennies for old ones to play the original machines. Other attractions include the Magical Mirror Maze and an enclosed passage of multiple image mirrors.

Wookey Hole, near Wells. ✆ 01749/672243. www.wookey.co.uk. 2-hr. tour £8.80 ($16) adults, £5.50 ($10) children 16 and under. Apr–Oct daily 10am–5pm; Nov–Mar daily 10:30am–4:30pm. Closed Dec 17–25. Follow the signs from the center of Wells for 3km (2 miles). Bus no. 172 from Wells.

WHERE TO STAY

The Crown ☆   This is one of the oldest and most historic hotels in the area, a tradition for overnighting since medieval times. William Penn was thrown in jail here in 1695. The charge? Preaching without a license. The landmark status building lies at the medieval Market Place in the heart of Wells, overlooking the splendid cathedral. The building still retains much of its 15th-century character, although the bedrooms are completely up to date—in fact, furnished with a

Nordic contemporary style. For more tradition, ask for one of a quartet of rooms graced with four-posters. Each unit comes with a well-maintained private bathroom with shower. Lunch or dinner can be enjoyed in either the Penn Bar, named in honor of that "jailbird," or else Anton's Bistrot, the latter named after the well-known cartoonist and former resident whose work was featured in *Punch* magazine. Some of his original drawings line the walls of the hotel.

Market Place, Wells, Somerset BA5 2RP. (C) **01749/673457.** Fax 01749/679792. www.crownatwells.co.uk. 15 units. £60–£80 ($111–$148) double; £95 ($176) suite. AE, MC, V. **Amenities:** Restaurant; pub; babysitting. *In room:* TV, coffeemaker, hair dryer, iron, trouser press, no phone.

The Swan Hotel Set behind a stucco facade on one of the town's main streets, this place was originally built in the 15th century as a coaching inn. Today, facing the west front of Wells Cathedral, it is the best of the inns within the town's central core. Rooms vary in style and size; a third of them have four-poster beds. Bathrooms are small but have a combination shower and tub. The spacious and elegant public rooms stretch out to the left and right of the entrance. Both ends have a blazing and baronial fireplace and beamed ceilings.

11 Sadler St., Wells, Somerset BA5 2RX. (C) **800/528-1234** in the U.S. and Canada, or 01749/836300. Fax 01749/836301. www.bhere.co.uk. 50 units. £110–£155 ($204–$287) double. Rates include English breakfast. AE, DC, MC, V. **Amenities:** Restaurant; bar; limited room service; laundry service; rooms for those with limited mobility. *In room:* TV, hair dryer, trouser press.

White Hart Opposite the cathedral, this is the best-located hotel in Wells. A former coaching inn, it dates from the 15th century. The Swan is more comfortable and remarkable, but the White Hart is an enduring favorite nonetheless. The creaky old bedrooms lie in the main house, or you can live in more modern surroundings in a converted stable block where horses and coaches from London were housed in olden times. Each bedroom is comfortably and tastefully furnished, with a tub-and-shower combination. Even if you're not staying here, drop in for a drink at the pub or a meal in the beamed restaurant. A fixed-price dinner is offered or you can order from a brasserie-style menu.

Sadler St., Wells, Somerset BA5 2RR. (C) **01749/672056.** Fax 01749/671074. www.whitehart-wells.co.uk. 15 units. £90 ($167) double. Rates include English breakfast. AE, MC, V. **Amenities:** Restaurant; bar; limited room service; laundry service. *In room:* TV, dataport, coffeemaker, hair dryer, iron/board.

WHERE TO DINE

The City Arms ENGLISH The former city jail, 2 blocks from the bus station, is now a pub with an open courtyard furnished with tables, chairs, and umbrellas. In summer it's a mass of flowers, and there's an old vine growing in the corner. Full meals may include homemade soup of the day followed by fresh salmon, lamb in burgundy sauce, or stuffed quail in Cointreau sauce. From the charcoal grill you can order rump steak or chicken with Stilton cheese, and longtime favorites include beef Wellington or steak-kidney-and-ale pie. Vegetarian dishes are also offered. Upstairs is an Elizabethan timbered restaurant. The food is a notch above the typical pub grub.

69 High St. (C) **01749/673916.** Reservations recommended. Main courses £3.95–£14 ($7.30–$25). MC, V. Daily 9am–10:30pm (closes at 9pm on Sun).

6 Glastonbury Abbey

219km (136 miles) SW of London; 42km (26 miles) S of Bristol; 9.5km (6 miles) SW of Wells

Glastonbury may be one of the oldest inhabited sites in Britain. Excavations have revealed Iron Age lakeside villages on its periphery (some of the discoveries that were dug up can be seen in a little museum on High St.). After the destruction of its once-great abbey, the town lost prestige; today it is just a market town with a rich history. The ancient gatehouse entry to the abbey is a museum, and its principal exhibit is a scale model of the abbey and its community buildings as they stood in 1539, at the time of the dissolution.

Where Arthurian myth once held sway, now exists a subculture of mystics, spiritualists, and hippies, all drawn to the kooky legends whirling around the town. Glastonbury is England's New Age center, where Christian spirituality blends with druidic beliefs. The average visitor arrives just to see the ruins and the monuments, but the streets are often filled with people trying to track down Jesus, if not Arthur and Lancelot.

ESSENTIALS

GETTING THERE   Go to Taunton, which is on the London-Penzance line that leaves frequently from London's Paddington Station. For rail information, call ℂ **0845/748-4950** or visit www.railtrack.co.uk. From Taunton, you'll have to take a bus the rest of the way. Take the Southern National bus (no. 17) to Glastonbury between Monday and Saturday. With six departures per day, the trip takes 1 hour. Call **Southern National** at ℂ **01823/272033** for details.

You can also leave London's Paddington Station for Bristol Temple Meads and go the rest of the way by First Bristol bus no. 376. It runs from Bristol via Wells to Glastonbury every hour Monday through Saturday; on Sunday, the schedule is reduced to every 3 hours. The trip takes 2 hours. For information about First Bristol bus service, call ℂ **01179/553231**.

One **National Express** bus a day (no. 403) leaves London's Victoria Coach Station at 6:30pm and arrives in Glastonbury at 10pm. For more information and schedules, call ℂ **0870/580-8080** or visit www.nationalexpress.com.

If you're driving, take the M4 west from London, then cut south on the A4 via Bath to Glastonbury.

VISITOR INFORMATION   The **Tourist Information Centre** is at The Tribunal, 9 High St. (ℂ **01458/832954**). It's open year-round Sunday through Thursday from 10am to 4pm, and Friday and Saturday from 10am to 4:30pm.

SEEING THE SIGHTS

Glastonbury Abbey ✦✦   Though no more than a ruined sanctuary today, Glastonbury Abbey was once one of the wealthiest and most prestigious monasteries in England. It provides Glastonbury's claim to historical greatness, an assertion augmented by legendary links to such figures as Joseph of Arimathea, King Arthur, Queen Guinevere, and St. Patrick.

Joseph of Arimathea is said to have journeyed to what was then the Isle of Avalon with the Holy Grail in his possession. According to tradition, he buried the chalice at the foot of the conical Glastonbury Tor, and a stream of blood burst forth. You can scale this more than 150m (500-ft.) high hill today, on which rests a 15th-century tower.

Joseph, so it goes, erected a church of wattle in Glastonbury. (The town, in fact, may have had the oldest church in England, as excavations have shown.) And at one point, the saint is said to have leaned against his staff, which was immediately transformed into a fully blossoming tree; a cutting alleged to have survived from the Holy Thorn remains on the grounds—it blooms at Christmastime. Some historians trace this particular story back to Tudor times.

Another famous chapter in the story, popularized by Tennyson in the Victorian era, holds that King Arthur and Queen Guinevere were buried on the abbey grounds. In 1191, the monks dug up the skeletons of two bodies on the south side of the Lady Chapel, said to be those of the king and queen. In 1278, in the presence of Edward I, the bodies were removed and transferred to a black marble tomb in the choir. Both the burial spot and the shrine are marked today.

A large Benedictine Abbey of St. Mary grew out of the early wattle church. St. Dunstan, who was born nearby, was the abbot in the 10th century and later became archbishop of Canterbury. Edmund, Edgar, and Edmund "Ironside," three early English kings, were buried at the abbey.

In 1184, a fire destroyed most of the abbey and its vast treasures. It was eventually rebuilt, after much difficulty, only to be dissolved by Henry VIII. Its last abbot, Richard Whiting, was hanged at Glastonbury Tor. Like the Roman forum, the abbey was used as a stone quarry for years.

Today, you can visit the ruins of the chapel, linked by an early English "Galilee" to the nave of the abbey. The best-preserved building on the grounds is a 14th-century octagonal Abbot's Kitchen, where oxen were once roasted whole to feed the wealthier pilgrims.

Magdalene St. © **01458/832267** for information. www.glastonburyabbey.com. Admission £4 ($7.40) adults, £3.50 ($6.50) students and seniors, £1.50 ($2.80) children 5–16 years, £10 ($19) family ticket. Daily Dec–Jan 10am–4:30pm, Feb 10am–5pm, Mar 9:30am–5:30pm, Apr–May and Sept 9:30am–6pm; June–Aug 9am–6pm, Oct 9:30am-5pm, Nov 9:30am–4:30pm.

Somerset Rural Life Museum   The history of the Somerset countryside since the early 19th century is chronicled here. Its centerpiece is the abbey barn, built around 1370. The magnificent timbered room, stone tiles, and sculptural details (including the head of Edward III) make it special. A Victorian farmhouse houses exhibits that illustrate farming in Somerset during the "horse age" as well as domestic and social life in Victorian times. In summer, you can watch demonstrations of butter making, weaving, basketwork, and many other traditional craft and farming activities that are rapidly disappearing.

Abbey Farm, Chilkwell St. © **01458/831197.** www.somerset.gov.uk/museums. Free admission. Apr–Oct Mon–Fri 10am–5pm, Sat–Sun 2–6pm; Nov–Mar Tues–Sat 10am–5pm. Closed New Year's Day, Good Friday, Dec 25–28.

WHERE TO STAY

George & Pilgrims 🏵   One of the few pre-Reformation hostelries still left in England, this inn in the center of town once offered hospitality to Glastonbury pilgrims. Its facade looks like a medieval castle, with stone-mullioned windows with leaded glass. Some rooms were formerly monks' cells; others have four-poster beds, veritable carved monuments of oak. You may be given the Henry VIII Room, from which the king watched the burning of the abbey in 1539. Rooms come in a variety of shapes and sizes, as befits a hotel of this vintage. Some bedrooms have recently been refurbished. Some rooms have just a shower, others a tub and shower combined.

1 High St., Glastonbury, Somerset BA6 9DP. © **01458/831146.** Fax 01458/832252. www.georgeandpilgrims. activehotels.com. 13 units. £55–£95 ($102–$176) double. Rates include English breakfast. MC, V. **Amenities:** Restaurant; bar; laundry service; dry cleaning. *In room:* TV, coffeemaker, hair dryer, trouser press.

Number 3 Hotel   This small property, adjoining the Glastonbury ruins, is housed in a Georgian structure in which Winston Churchill once resided. The double rooms are all tastefully and individually decorated. The bathrooms are small but well organized with adequate shelf space and shower-tub combinations. The entire property is nonsmoking.

3 Magdalene St., Glastonbury, Somerset BA6 9EW. ℂ **01458/834703.** www.numberthree.co.uk. 5 units. £100–£110 ($185–$204) double. Rates include continental breakfast. AE, DC, MC, V. Closed Dec–Jan. **Amenities:** Laundry service. *In room:* TV, coffeemaker.

WHERE TO DINE

The Brasserie ENGLISH/CONTINENTAL   This is a solid, reliable choice in a town not known for its dining. A reasonably priced a la carte menu with the chef's special of the day is posted on blackboards. Dishes may include peppered soup, warm avocado and walnuts in a light Stilton sauce, and vegetarian choices such as broccoli-and-cream-cheese bake or vegetable Stroganoff with a timbale of saffron and wild rice.

In the George & Pilgrims Hotel, 1 High St. ℂ **01458/831146.** Reservations recommended. Main courses £13–£15 ($23–$28). MC, V. Wed–Sun noon–2:30pm and 7–9:30pm.

7 Longleat House ★★★ & Stourhead Gardens ★★★

If you're driving, you can visit both Longleat and Stourhead in one busy day. Follow the directions to Longleat given below, then drive 9.5km (6 miles) down the B3092 to Stourton, a village just off the highway, 5km (3 miles) northwest of Mere (A303), to reach Stourhead.

Longleat House and Safari Park ★★★   A magnificent Elizabethan house built in the early Renaissance style, Longleat House was owned by the seventh marquess of Bath. On first glimpse, it's romantic enough, but once you've been inside, it's hard not to be dazzled by the lofty rooms and their exquisite paintings and furnishings.

From the Elizabethan Great Hall and the library to the State Rooms and the grand staircase, the house is filled with all manner of beautiful things. The walls of the State Dining Room are adorned with fine tapestries and paintings, whereas the room itself has displays of silver and plate. The library represents the finest private collection in the country. The Victorian kitchens are open, offering a glimpse of life "below the stairs" in a well-ordered country home. Various exhibitions are mounted in the stable yard.

Adjoining Longleat House is **Longleat Safari Park.** The park hosts several species of magnificent and endangered wild animals, including rhinoceroses and elephants, which are free to roam these bucolic surroundings. Here you can walk among giraffes, zebras, camels, and llamas, and view lions and tigers, as well as England's only white tiger, from your car. You can also ride on a safari boat around the park's lake to see gorillas and to feed sea lions. You can see the park by train for a railway adventure, or visit the tropical butterfly garden.

The park provides plenty of theme-park-like thrills as well, including an Adventure Castle, a *Doctor Who* exhibition, and the world's longest maze, **The Maze of Love.** Commissioned by the marquess of Bath and designed by Graham Burgess, the maze was inspired by the Garden of Love in Villandry, France, and Botticelli's painting *Primavera*. It lies between Longleat House and the Orangery, and at first appears to be a traditional parterre with gravel paths and small leafed box hedging; it's only on closer examination that its amorous shapes become apparent. The most obvious ones are the four giant hearts and a pair of women's lips, but there are many more. Love's symbolic flower, the rose, has been planted in the beds, and climbing roses trail over the heart-shaped arches. More than 1,300 rose bushes have been planted with names that enhance the symbolic story: First Kiss, Eve, Seduction, and more. The Maze of Love opened to the public on Valentine's Day, 2000, so now visitors can enjoy the scent of its roses in summer while finding their way through the maze.

Warminster, Wiltshire. ✆ **01985/844400.** www.longleat.co.uk. Admission to Longleat House £9 ($17) adults, £7 ($13) children. Safari Park £9 ($17) adults, £6 ($11) children. Special exhibitions and rides require separate admission tickets. Passport tickets for all attractions £16 ($30) adults, £13 ($24) seniors and children 4–14. House daily 10am–5:30pm. Park Apr–Oct 31 Mon–Fri 10am–4pm (last cars admitted at 5pm or sunset), Sat–Sun 10am–5pm. From Bath or Salisbury, take the train to Warminster; then take a taxi to Longleat (about 10 min.). Driving from Bath, take A36 south to Warminster; then follow the signposts to Longleat House. From Salisbury, take A36 north to Warminster, following the signposts to Longleat House.

Stourhead ★★★   In a country of superlative gardens and gardeners, Stourhead is the most fabled. It's certainly the most celebrated example of 18th-century English landscape gardening. More than that, it's a delightful place to wander— among its trees, flowers, and colorful shrubs, bridges, grottos, and temples are tucked away, almost hidden. Although Stourhead is a garden for all seasons, it is at its most idyllic in summer when rhododendrons are in full bloom.

A Palladian house, Stourhead was built in the 18th century by the Hoare banking family, who created 40 hectares (100 acres) of prime 18th-century land-scaped gardens, complete with classical temples, lakes, and grottos. Henry Hoare II (1705–85), known as "Henry the Magnificent," contributed greatly to the development of the landscape of this magnificent estate.

The Temple of Flora was the first building in the garden, designed by the architect Henry Flitcroft in 1744. The wooden seats are copies of those placed near the altar where images of pagan gods were laid. Marble busts of Marcus Aurelius and Alexander the Great can be seen in the niches on the wall.

The Grotto, constructed in 1748, is lined with tufa, a water-worn limestone deposit. The springs of the Stour flow through the cold bath where a lead copy of the sleeping Ariadne lies. In a cave beyond her, the white lead statue of the River God is seen dispensing justice to the waves and nymphs who inhabit his stream.

The Pantheon was built in 1753 to house Rysbrack's statues of Hercules and Flora and other classical figures. The temple was originally heated through brass grilles. The nearby Iron Bridge replaced a wooden one in 1860.

In 1765, Flitcroft built the **Temple of Apollo**, the route that takes the visitor over the public road via a rock-work bridge constructed in the 1760s. The Apollo Temple is copied from a round temple excavated at Baalbec: The statues that used to be in the niches are now on the roof of Stourhead House. The Turf Bridge was copied from Palladio's bridge in Vicenza.

The **Bristol High Cross** dates from the early 15th century and commemorates the monarchs who benefited the city of Bristol. It was removed from Bristol and set up by Henry Hoare at Stourhead in 1765.

The house at Stourhead, designed by Colen Campbell, a leader in the Palladian revival, was built for Henry Hoare I between 1721 and 1725. It closely resembles the villas Palladio built for wealthy Venetians. The magnificent interior hosts an outstanding library and picture gallery and a wealth of paintings, art treasures, and Chippendale furniture.

The three fine redbrick-walled terraces were built in the early 19th century to supply cut flowers, fresh fruit, salads, and vegetables to the mansion house. They were in use up to the deaths of Sir Henry and Lady Alda Hoare in 1947.

The lower combined an herbaceous garden with a peach and vine house. The pool was part of an irrigation system fed by rainwater from the greenhouses and stable yard.

Henry Hoare II's 18th-century redbrick folly, **Alfred's Tower,** is another feature at Stourhead. It sits 48m (160 ft.) above the borders of Wiltshire, Somerset, and Dorset and has 221 steps. **The Obelisk** was built between 1839 and 1840 of Bath stone and replaced the original of Chilmark stone constructed by William Privet for Henry Hoare in 1746.

The plant center is situated near the entrance to the main parking lot in part of the Old Glebe Farm—a small estate dairy farm. A working farm until the early 1970s, it's now a place where visitors buy plants they've just seen in the garden.

Lunches and suppers are served at the **Spread Eagle Inn,** near the garden entrance. Boxes are available to order for picnics in the grounds and garden. The Spread Eagle is noted for dinner, as well as for its Sunday lunches in the autumn, winter, and spring. A self-service buffet is available in the Village Hall tearoom.

© 01747/841152. Mar–Oct admission for garden and house £9.40 ($17) adults, £4.50 ($8.35) children; £22 ($41) family ticket; Nov–Feb garden only £4.10 ($7.60) adults, £2 ($3.70) children, £9.90 ($18) family ticket. Fri–Tues 9am–7pm (or until dusk). Last admission is at 4:30pm. A direct bus from Bath runs only on the 1st Sat of each month. Getting to Stourhead by public transportation is very difficult if you don't have a car. You can take the train from Bath to Frome, a 30-min. trip. From here it's still 16km (10 miles) away. Most visitors take a taxi from Frome to Stourhead. A direct bus from Bath runs only on the first Sat of each month.

8 Dunster ✦✦ & Exmoor National Park ✦✦

296km (184 miles) W of London; 5km (3 miles) SE of Minehead

The village of Dunster, in Somerset, lies near the eastern edge of Exmoor National Park. It grew up around the original Dunster Castle, constructed as a fortress for the de Mohun family, whose progenitor came to England with William the Conqueror. The village, about 6.5km (4 miles) from the Cistercian monastery at Cleeve, has an ancient priory church and dovecote, a 17th-century gabled yarn market, and little cobbled streets dotted with whitewashed cottages.

ESSENTIALS

GETTING THERE   The best route by rail is to travel to Minehead via Taunton, which is easily reached on the main London-Penzance line from Paddington Station in London. For rail information, call © **0845/748-4950** or visit www.railtrack.co.uk. From Minehead, a taxi or bus takes you to Dunster.

At Taunton, you can take one of the seven **Southern National** coaches (no. 28; © **01823/272033**) leaving hourly Monday through Saturday, with only one bus on Sunday. Trip time is 1 hour and 10 minutes. Buses (no. 38 or 39) from Minehead stop in Dunster Village at the rate of one per hour, but only from June to September. Off-season visitors must take a taxi.

If driving from London, head west along the M4, cutting south at the junction with the M5 until you reach the junction with the A39, going west to Minehead. Before your final approach to Minehead, cut south to Dunster along the A396.

VISITOR INFORMATION   Dunster doesn't have an official tourist office, but **Exmoor National Park Visitor Centre** is at Dunster Steep (© **01643/ 821835**), 3km (2 miles) east of Minehead. It's open from Easter to October daily from 10am to 5pm, plus limited hours in winter (call ahead).

EXPLORING THE AREA

Dunster Castle ✦✦   Dunster Castle is on a tor (high hill), from which you can see Bristol Channel. It stands on the site of a Norman castle granted to William de Mohun of Normandy by William the Conqueror shortly after the conquest of England. The 13th-century gateway, built by the de Mohuns, is all that remains of the original fortress. In 1376, the castle and its lands were bought by Lady Elizabeth Luttrell; her family owned it until it was given to the National Trust in 1976, together with 12 hectares (30 acres) of surrounding parkland.

The first castle was largely demolished during the civil war. The present Dunster Castle is a Jacobean house constructed in the lower ward of the original fortifications in 1620, then rebuilt in 1870 to look like a castle. From the terraced walks and gardens, you'll have good views of Exmoor and the Quantock Hills.

Some outstanding artifacts within include the 17th-century panels of embossed painted and gilded leather depicting the story of Antony and Cleopatra, and a remarkable allegorical 16th-century portrait of Sir John Luttrell (shown wading naked through the sea with a female figure of peace and a wrecked ship in the background). The 17th-century plasterwork ceilings of the dining room and the finely carved staircase balustrade of cavorting huntsmen, hounds, and stags are also noteworthy.

On A396 (just off A39). ℂ **01643/821314.** Admission to castle and grounds £6.80 ($13) adults, £3.40 ($6.30) children, family ticket £17 ($31); to grounds only £3.70 ($6.85) adults, £1.60 ($2.95) children, family ticket £9 ($17). Castle Apr–Sept Sat–Wed 11am–5pm; Oct Sat–Wed 11am–4pm; closed Nov–Mar. Grounds Jan–Mar and Oct–Dec daily 11am–4pm; Apr–Sept daily 10am–5pm. Take bus no. 28 or 39 from Minehead.

Exmoor National Park 🏃🏃 Between Somerset and Devon, along the northern coast of England's southwest peninsula, is Exmoor National Park, an unspoiled plateau of lonely moors. One of the most cherished national parks in Britain, it includes the wooded valleys of the rivers Exe and Barle, the Brendon Hills, a sweeping stretch of rocky coastline, and such sleepy but charming villages as **Culbone, Selworthy, Parracombe,** and **Allerford.** Bisected by a network of heavily eroded channels for brooks and streams, the park is distinctive for lichen-covered trees, gray-green grasses, gorse, and heather. The moors reach their highest point at Dunkery Beacon, 512m (1,707 ft.) above sea level.

Exmoor National Park is one of the smallest in Britain, yet it contains one of the most beautiful coastlines in England. Softly contoured, without the dramatic peaks and valleys of other national parks, the terrain is composed mostly of primeval layering of sandstone slate. Although noteworthy for its scarcity of trees, the terrain encompasses a limited handful of very old oak groves, which are studied by forestry experts for their growth patterns.

On clear days, you can spot the coast of South Wales, 32km (20 miles) away across the estuary of the Bristol Channel. The wildlife that thrives on the park's rain-soaked terrain includes a breed of wild pony (the Exmoor pony), whose bloodlines can be traced from ancient species.

Although the park boasts more than 1,127km (700 miles) of walking paths, most visitors stay on the **coastal trail** that winds around the bays and inlets of England's southwestern peninsula or along some of the shorter **riverside trails.**

The park's administrative headquarters is located in a 19th-century workhouse in the village of Dulverton, in Somerset, near the park's southern edge, where you can pick up the *Exmoor Visitor* brochure, listing events, guided walks, and visitor information. A program of walking tours is offered at least five times a week. Themes include Woodland Walks, Moorland Walks, Bird-Watching Excursions, and Deer Spottings. Most of the tours last from 4 to 6 hours, and all are free, with an invitation to donate. Wear sturdy shoes and rain gear.

Dulverton, Somerset TA22 9EX. ℂ **01398/323841.** www.exmoor-nationalpark.gov.uk. Free admission. Visitor center daily 10am–5pm.

NEARBY SIGHTS

Coleridge Cottage   The hamlet of Nether Stowey is on the A39, north of Taunton, across the Quantock Hills to the east of Exmoor. The cottage is at the west end of Nether Stowey on the south side of the A39. Here you can visit the home of Samuel Taylor Coleridge, where he penned "The Rime of the Ancient Mariner." During his 1797 to 1800 sojourn here, he and his friends, William Wordsworth and sister Dorothy, enjoyed exploring the Quantock woods. The parlor and reading room of his National Trust property are open to visitors.

35 Lime St., Nether Stowey, near Bridgwater. ✆ **01278/732662**. Admission £3.20 ($5.90) adults, £1.60 ($2.95) children. Apr 1–Oct 1 Thurs–Sun 2–5pm. From Minehead, follow A39 east about 48km (30 miles), following the signs to Bridgwater. About 13km (8 miles) from Bridgwater, turn right, following signs to Nether Stowey.

Combe Sydenham Hall ✸   This hall was the home of Elizabeth Sydenham, wife of Sir Francis Drake, and it stands on the ruins of monastic buildings that were associated with nearby Cleeve Abbey. Here you can see a cannonball that legend says halted the wedding of Lady Elizabeth to a rival suitor in 1585. The gardens include Lady Elizabeth's Walk, which circles ponds originally laid out when the knight was courting his bride-to-be. The valley ponds fed by spring water are full of rainbow trout (ask about getting fly-fishing lessons). You can also take a woodland walk to Long Meadow, with its host of wildflowers. Also to be seen are a deserted hamlet, whose population reputedly was wiped out by the Black Death, and a historic corn mill. In the hall's tearoom, smoked trout and pâté are produced on oak chips, as in days of yore, and there is a shop, working bakery, and parking lot.

Monksilver. ✆ **01984/656284**. Admission £5.50 ($10) adults, £2.30 ($4.25) children. Country Park Easter–Sept Sun–Fri 9am–5pm; courtroom and gardens May–Sept at 1:30pm for guided tours only, Mon and Wed–Thurs. From Dunster, drive on A39, following signs pointing to Watchet and/or Bridgwater. On the right, you'll see a minor zoo, Tropiquaria, at which you turn right and follow the signs pointing to Combe Sydenham.

WHERE TO STAY IN THE AREA

Luttrell Arms ✸✸   A hostelry for weary travelers has been on this site for more than 600 years. Simply the best choice around, this hotel is the outgrowth of a guesthouse the Cistercian abbots at Cleeve had built in the village of Dunster. It was named for the Luttrell lords of the manor, who bought Dunster Castle and the property attached to it in the 14th century. It has, of course, been updated with modern amenities, but from its stone porch to the 15th-century Gothic hall with hammer-beam roof, it still retains a feeling of antiquity. Bedrooms range in size and are attractively decorated in keeping with the hotel's long history; five of them have four-poster beds. Rooms in a section called the "Latches" are cottagelike in style, with tight stairways and narrow corridors. One room is big enough for use by a family, and nine of the bedrooms are non-smoking. Bathrooms are small and have a shower-and-tub combination.

32–36 High St., Dunster, Somerset TA24 6SG. ✆ **01643/821555**. Fax 01643/821567. www.bhere.co.uk. 28 units. £140–£170 ($259–$315) double. Dinner, B&B rates: Nov–Mar £100–£110 ($185–$204) double; Apr–Oct £130–£140 ($241–$259) double. 2-night minimum stay required for the Oct–Feb rate. AE, DC, MC, V. **Amenities:** 2 restaurants; bar; limited room service; babysitting; laundry service; dry cleaning. *In room:* TV, coffeemaker, minibar, hair dryer, iron/ironing board.

Devon

The great patchwork-quilt area of southwest England, part of the "West Countree," abounds in cliff-side farms, rolling hills, foreboding moors, semi-tropical plants, and fishing villages that provide some of the finest scenery in England. You can pony trek across moor and woodland, past streams and sheep-dotted fields, or soak up atmosphere and ale at a local pub.

The British approach sunny **Devon** with the same kind of excitement normally reserved for hopping over to the Continent. Especially along the coastline—**the English Riviera**—the names of the seaports, villages, and resorts are synonymous with holidays in the sun: Torquay, Clovelly, Lynton-Lynmouth. Devon is a land of jagged coasts—the red cliffs in the south face the English Channel. In South Devon, the coast from which Drake and Raleigh set sail, tranquillity prevails, and on the bay-studded coastline of North Devon, pirates and smugglers found haven.

Almost every village is geared to accommodate visitors. But many small towns and fishing villages don't allow cars; these towns have parking areas on the outskirts, with a long walk to reach the center of the harbor area. From mid-July to mid-September, the most popular villages are quite crowded, so make reservations for a place to stay well in advance.

Along the south coast, the best bases from which to explore the region are **Exeter, Plymouth,** and **Torquay.** Along the north coast, we suggest **Lynton-Lynmouth.** The area's most charming village (with very limited accommodations) is **Clovelly.** The greatest natural spectacle is **Dartmoor National Park,** northeast of Plymouth, a landscape of gorges and moors filled with gorse and purple heather—home of the Dartmoor pony.

If you're taking the bus around Devon, Stagecoach Devon and Western National bus lines combine to offer a discounted **"Explorer Ticket."** Adults can enjoy unlimited use of the lines at these rates: £6 ($11) adults, £4.25 ($7.85) children for 1 day, or £25 ($46) adults, £14 ($26) children for 7 days. You can plan your journeys from the maps and timetables available at any **Western National** office when you purchase your ticket (© **01209/719988**) or **Devon General Office** (© **01752/495250**). For further information, contact **Stagecoach Devon Ltd.,** Paris Street, Exeter, Devon FX1 2JP (© **01392/427711**).

1 Exeter ⭑⭑

324km (201 miles) SW of London; 74km (46 miles) NE of Plymouth

Exeter was a Roman city founded in the 1st century A.D. on the banks of the River Exe. Two centuries later it was encircled by a mighty stone wall, traces of which remain today. Conquerors and would-be conquerors, especially Vikings, stormed the fortress in later centuries; none was more notable than William the Conqueror, who brought Exeter to its knees on short notice.

Devon

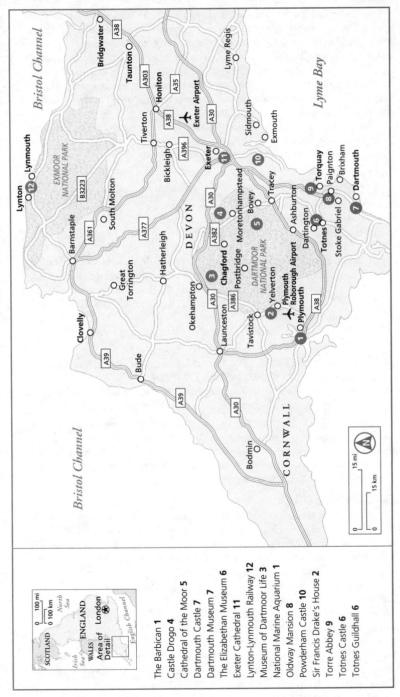

Bristol Channel

Lynton • Lynmouth 12

EXMOOR NATIONAL PARK

Barnstaple

Clovelly

Bude

CORNWALL

Bodmin

Bristol Channel

Bridgwater

Taunton

A303 Honiton A35

A38 Lyme Regis

Tiverton

A396 Bickleigh

South Molton

DEVON

Great Torrington

Hatherleigh

Okehampton

Launceston

Tavistock

Chagford 3

A382

Postbridge

Moretonhampstead

DARTMOOR NATIONAL PARK

Yelverton

Plymouth
Roborough Airport

2

Plymouth 1

Exeter Airport

Exeter 11

Tracey 10

Bovey 5

4

Ashburton

Dartington

Totnes 6

Stoke Gabriel

7 Dartmouth

9 Torquay
Paignton
8 Brixham

Sidmouth
Exmouth

Lyme Bay

North Sea

SCOTLAND

ENGLAND

WALES

London

Area of Detail

Irish Sea

English Channel

The Barbican 1
Castle Drogo 4
Cathedral of the Moor 5
Dartmouth Castle 7
Dartmouth Museum 7
The Elizabethan Museum 6
Exeter Cathedral 11
Lynton-Lynmouth Railway 12
Museum of Dartmoor Life 3
National Marine Aquarium 1
Oldway Mansion 8
Powderham Castle 10
Sir Francis Drake's House 2
Torre Abbey 9
Totnes Castle 6
Totnes Guildhall 6

Under the Tudors, the city grew and prospered. Sir Walter Raleigh and Sir Francis Drake were just two of the striking figures who strolled through Exeter's streets. In May 1942, the Germans bombed Exeter, destroying many of its architectural treasures. The town was rebuilt, but the new, impersonal-looking shops and offices can't replace the Georgian crescents and the black-and-white-timbered buildings with their plastered walls. Fortunately, much was spared, and Exeter still has its Gothic cathedral, a renowned university, some museums, and several historic houses.

Exeter is a good base for exploring both Dartmoor and Exmoor national parks, two of the finest England has to offer. It's also a good place to spend a day, with a lot to do in what's left of the city's old core.

ESSENTIALS

GETTING THERE   Trains from London's Paddington Station depart every hour during the day. The trip takes 2½ hours. For rail information, call ℭ **0845/748-4950** or visit www.firstgreatwestern.co.uk. Trains also run every 20 minutes during the day between Exeter and Plymouth; the trip takes 1 hour. Trains often arrive at Exeter St. David's Station at St. David's Hill.

A **National Express** coach departs from London's Victoria Coach Station every 2 hours during the day; the trip takes 4 hours. You can also take bus no. 38 or 39 between Plymouth and Exeter. During the day, two coaches depart per hour for the 1-hour trip. For information and schedules call ℭ **0870/580-8080** or visit www.nationalexpress.com.

If you're driving from London, take the M4 west, cutting south to Exeter on the M5 (junction near Bristol).

VISITOR INFORMATION   The **Tourist Information Centre** is at the Civic Centre, Paris Street (ℭ **01392/265700;** fax 01392/265260). It's open from September to June Monday to Saturday from 9am to 5pm, and in July and August Monday to Saturday from 9am to 5pm and Sunday from 10am to 4pm.

SPECIAL EVENTS   A classical music lover's dream, the **Exeter Festival,** held the first 2 weeks in July, includes more than 150 events, ranging from concerts and opera to lectures. Festival dates and offerings vary from year to year, and more information is available by contacting the **Exeter Festival Office,** Civic Center (ℭ **01392/265205;** www.exeter.gov.uk/festival).

EXPLORING EXETER

Exeter Cathedral ★★   The Roman II Augusta Legion made its camp on the site where the Cathedral Church of Saint Peter now stands in Exeter. It has been occupied by Britons, Saxons, Danes, and Normans. The English Saint Boniface, who converted northern Germany to Christianity, was trained here in A.D. 690. The present cathedral structure was begun around 1112, and the twin Norman towers still stand. Between the towers runs the longest uninterrupted true Gothic vault in the world, at a height of 20m (66 ft.) and a length of 90m (300 ft.). It was completed in 1369, and is the finest existing example of Decorated Gothic architecture. The Puritans destroyed the cathedral cloisters in 1655, and a German bomb finished off the twin Chapels of St. James and St. Thomas in May 1942. Now restored, it's one of the prettiest churches anywhere. Its famous choir sings evensong every day except Wednesday during school term. On school holidays, visiting choirs perform.

1 The Cloisters. ℭ 01392/255573. www.exeter-cathedral.org.uk. Free admission; a donation of £3.50 ($6.50) is requested of adults. Mon–Fri 8am–6:30pm; Sat 8am–5pm; Sun 8am–7:30pm.

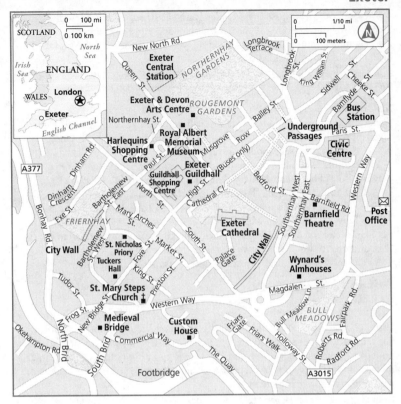

Exeter Guildhall This colonnaded building on the main street is the oldest municipal building in the kingdom—the earliest reference to the guildhall is in a deed from 1160. The Tudor front that straddles the pavement was added in 1593. Inside you'll find a fine display of silver, plus a number of paintings. The ancient hall is paneled in oak.

High St. ℂ **01392/665500.** Free admission. Mon–Fri 10:30am–1pm and 2–4pm. It's best to call before visiting.

Powderham Castle ⭐ This private house is occupied by the countess and earl of Devon, who let Ismail Merchant and James Ivory use their home as a setting for *The Remains of the Day*, starring Anthony Hopkins and Emma Thompson. It was built in the late 14th century by Sir Philip Courtenay, sixth son of the second earl of Devon, and his wife, Margaret, granddaughter of Edward I. Their magnificent tomb is in the south transept of Exeter Cathedral. The castle has many family portraits and fine furniture, including a remarkable clock that plays full tunes at 4pm, 8pm, and midnight; some 17th-century tapestries; and a chair used by William III for his first council of state at Newton Abbot. The chapel dates from the 15th century, with hand-hewn roof timbers and carved pew ends.

In Powderham, Kenton. ℂ **01626/890243.** www.powderham.co.uk. Admission £6.90 ($13) adults, £6.40 ($12) seniors, £3.90 ($7.20) children 5–17, free for children 4 and under, family ticket £18 ($33). Apr–Oct Sun–Fri 10am–5:30pm. Closed Nov–Mar. Take the A379 Dawlish Rd. 13km (8 miles) south of Exeter; the castle is signposted.

Underground Passages   The Underground Passages, accessible from High Street, were built to carry the medieval water supply into the city. By entering the new underground interpretation center, visitors can view a video and exhibition before taking a guided tour.

Boots Corner, off High St. ℂ **01392/665887**. Admission £3.75 ($6.95) adults, £2.75 ($5.10) children, £11 ($20) family ticket. June–Sept Mon–Sat 10am–5pm; Oct–May Tues–Fri noon–5pm, Sat 10am–5pm.

SHOPPING

Exeter has long been famous for its silver. If you seek, ye shall find old Exeter silver, especially spoons, sold in local stores. **Burfords,** 17 Guildhall, Queen St. (ℂ **01392/254901**), sells modern silver and jewelry.

You can find a number of antiques dealers in Exeter, many on the Quay off Western Way. **The Quay Gallery Antiques Emporium** (ℂ **01392/213283**) houses 10 dealers who sell furniture, porcelain, metalware, and other collectibles. **The Antique Centre** on the Quay (ℂ **01392/493501**) has 20 dealers.

The Edinburgh Woolen Mill, 23 Cathedral Yard (ℂ **01392/412318**), carries a large selection of woolen goods, including kilts, Aran jumpers, tartan travel rugs, and quality wool suits for women and trousers for men.

A daily market on Sidwell Street is Exeter's version of a flea market.

WHERE TO STAY
EXPENSIVE

Thistle Exeter   Though its history is far less impressive than the Royal Clarence Hotel, this great, old-fashioned, rambling Victorian hotel (renovated fairly recently) is also a traditional choice for those who want to stay in the center of town. Its small to medium bedrooms are comfortably furnished in a modern style. Units come with well-maintained private bathrooms equipped with tub-and-shower combinations.

Queen St. (opposite the central train station), Exeter, Devon EX4 3SP. ℂ **0870/333-9133**. Fax 0870/ 333-9233. www.thistlehotels.com/exeter. 90 units. £150 ($278) double; £190–£210 ($352–$389) suite. AE, DC, MC, V. **Amenities:** Restaurant; bar; 24-hr. room service. *In room:* TV, dataport, coffeemaker, hair dryer, safe (in some).

MODERATE

Barcelona ℛ *(Finds*   When it opened, Britain's *Good Hotel Guide* hailed this winning choice as "designer hotel of the year." A former hospital devoted to the treatment of eye problems, this hip, modern, and rather tony hotel was created from an old redbrick pile. The big corridors used for wheeling patients and the giant elevators are still here, but everything else is new. Many adornments and artifacts from past decades, notably the '30s and '60s, have been put in place, giving the hotel a distinctive look. The bedrooms, all of which are nonsmoking, are rather luxurious, each tastefully furnished and equipped with first-class aquamarine bathrooms with showers. Expect bold spreads and carpets in geometric

---

Moments   **A Relic from William the Conqueror**

Just off "The High," at the top of Castle Street, stands an impressive **Norman Gatehouse** from William the Conqueror's castle. Though only the house and walls survive, you can enjoy the panoramic view and surrounding gardens, and contemplate all the invasions that have assaulted Exeter, from the Romans to the Nazi bombers of World War II.

In Search of Traditional Devonshire Cream Tea

Cream teas are always associated with Devon. How did they come about? Think back to the traditional Devonshire farmer's wife laboring away on a faraway grange. These matriarchs perfected the medieval process of simmering a batch of whole cow's milk at very low temperatures, sometimes for a day or two, to create the region's famous Devonshire clotted cream. Silken-textured and rich, with just enough acidity to perk up the taste buds, it isn't clotted at all. It's a very English, very urbane, and very perishable version of what the French call crème fraîche.

What should accompany your clots of cream? A scone, preferably just out of the oven and made without baking soda. The resulting, slightly bitter, slightly sour taste seems to go better with the tangy cream. Preserves? Don't even think of asking for anything except strawberry preserves.

The tea itself seems to be less crucial than the items that accompany it. Most Devonites opt for strong, simple Indian tea, eschewing the more delicate Chinese blends as something too fancy to muck about with.

Here are our favorite spots to pause and take afternoon tea with clotted cream while you're exploring the byways and primrose paths of Devon.

While visiting the coastal towns of Devon, dart inland to **Honeybees,** High Street (© 01404/43392), in the town of Honiton, long famous for its lace made a century ago. The brick-fronted tearoom with a large bay window is known for its cream teas and "squidgy cakes." From Exeter, take the A30 straight into Honiton.

Southeast of Exeter, follow the A376 through Exmouth to **The Cozy Teapot,** Fore Street (© 01395/444016), in Budleigh Salterton. A cozy brick building, this tearoom is tucked away just past a small bridge with running water. It serves the best Devon cream tea in the area. You get bone china, lace cloths on the tables, and homemade cakes, too.

Our favorite name for a tearoom is **Four and Twenty Blackbirds,** 43 Gold St., Tiverton (© 01884/257055), reached by following the Old Road (now called the A396) from Exeter straight into Tiverton to the north. The black-and-white-timbered tearoom stands in a sunken square. An assortment of set teas and tea breads and homemade cakes await you.

patterns, large windows, and the original parquet floors, along with such conveniences as cordless phones. The on-site Café Paradiso, arranged like a big-top circus, features Mediterranean food, including Neapolitan pizzas and a brushwood grill for locally caught fish.

Magadalen St., Exeter, Devon EX2 4HY. © 01392/281000. Fax 01392/281001. www.hotelbarcelona-uk.com. 46 units. £90–£110 ($167–$204) double. Children stay free in parent's room. AE, MC, V. **Amenities:** Restaurant; bar; nightclub. *In room:* TV, dataport, beverage maker, hair dryer.

Buckerell Lodge Hotel   This country house originated in the 12th century, but it has been altered and changed beyond recognition over the years. The exterior is a symmetrical and severely dignified building with a Regency feel. Often hosting business travelers, it's also a tourist favorite, especially in summer. The bedrooms, in a range of styles and sizes, are well-decorated and nicely equipped. The best rooms are the executive accommodations in the main house, though most bedrooms are in a more sterile modern addition. Two units are large enough to accommodate families. All units contain well-kept bathrooms with shower-tub combinations.

Topsham Rd., Exeter, Devon EX2 4SQ. ✆ **800/528-1234** in the U.S. and Canada, or 01392/221111. Fax 01392/491111. www.corushotels.com. 53 units. £89–£105 ($165–$194) double. Rates include breakfast. AE, DC, MC, V. Free parking. Bus: S, T, or R. Take B3182 1.5km (1 mile) southeast, off Junction 30 of M5. **Amenities:** Restaurant; bar; 24-hr. room service; laundry service; dry cleaning; nonsmoking rooms; rooms for those with limited mobility. *In room:* TV, dataport, coffeemaker, hair dryer, trouser press.

Gipsy Hill *(Kids)* Affiliated with Best Western, this late Victorian country house stands on the eastern edge of the city and is close to the airport. (It's especially convenient if you're driving, as it's within easy reach of the M5.) Bedrooms, ranging from small to medium, are comfortably appointed; some have four-poster beds. Five accommodations are large enough for families. Bedrooms have more tradition and ambience in the main house, and the other 17 rooms are located in an annex.

Gipsy Hill Lane, via Pinn Lane, Monkerton, Exeter, Devon EX1 3RN. ✆ **800/528-1234** in the U.S., or 01392/465252. Fax 01392/464302. www.gipsyhillhotel.co.uk. 37 units. £90–£125 ($167–$231) double. Rates include English breakfast. AE, DC, MC, V. Bus: T. **Amenities:** Restaurant; bar; limited room service; babysitting; nonsmoking rooms; rooms for those with limited mobility. *In room:* TV, coffeemaker, hair dryer, trouser press.

Royal Clarence Hotel *✿* *(Kids)* Just a short walk from the rail station this hotel offers far more tradition and style than the sometimes better rated and more recently built Southgate at Southernhay East, or the Thistle on Queen Street. It dates from 1769 and escaped the Nazi blitz. Just a step away from the cathedral, it offers individually furnished rooms in Tudor, Georgian, or Victorian styling, each with a tub-and-shower bathroom. Five rooms are large enough for families; some rooms have four-poster beds.

A great two-star Michelin chef (Michael Caines) and a top-notch hotelier of south England (Andrew Brownsword) have joined in partnership to run this hotel. During the life of this edition, major refurbishments will take place, the hotel remaining open. Expect a remarkable transformation in the cuisine at the hotel's main restaurant, Michael Caines at the Royal Clarence. A chic little nook, The Moët et Chandon Champagne & Cocktail Bar, has also been added.

Cathedral Yard, Exeter, Devon EX1 1HD. ✆ **01392/319955.** Fax 01392/439423. www.michaelcaines.com. 56 units. £90–£130 ($167–$241) double; £140–£155 ($259–$287) suite. AE, DC, MC, V. **Amenities:** Restaurant; cafe; 2 bars; limited room service; laundry service; dry cleaning; babysitting; wheelchair accessible; nonsmoking rooms. *In room:* A/C, TV, coffeemaker, hair dryer, safe, trouser press.

St. Olaves Court Hotel *✿* This is our favorite place to stay in town. The location is ideal, within a short walk of the cathedral—you can hear the church bells. A Georgian mansion, it was constructed in 1827 by a rich merchant as a home. The house has been discreetly furnished, in part with antiques, and decorated with sporting prints. Each of the bedrooms, last renovated in 2001, is tastefully decorated; some have four-poster beds. All rooms have well-maintained bathrooms with shower-tub combinations.

Mary Arches St. (off High St.), Exeter, Devon EX4 3AZ. ✆ **800/544-9993** in the U.S., or 01392/217736. Fax 01392/413054. www.olaves.co.uk. 17 units. £115–£125 ($213–$231) double, £155 ($287) suite. Rates include continental breakfast. MC, V. **Amenities:** Restaurant; bar; limited room service. *In room:* TV, coffeemaker, hair dryer.

White Hart Hotel   In the center of town, this inn, a coaching inn in the 15th century, is one of the oldest in the city. Oliver Cromwell stabled his horses here. The hotel is a mass of polished wood, slate floors, oak beams, and gleaming brass and copper. The rooms, which combine old and new, are housed in either the old wing or a more impersonal modern one. Six rooms are large enough for families, and each comes with a bathroom equipped with a shower-tub combination.

65–66 South St., Exeter, Devon EX1 1EE. (*) 01392/279897. Fax 01392/250159. 54 units. Mon–Thurs £69 ($128) double. Fri–Sun £59 ($109) double. Family rooms year-round £89 ($165). Rates include English breakfast. AE, DC, MC, V. **Amenities:** 2 restaurants; 2 bars; limited room service; laundry service; nonsmoking rooms. *In room:* TV, coffeemaker, hair dryer, trouser press.

INEXPENSIVE

Claremont   This Regency-style 1840 town house is in a quiet residential area, close to the center of town. The rooms, much like those you would find in a private home and all nonsmoking, are well kept and tastefully decorated. Each room has a small bathroom with a shower unit (some have tubs). Kathy and Tony Gray, who run the property, assist visitors in many ways.

36 Wonford Rd., Exeter, Devon EX2 4LD. (*) 01392/426448. 4 units. £48 ($89) double. Rates include continental breakfast. No credit cards. Bus: H. **Amenities:** Breakfast room. *In room:* TV, coffeemaker.

Park View Hotel   This hotel lies near the heart of town and the train station. A landmark Georgian house, it offers comfortably but plainly furnished rooms, ranging in size from small to medium. The decor is regularly upgraded. Rooms with private bathroom usually have a shower (only two have a tub-and-shower combination). The public bathrooms available to other guests are convenient and well maintained. Guests take their breakfast in a cozy room opening onto the hotel's garden. Breakfast is the only meal served, but the staff will prepare a packed lunch for touring. All bedrooms are nonsmoking.

8 Howell Rd., Exeter, Devon EX4 4LG. (*) 01392/271772. Fax 01392/253047. www.parkviewexeter.co.uk. 13 units, 10 with bathroom. £50 ($93) double without bathroom, £55–£60 ($102–$111) double with bathroom. Rates include English breakfast. MC, V. *In room:* TV, dataport, coffeemaker.

IN NEARBY BICKLEIGH

Perhaps the finest way to enjoy the cathedral city of Exeter, especially if you have a car, is to stay on the outskirts, 16km to 31km (10–19 miles) from the heart of the city. In the Exe Valley, 6.5km (4 miles) south of Tiverton and 16km (10 miles) north of Exeter, lies Bickleigh, a hamlet with a river, arched stone bridge, millpond, and thatch-roofed cottages—the epitome of English charm and one of the finest spots in all of Devon.

Bickleigh Cottage Country Hotel 🖘🖘 *Finds*   This thatched, 17th-century hotel opens onto a riverside garden that leads down to the lovely Bickleigh Bridge, where swans and ducks glide by. Inside, the rooms are small, possessing oak beams and old fireplaces. Everything is comfortably cozy—like visiting your great-aunt. This is especially true when you snuggle into your comfy bed for the evening. Each unit comes with a small private bathroom; half have a tub and shower and half have a shower only. Mr. and Mrs. Stuart Cochrane, the owners, provide good and nourishing breakfasts.

Bickleigh Bridge, Bickleigh, Devon EX16 8RJ. (*) 01884/855230. 5 units. £25 ($46) double. Rates include English breakfast. MC, V. Closed Nov–Mar. Bus no. 55 from Exeter. *In room:* Coffeemaker.

WHERE TO DINE

Michael Caines at Royal Clarence 🖘🖘 FRENCH   Exeter at long last offers a restaurant worthy of itself, with an aura of smart, sophisticated brasserie. Try to get a table near one of the bay windows overlooking the cathedral. As is obvious by the name, Michael Caines, a skilled chef, is in charge of the overall operation. Excellent, not deluxe, raw materials are purchased and turned into an impressive array of dishes beautifully prepared and served. The dishes we've sampled have been filled with flavor and perfectly spiced, as in appetizers such as a terrine of game and winter vegetables with truffle vinaigrette. Another starter is a salad of scallops with celeriac purée and soy vinaigrette. Main dishes are likely to feature braised turbot with roasted red onions and mussels in a saffron sauce. Desserts are worth saving room for, especially banana parfait in a chocolate and lime coulis.

Cathedral Yard, Devon. © 01392/310031. www.michaelcaines.com. Reservations required. Main courses £15–£25 ($28–$46); 3-course menu £35–£55 ($65–$102). AE, DC, MC, V. Mon-Sat noon–2:30pm and 7–10pm.

St. Olaves Court Hotel Restaurant *Finds* CONTINENTAL At one of Exeter's finest restaurants, guests enjoy a before-dinner drink in a paneled bar that overlooks a verdant garden. The cuisine reflects the sophisticated palate of the congenial owners and includes grilled filet of beef and veal with vegetables and baby onions, baked scallop of salmon with langoustine mousse wrapped in filo pastry with saffron butter sauce, or a variety of vegetarian dishes.

In the St. Olaves Court Hotel, Mary Arches St. © 01392/217736. www.olaves.co.uk. Reservations recommended. Fixed-price 2-course dinner £23 ($43); fixed-price 3-course dinner £30 ($55); fixed-price "light lunch" (2-course) £15 ($28), 3-course £19 ($35). DC, MC, V. Daily noon–2pm and 7–9pm.

The Ship Inn *Finds* ENGLISH   Often visited by Sir Francis Drake, Sir Walter Raleigh, and Sir John Hawkins, this restaurant still provides tankards of real ale, lager, and stout. A large selection of snacks is offered in the bar every day, whereas the restaurant upstairs provides more substantial English fare. At either lunch or dinner, you can order French onion soup, whole grilled lemon sole, five different steaks, and more. Portions are large, as in Elizabethan times.

St. Martin's Lane. © 01392/272040. Reservations recommended. Restaurant main courses £4.45–£11 ($8.25–$20). Pub platters £2.35–£7 ($4.35–$13). MC, V. Mon–Fri noon–9pm; Sat noon–6pm; Sun noon–9pm.

EXETER AFTER DARK

Exeter is a lively university town offering an abundance of classical concerts and theater productions, as well as clubs and pubs. For information concerning cultural events and theaters, the **Exeter Arts Booking and Information Centre,** High St. (© 01392/493493), open Monday through Saturday from 9:30am to 5:30pm, provides a monthly brochure of upcoming events and sells tickets.

An abundance of concerts, opera, dance, and film can be found year-round at the **Exeter Phoenix,** Bradninch Place, Gandy St. (© 01392/667080; www.exeterphoenix.org.uk), and Exeter University's **Northcott Theatre,** Stocker Road (© 01392/493493; www.northcott-theatre.co.uk), which is also home to a professional theater company.

On the club scene, head to **Volts** and the **Hothouse,** The Quay (© 01392/211347; info line 01392/435820), a two-story club featuring funk, soul, dance, and alternative tunes on the first floor, and classic pop music on the second floor. The crowd is young, and a full bar and fast food is available. The cover charge varies from free to £3 ($5.55).

Attracting a more diverse crowd, **The Warehouse/Boxes Disco & Boogies,** Commercial Road (© 01392/259292), is another split club, with different musical styles featured throughout the week. The cover charge varies from free to £5 ($9.25) before 11pm, and £6 ($11) afterward, which gets you into all three clubs on Thursday and Saturday. Warehouse is only open Thursday to Saturday and Boxes is only open on Tuesday, Wednesday and Saturday.

Pubs vary from the ancient and haunted to haunts of folk-music fans, with the **Turks Head,** High Street (© **01392/256680**), offering a bit of local color, because it's housed in a 600-year-old dungeon allegedly haunted by the Turks who were tortured and killed here. The first two floors are unchanged from that bygone era, but the top three floors were turned into the existing pub more than 450 years ago. It was a favorite hangout and scribbling spot of Charles Dickens, whose favorite chair is still on display. Today, it's a lively pub with a computerized jukebox and a fast-food menu. There is a DJ on Saturday.

Well House Tavern, Cathedral Close (© **01392/223611**), is part of the Royal Clarence Hotel. It's housed in a building believed to have been constructed in the 14th century, though the Roman well in the basement predates that estimate. It, too, is said to be haunted—though the ghost here, affectionately called Alice, is said to be good-spirited when she appears in her flowing white dress. Join Alice and the other regulars for a pint or a light meal.

Featuring a great view of the canal, **Double Locks,** Canal Banks (© **01392/256947**), welcomes a varied crowd, largely students. It features live music (jazz, rock, and blues) with no cover charge, and you can get traditional pub grub to go with your pint. Though spaciously spread through a Georgian mansion, the **Imperial Pub,** New North Road (© **01392/434050**), is friendly to frugal travelers, with the cheapest brand-name beer in town, starting at £1.60 ($2.95), and a fast-food menu.

2 Dartmoor National Park ★★

343km (213 miles) SW of London; 21km (13 miles) W of Exeter

This national park lies northeast of Plymouth, stretching from Tavistock and Okehampton on the west to near Exeter in the east, a granite mass that sometimes rises to a height of 600m (2,000 ft.) above sea level. The landscape offers vistas of gorges with rushing water, spiny shrubs, and purple heather ranged over by Dartmoor ponies—a foreboding landscape for the experienced walker only.

ESSENTIALS

GETTING THERE Take the train from London to Exeter, then use local buses to connect you with the various villages of Dartmoor. **Transmoor Link,** a public transport bus service, usually operates throughout the summer, an ideal way to get onto the moor. Information on the Transmoor Link and on the bus link between various towns and villages on Dartmoor is available from the **Travel Line** (© **0870/608-2608**).

If you're driving, Exeter is the most easily reached gateway. From here, continue west on the B3212 to such centers of Dartmoor as Easton, Chagford, Moretonhampstead, and North Bovey. From these smaller towns, tiny roads—often not really big enough for two cars—cut deeper into the moor.

VISITOR INFORMATION The main source of information is the **Tourist Information Office,** Town Hall, Bedford Square, Tavistock (© **01822/612938**). It will book accommodations within an 80km (50-mile) radius for free. It's open April through October daily from 9:30am to 5pm. From November to March, it's open on Monday, Tuesday, Friday, and Saturday from 10am to 4:30pm.

EXPLORING THE MOORS

This region is as rich in myth and legend as anywhere else in Britain. Crisscrossed with about 805km (500 miles) of bridle paths and hiking trails and covering about 932 sq. km (360 sq. miles)—466 sq. km (180 sq. miles) of which comprise the Dartmoor National Park—the moors rest on a granite base with numerous rocky outcroppings.

The Dartmoor National Park Authority (DNPA) runs **guided walks** of varying difficulty, ranging from 1½ to 6 hours for a trek of some 14km to 19km (9–12 miles). All you have to do is turn up suitably clad at your selected starting point. The country is rough, and on the high moor you should always make sure you have good maps, a compass, and suitable clothing and shoes. Details are available from DNPA information centers or from the **Dartmoor National Park Authority,** High Moorland Visitor Centre, Tavistock Road, Princetown (near Yelverton) PL20 6QF (© **01822/890414;** www.dartmoor-npa.gov.uk). Information centers are open daily Easter through October 10am to 5pm; most (including the High Moorland Visitor Centre) are open daily off season 10am to 4pm. Guided tours cost £3 ($5.55) for a 2-hour walk, £4 ($7.40) for a 3-hour walk, £4.50 ($8.35) for a 4-hour walk, and £5 ($9.25) for a 6-hour walk. These prices are subsidized by the national park services.

Throughout the area are stables where you can arrange for a day's trek across the moors. For **horseback riding** in Dartmoor, there are too many establishments to list. All are licensed, and you are accompanied by an experienced rider/guide. The moor can be dangerous because sudden fogs descend on the treacherous marshlands without warning. Prices are around £11 ($20) per hour. Most riding stables are listed in a useful free publication, *The Dartmoor Visitor,* which also provides details on guided walks, places to go, accommodations, local events, and articles about the national park. *The Dartmoor Visitor* is obtainable from DNP information centers and tourist information centers or by mail. Send an International Reply Coupon to the DNPA headquarters (address above).

CHAGFORD: A GOOD BASE FOR EXPLORING THE PARK ℛ
351km (218 miles) SW of London; 21km (13 miles) W of Exeter; 32km (20 miles) NW of Torquay

At 180 meters (600 ft.) above sea level, romantic Chagford is an ancient town. With moors all around, it's a good base for exploring the often forlorn yet enchanting north Dartmoor. You're in Sir Francis Drake country now. Chagford overlooks the Teign River and is itself overlooked by the high granite *tors* (high craggy hills). There's good fishing in the Teign. From Chagford, the most popular excursion is to Postbridge, a village with a prehistoric clapper bridge.

To get here, take a train to Exeter, and then catch a local bus to Chagford (Transmoor Link National Express bus no. 82). If you're driving from Exeter, drive west on the A30, then south on the A382 to Chagford.

EXPLORING THE AREA
Castle Drogo ℛ *Kids*   This massive granite castle, in the hamlet of Drewsteignton, 27km (17 miles) west of Exeter, was designed and built between 1910 and 1930 by architect Sir Edwin Lutyens, then at the height of his powers, for his client, Julius Drewe. It was the last private country house built in the United Kingdom on a grand scale. Though constructed of granite and castellated and turreted like a medieval castle from the age of chivalry, it was never intended to be a military stronghold. The castle occupies a bleak but dramatic position high above the River Teign, with views sweeping out over the moors.

The tour covers an elegant series of formal rooms designed in the tradition of the Edwardian age. Two restaurants and a buffet-style tearoom are on premises.

Insider's tip: The castle is so overpowering it's easy to forget the secluded gardens. But they are wonderful, including a sunken lawn enclosed by raised walkways, a circular croquet lawn (sets are available for rent), geometrically shaped yew hedges, and a children's playroom based on a 1930s residence.

Drewsteignton, 6.5km (4 miles) northeast of Chagford and 9.5km (6 miles) south of the Exeter-Okehampton Rd. (A30). ℂ **01647/433306.** Admission (castle and grounds) £6.20 ($11) adults, £3 ($5.55) children, £15 ($28) family. Grounds only £3.15 ($4.90) adults, £1.60 ($2.95) children; no family ticket. Apr–Oct Wed–Mon 11am–5pm; grounds daily 10:30am–5:30pm. Closed Nov–Mar. Take A30 and follow the signs.

Sir Francis Drake's House 🐦 Constructed in 1278, Sir Francis Drake's House was originally a Cistercian monastery. The monastery was dissolved in 1539 and became the country seat of sailors Sir Richard Grenville and, later, Sir Francis Drake. The house remained in the Drake family until 1946, when the abbey and grounds were given to the National Trust. The abbey is now a museum, with exhibits including Drake's drum, banners, and other artifacts. There is also an audiovisual presentation about the history of the house.

Buckland Abbey, Yelverton. ℂ **01822/853607.** Admission £5 ($9.25) adults, £2.50 ($4.65) children. Apr–Oct Fri–Wed 10:30am–5:30pm; Nov–Mar Sat–Sun 2–5pm. Last admission 45 min. before closing. Go 5km (3 miles) west of Yelverton off A386.

WHERE TO STAY & DINE

Bovey Castle 🐦🐦🐦 The grandest address in Devon is an elegant 1906 estate within the national park which still pursues such "gentlemanly pursuits" as trout fishing, archery, and falconry. There's even a golf course whose revamped links were first laid out in 1926. It's all the creation of Peter de Savary, the British entrepreneur who restored Skibo Castle in the Scottish Highlands where Madonna married Guy. Luxury abounds at this castle, which seems to await the experience any minute of Agatha Christie or at least Hercule Poirot. The spacious bedrooms are the epitome of comfort, taste, and elegance. For those seeking the ultimate retreat, there is the North Lodge with an exquisite home standing in private gardens. The accommodations are virtual staterooms, including the most luxurious, the spa rooms.

North Bovey, Devon TQ13 8RE. ℂ **01647/445-016.** Fax 01647/445-020. www.boveycastle.com. 65 units. £180–£290 ($333–$537) double, £350–£550 ($648–$1,018) suite. AE, DC, MC, V. **Amenities:** Restaurant; bar; 24-hr. room service; golf course; fly-fishing; spa; 2 pools (1 indoor, 1 outdoor); equestrian center; movie theater; business services; falconry; 2 outdoor tennis courts; archery; laundry service; dry cleaning. *In room:* A/C, TV, dataport, minibar, hair dryer, safe.

Easton Court Hotel 🐦 *Finds* Established in the 1920s, this Tudor house, standing in 1.6 hectares (4 acres) of gardens and paddocks, is a longtime favorite of the literati and theatrical celebrities. Best known as the place where Evelyn Waugh wrote *Brideshead Revisited,* the atmosphere here is very English country house: ancient stone house with thatched roof, inglenook where log fires burn, and high-walled flower garden. Bedrooms are snug and comfortable, ranging in size from small to medium, and are all nonsmoking. Rooms are appointed with comfortable English beds where the greats of yesteryear slept; some have four-posters. Most rooms open onto views; all but two bathrooms have shower-tub combinations and the rest have showers only.

Easton Cross, Chagford, Devon TQ13 8JL. ℂ **01647/433469.** Fax 01647/433654. www.easton.co.uk. 5 units. £65–£70 ($120–$130) double. Rates include English breakfast. MC, V. No children 12 and under. Take A382 2.5km (1½ miles) northeast of Chagford. Bus no. 359 from Exeter. **Amenities:** Guest lounge. *In room:* TV, coffeemaker, hair dryer.

Gidleigh Park Hotel 🐦🐦🐦 This Tudor-style hotel, a Relais & Châteaux member, is country house supreme, the finest and most elegant place to stay in the Dartmoor area. On 1.8 hectares (4½ acres) the hotel lies in the Teign Valley, opening onto panoramic vistas of the Meldon and Nattadon Hills. Its American

---

Moments **A Cuppa & an Homage to Lorna Doone**

At teatime, drop in at **Whiddons,** High Street (© **01647/433406**), serving freshly baked scones and delectable cucumber sandwiches. After tea, visit the nearby Church of St. Michael, where a spurned lover killed Mary Whiddon on her wedding day (later fictionalized in R. D. Blackmore's classic *Lorna Doone*).

---

owners, Kay and Paul Henderson, have renovated and refurnished the house with flair and imagination. Most of the bedrooms are on the second floor and are reached by a grand staircase. Bedrooms are roomy and furnished in the most elegant English country-house tradition. Half-canopies usually crown the sumptuous English beds, and each well-appointed bathroom has Crabtree & Evelyn toiletries and Frette bathrobes. The hotel has a two-bedroom thatched cottage with two bathrooms across the river, available for two to four people.

Gidleigh Park (3km/2 miles outside town), Chagford, Devon TQ13 8HH. © **01647/432367.** Fax 01647/432574. www.gidleigh.com. 14 units, 1 cottage. £435–£575 ($805–$1,064) double; £575 ($1,064) cottage for 2; £775 ($1,434) cottage for 4. Rates include English breakfast, morning tea, and dinner. AE, DC, MC, V. To get here from Chagford Sq., turn right onto Mill St. at Lloyds Bank. After 135m (450 ft.), turn right and go down the hill to the crossroads. Cross straight over onto Holy St., following the lane passing Holy St. Manor on your right and shifting into low gear to negotiate 2 sharp bends on a steep hill. Over Leigh Bridge, make a sharp right turn into Gidleigh Park. A 1km (½-mile) drive will bring you to the hotel. **Amenities:** Restaurant; bar; putting green; tennis court; bowling green; croquet lawn; babysitting; laundry service. *In room:* TV, hair dryer.

OTHER TOWNS IN & AROUND DARTMOOR

Some 21km (13 miles) west of Exeter, the peaceful little town of **Moretonhampstead** is perched on the edge of Dartmoor. Moretonhampstead contains an old market cross and several 17th-century colonnaded almshouses.

The much-visited Dartmoor village of **Widecombe-in-the-Moor** is only 11km (7 miles) from Moretonhampstead. The fame of the village of Widecombe-in-the-Moor stems from an old folk song about Tom Pearce and his gray mare, listing the men who were supposed to be on their way to Widecombe Fair when they met with disaster. Widecombe also has a parish church worth visiting. Called the **Cathedral of the Moor,** with a roster of vicars beginning in 1253, the house of worship in a green valley is surrounded by legends. When the building was restored, a wall plate was found bearing the badge of Richard II (1377–99), the figure of a white heart. The town is very disappointing, tacky, and unkempt in spite of its fame.

The market town of **Okehampton** owes its existence to the Norman castle built by Baldwin de Bryonis, sheriff of Devon, under orders from his uncle, William the Conqueror, in 1068, just 2 years after the conquest. The Courtenay family lived here for many generations until Henry VIII beheaded one of them and dismantled the castle in 1538.

Museum of Dartmoor Life, at the Dartmoor Centre, 3 West St., Okehampton (© **01837/52295**), restored in 2004, is housed in an old mill with a water wheel and is part of the Dartmoor Centre, a group of attractions around an old courtyard. Also here are working craft studios, a Victorian Cottage Tearoom, and a tourist information center. Museum displays cover all aspects of Dartmoor's history from prehistoric times, including some old vehicles—a Devon box wagon of 1875 and a 1922 Bullnose Morris motorcar—and a reconstructed cider press and a blacksmith. The museum is open from October to Easter, Monday through Friday from 10am to 4pm, and from Easter to September, Monday through Saturday from 11am to

4:30pm. It also opens on Sunday June through September from 10am to 5pm. Admission is £2.50 ($4.65) for adults, £2 ($3.70) for seniors, £1.25 ($2.30) for children, and £6 ($11) for a family ticket (two adults, two children).

Let yourself drift back in time to the days when craftspeople were the lifeblood of thriving communities. Basket weavers, wood turners, and potters are among the traditional crafters that you can still see in the area. Indulge in with some genuine Devon pieces of craftsmanship. In the Dartmoor National Park in West Devon, you'll find that **The Yelverton Paperweight Centre,** Leg O'Mutton (✆ **01822/854250;** www.paperweightcentre.co.uk), presents an impressive display of more than 800 glass paperweights for sale along with paintings of Dartmoor scenes. Open daily April through October 10:30am to 5pm.

WHERE TO STAY & DINE IN THE AREA

The Castle Inn   A 12th-century structure next to Lydford Castle, this inn lies midway between Okehampton and Tavistock. With its pink facade and row of rose trellises, it is the hub of the village. The owners have maintained the character of the roomy old rustic lounge. One room, the Snug, has a group of high-backed oak benches arranged in a circle. Bedrooms are not large but are attractively furnished, often with mahogany and marble Victorian pieces. Half the bathrooms have showers only, the rest a tub-and-shower combination.

Lydford, near Okehampton (1.5km/1 mile off A386), Devon EX20 4BH. ✆ 01822/820241. Fax 01822/820454. www.castleinnlydford.co.uk. 7 units. £65–£90 ($120–$167) double. MC, V. **Amenities:** Restaurant; bar. *In room:* TV, coffeemaker.

Cherrybrook Hotel   This is a small family run hotel in the center of the Dartmoor National Park, on the high moor but within easy driving distance of Exeter and Plymouth. It was built in the early 19th century by a prince regent's friend who received permission to enclose a large area of the Dartmoor forest for farming. The lounge and bar with their beamed ceilings and slate floors are a reminder of those times. Andy and Margaret Duncan rent small to medium-size rooms with a traditional decor, often with a granite fireplace. A different group of bedrooms is redecorated each year. Bathrooms contain a shower stall.

On B3212 between Postbridge and Two Bridges, Yelverton, Devon PL20 6SP. ✆ and fax 01822/880260. www.cherrybrook-hotel.co.uk. 7 units. £100 ($185) double. Rates include English breakfast and dinner. No credit cards. Closed Dec 22–Jan 2. **Amenities:** Restaurant; bar. *In room:* TV, coffeemaker, hair dryer.

Holne Chase Hotel ✦ *(Kids)*   The hotel on 28 hectares (70 acres) is a white-gabled country house, 5km (3 miles) northwest of the center of town, within sight of trout- and salmon-fishing waters. You can catch your lunch and take it back to the kitchen to be cooked. Though the mood of the moor predominates, Holne Chase is surrounded by trees, lawns, and pastures—a perfect setting for walks along the Dart. The house is furnished in period style; a stable block has been converted into four sporting lodges. Rooms come in various shapes, sizes, and styles; some have their original fireplaces and four-poster beds, ideal for a romantic interlude. If assigned a room in the stable, don't be disappointed, as they are really delightful split-level suites. All the comforts of English country living are found here. Seven rooms are large enough for families. All units contain bathrooms with shower-tub combinations.

Two Bridges Rd., Ashburton, near Newton Abbot (off the main Ashburton-Princetown Rd., between the Holne Bridge and New Bridge), Devon TQ13 7NS. ✆ 01364/631471. Fax 01364/631453. www.holne-chase.co.uk. 16 units. £140–£160 ($259–$296) double; from £200 ($370) suite. Rates include English breakfast. Discount packages available. MC, V. **Amenities:** Restaurant; bar; limited room service; babysitting; laundry service. *In room:* TV, coffeemaker, hair dryer.

Lewtrenchard Manor   On the northwest edges of Dartmoor, near the popular touring center of Okehampton, this is a 17th-century Jacobean house with a certain charm and grace. It was at one time the residence of the Victorian hymn writer, the Rev. Sabine Baring Gould (hardly a household name today). It is set in a garden so lovely it is open to the general public as part of the National Gardens Scheme. Lovely walks are possible in several directions. As is typical of its time, the house features oak paneling, leaded windows, beautifully detailed ceilings, and antiques. Rooms come in various shapes and sizes, but each is exceedingly comfortable and equipped with a shower-tub combination.

Lewdown, Devon EX20 4PN. ℂ **01566/783256.** Fax 01566/783332. www.lewtrenchard.co.uk. **9 units.** £130–£185 ($241–$342) double; £195 ($361) suite. Rates include English breakfast. AE, DC, MC, V. **Amenities:** Restaurant; bar; limited room service; laundry service. *In room:* TV, hair dryer.

3 Torquay: The English Riviera ⋆

359km (223 miles) SW of London; 37km (23 miles) SE of Exeter

In 1968, Torquay, Paignton, and Brixham joined to form "The English Riviera" as part of a plan to turn the area into one of the super three-in-one resorts of Europe. The area today—the birthplace of mystery writer Agatha Christie—opens onto 35km (22 miles) of coastline and 18 beaches.

Torquay is set against a backdrop of the red cliffs of Devon, with many sheltered pebbly coves. With its parks and gardens, including numerous subtropical plants, it's often compared to the Mediterranean. At night, concerts, productions from the West End, vaudeville shows, and ballroom dancing keep the vacationers and many honeymooners entertained.

ESSENTIALS

GETTING THERE   Frequent trains run throughout the day from London's Paddington Station to Torquay, whose station is at the town center on the seafront. The trip takes 2½ hours. For rail information, call ℂ **0845/748-4950** or visit www.wessextrains.co.uk.

National Express coach links from London's Victoria Coach Station leave every 2 hours during the day for Torquay. For information and schedules, call ℂ **0870/580-8080** or visit www.nationalexpress.com.

If you're driving from Exeter, head west on the A38, veering south at the junction with the A380.

VISITOR INFORMATION   The **Tourist Information Centre** is at Vaughan Parade (ℂ **01803/297428**); open Monday through Thursday from 8:40am to 5:15pm and Friday from 8:40am to 4:15pm.

PALM TREES & AGATHA CHRISTIE

This area is known for offering one of the balmiest climates in Britain. It's so temperate, because of its exposure to the Gulf Stream, subtropical plants such as palm trees and succulents thrive.

Oldway Mansion   You'll see the conspicuous consumption of England's Gilded Age here. The mansion was built in 1874 by Isaac Merritt Singer, founder of the sewing-machine empire. His son, Paris, enhanced its decor, massive Ionic portico, and 6.8 hectares (17 acres) of Italianate gardens. The mansion's eclectic decor includes a scaled-down version of the Hall of Mirrors in the Palace of Versailles. During its Jazz Age heyday, Oldway served as a rehearsal space and performance venue for Isadora Duncan, who was having a not-very-discreet affair with Paris.

Torbay Rd., in Preston, near Paignton (a short drive south of the center of Torquay on the main Paignton-Torquay Rd.). ℂ 01803/207933. Tours available Easter–Oct 9am–1pm for £1 ($1.85). Free admission without guided tour. Year-round Mon–Fri 10am–5pm. Open weekends in summer; call to confirm times.

Torre Abbey   Originally built as a monastery in 1196, then converted into a private home in the 16th century, it has long been associated with Torquay's leading citizens. Today, the Torquay Town Council maintains it as a museum. The museum features a room outfitted in a close approximation of Agatha Christie's private study. After the mystery writer's death, her family donated for display her Remington typewriter, many of her original manuscripts, an oil portrait of Ms. Christie as a young woman, family photographs, and more.

Kings Dr. (.5km/¼ mile east of Torquay's center). ℂ 01803/293593. www.torre-abbey.org.uk. Admission £3.50 ($6.50) adults, £1.70 ($3.15) children. Apr–Oct daily 9:30am–6pm (last admission 1 hr. before closing); Nov–Mar by appointment only.

WHERE TO STAY
EXPENSIVE

The Imperial 𝒜𝒜𝒜   This leading government-rated five-star hotel in the West Country dates from 1866, but a major refurbishing has kept it abreast of the times and way ahead of its competition. It sits on 2.2 hectares (5½ acres) of subtropical gardens opening onto rocky cliffs, with views of the Channel. You'll follow the example of some of the characters of Agatha Christie if you check in here. She called it the Esplanade in *The Rajah's Emerald,* the Castle in *Partners in Crime,* and the Majestic in *Peril at End House.* Inside is a world of soaring ceilings, marble columns, and ornate plasterwork—enough to make a former visitor, Edward VII, feel at home. Rooms are studies in grand living, with beautiful reproduction pieces, striped wallpaper, and upholstered seating. Many have private balconies suspended high above a view that encompasses offshore islands with black rocks and sheer sides. Bathrooms are grandly appointed with deluxe toiletries and shower-tub combinations.

Park Hill Rd., Torquay, Devon TQ1 2DG. ℂ 800/225-5843 in the U.S. and Canada, or 01803/294301. Fax 01803/298293. www.paramount-hotels.co.uk. 153 units. £130–£200 ($241–$370) double; £205–£350 ($379–$648) suite. Rates include English breakfast, use of sporting facilities, and dancing in the ballroom Mon–Sat. AE, DC, MC, V. Garage parking £10 ($19); free parking lot. **Amenities:** 2 restaurants; bar; 2 heated pools (indoor, outdoor); 2 tennis courts; 2 squash courts; health club with sauna and beauty salon; concierge; 24-hr. room service; laundry service; dry cleaning; nonsmoking rooms; rooms for those with limited mobility. *In room:* TV, minibar, coffeemaker, hair dryer, safe, trouser press.

Orestone Manor 𝒜   Sometimes the best way to enjoy a bustling seaside resort is from afar, nestled in a country home. Orestone Manor is in nearby Maidencombe, a small village north of Torquay. In one of the loveliest valleys in South Devon, this gabled manor house, constructed in the early 19th century as a private home, enjoys a tranquil rural setting, situated on .8 hectares (2 acres) of well-landscaped gardens. All of the bedrooms are handsomely furnished. The

---

Moments **Under the Sheltering Palms on the Riviera**

Three seaside towns—Torquay, Brixham, and Paignton—combine to form the longest sweep of beachfront in Britain. This almost continuous sweep of sandy beach opening onto calm waters has earned the title "the English Riviera." The Gulf Stream climate allows for subtropical vegetation, and the palm trees imported from Australia in the 19th century still make for a Riviera-like backdrop.

gable rooms are a bit small but some offer sea views; all the superior rooms have sea views and complimentary sherry. Because this was once a country lodge, all the bedrooms have an individual character and aren't just square boxes. Some of the good-size bathrooms have claw-foot tubs with separate walk-in showers.

Rockhouse Lane, Maidencombe, Torquay, Devon TQ1 4SX. © **01803/328098.** Fax 01803/328336. www.orestone.co.uk. 12 units. £110–£180 ($204–$333) double. Rates include English breakfast. Winter discounts available. AE, DC, MC, V. Closed 2 weeks in Jan. Drive 5.5km (3½ miles) north of Torquay on A379. **Amenities:** Restaurant; bar; pool; limited room service; babysitting; laundry service; dry cleaning. *In room:* TV, coffeemaker, hair dryer, safe.

Palace Hotel ☆ In Torquay, only the Imperial is better. This 1921 hotel was built when life was experienced on a grand scale, an attitude reflected by spacious public rooms with molded ceilings and columns. With its recent improvements, the hotel has entered the 21st century in a premier position. Luxurious through and through, the bedrooms are well furnished, each with a well-maintained bathroom. The hotel occupies 10 choice hectares (25 acres) of real estate in Torquay, sweeping down to Anstey's Cove.

Babbacombe Rd., Babbacombe, Torquay, Devon TQ1 3TG. © **01803/200200.** Fax 01803/299899. www.palacetorquay.co.uk. 135 units. £196 ($363) double; £236–£280 ($437–$518) suite for 2. Rates include English breakfast. AE, DC, MC, V. Parking £5 ($9.25) for garage spaces. From the town center take B3199 east. Bus: 32. **Amenities:** Restaurant; 2 bars; 2 pools (heated indoor; outdoor); 9-hole golf course; 6 tennis courts; 2 squash courts; sauna; limited room service; babysitting; laundry service; dry cleaning. *In room:* TV, minibar, coffeemaker, hair dryer, trouser press.

INEXPENSIVE

Colindale This hotel is a good choice, centrally located, opening onto King's Garden, a 5-minute walk from Corbyn Beach and a 3-minute walk from the railway station. Rooms are cozily furnished, in a range of sizes and shapes, each in a Victorian style. Each room has a private shower (one has a bath). Colindale is one of a row of attached brick Victorian houses, with gables and chimneys.

20 Rathmore Rd., Chelston, Torquay, Devon TQ2 6NY. © **01803/293947.** www.colindalehotel.co.uk. 8 units. £50–£56 ($93–$104) double. Rates include English breakfast. MC, V. **Amenities:** Breakfast room; bar. *In room:* TV, coffeemaker, hair dryer.

Craig Court Hotel (Value) This hotel is in a large Victorian mansion with a southern exposure that lies a short walk from the heart of town. Owner Ann Box's modernized rooms, many with private facilities, offer excellent value. Bedrooms tend to be small and cozy, each with a compact private bathroom with a shower. In addition to enjoying the good, wholesome food served here, guests can also make use of a lounge or an intimate bar opening onto the grounds.

10 Ash Hill Rd., Castle Circus, Torquay, Devon TQ1 3HZ. © **01803/294400.** Fax 01803/212525. £41–£47 ($76–$87) double. Rates include English breakfast. Special packages available. No credit cards. Take St. Marychurch Rd. (signposted St. Marychurch, Babbacombe) from Castle Circus (the town hall), make the 1st right onto Ash Hill Rd., go 180m (600 ft.), and the hotel is on the right. **Amenities:** Coffee lounge; bar. *In room:* TV, coffeemaker, hair dryer.

Fairmount House Hotel ☆ (Finds) Standing on a perch overlooking the Cockington Valley, this little haven of tranquillity is far removed from the bustle of the resort, lying in the residential valley of Chelston, on the periphery of Torquay. A converted Victorian building has been turned into a winning little B&B, with its gardens facing south. Torquay Harbour is within easy reach, and the sea is less than .6km (1 mile) away. The family home, complete with cellars and servants' quarters, dates from the turn of the 20th century. For an inglorious period in the 1950s, it was turned into apartments, but after its restoration its original character has been returned. The aura is more of a large family home than a hotel. A highlight is the Victorian Conservatory Bar, with French doors opening onto the suntrap patio. Bedrooms are midsize and tastefully furnished, each with a well-maintained private bathroom with shower. Two garden rooms have a tub and shower. An evening dinner can be arranged in advance.

Herbert Rd., Chelston, Torquay, Devon TQ2 6RW. © **01803/605446.** Fax 01803/605446. www.fairmount househotel.co.uk. 8 units. £60–£62 ($111–$115) double. Rates include breakfast. MC, V. **Amenities:** Restaurant; bar; rooms for those with limited mobility. *In room:* TV, beverage maker, hair dryer, no phone.

WHERE TO DINE

Capers Restaurant ✦ INTERNATIONAL   This intimate, French-style bistro lies at Lisbourne Square, just off the main artery, Babbacombe Road. Torquay is not renowned for its dining, but this serious little restaurant is a bright note in a culinary wasteland. Families are among the regular patrons. The chef-owner, Robert Llewellyn, shops for the freshest of regional produce, when available, and serves locally caught fish and shellfish. A selection of vegetarian dishes is also available. The sauces that go with the fish are a perfect match to the catch of the day, as in the green peppercorn sauce that is zestily served with the monkfish or the caper sauce coming with the perfectly poached skate.

7 Lisbourne Sq. © **01803/291177.** Reservations required. Main courses £11–£17 ($20–$31). AE, MC, V. Mon–Sat 7–10pm. Closed 1 week in Aug.

Mulberry House ✦ *Value* TRADITIONAL ENGLISH   Lesley Cooper is an inspired cook, and she'll feed you well in her little dining room, seating some two dozen diners at midday. The restaurant is situated in one of Torquay's Victorian villas, facing a patio of plants and flowers, with outside tables for summer lunches. Vegetarians will find comfort here, and others can feast on Lesley's smoked ham rissoles, honey-roasted chicken, or grilled natural fried filets of sole with tartar sauce. Traditional roasts draw the Sunday crowds. The choice is wisely limited so that everything served will be fresh.

You can even stay here in one of three bedrooms, each comfortably furnished and well-kept, with private bathrooms. Bed-and-breakfast rates, from £35 ($65) per person daily, make this one of the best bargains of the whole area.

1 Scarborough Rd., Torquay, Devon TQ2 5UJ. © **01803/213639.** Reservations required. Main courses £13–£15 ($23–$28), 3-course meal £18–£25 ($33–$46). No credit cards. Fri–Sun noon–2pm; Wed–Sat 7:30–9:30pm. Bus: 32. From the Sea Front, turn up Belgrave Rd.; Scarborough Rd. is the 1st right.

TORQUAY AFTER DARK

Seven theaters in town, all open year-round, offer everything from Gilbert and Sullivan and tributes to Sinatra and Nat King Cole to Marine Band concerts and comedy shows. Among the most active are the **Palace Theatre,** Palace Avenue, Paignton (© **01803/665800**); and the **Princess Theatre,** Torbay Road (© **08702/414120**).

Fifteen area nightclubs cater to everyone from teenyboppers to the gay scene, but dancing rules the town, and there's virtually nowhere to catch live club acts. Among the better dance clubs are **Claires,** Torwood Street (© **01803/292079**), for its Thursday-, Friday- and Saturday-night house music, with a cover charge varying from £3 to £7 ($5.55–$13).

4 Totnes ✦

361km (224 miles) SW of London; 19km (12 miles) NW of Dartmouth

One of the oldest towns in the West Country, the ancient borough of Totnes rests quietly in the past, seemingly content to let the Torquay area remain in the vanguard of the building boom. On the River Dart, upstream from Dartmouth,

Totnes is so totally removed in character from Torquay that the two towns could be in different countries. Totnes has several historic buildings, notably the ruins of a Norman castle, an ancient guildhall, and the 15th-century Church of St. Mary, constructed of red sandstone. In the Middle Ages, the town was encircled by walls; the North Gate serves as a reminder of that period.

ESSENTIALS

GETTING THERE Totnes is on the main London–Plymouth line. Trains leave London's Paddington Station frequently throughout the day. For rail information, call © **0845/748-4950** or visit www.firstgreatwestern.co.uk.

Totnes is served locally by the Western National and Devon General bus companies (© **01752/402060** in Plymouth for information about routings).

If you're driving from Torquay, head west on the A385.

Many visitors approach Totnes by river steamer from Dartmouth. Contact **Dart Pleasure Craft,** River Link (© **01803/834488;** www.riverlink.co.uk), for information.

VISITOR INFORMATION The **Tourist Information Centre** is at the Town Mill, Coronation Road (© **01803/863168**). It's open in winter Monday through Friday from 9:30am to 5pm and Saturday from 10am to 4pm. Summer hours are Monday through Saturday from 9:30am to 5pm.

EXPLORING TOTNES

The Elizabethan Museum This 16th-century home of a wealthy merchant houses furniture, costumes, documents, and farm implements of the Elizabethan age. One room is devoted to local resident Charles Babbage (1792–1871), a mathematician and inventor. He invented a calculating machine whose memory capacity categorized it as an early version of the computer. His other inventions included the ophthalmoscope, a speedometer, and the cowcatchers later used to nudge cows off the tracks of railways around the world.

70 Fore St. © **01803/863821.** Admission £1.50 ($2.80) adults, £1 ($1.85) seniors, 25p (45¢) children. Easter–Oct Mon–Fri 10:30am–5pm. Closed Nov–Easter.

Totnes Castle Crowning the hilltop at the northern end of High Street, this castle was built by the Normans shortly after their conquest of England. It's one of the best examples of motte-and-bailey construction remaining in the United Kingdom. Although the outer walls survived, the interior is mostly in ruins.

Castle St. © **01803/864406.** Admission £1.80 ($3.35) adults, 90p ($1.65) children. Apr–Sept daily 10am–6pm; Oct daily 10am–5pm. Closed Nov–Mar.

Totnes Guildhall This symbol of Totnes, originally built as a priory (monastery) in 1553, contains an old *gaol* (jail), a collection of civic memorabilia, and the table Oliver Cromwell used to sign documents during his visit to Totnes in 1646.

Ramparts Walk. © **01803/862147.** Admission £1 ($1.85) adults, 50p (95¢) seniors, 25p (45¢) children. Easter–Oct Mon–Fri 10:30am–1pm and 2–4pm. Closed Nov–Easter.

Moments To Market with "the Elizabethans"

Totnes is known for its colorful **markets,** staged Friday and Saturday year-round in the center of town at Civic Square. On Tuesdays, May through September, many vendors wear Elizabethan costumes. You may want to wander throughout the town enjoying its old bookstores, antiques shops, and other gifts.

WHERE TO STAY IN THE TOTNES AREA

The Cott Inn *Finds* Built in 1320, this hotel is the second-oldest inn in England. It's a low, rambling two-story building of stone, cob, and plaster, with a thatched roof and 1m (3-ft.) thick walls. The owners rent low-ceilinged double rooms upstairs, with modern conveniences. The recently refurbished rooms (all nonsmoking) come in all shapes and sizes and include private bathrooms with shower-tub combinations. The inn is a gathering place for the people of Dartington, and you'll feel the pulse of English country life here.

Dartington, near Totnes (on the old Ashburton-Totnes turnpike), S. Devon TQ9 6HE. ✆ **01803/863777.** Fax 01803/866629. www.thecottinn.co.uk. 5 units. £65–£70 ($120–$130) double. Rates include breakfast. MC, V. Bus: X80 travels from Totnes to Dartington, but most people take a taxi for the 2.5km (1½-mile) journey. **Amenities:** Restaurant; bar. *In room:* TV, hair dryer, coffeemaker.

Gabriel Court Hotel *Value* In nearby Stoke Gabriel, this manor house was owned by the same family from 1487 until 1928, when it was converted into a hotel. Douglas Nicol and Sue Letchfont, the proprietors, offer good value and hospitality. The hotel, overlooking a pretty village on the banks of the River Dart, stands in a terraced Elizabethan garden. Each bedroom is in a modern extension that was converted from a hayloft; all have tub-and-shower combinations.

Stoke Gabriel, near Totnes, S. Devon TQ9 6SF. ✆ **01803/782206.** Fax 01803/782333. www.gabrielcourthotel. co.uk. 25 units. £86–£92 ($159–$170) double; £118–£126 ($218–$234) family room for 3. Rates include English breakfast. AE, DC, MC, V. Exit A38 at Buckfastleigh, taking A384 to Totnes, then A385 to Paignton; approximately 1.5km (1 mile) out of Totnes, turn right at the sign to Stoke Gabriel. **Amenities:** Restaurant; bar; heated outdoor pool; room service on request; laundry service; dry cleaning. *In room:* TV, coffeemaker, hair dryer.

Royal Seven Stars Hotel A historic former coaching inn in the center of Totnes, this hotel largely dates from 1660. The hotel overlooks a square in the town center, near the banks of the River Dart. The interior courtyard, once used for horses and carriages, is now enclosed in glass, with an old pine staircase. Decorated with antiques, paintings, and the hotel's own heraldic shield, the courtyard forms an inviting entrance to the inn. The bedrooms have been modernized and have built-in furniture. Two rooms have four-poster beds. All the rooms have compact bathrooms with shower-tub combinations, though in two cases you have to go outside your bedroom door to access the bathroom.

The Plains, Totnes, S. Devon TQ9 5DD. ✆ **01803/862125.** Fax 01803/867925. www.smoothhound.co.uk/ hotels/royal.html. 18 units, 14 with bathroom. £62–£76 ($115–$141) double without bathroom; £68–£84 ($126–$155) double with bathroom. Children under 16 £15 ($28). Rates include English breakfast. AE, DC, MC, V. **Amenities:** Restaurant; bar; limited room service. *In room:* TV, coffeemaker, hair dryer.

WHERE TO DINE

When it's teatime, **Greys Dining Room,** 96 High St. (✆ **01803/866369**), sets out its fine silver and china to welcome you in an atmosphere of wood paneling and antiques. About 40 different teas along with homemade cakes and scones will invite you to extend the afternoon.

Brutus Room ENGLISH For the kind of cuisine that pleased Grandpa, this old coaching inn delivers quite well. You can stick with the four-course table d'hôte menu or order a la carte. Begin with batter-crisp mushrooms with garlic mayonnaise or the soup of the day. Main dishes are always two-fisted selections such as grilled sirloin, grilled lemon sole, or halibut steak. The steak and kidney pie is also a favorite. Vegetables of the day are fresh and well prepared. Finish in the British manner with blue Stilton cheese or a fruited pie with clotted cream. The adjoining Saddle Room bar has a wide range of ales, wine, and spirits.

In the Royal Seven Stars Hotel. ✆ 01803/862125. Reservations recommended. Main courses £6.50–£14 ($12–$26); 4-course table d'hôte £19 ($35). AE, DC, MC, V. Daily 7–9:30pm.

5 Dartmouth ⟨★⟨★

380km (236 miles) SW of London; 56km (35 miles) SE of Exeter

At the mouth of the Dart River, this ancient seaport is home of the Royal Naval College. Traditionally linked to England's maritime greatness, Dartmouth sent out the young midshipmen who saw to it that "Britannia ruled the waves." You can take a river steamer up the Dart to Totnes (book at the kiosk at the harbor); the scenery along the way is panoramic, as the Dart is Devon's most beautiful river. Dartmouth's 15th-century castle was built during the reign of Edward IV. The town's most noted architectural feature is the Butter Walk, which lies below Tudor houses. A Flemish influence, acquired through trade during the Middle Ages, is pronounced in some of the houses.

ESSENTIALS

GETTING THERE   Dartmouth is not easily reached by public transport. Trains run to Totnes and Paignton. One bus a day runs from Totnes to Dartmouth. Call ✆ 0870/608-2608 for schedules.

If you're driving from Exeter, take the A38 southwest, cutting southeast to Totnes on the A381; then follow the A381 to the junction with the B3207.

Riverboats make the 16km (10-mile) run from Totnes to Dartmouth, but these trips depend on the tide and operate only from Easter to the end of October. See "Essentials," in the Totnes section above, for details on obtaining boat schedules.

VISITOR INFORMATION   The **Tourist Information Centre** is at the Engine House, Mayors Avenue (✆ 01803/834224), and is open April through October, Monday through Saturday from 9:30am to 5pm and Sunday from 10am to 4pm; off season Monday through Saturday 9:30am to 4:30pm.

EXPLORING DARTMOUTH

Many visitors come to Dartmouth for the bracing salt air and a chance to explore the surrounding marshlands, which are rich in bird life and natural beauty. The historic monuments here are steeped in much of the legend and lore of Channel life and historic Devon.

The town's most historic and interesting church is **St. Petrox,** on Castle Road, a 17th-century Anglican monument with an ivy-draped graveyard whose tombstones evoke the sorrows of Dartmouth's maritime past. The church is open daily from 7am to dusk.

It's also worth walking through **Bayard's Cove,** a waterfront, cobbled, half-timbered neighborhood that's quite charming. Set near the end of Lower Street, it prospered during the 1600s thanks to its ship-repair services. In 1620, its quays were the site for repairs of the Pilgrims' historic ships, the *Speedwell* and the *Mayflower,* just after their departure from Plymouth.

Dartmouth Castle   Originally built during the 15th century, the castle was later outfitted with artillery and employed by the Victorians as a coastal defense station. A tour of its bulky ramparts and somber interiors provides insight into the changing nature of warfare throughout the centuries, and you'll see sweeping views of the surrounding coast and flatlands.

Castle Rd. (1km/½ mile south of the town center). © 01803/833588. Admission £3.50 ($6.50) adults, £1.80 ($3.35) children. Apr–June and Sept daily 10am–5pm; July–Aug daily 10am–6 pm; Oct daily 10am–4pm; Nov–Mar Sat–Sun 10am–4pm.

Dartmouth Museum This is the region's most interesting maritime museum, focusing on the British Empire's military might of the 18th century. Built between 1635 and 1640, it's set amid an interconnected row of 17th-century buildings—The Butter Walk—whose overhanging, stilt-supported facade was originally designed to provide shade for the butter, milk, and cream sold there by local milkmaids. Today, the complex houses the museum, as well as shops selling wines, baked goods, and more.

The Butterwalk. © 01803/832923. Admission £1.50 ($2.80) adults, £1 ($1.85) seniors, 50p (95¢) children. Mar–Oct Mon–Sat 11am–5pm; Nov–Feb Mon–Sat noon–3pm.

WHERE TO STAY

Dart Marina Hotel ⓡ This hotel—the town's "second choice"—sits at the edge of its own marina, within a 3-minute walk from the center of town. It was originally built as a clubhouse for local yachties late in the 19th century and was then enlarged and transformed into a hotel just before World War II. It does not have as much charm or character as the Royal Castle. The bar, the riverside terrace, and each bedroom afford a view of yachts bobbing at anchor in the Dart River; 14 bedrooms have private balconies. The superior rooms also sport sofa beds, making them a good bet for families. All units are nonsmoking and come with bathrooms with shower-tub combinations.

Sandquay, Dartmouth, Devon TQ6 9PH. © 01803/832580. Fax 01803/835040. www.dartmarinahotel.com. 49 units. £149–£178 ($274–$329) double; £159–£203 ($294–$376) suite for 2. Rates include half board. MC, V. **Amenities:** Restaurant; bar; limited room service. *In room:* TV, coffeemaker, hair dryer, trouser press.

Royal Castle Hotel ⓡ A coaching inn on the town quay since 1639, this is the leading choice. The Royal Castle has hosted Sir Francis Drake, Queen Victoria, Charles II, and Edward VII. Horse-drawn carriages (as late as 1910) dispatched passengers in a carriageway, now an enclosed reception hall. The glassed-in courtyard, with its winding wooden staircase, has the original coaching horn and a set of 20 antique spring bells connected to the bedrooms. Three rooms open off the covered courtyard, and the rambling corridors display antiques. River-view rooms are the most sought after. All units have been recently restored and have central heating. Three rooms are air-conditioned, and eight units offer a Jacuzzi. Five rooms contain a four-poster bed, and each is individually decorated, although all reflect the age of the building. Four accommodations are large enough for families. All but four of the well-kept bathrooms have shower-tub combinations; the rest have showers only.

11 The Quay, Dartmouth, Devon TQ6 9PS. © 01803/833033. Fax 01803/835445. www.royalcastle.co.uk. 25 units. £126–£180 ($233–$333) double. Rates include English breakfast. AE, MC, V. **Amenities:** Restaurant; 2 bars; limited room service; babysitting; laundry service; dry cleaning. *In room:* A/C (in some), TV, coffeemaker, hair dryer, safe.

WHERE TO DINE

The Carved Angel ⓡⓡ CONTINENTAL The best restaurant in town, the stylishly simple Carved Angel is on the riverfront. The building's half-timbered, heavily carved facade rises opposite the harbor. Inside, there's a statue of a carved angel (hence the name).

The cooking is both innovative and interesting, more akin to the creative cuisine of the Continent than to the traditional cookery of England. Appetizers range from crawfish bisque to chicken liver parfait with red-onion confit and toasted brioche. Main dishes include roasted salt cod with bacon, leeks, and olives and pan-fried local sea bass served with a shellfish ravioli and braised fennel. It's worth saving room for the kumquat bavarois with poached rhubarb in ginger syrup.

2 S. Embankment. ⓒ **01803/832465.** Reservations recommended. 2-course lunch £12 ($22); 4-course fixed-price dinner £35 ($65). MC, V. Tues–Sun noon–2pm; Mon–Sat 7–9pm.

Carved Angel Café (Value) ENGLISH The low-budget cafe and brasserie is associated with the upscale and pricey restaurant reviewed above, The Carved Angel; you are guaranteed a well-prepared, fairly priced meal in an environment reeking of bucolic charm and traditional English wholesomeness. Menu items are listed on a blackboard and change every day according to the seasonality of the ingredients and the inspiration of the chef. Good cooking is the rule, as evoked by such dishes as chicken and mushroom casserole and such desserts as lemon-flavored cheesecake. Soups are rich and nutritious, and at least three traditional "puddings" are always available for dessert. The restaurant is fully licensed.

7 Foss St. ⓒ **01803/834842.** Reservations not necessary. Lunch main courses £5.50–£7 ($10–$13); dinner main courses £6–£12 ($11–$22). AE, DC, MC, V. Dec–Mar Tues–Sat 9am–5pm; Apr–Nov Mon–Thurs 9am–5pm, Fri–Sat 9am–5pm and 7–9pm.

Horn of Plenty ⓐ INTERNATIONAL As you drive from Tavistock to Callington, a small sign points north along a leafy drive to a solid Regency house where the owners operate what the French call a restaurant *avec chambres.* It was built by the duke of Bedford in the early 1800s as a private home on 5 acres (2h) of grounds. After a day of touring the country, guests enjoy well-prepared dinners at this award-winning restaurant, which may include terrine of duck foie gras with sweet-and-sour leeks as an appetizer, followed by the fresh fish of the day. Our party of three recently enjoyed such specialties as lightly coated medallion of beef, roast loin of venison, and an especially delectable grilled sea bass in a lobster-flavored sauce. Even though all meals are fixed-price arrangements, there is a choice in each category.

You can stay in one of the spacious, warm, and elegant bedrooms (10 in all) that have been installed over the old stables of the house. With a full English breakfast included, doubles range from £130 to £200 ($241–$370). All accommodations have TVs, beverage maker, phones, and well-stocked minibars.

In the Tamar View House, Gulworthy, Tavistock, Devon PL19 8JD. ⓒ **01822/832528.** www.thehornofplenty. co.uk. Reservations recommended. Fixed-price lunch £19–£23 ($34–$43); fixed-price dinner (Tues–Sun) £25–£40 ($46–$74). AE, MC, V. Tues–Sun noon–2pm; daily 7–9pm. Closed Dec 24–26. Drive 5km (3 miles) west of Tavistock on A390.

A FAVORITE LOCAL PUB

Just a 2-minute walk from Bayard's Cove is one of our favorite pubs, **The Cherub,** 13 Higher St. (ⓒ **01803/832571**). It was originally built in 1380 as the harbormaster's house. Today this charming pub is a great place to drink and dine on simple traditional British platters and bar snacks. There's a more formal dining room upstairs that serves a number of fish dishes, steaks, lamb, and duck.

6 Plymouth ⓐⓐ

390km (242 miles) SW of London; 259km (161 miles) SW of Southampton

The historic seaport of Plymouth is more romantic in legend than in reality. But this was not always so—during World War II, greater Plymouth lost at least

75,000 buildings to Nazi bombs. The heart of present-day Plymouth, including the municipal civic center on the Royal Parade, has been entirely rebuilt; however, the way it was rebuilt is the subject of much controversy.

For the old part of town, you must go to the Elizabethan section, known as **The Barbican,** and walk along the quay in the footsteps of Sir Francis Drake (once the mayor of Plymouth). From here, in 1577, Drake set sail on his round-the-world voyage. The Barbican also holds special interest for visitors from the United States as the final departure point of the Pilgrims in 1620. The two ships, *Mayflower* and *Speedwell,* that sailed from Southampton in August of that year put into Plymouth after suffering storm damage. The *Speedwell* was abandoned as unseaworthy; the *Mayflower* made the trip to the New World alone.

ESSENTIALS

GETTING THERE   Plymouth Airport lies 6.5km (4 miles) from the center of the city. **Brymon Airways** (© **01752/204090**) has direct service from the London airports, Heathrow and Gatwick, to Plymouth.

Frequent trains run from London's Paddington Station to Plymouth in 3¼ to 4 hours. For rail information, call © **0845/748-4950** or visit www.firstgreat western.co.uk. The **Plymouth Train Station** lies on North Road, north of the Plymouth Center. Western National Bus no. 83/84 runs from the station to the heart of Plymouth.

National Express has frequent daily bus service between London's Victoria Coach Station and Plymouth. The trip takes 4½ hours. Call © **0870/580-8080** for schedules and information or visit www.nationalexpress.com.

If you're driving from London, take the M4 west to the junction with the M5 going south to Exeter. From Exeter, head southwest on the A38 to Plymouth.

VISITOR INFORMATION   The **Tourist Information Centre** is at the Island House, The Barbican (© **01752/264849**). A second information center, **Plymouth Discovery Centre,** is at Crabtree Marsh Mills, Plymouth (© **01752/ 266030**). Both are open from Easter to October, Monday through Saturday from 9am to 5pm and Sunday from 10am to 4pm; and from November to Easter, Monday through Friday from 10am to 5pm and Saturday from 9am to 4pm.

SEEING THE SIGHTS

To commemorate the spot from which the *Mayflower* sailed for the New World, a white archway, erected in 1934 and capped with the flags of Great Britain and the United States, stands at the base of Plymouth's West Pier, on The Barbican. Incorporating a granite monument that was erected in 1891, the site is referred to as both the *Mayflower* **Steps** and the **Memorial Gateway.**

The **Barbican** is a mass of narrow streets, old houses, and quayside shops selling antiques, brass work, old prints, and books. It's a perfect place for strolling and browsing through shops at your leisure.

Fishing boats still unload their catch at the wharves, and passenger-carrying ferryboats run short harbor cruises. A trip includes views from the water of Drake's Island in the sound, the dockyards, naval vessels, and The Hoe—a greenbelt in the center of the city that opens onto Plymouth Harbour. A cruise of Plymouth Harbour costs £6 ($11) for adults and £3 ($5.55) for children. Departures are Easter to October, with cruises leaving every half-hour from 10am to 4pm daily. These **Plymouth Boat Cruises** are booked at 8 Anderton Rise, Millbrook, Torpoint (© **01752/822797**).

National Marine Aquarium ⚘   The best aquarium in the United Kingdom stands near the center of the harbor area, displaying both freshwater and seawater fish, even a shark theater. At least three times a week is shark feeding time, a grue-some *Jaws*-like horror. You can actually walk under the sharks in their holding tank. Fearing many sea creatures are being destroyed, the institution also engages in such work as a breeding program for sea horses. There are many other exhibits as well.

Rope Walk, Coxside. (✆ 01752/600301. www.national-aquarium.co.uk. Admission £8.75 ($16) adults, £7.25 ($13) students and seniors, £5.25 ($9.70) children ages 3–15, £25 ($46) family; free for children under 3. Apr–Oct daily 10am–6pm; Nov–Mar daily 10am–5pm.

Plymouth Gin Distillery   One of Plymouth's oldest surviving buildings, this is where the Pilgrims met before sailing for the New World. Plymouth Gin has been produced here for 200 years on a historic site that dates from a Dominican monastery built in 1425. Public guided tours (including a tasting) are offered, and a Plymouth Gin Shop is on the premises.

Black Friars Distillery, 60 Southside St. (✆ 01752/665292. www.plymouthgin.com. Admission £2.75 ($5.10) adults, £2.25 ($4.15) children 10–18, free for children 9 and under. Jan–Feb Mon–Sat 10am–5pm; Mar–Dec daily 10am–4pm. Closed Christmas and Easter. Bus: 54.

Prysten House   Built in 1490 as a town house close to St. Andrew's Church, this is now a church house and working museum. Reconstructed in the 1930s with American help, it displays a model of Plymouth in 1620 and tapestries depicting the colonization of America. At the entrance is the gravestone of the captain of the U.S. brig *Argus,* who died on August 15, 1813, after a battle in the English Channel.

Finewell St. (✆ 01752/661414. Admission £1 ($1.85) adults, 50p (95¢) children. Mon–Sat 9:30am–6:30pm.

WHERE TO STAY

Astor Hotel   This appealing and completely restored hotel is better than ever following massive improvements in 2001 to its structure, once the private home of a sea captain during the Victorian era. The best rooms are the so-called exec-utive suites with four-poster beds, and even better are the Bridal Suites with both four-posters and a Jacuzzi. Of course, you don't have to be a honeymooner to book any of these. Even the mostly midsize standard rooms are exceedingly com-fortable. All rooms have a private bathroom with shower or tub. You don't need to leave the premises at night as there is a cozy lounge bar and a first-class restau-rant serving both a traditional British and an international cuisine.

14–22 Elliott St., The Hoe, Plymouth, Devon PL1 2PS. (✆ 01752/225511. Fax 01752/251994. www.astor hotel.co.uk. 64 units. £80–£120 ($148–$222) double; from £200 ($370) suite. Rates include English break-fast. AE, DC, MC, V. Free parking overnight, £3.50 ($6.50) permit parking nearby. **Amenities:** Restaurant; 2 bars; limited room service; laundry service. *In room:* TV, coffeemaker, trouser press.

Duke of Cornwall Hotel 🅰   This hotel is a Victorian Gothic building that survived World War II bombings. Constructed in 1863, it was regarded by Sir John Betjeman as the finest example of Victorian architecture in Plymouth. The refurbished bedrooms are comfortable and well maintained. Four rooms contain antique four-poster beds, and all have bathrooms with shower-tub combina-tions. Six units are large enough for families.

Millbay Rd., Plymouth, Devon PL1 3LG. (✆ 800/528-1234 in the U.S., or 01752/275850. Fax 01752/275854. www.duke.activehotels.com/TUK. 72 units. £104 ($192) double. Rate includes English breakfast. AE, MC, V. free parking. **Amenities:** Restaurant; bar; 24-hr. room service; laundry service; dry cleaning; nonsmoking rooms; rooms for those with limited mobility. *In room:* TV, dataport, coffeemaker, hair dryer, trouser press.

Plymouth Hoe Moat House Hotel 🅰   One of the most distinguished hotels in the West Country, overlooking the harbor and The Hoe, the Plymouth Moat House is a midget high-rise. It is the town's finest address, superior to the long-standing Duke of Cornwall. The good-size rooms are well furnished with long double beds, and have wide picture windows, and compact bathrooms with shower-tub combinations. The decor is tasteful, and the overall atmosphere is casual and comfortable.

Armada Way, Plymouth, Devon PL1 2HJ. ℂ **01752/639988.** Fax 01752/673816. www.moathousehotels.com. 210 units. £140–£170 ($259–$315) double. AE, DC, MC, V. Parking £3.50 ($6.50) for duration of stay. **Amenities:** Restaurant; 2 bars; indoor pool; health club; spa; salon; limited room service; babysitting; laundry service; dry cleaning; nonsmoking rooms. *In room:* A/C, TV, coffeemaker, minibar in executive rooms, hair dryer, safe, trouser press.

WHERE TO DINE

The Plymouth Arts Centre Restaurant, 38 Looe St. (ℂ **01752/202616**), offers one of the most filling and down-home vegetarian meals in town. Prices range from £2.30 to £4.10 ($4.25–$7.60), and it's also ideal for a snack. You can even see a movie downstairs if you'd like. Food is served Monday to Saturday noon to 2pm and Tuesday to Saturday from 5:30pm to 8:30pm.

Duke of Cornwall Hotel Restaurant ⍟ MODERN BRITISH   This landmark hotel dining room is one of the finest in the area. Lit by a Victorian chandelier, your menu is illuminated in an elegant setting. Traditional and classic favorites are included on the menu, but the taste is definitely contemporary English. High-quality ingredients are seriously and professionally cooked. "West Countree" favorites appear including a perfectly roasted loin of pork with a sage-flavored fruit stuffing. Or else you may prefer loin of lamb cooked in the wok with tempura vegetables. Fresh fish and fine meats go into the dishes. For dessert, you can opt for the old-fashioned Treacle tart and custard which tastes as good as it always did. Service is first class, and there's also a good wine list.

Millbay Rd. ℂ **01752/275850.** Reservations recommended. Main courses £11–£18 ($20–$33). AE, DC, MC, V. Daily 7–10pm.

Kubes ⍟ *Value* CONTINENTAL   In the center of Plymouth, this new (in 2004) restaurant has quickly become the leading dining choice in town. A first-class dining experience, based on market-fresh ingredients, awaits you here. The cozy ambience is decorated with works by local artists. At night, candles are lit to create a romantic atmosphere for sophisticated dining. The chef-owner, John Powe, marries ingredients well, including Gressingham duck and pork stuffed with apricots and paired with exotic sauces. Showing a polished technique are such starters as seared scallops with a cauliflower fondant and gazpacho or a

---

⸲Moments Following the Seagulls & Fish

On a fair day, head down by the Barbican side of the Plymouth Harbour. Here you'll see a hungry line of locals queuing up at a kiosk called **Cap'n Jaspars,** dispensing fresh fish from the local catch. Enjoy a fish sandwich at one of the wooden picnic tables while seagulls fly overhead. This is such a fine little moment you wonder why the Pilgrims ever set sail.

Watching the fresh fish land on the Plymouth pier, we trailed it to the first restaurant where it was headed. The chef came out to inspect the catch of the day and purchased it on sight. The restaurant discovery turned out to be **Piermaster's,** 33 Southside St., right at the Barbican (ℂ **01752/229345**). The decor's your typical seaside nautical joint, but the fish dishes are excellent. And they're certainly fresh.

pressed ham hock with wild mushroom terrine with spicy pineapple chutney. Our party recently took delight in the baked John Dory with chive mash, saffron sauce, cherry tomatoes, and deep-fried leeks, and in the ballotine of guinea fowl leg and roasted breast flavored with a thyme and truffle *jus* and served with a potato cake and ratatouille. For desserts, nothing's finer than a glazed lemon tart, lemon curd ice cream, and a mango coulis—that is, if you choose not to order the chocolate and praline terrine with a cream sauce and kirsch-infused cherries.

13 Frankfort Gate. 🕐 **01752/266793**. Reservations required. Main courses £6.50–£7.95 ($12–$15); 3-course fixed-price lunch £6.50 ($12); 3-course fixed-price dinner £25 ($45). MC, V. Tues–Fri 12:30–2pm; Tues–Sat 7–10:30pm.

7 Clovelly

386km (240 miles) SW of London; 18km (11 miles) SW of Bideford

This is the most charming of all Devon villages and one of the main attractions of the West Country. Starting at a great height, the village cascades down the mountainside. Its narrow, cobblestone High Street makes driving impossible. You park your car at the top and make the trip on foot; supplies are carried down by donkeys. Every step of the way provides views of tiny cottages, with their terraces of flowers lining the main street. The village fleet is sheltered at the stone quay at the bottom.

The major sight of Clovelly is Clovelly itself. Charles Kingsley once wrote, "It is as if the place had stood still while all the world had been rushing and rumbling past it." The price of entry to the village (see below) includes a guided tour of a fisherman's cottage as it would have been at the end of the 1800s. For the same price, you can also visit the **Kingsley Exhibition.** Author of *Westward Ho!* and *Water Babies,* Kingsley lived in Clovelly while his father was curate at the church. This exhibition traces the story of his life.

Right down below the Kingsley Exhibition—and our shopping note for the town—is a **Craft Gallery** where you have a chance to see and buy a wide variety of works by local artists and craftspeople. Once you've reached the end, you can sit and relax on the quay, taking in the views and absorbing Clovelly's unique atmosphere from this tiny, beautifully restored 14th-century quay.

Once you've worked your way to the bottom, how do you get back up? Those in good shape will climb back up the impossibly steep cobbled streets to the top and the parking lot. For those who can't make the climb up the slippery incline, go to the rear of the Red Lion Inn and line up for a Land Rover. In summer, the line is often long, but considering the alternative, it's worth the wait.

To avoid the tourist crowd, stay out of Clovelly from around 11am until teatime. When the midday congestion is at its height, visit nearby villages such as Bucks Mills (5km/3 miles to the east) and Hartland Quay (6.5km/4 miles to the west).

ESSENTIALS

GETTING THERE   From London's Paddington Station, trains depart for Exeter frequently. At Exeter, you transfer to a train headed for the end destination of Barnstaple. Travel time from Exeter to Barnstaple is 1¼ hours. For rail information, call 🕐 **0845/748-4950** or visit www.wessextrains.co.uk. From Barnstaple, passengers transfer to Clovelly by bus.

From Barnstaple, about one bus per hour, operated by either the Red Bus Company or the Filers Bus Company, goes to Bideford. The trip takes 40 minutes. At Bideford, connecting buses (with no more than a 10-min. wait between arrival and departure) continue on for the 30-minute drive to Clovelly. Two Land Rovers make continuous round-trips to the Red Lion Inn from the top of the hill. The Clovelly Visitor Centre (see below) maintains up-to-the-minute transportation information about getting to Clovelly, depending on your location.

If driving from London, head west on the M4, cutting south at the junction with the M5. At the junction near Bridgewater, continue west along the A39 toward Lynton. The A39 runs all the way to the signposted turnoff for Clovelly.

VISITOR INFORMATION   Go to the **Clovelly Visitor Centre** (© 01237/ 431781), where you'll pay £4 ($7.40) adults, £2.75 ($5.10) for kids under 7, for the cost of parking, use of facilities, entrance to the village, and an audiovisual theater admission, offering a multiprojector show tracing the story of Clovelly back to 2000 B.C. Also included in the price is a tour of a fisherman's cottage and admission to the **Kingsley Exhibition** (see above). It's open Monday to Saturday 9am to 5:30pm April to June and October, daily from 10am to 3:30pm November to March, and daily from 9am to 6pm July to September.

WHERE TO STAY & DINE

New Inn   About halfway down High Street is the village pub, a good meeting place at sundown. It offers the best lodgings in the village, in two buildings on opposite sides of the steep street (but only a 3.5m/12-ft. leap between balconies). Each room is relatively small but comfortable, and two are large enough for a family. Only a few have a small private bathroom with a shower stall. Corridor bathrooms are adequate, however, and you rarely have to wait in line. If you're driving, you can park in the lot at the entrance to the town. It's advisable to pack a smaller overnight bag, because your luggage will have to be carried down (but is returned to the top by donkey).

High St., Clovelly, N. Devon EX39 5TQ. © 01237/431303. Fax 01237/431636. newinn@clovelly.co.uk. 19 units, 8 with bathroom. £35–£45 ($65–$83) double without bathroom, £74–£89 ($137–$164) double with bathroom. Rates include English breakfast. AE, MC, V. **Amenities:** Restaurant; bar. *In room:* TV, coffeemaker, trouser press.

Red Lion   At the bottom of the steep cobbled street, right on the stone seawall of the little harbor, Red Lion occupies the prime position in the village. Rising three stories with gables and a courtyard, it's actually an unspoiled country inn, where life centers around an antique pub and village inhabitants, including sea captains, who gather to satisfy their thirst over pints of ale. Most rooms look directly onto the sea with spectacular views, and they have recently been refurbished. Many are small, but two are spacious enough for a family. All units contain neatly kept bathrooms with shower-tub combinations.

The Quay, Clovelly, Devon EX39 5TF. © 01237/431237. Fax 01237/431044. www.redlion-clovelly.co.uk. 11 units. £68–£80 ($126–$148) double. Rates include English breakfast and dinner. AE, MC, V. **Amenities:** Restaurant; bar. *In room:* TV, coffeemaker, hair dryer, safe.

EN ROUTE TO LYNTON-LYNMOUTH: A STAY ON A WORKING FARM

Halmpstone Manor 𝒜 (Finds)   In the countryside, this working farm is operated by Charles and Jane Stanbury. Originally built in the 11th century as a manor house with 22 rooms, the structure has diminished in size because of two fires that occurred in the 15th and 16th centuries. The edifice was rebuilt in 1701 in its present form, with 15th-century paneling located in the dining room and high ceilings in the four-poster bedrooms. Family heirlooms are scattered throughout, and all the spacious bedrooms are a regal statement of English taste, luxuriously furnished with either four-poster or brass and coronet beds, along with deluxe bathrooms with shower-tub combinations and toiletries.

Chittlehampton Rd., Bishop's Tawton, Barnstaple, N. Devon EX32 OEA. ℂ **01271/830321.** Fax 01271/830826. www.halmpstonemanor.co.uk. 5 units. £50 ($93) double, £70 ($130) suite. Rates include English breakfast. AE, DC, MC, V. From Clovelly, take A39 east for 30–45 min., turning off the A39 when you see signs for Chittlehampton. About 3km (2 miles) after the turnoff, you'll see signs pointing to Halmpstone Manor. **Amenities:** Restaurant; bar; 24-hr. room service; babysitting; laundry; dry cleaning. *In room:* TV, coffeemaker, hair dryer, trouser press.

8 Lynton-Lynmouth ⟨★

332km (206 miles) W of London; 95km (59 miles) NW of Exeter

The north coast of Devon is particularly dramatic in Lynton, a village some 150m (500 ft.) high, which is a good center for exploring the Doone Valley and the part of Exmoor that overflows into the shire from neighboring Somerset. The Valley of the Rocks, west of Lynton, offers the most panoramic scenery.

ESSENTIALS
GETTING THERE   The town is rather remote, and the local tourist office recommends that you rent a car to get here. However, local daily trains from Exeter arrive at Barnstaple. For rail information, call ℂ **0845/748-4950** or visit www.wessextrains.co.uk.

From Barnstaple, bus service is provided to Lynton at a frequency of about one every hour. Call ℂ **01598/752225** for schedules.

If you're driving, take the M4 west from London to the junction with the M5, then head south to the junction with the A39. Continue west on the A39 to Lynton-Lynmouth.

VISITOR INFORMATION   The **Tourist Information Centre** is at the Town Hall, Lee Road (ℂ **01598/752225**), and is open from Easter to October daily from 8:30am to 6pm and from November to Easter from 10am to 4pm Monday through Saturday.

SEEING THE SIGHTS
Lynton is linked to its twin, Lynmouth—located about 150m (500 ft.) below, near the edge of the sea—by one of the most celebrated **railways** in Devon, the Lynton & Lynmouth Cliff Railway (ℂ **01598/753486**). The century-old train uses no electricity and no power. Instead, the railway covers the differences in distance and altitude by means of a complicated network of cables and pulleys, allowing cars to travel up and down the face of the rocky cliff. The length of the track is 259m (862 ft.) with a gradient of 1 inch, which gives it a vertical height of approximately 150m (500 ft.). The two passenger cars are linked together with two steel cables, and the operation of the lift is on the counterbalance system, which is simply explained as a pair of scales where one side, when weighted by a water ballast, pulls the other up. The train carries about 40 passengers at a time for 60p ($1.10) adults, 40p (75¢) children. Trains depart daily from February to October, at 2- to 5-minute intervals, from 9am to 7pm. From November to March, the train is shut down.

The East Lyn and West Lyn rivers meet in Lynmouth, a popular resort with the British. For a **panoramic view** of the rugged coastline, you can walk on a path that runs along the cliff halfway between the towns. From Lynton, or rather from Hollerday Hill, you can look out onto Lynmouth Bay, Countisbury Foreland, and Woody Bays in the west. From Hollerday Hill, the view encompasses the Valley of Rocks, formed during the Ice Age by towering rock formations with names such as "The Devil's Cheesewring." The Valley of Rocks' centerpiece, Castle Rock, is renowned for its resident herd of wild goats.

From Lynmouth harbor, regular boat trips go along what the English have dubbed "The Heritage Coast" of North Devon. You can cruise past nesting colonies of razorbills, guillemots, dunlin, and kittiwakes, with the gulls soaring in the thermals by the highest sea cliffs in England.

Other activities in the locale include fishing, putting, bowls, tennis, pony trekking, and golf courses lying within a 32km (20-mile) radius. The Tourist Information Centre (see above) also keeps abreast of the various outdoor pursuits (which change seasonally) available at the time of your visit.

WHERE TO STAY & DINE

Hewitt's at the Hoe Hewitt's is named for Sir Thomas Hewitt, who helped construct the funicular railway that links the twin resorts. In the 1860s, he also built a home for himself, and today that place is one of the most successful small hotels in Lynton. Situated on some 11 hectares (27 acres), it opens onto the beautiful vistas of Lynmouth Bay (best enjoyed while seated on a sunny terrace). The old house is filled with architectural character, as exemplified by its grand staircase, time-mellowed paneling, antiques, and stained-glass windows. All rooms are comfortably appointed and include such amenities as CD players; some have private balconies. All rooms have well-maintained bathrooms with shower-tub combinations. Many rooms have panoramic views across the channel to the Welsh coastline. The hotel is "for all seasons" and has a country-house atmosphere. It's a perfect Agatha Christie set.

The Hoe, N. Walk, Lynton, Devon EX35 6HJ. ℂ **01598/752293.** Fax 01598/752489. www.hewittshotel.com. 5 units. £140 ($259) double; £450 ($833) serviced apt. for 3. Rates include English breakfast. MC, V. **Amenities:** Restaurant; bar; Jacuzzi; limited room service; laundry service; dry cleaning. *In room:* TV, coffeemaker, hair dryer, trouser press.

The Rising Sun 🐾🐾 Bask in the wonder and warmth of an inn that has been in business for more than 600 years. Following a renovation and refurbishment in 2002 and 2003, under the direction of an international designer from London, the bedrooms and bathrooms look more glamorous and romantic than ever, many with four-poster beds or else "half-tester" beds. Stylish and tasteful fabrics were used extensively to give the rooms more elegance. Behind the inn, halfway up the cliff, a tiny garden brightens with flowers in summer. The owner has refurbished the place, and he has rooms available nearby in Shelley's Cottage, where the poet honeymooned in 1812. *Note:* The hotel discourages children under 7 and people with disabilities from staying here.

The Harbourside, Lynmouth, N. Devon EX35 6EQ. ℂ **01598/753223.** Fax 01598/753480. www.risingsun lynmouth.co.uk. 16 units, 1 cottage. £98–£138 ($181–$255) double; £150 ($278) Shelley's Cottage for 2. Rates include English breakfast. AE, DC, MC, V. **Amenities:** Restaurant; bar; limited room service; laundry service; dry cleaning; nonsmoking rooms. *In room:* TV, coffeemaker, hair dryer.

Tors Hotel Set high on a cliff, the Tors Hotel opens onto a view of the coastline and the bay. It was built in 1895 in the fashion of a Swiss château, with more than 40 gables, Tyrolean balconies jutting out to capture the sun (or the moon), and some 30 chimneys. The interior has been modernized, and much attention has been lavished on the comfortable bedrooms, five of which are large enough for families. The superior rooms all have sea views. All rooms contain well-managed bathrooms with shower-tub combinations.

Tors Park, Lynmouth, Lynton, N. Devon EX35 6NA. ℂ **01598/753236.** Fax 01598/752544. www.tors lynmouth.co.uk. 31 units. £96–£120 ($178–$222) double; £200 ($370) suite. Rates include English breakfast. AE, DC, MC, V. Closed Jan–Feb. **Amenities:** Restaurant; bar; heated outdoor pool; limited room service; babysitting; laundry service. *In room:* TV, coffeemaker, hair dryer, safe, trouser press.

11

Cornwall

The ancient duchy of **Cornwall** is in the extreme southwestern part of England, often called "the toe." This peninsula is a virtual island—culturally if not geographically. Encircled by coastline, it abounds in rugged cliffs, hidden bays, fishing villages, sandy beaches, and sheltered coves where smuggling was once rampant. Though many of the seaports with hillside cottages resemble towns on the Mediterranean, Cornwall retains its own distinctive flavor.

The ancient land had its own language until about 250 years ago, and some of the old words (*pol* for pool, *tre* for house) still survive. The Cornish dialect is more easily understood by the Welsh than by those who speak the queen's English.

We suggest basing yourself at one of the smaller fishing villages, such as **East or West Looe, Polperro,** or **Mousehole,** where you'll experience the true charm of the duchy. Many of the villages, such as **St. Ives,** are artists' colonies. Except for St. Ives and **Port Isaac,** some of the most interesting places lie on the southern coast, often called the **Cornish Riviera.** However, the north coast has its own peculiar charm as well. The majestic coastline is studded with fishing villages and hidden coves for swimming, with **Penzance** and St. Ives serving as the major meccas. A little further west is **Land's End,** where England actually comes to an end. And the **Isles of Scilly,** 43km (27 miles) off the Cornish coast, have only five islands inhabited out of more than 100. Here you'll find the **Abbey Gardens of Tresco,** 297 hectares (735 acres) with 5,000 species of plants. Finally, a trip to this region is incomplete without a visit to **Tintagel Castle,** linked with the legends of King Arthur, Lancelot, and Merlin.

1 The Fishing Villages of Looe & Polperro ⟨★⟩

Looe: 425km (264 miles) SW of London; 32km (20 miles) W of Plymouth. Polperro: 463km (271 miles) SW of London; 9.5km (6 miles) SW of Looe; 42km (26 miles) W of Plymouth.

The ancient twin towns of East and West Looe are connected by a seven-arched stone bridge that spans the Looe river. Houses on the hills are stacked one on top of the other in terrace fashion. In each fishing village are good accommodations.

The old fishing village of Polperro is reached by a steep descent from the top of a hill from the main road leading to Polperro. You can take the 7km (4½-mile) cliff walk from Looe to Polperro, but the less adventurous will want to drive. However, in July and August you're not allowed to take cars into town unless you have a hotel reservation, in order to prevent traffic bottlenecks. A large parking area charges according to the length of your stay. For those unable to walk, a horse-drawn bus will take visitors to the town center.

Fishing and sailing are two of the major sports in the area, and the sandy coves, as well as **East Looe Beach,** are spots for sea bathing. Beyond the towns are cliff paths and chalky downs worth a ramble. Looe is noted for its shark

Cornwall

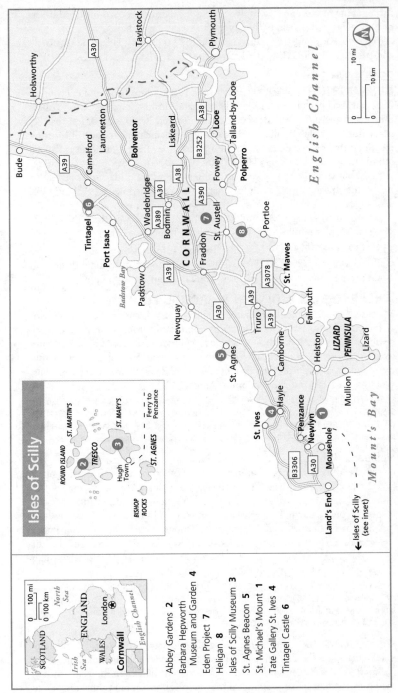

Isles of Scilly

ROUND ISLAND
ST. MARTIN'S
TRESCO
ST. MARY'S
Hugh Town
ST. AGNES
BISHOP ROCKS
Ferry to Penzance

English Channel

Plymouth
Tavistock
Holsworthy
A30
Bude
Launceston
Camelford
Bolventor
Liskeard
Loe
A39
A38
A38
B3252
Talland-by-Looe
Tintagel **6**
Port Isaac
Fowey
Polperro
Wadebridge
Bodmin
A389
A30
St. Austell **7**
A390
A38
8
C O R N W A L L
Fraddon
Portloe
Padstow
Padstow Bay
Newquay
A39
A30
St. Agnes **5**
St. Mawes
A3078
Falmouth
A39
Truro
A39
Camborne
St. Ives **4**
Hayle
Helston
LIZARD PENINSULA
Lizard
Penzance
Newlyn
Mullion
1
Mousehole
B3306
A30
Land's End
← Isles of Scilly (see inset)
Mount's Bay

10 mi
10 km

SCOTLAND
North Sea
Irish Sea
ENGLAND
WALES
London
English Channel
Cornwall
0   100 mi
0   100 km

Abbey Gardens **2**
Barbara Hepworth Museum and Garden **4**
Eden Project **7**
Heligan **8**
Isles of Scilly Museum **3**
St. Agnes Beacon **5**
St. Michael's Mount **1**
Tate Gallery St. Ives **4**
Tintagel Castle **6**

fishing, but you may prefer simply walking the narrow, crooked medieval streets of East Looe, with its old harbor and 17th-century guildhall.

Polperro, surrounded by Cliffs, is one of the handsomest villages in Cornwall, and parts of it hark back to the 17th century.

ESSENTIALS

GETTING THERE Daily trains run from Plymouth to Looe, and rail connections can also be made from Exeter (Devon) and Bristol (Somerset). Most visitors drive to Polperro, but the nearest main-line station is at Liskeard, less than 4½ hours from London's Paddington Station, with a branch line to Looe. Taxis meet incoming trains to take visitors to the various little villages in the area. For rail information in the area, call © **0845/748-4950** or visit www.wessextrains.co.uk.

Local bus companies have various routings from Plymouth into Looe. Ask at the Tourist Information Centre in Plymouth for a schedule (p. 417). You can take a local bus to Polperro from Liskeard or Looe.

If you're driving to Looe from Plymouth, take the A38 west, then the B3253. To get to Polperro, follow the A387 southwest from Looe.

VISITOR INFORMATION The **Tourist Information Centre** is at the Guildhall, Fore Street (© **01503/262072**), and is open in summer daily from 10am to 2pm, and in winter only on Saturdays from 10am to 2pm.

WHERE TO STAY & DINE IN & AROUND LOOE

Barclay House A family operated, country-house hotel on the edge of town at the entrance to Looe, it's about a 5-minute walk from the harbor and the center of the resort and stands on a wooded hillside surrounded by 2.4 hectares (6 acres) of private woodlands overlooking the Looe River Valley. Units are spacious and fitted with soft twin or king-size beds. Rooms have small bathrooms, usually with a tub-and-shower combination.

St. Martins Rd. (the main Plymouth-Looe Rd., B3253), E. Looe, Cornwall PL13 1LP. © **01503/262929.** Fax 01503/262632. www.barclayhouse.co.uk. 11 units, 8 cottages. £90–£120 ($167–$222) double; £250–£1,100 ($463–$2,035) cottage per week. Rates (except cottages) include English breakfast. AE, MC, V. **Amenities:** Restaurant; bar; outdoor pool; limited room service; babysitting. *In room:* TV, coffeemaker, hair dryer.

Fieldhead Hotel *(Kids* The Fieldhead, built in 1896 as a private home, is now one of the area's best hotels. Commanding a view of the sea, it is situated on .8 hectares (2 acres) of gardens. The rooms have a high standard of traditional furnishings and are continually maintained. Rooms are warm and inviting; most of them open onto panoramic views of St. George's Island and the bay. All rooms have well-kept bathrooms with shower-tub combinations; some rooms have balconies.

Note: Families like not only the kid-friendly management here, but also the location in a garden setting where even young children can play in safety. This is also one of the few hotels in the area with a pool.

Portuan Rd., Hannafore, W. Looe, Cornwall PL13 2DR. © **01503/262689.** Fax 01503/264114. www.chycor. co.uk/fieldhead/main.htm. 16 units. £60–£200 ($111–$370) double. Rates include English breakfast. MC, V. **Amenities:** Restaurant; bar; outdoor heated pool; limited room service; nonsmoking rooms; laundry service. *In room:* TV, coffeemaker, hair dryer, trouser press.

Klymiarven *(R (Kids* This is the finest place to stay in the area, a family run hotel perched on the East Cliff with panoramic views of the harbor some 450m (1,500 ft.) below. The original cellars of the building date from the 17th century; the present manor house was built in the early 1800s. An old tunnel discovered on the site was probably used by smugglers. A sun deck has been installed between the pool and the restaurant. All the roomy bedrooms are handsomely furnished. On the second floor is a series of family rooms with stunning views. In the new wing (built in the 1950s) are another attractive six bedrooms. Bathrooms contain tub-and-shower accommodations. All rooms are nonsmoking. The kitchen prepares an excellent three-course table d'hôte. The restaurant is renowned for its fresh seafood and steaks, using grass-fed Hereford steers or Angus beef from Scotland.

Barbican Hill, East Looe, PL13 1BH. ℭ **01503/262333.** Fax 01503/262333. www.klymiarven.co.uk. 14 units. £55–£72 ($102–$133) per person. Rates include half board. Children 7 and under stay free, ages 8–12 £14 ($26), and 12 and over pay half price of the B&B rate. MC, V. Closed Jan. Lies 3km (2 miles) from Looe by A387 off B3253 (can also be reached by foot from the harbor). **Amenities:** Restaurant; bar; pool. *In room:* TV, coffeemaker, hair dryer.

The Talland Bay Hotel ℱ   A country house dating from the 16th century, situated on 1 hectare (2½ acres), this hotel is the domain of George and Mary Granville, who will direct you to local beaches and the croquet lawn. Its rectangular swimming pool is ringed with flagstones and a semitropical garden. Views from the tastefully furnished bedrooms—last refurbished in 1995—include the sea and rocky coastline. Some bedrooms are in a comfortable annex. All rooms are nonsmoking and come with a private bathroom with tub-and-shower combination.

Talland-by-Looe, Cornwall PL13 2JB. ℭ **01503/272667.** Fax 01503/272940. www.tallandbayhotel.co.uk. 22 units. Nov–Apr £140–£190 ($259–$352) double; May–Oct £170–£230 ($315–$426) double. Rates include English breakfast and dinner. MC, V. Take A387 6.5km (4 miles) southwest of Looe. **Amenities:** Restaurant; bar; pool; limited room service. *In room:* TV, coffeemaker, hair dryer, safe.

The Well House ℱ *Kids*   Well House is one of those *restaurants avec chambres* found occasionally in the West Country, and it's one of the best. Located 5km (3 miles) from Liskeard, it has 2 hectares (5 acres) of gardens opening onto vistas of the Looe Valley. It offers beautifully furnished bedrooms, with many thoughtful extras, such as fresh flowers. Two beautiful terrace rooms are at the garden level.

Most rooms have a twin bed or else a large double. Families are welcomed into extralarge rooms; especially popular is the hotel's family suite with one large double bedroom plus a twin-bedded unit as well. Each unit in the hotel has a tidily kept bathroom with a tub-and-shower combination.

St. Keyne, Liskeard, Cornwall PL14 4RN. ℭ **01579/342001.** Fax 01579/343891. www.wellhouse.co.uk. 9 units. £115–£170 ($213–$315) double; £185–£205 ($342–$379) family room. Rates include English breakfast. MC, V. From Liskeard, take B3254 to St. Keyne, 5km (3 miles) away. **Amenities:** Restaurant; bar; heated outdoor pool; outdoor tennis court; croquet lawn; limited room service. *In room:* TV, hair dryer, safe.

WHERE TO STAY IN NEARBY PELYNT & LANREATH

If you want to get away from the busy activity of the two little harbors of Looe and Polperro, the pace of the nearby communities of Pelynt and Lanreath may be just right. The sleepy little village of Pelynt is just 5km (3 miles) north of Polperro. Peaceful Lanreath lies just 9.5km (6 miles) away from Polperro off the road to West Looe. Most visitors take a car or taxi from the Looe train station. The two places listed here rank among England's major inns of character.

Jubilee Inn ℱ   Built in the 16th century, this inn takes its name from Queen Victoria's Jubilee celebration, when it underwent restoration. It's a comment on, rather than a monument to, the past. A glass-enclosed circular staircase, built to serve as a combined tower and hothouse, takes you to the bedrooms. All but the three newest rooms have excellent 19th-century furnishings. Most rooms are

Cornwall's Geodesic Domed Eden

At first you think some space ship filled with aliens has invaded sleepy old Cornwall. A second look reveals one of England's newest and most dramatic attractions, the **Eden Project,** Bodelva, St. Austell (℃ **01726/ 811911;** www.edenproject.com), a 48km (30-mile) drive west of Plymouth. This sprawling attraction presents plants from the world over, including the major climates, on 51 hectares (125 acres) of a former clay quarry. One of the two conservatories is nearly 1.6 hectares (4 acres) in dimension, reaching 54m (180 ft.) high, housing tropical plants from some of the world's rainforests, including the Amazon. The smaller dome, covering .6 hectares (1½ acres), grows plants from everywhere from California to South Africa. A roofless biome houses plants that thrive in the Cornish climate, including species from every-where from India to Chile. The site takes in a small lake and offers a 2,300-seat amphitheater where special shows are staged. Within this biome is also a giant global garden planted in a crater. The crater is totally hidden from view until you walk through the visitor center, which is on the lip of the pit—very James Bondian.

Open daily from 10am to 6pm (last admission at 4:30pm), admission is £12 ($22) for adults, £9 ($17) for seniors, £6 ($11) for students, £5 ($9.25) for children 5 to 15, or £30 ($56) for a family ticket. The project lies 9.5km (6 miles) from the St. Austell train station, to which it is linked by frequent buses.

midsize, though two are large enough for families and all contain bathrooms with shower-tub combinations.

Jubilee Hill, Pelynt (6.5km/4 miles from Looe, 5km/3 miles from Polperro), Cornwall PL13 2JZ. ℃ **01503/ 220312.** Fax 01503/220920. www.jubileeinn.com. 11 units. £70–£84 ($130–$155) double. Rates include English breakfast. MC, V. **Amenities:** Restaurant; bar. In room: TV, coffeemaker, hair dryer.

The Punch Bowl Inn ⍟   Opened in 1620, the Punch Bowl has since served as a courthouse, coaching inn, and rendezvous for smugglers. Today its bed-rooms (all with four-poster beds) provide old-fashioned comfort. One of the kitchens here is one of the few licensed in Britain as a bar. Many bedrooms are quite small, though they come in various shapes and sizes, each with a small, compact bathroom fitted with a tub only and adequate shelf space.

Lanreath, near Looe, Cornwall PL13 2NX. ℃ **01503/220218.** Fax 01503/220788. 7 units. £50–£75 ($93–$139) double. Rates include English breakfast. MC, V. From Polperro, take B3359 north. **Amenities:** Restaurant; bar; lounge. In room: TV, coffeemaker, no phone.

WHERE TO DINE IN POLPERRO

The Kitchen SEAFOOD   This pink cottage halfway to the harbor from the parking area was once a wagon-builder's shop. Now a restaurant offering good English cooking, everything is homemade from fresh ingredients. The menu changes seasonally and features local fresh fish. Typical dishes include Fowey sea trout with lemon-and-herb butter and breast of duckling with blueberry-and-Drambuie sauce. Many vegetarian dishes are offered as main courses.

Fish na Bridge. ℃ **01503/272780.** Reservations required. Main courses £15–£20 ($28–$37). MC, V. Daily 7–9:30pm. Closed Oct–Easter.

Nelson's Restaurant SEAFOOD   Situated in the lower reaches of Polperro, near the spot where the local river meets the sea, this is the only structure in town specifically built as a restaurant. It features succulent preparations of regional fish and shellfish that arrive fresh from local fishing boats. The menu changes daily, but usually includes fresh crab, Dover sole, fresh lobster, and many other exotic fish. Fresh meat, poultry, and game, all from local suppliers, are also available and are prepared exceedingly well. A lower deck features a cafe-bar and bistro. A comprehensive wine list boasts some fine vintages.

Saxon Bridge. © **01503/272366**. Reservations advised. Main courses £6.50–£20 ($12–$37); 2-course table d'hôte lunch or dinner £15 ($27). MC, V. Tues–Sun 7pm to last customer; Thurs–Fri and Sun 11am–2pm. Closed mid-Jan to mid-Feb.

2 St. Mawes ⟨★⟩

483km (300 miles) SW of London; 3km (2 miles) E of Falmouth; 29km (18 miles) S of Truro

Overlooking the mouth of the Fal River, St. Mawes seems like a port on the French Riviera: It's sheltered from northern winds, and subtropical plants can grow here. From the town quay, you can take a boat to Frenchman's Creek and Helford River, as well as other places. St. Mawes is noted for its sailing, boating, fishing, and yachting, and half a dozen sandy coves lie within a 15-minute drive from the port. The town, built on the Roseland Peninsula, makes for interesting walks because of its colorful cottages and sheltered harbor.

GETTING THERE

Trains leave London's Paddington Station for Truro several times a day. The trip takes 4½ to 5 hours. For schedules and information, call © **0845/748-4950** or visit www.wessextrains.co.uk. Passengers transfer at Truro to one of the two buses that make the 45-minute bus trip from Truro to St. Mawes. It's much easier to take a taxi from either Truro or, even better, from the village of St. Austell, which is the train stop before Truro.

Buses leave London's Victoria Coach Station several times a day for Truro. The bus takes 6 hours. For schedules and information, call © **0870/580-8080** or visit www.nationalexpress.com.

If you're driving, to reach St. Mawes, turn left off the A390 (the main road along the southern coast of Cornwall), at a junction 6.5km (4 miles) past St. Austell, onto the Tregony road, which will take you into St. Mawes.

A ferry travels to St. Mawes from both Falmouth and Truro, but schedules are erratic, varying with the tides and the weather conditions.

WHERE TO STAY & DINE

Hotel Tresanton ⟨★★⟩   Laura Ashley and the designer of an ocean liner must have combined talents to create this country-house hotel, which lies above the sea overlooking the fishing harbor. Tresanton has quickly replaced Idle Rocks and Rising Sun as the premier address of town. The whole place casts an aura of a chic house party, 1930s style. A glamorous hotel, Tresanton offers a combination of beautiful old and new furnishings in its spacious, airy bedrooms. The views from the bedrooms are among the most panoramic on the coast, which you'll want to explore on long walks above *Rebecca*-like cliffs. The preferred units are nos. 22 through 27, each with its own terrace overlooking the churning waters. Most units have beautifully maintained bathrooms with shower-tub

The Lost Gardens of Heligan

Like taking a time capsule back to Victoria's day, Europe's largest garden restoration project sprawls over 32 hectares (80 acres) of pure enchantment, with award-winning gardens. Near the fishing village of Mevagissey, these gardens "slept" for nearly 7 decades before they were rediscovered and restored.

On the gardens were part of the 404-hectare (1,000-acre) Victorian estate of the Tremayne family, in residence here since the 16th century. As family fortunes declined after World War I, the gardens were allowed to decay, and the grand estate itself was converted to apartments.

As Cornwall enjoys a subtropical climate, it didn't take long for rampant weeds, brambles, and other unchecked growth to blanket the gardens, even "burying" the tall palm trees in time.

In 1990, composer Tim Smit, with his friend, builder John Nelson, rediscovered the garden along with the heir to the estate, John Willis. The estate had by then been reduced to 36 hectares (80 acres). The men became so enchanted with this secret garden that restoration was launched shortly thereafter.

Both professionals and volunteers began the gargantuan project of reclaiming the gardens. Greenhouses were rebuilt, ornamental pools cleaned and put into working order, pineapple pits redug, orchards replanted, and new plants put into the earth as they were in the 19th century. Part of the gardens encompasses a "Jungle," an extraordinary dell evocative of a Garden of Eden. Giant tree ferns, palms, bamboo, and other vegetation rise from the earth. All that is missing is a swinging appearance by Tarzan.

Beyond the jungle rises the "Lost Valley," with its woodland, flowers, and lakes. The location near the fishing village of Mevagissey is southwest of St. Austell, near Pentewan, off the Mevagissey Road or B3273. In summer the gardens are open from 10:30am to 6pm (they close at 5pm off season). Admission is £7.50 ($14) for adults, £7 ($13) for seniors, £4 ($7.40) for ages 5 to 16 (free 4 and under). A family ticket sells for £20 ($37). For more information, call ✆ 01726/845100 or check out **www.heligan.com**.

combinations. The hotel offers a large front terrace, which has exceptional nighttime views of the lights in the twinkling harbor.

St. Mawes, Cornwall TR2 5DR. ✆ 01326/270055. Fax 01326/270053. www.tresanton.com. 29 units. £165–£265 ($305–$490) double; from £365 ($675) suite. Rates include English breakfast. AE, MC, V. **Amenities:** Restaurant; bar; 24-hr. room service; babysitting; laundry service; movie theater. *In room:* TV, hair dryer, safe.

The Idle Rocks Hotel *(Kids)*   The second-best place to stay in St. Mawes is this solid old building, right on the seawall, sporting gaily colored umbrellas and tables all along the terrace. Water laps at the wall, and the site opens onto views over the river and the constant traffic of sailboats and dinghies. Most rooms have sea or river views; the 17 units in the main hotel building charge higher rates. Four rooms tout balconies and four-poster beds. Families flock here for the bustling harbor view, which kids love, and for the number of extralarge, comfortably appointed rooms.

Tredenham Rd., St. Mawes, Cornwall TR2 5AN. © **01326/270771.** Fax 01326/270062. www.idlerocks.co.uk. 27 units. £136–£198 ($252–$366) double. Rates include half board. AE, MC, V. Parking available in the town parking lot; cost will be refunded for 1st night. **Amenities:** Restaurant; bar; limited room service; babysitting. *In room:* TV, coffeemaker, hair dryer.

The Rising Sun 🎯   Converted from four 17th-century fishing cottages, with a flower-draped flagstone terrace out front, this colorful seafront inn in the center of town exudes charm. Known as one of Cornwall's best inns, it offers recently refurbished bedrooms that are functional and cozy. The small to midsize bedrooms are graced with specially commissioned watercolors by local artists. Each small bathroom has adequate shelf space and a shower-tub combination.

The Square, St. Mawes, Cornwall TR2 5DJ. © **01326/270233.** Fax 01326/270198. 8 units. £80–£120 ($148–$222) double. Children 4–15 receive 50% discount. Rates include English breakfast. MC, V. **Amenities:** Restaurant; bar; limited room service; laundry service. *In room:* TV, coffeemaker, hair dryer.

3 Penzance 🎯

451km (280 miles) SW of London; 124km (77 miles) SW of Plymouth

This little harbor town, which Gilbert and Sullivan made famous, is at the end of the Cornish Riviera. It's noted for its moderate climate (it's one of the first towns in England to blossom with spring flowers), and for the summer throngs that descend for fishing, sailing, and swimming. Overlooking Mount's Bay, Penzance is graced in places with subtropical plants including palm trees.

Those characters in *The Pirates of Penzance* were not entirely fictional. The town was raided by Barbary pirates, destroyed in part by Cromwell's troops, sacked and burned by the Spaniards, and bombed by the Germans. In spite of its turbulent past, it offers tranquil resort living today.

The most westerly town in England, Penzance is a good base for exploring Land's End, the Lizard peninsula, St. Michael's Mount, the old fishing ports and artists' colonies of St. Ives, Newlyn, Mousehole, and even the Isles of Scilly.

ESSENTIALS
GETTING THERE   Ten express trains leave daily from Paddington Station in London for Penzance. The trip takes 5½ hours. Call © **0845/748-4950** or visit www.wessextrains.co.uk.

The **Rapide,** run by National Express from Victoria Coach Station in London (© **0870/580-8080;** www.nationalexpress.com), costs £29 ($53) for the one-way trip from London, which takes about 8½ hours. The buses have toilets and reclining seats.

Drive southwest across Cornwall on the A30 all the way to Penzance.

VISITOR INFORMATION   The **Tourist Information Centre** is on Station Road (© **01736/362207**). It's open from the end of May to September, Monday through Friday from 9am to 5:30pm, Saturday from 10am to 5pm, and Sunday from 10am to 1pm; from October to May, hours are Monday to Friday from 9am to 5pm and Saturday from 10am to 1pm.

SEEING THE SIGHTS AROUND PENZANCE
Castle on St. Michael's Mount 🎯   Rising about 75m (250 ft.) from the sea, St. Michael's Mount is topped by a part medieval, part 17th-century castle. It's 5km (3 miles) east of Penzance and is reached at low tide by a causeway. At high

Moments   Trekking the Cornish Coast

Much of Cornwall is an evocatively barren landscape, composed of gray rocks, weathered headlands jutting seaward, and very few trees. The weather alternates between bright sunshine and the impenetrable fogs for which the English Channel is famous.

The land and seascapes provide a scenic backdrop for hiking around the Cornish peninsula's coastline. The government maintains a clearly signposted coastal path more than 966km (600 miles) long that skirts the edge of the sea, following the tortured coastline from Minehead (in Somerset, near Dunster) to Poole (in Dorset, near Bournemouth). En route, the path crosses some of the least developed regions of southern England, including hundreds of acres of privately owned land as well as the northern border of the Exmoor National Park.

Throughout is a sense of ancient Celtic mysticism and existential loneliness. Low-lying gorse, lichens, and heathers characterize the vegetation. In marked contrast to the windblown uplands, verdant subtropical vegetation grows in the tidal estuaries of the Fowey, Fal, Helford, and Tamar rivers.

Your options for exploring the coasts of Cornwall, Devon, and Dorset are numerous. It's a full 4 to 6 weeks of hard trekking to do the whole thing, though most people just pick a short section for a day hike. Although the route is sometimes arduous, no special equipment other than sturdy shoes, good stamina, and waterproof clothing is required.

You may also want to pick up a locally researched and annually revised book: The South West Way Association's *The Complete Guide to the South West Coast Path—Great Britain's Longest Trail*. This book divides the 966km (600-mile) coast path into manageable segments, rates them for degrees of difficulty, and contains a comprehensive accommodations section with addresses of pubs, bed-and-breakfasts, inns, hotels, and campsites en route. You can order the book from the **South West Way Association,** 1 Orchard Dr., Kingskerswell, Newton Abbot, Devon, England TQ12 5DG (© and fax **01752/896237;** www.swcp.org.uk), at a cost of £7 ($13) including postage.

The loneliness of the Cornish moors could be marred by hundreds of other people with exactly the same idea during Britain's school holidays. If possible, schedule your visit for relatively quiet periods, and remember that the weather between late October and early May is rainy, foggy, and windy—romantic, but no fun for hiking.

tide, the mount becomes an island, reached only by motor launch from Marazion. In winter, you can go over only when the causeway is dry.

A Benedictine monastery, the gift of Edward the Confessor, stood on this spot in the 11th century. The castle now has a collection of armor and antique furniture. A tea garden is on the island, as well as a National Trust restaurant, both open in summer. The steps up to the castle are steep and rough, so wear sturdy shoes. To avoid disappointment, call the number listed below to check on the tides, especially during winter.

On St. Michael's Mount, Mount's Bay. ℂ **01736/710507.** Admission £5.20 ($9.60) adults, £2.60 ($4.80) children, £13 ($24) family ticket. Apr–Oct Mon–Fri 10:30am–5:30pm (open weekends in summer); Nov–Mar Mon, Wed, and Fri by conducted tour only, which leaves at 11am, noon, 2, and 3pm, weather and tide permitting. Bus nos. 2 or 2A from Penzance to Marazion, the town opposite St. Michael's Mount. Parking £1.50 ($2.80).

Minack Theatre   One of the most unusual theaters in southern England, this open-air amphitheater was cut from the side of a rocky Cornish hill near the village of Porthcurno, 14km (9 miles) southwest of Penzance. Its legendary creator was Rowena Cade, an arts enthusiast and noted eccentric, who began work on the theater after World War I by physically carting off much of the granite from her chosen hillside. On the premises, an exhibition hall showcases her life and accomplishments. She died a very old woman in the 1980s, confident of the enduring appeal of her theater to visitors from around the world.

Up to 750 visitors at a time can sit directly on grass- or rock-covered ledges, sometimes on cushions if they're available, within sight lines of both the actors and a sweeping view out over the ocean. Experienced theatergoers sometimes bring raincoats for protection against the occasional drizzle. Theatrical events are staged by repertory theater companies that travel throughout Britain and performances are likely to include everything from Shakespeare to musical comedy.

Porthcurno. ℂ **01736/810694.** www.minack.com. Theater tickets £7 ($13) adults, £3.50 ($6.50) children; tour tickets £2.50 ($4.65) adults, £1.80 ($3.35) seniors, £1 ($1.85) children. Exhibition hall Oct–Mar daily 10am–4pm; Apr–Sept 9:30am–6pm. Performances end of May to mid-Sept, matinees Wed and Fri at 2pm, evening shows Mon–Fri at 8pm. Leave Penzance on A30 heading toward Land's End; after 5km (3 miles), bear left onto B3283 and follow the signs to Porthcurno.

WHERE TO STAY

Abbey Hotel   This small-scale hotel occupies a stone-sided house that was erected in 1660 on the site of a 12th-century abbey that was demolished by Henry VIII. On a narrow side street on raised terraces that overlook the panorama of Penzance Harbour, behind the hotel is a medieval walled garden that was part of the original abbey. Bedrooms are furnished with English country-house flair.

Abbey St., Penzance, Cornwall TR18 4AR. ℂ **01736/366906.** Fax 01736/351163. www.theabbeyonline.com. 6 units. Low season £86–£149 ($158–$275) double, £176–£212 ($325–$391) suite; high season £95–£165 ($176–$305) double, £195–£235 ($361–$435) suite. Rates include English breakfast. AE, MC, V. **Amenities:** Restaurant; limited room service; bar; laundry service. *In room:* TV, coffeemaker, hair dryer, iron/ironing board.

Camilla House Hotel ⟨⟩   This comfortable, nicely furnished house is located near the town promenade, within walking distance of shops and restaurants. A local mariner built this house for his family in 1836. The small to midsize bedrooms will give you the feeling of being "at home." Susan and Simon Chapman are most helpful in providing tourist information for attractions in Penzance and surrounding areas. They're also agents for the Skybus (airplane) and Scillonian III (ferry) and book day trips to the Isles of Scilly. A delicious English breakfast is served in a charming dining room. The facility is completely nonsmoking.

12 Regent Terrace, Penzance, Cornwall. ℂ and fax **01736/363771.** www.camillahouse-hotel.co.uk. 8 units. £50–£70 ($93–$130) double. Rates include English breakfast. AE, MC, V. **Amenities:** Breakfast room; bar; lounge. *In room:* TV, coffeemaker, hair dryer, no phone.

Ennys ⟨⟩ *Finds*   Once a flower farm, Ennys produces mainly vegetables today. Owned by Jill Charlton, this Cornish granite farmhouse has a slate roof; its front section dates back to the 17th century, and other portions are thought to be much

---

Finds A Fishing Village & Artists' Colony

From Penzance, a promenade leads to Newlyn, another fishing village of infinite charm on Mount's Bay. In fact, its much-painted harbor seems to have more fishing craft than Penzance. Stanhope Forbes founded an art school in Newlyn, and in recent years, the village has achieved a growing reputation for its artists' colony, attracting both serious painters and Sunday sketchers. From Penzance, the old fishing cottages and crooked lanes of Newlyn are reached by bus.

---

older. The bedrooms are furnished in an old-fashioned farmhouse style with patchwork quilts and four-poster beds; two have shower-only bathrooms and three have shower/tub combination bathrooms. The hostess prepares an afternoon Cornish-style cream tea. Guests can enjoy a large flower garden, a heated swimming pool, and a grass tennis court. This is a nonsmoking establishment.

St. Hilary, Penzance, Cornwall TR20 982. ✆ 01736/740262. www.ennys.co.uk. 5 units. £70–£95 ($130–$176) double, £100–£130 ($185–$241) family suite. Rates include English breakfast. MC, V. Closed Nov–Mar 15. **Amenities:** Dining room; outdoor pool; tennis court. *In room:* TV, coffeemaker, hair dryer, no phone.

Tarbert Hotel   This dignified granite-and-stucco house lies about a 2-minute walk northwest of the town center. Some of the small to midsize rooms retain original high ceilings and elaborate cove moldings. Each room has comfortable furniture and a well-kept shower-only bathroom. Recent improvements include a new reception area, a completely refurbished bar and lounge, and a sun patio.

11–12 Clarence St., Penzance, Cornwall TR18 2NU. ✆ 01736/363758. Fax 01736/331336. www.tarbert-hotel.co.uk. 12 units. £64–£84 ($118–$155) double. Rates include English breakfast. AE, MC, V. Closed Jan 5–Feb 15. **Amenities:** Restaurant; bar; laundry service. *In room:* TV, coffeemaker, hair dryer, safe.

WHERE TO DINE

The Nelson Bar, in the Union Hotel on Chapel Street in Penzance (✆ **01736/ 362319**), is known for its robust pub grub and collection of Nelsoniana. It's the spot where the admiral's death at Trafalgar was first revealed to the English people. Lunch is served Monday to Friday and dinner is served Monday to Saturday only.

Harris's Restaurant ₢ FRENCH/ENGLISH   Down a narrow cobblestone street off Market Jew Street, this warm, candlelit place has a relaxed atmosphere and is your best bet for a meal. A beacon of light against the culinary bleakness of Penzance, Harris's offers dining in two small rooms. The seasonally adjusted menu emphasizes local produce, including seafood and game. Dishes may include roast wild venison with caraway seeds, or John Dory in a bed of fresh spinach with a white wine and saffron sauce.

46 New St. ✆ 01736/364408. Reservations recommended. Main courses £15–£23 ($28–$43). AE, MC, V. Mon–Sat noon–2pm and 7–10pm. Closed 3 weeks in winter.

The Turk's Head ₢₢ ENGLISH/INTERNATIONAL   Dating from 1233, this inn, said to be the oldest in Penzance, serves the finest food of any pub in town. In summer, drinkers overflow into the garden. Inside, the inn is decorated in a mellow style, as befits its age, with flatirons and other artifacts hanging from its timeworn beams. Meals include fishermen's pie, local seafood, and chicken curry, and prime quality steaks including rib-eye. See the chalkboards for the daily specials.

49 Chapel St. ✆ 01736/363093. Reservations not needed. Main courses £6–£15 ($11–$28); bar snacks £3.50–£6 ($6.50–$11). AE, MC, V. Daily 11am–3pm. From the rail station, turn left just past Lloyd's Bank.

4 The Isles of Scilly ⭐

43km (27 miles) SW of Land's End

Several miles off the Cornish coast, the **Isles of Scilly** are warmed by the Gulf Stream to the point where semitropical plants thrive. In some winters they never see signs of frost. They're the first landfall most oceangoing passengers see on journeys from North America. Charles, the Prince of Wales (who is the duke of Cornwall as well), makes regular visits to Scilly, which he regards as a jewel in the duchy of Cornwall's crown.

Five inhabited and more than 100 uninhabited islands are in the group. Some are only a few square miles, whereas others, such as the largest, St. Mary's, encompass some 77 sq. km (30 square miles). Three of these islands—Tresco, St. Mary's, and St. Agnes—attract visitors from the mainland. Early flowers are the main export and tourism is the main industry.

The Isles of Scilly figured prominently in the myths and legends of ancient Greece and Rome; in Celtic legend, they were inhabited entirely by holy men. More ancient burial mounds are on these islands than anywhere else in southern England, and artifacts have clearly established that people lived here more than 4,000 years ago. Today little is left of this long history for visitors to see.

St. Mary's is the capital, with about seven-eighths of the total population of all the islands, and it's here that the ship from the mainland docks at Hugh Town. However, if you'd like to make this a day visit, we recommend the helicopter flight from Penzance to Tresco, the neighboring island, where you can enjoy a day's walk through 297 hectares (735 acres), mostly occupied by the Abbey Gardens.

ESSENTIALS

GETTING THERE   You can fly by plane or helicopter. **Isles of Scilly Skybus Ltd.** (© 01736/785220) operates 2 to 20 flights per day, depending on the season, between Penzance's Land's End Airport and Hugh Town on St. Mary's Island. Flight time on the eight-passenger fixed-wing planes is 15 minutes each way. The round-trip fare is £75 ($139) for a same-day return or £108 ($196) if you plan to stay overnight.

A helicopter service run by **British International Helicopters,** Penzance Heliport Eastern Green (© 01736/363871 for recorded information; www. scillyhelicopter.co.uk), operates, weather permitting, up to 26 helicopter flights, Monday through Saturday, between Penzance, St. Mary's, and Tresco. Flight time is 20 minutes from Penzance to either island. A same-day round-trip fare is £84 ($155); it's £122 ($222), if you choose to overnight on the island. A bus, whose timing coincides with the departure of each flight, runs to the heliport from the railway station in Penzance for £1.50 ($2.80) per person each way.

The rail line ends in Penzance (see "Getting There," in section 3, above).

Slower, but more cadenced and contemplative, is a ship leaving from the **Isles of Scilly Travel Centre,** on Quay Street in Penzance (© 0845/710-5555 toll-free from anywhere in the U.K., or 01736/362207; www.islesofscilly-travel.co.uk). It departs at least 6 days a week between April and October, requiring 2 hours and 40 minutes for the segment between Penzance and Hugh Town, with an additional 20 or so minutes for the second leg of the trip, which is from Hugh Town to Tresco. It departs Monday through Friday at 9:15am, returning from St. Mary's at 4:30pm. Saturday departures usually follow the Monday through Friday timing, but not always, as the managers sometimes add a second Saturday sailing to accommodate weekend holidaymakers, depending on the season. Between November and March there is no service. Depending on the time of year, a same-day round-trip ticket from Penzance to St. Mary's costs £32 ($59) for adults and £16 ($30) for children 15 and under.

VISITOR INFORMATION **St. Mary's Tourist Information Office,** at High Street, St. Mary's (© **01720/422536**), is open November to March, Monday to Friday 9am to 5pm; April to October, Monday to Friday 8:30am to 6pm, and Saturday from 8am to 6pm.

ST. MARY'S

To get around St. Mary's, cars are available but hardly necessary. The **Island Bus Service** charges £2 ($3.70) from one island point to another; children ride for half fare.

Bicycles are one of the most practical means of transport. **Buccabu Bicycle Rentals,** The Strand, St. Mary's (© and fax **01720/422289**), is the only bike-rental outfit. They stock "shopper's cycles" with 3 speeds, "hybrid" bikes with 6 to 12 speeds, and 18-speed mountain bikes. All are available at prices ranging from £4 to £6 ($7.40–$11) daily. A £10 ($19) deposit is required.

For the best selections of island crafts, visit **Phoenix,** Portmellon Industrial Estate, St. Mary's (© **01720/422900**). At this studio, you can watch original artifacts being made into stained glass. The shops also sell a wide assortment of gifts, including jewelry and leaded lights and souvenirs.

Isles of Scilly Perfumery, Porthloo Studios, St. Mary's (© **01720/423304**), a 10-minute walk from the center of Hugh Town, is packed with intriguing gifts, made from plants grown on the isles—everything from a delicate shell-shaped soap to fine fragrances, cosmetics, potpourri, and other accessories.

Isles of Scilly Museum, on Church Street in St. Mary's (© **01720/422337**), illustrates the history of the Scillies from 2500 B.C., with drawings, artifacts from wrecked ships, and assorted relics discovered on the islands. A locally themed exhibit changes annually. It's open from Easter to October, Monday through Saturday from 10am to noon and 1:30 to 4:30pm; and June through September, also daily from 7:30 to 9pm; off season, only on Wednesday from 2 to 4pm. Admission is £1.25 ($2.30) for adults and 60p ($1.10) for children.

WHERE TO STAY

Star Castle Hotel 𝕲 𝒦𝒾𝒹𝓈   This hotel, built as a castle in 1593 to defend the Isles of Scilly against Spanish attacks in retaliation for the 1588 defeat of the armada, offers views out to sea, and over town and harbor. The great kitchen has a huge fireplace where a whole ox could be roasted. A young Prince of Wales (later King Charles II) took shelter here in 1643 when he was being hunted by Cromwell and his parliamentary forces. In 1933, another Prince of Wales officiated at the opening of the castle as a hotel—the man who succeeded to the throne as King Edward VIII but was never crowned. The 18 rooms in the garden annex are extra-large units opening directly onto the gardens. Eight double rooms and four single rooms are in the castle. The rooms in the castle are full of more character, including 10 rooms with four-poster beds and beamed ceilings, although the garden apartments are more spacious and comfortable. Seventeen rooms are large enough for families. All units have a bathroom with a shower-tub combination.

The Garrison, St. Mary's, Isles of Scilly TR21 0JA. © **01720/422317.** Fax 01720/422343. www.star-castle. co.uk. 34 units. £55–£130 ($102–$241) per person. Rates include half board. MC, V. Closed Nov to mid-Mar. **Amenities:** 2 restaurants; bar; lounge; indoor pool; outdoor tennis court; game room; room service; laundry service. *In room:* TV, coffeemaker, hair dryer.

WHERE TO DINE

Chez Michel FRENCH   The finest dining outside the hotels is found at this warm and cozy 24-seat restaurant. The cooks emphasize fresh ingredients, whatever the season. In the heart of town, the restaurant sells beer and wine. Lunches are fairly light, including such standards as a Cornish crab sandwich or a fresh lobster salad made from seafood harvested right off the shores. At night, fare is more elaborate. Count on such delights as Cornish beef filet with white mushroom sauce or baked and crusted fresh sea bass. The breast of duckling with cranberry sauce is another taste treat.

Parade, Hugh Town, St. Mary's. © **01720/422871.** Reservation required for dinner. Lunch £4–£7 ($7.40–$13); dinner £10–£15 ($19–$28). No credit cards. Year-round Tues, Thurs, and Sat 10am–2pm; summer Mon–Sat 6:30–11pm; winter Sat 6:30pm–closing.

TRESCO

No cars or motorbikes are allowed on Tresco, but you can rent bikes by the day; the hotels use a special wagon towed by a farm tractor to transport guests and luggage from the harbor.

Abbey Gardens 🌾 *Finds*   The gardens are the most outstanding feature of Tresco, started by Augustus Smith in the mid-1830s. When he began his work, the area was a barren hillside, a fact visitors now find hard to believe.

The gardens are a nature-lover's dream, with more than 5,000 species of plants from 100 different countries. The old abbey, or priory, now in ruins, was allegedly founded by Benedictine monks in the 11th century, though some historians date it from A.D. 964. Of special interest in the gardens is Valhalla, a collection of nearly 60 figureheads from ships wrecked around the islands; the gaily painted figures from the past have a rather eerie quality, each one a ghost with a different story to tell.

After a visit to the gardens, take a walk through the fields, along paths, and across dunes thick with heather. Flowers, birds, shells, and fish are abundant. Birds are so fearless that they'll land within a foot or so of you and feed happily.

© **01720/424105.** www.tresco.co.uk. Admission £9 ($17) adults, free for children 16 and under. Daily 10am–4pm.

WHERE TO STAY & DINE

Island Hotel Tresco 🌾   This is the finest hotel in the Scillies, located at Old Grimsby near the northeastern shore of Tresco. It was established in 1960 when a late-19th-century stone cottage was enlarged with conservatory-style windows and a series of long and low extensions. Today, the plant-filled interior feels almost Caribbean. Some rooms overlook the sea; others face inland. All are comfortably furnished with easy chairs and storage spaces. Bedrooms range from medium to spacious, and nearly two dozen of them are large enough for families. All units contain well-managed bathrooms with shower-tub combinations. The hotel is noted for its subtropical garden.

Old Grimsby, Tresco, Isles of Scilly, Cornwall TR24 0PU. © **01720/422883.** Fax 01720/423008. www. tresco.co.uk. 48 units. £125–£202 ($231–$374) per person double; £143–£283 ($265–$524) per person suite. Rates include breakfast and dinner. MC, V. Closed Nov to early Mar. **Amenities:** Restaurant; bar; babysitting; laundry service; outdoor pool; tennis court; room service (9am–10pm); rooms for those with limited mobility. *In room:* TV, coffeemaker, hair dryer.

New Inn   An interconnected row of 19th-century fishermen's cottages and shops, the New Inn is situated at the center of the island, beside its unnamed main road. The rooms are tastefully decorated in a modern style in blue and creamy yellow hues; each features matching twin or double beds, and the more expensive units offer sea views. All rooms contain bathrooms with shower-tub combinations.

Tresco, Isles of Scilly, Cornwall TR24 0QQ. ✆ **01720/422844.** Fax 01720/423200. www.tresco.co.uk. 15 units. £87–£115 ($161–$213) per person double. Rates include half board. MC, V. **Amenities:** Restaurant; bar; pool; laundry service. *In room:* TV, coffeemaker, hair dryer.

ST. AGNES

St. Agnes lies farther southwest than any other community in Britain and, luck-ily, remains relatively undiscovered. Much of the area is preserved by the Nature Conservancy Council. Because the main industries are flower farming and fish-ing, it has little pollution; visitors can enjoy crystal-clear waters that are ideal for snorkeling and diving. Little traffic moves on single-track lanes crossing the island; the curving sandbar between St. Agnes and its neighbor, the island of Gugh, is one of the best beaches in the archipelago. The coastline is diverse and a walker's paradise. A simple trail leads to any number of sandy coves, granite outcroppings, flower-studded heaths and meadows, and even a freshwater pool. Sunsets are always romantic and are followed by a brilliant showcase of the night sky. This place of endless natural wonderment is truly soothing.

A boat leaves from the quay at St. Mary's every day April to late October at 10:15am, 12:15, and 2pm. then from November to March once a day at 9:20am, requiring a 15- to 20-minute transfer to St. Agnes, for a round-trip charge of about £6.20 ($11). Boats return on a schedule determined by the tides, usually at 2:15 and again at 4:30pm. The day's transportation schedule is chalked onto a blackboard on the quay at St. Mary's daily. Schedules generally allow you to visit St. Agnes for the day. The boat is operated by the family run company, **Hicks Boating** (✆ **01720/422541**).

WHERE TO STAY

Coastguards   The home of Wendy Hick opens onto excellent sea views from its location near St. Warna's Cove. One of the double rooms has two beds. Accom-modation is one adjacent and roomy cottage, and in two adjacent and roomy cot-tages, and furnished simply but pleasantly with interesting objects. One room has a shower stall and two have only tubs; housekeeping is excellent. The price of half board depends on whether you order a two- or three-course evening meal.

St. Agnes, Isles of Scilly, Cornwall TR22 0PL. ✆ 01720/422373. 2 units. £38 ($70) per person. No credit cards. Closed Nov–Mar. *In room:* Coffeemaker.

WHERE TO DINE

The Turks Head ENGLISH   In a solid-looking building that was constructed in the 1890s as a boathouse, this is the only pub on the island. Prominently located a few steps from the pier, it's run by John and Pauline Dart, who serve pub snacks and solid fare, including steaks and platters of local fish. The pub is the second building after the arrival point of the ferryboats from St. Mary's. Also here is a twin-bedded room with shower and tub, costing £32 ($59) per person including breakfast.

St. Agnes, Isles of Scilly, Cornwall TR22 0PL. ✆ 01720/422434. Main courses £4–£12 ($7.40–$22). AE, MC, V. Daily noon–2:30pm and 6–9pm. Pub daily 10:30am–4:30pm and 6:30–11pm.

5 Mousehole ⊛ & Land's End ⊛

Mousehole: 5km (3 miles) S of Penzance. Land's End: 14km (9 miles) W of Penzance.

Reached by traveling through some of Cornwall's most beautiful countryside, Land's End is literally the end of Britain. The natural grandeur of the place has been somewhat marred by theme-park-type amusements, but the view of the sea crashing against rocks remains undiminished. If you want to stay in the area, you can find accommodations in Mousehole, a lovely Cornish fishing village. If you visit in July and August, you'll need reservations far in advance, as Mousehole doesn't have enough bedrooms to accommodate the summer hordes.

GETTING THERE
From London, journey first to Penzance (see "Getting There," in section 3, earlier in this chapter), then take a local bus for the rest of the journey (Bus A to Mousehole and Bus no. 1 to Land's End). There is frequent service throughout the day.

If you're driving from Penzance, take the B3315 south.

MOUSEHOLE
The Cornish fishing village of Mousehole (pronounced *Mou*-sel) attracts hordes of tourists, who, fortunately, haven't changed it too much. The cottages still sit close to the harbor wall; the fishers still bring in the day's catch; the salts sit around smoking tobacco talking about the good old days; and the lanes are as narrow as ever. About the most exciting thing to happen here was the arrival in the late 16th century of the Spanish galleons, whose sailors sacked and burned the village. In a sheltered cove of Mount's Bay, Mousehole today has developed as the nucleus of an artists' colony.

WHERE TO STAY & DINE
Carn Du   Twin bay windows gaze over the top of the village onto the harbor with its bobbing fishing vessels. The hotel's rooms (all doubles or twins) offer much comfort. Five rooms were recently redecorated. Most units have a shower stall, though two come with a tub-and-shower combination. The owners will arrange sporting options for active vacationers but won't mind if you prefer to sit and relax.

Raginnis Hill, Mousehole, Cornwall TR19 6SS. ℭ and fax **01736/731233**. 4 units. £75–£100 ($139–$185) double. Rates include English breakfast. AE, MC, V. Take B3315 from Newlyn past the village of Sheffield (2.5km/1½ miles) and bear left toward Castallack; after a few hundred feet, turn left to Mousehole, which is signposted; coming down the hill, the Carn Du is on the left facing the sea. **Amenities:** Laundry service; babysitting; bar; rooms for those with limited mobility. *In room:* TV, coffeemaker, safe.

The Ship Inn   This charming pub is located on the harbor in this fishing village. The exterior has a stone facade, and the interior has retained much of the original rustic charm with its black beams and paneling, granite floors, built-in wall benches, and, of course, a nautical motif decorating the bars. The rooms, offering views of the harbor and the bay, have window seats. The rooms are simply furnished and tend to be small but are cozy, each with a compact bathroom with a shower stall or bath.

S. Cliff, Mousehole, Penzance, Cornwall TR19 6QX. ℭ **01736/731234**. 8 units. £60 ($111) double. Rates include English breakfast. MC, V. **Amenities:** Restaurant; 2 bars. *In room:* TV, coffeemaker, hair dryer.

LAND'S END
Craggy Land's End is where England comes to an end. America's coast is 5,299km (3,291 miles) west of the rugged rocks that tumble into the sea beneath Land's End. Some enjoyable cliff walks and panoramic views are available here.

WHERE TO STAY & DINE
Land's End Hotel   This hotel is situated behind a white facade in a complex of buildings rising from the rugged landscape at the end of the main A30 road, the very tip of England. The hotel has a panoramic cliff-top position and is

---

> **Fun Fact** **The End of the Earth**
>
> To ancient Cornish mariners, it was known as *Pen an Wlas* or "the end of the earth," a reference to what is today **Land's End,** the most westerly point on the British mainland. It is at the very tip of the granite peninsula of Penwith, one of the ancient kingdoms of Cornwall. The nearest town to Land's End is Penzance, 16km (10 miles) away. The A30 ends its run at Land's Inn, which is 1,407km (874 miles) from John O'Groats, which is the most northerly point of Britain, lying in Scotland.

---

exposed to the wind and sea spray. The rooms are attractively furnished and well maintained. Rooms range from small to spacious, especially the premier or family rooms. Three contain four-poster beds and offer sea views. Some rooms are reserved for nonsmokers. Bathrooms are small but have shower-tub combinations and adequate shelf space.

Land's End, Sennen, Cornwall TR19 7AA. ✆ **01736/871844.** Fax 01736/871599. 34 units. £96–£180 ($178–$333) double. Rates include dinner and breakfast. AE, MC, V. **Amenities:** Restaurant; bar; limited room service; nonsmoking rooms; laundry service. *In room:* TV, dataport, coffeemaker, hair dryer, iron, trouser press.

6 The Artists' Colony of St. Ives ★★

514km (319 miles) SW of London; 34km (21 miles) NE of Land's End; 16km (10 miles) NE of Penzance

This north-coast fishing village, with its sandy beaches, narrow streets, and well-kept cottages, is England's most famous artists' colony. The artists settled in many years ago and have integrated with the fishers and their families. They've been here long enough to have developed several schools or "splits," and they almost never overlap—except in the pubs. The old battle continues between the followers of the representational and the devotees of the abstract in art, with each group recruiting young artists all the time. In addition, potters, weavers, and other craftspeople all work, exhibit, and sell in this area.

St. Ives becomes virtually impossible to visit in August, when you're likely to be trampled underfoot by busloads of tourists, mostly the English themselves. However, in spring and early fall the pace is much more relaxed.

ESSENTIALS

GETTING THERE   There is frequent service throughout the day between London's Paddington Station and the rail terminal at St. Ives. The trip takes 8 hours and 20 minutes. Call ✆ **0845/748-4950** or visit www.wessextrains.co.uk for schedules and information.

Several coaches a day run from London's Victoria Coach Station to St. Ives. The trip takes 7 hours. Call ✆ **0870/580-8080** or visit www.nationalexpress. com for schedules and information.

If you're driving, take the A30 across Cornwall, heading northwest at the junction with the B3306, heading to St. Ives on the coast. During the summer, many streets in the center of town are closed to vehicles. You may want to leave your car in the Lelant Saltings Car Park, 5km (3 miles) from St. Ives on the A3074, and take the regular train service into town, an 11-minute journey. Departures are every half-hour. It's free to all car passengers and drivers, and the parking charge is £8 to £11 ($15–$20) per day. You can also use the large Trenwith Car Park, close to the town center, for £1.50 ($2.80), and then walk down to the shops and harbor or take a bus that costs 40p (75¢) per person.

VISITOR INFORMATION The **Tourist Information Centre** is at the Guildhall, Street-an-Pol (© **01736/796297**). From January to mid-May and from September to December, hours are Monday through Friday from 9am to 5pm, and Saturday from 10am to 4pm. From mid-May to August, hours are Monday through Saturday from 9am to 6pm and Sunday from 10am to 4pm.

SEEING THE SIGHTS

Barbara Hepworth Museum and Garden ⭐ Dame Barbara Hepworth lived at Trewyn from 1949 until her death in 1975 at the age of 72. In her will she asked that her working studio be turned into a museum where future visitors could see where she lived and created her world-famous sculpture. Today, the museum and garden are virtually just as she left them. On display are about 47 sculptures and drawings, covering the period from 1928 to 1974, as well as photographs, documents, and other Hepworth memorabilia. You can also visit her workshops, housing a selection of tools and some unfinished carvings.

Barnoon Hill. © **01736/796226**. Admission £4.25 ($7.85) adults, £2.25 ($4.15) students, free for seniors and children under 18. Mar–Oct daily 10am–5:30pm; Nov–Feb Tues–Sun 10am–4:30pm.

Tate Gallery St. Ives ⭐⭐ This branch of London's famous Tate Gallery exhibits changing groups of work from the Tate Gallery's preeminent collection of St. Ives painting and sculpture, dating from about 1925 to 1975. The gallery is administered jointly with the Barbara Hepworth Museum (see above). The collection includes works by artists associated with St. Ives, including Alfred Wallis, Ben Nicholson, Barbara Hepworth, Naum Gabo, Peter Lanyon, Terry Frost, Patrick Heron, and Roger Hilton. All artists shown here had a decisive effect on the development of painting in the United Kingdom in the second half of the 20th century. About 100 works are on display at all times.

Boasting dramatic sea views, the museum occupies a spectacular site overlooking Porthmear Beach, close to the home of Alfred Wallis and to the studios used by many of the St. Ives artists.

Porthmear Beach. © **01736/796226**. www.tate.org.uk. Admission £4.75 ($8.80) adults, £2.50 ($4.65) students, free for seniors and children under 18. Mar–Oct daily 10am–5:30pm; Nov–Feb Tues–Sun 10am–4:30pm. Closes occasionally to change displays; call for dates.

WHERE TO STAY

Garrack Hotel and Restaurant *Value* This small vine-covered hotel, once a private home, commands a panoramic view of St. Ives and Porthmear Beach from its .8-hectare (2-acre) knoll at the head of a narrow lane. This is one of the friendliest and most efficiently run mid-priced hotels on the entire coast, and each room is furnished in a warm, homey manner. Most units are midsize, but two rooms are large enough to accommodate families; one is suitable for persons with disabilities. The small bathrooms are well maintained and have shower-tub combinations.

Burthallan Lane, Higher Ayr, St. Ives, Cornwall TR26 3AA. © **01736/796199**. Fax 01736/798955. www.garrack.com. 18 units. Low season £135–£161 ($250–$298) double; high season £140–£167 ($259–$309) double. Rates include English breakfast. AE, DC, MC, V. Take B3306 to the outskirts of St. Ives; after passing a gas station on the left, take the 3rd road left toward Portmeor Beach and Ayr and after 180m (600 ft.) look for the hotel sign. **Amenities:** Restaurant; 2 bars; indoor pool; health club; sauna; spa; limited room service; laundry service. *In room:* TV, dataport, coffeemaker, hair dryer, iron/ironing board.

Pedn-Olva Hotel The panoramic view of the bay afforded from its restaurant and most rooms is the outstanding feature of this establishment. It was built in the 1870s as the home of the paymaster for the local mines, before being transformed into a hotel in the 1930s. The rooms are all nonsmoking and furnished in a modern style, with comfortable twin or double beds. Seven of the rooms are in a less desirable annex where the chambers are more sterile and lack the character of the main building. Five rooms are large enough for families. There are sun terraces with lounges, umbrellas, and a swimming pool for those who don't want to walk down the rocky path to Porthminster Beach. If you crave solitude, however, scramble down the rocks to sunbathe just above the gentle rise and fall of the sea.

The Warren, St. Ives, Cornwall TR26 2EA. ☏ **01736/796222.** Fax 01736/797710. www.westcountryhotel rooms.co.uk. 30 units. From £55–£68 ($102–$126) per person. Rates include English breakfast. Half board £65–£82 ($120–$152) per person. AE, MC, V. Parking £3 ($5.55). **Amenities:** Restaurant; bar; outdoor pool; coin-operated laundry; rooms for those with limited mobility. *In room:* TV, coffeemaker, hair dryer, iron/ironing board.

Porthminster Hotel ⓖ   This leading Cornish Riviera resort, the town's best address, stands on the main road into town amid a beautiful garden and within easy walking distance of Porthminster Beach. Large and imposing, the Porthminster is a traditional choice for visitors to St. Ives. With its 1894 Victorian architecture, it's warm and inviting. The spacious rooms are well furnished, although with a bland decor. All units have well-maintained bathrooms with mainly shower-tub combinations. Over the years the bedrooms have been considerably upgraded, and the standard of comfort is high here.

The Terrace, St. Ives, Cornwall TR26 2BN. ☏ **01736/795221.** Fax 01736/797043. www.porthminster-hotel. co.uk. 43 units. £62–£77 ($115–$142) per person. Rates include half board. AE, DC, MC, V. **Amenities:** Restaurant; bar; 2 pools; sauna; limited room service; laundry service. *In room:* TV, coffeemaker, hair dryer.

WHERE TO DINE

Garrack Hotel and Restaurant ENGLISH/INTERNATIONAL   The dining room at the Garrack Hotel produces excellent cuisine and, whenever possible, uses fresh ingredients from their own garden. The hotel dining room, which is open to nonguests, offers a set dinner, plus a cold buffet or snacks at the bar. The menu features some of the best English dishes, such as roast shoulder of lamb with mint sauce, plus a wide sampling of continental fare, perhaps including a roast roulade of salmon with sesame crust and a cucumber sauce. Live lobsters swim in the seawater tank—until they're removed for preparation and cooked to order. Cheese and dessert trolleys are at your service.

In the Garrack Hotel, Burthallan Lane, Higher Ayr. ☏ **01736/796199.** Reservations recommended. Main courses £12–£20 ($22–$37); fixed-price 4-course dinner £26 ($47). AE, DC, MC, V. Daily 7–9pm.

EN ROUTE TO PORT ISAAC

The stretch of coastline between St. Ives and Port Isaac doesn't have the charm of Cornwall's eastern coast. The fastest way to get to Port Isaac is to take the A30 northeast. However the B3301, hugging close to the Atlantic Ocean, is the more scenic route.

Heading north along the B3301, your first stop will be the estuary town of **Hayle,** once known for its tin and copper mines, but now a beach resort with miles of sand fronting the often wind-tossed Atlantic. Going north from here, the first attraction is **St. Agnes Beacon** (it's signposted). This is the most panoramic belvedere along this wild stretch of north Cornish coastline. At 191m (628 ft.), you can see all the way from Trevose Head in the northeast to St. Michael's Mount in the southwest—that is, if the weather's clear. It's often rainy and cloudy.

The first town of any importance is **Newquay,** a resort with sandy beaches at the foot of the cliffs, opening onto a sheltered bay. Taking its name from a new quay built in 1439, it attracts everyone from young surfers to elderly ladies who check into B&Bs along the harbor for long stays. Newquay is a rather commercial

---

Finds An Escape to Brigadoon

One of the loveliest spots in the west of England is **St. Just in Roseland** ⟨★★⟩, a tiny hamlet of stone cottage terraces and a church dating from the 1200s. It's as if time stood still here. Locals call it their Garden of Eden because of its subtropical foliage including rhododendrons and magnolias. There are even palm trees—in England, no less. St. Just lies 14km (9 miles) south of Truro. To visit it, drive to Trelissick, 9.5km (6 miles) north of Falmouth on B3289. Here you can take a chain-drawn car ferry, **King Harry Ferry** (ⓒ **01872/862312;** www.kingharryferry.co.uk), which makes several trips daily over to the isolated Roseland Peninsula and St. Just. The cost is £6 ($11) per car (same day return), 50p (95¢) per bicycle, and 20p (35¢) for passengers.

---

town, lacking the charm of St. Ives or Port Isaac, but its beaches attract families in summer. At night, pubs fill up with surfers ready to party.

If you'd like to stay over in Newquay, we recommend the **Hotel Bristol, Narrowcliff** (ⓒ **800/528-1234** in the U.S., or 01637/875181; fax 01637/879347; www.hotelbristol.co.uk). This redbrick hotel overlooking the beach has 74 well-furnished rooms that cost £92 to £176 ($170–$326) double, including an English breakfast. This friendly and inviting place is popular with families. Facilities include an indoor swimming pool, sauna, beauty salon, game room, and solarium; American Express, Diners Club, MasterCard, and Visa are accepted.

Back on the road again, the next important stop is **Padstow.** This town has a long and ancient history. It reached its heyday in the 19th century when it was an important port. Unfortunately, ships became too big to pass the sand bar (called "The Doom Bar") at the estuary mouth. Walk along its quay-lined harbor and explore its narrow streets. At the end of the quay stands **St. Petroc's Church** and **Prideaux Place,** a Tudor house with 18th-century battlements.

Try to arrive in Padstow in time for lunch, because a restaurant—simply called **Seafood** ⟨★⟩, at Riverside (ⓒ **01841/532700**)—offers the best cuisine along this stretch of coastline. Here, Rick Stein selects the best "fruits of the sea," which he crafts into French-influenced dishes such as grillade of monkfish and Dover sole with a sauce vierge of garlic, sun-dried tomatoes, and herbs. Stein also rents 13 rooms above the restaurant, bistro, and coffee shop for £110 to £200 ($204–$370) double per night including breakfast; two have private balconies opening onto harbor views. The bar is open all day; lunch is served from noon to 2pm and dinner is served from 7 to 10pm, Monday through Sunday; American Express, MasterCard, and Visa are accepted.

7 Port Isaac ⟨★⟩

428km (266 miles) SW of London; 23km (14 miles) SW of Tintagel; 14km (9 miles) N of Wadebridge

Port Isaac remains the most unspoiled fishing village on the north Cornish coastline, in spite of large numbers of summer visitors. By all means, wander through its winding, narrow lanes, gazing at the whitewashed fishing cottages with their rainbow trims.

ESSENTIALS
GETTING THERE   Bodmin is the nearest railway station. It lies on the main line from London (Paddington Station) to Penzance (about a 4½–5-hr. trip). Call

ℭ **0845/748-4950** or visit www.wessextrains.co.uk. Many hotels will send a car to pick up guests at the Bodmin station or you can take a taxi. If you take a bus from Bodmin, you'll have to change buses at Wadebridge, and connections are not good. Driving time from Bodmin to Port Isaac is 40 minutes.

A bus from Wadebridge goes to Port Isaac about six times a day. It's maintained by the Prout Brothers Bus Co. Wadebridge is a local bus junction to many other places in the rest of England.

If you're driving from London, take the M4 west, then drive south on the M5. Head west again at the junction with the A39, continuing to the junction with the B3267, which you follow until you reach the signposted cutoff for Port Isaac.

WHERE TO STAY & DINE

Port Gaverne Hotel ⭒   Built in the 17th century as a coastal inn for fishermen needing a rest from their seagoing labors, Port Gaverne, 1km (½ mile) east of Port Isaac, today caters to vacationing families and couples. It's the port's best bet for food and lodgings. The small to midsize bedrooms are traditionally furnished. The bathrooms have adequate shelf space and shower-tub combinations. Its painted facade is draped with vines. Clusters of antiques and early photographs of Cornwall add somewhat homey touches.

Port Gaverne, Port Isaac, Cornwall PL29 3SQ. ℭ **01208/880244.** Fax 01208/880151. www.chycor.co.uk/hotels/port-gaverne-inn/index.htm. 14 units. £75–£95 ($139–$176) double. Rates include English breakfast. MC, V. **Amenities:** Restaurant; bar; coin-operated laundry. *In room:* TV, coffeemaker, hair dryer, iron.

Slipway Hotel ⭒   Built in 1527, with major additions made in the early 1700s, this waterside building has seen more uses than any other structure in town, serving as everything from fishing cottages to the headquarters of the first bank here. The building was once a lifeboat station for rescuing sailors stranded on stormy seas. The cozy bedrooms have compact bathrooms with shower stalls.

The hotel is also known for its restaurant where ultrafresh seafood is the chef's specialty. Its main dining room contains a minstrel's gallery and lies adjacent to a popular bar frequented by both visitors and locals. At lunch, sandwich, fish and chips, and seafood pancakes are served. Dinner is more elaborate, featuring fish directly from the nets of local fisherman. *Note:* The hotel's steep and narrow staircases are not suitable for young kids or persons with limited mobility.

The Harbour Front, Port Isaac, Cornwall PL29 3RH. ℭ **01208/880264.** www.portisaac.com/slipwayhotel. 10 units. £90–£100 ($167–$185) double; £110–£140 ($204–$259) suite. Rates include English breakfast. AE, MC, V. Closed Jan to mid-Feb. **Amenities:** Restaurant; bar; lounge. *In room:* TV, dataport, coffeemaker, hair dryer, iron/ironing board.

8 Tintagel Castle: King Arthur's Legendary Lair ⭒⭒

425km (264 miles) SW of London; 79km (49 miles) NW of Plymouth

On a wild stretch of the Atlantic coast, **Tintagel** is forever linked with the legends of King Arthur, Lancelot, and Merlin. So compelling was this legend that medieval writers treated it as a tale of chivalry, even though the real Arthur, if he lived, probably did so around the time of the Roman or Saxon invasions. (Some scholars have speculated that if Arthur existed at all, he might not have been a king but a warlord; his reign may have lasted 3 decades, leading native Britons who were fighting off the Saxon invasion.)

Despite its universal adoption throughout Europe, the legend initially developed and blossomed in Wales and southern England. The story was polished and given a literary form for the first time by Geoffrey of Monmouth around

1135. Combining Celtic myth and Christian and classical symbolism (usually without crediting sources), Geoffrey forged a fictional history of Britain whose form, shape, and elevated values were centered around King Arthur. Dozens of other storytellers embellished the written and oral versions of the tale.

The Arthurian legend has captured the imagination of the British people like no other. Arthur supposedly still lies sleeping, ready to rise and save Britain in its greatest need. The version of the legend by Sir Thomas Malory has become the classic, but there were many others: Edmund Spenser's in the Tudor period; John Milton's in the 17th century; Tennyson's, William Morris's, and Swinburne's in the Victorian age; and T. H. White's and C. S. Lewis's in the 20th century, not to mention the many film treatments.

The legend of King Arthur gained considerable credibility in August 1998 when a stone bearing a Latin inscription referring to King Arthur was uncovered at the ancient ruined castle in Tintagel where he was supposed to have been born. The piece of slate, 35cm by 25cm (14 in. by 10 in.), was found in a drain at the castle. For Arthur fans this is the find of a lifetime and is all that is needed to verify the existence of the king.

The 13th-century ruins of the castle that stand here—built on the foundations of a Celtic monastery from the 6th century—are popularly known as King Arthur's Castle. They stand 90m (300 ft.) above the sea on a rocky promontory, and to get to them you must take a long, steep, tortuous walk from the parking lot. In summer, many visitors make the ascent to Arthur's Lair, up 100 rock-cut steps. You can also visit Merlin's Cave at low tide.

The castle is 1km (½ mile) northwest of Tintagel. It's open April through September daily from 10am to 6pm; October daily from 10am to 5pm; and November through March daily from 10am to 4pm. Admission is £3.70 ($6.85) for adults, £2.80 ($5.20) for students and seniors, and £1.90 ($3.50) for children. For information, call © **01840/770328** or go to www.english-heritage.org.uk.

ESSENTIALS

GETTING THERE   The nearest railway station is in Bodmin, which lies on the main rail line from London to Penzance. From Bodmin, you'll have to drive or take a taxi for 30 minutes to get to Tintagel (there's no bus service from Bodmin to Tintagel). For railway inquiries, call © **0845/748-4950** or visit www.wessex trains.co.uk.

By bus, you'll travel from London to Plymouth. One bus a day travels from Plymouth to Tintagel, at 4:20pm, but it takes twice the time (2 hr.) required for a private car, because the bus stops at dozens of small hamlets along the way. For bus schedule information, call © **01209/719988.**

If you're driving, from Exeter, head across Cornwall on the A30, continuing west at the junction with the A395. From this highway, various secondary roads lead to Tintagel.

VISITOR INFORMATION   In Truro, the **Municipal Building,** Boscawen Street (© **01872/274555**), has tourist information and is open from Easter to November, Monday through Friday from 9am to 5:30pm, and Saturday from 9am to 5pm; from November to Easter, it's Monday through Friday from 9am to 5pm.

WHERE TO STAY & DINE IN TINTAGEL

Bossiney House Hotel   The hotel, in its inviting location, is comfortable and in a fairly tranquil and idyllic setting. Bedrooms have a streamlined, modern feel, accompanied by small bathrooms with a combination tub and shower (or

---

Moments **The Haunting Daphne du Maurier Country**

Nothing captures the wild Cornish landscape more than the novels of **Daphne du Maurier** (1907–89), author of *Rebecca*. Beginning west of Tintagel, you can drive for hours, exploring a windswept land of Celtic legend and myth near the Cornish coast. Head for the village of **Bolventor;** du Maurier used the Jamaica Inn here (✆ **01566/86250**) as the setting for her novel of the same name. The name honors its one-time owner, who became prosperous from sugar on his Jamaican plantation; a room in the inn honors the author. Opposite the inn, a small road leads to Dozmary Pool, where "waves wap and the winds wan" and into which Sir Bedivere threw Excalibur at Arthur's behest.

---

else a shower stall). The hotel offers one of the best restaurants in the area, serving excellent Cornish cuisine based on fresh regional produce and especially seafood caught along the coast.

Bossiney Rd., Bossiney, Tintagel, Cornwall PL34 0AX. ✆ 01840/770240. Fax 01840/770501. www.bossiney house.co.uk. 19 units. £58–£70 ($107–$130) double. Rates include English breakfast. AE, MC, V. Closed Jan. Take B3263 1km (½ mile) northeast of Tintagel. **Amenities:** Restaurant; bar; indoor pool; sauna; solarium; rooms for those with limited mobility. *In room:* TV, coffeemaker, hair dryer.

Old Borough House Run by the Dale family, this Cornish house offers thick stone walls, low ceiling beams, and an illustrious history dating from 1558. Most of what stands today was completed in the late 1600s, when it served as the residence for the mayor of Bossiney, the hamlet in which it's situated. The all-nonsmoking accommodations are cozy, antique, and very comfortable. Many of the bedrooms have been recently refurbished and upgraded. Each comes with a well-kept bathroom with a shower-tub combination.

Bossiney, Tintagel, Cornwall PL34 0AY. ✆ 01840/770475. Fax 01840/779000. 8 units. £72–£80 ($133–$148) double. Rates include English breakfast. MC, V. Walk north from the ruins of Tintagel Castle for 10 min. **Amenities:** Restaurant (for guests only); lounge; bar. *In room:* TV, coffeemaker, hair dryer.

12

The Cotswolds

Between Oxford and the River Severn, about a 2-hour drive west of London, the pastoral **Cotswolds** occupy a stretch of grassy limestone hills, deep ravines, and barren plateaus known as *wolds,* Old English for "God's high open land." Ancient villages with names like **Stow-on-the-Wold, Wotton-under-Edge,** and **Moreton-in-Marsh** dot this bucolic area, most of which is in Gloucestershire, with portions in Oxfordshire, Wiltshire, and Worcestershire.

Made rich by wool from their sheep, the landowners here invested in some of the finest domestic architecture in Europe, distinctively built of honey-brown **Cotswold stone.** The gentry didn't neglect spiritual duties, for some of the simplest Cotswold hamlets have churches that, in style and architectural detail, seem far beyond their modest means.

You'll also see some **thatched cottages** in the Cotswolds, which are fiercely protected by local bylaws, yet endlessly impractical because of their need for frequent repair, maintenance, and replacement. (They also cost a fortune to insure against fire!) More common are Cotswolds roof shingles fashioned from split slabs of stone, which required massive buttressing from medieval carpenters as a means of supporting the weight of the roof. Buildings erected since the 1700s, however, usually have slate roofs.

You'll really want to rent a car and drive through the Cotswolds at your own pace. This way, you can spend hours viewing the land of winding goat paths, rolling hills, and sleepy hamlets. One of the reasons to visit the Cotswolds is to take advantage of its natural beauty.

Mobbed by tourists, **Broadway,** with its 16th-century stone houses and cottages, is justifiably the most popular base for touring this area, but we suggest you also head for **Bibury, Painswick,** or other small villages to capture the true charm of the Cotswolds. You'll find the widest range of hotels and facilities in **Cheltenham,** once one of England's most fashionable spas, with a wealth of Regency architecture. And families may head to **Birdland,** in Bourton-on-the-Water, where you can see some 1,200 birds of 361 different species.

Biking & Hiking through the Cotswolds Biking the country roads of the Cotswolds is one of the best ways to experience the quiet beauty of the area. **Country Lanes,** The Railway Station, Moreton-in-Marsh, Gloucestershire GL56 0AA (© **01608/650065;** www.countrylanes.co.uk), offers visitors that opportunity. The company rents 21-speed bicycles fully equipped with mudguards, a water bottle, lock and key, a rear carrier rack, and, of course, safety helmets. Daily rental rates are £15 ($28) for adult bikes and £10 ($19) for bikes for the younger folks, with reduced rate opportunities for longer hires.

Country Lanes also has self-guided day trips, so you can ride at your own pace. You'll get an easy-to-follow route sheet. As you explore, you pass manor farms and pretty cottages of honey-colored stone. Several villages are also on the path, and the Hidcote Manor Garden is a perfect spot to relax if your legs tire of pedaling. The 16km, 32km, or 45km (10-, 20-, or 28-mile) trips end at the Café Dijon, where you're served afternoon tea in the garden. The £30 ($56) price includes everything listed above. Advanced booking by credit card is essential, either by phone or online.

This is also one of the most famous regions of England for hiking. With such a large area in which to ramble, it's a good idea to know where you are (and aren't) welcome. The **Cotswold Voluntary Wardens Service,** Shire Hall, Gloucester (© **01451/862000**),

offers free brochures highlighting trails and paths.

The Wayfarers, 174 Bellevue Ave., Newport, RI 02840 (© **800/249-4620;** www.thewayfarers.com), sponsors about four Cotswold walks a year from May to October. The cost of a 1-week tour is $2,595 per person, including all meals and snacks, first-class accommodations with private bathroom along the route, and admission to attractions.

If you'd like to walk and explore on your own without a guide, you can get data from the **Cheltenham Tourist Information Centre,** 77 The Promenade (© **01242/522878**). The center sells a Cotswold Way map.

1 Tetbury

182km (113 miles) W of London; 42km (27 miles) NE of Bristol

In the rolling Cotswolds, Tetbury was out of the tourist mainstream until the heir to the British throne and his beautiful bride took up residence at the Macmillan Place, a Georgian building situated on nearly 141 hectares (350 acres). Then, crowds came here to catch a glimpse of Prince Charles riding horses and Princess Di shopping. (Today, folks keep an eye out for Charles and Camilla Parker-Bowles, who are occasionally spotted driving by en route to their homes.) Though it can't be seen from the road, the nine-bedroom Windsor mansion, **Highgrove,** is 2.5km (11/2 miles) southwest of Tetbury on the way to Westonbirt Arboretum.

Tetbury itself has a 17th-century market hall and a number of antiques shops and boutiques. The town's inns weren't cheap before royalty moved in, and the prices certainly have not dropped since then.

ESSENTIALS

GETTING THERE Frequent daily trains run from London's Paddington Station to Kemble, 11km (7 miles) east of Tetbury. For more information and schedules, call © **0845/748-4950** or visit www.wessextrains.co.uk. You can then take a bus from there to Tetbury.

National Express buses leave London's Victoria Coach Station with direct service to Cirencester, 16km (10 miles) northeast of Tetbury. For information, call © **0870/580-8080** or visit www.nationalexpress.com. Several buses a day connect Cirencester to Tetbury.

If you're driving from London, take the M40 northwest to Oxford, continuing along the A40 to the junction with the A429. Drive south to Cirencester, where you connect with the A433 southwest into Tetbury.

VISITOR INFORMATION The **Tourist Information Centre** in Tetbury, 33 Church St. (© **01666/503552**), is open March through October, Monday through Saturday from 9:30am to 4:30pm, and November through February, Monday through Saturday from 10am to 1pm.

The Cotswolds

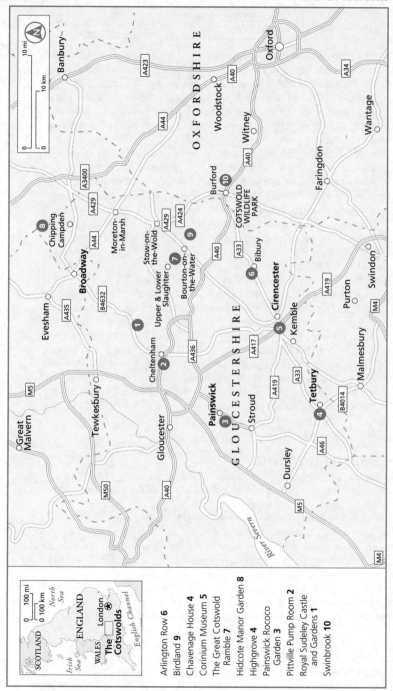

Arlington Row **6**
Birdland **9**
Chavenage House **4**
Corinium Museum **5**
The Great Cotswold Ramble **7**
Hidcote Manor Garden **8**
Highgrove **4**
Painswick Rococo Garden **3**
Pittville Pump Room **2**
Royal Sudeley Castle and Gardens **1**
Swinbrook **10**

Hiking the Cotswold Way

One of the under-publicized pleasures of a sojourn in the Cotswolds involves an overland pedestrian ramble, the Cotswold Way, that's only for the hardy or hardy wannabes. The idea for the establishment of such a walking trail originated in the 1950s, though formalized rights of way interconnecting the 167km (104-mile) path weren't finalized until 1968. Since then, the number of hikers trekking along the path has increased every year.

The path stretches from Chipping Campden, at the northern edge of the Cotswolds, to Bath, following a meandering route that's clearly marked with bright yellow signs at virtually every intersection en route. Know in advance that the topography abounds in rolling hills, whose interplay contributes so richly to the beauty of the area. Local statisticians say that the distance you ascend following the northbound route (Bath to Chipping Campden) is 3,990m (13,300 ft.), and the distance you ascend along the southbound route (Chipping Campden to Bath) is 3,870m (12,900 ft.).

We recommend the southbound route, because it's by far the less well traveled and you won't find yourself in "traffic jams" caused by groups of hikers meandering at speeds different from your own.

Regardless of the direction you follow, don't underestimate the effort it takes to walk along this path: Tourist officials in Chipping Campden report that most participants take between 7 and 8 days to walk the entire stretch of the path, and that many hikers emerge at the end of their experience blistered, sunburned, rain-drenched, and exhausted.

Despite its discomforts, the allure of the walking path is potent, the panoramas spectacular, and the sense of medieval England very

EXPLORING THE TOWN

Everything in Tetbury is conveniently located in the center of the village; you can easily spend a morning wandering in and out of the many antiques shops and gazing up at the old houses.

The **Parish Church of St. Mary the Virgin,** built between 1777 and 1781, has been hailed as the best Georgian Gothic church in the country. Extensive restoration has returned the interior to its original 18th-century appearance, and the spire is among England's tallest. For information, call ② **01666/502333;** it's more than likely the vicar himself will come on the line.

One of the finest examples of a Cotswold-pillared market house is the 1655 **Market House of Tetbury.** It's still in use, hosting one of the most interesting markets in the Cotswolds, in the antique stalls of its meeting hall. Try to schedule a Wednesday visit here to sift through the bric-a-brac.

After the market, head for **Chipping Steps.** The Chipping (market) was for centuries the site of "mop fairs," where farmhands and domestic staff offered themselves for employment. Many surrounding buildings have medieval origins.

Another place to explore is **Gumstoll Hill,** one of Tetbury's most ancient streets and now famous for its annual Woolsack Races. Legend has it that at the appealing. The planners who laid out the walk made every effort to avoid "road verge" walking, though for a small portion of the route, you will indeed be funneled to the shoulder of roads and highways. (Be alert to the fact that in England, for safety reasons, pedestrians are usually instructed to walk on the right side of the road, facing the oncoming traffic.) Most of the route, however, avoids traffic arteries completely, guiding you through forests and fields, and along rocky escarpments where views sweep out over medieval wool villages and along the periphery of historic villages. Whether you opt to detour a quarter-mile or so into any of at least a dozen historic villages en route depends on your level of interest, your time, and your energy.

If you're interested in navigating this trail, any tourist office at any village in the Cotswolds has shelves groaning under the weight of Ordnance Maps and specialized walking tour guides that cover all aspects of the Cotswold Way. One of the best sources of information is **The Ramblers' Association,** Camelford House, 87-90 Albert Embankment, London, SE1 7TW (© **020/7339-8500;** www.ramblers.org.uk). This organization publishes a *Yearbook* on walking in Britain, including the Cotswolds. Membership costs £20 ($37). You can get additional information from the tourist offices of Chipping Campden, Bath, or Broadway, or by calling the **Cotswold Voluntary Warden Service** at © **01451/862000.** Bring a raincoat, sturdy shoes, and a sense of humor. If you collect souvenirs, you'll have plenty to choose from en route, as the experience is not without its share of touristy overtones. Hundreds of shops will sell you an official-looking certificate announcing the way you've walked the path, as well as T-shirts, postcards, commemorative ashtrays, and beer mugs.

bottom of the hill, there was a pool where scolding wives and other miscreants were tied to a ducking stool and plunged underwater for punishment.

The Police Bygones Museum, Old Court House, 63 Long St., situated in the former police station and magistrates court, is worth a peek. The old cells house a collection of relics from centuries of Cotswold law enforcement. The location and hours are Monday through Friday from 9am to 3pm.

Chavenage House   The drama started with Colonel Nathaniel Stephens, who owned the house during the English civil war and met an unfortunate demise while living here. He was persuaded by Cromwell, a relative by marriage, to vote for the impeachment of King Charles. This angered Stephens's daughter to the point that she cursed him. Soon after, Stephens died, and it is rumored that his ghostly form can be seen being driven away from Chavenage by a headless coachman wearing royal vestments. The house has been a location shoot for several BBC television productions, including Agatha Christie's *Hercule Poirot.*

Aside from its fine Cromwell-era tapestries, furniture, and artifacts, this Elizabethan country house is worth a visit for its rich history and legends.

3km (2 miles) northwest of Tetbury. © **01666/502329.** www.chavenage.com. Admission £5 ($9.25) adults, £2.50 ($4.65) children. May–Sept Thurs and Sun 2–5pm; also open on Easter and bank holiday Mon.

Antiquing the 'Wolds

If ever there were an English fantasy, it's to drive the country back roads of the Cotswolds, stay in a manor house hotel, and spend your days browsing the villages, ignoring the touristy teddy-bear shops, and concentrating on the antiques shops densely packed into these old market towns.

These towns don't offer many bargains, but it makes for lovely browsing. Few stores sell inexpensive or junky antiques, though you'll find some great rummage sales on the weekends (ask your hotel for directions to the nearest and the best if you are into cheap thrills).

For the most part, antiques in the Cotswolds are about patina and provenance—really serious stuff. Most of the dealers are members of Britain's leading antiques associations (such as the British Antiques Dealers Association—BADA) so that stores displaying this logo in their window have reputations to safeguard and will only sell you the best merchandise. Naturally, the best is pricey.

Also, the **Cotswold Antique Dealer's Association (CADA)** publishes a free brochure of members and will happily guide you toward shippers and even hotels. Established in the mid-1970s, and with about 45 active dealers scattered throughout the region, it offers valuable help in organizing your antique-buying assault on a region known for its decorative treasures. Write to the Secretary, CADA, Broadwell House, Sheep Street, Stow-on-the-Wold, Gloucestershire, GL54 1JS, England (© **01451/810407,** or click on www.cotswolds-antiques-art.com).

Each of the Cotswolds' villages usually has an antiques center in the heart of town, with a variety of dealers, as well as a cafe or a place for tea, and clean bathrooms. They do not charge an entrance fee and are often open on Sundays.

In all Cotswold towns, the most expensive stores are clustered in the center of the high street. The further from this center, the less the rent and the more likely the possibility of finding affordable antiques shops.

The best town in the Cotswolds, especially for antiques shoppers, is **Stow-on-the-Wold;** with far more to it than a high street. **Moreton-in-Marsh** is an unusual town; its high street is Roman and unusually wide.

Some of the Cotswolds towns have been turned into tourist traps over the years; many shops in the area sell an artful mix of reproductions, foreign imports, and Asian junk. Buyers beware.

WHERE TO STAY

Calcot Manor ⊘⊘ (Kids)   Though The Close in town has a more refined atmosphere (see below), this inn is the finest place on the outskirts. The thick, stone walls of the main house shelter a flowering terrace where tea and drinks are served in good weather. The rooms are furnished with antiques and modern conveniences; two are equipped with whirlpool baths, and one has a four-poster bed. Bedrooms range from midsize to spacious, and some rooms, specially designed for families, are located in a refurbished granary near the main house and have small refrigerators. Bathrooms are adequate and well maintained, with tub and shower. Views from many of the rooms encompass the Cotswold countryside. The building has indoor and outdoor play areas for children in addition to child monitors in each room.

Calcot, near Tetbury, Gloucestershire GL8 8YJ. ⓒ 800/987-7433 in the U.S., or 01666/890391. Fax 01666/890394. www.calcotmanor.co.uk. 28 units. £175–£215 ($324–$398) double; from £230 ($426) suite. Rates include early morning tea and English breakfast. AE, DC, MC, V. Take A4135 5.5km (3½ miles) west of Tetbury. **Amenities:** Restaurant; bar; pool; spa; 2 tennis courts; limited room service; babysitting; laundry service. *In room:* TV, coffeemaker, fridge (family rooms and suites only), hair dryer, iron, trouser press.

The Close 🕊🕊🕊 The Close, which dates from 1596 and takes its name from a Cistercian monastery that was on this site, is the town's premier inn. Once the home of a wealthy wool merchant, the house was built of Cotswold stone, with gables and stone-mullioned windows. The ecclesiastical windows in the rear overlook a garden with a reflecting pool, a haven for doves. Most rooms are spacious and handsomely furnished with antiques. Three of the individually decorated rooms have four-poster beds. Bathrooms boast such extras as rubber ducks and bathrobes.

8 Long St., Tetbury, Gloucestershire GL8 8AQ. ⓒ 01666/502272. Fax 01666/504401. www.oldenglish.co.uk. 15 units. Sun–Thurs £140–£180 ($259–$333) double; Fri–Sat £160–£210 ($296–$389) double. Rates include English breakfast and dinner. AE, MC, V. **Amenities:** Restaurant; bar; concierge; car-rental desk; limited room service; babysitting; laundry service; dry cleaning. *In room:* TV, coffeemaker, hair dryer, trouser press.

The Snooty Fox 🕊 This desirable hotel stands in the commercial heart of Tetbury. It was originally a 16th-century coaching inn. Despite its name, it's a lot less snooty than The Close and is a popular local rendezvous. Two rooms have antique beds with canopies, and the rest are comfortably and tastefully furnished in a more modern style. The small to very spacious bedrooms are filled with English country house luxury, including sumptuous beds and fresh fruit. Each bathroom, most with tubs and showers, has luxury toiletries and bathrobes; some offer whirlpool baths.

Market Place, Tetbury, Gloucestershire GL8 8DD. ⓒ 01666/502436. Fax 01666/503479. www.snooty-fox.co.uk. 12 units. Sun–Thurs £97 ($179) double; Fri–Sat £145 ($268) double. Rates include English breakfast. AE, DC, MC, V. **Amenities:** Restaurant; bar; limited room service. *In room:* TV, coffeemaker, hair dryer, trouser press.

WHERE TO DINE

The Close Restaurant 🕊 ENGLISH This is a dining room of distinction, set with exquisite porcelain, silver, and glass that reflects the sumptuous but discreet atmosphere and friendly service. While sipping champagne on the terrace, take time to peruse the imaginative menu, which is complemented by the town's best wine list.

The a la carte menu is seasonally adjusted to take advantage of market-fresh ingredients. Starters and main courses reach out for the finest catch or harvest in England's fields and streams. An example is pressed terrine of foie gras and Bathhurst pigeon with a paprika biscuit and shallot marmalade. Main courses are likely to feature local venison, pan-fried sea bream, or filet of Scottish salmon. Pan-fried John Dory with oyster beignets, garlic mash, and a champagne-and-caviar-flavored *beurre blanc* sauce; and filet of beef "faggot of the blade," served with a fricassee of wild mushrooms and tarragon. Desserts sometimes reach back in England's culinary attic for inspiration, such as a parsnip-and-Cotswold-honey soufflé with whiskey and lime ice.

In The Close, 8 Long St. ⓒ 01666/502272. Reservations required. Main courses £25 ($45) each; fixed-price lunch £13–£17 ($23–$31); fixed-price dinner £28 ($52). AE, MC, V. Daily noon–2pm and 7–9:30pm.

2 Cirencester ★★

143km (89 miles) W of London; 26km (16 miles) S of Cheltenham; 27km (17 miles) SE of Gloucester; 58km (36 miles) W of Oxford

Cirencester is the unofficial capital of the Cotswolds, a throwback to the Middle Ages, when it flourished as the center of the great Cotswold wool industry. Then known as Corinium, five roads converged here during the Roman occupation. In size, it ranked second only to London. Today, it is chiefly a market town and a good base for touring. (And don't worry about how to pronounce *Cirencester*. Even the English disagree. Say *Siren*-cess-ter and you won't be too far off.)

ESSENTIALS

GETTING THERE Cirencester has no railway station, but trains depart several times a day from London's Paddington Station for the 80-minute trip to Kemble, which is 6.5km (4 miles) southwest of Cirencester. You may have to transfer trains at Swindon. For schedules and information, call ℂ **0845/748-4950** or visit www.wessextrains.co.uk. From Kemble, a bus travels to Cirencester four to five times a day.

National Express buses leave London's Victoria Coach Station with direct service to Cirencester. For schedules and information, call ℂ **0870/580-8080** or visit www.nationalexpress.com.

If driving from London, take the M40 northwest to Oxford, continuing along the A40 to the junction with the A429, which you'll take south to Cirencester.

VISITOR INFORMATION The **Tourist Information Centre** is at Corn Hall, Market Place (ℂ **01285/654180**). It's open April through October, Monday from 9:45am to 5pm and Tuesday through Saturday from 9:30am to 5:30pm. From November to March, it closes at 5pm.

EXPLORING CIRENCESTER

Cirencester has some of the greatest walks and scenic views of any town in the Cotswolds. You don't have to go miles out of town to enjoy a stroll—they are easily reached from the center at Market Place. On the grounds of the Church of St. John the Baptist (see below), attractive trees and shrubs highlight a well-manicured landscape. You can see swans and wild fowl on the River Churn and the lake, even remnants of the town's Roman walls. For a great stroll, take the riverside walk along the Churn from Barton Lane to the Abbey Grounds. For more, head west from Market Place until you reach **Cirencester Park,** 1,214 hectares (3,000 acres) of parkland with woodland walks. The park is open daily for horseback riding and walking. Pedestrian access is from Cecily Hill (no vehicles).

Brewery Arts Centre The living heart of this arts complex is the workshop area of 15 resident crafts workers who produce everything from baskets to chandeliers. Other components of the center include three galleries with exhibitions in both crafts and fine art, a theater, education classes, a shop selling the best in British crafts work, a cafe-bar, and a coffeehouse.

Brewery Ct. ℂ 01285/657181. Free admission. Year-round Mon–Sat 10am–5pm.

Church of St. John the Baptist A church may have stood here in Saxon times, but the present building overlooking the Market Place in the town center dates from Norman times and Henry I. In size, it appears more like a cathedral than a mere parish church, with a variety of styles, largely Perpendicular, as in the early-15th-century tower. Among the treasures inside are a 15th-century "wineglass" pulpit and a silver-gilt cup given to Queen Anne Boleyn 2 years before her execution. In the Trinity Chapel, you can rub some great 15th-century brasses.

Market Place. © 01285/659317. Free admission; donations invited. Mon–Fri 10am–1pm.

Corinium Museum ⭐⭐ The museum houses one of the finest collections of archaeological remains from the Roman occupation, found locally in and around Cirencester. Mosaic pavements excavated on Dyer Street in 1849 and other mosaics are the most important exhibits. Provincial Roman sculpture, including such figures as Minerva and Mercury, pottery, and artifacts salvaged from long-decayed buildings, provide a link with the remote civilization that once flourished here. The museum has been completely modernized to include full-scale reconstructions and special exhibitions on local history and conservation.

Park St. © 01285/655611. www.cotswold.gov.uk/museum. Admission £2.50 ($4.65) adults, £2 ($3.70) seniors, £1 ($1.85) students and children, £5 ($9.25) family ticket. Mon–Sat 10am–5pm; Sun 2–5pm.

SHOPPING

For antiques in Cirencester, try **William H. Stokes,** The Cloisters, 6–8 Dollar St. (© **01285/653907**), which specializes in furniture, tapestries, and other items from the 16th and 17th centuries. **Rankine Taylor Antiques,** 34 Dollar St. (© **01285/652529**), sells items from the 17th, 18th, and early 19th centuries, including silver, glass, and furniture.

The arts complex known as the **Brewery Arts,** Brewery Court (© **01285/657181**), has 15 independent workshops of area craftspeople ranging from jewelers and weavers to basket makers. Three galleries and a crafts shop recognized by the Crafts Council sell many of the artists' wares.

WHERE TO STAY & DINE IN & AROUND CIRENCESTER

Tatyan's, 27 Castle St. in Cirencester (© **01285/653529**), is a great place to dine. It serves Peking, Hunan, and Szechuan specialties, with nearly a dozen prawn dishes on the large menu. For a pint, head for the town favorite, **The Crown,** 17 West Market Place (© **01285/653206**), a friendly pub enjoyed by locals and students alike, with out-of-towners predominating in summer, with a tradition of serving ale and victuals on this site that goes back 400 years. It has the most convivial after-dark scene in town.

Barnsley House ⭐⭐⭐ *Finds* The gardens here, surrounding a 17th-century manor house, were always one of the major attractions of the Cotswolds. They were created by the late Rosemary Verey, the garden writer. Following her death in 2001, the property has been turned into a small inn of charm and grace. Although old-fashioned outside, its interiors are of the 21st century, with strong Italian and French influences. Each accommodation is individually designed with elegant, comfortable furnishings and such surprise features as complimentary homemade ice cream, 2.1m (7-ft.) beds, and chilled champagne. The food is among the finest in the area, much of it concocted from home-grown produce.

Even if the place weren't so fabulous, we'd stay here just to be able to walk through the gardens, with their sunny terraces, ancient meadows, and the famous laburnum walk, where chains of golden flowers hang over towering purple alliums. There's even a neo-classical temple and a neo-Gothic summer house.

Barnsley, Cirencester, Gloucestershire GL7 5EE. © 01285/740000. Fax 01285/740900. www.barnsleyhouse. com. 9 units. £250–£350 ($463–$648) double, £375–£450 ($694–$833) suite. Rates include continental breakfast. AE, MC, V. Lies 6.4km (4 miles) northeast of Cirencester on the B4425. **Amenities:** Restaurant; bar; 24-hr. room service; laundry service; dry cleaning; babysitting; pool. *In room:* A/C, TV, dataport, minibar, hair dryer.

The Fleece Hotel The half-timbered facade here hints at origins as an Elizabethan coaching inn, but it was enlarged by the Georgians and today has had many modernizations. The comfortable rooms feature old-fashioned hints of yesteryear including quilts. Rooms range from small to midsize, most containing small bathrooms with showers and tubs. Two rooms are large enough for families, and two have four-poster beds.

Market Place, Cirencester, Gloucestershire GL7 2NZ. © **01285/658507.** Fax 01285/651017. www.fleecehotel. co.uk. 26 units. £119–£139 ($220–$257) double. Rates include English breakfast. Children under 16 stay free in same room as 2 paying adults. AE, MC, V. **Amenities:** 2 restaurants; 2 bars; limited room service; nonsmoking rooms. *In room:* TV, coffeemaker, hair dryer, iron/ironing board, safe, trouser press.

The Pear Tree at Purton ⋆ *Finds* This English country hotel/restaurant, on 3h (7½ acres), offers individually styled rooms in various shapes and sizes, each equipped with extras such as sherry and mineral water. All accommodations (three with four-poster beds) have views of the traditional Victorian garden and countryside; some executive rooms have whirlpool baths. Rooms are named for characters associated with the village of Purton—Anne Hyde, for example, mother of Queen Mary and Queen Anne. Bathrooms are well supplied, each with a shower-tub combination. The Cotswold stone house was formerly the vicarage for the twin-towered parish Church of St. Mary.

Church End, Purton, near Swindon, Wiltshire SN5 4ED. © **01793/772100.** Fax 01793/772369. www. peartreepurton.co.uk. 17 units. £110–£135 ($204–$250) double; £135–£180 ($250–$333) suite. Rates include English breakfast. AE, DC, MC, V. Closed Dec 26–30. It's 13km (8 miles) southeast of Cirencester, 5km (3 miles) from Junction 16 of M4, and 8km (5 miles) from Swindon. To get here from Cirencester, follow route B419 in the direction of Swindon. Turn left when signs point to Cricklade, and from here, follow the signs to Purton. **Amenities:** Restaurant; bar; croquet lawn; limited room service; laundry service; dry cleaning. *In room:* TV, hair dryer, safe, trouser press.

Stratton House Hotel Built in several stages throughout the 18th century, with a modern wing added in the 1990s, this inviting country house is part Jacobean and part Georgian. It is surrounded by beautiful grounds with a walled garden and herbaceous borders. The rooms are large and well furnished (the "cozy" rooms being the smallest of the lot); some have four-poster beds. Two-thirds of the units lie within the most modern wing—designer-decorated, with an aura evoking a traditional private English country house. Bathrooms are small but tidy, each with a shower-tub combination.

Gloucester Rd., Cirencester, Gloucestershire GL7 2LE. © **01285/651761.** Fax 01285/640024. www.stratton househotel.co.uk. 40 units. £110–£140 ($204–$259) double. Rates include English breakfast. AE, DC, MC, V. Take A417 2km (1¼ miles) northwest of Cirencester. **Amenities:** Restaurant; bar; limited room service. *In room:* TV, coffeemaker, hair dryer, iron, trouser press.

3 Painswick ⋆

6.5km (4 miles) N of Stroud; 172km (107 miles) W of London; 16km (10 miles) SW of Cheltenham; 24km (15 miles) NW of Cirencester

This sleepy stone-built Cotswold wool town vies with Bibury for the title of the most beautiful in the Cotswolds. Painswick is a dream of England of long ago, the perfect escape from a string of dull market towns too often encountered. Its mellow gray stone houses and inns date from as early as the 14th century.

A visit to Painswick at any time of the year would be idyllic, in spite of the "day-trippers" and tourist buses, but there are two special occasions that make it an especially wonderful destination. One is the town's Victorian Market Day in early July. You can contact the **Tourist Information Centre** (see below) for the exact day, which is announced in the late spring. The other big occasion is the Clipping Feast (see "Special Events," below).

ESSENTIALS

GETTING THERE   Trains depart London's Paddington Station several times a day for Stroud, the nearest railway station, 5km (3 miles) away. The trip takes from 1½ to 2 hours, and you may have to change trains at Swindon. For rail information, call ℂ **0845/748-4950** or visit www.wessextrains.co.uk. From Stroud, buses run to Painswick, some as frequently as every hour. Many taxis also wait at the Stroud railway station.

Buses depart from Bath heading toward Cheltenham on Wednesday and Saturday, stopping in Painswick (and many other small towns) along the way. For schedules, call ℂ **0870/580-8080** or visit www.nationalexpress.com.

If you're driving from Cirencester, continue west along the A419 to Stroud, then head north on the A46 to Cheltenham and Painswick.

VISITOR INFORMATION   The Painswick **Tourist Information Centre** is at the Painswick Library, Stroud Road (ℂ **01452/813552**), and is open April through September, Monday through Saturday from 10am to 6pm. These hours are true at least in theory, but the staff volunteers manning the office don't always show up. In that case, you can visit the more reliably open tourist office at Stroud, located in Subscription Rooms, George Street (ℂ **01453/760960**). Hours are Monday through Saturday from 10am to 5pm.

SPECIAL EVENTS   The **Clipping Feast** of Painswick, also known as the Clipping Ceremony, is an unusual, early medieval ceremony that anthropologists think may have begun in the dim Celtic prehistory of Britain. Every September, a month that coincides with the harvest ceremonies of pagans, adults and as many children as can be mustered hold hands in a circle around St. Mary's Anglican Church. The circle moves first one way, then the other, and the participants sing hymns and pray out loud in a celebration of thanksgiving. Participants and observers come from all over the region to take part in this important rite.

EXPLORING THE TOWN

The charm of this town comes from its mellow Cotswold architecture with stone-built houses. Funded by wealthy farmers and merchants in the era when fluffy wool was called "white gold," the houses of Painswick represent a peak at English domestic architecture. The architecture is best seen by walking around New Street in the center of the village. This has to be one of the most misnamed streets in England, as it dates from 1450 and there isn't anything new about it.

The **Painswick Rococo Garden** ⟨⸮⟩, B4073, .8km (½ mile) north of Painswick (ℂ **01452/813204;** www.rococogarden.co.uk), is a rare English garden and is a throwback to the flamboyant English rococo period, which lasted only from 1720 to 1760. Originally laid out in the 18th century, the garden lies in a hidden Cotswold valley opening onto views of the countryside. By the 1970s the garden had become overgrown. Its owners discovered a 1748 painting by the artist, Thomas Robins, depicting the garden in its original glory, and they set out to return it to the charm of its heyday. Today the garden is best known for its spectacular display of snowdrops. The original architectural structures in the garden have been restored, and there is an on-site restaurant and gift shop. On certain summer evenings Shakespeare's plays are performed in the garden. Admission is £4 ($7.40) adults, £3.50 ($6.50) seniors, and £2 ($3.70) children 5 to 16, and visits are possible from mid-January until October daily from 11am to 5pm.

Finds   Owlpen Manor: A Journey to Brigadoon

As beautiful as Painswick is, nearby is a place even more lovely. The hamlet of **Owlpen Manor** near Dursley lies immediately to the south of Painswick, off the beaten track. "Owlpen in Gloucestershire" has been called the British version of Brigadoon, an English Shangri-la. Vita Sackville-West in 1941 rhapsodized, "Ah, what a dream is there." Even Prince Charles, who lives nearby at Highgrove, called it "the epitome of an English village," with its population of 35 lucky souls.

The hamlet centers on a medieval church, an Elizabethan manor, and a collection of stone-built cottages. In the center, you can stroll through the gardens of the triple-gabled manor, constructed between 1450 and 1720. Between April and September, it is open Tuesday to Sunday between 2 and 5pm; admission is £4.80 ($8.90) adults, £2 ($3.70) children 4 to 14, for a visit of the antique-filled house; £2.80 ($5.20), £1 ($1.85) children for access to the beautifully kept gardens and grounds only. A restaurant on-site, the Cyder House, serves English and Scandinavian food as part of lunches and high teas every Tuesday to Sunday from noon to 5pm.

If you'd like to really immerse yourself into this bucolic English setting, you can rent one of the nine cottages within the village, each of which was built sometime between 1620 and 1950. Each has been luxuriously converted into guest accommodations, including a studio apartment within the Tithe Barn, or our particular favorite, "Summerfield Cottage," which opens onto a murmuring brook—almost a cliché picture postcard of the Cotswolds. Weekly rentals range, double occupancy, from £250 to £895 ($463–$1,656). If you prefer a shorter stay, a 2-day break costs, double occupancy, £80 to £140 ($148–$259) for the full 2-day stopover.

This fairy-tale hamlet is administered by Nicholas Mander, a descendant of Sir Geoffrey and Lady Mander, fabled pre-Raphaelite patrons of the arts. For information about visits to the manor or grounds, or rentals of the cottages, call ✆ **01453/860261;** www.owlpen.com). From Painswick, go south on the A46, following the signposts to Stroud, until you reach the junction of the A419. There, follow the signs pointing to the M5, but before you reach the M5, turn onto the B4066 immediately adjacent to the Sinsbury Supermarket, following the signs pointing to Uley. Once you reach the village green of Uley, you'll see signposts pointing to Owlpen Manor.

St. Mary's Church, the centerpiece of the village, was originally built between 1377 and 1399, and it was reconstructed into its present form in 1480. Its churchyard contains 99 massive yew trees, each of which is at least 200 years old. Local legend states that no matter how hard well-meaning gardeners have tried, they've never been able to grow more than 99 of them.

WHERE TO STAY & DINE

Cardynham House 🎯 *Value*   Adjacent to St. Mary's Church, in the heart of Painswick, this small but choice house dates from 1498. It was later enlarged thanks to beams that were salvaged from the remains of a wrecked ship from the Spanish Armada. The owner has outfitted the interior with lots of cozy accessories (tartan blankets, leather armchairs, and antique books) that fit in well with a stylish hodgepodge of cabinets, wide floorboards, and an intricate network of ceiling beams built by the Elizabethans and the Jacobeans. Bedrooms are cramped but cozy, each with a different theme (Arabian Nights and Medieval Garden are good examples). One of them is a bit larger than the others and enjoys exclusive access to a 5m (16-ft.) indoor swimming pool, wherein you can swim against the current by throwing a switch for the simulation of a flowing stream. The Dovecote room is good for families. The small bathrooms are neatly organized; two come with baths and the rest have shower stalls.

The Cross, Painswick, Gloucestershire GL6 6XX. ℗ **01452/814006.** Fax 01452/812321. www.cardynham. co.uk. 9 units. £69–£175 ($128–$324) double. Rates include breakfast. AE, MC, V. Minimum stay of 2 nights Fri–Sun. **Amenities:** Restaurant. *In room:* TV, coffeemaker, hair dryer.

Painswick Hotel 🌟🌟   The best inn in the area is this beautiful, completely refurbished Georgian house behind the Painswick parish church. It was once a vicarage and is encircled by terraces of formal gardens. Many readers have reported that a stay here was the highlight of their Cotswold tour. For its accommodations, cuisine, and service, it merits a major detour. The bedrooms are what you dream about when you contemplate a stay in the Cotswolds. You'll feel like Henry VIII or Elizabeth I when you crawl in for the night in one of the luxurious beds, some of them four-posters. The bedrooms are enhanced by antiques, period furnishings, and objets d'art. The bathrooms are splendid, with plenty of fine toiletries and bathrobes. Thoughtful extras include baskets of fresh fruit, mineral water, books, and magazines about the English countryside.

Kemps Lane, Painswick, Gloucestershire GL6 6YB. ℗ **01452/812160.** Fax 01452/814059. www.painswick hotel.com. 19 units. £125–£210 ($231–$389) double. Rates include English breakfast. AE, MC, V. **Amenities:** Restaurant; bar; concierge; limited room service; babysitting; laundry service. *In room:* TV, hair dryer.

4 Cheltenham 🌟

159km (99 miles) NW of London; 14km (9 miles) NE of Gloucester; 69km (43 miles) W of Oxford

Legend has it that the Cheltenham villagers discovered a mineral spring by chance when they noticed pigeons drinking from a spring and observed how healthy they were (the pigeon has been incorporated into the town's crest). King George III arrived in 1788 and launched the town's career as a spa.

Cheltenham remains one of England's most fashionable spas; many visitors come just to see its gardens. The architecture is mainly Regency, with lots of ironwork, balconies, and verandas. Attractive parks and open spaces of greenery make the town especially inviting. The main street, the Promenade, has been called the most beautiful thoroughfare in Britain. Rather similar are Lansdowne Place and Montpellier Parade (with caryatids separating its stores, Montpellier Walk is one of England's most interesting shopping centers).

ESSENTIALS

GETTING THERE   Twenty-one trains depart daily from London's Paddington Station for the 2¼-hour trip. You may have to change trains at Bristol or Swindon. For information, call ℗ **0845/748-4950** or visit www.wessextrains.co.uk. Trains between Cheltenham and Bristol take an hour, with continuing service to Bath.

National Express offers nine buses daily from London's Victoria Coach Station to Cheltenham. The ride takes about 2½ hours. For schedules and information, call ℗ **0870/580-8080** or visit www.nationalexpress.com.

If you're driving from London, head northwest on the M40 to Oxford, continuing along the A40 to Cheltenham.

VISITOR INFORMATION The **Tourist Information Centre,** 77 The Promenade (*©* **01242/522878**), is open September through June, Monday through Saturday from 9:30am to 5:15pm.

SPECIAL EVENTS The **International Festival of Music** and the **Festival of Literature** take place each year in July and October, respectively, and attract internationally acclaimed performers and orchestras. For details, call *©* **01242/ 227979** or visit www.cheltenhamfestivals.co.uk.

EXPLORING THE TOWN

Cheltenham Art Gallery & Museum This gallery houses one of the foremost collections of the Arts and Crafts movement, notably the fine furniture of William Morris and his followers. One section is devoted to Edward Wilson, Cheltenham's native son, who died with Captain Scott in the Antarctic in 1912. The gallery is located near Royal Crescent and the Coach Station.

Clarence St. *©* **01242/237431.** www.cheltenhammuseum.org.uk. Free admission. Year-round Mon–Sat 10am–5:20pm; closed Sun and bank holidays.

Everyman Theatre Cheltenham is the cultural center of the Cotswolds, a role solidified by the Everyman Theatre. Designed in the 1890s as an opera house by Frank Matcham, Victorian England's leading theater architect, it retains its ornate cornices, sculpted ceilings, and plush velvets despite extensive renovations to its stage and lighting facilities. The theater has begun to attract some of England's top dramatic companies. Shakespeare, musicals, comedies, and other genres are performed in the small (658 seats) but charming hall.

Regent St. *©* **01242/572573.** www.everymantheatre.org.uk. Admission £5–£25 ($9.25–$46), depending on the event. Box office on performance days Mon–Sat 9:30am–8:30pm.

Pittville Pump Room Cheltenham Waters are the only natural, consumable alkaline waters in Great Britain and are still taken at one of the spa's finest Regency buildings. The Pittville Pump Room is open Sundays from the end of May until the end of September for a host of activities, including lunch, afternoon cream teas, live classical music, landau carriage rides around the city, and brass bands playing in Pittville Park.

East Approach Dr., Pittville Park. *©* **01242/523852.** Free admission. Year-round Wed–Mon 10am–4pm. From the town center, take Portland St. and Evesham Rd.

SHOPPING

The different quarters that make up Cheltenham's shopping district turn shopping into an unusually organized event. Start in the **Montpellier quarter** for individual boutiques and craft and specialty shops. Then, continue to the nearby **Suffolk quarter** to find most of the town's antiques stores.

And an enjoyable short stroll to the **Promenade** takes you by stores featuring attractive clothing and shoes, as well as several bookstores. From the Promenade, take Regent Street to **High Street,** which is mostly pedestrian-only, and you'll find several brand-name department stores in the **Beechwood Shopping Centre.**

The **weekly market** is in the Henrietta Street car park on Thursday. Weather permitting, the market is open from 9am to 4pm.

The **Courtyard,** on Montpellier Street in the heart of the Montpellier quarter, has become an award-winning shopping mall that offers a fun blend of shops specializing in unique fashion, furniture, and gift items. A good mix of restaurants, cafes, and wine bars rounds out the mall. **Hoopers** (☎ **01242/527505**) is a quality department store devoted to designer clothes for men and women. It also has a perfumery, hair and beauty salon, and fully air-conditioned restaurant.

Cavendish House, the Promenade (☎ **01242/521300**), is a long-established shopping landmark, housing two restaurants, a hair and beauty salon, an immense cosmetic and jewelry hall, and departments devoted to fine fashion, housewares, and furniture.

WHERE TO STAY

Central Hotel   Within easy reach of Cheltenham's range of attractions, this hotel consists of a pair of stone houses that were originally built in the 1700s and then combined. Today, it's a family run hotel, with a street-level public house. The small comfortable bedrooms are conservatively modern with everything you need. The private shower bathrooms are compact; the public bathrooms are adequately maintained, and you rarely have to wait in line.

7–9 Portland St., Cheltenham, Gloucestershire GL52 2NZ. ☎ 01242/582172 or 01242/524789. www.centralhotelcheltenham.co.uk. 18 units. £60 ($111) double. Rates include English breakfast. AE, DC, MC, V. **Amenities:** Restaurant; bar; nonsmoking rooms. In room: TV, coffeemaker.

The Greenway ☆☆   An elegant and beautifully furnished former Elizabethan manor house from the 1540s in a garden setting, this is an ivy-clad Cotswold showpiece. Restored with sensitivity, Greenway rents rooms in both its main house and a converted coach house. Bedrooms, midsize to spacious, are rather sumptuously outfitted. Bathrooms have deluxe toiletries, combination tub and shower, and bathrobes. This is the best English country-house living in the area.

Shurdington, near Cheltenham, Gloucestershire GL51 4UG. ☎ 01242/862352. Fax 01242/862780. www.thegreenway.co.uk. 21 units. £150–£195 ($278–$361) double, £230–£280 ($426–$518) suite. Rates include English breakfast. AE, DC, MC, V. Take A46 less than 6.5km (4 miles) southwest of Cheltenham. **Amenities:** Restaurant; bar; concierge; car-rental desk; limited room service; laundry service; dry cleaning. In room: TV, hair dryer.

Hotel de la Bere and Country Club   This 16th-century Cotswold-stone building stands near the Cheltenham race course and until its takeover by a nationwide chain a few years ago, it had been owned by the de la Bere family for 3 centuries. Converted into a hotel in 1972 it retains its original charm. All rooms are furnished to preserve their individual character, and most were refurbished since 2002. Five rooms have double four-poster beds. Bathrooms come with shower-tub combinations.

Southam, Cheltenham, Gloucestershire GL52 3NH. ☎ 01242/545454. Fax 01242/236016. www.corushotels.com. 57 units. £99 ($183) double. Half board (2-night minimum required) Mon–Thurs £134 ($248) double, Fri–Sun £122 ($226) double. AE, DC, MC, V. Take B4632 5km (3 miles) northeast of town, following the signs to Prestbury. **Amenities:** Restaurant; bar; outdoor heated pool; tennis court; health club; sauna; car-rental desk; squash court; limited room service; laundry service; dry cleaning. In room: TV, coffeemaker, hair dryer, trouser press.

Kandinsky ☆   This Georgian inn has been dramatically modernized and is today a stylish stopover in this rather staid spa town. Fashionable teak designer furnishings decorate the modern accommodations, which are both tasteful and comfortable with attractive little bathrooms with showers. Large potted plants and a choice of antiques grace the public bedrooms and throw rugs cover many of the floors. The on-site Café Paradiso serves the best antipasti in town, along with other continental offerings; it's like a cool 1950s bar where entertainment is often presented.

Bayshill Rd., Montpellier, Cheltenham, Gloucestershire GL50 3AS. ☎ 01242/527788. Fax 01242/226412. www.aliaskandinsky.com. 48 units. £90–£115 ($167–$213) double; £150 ($278) suite. AE, DC, MC, V. **Amenities:** Restaurant; bar; cafe/nightclub. In room: TV/VCR, CD player, dataport.

Lypiatt House ☆ *Value* This beautifully restored Victorian home stands in the Montpellier area, the most fashionable part of Cheltenham. A hotel of ambience and character, it offers a large elegant drawing room with a colonial-style conservatory with an "honesty bar." The bedrooms are beautifully furnished and of generous size, each with a well-equipped bathroom with private shower. The friendly owners are the most helpful in town. You may choose to use this B&B as your base for touring the Cotswolds.

Lypiatt Rd., Cheltenham, Gloucestershire GL50 2QW. ℭ **01242/224994.** Fax 01242/224996. www.lypiatt. co.uk. 10 units. £70–£90 ($130–$167) double. Rates include English breakfast. AE, MC, V. **Amenities:** Bar; laundry service. *In room:* TV, coffeemaker.

On the Park ☆☆ Opened in 1991, in what was formerly an 1830s private villa, this is one of the most talked-about hotels in town. It is located among similar terraced buildings in the once-prominent village of Pittville Spa, 1km (½ mile) north of Cheltenham's town center. Owned and operated by Darryl Gregory, who undertook most of the Regency-inspired interior design, it has received several awards. Each bedroom is named after a prominent 19th-century visitor who came here shortly after the villa was built. Comfortable and high-ceilinged, the rooms have stylish accessories and a tasteful assortment of antique and reproduction furniture. Bedrooms are beautifully appointed, with thoughtful extras such as sherry and mineral water. Bathrooms are laudable and roomy; each has deluxe toiletries and some have Jacuzzis.

Evesham Rd., Cheltenham, Gloucestershire GL52 2AH. ℭ **01242/518898.** Fax 01242/511526. www.hotel onthepark.com. 12 units. £112–£162 ($207–$300) double. AE, DC, MC, V. **Amenities:** Restaurant; bar; limited room service. *In room:* TV, coffeemaker, hair dryer.

WHERE TO DINE

Le Champignon Sauvage ☆☆☆ FRENCH This is among the culinary highlights of the Cotswolds. David Everitt-Matthias, a chef of considerable talent, limits the selection of dishes each evening for better quality control. Some evenings, his imagination roams a bit, so dining here is usually a pleasant surprise. You may begin with light cauliflower soup flavored with cumin. Main courses may include braised lamb dumplings with roasted carrots and shallots. On a more daring level, you can sample the pan-fried squid and scallops with a pumpkin purée and a squid ink sauce or the red-legged partridge with sour cabbage and black pudding. Matthias was recently named dessert chef of the year in England, so be sure to try one of the acclaimed sweet treats. Choices include iced licorice parfait with damson sorbet, and baked caramel cheesecake with caramelized banana.

24–26 Suffolk Rd. ℭ **01242/573449.** Reservations required. 2-course fixed-price lunch £18 ($33), 3-course fixed-price lunch £22 ($41); 2-course fixed-price dinner £19–£36 ($35–$67), 3-course fixed-price dinner £23–£44 ($43–$81). AE, DC, MC, V. Tues–Sat 12:30–1:30pm and 7:30–9pm.

Le Petit Blanc ☆ FRENCH Already a bit of a dining legend in Oxford, this offspring has invaded Cheltenham and is waking up the sleepy taste buds of the old-fashioned spa. Under the guidance of master chef Raymond Blanc, a celebrity chef whose more famous, and more expensive, gastronomic restaurant is known throughout England, this is a *brasserie de luxe*, with a decor inspired by turn-of-the-20th-century Paris, modern paintings, a row of unusual sculpture that runs up the middle, and a hip and knowledgeable staff. Cuisine is beautifully presented, and prepared with the freshest of the day's available ingredients. Examples include deep-fried goat cheese with a French bean salad and tomato chutney, char-grilled squid with soused vegetables and a rocket and parmesan salad, mussels marinière, and a superb version of fried filet of hake with mashed potatoes and a caper-flavored tomato sauce. Save room for the hot semisoft chocolate cake, served with pistachio ice cream and chocolate sauce.

In the Queen's Hotel. The Promenade. © **01242/266800.** Reservations recommended. Main courses £9.25–£17 ($17–$31); fixed-price lunch or dinner £14–£16 ($25–$30) for 2 and 3 courses. AE, DC, MC, V. Daily noon–3pm; Mon–Sat 6–10:30pm; Sun 6–10pm.

CHELTENHAM AFTER DARK

The major venue for entertainment is the **Everyman Theatre** (see above), which is the premier sightseeing attraction of Cheltenham. But there's a lot more theater at the **Playhouse,** Bath Road (© **01242/522852;** www.playhousecheltenham. org), with new local, amateur productions of drama, comedy, dance, and opera being staged at the dizzying pace of every 2 weeks. Tickets are £6 to £12 ($11–$22).

There are at least a dozen different nightspots in hard-partying Cheltenham, but the biggest and most durable of the lot is **Chemistry,** St. James Square (© **012242/527700**). Set within an amiably battered Regency-style mid-19th-century building in the heart of town, it offers four floors of dining, drinking, and music venues that include "urban, R&B sounds" in the cellar, party-oriented dance music on street level and immediately above, and a restaurant on the top floor. It's open Monday, Wednesday, Friday, and Saturday nights from 9pm to 2am. After 10pm, there's a cover charge of £10 ($19).

A SIDE TRIP TO SUDELEY CASTLE ⊛

Royal Sudeley Castle and Gardens   This 15th-century structure is one of England's finer stately homes. It has a rich history that begins in Saxon times, when the village was the capital of the Mercian kings. Later, Catherine Parr, the sixth wife of Henry VIII, lived and died here. Her tomb is in a chapel on the grounds, which include a host of formal gardens like the Queen's Garden, now planted with old-world roses and dating from the time of Catherine Parr. While exploring the gardens, you're sure to see the waterfowl and flamboyant peacocks that call Sudeley home. For the past 30 years, Lady Ashcombe, an American by birth, has owned the castle and welcomed visitors from the world over. The castle houses many works of art by Constable, Turner, Rubens, and Van Dyck, among others, and has several permanent exhibitions, magnificent furniture and glass, and many artifacts from the castle's past. In the area to the right of the keep, as you enter the castle, workshops are devoted to talented local artisans who continue to use traditional techniques to produce stained glass, textiles, wood and leather articles, and marbled paper.

In the village of Winchcombe (9.5km/6 miles northeast of Cheltenham). © **01242/604357.** www.sudeley castle.co.uk. Admission £6.85 ($13) adults, £5.85 ($11) seniors, £3.85 ($7.10) children 5–15 years, £19 ($34) family ticket. Castle Apr–Oct daily 11am–5pm (last entry at 4:30pm); gardens and grounds Mar–Oct daily 10:30am–5:30pm. From Cheltenham, take the regular bus to Winchcombe and get off at Abbey Terrace. Then, walk the short distance along the road to the castle. If you're driving, take B4632 north out of Cheltenham, through Prestbury, and up Cleve Hill to Abbey Terrace, where you can drive right up to the castle.

5 Bibury ⊛

138km (86 miles) W of London; 48km (30 miles) W of Oxford; 42km (26 miles) E of Gloucester

On the road from Burford to Cirencester, Bibury is one of the loveliest spots in the Cotswolds. In fact, the utopian romancer of Victoria's day, poet William Morris, called it England's most beautiful village. In the Cotswolds, it is matched only by Painswick for its scenic village beauty and purity. Both villages are still unspoiled by modern intrusions.

GETTING THERE

About five trains per day depart London's Paddington Station for the 1-hour-10-minute trip to Kemble, the nearest station, 21km (13 miles) south of Bibury. Some will require an easy change of train in Swindon (the connecting train waits across the tracks). For information, call © **0845/748-4950** or visit www. wessextrains.co.uk. No buses run from Kemble to Bibury, but most hotels will arrange transportation if you ask in advance.

Five buses leave London's Victoria Coach Station daily for Cirencester, 11km (7 miles) from Bibury. For information, call © **0870/580-8080** or visit www. nationalexpress.com. With no connecting buses into Bibury, local hotels will send a car, and taxis are available.

If driving from London, take the M4 to Exit 15, head toward Cirencester, then follow the A33 (on some maps this is still designated as the B4425) to Bibury.

EXPLORING THE TOWN

On the banks of the tiny Coln River, Bibury is noted for **Arlington Row,** a group of 17th-century gabled cottages protected by the National Trust. Originally built for weavers, these houses are its biggest and most-photographed attraction, but it's rude to peer into the windows, as many do, because people still live here.

To get a view of something a bit out of the ordinary for the Cotswolds, check out **St. Mary's Parish Church.** As the story goes, the wool merchants who had the power and money in the area were rebuilding the churches. However, they did not finish the restoration to St. Mary's, and, as a result, much of the original Roman-style architecture has been left intact. The 14th-century Decorated-style windows have even survived the years. This is an often-overlooked treasure.

WHERE TO STAY & DINE

Bibury Court Hotel ℛ (Finds)   You can feel the history when you stay at this Jacobean manor house, built by Sir Thomas Sackville in 1633 (parts of it date from Tudor times). Sackville, an illegitimate son of the first earl of Dorset, launched a family dynasty. His family occupied the house for several generations. Through the female line it passed to the Cresswells, who, eventually, owing to a disputed will and years of litigation, sold the house in the last century to Lord Sherborne. (Charles Dickens is said to have written *Bleak House* with this case in mind.) The house was a residence until it was turned into a hotel in 1968.

You enter the 2.4 hectares (6 acres) of grounds through a large gateway, and the lawn extends to the Coln River. The structure is built of Cotswold stone, with many gables, huge chimneys, and a formal graveled entryway. Many rooms have four-poster beds, original oak paneling, and antiques. Bedrooms are furnished in old English style but have modern comforts, plus bathrooms with a shower-and-tub combination (one has a shower stall instead).

Bibury, Gloucestershire GL7 5NT. © **01285/740337.** Fax 01285/740660. 18 units. £135–£155 ($250–$287) double; £220 ($407) suite. Rates include continental breakfast and VAT. AE, DC, MC, V. **Amenities:** 2 restaurants; bar; croquet lawn; limited room service. *In room:* TV, coffeemaker, hair dryer, iron.

The Swan ℛℛ   Well managed, upscale, and discreet, this hotel and restaurant is the finest in the village. It originated as a riverside cottage in the 1300s, was greatly expanded throughout the centuries, and received its latest major refurbishment early in the millennium when its ownership was transferred from the couple who had established it to a small-scale chain of upscale inns whose other members are scattered throughout the Cotswolds. Much of the interior is outfitted in a traditional, warm-toned design evocative of a discreetly upscale stately home, with tartan-patterned and flowered fabrics, autumn-inspired colors, and touches of regional charm. The bedrooms are outfitted with antique furniture and an individualized decor. Each contains an elegant bed—some are four-posters—with soft linens and a beautifully maintained bathroom with bathrobes and deluxe toiletries. Some bathrooms have Jacuzzi tubs.

Bibury, Gloucestershire GL7 5NW. (**C**) **01285/740695.** Fax 01285/740473. www.swanhotel.co.uk. 18 units. £140–£260 ($259–$481) double. Rates include English breakfast. AE, DC, MC, V. **Amenities:** 2 restaurants; bar; limited room service; laundry service; spa facilities. *In room:* TV, hair dryer, coffeemaker, trouser press.

6 Burford ★

122km (76 miles) NW of London; 32km (20 miles) W of Oxford

Built of Cotswold stone and serving as a gateway to the area, the unspoiled medieval town of Burford is largely famous for its Norman church (ca. 1116) and its High Street lined with coaching inns.

Burford was one of the last of the great wool centers, the industry bleating out its last breath during Queen Victoria's day. Be sure to photograph the bridge across the River Windrush where Queen Elizabeth I once stood. As the antiques shops along High Street testify, Burford today is definitely equipped for tourists.

The River Windrush, which toward Burford is flanked by willows through meadows, passes beneath the packhorse bridge and goes around the church and away through more meadows. Strolling along its banks is one of the most delightful experiences in the Cotswolds.

ESSENTIALS

GETTING THERE Many trains depart from London's Paddington Station to Oxford, a 45-minute trip. For information, call (**C**) **0845/748-4950** or visit www. firstgreatwestern.co.uk/link. From Oxford, passengers walk a short distance to the entrance of the Taylor Institute, from which about three or four buses per day make the 30-minute run to Burford.

A **National Express** bus runs from London's Victoria Coach Station to Burford several times a day, with many stops along the way. It's a 2-hour ride. For schedules and information, call (**C**) **0870/580-8080** or visit www.nationalexpress.com.

If you're driving from Oxford, head west on the A40 to Burford.

VISITOR INFORMATION The **Tourist Information Centre** is at the Old Brewery on Sheep Street ((**C**) **01993/823558**) and is open November through February, Monday through Saturday from 10am to 4:30pm; March through October, Monday through Saturday from 9:30am to 5:30pm (also open Sun 10:30am–3pm May–Sept).

SEEING THE SIGHTS

Approaching Burford from the south, you'll experience one of the finest views of any ancient market town in the country. The main street sweeps down to the River Windrush, past an extraordinary collection of houses of various styles and ages. Burford's ancient packhorse bridge still does duty at the bottom of the hill. Hills opposite provide a frame of fields, trees, and, with luck, panoramic skies.

Though the wool trade has long vanished, most of Burford remains unchanged in appearance, with old houses in the High Street and nearby side streets. Nearly all are built of local stone. Like many Cotswold towns, Burford has a Sheep Street, with many fine stone-built houses covered with roofs of Stonesfield slate. Burford Church (ca. 1175) is almost cathedral-like in proportion. It was enlarged throughout succeeding centuries until the decline of the wool trade. Little has changed here since about 1500.

Traders and vendors still set up their stalls under the Tolsey on Friday, where, from the 12th century, the guild has collected tolls from anyone wishing to trade in the town. It still stands at the corner of Sheep Street. On the upper floor is the minor Tolsey Museum, where you can see a medieval seal bearing Burford's insignia, the "rampant cat."

Three kilometers (2 miles) south of Burford on the A361 lies the **Cotswold Wildlife Park** (© **01993/823006;** www.cotswoldwildlifepark.co.uk). The 65 hectares (160 acres) of gardens and forests around this Victorian manor house have been transformed into a jungle of sorts, with a Noah's Ark consortium of animals ranging from voracious ants to rare Asiatic lions, rhinos, and leopards. Children can romp around the farmyard and the adventure playground. A narrow-gauge railway runs from April to October, and there are extensive picnic areas plus a cafeteria. Open March to September daily 10am to 5:30pm; October to February daily 10am to 4pm (last entry 1 hr. before closing). Admission is £8 ($15) for adults, £5.50 ($10) for seniors and children 3 to 16, and free for children 2 and under.

And before you leave Burford, we suggest a slight detour to **Swinbrook,** a pretty village by the River Windrush immediately to the east. It's best known as the one-time home of the fabled Mitford sisters. Visit the local parish church to see the grave of writer Nancy Mitford and the impressive tiered monuments to the Fettiplace family.

On High Street in Burford, you'll find several antiques shops, including **Manfred Schotten Antiques,** The Crypt, 109 High St. (© **01993/822302**). Sporting antiques and collectibles, they also carry library and club furniture. **Jonathan Fyson Antiques,** 50–52 High St. (© **01993/823204**), carries English and Continental furniture and porcelain, glass, and brass items. At the Burford Roundabout, on Cheltenham Road, **Gateway Antiques** (© **01993/823678**) has a variety of items displayed in large showrooms. English pottery, metalware, and 19th-century furniture dominate the inventory. Unique arts and crafts items and interesting decorative objects are fun to browse through, even if you don't buy.

WHERE TO STAY

Bay Tree Hotel 🐾🐾   This is the best and most atmospheric of Burford's many interesting old inns. The house was built for Sir Lawrence Tanfield, the unpopular lord chief baron of the Exchequer to Elizabeth I. The house has oak-paneled rooms with stone fireplaces, and a high-beamed hall with a minstrel's gallery. Modern comforts have been discreetly installed in the tastefully furnished rooms, some of which have four-poster beds. Some of the accommodations are in a comfortable annex, though the chambers in the main building—nine in all—have more character. Try to get a room overlooking the terraced gardens at the rear of the house. Each unit comes with a midsize bathroom, often with both tub and shower.

12–14 Sheep St., Burford, Oxfordshire OX18 4LW. © **01993/822791.** Fax 01993/823008. www.cotswold-inns-hotels.co.uk. 21 units. £165–£195 ($305–$361) double; £215–£270 ($398–$500) suite. Rates include English breakfast. AE, DC, MC, V. **Amenities:** Restaurant; bar; room service; babysitting; laundry service; dry cleaning. *In room:* TV, coffeemaker, hair dryer, trouser press.

Golden Pheasant Hotel 🐾   This inn is housed in what was once the 15th-century home of a prosperous wool merchant. It began serving food and drink in the 1730s when it was used both to brew and serve beer. Today, it's one of the best places to stay in town (though it lacks the rich furnishings of the best, the Bay Tree Hotel). Like many of its neighbors, the Golden Pheasant is capped with a slate roof and fronted with hand-chiseled stones. The cozy accommodations come in a range of sizes, many a bit small, and one room has a four-poster bed. Each, though, is stylishly appointed with period furniture. One room is large enough for a family; all but one come with a shower-and-tub combination (one has a shower stall).

91 High St., Burford, Oxfordshire OX18 4QA. ℂ 01993/823223. Fax 01993/822621. 10 units. £85–£110 ($157–$204) double. Rates include English breakfast. DC, MC, V. **Amenities:** Restaurant; bar. *In room:* TV, coffeemaker, hair dryer, iron, trouser press.

The Lamb Inn 𝕉𝕉   This thoroughly Cotswold house solidly built in 1430 offers thick stones, mullioned and leaded windows, many chimneys and gables, and a slate roof now mossy with age. Vying with the Bay Tree in antique furnishings, it opens onto a stone-paved rear garden, with a rose-lined walk and a shaded lawn. The bedrooms are a mixture of today's comforts and antiques, and prices depend on how recently the room was furnished. Rooms vary in size, and each has a compact bathroom with a tub-and-shower combination (one has a shower stall). The public living rooms have heavy oak beams, stone floors, window seats, Oriental rugs, and fine antiques.

Sheep St., Burford, Oxfordshire OX18 4LR. ℂ 01993/823155. Fax 01993/822228. www.lambinn-burford. co.uk. 15 units. Sun–Thurs £130–£175 ($241–$324) double; Fri–Sat £140–£200 ($259–$370) double. Rates include English breakfast. MC, V. **Amenities:** Restaurant; bar; limited room service; laundry service. *In room:* TV, hair dryer, beverage maker, baby monitor.

WHERE TO DINE

After you've browsed through the antiques shops, head to **Burford House** (ℂ **01993/823151**) for tea. This old Cotswold favorite serves non-residents Tuesday to Saturday from 9am to 5pm. Freshly baked goods, including flans, scones, cakes, and muffins, will tempt you.

Lamb Inn Restaurant MODERN BRITISH   A meal in this pretty pillared restaurant is the perfect way to cap off a visit to Burford. Good pub lunches dominate the agenda at midday; dinners are formal, candlelit affairs. The evening menu is beautifully cooked and served. You may begin with cream of broccoli and blue cheese soup before moving on to rack of lamb with parsnip, sage, and a port sauce, or medallions of venison with sautéed red cabbage and a beetroot coriander sauce. The pub here attracts folks from all walks of life. They seem to adore its mellow atmosphere and charm. Guinness, cider, and a carefully chosen collection of ales, including a local brew, Wadworth Hook Norton Ale, are on tap.

Sheep St. ℂ **01993/823155**. Reservations recommended for dinner. Lunch platters £11–£14 ($20–$25); dinner main courses £15–£22 ($28–$40). MC, V. Mon–Sat noon–2pm; Sun noon–4pm; daily 7–9:30pm.

7 Bourton-on-the-Water ⍣

137km (85 miles) NW of London; 58km (36 miles) NW of Oxford

Its fans call it the quintessential Cotswold village, with history going back to the Celts. Residents fiercely protect the heritage of 15th- and 16th-century architecture, though their town is singled out for nearly every bus tour that rolls through the Cotswolds. Populated in Anglo-Saxon times, Bourton-on-the-Water developed into a strategic outpost along the ancient Roman road, Fosse Way, which traversed Britain from the North Sea to St. George's Channel. During the Middle Ages, its prosperity came from wool, which was shipped all over Europe. During the Industrial Revolution, when the greatest profits lay in finished textiles, it became a backwater as a producer of raw wool—albeit with the happy result for us that it never "modernized," its traditional appearance preserved.

This scenic Cotswold village on the banks of the Windrush River has earned the title of "Venice of the Cotswolds," with its mellow stone houses, its village greens on the banks of the water, and its bridges. Don't expect gondoliers, however. This makes a good stopover, if not for the night, at least as a place to enjoy a lunch and a rest along the riverbanks. Afterwards, you can take a peek inside St. Lawrence's Church in the center of the village. Built on the site of a Roman temple, it has a crypt from 1120 and a tower from 1784.

GETTING THERE

Trains go from London's Paddington Station to nearby Moreton-in-Marsh, a trip of 2 hours. For information, call ℂ **0845/748-4950** or visit www.firstgreatwestern.co.uk/link. From here, take a Pulhams Bus Company coach (ℂ **01451/820369**) 9.5km (6 miles) to Bourton-on-the-Water. Trains also run from London to Cheltenham and Kingham; while somewhat more distant than Moreton-in-Marsh, both have bus connections to Bourton-on-the-Water.

National Express buses run from Victoria Coach Station in London to both Cheltenham and Stow-on-the-Wold. For schedules and information, call ℂ **0870/580-8080** or visit www.nationalexpress.com. Pulhams Bus Company operates about four buses per day from both towns to Bourton-on-the-Water.

If you're driving from Oxford, head west on the A40 to the junction with the A429 (Fosse Way). Take it northeast to Bourton-on-the-Water.

A TINY VILLAGE, THE BIRDS, VINTAGE CARS & MORE

Within the town are a handful of minor museums, each of which was established from idiosyncratic collections amassed over the years by local residents. They include the **Bourton Model Railway Exhibition and Toy Shop** (ℂ **01451/820686**) and **Birdland,** described below.

After you've seen them, stop by the quaint little tearoom called **Small Talk,** on High Street (ℂ **01451/821596**). It's full of dainty lace and fine china and appetizing scones and pastries. Sit at a table overlooking the water and enjoy a pot of tea and some good conversation.

Birdland   This handsomely designed attraction sits on 3.4 hectares (8½ acres) of field and forests on the banks of River Windrush, about 1.6km (1 mile) east of Bourton-on-the-Water. It houses about 1,200 birds representing 361 species, many on exhibition for the first time. Included is the largest and most varied collection of penguins in any zoo, with glass-walled tanks that allow observers to appreciate their agile underwater movements. There's also an enviable collection of hummingbirds. Birdland has a picnic area and a children's playground in a wooded copse.

Rissington Rd. ℂ **01451/820480.** www.birdland.co.uk. Admission £4.85 ($9) adults, £3.85 ($7.10) seniors, £2.85 ($5.25) children 4–14, £14 ($26) family ticket; free for children under 4. Apr–Oct daily 10am–6pm; Nov–Mar daily 10am–4pm (last admission 1 hr. before closing).

Cotswold Motor Museum   This museum is actually in a historic water mill from the 1700s. It has fun displays of cars, bikes, caravans from the 1920s, toys, and the largest collection of advertising signs in Europe. Visitors can also see village shops from the past.

The Old Mill. ℂ **01451/821255.** www.cotswold-motor-museum.com. Admission £3 ($5.55) adults, £2 ($3.70) children. Mid-Feb to Nov daily 10am–6pm. Closed Dec to mid-Feb.

Cotswold Perfumery   This permanent perfume exhibition details the history of the perfume industry and also focuses on its production. You'll find an audiovisual show in a "smelly vision" theater, a perfume quiz, a perfume garden full of plants grown exclusively for their fragrance, and a genealogy chart that can be used by visitors to select their own personal perfume. Perfumes are made on the premises and sold in the shop. Brand names manufactured here include *Muguet,* with its distinctive scent of lily-of-the-valley; *Viva,* a scent that's remarkably similar to (and less expensive than) Chanel No. 5; and *Pallas,* with the scent of jasmine. Flacons, depending on their size, of these fragrances range from £2 to £15 ($3.70–$28) each.

Victoria St. © **01451/820698.** www.cotswold-perfumery.co.uk. Admission £2 ($3.70) adults, £1.75 ($3.25) children ages 5-16 and seniors. Mon–Sat 9:30am–5pm (till 6pm July to mid-Sept); Sun 10:30am–5pm. Closed Dec 25–26.

The Model Village at the Old New Inn   Beginning in the 1930s, a local hotelier, Mr. Morris, whiled away some of the doldrums of the Great Depression by constructing a scale model (1:9) of Bourton-on-the-Water as a testimony to its architectural charms. This isn't a tiny and cramped display set behind glass— the model is big enough that you can walk through this near-perfect and most realistic model village.

High St. © **01451/820467.** www.theoldnewinn.co.uk/village.htm. Admission £2.75 ($5.10) adults, £2.50 ($4.65) seniors, £2 ($3.70) children. Daily 9am–6pm or dusk in summer; daily 10am–4pm in winter.

WHERE TO STAY & DINE

Chester House Hotel   This 300-year-old Cotswold-stone house, built on the banks of the Windrush River, is conveniently located in the center of town. The main building and its adjoining row of stables were converted into this comfortable hotel; the stables were completely renovated and turned into small to midsize bedrooms. Bathrooms are small and compact but with adequate shelf space. Most of them have a tub-and-shower combination.

Victoria St., Bourton-on-the-Water, Cheltenham, Gloucestershire GL54 2BU. © **01451/820286.** Fax 01451/ 820471. 22 units. £69–£105 ($128–$194) double. Rates include continental or English breakfast. AE, DC, MC, V. Closed mid-Dec to early Feb. **Amenities:** Restaurant; bar; limited room service; laundry service; dry cleaning. *In room:* TV, coffeemaker.

Dial House Hotel ♠   Our top choice in town, this 1698 house is constructed from yellow Cotswold stone and stands in the heart of the village center. Mr. and Mrs. Adrian Campbell-Howard, your hosts, offer not only a nostalgic retreat but some of the best cuisine in the area. Set on .6 hectares (1½ acres) of manicured gardens, the house overlooks the River Windrush. Each room has an individual character, and some boast four-poster beds. Two of the rooms, as charming as those in the main building, are in a converted coach house. All rooms have well-kept bathrooms with shower units and Penhaligons toiletries. This establishment is entirely nonsmoking.

Log fires burn on chilly nights, and there are two small dining rooms, one with an inglenook fireplace. Under oak beams and on flagstone floors, candlelit dinners consist of modern British fare, the best local game, and fish. Try pink salmon fish cakes with a pink champagne sauce or medallions of pork with a pistachio and apricot stuffing. Nonresidents can dine here but should call first for a reservation.

The Chestnuts, High St., Bourton-on-the-Water, Gloucestershire GL54 2AN. © **01451/822244.** Fax 01451/ 810126. www.dialhousehotel.com. 14 units. £110–£150 ($204–$278) double, £175 ($324) suite. Rates include English breakfast. MC, V. **Amenities:** 2 restaurants; bar; croquet lawn; limited room service. *In room:* TV, coffeemaker, hair dryer.

The Old Manse Hotel ⭐ *Finds*   An architectural gem, this hotel sits in the center of town by the river that wanders through the village green. Built of Cotswold stone in 1748, with chimneys, dormers, and small-paned windows, it has been frequently modernized, most recently in 2003. Rooms are midsized and cozy, much like something you'd find in the home of your favorite great-aunt. About half of the bathrooms have shower-tub combinations; the remainder contain just showers.

Victoria St., Bourton-on-the-Water, Cheltenham, Gloucestershire GL54 2BX. 𝒞 **01451/820082.** Fax 01451/810381. www.oldmansehotel.com. 15 units. £105–£140 ($194–$259) double. Rates include English breakfast. AE, DC, MC, V. **Amenities:** Restaurant; bar; laundry service; dry cleaning. *In room:* TV, hair dryer, iron/ironing board, trouser press.

Old New Inn   The Old New Inn originally built in 1793 is a landmark in the village. On the main street, overlooking the river, it's a good example of Queen Anne design (the miniature model village in its garden is reviewed above). Hungry or tired travelers are drawn to old-fashioned comforts and cuisine of this most English inn. Rooms are comfortable, with homey furnishings and soft beds. Some rooms are spacious, especially if they have a four-poster bed, but most are small and lie in a cottage annex. Bathrooms have shower stalls and adequate shelf space.

High St., Bourton-on-the-Water, Cheltenham, Gloucestershire GL54 2AF. 𝒞 **01451/820467.** Fax 01451/810236. www.theoldnewinn.co.uk. 9 units. £76 ($141) double. Rate includes English breakfast. MC, V. **Amenities:** Restaurant; 3 bars. *In room:* TV, hair dryer, coffeemaker.

8 Upper & Lower Slaughter

3km (2 miles) N of Bourton-on-the-Water; 6.5km (4 miles) SW of Stow-on-the-Wold

Midway between Bourton-on-the-Water and Stow-on-the-Wold are two of the prettiest villages in the Cotswolds: Upper and Lower Slaughter. Don't be put off by the name—"Slaughter" is actually a corruption of *de Sclotre,* the name of the original Norman landowner. Houses here are constructed of honey-colored Cotswold stone, and a stream meanders right through the street, providing a home for free-wandering ducks, which beg scraps from kindly passersby. Upper Slaughter has a fine example of a 17th-century Cotswold manor house.

The **Old Mill,** in Lower Slaughter (𝒞 **01451/820052**), is a sturdy 19th-century stone structure built on the River Eye with the sole purpose of grinding out flour. The river still turns the massive water wheel that powers this Victorian flourmill today. Visitors can enjoy an ice-cream parlor and tearoom while visiting the mill.

GETTING THERE
Lower Slaughter and Stow-on-the-Wold are 6.5km (4 miles) apart. From Stow, take the A429 (the Main Fosse Way) and follow signs to Cirencester and Bourton-on-the-Water. Turn off the highway when you see signs to Upper and Lower Slaughter. The road will then divide, and you can pick which hamlet you want to head to.

WHERE TO STAY & DINE
Lords of the Manor Hotel ⭐⭐⭐   A 17th-century house set on several acres of rolling fields, the Lords of the Manor offers gardens with a stream featuring brown trout. A quintessentially British hotel of great style and amenities, it's a showplace. It may be modernized, but it successfully maintains the quiet country-house atmosphere of 300 years ago. Half the rooms are in a converted old barn and granary, and many have lovely views. Each has a high standard of

The Great Cotswold Ramble

A walking tour between the villages of Upper and Lower Slaughter, with an optional extension to Bourton-on-the-Water, is one of the most memorable in England. A mile each way between the Slaughters, or 4km (2½ miles) from Upper Slaughter to Bourton-on-the-Water, the walk can take 2 to 4 hours.

The architecture of Upper and Lower Slaughter is so unusual that you're likely to remember this easy hike for many years. You'll also avoid some of the traffic that taxes the nerves and goodwill of local residents during peak season. En route, you're likely to glimpse the waterfowl that inhabit the rivers, streams, and millponds that criss-cross this much-praised region.

A well-worn footpath known as **Warden's Way** meanders beside the edge of the swift-moving River Eye. From its well-marked beginning in Upper Slaughter's central car park, the path passes sheep grazing in meadows, antique houses crafted from local honey-colored stone, stately trees arching over ancient millponds, and footbridges that have endured centuries of foot traffic and rain.

The rushing river powers a historic mill on the northwestern edge of Lower Slaughter. In quiet eddies, you'll see ample numbers of water-fowl and birds, such as wild ducks, gray wagtails, mute swans, coots, and Canada geese.

Most visitors turn around at Lower Slaughter, but Warden's Way con-tinues another 2.5km (1½ miles) to Bourton-on-the-Water by following the Fosse Way, route of an ancient Roman footpath. Most of it, from Lower Slaughter to Bourton-on-the-Water, is covered by tarmac; it's closed to cars, but ideal for walking or biking. You're legally required to close each of the several gates that stretch across the footpath.

Warden's Way will introduce you to Bourton-on-the-Water through the hamlet's northern edges. The first landmark you'll see will be the tower of St. Lawrence's Anglican Church. From the base of the church, walk south along The Avenue (one of the hamlet's main streets) and end your Cotswold ramble on the Village Green, directly in front of the War Memorial.

You can follow this route in reverse, but parking is more plentiful in Upper Slaughter than in Lower Slaughter.

---

comfort and elegant beds with sumptuous linens. The deluxe bathrooms are well appointed and contain tubs and showers.

Upper Slaughter, near Cheltenham, Gloucestershire GL54 2JD. ℭ **01451/820243.** Fax 01451/820696. www.lordsofthemanor.com. 27 units. £160–£310 ($296–$574) double; £270–£375 ($500–$694) suite. AE, DC, MC, V. Take A429 29km (18 miles) north of Cheltenham. **Amenities:** Restaurant; bar; limited room service; babysitting; laundry service. *In room:* TV, minibar, hair dryer, safe.

Lower Slaughter Manor ⭐⭐⭐   This hotel dates from 1658 when it was owned by Sir George Whitmore, high sheriff of Gloucestershire. It remained in the same family until 1964 when it was sold as a private residence. Today, it's one of the great inns of the Cotswolds, though its charms are matched in every way by Lords of the Manor. Standing on its own private grounds, it has spacious and sumptuously furnished rooms, some with four-poster beds. Bedrooms in the main building have more old English character, although those in the annex are equally comfortable and include the same luxuries. Each room is equipped with a beautifully maintained bathroom; some have tubs with separate shower units and twin sinks, the rest have tub-and-shower combinations.

Lower Slaughter, near Cheltenham, Gloucestershire GL54 2HP. (C) **01451/820456.** Fax 01451/822150. www.lowerslaughter.co.uk. 16 units. £220–£395 ($407–$731) double. Rates include English breakfast. AE, DC, MC, V. Take A429 turnoff at the sign for The Slaughters, and drive 1km (½ mile); manor is on right as you enter the village. No children under 12. **Amenities:** Restaurant; lounge; tennis court; limited room service; laundry service; dry cleaning. *In room:* TV, hair dryer.

9 Stow-on-the-Wold ✧

14km (9 miles) SE of Broadway; 16km (10 miles) S of Chipping Campden; 6.5km (4 miles) S of Moreton-in-Marsh; 34km (21 miles) S of Stratford-upon-Avon

As you pass through Shakespeare's "high wild hills and rough uneven ways," you arrive at Stow-on-the-Wold, its very name evoking the elusive spirit of the Cotswolds, one of the greatest sheep-rearing districts of England. Lying 240m (800 ft.) above sea level, it stands on a plateau where "the cold winds blow," or so goes the old saying. This town prospered when Cotswold wool was demanded the world over. Stow-on-the-Wold may not be the cognoscenti's favorite—Chipping Campden takes that honor—but it's even more delightful as it has a real Cotswold town atmosphere.

The town lies smack in the middle of the Fosse Way, one of the Roman trunk roads that cut a swath through Britain. Kings have passed through here, including Edward VI, son of Henry VIII, and they've bestowed their approval on the town. Stagecoaches stopped off here for the night on their way to Cheltenham.

A 14th-century cross stands in the large Market Square, where you can still see the stocks where "offenders" in the past were jeered at and punished by the townspeople who threw rotten eggs at them. The final battle between the Roundheads and the Royalists took place outside Stow-on-the-Wold, and mean old Cromwell incarcerated 1,500 Royalist troops in St. Edward's Market Square.

The square today teems with pubs and outdoor cafes. But leave the square at some point and wander at leisure along some of the narrowest alleyways in Britain. When the summer crowds get you down, head in almost any direction from Stow to surrounding villages that look like sets from a Merchant-Ivory film.

ESSENTIALS

GETTING THERE   Several trains run daily from London's Paddington Station to Moreton-in-Marsh (see below). For schedules and information, call (C) **0845/748-4950** or visit www.firstgreatwestern.co.uk/link. From Moreton-in-Marsh, Pulhams Bus Company makes the 10-minute ride to Stow-on-the-Wold.

National Express buses also run daily from London's Victoria Coach Station to Moreton-in-Marsh, where you can catch a Pulhams Bus Company coach to Stow-on-the-Wold. For schedules and information, call (C) **0870/580-8080** or visit www.nationalexpress.com. Several Pulhams coaches ((C) **01451/820369**) also run daily to Stow-on-the-Wold from Cheltenham.

If driving from Oxford, take the A40 west to the junction with the A424, near Burford. Head northwest along the A424 to Stow-on-the-Wold.

VISITOR INFORMATION   The **Tourist Information Centre** is at Hollis House, The Square ((C) **01451/831082**). It's open Easter through October,

Monday through Saturday from 9:30am to 5:30pm, Sunday from 9am to 5pm; from November to mid-February, Monday through Saturday from 9:30am to 4:30pm; and from mid-February to Easter, Monday through Saturday from 9:30am to 5pm.

ANTIQUES HEAVEN

Don't be fooled by the village's sleepy, country setting: Stow-on-the-Wold has developed over the last 20 years into the antiques-buyer's highlight of Britain and has at least 60 merchandisers scattered throughout the village and its environs.

Set within four showrooms inside an 18th-century building on the town's main square, **Anthony Preston Antiques, Ltd.,** The Square (© 01451/ 831586), specializes in English and French furniture, including some large pieces such as bookcases, and decorative objects that include paperweights, lamps, paintings on silk, and small objects designed to add a glossy accent to carefully contrived interior decors.

Located on Church Street, **Baggott Church Street, Ltd.** (© 01451/ 830370), is the smaller, and perhaps more intricately decorated, of two shops founded and maintained by a well-regarded local antiques merchant, Duncan ("Jack") Baggott, a frequent denizen at estate sales of country houses throughout Britain. The shop contains four showrooms loaded with furniture and paintings from the 17th to the 19th century.

More eclectic and wide-ranging is Baggott's second shop, **Woolcomber House,** on Sheep Street (© 01451/830662). Among the largest retail outlets in the Cotswolds, it contains about 17 rooms that during the 16th century functioned as a coaching inn, but today are lavishly decorated, each according to a particular era of English decorative history.

Covering about half a block in the heart of town, **Huntington's Antiques Ltd.,** Church Street (© 01451/830842), contains one of the largest stocks of quality antiques in England. Wander at will through 10 ground-floor rooms, then climb to the second floor where a long gallery and a quartet of additional showrooms bulge with refectory tables, unusual cupboards, and all kinds of finds.

WHERE TO STAY & DINE

Fosse Manor Hotel   Though lacking the charm of the Grapevine (see below), Fosse Manor is at least the second best in town, even more inviting than the Stow Lodge. The hotel lies near the site of an ancient Roman road that used to bisect England. Its stone walls and neo-Gothic gables are almost concealed by strands of ivy. From some of the high stone-sided windows, you can enjoy a view of a landscaped garden with a sunken lily pond and old-fashioned sundial. Inside, the interior is conservatively modern, with homey bedrooms. Some are large enough for a family; others have a four-poster bed. Six bedrooms, equal in comfort to the main building, are located in a converted coach house on the grounds. Bathrooms are small but well organized, most with a shower-tub combination.

Fosse Way, Stow-on-the-Wold, Cheltenham, Gloucestershire GL54 1JX. © 01451/830354. Fax 01451/832486. www.fossemanor.co.uk. 22 units. £125 ($231) double. Rates include English breakfast. Half board £165 ($305) double. Children under 10 stay free when sharing with paying adult. AE, DC, MC, V. Take A429 2km (1¼ miles) south of Stow-on-the-Wold. **Amenities:** Restaurant; bar; limited room service; babysitting; laundry service; dry cleaning. *In room:* TV, coffeemaker, hair dryer, trouser press.

The Grapevine Hotel ★ *Value*   Facing the village green, The Grapevine mixes urban sophistication with reasonable prices, rural charm, and intimacy. It's the best inn in town, although it doesn't have the charm and grace of Wyck Hill House on the outskirts (see below). It was named after the ancient vine whose tendrils shade and shelter the beautiful conservatory restaurant. Many of the bedrooms have recently been redecorated, and each varies in size—some quite small—but comfort is the keynote here. Ten rooms are in a comfortably appointed annex and lack the character of the stone-sided walls and crooked floors in the main building. Some rooms offer four-poster beds. Each unit comes with a small bathroom, most with a tub-and-shower combination.

Sheep St., Stow-on-the-Wold, Cheltenham, Gloucestershire GL54 1AU. ℂ **01451/830344.** Fax 01451/832278. www.vines.co.uk. 22 units. £130–£150 ($241–$278) double. Rates include breakfast. AE, DC, MC, V. **Amenities:** Restaurant; bar; limited room service; laundry service; dry cleaning. *In room:* TV, coffeemaker, hair dryer.

Stow Lodge Hotel   Stow Lodge dominates the marketplace but is set back far enough to avoid too much noise. Its gardens, honeysuckle growing over the stone walls, diamond-shaped windows, gables, and many chimneys capture the best of country living, even though you're right in the heart of town. The ample, well-furnished rooms vary in size; one has a four-poster bed. The main building has more character, though some equally comfortable rooms are in a converted coach house (most on the ground floor). Room nos. 17 and 18—the smallest in the hotel—share a private bathroom. Bathrooms are small but adequate, each with a shower-tub combination.

The Square, Stow-on-the-Wold, Cheltenham, Gloucestershire GL54 1AB. ℂ **01451/830485.** Fax 01451/831671. www.stowlodge.com. 21 units. £101–£115 ($187–$213) double. 2-night minimum stay on Sat–Sun. Rates include English breakfast. MC, V. Children under 5 not allowed. **Amenities:** Restaurant; bar; limited room service; laundry service; nonsmoking rooms. *In room:* TV, coffeemaker, hair dryer.

Wyck Hill House ✷✷✷   This is sleepy old Stow's pocket of posh. Parts of this otherwise Victorian country house on 40 hectares (100 acres) of grounds and gardens date from 1720, when its stone walls were first erected. It was discovered in the course of recent restoration that one wing of the manor house rests on the foundations of a Roman villa. Today, it is the showcase country inn of this area. The opulent interior adheres to 18th-century authenticity with room after room leading to paneled libraries and Adam sitting rooms. The well-furnished bedrooms are in the main hotel, in the coach-house annex, or in the Orangery, a building erected in the 1980s whose larger-than-usual bedrooms are outfitted in a vaguely Mediterranean theme. Some rooms offer four-poster beds and views of the surrounding countryside. Bathrooms are state of the art; some have Jacuzzi tubs with separate showers.

A424 Burford Rd., Stow-on-the-Wold, Cheltenham, Gloucestershire GL54 1HY. ℂ **01451/831936.** Fax 01451/832243. www.wyckhill.com. 32 units. £88–£127 ($162–$234) per person double; £139 ($257) per person suite. Children under 12 are charged £30 ($56) per night when sharing parent's room. Rates include English breakfast. AE, MC, V. Drive 4km (2½ miles) south of Stow-on-the-Wold on A424. **Amenities:** Restaurant; bar; croquet lawn; 24-hr. room service; laundry service; 1 unit for those with limited mobility. *In room:* TV, coffeemaker, hair dryer, trouser press.

10 Moreton-in-Marsh ✶

134km (83 miles) NW of London; 6.5km (4 miles) N of Stow-on-the-Wold; 11km (7 miles) S of Chipping Campden; 27km (17 miles) S of Stratford-upon-Avon

This is no swampland as the name implies. Marsh derives from an old word meaning "border," so you won't be wading through wetlands to get here. Moreton is a real Cotswold market town that is at its most bustling on Tuesday morning when farmers and craftspeople who live in the surrounding area flood the town to sell their wares and produce. Some of the scenes that take place then are evocative of the classic film *Brigadoon.*

An important stopover along the old Roman road, Fosse Way, as well as an important layover for the night for stagecoach passengers, Moreton-in-Marsh has one of the widest High Streets in the Cotswolds. Roman legions trudged through here centuries ago, but today visitors and antiques shops have replaced them.

The town is still filled with records of its past, including a Market Hall on High Street, built in Victorian Tudor style in 1887, and Curfew Tower on Oxford Street dating from the 17th century. Its bell was rung daily until the late 19th century.

For a fascinating lesson on birds of prey, stop by the **Cotswold Falconry Centre,** Batsford Park (© **01386/701043;** www.cotswold-falconry.co.uk). These great birds are flown daily by experienced falconers for visitors to see firsthand the remarkable speed and agility of eagles, hawks, owls, and falcons. It's open daily from mid-February to mid-November from 10:30am to 5:30pm. Flying displays are daily at 11:30am, 1:30, 3, and 4:30pm. Admission is £5 ($9.25) for adults and £2.50 ($4.65) for children 4 to 14 (free for kids 3 and under).

GETTING THERE

Trains run from London's Paddington Station to Moreton-in-Marsh, a nearly 2-hour trip. For schedules and information, call © **0845/748-4950** or visit www.firstgreatwestern.co.uk/link.

National Express buses run from London's Victoria Coach Station to Moreton-in-Marsh daily. For schedules and information, call © **0870/580-8080** or visit www.nationalexpress.com.

If you're driving from Stow-on-the-Wold (see above), take the A429 north.

WHERE TO STAY & DINE

The Bell Inn *Value*   This is a coaching inn from the 1700s. It has been well restored and is now a traditional and welcoming Cotswold inn for those desiring both a meal and a bed for the night. In summer, guests can enjoy a pint or two in the old courtyard or join the locals in the large bar. Even if you're passing through Moreton just for the day, the bar is ideal for filling, affordable English food. Their specialty is a traditional ploughman's lunch with English Stilton and home-cooked ham, along with a chicken-liver and wild mushroom pâté, crusty bread, a salad, a pickle, and an apple. Under beamed ceilings, bedrooms are comfortably and tastefully furnished in an old English styling, each with a small bathroom with shower. *Note:* The hotel publicizes that it caters to those with disabilities and while there are no entrance ramps, the entrance door is wide and there are some specially equipped bathrooms.

High St., Moreton-in-Marsh, Gloucestershire GL56 0AE. © 01608/651688. Fax 01608/652195. www.bellinn cotswold.com. 5 units. £85 ($157) double; £90 ($167) for 3. Rates include English breakfast. **Amenities:** Restaurant; pub. *In room:* TV, beverage maker, no phone.

The Falkland Arms *Finds*   Immerse yourself in old England with a meal or an overnight at this historic Cotswold village dating from the 1500s when it was known as the Hore & Groom. Many English inns claim to be "unspoiled," but this mellow old place actually is. You can smoke a clay pipe here, as many of the regulars do, and even purchase snuff as in olden days. The timeworn pub has the most awesome collection of jugs and mugs in the area, and they're displayed hanging from the oak beams. The original settle along with flagstone floors and an inglenook fireplace make this a warm, inviting place—that and the extensive range of malt whiskies. An on-site restaurant (reservations essential) offers an imaginative menu daily based on market-fresh ingredients.

A spiral stone staircase leads to the cozy accommodations, with brass steads and white covers. Rooms are beautifully furnished and look out over the countryside and the village green. Each comes with a well-kept bathroom with shower.

Great Tew, Oxfordshire OX7 4DB. © **01608/683653**. Fax 01608/683656. www.falklandarms.org.uk. 5 units. £65 ($130) double. Rates include breakfast. AE, MC, V. Lies 7.4km (12 miles) east of Moreton-in-Marsh. Take A44 to Chipping Norton, then follow A361 to B4022. **Amenities:** Restaurant; pub. *In room:* No phone.

Manor House Hotel ⭐ The town's best hotel, the Manor House comes complete with its own ghost, a secret passage, and a moot room used centuries ago by local merchants to settle arguments over wool exchanges. On the main street, it's a formal yet gracious house, and its rear portions reveal varying architectural periods of design. Inside are many living rooms, one especially intimate with leather chairs and a fireplace-within-a-fireplace, ideal for drinks and swapping "bump-in-the-night" stories. The cozy rooms are tastefully furnished, often with antiques or fine reproductions. Many have fine old desks set in front of window ledges, with a view of the garden and ornamental pond. The well-maintained bathrooms contain shower-tub combinations.

High St., Moreton-in-Marsh, Gloucestershire GL56 0LJ. © **01608/650501**. Fax 01608/651481. www.cotswold-inns-hotels.co.uk. 38 units, 1 family suite. £135–£175 ($250–$324) double; £170–£215 ($315–$398) suite. Rates include English breakfast. AE, MC, V. **Amenities:** Restaurant; bar; indoor pool; Jacuzzi; limited room service; babysitting; laundry service; dry cleaning. *In room:* TV, coffeemaker, hair dryer, iron, safe, trouser press.

Redesdale Arms Though the Manor House is better appointed and more comfortable, this is one of the largest and best-preserved coaching inns in Gloucestershire. Originally established around 1774 as the Unicorn Hotel, it functioned around 1840 as an important link in the Bath-Lincoln stagecoach routes, offering food and accommodations to both humans and horses during the arduous journey. Since then, the inn has been considerably upgraded, with modernized and comfortably furnished bedrooms, but much of the old-fashioned charm remains intact. The small to midsize bedrooms are appointed with either twin or double beds. Each room has a compact bathroom with a shower stall, and some have shower-tub combos.

High St., Moreton-in-Marsh, Gloucestershire GL56 0AW. © **01608/650308**. Fax 01608/651843. www.redesdalearms.com. 15 units. Mon–Thurs £65 ($120) double; Fri–Sun £85 ($157) double. Suite £120 ($222) all week long. Rates include breakfast. MC, V. **Amenities:** 2 restaurants; 2 bars; limited room service; laundry service; dry cleaning. *In room:* TV, dataport, coffeemaker, hair dryer, iron, trouser press.

The White Hart Royal Hotel A mellow old Cotswold inn graced by Charles I in 1644, the White Hart provides modern amenities without compromising the personality of yesteryear. It long ago ceased being the town's premier inn but is still a comfortable place to spend the night. The well-furnished rooms all have a few antiques mixed with basic 20th-century pieces. Much of the original character of the bedrooms remains intact, but you get comfort here, not a lot of style. Each unit is fitted with a small, shower-only bathroom, and some have shower-tub combinations.

High St., Moreton-in-Marsh, Gloucestershire GL56 0BA. © **01608/650731**. Fax 01608/650880. www.oldenglish.co.uk. 18 units. £95–£100 ($176–$185) double. Rates include English breakfast. AE, MC, V. **Amenities:** Restaurant; bar; laundry service; dry cleaning. *In room:* TV, coffeemaker.

11 Broadway ⭐⭐

24km (15 miles) SW of Stratford-upon-Avon; 150km (93 miles) NW of London; 24km (15 miles) NE of Cheltenham

The showcase village of the Cotswolds, if you don't mind the summer coach tours, Broadway's the most attractive spot to anchor for the night. Many prime attractions of the Cotswolds, including Shakespeare Country, are nearby. Flanked by honey-colored stone buildings, its High Street is a gem, remarkable for its harmonious style and design from a point overlooking the lovely Vale of Evesham.

Don't come here seeking a lot of museums and attractions. Show-stopping Broadway is its own attraction. When you see wisteria and cordoned fruit trees covering 17th-century cottages, fronted by immaculately maintained gardens, you'll understand why Henry James found it "delicious to be in Broadway."

ESSENTIALS

GETTING THERE   Rail connections are possible from London's Paddington Station via Oxford. The nearest railway stations are at Moreton-in-Marsh (11km/7 miles away) or at Evesham (8km/5 miles away). For schedules and information, call © **0845/748-4950** or visit www.firstgreatwestern.co.uk/link. Frequent buses arrive from Evesham, but you have to take a taxi from Moreton.

One **National Express** coach departs daily from London's Victoria Coach Station to Broadway, a 2½-hour ride. For schedules and information, call © **0870/580-8080** or visit www.nationalexpress.com.

If you're driving from Oxford, head west on the A40, then take the A434 to Woodstock, Chipping Norton, and Moreton-in-Marsh.

VISITOR INFORMATION   The **Tourist Information Centre** is at 1 Cotswold Ct. (© **01386/852937**), open February through December, Monday through Saturday from 10am to 1pm and 2 to 5pm.

SEEING THE SIGHTS

The **High Street** is one of the most beautiful in England—perhaps the most beautiful. Many of its striking facades date from 1620 or a century or two later. The most famous facade is that of the **Lygon Arms,** High Street (© **01386/852255**), a venerable old inn. It has been serving wayfarers since 1532, and it stands on its own 1.2 hectares (3 acres) of formal gardens. Even if you're not staying here, you may want to visit for a meal or a drink.

You may also seek out **St. Eadurgha's Church,** a place of Christian worship for more than 1,000 years. It's located just outside Broadway on Snowshill Road and is open most days, though with no set visiting hours. If it's closed at the time of your visit, a note on the porch door will tell you what house to go to for the key. Occasional Sunday services are held here.

Also along the street you can visit the **Broadway Magic Experience,** 76 High St. (© **01386/858323**), a showcase shop for teddy bear and doll artisans. The site is also the setting for a unique museum displaying hundreds of antique and collectors' teddy bears, toys, and dolls. This 18th-century stone shop offers a historical look at the world of teddy bears, ranging from Steiff to Pooh. Hours are Tuesday through Sunday from 10am to 5pm. Admission is £2.50 ($4.65) for adults, £1.75 ($3.25) for children under 14 and seniors, £7 ($13) for a family ticket.

On the outskirts of Broadway stands the **Broadway Tower Country Park** on Broadway Hill (© **01386/852390**), a "folly" created by the fanciful mind of the sixth Earl of Coventry. Today, you can climb this tower on a clear day for a panoramic vista of 12 shires. It's the most sweeping view in the Cotswolds. The tower is open from early April to late October daily from 10:30am to 5pm. Admission is £4 ($7.40) for adults and £3 ($5.55) for children. You can also bring the makings for a picnic here and spread it out for your lunch in designated areas.

South of Broadway, a final attraction is **Snowshill Manor,** at Snowshill (© **01386/852410**), a house that dates mainly from the 17th century. It was once owned by an eccentric, Charles Paget Wade, who collected virtually everything he could between 1900 and 1951. Queen Mary once remarked that Wade himself was the most remarkable artifact among his entire flea market. You'll find a little bit of everything here: Flemish tapestries, toys, lacquer cabinets, narwhal tusks, mousetraps, and cuckoo clocks—a glorious mess, like a giant attic of the 20th century. The property, owned by the National Trust, is open April to October, Wednesday to Sunday from noon to 5pm; also open Monday in July and August. Admission is £6.40 ($12) per person or £16 ($12) for a family ticket. *Note:* The Manor is closed for refurbishing during 2004 (reopening in 2005), but the gardens remain open; garden admission is £3.80 ($7.05) adults, £1.90 ($3.50) children, and £9.50 ($18) family.

WHERE TO STAY

The Broadway Hotel ★★   On the village green and one of the most colorful places in Broadway, this converted 15th-century house keeps its old-world charm while providing modern comforts. The recently refurbished rooms are tastefully and comfortably furnished. One room has a four-poster bed. Some guests seek out the more private bedrooms on the ground floor of a separate building, with its direct access to the garden. All but one room have a tub-and-shower combination in the bathroom.

The Green, Broadway, Worcestershire WR12 7AA. ℂ **01386/852401.** Fax 01386/853879. www.cotswold-inns-hotels.co.uk. 20 units. £125–£145 ($231–$268) double. Rates include English breakfast. AE, DC, MC, V. **Amenities:** Restaurant; bar; limited room service; laundry service. *In room:* TV, coffeemaker, hair dryer.

Buckland Manor Hotel ★★★   The Lygon Arms (see below) reigned supreme in Broadway for so long that people thought it had squatters' rights to the title of top inn in town, both for food and lodging. But along came Buckland Manor on the town's outskirts, topping The Lygon Arms in every way, especially in cuisine. This imposing slate-roofed manor house is ringed with fences of Cotswold stone. The core of the manor house was erected in the 13th century, with wings added in succeeding centuries. The Oak Room, with a four-poster bed and burnished paneling, occupies what used to be a private library. Leaded windows in the room overlook gardens and grazing land with Highland cattle and Jacob sheep. Some of the large bedrooms have four-poster beds and fireplaces, but all come with sumptuous beds. All rooms contain such luxuries as fresh fruit and flowers, bathrobes, and luxury toiletries. Each of the oversize bathrooms contains at least one antique, as well as carpeting. The bathrooms with shower-tub combinations use water drawn from the hotel's own spring.

Buckland, near Broadway, Worcestershire WR12 7LY. ℂ **01386/852626.** Fax 01386/853557. www.buckland manor.com. 13 units. £225–£360 ($416–$666) double. Rates include early morning tea and English breakfast. AE, DC, MC, V. Take B4632 about 3km (2 miles) south of Broadway, into Gloucestershire. No children under 12. **Amenities:** Restaurant; bar; heated pool; putting green; tennis court; croquet lawn; limited room service; laundry service; dry cleaning. *In room:* TV, hair dryer.

Dormy House ★   This manor house, high on a hill above the village, boasts views in all directions. Its panoramic position has made it a favorite place whether you're seeking a meal, afternoon tea, or lodgings. Halfway between Broadway and Chipping Campden, it was created from a sheep farm. The owners transformed it, furnishing the 17th-century farmhouse with a few antiques, good soft beds, shower-tub combinations, and full central heating; they also extended these luxuries to an old adjoining timbered barn, converted into studio rooms with open-beamed ceilings. Some rooms have four-poster beds. Bowls of fresh flowers adorn tables and alcoves throughout the hotel.

Willersey Hill, Broadway, Worcestershire WR12 7LF. ℂ **01386/852711.** Fax 01386/858636. www.dormyhouse. co.uk. 49 units. £155–£165 ($287–$305) double; £190 ($352) 4-poster room; £200 ($370) suite. Rates include

English breakfast. AE, DC, MC, V. Closed Dec 24–27. Take A44 3km (2 miles) southeast of Broadway. **Amenities:** Restaurant; bar; putting green; croquet lawn; sauna; limited room service; babysitting; laundry service. *In room:* TV, coffeemaker, hair dryer, trouser press.

The Lygon Arms ★★★ Despite the challenge of Buckland Manor, this many-gabled structure with mullioned windows still basks in its reputation as one of the great old English inns. It opens onto a private rear garden, with 1.2 hectares (3 acres) of lawns, trees, and borders of flowers, stone walls with roses, and nooks for tea or sherry. The oldest portions date from 1532 or earlier, and additions have been made many times since then. King Charles I reputedly drank with his friends in one of the oak-lined chambers, and later, his enemy Oliver Cromwell slept here the night before the Battle of Worcester. Today, many but not all of the bedrooms are in the antique style; a comfortable annex added in the 1970s offers more of a modern feel. In 2004, rooms in the annex were renovated for a total cost of around £4 million. Each room is furnished with a sumptuously comfortable bed. Bathrooms are kept in prime condition, most with tub and shower, and sport bathrobes and Floris toiletries. Some rooms are available for mobility-impaired travelers.

High St., Broadway, Worcestershire WR12 7DU. © **01386/852255.** Fax 01386/858611. www.thelygonarms. co.uk. 69 units. Sun–Fri £179–£200 ($331–$370) double; £279–£395 ($516–$731) suite. Sat £240–£275 ($444–$509) double, £395–£495 ($731–$916) suite. Rates include English breakfast. AE, DC, MC, V. **Amenities:** 2 restaurants; bar; indoor pool; health club; sauna; 24-hr. room service; massage; laundry service. *In room:* TV, dataport, coffeemaker, hair dryer, iron, safe, trouser press.

The Olive Branch Guest House *Value* In the heart of an expensive village, this is a terrific bargain. The house, dating from the 16th century, retains its old Cotswold architectural features. Behind the house is a large-walled English garden and parking area. Guests are given a discount for purchases at the owners' attached antiques shop. Furnishings are basic, but comfortable, and the bathrooms are tiny with a tub or shower. One family room can accommodate up to four people and one room has a four-poster bed.

78 High St., Broadway, Worcestershire WR12 7AJ. © **01386/853440.** Fax 01386/859070. www.theolive branch-broadway.com. 8 units, 7 with bathroom. £66–£78 ($122–$144) double with bathroom. Rates include English breakfast. MC, V. *In room:* TV, coffeemaker, hair dryer.

WHERE TO DINE

The best place in Broadway for a cup of tea is **Tisanes,** The Green (© **01386/ 852112**), offering perfectly blended teas with a variety of sandwiches and salads. Within the town itself, the finest cuisine is served at the previously recommended Lygon Arms (see above), which has both a formal dining room, The Great Hall, plus a less formal brasserie, Goblets. A classic British and French cuisine is featured. Dine on such fare as roast squab in Madeira sauce or Cornish turbot with fresh, handmade noodles and a drizzle of red pepper pesto.

The Tapestry Restaurant ★ MODERN BRITISH Set 3km (2 miles) from the center of Broadway, beside the highway to Moreton-in-Marsh and Oxford, this is one of the most charming and well-managed restaurants in the region. Elegant, though not as formal and stuffy as some competitors, the setting is as pastoral as a painting by Constable. You'll dine in a room ringed with Cotswold stone or in an adjacent glass-sided conservatory.

Chef Alan Cutler turns out an intelligent and interesting cuisine. Appetizers include thin slices of smoked and cured Scottish salmon with a chervil-and-dill-flavored vinaigrette; tempura-style deep-fried ravioli stuffed with white Cornish crabmeat and topped with grilled tiger prawns; and roasted tenderloin of

English duck wrapped in a *duxelle* of wild mushrooms, served with caramelized apples baked in puff pastry and served with a sweet-cider and cream sauce; and a dessert of hot vanilla soufflé with a warm dark chocolate sauce. The cellar houses a superb collection of wines.

In Dormy House, off A44, Willersey Hill, Broadway. (✆ **01386/852711**. Reservations recommended. Fixed-price Sun lunch £21 ($39); dinner main courses £20–£23 ($37–$43); fixed-price dinner £25 ($46). AE, DC, MC, V. Daily 7–9:30pm and Sun noon–2pm.

12 Chipping Campden ✶✶

58km (36 miles) NW of Oxford; 19km (12 miles) S of Stratford-upon-Avon; 150km (93 miles) NW of London

The wool merchants have long departed, but the architectural legacy of honey-colored stone cottages—financed by their fleecy "white gold"—remains to delight the visitor today. Try to tie in a stopover here as you rush from Oxford to Stratford-upon-Avon.

On the northern edge of the Cotswolds, it opens onto the dreamy Vale of Evesham that you've seen depicted in a thousand postcards. Except for the heavy traffic in summer, the main street still looks as it did centuries ago—in fact, the noted British historian, G. M. Trevelyan, called it "the most beautiful village street now left in the island." And so it is even today. You can tie in a stop here on the same day you visit Broadway, lying 6.5km (4 miles) to the west.

Arriving through beautiful Cotswold landscapes—called "seductive" by some—you come upon this country town, whose landmark is the soaring tower of the Church of St. James. You'll see it for miles around. Constructed in the Perpendicular style by the town's wool merchants in the 15th century, it is one of the finest churches in the Cotswolds.

The town's long High Street is curved like Oxford's, and it's lined with stone houses dating from the 16th century. A hundred years later, Chipping Campden was one of the richest wool towns of England. The Campden Trust, a determined group of dedicated conservationists, has preserved the town the way it should be.

Of special interest is the Silk Mill, Sheep Street, open Monday through Saturday from 9am to 5pm. The Guild of Handicrafts was established here in 1902, practicing such skills as bookbinding and cabinetmaking. It folded in 1920 but has been revived today with a series of craft workshops.

ESSENTIALS

GETTING THERE Trains depart from London's Paddington Station for Moreton-in-Marsh, a 1½- to 2-hour trip. For schedules and information, call (✆ **0845/748-4950** or visit www.firstgreatwestern.co.uk/link. A bus operated by Castleway's travels the 11km (7 miles) from Moreton-in-Marsh to Chipping Campden five times a day. Many visitors opt for a taxi from Moreton-in-Marsh to Chipping Campden.

The largest and most important nearby bus depot is Cheltenham, which receives service several times a day from London's Victoria Coach Station. For schedules and information, call (✆ **0870/580-8080** or visit www.nationalexpress.com. From Cheltenham, Barry's Coaches are infrequent and uncertain, departing three times per week at most. Call Gloucester Coach Station ((✆ **01452/527516**) for details.

If you're driving from Oxford, take the A40 west to the junction with the A424. Follow it northwest, passing by Stow-on-the-Wold. The route becomes the A44 until you reach the junction with the B4081, which you take northeast to Chipping Campden.

VISITOR INFORMATION   The **Tourist Information Centre** is at the Old Police Station, High Street (℗ **01386/841206**). It's open daily from 10am to 5pm.

SEEING THE SIGHTS

In 1907, American horticulturist Major Lawrence Johnstone created **Hidcote Manor Garden** ✿✿, 6.5km (4 miles) northeast of Chipping Campden and 14km (9 miles) south of Stratford-upon-Avon (℗ **01386/438333**). Set on 4 hectares (10 acres), this masterpiece is composed of small gardens, or rooms, that are separated by a variety of hedges, old roses, rare shrubs, trees, and herbaceous borders. April through September, the garden is open Saturday through Wednesday from 10:30am to 6pm; open until 5pm in October. Last admission is 1 hour before closing. Admission is £6.20 ($11) for adults, £3.10 ($5.75) for children, and £15 ($28) family ticket.

The poet, artist, and craftsman William Morris (1834–96) called the Cotswold countryside home for most of his life. The worldwide Arts and Crafts movement he led in the late 19th century still inspires artists and craftspeople in this area.

At the studio of **D. I. Hart Silversmiths,** The Guild, The Silk Mill, Sheep Street (℗ **01386/841100**), silver is expertly smithed by descendants of George Hart (born in the 1890s), an original member of the Guild of Handicraft, in the original Ashbee workshop. **Robert Welch Studio Shop,** Lower High Street (℗ **01386/840522**), is where William and Rupert Welch have been crafting silverware, stainless steel, and cutlery within an organization established more than 50 years ago. **Martin Gotrel,** The Square (℗ **01386/841360**), designs and makes fine contemporary and traditional jewelry.

If you're interested in antique porcelain and china, the best repository in Chipping Campden, with a special emphasis on antique and very fragile pieces of Royal Worcester china, is **Circa Antiques,** High St. (℗ **01386/840851**). If antiques and antiques hunting are your passion, visit **School House Antiques,** High Street (℗ **01386/841474**), or **The Barn Antiques Centre,** Long Marston on the Stratford-upon-Avon Road (℗ **01789/721399**). For new, secondhand, and antiquarian books, look up **Campden Bookshop,** High Street (℗ **01386/ 840944**), or **Draycott Books,** 2 Sheep St. (℗ **01386/841392**).

WHERE TO STAY

Charingworth Manor Hotel ✿✿✿   In nearby Charingworth, this elegant country home is the showpiece of the area, more luxurious than Cotswold House in town. A manor has stood on this spot since the time of the *Domesday Book*. The present Tudor-Jacobean house, in honey-colored stone with slate roofs, has 22 hectares (55 acres) of grounds. In the 1930s, it hosted such illustrious guests as T. S. Eliot. Its old-world charm has been preserved, in spite of modernization. Each spacious room is luxuriously furnished with antiques and English fabrics. Many of the period rooms have four-poster beds. Bathrooms are state of the art with tub-and-shower combos. Guests can also wander through a well-manicured garden.

Charingworth, near Chipping Campden, Gloucestershire GL55 6NS. ℗ 01386/593555. Fax 01386/593353. www.englishrosehotels.co.uk. 26 units. £200–£375 ($370–$694) double, £475 ($879) suite. Rates include English breakfast and dinner. AE, DC, MC, V. Take B4035 5km (3¼ miles) east of Chipping Campden. **Amenities:** Restaurant; bar; indoor heated pool; sauna; gym; tennis court; billiards room; limited room service; laundry service. *In room:* TV, coffeemaker, hair dryer, iron, safe, trouser press.

The Cotswold House Hotel ✿✿   This is the best place to stay in town. A stately, formal Regency house dating from 1800, right in the heart of the village opposite the old wool market, Cotswold House sits amid .6 hectares (1½ acres) of tended, walled gardens with shaded seating. The hotel has seen a number of improvements, including the addition of an Old Grammar School Suite, furnished with antiques and paintings, and ideal for a honeymoon retreat. All the bedrooms were refurbished in 2003 with such luxuries as Hypnos beds and crisp Frette linen, along with Hermès bath products in the thoroughly laid out, spacious bathrooms. Many guests prefer one of the more secluded Garden Cottages, each beautifully furnished, with more luxurious appointments than the main house bedrooms.

The Square, Chipping Campden, Gloucestershire GL55 6AN. © **01386/840330.** Fax 01386/840310. www.cotswoldhouse.com. 20 units. £125–£325 ($231–$601) double; £275 ($509) 4-poster bed; from £325 ($601) cottage. Rates include English breakfast. AE, MC, V. **Amenities:** 2 restaurants; bar; limited room service; babysitting; laundry service. *In room:* TV/DVD, minibar, coffeemaker, hair dryer, iron, trouser press.

Noel Arms Hotel   Long before more elegant country houses came along, this old coaching inn was famous, and it still is, with a history dating from the 14th century. Charles II rested here in 1651 after his defeat at the Battle of Worcester. Tradition is kept alive in the decor, which includes fine antiques, muskets, swords, and shields. Twelve rooms date from the 14th century; the others, comfortably furnished and well appointed, are housed in a modern wing built of Cotswold stone. Those bedrooms in the older part of the hotel are the most stylish—one has an exquisitely carved four-poster bed—although comfort is perhaps better in the more modern annex, where the units are more spacious. All the bathrooms, though small, are neatly organized and come with a tub and shower for the most part.

High St., Chipping Campden, Gloucestershire GL55 6AT. © **01386/840317.** Fax 01386/841136. www.cotswold-inns-hotels.co.uk. 26 units. £120–£140 ($222–$259) double. Rates include English breakfast. AE, DC, MC, V. **Amenities:** Restaurant; bar; limited room service; laundry service. *In room:* TV, coffeemaker, hair dryer, trouser press.

WHERE TO DINE

Traditionally, one dined at the grand old inns of the town, and that is still possible. However, today there is a choice outside the hotels.

Malt House 🍴 BRITISH   In the little hamlet bordering Chipping Campden, this classic Cotswold cottage has a well-manicured garden set against a backdrop of orchards. With its paneled walls, exposed beams, and leaded windows, it's a Cotswold cliché. Its fixed-price dinner is the finest in the area, with three selections per course offered. The menu is based on the best produce in any given season. Some veggies and herbs are grown in the house's garden. All dishes have flavor and are deftly handled, especially the seared duck breast with red onion marmalade or the pan-fried filet of Scottish salmon with gnocchi. The risotto with marinated artichokes is rich and creamy, and the filet of beef comes on a bed of wilted spinach and shallots. Save room for the rich desserts, including a chocolate fondant with homemade vanilla ice cream.

The inn also rents seven well-furnished bedrooms, costing £119 to £125 ($219–$231) double; £140 ($259) suite. To reach it, take the B4081 south of Chipping Campden for 2km (1¼ miles).

Broad Campden, GL55 6UU Gloucestershire. © **01386/840295.** Fax 01386/841334. www.malt-house.co.uk. Reservations required. Fixed-price dinner £35 ($64). AE, MC, V. Thurs–Mon 7:30–9pm.

13

Shakespeare Country &
the Heart of England

After London, **Shakespeare Country** is the most popular destination in England for North Americans. Many who don't recognize the county name, Warwickshire, know its foremost tourist town, **Stratford-upon-Avon,** birthplace of Shakespeare and one of the great meccas for writers, readers, and playgoers from around the world.

Shakespeare's hometown is the best center for touring this part of England. You'll want to take in some theater while in Stratford-upon-Avon and branch out for day trips—notably to **Warwick Castle** in nearby Warwick, to **Kenilworth Castle,** and to **Coventry Cathedral.**

And then you have the heart of England at your doorstep. The adventure can begin in nearby **Birmingham,** England's second largest city. Though abandoned warehouses and bleak factories remain, this industrial city, like the rest of England, is being spruced up. From here, you can branch out to any number of lovely old market towns and bucolic spots. There's the scenic **Malverns,** the historic town of **Shrewsbury,** and **Worcester,** of Royal Worcester Porcelain fame. Those who are truly passionate about porcelain flock to the fabled Potteries to visit towns like **Stoke-on-Trent.** Here, factory and outlet shops sell Wedgwood, Portmeirion, and other fine brands of English tableware at a discount.

1 Stratford-upon-Avon ★★

147km (91 miles) NW of London; 64km (40 miles) NW of Oxford; 13km (8 miles) S of Warwick

Crowds of tourists overrun this market town on the River Avon during the summer. In fact, today, **Stratford** aggressively hustles its Shakespeare connection—everybody seems to be in business to make a buck off the Bard. However, the throngs dwindle in winter, when you can at least walk on the streets and seek out the places of genuine historic interest.

Aside from the historic sites, the major draw for visitors is the **Royal Shakespeare Theatre,** where Britain's foremost actors perform during a long season that lasts from April to October. Other than the theater, Stratford is rather devoid of any rich cultural life, and you may want to rush back to London after you've seen the literary pilgrimage sights and watched a production of *Hamlet.* But Stratford-upon-Avon is also a good center for trips to Warwick Castle, Kenilworth Castle, and Coventry Cathedral (see below).

ESSENTIALS
GETTING THERE The journey from London's Paddington Station to Stratford-upon-Avon takes about 2 hours and a round-trip ticket costs £23 ($43). For schedules and information, call ✆ **0845/748-4950** or visit

www.firstgreatwestern.co.uk. The train station at Stratford is on Alcester Road. On Sundays from October to May, it is closed, so you'll have to rely on the bus.

Eight **National Express** buses a day leave from London's Victoria Station, with a trip time of 3¼ hours. A single-day round-trip ticket costs £13 ($24) except Friday when the price is £20 ($37). For schedules and information, call © **0870/580-8080** or visit www.nationalexpress.com.

If you're driving from London, take the M40 toward Oxford and continue to Stratford-upon-Avon on the A34.

VISITOR INFORMATION   The **Tourist Information Centre,** Bridgefoot, Stratford-upon-Avon, Warwickshire, CV37 6GW (© **01789/293127;** www.shakespeare-country.co.uk), provides details about the Shakespeare houses and properties and will assist in booking rooms (see "Where to Stay," below). Call and ask for a copy of their free *Shakespeare Country Holiday* guide. They also operate an American Express currency-exchange office. It's open from April to October, Monday through Saturday from 9am to 6pm and Sunday from 10:30am to 4:30pm; from November to March, Monday through Saturday from 9am to 5pm, and Sunday from 10am to 4pm.

To contact **Shakespeare Birthplace Trust,** which administers many of the attractions, call the Shakespeare Centre (© **01789/204016;** www.shakespeare. org.uk).

THE ROYAL SHAKESPEARE THEATRE

On the banks of the Avon, the **Royal Shakespeare Theatre,** Waterside, Stratford-upon-Avon CV37 6BB (© **01789/403403**), is a major showcase for the Royal Shakespeare Company and seats 1,500 patrons. The theater's season runs from April to October and typically features five Shakespearean plays. The company has some of the finest actors on the British stage.

You usually need **ticket reservations,** with two successive booking periods, each one opening about 2 months in advance. You can pick these up from a North American or English travel agent. A small number of tickets are always held for sale on the day of a performance, but it may be too late to get a good seat if you wait until you arrive in Stratford. Tickets can be booked through **Keith Prowse** (© **800/223-6108** in North America, or 020/7014-8550 in London; www.keithprowse.com).

You can also call the **theater box office** directly (© **0870/609-1110**) and charge your tickets. The box office is open Monday through Saturday from 9am to 8pm, although it closes at 6pm on days when there are no performances. Seat prices range from £8 to £50 ($15–$93). You can make a credit-card reservation and pick up your tickets on the performance day, but you must cancel at least 1 full week in advance to get a refund.

Opened in 1986, the **Swan Theatre** is architecturally connected to the back of its older counterpart and shares the same box office, address, and phone number. It seats 425 on three sides of the stage, as in an Elizabethan playhouse, an appropriate design for plays by Shakespeare and his contemporaries. The Swan presents a repertoire of about five plays each season, with tickets ranging from £10 to £36 ($19–$67).

Within the Swan Theatre is a **painting gallery,** which has a basic collection of portraits of famous actors and scenes from Shakespeare's plays by 18th- and 19th-century artists. It also operates as a base for **guided tours** with lively running commentary through the world-famous theaters. Guided tours are conducted Monday through Saturday at 1:30 and 5:30pm, and four times every

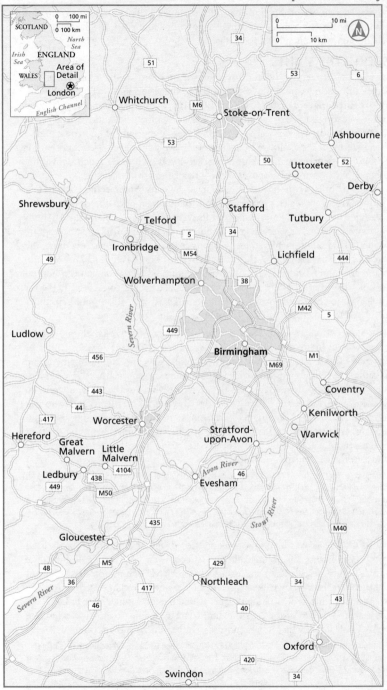

Sunday afternoon, production schedules permitting. Tours cost £4 ($7.40) for adults and £3 ($5.55) for students, seniors, or children. Call ahead for tour scheduling, which is subject to change.

SEEING THE SIGHTS

Besides the attractions on the periphery of Stratford, many Elizabethan and Jacobean buildings are in town, a number of them administered by the **Shakespeare Birthplace Trust** (© **01789/204016;** www.shakespeare.org.uk). One ticket—costing £13 ($24) adults, £12 ($22) for seniors and students, and £6.50 ($12) for children—lets you visit the five most important sights. You can also buy a family ticket to all five sights (good for two adults and three children) for £29 ($54)—a good deal. Pick up the ticket if you plan to do much sightseeing (obtainable at your first stopover at any one of the Trust properties).

Guided tours of the area are conducted by **City Sightseeing,** Civic Hall, Rother Street (www.city-sightseeing.com). In summer, open-top double-decker buses depart every 15 minutes daily from 9am to 6pm. You can take a 1-hour ride without stops, or you can get off at any or all of the town's five Shakespeare properties. Though the bus stops are clearly marked along the historic route, the most logical starting point is the sidewalk in front of the Pen & Parchment Pub, at the bottom of Bridge Street. Tour tickets are valid all day so you can hop on and off the buses as many times as you want. The tours cost £8.50 ($16) for adults, £6 ($11) for seniors or students, and £3.50 ($6.50) for children under 12. A family ticket sells for £20 ($36), and children under 5 go free.

Anne Hathaway's Cottage 🅰   Before she married Shakespeare, Anne Hathaway lived in this thatched, wattle-and-daub cottage in the hamlet of Shottery, 1.5km (1 mile) from Stratford-upon-Avon. It's the most interesting and the most photographed of the Trust properties. The Hathaways were yeoman farmers, and the cottage provides a rare insight into the life of a family in Shakespearean times. The Bard was only 18 when he married Anne, who was much older. Many of the original furnishings, including the courting settle and utensils, are preserved inside the house, which was occupied by descendants of Shakespeare's wife's family until 1892. After visiting the house, you'll want to linger in the garden and orchard.

Cottage Lane, Shottery. © **01789/292100.** Admission £5.20 ($9.60) adults, £2 ($3.70) children, £12 ($22) family ticket (2 adults, 3 children) for all 5 Shakespeare-related houses. Nov–Mar daily 10am–4pm; Apr–May Mon–Sat 9:30am–5pm, Sun 10am–5pm; June–Aug Mon–Sat 9am–5pm, Sun 9:30am–5pm; Sept–Oct Mon–Sat 9:30am–5pm, Sun 10am–5pm. Closed Dec 23–26. Take a bus from Bridge St. or walk via a marked pathway from Evesham Place in Stratford across the meadow to Shottery.

Hall's Croft   It was here that Shakespeare's daughter Susanna probably lived with her husband, Dr. John Hall. Hall's Croft is an outstanding Tudor house with a beautiful walled garden, furnished in the style of a middle-class home of the time. Dr. Hall was widely respected, and he built up a large medical practice in the area. Exhibits illustrating the theory and practice of medicine in Dr. Hall's time are on view. Visitors to the house are welcome to use the adjoining Hall's Croft Club, which serves morning coffee, lunch, and afternoon tea.

Old Town (near Holy Trinity Church). © **01789/292107.** Admission £3.50 ($6.50) adults, £1.70 ($3.15) children, £9 ($17) family ticket (2 adults, 3 children) for all 5 Shakespeare-related houses. Nov–Mar daily 11am–4pm; Apr–May daily 11am–5pm; June–Aug Mon–Sat 9:30am–5pm, Sun 10am–5pm; Sept–Oct daily 11am–5pm. Closed Dec 23–26. To reach Hall's Croft, walk west from High St., which becomes Chapel St. and Church St.; at the intersection with Old Town, go left.

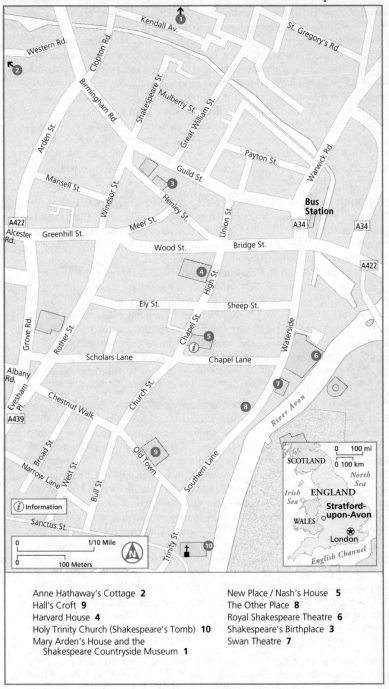

Stratford-upon-Avon

Anne Hathaway's Cottage **2**
Hall's Croft **9**
Harvard House **4**
Holy Trinity Church (Shakespeare's Tomb) **10**
Mary Arden's House and the
    Shakespeare Countryside Museum **1**

New Place / Nash's House **5**
The Other Place **8**
Royal Shakespeare Theatre **6**
Shakespeare's Birthplace **3**
Swan Theatre **7**

Harvard House   The most ornate home in Stratford, Harvard House is a fine example of an Elizabethan town house. Rebuilt in 1596, it was once the home of Katherine Rogers, mother of John Harvard, founder of Harvard University. In 1909, the house was purchased by a Chicago millionaire, Edward Morris, who presented it as a gift to the famous American university. Today, following a restoration, it has reopened a Museum of British Pewter. The museum displays trace the use of pewter from the Roman era until modern times. Pewter, as you learn, used to be the most common choice for household items. Even kiddie toys were made from pewter. Highlights include a tankard engraved with the images of William and Mary; a teapot inspired by the Portland Vase, and a rare bell-based Elizabethan candlestick. Two "hands-on" activities allow children to examine original items.

High St. ✆ **01789/204507.** £2 ($3.70) adults; free for children. May–Nov Tues–Sat and bank holiday Mon 11:30am–4:30pm; Sun 10:30am–4:30pm.

Holy Trinity Church (Shakespeare's Tomb)   In an attractive setting near the River Avon is the parish church where Shakespeare is buried ("and curst be he who moves my bones"). The Parish Register records his baptism in 1564 and burial in 1616 (copies of the original documents are on display). The church is one of the most beautiful parish churches in England.

Shakespeare's tomb lies in the chancel, a privilege bestowed upon him when he became a lay rector in 1605. Alongside his grave are those of his widow, Anne, and other members of his family. You can also see the graves of Susanna, his daughter, and those of Thomas Nash and Dr. John Hall. Nearby on the north wall is a bust of Shakespeare that was erected approximately 7 years after his death—within the lifetime of his widow and many of his friends.

Old Town. ✆ **01789/266316.** Church free; Shakespeare's tomb donation £1 ($1.85) adults, 50p (95¢) students. Apr–Oct Mon–Sat 8:30am–6pm, Sun 12:30–5pm; Mar Mon–Sat 9am–5pm, Sun 12:30–5pm; winter Mon–Sat 9am–4pm, Sun 12:30–5pm. Walk 4 min. past the Royal Shakespeare Theatre with the river on your left.

Mary Arden's House & the Shakespeare Countryside Museum ⟨⟩   So what if millions of visitors have been tricked into thinking this timber-framed farmhouse with its old stone dovecote and various outbuildings was the girlhood home of Shakespeare's mother, Mary Arden? It's still one of the most intriguing sights outside Stratford, even if local historian, Dr. Nat Alcock, discovered in 2000 that the actual childhood home of Arden was the dull looking brick-built farmhouse, Glebe Farm, next door. It was all the trick of an 18th-century tour guide, John Jordan, who decided Glebe Farm was too unimpressive to be the home of the Bard's mother, so he told tourists it was this farmstead instead. Actually the so-called Mary Arden's House wasn't constructed until the late 16th century, a little late to be her home. Nonetheless, visit it anyway as it contains country furniture and domestic utensils. In the barns, stable, cowshed, and farmyard is an extensive collection of farming implements illustrating life and work in the local countryside from Shakespeare's time to the present.

Wilmcote. ✆ **01789/204016.** Admission £5.70 ($11) adults, £5 ($9.25) students and seniors, £2.50 ($4.65) children, family ticket £13.50 ($25). Nov–Mar Mon–Sat 10am–4pm, Sun 10:30am–4pm; Apr–May Mon–Sat 10am–5pm, Sun 10:30am–5pm; June–Aug Mon–Sat 9:30am–5pm, Sun 10am–5pm; Sept–Oct Mon–Sat 10am–5pm, Sun 10:30am–5pm. Closed Dec 23–26. Take A3400 (Birmingham) for 5.5km (3½ miles).

New Place/Nash's House   Shakespeare retired to New Place in 1610 (a prosperous man by the standards of his day) and died here 6 years later. Regrettably, the house was torn down, so only the garden remains. A mulberry tree planted by the Bard was so popular with latter-day visitors to Stratford that the garden's owner chopped it down. The mulberry tree that grows here today is said to have been planted from a cutting of the original tree. You enter the gardens through Nash's House (Thomas Nash married Elizabeth Hall, a granddaughter of the poet). Nash's House has 16th-century period rooms and an exhibition illustrating the history of Stratford. The popular Knott Garden adjoins the site and represents the style of a fashionable Elizabethan garden.

Chapel St. Ⓒ **01789/204016.** Admission £3.50 ($6.50) adults, £3 ($5.55) seniors and students, £1.70 ($3.15) children, £9 ($17) family ticket (2 adults, 3 children) for all 5 Shakespeare-related houses. Nov–Mar daily 11am–4pm; Apr–May daily 11am–5pm; June–Aug Mon–Sat 9:30am–5pm, Sun 10am–5pm; Sept–Oct daily 11am–5pm. Closed Dec 23–26. Walk west down High St.; Chapel St. is a continuation of High St.

The Royal Shakespeare Theatre Summer House   This is a brass-rubbing center, where medieval and Tudor brasses illustrate the knights and ladies, scholars, merchants, and priests of a bygone era. The Stratford collection includes a large assortment of exact replicas of brasses. Entrance is free, but visitors are charged depending on which brass they choose to rub. According to size, the cost ranges from £1 ($1.85) to make a rubbing of a small brass, to a maximum of £19 ($35) for a rubbing of the largest.

Avonbank Gardens. Ⓒ **01789/297671.** Free admission. May–Oct daily 10am–6pm; Nov–Feb Sat–Sun 11am–4pm; Mar–Apr daily 10am–5pm.

Shakespeare's Birthplace ⚹   The son of a glover and whittawer (leather worker), the Bard was born on St. George's day, April 23, 1564, and died on the same date 52 years later. Filled with Shakespeare memorabilia, including a portrait and furnishings of the writer's time, the Trust property is a half-timbered structure, dating from the early 16th century. The house was bought by public donors in 1847 and preserved as a national shrine. You can visit the living room, the bedroom where Shakespeare was probably born, a fully equipped kitchen of the period (look for the "babyminder"), and a Shakespeare Museum, illustrating his life and times. Later, you can walk through the garden. You won't be alone: It's estimated that some 660,000 visitors pass through the house annually.

Built next door to commemorate the 400th anniversary of the Bard's birth, the modern **Shakespeare Centre** serves both as the administrative headquarters of the Birthplace Trust and as a library and study center. An extension houses a visitor center, which acts as a reception area for those coming to the birthplace.

Henley St. (in the town center near the post office, close to Union St.). Ⓒ **01789/204016.** Admission £6.50 ($12) adults, £5.50 ($10) students and seniors, £2.60 ($4.80) children, £15 ($28) family ticket (2 adults, 3 children) for all 5 Shakespeare-related houses. Nov–Mar Mon–Sat 10am–4pm, Sun 10:30am–4pm; Apr–May Mon–Sat 10am–4pm, Sun 10:30am–5pm; June–Aug Mon–Sat 9am–5pm, Sun 9:30am–5pm; Sept–Oct Mon–Sat 10am–5pm, Sun 10:30am–5pm. Closed Dec 23–26.

SHOPPING

Among the many tacky tourist traps are some quality shops, including the ones described below.

Set within an antique house with ceiling beams, **The Shakespeare Bookshop,** 39 Henley St., across from the Shakespeare Birthplace Centre (Ⓒ **01789/ 292176**), is the region's premier source for textbooks and academic treatises on the Bard and his works. It specializes in books for every level of expertise on Shakespearean studies, from picture books for junior high school students to weighty tomes geared to anyone pursuing a Ph.D. in literature.

The largest shop of its kind in the Midlands, **Arbour Antiques, Ltd.,** Poets Arbour, off Sheep Street (Ⓒ **01789/293453**), sells antique weapons from Britain, Europe, and India. If you've always hankered after a full suit of armor, this place can sell you one.

Everything in the **Pickwick Gallery,** 32 Henley St. (© **01789/294861**), is a well-crafted work of art produced by copper or steel engraving plates, or printed by means of a carved wooden block. Hundreds of botanical prints, landscapes, and renderings of artfully arranged ruins, each suitable for framing, can be purchased. Topographical maps of regions of the United Kingdom are also available if you're planning on doing any serious hiking.

WHERE TO STAY

During the long theater season, you'll need reservations way in advance. The **Tourist Information Centre** (© **01789/293127**), part of the national "Book-a-Bed-Ahead" service, will help find an accommodation for you in the price range you're seeking. The fee for room reservations is 10% of your first night's stay (B&B rate only), which is deductible from your final bill.

VERY EXPENSIVE

Welcombe Hotel & Golf Course ☆☆☆   For a formal, historic hotel, there is none better in Stratford. The Welcombe is rivaled only by Ettington Park at Alderminster (see below). One of England's great Jacobean country houses, it's a 10-minute ride from the heart of Stratford-upon-Avon. Situated on 63 hectares (157 acres) of grounds, its keynote feature is an 18-hole golf course. Guests gather for afternoon tea or drinks on the rear terrace, with its Italian-style garden and steps leading down to flowerbeds. The public rooms are heroic in size, with high mullioned windows providing views of the park. Regular bedrooms—some seemingly big enough for tennis matches—are luxuriously furnished; however, those in the garden wing, while comfortable, are small. The accommodations most recently refurbished and up-to-date are found in the Garden wings. The rooms with the greatest character of old England are found in the main house. Many of the bedrooms have four-poster beds. The bathrooms are clad in marble or else tiled and offer deluxe toiletries and bathrobes.

Warwick Rd., Stratford-upon-Avon, Warwickshire CV37 0NR. © 01789/295252. Fax 01789/414666. www. welcombe.co.uk. 66 units. £150–£250 ($278–$463) double; £275–£450 ($509–$833) suite. Rates include English breakfast. AE, DC, MC, V. Take A439 2km (1½ miles) northeast of the town center. **Amenities:** Restaurant; bar; golf course; outdoor tennis court; 24-hr. room service; laundry service; dry cleaning; rooms for those with limited mobility. *In room:* TV, hair dryer, iron/ironing board (in some).

EXPENSIVE

Alveston Manor Hotel ☆☆   This black-and-white timbered manor is perfect for theatergoers; it's just a 2-minute walk from the River Avon. The Welcombe and Ettington Park may have cornered the deluxe trade, but the Alveston, along with the Shakespeare (see below), are the most atmospheric choices in town. Mentioned in the *Domesday Book,* the building predates the arrival of William the Conqueror and has everything from an Elizabethan gazebo to Queen Anne windows. The 19 rooms in the manor house will appeal to those who appreciate old slanted floors, overhead beams, and antique furnishings; some have half-tester beds. Other accommodations—full of tour groups—are in a 3-decades-old motel-like wing. Furnishings here are fresher, but the ambience is lacking. Most bathrooms include a shower and tub. The lounges are in the manor; there's a view of the centuries-old tree at the top of the garden—said to have been the background for the first presentation of *A Midsummer Night's Dream.*

Clopton Bridge (off B4066), Stratford-upon-Avon, Warwickshire CV37 7HP. © 800/225-5843 in the U.S. and Canada, or 0870/400-8181. Fax 01789/414095. www.macdonaldhotels.co.uk. 113 units. £125–£160 ($231–$296) double; £195–£230 ($361–$426) suite. Rates include breakfast. AE, DC, MC, V. **Amenities:** Restaurant; bar; 24-hr. room service; babysitting; laundry service; dry cleaning; sauna; indoor pool; gym; nonsmoking rooms; rooms for those with limited mobility. *In room:* TV, minibar, coffeemaker, hair dryer, iron/ironing board.

Shakespeare Hotel ⚑⚑ Filled with historical associations, the original core of this hotel, dating from the 1400s, has seen many additions in its long life. Quieter and plusher than the Falcon (see below), it is equaled in the central core of Stratford only by Alveston Manor. Residents relax in the post-and-timber-studded public rooms, within sight of fireplaces and playbills from 19th-century productions of Shakespeare's plays. Bedrooms are named in honor of noteworthy actors, Shakespeare's plays, or Shakespearean characters. The oldest are capped with hewn timbers, and all have modern comforts. Even the newer accommodations are at least 40 to 50 years old and have rose-and-thistle patterns carved into many of their exposed timbers. Bathrooms range in size, but each is adequate and well appointed with a tub and shower.

Chapel St., Stratford-upon-Avon, Warwickshire CV37 6ER. *©* **800/225-5843** in the U.S. and Canada, or 0870/400-8182. Fax 01789/415411. www.macdonaldhotels.co.uk. 74 units. £138–£150 ($255–$278) double; £178–£190 ($329–$352) suite. Rates include breakfast. Children up to 16 stay free in parent's room. AE, DC, MC, V. **Amenities:** Restaurant; bar; 24-hr. room service; laundry service; nonsmoking rooms; rooms for those with limited mobility. *In room:* AC, TV, dataport, hair dryer, iron/ironing board.

Stratford Moat House ⚑ The Moat House stands on 2 hectares (5 acres) of landscaped lawns on the banks of the River Avon near Clopton Bridge. Although lacking the charm of the Alveston Manor or the Shakespeare, this modern hotel offers fine amenities and facilities. It is one of the flagships of the Queen's Moat House, a British hotel chain, and was built in the early 1970s and last renovated in 1995. The hotel hosts many conferences, so don't expect to have the place to yourself. Every bedroom has a high standard of comfort; bathrooms offer generous shelf space, large mirrors, and tubs and showers.

Bridgefoot, Stratford-upon-Avon, Warwickshire CV37 6YR. *©* **01789/279988**. Fax 01789/298589. www.moathousehotels.com. 251 units. £120 ($222) double; £200 ($370) suite. AE, DC, MC, V. **Amenities:** 2 restaurants; 2 bars; heated indoor pool; spa; sauna; exercise room; limited room service; laundry service. *In room:* TV, dataport, coffeemaker, hair dryer, iron/ironing board, safe, trouser press.

Thistle Stratford-upon-Avon ⚑ Theatergoers flock here, because the hotel is across the street from the main entrance of the Royal Shakespeare and Swan theaters. The Thistle chain completely refurbished the interior after buying the hotel in 1993. Its redbrick main section dates from the Regency period, although over the years a handful of adjacent buildings were included and an uninspired modern extension added. Today, the interior has a lounge and bar; a dining room with bay windows; a covered garden terrace; and comfortable but narrow bedrooms. Two rooms are graced with a four-poster bed. The small bathrooms are adequate and well maintained with a shower and tub.

44 Waterside, Stratford-upon-Avon, Warwickshire CV37 6BA. *©* **0870/333-9146**. Fax 0870/333-9246. www.stratfordthistle.co.uk. 63 units. £73–£179 ($135–$331) double. AE, DC, MC, V. **Amenities:** Restaurant; bar; 24-hr. room service; laundry service; dry cleaning. *In room:* TV, dataport, coffeemaker, hair dryer, iron, trouser press.

MODERATE

The Falcon Hotel Located in the heart of Stratford, the Falcon blends the very old and the very new. The inn was licensed a quarter of a century after Shakespeare's death. A 1970s bedroom extension is connected to its rear by a glass passageway. The recently upgraded bedrooms in the mellowed part have oak beams, diamond leaded-glass windows, some antique furnishings, and good reproductions. Each room is comfortable and clean, but there is not enough soundproofing to drown out your next-door neighbor's telly. Rooms in the newer section are also comfortable but are more sterile in tone. Carved headboards crown fine beds.

The small bathrooms come with shower stalls. The comfortable lounges, also recently upgraded, are some of the finest in the Midlands.

Chapel St., Stratford-upon-Avon, Warwickshire CV37 6HA. ℂ **01789/279953.** Fax 01789/414260. www.corushotels.com/thefalcon. 84 units. £80–£125 ($148–$231) double; from £140 ($259) suite. Rates include breakfast. AE, DC, MC, V. **Amenities:** Restaurant; 3 bars; 24-hr. room service; rooms for those with limited mobility. *In room:* TV, dataport, coffeemaker, hair dryer.

Grosvenor House Hotel   A pair of Georgian town houses, built in 1832 and 1843, respectively, join to form this hotel, which is one of the second-tier choices of Stratford on equal footing with the Thistle (see above). Situated in the center of town, with lawns and gardens to the rear, it is a short stroll from the intersection of Bridge Street and Waterside, allowing easy access to the River Avon, Bancroft Gardens, and the Royal Shakespeare Theatre. All small to mid-size bedrooms are nicely furnished and comfortable. Bathrooms are compact but well maintained, most with a shower-tub combination.

12–14 Warwick Rd., Stratford-upon-Avon, Warwickshire CV37 6YT. ℂ **01789/269213.** Fax 01789/266087. www.groshotelstratford.co.uk. 67 units. £88–£114 ($163–$211) double, £164 ($303) suite. AE, MC, V. **Amenities:** Restaurant; bar; free pass to nearby recreation center; 24-hr. room service; babysitting; laundry service; nonsmoking rooms; rooms for those with limited mobility. *In room:* TV, dataport, coffeemaker, hair dryer, iron/ironing board, safe (in some), trouser press.

The White Swan 👫   This cozy, intimate hotel is one of the most atmospheric in Stratford and is, in fact, the oldest building here. In business for more than a century before Shakespeare appeared on the scene, it competes successfully with the Falcon in offering an ancient atmosphere. The gabled medieval front would present the Bard with no surprises, but the modern comforts inside would surely astonish him, even though many of the rooms have been preserved. Bedrooms are comfortable but generally lack style. Except for an occasional four-poster or half-canopy bed, most are twins or doubles. Bathrooms are compact with shower and bath.

Rother St., Stratford-upon-Avon, Warwickshire CV37 6NH. ℂ **01789/297022.** Fax 01789/268773. www.e-travelguide.info/whiteswan. 41 units. £80 ($148) double. Rates include English breakfast. AE, DC, MC, V. **Amenities:** Restaurant; bar; limited room service. *In room:* TV, dataport (in some), coffeemaker, hair dryer, trouser press.

INEXPENSIVE

The Marlyn Hotel   The Marlyn is situated near Hall's Croft, just a 5-minute walk from the town center and the Royal Shakespeare Theatre. This Victorian house has welcomed guests since 1870; the Evans family, who have owned and managed it since 1994, endeavor to make their guests comfortable. The hotel's good-size bedrooms contain comfortable furnishings. Like Gideon's Bible, a copy of the Bard's complete works is in every bedroom. There's also a small lounge with a TV.

3 Chestnut Walk, Stratford-upon-Avon, Warwickshire CV37 6HG. ℂ and fax **01789/293752.** www.marlynhotel.co.uk. 8 units, 5 with shower only. £52 ($96) double with shower only. Rates include English breakfast. MC, V. **Amenities:** Breakfast room; massage; babysitting; laundry; nonsmoking rooms; room for those with limited mobility. *In room:* TV, coffeemaker, hair dryer, iron.

Sequoia House   This hotel opens onto its own beautiful garden on .3 hectare (¾ acre) across the Avon opposite the theater, conveniently located for visiting the major Shakespeare properties of the National Trust. Renovation has vastly improved the house, which was created from two late Victorian buildings. In its price range, bedrooms are some of the most comfortable in town, with upholstered chairs and desk space. Bathrooms are small but tidy; the superior rooms have full baths, the rest have showers only. Guests gather in a lounge that has a licensed bar and an open Victorian fireplace. The hotel also has a private parking area.

51–53 Shipston Rd., Stratford-upon-Avon, Warwickshire CV37 7LN. ℂ **01789/268852.** Fax 01789/414559. www.sequoiahotel.co.uk. 23 units. £79–£89 ($146–$165) double. Rates include English breakfast. MC, V. **Amenities:** Bar. *In room:* TV, coffeemaker, hair dryer.

Stratheden Hotel   A short walk north of the Royal Shakespeare Theatre, the Stratheden Hotel is tucked away in a desirable location. Built in 1673, and currently the oldest remaining brick building in the town center, it has a tiny rear garden and top-floor rooms with slanted, beamed ceilings. Under the ownership of the Wells family for the past quarter century, it has improved again in both decor and comfort with the addition of fresh paint, new curtains, and good beds. Most of the small bathrooms have a shower stall though a few have tubs.

5 Chapel St., Stratford-upon-Avon, Warwickshire CV37 6EP. ℂ and fax **01789/297119.** www.ukstay.com/ warwick/stratheden. 9 units. £66–£72 ($122–$133) double. Rates include full English breakfast. AE, MC, V. **Amenities:** Breakfast room. *In room:* TV.

Victoria Spa Lodge   This B&B is old-fashioned and atmospheric and still going strong. Opened in 1837, the year Queen Victoria ascended to the throne, this was the first establishment to be given her name. This lodge was originally a spa frequented by the queen's eldest daughter, Princess Vicky. The accommodating hosts offer tastefully decorated, comfortable bedrooms. The small bathrooms are neatly organized with a shower stall. The entire property is nonsmoking.

Bishopton Lane (2.5km/1½ miles north of the town center where A3400 intersects A46), Stratford-upon-Avon, Warwickshire CV37 9QY. ℂ **01789/267985.** Fax 01789/204728. www.stratford-upon-avon.co.uk/ victoriaspa.htm. 7 units. £65 ($120) double; £80 ($148) for 3; £100 ($185) for 5-person family suite. Rates include English breakfast. MC, V. *In room:* TV, coffeemaker, hair dryer.

NEARBY PLACES TO STAY

Ettington Park Hotel ✿✿✿   This Victorian Gothic mansion is one of the most sumptuous retreats in Shakespeare Country. It opened as a hotel in 1985 but has a history that spans 9 centuries. The land is a legacy of the Shirley family, whose 12th-century burial chapel is near the hotel. Like a grand private home, the hotel boasts baronial fireplaces, a conservatory, and a charming staff. Adam ceilings, stone carvings, and ornate staircases have been beautifully restored. A new wing, assembled with the same stone and neo-Gothic carving of the original house, stretches toward a Renaissance-style arbor entwined with vines. In the spacious and elegant bedrooms, the most modern comforts are concealed behind antique facades. The best units are deluxe doubles, which are larger than the standard units and open onto garden views. Some rooms have old-fashioned four-posters. Bathrooms have Victorian-style tiling, robes, and deluxe toiletries. Stay clear of the bookcase in the library; the ghost is very temperamental.

Alderminster, near Stratford-upon-Avon, Warwickshire CV37 8BU. ℂ **01789/450123.** Fax 01789/450472. www.handpicked.co.uk. 48 units. £100–£150 ($185–$278) double; £185–£335 ($342–$620) suite. Rates include English breakfast. AE, DC, MC, V. Drive 8km (5 miles) south along A3400 just past Alderminster, then take 2nd left (signposted) into Ettington Park. **Amenities:** Restaurant; bar; indoor pool; tennis court; Jacuzzi; sauna; 24-hr. room service; laundry service; babysitting; rooms for those with limited mobility. *In room:* TV, dataport, coffeemaker, hair dryer, iron, safe (in some), trouser press.

Mary Arden Inn ✿ *(Finds)*   This is an escapist's retreat for those who want to avoid the hordes descending on Stratford. Shakespeare's mother, Mary Arden, lived in the tiny village of Wilmcote, some 5.5km (3½ miles) northwest of Stratford. Actually an upgraded village pub-hotel, this place offers not only appealing and well-furnished bedrooms at moderate prices but also good meals. The inn is relatively unpretentious and offers a welcome respite from the hordes in the center of Stratford. All of the rooms were upgraded in 2002, and offer a variety of amenities ranging from CD players to the complete works of Shakespeare. Some of the rooms are quite small, others more midsize. Bathrooms are very small with a minimum of shelf space and a shower stall/tub or both. The Romeo and Juliet Suite features a four-poster bed and a Jacuzzi tub.

The Green, Wilmcote, Stratford-upon-Avon, Warwickshire CV37 9XJ. $\mathcal{C}$ **01789/267030.** Fax 01789/204875. www.maryarden.com. 10 units. £85 ($157) double; £100 ($185) suite. Rates include English breakfast. AE, MC, V. Take A3400 5.5km (3½ miles) northwest of Stratford. **Amenities:** Restaurant; bar. *In room:* TV, dataport, coffeemaker, hair dryer, iron/ironing board.

WHERE TO DINE

After visiting the birthplace of Shakespeare, pop across the street for tea at **Brasserie,** Henley Street ($\mathcal{C}$ **01789/295261**). This airy tearoom is tremendously popular, but the very attentive staff more than compensates for the throngs of patrons. Choose from an array of tea blends, cream teas, and various cakes, pastries, and tea cakes—all freshly baked in their own kitchen.

EXPENSIVE TO MODERATE

Callands ✦✦ ECLECTIC/INTERNATIONAL   At last Stratford boasts a restaurant worth writing home about. In the town center between the Shakespeare Centre and Market Place, Callands was installed in a 16th-century building. Here you find good food in what had been a gastronomic wasteland in England (except for our recommendations, of course!). Extremely professional cooking, vivid use of spices, imaginative menus, and reasonable prices attract a never-ending stream of visitors and locals alike. We like experiments with Asian flavors and spices that always get the balance right. Is this the Stratford of yore, you ask, as you taste the aromatic pumpkin and Cerny cheese tagliatelle with almond pesto, tomato, and candied eggplant? Grilled vegetables in lemon oil with rosemary chickpeas and saffron couscous are followed by cashew-nut and herb risotto with wilted rocket and shaved Parmesan. Even such English classics as bubble and squeak (cabbage and potatoes) are given added zest by an orange Dubonnet sauce.

13–14 Meer St. $\mathcal{C}$ **01789/269304.** Reservations required. Main courses £12–£18 ($22–$33); fixed-price 2-course lunch £19 ($35), 3-course £24 ($44). AE, DC, MC, V. Tues–Sat noon–2pm and 5:45–10:30pm.

Lambs ✦ CONTINENTAL/ENGLISH   A stone's throw from the Royal Shakespeare Theatre, this cafe-bistro is housed in a building dating from 1547 (and with connections to Lewis Carroll). For a quick light meal or pretheater dinner, it's ideal. The menu changes monthly. Begin with such starters as fish soup with rouille, quite tasty, or else smoked salmon with a potato cake and a chive crème fraîche. Our party recently enjoyed such delights as breast of chicken roasted with lime and served in a green curry sauce and a rack of lamb Provençal with dauphinoise potatoes. Look to the blackboard for daily specials. The chef takes chances (no doubt inspired by trips to the Continent), and it's a nice departure from the bland tea-room food served for decades in Stratford.

12 Sheep St. $\mathcal{C}$ **01789/292554.** Reservations required Sat night. Main courses £9–£16 ($17–$30); fixed-price menu £12 ($22) for 2 courses, £15 ($28) for 3. MC, V. Mon–Sat noon–2pm and 5–10pm; Sun noon–2pm.

The Quarto's Restaurant ✦ FRENCH/ITALIAN/ENGLISH   This restaurant enjoys the best location in town—in the theater itself, with glass walls providing an unobstructed view of swans on the Avon. You can purchase an intermission snack feast of smoked salmon and champagne, or dine by flickering candlelight after the performance. Many dishes, such as apple-and-parsnip soup, are definitely old English; others reflect a continental touch, such as fried polenta with filets of pigeon and bacon. For your main course, you may select Dover sole, pheasant supreme, or roast loin of pork. Homemade crème brûlée is an old-time favorite. The theater lobby has a special phone for reservations.

In the Royal Shakespeare Theatre, Waterside. (C) **01789/403415.** Reservations required. Matinee lunch £18 ($33); dinner £16–£22 ($30–$41). AE, MC, V. Thurs and Sat noon–2:30pm; Mon–Sat 5:30pm–midnight. Closed when theater is shut down.

Thai Boathouse ☆ THAI The only restaurant set on the Avon, this charming choice is reached by crossing Clopton Bridge toward Oxford and Banbury. The second-floor dining room opens onto vistas of the river. This restaurant, originally established 4 decades ago in Bangkok, has brought spice and zest to Stratford's lazy restaurant scene. The decor comes from Thailand itself, with elephants, woodcarvings, and Buddhas. Seasonal specialties such as wild duck and pheasant are a special feature of the menu. Fresh produce, great skill in the kitchen, and exquisite presentations are the hallmarks of this restaurant. Sample a selection of authentic Thai appetizers before going on to such a delectable main course as fresh sea bass in lemon grass. One of our favorites is their lamb in a yellow curry with potatoes, onions, and cashew nuts.

Swan's Nest Lane. (C) **01789/297733.** Reservations recommended. Main courses £5.50–£12 ($10–$22); fixed-price menus £21–£27 ($39–$50). MC, V. Daily noon–2:30pm and 5:30–10:30pm.

INEXPENSIVE

Hussain's INDIAN This restaurant has many admirers—it's one of the brighter spots on the bleak culinary landscape hereabouts. A well-trained and alert staff welcomes guests and advises them about special dishes. You can select from an array of northern Indian dishes, many from the tandoor, plus various curries with lamb or prawn. Offering a 10% discount on pre- and post-theater dinners, Hussain's is across from the Shakespeare Hotel and historic New Place.

6A Chapel St. (C) **01789/267506.** Reservations recommended. Main courses £6.75–£15 ($12–$27). AE, MC, V. Thurs–Sun 12:30–2:30pm; daily 5pm–midnight.

The Oppo INTERNATIONAL Located in the heart of Stratford within a 16th-century building, this refreshingly unpretentious restaurant serves up good bistro cooking at reasonable prices. Menu choices include breast of chicken with banana roasted in lime butter, basmati rice with a mild curry sauce, or salmon fish cakes served on a bed of spinach.

13 Sheep St. (C) **01789/269980.** Reservations recommended. Main courses £8.50–£18 ($16–$33). MC, V. Daily noon–2pm and 5–10:30pm.

Russons INTERNATIONAL Because the theater is a short stroll away, this is a great place for a pre-show meal. The restaurant is housed in a 400-year-old building and the two simply furnished dining rooms both feature inglenook fireplaces. The menu changes regularly to reflect the availability of seasonal ingredients. Fresh seafood is the specialty here. Daily specials are posted on a blackboard and include rack of lamb, guinea fowl, and numerous vegetarian dishes. Finish with one of the delicious homemade desserts.

8 Church St. (C) **01789/268822.** Reservations required. Main courses £8.50–£16 ($16–$30). AE, MC, V. Tues–Sat 11:30am–1:30pm and 5:15–9:30pm.

THE BEST PLACES FOR A PINT

The Black Swan ("The Dirty Duck") ☆☆ ENGLISH Affectionately known as The Dirty Duck, this has been a popular hangout for Stratford players since the 18th century. The wall is lined with autographed photos of its many famous patrons. Typical English grills, among other dishes, are featured in the Dirty Duck Grill Room, though no one has ever accused it of serving the best food in Stratford. You'll have a choice of a dozen appetizers, most of which would make a meal in themselves. In fair weather, you can have drinks in the front garden and watch the swans glide by on the Avon.

Waterside. ℂ **01789/297312.** Reservations required for dining. Main courses £8–£16 ($15–$30); bar snacks £5–£7.25 ($9.25–$13). AE, DC, MC, V (in the restaurant only). Daily 11am–11pm. No dinner Sun.

The Garrick Inn ENGLISH   Near Harvard House, this black-and-white timbered Elizabethan pub has an unpretentious charm. The front bar is decorated with tapestry-covered settles, an old oak refectory table, and an open fireplace that attracts the locals. The back bar has a circular fireplace with a copper hood and mementos of the triumphs of the English stage. The specialty is homemade pies such as steak and kidney or chicken and mushroom. Wild boar and venison are other specialties.

25 High St. ℂ **01789/292186.** Main courses £6.50–£13 ($12–$24). MC, V. Meals daily noon–9pm. Pub Mon–Sat 11am–11pm; Sun noon–10:30pm.

The White Swan ENGLISH   In the town's oldest building is this atmospheric pub, with cushioned leather armchairs, oak paneling, and fireplaces. You're likely to meet amiable fellow drinkers, who revel in a setting once enjoyed by Will Shakespeare himself when known as the Kings Head. At lunch, you can partake of hot dishes of the day, along with fresh salads and sandwiches.

In The White Swan hotel, Rother St. ℂ **01789/297022.** Dinner reservations recommended. Bar snacks £3.95–£15 ($7.30–$28); fixed-price 3-course Sun lunch £6.95 ($13). AE, DC, MC, V. Morning coffee daily 9am–noon; self-service bar snacks daily 12:30–3pm; afternoon tea daily 2–5:30pm; hot meals noon–2:30pm and 5:30–9:30pm.

2 Warwick: England's Finest Medieval Castle ✮✮✮

148km (92 miles) NW of London; 13km (8 miles) NE of Stratford-upon-Avon

Most visitors come to this town just to see Warwick Castle, the finest medieval castle in England. Some combine it with a visit to the ruins of Kenilworth Castle (see below), but the historic center of ancient Warwick has a lot more to offer.

Warwick cites Ethelfleda, daughter of Alfred the Great, as its founder. But most of its history is associated with the earls of Warwick, a title created by the son of William the Conqueror in 1088. The story of those earls—the Beaumonts and the Beauchamps (such figures as "Kingmaker" Richard Neville)—makes for an exciting episode in English history. A devastating fire swept through the heart of Warwick in 1694, but a number of Elizabethan and medieval buildings still survive, along with some fine Georgian structures from a later date.

ESSENTIALS

GETTING THERE   Trains run frequently between Stratford-upon-Avon and Warwick. Call ℂ **0845/748-4950** or visit www.firstgreatwestern.co.uk for schedules and information.

One **Stagecoach** bus per hour departs Stratford-upon-Avon during the day. The trip takes 15 to 20 minutes. Call the tourist office (ℂ **01789/293127**) for schedules.

Take the A46 if you're driving from Stratford-upon-Avon.

VISITOR INFORMATION   The **Tourist Information Centre** is at The Court House, Jury Street (ℂ **01926/492212**), and is open daily from 9:30am to 4:30pm; closed from December 24 to December 26 and January 1.

SEEING THE SIGHTS

Lord Leycester Hospital   The great fire also spared this group of half-timbered almshouses at the West Gate. The buildings were erected around 1400, and the hospital was founded in 1571 by Robert Dudley, earl of Leicester, as a home for old soldiers. It's still used by ex-service personnel and their spouses. On top of the West Gate is the attractive little chapel of St. James, dating from the 12th century but renovated many times since. Closed to the public since 1903, the gardens in back of the hospital were recently restored. Nathaniel Hawthorne wrote of his visits to the gardens in 1855 and 1857; the gardens were restored based on the observations he made in his writings.

High St. © 01926/491422. Admission £3.20 ($5.90) adults, £2.70 ($5) students and seniors, £2.20 ($4.05) children. Easter–Oct Tues–Sun 10am–5pm; Nov–Easter Tues–Sun 10am–4pm.

St. John's House Museum   At Coten End, not far from the castle gates, this early-17th-century house has exhibits on Victorian domestic life. A schoolroom is furnished with original 19th-century furniture and equipment. During the school term, Warwickshire children dress in period costumes and learn Victorian-style lessons. Groups of children also use the Victorian parlor and the kitchen. Because it's impossible to display more than a small number of items at a time, a study room is available where you can see objects from the reserve collections. The costume collection is a particularly fine one, and visitors can study the drawings and photos that make up the costume catalog. These facilities are available by appointment only. Upstairs is a military museum, tracing the history of the Royal Warwickshire Regiment from 1674 to the present.

St. John's, at the crossroads of the main Warwick-Leamington Rd. (A425/A429) and the Coventry Rd. (A429). © 01926/412132. Free admission. Tues–Sat and bank holidays 10am–5:30pm; Easter–Sept also Sun 2:30–5pm.

St. Mary's Church   Destroyed in part by the fire of 1694, this church, with rebuilt battlemented tower and nave, is among the finest examples of late-17th- and early-18th-century architecture. The Beauchamp Chapel, spared from the flames, encases the Purbeck marble tomb of Richard Beauchamp, a well-known earl of Warwick who died in 1439 and is commemorated by a gilded bronze effigy. Even more powerful than King Henry V, Beauchamp has a tomb that's one of the finest remaining examples of the Perpendicular Gothic style from the mid–15th century. The tomb of Robert Dudley, earl of Leicester, a favorite of Elizabeth I, is against the north wall. The Perpendicular Gothic choir dates from the 14th century; the Norman crypt and chapter house are from the 11th century.

Church St. © 01926/403940. www.saintmaryschurch.co.uk. Free admission; donations accepted. Apr–Sept daily 10am–6pm; Oct–Mar daily 10am–4pm. All buses to Warwick stop at Old Sq.

Warwick Castle 🏰🏰   Perched on a rocky cliff above the River Avon in the town center, a stately late-17th-century mansion is surrounded by a magnificent 14th-century fortress, the finest medieval castle in England. Even 3 hours may not be enough time to see everything. Surrounded by gardens, lawns, and woodland, where peacocks roam freely, and skirted by the Avon, Warwick Castle was described by Sir Walter Scott in 1828 as "that fairest monument of ancient and chivalrous splendor which yet remains uninjured by time."

Ethelfleda, daughter of Alfred the Great, built the first significant fortifications here in 914. William the Conqueror ordered the construction of a motte-and-bailey castle in 1068, 2 years after the Norman Conquest. The mound is all that remains today of the Norman castle, which Simon de Montfort sacked in the Barons' War of 1264.

The Beauchamp family, the most illustrious medieval earls of Warwick, is responsible for the appearance of the castle today; much of the external structure remains unchanged from the mid–14th century. When the castle was granted to Sir Fulke Greville by James I in 1604, he spent £20,000 (an enormous sum in those days) converting the existing castle buildings into a luxurious mansion. The Grevilles have held the earl of Warwick title since 1759.

The staterooms and Great Hall house fine collections of paintings, furniture, arms, and armor. The armory, dungeon, torture chamber, ghost tower, clock tower, and Guy's tower create a vivid picture of the castle's turbulent past and its important role in the history of England.

The private apartments of Lord Brooke and his family, who in recent years sold the castle to Tussaud's Group, are open to visitors. They house a display of a carefully reconstructed Royal Weekend House Party of 1898. The major rooms contain wax portraits of important figures of the time, including a young Winston Churchill. In the Kenilworth bedroom, a likeness of the Prince of Wales, later King Edward VII, reads a letter. The duchess of Marlborough prepares for her bath in the red bedroom. Among the most life-like of the figures is a uniformed maid bending over to test the temperature of the water running into a bathtub.

You can also see the Victorian rose garden, a re-creation of an original design from 1868 by Robert Marnock. Near the rose garden is a Victorian alpine rockery and water garden.

(C) 0870/442-2000. www.warwick-castle.co.uk. Admission £13 ($24) adults, £7.50 ($14) children 4–16, £9 ($17) seniors, free for children 4 and under, £32 ($59) family ticket. Apr–Sept daily 10am–6pm; Oct–Mar 10am–5pm. Closed Christmas Day.

WHERE TO STAY

Many people prefer to stay in Warwick and commute to Stratford-upon-Avon, though the accommodations here are not as special as those at Stratford.

The Glebe at Barford 𝄢 *(finds)*   This 1820s rectory to the Church of St. Peter has been welcoming wayfarers to either Stratford-upon-Avon or Warwick since it was successfully converted into a small country house hotel in 1948. The church still stands adjacent to the hotel's grounds. In recent years, much redecorating and many modern facilities have been added, including the Cedars Conservatory Restaurant looking out onto the gardens. A small swimming pool with hydro jets has been added as well. Each of the bedrooms has been individually designed, with either a tented ceiling, a four-poster, or a coronet-style bed. All the first-class bathrooms come with heated towel racks, and tubs and showers. The hotel lies only a 10-minute drive from the center of Warwick, and we suggest that motorists stay here instead of the center of town.

Church St., Barford, Warwickshire CV35 8BS. (C) 01926/624218. Fax 01926/624171. www.glebehotel.co.uk. 39 units. £118–£128 ($218–$237) double; £148 ($274) family unit; £153 ($283) Shakespeare Suite (with Jacuzzi corner bathroom). AE, DC, MC, V. **Amenities:** Restaurant; bar; heated indoor pool; fitness center; steam room; hot tub; sauna. *In room:* TV, beverage maker.

Hilton Warwick 𝄢   Though outside of town, the Hilton is the best choice in the area. Lying at the junction of a network of highways, it's popular with business travelers and hosts many conferences for local companies. But tourists also find that its comfort and easy-to-find location make it a good base for touring Warwick and the surrounding regions. It's a low-rise modern design with a series of interconnected bars, lounges, and public areas. Room furnishings are bland but comfortable. Units have well-kept bathrooms with shower-tub combinations.

Warwick Bypass (A429 Stratford Rd.), Warwick, Warwickshire CV34 6RE. ℂ **800/445-8667** in the U.S. and Canada, or 01926/499555. Fax 01926/410020. www.warwick.hilton.com. 181 units. £90–£175 ($167–$324) double. AE, DC, MC, V. Take A429 3km (2 miles) south of Warwick (11km/7 miles north of Stratford-upon-Avon). Junction 15 off M40 from London. **Amenities:** Restaurant; bar; pool; exercise room; sauna; 24-hr. room service; babysitting; laundry service; dry cleaning. *In room:* TV, coffeemaker, hair dryer, trouser press.

Lord Leycester Hotel   This affordable choice lies within walking distance of the castle and the other historic buildings of Warwick. In 1726, this manor house belonged to Lord Archer of Umberslade; in 1926, it was finally turned into this modest hotel. The rooms are small but offer reasonable comfort for the price with decent double or twin beds. Bathrooms are also small with a shower/tub or both.

17 Jury St., Warwick, Warwickshire CV34 4EJ. ℂ **01926/491481.** Fax 01926/491561. 49 units. £75–£90 ($139–$167) double. Rates include English breakfast. AE, DC, MC, V. **Amenities:** 2 restaurants; bar; room service. *In room:* TV, dataport, coffeemaker, hair dryer, trouser press.

Tudor House Inn & Restaurant   At the edge of town, on the main road from Stratford-upon-Avon to Warwick Castle, is a 1472 timbered inn. It's one of the few buildings to escape the fire that destroyed High Street in 1694. Off the central hall are two large rooms, each of which could be the setting for an Elizabethan play. All the simply furnished bedrooms have washbasins, and two contain doors only 1m (4 ft.) high. The compact bathrooms are equipped with a shower. In the corner of the lounge is an open turning staircase.

90–92 West St. (opposite the main Warwick Castle car park, 1km/½ mile south of town on A429), Warwick, Warwickshire CV34 6AW. ℂ **01926/495447.** Fax 01926/492948. www.thetudorhouse.co.uk. 10 units, 5 with bathroom. £65–£85 ($120–$157) double. Rates include English breakfast. AE, MC, V. **Amenities:** Restaurant; bar. *In room:* TV, coffeemaker.

WHERE TO DINE

For a break from sightseeing, it's hard to beat the ancient ambience of tea at **Brethren's Kitchen,** Lord Leycester Hospital (ℂ **01926/491422**). This tea-room is part of a 16th-century hospital the earl established in the year 1571. It has cool stone floors and wonderful exposed oak beams. Indian, Chinese, and herbal teas are all available, as well as scones with fresh cream, sponge cake, and fruit cake. It's closed in February and on Mondays but open on bank holidays.

Fanshaw's Restaurant BRITISH/FRENCH   In the heart of Warwick, at the edge of the city's commercial center, this restaurant occupies a late Victorian build-ing enlivened by flowered window boxes. Inside are only 32 seats in a well-main-tained, rather flouncy dining room lined with mirrors. A well-trained staff serves food from a menu that changes every 2 months, but usually includes sirloin steak; filet of beef Wellington with a red-wine and shallot sauce; and breast of pheasant with a shiitake and oyster mushroom brandy sauce. Especially elegant and usually offered during game season is a brace of quail with a hazelnut and apricot stuffing.

22 Market Place. ℂ **01926/410590.** Reservations recommended. Fixed-price menus £23 ($42). AE, MC, V. Mon–Sat 6:30–10pm.

Findon's Restaurant BRITISH   The building is authentically Georgian, constructed in 1700. You'll dine surrounded by original stone floors and cup-boards, within a setting for only 43 diners to dine in snug comfort. Michael Findon, owner and sometime chef, works hard at orchestrating a blend of traditional and modern British cuisine. Starters to tempt you include a salad of pan-fried pigeon breast with wild mushrooms or else a crispy filet of sea bass in tomato oil. A light, skilled hand is shown in such main courses as sautéed lamb's liver and kidneys in a port wine sauce (how very English) and a breast of Gressingham duck with a blackberry and green peppercorn sauce.

7 Old Sq. ℭ 01926/411755. Reservations recommended. Main courses £11–£19 ($20–$35). MC, V. Mon–Fri noon–2pm; Mon–Sat 6:30–9:30pm.

Vanilla *Value* BRITISH   It's the Castle that draws you to Warwick, not the cuisine, but this bistro is notable for serving affordable food that is both good-tasting and prepared with fresh ingredients. Launch your repast with a freshly made soup of the day or else something classic such as Parma ham and melon with a honey-and-mustard dressing. We recently dined very well on Gressingham duck breast, which was interestingly served with a fricassee of haricot vert and mushrooms. Our dinner companions preferred the roast cod, which came with buttery leeks, and the grilled Scottish rib-eye steak with wild mushrooms, roasted garlic, and a Claret jus. Save room for one of the old-fashioned desserts such as a vanilla crème brûlée with walnut shortbread or the warm dark chocolate tart with clotted cream.

6 Jury St. ℭ 01926/498930. Reservations recommended. Main courses £11–£15 ($20–$28). AE, MC, V. Tues–Sat 11am–2pm and 6:30–10pm; Sun 11:30am–6pm.

3 Kenilworth Castle ✰✰

164km (102 miles) NW of London; 8km (5 miles) N of Warwick; 21km (13 miles) N of Stratford-upon-Avon

The big attraction in the village of Kenilworth, an otherwise dull English market town, is Kenilworth Castle—and it's reason enough to stop here.

ESSENTIALS

GETTING THERE   InterCity train lines make frequent and fast connections from London's Paddington and Euston stations to either Coventry or Stratford-upon-Avon. For information, call ℭ 0845/748-4950 or visit www.firstgreat western.co.uk (for trains to Startford) or www.virgintrains.co.uk (for trains to Coventry). Midland Red Line buses make regular connections from both towns to Kenilworth.

If you're driving from Warwick, take the A46 toward Coventry.

VISITOR INFORMATION   The **Tourist Information Centre** is in the village at the Kenilworth Library, 11 Smalley Place (ℭ **01926/852595**). It's open Monday, Tuesday, Thursday, and Friday from 9:30am to 7pm; Saturday 9:30am to 4pm.

THE MAGNIFICENT RUINS OF KENILWORTH CASTLE

Kenilworth Castle ✰✰   The castle was built by Geoffrey de Clinton, a lieutenant of Henry I. At one time, its walls enclosed an area of 4.3 hectares (7 acres), but it is now in magnificent ruins. Caesar's Tower, with its 5m (16-ft.) thick walls, is all that remains of the original structure.

Edward II was forced to abdicate at Kenilworth in 1327 before being carried off to Berkeley Castle in Gloucestershire, where he was undoubtedly murdered. In 1563, Elizabeth I gave the castle to her favorite, Robert Dudley, earl of Leicester. He built the gatehouse, which the queen visited on several occasions. After the civil war, the Roundheads were responsible for breaching the outer walls and towers and blowing up the north wall of the keep. This was the only damage inflicted following the earl of Monmouth's plea that it be "Slighted with as little spoil to the dwelling house as might be."

The castle is the subject of Sir Walter Scott's romance, *Kenilworth*. In 1957, Lord Kenilworth presented the decaying castle to England and limited restoration has since been carried out.

© **01926/852078.** Admission £4.80 ($8.90) adults, £3.50 ($6.50) seniors, £2.40 ($4.45) children 5–16, £12 ($22) family; free for children under 5. Mar–Oct daily 10am–5pm (till 6pm June–Aug); Nov–Feb daily 10am–4pm. Closed Jan 1 and Dec 24–26.

WHERE TO STAY

Clarendon House Hotel A family-run hotel and restaurant, the Clarendon House is in the old part of Kenilworth. The oak tree around which the original alehouse was built in 1430 is still supporting the roof of the building today. The bedrooms vary greatly in size, but each is tastefully decorated with a comfortable bed—usually a double or twins, though there are two four-posters. Bathrooms are small and compact but well maintained, each with a shower-tub combination.

6–8 Old High St., Kenilworth, Warwickshire CV8 1LZ. *©* **01926/857668.** Fax 01926/850669. www.oldenglish. co.uk. 20 units. £180 ($333) double. Rates include English breakfast. AE, DC, MC, V. **Amenities:** Restaurant; bar; laundry service; rooms for those with limited mobility. *In room:* TV, dataport, coffeemaker, hair dryer, trouser press.

WHERE TO DINE

Restaurant Bosquet *©* FRENCH This narrow, stone-fronted town house from the late Victorian age is a culinary oasis. It's owned and operated by French-born Bernard Lignier, who does the cooking, and his English wife, Jane, who supervises the dining room. The a la carte menu changes every 2 months and may include such offerings as terrine of wild duck with foie gras and truffles, and a dessert specialty known as an *assiette* (plate) of chocolates.

97A Warwick Rd. *©* **01926/852463.** Reservations recommended. Main courses £18–£19 ($33–$35); 3-course lunch or dinner £28 ($52). AE, MC, V. Tues–Fri noon–1:15pm; Tues–Sat 7–9pm. Closed 1 week for Christmas and the last 3 weeks in Aug.

4 Coventry *©*

161km (100 miles) NW of London; 32km (20 miles) NE of Stratford-upon-Avon; 29km (18 miles) SE of Birmingham; 84km (52 miles) SW of Nottingham

Coventry has long been noted in legend as the ancient market town through which Lady Godiva took her famous ride in the buff (giving rise to the term Peeping Tom). The veracity of the Lady Godiva story is hard to pin down. It has been suggested that she never appeared nude in town but was the victim of scandalmongers. Coventry today is a Midlands industrial city. The city was partially destroyed by German bombers during World War II, but the restoration is miraculous.

ESSENTIALS

GETTING THERE Trains run every half-hour from London's Euston Station to Coventry (trip time: 1¼ hr.). For schedules and information, call *©* **0845/ 748-4950** or visit www.virgintrains.co.uk.

From London's Victoria Coach Station, buses depart every hour throughout the day for the 2-hour trip. From Stratford, bus no. X-16 runs from the town's bus station every hour for Coventry's bus station at Pool Meadow, Fairfax Street. This bus takes 60 to 90 minutes and stops at Kenilworth and Warwick en route. For schedules and information, call *©* **020/7529-2000.**

VISITOR INFORMATION   The **Coventry Tourist Office,** Bayley Lane (① **024/7683-2303**), is open from Easter to mid-October, Monday through Friday from 9:30am to 5pm, and Saturday through Sunday from 10am to 4:30pm; from mid-October to Easter, Monday through Friday from 9:30am to 4:30pm, Saturday and Sunday from 10am to 4:30pm.

TOURING COVENTRY CATHEDRAL

Coventry Cathedral ★★★   Consecrated in 1962, Sir Basil Spence's controversial Coventry Cathedral is the city's main attraction. The cathedral is on the same site as the 14th-century Perpendicular building, and you can visit the original tower. Many locals maintain that the structure is more likely to be appreciated by the foreign visitor, because Brits are more attached to traditional cathedral design. Some visitors consider the restored site one of the most poignant and religiously evocative modern churches in the world.

Outside is Sir Jacob Epstein's bronze masterpiece, *St. Michael Slaying the Devil.* Inside, the outstanding feature is the 21m (70-ft.) high altar tapestry by Graham Sutherland, said to be the largest in the world. The floor-to-ceiling abstract stained-glass windows are the work of the Royal College of Art. The West Screen (an entire wall of stained glass installed during the 1950s) depicts rows of stylized saints and prophets with angels flying among them.

In the undercroft of the cathedral is a visitor center, the Walkway of Holograms, whose otherwise plain walls are accented with three-dimensional images of the stations of the cross, created with reflective light. One of the most evocative objects here is a charred cross wired together by local workmen from burning timbers that crashed to the cathedral's floor during the Nazi bombing. An audiovisual exhibit on the city and church includes the fact that 450 aircraft dropped 40,000 firebombs on the city in 1 day.

Priory Row. ① **024/7652-1200.** www.coventrycathedral.org.uk. Suggested donation of £3 ($5.55) to cathedral. Admission to tower £1.50 ($2.80) adults, 75p ($1.40) children. Cathedral Easter–Sept daily 9am–5:30pm; Oct–Easter daily 9:30am–5pm.

5 Birmingham ★

193km (120 miles) NW of London; 40km (25 miles) N of Stratford-upon-Avon

England's second-largest city may lay claim fairly to the title "Birthplace of the Industrial Revolution." It was here that James Watt first used the steam engine with success to mine the Black Country. Watt and other famous 18th-century members of the Lunar Society regularly met under a full moon in the nearby Soho mansion of manufacturer Matthew Boulton. Together, Watt, Boulton, and other "lunatics," as Joseph Priestly, Charles Darwin, and Josiah Wedgwood cheerfully called themselves, launched the revolution that thrust England and the world into the modern era.

Today, this brawny, unpretentious metropolis still bears some of the scars of industrial excess and the devastation of the Nazi Luftwaffe bombing during World War II. But an energetic building boom has occurred recently, and Brummies have nurtured the city's modern rebirth by fashioning Birmingham into a convention city that hosts 80% of all trade exhibitions in the country.

Birmingham has worked diligently in recent decades to overcome the blight of over-industrialization and poor urban planning. New areas of green space and the city's cultivation of a first-rate symphony and ballet company, as well as art galleries and museums, have all made Birmingham more appealing.

Birmingham Museum and Art Gallery **4**
Council House **4**
Gas Street Basin **2**
Sherborne Wharf Heritage Narrowboats **1**
Museum of Science and Industry **3**

ⓘ Information

Though not an obvious tourist highlight, Birmingham serves as a gateway to England's north. With more than 1 million inhabitants, Birmingham has a vibrant nightlife and restaurant scene. Its three universities, 2,428 hectares (6,000 acres) of parks and nearby pastoral sanctuaries, and restored canal walkways also offer welcome quiet places.

ESSENTIALS

GETTING THERE By Plane Continental Airlines (© **800/525-0280;** www.continental.com) flies every evening from Newark to Birmingham International Airport (BHX). Details on other Birmingham flights and schedules are available through the airport (© **0870/733-5511;** www.bhx.co.uk).

Direct air service between Birmingham and London is almost nonexistent. Many air carriers, however, maintain a virtual air-shuttle service between London airports and nearby Manchester, which is a 1½-hour trip to Birmingham via ground transport. For example, British Airways (BA) operates 28 daily flights from London's Heathrow to Manchester, 17 daily flights from London's Gatwick, and six daily flights from Stansted to Manchester. BA runs even more return flights daily from Manchester to London.

Birmingham's airport lies about 13km (8 miles) southeast of the Birmingham City Centre and is easily accessible by public transportation. **AirRail Link** offers a free shuttle bus service every 10 minutes from the airport to the Birmingham International Rail Station and National Exhibition Centre (NEC). **InterCity** train services operate a shuttle from the airport to New Street Station in the City Centre, just a 10-minute trip.

By Train InterCity offers half-hourly train service (Mon–Fri) between London's Euston Station and Birmingham, a 90-minute rail trip. Trains depart every 2 hours for Birmingham. Birmingham's New Street Station in the City Centre and the airport's International Station link the city to the national rail network.

Trains leave Manchester's Piccadilly Station nearly every hour for Birmingham. The trip takes 90 minutes. Call © **0845/748-4950** or visit www.virgintrains. co.uk for train schedules and current fares.

By Bus **National Express** (© **0870/580-8080;** www.nationalexpress.com) provides regular bus service between Birmingham and London, Manchester, and regional towns.

By Car From London, the best route is via the M40, which leads onto the M42, the motorway that circles south and east of Birmingham. Once on the M42, any of the roads from junctions 4 to 6 will lead into the center of Birmingham.

The drive takes about 2 to 2½ hours from London, depending on traffic conditions. Parking is available at locations throughout Birmingham.

VISITOR INFORMATION The **Birmingham Convention & Visitor Bureau (BCVB),** 150 New St. in the City Centre (© **01212/025099**), is open Monday to Saturday 9:30am to 5:30pm, Sunday 10:30am to 4:30pm. The BCVB assists travelers in arranging accommodations, obtaining theater or concert tickets, and planning travel itineraries.

GETTING AROUND Birmingham's City Centre hosts a number of attractions within easy walking distance. **Centro** (© **01212/002700;** www.centro. org.uk) provides information on all local bus and rail services within Birmingham and the West Midlands area. A **Day Saver Pass** costs £5.20 ($9.60) and is an economical way to use the Centro bus and local train system. A weekly **Centro Card** costs £20 ($36). Exact change is required on one-way local bus and train trips.

Centro also links Birmingham and surrounding Midland towns with regular bus service. Taxis queue at various spots in the City Centre, rail stations, and the National Exhibition Centre. Travelers can also ring up a radio-cab operator like **BB's** (© **01216/933333**).

EXPLORING BIRMINGHAM

Stephenson Place, at the intersection of New and Corporation streets, is a good starting point for sampling the attractions of City Centre. A 5-minute stroll along New Street leads to Victoria Square, where **Council House,** Victoria Square (© **01213/032040**), the city's most impressive Victorian building, anchors the piazza. Built in 1879, it is still the meeting place for the Birmingham City Council and an impressive example of the Italian Renaissance style.

Along Broad Street is the **Gas Street Basin** (© **01212/369811**). Operated by Second City Canal Cruises, it forms the hub of the 3,220km (2,000-mile) canal network that runs in all directions from Birmingham to Liverpool, London, Nottingham, and Gloucester. From the Basin, you can take a cruise along the canals, or just walk by the towpaths.

Just a 10-minute walk from City Centre is the **Jewelry Quarter** at 75–79 Vyse St. (© **01215/543598**). This complex includes more than 100 jewelry shops. The skill of the jeweler's craft can be viewed at the Discovery Centre's restored Smith and Pepper factory displays or by visiting shop workbenches that still produce most of the jewelry made in Britain. A unique time capsule of the ancient craft of jewelry making and working with precious metals, the quarter offers bargain-hunters the opportunity to arrange repairs, design a custom piece, or just browse. Admission to the Museum of the Jewelry Quarter is free. Open April to October Tuesday to Sunday 11:30am to 4pm.

Sherborne Wharf Heritage Narrowboats (© **01214/556163;** www. sherbornewharf.co.uk), depart from the International Convention Centre Quayside, taking you on 1-hour tours to see Birmingham from the water. You cruise along quiet stretches of the canal, which first brought commercial life to the city at the start of the Industrial Revolution. Departures are daily from Easter to October at 11:30am, 1, 2:30, and 4pm, costing £4.25 ($7.85). Off season, tours are conducted only Saturday and Sunday if weather permits.

Blakesley Hall, Blakesley Rd., Yardley (© **01214/642193;** www.bmag.org. uk/blakesley_hall), is a restored Tudor farmhouse from 1590. The half-timbered structure is typical of buildings once common in the West Midlands. Its original architectural features, including a herringbone floor, are intact; the Great and Little Parlours on the ground floor have been restored. Oak furnishings include carved, panel-back armchairs, long refectory tables, and other period pieces. Among the many artifacts from the era are pewter goblets and candlesticks. In the painted Bedchamber, paintings on the walls from 1590 were uncovered after having been hidden for centuries. Admission free, the museum is open daily from Easter through October Tuesday to Sunday 11:30am to 4pm.

Thinktank at Millennium Point, Curzon St. (© **01212/022222;** www. thinktank.ac), combines science and history in 10 galleries where you can get active with the exhibits spread over four floors. The place is for both learning and for fun. Kids can do everything from grab a handful of polar bear blubber to take control of a digger. Various sections deal with such subjects as "Medicine Matters," exploring surgical instruments and health in general. Nature is uncovered in the "Wild Life" section, as you learn how scientists study the wild world and how animals adapt to change. "Futures" gives you a look into a living tomorrow. Open daily 10am to 5pm, costing £6.95 ($13) for adults, £4.95 ($9.15) for children 3 to 15 years old, and £5.50 ($10) for students and seniors.

Barber Institute of Fine Arts ★★   Don't be put off by the stark, stone-and-brick building that houses the Barber Institute collection. Some critics consider it the finest small art museum in England and the equal of any museum outside London. The choice selection of paintings includes works by Bellini, Botticelli, Brueghel, Canaletto, Delacroix, Gainsborough, Gauguin, Guardi, Murillo, Renoir, Rubens, Turner, van Gogh, and Whistler.

University of Birmingham (just off Edgbaston Park Rd., near the University's East Gate, 4km/2½ miles south of City Centre). © **01214/147333.** www.barber.org.uk. Free admission. Mon–Sat 10am–5pm; Sun noon–5pm. Bus: 61, 62, or 63 from City Centre.

Birmingham Museum and Art Gallery ★   Known chiefly for its collection of pre-Raphaelite paintings (including works by Ford Maddox Brown, Dante Gabriel Rossetti, Edward Burne-Jones, and Holman Hunt), the gallery also houses exceptional paintings by English watercolor masters from the 18th century. The BMAG is instantly recognized by its "Big Brum" clock tower.

Chamberlain Sq. © **01213/032834.** www.bmag.org.uk. Free admission; varying charges for special exhibitions. Mon–Thurs and Sat 10am–5pm; Fri 10:30am–5pm; Sun 12:30–5pm.

The Black Country Living Museum   Much of the area immediately surrounding Birmingham is called the Black Country (after the black smoke that billowed over the area during the iron-working era). That period is best preserved at the Black Country Living Museum in Dudley, a town about 16km (10 miles) northwest of Birmingham. The museum occupies a sprawling landscape in the South Staffordshire coalfields, an early forge of the Industrial Revolution, and re-creates what it was like to work and live in the Black Country of the 1850s. An electric tramway takes visitors to a thick underground coal seam, and trolleys move through a reconstructed industrial village with a schoolhouse, anchor forge, working replica of a 1712 steam engine, and trade shops.

Tipton Rd., Dudley (5km/3 miles north of Junction 2 exit on M5). ⓒ 01215/579643. www.bclm.co.uk. Admission £9.60 ($18) adults, £8.50 ($16) seniors, £5.50 ($10) children; family ticket £27 ($50). Mar–Oct daily 10am–5pm; Nov–Feb Wed–Sun 10am–4pm.

SHOPPING

In addition to exploring the **Jewelry Quarter** (see above), Birmingham is a great town for shopping. There are more than 700 retail stores, and many people in the Midlands come here just to shop, especially along **Cannon Street** and **New Street** with its recently opened top-brand designer stores. The city's **Mailbox** complex at Wharfside Street (ⓒ 01216/321123), was once used to sort the mail. But now it's becoming a big shopping center, with department stores like Harvey Nichols moving in. In the heart of town, **The Bullring,** near St. Martin's Square, is being developed into Europe's largest city-center retail area, based around the historic street patterns of the city and linking New Street and High Street.

The reinvention of "Brum" (as Britain's much-maligned second city is nick-named) is reflected by the opening of a grand department store, **Selfridges,** Bullring Centre (ⓒ 0870/837-7377). As a fashion emporium, its architecture was appropriately inspired by a dress. The curvaceous complex is adorned with 15,000 aluminum disks à la Paco Rabanne's 1960 chain-mail frocks.

WHERE TO STAY
VERY EXPENSIVE

New Hall ★★★   A 12th-century manor, reputedly the oldest in England, has been converted into a luxurious country house hotel residing outside the city of Birmingham. The location is in a leafy suburb where a tree-lined drive leaves to 10 hectares (26 acres) of gardens and this moated manor at a point 11km (7 miles) northeast of the center. This is one of the best places in England for a romantic escape. All the bedrooms are sumptuously and luxuriously furnished, with all the modern amenities, including state-of-the-art marble and tile bath-rooms with tub and shower. Most of the well-accessorized guest rooms are in a more contemporary addition. The public rooms are even more gracious, espe-cially the 16th-century oak-paneled dining room where an award-winning chef serves an innovative continental cuisine. The public rooms are lit by 18th-century chandeliers and a stone fireplace is from the 17th century.

Walmley Rd., Sutton Colffield, Birmingham B76 8QX. ⓒ 800/847-4385 in the U.S., or 0870/333-9147. Fax 0870/333-9247. www.thistlehotels.com/newhall. 60 units. £225–£290 ($416–$537) double; £300 ($555) suite. AE, DC, MC, V. **Amenities:** Restaurant; bar; coffee shop; indoor pool; pool; 9-hole golf course; tennis court; fitness center; sauna; spa; hot tub; 24-hr. room service; babysitting; nonsmoking rooms; 1 room for those with limited mobility. *In room:* TV, dataport, beverage maker, hair dryer.

EXPENSIVE

Hotel du Vin & Bistro ★ *Finds*   A former eye hospital, in a classy bit of recy-cling, has been converted into a stunning early Victorian building with a lot of style. Right in the city center, the hotel retains many of its original architectural features such as marble pillars and a double ironwork stairwell. An inner courtyard with a bubbling fountain and garden add a grace note. The midsize bedrooms are completely up-to-date and handsomely furnished with beautiful Egyptian linens, comfortable beds, and first-class bathrooms with tub and shower. The toiletries in the bathrooms here are the most luxurious in town, specially imported from the Isle of Arran in Scotland. The urban spa and gym is also one of the finest of any hotel in Birmingham. The Bubble Lounge is flamboyantly decorated in the style of the fabled Café Florin in Venice, offering a selection of more than 50 champagnes; the Cigar du Vin attracts stogie lovers.

25 Church St., Birmingham, West Midlands B3 2NR. ✆ 01212/000600. Fax 01212/360889. www.hotel duvin.com. 66 units. £120 ($222) double; £195–£225 ($361–$416) suite. AE, MC, V. **Amenities:** Restaurant; 2 bars; fitness room; limited room service; babysitting; sauna; laundry service; rooms for those with limited mobility. *In room:* TV, beverage maker, hair dryer, iron/ironing board.

Hyatt Regency 𝕉𝕉𝕉 *(Kids* The town's premier choice, this sheer, 24-story, glass-skinned hotel, linked by footbridge to the Convention Centre, affords one of the best views of Birmingham from its upper floors. In the heart of Birmingham, it opens onto a canal-side setting with a glazed atrium that's the epitome of elegance and style. Rooms are tastefully appointed with modern furnishings, marble-floored bathrooms, and an open design. Most beds are king or twins, and there are plain marble slabs for desks. Bathrooms are first-rate, with makeup mirrors, deluxe toiletries, and combination tubs and showers.

2 Bridge St., Birmingham B1 2JZ. ✆ 800/400-3319 in the U.S. and Canada, or 01216/431234. Fax 01216/ 162323. www.birmingham.hyatt.com. 319 units. Mon–Fri £125–£180 ($231–$333) double; Sat–Sun £85–£89 ($157–$165) double; £170–£215 ($315–$398) suite. AE, DC, MC, V. Parking: £10 ($19). **Amenities:** Restaurant; bar; indoor heated pool; spa; children's facilities; health club; business services; 24-hr. room service; babysitting; laundry service; dry cleaning; rooms for those with limited mobility. *In room:* TV w/pay movies, dataport, minibar, coffeemaker, hair dryer, trouser press, iron/ironing board.

Jonathans 𝕉𝕉 *(Finds* Filled with Victorian antiques, this charming choice features two highly rated restaurants, a tavern, and plenty of business amenities, all set within a classic 19th-century country-house hotel 8km (5 miles) from New Street Station in City Centre. Jonathans derives its name from its two owners, each of whom is named Jonathan (one cooks and the other attends to guests). Visitors enjoy a sojourn back to the 1880s, right down to the mock Victorian street, and the secret boardroom tucked behind a book-lined dining-room wall. The bedrooms—really like suites—are spacious. Each is furnished individually with antiques and quaint Victoriana. Some rooms have four-poster beds and some have fireplaces. Bathrooms feature thick towels and a wide range of plumbing; most have baths or showers, while the rest have both.

16–24 Wolverhampton Rd., Oldbury (at the crossroads of A456 and A4123, just off Exit 2 or 3 on M5), Birmingham B68 OLH. ✆ 01214/293757. Fax 01214/343107. www.jonathans.co.uk. 45 units. £125–£140 ($231–$259) double; £170 ($315) suite. Rates include English breakfast. AE, DC, MC, V. **Amenities:** 2 restaurants; bar; 24-hr. room service; laundry service; dry cleaning; rooms for those with limited mobility. *In room:* TV, dataport, coffeemaker, hair dryer, iron/ironing board, trouser press.

Malmaison 𝕉𝕉 *(Finds* This string of oh-so-chic hotels that stretches from London to Edinburgh has now invaded Birmingham. The "fab" hotel occupies part of "The Mailbox," a converted 1960s Royal Mail Sorting Office with a panoramic canal-side setting. Bedrooms have the latest designs and are sleekly modern and invitingly comfortable—great beds, slinky lights, bathrooms with tub and power showers, and luxe toilet articles along with CD players and libraries. You can relax in Le Petit Spa, called Birmingham's "sexiest," or else work out in Gymtonic. Some of the best shopping in town is right outside your door. If you're not a guest, you'll find sophisticated Continental cuisine served here.

1 Wharfside St., Birmingham B1 1RD. ℂ **01212/465000.** Fax 01212/465002. www.malmaison.com/ Birmingham/location.asp. 85 units. Mon–Thurs £129 ($239) double; Fri–Sun £99 ($183) double. All week £165 ($305) suite. AE, DC, MC, V. **Amenities:** Restaurant; bar; 24-hr. room service; laundry service; dry cleaning; gym; spa Jacuzzi; nonsmoking rooms; rooms for those with limited mobility. *In room:* A/C, TV, dataport, minibar, hair dryer, coffeemaker, iron/ironing board.

MODERATE

Apollo Hotel   A 5-minute drive from City Centre, this hotel offers comfortable modern rooms, a restaurant, and a location convenient to the convention centers or the countryside. Rooms are often a bit cramped, but all are equipped with twin or double beds. Bathrooms are small but tidily organized, with a shower-tub combination. Double-glazed windows cut down noise. The suites are a good value here, as they incorporate a minibar, private kitchen, and their own dining and lounge facilities.

Hagley Rd., Edgbaston, Birmingham B16 9RA. ℂ **01214/550271.** Fax 01214/562394. www.apollo-hotel-birmingham.com. 126 units. £85 ($157) double; from £150 ($278) suite. AE, DC, MC, V. Take Exit 3 from M5, or Exit 6 from M6. **Amenities:** Restaurant; bar; Internet cafe; limited room service; laundry service; dry cleaning; rooms for those with limited mobility. *In room:* TV, dataport, coffeemaker, hair dryer, trouser press.

INEXPENSIVE

Ashdale House Hotel *(Value*   A spacious Victorian terrace house, this is one of Birmingham's best B&Bs. Your host, Theresa Iomml, invites you to use her library with television. The cozy rooms range from small to midsize, and rooms with a bathroom contain a shower stall and adequate shelf space; the corridor bathrooms are well maintained for those who must share. Organic produce is offered at breakfast along with some vegetarian choices. Naturally in such an ecofriendly environment, smoking isn't allowed. It's a very inviting and homelike place for an affordable stay in Birmingham.

39 Broad Rd., Acock's Green B27 7UX. ℂ **01217/063598.** Fax 01217/072324. www.accommodation. uk.net/ashdalehouse.htm. 12 units, 7 with bathroom. £42 ($78) double without bathroom, £48 ($89) double with bathroom. Rates include continental breakfast. MC, V. **Amenities:** Laundry service. *In room:* TV, coffeemaker, iron/ironing board.

Awentsbury Hotel   University and Pebble Mill Studio visitors will find this lodging—installed in a restored 1882 house—convenient and comfortable. The place is kept spick-and-span, and the rooms, while not stylish, are acceptable in every other way. Two of the units are large enough for families. Bathrooms are small with a shower stall; otherwise, there are enough corridor bathrooms so you'll rarely have to wait.

21 Serpentine Rd., Selly Park B29 7HU. ℂ and fax **01214/721258.** www.awentsbury.com. 16 units, 11 with shower. £54 ($100) double without bathroom; £62 ($115) double with bathroom. Rates include English breakfast. AE, DC, MC, V. Take A38 from City Centre for about 3km (2 miles), turn left at Bournebrook Rd., then take the 1st right onto Serpentine Rd. **Amenities:** Rooms for those with limited mobility. *In room:* TV, coffeemaker.

Lyndhurst Hotel   Fourteen kilometers (9 miles) from the airport, this stone-exterior Victorian hotel in the northern suburbs is convenient to the Convention and City Centres and Aston University. Most units are small but well organized for your comfort. Bathrooms are small and only three have a tub-and-shower combination; the rest come with shower only. Though the house is Victorian, furnishings are contemporary. Those who have trouble with steep steps may prefer the ground-floor rooms.

135 Kingsbury Rd., Erdington B24 8QT. ☎ 01213/735695. Fax 01213/735697. www.smoothhound.co.uk/hotels/lyndhur.html. 15 units. £47–£58 ($87–$107) double. Rates include English breakfast. DC, MC, V. From junction 6 of M6, follow A5127, take the right signposted Minworth onto Kingsbury Rd. The hotel is on the right. **Amenities:** Restaurant; bar; limited room service; babysitting. *In room:* TV, coffeemaker, hair dryer, iron/ironing board.

WHERE TO DINE

Bank ⚡ FRENCH/BRITISH   You are likely to enjoy your finest meal at this relatively new restaurant, which is winning friends among the more discriminating palates of Birmingham. Affiliated with its even more famous sibling in London, chefs work feverishly in the open-plan kitchen. As you study the menu, you look up nervously at the glass shards hanging precariously from the ceiling. Start, perhaps, with delectable rock oysters or the mussels of the day, perhaps Scottish smoked salmon. For a main course, we'd recommend such well-prepared and flavorful dishes as fish cakes, or the baked hake with broad beans and clams flavored with fresh tomato and olive oil. Some desserts are contemporary; others hark back to olden days as evoked by the rhubarb-and-apple crumble with clotted cream ice cream.

4 Brindley Place. ☎ 01216/337001. Reservations recommended. Main courses £10–£18 ($19–$33); fixed-price lunch or dinner £12 ($22) for 2 courses, £14 ($26) for 3 courses. AE, DC, MC, V. Mon–Thurs noon–3pm and 5:30–11pm; Fri–Sat 5:30–11:30pm; Sun 11:30am–3:30pm and 5:30–10:30pm.

Chung Ying CHINESE   More than 400 flavor-filled items are on this predominantly Cantonese menu (40 dim sum items alone). Samples include pan-cooked Shanghai dumplings, stuffed crispy duck packed with crabmeat, steamed eel in bean sauce, and a variety of tasty casseroles. To go really authentic and sample some of the dishes the local Chinese community likes, try fried frogs' legs with bitter melon, steamed pork pie with dried or fresh squid, or fish cakes.

The **Chung Ying Garden,** another restaurant owned by the same proprietor, is at 17 Thorpe St. (☎ 01216/666622).

16 Wrottesley St., City Centre. ☎ 01216/225669. Reservations recommended. Meals around £14–£18 ($26–$33) per person. AE, DC, MC, V. Mon–Sat noon–10:30pm; Sun noon–11:30pm.

Le Petit Blanc ⚡ MODERN FRENCH   Gallic owner Raymond Blanc made his fame with Le Manoir aux Quat' Saisons outside Oxford. Since that time his empire has expanded, now taking in the city of Birmingham. In his latest outpost, he brings not haute cuisine but a brasserie-style regional French menu to Birmingham, and does so exceedingly well. It's one of your best bets for dining in the city. The setting is sophisticated and modern, with polished metal, lots of plate glass, and blond woods. You get not only an excellent cuisine, but fine service and good value for the money.

The cookery is competent, the presentation a strong point, and the ingredients are first-rate. Dip into such delights as duck confit with a butter-bean broth, or chargrilled scallops with mashed potatoes. The grilled loin of tuna is also an excellent choice, served in the southwestern French tradition with lentils. For an appetizer, you can do no better than the Roquefort soufflé with a walnut-and-pear dressing. In summer, a pumpkin risotto appears, or you may prefer a delectable soup made of Jerusalem artichoke. The smoothest finish is a passion fruit sorbet in mango "soup."

9 Brindley Pl. ☎ 01216/337333. Reservations required. Main courses £9.95–£17 ($19–$32); fixed-price 2- or 3-course lunch before 7pm £14–£16 ($25–$30). Mon–Sat 11am–11pm, Sun noon to 3pm and 5:30–10:30pm.

Moments **"Bucket Dining" Kashmiri Style**

A growing phenomenon, which we can only call the **Birmingham Balti Experience,** may interest those who love spicy food. *Balti* literally means bucket, but it refers to a Kashmiri style of cooking over a fast, hot flame. With the city's large Kashmiri population, there are now many *baltihouses* in Birmingham, most of which are bare-bones, BYOB affairs. One of the better ones is **Celebrity Balti,** 44 Broad St. (℃ **01216/326074**), close to the Convention Centre, which is open daily from 6pm to midnight.

Maharaja INDIAN   Set a few doors down from the Birmingham Hippodrome, this rather good restaurant specializes in Mughlai and North Indian dishes. Dining is on two floors, with framed fragments of Indian printed cloth on the walls. The menu features such dishes as lamb *dhansak* (cubes of lamb in thick lentil sauce), chicken *patalia* (chicken cooked in spices, herbs, and fruit), and prawn madras. The kitchen's balanced use of spices, herbs, and other flavorings lends most dishes an aromatic but delicate taste.

23 Hurst St., near the Hippodrome. ℃ 01216/222641. Reservations not needed. Main courses £7.45–£8.90 ($14–$17). AE, DC, MC, V. Mon–Sat noon–2pm and 6–11pm.

Shimla Pinks ✹✹ SOUTH ASIAN   In India this restaurant's name refers to "bright young things," but here it stands for the finest Indian cuisine in this part of England. A carefully selected menu featuring mostly Indian and Sri Lankan dishes is served by a very courteous staff in this relaxed, elegant restaurant. Special buffets complement the main menu on Sunday and Monday nights.

215 Broad St., City Centre. ℃ 01216/330366. Reservations not needed. Main courses £8.95–£15 ($17–$28). AE, MC, V. Mon–Fri noon–2:30pm and 6–11pm; Sat–Sun 6–11:30pm.

BIRMINGHAM AFTER DARK
THE PERFORMING ARTS

Connected to the Convention Centre, **Symphony Hall,** at Broad Street (℃ **01217/803333**), has been hailed as an acoustical gem since its completion in 1990. Home to the **City of Birmingham Symphony Orchestra,** it also hosts special classical music events.

The **National Indoor Arena,** King Edward's Road (℃ **01212/002202**), is a favorite site for jazz, pop, and rock concerts; sporting events; and conventions.

The **Birmingham Repertory Theatre** on Broad Street at Centenary Square (℃ **01212/364455;** www.birmingham-rep.co.uk), houses one of the top companies in England. Some of the world's greatest actors have performed with the repertory company over the years, including Lord Olivier, Albert Finney, Paul Scofield, Dame Edith Evans, and Kenneth Branagh. The widely known "Rep" comprises the **Main House,** which seats 800 theatergoers, and **The Door,** a more intimate 140-seat venue that often stages new and innovative works. The box office is open from 9:30am to 8pm Monday through Saturday. Tickets cost £8 to £22 ($15–$41).

Midlands Arts Centre (MAC) in Cannon Hill Park (℃ **01214/403838;** www.mac-birmingham.org.uk) is close to the Edgbaston Cricket Ground and reached by car or bus (route no. 1, 35, 42, 62, or 63). The MAC houses three performance areas and stages a lively range of drama, dance, and musical performances, as well as films. The box office is open daily from 9am to 8:45pm.

The **Alexandra Theatre,** Station Street (℃ **0870/607-7533**), hosts national touring companies, including productions from London's West End. Tickets for all theaters are available through Birmingham visitor offices. The theater serves as a temporary home to many of England's touring companies. Contact the box office for show details.

The restored **Birmingham Hippodrome,** Hurst Street (℃ **0870/730-1234** or 0870/730-4321), is home to the **Birmingham Royal Ballet** and visiting companies from around the world. It hosts a variety of events from the Welsh National Opera and musicals to dance. The box office is open Monday through Saturday from 10am to 8pm.

CLUBS & PUBS

Bobby Brown's The Club, 52 Gas St., along the City Centre canal (℃ **01216/ 432573**), is a converted warehouse with 3 small bars and a disco. **Liberty's,** 184 Hagley Rd. (℃ **01214/544444**), is a large, fashionable club, a champagne bar, vodka bar, and other smaller bars.

Goose O.V.T., 561 Bristol Rd. (℃ **01214/723186**), the third-largest pub in England, is popular with university students. One local fan says it's "good for dodgy music." Another laments that while it is "generally a good pub, there are vast numbers of wasted students."

6 Worcester ✶

200km (124 miles) NW of London; 42km (26 miles) SW of Birmingham; 98km (61 miles) N of Bristol

Awash with some of the most magnificent and lush river scenery in all of Europe, the River Wye Valley contains some of the most charming small villages in west-central England. Where wool used to be the main industry in this area, most of the locals today make their living by fruit growing, dairy farming, and, to an increasing degree, tourism.

Worcestershire has become a household name, thanks to the famous sauce that is used to accent myriad dishes and to perk up any respectable Bloody Mary. One of the quaintest of the Midland counties, it covers portions of the rich valleys of the Severn and Avon rivers. Between the two cathedral cities of Hereford and Worcester, the ridge of the Malverns rises from the Severn Plain.

The River Severn flows through the heart of Worcester, a world-famous porcelain center. In medieval times, the river—just a short distance away from the bustling High Street—served as the hub of the city's commercial life. Today, it plays host to more leisurely activities such as boat trips, fishing, and rowing. The river's bridge also affords the city's best views of 900-year-old Worcester Cathedral, with its 60m (200-ft.) high tower.

ESSENTIALS

GETTING THERE   Regular trains depart London's Paddington Station for Worcester, arriving about 2¼ hours later. For schedules and information, call ℃ **0845/748-4950** or visit www.centraltrains.co.uk.

National Express buses leave throughout the day from London's Victoria Coach Station. For schedules and information, call ℃ **0870/580-8080** or visit www.nationalexpress.com.

Driving from London, take the M5 to Junction 7 toward Worcester. Give yourself about 3 hours. From Hereford, it's a short drive to Worcester. Just take the A449 42km (26 miles) west.

VISITOR INFORMATION   The **Worcester Tourist Information Centre,** in Queen Anne's Guildhall on High Street (✆ **01905/726311**), is open from 9:30am to 5:30pm Monday through Saturday.

SEEING THE SIGHTS

Bickerline River Trips, 98 Christine Ave., Rushwick (✆ **01905/831639;** www.riverboattrips.co.uk), lets you see Worcester from the river aboard the 88-passenger *Marianne.* These 45-minute trips set sail daily on the hour from 11am to 5pm from March to October. Light refreshments are served and party bookings are available.

If you're interested in shopping, you might want to take a stroll down the architecturally important **Friar Street,** taking in the eclectic collection of individual timber-framed and brick shops. **G. R. Pratley & Sons,** Shambles (✆ **01905/22678** or 01905/28642), offers a smorgasbord of glass, china, and earthenware. You can also find finely woven Oriental rugs and carpets and top-quality furniture here.

Bygones of Worcester, 55 Sidbury and Cathedral Square (✆ **01905/23132** or 01905/25388), is actually two shops packed with an intriguing collection of antiques and odds and ends. Wander through this store to find furnishings for your home that range from the bizarre to the decorative and fanciful—all from cottages and castles in England.

The Commandery   Originally the 11th-century Hospital of St. Wulstan, the Commandery was transformed over the years into a sprawling 15th-century, medieval timber-framed building that served as the country home of the Wylde family. This was the headquarters of King Charles II during the Battle of Worcester in 1651, the last battle in the English Civil War. The Great Hall has a hammer-beam roof and a minstrel's gallery. England's premier **Civil War Centre** is now situated here. This exciting, interactive, and hands-on museum marvelously incorporates life-size figures, sound systems, and videos to take you through the bloody and turbulent years of England's civil war. You can even try on helmets, handle weapons, and pick up cannon balls. The Commandery also has canalside tearooms, a picnic area, and a Garden of Fragrance.

Sidbury. ✆ **01905/36182.** Admission £4 ($7.40) adults, £2.80 ($5.20) children and seniors, £10 ($19) family ticket. Year-round Mon–Sat 10am–5pm; Sun 1:30–5pm. The Commandery is a 3-min. walk from Worcester Cathedral.

Royal Worcester Porcelain Factory ✿   This factory has been achieving its goal of creating "ware of a form so precise as to be easily distinguished from other English porcelain" since its founding in 1751. It produces a unique range of fine china and porcelain that remains unsurpassed throughout the world. Behind-the-scenes tours last about 45 minutes and do not accept children under 11, very elderly visitors, or persons with disabilities, because of safety regulations.

The **Retail and Seconds Shops** at the factory are open to all and offer a unique chance to buy the beauty of Royal Worcester at bargain prices. Many of the pieces are marked as seconds, but most of the time you won't be able to tell why. The **Dyson Perrins Museum** is also located at the factory and houses the world's largest collection of Worcester Porcelain.

Severn St. ✆ **01905/746000.** www.royal-worcester.co.uk. Factory tours available Mon–Fri beginning at 10:30am; cost is £5 ($9.25). Call ahead to reserve (for a same-day tour, phone before 10am). Museum admission £3.50 ($6.50) adults, £2.75 ($5.10) seniors and children. Ticket for tour and museum £9 ($17) adults, £7.25 ($13) children. Museum open Mon–Sat 9am–5:30pm, Sun 11am–5pm.

Sir Edward Elgar's Birthplace Museum This charming and inviting red-brick country cottage, stable, and coach house is set on well-tended grounds. Elgar, perhaps England's greatest composer, was born in this early-19th-century house on June 2, 1857. Today, the cottage houses a unique collection of manuscripts and musical scores, photographs, and other personal memorabilia.

Crown East Lane, Lower Broadheath. ℂ **01905/333224**. www.elgarfoundation.org. Admission £4.50 ($8.35) adults, £4 ($7.40) seniors, £2 ($3.70) children, £11 ($20) family ticket. Year-round daily 11am–5pm. Drive out of Worcester on A44 toward Leominster. After 3km (2 miles), turn off to the right at the sign. The house is 1km (¾ mile) on the right.

Worcester Cathedral ⟨⟨ Historically speaking, the most significant part of Worcester Cathedral is its crypt, a classic example of Norman architecture that dates from 1084. It contains the tombs of King John, whose claim to fame is the Magna Carta, and Prince Arthur, the elder brother of Henry VIII. Both tombs can be found near the high altar. The 12th-century chapter house is one of the finest in England and, along with the cloisters, evokes the cathedral's rich monastic past. The cathedral is also known for a distinguished history of fine choral music, and, rotating with the cathedrals of Gloucester and Hereford, hosts the oldest choral festival in Europe, the Three Choirs Festival.

College Yard at High St. ℂ **01905/611002**. www.cofe-worcester.org.uk/cathedral. Admission free, but adults asked for a £3 ($5.55) donation. Daily 7:30am–6pm.

WHERE TO STAY

Diglis House Hotel ⟨ This is the town's best choice. Set within gardens at the edge of the Severn River, this mansion was built in the 1700s as a guesthouse for visitors to the nearby cathedral. Later, it was the family home of the noted landscape architect Benjamin Williams Leader, whose paintings of bucolic England have graced the cover of many English Christmas cards. The building's interior was upgraded to country-house hotel standards. Bedrooms, though small, are cozily and comfortably arranged, each fitted with twin or double beds. The compact bathrooms have adequate shelf space and a shower-tub combination.

Severn St., Worcester WR1 2NF. ℂ **01905/353518**. Fax 01905/767772. www.diglishousehotel.co.uk. 30 units. Mon–Thurs £95–£110 ($176–$204) double; £125 ($231) junior suite; Fri–Sun £85–£100 ($157–$185) double; £110 ($204) junior suite. Rates include English breakfast. AE, DC, MC, V. **Amenities:** Restaurant; bar; limited room service; laundry service; rooms for those with limited mobility. *In room:* TV, coffeemaker, hair dryer.

The Elms Hotel ⟨ *Finds* This is one of the most impressive hotels in the region, built in 1710 by Gilbert White, a disciple of Sir Christopher Wren. It is chic, fun, sophisticated, and international, and lies on the outskirts of Worcester. Surrounded by 4 hectares (10 acres) of field, park, and forest, it offers what some visitors consider a fantasy version of the best of England, complete with mahogany or walnut 18th- and 19th-century antiques, an intriguing collection of clocks and oil paintings, and log-burning fireplaces. The frequently redecorated bedrooms come in various shapes and sizes, and feature twin or double beds. The compact bathrooms have a shower or tub unit and Crabtree & Evelyn toiletries.

On A443 (3km/2 miles west of Abberley, near Worcester), Worcester WR6 6AT. ℂ **01299/896666**. Fax 01299/ 896804. www.theelmshotel.com. 21 units. £120–£160 ($222–$296) double. Rates include breakfast. AE, DC, MC, V. Take A443 for 9.5km (6 miles) west of Worcester, following the signs to Tenbury Wells. **Amenities:** Restaurant; bar; tennis court; room service (7am–11pm); babysitting; laundry service. *In room:* TV, hair dryer, trouser press.

Fownes Hotel A 5-minute walk west of Worcester's cathedral, this hotel occupies the industrial-age premises of the Fownes Glove Factory (ca. 1892). A civic monument, and source of income for many local residents until glove-wearing went out of fashion, it was converted in the 1980s into Worcester's most interesting large hotel. Public rooms are attractively outfitted and are unified by a decorating theme that includes gilt-edged photographs of the hotel during its glove-making heyday. Bedrooms are cozy and furnished in a conservative English style that includes the wide or tall many-paned windows of the factory's original construction. Each comes with a small bathroom featuring a combination tub and shower. Some 32 units are set aside for nonsmokers.

City Walls Rd., Worcester WR1 2AP. ✆ **01905/613151.** Fax 01905/23742. 61 units. £79–£140 ($146–$259) double; £115–£140 ($213–$259) suite. Children under 15 stay free in same room as 2 paying adults. AE, DC, MC, V. **Amenities:** Restaurant; bar; 24-hr. room service; laundry service; rooms for those with limited mobility. *In room:* TV, dataport, coffeemaker, hair dryer, trouser press.

WHERE TO DINE

Across from the cathedral, **The Pub at Ye Old Talbot Hotel,** Friar Street (✆ **0190/523-573**), contains lots of Victorian nostalgia and old-fashioned wood paneling that has been darkened by generations of cigarette smoke and spilled beer. It offers predictable pub grub that's a bit better than expected, especially when it's accompanied with a pint of the house's half-dozen ales on tap.

One of Worcester's most whimsical restaurant pubs is the **Little Sauce Factory,** London Road (✆ **01905/350159**). The entire place is a takeoff on Worcester's famous sauce, with posters advertising food flavorings, all the accessories of an old-fashioned kitchen, and an enormous ceiling map of Britain in ceramic tiles.

Benedictos ITALIAN   Set within 180m (600 ft.) of the cathedral in a half-timbered, 16th-century Elizabethan building, this restaurant has an ambience that's a lot more international and suave than the very English exterior suggests. The town's best antipasti selection features such delights as mussels sautéed in white wine, fresh tomatoes, and black olives or a fresh daily homemade soup. Pastas are succulent, especially the homemade cannelloni filled with fresh spinach and ricotta and the penne with salmon and a cream sauce. The chefs have a winning way with meats, especially the grilled rack of lamb and sliced duck breast in a rich orange and brandy sauce.

34 Sidbury. ✆ **01905/21444.** Reservations recommended. Main courses £12–£15 ($22–$28). AE, MC, V. Mon–Sat 11am–2pm and 6:30–10:30pm. Closed 2 weeks in late July.

7 The Malverns ✭

195km (127 miles) NW of London; 55km (34 miles) SW of Birmingham

Once part of the ancient and formidable kingdom of Mercia, the beautiful and historic Malvern Hills lie just west of Worcester, rising suddenly and drastically from the Severn Valley and stretching for 14km (9 miles). This tranquil area is rich in natural beauty. The towns are especially famous for their healing waters, refreshing air, and inspiring vistas.

Six townships cling to the Malvern Hills, making this an outstanding place to strike out for easy day hikes while in Worcester or Hereford. You can wander through Great Malvern, Malvern Link, West Malvern, Welldon, Malvern Wells, Little Malvern, and several other hamlets in a day's stroll. Great Malvern is resplendent with Victorian grandeur, much of which was gained from its importance as a 19th-century spa resort. The town boasts the largest priory church in the area, dating from the 15th century and boasting some fine stained-glass windows, as well as a great Gothic tower. The monks' stalls have superb misericords and medieval titles. The greatest and most beloved singer of the 19th century, the wildly talented "Swedish Nightingale" Jenny Lind, as well as that century's greatest English composer, Sir Edward Elgar, called this area home.

The Malvern Hills provide a breathtaking backdrop for hiking and biking. You can take in immense views, eastward to the Cotswolds and westward to the Wye Valley and the Welsh mountains, while exploring the most beautiful countryside in England. The Malverns Tourist Information Centre (see below) can provide you with detailed maps and route descriptions.

St. Wulstan's Church, 3km (2 miles) out of Great Malvern on the Ledbury Road, is where the composer Sir Edward Elgar is buried with his wife and daughter. You'll find a bronze bust of the composer in Priory Park, and he lived at Craeglea on the Malvern Wells Road and at Forli in Alexandra Road, where he composed the *Enigma Variations, Sea Pictures,* and the *Dreams of Gerontius.*

ESSENTIALS

GETTING THERE   From London, trains leave regularly from Paddington Station for the 2-hour trip to Great Malvern. For schedules and information, call (*C*) **0845/748-4950** or visit www.centraltrains.co.uk.

One **National Express** bus departs daily from Victoria Coach Station in London, arriving in Great Malvern 2½ hours later. Call (*C*) **0870/580-8080** or visit www.nationalexpress.com for more information.

If you're driving from London, take the M5 to the A4104 west, then the A449 north toward Great Malvern. Depending on traffic, the drive takes about 2 hours.

VISITOR INFORMATION   The **Malverns Tourist Information Centre,** 21 Church St., Malvern, Worcestershire WR14 2AA ((*C*) **01684/892289**), is open from 10am to 5pm Monday through Saturday and from 10am to 4pm Sunday.

WHERE TO STAY

The Cotford Hotel *(Kids)*   A 5-minute walk east of Malvern's town center, on an acre of lawns and rock gardens, this towering and stately home dates from 1851 when it was built as the local bishop's residence. Constructed of Cotswold stone and accented with lavish gingerbread, it retains a vaguely ecclesiastical air despite the modern-day furnishings. Views extend over the garden through elaborate windows carved from wood to resemble Gothic tracery. The main appeal of the place derives from its monumental historic premises, the warm welcome, and such Victorian touches as the tile-floored wide entrance hallway. The bedrooms, usually midsize, have been much improved in recent years, with excellent beds and good bathrooms, each with shower. Several rooms have been specifically set aside for families.

Graham Rd., Malvern, Worcestershire WR14 2HU. (*C*) **01684/572427.** www.cotfordhotel.co.uk. 15 units. £75 ($139) double, £85 ($157) family room. Rates include breakfast. AE, MC, V. **Amenities:** Restaurant; bar; free pass to nearby pool; limited room service; laundry service. *In room:* TV, dataport, coffeemaker, hair dryer.

The Cottage in the Wood *(R)*   There is indeed a cottage in the woods associated with this hotel (it contains four cozy bedrooms and dates from the 17th century). But most of the inn occupies a nearby Georgian house from the late 1700s. Originally built for the semiretired mother of the lord of a neighboring estate, it's referred to as "The Dower House" and is appropriately outfitted in an attractive Laura Ashley style. The bedrooms are quite small, but this place is so charming and offers such panoramic views that most visitors don't mind. The place is exceedingly well furnished with thoughtfully equipped bedrooms that include a tub and shower. Your hosts are John and Sue Pattin, whose skill is especially visible within their restaurant (see below).

Holywell Rd., Malvern Wells, Great Malvern, Worcestershire WR14 4LG. © 01684/575859. Fax 01684/560662. www.cottageinthewood.co.uk. 31 units. £99–£170 ($183–$315) double. Rates include full English breakfast. AE, MC, V. After leaving Great Malvern on A449, turn right just before the B4209 turnoff on the opposite side of the road. The inn is on the right. **Amenities:** Restaurant; bar; limited room service; babysitting; nonsmoking rooms; rooms for those with limited mobility. *In room:* TV/VCR, dataport, coffeemaker, hair dryer.

The Foley Arms   Home to one of the town's most bustling pubs, this is the oldest hotel in Malvern, with a Georgian pedigree from 1810 when it welcomed the affluent and exhausted for curative sessions at the nearby spa. Close to the town center, it rises from a very steep hillside, which makes it inconvenient for mobility-impaired guests, but also gives it glorious views over the Severn River to the edge of the Cotswolds from many of its bedroom windows. Rooms contain old, usually antique, furniture and heavy draperies; they have all the modern conveniences but offer old-fashioned character. Five rooms are set aside for nonsmokers. Bathrooms are small, but tidily arranged, each with a shower or tub/shower.

14 Worcester Rd., Malvern, Worcestershire WR14 4QS. © 01684/573397. Fax 01684/569665. www.foley armshotel.com. 27 units. £105–£145 ($194–$268) double. Rates include English breakfast. AE, DC, MC, V. **Amenities:** Restaurant; bar; limited room service; babysitting; laundry service. *In room:* TV, dataport, coffeemaker, hair dryer, iron/ironing board, trouser press.

WHERE TO DINE
The Cottage in the Wood MODERN BRITISH   An 18th-century, Georgian-style dower's house, on a steeply sloping, wooded plot of land with panoramic views over the Herefordshire countryside, the site manages to be elegant, cozy, and nurturing at the same time, thanks to the hard work and charm of resident owners John and Sue Pattin. They offer modern adaptations of traditional British favorites, including monkfish with five spices served with mascarpone risotto and red-wine sauce, and grilled lamb kidneys with wild mushrooms, red onions, and Worcestershire sauce butter. English cheeses or such desserts as a white chocolate soufflé, are particularly appealing. *Note:* The accommodations on the property are reviewed above.

Holywell Rd., Malvern Wells. © 01684/575859. Reservations recommended. Main courses £17–£19 ($31–$35); 2-course lunch £14 ($26); fixed-price Sun lunch £19 ($35). AE, MC, V. Daily 12:30–2pm and 7–9:30pm.

8 Hereford ⓧ
214km (133 miles) NW of London; 82km (51 miles) SW of Birmingham

Situated on the Wye River, the city of Hereford is one of the most colorful towns in England. It was the birthplace of both David Garrick—the actor, producer, and dramatist who breathed life back into London theater in the mid–18th century— and Nell Gwynne, an actress who was the mistress of Charles II. Dating from 1080, the red sandstone Hereford Cathedral contains an eclectic mix of architectural styles from Norman to Perpendicular.

Surrounded by pristine countryside, including orchards and lush pasturelands, Hereford is home to the world-famous, white-faced Hereford cattle and some of the finest cider around, best sampled in one of the city's traditional and atmospheric pubs.

ESSENTIALS
GETTING THERE   By train from London's Paddington Station, Hereford is a 3-hour trip. For schedules and information, call © 0845/748-4950 or visit www.centraltrains.co.uk.

To make the 4-hour-plus trip by bus from London, you'll need to catch a **National Express** bus from Victoria Coach Station. For schedules and information, call ✆ **0870/580-8080** or visit www.nationalexpress.com.

The trip to Hereford makes a scenic 3-hour drive from London. Take the M5 to either Ledbury or Romp-on-Wye, then turn onto the A49 toward Hereford.

VISITOR INFORMATION   Hereford's **Tourist Information Centre** (✆ **01432/268430**) is located at 1 King St. and is open Monday through Saturday from 9am to 5pm and on Sunday from 10am to 4pm in summer, and Monday through Saturday from 9am to 5pm off season.

EXPLORING THE TOWN

You can find interesting shopping within a labyrinth of historic buildings known collectively as **High Town.** Limited only to pedestrians, it's enhanced with street performers and visiting entertainers. Principal shopping streets include Widemarsh Street, Commercial Road, St. Owen's Street, and perhaps the most charming and artfully old-fashioned of them all, Church Street.

Also near the town center is **Hereford Market,** evoking West Country street fairs of old with its cornucopia of collectibles and junk displayed in an open-air setting. It's conducted throughout the year, every Wednesday and Saturday morning from 8am to 3:30pm. The area literally pulsates with life as vendors sell items ranging from sweatshirts and saucepans to paintings and pet food.

Andrew Lamputt, The Silver Shop, 28 St. Owen St. (✆ **01432/274961**), is the place to pick up the perfect silver gift. It boasts an extensive array of quality silverware and fine gold jewelry, and maintains a stable of skilled craftspeople who restore old pieces.

Cider Museum and King Offa Cider Brandy Distillery   This museum tells the story of traditional cider making from its heyday in the 17th century to modern factory methods. The King Offa Distillery has been granted the first new license to distill cider in the United Kingdom in more than 250 years; you can see it produced from beautiful copper stills brought from Normandy. The museum shop sells cider, cider brandy, cider brandy liqueur, and Royal Cider, the real wine of old England, as well as a good selection of gifts and souvenirs.

Pomona Place, Whitecross Rd. (a 5-min. walk from the city center and .5km/¼ mile from City Ring Rd. on A438 to Brecon). ✆ 01432/354207. www.cidermuseum.co.uk. Admission £2.70 ($5) adults, £2.20 ($4.05) children, seniors, and students. Museum Apr–Oct daily 10am–5:30pm; Nov–Mar Tues–Sun 11am–3pm.

Hereford Cathedral 🏛🏛   This is one of the oldest cathedrals in England (its cornerstone was laid in 1080). The cathedral is primarily Norman, and includes a 13th-century Lady Chapel erected in 1220, as well as a majestic "Father" Willis organ, one of the finest in the world.

Exhibited together in the new library building at the west end of the Hereford Cathedral are two of Hereford's unique and priceless historical treasures: the Mappa Mundi of 1290, which portrays the world oriented around Jerusalem, and a 1,600-volume library of chained books, with some volumes dating from the 8th century. The cathedral also contains the Diocesan Treasury and the St. Thomas à Becket Reliquary.

Hereford city center. ✆ 01432/374202. www.herefordcathedral.co.uk. Free admission to cathedral; guided tours £3.50 ($6.50) per person. Admission for exhibitions at Mappa Mundi and Chained Library exhibition £4.50 ($8.35) adults, £3.50 ($6.50) children and seniors, free for children under 5, £10 ($19) family ticket (2 adults and 3 children). Summer Mon–Sat 10am–4:15pm, Sun 11am–3:15pm; off season Mon–Sat 11am–3pm.

The Other Hampton Court

Cardinal Wolsey's splendid palace beside the Thames south of London is one of the most visited attractions in England. But there's another Hampton Court between Hereford and Leominster, 289km (180 miles) northwest of London. It's called the "best-kept secret in England."

Hampton Court (© **01568/797777;** www.hamptoncourt.org.uk) is open Tuesday through Sunday from March 29 to October 26, charging £5 ($9.25) for adults. £3 ($5.55) for children, and £4.75 ($8.80) for seniors, with a family ticket going for £14 ($26). It lies off the A417 near the junction of A49 between Hereford and Leominster.

With a history going back to the 15th century, it once extended over more than 24,281 hectares (60,000 acres). Henry IV granted the estate to Sir Rowland Lenthall following the granting of a knighthood to him at the Battle of Agincourt. The present owners, the Van Kampen family, restored the castle and its grounds, following decades of neglect. The deeply religious Van Kampen family are also known for holding the largest private collection of Bibles in the world.

The restored Herefordshire gardens are one of the most ambitious garden creations in our time. Original Victorian gardens enclose panoramic flower gardens divided by canals, island pavilions, and avenues.

Teas and lunches are served in a grand conservatory adjoining the castle. The late-medieval fortified manor house has been restored until it's the epitome of a fairytale castle. The castle is open only on special occasions but the gardens are here to view.

The Old House   This is a completely restored Jacobean-period museum with 17th-century furnishings on three floors. The painstakingly restored half-timbered building was constructed in 1621 and includes a kitchen, hall, and rooms with four-poster beds.

High Town. © **01432/260694.** Free admission. Apr–Sept Tues–Sun 10am–4pm; Oct–Mar Tues–Sat 10am–4pm.

WHERE TO STAY

Ancient Camp Inn   Perched 23m (75 ft.) above the Wye River, this little inn—known more for its food than its rooms—takes its name from an Iron Age hill fort that originally stood here. East of Hereford, and rather remotely located, it is a real discovery, and worth a visit even if you're not staying here. Filled with charm and character, the inn is the domain of Harry and Catherine MacKintosh. Bedrooms are roomy but not luxurious, and the beds are comfortable; bathrooms are small, with shower units.

Ruckhall, Herefordshire HR2 9QX. © **01981/250449.** Fax 01981/251581. 5 units. £60 ($111) double; £80 ($148) suite. Rates include English breakfast. MC, V. To reach the site, take the A465 from Hereford. Turn right at the signpost to Ruckhall and Belmont Abbey. The inn is 4km (2½ miles) along this road. **Amenities:** Restaurant; bar. *In room:* TV, coffeemaker, hair dryer.

The Green Dragon ⭐   The Green Dragon is the oldest, most historic hotel in Hereford, and the best. In 1857, this attractive inn, situated near the cathedral, had already been in business for 300 years when the then-owners decided to replace its front with the stately neoclassical facade you see today. Rooms are scattered over three upper floors, and have all the high ceilings, thick walls, and squeaky floors you'd expect from an old treasure like this. Each has reasonably modern furnishings and is comfortably appointed. All units come with a tub-and-shower combination.

Broad St., Herefordshire HR4 9BG. ℂ 01432/272506. Fax 01432/352139. 83 units. £101 ($187) double. Rates include English breakfast. AE, DC, MC, V. **Amenities:** Restaurant; bar; 24-hr. room service; laundry service. *In room:* TV, dataport, coffeemaker, hair dryer, iron/ironing board, trouser press.

Three Counties Hotel   This hotel is set 1.5km (1 mile) south of Hereford's center on the opposite bank of the River Wye. This hotel has a distinctive hip-roofed, barn-like design that's more common in central Europe than England. You can't miss its prominent tawny-colored tile roof from a distance. The hotel caters to business travelers and bus tours. Rooms are monochromatic and modern, nothing fussy. Comfort is the keynote, and some of the bedrooms are suitable for persons with disabilities. Not all of the rooms are in the main building; some lie in separate buildings opening onto the parking lot. Bathrooms are small and compact, each with shower-tub combination.

Belmont Rd. (Hwy. A465), Herefordshire HR2 7XB. ℂ 01432/299955. Fax 01432/275114. www.threecounties hotel.co.uk. 60 units. £67–£89 ($124–$165) double. Rates include English breakfast. AE, DC, MC, V. **Amenities:** Restaurant; bar; 24-hr. room service; laundry service; rooms for those with limited mobility. *In room:* TV, dataport, coffeemaker, hair dryer, trouser press.

WHERE TO DINE

Café @ All Saints 𝕽 VEGETARIAN   This coffee bar and restaurant is Hereford's number-one spot for casual dining. It occupies the west end of a local medieval church right in the center of Hereford. The cooks here serve a simple daily changing lunch menu combined with an all-day feature of coffee, home-made bread, cakes, and sandwiches. Some of their best dishes include a mushroom and Hereforde ale casserole with a smoked cheddar mash; and a pesto concoction that includes mozzarella and tomato with the cafe's own olive-oil bread. For dessert, try the likes of a prune and cider tart with crème fraîche, or a chocolate-and-marmalade tart. Occasional evenings also feature live music.

Eign St. ℂ 01432/370415. Reservations not needed. Main courses £4.65–£5.85 ($8.60–$11); sandwiches £4.25 ($7.85). MC, V. Mon–Sat 8:30am–5pm.

Shires Restaurant ENGLISH/FRENCH   Set on the street level of the town's most historic and prestigious hotel, this restaurant is sheathed with very old paneling, some of it from the 17th century, carved from Herefordshire oak. Everyone in town considers it the stateliest restaurant around, suitable for formal family celebrations. Main courses at lunchtime are selected from an all-English carvery table, where a uniformed attendant will carve from roasted joints of beef, turkey, or ham, garnished with all the traditional fixings. Dinners are more French in their flavor and are conducted with as much fanfare as anything else. Menu items include a pâté of duck meat and wild mushrooms served with a juniper chutney, and pan-fried filet of salmon with avocado.

In The Green Dragon Hotel, Broad St. ℂ 01432/272506. Reservations recommended. Main dinner courses £11–£20 ($20–$37); 3-course dinner £22 ($41). AE, DC, MC, V. Daily 7–10pm.

A FAVORITE LOCAL PUB

The **Orange Tree,** 16 King St. (ℂ **01432/267698**), a consistently popular pub, attracts beer lovers and tipplers from across the county. Nothing is particularly unusual about this woodsy pub (mostly a place to soak up local color), but its beers on tap include Buddington's and a changing roster of ales and lagers sent on spec from local breweries, sometimes as part of local sales promotions.

9 Ludlow ⓕ

261km (162 miles) NW of London; 47km (29 miles) S of Shrewsbury

An outpost on the Welsh border during Norman times, this mellow town on the tranquil Teme River is often referred to as "the perfect historic town." Indeed, a tremendous amount of history whispers through its quiet lanes and courts, all lined with Georgian and Jacobean timbered buildings. The two little princes who died in the Tower of London lived here, and it was once the refuge of Henry VIII's first wife, Catherine of Aragon. You can still visit the church where the unhappy queen prayed. The town's most colorful street is the "Broad," which rises from the old Ludford Bridge to Broadgate, the last remains of a wall erected in the Middle Ages. Be sure to visit the Butter Cross and Reader's House, in particular, as well as A. E. Housman's grave in the town cemetery.

ESSENTIALS

GETTING THERE Trains run hourly from Paddington Station in London to Ludlow, with a transfer at Newport. It's approximately a 3-hour journey. For schedules and information, call ⓒ **0845/748-4950** or visit www.arrivatrainswales.co.uk.

National Express buses depart London's Victoria Coach Station for Shrewsbury, where you must change to the local line to reach Ludlow. It's a slow journey, approximately 5½ hours, but for those who are still interested, call ⓒ **0870/580-8080** or visit www.nationalexpress.com for the current schedule.

By car, it's a much shorter, 3-hour drive. Follow the M25 out of London to the M40 at Oxford. Take the M40 to Bromsgrove. Once at Bromsgrove, follow the M42 until Kidderminster. From here, take the A456 to Ludlow.

VISITOR INFORMATION The **Ludlow Tourist Information Centre,** Castle Street (ⓒ **01584/875053**), is open December through March, Monday through Saturday from 10am to 1pm and 2 to 5pm; April through November, it is also open on Sunday from 10:30am to 5pm.

SPECIAL EVENTS The **Ludlow Festival,** held annually in late June and early July, is one of England's major arts festivals. The centerpiece is an open-air Shakespeare performance within the Inner Bailey of Ludlow Castle. Orchestral concerts, historical lectures, readings, exhibitions, and workshops round out the festival. From March onward, you can request a schedule from the box office (ⓒ **01584/872150;** www.ludlowfestival.co.uk). The box office is open daily beginning in early May.

EXPLORING THE TOWN

Whitcliffe Common was the common land of Ludlow during the Middle Ages. From here, you can enjoy panoramic views of Ludlow as you stroll. Leave town by one of two bridges across the River Teme and follow any of a number of paths through the Common.

A colorful Sunday **flea market** is held on Castle Square on alternate Sundays throughout the year from 9am to approximately 4pm.

In addition, the town is filled with traditional family businesses; of particular interest are the many antiques, book, arts-and-crafts, and gift shops. **The Marches Pottery,** 45 Mill St. (ⓒ **01584/878413**), produces a wide selection of hand-thrown tableware and individual pieces decorated with subtle Chinese glazes, including a host of terra-cotta flowerpots.

Ludlow Castle ⓕ   This Norman castle was built around 1094 as a frontier outpost to keep out the as-yet-unconquered Welsh. The original castle, or the inner bailey, was encircled in the early 14th century by a very large outer bailey and transformed into a medieval palace by Roger Mortimer, the most powerful man in England at the time. After the War of the Roses, the castle was turned into a royal residence, and Edward IV sent the Prince of Wales and his brother (the "Princes in the Tower") to live here in 1472. It was also the seat of government for Wales and the Border Counties. Catherine of Aragon and Mary Tudor and her court also spent time in this 900-year-old home. Norman, medieval, and Tudor architectural styles can be found throughout the castle. Many of the original buildings still stand, including the Chapel of St. Mary Magdalene, with one of England's last remaining circular naves. Excellent views of the castle can be spied from the banks of the River Teme.

Ludlow Town Centre. ℂ 01584/873355. www.ludlowcastle.com. Admission £3.50 ($6.50) adults, £3 ($5.55) seniors, £1.50 ($2.80) children, £9.50 ($18) family. Feb–Mar, Oct, and Dec daily 10am–4pm; Apr–July daily 10am–5pm; Aug daily 10am–7pm; Sept daily 10am–5pm (last admission 30 min. before closing).

Ludlow Museum *Kids*   This museum tells the story of Ludlow town: the construction of its castle 900 years ago, the prosperity gained from wool and agriculture during the Middle Ages, and its rise in political importance. The museum also houses natural history displays; the Norton Gallery contains "Reading the Rocks," an exhibit that celebrates Ludlow's unique contribution to international geology. There are several hands-on, interactive displays, including a video microscope that lets you examine geological specimens. Visitors can also try on helmets used in England's civil war. It's a great place for kids.

Castle Sq. ℂ 01584/875384. Free admission. Apr–Oct daily 10:30am–1pm and 2–5pm.

Secret Hills 🐾   This center depicts the geology, ecology, history, and culture of Shropshire. Engulfed by meadows and topped off with a green grass roof, the center in particular honors resident writers, such as Mary Webb who wrote *Gone to Earth*, published in 1917. Webb is still known today in the area as much so as the Brontë sisters who still haunt the Yorkshire Moors. Jennifer Jones filmed the story as a 1950 movie, retitled *Wild Heart* in the U.S. Another writer, A. E. Housman, is also honored by the exhibit.

Shropshire Hills Discovery Centre, School Lane, Craven Arms, Shropshire. ℂ 01588/676000. www.shropshire online.gov.uk/discover.nsf. Admission £4.25 ($7.85) adults, £3.75 ($6.95) students and seniors, £2.75 ($5.10) children, £12 ($23) family ticket (2 adults, 3 children). Apr–Oct daily 10am–5:30pm; off season daily 10am–4:30pm (last admission 1 hr. before closing) time. Lies beside A49 on the southern outskirts of Craven Arms, 11km (7 miles) northwest of Ludlow.

WHERE TO STAY

Dinham Hall Hotel   Not to be confused with a less desirable competitor, Ludlow's Dinham Weir Hotel, the Dinham Hall Hotel rises in severe gray-stoned dignity, across the road from Ludlow Castle. Especially popular with participants of the Ludlow Festival, it offers a kind of Georgian-era, stately ambience. Built in 1792 by the earl of Mortimer, it served through the 1960s and 1970s as a dormitory for the nearby public boys' school. Many of the comfortable but very simple bedrooms bear the names of that school's former headmasters. The hotel enjoys a well-deserved reputation for the quality of its bedrooms, two of which are in a converted cottage. Some of the rooms have four-poster beds; all the bathrooms have bathrobes, and all come with a combination tub and shower.

Dinham by the Castle, Ludlow, Shropshire SY8 1EJ. ℂ 01584/876464. Fax 01584/876019. www. dinhamhall.co.uk. 13 units. £130–£280 ($241–$518) double. Rates include English breakfast. AE, MC, V. **Amenities:** Restaurant; bar; limited room service; laundry service. *In room:* TV, dataport, coffeemaker, hair dryer, trouser press.

The Feathers Hotel ★★ The *New York Times* hailed this "the most handsome inn in the world," and after a glance at its lavishly ornate half-timbered facade, you may agree. Built as a private home in 1603, and enlarged many times since, it boasts a winning combination of formal, high-style plasterwork ceilings and rustic, Elizabethan half-timbering and exposed stone, especially in the pub (the Comus) and restaurant (the Housman). Only the suite and a few of the rooms have exposed Tudor-style beams; others are traditional and conservative, without the medieval vestiges of the building's exterior. Twelve rooms have recently been refurbished in an old Georgian style. Some of the spacious rooms have massive headboards skillfully fashioned from antique overmantels or mirror frames. Some rooms have four-poster bed and two are suitable for families. Bathrooms are tidily maintained, mostly with tub and shower; one room sports a Jacuzzi.

The Bull Ring, Ludlow, Shropshire SY8 1AA. ⓒ **01584/875261.** Fax 01584/876030. www.feathersatludlow. co.uk. 40 units. £90–£140 ($167–$259) double; £125–£150 ($231–$278) suite. Rates include breakfast. AE, DC, MC, V. **Amenities:** Restaurant; bar; limited room service; rooms for those with limited mobility. *In room:* TV w/pay movies, dataport, coffeemaker, hair dryer, trouser press.

WHERE TO DINE

The explosion of top-rated restaurants in this quaint little town of 9,000 is one of the mysteries of England, or, in the words of one critic, "one of the unexplained wonders of our age." How Ludlow came to boast three Michelin-starred restaurants remains a puzzle. Whatever the reason, Ludlow is fast coming Britain's "gastro capital."

Hibiscus ★★★ FRENCH Amazingly, the cuisine at Hibiscus equals the stellar ratings of Merchant House and Mr. Underhills (both reviewed below). Given certain variables at any one place, the race among the top three is too close to call. Don't judge this 17th-century place by its relatively spartan look with rough-stone walls and oak paneling. Claude Bosi worked under one of the world's most famous chefs, Alain Ducasse, but has forged ahead with his own creative culinary statements. Because Bosi was born in Lyons, the gastronomic capital of France, his cuisine is more French than the other two leading restaurants. He cooks for only eight tables, and every guest receives personal attention here.

The menu changes daily to allow for market-fresh ingredients. The cuisine is inventive, with a well-balanced and subtle blend of flavors. A first for many diners is the "foie gras ice cream" served on a toasted brioche. Follow that up with snails coated in a lusty garlic and lime foam, and a main course of pink spring lamb that has been perfectly seared. A particularly refreshing dessert is composed of a chilled soup made from yogurt and Jaffa oranges, in which nestles a scoop of oregano-flavored ice cream.

17 Corve St. ⓒ **01584/872325.** Reservations required. Fixed-price lunch £25 ($46); fixed-price dinner £36–£55 ($67–$102). MC, V. Tues–Sat 12:30–1:30pm; Mon–Sat 7–9:30pm.

Les Marches MODERN BRITISH/FRENCH This well-recommended and rather stylish restaurant has an ambitious menu that usually succeeds with flair. The richly oak-paneled dining room evokes the grand age of private dinner parties. Menu items are prepared by Olivier Bossut or his assistants, with straightforward but intelligent use of fresh ingredients. Examples include roasted Cornish lobster with pan-fried cauliflower, watercress purée, and sweet and sour sauce; or pan-fried squab with fresh dates and a lemon and apricot mousse. The wine list boasts more than 300 selections.

In the Overton Grange Hotel, Overton, near Ludlow. ⓒ **01584/873500.** Reservations recommended. Fixed-price lunch menus £35 ($65); fixed-price dinner menus £38 ($69). MC, V. Daily noon–2:30pm and 7–9:30pm.

The Merchant House 👫👫👫 MODERN BRITISH   The Merchant House is one of the three best restaurants in town. In virtually any other city in the world, much attention and fuss would be made over the half-timbered facade of this late-16th-century building (the former home of a wool merchant), but in Ludlow, it blends right in. In a room where you could imagine William Shakespeare concocting some of his sonnets, you'll enjoy a view over the River Corve. The only drawbacks are a comparatively small dining room (with seating for only 24) and limited hours.

The creative forces are Shaun (who prepares the food) and Anja (the manager) Hill, whose cuisine is based on a deep respect for fresh local ingredients. Enjoy roasted venison, or an artfully arranged chunk of brill with perfectly prepared vegetables and drizzled with a watercress-and-vermouth sauce. One of the best desserts is a chocolate-flavored *pativier* that elevates an old-fashioned almond tart to chocoholic heaven.

Lower Corve St. ✆ **01584/875438.** Reservations required. Fixed-price menu £35 ($65); fixed-price lunch £29 ($54). MC, V. Fri–Sat noon–1:30pm; Tues–Sat 7–9pm.

Mr. Underhill's at Dinham Weir 👫👫👫 BRITISH/MEDITERRANEAN Giving Merchant House and Hibiscus competition is Mr. Underhill's. Serious foodies think nothing of journeying here for dinner from Oxford or Birmingham. Weekends see many Londoners arriving at the place for a serious bitedown. Chris Bradley, the chef and owner, turned this threadbare inn, which looked like Fawlty Towers, into a charming inn beneath the ruins of an 11th-century castle overlooking an English garden above a dam on the River Teme. Dining here evokes the aura of a house party. In summer, tables are placed outside in the garden.

Since the menu changes every night, you don't know what you'll be served. Perhaps you'll start with undyed smoked haddock with a beurre blanc (white butter) sauce, or tarts of Brie, chives, and tomatoes, suffused with flavor. This is straightforward, not overly fancy cookery. Your main course may be a divine piece of brill with a flavor of cardamom and lime, or else marinated organic farm chicken set on a mushroom risotto. Bradley serves such desserts as homemade ice cream with praline oatmeal. The winter apple pudding deserves an award.

Many diners choose to overnight here, and we recommend you follow their example. The B&B rate is £98 to £110 ($181–$204), rising to £140 ($259) in a suite.

Dinham Weir. ✆ **01584/874431.** Reservations required. Fixed-price dinner £35 ($65). MC, V. Daily 7:30–8:30pm.

A FAVORITE LOCAL PUB

The town's most atmospheric and evocative pub, **The Church Inn,** Church Street, Buttercross (✆ **01584/872174**), is a favorite source for beer, gossip, and good cheer. Beer, mead, and wine have flowed here since at least 1446, and according to some historians, even earlier. Meals are served daily from noon to 2pm and Monday to Saturday from 6:30 to 9pm. Whether you eat informally in the bar or head for the more formal restaurant, the food and prices are exactly the same. Main courses range from £7.25 to £9.95 ($13–$19). Cuisine is straightforward, British, and rib-sticking, with traditional pub grub such as steak-and-kidney pie, fried prawns, and omelets. Some Italian dishes and a few Indian curries have also been added to the menu. The bar is open Monday through Saturday from 11am to 11pm, and Sunday from noon to 10:30pm.

10 Shrewsbury

264km (164 miles) NW of London; 63km (39 miles) SW of Stoke-on-Trent; 77km (48 miles) NW of Birmingham

The finest Tudor town in England, Shrewsbury is noted for its black-and-white buildings of timber and plaster, including Abbot's House (dating from 1450), and the tall gabled Ireland's Mansion (ca. 1575) on High Street. These houses were built by the powerful and prosperous wool traders, or drapers. Charles Dickens wrote of his stay in Shrewsbury's Lion Hotel, "I am lodged in the strangest little rooms, the ceilings of which I can touch with my hands. From the windows I can look all downhill and slantwise at the crookedest black-and-white houses, all of many shapes except straight shapes." The town also has a number of Georgian and Regency mansions, some old bridges, and handsome churches, including the Abbey Church of Saint Peter, and St. Mary's Church.

ESSENTIALS

GETTING THERE   Shrewsbury-bound trains depart London's Euston Station daily every half-hour. You change trains in Birmingham before you arrive in Shrewsbury 3 hours later. For information, call © **0845/748-4950** or visit www.arrivatrainswales.co.uk.

Three **National Express** buses depart daily from London's Victoria Coach Station for the 5-hour trip. For information, call © **0870/580-8080** or visit www.nationalexpress.com.

By car from London, the drive is 2½ hours; take the M1 to the M6 to the M54 to reach the A5, which will take you directly to Shrewsbury.

VISITOR INFORMATION   From Easter to September, the **Shrewsbury Tourist Information Centre,** The Square (© **01743/281200**), is open from 10am to 6pm Monday through Saturday and from 10am to 4pm Sunday. From October to Easter, its hours are from 10am to 5pm Monday through Saturday.

SEEING THE SIGHTS

Many tales and stories are locked within Shrewsbury's winding narrow streets and black-and-white buildings. The best way to learn this local lore is to take one of the many walking or coach tours hosted by official Shrewsbury guides. Special themed walking tours such as Ghosts, Brother Cadfael, and the Civil War are also available. A typical tour starts in the town center and lasts 1½ hours. Tickets can be purchased from the Tourist Information Centre (see above).

Attingham Park   This elegant classical house set on 100 hectares (250 acres) of woodlands and landscaped deer park is graced with superbly decorated state-rooms, including a red dining room and blue drawing room. Treasures of the house include Regency silver used at 19th-century ambassadorial receptions and elegant Italian furniture. A tearoom and gift shop on the grounds make a pleasant stop before or after you've toured the house.

Shrewsbury. © **01743/709203**. House admission £5.50 ($10) adults, £2.70 ($5) children, £14 ($25) families. Park and grounds £2.70 ($5) adults, £1.35 ($2.50) children, £6.50 ($12) families. House, tearoom, and shop Mar 19–Nov 3 Fri–Tues 1:30–4:30pm (the tearoom opens an hour earlier for lunch); park and grounds open daily 9am–5pm, until 9pm in summer.

Shrewsbury Abbey ⚘   Founded in 1083, Shrewsbury Abbey became one of the most powerful Benedictine monasteries in England. It's the setting of the Brother Cadfael tales, a series of mysteries written by Ellis Peters that have recently been adapted for television. The church remains in use to this day, and visitors can see displays devoted to the abbey's history as well as the remains of the 14th-century shrine of St. Winefride.

Abbey Foregate. (C) **01743/232723.** Admission free, but donations requested for the Abbey Fund. Easter–Oct daily 9:30am–5:30pm; Nov–Easter daily 10:30am–3pm.

Shrewsbury Castle   Built in 1083 by a Norman earl, Roger de Montgomery, this castle was designed as a powerful fortress to secure the border with Wales. The Great Hall and walls were constructed during the reign of Edward I, but 200 years ago, Thomas Telford extensively remodeled the castle. Today, it houses the Shropshire Regimental Museum, which includes the collections of the King's Shropshire Light Infantry, the Shropshire Yeomanry, and the Shropshire Royal Horse Artillery. These collections represent more than 300 years of regimental service, and include a lock of Napoleon's hair and an American flag captured during the seizure and burning of the White House during the War of 1812.

Castle St. (C) **01743/358516.** Admission £2 ($3.70), free students and children under 16. Feb 4–Mar 15 Wed–Sat 10am–4pm; Mar 18–Dec 19 Tues–Sat 10am–5pm, Sun–Mon 10am–4pm; Easter–Sept 26 10am–4:30pm. Closed Dec 20–Feb 3.

WHERE TO STAY

Albright Hussey Hotel 🏠🏠   Its unusual name derives from the feudal family (the Husseys) who occupied it between 1292 and the 1600s. Today, it's one of the best examples of an elaborate Tudor timber-frame building in Shrewsbury. The brick-and-stone wing was added around 1560. The interior has all the old-world charm and eccentricities you could hope for, including oak panels, fireplaces large enough to roast an ox, and a moated garden with several pairs of fiercely territorial black swans. Most furnishings date from the early 19th century, contrasting well with dozens of beams that have been artfully exposed in the ceilings and walls of bedrooms and public areas. Five rooms have four-poster beds. Rooms in the main house have more character, though those in the new wing are slightly more spacious with more up-to-date furnishings. Most rooms open onto views of the landscaped gardens. Bathrooms are small but well organized, mostly with tub and shower; suites have Jacuzzis.

Ellesmere Rd., Shrewsbury, Shropshire SY4 5TX. (C) **01939/290571.** Fax 01939/291143. www.albrighthussey. co.uk. 26 units. £110 ($204) double; £160 ($296) suite. Rates include breakfast. AE, DC, MC, V. 4km (2½ miles) northeast of Shrewsbury along A528. **Amenities:** Restaurant; bar; 24-hr. room service; babysitting; laundry service; rooms for those with limited mobility. *In room:* TV, dataport, coffeemaker, hair dryer, iron/ironing board, trouser press.

The Lion   Housed on the site of a 17th-century coaching inn that claims to have origins in the 14th century, this is easily the most evocative hotel in Shrewsbury itself. Since then, the rooms have been enlarged, and the setting has been lavishly gentrified with lots of patterned chintz and modern luxuries. Only the suite contains artfully gnarled oaken beams—other rooms are comfortable as well and are being refurbished in a style evocative of the 17th century. Beds are exceedingly comfortable; the shower-only bathrooms are small and compact.

Wyle Cop, Shrewsbury, Shropshire SY1 1UY. (C) **01743/353107.** Fax 01743/352744. www.corushotels.co.uk. 59 units. £99 ($183) double; £120 ($222) suite. Rates include breakfast. AE, DC, MC, V. **Amenities:** Restaurant; bar; 24-hr. room service; laundry service; rooms for those with limited mobility. *In room:* TV, dataport, coffeemaker, hair dryer, trouser press.

WHERE TO DINE

Country Friends MODERN BRITISH   Built in 1673 as a private home, this pleasant restaurant today boasts a much-restored Tudor facade amid attractive gardens. Inside, a hardworking kitchen concocts modern reinventions of such old-fashioned dishes as lamb noisettes roasted in mustard crust with mint hollandaise and filet of steak with a leek and horseradish topping and red-wine sauce. Some aspects of the menu change almost every week.

They also offer one comfortable bedroom at a rate of £135 ($250) double occupancy, including dinner and breakfast. There's no phone or TV; the medium-size room has a tub and a hair dryer.

Dorrington (9.5km/6 miles south of Shrewsbury via A49), Shropshire S45 7JD. © **01743/718707**. Reservations not needed. Light luncheon platters £3.90–£10 ($7.20–$19); 2-course fixed-price menus £29 ($54); 3-course fixed-price menus £32 ($59). MC, V. Wed–Sat noon–2pm and 7–9pm.

The Peach Tree ★ (Finds BRITISH/EUROPEAN   Its name derives from the hundreds of ripe peaches, peach trees, and peach boughs that someone laboriously stenciled onto the walls. The setting dates from the 15th century, when this was a weaver's cottage adjacent to the abbey. The food is based on solid, time-tested recipes made with fresh ingredients and loads of European savoir-faire. Main courses include medallions of venison and such vegetarian dishes as ragout of woodland mushrooms with filo pastry and a basil and crème fraîche. The dessert that keeps everyone coming back for more is homemade meringue with ice cream, traditional butterscotch sauce, and shreddings of roasted coconut. Though the upstairs restaurant is more fancy, you can have any of the platters informally in the street-level bar if you're alone or in a hurry.

21 Abbey Foregate. © **01743/355055**. Reservations recommended on weekends. Main courses £8.50–£16 ($16–$30). AE, DC, MC, V. Mon–Sat 9am–midnight; Sun 9am–11pm.

SHREWSBURY AFTER DARK

Quench your thirst or have a bite to eat at the **Lion & Pheasant Hotel** bar, 49–50 Wyle Cop (© **01743/236288**), where in colder months, an inviting firelight ambience presides. Or check out the **Boat House Pub,** New Street (© **01743/231658**), located beside a beautiful old park on the River Severn. In summer, they open up the terrace overlooking the river, and it becomes a popular date place. Couples enjoy a healthy selection of beers and ales, along with a tasty pub grub that ranges from soup and sandwiches to pies.

The **Buttermarket Nightclub** (© **01743/241455**), set in the old butter market on Howard Street, caters to the over-25 crowd. It has two theme nights: Saturday (disco) and Thursday (world music).

The Music Hall, The Square (© **01743/281281**), hosts musicals, plays, and concerts year-round. Tickets range from £5 to £15 ($9.25–$28).

11 Ironbridge

217km (135 miles) NW of London; 58km (36 miles) NW of Birmingham; 29km (18 miles) SE of Shrewsbury

Ironbridge, located in the Ironbridge Gorge, is famous for kicking off an early stage of the Industrial Revolution. Indeed, this stretch of the Severn River valley has been an important industrial area since the Middle Ages because of its iron and limestone deposits. But the event that clinched this area's importance came in 1709, when the Quaker ironmaster, Abraham Darby I, discovered a method for smelting iron by using coke as a fuel, instead of charcoal. This paved the way for the first iron rails, boats, wheels, aqueducts, and bridge, cast in Coalbrookdale in 1779. So momentous was this accomplishment that the area, originally called Coalbrookdale, was renamed Ironbridge. The area literally buzzed with the new transportation and engineering innovations that soon followed.

Today, you'll find an intriguing complex of museums that documents and brings to life the rich history of Ironbridge Gorge. The gift shops and other stores in town have plenty of unusual souvenirs to help you remember your visit.

ESSENTIALS

GETTING THERE Seven days a week, trains leave London's Euston Station hourly for Telford Central Station in Telford, with a transfer in Birmingham. From here, take a bus or taxi into Ironbridge. The entire journey takes about 3 hours. For schedules and information, call © **0845/748-4950** or visit www.centraltrains.co.uk.

Three buses daily depart London's Victoria Coach Station, arriving in Telford about 5 hours later. Call © **020/7529-2000** for information. Local buses that leave Telford for the 20-minute ride to Ironbridge include nos. 6, 8, 9, and 99.

If you're driving a car from London, take the M1 to the M6 to the M54, which leads directly to Ironbridge.

VISITOR INFORMATION The **Ironbridge Gorge Tourist Information Centre,** 4 The Wharfage (© 01952/432166), is open Monday through Friday from 9am to 5pm and Saturday and Sunday from 10am to 5pm.

EXPLORING THE AREA

The Ironbridge Valley plays host to seven main museums and several smaller ones, collectively called the **Ironbridge Gorge Museums** *ᏇᏇ*, Ironbridge, Telford (© **01952/433522** weekdays, or 01952/432166 Sat–Sun; www.ironbridge.org.uk). Museums include the **Coalbrookdale Museum,** with its Darby Furnace of Iron and sound-and-light display, as well as restored 19th-century homes of the Quaker ironmasters; the **Iron Bridge,** with its original tollhouse; the **Jackfield Tile Museum,** where you can see demonstrations of tile-pressing, decorating, and firing; the **Blists Hill Open Air Museum,** with its re-creation of a 19th-century town; and the **Coalport China Museum.** A passport ticket to all museums in Ironbridge Gorge is £13 ($24) for adults, £11 ($21) for seniors, £8.25 ($15) for students and children, and £40 ($74) for a family of two adults and up to five children. The sites are open from Easter to November daily from 10am to 5pm. The Iron Bridge Tollhouse and Rosehill House are closed from November to March.

You can also find some good shopping. You can buy Coalport china at the **Coalport China Museum** and decorative tiles at the **Jackfield Tile Museum.** Another place worth visiting is just beyond the Jackfield Museum: **Maws Craft Center** (© **01952/883923**) is the site of 20 workshops situated in an old Victorian tile works beside the River Severn. Here, you can browse for glass sculptures, dollhouses, original and Celtic art, pictures with frames made while you wait, jewelry, and stained glass. There's also a tearoom on-site that's open for lunch and afternoon tea.

WHERE TO STAY

Bridge House Set 2.5km (1½ miles) west of Ironbridge, on the outskirts of the hamlet of Buildwas, this ivy-draped, half-timbered coaching inn is from 1620. Resident proprietor Janet Hedges will tell you unusual stories about the house, such as the 365 nails (one for every day of the year) that hold together the planks of the front door, or the fact that the building's front porch was removed from the nearby abbey. Rooms are genteel and comfortable, sometimes with touches of Edwardian drama (lavishly draped beds, in some cases). Others have exposed beams, and all have creaking floors and uneven walls that testify to the age of the building. Rooms are small but snug, and each is individually decorated. The compact bathrooms are efficiently organized, each with a shower or tub.

Buildwas, Telford, Shropshire TF8 7BN. © **01952/432105.** Fax 01952/432105. 4 units. £65 ($120) double; £90 ($167) family unit. Rates include breakfast. MC, V. Closed for 2 weeks at Christmas. *In room:* TV, coffeemaker, hair dryer.

Library House ☆ *(Finds* This restored landmark building lies only 18m (60 ft.) from Ironbridge itself, convenient for all the museums. The building, parts of which date back to 1752, has been used for many purposes, including a doctor's surgery and even the village library, from which the B&B takes its name. Breakfast is served in a room with a rich collection of copper. The breakfast is the best in the area, and the house was in the running for the Automobile Association's best breakfast award. The delightful bedrooms are individually designed and decorated, and named after such birds as the Bluebird or the Chaffinch. The bathrooms have either tub or shower and are beautifully maintained. All guest bedrooms have their own teddy bears if you want to cuddle up. There is also a pretty terraced garden.

11 Severn Bank, Ironbridge, Telford, Shropshire TF8 7AN. © **01952/432299.** Fax 01952/433967. www.library house.com. 4 units. £60 ($111) double; £80–£85 ($148–$157) family rooms. Rates include breakfast. No credit cards. **Amenities:** Breakfast room, garden; nonsmoking rooms. *In room:* TV, coffeemaker, hair dryer, no phone.

The Valley Hotel This hotel was originally built as a private home around 1750. This riverside inn was enlarged over the years into the sprawling, light-brown brick design you see today. The high-ceilinged interior contains hints of its original grandeur, including a worthwhile restaurant, the Chez Maw (see below). Fifteen of the hotel's rooms lie within the original stable and are accessible via a glass-roofed courtyard. Although rooms in the main house usually have more panoramic views, many visitors prefer the coziness of the former stables. All rooms are clean and modern; some have four-poster beds. The small bathrooms are adequate and well maintained, each with a shower.

Ironbridge, Telford, Shropshire, TF8 7DW. © **800/528-1234** in the U.S., or 01952/432247. Fax 01952/432308. www.thevalleyhotel.co.uk. 35 units. £121–£145 ($224–$268) double. Rates include breakfast. AE, DC, MC, V. **Amenities:** Restaurant; 3 bars; 24-hr. room service; laundry service; rooms for those with limited mobility. *In room:* TV, dataport, coffeemaker, hair dryer, iron/board, trouser press.

WHERE TO DINE

Restaurant Chez Maw BRITISH The name refers to Arthur Maw, long-ago owner of the house, and founder of a nearby factory that produced decorative tiles during the 19th century. Prized examples of his ceramic creations line the reception area and the monumental staircase. Outfitted with crisp napery, Windsor-style chairs, and a high ceiling, the restaurant serves such updated British food as tortellini laced with cream, herbs, and slices of Parma ham; platters of smoked tuna and marinated salmon; and filets of pork and beef drizzled with sauce made from Shropshire blue cheese.

In The Valley House Hotel. © **01952/432247.** Reservations recommended. Main courses £5–£15 ($9.25–$28); fixed-price menu £28 ($51). AE, DC, MC, V. Sun–Fri noon–2pm and 7–9:30pm.

A FAVORITE LOCAL PUB

A rebuilt Victorian pub, complete with a chicken coop in the backyard? Yes, it's the **New Inn,** in the Blists Hill Museum complex (© **01952/586063**). It has atmosphere galore, with its gas lamps, sawdust floors, and knowledgeable and friendly staff sporting vintage Victorian garb. You'll find a good selection of ales; hearty, rib-sticking home-cooked meals; and plenty of pub games.

12 Stoke-on-Trent: The Potteries

261km (162 miles) NW of London; 74km (46 miles) N of Birmingham; 95km (59 miles) NW of Leicester; 66km (41 miles) S of Manchester

Situated halfway between the Irish and the North seas, Staffordshire is a county of peaceful countryside, rugged moorlands, and Cheshire plains. While there are several charming country inns here, pottery is Staffordshire's real claim to fame. Although it has been created in the area since 2000 B.C., it wasn't until the Romans rolled through in A.D. 46 that the first pottery kiln was set up at Trent Vale. Now it's **Stoke-on-Trent,** a loose confederation of six towns (Tunstall, Burslem, Stoke, Fenton, Longton, and Hanley, the most important town) covering an 11km (7-mile) area, that's the real center of the pottery trade. During the Industrial Revolution, the area known collectively as Stoke-on-Trent became the world's leading producer of pottery, and today it is a tourist attraction.

ESSENTIALS

GETTING THERE   It's a direct train ride of 2 hours to Stoke-on-Trent from London's Euston Station. Trains make hourly departures daily. For schedules and information, call ✆ **0845/748-4950** or visit www.virgintrains.co.uk.

Six **National Express** buses leave London's Victoria Coach Station daily for the 4- to 5-hour trip to Stoke. For information, call ✆ **0870/580-8080** or visit www.nationalexpress.com.

By car from London, drive along the M1 to the M6 to the A500 at Junction 15. It will take you 2 to 3 hours by car.

VISITOR INFORMATION   The **Stoke-on-Trent Tourist Information Centre,** Quadrant Road, Hanley, Stoke-on-Trent (✆ **01782/236000**), is open Monday through Saturday from 9:15am to 5:15pm. You can pick up a China Experience visitor map, noting most potteries, shops, and museums in the area.

HISTORY FIRST: TWO WORTHWHILE MUSEUMS

The Gladstone Pottery Museum ⚐   This is the only Victorian pottery factory that has been restored as a museum, with craftspeople providing daily demonstrations in original workshops. Various galleries depict the rise of the Staffordshire pottery industry, tile history, and so on (check out the toilets of all shapes, sizes, colors, and decoration). Great hands-on opportunities for plate painting, pot throwing, and ornamental-flower making.

Uttoxeter Rd. at Longton. ✆ 01782/319232. Admission £4.95 ($9.15) adults, £3.95 ($7.30) seniors and students, £3.50 ($6.50) children, £14 ($26) family ticket. Daily 10am–5pm; last admission at 4pm.

The Potteries Museum and Art Gallery ⚐   Start here for an overview of Stoke-on-Trent history. It houses departments of fine arts, decorative arts, natural history, archaeology, and social history. It also has one of the largest and finest collections of ceramics in the world. It's a great place for training your eyes before exploring the factories and shops of Stoke-on-Trent.

Bethesda St., Hanley. ✆ 01782/232323. www2002.stoke.gov.uk/museums/pmag/index.html. Free admission. Nov–Feb Mon–Sat 10am–5pm, Sun 2–5pm; Mar–Oct Mon–Sat 10am–4pm, Sun 2–5pm.

TOURING & SHOPPING THE POTTERIES

With over 40 factories in Stoke-on-Trent—all with gift shops and seconds shops on-site—you need to be in shape for this adventure. In fact, some have several shops, selling everything from fine china dinner services to hand-painted tiles.

Seconds are always a great bargain. They're still high-quality pieces with imperfections that only the professional eye can detect. But don't expect bargains on top-of-the-line pieces. Shops discount their best wares once in a while, but most of the time, prices for first-quality items are the same here as they are in London, elsewhere in England, or in America.

During the big January sales in London, many department stores, including Harrods, truck in seconds from the factories in Stoke, so if you're in London then, you don't have to visit here to bring home a bargain.

Each factory discussed below offers shipping and can help with value-added tax (VAT) refund. Expect your purchases to be delivered within 1 to 3 months. (Chapter 3 has more details about getting your VAT refund.)

Moorcroft Pottery   Moorcroft is a welcome change from the world-famous names you've just seen. It was founded in 1898 by William Moorcroft, who produced his own special brand of pottery and was his own exclusive designer until his death in 1945. Decoration is part of the first firing here, giving it a higher quality of color and brilliance than, say, Spode, creating floral designs in bright, clear colors (think of it as the Art Nouveau of the pottery world). There is much to admire and buy in the factory seconds shop. There is always someone around to explain the various processes and to show you around the museum, with its collections of early Moorcroft.

West Moorcroft, Sandbach Rd., Burslem, Stoke-on-Trent. ℂ 01782/207943. www.moorcroft.com. Factory tours Mon, Wed, and Thurs at 11am and 2pm, Fri at 11am. Tours must be booked in advance; cost is £2.50 ($4.65) adults, £1.50 ($2.80) seniors and children under 16. Museum and shop open Mon–Fri 10am–5pm, Sat 9:30am–4:30pm. A taxi from the Stoke-on-Trent train station will run about £6 ($11). If you're driving from London, follow M1 north to M6. Take it north to Junction 15, which becomes A500. Follow the signs.

Royal Doulton Pottery Factory ⋆   Wear some comfortable shoes for the tour here—you'll walk nearly a mile and tackle over 250 steps, but you will see plates, cups, and figures made from start to finish. Live demonstrations of how figures are assembled from a mold and decorated are given at the **Visitor Centre,** which also has the world's largest collection of Royal Doulton figures. Next door to the Visitor Centre is the **Minton Fine Art Studio,** where plates and pillboxes are hand-painted and richly decorated with gold before your eyes.

The Gallery Restaurant serves cakes and coffee, light lunches, and afternoon tea, everything, of course, on the finest bone china. The gift shop is stocked with a full range of Royal Doulton figures and tableware, and a selection of bargains.

Nile St. Burslem, near Stoke-on-Trent. ℂ 01782/292434. Admission for both tour and Visitor Centre £6.50 ($12) adults; £5 ($9.25) children ages 10–16, students, and seniors; £17 ($31) family tickets. Admission to just Visitor Centre £3 ($5.55) adults; £2.25 ($4.15) children ages 5–9; £2.25 ($4.15) children ages 10–16, students, and seniors; £7 ($13) family tickets. Tours offered Mon–Thurs 10:30am and 2pm; Fri 10:30am and 1pm; they must be booked in advance. Visitor Centre open Mon–Sat 9:30am–5pm, Sun 10:30am–4:30pm; shop open Mon–Sat 9am–5:30pm, Sun 10:30am–4:30pm. A taxi from the Stoke-on-Trent train station will cost about £5 ($9.25). If you're driving from London, follow M1 north until you reach M6. Take it to Junction 15, which becomes A500. Follow A500 to its junction with A527, then follow the brown signs to the factory.

Spode ⋆   The oldest English pottery company operating on the same site since 1770 and the birthplace of fine bone china, Spode offers regular factory tours lasting about 1½ hours and connoisseur tours lasting 2½ hours. In the **Craft Centre,** visitors can see demonstrations of engraving, lithography, hand painting, printing, and clay casting. An unrivaled collection of Spode's ceramic masterpieces is on display in the **Spode Museum.** The Blue Italian Restaurant cooks

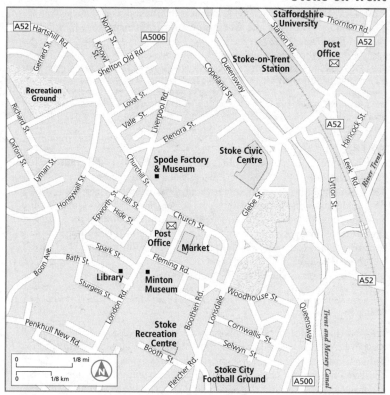

up refreshments and lunch—all served on Spode's classic blue tableware, Blue Italian. The Factory Shop sells seconds at reduced prices.

Church St., Stoke-on-Trent. ☎ 01782/744011. www.spode.co.uk. Basic factory tour £4.50 ($8.35) adults, £4 ($7.40) children 12 years and older, students, and seniors. Connoisseur factory tour £7.50 ($14) adults, £6.50 ($12) children 12 years and older, students, and seniors. Tours Mon–Thurs at 10am and 11:30am, Fri at 10am. Tours must be booked in advance. Admission for Spode Visitor Centre and Museum is free. Visitor Centre open Mon–Sat 9am–5pm; Sun 10am–4pm. Spode is a 10-min. walk from the Stoke-on-Trent train station. If you're driving from London, follow M1 north until you reach M6. Take it north to Junction 15, which becomes A500. Follow the signs.

Wedgwood Visitor Centre ☙ The visitor center includes a demonstration hall to watch clay pots being formed on the potter's wheel, and witness plates being turned and fired, then painted. Highly skilled potters and decorators are happy to answer your questions. An art gallery and gift shop showcase samples of factory-made items that also can be purchased. (Note that the prices at this shop are the same as those found elsewhere.) Tours must be booked in advance.

Also located at the Wedgwood Centre, the **Wedgwood Museum** covers 3 centuries of design and features living displays including Josiah Wedgwood's Etruria factory and his Victorian showroom. Other room settings can also be seen at the museum. The Josiah Wedgwood Restaurant is the perfect place to relax with a cup of coffee or a full meal.

Wedgwood seconds, which are available at reduced prices, are not sold at the center, but are available at the **Wedgwood Group Factory Shop,** King Street, Fenton (ⓒ **01782/316161**).

Barlaston. ⓒ **01782/204218.** www.thewedgwoodstory.com. Admission £7.25–£8.95 ($13–$17) adults; £5.25–£6.95 ($9.70–$13) seniors, students, and children; £24–£30 ($44–$56) family ticket (up to 2 adults and 3 children). Factory tours Mon–Thurs at 10am and 2pm; they last 2 hr. and must be booked in advance. Centre open Mon–Fri 9am–5pm; Sat–Sun 10am–5pm. It's easiest to get here by taxi from the Stoke-on-Trent train station, a 9.5km (6-mile) trip that will cost around £7.75 ($14). If you're driving from London, head north along M1 until you reach M6. Continue north to Junction 14, which becomes A34. Follow A34 to Barlaston and follow the signs to Wedgwood.

WHERE TO STAY & DINE

George Hotel   This is one of the most upscale, formal, and dignified hotels in town, the kind of place where the mayor would invite some cronies or a businessperson might bring an important client. Built in 1929 of red brick, it rises three floors above the hamlet of Burslem, one of the six villages comprising the Stoke-on-Trent district. Public areas are outfitted with traditional furniture and large 19th-century oil paintings of the town and region. The conservative but comfortable bedrooms are well furnished and generally spacious. Each small bathroom is well maintained with a shower.

Swan Sq., Burslem, Stoke-on-Trent ST6 2AE. ⓒ **01782/577544.** Fax 01782/837496. www.georgehotelstoke. cwc.net. 40 units. £60–£85 ($111–$157) double. Rates include breakfast. AE, DC, MC, V. **Amenities:** Restaurant; bar; limited room service; laundry service. *In room:* TV, dataport, coffeemaker, hair dryer, iron/ironing board, trouser press.

Haydon House Hotel   This imposing late Victorian house is the home of the Machin family. They've added a collection of built-in mahogany furniture to the bedrooms and reconfigured their home and their lives to welcome overnight guests. You'll find many of the original Victorian fittings, an unusual collection of clocks, and many modern amenities that will make your stay comfortable. Quality beds are in the roomy bedrooms, and the small bathrooms have a tub-and-shower combination. Suites have efficiently arranged kitchenettes and private entrances.

1–9 Haydon St., Basford, Stoke-on-Trent, Staffordshire ST4 6JD. ⓒ **01782/711311.** Fax 01782/717470. www. touristnetuk.com/wm/haydon-house. 30 units. Mon–Thurs £85 ($157) double, £120 ($222) suite; Fri–Sun £60 ($111) double, £100 ($185) suite. AE, DC, MC, V. **Amenities:** Restaurant; bar; limited room service; laundry service. *In room:* TV, coffeemaker, hair dryer, trouser press.

Stoke-on-Trent Moat House ⟨★⟩   This is the town's leading accommodation. Originally built in the 18th century as the home of Josiah Wedgwood, father of the ceramics company that still bears his name today, this redbrick house functioned for many years as an administrative office for British Steel. By the time the Queen's Moat House chain bought it in the late 1980s, many of the architectural nuances had been removed, except for the sweeping staircase and a few remnants. The new owners subsequently began the laborious process of enlarging and restoring the premises. The result is a four-story annex wing—joined to the historic core by a glass-sided corridor—in which the bulk of the accommodations lie. Its redbrick walls more or less match those of the original premises. The result is a modern, chain-style hotel that retains a sense of history, which its hardworking staff strives to maintain. All the midsize rooms have been redecorated and furnished to a comfortable standard. Bathrooms are small but have adequate shelf space and tubs with showers.

Etruria Hall, Festival Way, Etruria, Stoke-on-Trent, Staffordshire ST1 5BQ. ⓒ **01782/609988.** Fax 01782/284500. www.moathousehotels.com. 143 units. £149 ($276) double; £199 ($368) suite. AE, DC, MC, V. **Amenities:** Restaurant; 2 bars; indoor pool; health club; sauna; 24-hr. room service; laundry service; dry cleaning; rooms for those with limited mobility. *In room:* TV, dataport, coffeemaker, hair dryer, safe.

14

Cambridge & East Anglia

The four essentially bucolic counties of **East Anglia** (Essex, Suffolk, Norfolk, and Cambridgeshire) were once an ancient Anglo-Saxon kingdom dominated by the Danes. In part, the region is a land of heaths, fens, marshes, and inland lagoons known as "broads." Many old villages and market towns abound; anglers, walkers, cyclists, and bird-watchers are drawn to the area.

Suffolk and Essex are Constable Country and boast some of England's finest landscapes. Many visitors drive through Essex on the way to **Cambridge.** Though close to London and industrialized in places, this land of rolling fields has rural areas and villages, many on the seaside. Essex stretches east to the English Channel, where its major city, **Colchester,** is known for oysters and roses. Eighty kilometers (50 miles) from London, Colchester was the first Roman city in Britain and is the oldest recorded town in the kingdom.

Because Colchester is not on the route of most visitors, we have focused instead on tiny villages in the western part of Essex, such as Thaxted, just south of Cambridge, and easily explored on your way from London.

The easternmost county of England, Suffolk is a refuge for artists, just as it was in the day of its famous native sons, Constable and Gainsborough, who preserved its landscapes on canvas. Though a fast train can whisk visitors from London to East Suffolk in approximately 1½ hours, its fishing villages, historic homes, and national monuments remain off the beaten track for most tourists. To capture the true charm of Suffolk, you must explore its little market towns and villages. Beginning at the Essex border, we head toward the North Sea, highlighting the most scenic villages as we move eastward across the shire.

Seat of the dukes of Norfolk, **Norwich** is less popular, but those who venture toward the North Sea are rewarded with some of England's most beautiful scenery. An occasional dike or windmill reminds one of the Netherlands. From here you can branch out and visit the **Broads.**

The resort town of **Wroxham,** capital of the Broads, is easily reached from Norwich, only 13km (8 miles) to the northeast. Motorboats regularly take parties on short trips from Wroxham. Some of the best scenery of the Broads is on the periphery of Wroxham. From Norwich you can also make a trip to **Sandringham,** the country home of four generations of British monarchs.

1 Cambridge: Town & Gown ★★★

89km (55 miles) N of London; 129km (80 miles) NE of Oxford

The university town of Cambridge is a collage of images: the Bridge of Sighs; spires and turrets; drooping willows; dusty secondhand bookshops; carol-singing on Christmas Eve in King's College Chapel; dancing until sunrise at the May balls; Elizabethan madrigals; narrow lanes upon which Darwin, Newton, and Cromwell once walked; the "Backs" where the college lawns sweep down to the River Cam; tattered black robes of hurrying upperclassmen flying in the wind.

Along with Oxford, Cambridge is one of Britain's ancient seats of learning. In many ways their stories are similar, particularly the age-old conflict between town and gown. As far as the locals are concerned, alumni such as Isaac Newton, John Milton, and Virginia Woolf aren't from yesterday. Cambridge continues to graduate many famous scientists such as physicist Stephen Hawking, author of *A Brief History of Time*.

In the 1990s, Cambridge became known as a high-tech outpost, or "a silicon fen," if you will. High-tech ventures continue to base themselves here to produce new software—start-up companies producing $3 billion a year in revenues. Even Bill Gates, in 1997, financed an £80 million research center here, claiming that Cambridge was becoming "a world center of advanced technology."

ESSENTIALS

GETTING THERE   Trains depart frequently from London's Liverpool Street and King's Cross stations, arriving an hour later. For inquiries, call © **0845/748-4950** or visit www.railtrack.co.uk. A one-way ticket costs £16 ($29).

National Express buses leave hourly from London's Victoria Coach Station for the 2-hour trip to Drummer Street Station in Cambridge. A one-way ticket costs £9 ($17). For schedules and information, call © **0870/580-8080** or visit www.nationalexpress.com.

If you're driving from London, head north on the M11.

VISITOR INFORMATION   In back of the guildhall, the **Cambridge Tourist Information Centre,** Wheeler Street (© **01223/457577;** www.tourism cambridge.com), has a wide range of information, including data on public transportation and sightseeing attractions. From April to October, hours are Monday to Saturday from 10am to 6pm and Sunday from 11am to 4pm. In July and August, the office is open daily from 10am to 7pm. From November to March, hours are Monday through Saturday from 10am to 5:30pm.

A tourist reception center for Cambridge and Cambridgeshire is operated by **City Sightseeing** at Cambridge Railway Station (© **01223/362444;** www.city-sightseeing.com). The center, on the concourse of the railway station, sells brochures and maps. Also available is a full range of tourist services, including accommodations booking. Open in summer daily from 8:45am to 7pm (closes at 5pm off season). Guided tours of Cambridge leave the center daily.

GETTING AROUND   The center of Cambridge is made for pedestrians, so leave your car at one of the many parking lots (they get more expensive as you approach the city center) and stroll to some of the colleges spread throughout the city. Follow the courtyards through to the "Backs" (the college lawns) and walk through to Trinity (where Prince Charles studied) and St. John's College, which is home to the Bridge of Sighs.

Another popular way of getting around is bicycling. **Station Cycles** (© **01223/307125;** www.stationcycles.co.uk), has bicycles for rent for £6 ($11) for half day, £8 ($15) per day, or £16 ($30) per week. A deposit of £50 ($93) is required. Call their number to reserve a bike. At that time you'll be told the address at which to pick up the cycle. Open Monday through Friday from 7am to 8pm, Saturday from 9am to 5pm, and Sunday 10am to 4pm.

Stagecoach Cambus, 100 Cowley Rd. (© **01223/423578;** www.stagecoach bus.com), services the Cambridge area with a network of buses, with fares ranging

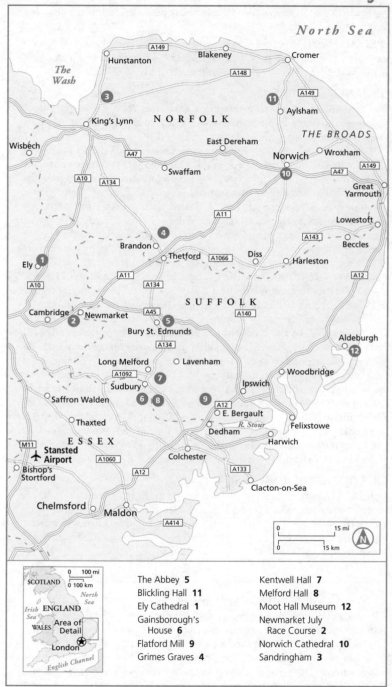

East Anglia

North Sea

The Wash

Hunstanton · Blakeney · Cromer · **11** · A149 · Aylsham

3 · A148

NORFOLK

Wisbech · King's Lynn · East Dereham · Norwich · Wroxham · *THE BROADS*

A47 · Swaffam · **10** · A47 · A149

A10 · A134 · Great Yarmouth

Lowestoft

A11 · **4** · Beccles

Ely · **1** · Brandon · Thetford · A1066 · Diss · Harleston · A143

A10 · A11 · A134 · **SUFFOLK** · A12

Cambridge · **2** · Newmarket · A45 · **5** · A140

Bury St. Edmunds

A134 · Aldeburgh

Long Melford · Lavenham · **12**

A1092 · **7** · Woodbridge

Sudbury · Ipswich

Saffron Walden · **6** · **8** · **9** · A12

Thaxted · E. Bergault · Felixstowe

ESSEX · Dedham · *R. Stour* · Harwich

M11 · Stansted Airport · A1060

Bishop's Stortford · Colchester

Chelmsford · Maldon · A133 · Clacton-on-Sea

A414

0 — 15 mi
0 — 15 km

SCOTLAND · 0 — 100 mi · 0 — 100 km

North Sea

Irish Sea · **ENGLAND**

WALES · Area of Detail

London

English Channel

The Abbey **5**
Blickling Hall **11**
Ely Cathedral **1**
Gainsborough's House **6**
Flatford Mill **9**
Grimes Graves **4**

Kentwell Hall **7**
Melford Hall **8**
Moot Hall Museum **12**
Newmarket July Race Course **2**
Norwich Cathedral **10**
Sandringham **3**

in price from 65p to £3 ($1.20–$5.55) for a day pass. The local tourist office has bus schedules.

SPECIAL EVENTS   Cambridge's artistic bent peaks from the end of June to the end of July during **Camfest** (© **01223/359547**), a visual and performing arts festival. Event tickets are generally from £6 to £12 ($11–$22).

ORGANIZED TOURS

The **Cambridge Tourist Information Centre** (see above) sponsors 2-hour walking tours, taking in the highlights of the city, costing £13 ($23) for adults or £6 ($11) for children. Call for opening times.

For an informative spin on Cambridge, join a **Guided Walking Tour** given by a Cambridge Blue Badge Guide (© **01223/457574**). Two-hour tours leave the Tourist Information Centre (see above) and wind through the streets of historic Cambridge, visiting at least one college and the famous "Backs." From mid-June to August, drama tours are conducted, during which participants may see various costumed characters walk in and out of the tour. Henry VIII, Queen Elizabeth I, Isaac Newton, and others help to breathe life into the history of Cambridge during these tours. Regular tours are from April to mid-June, daily at 11:30am and 1:30pm; from mid-June to September, daily at 11:30am, 1:30, and 2:30pm; October through March, daily at 1:30pm and Saturday at 11:30am. Drama tours are July and August on Tuesday at 6:30pm. Admission for regular tours is £7.85 ($15) per person, £4.50 ($8.35) per person for drama tours.

In addition to its visitor information services (see "Essentials," above), **City Sightseeing,** on the concourse of Cambridge Railway Station (© **01223/ 362444**; www.city-sightseeing.com), offers daily guided tours of Cambridge via open-top, double-decker buses. In summer, they depart every 15 minutes from 9:30am to 4pm. Departures are curtailed off season depending on demand. The tour can be a 1-hour ride, or you can get off at any of the many stops and rejoin the tour whenever you wish. Tickets are valid all day. The fare is £7.50 ($14) for adults, £5.50 ($10) for students and seniors, £3 ($5.55) for children 6 to 12, and free for kids 5 and under. A family ticket for £20 ($37) covers two adults and up to three children. Office hours are daily from 8:45am to 7pm in summer and from 9:30am to 5pm during off season.

EXPLORING THE UNIVERSITY

Oxford University predates Cambridge, but by the early 13th century, scholars began coming here, too. Eventually, Cambridge won partial recognition from Henry III, rising or falling with the approval of subsequent English monarchs. Cambridge consists of 31 colleges for both men and women. Colleges are closed for exams from mid-April until the end of June.

Tips **Caution: Students at Work**

Because of disturbances caused by the influx of tourists, Cambridge limits visitors, or excludes them altogether, from various parts of the university. In some cases, a small entry fee is charged. Small groups of up to six people are generally admitted with no problem; you can inquire with the local tourist office about visiting hours. All colleges are closed during exams and graduation, on Easter and all bank holidays, and other times without notice.

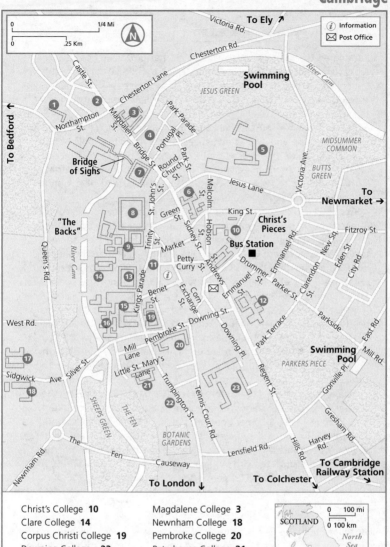

Cambridge

0 1/4 Mi

0 .25 Km

To Ely ↗

Victoria Rd.

Chesterton Rd.

ⓘ Information
✉ Post Office

River Cam

Swimming Pool

JESUS GREEN

Castle St.

Chesterton Lane

Northampton St.

Magdalene St.

Bridge St.

Park Parade

Portugal Pl.

Round Church St.

Park St.

MIDSUMMER COMMON

To Bedford ←

Bridge of Sighs

Jesus Lane

BUTTS GREEN

Victoria Ave.

To Newmarket →

St. John's St.

Green St.

Sidney St.

Malcolm St.

Hobson St.

King St.

Christ's Pieces

Fitzroy St.

New Sq.

"The Backs"

River Cam

Queen's Rd.

Trinity St.

Market

Petty Curry

St. Andrew's St.

Bus Station

Emmanuel Rd.

Clarendon St.

Eden St.

City Rd.

Kings Parade

Benet St.

Corn Exchange St.

Drummer St.

Emmanuel St.

Parker St.

Parkside

East Rd.

Pembroke St.

Downing St.

Park Terrace

Swimming Pool

West Rd.

Mill Lane

Little St. Mary's Lane

Trumpington St.

Downing Pl.

PARKERS PIECE

Mill Rd.

Gonville Pl.

Sidgwick Ave.

Silver St.

Tennis Court Rd.

Regent St.

Gresham Rd.

SHEEPS GREEN

THE FEN

BOTANIC GARDENS

Lensfield Rd.

Hills Rd.

Harvey Rd.

To Cambridge Railway Station

Newnham Rd.

The Fen

Causeway

To London ↓

To Colchester →

Christ's College **10**
Clare College **14**
Corpus Christi College **19**
Downing College **23**
Emmanuel College **12**
The Fitzwilliam Museum **22**
Folk Museum **2**
Gonville & Caius College **9**
Great St. Mary's **11**
Jesus College **5**
King's College **13**

Magdalene College **3**
Newnham College **18**
Pembroke College **20**
Peterhouse College **21**
Punts **4**
Queens' College **16**
St. Catharine's College **15**
St. John's College **7**
Selwyn College **17**
Sidney Sussex College **6**
Trinity College **8**
Westminster College **1**

0 100 mi

0 100 km

SCOTLAND

North Sea

Irish Sea

ENGLAND

Cambridge

WALES

London

English Channel

Moments Punting on the Cam

Punting on the River Cam in a wood-built, flat-bottomed boat (which looks somewhat like a Venetian gondola) is a traditional pursuit of students and visitors to Cambridge. Downstream, you pass along the ivy-covered "Backs" of the colleges, their lush gardens sweeping down to the Cam.

People sprawl along the banks of the Cam on a summer day to judge and tease you as you maneuver your punt with a pole about 4.5m (15 ft.) long. The river's floor is muddy, and many a student has lost his pole in the riverbed shaded by the willows. If your pole gets stuck, it's better to leave it sticking in the mud instead of risking a plunge into the river.

About 3km (2 miles) upriver lies Grantchester, immortalized by Rupert Brooke. Literary types flock to Grantchester, either by punting or by taking the path following the River Granta for less than an hour to Grantchester Meadows (the town lies about a mile from the meadows). When the town clock stopped for repairs in 1985, its hands were left frozen "for all time" at 10 minutes to 3, in honor of Brooke's famed sonnet "The Soldier."

After so much activity, you're bound to get hungry or thirsty, so head to **The Green Man,** 59 High St. (*©* **01223/841178**), a 400-year-old inn named in honor of Robin Hood, where a crackling fire warms you in cold weather and summer features a back beer garden, leading off toward the river, where your punt is waiting to take you back to Cambridge.

Scudamore's Boatyards, Granta Place (*©* **01223/359750**), by the Anchor Pub, has been in business since 1910. Punts and rowboats rent for £12 to £14 ($22–$26) per hour (maximum of six persons per punt). A £60 ($111) cash or credit-card deposit is required. They are open year-round, although March through October is the high season. You may prefer a chauffeur, with a minimum cost of £40 to £45 ($74–$83) for two people and £10 ($19) per person after that.

The following listing is only a sample of the colleges. If you're planning to be in Cambridge a while, you may also want to visit **Magdalene College,** on Magdalene Street, founded in 1542; **Pembroke College,** on Trumpington Street, founded in 1347; **Christ's College,** on St. Andrew's Street, founded in 1505; and **Corpus Christi College,** on Trumpington Street, which dates from 1352.

KING'S COLLEGE 𝒦𝒦   The adolescent Henry VI founded King's College on King's Parade (*©* **01223/331212;** www.kings.cam.ac.uk) in 1441. Most of its buildings are from the 19th century, but its crowning glory, the Perpendicular **King's College Chapel** 𝒦𝒦𝒦, dates from the Middle Ages and is one of England's architectural gems. Its most characteristic features are the magnificent fan vaulting, all of stone, and the great windows, most of which were fashioned by Flemish artisans between 1517 and 1531. The stained glass portrays biblical scenes in hues of red, blue, and amber. The chapel also houses Rubens's *The Adoration of the Magi.* The rood screen is from the early 16th century. ***Insider's***

tip: For a classic view of the chapel, you can admire the architectural complex from the rear, which would be ideal for a picnic along the river. E. M. Forster came here to contemplate scenes for his novel *Maurice.*

The college is open during term time, Monday through Friday from 9:30am to 3:30pm, Saturday from 9:30am to 3:15pm, and Sunday from 1:15 to 2:15pm and 5 to 5:30pm. During vacation time, college hours are Monday through Saturday 9:30am to 4:30pm and Sunday 10am to 5pm. The public is welcome to attend chapel services Monday through Saturday at 5:30pm and on Sunday at 10:30am and 3:30pm. Call ahead for open times for the chapel, which is closed at various times throughout the year for recording sessions, broadcasts, and concerts.

An exhibition in the seven northern side chapels shows why and how the chapel was built. Admission to the college and chapel, including the exhibition, is £4 ($7.40) for adults, £3 ($5.55) for students and children 12 to 17, and free for children under 12.

PETERHOUSE   This college, on Trumpington Street (© **01223/338200;** www.pet.cam.ac.uk), is the oldest Cambridge college, founded in 1284 by Hugh de Balsham, the bishop of Ely. Of the original buildings, only the hall remains, but this was restored in the 19th century and now boasts stained-glass windows by William Morris. Old Court, constructed in the 15th century, was renovated in 1754; the chapel dates from 1632. Ask permission to enter at the porter's lodge. *Insider's tip:* Almost sadly neglected, the Little Church of St. Mary's next door was the college chapel until 1632. Pay it the honor of a visit.

EMMANUEL COLLEGE   On St. Andrew's Street, Emmanuel (© **01223/ 334200;** www.emma.cam.ac.uk) was founded in 1584 by Sir Walter Mildmay, a chancellor of the exchequer to Elizabeth I. You can take a nice stroll around its attractive gardens and visit the chapel designed by Sir Christopher Wren and consecrated in 1677. Both the chapel and college are open daily from 9am to 6pm (closed during exam time).

QUEENS' COLLEGE   On Queens' Lane, Queens' College (© **01223/ 335511;** www.quns.cam.ac.uk) is the loveliest of Cambridge's colleges. Dating from 1448, it was founded by two English queens, one the wife of Henry VI, the other the wife of Edward IV. Its second cloister is the most interesting, flanked by the early-16th-century President's Lodge. Admission is £1.50 ($2.80), free for children under 12 accompanied by parents. A printed guide is issued. Hours vary depending on the time of year; call for details. Entry and exit is by the old porter's lodge in Queens' Lane only. The old hall and chapel are usually open to the public when not in use.

ST. JOHN'S COLLEGE   On St. John's Street, this college (© **01223/ 338600;** www.joh.cam.ac.uk) was founded in 1511 by Lady Margaret Beaufort, mother of Henry VII. A few years earlier she had founded Christ's College. Before her intervention, an old hospital had stood on the site of St. John's. The

---

(Fun Fact **The Harvard Link**

Harvard men and women, and those who love them, can look for a memorial window in Wren's chapel dedicated to John Harvard, an alumnus of Emmanuel who lent his name to that other university in Cambridge, Massachusetts.

impressive gateway bears the Tudor coat of arms, and Second Court is a fine example of late Tudor brickwork. Its best-known feature is the **Bridge of Sighs** crossing the Cam, built in the 19th century and patterned after the bridge in Venice. It connects the older part of the college with New Court, a Gothic Revival on the opposite bank with an outstanding view of the famous Backs. The Bridge of Sighs is closed to visitors but you can see it from the neighboring Kitchen Bridge. The college is open from March to October daily from 9:30am to 5:30pm. Admission is £2 ($3.70) for adults and £1.50 ($2.80) for children. Visitors are welcome to attend choral services in the chapel. *Insider's tip:* The Bridge of Sighs links the old college with an architectural "folly" of the 19th century, the elaborate New Court, which is a crenellated neo-Gothic fantasy. It's adorned with a "riot" of pinnacles and a main cupola. Students call it "the wedding cake."

TRINITY COLLEGE 🕉🕉 On Trinity Street, Trinity College (not to be confused with Trinity Hall) is the largest college in Cambridge. It was founded in 1546 by Henry VIII, who consolidated a number of smaller colleges that had existed on the site. The courtyard is the most spacious in Cambridge, built when Thomas Nevile was master. Sir Christopher Wren designed the library. For entry to the college, apply at the Great Gate, or call ✆ **01223/338400** or check out the website, www.trin.cam.ac.uk, for information. There is a charge of £2 ($3.70) from March to November. *Insider's tip:* What's fun to do here is to contemplate what has gone on before you arrived. Pause at Nevile's Court where Isaac Newton first calculated the speed of sound. Take in the delicate fountain of the Great Court where Lord Byron used to bathe naked with his pet bear. Why a bear? The university forbade students from having a dog but had no proviso for bears. Through the same courtyard years later walked Vladimir Nabokov dreaming of that sexy little pubescent he would later immortalize as *Lolita*.

CAMBRIDGE'S OTHER ATTRACTIONS

The Fitzwilliam Museum 🕉🕉 One of the finest museums in Britain is worth the trip here. Though it features temporary exhibitions, its permanent collections are noted for their antiquities from ancient Egypt, Greece, and Rome. The Applied Arts section features English and European pottery and glass, along with furniture, clocks, fans, and armor; Chinese jades; ceramics from Japan and Korea; plus rugs and samplers. The museum is also noted for its rare-coin collection. Many rare printed books and illuminated manuscripts, both literary and musical, are also on display.

But the best we've saved for last: The paintings include masterpieces by Simone Martini, Domenico Veneziano, Titian, Veronese, Rubens, Van Dyck, Canaletto, Hogarth, Gainsborough, Constable, Monet, Degas, Renoir, Cézanne, and Picasso. There is also a fine collection of other 20th-century art, miniatures, drawings, watercolors, and prints.

Insider's tip: Occasional musical events, including evening concerts, and some of the best lectures in England are staged here throughout the year. For more details, call ✆ **01223/332900.**

Trumpington St., near Peterhouse. ✆ **01223/332900.** www.fitzmuseum.cam.ac.uk. Free admission, donations appreciated. Tues–Sat 10am–5pm; Sun 2:15–5pm. Guided tours £3 ($5.55) per person, Sun 2:45pm. Closed Jan 1, Good Friday, May Day, and Dec 24–31.

Great St. Mary's Church Cambridge's central church was built on the site of an 11th-century church, but the present building dates largely from 1478. It was closely associated with events of the Reformation. The cloth that covered the hearse of King Henry VII is on display in the church. There is a fine view of Cambridge from the top of the tower.

King's Parade. (✆ **01223/741716.** Admission to tower £2 ($3.70) adults, £1 ($1.85) children. Tower summer Mon–Sat 9:30am–5pm, Sun 12:30–5pm; church daily 9am–6pm.

SHOPPING

Forage around the shops lining St. John's Street, Trinity Street, King's Parade, and Trumpington Street.

Check out **English Teddy Bear Company,** 1 King's Parade (✆ **01223/ 300908**), which sells teddy bears handmade in cottages all over the United Kingdom—a real British souvenir.

Primavera, 10 King's Parade (✆ **01223/357708**), is a showplace of British crafts, featuring pottery, glass, ceramics, jewelry, ironwork, and fabric crafts ranging from ties to wall hangings. Be sure to explore the basement exhibition of paintings and crafts items.

Another well-defined shopping district is comprised of Bridge Street, Sidney Street, St. Andrew's Street, and Regent Street. Particularly worth noting in this area is **James Pringle Weavers,** 11 Bridge St. (✆ **01223/361534**), a Scottish haven. You'll find a mind-boggling array of Scottish tartans, kilts, tweeds, fine knitwear, Scottish food, and of course, postcards.

A posh area of extremely chic, small, and exclusive shops runs between Market Square and Trinity Street and is called **Rose Crescent.** Here, you can buy leather goods, smart women's clothing, and fine hats as well as jewelry and a host of very expensive gift items.

Cambridge's pedestrian shopping district runs between Market Square and St. Andrew's Street and is known as the Lion Yard. **Culpepper the Herbalists,** 25 Lion Yard (✆ **01223/367370**), carries a complete herbal line that includes everything from extracts of plants to jellies, honeys, teas, cosmetics, bath products, pillows, and potpourri.

For book lovers, Cambridge's bookstores will truly delight you. **Heffers of Cambridge** is a huge book, stationery, and music store with six branches, al of which can be contacted through one central phone number (✆ **01223/ 568568**). The main store, at 20 Trinity St., carries academic books; an art-and-graphics shop has an address of 15–21 King St.; and the music store at 19 Trinity St. features classical and popular cassettes, CDs, and choral college music. Heffers also has a shop in the mall at Grafton Centre that carries new fiction and nonfiction titles.

G. David, 16 St. Edward's Passage (✆ **01223/354619**), hawks secondhand books, publishers' overruns at reduced prices, and antiquarian books. **Waterstone,** 22 Sydney St. (✆ **01223/351688**), deals exclusively in new books on a variety of subjects. **The Haunted Bookshop,** 9 St. Edward's Passage (✆ **01223/ 312913**), specializes in out-of-print children's books and first editions.

WHERE TO STAY
EXPENSIVE

Cambridge Garden House Moat House 🐦🐦   This modern hotel, the best in Cambridge, sits between the riverbank and a cobblestone street in the oldest part of town, a short stroll from the principal colleges. (Because of its riverside location, we prefer it over its nearest competitor, the University Arms, which is in the center of town.) It offers ample parking. You can rent punts at a boatyard next door. Visitors can relax on comfortable sofas and chairs in the bars and lounge. The soundproof bedrooms have glass-topped nightstands, adequate desk space, and private balconies. The expensive units (premium rooms) are very spacious with large sitting areas with face-to-face sofas. The river-view rooms are the most desirable. Bathrooms are large with shower-tub combinations.

Overlooking the river and gardens, the hotel's restaurant, called simply "The Restaurant," offers fixed-price and a la carte menus, including vegetarian meals. The Riverside Lounge provides light meals, accompanied in the evening by piano music. The hotel has a series of outdoor terraces where drinks and afternoon tea are served in nice weather.

Granta Place, Mill Lane, Cambridge, Cambridgeshire CB2 1RT. ✆ **01223/259988.** Fax 01223/316605. www. moathousehotels.com. 120 units. £172–£255 ($318–$472) double. AE, DC, MC, V. **Amenities:** Restaurant; bar; indoor pool; health club; Jacuzzi; sauna; business center; 24-hr. room service; laundry service; dry cleaning; nonsmoking rooms; rooms for those with limited mobility. *In room:* TV, dataport, minibar, coffeemaker, hair dryer, safe.

De Vere University Arms Hotel ✪
This 1834 hotel maintains much of its antique charm and many original architectural features despite modernization over the years. The only real rival in town to the Garden House, it lacks the river location and timeworn Edwardian elegance of the former. Near the city center and the university, it offers suitable bedrooms. Rooms range from small to midsize, each with bedside controls; the premium rooms also have slippers and robes. Many of the bedrooms have been recently refurbished; eight have four-poster beds. Rooms in front are smaller but more up-to-date and have double-glazed windows. Each room comes with a king-size or twin beds, and bathrooms have a shower-and-tub combo (except the single rooms, which have showers only). Three rooms are suitable for families.

Regent St., Cambridge, Cambridgeshire CB2 1AD. ✆ **01223/351241.** Fax 01223/273037. www.devere online.co.uk. 118 units. £200–£250 ($370–$463) double; from £350 ($648) suite. Rates include English breakfast. AE, DC, MC, V. Parking £8 ($15). Bus: 1. **Amenities:** Restaurant; bar; 24-hr. room service; babysitting; laundry service; dry cleaning; nonsmoking rooms; rooms for those with limited mobility. *In room:* TV, dataport, minibar, coffeemaker, hair dryer, iron/ironing board.

MODERATE

Arundel House Hotel   The Arundel enjoys a great location. Until recently, it consisted of six identical Victorian row houses, connected many years ago. In 1994, after two additional row houses were purchased from the university, the hotel was enlarged and upgraded into the current well-maintained place. Rooms overlooking the River Cam and Jesus Green cost more than those facing the other way; and with no elevator, rooms on lower floors go for more than those upstairs. Regardless of location, all rooms are clean and comfortable, fitted with king-size or twin beds, plus compact bathrooms with shower-tub combinations. With a bar and restaurant (see "Where to Dine," below) and a garden with outdoor tables for drinks in warm weather, the Arundel offers the best dining of any hotel in town.

53 Chesterton Rd., Cambridge, Cambridgeshire CB4 3AN. ✆ **01223/367701.** Fax 01223/367721. www. arundelhousehotels.co.uk. 102 units. £95–£125 ($176–$231) double; £120–£135 ($222–$250) family bedroom. Rates include continental breakfast. AE, DC, MC, V. Bus: 1 or 3. **Amenities:** Restaurant; bar; laundry; nonsmoking rooms. *In room:* A/C, TV, coffeemaker, hair dryer.

Cambridgeshire Moat House   This place, a more affordable member of the same chain that manages the Cambridge Garden House Moat House (reviewed above), offers the best sports facilities in the Cambridge area. Built around 1977, it has comfortable bedrooms with shower-tub combinations and nice views, a putting green, and an 18-hole championship golf course where greens fees range from £15 to £30 ($28–$56). There's a restaurant in the hotel, although the food is just standard stuff. Meals are also served daily in the bar.

Huntingdon Rd., Bar Hill, Cambridge, Cambridgeshire CB3 8EU. ℂ **01954/249988.** Fax 01954/780010. www.moathousehotels.com. 134 units. £130–£167 ($241–$309) double. Children 15 and under stay free in parent's room. AE, DC, MC, V. Take A14 9km (5½ miles) northwest of the town center. **Amenities:** Restaurant; bar; indoor heated pool; golf course; gym; sauna; laundry service; dry cleaning; nonsmoking rooms; rooms for those with limited mobility. *In room:* TV, dataport, coffeemaker, hair dryer, trouser press.

Gonville Hotel   A 5-minute walk from the center of town, this Best Western hotel and its grounds are opposite Parker's Piece. The Gonville has been much improved in recent years. It's not unlike a country house, with shade trees and a formal car entry, and it attracts businesspeople as well as tourists. The recently refurbished rooms are comfortable and furnished in a modern style. The compact bathrooms contain shower-tub combinations. The restaurant is air-conditioned.

Gonville Place, Cambridge, Cambridgeshire CB1 1LY. ℂ **800/528-1234** in the U.S. and Canada, or 01223/ 366611. Fax 01223/315470. www.gonvillehotel.co.uk. 78 units. £120 ($222) double. AE, DC, MC, V. **Amenities:** Restaurant; bar; limited room service; laundry service; dry cleaning; nonsmoking rooms. *In room:* TV, coffeemaker, hair dryer, iron/ironing board.

Holiday Inn Cambridge   Located a short walk from a small artificial lake, which the bedrooms overlook, this modern two-story hotel is vaguely influenced by the designs of nearby country houses. Like the Moat House, it emphasizes leisure facilities (though it doesn't offer golf), and of the two, it has better bedrooms. There's a grassy courtyard partially enclosed by the hotel's wings. Public rooms with peak ceilings are furnished with scattered clusters of sofas and chairs. The small yet comfortable bedrooms have large windows with pleasant views. The bathrooms are compact and contain shower-tub combinations. The restaurant has reproductions of paintings created by Sir Winston Churchill.

Lakeview, Bridge Rd., Lakeview Bridge, Impington, Cambridge, Cambridgeshire CB4 9PH. ℂ **800/225-5843** in the U.S. and Canada, or 08704/009015. Fax 01223/233426. www.holiday-inn.com. 165 units. £100–£156 ($185–$289) double. AE, DC, MC, V. Bus: 104, 105, or 106. Drive 3km (2 miles) north of Cambridge on B1049 (Histon Rd.) to A45 intersection. **Amenities:** Restaurant; bar; indoor heated pool; health club; Jacuzzi; sauna; 24-hr. room service; babysitting; laundry service; dry cleaning; nonsmoking rooms; rooms for those with limited mobility. *In room:* TV, dataport, minibar, hair dryer, safe.

INEXPENSIVE

Hamilton Hotel *Value*   One of the better and more reasonably priced of the small hotels of Cambridge, this redbrick establishment lies about a mile northeast of the city center, close to the River Cam. Well run and modestly accessorized, the hotel stands on a busy highway, but there's a parking area out back. The well-furnished bedrooms contain reasonably comfortable twin or double beds. Bathrooms are compact with shower stalls. The hotel has a small, traditionally styled licensed bar, offering standard pub food and snacks.

156 Chesterton Rd., Cambridge, Cambridgeshire CB4 1DA. ℂ **01223/365664.** Fax 01223/314866. www. hamiltonhotelcambridge.co.uk. 26 units, 21 with bathroom. £50 ($93) double without bathroom, £65 ($120) double with bathroom. Rates include English breakfast. AE, DC, MC, V. Bus: 3 or 3A. **Amenities:** Bar. *In room:* Dataport.

Regency Guest House   In a desirable location near the town center, overlooking the verdant city park known as Parker's Piece, this nonsmoking hotel dates from 1850. Set behind a stone facade, and similar in design to many of its neighbors, it offers small bedrooms with 1950s-style retro furniture. The rooms are painted about every 6 months and have a bright, fresh look. Those rooms with compact bathrooms contain adequate shelf space and a shower.

7 Regent Terrace, Cambridge, Cambridgeshire CB2 1AA. ℂ **01223/329626.** Fax 01223/301567. www.regency guesthouse.co.uk. 8 units, 3 with bathroom. £68 ($126) double without bathroom, £75 ($139) double with bathroom. Rates include continental breakfast. AE, MC, V. Bus: 5. *In room:* TV, coffeemaker.

WHERE TO DINE

Drop down into the cozy **Rainbow Vegetarian Bistro,** King's Parade, across from King's College (✆ **01223/321551**), for coffee, a slice of fresh-baked cake, or a meal from their selection of whole-food and vegetarian offerings. A main course lunch or dinner goes for only £7.25 ($13). Open Monday through Saturday from 11am to 10:30pm. The cafe lies at the end of a lily-lined path.

VERY EXPENSIVE

Midsummer House ✸✸ *Finds* MEDITERRANEAN   Located in an Edwardian-era cottage near the River Cam, the Midsummer House is a real find. We prefer to dine in the elegant conservatory, but you can also find a smartly laid table upstairs. The fixed-price menus are wisely limited, and quality control and high standards are much in evidence here. Daniel Clifford is the master chef, and he has created such specialties as filet of beef Rossini with braised winter vegetables and sauce Perigourdine; and roast squab pigeon, pomme Anna, tart tatin of onions, caramelized endives, and jus of morels.

Midsummer Common. ✆ **01223/369299.** Reservations required. 3-course fixed-price lunch £26 ($66); 3-course fixed-price dinner £45 ($83). AE, MC, V. Tues–Sat noon–2pm and 7–10pm.

MODERATE

Arundel House Restaurant ✸ FRENCH/BRITISH/VEGETARIAN   One of the best and most acclaimed restaurants in Cambridge is in a hotel overlooking the River Cam and Jesus Green, a short walk from the city center. Winner of many awards, it's noted not only for its excellence and use of fresh produce, but also for its good value. The decor is warmly inviting with Sanderson curtains, Louis XV–upholstered chairs, and spacious tables. The menu changes frequently, and you can dine both a la carte or from the set menu. Perhaps you'll begin with a homemade golden-pea-and-ham soup or a white-rum-and-passion-fruit cocktail. Fish choices include plaice or salmon; try the pork-and-pigeon casserole or the Japanese-style braised lamb.

53 Chesterton Rd. ✆ **01223/367701.** Reservations required. Main courses £10–£16 ($19–$30); fixed-price dinner £20 ($37); fixed-price Sun lunch £16 ($30). AE, DC, MC, V. Daily 12:30–2pm and 6:30–9:30pm. Bus: 3 or 5.

Finds The Gastronomic Center of East Anglia

The little town of Melbourn, on the A10 between Royston and Cambridge, 16km (10 miles) away, has just emerged as a gastronomic center in the minds of food lovers from London. Just ask Prince Charles, a longtime fan. The revolution was started by flamboyant Steven Saunders, who launched **The Pink Geranium,** 25 Station Rd. (✆ **01763/260215**), and is one of the hot new chefs credited with ushering in a renaissance in British cuisine. Before Saunders sold it in 2000, it was hailed as one of the top restaurants in the country. It still is, even with the departure of its famed chef. The chef, Gordon Campbell, oversees the luxury-strewn menu. Saunders, known by all BBC watchers for his culinary TV shows, is still around, owning and running nearby **Sheene Mill Hotel & Brasserie,** Station Road (✆ **01763/261393**), where modern England meets the Pacific Rim in an historic water mill. A champion of organic food, Saunders experiments with different styles and different cuisines, so you never know what's going to be on his menu, except he admits his favorite food is shellfish.

Browns ☆ *Value* ENGLISH/CONTINENTAL   With a neoclassical colonnade in front, Browns has all the grandeur of the Edwardian era, but inside, it's the most lighthearted restaurant in the city, with wicker chairs, high ceilings, pre–World War I woodwork, and a long bar covered with bottles of wine. The extensive bill of continually varied fare includes pasta, scores of fresh salads, several selections of meat and fish (from charcoal-grilled leg of lamb with rosemary to fresh fish in season), hot sandwiches, and the chef's daily specials posted on a blackboard. If you drop by in the afternoon, you can also order thick milkshakes or natural fruit juices. In fair weather, there's outdoor seating.

23 Trumpington St. (5 min. from King's College and opposite the Fitzwilliam Museum). ✆ **01223/461655.** Main courses £7–£14 ($13–$26). AE, MC, V. Mon–Thurs 11am–11pm; Fri–Sat 11am–11:30pm; Sun noon–10:30pm. Bus: 2.

Twenty Two ☆ ENGLISH/CONTINENTAL   One of the best in Cambridge, this restaurant is located in a quiet district near Jesus Green, and is a secret jealously guarded by the locals. The homelike but elegant Victorian dining room offers an ever-changing fixed-price menu based on fresh market produce. Owners David Carter and Louise Crompton use time-tested recipes along with their own inspirations, offering creations such as white onion soup with toasted goat's cheese or sautéed breast of chicken on braised celery with thyme jus.

22 Chesterton Rd. ✆ **01223/351880.** Reservations required. Fixed-price menu £25 ($46). AE, MC, V. Tues–Sat 7–9:30pm.

INEXPENSIVE

Cambridge Arms ENGLISH   This no-nonsense pub in the center of town bustles with atmosphere and dispenses endless platters of food to customers over the bar's countertop. Favorites include the chef's daily specials, grilled steaks, vegetarian meals, and an array of both hot and cold dishes.

The pub was recently refurbished and now is a music-oriented theme pub. Guitars and various music paraphernalia adorn the walls.

4 King St. ✆ **01223/505015.** Reservations not accepted. Bar snacks £1.50–£3 ($2.80–$5.55), main courses £4–£10 ($7.40–$19). MC, V. Mon–Sat noon–3pm, 6–9pm; Sun noon–4pm. Pub Mon–Sat 11am–11pm, Sun noon–10:30pm.

Charlie Chan CHINESE   Most people agree that this is the finest Chinese restaurant in Cambridge, and so do we. We've always found Charlie Chan reliable and capable, which is remarkable given its huge menu. Downstairs is a long corridor-like restaurant, with pristine decor. The ambience is more lush in the Blue Lagoon upstairs. Most of the dishes here are inspired by the traditional cuisine of Beijing. The specialties we've most enjoyed include an aromatic and crispy duck, lemon chicken, and prawn with garlic and ginger.

14 Regent St. ✆ **01223/361763.** Reservations recommended. Main courses £6–£35 ($11–$65). AE, MC, V. Daily noon–5pm and 6–11pm.

The Green Man ENGLISH   Named in honor of Robin Hood, this 400-year-old inn is the most popular pub for outings from Cambridge. It's located on A604, 3km (2 miles) south of Cambridge in the hamlet of Grantchester, made famous by poet Rupert Brooke (see "Punting on the Cam," earlier in this chapter). Even if you haven't heard of Brooke, you may enjoy a late afternoon wandering through the old church and then heading, as everybody does, to the Green Man. In winter, a crackling fire welcomes the weary, but in summer it's more tempting to retreat to the beer garden, from which you can stroll to the edge of the River Cam. Place your order at the counter; a server will bring your food to your table. The fare ranges from fish cakes in a Thai curry sauce to chicken Kiev and even traditional English pies and bangers and mash, as well as various vegetarian choices.

59 High St., Grantchester. © 01223/841178. Reservations recommended. Main courses £8–£15 ($15–$28). MC, V. Mon–Fri 11am–2:30pm and 5:30–11pm; Sat 11am–11pm; Sun noon–10:30pm. Pub Mon–Sat noon–3pm and 6–9pm, Sun noon–10:30pm. Bus: 118 from Cambridge.

CAMBRIDGE AFTER DARK

You can take in a production where Emma Thompson and other well-known thespians got their start at **The Amateur Dramatic Club,** Park Street near Jesus Lane (© **01223/359547;** box office 01223/503333; www.cuadc.org). It presents two student productions nightly, Tuesday through Saturday, with the main show tending toward classic and modern drama or opera, and the late show being of a comic or experimental nature. The theater is open nearly year-round, closing in September, and tickets run from £3.50 to £8 ($6.50–$15).

The most popular Cantabridgian activity is the **pub crawl.** With too many pubs in the city to list, you may as well start at Cambridge's oldest pub, the **Pickerel,** on Bridge Street (© 01223/355068), dating from 1432. English pubs don't get more traditional than this. If the ceiling beams or floorboards groan occasionally—well, they've certainly earned the right over the years. Real ales on tap include Bulmer's Traditional Cider, Old Speckled Hen, or Theakston's 6X, Old Peculiar, and Best Bitter. **The Maypole,** Portugal Place at Park Street (© **01223/352999**), is the local hangout for actors from the nearby ADC Theatre. Known for cocktails and not ales, you can still get a Tetley's 6X or Castle Eden.

The Eagle, Benet Street off King's Parade (© **01223/505020**), will be forever famous as the place where Nobel Laureates Watson and Crick first announced their discovery of the DNA double helix. Real ales include Icebreaker and local brewery Greene King's Abbott, so make your order and raise a pint to the wonders of modern science.

To meet up with current Cambridge students, join the locals at the **Anchor,** Silver Street (© **01223/353554**), or **Tap and Spiel (The Mill),** 14 Mill Lane, off Silver Street Bridge (© **01223/357026**), for a pint of Greene King's IPA or Abbott. The crowd at the Anchor spills out onto the bridge in fair weather, whereas the Tap and Spiel's clientele lay claim to the entire riverside park.

For musical entertainment, you can find out who's playing by checking out flyers posted around town, or by reading the *Varsity.* **The Corn Exchange,** Wheeler Street and Corn Exchange (© **01223/357851**), hosts everything from classical concerts to bigger-name rock shows. **The Graduate,** 16 Chesterton Rd. (© **01223/301416**), a pub located in a former movie theater, is open from noon to 11pm with no cover charge.

Entertainment in some form can be found nightly at **The Junction,** Clifton Road, near the train station (© **01223/511511**), where an eclectic mix of acts take to the stage weeknights to perform all genres of music, comedy, and theater, and DJs take over on the weekend. Cover charges vary from £7 to £13 ($13–$24), depending on the event.

Ballare, Lion Yard (© **01223/364222**), a second-story club, has a huge dance floor and plays everything from house to the latest pop hits, Monday through Saturday from 9pm until 2am. Sometimes they even DJ the old-fashioned way, by taking requests. The cover charge ranges from £3 to £8 ($5.55–$15), depending on what night you're here.

2 Ely

113km (70 miles) NE of London; 26km (16 miles) N of Cambridge

Ely Cathedral is the top attraction in the fen country, outside of Cambridge. After you've seen the cathedral, you can safely be on your way; Ely is simply a sleepy market town that can't compete with the life and bustle found at Cambridge.

ESSENTIALS

GETTING THERE   Ely is a major railway junction served by express trains to Cambridge. Service is frequent from London's Liverpool Street Station. For schedules and information, call ✆ **0845/748-4950** or visit www.railtrack.co.uk.

Campus buses run frequently between Cambridge and Ely. Call ✆ **01223/ 423554** for schedules and information.

If you're driving from Cambridge, take the A10 north.

VISITOR INFORMATION   The **Tourist Information Centre** is at Oliver Cromwell's House, 29 St. Mary's St. (✆ **01353/662062;** www.ely.org.uk/tic. htm); open April through October daily from 10am to 5pm; November through March, Monday through Saturday from 10am to 5pm and Sunday 11:15am to 4pm.

SEEING THE SIGHTS

Ely Cathedral 𝕽𝕽   The near-legendary founder of this cathedral was Ethel-dreda, the wife of a Northumbrian king who established a monastery on the spot in 673. The present structure dates from 1081. Visible for miles around, the landmark octagonal lantern is the crowning glory of the cathedral. Erected in 1322 following the collapse of the old tower, it represents a remarkable engineering achievement. Four hundred tons of lead and wood hang in space, held there by timbers reaching to the eight pillars.

You enter the cathedral through the Galilee West Door, a good example of the Early English style of architecture. The lantern tower and the Octagon are the most notable features inside, but visit the Lady Chapel, too. Although its decor has deteriorated over the centuries, it's still a handsome example of the Perpendicular style, having been completed in the mid–14th century. The entry fee goes to help preserve the cathedral. Monday through Saturday, guided tours gather at 11:15am and 2:15pm; in the summer, tours occur throughout the day.

At a Brass Rubbing Centre, a large selection of replica brass is available for you to rub. These can produce remarkable results for wall hangings or special gifts. It's open year-round in the North Aisle, outside the Cathedral Shop.

✆ 01353/667735. www.cathedral.ely.anglican.org. Admission £4.80 ($8.90) adults, £4.20 ($7.75) students and seniors; free for children under 16. Apr–Oct daily 7am–7pm; Nov–Mar Mon–Sat 7:30am–6pm, Sun 7:30am–5pm.

Ely Museum   A gallery presents a chronological history of Ely and the Isle from the Ice Age to the present day. Displays include archaeology, social history, rural life, local industry, and military history, as well as a tableau of the debtor's cell and condemned cell, which are also on view.

The Old Gaol, Market St. ✆ 01353/666655. Admission £3 ($5.55) adults; £2 ($3.70) children, students, and seniors; free for children 6 and under. Daily 10:30am–4:30pm. Closed Dec 20–Jan 2.

Grimes Graves   This is the largest and best-preserved group of Neolithic flint mines in Britain; they produced the cutting edges of spears, arrows, and knives for prehistoric tribes throughout the region. Because of its isolated location within sparsely populated, fir-wooded countryside, it's easy to imagine yourself transported back through the millennia.

A guardian will meet you near the well-signposted parking lot. After determining that you are not physically impaired, he or she will open one or several of the mineshafts, each of which requires a descent down an almost-vertical 9m (30-ft.) ladder (a visit here is not recommended for very young children, elderly travelers, or those with disabilities). Because the tunnel and shaft have been restored and reinforced, it's now possible to see where work took place during Neolithic times. Although it's not essential, many archaeologists, professional and amateur, bring their own flashlights with them. The mines, incidentally, are situated close to the military bases that housed thousands of American air-force personnel during World War II.

On B1107, 4km (2¾ miles) northeast of Brandon, Norfolkshire. ℂ 01842/810656. Admission £1.75 ($3.25) adults, 90p ($1.65) students, seniors, and children 5–15, free for children 4 and under. Apr–Oct daily 10am–1pm and 2–6pm; Nov–Mar Wed–Sun 10am–1pm and 2–4pm. Take A134 for 11km (7 miles) northwest of Thetford, then transfer to B1107.

Oliver Cromwell's House This recently restored house was owned by the Puritan Oliver Cromwell, a name hardly beloved by the royals, even today. He rose to fame as a military and political leader during the English civil wars of 1642 to 1649, which led to the execution of Charles I and the replacement of the monarchy by the Commonwealth. In 1653, Cromwell was declared lord protector; and the local farmer was the most powerful man in the land until his death in 1658. Exhibitions, displays, and period rooms offer insight into Cromwell's character and 17th-century domestic life. A tourist center is also located here.

29 St. Mary's St. (next to St. Mary's Church). ℂ 01353/662062. Admission £3.50 ($6.50) adults; £3 ($5.55) children, students, and seniors; £8.50 ($16) family ticket. Apr–Oct daily 10am–5pm; off season Mon–Sat 10am–5pm, Sun 11:15am–4pm.

WHERE TO STAY

Lamb Hotel Right in the center of town, this hotel is a former 14th-century coaching inn whose ground-floor areas, including the lounge and bars, were completely refurbished in the '90s. In the shadow of the cathedral, this hotel offers renovated bedrooms furnished traditionally but with modern comfort. Each contains a good English bed, usually king-size or twin. Bathrooms offer adequate shelf space and tub-and-shower combinations. In the 1400s, this place was known as the "Holy Lambe," a stopping-off spot for wayfarers, often pilgrims, passing through East Anglia. Rather standard English meals are served.

2 Lynn Rd., Ely, Cambridgeshire CB7 4EJ. ℂ 01353/663574. Fax 01353/662023. www.oldenglish.co.uk. 32 units. £95 ($176) double. Rates include English breakfast. AE, DC, MC, V. Bus: 109. **Amenities:** Restaurant; bar; limited room service; laundry service; dry cleaning. *In room:* TV, coffeemaker, hair dryer, trouser press.

WHERE TO DINE

Around the corner from St. Mary's Church is **Steeplegate,** 16–18 High St. (ℂ 01353/664731), a tearoom and craft shop with wooden tables and ancient windows. There are tea selections plus light lunch items, scones, and creamy gâteaux. After tea, venture downstairs to the craft shop and have a look at the variety of handmade pottery, glass, and baskets.

An unusual choice is **The Almonry Restaurant & Tea Rooms in The College,** Ely Cathedral, High St. (ℂ 01353/666360). Housed in the medieval college buildings on the north side of the Cathedral, this is a comfortable tearoom with table service in a beautiful 12th-century undercroft licensed to sell drinks.

You can take your tea out to a garden seat in good weather. It is open for late morning coffee, lunches, and afternoon teas. Meals start at £6.25 ($12).

The Old Fire Engine House *(Finds* ENGLISH   It's worth a special trip to this converted fire station in a walled garden, within a building complex that includes an art gallery. Soups are served in huge bowls, accompanied by coarse-grained crusty bread. Main dishes include lamb noisettes in pastry with tomato and basil, jugged hare, casseroled pheasant, and rabbit with mustard and parsley. In summer, you can dine outside in the garden and even order a cream tea.

25 St. Mary's St. (opposite St. Mary's Church). **01353/662582.** Reservations required. Main courses £14–£17 ($26–$31). MC, V. Daily 12:30–2pm; Mon–Sat 7:30–9pm (last entry). Bus: 109.

3 Newmarket
100km (62 miles) NE of London; 21km (13 miles) NE of Cambridge

This old Suffolk town has been famous as a horseracing center since the time of James I. Visitors can see Nell Gwynne's House, but mainly they come to visit Britain's first and only equestrian museum.

GETTING THERE
Trains depart from London's Liverpool Street Station every 45 to 60 minutes for Cambridge (see earlier in this chapter). In Cambridge, passengers change trains and head in the direction of Mildenhall. Three stops later, they arrive at Newmarket.

About eight National Express buses leave London's Victoria Coach Station for Norwich every day, stopping at Stratford, Stansted, and (finally) Newmarket along the way. For schedules and information, call **0870/580-8080** or visit www.nationalexpress.com.

If you're driving from Cambridge, head east on the A133.

OFF TO THE RACES
Britain's most prestigious racecourse lies at **Newmarket,** a small country town whose main tourist draw is the series of warm-weather horse races with origins dating from the days of James I and Charles II. Charles II was so enthusiastic about racing that he frequently ordered most of his Restoration-era court up from London to attend the races.

The headquarters of British racing, and the venue where precedents and policies are hammered out before being applied to the more formal venue of Ascot, Newmarket is the only racecourse in Britain with two separate racetracks.

The more bucolic of these is the July Race Course, where races are held during the heat and glare of June, July, and August. It's the site of the prestigious July Cup. The Rowley Mile, smaller than the other course, is known for its rows of beech trees that shade the saddling boxes and promenade grounds, as well as the thatched roofs that add an old-English charm to ornamental entranceways and some of the showcase buildings used by investors, owners, and fans. The grandstands have conventional roofs shielding fans from the sun and the rain.

The more industrial-looking racetrack is the Rowley Mile, used during the racing season's cooler months (mid-Apr to late May and early Sept to Nov 2). Dress codes are less strictly observed here and at the July Race Course, where men wear jackets and ties, but the venue at Rowley Mile attracts a bigger and brasher crowd. At the Rowley Mile, prestigious races such as the Guineas Races, the Cesarewitch Handicap, and the Champion Stakes are run.

The two courses lie within 1km (½ mile) of each other and share the same administration. For information, contact The **Clerk of the Course,** Westfield House, The Links, Newmarket, Suffolk CB8 0TG (© **01638/663482;** www. newmarketracecourses.co.uk).

National Horseracing Museum   Visitors can see the history of horse racing over 300 years in this museum housed in the old subscription rooms, early-19th-century betting rooms. There are fine paintings of famous horses, paintings on loan from Queen Elizabeth II, and copies of old parliamentary acts governing races. A 53-minute audiovisual presentation shows races and racehorses.

To make history come alive for visitors, they also offer equine tours of this historic town. Guides take you to watch morning gallops on the heath where you'll see bronzes of horses from the past.

99 High St. © **01638/667333.** www.nhrm.co.uk. Admission £4.50 ($8.35) adults, £2.50 ($4.65) children, £3.50 ($6.50) seniors. Tues–Sun 11am–5pm. Closed Nov–Mar.

The National Stud   Next to Newmarket's July Race Course, 3km (2 miles) southwest of the town, this place is home to some of the world's finest horses, and a renowned breeding stud operation. A tour lasting about 75 minutes lets you see many mares and foals, plus top-class stallions. Reservations for tours must be made at the National Stud office or by phoning the number given below.

July Race Course. © **01638/666789.** www.nationalstud.co.uk. Admission £5 ($9.25) adults, £4 ($7.40) seniors, £3.50 ($6.50) students and children. Mar–Sept and Oct race day only. Guided tours Mon–Sat 11:15am and 2:30pm; Sun 2:30pm. Closed Nov–Feb.

WHERE TO STAY & DINE

Heath Court Hotel   A member of the Queen's Moat House hotel chain, this brick-fronted hotel is near The Gallops, the exercise area for the stables at the Newmarket Heath racetrack, about a 5-minute walk from the center of town. Built in the mid-1970s, it's a favorite of the English horseracing world and is fully booked during the racing season. Its public rooms are decorated in an appropriate country-elegant style, including oil portraits of horses and souvenirs of the racing life in its bar and restaurant. The bedrooms are well appointed, conservatively modern, and comfortable. Most of the units are spacious and in the more expensive units, called executive rooms, there are also bathrobes and a small refrigerator. Most bathrooms are equipped with both tub and shower.

Moulton Rd., Newmarket, Suffolk CB8 8DY. © **01638/667171.** Fax 01638/666533. www.heathcourt-hotel. co.uk. 41 units. Mon–Thurs £112–£137 ($207–$253) double; Fri–Sun £79–£102 ($146–$189) double. Family room £120–£137 ($222–$253), from £182 ($337) suite. Extra bed £35 ($65). Rates include English breakfast. AE, DC, MC, V. **Amenities:** Restaurant; bar; limited room service; laundry service. *In room:* A/C, TV, coffeemaker, hair dryer, safe, trouser press.

Swynford Paddocks   This well-appointed country house, one of the finest in the area, is situated on a 24-hectare (60-acre) stud farm surrounded by beautiful grounds. Once a retreat of Lord Byron, he wrote many of his works at the foot of a now-felled beech. The house then became the home of Lord and Lady Halifax until 1976, when it was converted into a luxury hotel. Many guests use it as a base for exploring both Newmarket and Cambridge. Each spacious bedroom, opening onto scenic views, is decorated with a special character; some have four-poster beds and are quite romantic. The ample bathrooms are handsomely equipped with adequate shelf space, toiletries, and most often a tub and shower. For extraspecial occasions, try for a suite of rooms or the two sumptuous four-poster rooms. The rates are expensive, but the quality is excellent.

Six Mile Bottom, Cambridgeshire CB8 0UE. © **01638/570234.** Fax 01638/570283. www.swynfordpaddocks. com. 15 units. £135–£175 ($250–$324) double. Rates include English breakfast. AE, DC, MC, V. Take A1304 9.5km (6 miles) southwest of Newmarket. **Amenities:** 2 restaurants; bar; limited room service; laundry service; dry cleaning; nonsmoking rooms; rooms for those with limited mobility. *In room:* TV, dataport, coffeemaker, hair dryer, trouser press.

4 Bury St. Edmunds ✶

127km (79 miles) NE of London; 43km (27 miles) E of Cambridge; 19km (12 miles) N of Lavenham

Bury St. Edmunds is "a handsome little town, of thriving and cleanly appearance." That's how Charles Dickens described it in *Pickwick Papers,* and it remains true. This historical town, founded around the powerful Benedictine Abbey in 1020, derives its name from St. Edmund, King of the East Angles in the mid–9th century. In the Abbey Church, the barons of England united and forced King John to sign the Magna Carta in 1214. Though sometimes hard to tell, Bury is filled with many original medieval buildings. (Many buildings were given face-lifts in the 17th and 18th c.; it's only when you step inside that their medieval roots become clear.) During the 18th century, this market town was quite prosperous and had a thriving cloth-making industry. The large number of fine Georgian buildings bear testament to the wealth of the day.

Upon the Vikings' arrival to the area, they dubbed it "The Summer Country." And, indeed, the summer, when the town bursts into bloom, is the best time to visit. Most of the historic sites and gardens open for the season on Easter.

ESSENTIALS

GETTING THERE   Trains leave regularly from either Liverpool Street Station or King's Cross Station in London; however, none are direct. Leaving from Liverpool Street, you will change at Ipswich. And from King's Cross Station, you'll have to switch trains at Cambridge. The trip takes approximately 1½ hours. For schedules and information, call © **0845/748-4950** or visit www.railtrack.co.uk.

National Express runs several direct buses every day from London's Victoria Coach Station, which reach Bury in 2 hours. For schedules and information, call © **0870/580-8080** or visit www.nationalexpress.com.

By car, take the M11 north out of London. As you near Cambridge, get on the A45 and continue on to Bury. The drive takes about 1½ hours.

It's also possible to get here by train or bus from Cambridge. Regular trains leave from the Cambridge Rail Station and arrive about 45 minutes later in Bury St. Edmunds. **Cambus Bus Company** runs five buses a day to Bury from the Drummer Street Bus Station in Cambridge; it's a 1-hour ride. Call © **01223/ 423578** for information and schedules. By car from Cambridge, simply take the A45 directly. It's a 45-minute drive.

VISITOR INFORMATION   The **Bury St. Edmunds Tourist Information Centre,** 6 Angel Hill (© **01284/764667**), is open November to Easter, Monday through Friday from 10am to 4pm and Saturday from 10am to 1pm; and from Easter to October, Monday through Saturday 9:30am to 5:30pm, Sunday from 10am to 4pm.

SPECIAL EVENTS   The **Bury St. Edmunds Festival** (© **01284/757099**) is held annually in May. The 17-day festival includes performances from leading ensembles and soloists ranging from classical to contemporary. Exhibitions, talks, walks, films, plays, and a fireworks display are integral parts of this internationally renowned festival.

EXPLORING THE TOWN

For a bit of easy and always interesting sightseeing, take one of the hour-long **guided walks** around Bury St. Edmunds. Choices include a Blue Badge Guided Tour and theme tours with Bury's historical monk, Brother Jocelin, or gravedigger William Hunter. Tours leave from the Tourist Information Centre (see above) where tickets can also be purchased.

The normally quiet town center is a hub of hustle and bustle on Wednesday and Saturday mornings when the market arrives. Weather permitting, hours are approximately from 9am to 4pm. You'll find a pleasing mix of family-run businesses and High Street names for shopping in and around town and its pedestrian zones.

Bury St. Edmunds Art Gallery, Market Cross, Cornhill (℃ **01284/ 762081**), hosts eight fine art and craft exhibitions each year and serves as a venue for local craftspeople and artists. A craft shop located in the gallery sells ceramics, prints, books, glassware, and jewelry. **The Parsley Pot,** 17 Abbeygate St. (℃ **01284/760289**), sells an assortment of gift items, including china and porcelain.

Several parks are located just outside of town. Eleven kilometers (7 miles) north of Bury is the 51-hectare (125-acre) **West Stow Country Park** with heathland, woodland, and a large lake bordered by the River Lark. This diverse area is perfect for the proverbial "walk in the park" with a rustic twist. **The West Stow Anglo-Saxon Village** (℃ **01284/728718**) is part of West Stow Country Park. This reconstructed village is built on the excavated site of an ancient Anglo-Saxon village, and period re-enactments take place throughout the year. The park is open daily from 9am to 5pm. Admission is free. The village is open year-round from 10am to 5pm. Admission is £5 ($9.25) for adults and £4 ($7.40) for children. Family tickets are also available for £15 ($28).

Nowton Park (℃ **01284/763666**) is 2.5km (1½ miles) outside of Bury on 200 acres (81h) of Suffolk countryside. Landscaped a century ago, the park is typically Victorian and has many country estate features. In the springtime, walk the avenue of lime trees with its masses of bright yellow daffodils. Marked walking paths snake through the park. Depending on the path, walks take between 20 and 75 minutes. It's open daily from 8:30am to dusk; free admission.

The Abbey 👷👷   The Visitor Centre is a good starting point for a visit to the entire Abbey precinct. (The Abbey itself is in ruins today and sits in the middle of the Abbey Gardens.) The Visitor Centre is housed in the west front of the Abbey of St. Edmunds's remains and uses a clever series of displays to give the visitor an idea of what life was like in this powerful abbey from its beginnings in 1020 to its dissolution in 1539.

Moving on to the formal Abbey Gardens with its flowerbeds and well-kept lawns, you'll see the ruins of the abbey. When the long shadows cast themselves across the weathered ruins, the landscape becomes surreal and looks much like a Dalí masterpiece. In reality, the abandoned abbey was used as a quarry for the townspeople down through the ages, and that is the reason for the extremely worn condition and melted character of the ruins. A rather interesting tour of the Abbey Gardens is led by medieval monk Brother Jocelin; book it through the town's Tourist Information Centre at ℃ **01284/764667.**

Samson's Tower. ℃ **01284/757490** for Visitor Centre. Free admission. Visitor Centre Easter–Oct daily 10am–5pm. Abbey Gardens and ruins year-round Mon–Sat 7:30am to ½ hr. before dusk, Sun 9am to ½ hr. before dusk.

St. Edmundsbury Cathedral   This 16th-century church has a magnificent font, beautiful stained-glass windows, and a display of 1,000 embroidered kneelers.

Angel Hill. ✆ **01284/754933**. Free admission. Daily 8:30am–dusk.

Ickworth House   This National Trust property was built in 1795 and contains an impressive rotunda, staterooms, and art collections of silver and paintings. An Italian garden surrounds the house, and all is set in a peaceful, landscaped park.

5km (3 miles) south of Bury at Horringer. ✆ **01284/735270**. Admission £6.10 ($11) adults, £2.75 ($5.10) children. Easter–Oct Fri–Wed 1–5pm.

Manor House Museum   Housed in a restored Georgian mansion, this museum uses touch-screen computers to help interpret its displays of fine and decorative art.

Honey Hill. ✆ **01284/757076**. Admission £2.50 ($4.65) adults, £2 ($3.70) seniors and children, £8 ($15) family ticket. Wed–Mon 11am–4pm.

Moyse's Hall Museum   Located in one of England's last surviving Norman stone houses, this museum has nationally important archaeological collections and local artifacts.

Cornhill. ✆ **01284/757488**. Admission £2.50 ($4.65) adults, £2 ($3.70) seniors and children. Mon–Sat 10:30am–4:30pm; Sun 11am–4pm.

St. Mary's Church   St. Mary's was built on the site of a Norman church in 1427. Note its impressive roof and nave. It is also where Henry VIII's sister, Mary "the Tudor Rose," is buried.

Angel Hill. ✆ **01284/706668**. Call the church to arrange a tour. Free admission.

WHERE TO STAY

The Angel Hotel ✿   Originally a 1452 coaching inn, the hotel received an exterior face-lift during the Georgian era, and its front facade is now completely covered with lush ivy. The location is ideal for sightseeing and shopping, as both are only a short walk from the hotel. Look out the window of any of the front-facing rooms, and you'll see the romantic Abbey Gardens. Each of the rooms is individually decorated with freestanding furnishings and some have four-poster beds. Room 36 is one of the more popular rooms with its four-poster bed, bold peach-colored walls (a shade you can almost taste), and armchairs. Ten of the bedrooms have been recently refurbished. Bathrooms are compact but well maintained, with tubs and showers.

Angel Hill, Bury St. Edmunds, Suffolk IP33 1LT. ✆ **01284/714000**. Fax 01284/714001. www.angel-halesworth.co.uk. 66 units. £119–£165 ($220–$305) double; £230 ($426) suite. AE, DC, MC, V. **Amenities:** 2 restaurants; bar; limited room service; babysitting; laundry service; dry cleaning; access for those with disabilities. *In room:* A/C (23 rooms only), TV, coffeemaker, hair dryer, iron, trouser press.

Butterfly Hotel   This standard, rather ordinary hotel, built relatively recently, is located 10 minutes from Bury on the A14 motorway. The grassy grounds are landscaped, and there is a sunny patio for dining alfresco. All the rooms are decorated in the same bland style with landscape pictures and an armchair or two, along with an accompanying desk. Because of the proximity to the motorway, the windows are double-paned to reduce traffic noise and to help guests get a better night's rest. The compact bathrooms are clean, equipped mainly with shower-tub combinations.

Symonds Rd., Bury St. Edmunds, Suffolk IP32 7DZ. ✆ **01284/760884**. Fax 01284/755476. www.butterflyhotels.co.uk. 66 units. Sun–Thurs £80 ($148) double; Fri–Sat £55 ($102) double, £95 ($176) suite. AE, DC,

MC, V. **Amenities:** Restaurant; bar; limited room service; laundry service; dry cleaning; nonsmoking rooms. *In room:* TV, dataport, coffeemaker, hair dryer, safe, trouser press.

Ravenwood Hall *★★ (Finds)*   Located 5km (3 miles) outside of town, this Tudor hall dates from the 1500s, and is set in a peaceful 2.8-hectare (7-acre) park with well-manicured lawns, gardens, and forest. This rustic country place has a magnificent fireplace that is the focal point of the restaurant, where diners enjoy an a la carte menu. The individually decorated rooms are full of atmosphere. If you're a fancier of fine beds, check out the Oak Room with its four-poster bed and the bridal suite with its brass bed. Some rooms are in the main house, others in a converted stable mews; all are equally comfortable. Bathrooms are exceedingly fine here, with adequate shelf space and a tub-and-shower combination.

Rougham, Bury St. Edmunds, Suffolk IP30 9JA. © **01359/270345.** Fax 01359/270788. www.ravenwoodhall. co.uk. 14 units. £105–£149 ($194–$276) double. Rates include breakfast. AE, DC, MC, V. **Amenities:** Restaurant; bar; outdoor heated pool; outdoor tennis court; limited room service; babysitting; laundry service. *In room:* TV, coffeemaker, hair dryer, safe.

WHERE TO DINE

Maison Blue SEAFOOD   This restaurant is the town's best. The open and airy dining room has a nautical theme, in keeping with the fresh seafood that's served. The same menu is available for both lunch and dinner and changes regularly with the season. Favorites include filet of sea bass in a fennel sauce; boneless wing of skate with bacon, onion, and mushrooms; and lobster in a cream and brandy sauce. All main courses are presented with new potatoes.

31 Churchgate St. © **01284/760623.** Reservations recommended for dinner. Main courses £10–£18 ($19–$33); fixed-price lunch £14.95 ($28); 3-course fixed-price dinner £22 ($41). AE, MC, V. Tues–Sat noon–2:30pm and 7–9:30pm (open until 10pm Fri–Sat).

BURY ST. EDMUNDS AFTER DARK

Throughout the centuries, Bury has enjoyed a well-deserved reputation as a small center of arts and entertainment. The **Theatre Royal,** Westgate Street, is the oldest purpose-built theater in England. Its Georgian building has been lovingly and richly restored to its original grandeur. Programs include opera, dance, music, and drama from the best touring companies. Tickets are £10 to £35 ($19–$65) and can be purchased at the **box office** (© **01284/769505;** www. theatreroyal.org).

Stop by the 17th-century pub **Dog and Partridge,** 29 Crown St. (© **01284/ 764792**), and see where the bar scenes from the BBC hit series *Lovejoy* were filmed while you sample one of the region's Greene King Ales. Also try wiggling your way into the **Nutshell,** corner of The Traverse and Abbeygate Street (© **01284/764867**). This pub has been notoriously dubbed the smallest pub in all of England and is a favorite tourist stop. **The Masons Arms,** 14 Whiting St. (© **01284/753955**), features more of a family atmosphere and welcomes children. Home-cooked food is served along with a standard selection of ales. There's a patio garden in use in summer.

A SIDE TRIP TO SUDBURY

Thirty-two kilometers (20 miles) south of Bury St. Edmunds along the A134 is Sudbury, a town that has prospered through the ages thanks to its sheep (the wool industry) and prime location along the banks of the River Stour. A handful of medieval half-timbered buildings and Georgian homes attest to the town's ripe old age. Its most famous native son is Thomas Gainsborough, who was born in 1727 and went on to become one of England's most beloved painters.

His birthplace, **Gainsborough's House,** 46 Gainsborough St. (© **01787/ 372958;** www.gainsborough.org), is a museum and arts center that has many of his works of art on display. Visitors will notice that several different architectural styles make up the house, and there is a walled garden in back worth seeing. It's open from mid-April to October, Tuesday to Saturday from 10am to 5pm and Sunday from 2 to 5pm; from November to mid-April, Tuesday to Saturday from 10am to 4pm and Sunday from 2 to 4pm. Admission is £3 ($5.55) adults, £2.80 ($5.20) seniors, £1.50 ($2.80) children and students, during the year, but it is free during the month of December.

WHERE TO STAY

The Mill Hotel ⋒ *Finds*   As its name implies, this four-story hotel is located in the shell of an old mill. In fact, the River Stour, which runs under the hotel, still turns the mill's 5m (16-ft.) water wheel, now encased in glass and on display in the hotel's restaurant and bar. Rooms vary in size; some have heavy oak beams and massive columns, but all are outfitted with comfortable furnishings, including well-kept bathrooms with shower-tub combinations. You may even be able to watch the local cows occasionally pass by the water's edge, as many of the rooms have a river or millpond view. *Note:* The hotel has no elevator.

Walnut Tree Lane, Sudbury CO10 1BD. © 01787/375544. Fax 01787/373027. www.millhotelsuffolk.co.uk. 56 units. £79 ($146) double. AE, DC, MC, V. **Amenities:** Restaurant; bar; limited room service; laundry service; nonsmoking rooms. *In room:* TV, dataport, coffeemaker, hair dryer, iron.

5 Lavenham ⟨★

106km (66 miles) NE of London; 56km (35 miles) SE of Cambridge

Once a great wool center, Lavenham is the classic Suffolk village, beautifully preserved today. It features a number of half-timbered Tudor houses washed in the characteristic Suffolk pink. The town's wool-trading profits are apparent in its guildhall, on the triangular main "square." Inside, exhibits on Lavenham's textile industry show how yarn was spun, then "dyed in the wool" with woad (the plant used by ancient Picts to dye themselves blue), following on to the weaving process. Another display shows how half-timbered houses were constructed.

The Church of St. Peter and St. Paul, at the edge of Lavenham, has interesting carvings on the misericords and the chancel screen, as well as ornate tombs. This is one of the "wool churches" of the area, built by pious merchants in the Perpendicular style with a landmark tower.

ESSENTIALS

GETTING THERE   Trains depart London's North Street Station at least once an hour, sometimes more often, for Colchester, where they connect quickly to the town of Sudbury. For information, call © **0845/748-4950** or visit www. railtrack.co.uk. From Sudbury, **Beestons Coaches, Ltd.,** (© **01473/212521;** www.beestons.co.uk) has about nine daily buses making the short run to Lavenham. The trip from London takes between 2 and 2½ hours.

National Express buses depart from London's Victoria Coach Station, carrying passengers to the town of Bury St. Edmunds, some 14km (9 miles) from Lavenham. For information, call © **0870/580-8080** or visit www.national express.com. From Bury St. Edmunds, you can take another bus onto Lavenham. The trip takes about 2½ hours.

If you're driving from Bury St. Edmunds, continue south on the A134 toward Long Melford, but cut southeast to Lavenham at the junction with the A1141.

VISITOR INFORMATION The **Tourist Information Centre** is on Lady Street (© **01787/248207**) and is open Monday through Friday from 9am to 5pm, Saturday from 10am to 3pm; April through September Saturday hours are extended until 5pm.

SHOPPING & TEATIME

Shoppers from all over East Anglia flock to **Timbers,** 6 High St. (© **01787/ 247218**), a center housing 24 dealers specializing in antiques and collectibles, including books, toys, military artifacts, glass, porcelain, and much more. It's open daily.

After strolling the medieval streets of Lavenham, stop by **Tickle Manor Tea Rooms,** 17 High St. (© **01787/248438**). This two-story timber-frame home was built by the son of a priest in 1530 and provides an ample dose of history for patrons to absorb while sipping any one of a selection of teas that are served with English breakfast, sandwiches, or a piece of cake.

WHERE TO STAY

The Great House (see "Where to Dine," below) also rents rooms.

Lavenham Priory ☆ *Finds* The Tudor age lives again in this building dating from the 13th century and once owned by Benedictine monks. In time the mansion became the property of the Earls of Oxford before being sold to rich cloth merchants. Today it's been restored to its appearance during its Elizabethan period. It was first put on the map when the Automobile Association named it "accommodation of the year" for Britain. Since that time, it has enjoyed immense popularity. The timber-framed house has been beautifully restored and sensitively modernized to offer guests grand comfort. An oak Jacobean staircase leads to the bedchambers featuring four-posters, Tudor wall paintings, and oak floors. Each room is furnished individually, and all the well-maintained bathrooms contain either a tub or shower. You can enjoy a chair by an inglenook fireplace or order a summer breakfast in the herb garden. The hotel stands in 1.2 hectares (3 acres) of grounds in the center of the village.

Water St., Lavenham, Suffolk CO10 9SH. © **01787/247404.** Fax 01787/248472. www.lavenhampriory.co.uk. 6 units. £90–£130 ($167–$241). MC, V. **Amenities:** Sitting room; breakfast lounge. *In room:* TV, beverage maker.

The Swan Lavenham ☆☆☆ This lavishly timbered inn, the best accommodation in Suffolk, is one of the oldest and best-preserved buildings in a relatively unspoiled village. It has been so successful that it has expanded into an adjoining ancient wool hall, which provides a high-ceilinged guesthouse and raftered, second-story bedrooms opening onto a tiny cloistered garden. The bedrooms vary in size, according to the eccentricities of the architecture. Most have beamed ceilings and a mixture of traditional pieces that blend well with the old. The more expensive rooms feature four-poster beds. Bathrooms are immaculately maintained, with tub-and-shower combinations.

High St., Lavenham, Sudbury, Suffolk CO10 9QA. © **01787/247477.** Fax 01787/248286. 51 units. £110–£150 ($204–$278) double; £160–$200 ($296–$370) suite. Rates include breakfast and dinner. AE, DC, MC, V. **Amenities:** Restaurant; lounge; bar; limited room service; laundry service; nonsmoking rooms. *In room:* TV, dataport, minibar, coffeemaker, hair dryer, iron, safe, trouser press.

WHERE TO DINE

The Great House Hotel ☆ FRENCH With its Georgian facade and location near the marketplace, The Great House is the town's finest place to dine, a quintessentially French hotel in a beautiful English town. The interior is also attractively decorated, with Laura Ashley prints, an inglenook fireplace, and old oak beams. Assisted by his wife, Martine, owner Régis Crépy does double duty as the *chef de cuisine*. He is an inventive, quixotic cook, as reflected by such dishes as roasted magret of duck served with wild mushrooms and a green peppercorn sauce; roasted rack of English lamb served with sautéed garnish Provençale, fried garlic, and an eggplant and coriander coulis; and stuffed filet of sea bass perfumed with licorice and served with aromatic rice.

The house also rents five elegantly decorated suites for £76 to £96 ($141–$178) for a double, including an English breakfast. The units have TVs, phones, and private bathrooms or showers.

Market Place. ℂ **01787/247431.** Fax 01787/248007. www.lavenham.co.uk/greathouse. Reservations recommended. Snacks £2.95–£10 ($5.45–$19); fixed-price lunch £17 ($31) Tues–Sat; £22 ($41) Sun lunch; £22 ($41) dinner Tues–Fri. AE, MC, V. Tues–Sun noon–2:30pm; Tues–Sat 7–9:30pm.

6 Two Stately Homes in Long Melford

98km (61 miles) NE of London; 55km (34 miles) SE of Cambridge

Long Melford has been famous since the days of the early cloth makers. Like Lavenham, it attained prestige and importance during the Middle Ages. Of the old buildings remaining, the village church is often called "one of the glories of the shire." Along its 5km (3-mile) long High Street—said to boast the highest concentration of antiques shops in Europe—are many private homes erected by wealthy wool merchants of yore. Of special interest are Long Melford's two stately homes, Melford Hall and Kentwell Hall.

ESSENTIALS

GETTING THERE Trains run from London's Liverpool Street Station toward Ipswich and on to Marks Tey. Call ℂ **0845/748-4950** or visit www.railtrack.co.uk for information. Here, you can take a shuttle train going back and forth between that junction and Sudbury. From the town of Sudbury, it's a 5km (3-mile) taxi ride to Long Melford.

From Cambridge, take a Cambus Bus Company coach (ℂ **01223/423578;** www.stagecoachbus.com) to Bury St. Edmunds, then change for the final ride into Long Melford. These buses run about once an hour throughout the day and early evening.

If driving from Newmarket, continue east on the A45 to Bury St. Edmunds, but cut south on the A134 (toward Sudbury) to Long Melford.

VISITOR INFORMATION   There is a **Tourist Information Office** in the Town Hall, Sudbury (ℂ **01787/881320**), that's open Monday through Friday from 9am to 5pm and Saturday from 10am to 4:45pm during summer, and Monday through Friday from 9am to 5pm and Saturday from 10am to 2:45pm during winter.

BEATRIX POTTER'S ANCESTRAL HOME & A TUDOR MANSION

Kentwell Hall   At the end of an avenue of linden trees, the redbrick Tudor mansion called Kentwell Hall, surrounded by a broad moat, has been restored by its owners, Mr. and Mrs. Patrick Phillips. A 15th-century moat house, interconnecting gardens, a brick-paved maze, and a costume display are of interest. There are also rare-breed farm animals here. Two gatehouses are constructed in 16th-century style. The hall hosts regular re-creations of Tudor domestic life, including the well-known annual events for the weeks of June 16 to July 7 when admission prices tend to escalate slightly.

On A134 between Sudbury and Bury St. Edmunds. ℭ **01787/310207**. www.kentwellhall.co.uk. Admission £7 ($13). July–Sept daily noon–5pm; Apr–June Sun, Wed, and Thurs noon–5pm; Oct Sun noon–5pm. The entrance is north of the green in Long Melford on the west side of A134, about 1km (½ mile) north of Melford Hall.

Melford Hall This is the ancestral home of Beatrix Potter, who often visited. Jemima PuddleDuck still occupies a chair in one of the bedrooms upstairs, and some of her other figures are on display. The house, built between 1554 and 1578, has paintings, fine furniture, and Chinese porcelain. The gardens alone make a visit here worthwhile.

Long Melford (off A135), Sudbury, Suffolk. ℭ **01787/880286**. Admission £4.60 ($8.50) adults, £2.25 ($4.15) children. May–Sept Wed–Sun and bank holiday Mon 2–5:30pm; Apr and Oct Sat–Sun and bank holiday Mon 2–5:30pm.

WHERE TO STAY

Black Lion The Bull has the edge, but this place is doing something right, as an inn has stood here since the 12th century. Fourteenth-century documents mention it as the spot where drinks were dispensed to revolutionaries during one of the peasants' revolts. The present building dates from the early 1800s and has been richly restored by its new owners. All rooms are of a high standard with antique furnishings and well-kept bathrooms with shower-tub combinations. The Black Lion overlooks one of the loveliest village greens in Suffolk.

The Green, Long Melford, Suffolk CO10 9DN. ℭ **01787/312356**. Fax 01787/374557. www.ravenwoodhall. co.uk/blacklion. 10 units. £109–£120 ($202–$222) double; from £146 ($270) suite. Rates include English breakfast. AE, MC, V. **Amenities:** Restaurant; bar; limited room service; babysitting; laundry service. *In room:* TV, coffeemaker, hair dryer, iron, safe.

Bull Hotel ⟨⟩ Here is an opportunity to experience life in one of the great old inns of East Anglia. Built by a wool merchant in 1540, this is Long Melford's finest hotel and its best-preserved building, with lots of improvements and modernizations added over the years. The rooms here are a mix of the old and the new. The interior and exterior of the hotel have been refurbished, and the beds are usually king-size or twins. Bathrooms are well kept, with a tub and shower. A medieval weavers' gallery and an open hearth with Elizabethan brickwork have been incorporated into the hotel's design.

Hall St., Long Melford, Sudbury, Suffolk CO10 9JG. ℭ **01787/378494**. Fax 01787/880307. www.oldenglish. co.uk. 25 units. £120–£140 ($222–$259) double; £140–£160 ($259–$296) suite. Leisure breaks (2-night minimum) £73 ($134) per person double, including half board. AE, DC, MC, V. **Amenities:** Restaurant; bar; limited room service; nonsmoking rooms. *In room:* TV, dataport, coffeemaker, hair dryer, iron, trouser press.

WHERE TO DINE

Chimneys ⟨⟩ BRITISH/TRADITIONAL This is the most venerable restaurant in town, with a more refined cuisine than that served at Scutchers Bistro (see below). The building here was erected in the 16th century and retains its original dark-stained oaken beams and mellow brick walls in the dining room. A walled garden is in back. The menus offer a wide choice of foods, influenced by the best modern British cuisine trends. Begin with a warm salad of duck confit and orange, or a gratin of king prawns with chile and cheese. Main courses are equally sumptuous, such as baked filet of Scottish salmon with a brioche and herb crust, or braised lamb shank with red onion and rosemary. For dessert, try the mango Bavarois set on a forest fruit purée. Chimneys also has one of the most extensive wine lists in town.

Hall St. ℭ **01787/379806**. Reservations recommended. Main courses £12–£23 ($22–$43). AE, MC, V. Mon–Sat noon–2pm and 7–9pm.

Scutchers Bistro BRITISH   This upscale bistro earns favorable recommendations from many locals. The building was erected in stages between the 1600s and the 1800s and was named after the workers (scutchers) who, in olden days, rendered flax into linen. As The Scutchers Arms, it was a favorite pub—until the new owners painted its facade bright yellow and filled its heavily beamed interior with vivid Mediterranean colors. Menu choices change daily. Your meal might include sautéed tiger prawns with mushrooms, bacon, and garlic; steamed scallops with asparagus and lemon-flavored hollandaise; and a very English version of steamed fruit pudding with custard.

Westgate St. ⓒ **01787/310200.** Reservations recommended. Main courses £12–£19 ($22–$35). AE, MC, V. Tues–Sat noon–2pm and 7–9:30pm.

7 Dedham

101km (63 miles) NE of London; 13km (8 miles) NE of Colchester

Remember Constable's *Vale of Dedham?* The Vale of Dedham lies between the towns of Colchester and Ipswich in a wide valley through which runs the River Stour, the boundary between Essex and Suffolk. It's not only the link with Constable that has made this vale so popular. It is one of the most beautiful, unspoiled areas left in southeast England. In this little Essex village on the Stour River, you're in the heart of Constable Country. Flatford Mill is only 1.5km (1 mile) farther down the river. The village, with its Tudor, Georgian, and Regency houses, is set in the midst of the water meadows of the Stour. Constable painted its church and tower. Dedham is right on the Essex-Suffolk border and makes a good center for exploring both North Essex and the Suffolk border country.

GETTING THERE

Trains depart every 20 minutes from London's Liverpool Street Station for the 50-minute ride to Colchester. For schedules and information, call ⓒ **0845/748-4950** or visit www.railtrack.co.uk. From Colchester, it's possible to take a taxi from the railway station to the bus station, then board a bus run by the Eastern National Bus Company for the 8km (5-mile) trip to Dedham. (Buses leave about once an hour.) Most people take a taxi from Colchester directly to Dedham.

National Express buses depart from London's Victoria Coach Station for Colchester, where you have the choice of taking either another bus or a taxi to Dedham. For schedules and information, call ⓒ **0870/580-8080** or visit www. nationalexpress.com.

If you're driving from the London ring road, travel northeast on the A12 to Colchester, turning off at East Bergholt onto a small secondary road leading east to Dedham.

VISITING THE PAINTERS' HOMES

Less than a mile from the village center is **The Sir Alfred Munnings Art Museum,** East Lane (ⓒ **01206/322127;** www.siralfredmunnings.co.uk), home of Sir Alfred Munnings, president of the Royal Academy from 1944 to 1949, and painter extraordinaire of racehorses and other animals. The house and studio, which have sketches and other works, are open from early April to early October, on Sunday, Wednesday, and bank holidays (plus Thurs and Sat during Aug) from 2 to 5pm. Admission is £3 ($5.55) for adults, £2 ($3.70) students and seniors, and 50p (95¢) for children.

The English landscape painter John Constable (1776–1837) was born at East Bergholt, north of Dedham. Near the village is **Flatford Mill,** East Bergholt

(© **01206/298283**), the subject of one of his most renowned works. The mill was given to the National Trust in 1943 and has since been leased to the Field Studies Council for use as a residential center. The center offers more than 170 short courses each year in all aspects of art and the environment. Fees are from £136 ($252) for a weekend and from £380 ($703) for a full week. The fee includes accommodations, meals, and tuition. Write to Field Studies Council, Flatford Mill Field Centre, East Bergholt, Colchester CO7 6UL.

WHERE TO STAY

Dedham Hall/Fountain House Restaurant   A 3-minute walk east of the center of town, this well-managed hotel flourishes under the direction of Jim and Wendy Sarton. Set on 2 hectares (5 acres) of grazing land whose centerpiece is a pond favored by geese and wild swans, it consists of a 400-year-old brick-sided cottage linked to a 200-year-old home of stately proportions. The older section is reserved for the breakfast room, a bar, and a sitting room for residents of the six second-floor bedrooms. Each cozy room comes with a compact bathroom with a shower-tub combination. A cluster of three converted barns provides accommodations for many artists who congregate here several times throughout the year for painting seminars and art workshops.

Brook St., Dedham CO7 6AD. © **01206/323027**. Fax 01206/323293. www.dedhamhall.demon.co.uk. 16 units. £130 ($241) double. Rate includes half board. MC, V. **Amenities:** Restaurant; bar; limited room service. *In room:* TV, minibar, coffeemaker, hair dryer, iron, safe.

Maison Talbooth 🌟🌟🌟   This small, exclusive hotel is in a handsomely restored Victorian country house on a bluff overlooking the river valley, with views that stretch as far as the medieval Church of Stratford St. Mary. Accommodations consist of spacious suites distinctively furnished by one of England's best-known decorators. High-fashion colors abound, antiques are mixed discreetly with reproductions, and the original architectural beauty has been preserved. The sumptuous beds feature fine linens and the bathrooms are luxurious; some have tubs (even Jacuzzis) and others have showers only. A superluxury suite has a sunken Jacuzzi bath and a draped bed. Fresh flowers, fruit, and a private bar are standard amenities in the suites. If accommodations are not available here, the staff can book you into neighboring hotels with which they are affiliated.

Stratford Rd., Dedham, Colchester, Essex CO7 6HN. © **01206/322367**. Fax 01206/322752. www.talbooth. com. 10 units. £180–£220 ($333–$407) double. Rates include continental breakfast. AE, DC, MC, V. Take Stratford Rd. 1km (½ mile) west of the town center. **Amenities:** Bar; limited room service; babysitting; laundry service. *In room:* TV, dataport, minibar, hair dryer.

WHERE TO DINE

Le Talbooth 🌟🌟🌟   ENGLISH/FRENCH   A hand-hewn, half-timbered weaver's house is the setting for this restaurant standing amid beautiful gardens on the banks of the River Stour. Le Talbooth was featured in Constable's *Vale of Dedham.* You descend a sloping driveway leading past flowering terraces. A well-mannered staff will usher you to a low-ceilinged bar for an aperitif.

Owner Gerald Milsom has brought a high standard of cooking to this rustically elegant place, where a well-chosen wine list complements the good food. An a la carte menu changes six times a year, and special dishes are altered daily, reflecting the best produce available at the market. You'll get off to a fine start with half a dozen native oysters from nearby Colchester. The velvety smooth parfait of foie gras and duck livers is hard to resist. Each night a different roast is featured, ranging from honey-coated ham to leg of lamb. Your main course, inevitably a delight, might be roast breast of guinea fowl with tarragon-scented sausage, shiitake mushrooms, and broad beans in a creamy sauce.

Gun Hill. ✆ **01206/323150.** www.talbooth.com. Reservations recommended. Main courses £17–£25 ($31–$46); fixed-price lunch £20 ($36) for 2 courses, £24 ($44) for 3 courses. AE, DC, MC, V. Daily noon–2pm and 7–9:30pm.

8 Woodbridge & Aldeburgh

Woodbridge: 130km (81 miles) NE of London; 76km (47 miles) S of Norwich. Aldeburgh: 156km (97 miles) NE of London; 66km (41 miles) SE of Norwich

On the Deben River, the market town of Woodbridge is a yachting center. Its best-known, most famous resident was Edward FitzGerald, Victorian poet and translator of the "Rubaiyat of Omar Khayyam." Woodbridge is a good base for exploring the East Suffolk coastline, particularly the small resort of Aldeburgh, noted for its Moot Hall.

On the North Sea, 24km (15 miles) from Woodbridge, Aldeburgh is an exclusive resort, and it attracts many Dutch visitors, who make the sea crossing via Harwich and Felixstowe, both major entry ports for traffic from the Continent. Aldeburgh dates from Roman times and has long been known as a small port for North Sea fisheries. The Aldeburgh Festival, held every June, is the most important arts festival in East Anglia, and one of the best attended in England.

ESSENTIALS

GETTING THERE   Woodbridge is on the rail line to Lowestoft from either Victoria Station or Liverpool Street Station in London. Get off two stops after Ipswich. For schedules and information, call ✆ **0845/748-4950** or visit www. railtrack.co.uk. The nearest rail station to Aldeburgh is on the same line, at Saxmundham, six stops after Ipswich. From Saxmundham, you can take a taxi or one of six buses that run the 9.5km (6 miles) to Aldeburgh during the day.

One National Express bus a day passes through Aldeburgh and Woodbridge on the way from London's Victoria Coach Station to Great Yarmouth. It stops at every country town and narrow lane along the way, so the trip to Aldeburgh takes a woeful 4½ hours. For information, call ✆ **0870/580-8080** or visit www. nationalexpress.com. Many visitors reach both towns by Eastern County Bus Company's service from Ipswich. That company's no. 80/81 buses run frequently between Woodbridge and Aldeburgh.

If driving from London's ring road, take the A12 northeast to Ipswich, then continue northeast on the A12 to Woodbridge. To get to Aldeburgh, stay on the A12 until you reach the junction with the A1094, then head east to the North Sea.

VISITOR INFORMATION   The **Tourist Information Centre** is at the Cinema, 152 High St., Aldeburgh (✆ **01728/453637**), and is open daily year-round from 9am to 5pm.

SPECIAL EVENTS   Aldeburgh was the home of Benjamin Britten (1913–76), renowned composer of the operas *Peter Grimes* and *Billy Budd,* as well as many orchestral works. Many of his compositions were first performed at the **Aldeburgh Festival,** which he founded in 1946. The festival takes place in June, featuring internationally known performers. There are other concerts and events throughout the year. Write or call the tourist office for details, or check out www. aldeburgh.co.uk. The Snape Maltings Concert Hall nearby is one of the more successful among the smaller British concert halls; it also houses the Britten-Pears School of Advanced Musical Studies, established in 1973.

SEEING THE SIGHTS IN ALDEBURGH

There are two local golf courses, one at Aldeburgh and another at Thorpeness, 3km (2 miles) away. A yacht club is situated on the River Alde, 14km (9 miles) from the river's mouth. There are also two bird sanctuaries nearby, **Minsmere** and **Havergate Island.** Managed by the Royal Society for the Protection of Birds, they are famous for their waterfowl.

Insider's tip: Seek out Crag Path, running along Aldeburgh's wild shore. It is unusually attractive, with its two lookout towers built early in the 19th century to keep watch for vessels putting down or needing pilots.

Constructed on a shelf of land at the sea level, the High Street runs parallel to the often-turbulent waterfront. A cliff face rises some 89m (55 ft.) above the main street. A major attraction is the 16th-century **Moot Hall Museum,** Market Cross Place, Aldeburgh (**© 01728/453295**). The hall dates from the time of Henry VIII, but its tall twin chimneys are later additions. The timber-frame structure displays old maps, prints, and Anglo-Saxon burial urns, as well as other items of historical interest. It is open July and August daily from 10:30am to 12:30pm and 2:30 to 5pm. It is also open from Easter to May, Saturday and Sunday from 2:30 to 5pm, and in June, September, and October daily from 2:30 to 5pm. Admission is £1 ($1.85) for adults and free for children.

Aldeburgh is also the site of the nation's northernmost martello tower, erected to protect the coast from a feared invasion by Napoleon.

WHERE TO STAY & DINE
NEAR WOODBRIDGE

Seckford Hall 😊😊😊   This ivy-covered estate's pure Tudor, crow-stepped gables, mullioned windows, and ornate chimneys capture the spirit of the days of Henry VIII and his strong-willed daughter Elizabeth (the latter may have held court here). Today, it provides some of the finest accommodations in Suffolk, rivaling those at The Swan in Lavenham (see review, earlier in this chapter). You enter through a heavy, studded Tudor door into a flagstone hallway with antiques. The butler will show you to your bedroom. Many rooms have four-poster beds, one of them a monumental 1587 specimen. Bedrooms are statements in luxury and elegance. Bathrooms are lavish and some of them have Jacuzzi tubs.

If you arrive before sundown, you may want to stroll through the 14-hectare (34-acre) gardens, which include a rose garden, herbaceous borders, and greenhouses. At the bottom of the garden is an ornamental lake, complete with weeping willows and paddling ducks.

On A12 (2.5km/1½ miles from the Woodbridge rail station), Woodbridge, Suffolk IP13 6NU. **© 01394/ 385678.** Fax 01394/380610. www.seckford.co.uk. 32 units. £130–£140 ($241–$259) double; £170–£200 ($315–$370) suite. Rates include English breakfast. AE, DC, MC, V. **Amenities:** 2 restaurants; 2 bars; indoor pool; golf course; Jacuzzi; health club; babysitting; limited room service; laundry service; nonsmoking rooms; rooms for those with limited mobility. *In room:* TV, dataport, minibar in some rooms, coffeemaker, hair dryer, iron.

IN ALDEBURGH

The Brudenell Hotel   Located on the waterfront, this hotel is no match for the Wentworth (see below) but is a good choice. It was built at the beginning of the 20th century and was remodeled and redecorated in 2003 to achieve a pleasant interior. Many of the bedrooms face the sea, and each has comfortable beds. Bathrooms are well equipped, each with a shower.

The Parade, Aldeburgh, Suffolk IP15 5BU. **© 01728/452071.** Fax 01728/454082. www.aldeburgh-breaks.co. uk/brudenell/brudenell.html. 47 units. £96–£142 ($178–$263) double. Rates include breakfast. AE, MC, V.

Amenities: Restaurant; bar; limited room service; babysitting; laundry service; dry cleaning; nonsmoking rooms; rooms for those with limited mobility. *In room:* TV, coffeemaker, hair dryer, iron.

The Wentworth Hotel 🎧 A traditional country-house hotel with tall chimneys and gables, the Wentworth overlooks the sea. Built in the early 19th century as a private residence, it was converted into a hotel around 1900. The Pritt family has welcomed the world since 1920, including Sir Benjamin Britten and novelist E. M. Forster. In summer, tables are placed outside so that guests can enjoy the sun; in winter, open fires in the lounges, even the cozy bar, are a welcome sight. Many guest rooms have panoramic views. A 19th-century building across the road from the main house offers a comfortable, seven-room annex. The standards here match those of the main house.

Wentworth Rd., Aldeburgh, Suffolk IP15 5BD. 🕐 **01728/452312.** Fax 01728/454343. www.wentworth-aldeburgh.com. 37 units. £140–£198 ($259–$366) double. Rates include English breakfast and dinner. AE, DC, MC, V. Closed Dec 27–Jan 9. **Amenities:** Restaurant; bar; limited room service; laundry service; nonsmoking rooms; rooms for those with limited mobility. *In room:* TV, dataport, coffeemaker, hair dryer.

9 Norwich 🎧🎧

175km (109 miles) NE of London; 32km (20 miles) W of the North Sea

Norwich still holds to its claim as the capital of East Anglia. Despite its partial industrialization, it's a charming and historic city. In addition to its cathedral, it has more than 30 medieval parish churches built of flint. It's also the most important shopping center in East Anglia and has a lot to offer in the way of entertainment and interesting hotels, many of them in its narrow streets and alleyways. A big open-air market is busy every weekday, with fruit, flowers, vegetables, and other goods sold from stalls with colored canvas roofs.

ESSENTIALS

GETTING THERE   Hourly train service from London's Liverpool Street Station takes nearly 2 hours. For information, call 🕐 **0845/748-4950** or visit www.railtrack.co.uk.

National Express buses depart London's Victoria Coach Station once each hour for the 3-hour ride. For schedules and information, call 🕐 **0870/580-8080** or visit www.nationalexpress.com.

If driving from London's ring road, head north toward Cambridge on the M11. Turn northeast at the junction with the A11, which takes you to Norwich.

GETTING AROUND   For information about buses serving the area, go to the **Norfolk Bus Information Centre** at Castle Meadow (🕐 **0870/608-2608**). The office there can answer your transportation questions; open Monday through Saturday from 8:30am to 5pm.

VISITOR INFORMATION   The Tourist Information Centre is located in the **Millennium Plain,** Norwich, near the marketplace in the center of town (🕐 **01603/727927**). It's open April through October Monday through Saturday from 10am to 6pm and Sunday from 10:30am to 4:30pm; November through March Monday through Saturday from 10am to 5:30pm.

SEEING THE SIGHTS

Blickling Hall 🎧🎧   Massive yew hedges bordering a long drive frame your first view of Blickling Hall, a great Jacobean house built in the early 17th century, one of the finest examples of such architecture in the country. The long gallery has an elaborate 17th-century ceiling, and the Peter the Great Room, decorated later, has a fine tapestry on the wall. The house is set in ornamental parkland with a formal garden and an orangery.

Blickling, near Aylsham. ℂ **01263/738030.** House and gardens Tues–Sat £6.90 ($13) adults, £3.45 ($6.40) children. Gardens only Tues–Sat £3.90 ($7.20) adults, £1.95 ($3.60) children. Late Mar to Oct Wed–Sun and bank holiday Mon 1–4:15pm. (Garden, shop, restaurant, and Plant Centre open Thurs–Sun and bank holiday Mon 10:15am–5:15pm.) Blickling Hall lies 23km (14 miles) north of the city of Norwich, 2.5km (1½ miles) west of Aylsham on B1354; take A140 toward Cromer and follow the signs. Telephone before visiting to confirm opening arrangements.

The Mustard Shop Museum   The Victorian-style Mustard Shop displays a wealth of mahogany and shining brass. The standard of service and pace of life reflect the personality and courtesy of a bygone age. The Mustard Museum features exhibits on the history of the Colman Company and the making of mustard, including its properties and origins. There are old advertisements, as well as packages and tins. You can browse in the shop, selecting whichever mustards you prefer, including the really hot English type. The shop also sells aprons, tea towels, pottery mustard pots, and mugs.

15 Royal Arcade. ℂ **01603/627889.** Free admission. Mon–Sat 9:30am–5pm. Closed bank holidays.

Norwich Cathedral ⍟⍟   Dating from 1096, and principally of Norman design, Norwich Cathedral is noted for its long nave with lofty columns. Built in the late Perpendicular style, the spire rises 95m (315 ft.); together with the keep of the castle, it forms a significant landmark on the Norwich skyline. More than 300 *bosses* (knoblike ornamental projections) on the ceiling depict biblical scenes. The impressive choir stalls with handsome misericords date from the 15th century. Edith Cavell, an English nurse executed by the Germans during World War I, is buried on the cathedral's Life's Green. The quadrangular cloisters, which date from the 13th century, are the largest monastic cloisters in England.

The cathedral visitor center includes a refreshment area and exhibition and film room with tape/slide shows about the cathedral. Ask at the information desk about guided tours from June to September. A short walk from the cathedral is Tombland, one of the most interesting old squares in Norwich.

62 The Close. ℂ **01603/764385.** Free admission, £3 ($5.55) donation suggested. Oct–May daily 7:30am–6pm; June–Sept daily 7:30am–7pm.

Sainsbury Centre for Visual Arts   The center was the gift of Sir Robert and Lady Sainsbury, who, in 1973, contributed their private collection to the University of East Anglia, 5km (3 miles) west of Norwich on Earlham Road. Together with their son David, they gave an endowment to provide a building to house the collection. Designed by Foster Associates, the center was opened in 1978 and has since won many national and international awards. The prominent features of the structure are its flexibility, allowing solid and glass areas to be interchanged, and the superb quality of light, which permits optimum viewing of works of art. Special exhibitions are often presented in the 1991 Crescent Wing extension. The Sainsbury Collection is one of the foremost in the country, including modern, ancient, classical, and ethnographic art. Its most prominent works are those by Francis Bacon, Alberto Giacometti, and Henry Moore.

University of East Anglia, Earlham Rd. ℂ **01603/593199.** Admission £2 ($3.70) adults, £1 ($1.85) children and students. Tues–Sun 11am–5pm. Bus: 25, 26, 27, or 76 from Castle Meadow.

Second Air Division Memorial Library   A memorial room honoring the Second Air Division of the Eighth U.S. Army Air Force is part of the central

The Royal Residence of Sandringham

Some 177km (110 miles) northeast of London, 2,833-hectare (7,000-acre) Sandringham has been the country home of four generations of British monarchs; Queen Victoria's son, the Prince of Wales (later King Edward VII), purchased it in 1861. He and his Danish wife, Princess Alexandra, rebuilt the house, which became a popular meeting place for British society. The redbrick and stone Victorian-Tudor mansion has more than 200 rooms, some of which are open to the public, including two drawing rooms, the ballroom, and a dining room. The atmosphere of a well-loved family home is a contrast to the formal splendor of Buckingham Palace. Guests can also view a loft salon with a minstrel's gallery used as a sitting room by the royal family and full of photographs and mementos.

A Land Train designed and built on the estate makes it easy for visitors to reach Sandringham House, which sits at the heart of 24 hectares (60 acres) of beautiful grounds. The train's covered carriages have room for wheelchairs.

The Sandringham Museum holds a wealth of rare items relating to the history of the royal family's time here and displays tell the story of the monarchs who have owned the estate since 1862. Visitors can see the big-game trophies in settings that include a safari trail.

Sandringham is some 80km (50 miles) west of Norwich and 13km (8 miles) northeast of King's Lynn (off the A149). King's Lynn is the end of the main train route from London's Liverpool Street Station that goes via Cambridge and Ely. Trains from London arrive at King's Lynn every 2 hours, a trip of 2½ hours. From Cambridge, the train ride takes only 1 hour. Buses from both Cambridge and Norwich run to King's Lynn, where you can catch bus no. 411 to take you the rest of the way to Sandringham.

The grounds and museum of Sandringham (© **01553/772675**; www.andringhamestate.co.uk) are open from April 10 to July 23 and from August 1 to October 31 daily from 11am to 5pm (in Oct, the house closes at 4:45pm). Admission to the house, grounds, and museum is £6.50 ($12) for adults, £5 ($9.25) for seniors, and £4 ($7.40) for children 5 to 15 years. Admission to the grounds and museum only is £4.50 ($8.35) for adults, £3.50 ($6.50) for seniors, and £2.50 ($4.65) for children 5 to 15 years.

library. The library staff will assist veterans who wish to visit their old air bases in East Anglia. At the library, you can find pertinent books, audiovisual materials, and records of the various bomber groups.

The Forum, Millennium Plain. © 01603/774747. Free admission. Mon–Fri 9am–5pm; Sat 9am–5pm.

EXPLORING THE BROADS

Wroxham, 11km (7 miles) northeast of Norwich, is the best center for exploring the Broads, mostly shallow lagoons connected by streams. These are fun to explore by boat, of course, but some folks prefer to ride their bikes along the Broads.

To get to Wroxham from Norwich, take bus no. 51. The 30-minute ride costs £2.25 ($3.70) for a return ticket. Information about touring the Broads is provided by the **Hoveton Tourist Office,** Station Road (© **01603/782281**), open from Easter to October daily from 9am to 1pm and 2 to 5pm. At this office you can get a list of boat-rental facilities. During the winter months contact the office of the Broads Authority (© **01603/610734**) in Norwich for information around town.

If you don't want to handle your own boat, you can take an organized tour. The best ones are offered by **Broads Tours,** near the Wroxham bridge (© **01603/ 782207;** www.broads.co.uk). Their cruises last 1½ to 3½ hours. In summer, most departures are at either 11:30am or 2:30pm. The cost ranges from £6 to £7 ($11–$13) for adults, and from £4 to £5.50 ($7.40–$10) for children 5 to 15 years.

SHOPPING

For the best in antiques, books, and crafts, shoppers can search out the historic lanes and alleys of the town center.

Norwich Antiques Centre, 14 Tombland (© **01603/619129**), is a three-floor house opposite the cathedral where 60-plus dealers set up shop. The selection is wide and varied and includes everything from small collectibles to antique furniture.

WHERE TO STAY
EXPENSIVE

De Vere Dunston Hall ☆☆   Surrounded by parkland and its own golf course, this gabled house is imbued with an Elizabethan aura, even though the redbrick mansion dates from 1859. With its soaring chimneys, it has been sensitively converted and extended, and is now elegantly furnished and imbued with grand character and comfort. Many of its original 19th-century features are still intact. A wide range of bedrooms is available, including some family rooms with double sofa beds for children and rooms specially equipped for the mobility impaired; all rooms but one have both a bath and shower. You can stay in elegant four-poster comfort or try one of the attic rooms, which still boast their original beamed low ceilings. Guests also have several dining options the best being the exquisite La Fontaine restaurant with its a la carte menu. From a golf course to an indoor pool and aerobics studios, Dunston Hall also has the best facilities in the area.

Ipswich Rd., Norfolk NR14 8PQ. © **01508/470444.** Fax 01508/470689. www.devereonline.co.uk. 130 units. £160–£200 ($296–$370) double; £220 ($407) suite. AE, DC, MC, V. **Amenities:** 3 restaurants; bar; indoor pool; 18-hole golf course; 2 outdoor tennis courts; aerobics studio; fitness center; nonsmoking rooms; rooms for those with limited mobility. *In room:* TV, dataport, coffeemaker, hair dryer, trouser press.

Sprowston Manor Marriott Hotel and Country Club ☆☆☆   Norfolk's premier hotel enjoys a long and illustrious history. It was once a private home before it became a hotel in the 1970s. Built in 1559 by a Protestant family prominent in the civil war of the 1640s, it was eventually sold to the lord mayor of Norwich in the late 1800s. It wasn't until 1991, however, that a comprehensive redevelopment added 87 new bedrooms and leisure and conference facilities.

Now owned by Marriott, the hotel lies in 4 hectares (10 acres) of parkland surrounded by the 18-hole Sprowston Park Golf Course. Elegance and informality are its hallmarks. The bedrooms are spacious, quiet, and filled with stylish furniture; some rooms have four-poster beds and others have fireplaces. All rooms have views, and most bathrooms are equipped with a tub and shower.

Sprowston Park, Wroxham Rd., Norwich, Norfolk NR7 8RP. © 01603/410871. Fax 01603/423911. www. marriotthotels.com. 94 units. £135–£165 ($250–$305) double; from £140 ($259) suite. Children under 15 stay free in parent's room. Rates include breakfast. AE, DC, MC, V. **Amenities:** 2 restaurants; 2 bars; indoor pool; health club; spa; salon; limited room service; laundry room; nonsmoking rooms; rooms for those with limited mobility. *In room:* TV, dataport, minibar, coffeemaker, hair dryer, iron/ironing board, safe, trouser press.

MODERATE

The Maid's Head Hotel   In business since 1272, the Maid's Head claims to be the oldest continuously operated hotel in the United Kingdom. Located next to Norwich Cathedral in the oldest part of the city, it has Elizabethan and Georgian architectural styles. The Georgian section has a prim white entry and small-paned windows. Many of the bedrooms have oak beams evocative of the hotel's earlier days. Each is supplied with bowls of fresh fruit and a complimentary newspaper. All units have well-maintained bathrooms with shower-tub combinations. Traditional services such as shoe cleaning, breakfast in bed, and afternoon cream teas are offered. The four-poster Queen Elizabeth I Suite (where the Tudor monarch allegedly once slept) is much sought after.

Palace St., Tombland, Norwich, Norfolk NR3 1LB. © 0870/6096110. Fax 01603/613688. www.corushotels. co.uk. 84 units. £94–£109 ($174–$202) double; £124–£145 ($229–$268) suite. AE, DC, MC, V. **Amenities:** 2 restaurants; bar; limited room service; babysitting; laundry service; dry cleaning; nonsmoking rooms. *In room:* TV, dataport, coffeemaker, hair dryer, iron, trouser press.

The Swallow Nelson Hotel ®   Located by the water near Thorpe Station and Foundry Bridge, this four-story hotel offers the best modern amenities and facilities in town, although it lacks the character and atmosphere of the Maid's Head (see above). Each of the bedrooms provides a view of either the river or a pleasant courtyard. All the bedrooms are well furnished, but some are a bit more spacious than others. Four-poster rooms are available, and bathrooms are excellent, often with both tub and shower.

121 Prince of Wales Rd., Norwich, NR1 1DX. © 01603/760260. Fax 01603/620008. www.swallowhotels. co.uk. 132 units. £100–£147 ($185–$272) double; £120–£162 ($222–$300) suite. Rates include breakfast. AE, DC, MC, V. **Amenities:** 2 restaurants; 2 bars; indoor heated pool; health club; sauna; limited room service; laundry service; dry cleaning; nonsmoking rooms; rooms for those with limited mobility. *In room:* TV, dataport, fridge, coffeemaker, hair dryer, iron/ironing board.

INEXPENSIVE

Holiday Inn   Situated on a sloping hillside about 3km (2 miles) from the city center, this redbrick building offers comfortable contemporary accommodations

---

(Finds Manor House Meets the Raj

Other than an invite from her Majesty to Sandringham Castle, your second best choice is to stay with Viscount and Viscountess Coke at **Victoria,** Park Road (© 01328/711008; www.holkham.co.uk/victoria), in the little town of Holkham, 39km (24 miles) northwest from Norwich. On the grounds of the coastal Holkham Estate, it offers 11 bedrooms in the style of a "manor house meets the Raf" motif. Against a backdrop of beautifully dark wood furniture, each bedroom has its own theme—in fact, it's hard to imagine that this was once a former run-down pub. With furniture and accessories from Rajasthan, including rugs, hand-carved lattice doors, and velvet and cane day beds—a real colonial feeling. The property is still owned by the present earl of Leicester. Bedrooms range from £120 to £170 ($222–$315) and the on-site restaurant is one of the best in the area.

for business travelers and visitors. Although uninspired, it's a good and safe haven. Many of the bedrooms feature sitting areas with sofas and armchairs. The superior rooms offer extras such as Neutrogena toiletries and bathrobes. The small bathrooms have a shower-tub combination and adequate shelf space.

Ipswich Rd., Norwich, Norfolk NR4 6EP. ✆ **0870/400-9060.** Fax 01603/506400. www.holiday-inn.com. 120 units. £95–£115 ($176–$213) double. AE, DC, MC, V. Take A140 (Ipswich Rd.) 3km (2 miles) from city center and 1.5km (1 mile) from A11 (London Rd.). **Amenities:** Restaurant; bar; indoor pool; health club; Jacuzzi; sauna; 24-hr. room service; business services; laundry service; dry cleaning; nonsmoking rooms; rooms for those with limited mobility. *In room:* TV w/pay movies, dataport, coffeemaker, hair dryer, safe in some rooms, trouser press.

Pearl Continental Hotel   The 18th-century former home of Norwich's Lord Mayor is now an affordable hotel. The refurbished bedrooms are in the main building and in two semidetached cottages. The cottages have bay windows and wooden beams, as well as a private garden. Most bedrooms are midsize, each with a comfortable bed, plus a bathroom with a shower-tub combination; some are big enough for families.

116 Thorpe Rd., Norwich, Norfolk NR1 1RU. ✆ **01603/620302.** Fax 01603/761706. www.pc-hotels.co.uk. 37 units. £76 ($141) double. Rates include English breakfast. AE, MC, V. Take Thorpe Rd. 1km (½ mile) east of city center. **Amenities:** Restaurant; bar; limited room service; babysitting; laundry service; dry cleaning; non-smoking rooms. *In room:* TV, dataport, coffeemaker.

WHERE TO DINE

Adlard's 🏵🏵🏵 MODERN BRITISH   Chef/proprietor David Adlard and his head chef, Tom Kerridge, are clearly the culinary stars of Norwich. This stylish dining room has a clean crisp decor of green and white, with candlelit tables and a collection of paintings. David sees to it that service is correct in every way but also relaxed enough to make diners comfortable. The chef specializes in modern British cookery, bringing his own interpretation to every dish. These might include cannelloni stuffed with ratatouille and tomato coulis, or breast of duck with confit of cabbage and wild mushroom.

79 Upper St. Giles St. ✆ **01603/633522.** Reservations recommended. Lunch main courses £7–£20 ($13–$37); dinner main courses £17–£20 ($31–$37); 2-course lunch £12 ($22); 3-course lunch £17 ($31). AE, MC, V. Tues–Sat 12:30–2pm; Mon–Sat 7–10pm.

The Belgian Monk BELGIAN   Set in the heart of Norwich, within an antique building very close to the Madderhouse Theatre, this restaurant focuses on the hearty, heady grills, stews, and shellfish of Belgium. Menu items include at least five different preparations of mussels; grilled monkfish with hollandaise sauce; a richly scented version of beef and Belgian beer pie; and pan-fried cray-fish with a Pernod-flavored cream sauce. Any of these may be preceded with Belgian-style pâté or smoked herring and white bean salad. There's a wine list here but most of the locals tend to avoid it in favor of beer, which you'll order from a comprehensive list of dark and blond Belgian beers. Most visitors opt for a seat beneath the massive ceiling beams of the street-level dining room, but there's additional seating upstairs if you prefer.

7 Pottergate. ✆ **01603/767222.** Reservations recommended. Main courses £6.95–£17 ($13–$31); daily specials, at lunch and dinner, cost £6.95 ($13) for 2 main courses, served only to tables of 2 or more diners at a time. AE, MC, V. Mon–Fri noon–3pm and 5:30–10pm; Sat noon–10pm.

St. Benedict's ENGLISH/FRENCH   This modern brasserie gives patrons a warm greeting in a contemporary and rather simple setting, along with afford-able and well-prepared food. The chef, Nigel Raffles, shops for some of the freshest of market produce and fashions it into a series of tasty dishes. We recently took delight in his double-baked vegetarian and cheese soufflé and found the slow-cooked crispy duck perfection itself. It came with a cinnamon sauce and a side of sweet-and-sour red cabbage. The filet of lemon sole is dusted in bread crumbs and pan seared, and made extra enjoyable by the Café de Paris butter and a timbale of watercress and local brown shrimp. The lip-smacking desserts include a luxurious ice praline parfait.

St. Benedict's St. (© **01603/765377.** Reservations recommended. Main courses £9–£12 ($17–$22). AE, DC, MC, V. Tues–Sat noon–2pm and 7–10pm.

NORWICH AFTER DARK

From fine art to pop art, there's quite a lot happening around Norwich at night. Information on almost all of it can be found at the box office of the Theatre Royal, Theatre Street (© **01603/630000;** www.theatreroyalnorwich.co.uk), where you can also pick up tickets to just about any event.

The Theatre Royal hosts touring companies performing drama, opera, ballet, and modern dance. The reduced Shakespeare Company troupe are among the regular visitors. Ticket prices run from £4 to £15 ($7.40–$27), with senior and student discounts usually available for Wednesday, Thursday, and Saturday matinees. The box office is open Monday through Saturday from 9:30am to 8pm on performance days, closing at 6pm on nonperformance days.

Hosting productions of classic drama on most evenings, the **Norwich Playhouse,** Gun Wharf, 42–58 St. George's St. (© **01603/598598;** www.norwich playhouse.co.uk), offers tickets ranging from £6 to £15 ($11–$28). The box office is open daily from 9:30am until 8pm.

An Elizabethan-style theater, the **Maddermarket Theatre,** 1 St. John's Alley (© **01603/620917;** www.maddermarket.co.uk), is home to the amateur Norwich Players' productions of classical and contemporary drama. Tickets, ranging from £5 to £15 ($9.25–$28), and schedules are available at the box office, Monday through Saturday from 10am to 9pm and from 10am to 5pm on nonperformance days.

The city's **Theatre in the Parks** (© **01603/212137**) includes about 40 outdoor performances every summer in various outdoor venues.

Located in a converted medieval church, **Norwich Puppet Theatre,** St. James, Whitefriars (© **01603/629921;** www.puppettheatre.co.uk), offers original puppet shows most afternoons and some mornings in an octagonal studio that holds about 50 people. Tickets are £5.50 ($10) for adults, £4 ($7.40) students and seniors, and £3.75 ($6.95) for children 16 and under, and are available at the box office Monday through Friday from 9:30am to 5pm, and on Saturday on days of performances.

The most versatile entertainment complex in town, the **Norwich Arts Centre,** Reeves Yard, St. Benedict's Street (© **01603/660352;** www.norwichartscentre. co.uk), hosts performances of ballet, comedy, and poetry, and has an emphasis on ethnic music. Tickets are £6 to £15 ($11–$28), and the box office is open Monday through Friday from 9:30am to 5pm, and Saturday from 11am to 4pm. On days of performances, the box office is open until 9pm.

Before or after your cultural event, check out the local culture at **Adam and Eve,** 17 Bishopgate (© **01603/667423**), the oldest pub in Norwich, founded in 1249, which serves a well-kept John Smith's or Old Peculiar. **The Gardener's Arms,** 2–4 Timberhill (© **01603/621447**), pours Boddington's and London Pride to a lively crowd of locals and students.

The East Midlands

This region is a mix of dreary industrial sections and incredible scenery, particularly in the **Peak District National Park,** centered in Derbyshire. Byron said that the landscapes in the Peak District rivaled those of Switzerland and Greece. In the East Midlands, you'll also find the tulip land of **Lincolnshire,** the 18th-century spa of **Buxton** in Derbyshire, and the remains of Robin Hood's **Sherwood Forest** in Nottinghamshire. George Washington looked to **Sulgrave Manor** in Northamptonshire as his ancestral home. If you have Pilgrims in your past, you can trace your roots to the East Midlands.

Except for Sulgrave Manor and **Althorp House,** where Princess Di spent her girlhood, Northamptonshire is not on the tourist circuit. If you do decide to stop here, the best place to base is in **Northampton,** the capital.

In **Leicestershire,** you can use the industrialized county town of Leicester as a base to explore many sights in the countryside, including **Belvoir Castle,** the setting for Steven Spielberg's movie *Young Sherlock Holmes,* and **Bosworth Battlefield,** site of one of England's most important battles.

Derbyshire is noted primarily for the Peak District National Park, but it also has a number of historic homes—notably **Chatsworth,** the home of the 11th duke of Devonshire. The best places to base yourself here are in **Buxton** and **Bakewell.**

In Nottinghamshire, the city of **Nottingham** is a good center for exploring what's left of Sherwood Forest, the legendary stomping grounds of Robin Hood.

If you're headed for Lincolnshire, the highlight is the cathedral city of **Lincoln** itself, with stopovers at the old seaport of **Boston,** which lent its name to the famous American city.

1 Northampton

111km (69 miles) NW of London; 66km (41 miles) NE of Oxford

In the heart of the Midlands, Northamptonshire has been inhabited since Paleolithic times. Traces have been found here of Beaker and other Bronze Age people, and you can still see remains of a number of Iron Age hill-forts. Two Roman roads—now Watling and Ermine streets—ran through the county, and relics of Roman settlements have been discovered at Towcester, Whilton, Irchester, and Castor. West Saxons and Anglicans invaded in the 7th century. In 655, the first abbey was established at Medehamstede, now Peterborough. In the Middle Ages, castles and manor houses dotted a country rich in cattle, sheep farms, and the production of leatherwork.

American visitors mostly come today to see Sulgrave Manor, George Washington's ancestral home.

Fortified after 1066 by Simon de Senlis (St. Liz), Northampton, the administrative and political center of Northamptonshire was a favorite meeting place of Norman and Plantagenet kings.

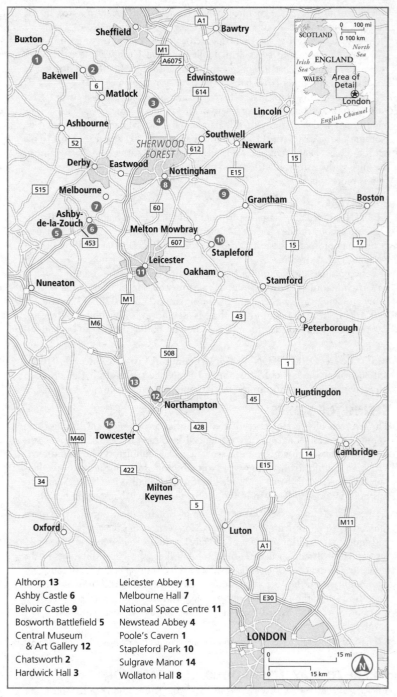

The East Midlands

Buxton
Sheffield
A1
Bawtry
M1
A6075
Bakewell
Chatsworth 2
6
Matlock
Edwinstowe
614
Ashbourne
3
Lincoln
52
4
Southwell
SHERWOOD
FOREST
612
Newark
Derby
Eastwood
15
515
Melbourne
Nottingham
E15
7
8
60
9
Grantham
Boston
Ashby-
de-la-Zouch
6
Melton Mowbray
5
453
607
10
Stapleford
15
17
Leicester
11
Oakham
Nuneaton
M1
Stamford
M6
43
Peterborough
508
1
13
12
Huntingdon
Northampton
45
14
428
Towcester
M40
14
Cambridge
422
E15
34
Milton
Keynes
5
M11
Oxford
Luton
A1
E30
LONDON

Area of Detail inset
SCOTLAND
ENGLAND
WALES
Area of Detail
London
Irish Sea
North Sea
English Channel
0   100 mi
0   100 km

0   15 mi
0   15 km

N

Althorp **13**
Ashby Castle **6**
Belvoir Castle **9**
Bosworth Battlefield **5**
Central Museum
 & Art Gallery **12**
Chatsworth **2**
Hardwick Hall **3**

Leicester Abbey **11**
Melbourne Hall **7**
National Space Centre **11**
Newstead Abbey **4**
Poole's Cavern **1**
Stapleford Park **10**
Sulgrave Manor **14**
Wollaton Hall **8**

The barons who tried to force policy changes that finally resulted in the Magna Carta besieged King John here. During the War of the Roses, Henry VI (before he achieved that title) was defeated and taken prisoner, and during the civil war, Northampton stuck with Parliament and Cromwell. On the River Nene, Northampton has long been an important center for the production of boots, shoes, and other leatherwork.

Historical records show that, before a fire destroyed the medieval city in 1675, Northampton was a fascinating town architecturally. Defoe once called it "the handsomest and best town in this part of England." That is no longer true. Nothing of the castle (ca. 1100) where Thomas à Becket stood trial in 1164 is left standing. The town of today was created essentially after the railway came in the mid–19th century. If ancient and medieval architecture is your interest, Lincoln is more appealing.

ESSENTIALS

GETTING THERE Trains depart from London's Euston Station every 30 minutes throughout the day for the 1-hour trip to Northampton. For information in Northampton and the rest of the Midlands, call ℂ **0845/748-4950** or visit www.railtrack.co.uk.

Between three and five motor coaches depart every day from London's Victoria Coach Station, requiring about 2 hours for the ride to Northampton, with many annoying stops in between. For information, call ℂ **020/7529-2000.**

If driving from London, follow the M1 due north to junction 15, then follow the signs into Northampton. Depending on traffic, the trek takes about an hour.

VISITOR INFORMATION The **Northampton Visitor Centre** (ℂ **01604/ 838800**) is at the Central Museum and Art Gallery, Guildhall Rd. It's open Monday through Saturday from 10am to 5pm and Sunday from 2 to 5pm.

SEEING THE SIGHTS

The **Church of the Holy Sepulchre,** on Sheep Street, is one of five Norman round churches in England. It was founded by Simon de Senlis, a famous veteran of the First Crusade. You can see its circular ambulatory and round nave. Victorian Gothic architecture swept Northampton after the coming of the railway, and the style is best exemplified by the **Guildhall** on St. Giles Square. It was built by Edward Godwin in the 1860s, an architect then only in his 20s.

Central Museum & Art Gallery One of Britain's most unusual provincial museums—and Northampton's key attraction—celebrates the city's rich cultural and industrial traditions. Proud of the city's status as the boot- and shoe-making capital of Britain, it devotes much of its gallery space to exhibitions of the largest collection of antique shoes in the world, spanning centuries of footwear, with emphasis on the Victorian era. Also on display: artworks from Italy spanning the 15th to the 18th centuries, a wide spectrum from the history of British art, and objects uncovered from nearby archaeological sites dating from the Stone Age.

Guildhall Rd. ℂ **01604/238548.** www.northampton.gov.uk/museums. Free admission. Mon–Sat 10am–5pm; Sun 2–5pm.

WHERE TO STAY IN & AROUND NORTHAMPTON

Crossroads and Daventry Premier Lodge A fine and decent choice, this hotel was acquired in the early 1990s by a competent but unpretentious nationwide chain, which enlarged and renovated it into a simple and rather standard format suited to business travelers. Hints of the building's original antique core are visible in the stone facade, which originally sheltered a tollbooth that taxed travelers between Northampton and nearby Daventry. Bedrooms are boxy and have the standard comforts, plus compact bathrooms with shower.

High St., Weedon, Northamptonshire NN7 4PX. (℃ **0870/700-1520.** Fax 0870/990-6365. www.premierlodge. co.uk. 46 units. £50 ($93) double. AE, DC, MC, V. Take A45 13km (8 miles) west of Northampton. **Amenities:** Restaurant; bar; nonsmoking rooms; rooms for those with limited mobility. *In room:* TV, dataport, coffeemaker, hair dryer.

Northampton Marriott Hotel (Kids)

Unlike the Moat House (see below), this 1980s-vintage hotel, 5km (3 miles) east of Northampton's center, offers a country setting and easy access to a golf course. Bedrooms are comfortably outfitted with monochromatic modern furnishings. Twelve rooms are large enough for families. All units come with shower, and some have a combination tub and shower. With a renovation completed in 2001, this hotel is better maintained than any other lodgings in town. The staff is friendly and the hotel competently run.

Eagle Dr., Northampton, Northamptonshire NN4 7HW. (℃ **01604/768700.** Fax 01604/769011. www.marriott. com. 120 units. Mon–Thurs £140 ($259) double, £180 ($333) studio king. Fri–Sun £80 ($148) double, £120 ($222) studio king. Rates include English breakfast. AE, DC, MC, V. **Amenities:** Restaurant; bar; indoor pool; Jacuzzi; 24-hr. room service; massage; laundry service. *In room:* TV w/pay movies, minibar, coffeemaker, hair dryer, iron/ironing board, trouser press.

Northampton Moat House (Kids)

The Moat House is often booked by conventioneers and business travelers who appreciate its comfort and its location near the heart of town. Built in the mid-1970s in an efficient, no-nonsense format of concrete and glass, it lies close to the western edge of the Inner Ring Road. The restaurant and bar have exposed stone, flickering candles, and varnished wood trim. The level of comfort in the renovated bedrooms is what you'd expect from an upscale chain hotel. Four units are large enough for families. Bathrooms are well equipped mainly with tub and shower. Overall, it's a fine if not particularly historic choice for an overnight stay.

Silver St., Northampton, Northamptonshire NN1 2TA. (℃ **01604/739988.** Fax 01604/230614. www.moat househotels.com. 145 units. £96–£132 ($178–$244) double. AE, DC, MC, V. Free parking. **Amenities:** Restaurant; bar; indoor pool; health club; Jacuzzi; sauna; 24-hr. room service; laundry service; nonsmoking rooms; rooms for those with limited mobility. *In room:* TV, dataport, coffeemaker, hair dryer, trouser press.

WHERE TO DINE

The restaurant situation in Northampton's center is pretty dismal, with an exception or two. Many visitors prefer to dine at the Marriott (see above).

Blue Plate Café (Finds) BRITISH/INTERNATIONAL One of our favorite restaurants in Northampton is hip, alive, and permeated with a spirit you may expect in big-city London. Sheathed with blue tiles and ringed with black-upholstered banquettes, it occupies what was originally conceived as a bakery. Large-scale ovens still provide decorative interest, and an overhead skylight floods part of the interior with sunlight. An accommodating staff proposes menu items that change every 2 weeks, but which may include Caesar salad, filet of beef with black peppercorn sauce; blinis stuffed with smoked haddock and salmon; bang-bang salad garnished with noodles, satay sauce, and spicy chicken; and such comfort food as macaroni and cheese and fish and chips.

The Ridings. (℃ 01604/620020. Reservations recommended for dinner. Main courses £8.50–£17 ($16–$31); fixed-price 2-course lunch £9.50 ($18), fixed-price 3-course lunch £13 ($23). AE, DC, MC, V. Mon–Fri noon–2:30pm and 5:30–10:30pm; Sat noon–11pm.

SULGRAVE MANOR:
GEORGE WASHINGTON'S ANCESTRAL HOME $\mathcal{R}$

Sulgrave Manor $\mathcal{R}$ American visitors will be especially interested in this small mid-16th-century Tudor manor, the ancestral home of George Washington. As part of a plan to dissolve the monasteries, Henry VIII sold the priory-owned manor in 1539 to Lawrence Washington, who had been mayor of Northampton. The Washington family occupied Sulgrave for more than a century, but in 1656, Colonel John Washington left for the New World. Born in Virginia, George Washington was a direct descendant of Lawrence (seven generations removed).

A group of English people bought the manor in 1914 in honor of the friendship between Britain and the United States. Appropriate furnishings and portraits, including a Gilbert Stuart original of the first president, have been donated from both sides of the Atlantic. The Washington family coat of arms on the main doorway—two bars and a trio of mullets—is believed to have been the inspiration for the Stars and Stripes.

Manor Rd. $\copyright$ **01295/760205.** www.stratford.co.uk/sulgrave. Admission £5.75 ($11) adults, £2.75 ($5.10) children ages 5–16, free for children under 5. Apr–Oct Tues–Thurs and Sat–Sun 2–5:30pm. From Northampton, drive 29km (18 miles) southwest on A43, then B4525 to Sulgrave. From Stratford-upon-Avon, take A422 via Banbury (whose famous cross entered nursery-rhyme fame) and continue to Brackley; 9.5km (6 miles) from Brackley, leave A422 and join B4525, which goes to the tiny village of Sulgrave. Signs will lead you to Sulgrave Manor.

ALTHORP: THE GIRLHOOD HOME &
FINAL RESTING PLACE OF PRINCESS DIANA $\mathcal{R}$

Althorp   Built in 1508 by Sir John Spencer, Althorp has brought a sometimes unwelcome dose of fame to the surrounding rural area as the girlhood home of Princess Diana. It was glamorously revived by Raine Spencer, Diana's step-mother. At least part of the beauty and historical authenticity of this frequently renovated site is the result of her efforts.

Since the death of Lord Spencer, Diana's father, the house has been under the jurisdiction of Charles Spencer, Diana's older brother. Its collection includes paintings by Van Dyck, Reynolds, Gainsborough, and Rubens, an assortment of rare French and English furniture, and porcelain by Sèvres, Bow, and Chelsea.

Following the tragic death of Princess Diana in August 1997, a ticket to Althorp House became extremely difficult to obtain. More than 200 24-hour telephone lines handle orders for tickets. Althorp is open to the public only from July 1, Diana's birthday, to September 30.

Diana was buried on an island in an artificial lake on the property. Visitors do not have access to the island but have a clear view of it across the lake. A museum celebrates Diana's life, complete with schoolgirl letters, her stunning silk wedding dress, and some of her haute couture clothes.

The museum also shows poignant films of her as a carefree child dancing in the gardens and later as a mother riding with her sons, William and Harry, plus videos that include the moving footage of her funeral. The museum makes no mention of Dodi al-Fayed, who died with her in the Paris car crash, and certainly no mention of her former lover, James Hewitt. Her estranged husband is also not featured prominently in the exhibition.

Facilities on-site include a restaurant and a shop selling a range of souvenirs associated with Diana. The estate states that these souvenirs do not "cheapen her memory in any way." You decide.

9.5km (6 miles) northwest of Northampton on A428 in Althorp, near Harlestone. ☎ **1604/772110.** www. althorp.com. Admission £12 ($21) adults, £9.50 ($18) seniors, £6 ($11) children 5–17, free for children under 5, £29 ($53) family ticket. July 1–Sept 30 daily 11am–5pm (last admission 1 hr. earlier). Closed Aug 31.

2 Leicester

172km (107 miles) NW of London; 69km (43 miles) NE of Birmingham; 39km (24 miles) NE of Coventry; 42km (26 miles) S of Nottingham

Hang on to your hats, because this county town is definitely no Sleepy Hollow. Leicester, pronounced *Les*-ter, one of the 10 largest cities in England, overflows with hustle and bustle and is by far the most cosmopolitan city in the East Midlands. This city of firsts—Beethoven's music was first performed here, the BBC's first local radio station was BBC Radio Leicester—thrives on the spirit of discovery and adventure. More recently, it gave birth to genetic fingerprinting.

Though it has some historic attractions, think of Leicester as a base for exploring the surrounding countryside. Its real lure with locals and tourists alike is its shopping, art scene, and nightlife.

ESSENTIALS

GETTING THERE   Trains depart from London's St. Pancras Station every 25 minutes throughout the day for Leicester, a trip of about 90 minutes. The fare costs £37 ($68) each way on the day of your trip. For schedules and information, call ☎ **0845/748-4950** or visit www.railtrack.co.uk.

About eight buses a day leave London's Victoria Coach Station for Leicester. They call at several secondary stops en route, thus taking 2 hours and 45 minutes each way. The round-trip fare is £33 ($61) if you stay overnight but only £15 ($27) if you return the same day. For information, call ☎ **0870/580-8080** or visit www.nationalexpress.com.

If you're driving from London, follow the M1 north to junction 21 toward Leicester. The drive takes 2 hours.

VISITOR INFORMATION   The main tourist information office is at 7–9 Every St., Town Hall Square (☎ **01162/998888**). It's open Monday through Wednesday and Friday from 9am to 5:30pm, Thursday from 10am to 5:30pm, and Saturday from 9am to 5pm. They'll supply a useful map. You can book Blue Badge guided walks by calling ☎ **01162/862252.**

SPECIAL EVENTS   The **Leicester Early Music Festival** (☎ **01162/709984;** www.earlymusicleicester.co.uk) takes place in May and June. Tickets for the whole series cost £20 to £25 ($37–$46). Also in June, the **Leicester International Music Festival** (☎ **01162/254916;** www.musicfestival.co.uk) attracts some of the biggest names in classical music. Ticket prices vary, but average £5 to £15 ($9.25–$28).

EXPLORING THE TOWN

Leicester is worth a look if you have an afternoon to spare. In addition to the sights mentioned below, the town has a boating lake, riverside walks, and ornamental gardens.

An exciting wave of new shops has opened in Leicester. In addition to Victorian-style **Shires Shopping Centre,** High Street, with its designer and collectible stores, wide walkways, fountains, and sunny skylights, there's **St. Martins Square** in the city center, which has given new life to old restored buildings, with new retailers, cafes, and teashops. A wealth of specialty shops—out .5km (¼ mile) on either side of the railway station—and several antiques stores line Oxford Street and Western Boulevard.

Venture out from the center of town to Belgrave Road, and you'll discover the **Golden Mile.** This neighborhood sells more gold than any other of its size in all of Europe, and the store windows along Belgrave Road overflow with fine Indian silks, organzas, and cottons. Sari shops also generally carry a variety of accessories including bags, jewelry, shoes, and shawls.

Jewry Wall and Archeology Museum   Set near the excavation of an ancient Roman bath, this museum has nothing at all to do with Jewish history. Its name derives from a corruption of the Norman French "Jurad," which referred to the governing magistrates of an early medieval town, who used to gather in the shadow of this wall for their municipal decisions. More than 12m (40 ft.) high, the wall is higher than any other piece of ancient Roman architecture in Britain. Exhibits within the museum include a pair of ancient Roman mosaics, the Peacock Pavement and the Blackfriars Mosaic, which are the finest of their kind in the British Midlands. Each was laboriously sliced from the masonry of ancient villas within the district and set into new masonry beds here.

St. Nicholas Circle (about .5km/¼ mile from the town center, adjacent to the Holiday Inn). ✆ **01162/473021.** Free admission. Daily dawn–dusk during summer. Winter Mon–Sat 10am–4pm, Sun 1–4pm.

Leicester Abbey   In a verdant public park favored by joggers and picnickers, about 1km (¾ mile) north of Leicester's historic core, these evocative, poetically shattered remains are all that's left of the richest Augustinian monastery in England, built in 1132. In 1530, Cardinal Wolsey came here to die, demoralized and broken after his political and religious conflicts with Henry VIII. The abbey was torn down during the Reformation, and stones were used in the construction of Cavendish House next door.

Abbey Park, Abbey Park Rd. ✆ **01162/221000.** Free admission. Daily dawn–dusk during summer. Winter daily 8am–4pm.

Leicester Guildhall   Built in stages between the 14th and 16th centuries, the city's most prominent public building was Leicester's first town hall and contains one of the oldest libraries in Britain. Plaques commemorate its role as a die-hard last bastion of the Parliamentarians during the civil war. On its ground floor, you'll see a 19th-century police station with a pair of original prison cells, whose mournful effigies afford a powerful testimony to the horrors of the Victorian penal system. Shakespeare's troupe is said to have appeared here.

Guildhall Lane. ✆ **01162/532569.** Free admission. Winter Mon–Sat 10am–4pm, Sun 1–4pm; summer Mon–Sat 10am–5pm, Sun 1–5pm.

Leicestershire Museum and Art Gallery   This multipurpose museum has two distinctly separate features. The street level contains exhibits of archaeology and natural history: a dinosaur bone found in a field near Leicester; a collection of Egyptian mummies and artifacts brought back to the Midlands by Thomas Cook, the 19th-century travel mogul; and geological exhibits. One floor above is a collection of paintings by British and European artists (including some by Gainsborough) from the 18th through 20th centuries. The collection of early-20th-century canvasses by German expressionists is one of the largest in Europe.

53 New Walk. ✆ **01162/554100.** Free admission but donations accepted. Oct–Mar Mon–Sat 10am–4pm, Sun 1–4pm; Apr–Sept Mon–Sat 10am–5pm, Sun 1–5pm. Closed Dec 24–26 and Jan 1.

St. Martin's Cathedral (Leicester Cathedral)   It may not have the soaring grandeur of the cathedrals of York or Lincoln, but this is the most venerated and

> ### ⟨ Moments   Launch Yourself into Space
>
> The latest attraction in Leicester is the **National Space Centre,** Exploration Drive (✆ **0870/607-7223;** www.nssc.co.uk), Britain's only attraction dedicated to space science and astronomy. It is crowned by a futuristic Rocket Tower. Allow 3 hours for a journey of discovery where stories, personalities, and technology of the past and present are used to explain space and how it will affect your future. You're taken through five theme galleries, seeing space rockets, satellites, and capsules, and taking part in hands-on activities. Admission is £8.95 ($17) for adults, £6.95 ($13) students and ages 4 to 16. Free 3 and under. A family ticket costs £28 to £34 ($52–$63). Hours year-round are Tuesday through Friday from 10am to 5pm, Saturday and Sunday 10am to 6pm (last admission half-hour earlier).

historic church in Leicester. In 1086, it was one of the region's parish churches, enlarged during the 1300s and 1500s. In 1927, it was designated as the cathedral of Leicester, adding considerably to its pomp and circumstance. The oak vaulting beneath the building's north porch is one of the most unusual treatments of its kind in England. For walking tours, contact the tourist office.

1 St. Martin's Lane E. ✆ **01162/625294.** Free admission. Daily 7:30am–4:30pm.

WHERE TO STAY

Ramada Jarvis Hotel ✪   This is one of the finest choices in the city itself. When it was built in 1898, no expense was spared. The original oak and mahogany paneling has been retained, and even though the building was enlarged in the 1970s. Bedrooms are more streamlined and contemporary than the semi-antique public areas suggest. All units come with well-kept bathrooms containing shower units.

73 Granby St., Leicester, Leicestershire LE1 6ES. ✆ **01162/555599.** Fax 01162/544736. www.ramadajarvis. co.uk. 104 units. Mon–Thurs £125 ($231) double, £165 ($305) suite. Fri–Sun £88 ($163) double, £165 ($305) suite. Weekend rates include English breakfast. AE, DC, MC, V. **Amenities:** Restaurant; bar, health club nearby (sauna, pool, massage complimentary for guests), 24-hr. room service, laundry service; dry cleaning; nonsmoking rooms; rooms for those with limited mobility. *In room:* TV, dataport, coffeemaker, hair dryer, trouser press.

Rothley Court Hotel ✪ *Finds*   This hotel stands on the edge of Charnwood Forest, a royal hunting ground for centuries. In 1231, Henry III granted the manor and "soke" (right to hold court under feudal law) to the Knights Templar. The chapel erected next to the existing abbey around 1240 is second only to the Temple in London as the best-preserved Templar chapel in Britain.

On 2.4 hectares (6 acres) of grounds, the hotel is surrounded by open farmland. Stone fireplaces, oak paneling, and stained-glass windows evoke its rich historical associations. Bedrooms have been handsomely restored and are comfortable, with modern conveniences and a number of antique furnishings. The less desirable rooms with standard furnishings are in a modern annex. Each comes with a compact private bathroom with adequate shelf space and a shower stall.

Westfield Lane, Rothley, Leicester, Leicestershire LE7 7LG. ✆ **01162/374141.** Fax 01162/374483. www.old english.co.uk. 32 units. £125 ($231) double; £150 ($278) suite. Rates include English breakfast. AE, MC, V. Head 9.5km (6 miles) north of Leicester on B5328 Rd., just off A6 between Leicester and Loughborough. **Amenities:** Restaurant; bar; limited room service; babysitting; laundry service; dry cleaning; nonsmoking rooms. *In room:* TV, dataport, coffeemaker, hair dryer, trouser press.

Finds Two Great Country-House Hotels

Outside Melton Mowbray are two of the great country houses of England, and the finest places to stay or dine in Leicestershire itself.

Stapleford Park ★★★, 8km (5 miles) east of Melton Mowbray on Highway B676 (Stapleford Road; ⓒ **01572/787522;** www.stapleford. co.uk), has just completed a multi-million dollar renovation—and has it all. Capability Brown laid out the 202 hectares (500 acres) of parkland surrounding the mansion, with parts dating from the 16th century. The site has a school of falconry, colonies of trained hawks and owls, a state-of-the-art gym and health club, and a group of hunt masters who take guests out on game shoots. Golfers can tee up at the Scottish-style 18-hole course, and those who prefer pampering can head for the brand-new Clarins spa. The hotel's lush bedrooms are outfitted with modern comforts and 18th-century antiques, and offer 24-hour room service. Rates for the 52 units, which have televisions and telephones, are £233 to £488 ($431–$903) for a double, with suites priced from £522 ($966). Bedrooms are truly splendid and eclectic, each designed by a sponsor, such as Wedgwood, MGM, or Tiffany. Bathrooms are equally sumptuous with deluxe toiletries. Major credit cards are accepted.

Three restaurants under the auspices of chef Wayne Vicarage serve elegant British cuisine with Caribbean and Asian accents. The main dining room here is opulent and highly acclaimed. You'll dine in a lavishly outfitted dining room that's as spectacular as 400 years of British tradition and gobs of money can provide. The spa restaurant, located in the golf clubhouse, serves up a dietician-aided menu of organic food and other tasty creations for the health minded.

Another great country house with a fabulous restaurant is **Hambleton Hall** ★★★, on the A606, 5km (3 miles) east of Oldham and 24km (15 miles) east of Leicester, in the small village of Hambleton, near Oakham, Leicestershire (ⓒ **01572/756991;** www.hambletonhall.com).

Built in 1881 as a hunting lodge by Victorian industrialist Walter Marshall, it sits on 4.8 hectares (12 acres) of landscaped park at the edge of an artificial lake, Rutland Water. Everything about the place evokes a Victorian/Edwardian country house. Bedrooms have the chintz curtains and Victorian antiques you'd expect. Each comes with a sumptuous bed and a luxurious bathroom with a combination tub and shower. Terraced gardens run down to the edge of the lake. Rates for the 17 rooms, which have televisions and telephones, are £186 to £355 ($344–$657) for a double, including continental breakfast. A charming cottage is also available, starting at £500 ($925). Major credit cards are accepted.

You dine here amid walls upholstered in russet-colored silk and order from a menu that changes according to the practiced but imaginative whims of chef Aaron Patterson, who takes full advantage of the game available from the surrounding countryside. Menu items include filet of red mullet with sweet pepper sauce, or ravioli of langoustines. Open daily from noon to 1:30pm and 7 to 9:30pm; reservations are strongly recommended.

WHERE TO DINE

Rothley Court Hotel Restaurant ENGLISH   Part of the fun of dining at this hotel (see above) involves a pre- or postmeal visit to one of Britain's best-preserved strongholds of the Knights Templar, a 13th-century semifanatical sect that played an important role in the Crusades. Within the venerable walls of a historic manor house surrounded with parks and farmland, you can enjoy a sophisticated blend of modern and traditional English cuisine—say, a medley of monkfish and crayfish with lime juice, coriander, and artichoke hearts; steak Diane with Dijon mustard, shallots, mushrooms, tomatoes, and a cognac sauce; or seared filet of Scottish salmon with nut-brown butter sauce. Not all dishes reach gastronomic heights, but this is as good as it gets in the Leicester area.

Westfield Lane, Rothley. ✆ 01162/374141. Reservations recommended. Fixed-price lunch £10–£13 ($19–$25); fixed-price dinner £20 ($37) for 2 courses, £23 ($43) for 3 courses. AE, MC, V. Daily 7–9:30am, noon–2:30pm, and 6:30–9:30pm.

LEICESTER AFTER DARK

Haymarket Theatre, Wote Street, Basingstoke (✆ **01256/465566;** www. haymarket.org.uk), one of the nation's leading provincial theaters, has been the launching point for many successful West End productions, including *Hot Stuff, Me and My Girl,* and *Mack & Mabel.* Popular musicals such as these are the house specialty, but you'll find anything from contemporary drama to visiting dance companies gracing the stage.

Phoenix Arts Centre, Newarke Street (✆ **01162/554854;** www.phoenix. org.uk), hosts dance, music, and theatrical productions from around the world; local dancers, musicians, and actors also perform on its stage, and there's even an occasional film screening.

On weekends, the area around the **Clock Tower** in the center of town is alive with bustling crowds headed out to the clubs and bars on Church Gate, Silver Street, and High Street. **Creations,** 97 Church Gate (✆ **01162/629720**), is a popular club pumping out dance music until the wee hours. Open Monday, Wednesday, Friday, and Saturday only. Free before 10pm; after that, the cover ranges from £4 to £8 ($7.40–$15).

As you may expect of a university town, Leicester has a variety of pubs, but the one favored most by locals is the **Pump and Tap,** Duns Lane (✆ **01162/540324**). Stop by to sample ales by Leicestershire's two home brewers: Everards and Hoskins.

HISTORIC SIGHTS NEAR LEICESTER

Ashby Castle   If you've read Sir Walter Scott's *Ivanhoe,* you will remember Ashby-de-la-Zouch, a town that retains a pleasant country atmosphere. The main attraction here is the ruined Norman manor house, Ashby Castle, where Mary Queen of Scots was imprisoned. The building was already an antique in 1464 when its thick walls were converted into a fortress.

Ashby-de-la-Zouch (29km/18 miles northwest of Leicester). ✆ 01530/413343. Admission £3.50 ($6.50) adults, £2.75 ($5.10) students and seniors, £1.80 ($3.35) children under 16. Apr–Oct daily 10am–6pm; off season Wed–Sun 10am–4pm.

Belvoir Castle   On the northern border of Leicestershire overlooking the Vale of Belvoir (pronounced *Beaver*), Belvoir Castle has been the seat of the dukes of Rutland since the time of Henry VII. Rebuilt by Wyatt in 1816, the castle contains paintings by Holbein, Reynolds, and Gainsborough, as well as tapestries in its magnificent staterooms. The castle was the location of the movies *Little Lord*

Fauntleroy and *Young Sherlock Holmes*. In summer, it's the site of medieval joust-ing tournaments.

11km (7 miles) southwest of Grantham, between A607 to Melton Mowbray and A52 to Nottingham. ℂ 01476/870262. www.belvoircastle.com. Admission castle and grounds £8 ($15) adults, £7 ($13) stu-dents and seniors, £5 ($9.25) children 5–16, £21 ($39) family ticket (2 adults, 2 children). Mar and Oct Sun only 11am–5pm; Apr–Sept Tues–Thurs and Sat–Sun 11am–5pm.

Bosworth Battlefield Visitor Centre and Country Park   This site com-memorates the 1485 battle that ended one of England's most important con-flicts. The Battle of Bosworth ended the War of the Roses between the houses of York and Lancaster. When the fighting subsided, King Richard III, last of the Yorkists, lay dead, and Henry Tudor, a Welsh nobleman who had been banished to France to thwart his royal ambition, was proclaimed the victor. Henry thus became King Henry VII, and the Tudor dynasty was born.

Today, the appropriate standards fly where the opponents had their positions. You can see the whole scene by taking a 2km (1¾-mile) walk along the marked battle trails. In the center are exhibitions, models, book and gift shops, a cafe-teria, and a theater where an audiovisual introduction with an excerpt from the Lord Laurence Olivier film version of Shakespeare's *Richard III* is presented.

29km (18 miles) southwest of Leicester between M1 and M6 (near the town of Nuneaton). ℂ 01455/290429. Admission £3.25 ($6) adults, £2.25 ($4.15) children under 16 and seniors, family ticket £8.50 ($16). Visitor center: Apr–Oct daily 11am–5pm; Nov–Dec and Mar Sat and Sun only 11am–5pm. Closed Jan–Feb.

Melbourne Hall 🅐   Built by the bishops of Carlisle in 1133, Melbourne Hall stands in one of the most famous formal gardens in Britain. The ecclesiastical structure was restored in the 1600s by one of the cabinet ministers of Charles I and enlarged by Queen Anne's vice chamberlain. It was the home of Lord Mel-bourne, who was prime minister when Victoria ascended to the throne. Lady Palmerston later inherited the house, which contains an important collection of antique furniture and artwork. A special feature is the beautifully restored wrought-iron pergola by Robert Bakewell, noted 18th-century ironsmith.

24km (15 miles) southwest of Leicester on A50, on Church Square. ℂ 01332/862502. www.melbourne hall.com. Admission to house and garden £5 ($9.25) adults, £4 ($7.40) students and seniors, £3 ($5.55) chil-dren 6–15, free for children 5 and under. House only, £3 ($5.55) adults, £2.50 ($4.65) students and seniors, £1.50 ($2.80) children 5–15. Gardens only, £3 ($5.55) adults, £2 ($3.70) students, children 5–15, and seniors. House open Aug only, daily 2–5pm (closed the first 3 Mon of the month). Gardens Apr–Sept Wed, Sat–Sun, and bank holidays 1:30–5:30pm.

3 Derbyshire & Peak District National Park

The most magnificent scenery in the Midlands is found in Derbyshire, between Nottinghamshire and Staffordshire. Some travelers avoid this part of the coun-try because it's ringed by the industrial sprawl of Manchester, Leeds, Sheffield, and Derby. But missing this area is a pity, for Derbyshire has actually been less defaced by industry than its neighbors.

The north of the county, with Peak District National Park, contains water-falls, hills, moors, green valleys, and dales. In the south, the land is more level, with pastoral meadows. Dovedale, Chee Dale, and Millers Dale are worth a detour.

EXPLORING PEAK DISTRICT NATIONAL PARK 🅐🅐

Peak District National Park covers some 1,404 square km (542 sq. miles), most of it in Derbyshire, with some spilling over into South Yorkshire and

Staffordshire. It stretches from Holmfirth in the north to Ashbourne in the south, and from Sheffield in the east to Macclesfield in the west. The best central place to stay overnight is Buxton (see below).

The peak in the name is a bit misleading, because there is no actual peak— the highest point is just 630m (2,100 ft.). The park has some 4,000 walking trails that cover some of the most beautiful hill country in England.

The southern portion of the park, called **White Peak,** is filled with limestone hills, tiny villages, old stone walls, and hidden valleys. August and September are the best and most beautiful times to hike these rolling hills.

In the north, called **Dark Peak,** the scenery changes to rugged moors and deep gullies. This area is best visited in the spring when the purple heather, so beloved by Emily Brontë, comes into bloom.

Many come to the park not for its natural beauty but for the **"well dressings."** A unique park tradition held between May and August, this festival with pagan origins is best viewed in the villages of Eyam, Youlgrave, Monyash, and Worksworth, which lie within the park's parameters. Local tourist offices will supply details. The dressings began as pagan offerings to local "water spirits," but later became part of Christian ceremonies. Dressings of the wells take place from early May to August of every year. Designs are pricked on large boards covered in clay. The board is then decorated with grasses, lichens, bark, seeds, and flowers and placed by the spring or well and blessed.

If you're planning an extensive visit to the park, write for details to the **Peak Park Joint Planning Board,** National Park Office, Aldern House, Bakewell, Derbyshire DE45 1AE (© **01629/816200**). A list of publications will be sent to you, and you can order according to your wishes.

GETTING TO THE PARK   You can reach Buxton (see below) by train from Manchester. It's also possible to travel by bus, the Transpeak, taking 3½ hours from Manchester to Nottingham, with stops at such major centers as Buxton, Bakewell, Matlock, and Matlock Bath. If you're planning to use public transportation, consider the **Derbyshire Wayfarer,** sold at various rail and bus stations; for £7.50 ($14) for adults or £3.75 ($6.95) for students and children, you can ride all the bus and rail lines within the peak district for a day.

If you're driving, the main route is the A515 north from Birmingham, with Buxton as the gateway. From Manchester, Route 6 heads southeast to Buxton.

GETTING AROUND THE PARK   Many visitors prefer to walk from one village to another. If you're not so hearty, you can take local buses, which connect various villages. Instead of the usual Sunday slowdown in bus service, more buses run on that day than on weekdays because of increased demand, especially in summer.

Another popular way to explore the park is by bicycle. Park authorities operate six **Cycle Hire Centres,** renting bikes for £13 ($23) a day for adults and £7.50 ($14) for children 15 and under, with a £20 ($37) deposit, helmet included. Centers are at Mapleton Lane in Ashbourne (© **01335/343156**); near the Fairholmes Information Centre at Derwent (© **01433/651261**); near New Mills on Station Road in the Sett Valley at Hayfield (© **01663/746222**); near Matlock on the High Peak Trail at Middleton Top (© **01629/823204**); at the junction of Tissington and High Peak Trails at Parsley Hay (© **01298/ 84493**); and between Ashbourne and Leek on the A523 near the southern tip of the Manifold Trail at Waterhouses (© **01538/308609**).

BUXTON: A LOVELY BASE FOR EXPLORING THE PARK

277km (172 miles) NW of London; 61km (38 miles) NW of Derby; 40km (25 miles) SE of Manchester

One of the loveliest towns in Britain, Buxton rivaled the spa at Bath in the 18th century. Its waters were known to the Romans, whose settlement here was called *Aquae Arnemetiae*. The thermal waters were pretty much forgotten from Roman times until the reign of Queen Elizabeth I, when the baths were reactivated. Mary Queen of Scots took the waters here, brought by her caretaker, the Earl of Shrewsbury.

Buxton today is mostly the result of 18th-century development directed by the duke of Devonshire. Its spa days have come and gone, but it's still the best center for exploring the peak district. The climate is amazingly mild, considering that at 300m (1,000 ft.) altitude, Buxton is the second highest town in England.

ESSENTIALS

GETTING THERE   Trains depart from Manchester (see chapter 16) at least every hour during the day. It's a 50-minute trip.

About half a dozen buses also run between Manchester and Sheffield, stopping in Buxton en route, after a 70-minute ride.

To arrive by car, take the A6 from Manchester, heading southeast into Buxton.

VISITOR INFORMATION   The **Tourist Office** is at The Crescent (© **01298/ 25106**) and is open between March and October daily from 9:30am to 5pm; off season daily from 10am to 4pm. It provides a free pamphlet, entitled "Buxton Town Trail," that offers a map and detailed instructions for a walking tour, lasting between 75 and 90 minutes, from the town center.

SPECIAL EVENTS   The town hosts the **Buxton Festival** (© **01298/70395;** www.buxtonfestival.co.uk), a well-known opera festival, during a 2½-week period in July and August, followed by the 2½-week **Gilbert and Sullivan Festival** (© **01422/323252;** www.gs-festival.co.uk).

SEEING THE SIGHTS

Water from nine thermal wells is no longer available for spa treatments except in the hydrotherapy pool at the 9.3-hectare (23-acre) **Pavilion Gardens** (which are open at all times; admission is free). You can purchase a drink of spa waters at the tourist information center or help yourself at the public fountain across the street.

Another sight, **Poole's Cavern,** Buxton Country Park, Green Lane (© **01298/ 26978;** www.poolescavern.co.uk), is a cave that was inhabited by Stone Age people, who may have been the first to marvel at the natural vaulted roof bedecked with stalactites. Explorers can walk through the spacious galleries, viewing the incredible horizontal cave, which is electrically lighted. It is open daily mid-February to October from 10am to 5pm. Admission is £5.50 ($10) for adults, £4.50 ($8.35) for students and seniors, £3 ($5.55) for children 5 to 16, and free for kids 4 and under. A family ticket costs £14 ($26).

Set about 2km (1¼ miles) south of Buxton's town center is one of the oddest pieces of public Victorian architecture in the Midlands, **Solomon's Temple,** whose circular design may remind you of a straight castellated Tower of Pisa as interpreted by the neo-Gothic designers of Victorian England. Conceived as a folly in 1895 and donated to the city by a prominent building contractor, Solomon Mycock, it sits atop a tumulus (burial mound) from Neolithic times. Climb a small spiral staircase inside the temple for impressive views over Buxton and the surrounding countryside. It's open all the time, day and night, and admission is free.

WHERE TO STAY

Buxton's Victorian Guest House *(Finds)*   Commissioned by the duke of Devonshire in 1860, this is one of a row of elegant terraced houses lying on a promenade overlooking a lake and the 16-hectare (40-acre) Pavilion Gardens. It is also only a 2-minute walk to the Buxton Opera House. The house is spectacularly decorated and furnished with art, prints, and antiques from both the Victorian and Edwardian eras. All of the bedchambers are individually designed with soft furnishings and bedding. The standard rooms are themed and include the Victorian Craftman's Room and the Egyptian Room. There's also a family suite consisting of two bedrooms and a private bathroom. The finest accommodation is the premier room decorated in a classical Victorian style and housing a four-poster bed. Breakfast is taken in The Oriental Dining Room, the most imaginatively decorated in the Buxton area.

3A Broad Walk, Buxton, Derbyshire SK17 6JE. © **01298/78759.** Fax 01298/74732. www.buxtonvictorian. co.uk. 10 units. £65–£83 ($120–$154) double; £100 ($185) suite. MC, V. **Amenities:** Breakfast room; laundry. *In room:* TV, beverage maker, hair dryer, iron/ironing board.

Fischer's Baslow Hall ***   At the edge of the Chatsworth Estate, at the end of a winding chestnut tree-lined drive, this stately Edwardian country house is the finest choice in the area for either food or lodgings. The six bedrooms in the main house are decorated with lavish fabrics and contain ornate plasterwork ceilings, along with Egyptian cotton bedding and traditionally styled bathrooms with tub and shower. We prefer these accommodations, although you can also rent a large double in the Garden House, built of locally quarried stone with high ceilings and exposed timber joists. In contrast to the main house, the garden rooms are more modern and more minimalist. The kitchen is presided over by Max Fischer, one of the area's finest chefs.

Baslow Hall, Calver Rd., Baslow, Derbyshire DE45 1RR. © **01246/583259.** Fax 01246/583818. www. fischers-baslowhall.co.uk. 11 units. £150–£180 ($278–$333) double. AE, DC, MC, V. **Amenities:** Restaurant; bar. *In room:* TV, safe (in some).

Old Hall *   This is one of the most historic old inns of Derbyshire. Although other hostelries make the same claim, this is reputed to be the oldest hotel in England, a 16th-century building overlooking the Buxton Opera House. Mary Queen of Scots stayed here on several occasions between 1573 and 1582. Daniel Defoe, writing as a guest in 1727, called Old Hall "indeed a very special place," and it remains so in its restored form today. Its mellowed walls and ancient rooms evoke the past, yet it is modernized inside and has kept up-to-date with the times. The bedrooms are generally spacious and each is comfortably furnished with a well-maintained bathroom with tub and shower. Nostalgia buffs seek out Queen Mary's Bower in the oldest part of the hotel, still with its original moldings and a four-poster bed. Even if not a guest, you may want to visit to enjoy an excellent table d'hôte menu in the stately dining room.

The Square, Buxton, Derbyshire SK17 6BD. © **01298/22841.** Fax 01298/72437. www.oldhallhotelbuxton. co.uk. 38 units. £112–£140 ($207–$259) double. AE, DC, MC, V. **Amenities:** Restaurant; 3 bars; fitness center; 24-hr. room service; babysitting; laundry. *In room:* TV, coffeemaker, hair dryer, iron/ironing board.

The Palace **   The beautiful restored Victorian architecture of this landmark returns Buxton to its heyday as a spa. For service, cuisine, and comfort, this is the premier choice within the town itself. It maintains tradition but with all the modern facilities such as a large swimming pool. In fact, the comfort is so grand you may want to make The Palace your base for touring the area instead of treating it like a 1-night stopover. The bedrooms are comfortably well furnished, though often falling short in style. Sometimes they are equipped with half-tester beds, and they are generally spacious, with newly restored bathrooms with tub and shower. You don't have to leave the premises for good food, which you can enjoy along with fine wines at the Dovedale restaurant, preceded, perhaps, by an aperitif in either the Robert Rippon Duke or Derby Bars.

Palace Rd., Buxton, Derbyshire SK17 6AG. (℘ **01298/22001.** Fax 01298/72131. www.paramount-hotels. co.uk. 122 units. £120–£130 ($222–$241) double; £180–£250 ($333–$463) triple. Rates include breakfast. AE, DC, MC, V. **Amenities:** Restaurant; 2 bars; indoor pool; 24-hr. room service; fitness center; solarium; sauna; nonsmoking rooms; rooms for those with limited mobility. *In room:* TV, coffeemaker, hair dryer, trouser press.

WHERE TO DINE

The Columbine ℘ *Value* CONTINENTAL/MODERN ENGLISH   Here is Buxton's most charming restaurant, serving the town's best food. It's reasonably priced but still rivals some of the more formal and expensive country-house hotels outside the center of town. Set behind a facade of gray Derbyshire stone, it was built during the Victorian age as a private home and retains some of its oldest vestiges within an atmospheric cellar. The place is especially popular during the town's annual music festivals; it sometimes prepares pre- and post-theater suppers. Menu items are straightforward and unpretentious, but fresh and flavorful, served in a bistro-style setting. Dishes may include pan-fried sirloin steak glazed with local Stilton cheese on a port-wine-and-mushroom sauce, or grilled tuna steak with a black olive, red onion, and fresh basil butter.

7 Hallbank. (℘ **01298/78752.** Reservations recommended. Main courses £11–£13.50 ($20–$25). MC, V. Mar–Oct Thurs–Sat noon–1:45pm, Mon–Sat 7–10pm; Nov–Apr Mon and Wed–Sat 7–10pm.

BAKEWELL

258km (160 miles) NW of London; 42km (26 miles) N of Derby; 60km (37 miles) SE of Manchester; 53km (33 miles) NW of Nottingham

Lying 19km (12 miles) southeast of Buxton, Bakewell is yet another possible base for exploring the southern Peak District, especially the beautiful valleys of Ashwood Dale, Monsal Dale, and Wyedale. On the River Wey, Bakewell is just a market town, but its old houses constructed from gray-brown stone and its narrow streets give it a picture-postcard look. Its most spectacular feature is a medieval bridge across the river with five graceful arches.

Still served in local tearooms is the famous Bakewell Pudding, which was supposedly created by accident. One day, a chef didn't put the proper proportions of ingredients into her almond sponge cake batter, and it remained gelatinous and runny. Served apologetically, as a mistake, everyone said it was wonderful, and the tradition has remained ever since. The pudding, made as it is with a rich puff pastry that lies at the bottom of the pudding, and covered with a layer first of jam and then the gelatinous version of the almond sponge cake, is richer than the tarts, and relatively difficult to find outside of Bakewell.

The best time to be here is on Monday, **market day,** when local farmers come in to sell their produce. Entrepreneurs from throughout the Midlands also set up flea market stands in the town's main square, The Market Place. Sales are conducted from 8:30am until 5:30pm in winter and until 7:30pm in summer.

ESSENTIALS

GETTING THERE   To reach Bakewell from Derby, take the A6 north to Matlock, passing by the town and continuing on the A6 north toward Rowsley. Just past Rowsley, you'll come to a bridge. Follow the signpost across the bridge into Bakewell.

From London, take the M1 motorway north to Junction 28. Then follow the A38 for 5km (3 miles), connecting with the A615 signposted to Matlock. Once you're at Matlock, follow the A6 into Bakewell.

VISITOR INFORMATION   The **Bakewell Information Centre,** Old Market Hall, Bridge Street (© **01629/813227**), is open from Easter to October daily from 9am to 5:30pm; from November to Easter daily from 10am to 5pm.

WHERE TO STAY & DINE IN THE AREA

For a look at a working 19th-century flour mill, stop in at **Caudwell's Mill,** Bakewell Road (© **01629/734374**). Here, you can have afternoon tea with freshly baked cakes, breads, and pastries made right here at the mill, and then stroll through a variety of shops, including a handcrafted furniture store, glass blowing studio, jewelry shop, and art gallery.

The Cavendish Hotel ✦✦   Located 6.5km (4 miles) east of Bakewell, the Cavendish is one of the most stately country hotels of England. The stone-sided building was constructed in the 1780s as the Peacock Inn and is located on the duke of Devonshire's private estate.

The duke and duchess took personal charge of the hotel and its lavish restoration in 1975, furnishing its public areas and more expensive bedrooms with antiques from nearby Chatsworth, a 15-minute walk to the south. The hotel remains aristocratic and charming. Beds are sumptuous with elegant fabrics, and each room includes a well-designed bathroom with deluxe toiletries and a shower-tub combination.

Baslow, Bakewell, Derbyshire DE4 1SP. © **01246/582311.** Fax 01246/582312. www.cavendish-hotel.net. 24 units. £130–£160 ($241–$296) double; £205 ($379) suite. AE, DC, MC, V. **Amenities:** 2 restaurants; bar; limited room service; laundry service; nonsmoking rooms. *In room:* TV, minibar, coffeemaker, hair dryer, trouser press.

Riber Hall ✦   South of Bakewell on Route 6, this symmetrically gabled structure is built of gray-toned Derbyshire stone. It's from 1450 but was enlarged and discreetly altered by the Jacobeans, and then intricately restored to what you'll see today by the present owners. Public areas are as richly historic and atmospheric as anything in the district. Bedrooms occupy the premises of a converted stable and are charmingly furnished, each with a four-poster bed and tasteful chintzes and antiques.

Riber, Matlock, Derbyshire DE4 5JU. © **01629/582795.** Fax 01629/580475. www.riber-hall.co.uk. 14 units. £136–£182 ($252–$337) double. Rates include continental breakfast. AE, DC, MC, V. **Amenities:** Restaurant; bar; tennis court; limited room service; laundry service; nonsmoking rooms. *In room:* TV, dataport, coffeemaker, hair dryer, trouser press.

Rutland Arms Hotel   A dignified early Georgian building set behind a gray stone facade built in 1804, this town landmark is a good base for visiting nearby Haddon Hall and Chatsworth House. Its original owner operated a prosperous livery stable; some of the bedrooms are in the old stable block in back. Last renovated in 1999, the hotel offers cozy, well-maintained bedrooms. Bathrooms are small; 10 come with a tub-and-shower combination, the rest with shower stalls.

The Square, Bakewell, Derbyshire DE45 1BT. © **01629/812812.** Fax 01629/812309. www.bakewell.demon. co.uk. 35 units. £89–£99 ($165–$183) double; £115–£125 ($213–$231) premier room. Rates include breakfast. AE, DC, MC, V. **Amenities:** Restaurant; bar; limited room service; laundry service; nonsmoking rooms. *In room:* TV, dataport, coffeemaker, hair dryer.

HISTORIC HOMES NEAR BAKEWELL

The tourist office in Bakewell (see above) will provide you with a map outlining the best routes to take to reach each of the attractions below.

Chatsworth ⭐⭐⭐   Here stands one of the great country houses of England, the home of the 11th duke of Devonshire and his duchess, the former Deborah Mitford. With its lavishly decorated interior and a wealth of art treasures, it has 175 rooms, the most spectacular of which are open to the public.

Dating from 1686, the present building stands on a spot where the eccentric Bess of Hardwick built the house in which Mary Queen of Scots was held prisoner upon orders of Queen Elizabeth I. Capability Brown (who seems to have been everywhere) worked on the landscaping of the present house. But it was Joseph Paxton, the gardener to the sixth duke, who turned the garden into one of the most celebrated in Europe. Queen Victoria and Prince Albert were lavishly entertained here in 1843. The house contains a great library and such paintings as the *Adoration of the Magi* by Veronese and *King Uzziah* by Rembrandt. On the grounds are spectacular fountains and a playground for children in the farmyard.

6.5km (4 miles) east of Bakewell, beside the A6 (16km/10 miles north of Matlock). ⓒ **01246/582204.** www. chatsworth-house.co.uk. Admission £8.50 ($16) adults, £6.50 ($12) students and seniors, £3 ($5.55) children 4–15, free for children 3 and under. Mar 21–Oct 28 daily 11am–4:30pm.

Hardwick Hall   Built in 1597 for Bess of Hardwick, a woman who acquired an estate from each of her four husbands, it's particularly noted for its "more glass than wall" architecture. The high great chamber and long gallery crown an unparalleled series of late-16th-century interiors, including an important collection of tapestries, needlework, and furniture. The house is surrounded by a 125-hectare (300-acre) country park, featuring walled gardens, orchards, and an herb garden.

Doe Lea, 15km (9½ miles) east of Chesterfield. ⓒ **01246/850430.** Admission £6.60 ($12) adults, £3.50 ($6.50) children. House Mar–Oct Wed–Sun 12:30–5pm. Grounds open daily year-round; gardens open Apr–Oct Wed–Sun 11am–5:30pm. Take junction 29 from M1.

4 Nottinghamshire: Robin Hood Country

"Notts," as Nottinghamshire is known, lies in the heart of the East Midlands. Its towns are rich in folklore or have bustling markets. Many famous people have come from Nottingham, notably those 13th-century outlaws from Sherwood Forest, Robin Hood and his Merry Men. It also was home to the romantic poet Lord Byron; you can visit his ancestral home at Newstead Abbey. D. H. Lawrence, author of *Sons and Lovers* and *Lady Chatterley's Lover,* was born in a tiny miner's cottage in Eastwood, which he later immortalized in his writings.

NOTTINGHAM
195km (121 miles) N of London; 116km (72 miles) SE of Manchester

Though an industrial center, Nottingham is a good base for exploring Sherwood Forest and the rest of the shire. Nottingham is known to literary buffs for its association with author D. H. Lawrence and its medieval sheriff, who played an important role in the Robin Hood story.

It was an important pre-Norman settlement guarding the River Trent, the gateway to the north of England. Followers of William the Conqueror arrived in 1068 to erect a fort here. In a later reincarnation, the fort saw supporters of Prince John surrender to Richard the Lionheart in 1194. Many other exploits occurred here—notably Edward III's capture of Roger Mortimer and Queen Isabella, the assassins of Edward II. From Nottingham, Richard III marched out with his men to face defeat and his own death at Bosworth Field in 1485.

With the arrival of the spinning jenny in 1768, Nottingham was launched into the forefront of the Industrial Revolution. It's still a center of industry and home base to many well-known British firms, turning out such products as John Player cigarettes, Boots pharmaceuticals, and Raleigh cycles.

Nottingham doesn't have many attractions, but it's a young and vital city, and is very student-oriented thanks to its two large universities. Its Hockley neighborhood is as hip as anything this side of Manchester or London. A look at one of the alternative newspapers or magazines freely distributed around town can connect you with the city's constantly changing nightlife scene.

ESSENTIALS

GETTING THERE The best rail connection is via Lincoln, from which 28 trains arrive Monday through Saturday and about 8 trains on Sunday. The trip takes about 45 minutes. Trains also leave from London's St. Pancras Station; the trip takes about 2½ hours. For information, call ✆ **0845/748-4950** or visit www.railtrack.co.uk.

Buses from London arrive at the rate of about seven per day. For schedules and information, call ✆ **0870/580-8080** or visit www.nationalexpress.com.

If you're driving from London, the M1 motorway runs to a few miles west of Nottingham. Feeder roads, including the A453, are well marked for the short distance into town. The drive takes about 3 to 3½ hours.

VISITOR INFORMATION Information is available at the **City Information Centre,** 1–4 Smithy Row (✆ **01159/155330**). It's open Monday through Friday from 9am to 5:30pm and Saturday from 9am to 5pm.

SPECIAL EVENTS Nottingham still gets a lot of reflected glory from its association with Robin Hood and his gang. The **Robin Hood Festival** is a family friendly, mock-medieval festival scheduled for the first week in August every year. Diversions include food and souvenir stands, jousting and falconry exhibitions, Maypole dances, crowd-pleasing jesters juggling their way through crowds, and lots of medieval costume. For information, call ✆ **01623/823202.**

EXPLORING THE AREA

Put on your most comfortable shoes and prepare to tackle the more than 800 shops in and around town—Nottingham boasts some of England's best shopping. Start in the city center, with its maze of pedestrian streets, and work your way out toward the two grand indoor shopping malls, the Victoria and the Broad Marsh, located to the north and to the south of the center of town. Then, head over to Derby Road for your fill of antiques.

Fine Nottingham lace can be found in the **Lace Centre,** Castle Road, across the street from Nottingham Castle (✆ **01159/413539**), or in the shops around the area known as the **Lace Market** along High Pavement.

Then, to catch up on the hippest and latest in fashion and furnishing trends, explore the many boutiques in the Hockley area, the Exchange Arcade, and the Flying Horse Mall, all in the city center.

Patchings Farm Art Centre, Oxton Road, near Calverton (✆ **01159/653479**), is a 24-hectare (60-acre) art haven. Restored farm buildings house three galleries, working art and pottery studios, a gift shop, and art and framing shops.

And long known as Britain's first real crafts center, **Longdale Craft Centre,** Longdale Lane, Ravenshead (✆ **01623/794858**), is a labyrinth of re-created Victorian streets where professional craftspeople work on a whole range of craft items, including jewelry, pottery, and prints.

Nottingham Castle Museum and Art Gallery ⚡ Overlooking the city, Nottingham Castle was built in 1679 by the duke of Newcastle on the site of an old Norman fortress. After restoration in 1878, it opened as a provincial museum surrounded by a charmingly arranged garden. Of particular note is the History of Nottingham Gallery, re-creating the legends associated with the city, plus a rare collection of ceramics and a unique exhibition of medieval alabaster carvings, which were executed between 1350 and 1530. These delicately detailed scenes illustrate the life of Christ, the Virgin Mother, and various saints. Paintings cover several periods but are strong on 16th-century Italian, 17th-century French and Dutch, and the richest English paintings of the past 2 centuries.

The only surviving element of the original Norman castle is a subterranean passage called Mortimer's Hole. The passage leads to **Ye Olde Trip to Jerusalem,** 1 Brewhouse Yard at Castle Rd. (© **01159/473171**), dating from 1189 and said to be the oldest inn in England (today it's a pub and restaurant). King Edward III is said to have led a band of noblemen through these secret passages, surprising Roger Mortimer and his queen, killing Mortimer and putting his lady in prison. A statue of Robin Hood stands at the base of the castle.

Castle Rd. © **01159/153700.** Admission Sat–Sun £2 ($3.70) adults, £1 ($1.85) children; free Mon–Fri. Mar–Oct daily 10am–5pm; Nov–Feb Sat–Thurs 10am–4pm.

HISTORIC HOMES NEAR NOTTINGHAM

Newstead Abbey ⚡ Lord Byron once made his home at Newstead Abbey, one of eight museums administered by the city of Nottingham. Some of the original Augustinian priory, purchased by Sir John Byron in 1540, still survives. In the 19th century, the mansion was given a neo-Gothic restoration. Mementos, including first editions and manuscripts, are displayed inside. You can explore the parkland of some 121 hectares (300 acres), with waterfalls, rose gardens, a Monk's Stew Pond, and a Japanese water garden.

On A60 (Mansfield Rd.), 19km (12 miles) north of Nottingham center in Ravenshead. © **01623/455900.** www.newsteadabbey.org.uk. Admission to house and grounds £4 ($7.40) adults, £2 ($3.70) students and seniors, £1.50 ($2.80) children. Gardens only £2 ($3.70) adults, £1.50 ($2.80) children. House Apr–Sept daily noon–5pm; gardens open year-round daily 9am–dusk.

Wollaton Hall ⚡ This well-preserved Elizabethan mansion, finished in 1588, is the most ornate in England and a tourist-drawing attraction itself. Today, it houses a natural history museum with lots of insects, invertebrates, British mammals, birds, reptiles, amphibians, and fish. The hall is surrounded by a deer park and garden. See the camellia house with the world's earliest cast-iron front dating from 1823. The bird dioramas here are among the best in Britain.

In Wollaton Park, 5km (3 miles) southwest from Nottingham center. © **01159/153900.** www.wollatonhall. org.uk. Admission Sat–Sun and bank holiday Mon £1.50 ($2.80) adults, 80p ($1.50) children. Free other days. Apr–Oct daily 11am–5pm; Nov–Mar daily 11am–4pm. Drive southwest along A609 (Ilkeston Rd.), which will become Wollaton Rd.

WHERE TO STAY

Nottingham Moat House *Kids* If you're driving, you'll appreciate this chain hotel's easy access from the A60 highway, and its location less than 1.5km (1 mile) north of the city center. It was built in 1968 as a modern alternative to the town's B&Bs. The rooms are standardized and dull but are well maintained; most contain twin beds. Thirty of the bedrooms are suitable for rental to families. Each compact bathroom comes with a combination tub and shower.

If this hotel is full, a desk employee will gladly refer you to the hotel's sibling, the **Royal Moat House Nottingham,** Wollaton Street (© **01159/369988**), where a double room costs £134 to £167 ($248–$309), suites cost £120 to £210 ($222–$389). Though the bedrooms are a bit more modern, many travelers prefer to save a few pounds by staying at the Nottingham Moat House.

296 Mansfield Rd., Nottingham, Nottinghamshire NG5 2BT. ℂ **01159/359988.** Fax 01159/969-1506. www.moathousehotels.com. 210 units. £80–£130 ($148–$241) double; £200–£210 ($370–$389) suite. Rates include breakfast. Parking £7 ($13). AE, DC, MC, V. **Amenities:** 2 restaurants; 2 bars; indoor heated pool; health club; Jacuzzi; sauna; limited room service; laundry service; dry cleaning; nonsmoking rooms; rooms for those with limited mobility. *In room:* TV, dataport, coffeemaker, hair dryer, trouser press.

Strathdon Hotel　This is a solid and unpretentious member of a nationwide chain. Built in the 1970s of gray-colored brick in the heart of town, it has seven floors, neutral public areas, and two bars. The nondescript bedrooms are equipped to a high standard, evocative of a first-class roadside motel. Forty-six units have a tub-and-shower combination, the rest have shower stalls.

44 Derby Rd., Nottingham, Nottinghamshire NG1 5FT. ℂ **01159/418501.** Fax 01159/483725. www.strathdon-hotel-nottingham.com. 68 units. £98–£125 ($181–$231) double. AE, DC, MC, V. **Amenities:** Restaurant; 2 bars; limited room service; laundry service. *In room:* TV, coffeemaker, hair dryer, trouser press.

WHERE TO DINE

Sonny's INTERNATIONAL　This choice, in the fashionable neighborhood of Hockley, seems almost like a hip London restaurant of the moment. Dishes include charcoal-grilled peppered duck with mango and sesame-seed oil; and roast rack of lamb with butter bean jus and rosemary. Desserts include an exotic fruit salad with soft cheese flavored with lime juice and ginger and are deliberately conceived to raise eyebrows; many are delicious.

3 Carlton St. ℂ **01159/473041.** Reservations required. Main courses £12–£18 ($22–$33). AE, MC, V. Sun–Fri noon–2:30pm; Sat noon–2:30pm and 7–10pm.

SHERWOOD FOREST 🖈🖈

Second only to Germany's Schwarzwald in European lore and legend, **Sherwood Forest** comprises 182 hectares (450 acres) of oak and silver birch trees owned and strictly protected by a local entity, the Thoresby Estate, and maintained by the county of Nottinghamshire. Actually, very little of this area was forest even when it provided cover for Robin Hood, Friar Tuck, and Little John.

Robin Hood, the folk hero of tale and ballad, fired the imagination of a hardworking, impoverished English people, who particularly liked his adopted slogan: "Take from the rich and give to the poor."

Celebrating their freedom in verdant Sherwood Forest, Robin Hood's eternally youthful band rejoiced in "hearing the twang of the bow of yew and in watching the gray goose shaft as it cleaves the glistening willow wand or brings down the king's proud buck." Life was one long picnic beneath the splendid oaks of a primeval forest, with plenty of ale and flavorful venison poached from the forests of an oppressive king. The clever rebellion Robin Hood waged against authority (represented by the haughty, despotic, and overfed sheriff of Nottingham) was full of heroic exploits and a desire to win justice for victims of oppression.

Now, as then, the forest consists of woodland glades, farm fields, villages, and hamlets. But the surroundings are so built up that Robin Hood wouldn't recognize them today.

Sherwood Forest Visitor Centre (ℂ **01623/823202**) is in Sherwood Forest Country Park at Edwinstowe, 29km (22 miles) north of Nottingham off the A614, or 13km (8 miles) east of Mansfield on the B6034. It stands near the Major Oak, popularly known as Robin Hood's tree, although analysis of its bark reveals that it wasn't around in the 13th century. Many marked walks and footpaths lead from the visitor center through the woodland. There's an exhibition of life-size models of Robin and the other well-known outlaws, as well as a shop with books, gifts, and souvenirs. The center provides as much information as is known about the Merry Men and Maid Marian, whom Robin Hood is believed to have married at Edwinstowe Church near the visitor center. Little John's grave is at Hathersage 58km (36 miles) away, and Will Scarlet's grave is at Blidworth (15km/9½ miles away).

The center also has a visitor information facility and the **Forest Table,** with cafeteria service and meals emphasizing traditional English country recipes.

Opening times for the country park are from dawn to dusk, and for the visitor center, April through October daily from 10:30am to 5pm and November through March from 10:30am to 4:30pm. Entrance to the center is free, and "Robin Hood's Sherwood" exhibition is also free. A year-round program of events is presented, mainly on weekends and during national and school holiday periods. Parking costs £1.50 ($2.80) per car per day from April to October.

An odd and somewhat archaic holdover from medieval times are **The Dukeries,** large country estates that contain privately owned remnants of whatever trees and vales remain of Sherwood Forest. Most lie on the edge of heavily industrialized towns and may or may not have privately owned houses of historic merit. Very few can actually be visited without special invitations from their owners. On the other hand, **Clumber Park,** a 1,537-hectare (3,800-acre) tract of park and woodland maintained by National Trust authorities, is favored by local families for picnics and strolls. It contains a 32-hectare (80-acre) lake at its center, a monumental promenade flanked with venerable lime (linden) trees, and the Gothic Revival **Clumber Chapel.** Built between 1886 and 1889 as a site of worship for the private use of the seventh duke of Newcastle, it's open from early March to mid-January, daily from 10am to 4pm.

The park itself is open year-round during daylight hours, though its allure and services are at their lowest ebb during November and December. The gift shop and tearoom are open daily January through March from 10:30am to 4pm, and from April to late October from 10am to 6pm. Admission to the park, including the chapel, ranges from £4 to £15 ($7.40–$28), depending on your vehicle.

If you're specifically interested in the botany and plant life, head for the park's **Conservation Centre,** a walled garden with extensive greenhouses, open from April 1 to late September on Saturday, Sunday, and bank holiday Mondays from 1 to 4pm. For information about the park and its features, contact the **Clumber Park Estate Office,** Worksop, Nottingham SKO 3AZ (✆ **01909/476592**).

5 Lincoln ★★

225km (140 miles) N of London; 151km (94 miles) NW of Cambridge; 132km (82 miles) SE of York

The ancient city of Lincoln was the site of a Bronze Age settlement, and later, in the 3rd century, one of four provincial capitals of Roman Britain. In the Middle Ages, it was the center of Lindsey, a famous Anglo-Saxon kingdom. After the Norman conquest, it grew increasingly important, known for its cathedral and castle. Its merchants grew rich by shipping wool directly to Flanders.

Much of the past remains in Lincoln today to delight visitors who wander past half-timbered Tudor houses, the Norman castle, and the towering Lincoln Cathedral. Medieval streets climbing the hillsides and cobblestones re-create the past. Lincoln, unlike other East Midlands towns such as Nottingham and

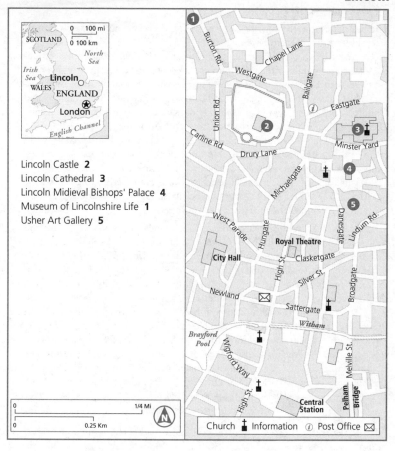

Lincoln Castle **2**
Lincoln Cathedral **3**
Lincoln Midieval Bishops' Palace **4**
Museum of Lincolnshire Life **1**
Usher Art Gallery **5**

Leicester, maintains somewhat of a country town atmosphere. But it also extends welcoming arms to tourists, the mainstay of its economy.

ESSENTIALS

GETTING THERE Trains arrive every hour during the day from London's King's Cross Station, a 2-hour trip usually requiring a change of train at Newark. Trains also arrive from Cambridge, again requiring a change at Newark. For schedules and information, call ℭ **0870/484950.**

National Express buses from London's Victoria Coach Station service Lincoln, a 4-hour ride. For schedules and information, call ℭ **0870/580-8080** or visit www.nationalexpress.com. Once in Lincoln, local and regional buses service the county from the City Bus Station, off St. Mary's Street opposite the train station.

If you're driving from London, take the M1 north to the junction with the A57, then head east to Lincoln.

VISITOR INFORMATION Lincoln has two separate tourist information offices. The larger of the two is at 9 Castle Sq. (ℭ **01522/529828**), open Monday to Thursday 9:30am to 5:30pm and Friday 9:30am to 5pm.

EXPLORING THE CITY

The best lanes for strolling are those tumbling down the appropriately named Steep Hill to the Witham River.

The cathedral is a good starting point for your shopping tour of Lincoln, as the streets leading down the hill (you won't be working against gravity this way) are lined with a mélange of interesting stores. Wander in and out of these historic lanes, down Steep Hill, along Bailgate, around the Stonebow gateway and Guildhall, and then down High Street. Following this route, you'll find all sorts of clothing, books, antiques, arts and crafts, and gift items.

While walking down Steep Hill, stop in the **Harding House Gallery,** 53 Steep Hill (© **01522/523537**), to see some of the best local crafts: ceramics, teddy bears, textiles, wood, metal sculptures, and jewelry. You can peek down St. Paul's Lane, just off Bailgate, to investigate **Cobb Hall Centre,** St. Paul's Lane (© **01522/527317**), a small cluster of specialty shops selling outdoor gear, candies and gift items, German figures, and antiques.

Lincoln Castle   A short walk from the cathedral, this 900-year-old fortress was once one of the most powerful strongholds in medieval England. Lincoln Castle dates from the time of William the Conqueror in 1068. Nothing remains of his original fortress. On one of the mounds where the original castle stood is the Lucy Tower dating from the late 12th century. The East Gate also dates from the 12th century. The castle came under siege in the wars of 1135–54 and again in 1216–17. During the 19th century, it functioned as a prison. You can see the Prison Chapel with its self-locking cubicles; these cages kept prisoners from seeing each other. Inside its exhibition rooms is displayed one of only four surviving copies of the Magna Carta. Much of the appeal of a visit here involves walking along the top of the wall that surrounds the fortress, overlooking the castle's grassy courtyard, the city of Lincoln, and its cathedral.

© **01522/511068.** Admission £3.50 ($6.50) adults, £2.50 ($4.65) students, £1.50 ($2.80) children under 16. Mon–Sat 9:30am–5:30pm; Sun 11am–5:30pm. Oct–Mar closes at 4pm.

Lincoln Cathedral 😊😊😊   No other English cathedral dominates its surroundings as does Lincoln's. Visible from up to 48km (30 miles) away, the central tower is 81m (271 ft.) high, which makes it the second tallest in England. The central tower once carried a huge spire, which, before heavy gale damage in 1549, made it the tallest in the world at 158m (525 ft.).

Construction on the original Norman cathedral was begun in 1072, and it was consecrated 20 years later. It sustained a major fire and, in 1185, an earthquake. Only the central portion of the West Front and lower halves of the western towers survive from this period.

The present cathedral is Gothic in style, particularly the Early English and Decorated periods. The nave is 13th century, but the black font of Tournai marble originates from the 12th century. In the Great North Transept is a rose medallion window known as the Dean's Eye. Opposite it, in the Great South Transept, is its cousin, the Bishop's Eye. East of the high altar is the Angel Choir, consecrated in 1280, and so called after the sculpted angels high on the walls. The exquisite woodcarving in St. Hugh's Choir dates from the 14th century. Lincoln's roof bosses, dating from the 13th and 14th centuries, are handsome, and a mirror trolley assists visitors in their appreciation of these features, which are some 21m (70 ft.) above the floor. Oak bosses are in the cloister.

In the Seamen's Chapel (Great North Transept) is a window commemorating Lincolnshire-born Captain John Smith, one of the pioneers of early settlement in America and the first governor of Virginia. The library and north walk of the cloister were built in 1674 to designs by Sir Christopher Wren. In the Treasury is fine silver plate from the churches of the diocese.

ⓒ **01522/544544**. www.lincolncathedral.com. Admission £4 ($7.40) adults, £3 ($5.55) seniors, students, and children. June–Aug Mon–Sat 7:15am–8pm, Sun 7:15am–6pm; Sept–May Mon–Sat 7:15am–6pm, Sun 7:15am–5pm.

Lincoln Medieval Bishops' Palace   On the south side of the Cathedral, this site was the headquarters of the biggest diocese in England during the Middle Ages. Launched in 1150, it held great power until it was sacked during the Civil War in the 1640s. Allowed to ruin over the centuries, it has been opened to the public, who can explore its ruins, including an intact entrance tower, a public hall, and a vaulted undercroft. You can also wander its grounds, taking in panoramic views of the city itself.

Minster Yard. ⓒ **01522/527468**. Admission £3.20 ($5.90). Apr–Oct daily 10am–6pm; off season Sat–Sun 10am–4pm.

Museum of Lincolnshire Life   This is the largest museum of social history in the Midlands. Housed in what was originally built as an army barracks in 1857, it's a short walk north of the city center. Displays here range from a Victorian schoolroom to a collection of locally built steam engines.

Burton Rd. ⓒ **01522/528448**. Admission £2.50 ($4.65) adults, £1 ($1.85) children. Mon–Sat 10am–5:30pm; Sun 2–5:30pm (opens at 10am May–Sept). Closed Good Friday, Dec 24–27, and New Year's Day.

Usher Art Gallery   Established in 1927 at the bequest of its founder, James Ward Usher (one of the city's prominent jewelers), the gallery is a repository for paintings and an impressive collection of antique clocks, 20th-century ceramics, and artifacts and literary mementos, plus portraits of Lincolnshire-born Alfred Lord Tennyson. Most impressive is the collection of miniatures from the 16th to 19th centuries, and an exhibition of 17th-century Dutch and Italian paintings. Our favorites are the works of Peter de Wint (1784–1849), including his moving depiction of *Lincoln Cathedral.*

Lindum Rd. ⓒ **01522/527980**. Admission £2 ($3.70). Tues–Sat 10am–5:30pm; Sun 2:30–5pm.

WHERE TO STAY

The Castle Hotel   This redbrick, three-story, traditional English hotel is situated in old Lincoln. It has been carefully converted from what was the North District National School, dating from 1858. It boasts splendid views of the castle and cathedral, which are just a 3-minute walk away. The bedrooms have been individually decorated—one has a four-poster bed—and are named after British castles. Most bathrooms have a tub-and-shower combination. Children under 10 are not permitted.

Westgate, Lincoln, Lincolnshire LN1 3AS. ⓒ **01522/538801**. Fax 01522/575457. www.castlehotel.net. 20 units. £88 ($163) double. Rates include English breakfast and newspaper. AE, DC, MC, V. **Amenities:** Restaurant; bar; limited room service; laundry service. *In room:* TV, coffeemaker, hair dryer.

D'Isney Place Hotel ⓕ *Value*   This family owned hotel is close to the cathedral, the minster yard, the castle, and the Bailgate shops. It was built in 1735 and later enlarged. The southern boundary of the house gardens is formed by the wall of the cathedral close and towers, which were constructed in 1285. Not nearly as luxurious as the White Hart Hotel, it is nevertheless one of the best bets in Lincoln. Each room is uniquely decorated, and some units have four-poster beds and Jacuzzi tubs. Many of the bedrooms have just recently been redecorated, and standards of comfort are high here. Bathrooms are small but well designed; most of them have a tub-and-shower combination.

Eastgate, Lincoln, Lincolnshire LN2 4AA. ⓒ **01522/538881.** Fax 01522/511321. www.disneyplacehotel. co.uk. 17 units. £92–£112 ($170–$207) double. Rates include English breakfast. AE, DC, MC, V. **Amenities:** Jacuzzi; laundry service; dry cleaning. *In room:* TV, hair dryer, iron/ironing board.

Hillcrest Hotel *(Value* This is a fine redbrick house built in 1871 as the private home of a local vicar. Though converted into a comfortable, small, licensed hotel, it retains many of its original features. It's on a quiet, tree-lined road overlooking 10 hectares (26 acres) of parkland, in the old high town and within easy walking distance of Lincoln Cathedral and the Roman remains. The bedrooms are well furnished and kept in shape; some rooms have a four-poster bed and nearly all open onto a view. The compact bathrooms have shower-tub combinations.

15 Lindum Terrace, Lincoln, Lincolnshire LN2 5RT. ⓒ **01522/510182.** Fax 01522/538009. www.hillcrest-hotel.com. 14 units. £83 ($154) double. Children under 2 stay free with 2 paying adults; children 2–12 pay £6 ($11) per night; ages 13–18 £12 ($22) per night. Rates include English breakfast. AE, DC, MC, V. From Wragby Rd., connect with Upper Lindum St.; continue to the bottom of this street, make a left onto Lindum Terrace, and the hotel is 180m (600 ft.) along on the right. **Amenities:** Restaurant; bar; limited room service; babysitting; laundry service; nonsmoking rooms. *In room:* TV, coffeemaker, hair dryer.

The Lincoln Hotel Lacking the charm of the White Hart, this is still one of the town's leading hotels. When workmen were digging the foundations here in the mid-1960s, they discovered remnants of the north tower of the East Gate of the Roman city wall, a preserved part of which is included in the hotel's rear garden. The hotel faces Lincoln Cathedral and is attached to a Victorian mansion (now the Eastgate Bar). The recently refurbished bedrooms are nicely decorated and comfortable. Bathrooms are small with adequate shelf space and showers.

Eastgate, Lincoln, Lincolnshire LN2 1PN. ⓒ **01522/520348.** www.thelincolnhotel.com. 72 units. Mon–Thurs £100–£120 ($185–$222) double; Fri–Sun £80–£100 ($148–$185) double. AE, DC, MC, V. **Amenities:** Restaurant; bar; limited room service; laundry service; nonsmoking rooms; rooms for those with limited mobility. *In room:* TV, dataport, coffeemaker, hair dryer, trouser press.

White Hart Hotel 🏨🏨 The White Hart is named after the emblem of Richard II, who visited this region shortly before this hotel was constructed and probably stayed at an inn on the site. A letter written in 1460 by a London woman who paid sixpence for her room complains that her bed was lumpy. The inn's facade dates from the 1700s, when it was a luxurious private home. Its life as a modern hotel began in 1913 when the live-in owners started accepting paying guests (only if they came with ironclad references). The hotel also hosted several meetings between Churchill and Eisenhower in the darkest days of World War II. Other guests have included Edward VIII and Baroness Margaret Thatcher.

The inn still goes strong today and is still the best choice in town. The lumpy beds are long gone, though the inn has a superb collection of antiques. Enter through a revolving mahogany door into a large and finely proportioned lounge filled with fine antiques, rare and unusual clocks, and display cabinets of rare silver, glass, and porcelain. Each of the accommodations, many restored in 1995, has some antique furniture, a well-accessorized bathroom, and views of the old city. Try for an accommodation in the older structure where the units are more spacious and stylish than those in the lackluster annex. Bathrooms are sparkling new with sinks set in marble counters, and power showers over the tubs. You have to negotiate a labyrinth of narrow halls and stairways to reach your room.

Bailgate, Lincoln, Lincolnshire LN1 3AR. ⓒ **01522/526222.** Fax 01522/531798. 48 units. £120–£140 ($222–$259) double; £150 ($278) suite. AE, DC, MC, V. .5km (¼ mile) from Lincoln Station. **Amenities:**

Restaurant; bar; 24-hr. room service; laundry service; nonsmoking rooms. *In room:* TV, dataport, coffeemaker, hair dryer, trouser press.

WHERE TO DINE

Restaurant in the Jews House ⍟ CONTINENTAL   Constructed around 1150, this stone-fronted building is said to be the oldest occupied house in Europe. Today, it offers the finest food in Lincoln. The dining room has a low-beamed ceiling, a cast-iron fireplace, and medieval features. Two of the massive ceiling beams date from the construction of the original house. Seating about 28 diners, the menu features stylish dishes that change every 4 weeks according to market ingredients and the inspiration of the chef—perhaps grilled goat cheese served on a bed of fresh spinach with croutons and bacon, or roast rack of lamb with a pesto crust. All these dishes are savory and prepared in an up-to-date, modern style without heavy saucing. The main restaurant is nonsmoking.

The Jews House, 15 The Strait. ⏣ **01522/524851.** Reservations required on weekends. Main courses £13.50–£18 ($25–$33); fixed-price lunch £13 ($24) for 2 courses, £15 ($28) for 3 courses. AE, DC, MC, V. Daily 11:30am–1:30pm; Mon–Sat 6:30–9pm.

Wig & Mitre ⍟ *Finds* INTERNATIONAL   This is not only the best pub in old Lincoln, but it serves fine food, too. Sitting on the aptly named Steep Hill near the cathedral and loaded with an Old English atmosphere, it operates somewhat like a pub-brasserie. The main restaurant, behind the bar on the second floor, has oak timbers, Victorian armchairs, and settees. This 14th-century pub has been substantially restored over the years. If the restaurant is full, you can dine in the bar downstairs. The menu is sophisticated and constantly kept up-to-date, like in a trendy London wine bar. Menu items may include a baked cheese soufflé, served with ham, leeks and a zesty cream sauce or pan-roasted duck with red Thai curry sauce and jasmine rice.

30-32 Steep Hill. ⏣ **01522/535190.** Reservations recommended. Main courses £11–£18 ($19–$32); sandwiches £5.75–£17 ($11–$31); fixed-price 3-course menu £14 ($26) served noon–6pm. AE, DC, MC, V. Daily 8am–11pm (closes 10:30pm Sun).

FAVORITE LOCAL PUBS

Drop by the **Adam & Eve Tavern,** Lindum Hill (⏣ **01522/537108**), the oldest pub in Lincoln, dating from 1701, to knock back a Magnet, Old Speckled Hen, or Theakston's Best Bitter in a homey, cottage atmosphere complete with gas fires and a large front garden for warm-weather drinking and browsing.

The **Jolly Brewer,** 27 Broadgate (⏣ **01522/528583**), dates from 1850, and it's a basic wooden-floorboards place where you'll be welcomed into a friendly crowd. If you're hungry, there's pub grub at lunchtime only, and draft ales include Tiger Bitter and Robinson's, as well as rotating guests.

16

The Northwest

The great industrial shadow of the 19th century cast such a darkness over England's northwest that the area has been relatively neglected by visitors. Most Americans rush through, heading for the Lake District and Scotland. But in spite of its industry and bleak commercial area, the northwest still has a lot to offer, including some beautiful countryside that remains unspoiled.

We will concentrate, however, on only three of its more important cities—**Manchester, Liverpool,** and **Chester**—plus a side trip to **Blackpool,** a huge Coney Island–style resort. You may want to visit it not so much for its beaches as for its kitschy, old-world appeal.

1 Manchester: Gateway to the North ★★

325km (202 miles) NW of London; 138km (86 miles) N of Birmingham; 56km (35 miles) E of Liverpool

One of the largest cities in England, **Manchester** is becoming increasingly important, as major airlines now fly here from North America, making the city a gateway to northern England. In recent years, Manchester has made great strides to shake its image as an industrial wasteland. Though chimneys still spike the skyline, they no longer make the metropolitan sky an ash-filled canopy. Abandoned warehouses are being renovated to provide sleek new loft apartments for yuppies. Rustic factory equipment turns up in museums rather than piling up in salvage yards. Even the old Victorian architecture has been given a face-lift. The overall effect is a gritty kind of charm.

Manchester's roots date from A.D. 79, when the Romans settled here. It remained under Roman occupation until A.D. 410 when the empire began its storied fall. The west gate has since been reconstructed upon its original site. Little is known of Manchester's Middle Ages.

But then in the mid–17th century, the city began to capitalize on the wealth of opportunity that the burgeoning textile industry offered. Manchester eventually became the Dickensian paradigm of the industrial complex and the plight of cities. The railways were equally responsible for catapulting the city to the forefront of the industrial movement. England found Manchester both a convenient terminus and refinement center through which raw goods became viable exports. It is apt indeed that the Museum of Science and Technology resides here.

Many of the factory laborers were immigrants who flocked to the city for the promise of work. The atrocity of their conditions is well documented. But these immigrants had a profound effect on the city's culture. Today, Manchester's nearly 20,000 descendants of Chinese immigrants constitute England's highest Chinese population outside London. The Chinese residents have amalgamated their surroundings to fit their heritage. Falkner Street, particularly the monumental Imperial Chinese Archway, is brought to life by the murals, gardens, and vibrant decor that pay homage to the once-displaced working force.

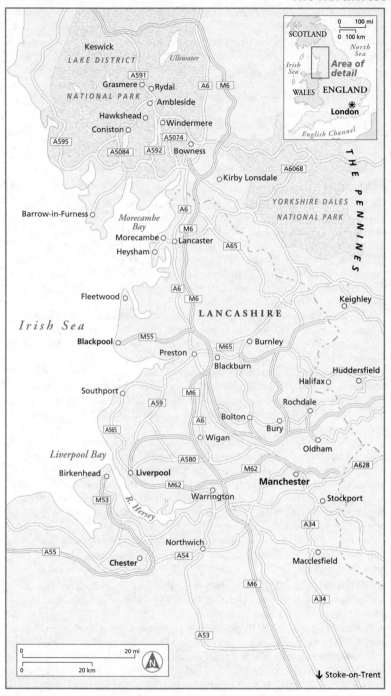

SCOTLAND

North
Sea

Irish
Sea

Area of
detail

WALES   ENGLAND

London

English Channel

0   100 mi

0   100 km

Keswick

LAKE DISTRICT

Ullswater

A591

Grasmere ○ Rydal

NATIONAL PARK

Ambleside

Hawkshead ○

Coniston ○

○ Windermere

A595

A5084   A592   Bowness

A5074

A6   M6

Kirby Lonsdale

A6068

YORKSHIRE DALES

NATIONAL PARK

Barrow-in-Furness ○

*Morecambe
Bay*

Morecambe ○

Heysham ○

A6

M6

○ Lancaster

A65

T
H
E

P
E
N
N
I
N
E
S

Fleetwood ○

A6

M6

LANCASHIRE

Keighley

Irish Sea

Blackpool ○

M55

Preston ○

M65   ○ Burnley

○
Blackburn

Huddersfield

Halifax ○   ○

Southport ○

A59

A565

M6

A6

Bolton ○

○ Wigan

Rochdale
○

Bury

Oldham
○

Liverpool Bay

Birkenhead ○

M53

A580

○ **Liverpool**

M62

Warrington

R. Mersey

M62

A628

Manchester
○

○ Stockport

A55

Chester ○

A54

Northwich ○

A34

Macclesfield ○

M6

A34

A53

0   20 mi

0   20 km

N

↓ Stoke-on-Trent

The most recent stars of Manchester have been Oasis, best known in America for their album *(What's the Story) Morning Glory.* These rock stars haven't exactly done for Manchester what the Beatles did to put Liverpool on the map, but they certainly have made an impression. Of course, these self-styled "hard-drinking, groupie-shagging, drug-snorting geezers" make the Beatles seem like choirboys. As Manchester is increasingly cited for its hipness, Oasis, whose *Definitely Maybe* was the fastest-selling debut album in British history, helped make it so.

The once-dreary Manchester Docklands, evoking a painting of L. S. Lowry, has a spiffy new life following a $200 million restoration. It's called simply "the Lowry," and the complex is filled with theaters, shops, galleries, and restaurants. A plaza provides space for up to 10,000 at outdoor performances.

ESSENTIALS

GETTING THERE BY PLANE   More and more North Americans are flying directly to Manchester to begin their explorations of the United Kingdom. **British Airways** (BA; *©* **800/247-9297** in the U.S. and Canada, or 0161/489-2437 in the U.K.; www.british-airways.co.uk) has daily flights departing New York's JFK airport for Manchester at 6pm, arriving after 7 hours in the air. You can also fly from BA's many North American gateways nonstop to London, and from here take the almost shuttlelike service from either Gatwick or Heathrow airports to Manchester, a 50-minute flight.

American Airlines (*©* **800/433-7300** in the U.S. and Canada; www.aa.com) offers a daily nonstop flight to Manchester from Chicago's O'Hare Airport that departs at 6:10pm, arriving the following morning. American also flies from London's Heathrow back to Chicago.

Manchester is also served by flights from the Continent. For example, **Lufthansa** (*©* **800/645-3880;** www.lufthansa.com) has frequent nonstop flights each week between Frankfurt and Manchester, depending on the season. Flight time is 1 hour and 45 minutes. For airport information, call *©* **01614/893000** or 090/1010-1000.

Manchester's airport, 24km (15 miles) south of the town center, is served by both public transportation and a motorway network. The **Airport Link,** a modern aboveground train, connects the airport terminal to the Piccadilly Railway Station downtown in Manchester. Trains leave every 15 minutes from 5:15am to 10:10pm, sometimes through the night. The ride takes 25 minutes. Direct rail lines link the airport to surrounding northern destinations such as Edinburgh, Liverpool, and Windermere.

Bus nos. 44 and 105 run between the airport and Piccadilly Gardens Bus Station every 15 minutes (hourly during the evenings and on Sun). The bus ride takes 55 minutes.

GETTING THERE BY TRAIN, BUS & CAR   Trains from London's Euston Station travel directly to Manchester (*©* **0845/748-4950;** www.railtrack.co.uk). The trip takes 2½ to 3 hours.

National Express (*©* **0870/580-8080;** www.nationalexpress.com) buses serve the Manchester region from London's Victoria Coach Station.

If you're driving from London to Manchester, go north on the M1 and the M6. At junction 21A, go east on the M62, which becomes the M602 as you enter Manchester. The trip from London to Manchester usually takes from 3 to 3½ hours, but it could be longer because of traffic and construction.

Manchester

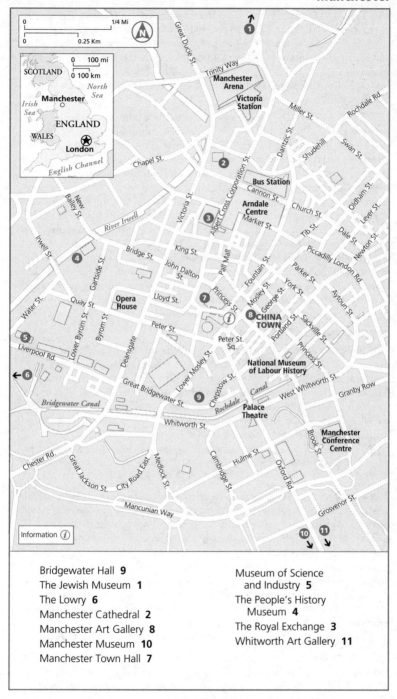

Bridgewater Hall **9**
The Jewish Museum **1**
The Lowry **6**
Manchester Cathedral **2**
Manchester Art Gallery **8**
Manchester Museum **10**
Manchester Town Hall **7**

Museum of Science
  and Industry **5**
The People's History
  Museum **4**
The Royal Exchange **3**
Whitworth Art Gallery **11**

VISITOR INFORMATION The **Manchester Visitor Centre,** Town Hall Extension, Lloyd Street (℡ **01612/343157;** www.manchester.gov.uk/visitor centre), is open Monday through Saturday from 10am to 5:30pm and Sunday and bank holidays from 10:30am to 4pm. To reach it, take the Metrolink tram to St. Peter's Square. Especially useful is a series of four free pamphlets with information on accommodations, dining, city attractions, and cultural/entertainment options.

GETTING AROUND It's not a good idea to try to hoof it in Manchester. It's better to take the bus and Metrolink. Timetables, bus routes, fare information, and a copy of a helpful leaflet, the *Passenger's Guide,* are available from **The Kiosk,** a general information booth within the Piccadilly Gardens Bus Station, Portland Street (℡ **01612/287811**), open daily from 8am to 8pm.

Buses begin running within Manchester at 6am and operate in full force until 11pm, then continue with limited routes until 3am. Tickets are sold at a kiosk at Piccadilly Gardens Bus Station. A day pass, the **Wayfarer** (℡ **01612/287811**), costs £3.30 ($6.10) and is valid for a complete day of public bus travel. Another source of bus information is **Stagecoach** (℡ **01612/733377**).

Metrolink (℡ **01612/052000;** www.metrolink.co.uk) streetcars connect the bus stations and provide a useful north–south conduit. Self-service ticket machines dispense zone-based fares. The streetcars operate Monday to Thursday from 6am to midnight, Friday and Saturday from 6am to 1am, and on Sunday from 7am to 11pm. They are wheelchair accessible.

SEEING THE SIGHTS

The Jewish Museum The premises here were originally built in the Moorish revival style in 1874 as a Sephardic synagogue. It's one of only two such museums in Britain (the other is in London). It traces the culture and history of Manchester's Jewish community, estimated today at around 27,000. Part of the emphasis is on the experiences of immigrants, many from Eastern Europe, whose recorded voices describe the experience of life in Manchester's Jewish quarter in the years before World War II.

Cheetham Hill Rd. ℡ **01618/349879.** www.manchesterjewishmuseum.com. Admission £3.95 ($7.30) adults; £2.95 ($5.45) children, students, and seniors; £9.50 ($18) family. Mon–Thurs 10:30am–4pm; Sun 10:30am–5pm. Closed Sat and Jewish holidays. Bus: 21, 56, 59, 89, 134, 135, or 167.

The Lowry ✪ At the newly restored docklands area, the Lowry, the industrial city landscapes of the artist, L. S. Lowry (1887–1976), are showcased as never before. Lowry depicted the horror of the industrial north of England, before it disappeared forever. His matchstick people are dwarfed by the smokestacks and viaducts in his paintings. Lowry's paintings, as seen here, imposed a vision on a grim and gloomy urban sprawl. Lowry found a cohesion and lyric beauty in these industrial landscapes. His best-known paintings are from 1905 to 1925. The artist was especially fond of depicting the crudeness of capitalism, forcing workers into box-like row houses, as railroads nearby rattled across viaducts belching smoke.

The Lowry. ℡ **01618/762000.** www.thelowry.com. Free admission. Sun–Fri 11am–5pm; Sat 10am–5pm. Bus: 51, 52, 71, 73, or M11.

Manchester Art Gallery ✪✪ Following an extensive expansion and rejuvenation, this gallery today is the proud owner of one of the best and most prestigious art collections in the north of England. Literally doubled in size, the new gallery displays works that are wide-ranging—from the pre-Raphaelites to old

Dutch masters, from the land- and seascapes of Turner to Lowry's industrial panoramas.

Designed by Sir Charles Barry, this gallery has been a landmark since 1882. Today's fine collection is also noted for its paintings by Ford Madox Brown, Holman Hunt, and its bevy of 18th- and early-19th-century art, including High Victorian, Edwardian, and British modern. A highlight for us is the magnificent collection of Turner watercolors.

The gallery's decorative art collection is one of the finest outside London, especially in its 17th- and 18th-century pieces, its metalwork, and porcelain. The silver, in particular the Assheton Bennett collection, is especially distinguished.

If you're here between Easter and September, consider a visit to **Heaton Hall** (✆ **01617/731231;** www.manchestergalleries.org), the museum's annex, 6.5km (4 miles) to the east. It's the centerpiece of 263 hectares (650 acres) of rolling parkland, and accessible via the Metrolink tram (get off at Heaton Park). Built of York stone in 1772, and filled with furniture and decorative art of the 18th and 19th centuries, it is open only between Easter and September. Opening hours may vary, however they are generally Tuesday to Sunday from 10am to noon and 1 to 5pm. Call the Visitor Centre to confirm. Admission is free.

Mosley St. ✆ **01612/358888.** www.manchestergalleries.org. Free admission. Tues–Sun 10am–5pm.

Manchester Cathedral ✦ Originally just a medieval parish in 1421, Manchester achieved cathedral status in 1847 with the creation of the new diocese. The cathedral's nave, the widest of its kind in Britain, is formed by six bays, as is the choir. The choir stall features unique 16th-century misericord seats—caricatures of medieval life. The choir screen is a woodcarving from the same era. Carel Weight provides her 20th-century canvas rendition of the beatitudes, and there's also a sculpture by typographer Eric Gill.

Victoria St. ✆ **01618/332220.** www.manchestercathedral.org. Free admission. Daily 8am–6pm.

Manchester Museum This venerable museum showcases an eclectic and sometimes eccentric collection of the spoils brought back by local industrialists from their adventurous forays outside of England, displaying archaeological finds from all over the world, including England's largest collection of ancient Egyptian mummies outside the British Museum in London. The museum underwent a major refurbishment, which was completed by fall of 2003, all of its exhibits better lit and presented than before.

University of Manchester, Oxford Rd., near Booth St. ✆ **01612/752634.** www.museum.man.ac.uk. Free admission. Mon–Sat 10am–5pm; Sun 11am–4pm. Metrolink tram to St. Peter's Sq., then bus 41, 42, 45, 16, or 11.

Manchester Town Hall ✦ Alfred Waterhouse designed this neo-Gothic structure that first opened in 1877, and extensions were added just before World War II. The tower rises nearly 90m (300 ft.) above the town. The Great Hall and its signature hammer-beam roof houses 12 pre-Raphaelite murals by Ford Madox Brown, commissioned between 1852 and 1856. The paintings chronicle the town's storied past, from the 1st-century Roman occupation to the Industrial Revolution of the 19th century.

Albert Square. ✆ **01612/343157.** Free admission. Mon–Fri 8am–5pm; Sun 10am–4pm. In winter call for times. Closed Dec 25–26 and New Year's Day.

The People's History Museum Few other museums in Europe catalog and commemorate the social history of the working class as carefully and with as much objectivity as this one. The museum began to take shape in 1990 when this was designated as the archive of Britain's communist party. Despite the fact that every exhibit is carefully couched in apolitical terms, it remains the most controversial museum in the Midlands. Of special note are exhibitions that describe the 1819 Peterloo Massacre of trade union activists by government forces and the ongoing struggles of the coal miners of Yorkshire in their fight for higher wages and better working conditions.

Left Bank, Bridge St. Ⓒ **01618/396061**. www.nmlhweb.org. Admission £1 ($1.85) adults Sat–Thurs; free for students, seniors, and children. Free to everyone on Fri. Tues–Sun 11am–4:30pm. Tram: Metrolink to St. Peter's Sq.

EXPLORING CASTLEFIELD

Manchester had its origins in Castlefield, the city's historic core that local authorities have recently designated an "urban heritage park." It comprises the densely populated neighborhood that housed as many as 2,000 civilians beginning in A.D. 79, when Manchester was *Mancestra,* a fortified Roman camp strategically positioned between other Roman outposts, Chester and Carlisle. The roots of modern-day Manchester grew from here, providing the basic goods and services that supplied the soldiers in the nearby fort. After the Romans abandoned their fortress in A.D. 411, the settlement stood alone throughout the Dark Ages.

Castlefield's next major development was the **Bridgewater Canal,** which transferred coal from Worsley. Many other goods passed through this center because of the ease of transportation. Warehouses arose around the wharves, their names suggesting their wares (for example, Potato Wharf). Later, Liverpool Road housed the world's first passenger railway station, today home to the Museum of Science and Industry.

Though the city atrophied for decades after its reign as industrial capital of the world, an interest in urban renewal emerged in the 1970s. Many of the grand canals and warehouses have been restored, and Castlefield is once again a thriving, vibrant area full of attractions.

The Museum of Science and Industry   Set within five separate and antique buildings, the premises were built in 1830 as the first railway station in the world. Its many exhibits celebrate the Industrial Revolution and its myriad inventions and developments, such as printing, the railway industry, electricity, textile manufacturing, and industrial machinery, plus the history of flight and aerospace exploration.

Liverpool Rd. (1.5km/1 mile north of Manchester's center), Castlefield. Ⓒ **01618/832-2244**. www.msim. org.uk. Free admission. Daily 10am–5pm. Closed Dec 24–26. Parking £4 ($7.40). Bus: 33. Tram: G-Mex, Deans Gate.

Whitworth Art Gallery   Whitworth was originally established in 1889 with a bequest to the city from a wealthy industrialist. The gallery was opened to the public in 1908. Behind the magnificent redbrick facade lies a light and spacious interior. The gallery is one of the richest research sources in England for antique patterns of wallpaper and textiles and the weaving techniques that produced them. It also features a superb collection of 18th- and 19th-century watercolors on display, including many by Turner.

South of the University of Manchester, on Oxford Rd., near the corner of Denmark Rd. Ⓒ **01612/757450**. www.whitworth.man.ac.uk. Free admission. Mon–Sat 10am–5pm; Sun 2–5pm. Metrolink to St. Peter's Sq., then bus 41, 42, or 45.

SHOPPING

Not only does Manchester offer a vast number and variety of boutiques, shops, galleries, and crafts centers, but it's also one of the best hunting grounds for bargains in all of England.

Most of the larger shopping areas in the city are pedestrian-only. These include **King Street** and **St. Ann's Square,** full of exclusive boutiques and designer stores; **Market Street,** with its major chain and department stores; **Arndale Centre,** Manchester's largest covered shopping center; and the recently revitalized **Piccadilly** and **Oldham streets,** for fashion, music, and plenty of bargains. **Deansgate Street** is not pedestrian-only but does have a lot of adventure-sports shops.

For the young at heart, interested in everything from World War II RAF bomber pilot gear to outrageous club wear, it's one-stop shopping at **Affleck Palace,** 52 Church St. This complex provides 50 of the most widely varied shops in the city divided among four floors.

ANTIQUES & FINE ART Those who like rooting through dusty stacks of stuff in search of treasures will find Manchester and the greater Manchester area prime hunting grounds. More pricey antiques can be found along **Bury New Road** in Prestwich village, just outside of Manchester.

ARTS & CRAFTS You can really rack up a lot of one-of-a-kind items while exploring the many shops devoted to craftspeople and their art. For ceramics, glass, textiles, jewelry, toys, dollhouses, and the like, visit the exquisite Victorian building that houses **Manchester Craft Centre,** 17 Oak St. (© **01618/324274**); and **St. George's Craft Centre,** St. George's Road, Bolton (© **01204/398071**).

MARKETS Here in the north, markets are a tradition and offer you a chance to jump in and barter with the locals. Tourists tend to steer clear of them, so this is a great chance for a really authentic experience.

Though markets tend to sell everyday items and foodstuff, some stalls are devoted to flea-market goods and "antiques." Market days vary throughout the city, but you're bound to find at least one in full swing each day of the workweek.

The major ones include Arndale Market and Market Hall in Manchester Arndale Centre, Grey Mare Lane Market and Beswick District Shopping Centre in Beswick, and Moss Side Market and Moss Lane East in Moss Side.

MILL SHOPS Manchester is an industrial stronghold with lots of textile mills. Most mills used to have a store, or mill shop, on-site where customers could come to buy mill goods. Today, more and more of the mills are setting up shop in towns across the country.

Bury New Road in Cheetham Hill, near Boddington's Brewery, has a great selection of factory shops, discount stores, warehouses, cash-and-carry outlets, and street stalls on Sunday mornings. Some of the stores along this road do not sell to the general public and others require a minimum purchase.

A. Sanderson & Sons, 2 Pollard St., Ancoats (© **01612/728501**), is one of England's most famous brands. The shop is right outside the heart of downtown and easy to get to. It's clean, modern, and fun to shop for fabrics by the yard, as well as bed linen, draperies, wallpaper, lampshades, and cushions.

WHERE TO STAY
EXPENSIVE
Hilton Manchester Airport ✦ This is the best of the many modern hotels that flank Manchester's airport. Built during the mid-1980s, it features

conservative but modern bedrooms with soundproof windows. Plush carpets and pickled pine furnishings are inviting, and padded headboards back the comfortable beds. Bathrooms have adequate shelf space, plus a combination pseudo-marble tub and shower. The 60 more expensive "Plaza Club" rooms feature a wider assortment of perks and amenities than the less expensive accommodations.

Outwood Lane (near Junction 5 of M56), Manchester Airport, Manchester M90 4WP. © 800/445-8667 in the U.S. and Canada, or 01614/353000. Fax 01614/353040. www.hilton.com. 223 units. £119–£165 ($220–$305) double; £325–£400 ($601–$740) suite. AE, DC, MC, V. **Amenities:** Restaurant; bar; pool; health club; sauna; shuttle service; business center; limited room service; laundry service; dry cleaning; nonsmoking rooms; rooms for those with limited mobility. *In room:* A/C, TV, dataport, minibar, coffeemaker, hair dryer, trouser press.

The Lowry Hotel ★★★ *Finds*

Sexy and sinuous, this hotel rises on the banks of the Irwell River in an increasingly gentrified section of Manchester, Salford, which is most often compared to New York's SoHo. The windows of the bedrooms open onto a modern footbridge linking this once blighted industrial zone to the heart of town. The glass edifice exudes a sense of airy, spacious luxury living. This government-rated five-star hotel (rare in this part of England) is part of the new Chapel Wharf development. The Lowry offers bedrooms of maximum comfort with deluxe furnishings and state-of-the-art marble bathrooms with tub and shower. The sleek design was directed by Olga Polizzi, who has helped redefine chic in the U.K. Polizzi's trademarks are wedge-wood paneling, built-in furniture, and floor-to-ceiling windows. Many patrons visit just to sample the international cuisine of the hotel's brasserie-style restaurant, The River Room Marco Pierre White, which overlooks the water.

50 Deadmans Place, Chapel Wharf. © 01618/274000. Fax 01618/274001. www.thelowryhotel.com. 165 units. £209–£269 ($387–$498) double; from £550 ($1,018) suite. AE, DC, MC, V. **Amenities:** Restaurant; bar; 24-hr. room service; fitness center; spa; sauna; steam room; business center; rooms for those with limited mobility. *In room:* TV, dataport, minibar, hair dryer, safe, trouser press.

The Midland ★

This is one of the leading hotels in Manchester, a six-story, redbrick structure originally built in 1903 as the city's railway station hotel. Holiday Inn acquired it in 1985 and radically renovated and upgraded it as one of its top-of-the-line offerings. In 2004, it became part of the Paramount Group of Hotels. Though comfortable, bedrooms are rather anonymous looking, with none of the Edwardian flair retained in some of the public areas, which have the high ceilings, skylights, arches, and majestic columns of their original construction. The small tiled bathrooms have shower-tub combinations. One room is equipped for guests with mobility impairments.

Peter St., Manchester M60 2DS. © 01612/363333. Fax 01619/324100. www.paramount-hotels.co.uk. 303 units. £99–£195 ($183–$361) double; £250–£600 ($463–$1,110) suite. Fri–Sun double rates include breakfast. AE, DC, MC, V. Tram: Metrolink to Piccadilly. **Amenities:** 3 restaurants; 2 bars; indoor pool, health club; sauna; business center; salon; 24-hr. room service; laundry service; dry cleaning; nonsmoking rooms; rooms for those with limited mobility. *In room:* A/C, TV w/pay movies, dataport, minibar, coffeemaker, hair dryer, safe, iron/ironing board, trouser press.

Victoria and Albert Hotel Manchester ★★★ *Finds*

One of the most unusual hotels in Britain occupies a renovated brick-sided pair of warehouses, originally conceived in 1843 to store bales of cotton being barged along the nearby Irwell River and the Manchester Ship Canal to looms and mills throughout the Midlands. About a decade ago, Granada TV transformed the then-decrepit buildings into lodgings for their out-of-town guests, and a showcase for many of their creative ideas.

Bedrooms drip with the authenticity and charm of the Victorian age. Each has exposed brick walls, massive ceiling beams, an individualized shape and themed decor, and in many cases, the ornate cast-iron columns of its earlier warehouse manifestation. Each room carries the name of a Granada TV show or series, all instantly recognizable to millions of Brits. Rooms are well equipped, most often with one double bed, and the bathrooms have such touches as yellow ducks ready to float in the tubs with you. The best and most spacious accommodations are called the Sovereign Rooms and offer extra amenities such as bathrobes and slippers. Some rooms on the street-level floor are rented to women only for security reasons.

Water St., Castlefield, Manchester M3 4JQ. ℂ 800/228-9290 in U.S. and Canada, or 01618/384130. Fax 01618/342484. www.marriott.com. 158 units. £180 ($333) double; from £280 ($518) suite. Rates include full English breakfast Fri–Sun only. AE, DC, MC, V. **Amenities:** Restaurant; bar; 24-hr. room service; laundry service; dry cleaning; nonsmoking rooms; rooms for those with limited mobility. *In room:* A/C, TV w/pay movies, minibar, coffeemaker, hair dryer, iron, safe, trouser press.

EXPENSIVE

Etrop Grange Hotel ✦   This is the most historic of the many hotels near Manchester Airport. Originally built of redbrick in 1760, with a modern wing added in the late 1980s in the same architectural style as the original bedrooms, it lies only a couple of minutes drive east of the airport. Don't expect lush meadows and views of fen and forest: The setting is one of sprawling parking lots and industrial-looking warehouses. But inside you'll find open fireplaces, ornate chandeliers, Edwardian windows, and many of the architectural features of the building's original construction. Bedrooms are often small but comfortably appointed; many have antique beds, but all beds are ensconced in brass or else canopied. Black-and-white tiled bathrooms have brass fittings and toiletries and are equipped with antique-style tubs without showers or else stalls with cascading showerheads. The gem here is a series of four-poster master bedrooms with sitting areas and bathrooms fitted with whirlpool tubs.

Thorley Lane, Manchester Airport M90 4EG. ℂ 01614/990500. Fax 01614/990790. www.corushotels.com. 64 units. £99–£149 ($183–$276) double; £169–£230 ($313–$426) suite. AE, DC, MC, V. **Amenities:** Restaurant; bar; 24-hr. room service; laundry service. *In room:* TV, dataport, coffeemaker, hair dryer, iron.

Malmaison ✦   This is one of the best examples in Manchester of combining old architectural features with the new. Behind an Edwardian facade, a dramatic and strikingly modern design reigns, enough of a statement that pop stars visiting from London often stop off here. In the heart of the city, only a minute's walk from Piccadilly Station, individually designed and "modern-as-tomorrow" bedrooms await you. The accommodations are quite stunning in red, black, and ivory. Expect great big beds, CD players, and very contemporary bathrooms with power showers. The Brasserie and bar is a sleek rendezvous, with a contemporary French menu. The setting evokes a Belle Epoque brasserie.

Piccadilly, Manchester M1 3AQ. ℂ 01612/781000. Fax 01612/781002. www.malmaison.com. 167 units. £129 ($239) double; from £165 ($305) suite. AE, DC, MC, V. **Amenities:** Restaurant; bar; health club; sauna; spa; steam room; business center; nonsmoking rooms; rooms for those with limited mobility. *In room:* TV, dataport, minibar, coffeemaker, hair dryer, iron.

Manchester Airport Marriott Hotel   Of the many airport accommodations, this one most closely emulates an American-style courtyard hotel, with an attractive, verdant oasis surrounded by a two-story block of motel-style bedrooms. Rooms are done in the modern chain-hotel style you'd expect. Each comes with a small tiled bathroom with a shower. It's just fine for a 1-night stopover, though you may not want to linger after that.

Hale Rd., Hale Barns, near Altrincham (3km/2 miles from the airport, near Exit 6 of M56), Manchester WA15 8XW. ℂ **01619/040301.** Fax 01619/801787. www.marriott.com. 142 units. Mon–Thurs £125 ($231) double, £200 ($370) suite; Fri–Sun £78 ($144) double, £128 ($237) suite. AE, DC, MC, V. **Amenities:** 2 restaurants; 2 bars; indoor pool; health club; 24-hr. room service; sauna; laundry service. *In room:* TV, dataport, coffeemaker, minibar, hair dryer, iron/ironing board.

INEXPENSIVE

Kempton House Hotel   A large Victorian house located 4km (2½ miles) south of the city center, this hotel offers basic, centrally located accommodations at a reasonable rate. You don't get much in the way of grand comfort in the rather smallish rooms here, but you do get a good bed for the night at a reasonable rate. Several buses go by the hotel on a regular basis.

400 Wilbraham Rd., Chorlton-Cum-Hardy M21 0UH. ℂ **01618/818766.** www.thekempton.co.uk. 8 units. £50–£55 ($93–$102) double. Rates include English breakfast. AE, MC, V. **Amenities:** Bar. *In room:* TV, coffeemaker, hair dryer.

New Central Hotel   Located just off the A665 Cheerham Hill Road, 2.5km (1½ miles) from Victoria Station, this hotel offers simple but comfortable accommodations. Rooms are smallish but decently maintained with comfortable beds. You stay here for the price, not any grand luxury. Be sure and specify your needs when booking a room, because three rooms share all bathroom facilities, and none has private toilet facilities. Some rooms have a shower unit.

144–146 Heywood St., Cheetham, M8 0PD. ℂ and fax **01612/052169.** 10 units. £45 ($83) double without shower, £50 ($93) double with shower. Rates include English breakfast. AE, MC, V. **Amenities:** Restaurant. *In room:* TV, coffeemaker.

WHERE TO DINE
EXPENSIVE

Juniper ⭑⭑⭑ ECLECTIC   Many of Britain's good food guides quite rightly hail this winning choice as one of the country's finest restaurants. It lies 4.9km (8 miles) outside Manchester. The chef, Paul Kitching, is often cited for "the menu's playful way with ingredients." In some cases, that could mean bad news. Not so with the offerings of Kitching, whose signature dishes include roast saddle of Cumbrian hare with foie gras, watercress, yogurt, spices, sugared cashews, and melon syrup juice. We sampled the concoction and found it quite wonderful. The setting isn't glamorous—in a parade of shops—but the food certainly is, especially the seafood, such as Dover sole filets served with preserved lemon and parsley in a creamy broth. For starters, try such divine concoctions as pieces of chicken breast, red pepper, carrots, and mushrooms bound together in a light jelly and topped with an intense tomato custard. By now, you surely have gotten the point: Expect dishes you possibly have never tried before. Ever had chocolate mayonnaise? For dessert, we endorse the locally famed lemon tart with rosemary sorbet.

21 The Downs, Altrincham, Greater Manchester. ℂ **01619/294008.** Reservations required. Main courses £15–£20 ($28–$37). AE, MC, V. Tues–Fri noon–2pm; Tues–Sat 7–9:30pm.

The Lincoln ⭑ BRITISH/INTERNATIONAL   One of the best of the city center restaurants, The Lincoln continues to win new friends since its opening. Fine wine, excellent ingredients, affordable platters, and an imaginative menu have combined to form a winning combination. The chef, Ashley Clarke, is a whiz in the kitchen, concocting delightful dishes that not only look good in presentation, but are good. The menu changes weekly, but you can generally count on such delights as roast rib-eye of beef with Yorkshire pudding; roast loin of lamb with French beans, feta cheese, olives, and a sun-dried tomato sauce; and the market fish of the day. Also anticipate seasonal delights such as oven-roasted breast of wood pigeon.

1 Lincoln Sq. ⓒ **01618/349000.** Reservations required. Main courses £10–£16 ($19–$30); fixed-price 2-course lunch £13 ($23); fixed-price 3-course lunch £15 ($27); Sun lunch £17 ($31). AE, MC, V. Sun–Fri noon–3pm; Mon–Sat 6–10:30pm (11pm Fri–Sat).

Market Restaurant ENGLISH   Few other restaurants capitalize as successfully on a sense of old-fashioned English nostalgia as this one. Set in the heart of town, it promotes itself with an allegiance to very fresh ingredients, and a slightly dowdy but homelike decor that hasn't changed very much since the beginning of World War II. About a third of the dishes are vegetarian; others include smoked breast of duck with chicory, orange, and olive salad; filet of beef with horseradish pancakes and Madeira-based gravy; and a dessert specialty they refer to as a pistachio pavlova crafted with bananas, passion fruit, and whipped Jersey cream. The rhubarb crumble ice cream served with a compote of ice cream is as delicious as it is British.

104 High St. ⓒ **01618/343743.** Reservations recommended. Main courses £12–£16 ($22–$30). AE, DC, MC, V. Wed–Fri noon–2:30pm and 6–9:30pm; Sat 7–9:30pm. Tram: Metrolink to Shudehill (best to take a taxi).

Moss Nook FRENCH   This restaurant, named after the village where it is located, is a favorite local choice for an upscale dinner. The setting, complete with red suede wallpaper, hefty cutlery, and elaborate table settings, is rather formal and heavy. The service is professional but warm and friendly. Menu choices include everything from the standard to the exotically imaginative—breast of duckling can be served in an orange sauce or with red-currant-and-elderflower dressing. Especially good is a soufflé of Swiss cheese with chives and red-pepper sauce or halibut with scallops prepared in a parsley sauce.

Ringway Rd., Moss Nook, 1km (¾ mile) from the Manchester Airport. ⓒ **01614/374778.** Reservations recommended. Main courses £20–£28 ($37–$52); fixed-price 5-course lunch £20 ($37); fixed-price 7-course dinner £37 ($68). AE, MC, V. Tues–Fri noon–1:30pm (last order); Tues–Sat 7–9:30pm (last order).

MODERATE

Cafe Istanbul TURKISH   This restaurant evokes an old Marlene Dietrich flick on the late, late show but is in fact the most savory spot for Turkish cuisine in Manchester. Decorated in a vague Mediterranean style, it draws a hip, young crowd, many who have traveled abroad and are in search of those exotic flavors discovered in their travels. The selection of *meze* (Turkish appetizers) alone is worth the trek here, and the wine list is extensive but without price gouging. Try any of the lamb kabobs (the house specialty) or the grilled seafood.

79 Bridge St. ⓒ **01618/339942.** Reservations recommended. Main courses £10–£13 ($19–$24). MC, V. Daily noon–3pm and 5–11pm.

Dimitri's GREEK   This bistro is a warm and friendly place, like the Greeks themselves. In the city center, it's so popular, especially with a young crowd, that you should call a day in advance for a table. Greek delicacies are the way to go, though Spanish and Italian dishes, including a tapas bar, are dished out nightly. Dimitri's also serves up some of the best veggie dishes in Manchester. On weekends, sit at the bar with a savory blend of Greek coffee and listen to a live jazz band.

1 Campfield Arcade. ⓒ **01618/393319.** Reservations recommended. Main courses £8–£11 ($15–$20). AE, MC, V. Mon–Sat 11am–midnight; Sun 11am–11pm.

The Lowry Restaurant ☆ MODERN BRITISH   Steven Saunders is one of England's best-known chefs. His latest offering is installed at The Lowry museum (p. 600) in Manchester's restored dockland area. In an avant-garde split-level dining area, you can select a table with views over the quay. You can take comfort here in knowing that you'll be served market-fresh ingredients prepared with skill and flair by a well-trained staff. Most dishes are light and totally in step with the tenets of modern British cookery.

A recently sampled main course was a first for us—hot *vichyssoise* (leek-and-potato soup) with Gorgonzola and truffle oil. Other delights on the ever-changing menu include a chargrilled rib-eye steak or a breast of herb-infused chicken with a lemon-and-herb risotto. From the tuna carpaccio with mango salsa and soy dressing, to such puddings as bread and butter with orange custard, the food here is colorful, fresh, and honest.

Pier 8, Salford Quays. ✆ **01618/762121.** Reservations recommended. Main courses £8–£14 ($15–$26); 2-course fixed-price lunch £13–£14 ($24–$26); fixed-price pretheater dinner 5–7:45pm £14–£18 ($26–$33). Daily noon–3pm; Mon–Thurs 5:45–7:45pm; Fri–Sat 5–10pm. Bus: 51, 52, 71, 73, or M11.

Mr. Thomas's Chophouse TRADITIONAL BRITISH   This mellow Manchester pub is also the city's oldest restaurant, established in 1872. Tall and thin, the building is squeezed into a narrow plot of land. The structure itself is a good example of the British Art Nouveau style in the ceramic cladding on the exterior and the provision of green tiles inside. Under brown ceilings, guests dine at tables placed on the checkerboard floors. Real ales are very popular here, including Boddingtons and Timothy Taylor's. The most traditional British food served in the city center is offered here at lunch, including dishes such as braised oxtail with cabbage and dumplings, and steak-and-kidney pudding. We recently dined on a very good pan-fried plaice with mushy peas. The French onion soup is the favorite starter of local diners, and it's always reliable.

52 Cross St. ✆ **01618/322245.** Reservations not needed. Main courses £9–£12 ($17–$22). AE, MC, V. Mon–Sat 11:30am–3pm (bar serves till 11pm).

Yang Sing ☆ *Finds* CANTONESE   Manchester's large population of Asian immigrants considers Yang Sing their favorite restaurant, as proven by the cacophony of languages spoken within its basement dining room. It's loud but efficient, with a fast turnover of tables. Dim sum, those delicate dumplings, are served in a blissful array of choices from a pair of oversize carts in the dining room's center. Menu items cover the gamut of the Cantonese repertoire.

Yang Sing also offers a street-level "steamboat restaurant," where containers of bubbling broth are brought to your table accompanied with an assortment of raw chicken, fish, chopped vegetables, and beef. Use your chopsticks to dunk the tidbits into the hot broth (think of it as a Chinese version of a Swiss fondue).

34 Princess St. ✆ **01612/362200.** Reservations required. Main courses £9–£12 ($17–$22). AE, MC, V. Daily noon–11:30pm. Metrolink tram to Piccadilly.

MANCHESTER AFTER DARK
THE CLUB & MUSIC SCENE
Above all else, Manchester is known for its recent contributions to pop music. From The Smiths and New Order to Oasis and the Stone Roses, the "Manchester sound" has been known throughout the world for over a decade. Yet surprisingly enough, live music went by the wayside in the early 1990s, and clubs were in short supply until they started making a steady comeback in the last couple of years.

Auto Bahn, 10 Canal St. (© **01612/366005**), is known for its design, with artwork displayed on the bright glow of the walls. On weekends, DJs play house and disco for the young crowd of all sexual persuasions. Sometimes a live funk band provides the hottest show in town. The club is a 2-minute walk west of the town center, and the bar serves tasty tapas.

The Attic, 50 New Wakefield (© **01612/366071**), just southwest of the town center, offers the best of both worlds. Downstairs is a relaxing pub aptly named Thirsty Scholar, with a lot of gorgeous guys and dolls. Upstairs you descend into the funk/soul chaos of a club, The Attic, drawing a hip young crowd to dance to reggae, house music, and techno.

South, 4A King St. (© **01618/317756**), is a small industrial-style club. A 10-minute walk north of Piccadilly Gardens, this club has a sophisticated young aura, with '60s and '70s music on Friday and a hot house DJ on Saturday.

Dry Bar, 28–30 Old Oldham St. (© **01612/369840**), was launched by the band New Order and Factory Records. A lot of young, hip media people are drawn here to this "stretch" bar with its ultramodern industrial steel look. A 5-minute walk north of the town center, it features live music every weekend and on some weekdays, too, ranging from hip-hop to acid jazz.

The Roadhouse, Newton Street (© **01612/281789**), the hottest small venue in Manchester, hosts bands up to 7 nights a week. Monday through Saturday check out **Band on the Wall,** 25 Swan St. at Oak Street (© **01618/326625**), where you can hear live blues, jazz, and reggae. For edgier music, check the stage at **Star & Garter,** Farefield Street (© **01612/736726**), on Wednesday through Friday, when harder rock and hard-core acts will get in your face.

Dance clubs here are still going strong. Just stroll through the Castlefield district on a weekend night and check out all the bars featuring a DJ. Located in the old three-story headquarters of Factory Records, **Industry,** 112–116 Princess St. (© **01612/735422**), offers up techno and disco to a mainly gay crowd.

Peveril of the Peak, Great Bridgewater Street (© **01612/366364**), is easy enough to find—just look for a 380-year-old triangular building covered in tile from top to bottom. No one seems to know why it was designed or built that way, but you can step inside and enjoy a pint of Theakston's Best Bitter, Yorkshire Terrier, or Webster's Best Bitter while you puzzle over it.

THE PERFORMING ARTS

Everyone knows about the rock scene in Manchester, but the fine arts thrive as well.

For drama with an unobstructed view, go to the nation's largest theater-in-the-round, **The Royal Exchange,** St. Ann's Square (© **01618/339833;** www.royalexchange.co.uk), which is housed in a futuristic glass-and-steel structure built within the Great Hall of Manchester's former Cotton Exchange and offers 48 weeks of in-house dramaturgy every year.

Home of the renowned **Halle Orchestra, The Bridgewater Hall,** Lower Mosley Street (© **01619/079000;** www.bridgewater-hall.co.uk), is a state-of-the-art, 2,400-seat concert hall. In addition to the orchestra's season, it also presents other classical performances as well as some pop and comedy, too.

The University of Manchester's Department of Music, Coupoand Street (© **01612/754982**), is home to one of the nation's most distinctive classical string quartets, the **Lindsay String Quartet,** which performs a series of eight evening concerts in the department's auditorium during the year. For a real bargain, check out its luncheon recital series, which is free.

The internationally acclaimed **BBC Philharmonic** usually performs Friday and Saturday evening concerts 12 times a year at Bridgewater Hall (box office ✆ **01619/079000**).

2 Liverpool ✯

353km (219 miles) NW of London; 166km (103 miles) NW of Birmingham; 56km (35 miles) W of Manchester

Liverpool, with its famous waterfront on the River Mersey, is a great shipping port and industrial center. King John launched it on its road to glory when he granted it a charter in 1207. Before that, it had been a tiny 12th-century fishing village, but it quickly became a port for shipping men and materials to Ireland. In the 18th century, it grew to prominence because of the sugar, spice, and tobacco trade with the Americans. By the time Victoria came to the throne, Liverpool had become Britain's biggest commercial seaport.

Recent refurbishing of the Albert Dock, the establishment of a Maritime Museum, and the conversion of warehouses into little stores similar to those in Ghirardelli Square in San Francisco have made this an up-and-coming area once again, with many attractions for visitors. Liverpudlians are proud of their city, with its new hotels, two cathedrals, shopping and entertainment complexes, and parks. And of course, whether they're fans of the Fab Four or not, most visitors to Liverpool want to see where Beatlemania began.

ESSENTIALS

GETTING THERE   Liverpool has its own airport, John Lennon Airport (✆ **0870/7508484;** www.liverpooljohnlennonairport.com), which has frequent daily flights from many parts of the United Kingdom, including London, the Isle of Man, and Ireland.

Frequent express trains depart London's Euston Station for Liverpool, a 3-hour trip. For schedules and information, call **0845/748-4950** or visit www.railtrack.co.uk. There is also frequent service from Manchester, a 45-minute ride away.

National Express buses depart London's Victoria Coach Station every 3 hours for the 4½-hour trip to Liverpool. Buses also arrive every hour from Manchester, a 1-hour ride away. For schedules and information, call ✆ **0870/580-8080** or visit www.nationalexpress.com.

If you're driving from London, head north on the M1, then northwest on the M6 to the junction with the M62, which heads west to Liverpool.

VISITOR INFORMATION   The **Tourist Information Centre** is at the Maritime Museum, Albert Dock (✆ **01517/088854**), and is open daily from 10am to 5:30pm. Another Tourist Information Centre in the City Centre, **Queen's Square Centre,** Roe Street (✆ **01517/095111**), is open Monday through Saturday from 9am to 5:30pm, and Sunday from 10am to 4:30pm.

SPECIAL EVENTS   At the end of August and running into the first couple of days of September, the annual **International Beatles Week** attracts about 100,000 fans to Liverpool for a 7-day celebration highlighted by concerts from bands from Argentina to Sweden (with names such as Lenny Pane, Wings Over Liverpool, and The Beats). You can hear the news today at the Sgt. Pepper concert, and take in many other Beatles tributes, auctions, and tours. **Cavern City Tours,** a local company, offers hotel and festival packages that include accommodations and tickets to tours and events, starting around £99 ($183) for 2 nights. For information, contact Cavern City Tours (✆ **01512/369091;**

Liverpool

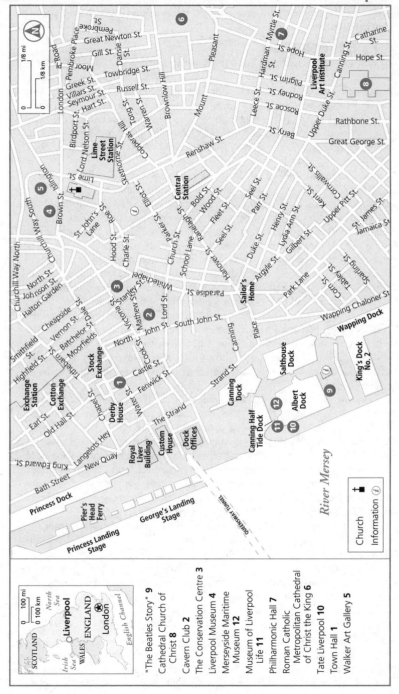

Map legend (1/8 mi, 1/8 km scale):

Church
Information ⓘ

Numbered locations:

"The Beatles Story" 9
Cathedral Church of Christ 8
Cavern Club 2
The Conservation Centre 3
Liverpool Museum 4
Merseyside Maritime Museum 12
Museum of Liverpool Life 11
Philharmonic Hall 7
Roman Catholic Metropolitan Cathedral of Christ the King 6
Tate Liverpool 10
Town Hall 1
Walker Art Gallery 5

www.cavern-liverpool.co.uk) or the Tourist Information Centre in Liverpool at
© **01517/088854.**

SEEING THE SIGHTS

If you'd like a Beatles-related bus tour, **Cavern City Tours** (© **01512/369091;**
www.cavern-liverpool.co.uk) presents a daily 2-hour Magical Mystery Tour,
departing from Albert Dock at 2:20pm and from Roe Street at 2:30pm. This
bus tour covers the most famous attractions associated with the Beatles. Tickets
cost from £11 ($20) and are sold at the Tourist Information Centre at the Mar-
itime Museum on Albert Dock or at the Queen's Square Centre on Roe Street.
For more information about tickets, call either © **01517/098111** or 01517/
088574.

In the Britannia Pavilion at Albert Dock, you can visit **"The Beatles Story"**
(© **01517/091963;** www.beatlesstory.com), a museum housing memorabilia of
the famous group, including a yellow submarine with live fish swimming past
the portholes. From April to September, it's open daily from 10am to 6pm;
October to March from 10am to 5pm. Admission is £7.95 ($15) for adults and
£4.95 ($9.15) for children and students, and a family ticket is £23 ($43).

Everyone's curious about **Penny Lane** and **Strawberry Field.** Actually, the
Beatles' song about Penny Lane didn't refer to the small lane itself but to the area
at the top of the lane called Smithdown Place. Today, this is a bustling thoroughfare for taxis and buses—hardly a place for nostalgic memories.

John Lennon lived nearby and attended school in the area. When he studied
at Art College, he passed here almost every day. To reach Penny Lane and the
area referred to, head north of Sefton Park. From the park, Green Bank Lane
leads into Penny Lane itself, and at the junction of Allerton Road and Smithdown Road stands the Penny Lane Tramsheds. This is John Lennon country—
or what's left of it.

Only the most diehard fans will want to make the journey to **Strawberry
Field** along Beaconsfield Road, which is reached by taking Menlove Avenue east
of the center. Today, you can stand at the iron gates and look in at a children's
home run by the Salvation Army. As a child, John played on the grounds, and
in 1970 he donated a large sum of money to the home. A garden party held
every summer here was attended by John. His son, Sean, and Yoko Ono made
two visits here in 1984. The first was a media circus, but the second was conducted in secrecy. Yoko spent many hours talking to the children and bringing
them gifts, along with $80,000 to help run their home.

Because these sights are hard to reach by public transport and lie outside the
center, you may want to take one of the Cavern City Tours (see above) that feature both Strawberry Field and Penny Lane.

A fun thing to do is to take the famous **Mersey Ferry** that travels from the
Pier Head to both Woodside and Seacombe. Service operates daily from early
morning to early evening throughout the year. Special cruises run throughout
the summer including trips along the Manchester Ship Canal. For more information, contact **Mersey Ferries,** Victoria Place, Seacombe, Wallasey (© **01516/
301030;** www.merseyferries.co.uk).

Albert Dock ✲   Built of brick, stone, and cast iron, this showpiece development on Liverpool's waterfront opened in 1846, saw a long period of decline,
and has now been extensively renovated and refurbished. The dockland warehouses now house shops, restaurants, cafes, an English pub, and a cellar wine
bar. One pavilion encompasses the main building of the Merseyside Maritime

Museum (see below) and another is the home of the Tate Liverpool (see below). Parking is available.

Albert Dock Co. Ltd. ⓒ 01517/087334. www.albertdock.com. Free admission. Shops daily 10am–6pm. Bars and restaurants daily 11am–11pm. Smart Bus from city center.

Cathedral Church of Christ ★★
The great new Anglican edifice overlooking the River Mersey was begun in 1904 and was largely completed 74 years later; it was the last Gothic-style cathedral to be built worldwide. Dedicated in the presence of Queen Elizabeth II in 1978, it is the largest church in England and the fifth-largest in the world. Its vaulting under the tower is 53m (175 ft.) high, the highest in the world, and its length, 186m (619 ft.), makes it one of the longest cathedrals in the world. The organ has nearly 10,000 pipes, the most found in any church. The tower houses the highest (66m/219 ft.) and the heaviest (31 tons) bells in the world, and the Gothic arches are the highest ever built. From the tower, you can see to North Wales.

A Visitor Centre and Refectory features an aerial sculpture of 12 huge sails, with a ship's bell, clock, and light that changes color on an hourly basis. You can enjoy full meals in the charming refectory.

St. James Mt. ⓒ 01517/096271. www.liverpoolcathedral.org.uk. Admission to cathedral free; tower and embroidery gallery £2.50 ($4.65) adults, £1.50 ($2.80) children. Cathedral daily 8am–6pm. Tower open daily Mar–Oct 11am–4pm; closed during winter.

The Conservation Centre
The Conservation Centre, in the heart of Liverpool, is the first of its kind in Europe. The Caught in Time exhibition uncovers the secret world of museum conservation and reveals how the 1.2 million artifacts in national museums and galleries on Merseyside collections are kept from the ravages of time. Using state-of-the-art hand-held audio guides, video linkups, demonstrations, behind-the-scenes tours, and interactive displays, visitors can see how everything from fine art and a Beatles gold disc to a mummified crocodile are saved from decay by expert conservators.

Whitechapel, Liverpool. ⓒ 01514/784999. www.nmgm.org.uk/conservation. Free admission. Mon–Sat 10am–5pm; Sun noon–5pm. Closed Dec 23–26 and Jan 1.

Liverpool Museum ★
One of Britain's finest museums features collections from all over the world—from the earliest beginnings with giant dinosaurs through centuries of great art and inventions. At the Natural History Centre, you can use microscopes and video cameras to learn about the natural world. Living displays from the vivarium and aquarium form a large part of the collections, and a planetarium features daily programs covering modern space exploration—an armchair tour toward the beginning of the universe and the far-flung reaches of the cosmos. There is a small charge for the planetarium and temporary exhibitions.

William Brown St. ⓒ 01514/784399. www.liverpoolmuseum.org.uk. Free admission. Mon–Sat 10am–5pm; Sun noon–5pm.

The McCartney House
The house where the McCartneys lived in Liverpool before Paul's meteoric rise to superstardom has been purchased by the National Trust. Working from old photographs taken by Paul's brother Michael, the house has been restored to its original 1950s appearance, complete with patterned brown sofa and armchair with white linen antimacassars, where Paul and John scribbled out their first songs. The Chinese willow print wallpaper doesn't reach the corners because the family was too poor to buy enough. Hardly Graceland, it does give an insight into the humble beginnings of one of the world's most famous and influential entertainers. The house is open to the public only

through tours organized by the National Trust. Four tours a day each depart from the Albert Dock or Speke Hall, The Walk. Groups are limited to 14 people at any one time. Book well in advance.

20 Forthlin Rd., Allerton 16. ⓒ **01517/088574** booking office; 0870/900-0256 information line. www.speke hall.org.uk/beatles.htm. Admission £12 ($22) adults and free for children under 16. Apr–Oct Wed–Sun 10:30 and 11:20am (Albert Dock), 2:15pm, and 4pm (Speke Hall). Closed Nov–Mar.

Mendips The stucco house where John Lennon lived as a boy was purchased by his wife, Yoko Ono, and was restored by the National Trust. Curators have recreated the late 1950s look of the house, right down to the vintage cleansers in the kitchen and the posters of Rita Hayworth, Elvis Presley, and Brigitte Bardot in Lennon's tiny bedroom. The future music great lived here with his Aunt Mimi and Uncle George, composing his early songs on the front porch and in his bedroom.

251 Menlove Ave. ⓒ **01517/427-7231**. www.spekehall.org.uk/mendips.htm. Admission £9.50 ($18) adults, free for children under 16. Tours (subject to change) leave daily at 10:30am and 11:20am from Albert Dock. No direct access to this property unless you book a tour.

Merseyside Maritime Museum ⚓ Set in the historic heart of Liverpool's waterfront, this museum provides a unique blend of floating exhibits, craft demonstrations, working displays, and special events. In addition to restored waterfront buildings, exhibitions present the story of mass emigration through Liverpool in the last century, shipbuilding on Merseyside, the Battle of the Atlantic Gallery, and Transatlantic Slavery. There is wheelchair access.

Albert Dock. ⓒ **01514/784499**. www.liverpoolmuseums.org.uk. Free admission. Daily 10am–5pm. Bus: Albert Dock Shuttle from city center.

Museum of Liverpool Life This museum of Mersey culture tells the story of Liverpudlians and their contribution to British life. On the banks of the Mersey River, the museum is installed in a former boat hall and building once used by river pilots. You can do everything here from listening to Liverpool bands on a jukebox to learning how Chinese sailors created the oldest Chinese community in Liverpool in the 18th century. Also present is the King's regiment gallery, "City Soldiers," with its medal collection. A new gallery, "City Lives," traces the richness of the city's cultural diversity, and another new gallery, the "River Room," celebrates the role of the River Mersey, including an exhibition of swimwear from a bygone age. If it pertains to Liverpool, it's all here, though it may be more than you want to know.

Albert Dock. ⓒ **01514/784080**. www.liverpoolmuseums.org.uk. Free admission. Daily 10am–5pm.

Roman Catholic Metropolitan Cathedral of Christ the King ⚓⚓ About 1km (½ mile) away from the Anglican cathedral stands the Roman Catholic cathedral—the two are joined by a road called Hope Street. The construction of the cathedral, designed by Sir Edwin Lutyens, was started in 1930, but when World War II interrupted in 1939, not even the granite-and-brick vaulting of the crypt was complete. At the end of the war it was estimated that the cost of completing the structure as Lutyens had designed it would be some £27 million. Architects throughout the world were invited to compete to design a more realistic project to cost about £1 million and to be completed in 5 years. Sir Frederick Gibberd won the competition and was commissioned to oversee the construction of the circular cathedral in concrete and glass, pitched like a tent at one end of the piazza that covered all of the original site, crypt included.

Construction was completed between 1962 and 1967, and today the cathedral offers seating for more than 2,000. Above the altar rises a multicolored glass lantern weighing 2,000 tons and rising to a height of 87m (290 ft.). Called a space-age cathedral, it has a bookshop, a tearoom, and tour guides.

Mount Pleasant. ✆ **0151/709-9222**. www.liverpool-rc-cathedral.org.uk. Free admission. Daily 8am–6pm (until 5pm in winter). Bus: Albert Dock Shuttle from city center.

Tate Liverpool ⭐ This museum displays much of the National Collection of 20th-century art, complemented by changing art exhibitions of international standing. Three- and 4-month special exhibitions are frequently mounted here, perhaps the prints of Joan Miró or the sculptures of the iconoclastic British sculptress Rachel Whiteread. The tourist office has full details on all special exhibitions, or you can call the museum directly.

Albert Dock. ✆ **01517/027400**. www.tate.org.uk/liverpool. Free admission except special exhibitions. Tues–Sun 10am–5:50pm. Bus: Albert Dock Shuttle from city center.

Walker Art Gallery ⭐⭐ One of Europe's finest art galleries offers an outstanding collection of European art from 1300 to the present day. The gallery is especially rich in European old masters, Victorian and pre-Raphaelite works, and contemporary British art. It also has an award-winning sculpture gallery, featuring works from the 18th and 19th centuries. Seek out, in particular, Simone Martini's *Jesus Discovered in the Temple* and Salvator Rosa's *Landscape with Hermit*. Rembrandt is on show, as is an enticing *Nymph of the Fountain* by Cranach. The work of British artists is strongest here, ranging from *Horse Frightened by a Lion* by Stubbs to *Snowdon from Llan Nantlle* by Richard Wilson. Among the pre-Raphaelites are Ford Madox Brown and W. R. Yeames. The French Impressionists represented include Monet, Seurat, and Degas, among others. Modern British paintings include works by Lucian Freud and Stanley Spencer.

William Brown St. ✆ **01514/784199**. www.liverpoolmuseums.org.uk. Free admission. Mon–Sat 10am–5pm; Sun noon–5pm. Closed Dec 23–26 and Jan 1.

SHOPPING

Pedestrian shopping areas with boutiques, specialty shops, and department stores include Church Street, Lord Street, Bold Street, Whitechapel, and Paradise Street. On the river, Albert Dock also houses a collection of small shops.

For shopping centers, go to **Cavern Walks** on Mathew Street, the heart of Beatleland (✆ **01512/369082**), or **Quiggins Centre,** 12–16 School Lane (✆ **01517/092462**).

If you want to buy that special piece of Beatles memorabilia, wander through the **Beatles Shop,** 31 Mathew St. (✆ **01512/368066**), or the **Heritage Shop,** 1 The Colonnades, Albert Dock (✆ **01517/097474**).

For a huge selection of British crafts, visit **Bluecoat Display Centre,** College Lane (✆ **01517/094014**), with its gallery of metal, ceramics, glass, jewelry, and wood pieces by some 350 British craftspeople.

Frank Green's, 97 Oakfield Rd., Anfield (✆ **01512/603241**), is where you'll find prints by this famous local artist who has been capturing the Liverpool scene on canvas since the 1960s. His work includes city secular buildings, churches, and street life.

A couple of other specialty shops that warrant a visit include **William Forbes,** Unit 19, Setton Lane Industrial Estate, Maghull (✆ **0870/752-2444**), which has been making nautical instruments longer than anyone in the known world; and **Thornton's,** 16 Whitechapel (✆ **01517/086849**), where you can choose from a dizzying selection of continental and traditional English chocolates, toffees, and mints.

Tips   **In the Footsteps of the Fab Four**

Wherever you turn in Liverpool today, somebody is hawking a Beatles tour. But if you'd like to see a few of the famous spots on your own, stop in at the **Cavern Club,** 8–10 Mathew St., now touted as "The Most Famous Club in the World," and pick up a Cavern City Tour map to find famous Beatles locations in the city center. The Beatles played 292 gigs here between 1961 and 1963. Manager Brian Epstein first saw them here on November 9, 1961, and by December 10, he had signed a contract with the band.

WHERE TO STAY

Beatles fans and others will want to book themselves into Liverpool's newest hotel, **Hard Day's Night,** North John St., slated to open some time during the life of this edition. It will occupy a restored downtown building near the site of the Cavern Club where the Fab Four played some of their earliest gigs, and will be connected at basement level with the new cavern, a replica of the original club. The hotel will feature 120 rooms, each with a mural relating to the Beatles. Prospective visitors will be able to stay in a Yellow Submarine or relax in a Lucy in the Sky with Diamonds Suite.

Britannia Adelphi Hotel ⭐   This grand hotel, built in 1914, is known for its fine Edwardian rooms and good cuisine. Past the elegant entrance, you enter an overblown world of marble corridors, molded ceilings, and dark polished wood. These traditional features are complemented by modern luxuries, because the hotel has been completely refurbished. Many still view this as the best address in town, but we rank it number three, after the Liverpool Moat House and the Thistle. Each recently refurbished bedroom is well furnished and comes with double-glazed windows. The mezzanine bedrooms are likely to be noisy. Sixteen bathrooms are fitted with whirlpool tubs; all rooms have shower-and-tub combinations.

Ranelagh Place, Liverpool, Merseyside L3 5UL. ℂ **01517/097200.** Fax 01517/088326. www.britannia-hotels. co.uk. 402 units. £50–£195 ($93–$361) double; £195 ($361) suite. Children under 12 stay free in parent's room. AE, DC, MC, V. Parking £10 ($19). **Amenities:** 3 restaurants, 2 bars; sauna; heated indoor pool; health club; Jacuzzi; salon; 24-hr. room service; laundry service; dry cleaning; nonsmoking rooms; rooms for those with limited mobility. *In room:* TV, coffeemaker, hair dryer, trouser press.

The Feathers Hotel   This brick-fronted hotel is composed of four separate Georgian-style town houses. It sits in the heart of the city, adjacent to the modern Metropolitan Cathedral. The bedrooms are comfortable, with simple traditional furniture—there are some four-poster beds—but don't expect much charm. Executive bedrooms offer additional amenities such as CD players and Sony PlayStations. Some 40 units come with both tub and shower.

119–125 Mt. Pleasant, Liverpool, Merseyside L3 5TF. ℂ **01517/099655.** Fax 01517/093838. www.feathers. uk.com. 66 units. £79–£90 ($146–$167) double. Rates include buffet breakfast. AE, MC, V. Bus: 80 (the airport bus). **Amenities:** Restaurant; bar; 24-hr. room service; dry cleaning; free spa pass. *In room:* TV, dataport (in some), coffeemaker, hair dryer, iron, trouser press.

Liverpool Moat House ⭐ *Kids*   This hotel may have zoomed past the Thistle in the race for the title of Liverpool's best hotel, but that doesn't mean it's a world-class hotel like you'll find in Manchester, or even Chester. Located in the center of the city, it is nonetheless one of the most comfortable, efficient hotels in Merseyside. The spacious bedrooms are spread across eight floors, and many have recently been refurbished. An astonishing 200 bedrooms are large enough to be used as family rooms, and each comes with a combination tub and shower. Typically favored by businesspeople, the hotel is also a perfectly nice choice for sightseers.

Paradise St., Liverpool, Merseyside O1 8JD. ✆ **01514/719988.** Fax 01517/092706. www.moathousehotels. com. 263 units. £130–£148 ($241–$274) double; £287 ($531) suite. AE, DC, MC, V. **Amenities:** Restaurant; bar; indoor pool; health club; 24-hr. room service; sauna; laundry service. *In room:* A/C, TV, dataport, coffeemaker, iron, hair dryer, safe, trouser press.

Thistle Liverpool ✨ Showcased in an austere high-rise evoking the bow of a great luxury liner, this first-class hotel is one of the top three in the city (with Liverpool Moat House and Brittania Adelphi). It caters largely to business travelers. You check in to a spacious lobby and are shown to one of the well-furnished but fairly standard bedrooms. Many bedrooms, though quite small, provide views of the River Mersey, and you can request a minibar. Average—not grand—comfort can be found here. The best units are the corner bedrooms, which are triangular in shape and face the river. Bedrooms are frequently renovated as the need arises. Each small bathroom comes with a combination tub and shower and adequate shelf space.

30 Chapel St., Liverpool, Merseyside L3 9RE. ✆ **800/847-4358** in the U.S., or 01512/274444. Fax 01512/363973. www.thistlehotels.com/liverpool. 226 units. £120 ($222) double; £160 ($296) suite. Rates include breakfast. Weekends £118 ($218) double including breakfast. AE, DC, MC, V. **Amenities:** Restaurant; bar; 24-hr. room service; laundry service; dry cleaning; nonsmoking rooms. *In room:* TV, dataport, coffeemaker, hair dryer, trouser press.

Trials Hotel ✨ *Finds* Though it's small, this rather luxurious hotel has charm and character. It was created in 1986 from a centrally located Victorian structure that had once been a bank. Now beautifully converted, it's often the choice of discriminating visitors. The plush accommodations are all individually decorated split-level suites. Each offers roomy comfort, plus a well-maintained bathroom with a Jacuzzi tub and shower.

56–62 Castle St., Liverpool, Merseyside L2 7LQ ✆ **01512/271021.** Fax 01512/360110. www.trialshotel.com. 20 suites. £110–£130 ($204–$241) suite. AE, MC, V. Parking £8 ($15). **Amenities:** Bar; limited room service; laundry service; dry cleaning. *In room:* TV, minibar, coffeemaker, hair dryer, iron/ironing board, trouser press, Jacuzzi.

WHERE TO DINE

For such a world-famous city, Liverpool has yet to play host to a world-class restaurant. Here are the best nonhotel restaurants it has to offer.

Bar Italia ITALIAN/CONTINENTAL In the center of the business district, this bustling little trattoria serves affordable and tasty dishes with a certain continental flair. Roman art on the walls evokes a Mediterranean feel, and on wintery nights, the brick fireplace adds a cozy touch. The chefs here select the choicest ingredients to turn out savory dishes, such as our favorite pasta, served with fresh prosciutto balls glazed with Parmesan. Always reliable is the steak with a creamy mushroom-and-brandy sauce. For a zesty main dish, opt for king prawns with flakes of hot chile pepper and a fresh tomato sauce.

48A Castle St. ✆ **01512/363375.** Reservations recommended. Main courses £8–£15 ($15–$28). MC, V. Mon–Fri 11:30am–3pm; Tues–Sat 5:30–11pm.

Far East CANTONESE/BEIJING Liverpool is famous for its Chinese restaurants—not surprising because the city has one of the largest Chinese populations in Europe, and Far East is a great Chinese restaurant. You may enjoy a dim sum lunch, later returning in the evening for more haute Chinese fare. You face a vast array of Cantonese specialties, including our favorite chile-flavored large prawns. The chefs also do marvelous things with duck.

27–35 Berry St. ✆ 01517/093141. Reservations required. Main courses £9–£22 ($17–$41); fixed-price meals £15–£21 ($28–$39). AE, DC, MC, V. Sun–Thurs noon–11:15pm; Fri–Sat noon–12:45am; Sun noon–11pm.

Shangri-La CANTONESE   One of the biggest and most consistently popular restaurants in the city center serves a wide-ranging choice of mostly Cantonese food, with special emphasis on the cuisine of Shanghai. With room for around 300 guests, it contains two separate dining rooms, each with its own bar, and a red, gold, and green decor that may remind you of some aspects of a Confucian temple. Many regulars opt to begin a meal with dim sum, the delicate steamed or fried dumplings whose variations are almost infinite. Expect well-flavored treatments of virtually every succulently stir-fried vegetable that's in season at the moment and myriad preparations of fish, shellfish, duck, pork, chicken, and beef.

In the Ashcroft Building, 37 Victoria St. ✆ 01512/272707. Reservations not necessary. Main courses £8–£12 ($15–$22); fixed-price lunch £6 ($11). AE, DC, MC, V. Daily noon–2:30pm and 6–11:30pm.

Simply Heathcote's BRITISH   An outpost of the "chef of the north," Paul Heathcote, who brings his Lancashire hot pot to the center of Liverpool. It's been an immediate success since its opening. The stylish decor is designed along clean, modern lines, and the freshest of ingredients are used. Try his filet of Torbay sole with "crushed potatoes," asparagus, and lemon pickle, or else his roast breast of Goosnargh duckling with summer vegetables and a red-wine sauce. Of course, those old favorites such as black pudding hash browns also appear on the menu. More modern dishes include linguine with crispy bacon and spring onions and spring vegetables with a herb risotto.

25 The Strand. ✆ 01512/363536. Reservations not needed. Main courses £8.75–£15 ($16–$28); fixed-price 2-course dinner £14 ($26); fixed-price 3-course meals £16 ($30) served daily noon–2:30 and 6–7pm. AE, MC, V. Mon–Fri noon–2:30pm and 6–10pm; Sat 6–11pm; Sun 6–9:30pm.

60 Hope St. ✦ MODERN EUROPEAN   In a double-fronted Georgian house, close to the Philharmonic Hall, this enticing restaurant, among the best in Liverpool, gives you both a ground floor restaurant and a basement cafe and bar. It's really like a brasserie you'd find on the Continent. For the most part, the food is light in texture and full of flavor. A certain robustness permeates the cuisine, as evoked by the ravioli stuffed with goat cheese and red pepper or the tea-smoked duck with a pear relish. The menu is inspired by many other cuisines, including an Asian crab omelet with soy dressing. A house specialty is treacle roast Welsh black beef with wild mushrooms, potatoes, spinach, and a foie gras crème sauce. For dessert, we dare you to try the deep-fried ham sandwich with Carnation milk ice cream.

60 Hope St. ✆ 01517/076060. Reservations required. Main courses £14–£25 ($26–$46). MC, V. Mon–Fri noon–2:30pm; Mon–Sat 7–10:30pm.

Tate Café BRITISH   When we're in Liverpool, we like to lunch at this cafe connected with its famous gallery. You can launch your day here with a late breakfast or else indulge in a hearty and delightful lunch, with as many cups of freshly brewed coffee as you wish. On summer days try for one of the dockside seats. Freshly made salads with crisp greens and well-stuffed sandwiches are regularly featured, though you may also want to opt for more substantial fare, such as a tender lamb shank with sweet potatoes or grilled salmon with an assortment of vegetables julienne. The grilled chicken breast is another pleasing favorite. Beer, lager, and wines are also served. Recorded light jazz is played in the background. The Colonnades, Albert Dock. (© **01517/027580.** Reservations not needed. Main courses £6–£10 ($11–$19); sandwiches £6–£10 ($11–$19). AE, MC, V. Tues–Sat 10am–6pm.

LIVERPOOL AFTER DARK

Liverpool's nightlife is nothing if not diverse. Several publications and places will help you get a handle on the entertainment options around town. The evening *Liverpool Echo* is a good source of daily information about larger and fine-arts events; the youth-oriented *L: Scene* magazine will provide you with a thorough calendar of club dates and gigs; and the free *City X Blag,* available in most clubs and pubs, will do the same. Available free in gay clubs and pubs, *Pulse* lists gay activities and events throughout the region.

The **Student Entertainment Office** (© **01517/944143**) at the University of Liverpool can tell you about the range of activities sponsored by the school, or you can stop by the student union on Mount Pleasant and check out the bulletin board. Two other good places for finding out about the underground scene are **The Palace,** Slater Street (© **01517/088515**), and **Quiggins Centre,** School Lane (© **01517/092462**). Each is overflowing with flyers advertising local events.

Open year-round, the **Liverpool Empire,** Lime Street, hosts visiting stage productions ranging from dramas and comedies to ballets and tributes. Book through Ticketmaster at © **0870/606-3541.**

Philharmonic Hall, Hope Street (© **01512/102895;** www.liverpoolphil. com), is home to **The Royal Philharmonic Orchestra,** one of the best orchestras outside of London, which usually performs twice weekly. When the orchestra is not on, there are often concerts by touring musicians, and films are sometimes shown as well.

At the **Zanzibar Club,** 43 Seel St. (© **01517/070633**), DJs spin drum and bass and hip-hop Monday through Saturday nights, with the occasional rock or pop booking thrown in for good measure.

Beatles fans flock to the **Cavern Club,** 8–10 Mathew St. (© **01512/361965;** www.cavern-liverpool.co.uk), thinking that this is where the Fab Four appeared. Demolished years ago, the old Cavern Club has faded into history. However, locals still go to this new version to hear live bands (regrettably, not as good as the dear, departed ones). There's no cover until 11pm; after that you pay a £2 ($3.70) door charge. For a more nostalgic evening, head for the **Cavern Pub,** also on Mathew Street (© **0151/236-4041**). This is where many groups in England got their start before going on to greater glory. The names of the groups who appeared here from 1957 to 1973 are recorded.

A cafe by day, **Baa Bar,** 43–45 Fleet St. (© **01517/070610**), serves an eclectic menu, and free dancing to a DJ brings in a lot of the evening's business.

A pub with a Fab Four spin, **Ye Cracke,** Rice Street (© **01517/094171**), was a favorite watering hole of John Lennon in pre- and early Beatles days (but expect regulars to suggest you quit living in the past if you ask about it). Better just soak up the little-changed atmosphere over a pint of Oak Wobbly Bob, Cains, or Haywood Oak.

GAY BARS IN LIVERPOOL

You won't find as frenetic or as varied a nightlife scene in Liverpool as you will in, say, Manchester or Leeds. But something about the rough-and-tumble streets of this monument to the Industrial Revolution makes for hard-party times at some of the city's gay bars. At **Masquerade,** 10 Cumberland St. (© **01512/367786**), a gay version of a Victorian pub, the scene is the most consistently crowded and animated of the several gay bars in its neighborhood near the Moorfields Railway Station, off Dale Street. Come to the street-level bar to drink, talk, and watch the occasional cabaret *artiste*, whose acts are presented after 8pm every Friday and Saturday. Head for the basement-level dance floor for a bit of boogeying with the 'Pudlians. At **G-Bar,** Eberle Street (© **01512/258-1230**), the street level is a pseudo-Gothic piece of kitsch that only a rave party could fully appreciate. The cellar has a floor where crowds of gay and sexually neutral fans dance, dance, dance. There's even a "love lounge" where you may catch up on a bit of dialogue, or whatever, in circumstances that are highly relaxing. Cover is from £3 to £5 ($5.55–$9.25), depending on the night of the week.

The Lisbon, 35 Victoria St. (© **01512/316831**), is set close to Moorfield railway station. This is the quietest and calmest of the four pubs listed in this section, alluring a nicer blend of men than at some of the seedier gay dives nearby.

3 The Walled City of Chester ★/★

333km (207 miles) NW of London; 31km (19 miles) S of Liverpool; 147km (91 miles) NW of Birmingham

A Roman legion founded Chester on the Dee River in the 1st century A.D. It reached its pinnacle as a bustling port in the 13th and 14th centuries but declined following the gradual silting up of the river. While other walls of medieval cities of England were either torn down or badly fragmented, Chester still has 3km (2 miles) of fortified city walls intact. The main entrance into Chester is Eastgate, which dates only from the 18th century. Within the walls are half-timbered houses and shops, though not all of them date from Tudor days. Chester is unusual in that some of its builders used black-and-white timbered facades even during the Georgian and Victorian eras.

Chester today has aged gracefully and is a lovely old place to visit, if you don't mind the summer crowds who overrun the place. It has far more charm and intimacy then either Liverpool or Manchester and is one of the most interesting medieval cities in England.

ESSENTIALS

GETTING THERE   About 21 trains depart London's Euston Station every hour daily for the 2½-hour trip to Chester. Trains also run every hour between Liverpool and Chester, a 45-minute ride. For schedules and information, call © **0845/748-4950** or visit www.railtrack.co.uk.

Three **National Express** buses run between Birmingham and Chester; the trip takes 2½ hours. The same bus line also offers service between Liverpool and Chester. It's also possible to catch a National Express coach from London's Victoria Coach Station to Chester. For schedules and information, call © **0870 580-8080** or visit www.nationalexpress.com.

If you're driving from London, head north on the M1, then take the M6 at the junction near Coventry. Continue northwest to the junction with the A54, which leads west to Chester.

VISITOR INFORMATION   The **Tourist Information Centre** is at the Town Hall, Northgate Street (© **01244/402385**). It offers a hotel-reservation service as well as information. Arrangements can also be made for coach tours or walking tours of Chester (including a ghost-hunter tour). It's open May through October Monday through Saturday from 9:30am to 5:30pm and Sunday from 10am to 4pm; off season, Monday through Saturday from 9:30am to 5pm.

Chester

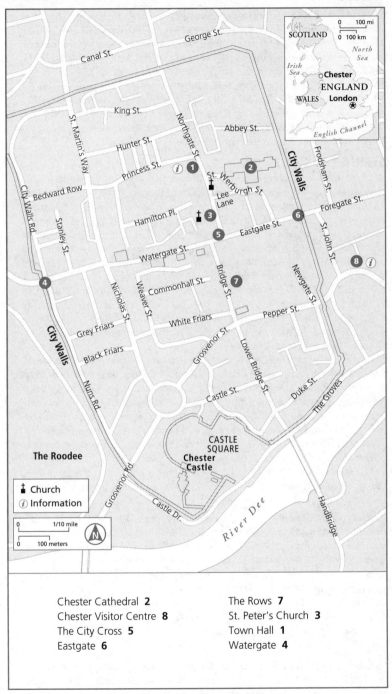

Chester Cathedral **2**
Chester Visitor Centre **8**
The City Cross **5**
Eastgate **6**

The Rows **7**
St. Peter's Church **3**
Town Hall **1**
Watergate **4**

SPECIAL EVENTS The last 2 weeks of July are an active time in Chester, as the **Chester Summer Music Festival** (© **01244/320700** and fax 01244/341200; Mon–Fri 9am–5:30pm, Sat 10am–4pm) hosts orchestras and other classical performers from around Britain in lunch concerts, with tickets averaging £6 ($11); small indoor evening concerts, where tickets cost from £6 to £30 ($11–$56). For additional information about the music festival, you can also write to the Chester Summer Music Festival Office, 8 Abbey Square, Chester CH1 2HU.

Occurring simultaneously, the **Chester Fringe Festival** (© **01244/321497**) focuses on other musical genres, offering Latin, rock, Cajun, folk, and jazz concerts. Ticket prices vary widely, depending on the performer.

SEEING THE SIGHTS

In a big Victorian building opposite the Roman amphitheater, the largest uncovered amphitheater in Britain, the **Chester Visitor Centre,** Vicars Lane (© **01244/ 351609**), offers a number of services to visitors. A 20-minute video presentation helps your appreciation of Chester. The center has a gift shop and a licensed restaurant serving meals and snacks. Admission is free, and the center is open May through October, Monday through Saturday from 9:30am to 5:30pm and Sunday from 10am to 4pm; November through April, Monday to Saturday from 9:30am to 5pm and Sunday from 10am to 4pm. Guided walking tours of the city depart daily at 10:30am in the winter and at 10:30am and 2pm in the summer.

To the accompaniment of a hand bell, the **town crier** appears at the City Cross—the junction of Watergate, Northgate, and Bridge streets—from May to August at noon Tuesday through Saturday to shout news about sales, exhibitions, and attractions in the city.

In the center of town, you'll see the much-photographed **Eastgate clock.** Climb the nearby stairs and walk along the top of the **city wall** for a view down on Chester. Passing through centuries of English history, you'll go by a cricket field, see the River Dee, formerly a major trade artery, and get a look at many 18th-century buildings. The wall also goes past some Roman ruins, and it's possible to leave the walkway to explore them. The walk is charming and free.

Eastgate Street is now a pedestrian way, and musicians often perform for your pleasure beside St. Peter's Church and the Town Cross.

The Rows 🐱🐱 are double-decker layers of shops, one tier on the street level, the others stacked on top and connected by a footway. The upper tier is like a continuous galleried balcony—walking in the rain is never a problem here.

Chester Cathedral 🐱 The present building, founded in 1092 as a Benedictine abbey, was made an Anglican cathedral church in 1541. Many architectural restorations were carried out in the 19th century, but older parts have been preserved. Notable features include the fine range of monastic buildings, particularly the cloisters and refectory, the chapter house, and the superb medieval woodcarving in the choir (especially for misericords). Also worth seeing are the long south transept with its various chapels, the consistory court, and the medieval roof bosses in the Lady Chapel.

St. Werburgh St. © **01244/324756.** www.chestercathedral.org.uk. £3 ($5.55) donation suggested. Daily 9am–5pm.

Chester Zoo 🐱 *Kids* The Chester Zoo is the largest repository of animals in the north of England. It is also the site of some of the most carefully manicured gardens in the region—44 hectares (110 acres) that feature unusual shrubs, rare trees, and warm-weather displays of carpet bedding with as many as 160,000 plants timed to bloom simultaneously.

Many rare and endangered animal species breed freely here; the zoo is particularly renowned for the most successful colonies of chimpanzees and orangutans in Europe. The water bus, a popular observation aid that operates exclusively in summer, allows you to observe hundreds of water birds that make their home on the park's lake. Also, a monorail stops at the extreme eastern and western ends of the zoo, making visits less tiring. Youngsters love the Monkey's Island exhibit.

Off A41, Upton-by-Chester, 3km (2 miles) north of the town center. © 01244/380280. www.chesterzoo.org. Admission £11 ($20) adults, £8.50 ($16) seniors and children 3–15. Family ticket £37 ($68). Monorail £1.80 ($3.35) adults, £1.40 ($2.60) children. Free for kids under 3. Opens daily 10am; closing times vary, call for details. Closed Dec 25. From Chester's center, head north along Liverpool Rd.

SHOPPING

Chester has three main shopping areas.

The **Grosvenor Precinct** is filled with classy, expensive shops and boutiques that sell a lot of trendy fashion and art items. This area is bordered on three sides by Eastgate, Bridge, and Pepper streets.

For stores with more character and lower prices, explore **the Rows,** a network of double-layered streets and sidewalks with an assortment of shops. The Rows runs along Bridge, Watergate, Eastgate, and Northgate streets. Shopping upstairs is much more adventurous than down on the street. Thriving stores operate in this traffic-free paradise: tobacco shops, restaurants, department stores, china shops, jewelers, and antiques dealers. For the best look, take a walk on arcaded Watergate Street.

Another shopping area to check out is **Cheshire Oaks,** a huge retail village of 60 shops, mainly clothing, perfume, and shoe outlet stores. Cheshire Oaks is located about 13km (8 miles) north of Chester on the M53.

Chester has a large concentration of antiques and craft shops. Some better ones include **Lowe & Sons,** 11 Bridge St. Row (© **01244/325850**), with antique silver and estate jewelry; **The Antique Shop,** 40 Watergate St. (© **01244/316286**), specializing in brass, copper, and pewter items; **Adam's Antiques,** 65 Watergate Row (© **01244/319421**), focusing on 18th- and 19th-century antiques.

One of the better shops for jewelry is **Boodle and Dunthorne,** 52 Eastgate St. (© **01244/326666**). Since the days of George III, **Brown's of Chester,** 34–40 Eastgate Rd. (© **01244/350001**), has carried women's fashions, perfumes, menswear, and children's clothes.

WHERE TO STAY
VERY EXPENSIVE

Chester Grosvenor Hotel ★★★ This fine, half-timbered, five-story building in the heart of Chester is one of the most luxurious hotels in northern England, a reputation well deserved. Owned and named after the family of the

---

Finds **Following the Antique Experts**

To find a good deal on antiques, try a quick trip to the town of **Boughton;** every transatlantic dealer seems to go here. Along the A41, a mile from the heart of town, Boughton is filled with antiques shops along Christledon Road. It doesn't have the charm of Chester, but shopping values are often better here than in the more historic city. Some outlets have as many as a dozen showrooms, even though they often are hidden behind rather dreary facades.

dukes of Westminster, its origin can be traced from the reign of Queen Elizabeth I. Started as a Tudor inn, it became a political headquarters in Hanoverian days, was later transformed into a glittering mecca for the Regency and Victorian set, and continued to be a social center during the Edwardian era. It's hosted its share of royalty, including Prince Albert, Princess Diana, and Prince Rainier.

The high-ceilinged, marble-floored foyer of the hotel, with its 200-year-old chandelier, carved wooden staircase, and antiques sets the tone. Each large, well-furnished bedroom is individually styled, with silks from France and handmade furnishings from Italy. Amenities include huge closets, CD players, and double-glazed windows. Some of the bathrooms are marble, but, regrettably, others are still a sorry sight with white laminate and linoleum. Each comes with heated towel racks, Floris toiletries, and bathrobes.

Eastgate, Chester, Cheshire CH1 1LT. © **01244/324024.** Fax 01244/313246. www.chestergrosvenor.co.uk. 80 units. £185–£265 ($342–$490) double; £425–£550 ($786–$1,018) suite. Weekend rates include breakfast. 1 child under 15 stays free in parent's room. AE, DC, MC, V. **Amenities:** 2 restaurants; 2 bars; health club; sauna; business center; 24-hr. room service; laundry service; dry cleaning; nonsmoking rooms; rooms for those with limited mobility. *In room:* A/C, TV, minibar, hair dryer, iron, safe, trouser press.

EXPENSIVE

Chester Crabwall Manor ★★ Chester's premier country-house hotel, the imposing crenellated Crabwall Manor traces its origins from the 16th century, though most of the present building dates from the early 1800s. It has a more peaceful location than the Chester Grosvenor, though it lacks the facilities and the top-notch service of its more highly rated competitor. Standing amid 4.4 hectares (11 acres) of private grounds and gardens, the capably managed hotel rents quite large, well-furnished bedrooms. Three rooms have four-poster beds. The bathrooms are first-class; most have bidets and separate showers. Relax in the full-service spa after working out in the hotel's aerobics studio.

Parkgate Rd., Mollington, Chester, Cheshire CH1 6NE. © **01244/851666.** Fax 01244/851400. www.marston hotels.com. 48 units. £181 ($335) double; £231 ($427) suite. Weekend rates include breakfast. Children under 16 stay free when sharing room with 2 paying adults. AE, DC, MC, V. Take A540 3.5km (2¼ miles) northwest of Chester. **Amenities:** Restaurant; bar; indoor pool; health club; Jacuzzi; sauna; limited room service; laundry service; dry cleaning; nonsmoking rooms; rooms for those with limited mobility. *In room:* A/C, TV, dataport (in some), coffeemaker, hair dryer, iron, trouser press.

MODERATE

Blossoms Hotel This hotel enjoys an ideal location in the very heart of Chester. Blossoms Hotel has been in business since the mid–17th century, though the present structure was rebuilt late in Victoria's day. An old open stair-case in the reception room helps set the tone here, but otherwise the public rooms are uninspired. Bedrooms are fitted with dark wood pieces and firm beds—some of them four-posters—and many rooms have recently been refurbished. Bathrooms are carpeted and beautifully maintained with luxury toiletries and generous shelf space, and most often a tub-and-shower combination.

St. John's St., Chester, Cheshire CH1 1HL. © **01244/323186.** Fax 01244/346433. 64 units. £118 ($218) double; £148 ($274) suite. AE, DC, MC, V. **Amenities:** Restaurant; bar; 24-hr. room service; laundry service; dry cleaning. *In room:* TV, dataport, coffeemaker, hair dryer, trouser press.

Green Bough Hotel & Olive Tree Restaurant ★★★ *Condé Nast* awarded this property the Johansens Award for "The Most Excellent City Hotel 2004." Hoteliers Janice and Philip Martin have turned this establishment into the most exclusive small luxury hotel in Chester, both for cuisine and accommodations. Each bedroom has been restored and beautifully furnished, each individually designed with elegant fabrics, beautiful wallpapers, Italian tiles, and antique cast iron or carved wooden beds. A Roman-themed junior suite boasts a four-poster dating from 1890 and draped in *eau-de-nil voiles*. There is also a Louis XV carved wooden antique bed in the French-themed master suite. Each unit comes with a well-equipped private bathroom with tub and shower. Delightful on-site facilities feature the Champagne Lounge Bar and the award-winning Olive Tree Restaurant, known for serving imaginatively conceived local produce. Smoking is not permitted anywhere on the hotel premises.

60 Hoole Rd., Chester CH2 3NL. (℃) **01244/326241.** Fax 01244/325265. www.greenbough.co.uk. 16 units. £125–£145 ($231–$268) double; £195–£250 ($361–$463) suite. Rates include English breakfast. AE, DC, MC, V. **Amenities:** Restaurant; bar; limited room service; laundry service; dry cleaning; rooms for those with limited mobility. *In room:* TV, beverage maker, hair dryer, safe (in some), trouser press.

Mollington Banastre ★ *Kids*   This Victorian mansion is a gabled house surrounded by gardens. It has been successfully converted into one of the leading country-house hotels in Cheshire, now affiliated with the Best Western reservation system. Rooms have comfortable doubles or twin beds; eight are spacious enough for families and two have four-poster beds. Each comes with a shower or tub-and-shower combination. It's not the most opulent choice in town, but it's a great value for the money.

Parkgate Rd., Chester, Cheshire CH1 6NN. (℃) **800/528-1234** in the U.S. and Canada, or 01244/851471. Fax 01244/851165. www.mollingtonbanastrehotel.com. 63 units. £105–£150 ($194–$278) double. Rates include breakfast. Children 15 and under stay free in parent's room. AE, DC, MC, V. Take A540 3km (2 miles) northwest of the center of Chester. Or take Junction 16 of M56 and continue for 2.5km (1½ miles). **Amenities:** 2 restaurants; 2 bars; coffee shop; indoor pool; health club; sauna; Jacuzzi; salon; 24-hr. room service; croquet; squash courts; laundry service; dry cleaning. *In room:* TV, minibar, coffeemaker, hair dryer, trouser press.

Rowton Hall Hotel   This stately home stands on the site of the Battle of Rowton Moor, which was fought in 1643 between the Roundheads and the Cavaliers. Built in 1779, with a wing added later, the house has a 3.2-hectare (8-acre) garden, with a formal driveway entrance. Rowton Hall has comfortable traditional and contemporary furnishings. The better and more stylish luxury rooms are in the old house and offer amenities such as bathrobes. An adjoining wing contains more sterile and uninspired units, which some readers have complained about. Regardless of room assignment, each has a comfortable bed; four rooms are large enough for families. The shower-only bathrooms are small.

Whitchurch Rd., Rowton, Chester, Cheshire CH3 6AD. (℃) **01244/335262.** Fax 01244/335464. www.rowton hallhotel.co.uk. 38 units. £90–£150 ($167–$278) double; £150 ($278) junior suite; £200–£220 ($370–$407) suite. AE, DC, MC, V. Take A41 3km (2 miles) from the center of Chester. **Amenities:** Restaurant; 2 bars; pool; 2 outdoor tennis courts; health club; limited room service; laundry service. *In room:* TV, coffeemaker, hair dryer, iron, safe.

WHERE TO DINE

Arkle Restaurant ★★★ *Finds* BRITISH/CONTINENTAL   Arkle is the premier restaurant in this part of England. The 45-seat formal, gourmet restaurant has a superb *chef de cuisine* and a talented 40-strong team that uses the freshest ingredients to create modern British and continental dishes prepared with subtle touches and a certain lightness. Main courses include langoustine ravioli, and Welsh black beef filet topped with fresh horseradish. Desserts are equally luscious and tempting. Arkle has an award-winning cheese selection and a choice of at least six unique breads daily.

In the Chester Grosvenor Hotel, Eastgate. (℃) **01244/324024.** Reservations required. 2-course fixed-price menu £45 ($83); 3-course fixed-price menu £52 ($96); fixed-price menu gourmand £60 ($111). AE, DC, MC, V. Tues–Sun noon–2:30pm; Tues–Sat 7–9:30pm.

La Brasserie *(Value* ENGLISH/FRENCH   This is perhaps the best all-around dining choice in Chester for convenience, price, and quality. In a delightful Art Nouveau setting, the Brasserie has an extensive a la carte menu to suit most tastes and pocketbooks. You get robust flavors and hearty ingredients. Main dishes include roast loin of cod with scallops in a red wine and mushroom sauce; baked chicken with potato pancakes and garlic cheese; and other hearty brasserie food.

In the Chester Grosvenor Hotel, Eastgate St. ℂ 01244/324024. Reservations recommended. Main courses £9.75–£25 ($18–$46). AE, DC, MC, V. Mon–Fri 7am–10pm; Sat 7:30am–10:30pm; Sun 7:30am–10pm.

CHESTER AFTER DARK

If you want to relax in a pub, grab a pint of Marston's at the **Olde Custom House,** Watergate Street (℃ 01244/324435), a 17th-century customhouse with many original features still intact. The **Pied Bull,** Northgate Street (℃ 01244/ 325829), is an 18th-century coaching inn where you can still eat, drink, or rent a room. Real ales on tap include Bitter and Traditional. At **Ye Olde King's Head,** Lower Bridge Street (℃ 01244/324855), ales are not the only spirits you may encounter. This B&B pub, built in 1622, is said to be haunted by three ghosts; a crying woman and baby in room no. 6, and the ghostly initials "ST" that appear in steam on the bathroom mirror of room no. 4. If you prefer your spirits in a glass, stick to the pub, where you can sip on a Pedigree, or Greenall's Original or Local.

Live Irish music and atmosphere can be sampled at **The Red Lion,** 59 Northgate St. (℃ 01244/321750), where you can hear traditional music on Sunday nights for the price of a pint of Guinness. **Alexandre's,** Rufus Court off Northgate Street (℃ 01244/340005), offers more varied entertainment.

4 Blackpool: Playground of the Midlands

396km (246 miles) NW of London; 142km (88 miles) W of Leeds; 90km (56 miles) N of Liverpool; 82km (51 miles) NW of Manchester

This once-antiquated Midlands resort is struggling to make a comeback by marketing itself to a new generation of vacationers. The result may remind you of Atlantic City or even Las Vegas (with a weird Victorian twist). The city has a midwinter population of 125,000 that swells to three or four times that in midsummer.

The country's largest resort makes its living from conferences, tour groups, families, and couples looking for an affordable getaway. Its 11km (7 miles) of beaches, 9.5km (6 miles) of colored lights, and dozens of Disneylike attractions and rides make Blackpool one of the most entertaining (and least apologetic) pieces of razzle-dazzle in England.

Disadvantages include unpredictable weather that brews over the nearby Irish Channel; a sandy, flat-as-a-pancake landscape that's less than inspiring; and a (sometimes undeserved) reputation for dowdiness. But some people love the brisk sea air, the architectural remnants of Britain's greatest Imperial Age, the utter lack of pretentiousness, and the poignant nostalgia that clings to the edges of places like Coney Island, where people look back fondly on the carefree fun they had in a simpler time.

ESSENTIALS

GETTING THERE   Two trains from Manchester arrive every hour (trip time: 1½ hr.), and one every 2 hours from Liverpool (trip time: 1½ hr.). For information, call ℂ 0845/748-4950 or visit www.railtrack.co.uk.

National Express buses arrive from Chester at the rate of three per day (trip time: 4 hr.); from Liverpool at the rate of six per day (trip time: 3½ hr.); from Manchester, five per day (trip time: 2 hr.); and from London, six per day (trip time: 6½ hr.). For schedules and information, call ℂ **0870/580-8080** or visit www.nationalexpress.com.

If you're driving from Manchester, take the M61 north to the M6 then the M55 toward Blackpool. The trip takes about 1 hour.

VISITOR INFORMATION   The helpful **Tourist Office,** located at 1 Clifton St. (ℂ **01253/478222**), is open November through March Monday through Friday from 9am to 4:45pm, and Saturday from 9am to 4:30pm; April through October, Monday through Saturday from 9am to 5pm and Sunday from 10am to 4pm.

WHERE TO PLAY

Blackpool is famous for the **Illuminations,** an extravaganza of electric lights affixed to just about any stationary object along the Promenade. It features hundreds of illuminated figures, including Diamonds Are Forever, Santa's Workshop, Lamp Lighters, and Kitchen Lites. The tradition began in 1879 with just eight electric lights, and has grown with time and technology to include 9.5km (6 miles) of fiber optics, low-voltage neon tubes, and traditional lamps. The illuminations burn bright into the night from the end of August to the beginning of November. Take a tram ride down the Promenade for a great view of these tacky but festive lights.

Without a doubt, the most famous landmark in this town is the **Tower** along the Central Promenade (ℂ **01253/622242**). In 1891, during the reign of Queen Victoria, a madcap idea started floating around to construct a 155m (518-ft.) tower that resembled a half-size version of Paris's Eiffel Tower. The idea was first formally presented to the town leaders of Brighton, who laughed at the idea, thinking it was a joke. But the forward-thinking leaders of Blackpool, when presented the plan, immediately saw the advantages of having such an attraction and quickly approved the tower's construction. You be the judge.

Lighted by more than 10,000 bulbs, this landmark has become a tower of fun. It is truly an indoor entertainment complex both day and night and features the Tower Ballroom (one of the great Victorian ballrooms of Britain), the Tower Circus, the Hornpipe Galley, and the Dawn of Time dinosaur ride for kids, as well as the Tower Aquarium. An elevator takes visitors to the top of the Tower for a 97km (60-mile) view. The Tower is open from Easter to May, Saturday and Sunday from 10am to 6pm; and June through October daily from 10am to 11pm. The circus has two to three shows daily (except Fri evening). Tower admission is £7 to £11 ($13–$20).

WHERE TO STAY

De Vere Herons' Reach ✿   This hotel symbolizes Blackpool's renewal. It was erected on 96 flat and sandy hectares (236 acres) in 1992, adjacent to the town's zoo and Stanley Park. Designed in a postmodern style that some visitors liken to a mansard-roofed French château, it evokes Las Vegas with a Midlands accent, partly because of the cheerful razzle-dazzle its hardworking staff throws into their jobs, and partly because of the many diversions on hand. Bedrooms are traditional but modern, done with light woods; despite their relative youth, they were renovated early in 2003 and offer such extras as Sony PlayStations. Most rooms open onto views of a golf course, and each offers the most comfortable beds in Blackpool hoteldom. Eight rooms are large enough to rent to families;

several rooms are equipped for guests with disabilities. Bathrooms have first-rate toiletries, generous shelf space, and a combination tub and shower.

E. Park Dr., Blackpool, Lancashire FY3 8LL. ✆ **01253/838866.** Fax 01253/798800. www.devereonline.co.uk. 172 units. £89–£160 ($165–$296) double; £215 ($398) suite. Rates include breakfast. AE, DC, MC, V. **Amenities:** 2 restaurants; 3 bars; indoor pool; 18-hole golf course; 3 outdoor tennis courts; 3 squash courts; 3 pool tables; exercise room; spa; limited room service; laundry service; dry cleaning. *In room:* TV, coffeemaker, hair dryer, trouser press.

The Imperial Hotel ★★ This is Blackpool's choice address. Noted as a stylish venue for group conferences, this hotel was built by the Victorians—Charles Dickens was a guest—as a massive redbrick pile, and it's still a major landmark in town. Recent renovations added vestiges of 19th-century country house stateliness to the public areas and some of the bedrooms, and a scattering of artwork related to such genteel pleasures as "the hunt." Accommodations are well appointed and some offer sea views. Most of the tidy bathrooms have a tub-and-shower combination.

N. Promenade, Blackpool, Lancashire FY1 2HB. ✆ **01253/623971.** Fax 01253/751784. www.paramount-hotels.co.uk. 180 units. £114–£144 ($211–$266) double; £224–£244 ($414–$451) suite. Rates include breakfast. AE, DC, MC, V. **Amenities:** 2 restaurants; bar; indoor pool; health club; Jacuzzi; sauna; 24-hr. room service; laundry service; nonsmoking rooms; rooms for those with limited mobility. *In room:* TV, dataport, coffeemaker, hair dryer, safe, trouser press.

The Savoy Hotel *Kids* The roots of this hotel stretch back to the late 19th century, when its redbrick tower and bay windows beckoned vacationers to its seaside location near the North Pier. Since then, ongoing refurbishment has kept the place well carpeted, well painted, and well upholstered. Bedrooms are conservatively up-to-date and restful. Most rooms are quite spacious, many offering sea views, though individual shape and size can vary considerably. Fourteen are large enough to rent to families. Each room has twin or double beds, and most bathrooms have a tub-and-shower combination.

Queens Promenade, Blackpool FY2 9SJ. ✆ **01253/352561.** Fax 01253/500735. 130 units. £97–£137 ($179–$253) double; £180 ($333) suite. Rates include breakfast. AE, DC, MC, V. **Amenities:** Restaurant; bar; 24-hr. room service; laundry service; rooms for those with limited mobility. *In room:* TV, coffeemaker, hair dryer, trouser press.

WHERE TO DINE

September Brasserie ★ MODERN BRITISH/INTERNATIONAL Set in a three-story building that originally functioned as a Victorian-era haberdashery, this noteworthy restaurant is Blackpool's finest. It developed from the core of a hairdressing salon that still flourishes on the street level today. Both establishments are the domain of the Golowicz family, which maintains (with a smile) that the staff members who work inside are probably the best-coiffed restaurant employees in the west of England. The restaurant prides itself on its sophisticated, modern, British cuisine (a step up from the pub grub and fish-and-chip parlors that proliferate in the surrounding neighborhood). Menu items include roasted organic salmon filet with tapenade noodles and saffron sauce; and breast of local pheasant and teal with creamed mushrooms and mashed potato.

15–17 Queen St. ✆ 01253/623282. Reservations recommended. Main courses £8–£14 ($15–$26); 2-course fixed-price dinner £20 ($37); 3-course fixed-price dinner £23 ($42); lunch £8–£10 ($15–$19). AE, DC, MC, V. Tues–Sat noon–2pm and 7–10pm.

17

The Lake District

The Lake District, one of the most beautiful parts of Great Britain, is actually quite small, measuring about 56km (35 miles) wide. Most of the district is in Cumbria, though it begins in the northern part of Lancashire.

Bordering Scotland, the far-north-western part of the shire is generally divided geographically into three segments: the **Pennines,** dominating the eastern sector (loftiest point at Cross Fell, nearly 900m/3,000 ft. high); the **Valley of Eden;** and the **lakes and secluded valleys of the west,** by far the most interesting.

So beautifully described by the romantic poets, the area enjoys literary associations with William Wordsworth, Samuel Taylor Coleridge, Charlotte Brontë, Charles Lamb, Percy Bysshe Shelley, John Keats, Alfred Lord Tennyson, and Matthew Arnold. In Queen Victoria's day, the district was one of England's most popular summer retreats.

The largest town is Carlisle, by the Scotland border, which is a possible base for exploring Hadrian's Wall (p. 695)—but for now, we concentrate on the district's lovely lakeside villages. **Windermere** is the best base for exploring the Lake District.

1 Kendal

435km (270 miles) NW of London; 103km (64 miles) NW of Bradford; 116km (72 miles) NW of Leeds; 14km (9 miles) SE of Windermere

The River Kent winds its way through a rich valley of limestone hills and cliffs, known as *fells,* and down through the "Auld Grey Town" of Kendal, whose moniker refers to the large number of gray stone houses found in and about the town. Many visitors to the Lake District simply pass through Kendal on their way to more attractive destinations—the town is a gateway rather than a true stopping place. It has never depended entirely on the tourist dollar. This fact should not deter you, however, from taking a bit of time to discover some of this market town's more intriguing areas.

Kendal contains the ruins of a castle where Catherine Parr, the last wife of Henry VIII, was allegedly born. Recent speculation about her actual birthplace has led to a clouding of the historic record. Even if she wasn't born here, it is still said that she most likely lived at the castle at some time in her life. Among other historic sites, Kendal has a 13th-century parish church that merits a visit.

Today, Kendal is famous for its mint cake and its surrounding limestone fells, which offer excellent vistas of the area and make for great hikes.

ESSENTIALS
GETTING THERE   Trains from London's Euston Station do not go directly to Kendal; seven daily trains arrive in Oxenholme, about 2.5km (1½ miles) away. From here, you'll be able to take a cab or board one of the local trains that leave

> ## (Moments) Walks & Rambles
>
> Driving in the wilds of this scenic shire is fine for a start, but the best way to take in its beauty is by walking. Pack some good waterproof hiking boots and a lightweight rain jacket—even if you set out on a nice morning, you need to be prepared for changing conditions and sunny days are few. When the mist starts to fall, do as the locals do and head for the nearest inn or pub, where you can drop in and warm yourself beside an open fireplace.
>
> If you want to make hiking in the Lake District a focus of your entire vacation, you may prefer an organized outing. **Countrywide Holidays,** Miry Lane, Wigan, Lancashire, WN3 4AG (© **01942/823456;** www.countrywidewalking.com), has offered walking and special-interest vacations for more than 100 years. Safe and sociable guided walks are led by experienced guides for all ages and abilities. It's ideal for independent walkers, with boot-drying rooms provided. They have four comfortable, informal, and welcoming guesthouses set in beautiful Lakeland locations.

approximately every hour to Kendal proper (trip time: 3½ hr.). For information, call © **0845/748-4950** or visit www.railtrack.co.uk.

To Kendal from London by bus, take one of the three daily National Express buses (trip time: 7 hr.). For schedules and information, call **National Express** at © **0870/580-8080** or visit www.nationalexpress.com.

If driving, take the M1 out of London, then the M6 to Kendal (trip time: 5 hr.).

VISITOR INFORMATION   The **Tourist Information Centre of Kendal,** Town Hall, Highgate (© **01539/725758**), is open September through December and March through June, Monday through Saturday from 9am to 5pm and Sunday from 10am to 4pm; January and February Monday through Saturday from 9am to 5pm; July and August Monday through Saturday from 9am to 6pm and Sunday from 10am to 5pm.

SEEING THE SIGHTS

Abbot Hall Art Gallery   The Georgian elegance of Kendal's Abbot Hall Art Gallery has created an ideal setting for its display of fine art. Paintings by the town's famous son, 18th-century portrait painter George Romney, fill the walls of rooms furnished by Gillows of Lancaster. A major display of work by 20th-century British artists such as Graham Sutherland, John Piper, and Ben Nicholson is on permanent display. Visitors can see the region through the eyes of the many painters who have been inspired by the landscapes in another of the gallery's permanent exhibitions housed in the Peter Scott Gallery.

Kirkland. © 01539/722464. www.abbothall.org.uk. Admission £4.75 ($8.80) adults, £3.75 ($6.95) children, £14 ($26) family ticket. Apr to late Oct Mon–Sat 10:30am–5pm; Mid-Jan to Mar and Nov to mid-Dec Mon–Sat 10:30am–4pm. Closed mid-Dec to mid-Jan.

Kendal Museum   One of England's oldest museums offers a journey of discovery from Roman times to the present. A natural history section includes a nature trail from mountaintop to lakeside, bringing you face to face with many of the

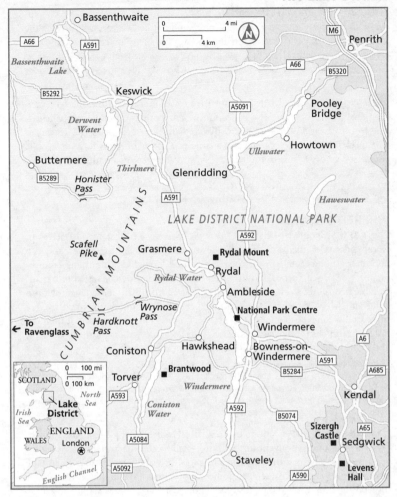

inhabitants of the area. The World Wildlife Gallery displays a vast collection of exotic animals. One of the exhibitions introduces visitors to the fell-tops' best-known visitor, Alfred Wainwright, who walked, talked, and wrote with a passion and flair about the region. Wainwright worked diligently until his death in 1991.

Station Rd. ✆ **01539/721374.** www.kendalmuseum.org.uk. Admission £2.50 ($4.65) adults, £2 ($3.70) seniors, free for children. Mid-Feb to mid-Dec Mon–Sat 10:30am–5pm (till 4pm Feb–Mar, Nov–Dec).

Levens Hall This Elizabethan mansion was constructed in the 1500s by James Bellingham. Today, the house is filled with Jacobean furniture and a working model of steam collection. The estate also has a **topiary garden** 🎐🎐 dating from 1692, with a host of yews and box hedges clipped into a variety of intriguing shapes.

Levens Park, Levens (6.5km/4 miles south of Kendal). ✆ **01539/560321.** www.levenshall.co.uk. Admission house and gardens £7.50 ($14) adults, £3.70 ($6.85) children, £21 ($39) family ticket (2 adults, 3 children); gardens only £5.80 ($11) adults, £2.60 ($4.80) children, £16 ($30) family ticket (2 adults, 3 children). Apr to mid-Oct Sun–Thurs noon–5pm (gardens open at 10am). Last entry at 4:30pm.

Museum of Lakeland Life and Industry   From the re-creation of a Victorian Kendal street, complete with pharmacy and market, visitors can discover the lost crafts and trades of the region and the ways of life that accompanied them.

Kirkland. ✆ **01539/722464.** www.lakelandmuseum.org.uk. Admission £3.50 ($6.50) adults, £2 ($3.70) children, £9.50 ($18) family (2 adults, 4 children). Mon–Sat 10:30am–4pm (till 5pm Apr–Oct). Closed mid-Dec to mid-Jan.

Sizergh Castle   The castle has a fortified tower that dates from the 14th century. Inside, visitors can see a collection of Elizabethan carvings and paneling, fine furniture, and portraits. The complete garden, largely from the 18th century, incorporates a rock garden and a famous planting of hardy ferns and dwarf conifers. The castle is surrounded by a show of fiery colors in autumn.

5.5km (3½ miles) south of Kendal (northwest of interchange A590/591). ✆ **01539/560070.** Admission £5 ($9.25) adults, £2.50 ($4.65) children, £13 ($23) family ticket (2 adults, 2 children). Apr–Oct Sun–Thurs 1:30–5:30pm (last admission 5pm). The shop and gardens open at 12:30pm.

WHERE TO STAY

The Castle Green Hotel in Kendal ✿   Set on 5.6 hectares (14 acres) of woodlands and gardens, this Best Western affiliate is one of the newest and also one of the finest hotels in the area. Though it looks like a rambling country estate, it was once a series of offices that have been cleverly converted into comfortable bedrooms. Each room is stylish and well furnished, many opening onto panoramic views. The best, albeit most expensive, accommodations are the executive studio suites with a lot of extra space. Guests enjoy free membership in the hotel's health club. The Castle Green also has one of the best pubs, Alexander's, and one of the best restaurants, Guesthouse, in the area.

Signposted from the M6, Junction 37. Kendal, Cumbria LA9 6BH. ✆ **01539/734000.** Fax 01539/735522. www.castlegreen.co.uk. 100 units. £118 ($218) double; £158 ($292) suite. Rates include English breakfast. AE, DC, MC, V. **Amenities:** Restaurant; pub; indoor heated pool; gym; solarium; steam room; fitness center; salon; 24-hr. room service; laundry service; dry cleaning; rooms for those with limited mobility; nonsmoking rooms. *In room:* TV, dataport, coffeemaker, hair dryer.

Garden House Hotel   Built in 1812, this is an inviting Georgian country house. It was once a convent for local nuns and has been a hotel for the past 30 years or so. It's nestled in .8 hectares (2 acres) of walled garden and green pastureland, and is perfectly serene. Some guest rooms have fireplaces; one has a four-poster bed. Each tiled bathroom, quite compact, comes with a tub-and-shower combination. The public areas include a somewhat formal sitting room, an informal lounge and bar with lots of seating, an elegant breakfast room with a dark mahogany fireplace, and a restaurant conservatory.

Fowling Lane, Kendal, Cumbria LA9 6PH. ✆ **01539/731131.** Fax 01539/740064. www.gardenhousehotel. co.uk. 11 units. £79 ($146) double; £85 ($157) for 4-poster bed. £5 ($9.25) extra bed. Rates include English breakfast. MC, V. **Amenities:** Restaurant; bar; putting green; croquet lawn; breakfast-only room service; car rental; limited laundry service; nonsmoking rooms. *In room:* TV, coffeemaker, hair dryer, trouser press.

WHERE TO DINE

Déjà Vu TRADITIONAL & MODERN FRENCH   The interior of this small and cozy French cabaret is inspired by one of van Gogh's landscape paintings. People come for good food and a fun time. A wide range of appetizers evoke a taste of Paris, featuring fresh scallops mille feuille with a basil cream sauce, or filet of venison with a red-wine and raspberry sauce. Follow with such mains as fresh monkfish filet on eggplant with a basil and fennel sauce, or Aberdeen Angus filet of beef with a port and pink peppercorn mousse. Desserts feature many classic French favorites, including the delicious peach tartlet.

124 Stricklandgate. ✆ **01539/724843.** Reservations recommended. Main courses £9.50–£15 ($18–$28). AE, DC, MC, V. Mon–Sat 5:30–10pm; Fri–Sat noon–2pm.

Moon INTERNATIONAL   This bistro cooks up the best food in Kendal. Set in a building that's more than 250 years old and was once a grocery store, the dining room offers patrons a close, friendly, and informal environment. The food is interesting without being gimmicky. The owners take pride in offering market-fresh ingredients when available. Main courses include lamb shank with either a mustard and Soya sauce or a cream, leek, and white-wine sauce; or for vegetarians, goat's cheese, red pepper, and mango wrapped in filo pastry with an apple, gooseberry, and honey sauce.

129 Highgate. ✆ **01539/729254.** Reservations not needed. Main courses £9–£15 ($17–$28). MC, V. Tues–Sun 6–10pm (closed Tues in winter).

Punch Bowl Inn ⋆⋆ (Finds) BRITISH   This is one of the best pubs for dining in the Lake District. The quality food is prepared and supervised by Steven Doherty, formerly executive chef for the Roux brothers, who are acclaimed as the finest chefs in Britain. Top-notch cuisine is served in a 17th-century coaching inn lying in the Lyth Valley, with black painted timbers, log fires, and walls covered with pictures of local artists. An old-world atmosphere permeates the restaurant with its low ceilings, beams, and open log fires. On summer evenings al fresco dining is enjoyed on the patio. The starters here may change your idea of pub grub forever, particularly if you sample the oven-baked beetroot tart with crumbled goat's cheese and honey or the fresh seared sea bass on pesto potatoes. For a main course, we suggest you dig into the sliced roasted chump of Cumbrian fell-bred lamb served sliced on a horseradish mash with a salad of mixed beans in a mint dressing and thyme jus, or else a chargrilled Cumbrian fell-bred rib-eye steak with a creamy pepper sauce. For dessert, the chocolate and ginger tart with homemade honey ice cream will make you want to return the following night.

The inn also rents three simply furnished bedrooms, with tub or shower, each with beverage maker, TV, and hair dryer. The cost is £65 ($120) in a double with an English breakfast.

Crosthwaite, near Kendal. ✆ **015395/68237.** Reservations recommended. Main courses £12–£14 ($22–$26). MC, V. Tues–Sun noon–2pm; Tues–Sat 6–9pm.

KENDAL AFTER DARK

One of the best entertainment centers in the Lake District is the **Brewery Arts Centre,** Highgate (✆ **01539/725133;** www.breweryarts.co.uk), which includes 2 cinemas, a theater, the Green Room restaurant, two cafe bars, and other venues in a converted brewery. The box office for all attractions is open Monday through Saturday from 10am to 8:30pm and Sunday from 11am to 8:30pm.

2 Windermere & Bowness ⋆⋆

441km (274 miles) NW of London; 16km (10 miles) NW of Kendal; 89km (55 miles) N of Liverpool

The largest lake in England is Windermere, whose eastern shore washes up on the town of Bowness (or Bowness-on-Windermere), with the town of Windermere 2.5km (1½ miles) away. From either town, you can climb **Orrest Head** in less than an hour for a panoramic view of the Lakeland. From that vantage point, you can even view **Scafell Pike,** rising to a height of 963m (3,210 ft.)—it's the tallest peak in all of England.

ESSENTIALS

GETTING THERE   Trains to Windermere meet the main line at Oxenholme for connections to both Scotland and London. You can obtain information about rail services in the area calling the railway information line at $©$ **0845/748-4950** or visiting www.railtrack.co.uk. Frequent connections are possible throughout the day. To get to Bowness and its ferry pier from Windermere, turn left from the rail terminal and cross the center of Windermere until you reach New Road, which eventually changes its name to Lake Road before it approaches the outskirts of Bowness. It's about a 20-minute walk downhill. The CMS Lakeland Experience bus also runs from the Windermere Station to Bowness every 20 minutes.

The **National Express** bus link, originating at London's Victoria Coach Station, serves Windermere, with connections also to Preston, Manchester, and Birmingham. For schedules and information, call $©$ **0870/580-8080** or visit www.nationalexpress.com. Local buses operated mainly by **Stagecoach** ($©$ **0870/608-2608;** www.stagecoachbus.com) go to Kendal, Ambleside, Grasmere, and Keswick. Call for information on various routings within the Lake District.

If you're driving from London, head north on the M1 and the M6 past Liverpool until you reach the A685 junction heading west to Kendal. From Kendal, the A591 continues west to Windermere.

VISITOR INFORMATION   The **Tourist Information Centre** at Windermere is on Victoria Street ($©$ **01539/446499**). It's open November through March daily from 9am to 5pm and April through October daily from 9am to 6pm (Fri–Sat until 6:30pm).

EXPLORING THE AREA

There is regular **steamer service** around Windermere, the largest of the lakes (about 17km/11 miles long). It's also possible to take a steamer on Coniston Water, a small lake that Wordsworth called "a broken spoke sticking in the rim." Coniston Water is a smaller and less heavily traveled lake than Windermere.

Launch and steamer cruises depart from Bowness daily throughout the year operated by **Windermere Lake Cruises Ltd.** ($©$ **01539/443360;** www.windermere-lakecruises.co.uk). Round-trip service is available among Bowness, Ambleside, and Lakeside at rates ranging from £6.65 to £12 ($12–$22) for adults and £3.45 to £6 ($6.40–$11) for children, £18 to £30 ($34–$56) family ticket. There is a 45-minute Island Cruise for £5 ($9.25) for adults and £2.50 ($4.65) for children, £14 ($26) family ticket.

At Lakeside, you can ride a steam train to Haverthwaite. A combination boat/train ticket is £11 ($20) for adults and £5.50 ($10) for children, £29 ($54) family ticket.

An attraction at Lakeside, near Newby Bridge, is the **Aquarium of the Lakes** ($©$ **01539/530153;** www.aquariumofthelakes.co.uk), with an exhibit of fish and wildlife. The aquarium is open daily from 9am to 4pm November through March, and from 9am to 5pm April through October. Combination boat/admission tickets from Ambleside are £16 ($29) for adults, £8.90 ($16) for children, and £46 ($84) for a family ticket; from Bowness, tickets are £12 ($22) for adults, £6.50 ($12) for children, and £35 ($65) for a family ticket. Aquarium-only admission is £5.95 ($11) for adults, £3.75 ($6.95) for children, and £17 ($31) for a family ticket (two adults and two children).

Directly south of Windermere, **Bowness** is an attractive old lakeside town with lots of interesting architecture, much of it dating from Queen Victoria's day. This has been an important center for boating and fishing for a long time, and you can rent boats of all descriptions to explore the lake.

Windermere Steamboat Centre   This museum houses the finest collection of steamboats in the world. Important examples of these elegant Victorian and Edwardian vessels have been preserved in working order. The steamboats are exhibited in a unique wet dock where they are moored in their natural lakeside setting. The fine display of touring and racing motorboats in the dry dock links the heyday of steam with some of the most famous names of powerboat racing and the record-breaking attempts on Windermere, including Sir Henry Segrave's world water-speed record set in 1930.

Each boat has an intriguing story, including the SL *Dolly*, built around 1850 and probably the oldest mechanically driven boat in the world. The vessel was raised from the lakebed of Ullswater in 1962 and, following restoration, ran for 10 years with its original boiler. The *Dolly* is still steamed on special occasions.

The SL *Swallow* (1911) is steamed most days; a 50-minute trip on the lake costs £5 ($9.25) for adults and £2.50 ($4.65) for children, with the crew serving tea or coffee made using the Windermere steam kettle.

Rayrigg Rd. Ⓒ 01539/445565. www.steamboat.co.uk. Admission £3.50 ($6.50) adults, £2 ($3.70) children, £8.50 ($16) family ticket. Daily 10am–5pm. Closed Nov to mid-Mar.

The World of Beatrix Potter   This exhibit uses the latest technology to tell the story of Beatrix Potter's fascinating life. A video wall and special film describe how her tales came to be written and how she became a pioneering Lakeland farmer and conservationist. There is also a shop with a wealth of top-quality Beatrix Potter merchandise, from Wedgwood ceramics to soft toys. It's mobbed on summer weekends; try to come at any other time.

The Old Laundry, Bowness-on-Windermere. Ⓒ **01539/488444**. www.hop-skip-jump.com. Admission £3.90 ($7.20) adults, £2.90 ($5.35) children. Easter–Oct daily 10am–5:30pm; rest of year daily 10am–4:30pm. Take A591 to Lake Rd. and follow the signs.

WHERE TO STAY
VERY EXPENSIVE

Holbeck Ghyll 🏵🏵🏵   This is the most tranquil oasis in the area and offers the most refined cuisine. Overlooking Lake Windermere, this country-house hotel was once a 19th-century hunting lodge owned by Lord Lonsdale, one of the richest men in Britain, and has a high price tag but offers a lot for the money. An inglenook fireplace welcomes visitors. The most elaborate room is a honeymoon and anniversary room that has a four-poster bed and a bathroom with a spa bath for two. But each unit is fitted with a luxury bed, often crowned by a canopy or a padded headboard. Rooms are individually designed, coming in various shapes and sizes, and most of them open onto a view of the lake. Six rooms are in a separate nonsmoking lodge added in 1998, and these are even finer than the rooms in the main building. Lodge rooms are interconnecting with panoramic lake views, individual balcony or patio areas, fresh flowers, and CD players; four units have kitchenettes. Luxurious bathrooms have separate shower cubicles, as well as a tub. Children under 8 are not welcome in the restaurant.

Holbeck Lane (on A591 5.5km/3½ miles northwest of town center), Windermere, Cumbria LA23 1LU. Ⓒ **01539/432375**. Fax 01539/434743. www.holbeckghyll.com. 21 units. £105–£135 ($194–$250) per person double; from £135 ($250) per person suite. Rates include English breakfast and dinner. Children under 17 stay for half price when sharing parent's room. AE, DC, MC, V. **Amenities:** Restaurant; bar; putting green; tennis court; croquet lawn; spa; gym; limited room service; laundry service; dry cleaning; nonsmoking rooms. *In room:* TV, kitchenette (4 rooms only), coffeemaker, hair dryer, trouser press.

Lake District National Park

Despite the reverence with which the English treat the Lake District, it required an act of Parliament in 1951 to protect its natural beauty. Sprawling over 885 square miles of hills, eroded mountains, forests, and lakes, the **Lake District National Park** ⭐⭐⭐ is the largest and one of the most popular national parks in the United Kingdom, with 14 million visitors a year. Lured by descriptions from the romantic lake poets, visitors come for the mountains, wildlife, flora, fauna, and secluded waterfalls. Much of the area is privately owned, but landowners work with the national park to preserve the landscape and its 2,898km (1,800 miles) of footpaths.

Alas, the park's popularity is now one of its major drawbacks. Hordes of weekend tourists descend, especially in summertime and on bank holiday weekends. But despite the crowds, great efforts are made to maintain the trails that radiate in a network throughout the district preserving the purity of a landscape that includes more than 100 lakes and countless numbers of grazing sheep.

Before setting out to explore the lake, stop in at the **National Park Visitor Centre** (© 01539/446601; www.lake-district.gov.uk), located on the lakeshore at Brockhole, on the A591 between Windermere and Ambleside. It can be reached by bus or by one of the lake launches from Windermere. Here, you can pick up useful information and explore 12 hectares (30 acres) of landscaped gardens and parklands; lake cruises, exhibitions, and film shows are also offered. Lunches and teas are served in Gaddums tearooms with terrace seating. Normally, admission is free, except for special events staged here. Parking costs £3.50 ($6.50) for 3 hours or £4 ($7.40) for a full day. The Brockhole tourist information centre is open from March 23 to November 3, daily 10am to 5pm.

When setting out anywhere in the Lake District, it's wise to take adequate precautions. Weather conditions can change rapidly in this area, and in the high fells it can be substantially different from that found at lower levels. A **weather** line (© 01768/775757) provides the latest conditions.

Be aware before you go that the Lake District receives more rainfall than any other district of England, and sturdy walking shoes and rain gear are essential. Hiking after dark is not recommended under any circumstances.

Tourist information offices within the park are richly stocked with maps and suggestions for several dozen bracing rambles. Regardless of the itinerary you select, you'll spot frequent green-and-white signs, or their older equivalents in varnished pine with Adirondack-style routed letters, announcing FOOTPATH TO . . . .

Any tourist information office within the park can provide leaflets describing treks through the park. The **Windermere Tourist Information Centre,** Victoria Street, Windermere, Cumbria LA23 1AD (© 01539/446499), is especially helpful.

See also section 5 of this chapter, "Coniston & Hawkshead," for additional details about boating in the national park.

Langdale Chase Hotel ✦✦   A grand old lakeside house, this hotel resembles a villa on Italy's Lake Como. It has better rooms than Miller Howe (see below), though the food is not as good. The bedrooms contain excellent furniture, and many were recently refurbished. Most of the bedrooms open onto panoramic views of the lake. Five bedrooms are in a converted cottage on the grounds, and these are equal in comfort to those units in the main building. Another bedroom lies over the boathouse on the lake, and this one is often requested. Bathrooms are tiled and come with adequate shelf space and combination tub and shower. The interior of the Victorian stone château, with its many gables, balconies, large mullioned windows, and terraces, is a treasure trove of antiques. The main lounge hall looks like a setting for one of those English drawing-room comedies. On the walls are distinctive paintings, mostly Italian primitives, though one is alleged to be a Van Dyck.

On A591 (3km/2 miles north of town, toward Ambleside), Windermere, Cumbria LA23 1LW. ✆ 01539/432201. Fax 01539/432604. www.langdalechase.co.uk. 27 units. £99–£129 ($183–$239) per person double. Rates include breakfast and dinner. AE, DC, MC, V. **Amenities:** Restaurant; bar; croquet lawn; 24-hr. room service; babysitting; laundry service; rooms for those with limited mobility; nonsmoking rooms. *In room:* TV, dataport, coffeemaker, hair dryer, iron/ironing board.

Lindeth Fell Hotel ✦   High above the town is this traditional large Lakeland house, built of stone and brick in 1907. Many of its rooms overlook the handsome gardens and the lake. The owners, the Kennedys, run the place more like a country house than a hotel, achieving an atmosphere of comfort in pleasingly furnished surroundings. Bedrooms open onto beautiful views, especially on the lakeside of the house; many are quite spacious, others are snug, but all have comfortable beds. The shower-only bathrooms are neatly kept.

Lyth Valley Rd. (on A5074 1.5km/1 mile south of Bowness), Bowness-on-Windermere, Cumbria LA23 3JP. ✆ 01539/443286. Fax 01539/447455. www.lindethfell.co.uk. 14 units. £120–£160 ($222–$296) double. Rates include breakfast and dinner. MC, V. Closed Jan–Feb 14. **Amenities:** Restaurant; bar; putting green; croquet lawn; limited room service; laundry service; dry cleaning; rooms for those with limited mobility; nonsmoking rooms. *In room:* TV, coffeemaker, hair dryer, trouser press.

The Linthwaite House Hotel ✦   This hotel, built in 1900, is surrounded by woodlands and gardens, with a panoramic view of Lake Windermere, Bell Isle, and the distant mountains. The bedrooms are beautifully decorated and offer many amenities, including bathrobes and satellite TVs. As befits its former role as an Edwardian gentleman's house, this hotel has individually decorated bedrooms that come in various shapes and sizes. All rooms are nonsmoking and are fitted with sumptuously comfortable beds and come with combination tub and shower.

Crook Rd., Bowness-on-Windermere, Cumbria LA23 3JA. ✆ 01539/488600. Fax 01539/488601. www.linthwaite.com. 26 units. £100–£260 ($185–$481) double, £266–£315 ($492–$583) suite. Rates include English breakfast. AE, DC, MC, V. **Amenities:** Restaurant; bar; complimentary use of nearby spa; limited room service; laundry service; dry cleaning; 1 room for those with limited mobility. *In room:* TV, coffeemaker, hair dryer, trouser press.

Miller Howe Hotel ✦✦   International guests come to this inn, which bears the unique imprint of its creator, former actor John Tovey, who treats his guests as if they had been invited to a house party. His country estate overlooks Lake Windermere (with views of the Langdale Pikes) and offers stylish accommodations and exquisite cuisine. The house was built in 1916 in the Edwardian style, sitting on 1.8 hectares (4½ acres) of statue-dotted garden and parkland. Each of the large, graciously furnished rooms is supplied with binoculars to help guests fully enjoy the view; other amenities include CD players and umbrellas. Beds are sumptuous, often canopy-draped, each with colorful spreads, soft comfortable mattresses, and padded headboards. Bathrooms have generous shelf space and a combination tub and shower; four rooms have Jacuzzis. There are even copies of *Punch* from the 1890s.

Rayrigg Rd. (on A592 between Windermere and Bowness), Windermere, Cumbria LA23 1EY. ℂ **01539/ 442536.** Fax 01539/445664. www.millerhowe.com. 16 units. Winter £85–£135 ($157–$250) per person per night; high season £93–£175 ($172–$324). Rates include English breakfast and 6-course dinner. AE, MC, V. **Amenities:** Restaurant; 3 lounges; conservatory room; croquet lawn; limited room service; laundry service; dry cleaning; nonsmoking rooms. *In room:* TV, hair dryer, trouser press.

MODERATE

Cedar Manor 🎗 One of the most desirable country-house hotels in the area is Cedar Manor, which completed a renovation in 2003. Originally built in 1860, with gables and chimneys, it was the summer getaway home for a wealthy industrialist from Manchester. But since those times, it has been converted into a hotel of exceptional merit with well-furnished and spacious bedrooms, all of which are nonsmoking. Each room is individually designed and well maintained; some have canopied or four-poster beds. Bathrooms are small and compact, mainly with tub-and-shower combinations. The hotel takes its name from a cedar tree, perhaps from India, which has grown in the garden for some 2 centuries.

Ambleside Rd. (A591), Windermere, Cumbria LA23 1AX. ℂ **01539/443192.** Fax 01539/445970. www.cedar manor.co.uk. 11 units. £74–£86 ($137–$159) double, £114–£140 ($211–$259) suite. Rates include breakfast. MC, V. **Amenities:** Restaurant; lounge; complimentary use of nearby health club; laundry service; dry cleaning. *In room:* TV, coffeemaker, hair dryer.

Lindeth Howe 🧒 This is a country house in a scenic position above Lake Windermere, with 2.4 hectares (6 acres) of garden. Part stone and part red brick, with a roof of green Westmoreland slate, the house was built for a wealthy mill owner in 1879, but its most famous owner was Beatrix Potter, who installed her mother here while she lived across the lake at Sawrey. The present owner, John A. Tiscornia, has furnished it in fine style. Nine of the bedrooms have lake views and are comfortably furnished. Three rooms have handsome four-poster beds, and some rooms have spa bathrooms. Three rooms are large enough for families. Most rooms have shower-tub combinations in the bathrooms.

Longtail Hill, Storrs Park, Bowness-on-Windermere, Cumbria LA23 3JF. ℂ **01539/445759.** Fax 01539/ 446368. www.lindeth-howe.co.uk. 36 units. £50–£89 ($93–$165) per person double with breakfast, £60–£109 ($111–$202) per person double with breakfast and dinner. AE, MC, V. Take B5284 south of Bowness. **Amenities:** Restaurant; bar; indoor heated pool; health club; sauna; limited room service; laundry service; dry cleaning; solarium; rooms for those with limited mobility; nonsmoking rooms. *In room:* TV, dataport, hair dryer, iron/ironing board (in some rooms), trouser press.

INEXPENSIVE

Beaumont Hotel This stone-sided Lakeland villa, originally built in the 1850s, is on a quiet residential street about a minute's walk from Windermere's commercial center. Mr. and Mrs. James C. Casey massively upgraded what had been a rather dowdy interior. Each of the bedrooms is named after one of the characters in the Beatrix Potter sagas (our favorite is Jemima PuddleDuck) and contains either some kind of elaborate canopy or a four-poster bed, fitted with a quality mattress. All the accommodations have recently been refurbished, with new showers, carpets, and curtains. No meals are served other than breakfast, so the owners keep local restaurant menus on hand for their guests to consult. The entire property is nonsmoking, and children under 10 are not accepted.

Holly Rd., Windermere, Cumbria LA23 2AF. ℂ **01539/447075.** Fax 01539/488311. www.lakesbeaumont. co.uk. 10 units. £65–£105 ($120–$194) double. Rates include English breakfast. MC, V. *In room:* TV, coffeemaker, hair dryer.

Fir Trees 🐸 *Value* One of the finest guesthouses in Windermere, this well-run inn provides hotel-like standards at B&B prices. Opposite St. John's Church, halfway between the villages of Bowness and Windermere, Fir Trees is a Victorian house furnished with antiques. Proprietors Mark and Jill Drinkall offer a warm welcome and beautifully maintained bedrooms. The attractive tiled bathrooms are equipped with a shower (some have shower-and-tub combinations). Some units are large enough for families; a few have four-poster beds. The Drinkalls provide their guests with information on restaurants, country pubs, or where to go and what to see. The property is entirely nonsmoking.

Lake Rd., Windermere, Cumbria LA23 2EQ. ℂ **01539/442272.** Fax 01539/442512. www.fir-trees.com. 9 units. £46–£84 ($85–$155) double. Rates include English breakfast. MC, V. **Amenities:** Free use of nearby health club. *In room:* TV, coffeemaker, hair dryer.

WHERE TO DINE

Miller Howe Café 🐸🐸 INTERNATIONAL Owned by Ian and Annette Dutton, this charming little cafe lies at the back of a shop that is known as one of the largest retailers of "creative kitchenware" in Britain. Amid a very modern decor, clients place their food orders at a countertop, and then wait until waitresses bring the dishes to their tables. The cuisine draws upon culinary traditions from around the world and includes such dishes as diced and curried beef in a spicy sauce, filet of salmon with a fresh garden herb sauce, crispy salad bowl with an orange and honey vinaigrette, and breast of chicken served in a red-wine gravy. The restaurant is adjacent to the town's railway station.

Lakeland Limited, Station Precinct. ℂ **01539/446732.** Reservations not needed. Main courses £7–£10 ($13–$19). MC, V. Mon–Fri 9am–6pm; Sat 9am–5pm; Sun 10:30am–4pm.

Porthole Eating House FRENCH/ITALIAN/ENGLISH In a white-painted Lakeland house near the center of town, this restaurant, owned and operated by Gianni and Judy Barten for the last quarter of a century, serves French, English, and Italian cuisine inspired by Italian-born Gianni. Amid a decor enhanced by rows of wine and liqueur bottles and nautical accessories, you can enjoy well-flavored specialties that change with the seasons. Examples include lobster-and-crab bisque; vegetarian lasagna made with mixed vegetables, fresh herbs, and a fresh tomato coulis and basil sauce; baked sea bass with a dill and white-wine sauce, and filet of beef lightly grilled and served with a reduction of butter, fresh herbs, and a touch of white wine.

3 Ash St. ℂ **01539/442793.** Reservations recommended. Main courses £11–£17 ($20–$31). AE, DC, MC, V. Thurs–Sat noon–2pm; Wed–Mon 6:30–10pm.

FAVORITE LOCAL PUBS

Drive a short distance south of Windermere to Cartmel Fell, situated between the A592 and the A5074, and you'll find a pub-lover's dream. The **Mason Arms,** Strawberry Bank (ℂ **01539/568486**), is a Jacobean pub with original oak paneling and flagstone floors. Sturdy, comfortable wooden furniture is spread through a series of five rooms in which you can wander or settle. The outside garden, attractive in its own right, offers a dramatic view of the Winster Valley beyond. The pub offers so many beers that they have a 24-page catalog to help you order, plus a creative, reasonable menu that includes several tasty vegetarian options. Beer prices start at £2 ($3.70).

Southeast of the village, off the A5074 in Crosthwaite, the **Punch Bowl** (ℂ **01539/568237**) is a 16th-century pub; the central room features a high-beamed ceiling with upper minstrel galleries on two sides. Outdoors, a stepped terrace on the hillside offers a tranquil retreat. Theakston's Best Bitter, Jennings Cumberland, and Cocker Hoop are available on tap.

A popular 17th-century pub, **The Queens Head,** on the A592 north of Windermere (© **01539/432174**), uses a gigantic Elizabethan four-poster bed as its serving counter, and has an eclectic mix of antiques strewn in with basic bar furnishings. There are 14 rooms in which you can settle with a pint of Mitchell's Lancaster Bomber, Tetley's, or Boddington's.

Established in 1612, the **Hole in t' Wall,** Lowside (© **01539/443488**), is the oldest pub in Bowness, a real treasure for its character and friendliness. The barroom is decorated with a hodgepodge of antiquated farming tools, and there's a large slate fireplace lending warmth on winter days plus a good selection of real ales on tap. The menu is determined daily, and there's real ingenuity illustrated in an eclectic mix of vegetarian, seafood, and local game dishes. A small flagstoned terrace in the front offers lingering on warmer days and evenings.

3 Ambleside & Rydal

448km (278 miles) NW of London; 23km (14 miles) NW of Kendal; 6.5km (4 miles) N of Windermere

An idyllic retreat at the north end of Lake Windermere, Ambleside is just a small village, but it's one of the major places to stay in the Lake District, attracting pony trekkers, hikers, and rock climbers. It's wonderful in warm weather and even through late autumn, when it's fashionable to sport a raincoat.

Between Ambleside and Wordsworth's former retreat at Grasmere is Rydal, a small village on one of the smallest lakes, Rydal Water. The village is noted for its sheepdog trials at the end of summer. It's 2.5km (1½ miles) north of Ambleside on the A591.

ESSENTIALS

GETTING THERE   Take a train to Windermere (see earlier in this chapter), then continue the rest of the way by bus.

Stagecoach (© **0870/608-2608;** www.stagecoachbus.com) has hourly bus service from Grasmere and Keswick (see later in this chapter) and from Windermere. All these buses into Ambleside are labeled either no. 555 or 556.

If you're driving from Windermere, continue northwest on the A591.

VISITOR INFORMATION   The **Tourist Information Centre** is at Market Cross Central Building, in Ambleside (© **01539/432582**), and is open daily from 9am to 5pm.

EXPLORING THE AREA

At **Lakeland Safari Tours,** 23 Fisherbeck Park, Ambleside (© **01539/433904;** www.lakesafari.co.uk), you can discover the Lakeland's hidden beauty, heritage, and traditions. The owner, a qualified Blue Badge Guide, provides an exciting selection of full-day and half-day safaris in his luxury six-seat vehicle. A half-day safari is £22 ($41) per person; a daylong trek is £33 ($61) per person.

Rydal Mount ⚐   This was the home of William Wordsworth from 1813 until his death in 1850. Part of the house was built as a farmer's lake cottage around 1575. A descendant of Wordsworth now owns the property, which displays numerous portraits, furniture, and family possessions, as well as mementos and the poet's books. A 1.8-hectare (4½-acre) garden, landscaped by Wordsworth, is filled with rare trees, shrubs, and other features of interest.

Off A591, 2.5km (1½ miles) north of Ambleside. © **01539/433002.** Admission house and garden £4.50 ($8.35) adults, £3.50 ($6.50) seniors, £3.25 ($6) students, £10 ($19) family ticket £1.50 ($2.80) children ages 5–16, free for kids 4 and under. Mar–Oct daily 9:30am–5pm; Nov–Feb Wed–Mon 10am–4pm.

WHERE TO STAY
EXPENSIVE

Kirkstone Foot ☆   This country house is one of the finest places to stay in the area. There's the main 17th-century manor house plus several apartments for rent in the surrounding parklike grounds. The original building is encircled by a well-tended lawn, whereas the interior is cozily furnished with overstuffed chairs and English paneling. The comfortable accommodations—11 in the main house and 16 in the less desirable outlying units—are tastefully decorated. The rooms that face the front are the most sought after. Each bathroom has a tub-and-shower combination. One room is spacious enough for families.

Kirkstone Pass Rd., Ambleside, Cumbria LA22 9EH. © **01539/432232.** Fax 01539/432805. www.kirkstone foot.co.uk. 27 units. £166 ($307) double. Rates include English breakfast. MC, V. Take Rydal Rd. north, turning right onto Kirkstone Pass Rd. **Amenities:** Restaurant; bar; babysitting; 1 room for those with limited mobility. *In room:* TV, coffeemaker, hair dryer.

Rothay Manor ☆☆ *(Kids)*   At this spot, which is reminiscent of a French country inn, the stars are the cuisine, the well-chosen French and American wines, and comfortable, centrally heated bedrooms and suites. It's our top choice in an area where the competition is stiff in the country-house race. Most bedrooms have shuttered French doors opening onto a sun balcony and a mountain view (two are wheelchair accessible). Throughout the estate you'll find an eclectic combination of antiques (some Georgian blended harmoniously with Victorian), flowers, and enticing armchairs.

The manor is a great place for families, renting both family rooms and family suites (big enough for a brood of six), and also providing cots free. "Baby-listening" devices are available, and there's a children's "high tea" served around 6 to 6:30pm, which is really a dinner, with burgers, fish sticks, pizzas, and the like. A children's play park is nearby. All rooms are nonsmoking.

Rothay Bridge, Ambleside, Cumbria LA22 0EH. © **01539/433605.** Fax 01539/433607. www.rothaymanor. co.uk. 17 units. £135–£155 ($250–$287) double; £180 ($333) suite. Rates include English breakfast. AE, DC, MC, V. Take A593 1km (½ mile) south of Ambleside. **Amenities:** Restaurant; bar; limited room service; babysitting; laundry service; rooms for those with limited mobility. *In room:* TV, coffeemaker, hair dryer.

Wateredge Inn ☆   This is a winning little choice with an idyllic lakeside setting. The center of this hotel was formed long ago from two 17th-century fishing cottages. Wateredge was, in fact, listed as a lodging house as early as 1873, and further additions were made in the early 1900s. Situated in a beautiful garden overlooking Lake Windermere, the hotel also serves some of the best food in the area. Public rooms have many little nooks for reading and conversation. However, on sunny days guests prefer to relax in the chairs on the lawn. The rooms vary in size and appointments; some are spacious, others much smaller. Furnishings are continually renewed and upgraded as the need arises. Bathrooms are tiled and compact; most come with a tub-and-shower combination; the Windermere room has a two-person tub with a separate walk-in shower.

Borrans Rd. (on A591, 1.5km/1 mile south of Ambleside), Waterhead, Ambleside, Cumbria LA22 0EP. © **01539/432332.** Fax 01539/431878. www.wateredgeinn.co.uk. 21 units. £70–£120 ($130–$222) double. Rates include English breakfast. AE, MC, V. **Amenities:** Restaurant; bar; nearby health club. *In room:* TV, coffeemaker, hair dryer.

MODERATE TO INEXPENSIVE

Glen Rothay Hotel   Built in the 17th century as a wayfarer's inn, this hotel adjoins Dora's Field, immortalized by Wordsworth. Set back from the highway, it has a stucco-and-flagstone facade. Inside, the place has been modernized, but original details remain, including beamed ceilings and paneling. The comfortable bedrooms upstairs are tastefully furnished. Most rooms have twin or double beds, but a couple offer four-posters. The tiled bathrooms are small and compact, each with a shower.

On A591, Rydal, Ambleside, Cumbria LA22 9LR. (✆ **01539/434500.** Fax 01539/431079. www.theglenrothay. com. 8 units. £70 ($130) double; from £160 ($296) suite. Rates include English breakfast and dinner. MC, V. On A591 2.5km (1½ miles) northwest of Ambleside. **Amenities:** Restaurant; bar; limited room service; non-smoking rooms. *In room:* TV, dataport, coffeemaker, hair dryer.

Queens Hotel   In the heart of this area is the Queens, an old-fashioned family-run hotel where guests are housed and fed well. It began as a private home in the Victorian era and was later transformed into a hotel, with some restoration completed in 1992. Bedrooms are a bit smallish but reasonably comfortable, and the small bathrooms have shower stalls and tubs.

Market Place, Ambleside, Cumbria LA22 9BU. (✆ **01539/432206.** Fax 01539/432721. www.queenshotel ambleside.com. 26 units. Sun–Thurs £64–£74 ($118–$137) double; Fri–Sat £64–£90 ($118–$167) double. AE, MC, V. **Amenities:** 2 restaurants; 2 bars. *In room:* TV, coffeemaker, hair dryer.

Riverside Hotel ⚘   Secluded on a quiet lane, this is a small country hotel formed by combining three adjoining riverside houses dating from the 1820s. It has the solid slate-block walls and slate roof common to Cumbria and, despite its peaceful location, lies a few minutes' walk from the center of Ambleside. Each of the painstakingly decorated rooms is comfortably furnished—one features a four-poster bed, and two suites have a Jacuzzi. One room is large enough for families.

Near Rothay Bridge, Under Loughrigg, Ambleside, Cumbria LA22 9LJ. (✆ **01539/432395.** Fax 01539/442041. www.riverside-at-ambleside.co.uk. 6 units. £64–£90 ($118–$167) double. Rates include breakfast. MC, V. Closed 2 weeks in Dec. From Windermere on A591, take the left fork at Waterhead toward Coniston. Follow Coniston Rd. for about 1.5km (1 mile) until you come to the junction at Rothay Bridge. Turn left across the bridge and then immediately make a sharp right along the small lane signposted Under Loughrigg. **Amenities:** Access to nearby health club. *In room:* TV, coffeemaker, hair dryer.

WHERE TO DINE

Glass House ⚘ MODERN BRITISH/MEDITERRANEAN   In the early 1990s, the owners of this popular restaurant renovated what had originally been built in the 1400s as a water-driven mill for the crushing of wheat into flour. Today, you'll find a split-level combination of medieval and postmodern architecture, with big sunny windows, interior views of the mill's original cogs and gears, lots of oaken interior trim, and on the buildings outside, a moss-covered, full-scale replica of the original water wheel. Menu items are more sophisticated and elegant than what's served by any of its competitors. Examples include a locally smoked, braised lamb shank in a red-wine sauce; a delectable grilled red snapper with a crushed potato cake; and a tantalizing warm feta cheese and polenta tart with rocket, French beans, beet, and fig-based salsa.

Rydal Rd. (✆ **01539/432137.** Reservations recommended. Main courses £11–£19 ($20–$35). MC, V. Wed–Mon noon–2pm and 6:30–10pm.

WHERE TO SHARE A PINT

The friendliest pub in Ambleside is the **Golden Rule,** Smithy Brow ((✆ **01539/ 432257**), named for the brass yardstick mounted over the bar. A country hunt theme in the barroom, it features comfortable leather furniture and cast-iron tables. You can step into one side room and throw darts, or go into the other for a quiet, contemplative pint. Behind the bar, a small but colorful garden provides a serene setting in warm weather. There's inexpensive pub grub if you get hungry.

Located 5km (3 miles) west of town, off the A593 in Little Langdale, **Three Shires** (© 01539/437215), a stone-built pub with a stripped timber-and-flagstone interior, offers stunning views of the valley and wooded hills. You can get good pub grub here, as well as a pint of Black Sheep Bitter, Ruddles County, or Webster's Yorkshire. Malt whiskies are well represented.

4 Grasmere ⊙⊙

454km (282 miles) NW of London; 29km (18 miles) NW of Kendal; 69km (43 miles) S of Carlisle

On a lake of the same name, **Grasmere** was the home of Wordsworth from 1799 to 1808. He called this area "the loveliest spot that man hath ever known."

ESSENTIALS
GETTING THERE   Take a train to Windermere (see earlier in this chapter) and continue the rest of the way by bus.

Stagecoach (© 0870/608-2608; www.stagecoachbus.com) runs hourly bus service to Grasmere from Keswick (see later in this chapter) and Windermere (see earlier in this chapter). Buses in either direction are marked no. 555 or 556.

If you're driving from Windermere (see earlier in this chapter), continue northwest along the A591.

VISITOR INFORMATION   The summer-only **Tourist Information Centre** is on Red Bank Road (© 01539/435245) and is open mid-March through October daily from 9:30am to 5:30pm; and November through mid-March Friday, Saturday, and Sunday only from 10am to 3:30pm.

A LITERARY LANDMARK
Dove Cottage/The Wordsworth Museum ⊙   Wordsworth lived with his writer-and-diarist sister, Dorothy, at Dove Cottage, which is now part of the Wordsworth Museum and administered by the Wordsworth Trust. Wordsworth, the poet laureate, died in the spring of 1850 and was buried in the graveyard of the village church at Grasmere. Another tenant of Dove Cottage was Thomas De Quincey *(Confessions of an English Opium Eater)*. The Wordsworth Museum houses manuscripts, paintings, and memorabilia. Various special exhibitions throughout the year explore the art and literature of English romanticism.

Afternoon tea is served in the **Dove Cottage Tearoom and Restaurant** (© 01539/435268). A good selection of open sandwiches, scones, cake, and tea breads is offered along with Darjeeling, Assam, Earl Grey, and herbal teas. The tearoom is open daily from 10am to 5pm and the restaurant from 6:30 to 9pm Wednesday through Sunday.

On A591, south of the village of Grasmere on the road to Kendal. © 01539/435544. www.wordsworth. org.uk. Admission to both Dove Cottage and the adjoining museum £5.95 ($11) adults, £3 ($5.55) children. Daily 9:30am–5:30pm. Closed Dec 24–26 and mid-Jan to early Feb.

WHERE TO STAY & DINE
EXPENSIVE
Swan Hotel   Sir Walter Scott used to slip in here for a secret drink early in the morning, and Wordsworth mentioned the place in "The Waggoner." In fact, the poet's wooden chair is in one of the rooms. Many bedrooms are in a modern wing, added in 1975, that fits gracefully onto the building's older core (only the

shell of the original 1650 building remains). Bedrooms are comfortably furnished, each with a twin or double bed (one room has a four-poster bed). Bathrooms are midsize, with combination tub and shower for the most part.

On A591 (on the road to Keswick, 1km/½ mile outside Grasmere), Grasmere, Cumbria LA22 9RF. ℂ **01539/ 435551.** Fax 01539/435741. 38 units. £134–£180 ($248–$333) double. Rates include breakfast and dinner. AE, DC, MC, V. **Amenities:** Restaurant; bar; limited room service; laundry service; dry cleaning; nonsmoking rooms. *In room:* TV, dataport, coffeemaker, hair dryer, trouser press.

White Moss House ♠ This 1730 Lakeland cottage, once owned by Wordsworth, overlooks the lake and the fells. You'll be welcomed here by Peter and Susan Dixon, who will pamper you with morning tea in bed, turn down your bedcovers at night, and cater to your culinary preferences. The rooms are individually decorated, comfortably furnished, and well heated in nippy weather. All the bathrooms are well appointed, each with shower. Brockstone, a cottage annex that is a 5-minute drive along the road, can accommodate two, three, or four guests comfortably in utter peace.

On A591 (2.5km/1½ miles south of town), Rydal Water, Grasmere, Cumbria LA22 9SE. ℂ **01539/435295.** Fax 01539/435516. www.whitemoss.com. 6 units. £150–£184 ($278–$340) double. Rates include breakfast and dinner. AE, MC, V. Closed Dec–Jan. **Amenities:** Restaurant; bar; access to nearby health club; breakfast only room service; laundry service; dry cleaning. *In room:* TV, coffeemaker, hair dryer, trouser press.

Wordsworth Hotel ♠♠ This choice in the heart of the village is situated in a 1.2-hectare (3-acre) garden next to the churchyard where Wordsworth is buried. An old stone Lakeland house that was once the hunting lodge of the earl of Cadogan, the Wordsworth has been completely refurbished to provide luxuriously appointed bedrooms with views of the fells, as well as modern bathrooms. Three rooms have four-poster beds. The original master bedroom contains a Victorian bathroom with a brass towel rail and polished pipes and taps. Bedrooms come with character and comfort, and the canopied beds are rather sumptuous. Three rooms are spacious enough for families. All contain beautifully maintained bathrooms with combination tub and shower; the suites have Jacuzzis.

Grasmere, Cumbria LA22 9SW. ℂ **01539/435592.** Fax 01539/435765. www.grasmere-hotels.co.uk. 37 units. £250 ($463) double; from £330 ($611) suite. Rates include English breakfast and dinner. AE, DC, MC, V. Turn left on A591 at the Grasmere Village sign and follow the road over the bridge, past the church, and around an S-bend; the Wordsworth is on the right. **Amenities:** Restaurant; bar; heated indoor pool; exercise room; sauna; 24-hr. room service; laundry service. *In room:* TV, dataport, coffeemaker, hair dryer, trouser press.

MODERATE

Gold Rill ♠♠ Paul and Cathy Jewsbury operate the best-located hotel in Grasmere, alongside the lake yet only a 2-minute walk to the center of the village. Surrounded by well-maintained gardens, the hotel stands on .8 hectares (2 acres) of land with its own heated outdoor pool and a private pier. It's really a sprawling country house of grand comfort and taste. Each midsize to spacious bedroom is individually furnished, including a king-size bed in some. Those who consider themselves romantics can arrange in advance for champagne, strawberries, and fresh flowers to be placed in the room. The well-maintained private bathrooms come with either tubs and showers or showers only. Guests can enjoy pub lunches or else a fine evening dinner, often prepared with local produce.

Red Bank Rd. Grasmere, Cumbria LA22 9PU ℂ 01539/435486. www.gold-rill.com. 31 units. £126–£148 ($233–$274) double. MC, V. **Amenities:** Restaurant; bar; heated outdoor pool; limited room service; laundry service; nonsmoking rooms. *In room:* TV, coffeemaker, hair dryer.

Grasmere Red Lion Hotel *(Kids* This 200-year-old coaching inn is only a short stroll from Wordsworth's Dove Cottage, and it's assumed that the poet often stopped here for a meal, drink, or to warm himself by the fire. Recently refurbished, the hotel offers comfortably furnished bedrooms, half with Jacuzzis in the bathrooms. In 1999, the hotel opened eight rather snug new bedrooms. The older rooms are fine as well, each fitted with firm mattresses. Four rooms are spacious enough for families and offer bunk beds. Each has a well-maintained bathroom with adequate shelf space and a shower and many have a Jacuzzi.

Red Lion Sq., Grasmere, Cumbria LA22 9SS. © **01539/435456.** Fax 01539/435579. www.hotelgrasmere. uk.com. 47 units. Sun–Thurs £90–£118 ($167–$218) double; Fri–Sat £100–£123 ($185–$228) double. Rates include English breakfast. AE, DC, MC, V. **Amenities:** Restaurant; 2 bars; indoor heated pool; exercise room; Jacuzzi; sauna; limited room service; laundry service. *In room:* TV, dataport, coffeemaker, hair dryer, trouser press.

INEXPENSIVE

Riversdale *(Value* This lovely old house, built in 1830 of traditional Lakeland stone, is situated on the outskirts of the village of Grasmere along the banks of the River Rothay. The bedrooms, all of which are nonsmoking, are tastefully decorated and offer every comfort, including hospitality trays, as well as views of the surrounding fells. Bedrooms, most often midsize, have quality furnishings. Each unit has a small bathroom; two have tub-and-shower combinations and the other a shower only. The staff has a wealth of information on day trips, whether by car or hiking. The delightful breakfasts offered here are served in a dining room overlooking Silver How and the fells beyond Easdale Tarn.

Grasmere, Cumbria LA22 9RQ. © **01539/435619.** www.riversdalegrasmere.co.uk. 3 units. £50–£64 ($93–$118) double. Rates include English breakfast. Children not accepted. No credit cards. Drive 16km (10 miles) north of Windermere along A591 (signposted to Keswick), then turn left by the Swan Hotel. In 360m (1,200 ft.), you'll find the inn on the left side of the road facing the river. *In room:* Coffeemaker, hair dryer, no phone.

5 Coniston & Hawkshead

423km (263 miles) NW of London; 84km (52 miles) S of Carlisle; 31km (19 miles) NW of Kendal

At Coniston, you can visit the village famously associated with John Ruskin. It's also a good place for hiking and rock climbing. The Coniston "Old Man" towers in the background, at 790m (2,633 ft.), give mountain climbers one of the finest views of the Lake District.

Just 6.5km (4 miles) east of Coniston, discover for yourself the village of Hawkshead, with its 15th-century grammar school where Wordsworth studied for 8 years (he carved his name on a desk that is still there). Nearby, in the vicinity of Esthwaite Water, is the 17th-century Hill Top Farm, former home of author Beatrix Potter.

ESSENTIALS

GETTING THERE Take a train to Windermere (see earlier in this chapter) and proceed the rest of the way by bus. From April to September, **Mountain Goat** (© **01539/445161**) operates eight buses per day to Hawkshead.

By car from Windermere, proceed north on the A591 to Ambleside, cutting southwest on the B5285 to Hawkshead.

Windermere Lake Cruises Ltd. (© **01539/443360;** www.windermere-lake-cruises.co.uk) operates a ferry service in summer from Bowness, directly south of Windermere, to Hawkshead. It reduces driving time considerably (see "Windermere & Bowness," earlier in this chapter).

VISITOR INFORMATION   The **Tourist Information Centre** (© **01539/ 436525**) is at Hawkshead in the Main Car Park and is open daily from 9:30am to 5:30pm during high season, and daily from 10am to 3:30pm during winter.

EXPLORING THE AREA

Of the many places to go boating in the Lake District, Coniston Water in the Lake District National Park may be the best. Coniston Water lies in a tranquil wooded valley between Grisedale Forest and the high fells of Coniston Old Man and Wetherlam. The **Coniston Boating Centre,** Lake Road, Coniston LA21 (© **01539/441366**), occupies a sheltered bay at the northern end of the lake. The center provides launching facilities, boat storage, and parking. You can rent row boats that carry two to six people, sailing dinghies carrying up to six passengers, or Canadian canoes that transport two. There is a picnic area and access to the lakeshore. From the gravel beach, you may be able to spot the varied water birds and plants that make Coniston Water a valuable but fragile habitat for wildlife.

You can also cruise the lake in an original Victorian steam-powered yacht, the *Gondola.* Launched in 1859, and in regular service until 1937, this unique boat was rescued and completely restored by the National Trust. Since 1980 it has become a familiar sight on Coniston Water; sailings to Park-a-Moor and Brantwood run throughout the summer. Service is subject to weather conditions, of course. Trips are possible from April to October costing £4.80 ($8.90) round-trip for adults or £2.80 ($5.20) for children. For more information, call © **01539/436216.**

Coniston Launch (© **01539/436216;** www.conistonlaunch.co.uk) is a traditional timber boat that calls at Coniston, Monk Coniston, Torver, and Brantwood. (Discounts are offered in combination with admission to Brantwood house; see below.) This exceptional boating outfitter offers special cruises in summer (a "Swallows and Amazons" tour was inspired by Arthur Ransome's classic story).

Summitreks operates from the lakeside at Coniston Boating Centre, offering qualified instruction in canoeing and windsurfing. You can rent a wide range of equipment from the nearby office at Lake Road (© **01539/441212;** www. summitreks.co.uk).

In Hawkshead, the **Beatrix Potter Gallery** (© **01539/436355**) has an annually changing exhibition of Beatrix Potter's original illustrations from her children's storybooks. The building was once the office of her husband, solicitor William Heelis, and the interior remains largely unaltered since his day. To get here, take bus no. 505 from Ambleside and Coniston to the square in Hawkshead.

Brantwood ⟨★⟩   John Ruskin, poet, artist, and critic, was one of the great figures of the Victorian age and a prophet of social reform, inspiring such diverse men as Proust, Frank Lloyd Wright, and Gandhi. He moved to his home, Brantwood, on the east side of Coniston Water, in 1872 and lived here until his death in 1900. The house today is open for visitors to see his memorabilia, including some 200 of his pictures.

Part of the 101-hectare (250-acre) estate is open as a nature trail. The Brantwood stables, designed by Ruskin, have been converted into a tearoom and restaurant, the Jumping Jenny. Also in the stable building is the Coach House Craft Gallery, which follows the Ruskin tradition of encouraging contemporary craftwork of the finest quality.

Literary fans may want to pay a pilgrimage to the graveyard of the village church, where Ruskin was buried; his family turned down the invitation to have him interred at Westminster Abbey.

Coniston. ℂ **01539/441396.** www.brantwood.org.uk. Admission £5.50 ($10) adults, £4 ($7.40) students, £1 ($1.85) children 5–16, £12 ($21) family ticket (2 adults, 3 children). Garden walk £3.75 ($6.95). Mid-Mar to mid-Nov daily 11am–5:30pm; mid-Nov to mid-Mar Wed–Sun 11am–4:30pm. Closed Dec 25–26.

John Ruskin Museum   At this institute, in the center of the village, you can see Ruskin's personal possessions and mementos, pictures by him and his friends, letters, and his collection of mineral rocks.

Yewdale Rd., Coniston. ℂ **01539/441164.** www.ruskinmuseum.com. Admission £3.50 ($6.50) adults, £1.75 ($3.25) children, £9 ($17) family ticket (2 adults, 2 or 3 children). Mid-Mar to mid-Nov daily 10am–5:30pm; mid-Nov to mid-Mar Wed–Sun 10:30am–3:30pm.

WHERE TO STAY

Coniston Lodge Hotel   A third generation of Lakeland hoteliers, Elizabeth and Anthony Robinson, invite you into their well-run lodge, which is almost as much a home as it is a small hotel. All of its bedrooms are individually furnished, one with a four-poster. Each room is comfortable and attractive, and carries the name of a local mountain tarn. The compact bathrooms have both tubs and showers. The entirely nonsmoking hotel has a garden and a communal sitting room where guests gather to watch the "telly." The dining room is furnished in a country cottage style with antique accessories. Home-cooked English and Lakeland dishes are served, using fresh local produce.

Station Rd., Coniston, Cumbria LA21 8HH. ℂ **01539/441201.** Fax 015394/41201. www.coniston-lodge.com. £82–£98 ($152–$181) double. AE, MC, V. **Amenities:** Restaurant. *In room:* TV, beverage maker, hair dryer, trouser press.

Grizedale Lodge   This is one of the better B&Bs in the area. It was built in 1902 as a hunting lodge for the chairman of the Cunard Line. Mr. and Mrs. Aspey offer handsomely furnished bedrooms with a compact private bathroom with shower. Some of the rooms have four-poster beds and offer lovely views; all of the rooms are nonsmoking.

Grizedale Hawkshead LA22 0QL. ℂ **01539/436532.** Fax 01539/436572. www.grizedale-lodge.com. 8 units. £70–£90 ($130–$167) double. Rates include breakfast. AE, MC, V. From Hawkshead take Newby Bridge Rd. for about 450m (1,500 ft.), then turn right (signposted GRIZEDALE & FOREST PARK CENTER) and follow this road for 3km (2 miles). **Amenities:** Bar; limited room service. *In room:* TV, coffeemaker, hair dryer, no phone.

The Sun Hotel   This is the most popular, traditional, and attractive pub, restaurant, and hotel in Coniston. It's a country-house hotel of much character, dating from 1902, though the inn attached to it is from the 16th century. Situated on beautiful grounds above the village, 135m (450 ft.) from the town center, it lies at the foot of the Coniston "Old Man." Each bedroom, ranging in size from small to midsize, is decorated with style and flair; one has a four-poster bed. Eight of the rooms contain a tub-and-shower combination; three are big enough for families. And all the rooms are nonsmoking.

Brow Hill (off A593), Coniston, Cumbria LA21 8HQ. ℂ **01539/441248.** Fax 01539/441219. 10 units. £90 ($167) double. Rate includes English breakfast. MC, V. **Amenities:** Restaurant; bar; limited room service. *In room:* TV, coffeemaker, hair dryer.

WHERE TO DINE

Queen's Head   ENGLISH/INTERNATIONAL   This is the most famous pub in town. Behind a mock black-and-white timber facade, it's a 17th-century structure of character. It serves a special brew, Robinson's Stockport, from old-fashioned wooden kegs. Try a sizzling sirloin steak, local Cumberland sausages, grilled rainbow trout, or duck in orange sauce. More exotic cuisine ranges from Thai curry to Moroccan chicken. Vegetarians are catered to with several dishes.

The Queen's Head may be more inn than pub; it rents 14 bedrooms with a private bathroom, TV, and phone. The comfortably old-fashioned bedrooms rent for £64 to £114 ($118–$211) for a double (two with four-poster beds). English breakfast is included.

Main St., Hawkshead. © **01539/436271.** Fax 01539/436722. www.queensheadhotel.co.uk. Reservations recommended. Main courses £11–£17 ($20–$31). AE, MC, V. Daily noon–2:30pm and 5-9:30pm.

WHERE TO ENJOY A PINT

A display case of fishing lures is the first tip-off, then there's the pond itself—yes, it's true, you can fish while you drink at the **Drunken Duck,** Barnsgate (© **01539/436347**). Or you can just sit on the front porch and gaze at Lake Windermere in the distance. Inside, you can choose from an assortment of cushioned settees, old pews, and tub or ladder-back chairs, then order a beef filet in red-wine sauce or minted lamb casserole to go with a pint of Mitchell's Lancaster Bomber, Yates Bitter, or Yates Drunken Duck Bitter, brewed especially for the pub. If you want stronger spirits, there are more than a dozen malt whiskies to choose from.

Overlooking the central square of the village, the **Kings Arms** (© **01539/436372**) offers a pleasant front terrace or lots of plush leather-covered seating inside the cozy barroom. Traditional pub grub is supplemented with a few pasta dishes, burgers and steaks, and ales include Greenall's Original, Tetley's, and Theakston's XB. Malt whiskies are also well represented.

6 Keswick

35km (22 miles) NW of Windermere; 473km (294 miles) NW of London; 50km (31 miles) NW of Kendal

Keswick opens onto Derwentwater, one of the loveliest lakes in the region, and the town makes a good base for exploring the northern half of Lake District National Park. Keswick has two landscaped parks, and above the small town is an historic stone circle thought to be some 4,000 years old.

St. Kentigern's Church dates from A.D. 553, and a weekly market held in the center of Keswick can be traced from a charter granted in the 13th century. It's a short walk to Friar's Crag, the classic viewing point on Derwentwater. The walk will also take you past boat landings with launches that operate regular tours around the lake.

Around Derwentwater are many places with literary associations that evoke memories of Wordsworth, Robert Southey, Coleridge, and Hugh Walpole. Several of Beatrix Potter's stories were based at Keswick. The town also has a professional repertory theater that schedules performances in the summer, a swimming pool complex, and an 18-hole golf course at the foot of the mountains 6.5km (4 miles) away.

ESSENTIALS

GETTING THERE   Take a train to Windermere (see earlier in this chapter) and proceed the rest of the way by bus.

Stagecoach(© **0870/608-2608;** www.stagecoachbus.com) has a regular bus service from Windermere and Grasmere (bus no. 555).

If driving from Windermere, drive northwest on the A591.

VISITOR INFORMATION The **Tourist Information Centre,** at Moot Hall, Market Square (℃ **01768/772645**), is open daily April through September from 9:30am to 5:30pm, and October through March daily from 9:30am to 4:30pm. It's closed Christmas and New Year's days.

SEEING THE SIGHTS

Mirehouse A tranquil Cumbrian family home that has not been sold since 1688, Mirehouse has unusually wide-ranging literary and artistic connections. The piano is played on afternoons when guests stop by to visit. The park around it stretches to Bassenthwaite Lake, and has extensive gardens, plus woodland adventure playgrounds. It is in easy reach of the ancient lakeside church and the Old Sawmill Tearoom, which is known for its generous Cumbrian cooking.

On A591, 5.5km (3½ miles) north of Keswick. ℃ **01768/772287**. www.mirehouse.com. Admission to house and gardens plus a lakeside walk £4.60 ($8.50) adults, £2.30 ($4.25) children and seniors, £14 ($26) family ticket (2 adults plus 4 kids ages 5–16). Gardens alone £2.20 ($4.05) adults, £1.10 ($2.05) children. House open Apr–Oct Sun and Wed (also Fri in Aug) 2–4:30pm. Tearoom and grounds Apr–Oct daily 10am–5:30pm.

WHERE TO STAY

Grange Country House A tranquil retreat, this charming hotel and gardens are situated on a hilltop. Dating from the 1840s, it is furnished in part with antiques. Guests enjoy the crackling log fires in chilly weather. Many of the attractively furnished, well-kept rooms have scenic views of the Lakeland hills. There is continual upgrading of the bedrooms, which come in various shapes and sizes; each is individually decorated and most have double or twin beds. The compact bathrooms are well organized, each with shower (some have tubs).

Manor Brow, Ambleside Rd. (on the southeast side of Keswick, overlooking the town, just off A591), Keswick, Cumbria CA12 4BA. ℃ **01768/772500**. www.grangekeswick.com. 10 units. £46–£82 ($85–$152) double. Rates include English breakfast. MC, V. Closed Dec–Feb. **Amenities:** Breakfast room; lounge; breakfast-only room service; nonsmoking rooms. *In room:* TV, coffeemaker, hair dryer.

Highfield Hotel ⭐ *(Value* Constructed in the late 1880s, two former private residences have been skillfully converted into a well-run hotel. The houses were built to take full advantage of mountain and lake views. A veranda, balconies, turrets, and bay windows characterize the architecture. A 5-minute walk from the center of town, the house is furnished in a traditional British way. All the bedrooms are nonsmoking, good-size, and handsomely decorated, many with bay windows where you can sit and soak up the view. Each accommodation comes with a well-maintained private bathroom with shower. The most magnificent room is the spacious and elegant Woodford Room with a four-poster bed and raised seating area. The main dining room is elegant yet informal with daily changing menus, using, whenever possible, the best of local produce, such as Borrowdale salmon.

The Heads, Keswick, Cumbria CA12 5ER. ℃ **01768/772508**. Fax 01768/772508. www.highfieldkeswick. co.uk. 19 units. £100–£126 ($185–$233) double. Rates include breakfast and dinner. AE, MC, V. Closed mid-Nov to Jan. **Amenities:** Restaurant; bar. *In room:* TV, beverage maker.

Skiddaw Hotel *(Kids* This hotel lies behind an impressive facade and entrance marquee built right onto the sidewalk in the heart of Keswick at the market square. The owners have refurbished the interior, retaining the best features. Bedrooms are compact and eye-catching, and have been refurbished. Seven rooms are large enough for families. Bathrooms are well appointed, each with a shower and tub. The upgraded Summit rooms offer extras such as bathrobes and mineral water. Guests may use the indoor pool and spa at Armathwaite Hall and golf at Keswick Golf Club during the week.

Market Sq., Keswick, Cumbria CA12 5BN. ℂ **01768/772071.** Fax 01768/774850. www.skiddawhotel.co.uk. 40 units. £106–£130 ($196–$241) double. Rates include English breakfast. AE, MC, V. **Amenities:** Restaurant; bar; limited room service; laundry service; dry cleaning; 1 room for those with limited mobility; nonsmoking rooms. *In room:* TV, coffeemaker, hair dryer.

Swinside Lodge 🦌 Isolated on a knoll that overlooks Lake Derwentwater, and solidly built in the 1850s as a home for the manager of the enormous estate that surrounded it at the time, this is a cozy, well-managed bed-and-breakfast hotel where evening meals are better than the norm. The nonsmoking venue belongs to Susan and Kevin Kniveton, with cuisine prepared by Andrew Carter. Bedrooms are outfitted with painted, cream-colored furniture, and pastel-colored fabrics that deliberately don't convey a sense of the Edwardian age. Each unit comes with a compact bathroom with tiled shower (some have tubs). Several public rooms and lounges have shelves of books and diversionary games that take the boredom off any rainy day. Children under 5 are not encouraged.

Grange Rd., Newlands, Cumbria CA12 5UE. ℂ and fax **01768/772948.** www.swinsidelodge-hotel.co.uk. 7 units. £140–£170 ($259–$315) double. Rates include dinner and breakfast for 2 occupants. MC, V. From Keswick, take A66 SW for 5km (3 miles), following the signs to Portinscale and to Grange. **Amenities:** Restaurant; 3 lounges. *In room:* TV, coffeemaker, hair dryer.

A NEARBY PLACE TO DINE

The Yew Tree Restaurant BRITISH This restaurant in the Borrowdale region lies in the hamlet of Seatoller. Named after the 500-year-old yew that broods timelessly near the front entrance, this restaurant occupies an interconnected pair of stone-sided cottages that were built in 1628 as the home of two German-born miners. If you've been out hiking, fortify yourself with simple but nourishing dishes that include soup, Cumberland sausages with salads, and a homemade lamb burger with baked potato. The interior of the place, loaded with oaken beams and memorabilia, is about as evocative as it gets.

Seatoller. ℂ **01768/777634.** Reservations recommended. Main courses £4.25–£7.95 ($7.85–$15). Daily 10am–6pm. Closed 3 weeks in Jan. MC, V. Take B5289 13km (8 miles) south of Keswick.

SIDE TRIPS FROM KESWICK
BORROWDALE

One of the most scenic parts of the Lake District, Borrowdale stretches south of Derwentwater to Seathwaite in the heart of the county. The valley is walled in by fell sides, and it's an excellent center for exploring, walking, and climbing. Many use it as a center for exploring **Scafell,** England's highest mountain, at 963m (3,210 ft.).

This resort is in the Borrowdale Valley, the southernmost settlement of which is Seatoller. The village of Seatoller, at 353m (1,176 ft.), is the terminus for buses to and from Keswick. It's also the center for a **Lake District National Park Information Centre** at Dalehead Base, Seatoller Barn (ℂ **01768/777294**). Open April to October 10am to 5pm.

After leaving Seatoller, the B5289 takes you west through the Honister Pass and Buttermere Fell, one of the most dramatic drives in the Lake District. The road is lined with towering boulders. The lake village of Buttermere also merits a stopover.

Where to Stay & Dine

Borrowdale Gates Hotel 🦌 The proprietors of this hotel, Terry and Christine Parkinson, welcome travelers from around the world; even former prime minister John Major has dropped in for afternoon tea. Their 1860 Victorian country house, built of Lakeland stone, received an addition of nine rooms that faithfully matches the Victorian style. All the rooms range in size from medium to large, and are decorated with rich Victorian colors and period reproductions. Every year some rooms are upgraded and refurbished. The place is warm, cozy, and inviting, and the shower-only bathrooms are well maintained. The public areas, with their antiques and open-log stone fireplaces, sprawl along the ground floor and include a bar, restaurant and dining area, and four sitting lounges. They are all airy and bright with views of the surrounding gardens.

Grange-in-Borrowdale, Keswick CA12 5UQ. ⓒ **01768/777204.** Fax 01768/777254. www.borrowdale-gates. com. 29 units. Sun–Thurs £126 ($233) double; Fri–Sat £142 ($263) double. Rates include English breakfast and dinner. AE, MC, V. From Keswick, take B5289 6.5km (4 miles) south to Grange, go over the bridge, and the inn sits on the right, just beyond the curve in the road. **Amenities:** Restaurant; bar. *In room:* TV, coffeemaker, hair dryer.

Borrowdale Hotel *&*   When the weather is damp, log fires welcome guests in this Lakeland stone building, which was originally a coaching inn (ca. 1866). The rooms are comfortable and many have fine views. All have intercom units. Each of the midsize to spacious bedrooms is well designed and furnished. Four rooms contain four-poster beds; several rooms are suitable for families. Bathrooms are well maintained; most offer a tub-and-shower combination.

Borrowdale Rd. (B5289), Borrowdale, Keswick, Cumbria CA12 5UY. ⓒ **01768/777224.** Fax 01768/777338. www.theborrowdalehotel.co.uk. 33 units. Summer and winter £65–£78 ($120–$144) per person double; spring and fall £69–£84 ($128–$155) double. Rates include English breakfast and dinner. MC, V. On B5289, 5.5km (3½ miles) south of Keswick. **Amenities:** Restaurant; bar; access to nearby health club; limited room service; laundry service; 1 room for those with limited mobility. *In room:* TV, dataport; coffeemaker, hair dryer, trouser press.

Lodore Falls Hotel *&*   This hotel overlooks Derwentwater from fields where cows graze. With its spike-capped mansard tower, symmetrical gables, and balcony-embellished stone facade, it seems straight out of the Swiss Alps. (Ironically, the Swiss owners who built this place in the 19th century were named England. Their tradition of good rooms, food, and service continues today.) The interior has been completely modernized, and the well-furnished bedrooms vary in size; it's worth opting for one of the larger ones. The tiled bathrooms are small, each with shower.

Borrowdale Rd. (B5289), Borrowdale, Keswick, Cumbria CA12 5UX. ⓒ **01768/777285.** Fax 01768/777343. www.lodorefallshotel.co.uk. 71 units. £114–£242 ($211–$448) double. Rates include breakfast. Winter discounts available. AE, DC, MC, V. Indoor parking £5 ($9.25); outdoor, free. On B5289 5.5km (3½ miles) south of Keswick. **Amenities:** Restaurant; bar; 2 heated pools (1 indoor, 1 outdoor); 24-hr. room service; laundry service; outdoor tennis court; rooms for those with limited mobility; nonsmoking rooms. *In room:* TV, dataport, coffeemaker, hair dryer.

BASSENTHWAITE

In the Lake District National Park, 9.5km (6 miles) north of Keswick, Bassenthwaite is one of the most beautiful of Lakeland villages and makes the best center for exploring the woodlands of Thornthwaite Forest and Bassenthwaite Lake nearby. Bassenthwaite Lake is the northernmost and only true "lake" in the Lake District, and it's visited yearly by many species of migratory birds from the north of Europe.

Where to Stay & Dine

Armathwaite Hall Hotel *&& (Kids*   Rich in history, this hotel goes back to the 1300s when it was built as a house for Benedictine nuns. During the Middle Ages, it was plundered frequently, leaving the sisters wretchedly poor. By the 17th century, a series of wealthy landowners had completed the severe Gothic design of its stately facade, and an architecturally compatible series of wings were added in 1844. It was converted into a hotel during the 1930s. Sir Hugh Walpole, who once stayed here, found it "a house of perfect and irresistible charm." Ringed with almost 160 hectares (400 acres) of woodland (some bordering the lake), the place offers a magnificent entrance hall sheathed with expensive paneling. The bedrooms are also handsomely furnished, with padded headboards crowning comfortable beds fitted with fine linen. Four-poster and family rooms are available. Bathrooms are excellently maintained and equipped with combination tub and shower.

A small but diverting attraction on its premises is a minizoo featuring unusual breeds of both barnyard and wild animals. The collection includes potbellied pigs, llamas, goats, rabbits, and owls. They also have a reptile house, bird-of-prey center, animated display, tearoom, and wet-weather facilities. Only a 5-minute walk from the hotel, **Trotters World of Animals** is open February through October daily from 10am to 5:30pm, and on weekends only from November to January. Adults pay £4.75 ($8.80); children ages 3 to 14, £3.50 ($6.50). Kids 3 and under enter free.

Bassenthwaite Lake (on B5291, 11km/7 miles northwest of Keswick, 2.5km/1½ miles west of Bassenthwaite), Keswick, Cumbria CA12 4RE. © **01768/776551.** Fax 01768/776220. www.armathwaite-hall.com. 43 units. £140–£230 ($259–$426) double; £280–£320 ($518–$592) suite. Rates include English breakfast. AE, DC, MC, V. **Amenities:** Restaurant; bar; indoor heated pool; outdoor tennis court; billiard room; health club; sauna; salon; 24-hr. room service; babysitting; laundry service; nonsmoking rooms; rooms for those with limited mobility. *In room:* TV, coffeemaker, hair dryer, trouser press.

The Castle Inn Hotel   Don't expect a castle. Though this place plays up its historical importance, you'll find there is an "old" core (no one on the staff is sure of how old), with many newer additions that don't exactly gracefully merge into a unified whole. The result is a hotel that's neither whimsically antique nor strikingly modern—but it is not dowdy. Bedrooms come in various shapes and sizes, including some beautifully appointed and spacious "superior" units. Five are large enough for families. The more modern but equally comfortable rooms are in a new wing. Two of the old-fashioned rooms contain a four-poster bed. All units contain bathrooms with shower-tub combinations.

Bassenthwaite (9.5km/6 miles north of Keswick on A591), Cumbria CA12 4RG. © **01768/776401.** Fax 01768/ 776604. www.regalhotels.co.uk/castleinn. 48 units. £64–£116 ($118–$215) double. Rates include half board. AE, DC, MC, V. From Keswick, take A591 9.5km (6 miles) north of town; the inn is on the left. **Amenities:** Restaurant; bar; indoor heated pool; health club; sauna; bike rental; 24-hr. room service; laundry service; nonsmoking rooms; 1 room for those with limited mobility. *In room:* TV, coffeemaker, hair dryer.

Overwater Hall ⊀   Built in the late 18th century, this is a Georgian mansion with battlements added to it by the Victorians. It is reminiscent of a castle and comes complete with a tragic ghost story. When the house was still new, its owner became involved with an alluring Jamaican mistress who became too much of an embarrassment to him. So in a fit of desperation, he threw her to the depths of the nearby lake, cutting off her hands so she could not climb back into the boat. According to reports, her handless spirit wanders the guest rooms during the night in a harmless manner.

Despite its sad past, this B&B is anything but somber. All the bedrooms, though standard in size, are extremely ritzy (which may be why Overwater's phantom has chosen to stay), having been furnished with top-quality antiques. One room has an oak-paneled four-poster bed. All of the tiled bathrooms have been recently renovated and have a tub-and-shower combination. Guests can enjoy the regal surroundings of the public rooms with their intricate and rich cove molding and formal Victorian antiques. The drawing room is a great place for afternoon tea, and the piano bar actually has a baby grand piano.

Overwater, Ireby, near Keswick CA5 1HH. © **01768/776566.** www.overwaterhall.co.uk. 13 units. £160–£170 ($296–$315) double. Rates include English breakfast and dinner. MC, V. **Amenities:** Restaurant; bar; lounge; limited room service; putting green. *In room:* TV, dataport, coffeemaker, hair dryer.

The Pheasant ✦ This former 17th-century coaching inn sets near the north-western tip of Bassenthwaite Lake. A series of extensions were later added. Everything about it evokes old-fashioned English coziness. Fireplaces warm a moderately eccentric bar area, a mishmash of antique and merely old-fashioned furniture, and individually decorated bedrooms whose windows overlook 24 hectares (60 acres) of forest and parkland associated with the hotel. All rooms are nonsmoking, and two offer sitting areas. Bathrooms are modern and contain tubs and "power" showers.

Bassenthwaite Lake near Cockermouth, Cumbria CA13 9YE. © **01768/776234.** Fax 01768/776002. www. the-pheasant.co.uk. 16 units. Nov–Mar £124–£134 ($229–$248) double, £150–£160 ($278–$296) suite; Apr–Oct £140–£150 ($259–$278) double, £160–£170 ($296–$315) suite. Rates include breakfast. MC, V. **Amenities:** Restaurant; bar; limited room service; limited laundry service; rooms for those with limited mobility. *In room:* TV (on request), coffeemaker, hair dryer.

7 Ullswater ✦

477km (296 miles) NW of London; 42km (26 miles) SE of Keswick

Set in a region that is home to contrasting vistas of gently rolling fields and dra-matic mountain rises, Ullswater is a favorite with those who enjoy spectacular natural beauty. Ullswater itself is a 14km (9-mile) expanse of water stretching from Pooley Bridge to Patterdale, and is the second-largest lake in the district. It is a magnet for outdoor types of all levels of ability, offering activities that range from walks and hikes around the shore to rock climbing, mountain biking, canoeing, sailing, and even windsurfing.

This part of the Lakeland, where the majesty of nature tends to entrance and envelope, has always held a special attraction for artists and writers. The area gained most of its fame from writings by the likes of Wordsworth during the early 19th century. It was on the shores of Ullswater that Wordsworth saw his "host of golden daffodils." Aira Force waterfall, near the National Trust's Gowbarrow, inspired both Wordsworth and Coleridge by its beauty. While using this area as a base for outdoor activities, you can also easily explore the many places of prehistoric and historic significance, from the times of the ancient Celts right through to modern day. Two noteworthy sites include Long Meg and her "daughters," an ancient stone circle near Penrith, and Hadrian's Wall, marking the northern extent of the Roman empire, east of Carlisle (see chapter 18).

In Ullswater, two 19th-century **steamers** provide the best way to see the area's panoramic mountain scenery around the lake. In season, there are two sched-uled services daily between Glenridding, Howtown, and Pooley Bridge as well as five shorter 1-hour cruises. Passengers may choose to walk back along the lakeside path or break for lunch at either end of the lake. The steamers run every day but December 25 and January 1, and cost £3.90 to £24 ($7.20–$44) per person. For more information, call © **01768/482229** or see **www.ullswater-steamers.co.uk**. Glenridding is on the A592 at the southern end of Ullswater. Pooley Bridge is 8km (5 miles) from the M6 junction 40 to Penrith.

ESSENTIALS

GETTING THERE About three trains from London's Euston Station arrive daily in Penrith, this region's main rail junction. Usually, a change of trains isn't necessary. For schedules and information, call ℭ **0845/748-4950** or visit www. railtrack.co.uk. Once in Penrith, passengers usually take a taxi to Ullswater.

Two **Stagecoach** buses (ℭ **0870/608-2608;** www.stagecoachbus.com) stop at the Penrith Bus Station daily on their way between Carlisle and Keswick. Passengers must take a taxi from Penrith to Ullswater.

If you're driving from Penrith, go southeast on the B5320.

VISITOR INFORMATION   The summer-only **Tourist Information Centre** for the lake is at The Square, Pooley Bridge (ℭ and fax **01768/486530**); it's open daily from Easter to November from 9:30am to 3:30pm.

WHERE TO STAY & DINE

Gowbarrow Lodge   This inn is named for the large limestone fell running behind the hotel. The lodge was a filling station a few years ago, but you could never tell that today by looking at its stone facade. The lodge affords views of the green fields, large lake, and distant fells across the road. This view was part of the reason the Whitehead family decided to convert their filling station, which people often described as being "the best filling station around simply because of its view." The bedrooms upstairs are decorated with contemporary, functional furnishings. The tiled bathrooms are small and compact, each with a shower stall (two have tubs). Downstairs, the public rooms are full of dark, polished wood with local maps and photographs adorning the walls.

Watermillock, Ullswater, Cumbria CA11 0JP. ℭ **01768/486286.** www.gowbarrowlodge.co.uk. 8 units. £55 ($102) double. Rates include English breakfast. MC, V. **Amenities:** Bar; lounge; limited room service. *In room:* TV, coffeemaker.

Sharrow Bay Country House Hotel ℛℛℛ   This was Britain's first country-house hotel, and it's the oldest British member of Relais & Châteaux. Sitting on 4.8 hectares (12 acres), it's an unusual Victorian house with a low angled roof and wide eaves. It was a private home until purchased by Francis Coulson in 1948. Realizing its potential, Coulson restored the structure, sleeping on the floor while work was in progress. Three years later he was joined by Brian Sack, and together they turned Sharrow into one of England's finest places to dine. Today, the hotel offers 26 antique-filled bedrooms, 17 of them in the gatehouse and cottages. Individually decorated, each is named after one or another of the glamorous (and often famous) women who have swept in and out of the lives of the articulate owners. Some of the rooms offer views of the lakes, trees, or Martindale Fells. Beds are sumptuous with cushiony pillows and quality linen. Each bathroom is well appointed with deluxe toiletries, generous shelf space, and a combination tub and shower.

Howtown Rd., Lake Ullswater, near Penrith, Cumbria CA10 2LZ. ℭ **01768/486301.** Fax 01768/486349. www.sharrow-bay.com. 26 units. £320–£400 ($592–$740) double; £380–£420 ($703–$777) suite for 2. Rates include half board. MC, V. Howtown Rd. 3km (2 miles) south of Pooley Bridge. **Amenities:** Restaurant; bar; limited room service; laundry service; dry cleaning; 1 room for those with limited mobility. *In room:* TV, mini-bar, hair dryer, trouser press.

8 Penrith

467km (290 miles) NW of London; 50km (31 miles) NE of Kendal

This one-time capital of Cumbria, in the old Kingdom of Scotland and Strathclyde, takes its name, some say, from the Celts who called it "Ford by the Hill." The namesake hill is marked today by a red-sandstone beacon and tower. Because of Penrith's central location above the northern Lake District and beside the Pennines, this thriving market center was important to Scotland and England from its very beginning, eventually prompting England to take it over in 1070.

The characteristically red-sandstone town has been home to many famous and legendary figures, including Richard, duke of Gloucester; William Cookson, the grandfather of poet William Wordsworth; and Dorothy Wordsworth, William's sister. Today, Penrith remains best known as a lively market town.

ESSENTIALS

GETTING THERE   Trains from London's Euston Station arrive in Penrith four times a day. The trip takes 4 hours. For train schedules and information, call ℂ **0845/748-4950** or visit www.railtrack.co.uk.

To take a bus from London to Penrith, hop on one of the two daily National Express buses to Carlisle and then take a Stagecoach Cumberland bus to Penrith, a total journey of 8 hours. The Stagecoach Cumberland buses leave every hour. For schedules and information, contact **National Express** (ℂ **0870/580-8080;** www.nationalexpress.com) or **Stagecoach** ℂ **0870/608-2608;** www.stagecoachbus.com).

To drive, take the M1 out of London, getting on the M6 to Penrith. The trip should take no more than 6 hours.

VISITOR INFORMATION   The **Tourist Information Centre,** Robinson's School, Middlegate, Penrith (ℂ **01768/867466**), is open from November to Easter, Monday through Friday from 10am to 4pm, Saturday from 10:30am to 4:30pm; from Easter to May and the month of October, Monday through Saturday from 9:30am to 4:45pm and Sunday from 1 to 5pm; June through September, Monday through Saturday from 9:30am to 5pm and Sunday from 1 to 4:45pm.

EXPLORING THE AREA

It's a small town of 12,500 people, but it has lots of shops to explore. Major shopping areas include the covered **Devonshire Arcade** with its name-brand stores and boutiques, the pedestrian-only **Angel Lane** and **Little Dockray,** with an abundance of family-run specialty shops, as well as **Angel Square** just south of Angel Lane.

For handmade earthenware and stoneware from the only remaining steam-powered pottery in Britain, stop by **Wetheriggs Country Pottery,** Clifton Dykes, 3km (2 miles) south of Penrith on the A6 (ℂ **01768/892733**).

The 130-year-old **Briggs & Shoe Mines,** Southend Road (ℂ **01768/899001**), is a shoe-shopping extravaganza. It is the largest independent shoe shop in the Lakelands, carrying famous names and offering great bargains, including sportswear, walking boots, clothing, and accessories.

Acorn Bank Garden   For a stroll in an English garden, see the Acorn Bank Garden with its varied landscape of blooming bulbs, plants, and walled spaces. Its claim to fame is its extensive herb garden, said to be the best in all of northern England. The Acorn Bank Garden is part of an estate dating from 1228. Buildings on the estate include a partially restored water mill, parts of which also date from the 13th century and a red-sandstone house—presently not open to the public—that is primarily from the Tudor period.

Temple Sowerby, 9.5km (6 miles) east of Penrith on A6. ℂ 017683/61893. Admission £2.75 ($5.10) adults, £1.30 ($2.40) children, family ticket (2 adults, 2 children) £6.80 ($13). Wed–Mon 10am–5pm (last admission at 4:30pm). Closed Nov to late Mar.

Penrith Castle This park contains the massive ruins of the castle, whose construction began in 1399, ordered by William Strickland, the bishop of Canterbury. For the next 70 years, the castle continued to grow in size and strength until it finally became the royal castle and oftentimes residence for Richard, duke of Gloucester.

Just across from the train station along Ullswater Rd. No phone. Free admission. Always accessible.

Penrith Museum For perspective on Penrith and the surrounding area, a visit here isn't a bad idea. Originally constructed in the 1500s, the museum building was turned into a poor girls school in 1670. Today, the museum offers a survey of the archaeology and geology of Penrith and the Eden Valley, which was a desert millions of years ago.

Robinson's School, Middlegate. ✆ **01768/212228.** Free admission. June–Sept Mon–Sat 10am–5pm, Sun 1:30–4pm; Oct–May Mon–Sat 10am–4pm.

WHERE TO STAY

George This is a 300-year-old coaching inn, built right in the heart of town. It welcomed Bonnie Prince Charlie in 1745. The front of the George looks out on a street of small specialty shops, and the guest rooms are spread among three floors and are individually decorated with light colors and up-to-date furnishings. The owners are gradually upgrading all the bedrooms, so standards here will be higher than before. Each small bathroom has a tub and shower or else a shower stall.

Devonshire St., Penrith, Cumbria CA11 7SU. ✆ **01768/862696.** Fax 01768/868223. www.georgehotel penrith.co.uk. 34 units. £86–£104 ($159–$192) double; £142 ($263) suite. Rates include full Cumbrian breakfast. AE, MC, V. **Amenities:** Restaurant; bar; 24-hr. room service; laundry service; nonsmoking rooms. *In room:* TV, coffeemaker, hair dryer, trouser press.

North Lakes Hotel 🐕 *(Kids)* This is Penrith's finest accommodation and the most family friendly hotel in the area. The exterior may lack character, but you'll find compensation inside. A member of the Shire Inns chain, this hotel is designed to meet the needs of businesspeople during the week and vacationers on weekends. Rooms are bright and spacious, decorated with classic wood furniture, large couches, and soft pastel accents. Six rooms are large enough for rental to families, and some have bunk beds. Bathrooms are well appointed, some with a combination tub and shower. Guests enjoy an inviting lobby sitting area with a grand, barn-style, open ceiling with rustic beams, and a huge stone fireplace.

Ullswater Rd., Penrith, Cumbria CA11 8QT. ✆ **01768/868111.** Fax 01768/868291. www.shirehotels.co.uk. 84 units. £130–£145 ($241–$268) double; £165 ($305) suite. Rates include English breakfast. AE, DC, MC, V. **Amenities:** Restaurant; bar; indoor heated pool; children's pool; 2 squash courts; health club; sauna; 24-hr. room service; babysitting; laundry service; dry cleaning; rooms for those with limited mobility; nonsmoking rooms. *In room:* TV, dataport, coffeemaker, hair dryer, trouser press.

Queen's Head Inn 🐕 Lying 4km (2½ miles) south of Penrith, this is a discovery from 1719, once the property of the Wordsworths. Today it is an inviting country pub and restaurant with overnight accommodations. It is found in the center of the village of Tirril, nestled on the edge of the Lake District National Park. Filled with bric-a-brac and memorabilia, the country inn is full of character. Expect oak beams, wooden settles, and even a roaring fire in the often chilly month of June. It's an atmosphere of hunting prints and horse brasses along with farm tools and hunting horns. Most patrons come here to enjoy the Tirril beers on tap, although you may also enjoy wines from the family owned vineyards.

Good food has always been a tradition of the inn, and you can enjoy traditional British food here, including such noteworthy dishes as braised shoulder of Lakeland lamb in its own red-currant gravy. Local venison and pheasant appear in winter or locally smoked Ullswater trout in summer. The bedrooms are fresh and well maintained and most comfortable, each with a private shower.

Tirril, near Penrith, Cumbria CA10 2JF. © **01768/863219.** Fax 01768/863243. www.queensheadinn.co.uk. 7 units. £70 ($130) double. Rates include breakfast. MC, V. **Amenities:** Restaurant; pub. *In room:* No phone.

WHERE TO DINE

A Bit on the Side BRITISH/INTERNATIONAL   Set "a bit on the side" from the center of Penrith, this restaurant resembles the brick-built interior of a high-ceilinged, authentically antique barn. The owners manage to squeeze 32 seats into this evocative, well-scrubbed setting, bustling to produce dishes whose derivation comes from all parts of what used to be the British Empire. The best examples include king prawns sautéed in garlic, ginger, lemon grass, and coriander; twice-baked cheese soufflé that's served with a salad made from watercress, roasted pears, and walnut oil; duck in port-wine sauce; and filet of Scottish beef with a Madeira-flavored tarragon sauce.

Brunswick Square. © **01768/892526.** Reservations recommended. Fixed-price menu £18–£20 ($33–$37). MC, V. Tues–Thurs 7–8:30pm; Fri–Sat 8pm–midnight (9pm last order).

18

Yorkshire & Northumbria

Yorkshire, known to readers of *Wuthering Heights* and *All Creatures Great and Small,* embraces the moors of North Yorkshire and the dales.

Across this vast region came Romans, Anglo-Saxons, Vikings, monks of the Middle Ages, kings of England, lords of the manor, craftspeople, hill farmers, and wool growers, all leaving their own mark. You can still see Roman roads and pavements, great abbeys and castles, stately homes, open-air museums, and crafts centers, along with parish churches, old villages, and cathedrals.

Some cities and towns still carry the taint of the Industrial Revolution, but you can also find wild and remote beauty—limestone crags, caverns along the Pennines, mountainous uplands, rolling hills, chalk land wolds, heather-covered moorlands, broad vales, and tumbling streams. Yorkshire offers not only beautiful inland scenery but also 161km (100 miles) of shoreline, with rocky headlands, cliffs, sandy bays, rock pools, sheltered coves, fishing villages, bird sanctuaries, former smugglers' dens, and yachting havens. And in the summer, the moors in **North York Moors National Park** bloom with purple heather. You can hike along the 177km (110-mile) **Cleveland Way National Trail,** encircling the park.

Yorkshire's most visited city is the walled city of **York. York Minster,** part of the cathedral circuit, is noted for its 100 stained-glass windows. In West Yorkshire is the literary shrine of **Haworth,** the home of the Brontës.

Northumbria is made up of the counties of Northumberland, Cleveland, and Durham. The Saxons, who came to northern England centuries ago, carved out this kingdom, which at the time stretched from the Firth of Forth in Scotland to the banks of the Humber in Yorkshire. Vast tracts of that ancient kingdom remain natural and unspoiled. Again, this slice of England has more than its share of industrial towns, but you should explore the wild hills and open spaces and cross the dales of the eastern Pennines.

The whole area evokes ancient battles and bloody border raids. Space constraints don't permit us to cover this area in great detail, and it's often overlooked by the rushed North American visitor, but we suggest at least a venture to **Hadrian's Wall,** a Roman structure that was one of the wonders of the Western world. The finest stretch of the wall lies within the **Northumberland National Park,** between the stony North Tyne River and the county boundary at Gilsland. And about 64km (40 miles) of the 242km (150-mile) **Pennine Way** meanders through the park; Pennine Way is one of Britain's most challenging hiking paths.

On the way north to Hadrian's Wall, we suggest you spend the night in the ancient cathedral city of **Durham.** This great medieval city is among the most dramatically sited and most interesting in the north.

Yorkshire & Northumbria

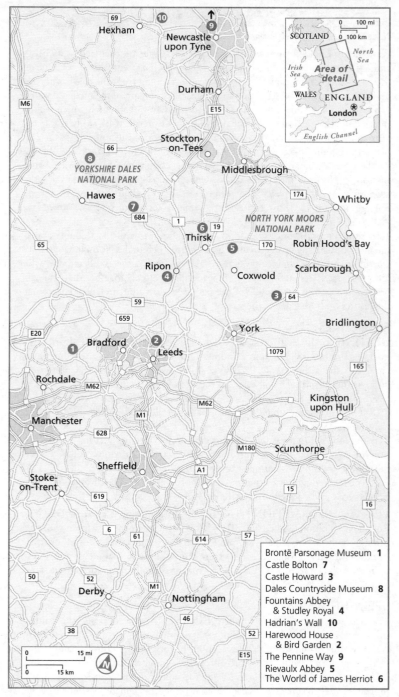

SCOTLAND

North Sea

Irish Sea

Area of detail

WALES

ENGLAND

★ London

English Channel

0 — 100 mi
0 — 100 km

69 Hexham

10 9 Newcastle upon Tyne

Durham

M6

E15

66 Stockton-on-Tees

8 *YORKSHIRE DALES NATIONAL PARK*

Middlesbrough

174 Whitby

Hawes

7 684

1

6 19 Thirsk

NORTH YORK MOORS NATIONAL PARK

5 170 Robin Hood's Bay

65

Ripon **4**

5 Scarborough

Coxwold

3 64

59

Bridlington

659

E20

York

1 Bradford

2 Leeds

1079

165

Rochdale

M62

M62

Kingston upon Hull

M1

Manchester

628

M180

Scunthorpe

Sheffield

A1

15

16

Stoke-on-Trent

619

6

61

614

57

50

52

Derby

M1

38

Nottingham

46

52

E15

0 — 15 mi
0 — 15 km

Brontë Parsonage Museum **1**
Castle Bolton **7**
Castle Howard **3**
Dales Countryside Museum **8**
Fountains Abbey & Studley Royal **4**
Hadrian's Wall **10**
Harewood House & Bird Garden **2**
The Pennine Way **9**
Rievaulx Abbey **5**
The World of James Herriot **6**

1 York (★(★(★

327km (203 miles) N of London; 42km (26 miles) NE of Leeds; 142km (88 miles) N of Nottingham

Few cities in England are as rich in history as York. It is still encircled by its 13th- and 14th-century city walls, about 4km (2½ miles) long, with four gates. One of these, Micklegate, once grimly greeted visitors coming from the south with the heads of traitors. To this day, you can walk on the footpath of the medieval walls.

The crowning achievement of York is its minster, or cathedral, which makes the city an ecclesiastical center equaled only by Canterbury. It's easily visible on a drive up to Edinburgh in Scotland. Or, after visiting Cambridge, you can make a swing through the great cathedral cities of Ely, Lincoln, York, and Ripon.

There was a Roman York (Hadrian came this way), then a Saxon York, a Danish York, a Norman York (William the Conqueror slept here), a medieval York, a Georgian York, and a Victorian York (the center of a flourishing rail business). A large amount of 18th-century York remains for visitors to explore today, including Richard Boyle's restored Assembly Rooms.

At some point in your exploration, you may want to visit the Shambles; once the meat-butchering center of York, it dates from before the Norman Conquest. The messy business is gone now, but the ancient street survives, filled today with jewelry stores, cafes, and buildings that huddle so closely together that you can practically stand in the middle of the pavement, arms outstretched, and touch the houses on both sides of the street.

ESSENTIALS

GETTING THERE   British Midland flights arrive at **Leeds/Bradford Airport,** a 50-minute flight from London's Heathrow Airport. For schedules and fares, call the airline at ℂ **0870/607-0555** (www.flybmi.com). Connecting buses at the airport take you east and the rest of the distance to York.

From London's King's Cross Station, York-bound trains leave every 30 minutes. The trip takes 2 hours. For information, call ℂ **0845/748-4950** or visit www.railtrack.co.uk.

Four **National Express** buses depart daily from London's Victoria Coach Station for the 4½ hour trip to York. For schedules and information, call ℂ **0870/580-8080** or visit www.nationalexpress.com.

If you're driving from London, head north on the M1, cutting northeast below Leeds at the junction with the A64, heading east to York.

VISITOR INFORMATION   The **Tourist Information Centre** at De Grey Rooms, Exhibition Square (ℂ **01904/621756**), is open in winter Monday through Saturday from 9am to 5pm and Sunday from 10am to 4pm; open in summer Monday through Saturday from 9am to 6pm and Sunday from 10am to 5pm. Another Tourist Information Centre at the railway station has the same hours.

SEEING THE SIGHTS

The best way to see York is to go to Exhibition Square (opposite the Tourist Information Centre), where a volunteer guide will take you on a **free 2-hour walking tour** of the city. You'll learn about history and lore through numerous intriguing stories. Tours run April through September, daily at 10:15am and 2:15pm, plus 6:45pm from June to August; from November to March, a daily tour starts at 10:15am. Groups can book by prior arrangement by contacting the **Association of Volunteer Guides,** De Grey Rooms, Exhibition Square, York YO1 2HB (ℂ **01904/640780**).

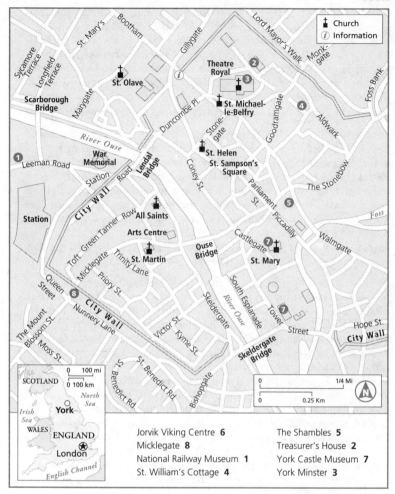

†	Church
ⓘ	Information

Jorvik Viking Centre **6**
Micklegate **8**
National Railway Museum **1**
St. William's Cottage **4**

The Shambles **5**
Treasurer's House **2**
York Castle Museum **7**
York Minster **3**

Jorvik Viking Centre ⭐ This Viking city, discovered many feet below present ground level, was reconstructed as it stood in 948, and underwent major refurbishment in 2001. In a "time car," you travel back through the ages to 1067, when Normans sacked the city, and then you ride slowly through the street market peopled by faithfully modeled Vikings. You also go through a house where a family lived and down to the river to see the ship chandlers at work and a Norwegian cargo ship unloading. At the end of the ride, you pass through the Finds Hut, where thousands of artifacts are displayed. The time car departs at regular intervals.

Coppergate. ☎ **01904/643211.** www.jorvik-viking-centre.co.uk. Admission £7.20 ($13) adults, £5.10 ($9.45) children 5–15 years, £6.10 ($11) students and seniors, £22 ($41) family ticket. Rates may change depending on the event. Apr–Oct daily 10am–5pm; Nov–Mar daily 10am–4:30pm.

National Railway Museum ⭐⭐⭐ This was the first national museum to be built outside London, and it has attracted millions of train buffs. Adapted from an original steam-locomotive depot, the museum gives visitors a chance to see how Queen Victoria traveled in luxury, and to look under and inside steam loco-motives. In addition, there's a collection of railway memorabilia, including a penny machine for purchasing tickets on the railway platform and an early-19th-century clock. More than 40 locomotives are on display. One, the *Agenoria,* dates from 1829 and is a contemporary of Stephenson's well-known *Rocket.* Of several royal coaches, the most interesting is Queen Victoria's Royal Saloon; it's like a small hotel, with polished wood, silk, brocade, and silver accessories.

Leeman York Rd. ☎ 01904/621261. www.nrm.org.uk. Free admission. Daily 10am–6pm. Closed Dec 24–26.

Treasurer's House   The Treasurer's House lies on a site where a continuous succession of buildings has stood since Roman times. The main part of the house, built in 1620, was refurbished by Yorkshire industrialist Frank Green at the turn of the 20th century; he used this elegant town house to display his col-lection of 17th- and 18th-century furniture, glass, and china. An audiovisual program and exhibit explain the work of the medieval treasures and the subse-quent fascinating history of the house. It has an attractive small garden in the shadow of York Minster.

Minster Yard. ☎ 01904/624247. Admission £4.50 ($8.35) adults £2.50 ($4.65) children, £11 ($20) family ticket. Apr–Oct Sat–Thurs 11am–4:30pm. Closed Nov–Mar.

York Castle Museum ★   On the site of York's Castle, this is one of the finest folk museums in the country. Its unique feature is a re-creation of a Victorian cobbled street, Kirkgate, named for the museum's founder, Dr. John Kirk. He acquired his large collection while visiting his patients in rural Yorkshire at the beginning of this century. The period rooms range from a neoclassical Georgian dining room to an overstuffed and heavily adorned Victorian parlor to the 1953 sitting room with brand-new television set purchased to watch the coronation of Elizabeth II. In the Debtors' Prison, former prison cells display crafts work-shops. There is also a superb collection of arms and armor. In the Costume Gallery, displays are changed regularly to reflect the collection's variety. Half Moon Court is an Edwardian street, with a gypsy caravan and a pub (sorry, the bar's closed!). During the summer, you can visit a water mill on the bank of the River Foss.

The Eye of York off Tower St. ☎ 01904/687687. www.yorkcastlemuseum.org.uk. Admission £6 ($11) adults, £3.50 ($6.50) children, £16 ($30) family ticket. Daily 9:30am–5pm. Closed Dec 25, 26, and Jan 1.

York Minster ★★★   One of the great cathedrals of the world, York Minster traces its origins from the early 7th century; the present building, however, dates from the 13th century. Like the cathedral at Lincoln, York Minster is character-ized by three towers built in the 15th century. The central tower is lantern-shaped in the Perpendicular style, and on a clear day, the top of the tower offers panoramic views of York and the Vale of York. The climb up a stone spiral stair-case is steep and not recommended for very elderly or very young visitors or any-one with a heart condition or breathing difficulties.

The outstanding characteristic of the cathedral is its **stained glass** ★★★ from the Middle Ages, in glorious Angelico blues, ruby reds, forest greens, and honey-colored ambers. See especially the Great East Window, the work of a 15th-cen-tury Coventry-based glass painter. In the north transept is an architectural gem of the mid–13th century: the Five Sisters Window, with its five lancets in gri-saille glass. The late-15th-century choir screen in its Octagonal Chapter House has an impressive lineup of historical figures—everybody from William the Conqueror to the overthrown Henry VI.

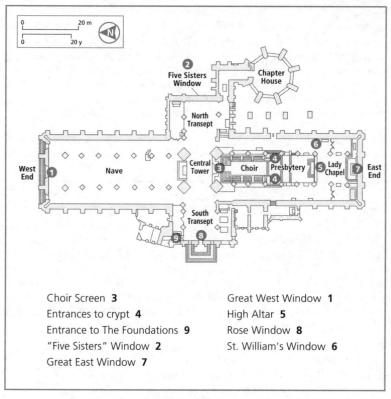

Choir Screen **3**

Entrances to crypt **4**

Entrance to The Foundations **9**

"Five Sisters" Window **2**

Great East Window **7**

Great West Window **1**

High Altar **5**

Rose Window **8**

St. William's Window **6**

At a reception desk near the entrance to the minster, groups can arrange a guide, if one is available. Conducted tours are free, but donations toward the upkeep of the cathedral are requested.

Insider's tip: Check out **St. William's Restaurant** at the front of St. William's Cottage (© **01904/634830**), close to the east end of the minster. This splendid timbered building provides a setting for coffee, affordable lunch, or tea. Here you can get tasty quiches, homemade soups, and luscious desserts. And if you can arrange for a party of 35 or more, you can have a medieval banquet staged on your behalf, complete with minstrels, jesters, and jugglers. One way to do this is to post a notice at your hotel and get people to sign up and invite their newly made acquaintances. In 1 day our party swelled to nearly 50, and we were regally fed and entertained.

At the converging point of Deangate, Duncombe Place, Minster Yard, and Petergate. © **01904/557216**. www.yorkminster.org. Chapter House £4.50 ($8.35); free for children under 16; crypt, foundations, and treasury £3 ($5.55) adults, £1.50 ($2.80) children. Chapter House, undercroft, and tower Mon–Sat 9am–5:30pm, Sun noon–5:30pm (closing time in winter 5pm). Call ahead to verify times, as they are subject to change.

SHOPPING

Several of the main areas to explore include **Gillygate** for antiques dealers, **St. Mary's Square** and its **Coppergate** pedestrian mall for name brands and chain stores, and **Newgate Marketplace** for local vendors selling a variety of wares Monday through Saturday.

Moments Is York Haunted?

After London, York has been the site of more beheadings, medieval tortures, and human anguish than any other city in Britain. Psychics and mystics insist that dozens of lost souls wander among the city's historic core reliving the traumatic moments of their earthly lives. Ghost walks are held every evening in York, allegedly England's most haunted city.

Several outfits conduct these tours, but the most charming one, **"The Ghost Hunt of York"** (© **01904/608700**; www.ghosthunt.co.uk), leaves at 7:30pm every night from The Shambles. The 75-minute tour costs £3 ($5.55) for adults and £2 ($3.70) for children. Be prepared for lively commentary and more ghoulishness than you may expect.

Several specialty shops that have ideal gift items include **Maxwell and Kennedy,** 79 Low Petergate (© **01904/610034**), a candy store specializing in both Belgian chocolate and Cambridge Wells dark, milk, and white chocolate; **Mulberry Hall,** 17 Stonegate (© **01904/620736**), housed in a medieval house from 1436, with 16 showrooms on three floors devoted to the best in British and European porcelain, fine china, crystal, and some antiques; and **Wooden Horse,** 9 Goodramgate (© **01904/626012**), featuring an eclectic mixture of ethnic items such as shirts, tops, jewelry, cushions, rugs, and throws from Africa, India, China, and Mexico.

WHERE TO STAY
EXPENSIVE

Dean Court Hotel ⚜   This 1850 building lies right beneath the towers of the minster. It was originally constructed to provide housing for the clergy of York Minster and then converted to a hotel after World War I. It may not be the most atmospheric choice in York, but recent refurbishments have vastly improved the accommodations. The rooms are very comfortable, with quality linens on the beds and bathrooms equipped with shower-tub combinations. Two rooms are spacious enough for use by families.

Duncombe Place, York, N. Yorkshire YO1 7EF. © **800/528-1234** in the U.S., or 01904/625082. Fax 01904/ 620305. www.deancourt-york.co.uk. 39 units. £120–£175 ($222–$324) double. Rates include English breakfast. AE, DC, MC, V. Parking £5 ($9.25). **Amenities:** Restaurant; bar; 24-hr. room service; babysitting; laundry service; dry cleaning; nonsmoking rooms. *In room:* TV, dataport, coffeemaker, hair dryer, trouser press.

Middlethorpe Hall Hotel ⚜⚜⚜   Set on a 11-hectare (26-acre) park, this hotel is on the outskirts of York, near the racecourse and away from the traffic. It's clearly York's leading hotel. Built in 1699, the stately, redbrick William-and-Mary country house was purchased by Historic House Hotels and beautifully restored, both inside and out. Fresh flowers are displayed profusely and lots of antiques create the ambience of a classic manor house. The rooms are located in the main house and restored outbuildings. Accommodations in the annex (a converted stable block) have slightly less drama and flair, though you can enjoy greater privacy there. Rooms have such niceties as homemade cookies and bottles of mineral water, as well as bathrobes. All the bedrooms have been styled to evoke the aura of a country house, though all the modern comforts have been installed as well. Each bedroom is decorated individually with four-poster beds or padded or canopied headboards. Bathrooms come with tub-and-shower combinations.

Bishopthorpe Rd. (on A64, 2.5km/1½ miles south of town), York, N. Yorkshire 4023 2GB. ✆ **800/735-2478** in the U.S. and Canada, or 01904/641241. Fax 01904/620176. www.middlethorpe.com. 30 units. £160–£210 ($296–$389) double, £280–£370 ($518–$685) suite. MC, V. **Amenities:** 2 restaurants; bar; spa; limited room service; laundry service; dry cleaning; nonsmoking rooms; 1 room for those with limited mobility. *In room:* TV, hair dryer, trouser press.

York Moat House ★ Within the ancient city walls, this modern hotel overlooks the River Ouse and is the leading hotel within the center of York. Built in the 1970s, the hotel is the largest in town and is conveniently located for sightseeing. Many of the well-furnished and modern bedrooms have views looking toward the minster. Ten rooms are spacious enough for families. Each comes with a well-maintained private bathroom with shower stall and tub.

North St., York, N. Yorkshire YO1 6JF. ✆ 01904/459988. Fax 01904/641793. www.moathousehotels.com. 200 units. £156 ($289) double; £180 ($333) suite. Rates include English breakfast. AE, DC, MC, V. Parking £10 ($19). **Amenities:** Restaurant; 2 bars; health club; sauna; 24-hr. room service; laundry service; dry cleaning; rooms for those with limited mobility; nonsmoking rooms. *In room:* TV, dataport, coffeemaker, hair dryer, trouser press.

MODERATE

The Judges Lodging ★ *Finds* The earliest historical fact about this charming house is that it was the home of a certain Dr. Wintringham in 1711. It is listed as having been a judges' lodging at the beginning of the 19th century. To get to your room, you'll climb a circular wooden staircase, the only one of its type in the United Kingdom. Four bedrooms have four-poster beds. If you want to spoil yourself, book the large Prince Albert room, a twin-bedded room with three large windows overlooking the minster (Prince Albert actually slept in the room once). Bedrooms, all of which are nonsmoking, range from small to midsize, and have been thoughtfully renovated, many with antiques, four-poster beds, and open fireplaces. The tiled bathrooms are well equipped, each with shower-tub combination (some have a spa bath). Many rooms have a view of York Minster.

9 Lendal, York, N. Yorkshire YO1 8AQ. ✆ **01904/638733.** Fax 01904/679947. www.judgeslodgings.com. 15 units. £100–£150 ($185–$278) double. Rates include English breakfast. AE, MC, V. **Amenities:** Restaurant; bar; breakfast-only room service; babysitting; laundry service. *In room:* TV, coffeemaker, hair dryer.

Mount Royale Hotel ★ A short walk west of York's city walls, in a neighborhood known as The Mount, this hotel is the personal statement of two generations of the Oxtaby family. They work hard to create a friendly, homey atmosphere. The main house was built as a private home in 1833, though several years ago the owners merged a neighboring house of the same era into the original core. Accommodations and public rooms are furnished with both modern pieces and antiques. Garden suites have private terraces leading to the garden. Bathrooms are small but well organized, each with a shower-tub combination.

119 The Mount, York, N. Yorkshire YO2 2DA. ✆ **01904/628856.** Fax 01904/611171. www.mountroyale. co.uk. 23 units. £98–£100 ($181–$185) double; £151 ($279) suite. Rates include English breakfast. AE, DC, MC, V. **Amenities:** Restaurant; bar; outdoor heated pool; sauna; limited room service; laundry service; nonsmoking rooms. *In room:* TV, dataport (in some), coffeemaker, hair dryer, trouser press.

INEXPENSIVE

Beechwood Close Hotel Beechwood is a large house that is surrounded by trees, a garden with a putting green, and a parking area. Mr. and Mrs. Blythe run the small hotel, which offers comfortable bedrooms with tasteful furnishings. Each small bathroom is well maintained; most have a tub-and-shower combination. The hotel is a 15-minute walk to the minster, either by road or along the river.

19 Shipton Rd. (on A19 north of the city), Clifton, York, N. Yorkshire YO30 5RE. ☎ **01904/658378.** Fax 01904/647124. www.beechwood-close.co.uk. 14 units. £80 ($148) double. Rate includes English breakfast. AE, DC, MC, V. **Amenities:** Restaurant; bar; breakfast-only room service. *In room:* TV, coffeemaker, hair dryer, iron/ironing board.

Cottage Hotel *Value*   About a 10-minute walk north of York Minster, this hotel comprises two refurbished and extended Victorian houses overlooking the village green of Clifton. The hotel offers cozy, small bedrooms with simple furnishings. Three rooms have four-poster beds. Each comes with a well-maintained bathroom with a shower stall and tub. Some 400-year-old timbers rescued from the demolition of a medieval building in one of the city's historic streets (Micklegate) grace the restaurant and bar, which does a thriving business in its own right.

3 Clifton Green, York, N. Yorkshire YO3 6LH. ☎ **01904/643711.** Fax 01904/611230. 25 units. £70–£80 ($130–$148) double. Rates include English breakfast. MC, V. Free parking. **Amenities:** Restaurant; bar. *In room:* TV, coffeemaker, hair dryer.

Heworth Court   Just a 10- to 15-minute walk east of the city center is this three-story redbrick Victorian structure (many of its bedrooms are located in a modern extension added during the 1980s). The rooms are agreeably furnished, and some open onto the courtyard. Each comes with a comfortable bed, plus a compact bathroom with a shower stall (some have tubs).

76 Heworth Green, York, N. Yorkshire YO3 7TQ. ☎ **01904/425156.** Fax 01904/415290. www.heworth.co.uk. 28 units. £66–£99 ($122–$183) double. Rates include English breakfast. Free parking. AE, DC, MC, V. Take the A1036 to the east side of the city. **Amenities:** Restaurant; bar; laundry service; nonsmoking rooms. *In room:* TV, dataport, coffeemaker, hair dryer.

WHERE TO DINE

Oscar's Wine Bar & Bistro, 8A Little Stonegate (☎ **01904/652002**), offers heaping plates of meats and salads, attracting a young crowd (often because of the inexpensive beer). With a courtyard and a large menu, it's open Monday through Saturday from 11:30am to 11pm, and Sunday from 11am to 10:30pm.

The best place for afternoon tea is **Betty's Café & Tea Rooms,** 6–8 St. Helen's Sq. (☎ **01904/659142**). We also recommend **St. William's College Restaurant,** 3 College St. (☎ **01904/634830**), and **Theatre Royal Café Bar,** St. Leonard's Place (☎ **01904/632596**).

The Ivy/The Seafood Bar/The Brasserie *☆* FRENCH/ENGLISH   A 10-minute walk west of York Minster, this dining complex is the most appealing in town. It is within an ivy-covered Regency town house that's also a 30-room hotel.

The least formal venue is The Brasserie, a paneled, candlelit hideaway in the cellar. The hearty menu items include steaks, fish, and ale. It's the most crowded of the complex's three restaurants.

On the ground level, The Ivy restaurant and The Seafood Bar are set adjacent to one another. Cuisine in The Ivy is more upscale than that in the cellar and includes dishes such as a whole grilled Dover sole.

A few steps away, The Seafood Bar has a great *trompe l'oeil* panoramic mural of York's Racecourse, complete with views of the city's skyline. The menu here features mostly seafood prepared in many ways. Examples include grilled sea scallops, with sesame, soy, and a spring onion dressing.

In the Grange Hotel, 1 Clifton (off Bootham Rd.), York, N. Yorkshire YO30 6AA. ☎ **01904/644744.** Fax 01904/612453. Reservations recommended in The Ivy and The Seafood Bar; not necessary in The Brasserie. Fixed-price 3-course menu in The Ivy £28 ($52); main courses in The Seafood Bar £15–£24 ($28–$44); main courses in The Brasserie £8–£16 ($15–$30). AE, DC, MC, V. The Ivy Mon–Sat 7–10pm, Sun noon–2pm; The Seafood Bar Tues–Sat 7–10pm; The Brasserie Mon–Sat noon–2pm and 6-10pm, Sun 7–10pm.

Kites INTERNATIONAL   About a 5-minute walk from the minster, this restaurant is in the heart of York, on a small street near Stonegate (walk up a narrow staircase to the second floor). This is a simple York bistro where the food is good and the atmosphere and service are unpretentious. Kites's many fans are attracted to its eclectic brand of cooking. One recipe might have been a dish served in the Middle Ages in England (perhaps with adaptations); the next might come from Thailand. Meals may feature trout, game, tuna, or pork depending on what the hunters and gatherers return with. Fondues, fresh salads, and vegetarian meals are also available.

13 Grape Lane. *Ⓒ* **01904/641750.** Reservations required. Main courses £12–£17 ($22–$31). AE, DC, DISC, MC, V. Daily noon–2pm and 6:30–10:30pm.

Melton's Restaurant *Kids* CONTINENTAL/ENGLISH   Some local food critics claim that Michael and Lucy Hjort serve the finest food in York, though we give that honor to The Ivy. Their small and unpretentious restaurant is approximately 1.5km (1 mile) from the heart of the city. Mr. Hjort trained with the famous Roux brothers of Le Gavroche in London, but he doesn't charge their astronomical prices. His cuisine reflects his own imprint.

In what has always been known as a culinary backwater town, the Hjorts have created some excitement with this family friendly place. Their menu changes frequently but could include roast monkfish with tiger prawns and eggplant "caviar"; roast venison with mixed vegetables such as kale and parsnips; and roast confit of duck. Vegetarian meals are available, and children are welcome.

7 Scarcroft Rd. *Ⓒ* **01904/634341.** Reservations required. Main courses £13–£18 ($24–$33); fixed-price menu (available on limited basis) £17 ($31). MC, V. Tues–Sat noon–2pm; Mon–Sat 5:30–10pm. Closed 1 week in early Aug and Dec 24–Jan 14.

19 Grape Lane ENGLISH   In the heart of York, on a cobbled lane off Petergate, this restaurant occupies two floors of a timbered building with a wealth of its original features. With such a name, you would expect a very British restaurant, and it is, but with a very contemporary touch. You can begin with a Jamaican cocktail, which is their own blend of poached salmon, banana, prawns, and pineapple served with a spiced mayonnaise; follow with filets of trout stuffed with crabmeat and wrapped in lettuce leaves. The menus are wisely limited to about 10 main courses so that every dish will be fresh. The cooking is kept simple, without excessive adornment. The wine list is ever growing, and service is thoughtful and considerate.

19 Grape Lane. *Ⓒ* **01904/636366.** Reservations recommended for dinner. Main courses £8–£17 ($15–$31). AE, MC, V. Tues–Sat noon–2pm and 6–10pm.

A YORK PUB CRAWL

One of the city's oldest inns, **The Black Swan,** Peaseholme Green (*Ⓒ* **01904/ 686911**), is a fine, timber-framed house that was once the home of the lord mayor of York in 1417; the mother of General James Wolfe of Quebec also lived here. In front of a log fire in a brick inglenook, you can enjoy pub meals such as fish and chips, burgers, and steaks. This is one of York's "musical pubs," featuring live folk music on Monday and Thursday and jazz on Wednesday and Sunday, hip-hop, every second and fourth Friday, with a small cover charge starting at £4 ($7.40).

Situated at the base of the Ouse Bridge, a few steps from the edge of the river, the 16th-century **Kings Arms Public House,** King's Staith (*Ⓒ* **01904/659435**), is boisterous and fun. An historic monument in its own right, it's filled with charm and character and has the ceiling beams, paneling, and weathered brickwork you'd expect. Because of its location by the river, the pub can flood if rain is heavy enough. Expect a virtually indestructible decor, the kind that can (and often does) sit under water for days at a time. In summer, rows of outdoor tables are placed beside the river. Your hosts serve a full range of draft and bottled beers, the most popular of which (Samuel Smith's) is still brewed in Tadcaster, only 16km (10 miles) away. The ghost walk we recommend leaves here every night at 7:30pm (see the sidebar, "Is York Haunted?" on p. 664).

On a pedestrian street in Old York, **Ye Olde Starre Inne,** 40 Stonegate (© **01904/623063**), dates from 1644 and is York's oldest licensed pub. An inn (of one kind or another) has stood on this spot since A.D. 900. In a pub said to be haunted by an old woman, a little girl, and a cat, you enter into an atmosphere of cast-iron tables, open fireplace, oak Victorian settles, and time-blackened beams. Recently, the owners have added a year-round glassed-in garden. In all types of weather, guests can enjoy the plants and view of the minster from their tables.

2 Leeds ⍟

328km (204 miles) NW of London; 121km (75 miles) NE of Liverpool; 69km (43 miles) NE of Manchester; 119km (74 miles) N of Nottingham

The foundations for a permanent community were laid nearly 2,000 years ago when the Romans set up a small camp here called Cambodunum, but the next step toward modern Leeds didn't come until the 7th century when the Northumbrian King Edwin established a residence. Kirkstall Abbey was founded in 1152, and in 1207 Leeds finally obtained its charter.

During the medieval era, Leeds took the golden fleece as its coat of arms, representative of its growth and importance as a wool town. In time, it became the greatest center of cloth trade in the region. Industrial advancements have played a great role in the development of the city, with the introduction of steam power leading to the development of the coalfields to the south. Other innovations allowed the continued growth of its textile industry, as well as the rapid development of such upstart industries as printing, tailoring, and engineering. The Victorian era marked the city's glory days.

After languishing for years and being dismissed for its industrial blight, the city is moving progressively forward again today. It's experiencing some economic growth, and many of the great Victorian buildings have been renovated in its bustling central core: The Corn Exchange, The Grand Theatre, and the Victoria Quarter. A "24-Hour City Initiative" makes Leeds the only U.K. location that not only allows but also encourages around-the-clock work and entertainment options; it's an up-and-coming city with a lot of new energy.

ESSENTIALS

GETTING THERE **Leeds-Bradford International Airport** (© **01132/ 509696;** www.lbia.co.uk) about 14km (9 miles) north of town has daily flights to and from London, with air transport taking less than an hour. There is also a 24-hour direct rail link between Manchester airport and Leeds.

Trains from London's King's Cross Station arrive hourly during the day, with the trip taking about 2 hours. For information, call © **0845/748-4950** or visit www.railtrack.co.uk.

Leeds is also serviced daily by **National Express** buses from London. For schedules and information, call © **0870/580-8080** or visit www.national express.com.

Craft Centre and Design
Gallery **1**
Leeds City Art Gallery **1**
Leeds City Museum **1**
The Henry Moore Institute **2**
Royal Armouries Museum **3**

Leeds lies at the crossroads of the North–South M1 and the East–West M62 routes, making it easily accessible by car from anywhere in England or Scotland.

VISITOR INFORMATION   The **Gateway Yorkshire Regional Travel & Tourist Information Centre,** The Arcade, City Station (© **01132/425242**), is open Monday through Saturday from 9am to 5:30pm and Sunday from 10am to 4pm. Leeds also has a website (www.leeds.gov.uk) with information on transportation, lodging, dining, shopping, and entertainment in the city.

Information on local bus and train routes and times is available by calling **Metroline** at © **01132/457676.**

SPECIAL EVENTS   In July, more than 40,000 opera lovers turn out at **Temple Newsam,** Temple Newsam Road, off Selby Road (© **01132/425242**), for the single performance of **Opera in the Park,** the largest free outdoor opera concert in the United Kingdom. The gargantuan **Party in the Park** (© **01132/ 478222**), also held at Temple Newsam, is one of the largest free pop and rock concerts in the United Kingdom. It's usually held the day following Opera in the Park and features some of the hottest acts in rock music.

Film buffs turn out in droves for the annual **Leeds International Film Festival** (© **01132/478308;** www.leedsfilm.com). Screened the first two weeks in October at cinemas throughout Leeds, it's the only theme-based film festival in the United Kingdom. It regularly features British as well as world-premiere films and hosts film-related lectures, seminars, and workshops.

EXPLORING LEEDS

Despite its longtime reputation as a grimy northern industrial city, Leeds will surprise you with the beauty and diversity of its **City Centre,** where £400 million has been invested during the past decade in both new construction and renovation of warehouses and landmark Victorian structures into homes, lodging, shops, and restaurants along The Waterfront and in the central shopping district.

The Henry Moore Institute 🐾 Located next door to the City Art Gallery, this is one of the largest sculpture galleries in Europe, as well as the first devoted to the display, study, and research of sculpture from all periods and cultures. The institute is named after the greatest British sculptor of the 20th century, Henry Moore (1898–1986), who was a Yorkshireman. This center shows the range of his accomplishments, from his early *Reclining Figure* (1929) to his most powerful postwar statements like *Meat Porters.* The works of many of Moore's contemporaries are also displayed. Lectures throughout the year supplement the institute's exhibitions.

74 The Headrow. 📞 **01132/467467.** www.henry-moore-fdn.co.uk. Free admission. Mon–Tues and Thurs–Sun 10am–5:30pm; Wed 10am–9pm.

Leeds City Art Gallery 🐾 Spread over three floors, this gallery, founded in 1888, houses England's best collection of 20th-century art outside of London, including collections of French post-Impressionist paintings, contemporary British sculpture, prints, watercolors, and drawings. Throughout the year it also hosts visiting exhibits, enhanced by workshops, talks, and other related events.

Located within the gallery, the **Craft Centre and Design Gallery** (📞 **01132/ 478241**), showcases contemporary ceramics, jewelry, prints, textiles, and applied arts from around the world, as well as hosts openings and exhibits by local and regional artists working within these mediums.

74 The Headrow. 📞 **01132/478248.** www.leeds.gov.uk/artgallery. Free admission. Mon–Tues and Thurs–Sat 10am–5pm; Wed 10am–8pm; Sun 1–5pm.

Royal Armouries Museum 🐾 A notable construction along The Waterfront, this £42 million facility is the home of London Tower's Royal Armouries, England's oldest museum, with exhibits that include the working arsenal of the medieval kings. It is designed to exhibit the many pieces that have been in perpetual storage because of inadequate facilities in London. The museum illustrates the development and use of arms and armor for war, sport, hunting, self-defense, and fashion.

Armouries Dr. 📞 **01132/201999.** www.armouries.org.uk. Free admission. Daily 10am–5pm. Closed Dec 24–25.

Temple Newsam House This was the birthplace, in 1545, of the ill-fated Lord Darnley, husband of Mary Queen of Scots. Construction began on this Tudor-Jacobean mansion in 1521, and substantial remodeling occurred in both the 17th and late 18th centuries. It stands as an odd but beautiful tribute to several eras of architecture. Today, it houses a splendid collection of silver and Chippendale furniture. The surrounding 480 hectares (1,200 acres) of parkland includes Home Farm, a breeding ground for rare farm animals, and the venue for Opera in the Park.

Temple Newsam Rd. (off Selby Rd.; 6.5km/4 miles from Leeds City Centre off the A63). 📞 **01132/647321.** Admission £3 ($5.55) for adults, students and seniors, £2 ($3.70) for children. Apr–Oct Tues–Sun 10:30am–5pm (last admission at 4:15pm); Nov–Mar Tues–Sun 10:30am–4pm (last admission at 3:15pm).

WHERE TO STAY

If you'd like advice on local lodging, or if you'd just like to tell someone your price range and requirements and let them book you a room, contact the **Gateway Yorkshire Accommodation Booking Line** (© **0800/808050** or 01132/425242). For a £3 ($5.55) handling fee and a refundable deposit of 10% of your first night's stay, they'll find you a bed for the night.

Aragon Hotel   Located only 3km (2 miles) north of City Centre, this small family-run hotel is set well back from the road on an acre of gardens. The surrounding properties stretch out in open fields and woods. Accommodations, while not luxurious, are neat and comfortable. Bedrooms range from small to midsize, and each has a small bathroom with a shower stall. A pleasant lounge for residents features a large marble fireplace as well as a full bar, both of which look out over the gardens. The hotel is completely nonsmoking.

250 Stainbeck Lane, Leeds LS7 2PS. © **01132/759306.** Fax 01132/757166. www.aragonhotel.co.uk. 12 units. £60–£70 ($111–$130) double. Rates include English breakfast. AE, DC, MC, V. From Leeds, follow A61 Harrogate signs out of the city. This becomes Scott Hall Rd. (A61). Take the 2nd roundabout, turning left onto Stainbeck Lane, and follow it down one hill and up another. The hotel is on the right. It is also conveniently located about 180m (600 ft.) from a bus stop with routes to Leeds and the surrounding area. **Amenities:** Dining room; bar. *In room:* TV, coffeemaker, hair dryer, trouser press.

42 The Calls ✿✿✿   Overlooking the River Aire in the heart of Leeds, this small but deluxe hotel is the city's most tranquil and elegant choice, created from an 18th-century grain mill in a once dilapidated waterfront area that's all high-tech and high-comfort now. Rooms range from the more traditional to units such as the Black Room, with a huge black bed and black-striped walls, or room no. 303, with an original winch hanging from the ceiling—a nod to the building's origins. Business travelers will appreciate the three phones in every room, full-size work desk, individual fax machine on request, and dictation by arrangement. Bathrooms feature deluxe toiletries, combination tub and shower, and bathrobes.

42 The Calls, Leeds LS2 7EW. © **01132/440099.** Fax 01132/344100. www.42thecalls.co.uk. 41 units. £99–£175 ($183–$324) double; from £230 ($426) suite. AE, DC, MC, V. **Amenities:** 2 restaurants; bar; access to nearby health club; concierge; car-rental desk; courtesy car; 24-hr. room service; babysitting; laundry service; dry cleaning; nonsmoking rooms. *In room:* TV, dataport, coffeemaker, hair dryer, iron/ironing board, trouser press.

Haley's Hotel & Restaurant ✿ *(Value*   Located in a quiet, tree-lined cul-de-sac just off the main Otley-Leeds road (A660), this town-house hotel, set up in a Victorian mansion, makes it easy to forget you're in the suburbs of a major metropolitan area. The hotel's rooms are comfortably laid out and opt for tasteful individuality, each with its own period-specific, polished, natural wood antiques. Features include a work desk with telephone and efficiently organized private bathrooms, many with tub or shower. As for the beds, management accurately quotes Charles Dickens: "It would make anyone go to sleep, that bedstead would, whether they wanted to or not." The staff is diligent, accommodating guests with such options as a late supper or shoe-cleaning service.

Shire Oak Rd. (3km/2 miles from Leeds City Centre and 11km/7 miles from Leeds-Bradford International Airport), Headingley, Leeds LS6 2DE. © **01132/784446.** Fax 01132/753342. www.haleys.co.uk. 29 units. £95–£155 ($176–$287) double; £230–£250 ($426–$463) suite. Rates include English or continental breakfast. AE, MC, V. **Amenities:** Restaurant; bar; 24-hr. room service; babysitting; laundry service; dry cleaning; nonsmoking rooms. *In room:* TV, dataport, coffeemaker, hair dryer, trouser press.

Malmaison ✿ *(Finds*   England, more so than any other country, continues its amazing program of recycling old, aging, and decrepit industrial and commercial sites and putting them to new uses. One of the most stunning examples of this trend is this former tram and bus garage, which has been given an amazing renaissance and is today a hotel of charm and character. The local newspaper hailed its rebirth as "sexy, cool, and slinky," and so it is, a stylish hotel that is intimate and cool. A great range of well-styled and individually designed bedrooms awaits you, some of them in subtle taupes with contrasting deep tones, such as autumn plum, "charcoal grill," and Austria ocher. You get some of the best beds in town and totally modern bathrooms with power showers, along with an exclusive set of toiletries for your use. The hotel also has a high-tech fitness suite. Downstairs is a super little Bar and Brasserie under a vaulted ceiling, serving an array of tantalizing platters such as wild rabbit cassoulet with red garlic confit and white risotto with lemon thyme and prosciutto.

Sovereign Quay, Leeds LS1 1DQ. © **01133/981000.** Fax 0113/398-1002. www.malmaison.com. 100 units. £129 ($239) double; £165 ($305) suite. AE, DC, MC, V. **Amenities:** Restaurant; bar; 24-hr. room service; fitness center; laundry service; dry cleaning; rooms for those with limited mobility; nonsmoking rooms. *In room:* TV, dataport, minibar, coffeemaker, hair dryer, trouser press, CD player.

Oulton Hall ★★ A painstakingly restored 1850s Italianate mansion, this hotel offers an atmosphere of pure elegance, from the black-and-white tiled front entrance and the damask-hung walls of the public rooms with their great crystal chandeliers, to the library with its mahogany wall paneling and window seat. You can enjoy butler service in the drawing room, a drink in the plush red-leather interior of the Calverley Bar, or stroll through formal gardens re-created from the original 19th-century plans. Most of the well-furnished bedrooms are in the modern wing; the grand suites are in the original house. Bedrooms enjoy views of the well-manicured grounds and championship golf course. Bathrooms are well maintained, each with tub and shower.

Rothwell Lane (9km/5½ miles east from Leeds by A61 and A639), Oulton, Leeds LS26 8HN. © **01132/821000.** Fax 01132/828066. www.devereonline.co.uk/hotel_oulton. 152 units. £170 ($315) double; from £245 ($453) suite. Rates include English breakfast. AE, DC, MC, V. **Amenities:** 3 restaurants; bar; indoor heated pool; 9- and 18-hole golf courses; driving range; croquet lawn; health club; Jacuzzi; sauna; salon; 24-hr. room service; laundry service; dry cleaning; nonsmoking rooms; rooms for those with limited mobility. *In room:* TV, dataport, minibar, coffeemaker, hair dryer, trouser press.

Quebecs ★★ (*Finds*) As a sign of the Renaissance of the city of Leeds, this gorgeous 1891 neo-Renaissance pile of red brick has been glamorously restored and converted into a hotel. The Victorian shell has been preserved; otherwise, the hotel is imbued with state-of-the-art amenities. The broad winding oak staircase and the ornate stained-glass windows are still there, along with handcrafted oak panels. A few minutes' walk from City Square and the main train station, the central hotel offers bedrooms that are beautifully and traditionally decorated in chic colors like camel brown and Wedgewood blue. The best accommodations are two mezzanine suites with spiral staircases leading to the sleeping quarters.

9 Quebec St., Leeds LS1 2HA. © **01132/448989.** www.summithotels.com. 45 units. £125–£170 ($231–$315) double; £170–£250 ($315–$463) suite. AE, DC, MC, V. Parking: £7 ($13). **Amenities:** Restaurant; bar; 24-hr. room service; laundry service; dry cleaning; nonsmoking rooms; rooms for those with limited mobility. *In room:* A/C, TV, dataport, minibar, coffeemaker, hair dryer, iron/ironing board, safe.

WHERE TO DINE

Haley's Restaurant BRITISH This hotel restaurant, in a beautifully restored Victorian mansion, is so popular among locals that even the guests have to reserve long in advance. Chef John Vennell changes his menu monthly to take advantage of the freshest and best market ingredients. Starters may feature a tantalizing "tasting" of quail with an autumn plum chutney, or a terrine of chicken, ham, and rabbit. We've found that some of the best main courses include chargrilled breast of Gressingham duck leg with braised cabbage and shallots, and a pan-seared sea bass with eggplant "caviar" and a tomato confit. You may finish off with a chocolate and Grand Marnier cake. The wine cellar has interesting offerings from around the world.

In Haley's Hotel, Shire Oak Rd., Headingley. © 01132/784446. Reservations required well in advance. Fixed-price dinner £28 ($52) for 3 courses; fixed-price Sun lunch £23 ($42) for 3 courses. AE, DC, MC, V. Mon–Sat 7:15–9:30pm; Sun 12:15–1:45pm. Closed Dec 26–30.

Heathcotes ★★ CONTINENTAL   Acquired in 2002 by a small and relatively upscale restaurant chain, this popular restaurant occupies what was built as a granary in the early 19th century. Set beside the water in the city's revitalized canal-front district, it boasts theatrical lighting, postmodern and minimalist accessories, and a showcasing of the massive beams and trusses that formed the skeleton of the building's original architecture. Menu items include a pleasing mixture of comfort food and more innovative cuisine. The best examples include seared salmon marinated with lemon and thyme, chargrilled rib-eye of beef with fondant potatoes and a broccoli hollandaise and peppercorn sauce, or poached chicken flavored with oven-dried tomatoes. Menus change frequently with the seasons.

Canal Wharf, Water Lane. © 01132/446611. Reservations recommended. Fixed-price menus 2 courses £14 ($25), 3 courses £16 ($29). AE, MC, V. Daily noon–2:30pm and 6–10pm (until 11pm on Sat and 9:30pm in Sun).

Leodis Brasserie BRITISH/FRENCH   Another fine choice in the revitalized canal district, Leodis is housed in an artfully renovated paint mill (ca. 1853). You dine in a comfortable space created from the mill's original cast-iron columns and new glass screens. The menu here changes weekly. At lunch, you have four three-course set meals to choose from, plus several a la carte options. Dishes are simple, yet incredibly well prepared. Starters may include fish cakes in tomato-lime salsa, followed by a main course of roast salmon with spinach and rösti or an old fashioned steak pudding. There's a full bar and a lengthy wine list as well.

Victoria Mill, Sovereign St. © 01132/421010. Reservations recommended. Main courses £9–£17 ($17–$31); fixed-price lunch £17 ($31). AE, DC, MC, V. Mon–Fri noon–2pm and 6–10pm; Sat 6–10pm.

Pool Court at 42 ★★ CONTINENTAL   This small, elegant restaurant, with its popular riverside terrace, is built into the lodging at 42 The Calls, but functions independently and has a private street entrance. It's an intimate space, seating only 38 diners, and the modern decor is stylish and refined. It's a comfortable spot, with great attention to detail and delectable food.

The menu is entirely a fixed-price affair, though you'll have a few choices for each course. Chef Jeff Baker scours the markets to see what's freshest and most abundant, then updates his menu often with creations such as roast scallops of peppered-duck foie gras, or sea scallops with braised fennel in a red-wine and lobster sauce. You can finish with one of the *assiettes,* a combination of three desserts, usually with a central theme, such as assiette of chocolate. There are some unusual selections on the wine list as well.

42–44 The Calls. © 01132/444242. Reservations recommended. Fixed-price 3-course lunch £19 ($35); fixed-price 3-course dinner £32–£55 ($59–$102). AE, DC, MC, V. Mon–Fri noon–2pm; Mon–Thurs 7–9pm; Fri–Sat 7–9pm.

LEEDS AFTER DARK

Thanks to a city initiative aimed at relaxing licensing restrictions and increasing late-night entertainment options, it's safe to say that Leeds now rocks around the clock. And it was already humming with classical concerts, opera, jazz, dance, theater, cinema, rock and dance clubs, cafes, and pubs.

THE CLUB & MUSIC SCENE Leeds has a thriving rock scene, with recent bands such as Sisters of Mercy and The Mission rising out of the music scene at **The Warehouse** (see below). Today's up-and-coming music scene is, not surprisingly, very influenced by the Manchester scene (see chapter 16), but innovative bands such as Black Star Liner, Bedlam A Go Go, and Embrace show that Leeds still has a musical voice all its own.

The **Cockpit/The Rocket,** Bridge House, Swinegate (✆ **01132/441573**), can host about 600 fans, who turn out to hear the latest indie bands in a converted railway arch setting. Usually open Monday through Saturday night with a cover charge ranging from £3 to £10 ($5.55–$19).

When you feel like grooving to the beat, you can head to a vast array of dance clubs around town. Leeds' dance music scene is thriving, as is evident by the presence of such internationally acclaimed clubs as **The Warehouse,** Somers Street (✆ **01132/468287**), on Tuesday through Saturday, with admission ranging from £3 to £10 ($5.55–$19), depending on the night.

You'll find the jazz you're looking for at **Arts Café,** 42 Call Lane (✆ **01132/438243**), a European-style cafe bar that offers tapas, bottled beers, and coffees.

Considering its size, there is a substantial gay scene in Leeds. The most popular club at the moment is **Queens Court,** Lower Briggate (✆ **01132/459449**). Downstairs is a restaurant and bar which is open daily from noon to 7pm; after which, head upstairs for the disco which is open daily from 11pm to 2am with a cover charge ranging from £2 to £4 ($3.70–$7.40). Another hot spot for gay men at the moment is **The Bridge Inn,** 1–5 Bridge Inn (✆ **01132/444734**), which has a friendly local pub atmosphere and becomes increasingly clubby as the night progresses (no cover).

PUBS Stop by **Whitelocks,** Turks Head Yard (✆ **01132/453950**), in the alley of Briggate, next to Marks & Spencer. There's a copper-topped bar with a handmade ceramic-tile front, a marble sandwich bar, old advertising mirrors, and stained-glass windows. Locals keep the conversation flowing in a thick, northern accent. If you get hungry, there's cheap traditional pub grub. Tap selections are varied and quite good, including McEwan's 80, Younger's IPA, and Theakston's Old Peculiar.

Hearkening back to Leeds's glory days, **Victoria,** Great George Street (✆ **01132/451386**), is every bit as Victorian as its name suggests, with ornate globe lamps, etched mirrors, and a well-adorned bar. Politicians and lawyers frequent the place. Join in the conversation or sit back and listen while you enjoy a pint of Tetley's Mild and maybe a bar snack or two.

THE PERFORMING ARTS **Leeds Town Hall,** The Headrow (✆ **01132/477989**), hosts orchestras from around the globe as part of the city's annual **International Concert Season,** and is also home to the world-famous **Leeds International Pianoforte Competition,** held every 3 years, with the next scheduled competition in September 2006. Opera North offers three to four productions during its season from October to April at the **Leeds Grand Theatre and Opera House,** New Briggate (✆ **01132/226222**), featuring a well-renovated 1,500-seat auditorium behind its original 1878 Victorian facade.

Theatergoers are much impressed by the facilities at the £12 million **West Yorkshire Playhouse,** Playhouse Square, Quarry Hill (© **01132/137700;** www.wyplayhouse.com), home to the "national theatre of the north." Playhouse artistic director Jude Kelly started out strong in the early inaugural seasons, with 17 productions, including eight British or world premieres. There has been no slowing down since then, and you can find a dramatic offering at most any time in either The Playhouse's Quarry Auditorium, which seats 750, or The Courtyard, which seats 350. The Playhouse, which is the cornerstone of a proposed £70 million Quarry Hill arts complex, also hosts other events throughout the year, including the annual Jazz at the Playhouse series.

The **Yorkshire Dance Centre,** St. Peters Building, York Street (© **01132/ 439867**), houses the internationally renowned **Phoenix Dance Troupe.**

3 Bradford ⟨★⟩

341km (212 miles) N of London; 52km (32 miles) NE of Manchester; 14km (9 miles) W of Leeds

This city of nearly half a million souls retains a rich ethnic heritage from the succession of immigrants who came to work the mills beginning in the mid–19th century. Generations of Irish, German, Italian, Eastern European, and later, Asian and African Caribbean immigrants, today give this West Yorkshire town an international flavor.

Bradford boosters like to say the town is one of the best-kept secrets in the United Kingdom. High-tech firms, galleries, and museums have displaced many of the textile factories of the past. Centrally located between the Yorkshire Dales and the Pennines, Bradford provides a nice diversion and is convenient to a historic countryside where the Brontës once dwelled and armor-covered soldiers clashed in the Wars of the Roses.

ESSENTIALS

GETTING THERE   Bradford is reached by car via the M62 and the M606.

Most rail links go through nearby Leeds (see section 2, above), but at least one direct train each day connects London's Kings Cross Station with Bradford (a 3-hr. trip). Train travel from Manchester takes about 1 hour; it's 3 hours from Birmingham.

Leeds/Bradford Airport (© **01132/509696**) is located about 16km (1 miles) from Bradford, and a number of scheduled flights connect to London's Heathrow and Gatwick airports and most major regional U.K. airports. A taxi from the airport to town costs about £10 ($19).

VISITOR INFORMATION   Call the **Bradford Tourist Information Centre,** City Hall, Centenary Square (© **01274/433678**). The center assists visitors in selecting accommodations and provides public transit timetables and city guides. Hours are Monday through Saturday from 9:30am to 5pm in winter, and until 5:30pm in summer.

EXPLORING BRADFORD

Bradford's museums, mill shops, and restaurants provide the main attractions for tourists. The city also boasts Bradford University, one of the better regional universities in the United Kingdom.

The **Industrial Museum and Horse at Work,** Moorside Mills, Moorside Road (© **01274/435900**), depicts mill life for worker and owner in the 1870s and offers Shire horse rides for kids and adults. The **Saltaire,** Salt's Mill, is the restored model factory-community developed in the mid–19th century by mill owner and philanthropist Titus Salt. The **1853 Gallery** at Saltaire (© **01274/ 531163**) exhibits more than 400 works by local artist David Hockney, among others.

Visitors can travel by steam-driven train on the **Keighley & Worth Valley Railway** (© **01535/645214**; www.kwvr.co.uk) for a tour of Brontë Country in Haworth, through Oakworth's Edwardian station, and Damen's Station, billed as Britain's smallest rail station. It operates daily in summer and only on Saturday in the winter.

National Museum of Photography, Film & Television, Little Horton Lane (© **0870/7010200;** www.nmpft.org.uk), captures the history of photography, film, and television in audiovisual presentations that span 150 years. The five-story-high IMAX screen, the largest in England, explores a dazzling variety of cinematic images in a series of new and continuing exhibitions. Admission to the museum is free; the IMAX movie costs £5.95 ($11) for adults, £4.20 ($7.75) for children, £17 ($32) family ticket (two adults and two children), and advance booking is recommended. Open Tuesday through Sunday from 10am to 6pm.

Bradford's textile industry is still represented in dozens of area mill shops where bargain hunters may find a great variety of mohair, pure-wool yarns, fabrics, sportswear, and other clothing and accessories. Some mill shops provide tours of factory spinning, weaving, and textile finishing.

Suit Length & Fabric Centre, Wakefield Road, Dudley Hill (© **01274/ 729103**), will customize suits and garments for the individual tastes and fit of shoppers. **British Mohair Spinners,** Louler Holme Mills, Shipley (© **01274/ 583111**), showcases the art of spinning hair and cotton into the heavy, shiny mohair fabric.

WHERE TO STAY

Beeties ⭑ *(Finds)*   This is an offbeat oddity for those who feel that an overnight stopover should be something of an adventure. A fish vendor once occupied the premises but today it's been turned into a cozy enclave for B&B stopovers with a tapas bar and brasserie downstairs. Jayne Dixon and Wayne Brimicombe are your hosts, welcoming you to their world, and doing so exceedingly well. Beeties lies in the heart of Saltaire Village, which enjoys World Heritage Status, as a historical "model" village built by wool baron Sir Titus Salt between 1851 and 1871 for his textile mill workers.

A landmark Victorian building, the Beeties exudes charm and character. Even if you're not staying here, we recommend a call on the tapas bar where we recently enjoyed a platter of seven tasty appetizers for £13 ($24), including such culinary highlights as hot prawns in chile and garlic and a Toulouse sausage with tomato dip. Bedrooms are modernized but decorated in an old-fashioned style with quilts and brass bedsteads, each with a small bathroom with shower.

7 Victoria Rd., Saltaire Village, Shipley, W. Yorkshire BD18 3LA. © **01274/595988.** Fax 01274/58218. www.beeties.co.uk. 5 units. £55 ($102) double. Rates include English breakfast. MC, V. Lies 1.2km (2 miles) west of Bradford. **Amenities:** Restaurant; tapas bar. *In room:* TV, coffeemaker, hair dryer, iron/ironing board.

Best Western Guide Post Hotel *(Kids)*   Catering to both business and leisure travelers, this is a winning choice. You get a warm welcome as you're shown to your spacious, well-furnished room, each equipped with a compact bathroom with shower. The more expensive executive rooms have a spacious lounge area. The reasonable price combined with the size of the rooms makes this a good choice for families as well.

Common Rd. (5km/3 miles from Junction 26 of M62), Low Moor, Bradford, W. Yorkshire BD12 0ST. ℂ 01274/607866. Fax 01274/671085. www.guideposthotel.net. 43 units. Sun–Thurs £85–£105 ($157–$194) double, £95 ($176) suite; Fri–Sat £60–£80 ($111–$148) double, £70 ($130) suite. Rates include English or continental breakfast. AE, DC, MC, V. **Amenities:** Restaurant; bar; 24-hr. room service; laundry service; dry cleaning; nonsmoking rooms; rooms for those with limited mobility. *In room:* TV, dataport, coffeemaker, hair dryer, iron/ironing board, trouser press.

Quality Victoria Hotel   Built in 1875, the Victoria in the city center is now entirely restored. Once the showpiece of the Lancashire and Yorkshire Railway, the hotel provides stylish accommodations at affordable rates. The well-furnished and recently renovated bedrooms all are comfortable and clean. Bathrooms are equipped with power showers. Four rooms are large enough for families.

Bridge St., Bradford, W. Yorkshire BD1 1JX. ℂ 01274/728706. Fax 01274/736358. www.brook-hotels.co.uk. 60 units. £75–£95 ($139–$176) double; £95–£120 ($176–$222) suite. Rates include breakfast. AE, DC, MC, V. From M62, take Junction 26 to M606, then to A6177 and A611, and exit at roundabout to Hallings; turn right at traffic light, and hotel is on left. **Amenities:** Restaurant; bar; sauna; limited room service; laundry service; dry cleaning; nonsmoking rooms; 1 room for those with limited mobility. *In room:* TV/VCR, dataport, coffeemaker, hair dryer, trouser press, CD player.

WHERE TO DINE

Bradford is called "the curry capital of the U.K.," boasting a vast array of Asian restaurants featuring dishes from Kashmir, Gujarat, the Punjab, and beyond. Many of the best of these curry houses are found along Morley Street near the National Museum of Photography, Film & Television. Our favorite along this street is **Kashmir,** 27 Morley St. (ℂ **01274/726513**), which, although a very simple place, serves authentic and excellently prepared Indian food.

Vic and Bert's CONTINENTAL   This elegant brasserie offers wood-grill cooking with an Oriental flavor. The clever chefs here have managed to lighten and modernize many dishes, though still showing a respect for traditional favorites. Their eclectic menu may include filet of steak slathered in mushrooms or any other number of courses such as beef bourguignon, and confit of duck.

In the Victoria Hotel, Bridge St. ℂ 01274/728706. Reservations recommended. Fixed-price menus £9.95–£15 ($18–$28). AE, DC, MC, V. Daily noon–2pm and 6–9:30pm.

BRADFORD AFTER DARK

Alhambra Theatre, Morley Street (ℂ **01274/43200;** www.bradford-theatres. co.uk), offers a variety of presentations ranging from amateur to professional. At certain times of the year, leading actors of the English stage and screen may appear here. You can also see children's theater, ballet, and musicals. Ticket prices vary depending upon the type of performance. The theater is closed for a few weeks in August.

But perhaps you're just looking for a local pub. In the city center, the **Shoulder of Mutton,** 28 Kirkgate (ℂ **01274/726038**), has a beer garden that comes complete with flowerbeds and hanging baskets. The oldest brewery in Yorkshire, it was originally Samuel Smith's Old Brewery. Lunch is available, and they also sell real ale here. As many as 200 drinkers can crowd in here on a summer night.

As an alternative choice, try the **Fighting Cock,** 21–23 Preston St. (ℂ **01274/726907**), an old-fashioned alehouse with bare floors and 12 different bitters. The best ales are Exmoor Gold, Timothy Taylor's, Black Sheep, and Green King Abbott, but they also sell foreign-bottled beers and farm ciders. On nippy nights, coal fires keep the atmosphere mellow. Bar snacks are among the most reasonable in town; the house specialty is chili (the chef guards the recipe).

4 Haworth: Home of the Brontës ★★

72km (45 miles) SW of York; 34km (21 miles) W of Leeds

Haworth, on the moor of the Pennines, is the famed home of the Brontës, the most visited literary shrine in England after Stratford-upon-Avon.

ESSENTIALS

GETTING THERE To reach Haworth by rail, take the Arriva Train from Leeds City Station to Keighley (it leaves approximately every 30 min.). Change trains at Keighley and take the Keighley and Worth Valley Railway to Haworth and Oxenhope. Train services operate every weekend year-round, with 7 to 12 departures. From late June to September, trains also run four times a day Monday through Friday. For general inquiries, call ℭ **01535/645214** (www.kwvr. co.uk); for a 24-hour timetable, dial the tourist office at ℭ **01535/642329.**

Keighley & District Bus Co., offers bus service between Keighley and Haworth. Bus nos. 663, 664, and 665 will get you there. For information, call ℭ **01535/603284.**

If you're driving from York, head west toward Leeds on the A64 approaching the A6120 Ring Road to Shipley; then take the A650 to Keighley, to the A629 to Halifax, and finally link up with the B6142 south to Haworth.

VISITOR INFORMATION The **Tourist Information Centre** is at 2–4 West Lane in Haworth (ℭ **01535/642329**). It's open April through October daily from 9:30am to 5:30pm, November through March daily from 9:30am to 5pm (closed Dec 24–26).

LITERARY LANDMARKS

Anne Brontë wrote two novels, *The Tenant of Wildfell Hall* and *Agnes Grey;* Charlotte wrote two masterpieces, *Jane Eyre* and *Villette,* which depicted her experiences as a teacher, as well as several other novels; and Emily is the author of *Wuthering Heights,* a novel of passion and haunting melancholy. Charlotte and Emily are buried in the family vault under the **Church of St. Michael** (Anne is buried at the **Church of St. Mary** in Scarborough).

While in Haworth, you'll want to visit the **Brontë Weaving Shed,** Townend Mill (ℭ **01535/646217**). The shop is not far from the Brontë Parsonage and features the famous Brontë tweed, which combines browns, greens, and oranges to evoke the look of the local countryside.

Brontë Parsonage Museum ★ The parsonage where the Brontë family lived has been preserved as this museum, which houses their furniture, personal treasures, pictures, books, and manuscripts. The stone-sided parsonage, built near the top of the village in 1777, was assigned for the course of his lifetime as the residence of the Brontës' father, Patrick, the Perpetual Curator of the Church of St. Michael and All Angel's Church. Regrettably, the church tended by the Brontës was demolished in 1870; it was rebuilt in its present form the same year. The parsonage contains a walled garden very similar to the one cultivated by the Brontës, five bedrooms, and a collection of family furniture (some bought with proceeds from Charlotte's literary success), as well as personal effects, pictures and paintings, and original manuscripts. It also contains the largest archive of family correspondence in the world.

The museum is maintained by a professional staff selected by the Brontë Society, an organization established in 1893 to perpetuate the memory and legacy of Britain's most famous literary family. Contributions to the society are welcomed. The museum tends to be extremely crowded in July and August.

Church St. ℂ **01535/642323**. www.bronte.org.uk. Admission £4.80 ($8.90) adults, £3.50 ($6.50) students and seniors, £1.50 ($2.80) children 5–16, free for children under 5, £11 ($19) family ticket (2 adults and 3 children). Oct–Mar daily 11am–5pm; Apr–Sept daily 10am–5pm. Closed in Jan and at Christmastime.

WHERE TO STAY

Old White Lion Hotel   At the top of a cobblestone street, this hotel dates from 1700 when it was built with a solid stone roof. It's almost next door to the church where the Reverend Brontë preached, as well as the parsonage where the family lived. Paul and Christopher Bradford welcome visitors to their warm, cheerful, and comfortable hotel. Though full of old-world charm, all rooms are completely up-to-date. Room size varies considerably, but each room is attractively furnished and has a comfortable bed and a small bathroom, most contain shower-tub combinations. Two rooms are large enough for families.

6–10 West Lane, Haworth near Keighley, W. Yorkshire BD22 8DU. ℂ **01535/642313**. Fax 01535/646222. www.oldwhitelionhotel.com. 14 units. £67 ($123) double. Rates include English breakfast. AE, DC, MC, V. **Amenities:** Restaurant; bar; limited room service; nonsmoking rooms. *In room:* TV, coffeemaker, hair dryer.

WHERE TO DINE

Weaver's Restaurant ★ *Value* MODERN BRITISH   The best restaurant in the Brontë hometown, this spot is British to the core. In an inviting, informal atmosphere, it serves excellent food made with fresh ingredients. Jane and Colin Rushworth are quite talented in the kitchen. Dinners may include such classic dishes as slow-cooked Yorkshire lamb. If available, try one of the Gressingham ducks, which are widely praised in the United Kingdom. For dessert, try a British cheese or one of the homemade delicacies. The restaurant is likely to be closed for vacation for a certain period each summer, so call in advance to check. They also rent four bedrooms of high caliber that cost £80 ($148) for a double, including breakfast.

15 West Lane. ℂ **01535/643822**. Reservations recommended. Main courses £12–£17 ($22–$31); 3-course fixed-price menu £16 ($30). AE, DC, MC, V. Wed–Sat noon–2pm; Tues–Sat 6:30–9:30pm.

5 Yorkshire's Country Houses, Castles & More

Yorkshire's battle-scarred castles, Gothic abbeys, and great country manor houses are unrivaled anywhere in Britain. Here are some of the highlights.

IN NORTH YORKSHIRE

Castle Howard ★★   In its dramatic setting of lakes, fountains, and extensive gardens, Castle Howard, the 18th-century palace designed by Sir John Vanbrugh, is undoubtedly the finest private residence in Yorkshire. This was the first major achievement of the architect who later created the lavish Blenheim Palace near Oxford. The Yorkshire palace was begun in 1699 for the third earl of Carlisle, Charles Howard.

The striking facade is topped by a painted and gilded dome, which reaches more than 24m (80 ft.) into the air. The interior boasts a 58m (192-ft.) long gallery, as well as a chapel with magnificent stained-glass windows by the 19th-century artist Sir Edward Burne-Jones. Besides the collections of antique furniture and sculpture, the castle has many important paintings, including a portrait of Henry VIII by Holbein and works by Rubens, Reynolds, and Gainsborough.

The seemingly endless grounds, including two rose gardens, also offer the visitor some memorable sights, including the domed Temple of the Four Winds, by Vanbrugh, and the richly designed family mausoleum, by Hawksmoor.

Malton (24km/15 miles northeast of York, 5km/3 miles off A64). ℂ **01653/648333.** www.castlehoward. co.uk. Admission £9.50 ($18) adults, £8.50 ($16) students and seniors, £6.50 ($12) children 4–16. Mid-Feb to Oct grounds daily 10am–4:30pm, house daily 11am–4pm (during winter, call to verify times).

Fountains Abbey & Studley Royal ⭐⭐⭐   On the banks of the Silver Skell, the abbey was founded by Cistercian monks in 1132 and is the largest monastic ruin in Britain. In 1987, it was awarded World Heritage status. The ruins provide the focal point of the 18th-century landscape garden at Studley Royal, one of the few surviving examples of a Georgian green garden. It's known for its conservation work in the water gardens, ornamental temples, follies, and vistas. The garden is bounded at its northern edge by a lake and 160 hectares (400 acres) of deer park.

At Fountains, 6.5km (4 miles) southwest of Ripon off B6265. ℂ **01765/608888.** www.fountainsabbey. org.uk. Admission £5 ($9.25) adults, £3 ($5.55) children, £14 ($26) family. Oct–Mar daily 10am–4pm; Apr–Sept daily 10am–6pm. Closed Dec 24–25, Fri in Nov–Jan. It's best to drive, though it can be reached from York by public transportation. From York, take bus no. 142 leaving from the York Hall Station to Ripon, 37km (23 miles) to the northwest (A59, A1, and B6265 lead to Ripon). From Ripon, it will be necessary to take a taxi 6.5km (4 miles) to the southwest, though some prefer to take the scenic walk.

IN WEST YORKSHIRE

Harewood House & Bird Garden ⭐⭐ *Kids*   Thirty-five kilometers (22 miles) west of York, the home of the earl and countess of Harewood is one of England's great 18th-century houses. It has always been owned by the Lascelles family. The fine Adam interior has superb ceilings and plasterwork and furniture made especially for Harewood by Thomas Chippendale. There are also important collections of English and Italian paintings and Sèvres and Chinese porcelain.

The gardens, designed by Capability Brown, include terraces, lakeside and woodland walks, and a 1.8-hectare (4½-acre) bird garden with exotic species from all over the world, including penguins, macaws, flamingos, and snowy owls. Other facilities include an art gallery, shops, a restaurant, and cafeteria. Parking is free, and there is a picnic area, plus an adventure playground for the children.

At the junction of A61 and A659, midway between Leeds and Harrogate, at Harewood Village. ℂ **01132/ 886331.** www.harewood.org. House, grounds, bird garden, and the terrace gallery £10 ($19) adults (Sun £11/$20), £8.25 ($15) seniors (£9.25/$17 Sun), £5.50 ($10) children (£6/$11 Sun), family ticket £31 ($56) (£34/$62 Sun). Grounds only £7.25 ($13) adults (£8.25/$15 Sun), £6.25 ($12) seniors (£7.25/$13 Sun), £4.50 ($8.35) children 15 and under (£5/$9.25 Sun), family ticket £23 ($43), (£26/$48 Sun). Mid-Feb to mid-Nov daily house, bird garden, and adventure playground 11am–4:30pm, terrace gallery 11am–5pm. Mid-Nov to mid-Dec daily garden and grounds 10am–4pm, bird garden 10am–3pm. From York, head west along B1224 toward Wetherby and follow the signs to Harewood from there.

6 Yorkshire Dales National Park ⭐

The national park consists of some 1,812.9 sq. km (700 sq. miles) of water-carved country. In the dales, or valleys, you'll find dramatic white limestone crags, roads and fields bordered by dry-stone walls, fast-running rivers, isolated sheep farms, and clusters of sandstone cottages.

Malhamdale receives more visitors annually than any dale in Yorkshire. Two of the most interesting historic attractions are the 12th-century ruins of Bolton Priory and the 14th-century Castle Bolton, to the north in Wensleydale.

Richmond, the most frequently copied town name in the world, stands at the head of the dales and, like Hawes (see below), is a good center for touring the surrounding countryside.

EXPLORING THE DALES

For orientation purposes, head first for **Grassington,** 16km (10 miles) north of Skipton and 40km (25 miles) west of Ripon. Constructed around a cobbled marketplace, this stone-built village is ideal for exploring Upper Wharfedale, one of the most scenic parts of the Dales. In fact, the Dales Way footpath passes right through the heart of the village.

Drop in to the **National Park Centre,** Colvend, Hebden Road (© 01756/752774; www.yorkshiredales.org.uk), which is open April through October daily from 10am to 5pm. From November to March, hours are Wednesday, Friday, Saturday, and Sunday 10am to 4pm. Maps, bus schedules through the dales, and a choice of guidebooks are available here to help you navigate your way. If you'd like a more in-depth look than what you can do on your own, you can arrange for a qualified guide who knows the most beautiful places and can point out the most interesting geological and botanical features of the wilderness.

Sixteen kilometers (10 miles) west of Grassington (reached along the B6265), **Malham** is a great place to set out on a hike in summer. Branching out from here, you can set out to explore some of the most remarkable limestone formations in Britain. First, it's best to stop in for maps and information at the **National Park Centre** (© 01729/830363), which is open from Easter to October daily from 9:30am to 5pm; off season, only Saturday and Sunday from 10am to 4pm. Amazingly, this village of 200 or so souls receives a half-million visitors annually. May or September are the times to come; the hordes descend from June to August.

The scenery in this area has been extolled by no less an authority than Wordsworth, and it has been painted by Turner. You can explore a trio of scenic destinations, **Malham Cove, Malham Tarn,** and **Gordale Scar,** on a circular walk of 13km (8 miles) that takes most hikers 5 hours. If your time (and your stamina) is more limited, you can take a circular walk from the heart of the village to Malham Cove and Gordale Scar in about 2 hours. At least try to walk 1.5km (1 mile) north of the village to Malham Cove, a large natural rock amphitheater. Gordale Scar is a deep natural chasm between overhanging limestone cliffs, and Malham Tarn is a lake in a desolate location.

Kettlewell lies 13km (8 miles) northwest of Malham and 9.5km (6 miles) north of Grassington. This is the main village in the Upper Wharfedale and is a good base for hiking through the local hills and valleys, which look straight out of *Wuthering Heights.* Narrow pack bridges and riverside walks characterize the region, and signs point the way to **The Dales Way** hiking path.

After Kettlewell, you can drive for 6.5km (4 miles) on B6160 to the hamlet of **Buckden,** the last village in the Upper Wharfedale. Once here, follow the sign to **Kidstone Pass,** still staying on B6160. At **Aysgarth,** the river plummets over a series of waterfalls, one of the dramatic scenic highlights of the Yorkshire Dales.

MASHAM: A ROOM IN A CASTLE

For luxury lovers, the little village of Masham makes the best base for overnight stay—certainly the most luxurious—for exploring the Yorkshire Dales. Swinton Parks stands at the gateway to the Dales.

Swinton Park ★★★   If you weren't born in an aristocrat's vine-covered castle, you can stay here and have the experience after all. Mark Cunliffe-Lister, nephew of the Earl and Countess of Swinton, along with his wife, Felicity, have converted this historic manor into a luxury hotel, one of our preferred stopovers in the northeast of England. Set in 80 hectares (200 acres) of parkland, lakes, and gardens, this family estate is a good base for exploring the Yorkshire Dales National Park, lying 52km (32 miles) northwest of York. Even with a pedigree going back to the 1500s, the castle is up-to-date with a spa and fitness area in a conservatory. There is also a bar in the family museum, a private cinema, and even a Victorian games room. Each of the spacious and beautifully designed bedrooms is individually designed, taking the theme of a Yorkshire dale, castle, abbey, or town. The Harrogate Room, for example, opens toward the south with a view of the lake and a deer park. Romantics book into the turret room, which is on two floors and reached by one of Yorkshire's steepest staircases. The beautifully restored bathrooms come with tub and shower. Rooms and suites are assigned based on your royal rank, with knights and barons paying the cheapest tariff, the most expensive tabs being assessed from dukes and earls. The hotel's superb restaurant, Samuel's, serves a modern British cuisine with an emphasis on game. In its heyday, many famous guests came here, including Prime Minister Harold Macmillan and crooner Bing Crosby.

Swinton Park, Masham, N. Yorkshire HG4 4JH. ✆ 01765/680900. Fax 01765/680901. www.swintonpark.com. 30 units. £100–£250 ($185–$463) double, £275 ($509) suite. Rates include Yorkshire breakfast. **Amenities:** Restaurant; bar; fitness center; spa; 24-hr. room service; babysitting; laundry service; dry cleaning; nonsmoking rooms; rooms for those with limited mobility. *In room:* TV, dataport, coffeemaker, iron/ironing board, trouser press, CD player.

HAWES: A BASE FOR EXPLORING YORKSHIRE DALES NATIONAL PARK

About 105km (65 miles) northwest of York, on the A684, Hawes is the natural center of Yorkshire Dales National Park and a good place to stay. On the Pennine Way, it's England's highest market town and the capital of Wensleydale, which is famous for its cheese. Trains from York take you to Garsdale, which is 8km (5 miles) from Hawes. From Garsdale, bus connections will take you into Hawes.

While you're there, you may want to check out the **Dales Countryside Museum,** Station Yard (the old train station; ✆ 01969/667494), which traces folk life in the Dales, a story of 10,000 years of human history. Peat cutting and cheese making, among other occupations, are depicted. The museum is open April through October daily from 10am to 5pm. Winter hours vary; you'll have to check locally. Admission is £3.50 ($6.50) for adults and £2.50 ($4.65) for children, students, and seniors.

WHERE TO STAY

Cockett's Hotel & Restaurant   This is an atmospheric choice, still sporting many remnants of its construction in 1668. In case you need reminding, the date of its construction is carved into one of its lintels. Set in the center of town, it's a two-story, slate-roofed, stone cottage whose front yard is almost entirely covered with flagstones. Rooms are done in an old-world style with exposed wooden beams; they're snug, cozy, and well maintained, some with a small shower-only bathroom, and some with tubs. Two rooms have four-poster beds. Smoking is not allowed in the bedrooms and in the restaurant.

Market Place, Hawes, North Yorkshire DL8 3RD. ✆ 01969/667312. Fax 01969/667162. www.cocketts.co.uk. 8 units. £59–£74 ($109–$137) double. Rates include English breakfast. MC, V. **Amenities:** Restaurant; bar. *In room:* TV, coffeemaker, hair dryer, trouser press.

Simonstone Hall   Just north of Hawes, you can stay and dine at Simonstone Hall. Constructed in 1733, this building has been restored and converted into a comfortable, family run, country-house hotel with a helpful young staff. It's the former home of the earls of Wharncliffe. The public rooms and the bed-rooms are equally ideal for relaxation and comfort. Most bedrooms are spacious, and all are furnished tastefully with antiques. Each comes with a quality bed and an efficiently organized shower bathroom.

2.5km (1½ miles) north of Hawes on the road signposted to Muker, Hawes, North Yorkshire DL8 3RD. ℂ **01969/667255.** Fax 01969/667741. www.simonstonehall.co.uk. 18 units. £110–£170 ($204–$315) per person double. Rates include breakfast. AE, MC, V. **Amenities:** Restaurant; bar; breakfast-only room service; nonsmoking rooms. *In room:* TV, coffeemaker, hair dryer.

7 North York Moors National Park (★

The moors, on the other side of the Vale of York, have a wild beauty all their own, quite different from that of the dales. This rather barren moorland blossoms in summer with purple heather. Bounded on the east by the North Sea, it embraces a 1,440-sq.-km (554-sq.-mile) area, which has been preserved as a national park.

If you're looking for a hot, sunny beach vacation where the warm water beckons, the North Yorkshire Coast isn't for you—the climate is cool because of the brisk waters of the North Sea. Even summer months aren't extremely hot. Many Britons do visit North Yorkshire for beach vacations, however, so you will find a beach-town atmosphere along the coast. Brightly colored stalls line the seafront and people seem to be a bit more relaxed than their inland counterparts.

The beauty and history of the area are the real reasons to visit North Yorkshire. The national park is perfect for solitary strolls and peaceful drives. For remnants of the area's exciting days of smugglers and brave explorers, visitors can follow the Captain Cook Heritage Trail along the coast. The fishing industry is still alive in the area, though the whaling ships of yesteryear have been anchored and the fishmongers now concentrate on smaller trappings.

ESSENTIALS

GETTING THERE   Because the park sprawls over such a large area, you can access it from five or six different gateways. Most visitors enter it from the side closest to York, by following either the A19 north via the hamlet of **Thirsk,** or by detouring to the northeast along the A64 and entering via **Scarborough.** You can also get in through **Helmsley,** where the park's administrative headquarters are located; just follow the roads from York that are signposted Helmsley. Gateways along the park's northern edges, which are less convenient to York, include the villages of **Whitby** (accessible via A171) and **Stokesley** (accessible via A19).

VISITOR INFORMATION   For information on accommodations and transportation before you go, contact **North York Moors National Park,** The Old Vicarage, Bondgate, Helmsley, York YO62 5BP (ℂ **01439/770657;** http://moors.uk.net). You can get advice, specialized guidebooks, maps, and information at the **Sutton Bank Visitor Centre,** Sutton Bank, near Thirsk, North Yorkshire YO7 2EK (ℂ **01845/597426**). Another well-inventoried information source, which unlike the others is open year-round, is **The Moors Centre,** Danby Lodge, Lodge Lane, Danby, near Whitby, YO21 2JE (ℂ **01439/772737**).

EXPLORING THE MOORS

Bounded by the Cleveland and Hambleton hills, the moors are dotted with early burial grounds and ancient stone crosses. **Pickering** and **Northallerton,** both market towns, serve as gateways to the moors.

The North York Moors will always be associated with doomed trysts between unlucky lovers, and ghosts who wander vengefully across the rugged plateaus of their lonely and windswept surfaces. Though the earth is relatively fertile in the river valleys, the thin, rocky soil of the heather-clad uplands has been scorned by local farmers as wasteland, suitable only for sheep grazing and healthy (but melancholy) rambles. During the 19th century, a handful of manor houses were built on their lonely promontories by moguls of the Industrial Revolution, but not until 1953 was the 1,440-sq.-km (554-sq.-mile) district designated the North York Moors National Park.

Encompassing England's largest expanse of moorland, the park is famous for the diversity of heathers, which thrive between the sandstone outcroppings of the uplands. If you visit between October and February, you'll see smoldering fires across the landscape—deliberately controlled attempts by shepherds and farmers to burn the omnipresent heather back to stubs. Repeated in age-old cycles every 15 years, the blazes encourage the heather's renewal with new growth for the uncounted thousands of sheep that thrive in the district.

Though public bridle and footpaths take you to all corners of the moors, two noteworthy and clearly demarcated trails make up the most comprehensive moor walks in Europe. The shorter of the two is the **Lyle Wake Walk,** a 64km (40-mile) east-to-west trek that connects the hamlets of Osmotherly and Ravenscar. It traces the rugged path established by 18th-century coffin bearers. The longer trek (the **Cleveland Walk**) is a 177km (110-mile) circumnavigation of the national park's perimeter. A good section skirts the edge of the Yorkshire coastline; other stretches take climbers up and down a series of steep fells in the park's interior.

Don't even consider an ambitious moor trek without good shoes, a compass, an ordinance survey map, and a detailed park guidebook. With descriptions of geologically interesting sites, safety warnings, and listings of inns and farmhouses (haunted or otherwise) offering overnight stays, the guidebooks sell for less than £4 ($7.40) each at any local tourist office.

The isolation and the beauty of the landscape attracted the founders of **three great abbeys:** Rievaulx near Helmsley, Byland Abbey near the village of Wass, and Ampleforth Abbey. Nearby is **Coxwold,** one of the most beautiful villages in the moors. The Cistercian Rievaulx and Byland abbeys are in ruins, but the Benedictine Ampleforth still functions as a monastery and well-known Roman Catholic boys' school. Though many of its buildings date from the 19th and 20th centuries, they do contain earlier artifacts.

The old market town of Thirsk, in the Vale of Mowbray, 39km (24 miles) north of York on the A19, is near the western fringe of the park. It has a fine parish church, but what makes it such a popular stopover is its association with the late James Herriot (1916–95), author of *All Creatures Great and Small.* Mr. Herriot used to practice veterinary medicine in Thirsk. You can drop in at a visitor center, **The World of James Herriot,** 23 Kirkgate (© **01845/524234**), which is dedicated to his life and to veterinary science. The Kirkgate surgery where he practiced from 1930 until his death in 1995 and the house next door have been transformed into *The Herriot Experience.* You can view the surgery and see various exhibitions and displays on veterinary science. Open daily from Easter to September from 10am to 5pm, and from October to Easter from 11am to 4pm (last admission is always 1 hour before closing). Admission is £4.70 ($8.70) adults, £3.70 ($6.85) children 5 to 15, family ticket £13 ($24).

EXPLORING THE NORTH YORKSHIRE COAST

Along the eastern boundary of the park, North Yorkshire's 72km (45-mile) coastline shelters such traditional seaside resorts as Filey, Whitby, and Scarborough, the latter claiming to be the oldest seaside spa in Britain, located supposedly on the site of a Roman signaling station. The spa was founded in 1622, when mineral springs with medicinal properties were discovered. In the 19th century, its Grand Hotel, a Victorian structure, was acclaimed the best in Europe. The Norman castle on the big cliffs overlooks the twin bays.

It's easy to follow the main road from Bridlington north to Scarborough and on to Robin Hood's Bay and Whitby. As you drive up the coast, you'll see small fishing ports and wide expanses of moorland.

BRIDLINGTON
29km (18 miles) SE of Scarborough

Bridlington is a good starting point for a trip up the North Yorkshire Coast. A fishing port with an ancient harbor, the wide beach and busy seafront markets draw crowds who enjoy relaxing on the sand or browsing through the gift shops and stalls that line the streets. Flamborough Head is one of the most distinguishable features on England's east coast. Jutting out into the North Sea, it features an 26m (85-ft.) tall lighthouse that stands atop a chalk cliff towering 51m (170 ft.) above the sea. A path that winds up the cliffs ends at Bempton, site of a bird sanctuary that is one of the finest reserves on the coast. You can enjoy watching the seabirds or simply take in the view of the sea off Flamborough, the final resting place of more than a few ships. Bridlington also has many country houses that are open for tours, in addition to Pickering and Helmsley castles and the deserted village of Wharram Percy.

Where to Stay
Flamborough Manor   The current manor house of Flamborough dates from 1800. It was fully restored by local craftspeople and now boasts comfortable accommodations and a friendly atmosphere. Bedrooms are tastefully appointed and have small bathrooms equipped with showers and adequate shelf space. Many visitors come to the house to browse through the variety of antiques sold in the converted stable block or to purchase a Gansey sweater. (These intricate fishermen's sweaters are handmade in the traditional way, an almost-lost process that has been revived by Lesley Berry, the house's proprietor.)

Flamborough, Bridlington, E. Yorkshire, YO15 1PD. ℂ and fax **01262/850943**. www.flamboroughmanor. co.uk. 2 units. £35–£40 ($65–$74) per person double. Rates include English breakfast. AE, MC, V. **Amenities:** Nonsmoking rooms. *In room:* TV, coffeemaker, hair dryer, no phone.

SCARBOROUGH
29km (18 miles) NW of Bridlington; 55km (34 miles) NE of York; 407km (253 miles) N of London

Scarborough, one of the first seaside resorts in Britain, has been attracting visitors for more than 3 centuries. A mineral spring discovered in the early 17th century led to the establishment of a spa that lured clients with promises of its water's healing benefits. In the 18th century, swimmers were attracted to the waters off the coast—sea bathing had come in vogue, and the beaches of England swarmed with tourists taking part in the craze.

The city of Scarborough is divided into two unique districts separated by a green headland that holds the remains of Scarborough Castle, which dates from Norman times. South of the headland, the town conforms to its historical molds. High cliffs and garden walks interspersed with early Victorian residences dominate the landscape. The north side is more touristy; souvenir shops and fast-food stands line the promenade. *Rock* (brightly colored hard candy that can be etched with the saying of your choice) and *candy floss* (cotton candy) satisfy even the most die-hard sweet tooth.

For more information about what to see and do while you're in Scarborough, visit the **Tourist Information Centre,** Pavillion House, Valley Bridge Road (© **01723/373333**), open May through September daily from 9:30am to 6pm; the rest of the year it's open Monday through Saturday from 10am to 4:30pm.

Trains leave London approximately every 30 minutes headed for York, where you'll have to transfer to another train. The entire trip takes just 2 hours and 10 minutes. For more information on schedules and prices, call © **0845/748-4950** or visit www.railtrack.co.uk. Three buses a day leave London heading for York, another will take you from York to Scarborough. If you're taking the bus, plan on spending most of a day riding. For **National Express** bus service, call © **0870/580-8080** or visit www.nationalexpress.com.

Exploring the Town

The ruins of **Scarborough Castle,** Castle Road (© **01723/372451**), stand on the promontory near a former Viking settlement. From the castle, you can look out over the North Bay, the beaches, and the gardens along the shore. Throughout the summer, fairs and festivals celebrate days of yore with mock battles, pageantry, and falconry displays. The castle is open April through September daily from 10am to 6pm; in October it closes at 5pm. From November to March, Scarborough Castle is open daily from 10am to 4pm. Admission is £3 ($5.55) for adults, £2.30 ($4.25) for seniors and persons with disabilities, and £1.50 ($2.80) for children. Children under 5 years enter free.

Nearby is the medieval **Church of St. Mary,** Castle Road (no phone), where Anne Brontë, the youngest of the three sisters of literary fame, was buried in 1849. She died in Scarborough after being brought from her home in Haworth in hopes that the sea air would revive her health.

Wood End Museum, The Crescent (© **01723/367326**), was once the vacation home of writers Edith, Osbert, and Sacheverell Sitwell. It now houses a library of their works as well as the collections of the **Museum of Natural History.** The house is open from June to September, Tuesday through Sunday from 10am to 5pm. The rest of the year it is open Wednesday, Saturday, and Sunday from 11am to 4pm. Admission is £2.50 ($4.65) adults, £1.50 ($2.80) seniors and children 5 to 16, £6 ($11) family ticket. Children under 5 enter free. This ticket also allows entry to the Art Gallery and the Rotunda Museum.

Also located at The Crescent is **The Art Gallery** (© **01723/374753**). The gallery's permanent collection features pieces ranging from 17th-century portraits to 20th-century masterworks. Many of the works relate to the Scarborough area. Changing exhibitions by young artists and local craftspeople are also displayed. If you're interested in learning how to create your own works of art, you may want to spend a while at the **Crescent Arts Workshop,** located in the basement of the gallery. Local artists offer courses and demonstrations in their respective mediums. The Art Gallery is open from May to mid-October, Tuesday through Sunday from 10am to 5pm. The rest of the year it is open Thursday through Saturday from 11am to 4pm. Admission is £2.50 ($4.65) for adults, £1.50 ($2.80) for seniors and children, and £6 ($11) for a family ticket. Children under 5 are admitted free. This ticket also allows entry to the Wood End Museum and the Rotunda Museum. For information about workshop offerings, call © **01723/351461.**

Local history collections and displays of important archaeological finds can be found at the **Rotunda Museum,** Vernon Road, down the street from Wood End (© **01723/374839**). The museum is housed in a circular building, constructed in 1829 for William Smith, the "Father of English Geology," to display his collection; it was one of the first public buildings in England built specifically for use as a museum. The Rotunda is open from May to September, Tuesday through Sunday from 10am to 5pm; from October to April, Tuesday, Saturday, and Sunday from 11am to 4pm. Admission is £2.50 ($4.65) for adults, £1.50 ($2.80) for seniors and children 5 to 16, and £6 ($11) for a family ticket. Children under 5 are admitted free. Admission is to both the Wood End Museum and the Art Gallery.

More than 70 species of sea creatures are housed at the **Sea Life Centre,** Scalby Mills, North Bay (© **01723/376125;** www.sealifeeurope.com). An acrylic tunnel passes under the watery habitat of rays and sharks and feeding pools; hands-on displays encourage interaction with the animals. A favorite of children and adults alike is the Seal Rescue and Rehabilitation Centre, which takes in and cares for stray pups and provides a haven for resident adult gray seals. The center is open daily from 10am to 6pm in the summer and from 10am to 4pm the rest of the year. Admission is £7.50 ($14) for adults, £6.50 ($12) for students and seniors, and £5 ($9.25) for children aged 3 to 14, free for children under 3.

Of course, Scarborough still has the springs that established its popularity. **The Spa,** South Bay (© **01723/376774**), no longer offers guests the opportunity to partake of the waters; it is now an entertainment and conference center in the midst of elegant gardens and buildings dating from several eras. In summer, there is a concert of some kind every day (usually classical and often held outdoors). Unless you just want to wander through the grounds, which is entertaining in itself, you may want to call ahead for concert times and prices.

Where to Stay

The Crown Hotel   Maintained in a style that's in keeping with its "Grand Hotel" origins in 1844, this hotel overlooks South Bay and Scarborough Castle from its setting above a cliff top, just above the quieter side of the town's beachfront. In recent years, extensive renovations have brought everything up-to-date. The accommodations are comfortable, with many rooms offering pleasant views over the sea. Most of the rooms, ranging from midsize to spacious, have been rejuvenated, and include roomy bathrooms, often with tub and shower. Nine bedrooms are rented to nonsmokers, and seven are large enough for families.

Esplanade, Scarborough, N. Yorkshire YO11 2AG. © **01723/373491.** Fax 01723/362271. www.chariet hotels.co.uk. 78 units. £104–£144 ($192–$266) double, £175 ($324) suite. Rates include breakfast. AE, MC, V. **Amenities:** 2 restaurants; bar; indoor heated pool; gym; sauna; Jacuzzi. *In room:* TV, coffeemaker, hair dryer, trouser press.

Palm Court Hotel   This inn provides guests with modern amenities in an elegant, old-world atmosphere. Inviting common areas, such as the lounge and cocktail bar, provide ideal settings for sharing a drink with friends. Rooms are tastefully furnished and among the most comfortable at the resort. Most accommodations are generally spacious, and six are rented to families. Bathrooms are well organized, each with a shower (some have bathtubs).

St. Nicholas Cliff, Scarborough, N. Yorkshire YO11 2ES. © **01723/368161.** Fax 01723/371547. www.palm court.scarborough.co.uk. 44 units. £82–£92 ($152–$170) double. Rates include English breakfast. AE, DC, MC, V. **Amenities:** Restaurant; bar; indoor heated pool; 24-hr. room service; babysitting; laundry service; dry cleaning. *In room:* TV, coffeemaker, hair dryer, trouser press.

Wrea Head Country House Hotel ★ This Victorian country house is situated just north of Scarborough on 5.6 hectares (14 acres) of beautifully kept grounds. There are several very compelling common rooms, such as a library and comfortable bar, which entice guests to sit and relax. The rooms vary in size and are individually styled with tasteful furnishings, including first-rate beds and well-maintained bathrooms with tub-and-shower combinations. Two rooms are ideal for families.

Barmoor Lane, Scalby, Scarborough, N. Yorkshire YO13 0PB. ℂ 01723/378211. Fax 01723/355936. www. englishrosehotels.co.uk. 20 units. £130 ($241) double, £190 ($352) suite. Rates include breakfast. AE, DC, MC, V. **Amenities:** Restaurant; bar; 24-hr. room service; babysitting; laundry service; nonsmoking rooms. *In room:* TV, coffeemaker, hair dryer, trouser press.

Where to Dine

Lanterna ★ ITALIAN Small, straightforward, and charming, this is a high-quality Italian restaurant whose owners, the Alessio family, maintain a strict allegiance to the recipes and ingredients (especially truffles) of their original home in northern Italy. Set in the center of old town, without any view of the sea, it offers places for 30 diners at a time in a room that's ringed with art photographs of Italian wine, food products and, of course, truffles. Menu items include lots of fresh fish (the owners make a trip to the fish market every morning at 7:30am), including whole sea bass roasted "on its bone" with olive oil and herbs. Pastas are made fresh almost every day and may include a succulent version of venison ravioli. A particularly unctuous starter is *tajarin* (strips of flat pasta), served with a relatively bland sauce of mushrooms and cream. The intent of this mild dish involves allowing the nutty, woodsy flavor of the truffles—added table side at the last minute—to emerge, unencumbered by other, more strident flavors.

33 Queen St. ℂ 01723/363616. Reservations recommended. Main courses £13–£30 ($24–$56). MC, V. Mon–Sat 7–11pm.

Scarborough After Dark

Alan Ayckbourn, a popular contemporary playwright, calls Scarborough home. **The Stephen Joseph Theatre,** Westborough, performs many of his plays as well as other favorites. Call the box office at ℂ **01723/370541** for information about shows and prices, or check out www.sjt.uk.com.

The Hole in the Wall, Vernon Road (ℂ **01723/373746**), is a well-stocked, lively pub where both locals and visitors gather to share drinks. Sheppard Neame's Master Brew, Fuller's ESB, and Durham's Margus are among the ales served at the long bar, and basic meals are served from noon to 3pm and 5 to 8pm.

ROBIN HOOD'S BAY

21km (13 miles) NW of Scarborough

Though Robin Hood's Bay was once a notorious port for smugglers, it has no connection with the well-known outlaw who shares the village's name. The tiny fishing port is tucked into a deep ravine; in fact, space is so limited that cars can't enter the village center. The villagers live in cottages precariously balanced on the steep cliffs, where narrow roads curve between the dwellings.

Where to Stay

Raven Hall Hotel *Kids* Many guests never leave the grounds of the hotel for entertainment, though Raven Hall makes a good base from which to venture out into Scarborough and nearby Robin Hood's Bay. The rooms have pleasant views of the water, the moors, or the garden. Each of the traditionally furnished bedrooms was renovated in 2001 and comes with a comfortable bed. Nearly half of the rooms here are large enough for families. Two rooms have four-poster beds. Bathrooms are well maintained with adequate shelf space and showers.

Ravenscar, N. Scarborough YO13 0ET. © 01723/870353. Fax 01723/870072. www.ravenhall.co.uk. 53 units. £77–£150 ($142–$278) double, £170 ($315) suite. Rates include English breakfast. AE, DC, MC, V. **Amenities:** Restaurant; bar; indoor heated pool; 9-hole golf course; putting green; 2 outdoor tennis courts; lawn bowling; gym; games room; sauna; 24-hr. room service; laundry service; 1 room for those with limited mobility. *In room:* TV, coffeemaker, hair dryer, trouser press.

WHITBY
11km (7 miles) NW of Robin Hood's Bay; 564km (350 miles) NE of London

The resort town of Whitby, at the mouth of the River Esk, has a rich and interesting history. It began as a religious center in the 7th century when Whitby Abbey was first founded. Later, Whitby became a prominent whaling port and eventually, like most coastal towns, an active participant in the smuggling trade.

Several famous explorers have pushed off from the beaches of Whitby, including Captain James Cook. Captain Cook, as the king's surveyor, circumnavigated the globe twice in ships constructed by local carpenters and craftsmen. He also claimed Australia and New Zealand for Great Britain.

Literary references to Whitby add intrigue to the town. Herman Melville paid tribute to William Scoresby, captain of some of the first ships that sailed to Greenland and inventor of the crow's nest, in his novel *Moby-Dick,* and Bram Stoker found his inspiration for *Dracula* in the quaint streets of Whitby.

Whitby Tourist Information Centre, Langbourne Road (© **01947/602674**), is open daily May through September from 9:30am to 6pm. The rest of the year it opens daily from 10am to 12:30pm and 1 to 4:30pm.

One bus a day travels between London and Whitby. The trip takes approximately 7 hours and is a direct route. Call the **National Express** bus service at © **0870/580-8080** or visit www.nationalexpress.com for more details. To get to Whitby from London by train, you'll have to ride to Middlesborough or Scarborough, then transfer to the train or bus to Whitby. The number of trains to Whitby varies, so call ahead. The number for rail information is © **0845/748-4950** (www.railtrack.co.uk).

Seeing the Sights
The ruins of **Whitby Abbey,** Abbey Lane (© **01947/603568**), lie high on the East Cliff, where they are visible from almost anywhere in town. The abbey dates from the 12th century and adjoins the site of a Saxon Monastery that was established in A.D. 657. Caedmon, the first identifiable English-language poet, was a monk here. On this site in A.D. 664, the date for Easter was decided. The abbey is open from Easter to September daily from 10am to 6pm; October from 10am to 5pm; and the rest of the year it closes at 4pm. Admission is £4 ($7.40) for adults, £3 ($5.55) for seniors, and £2 ($3.70) for children 5 to 16, £10 ($19) family ticket.

Another religious site is the uniquely designed **Church of St. Mary** (© **01947/603421**). Stairs (199 of them) leading to the church begin at the end of Church Street. If you have the stamina to climb them, you can walk through the rather spooky churchyard; it was here that Lucy was taken as Dracula's victim in Bram Stoker's novel. The church itself is an eclectic mix of architectural styles.

Whitby Museum, Pannett Park (© **01947/602908**), features exhibits that center around the city's history. Of course, ship models and details of Captain Cook's adventures are essential to the museum, but there are also displays about the archaeology and natural history of the area. The Pannett Art Gallery has a permanent collection featuring paintings by George Weatherill. There are also constantly changing special exhibits. The museum and gallery are open May through September, from 9:30am to 5:30pm Monday through Saturday and from 2 to 5pm Sunday. From October through April, they're open Tuesday from 10am to 1pm, Wednesday through Saturday from 10am to 4pm, and Sunday from 2 to 4pm. Admission to the museum is £2.50 ($4.65) for adults, £1 ($1.85) for children, and £6 ($11) for a family ticket; no charge for the gallery.

The **Captain Cook Memorial Museum,** Grape Lane (© **01947/601900;** www.cookmuseumwhitby.co.uk), deals more specifically with the life and achievements of the famous explorer James Cook. It is open daily April through October from 9:45am to 5pm (11am-5pm in March). Last entry is 30 minutes before closing. Admission is £3 ($5.55) for adults, £2.50 ($4.65) for students and seniors, £2 ($3.70) for children, and £8.50 ($16) for a family ticket.

The **Whitby Tourist Information Centre** (© 01947/602674) can give anglers information about fishing along the town's coastline. Fishing is free all along the Whitby shore. If you'd rather go out to sea to reel in a big one, there are boats for hire at points throughout the city. The cost usually includes tackle and bait.

Golfers should visit the **Whitby Golf Club,** Low Straggleton (© **01947/ 600660**). The 5,521m (6,134-yard) course is open to visiting golfers daily. **Raven Hall Hotel Golf Course,** Ravenscar (© **01723/870353**), is open to nonguests all day, every day. The nine-hole course is well tended and offers panoramic views of the moors and the sea. This is also the best place in the area for tennis.

Where to Stay

Dunsley Hall *Kids*   Five kilometers (3 miles) north of Whitby in the small hamlet of Dunsley, Dunsley Hall is from the turn of the 20th century when it was built by a Hartlepool shipping magnate who lived here with his family until 1940. Some of the original carpets and furnishings remain, and they now add historical charm to the well-appointed hotel. Guests can enjoy a stroll through carefully tended gardens around the house. Two of the spacious bedrooms are set aside for families, and bathrooms are small but well maintained, each with a shower unit (some have bathtubs).

Dunsley, Whitby, N. Yorkshire YO21 3TL. © **01947/893437.** Fax 01947/893505. www.dunsleyhall.com. 18 units. £130 ($241) double; £151 ($279) 4-poster room; £174 ($322) minisuite. Rates include breakfast. AE, MC, V. **Amenities:** Restaurant; bar; indoor heated pool; exercise room; sauna; breakfast-only room service; laundry service; dry cleaning. *In room:* TV, dataport, coffeemaker, hair dryer, trouser press.

Stakesby Manor   From your room at Stakesby Manor, a converted 1710 Georgian manor, you can view either the old town of Whitby or the surrounding moorland. The guesthouse is located within 1.5km (1 mile) of the beach, the golf course, and the town center. Though bedrooms vary in shape and size, each is modernized with comfortable furnishings. One is large enough for families, and each small bathroom comes with adequate shelf space and for the most part a shower-tub combination. Rod and Jill Hodgson are responsible for the day-to-day running of the hotel and are happy to arrange theater bookings or other entertainment for their guests.

Manor Close, High Stakesby, Whitby, N. Yorkshire YO21 1HL. © **01947/602773.** Fax 01947/602140. www. stakesby-manor.co.uk. 13 units. £92 ($170) double. Rate includes breakfast. AE, MC, V. **Amenities:** Restaurant; bar; limited room service; nonsmoking rooms. *In room:* TV, coffeemaker, hair dryer.

Where to Dine

Many hotels in the area offer half-board plans (with dinner) in addition to bed-and-breakfast rates; it may save you time and money if you take advantage of these. If you don't, or if you're looking for lunch, try **Trencher's,** New Quay Road (© **01947/603212**), for terrific fish and chips. Fresh filets of haddock or cod are fried in a crispy batter and served with thick-cut fries. For good food in an even better atmosphere, stop by **White Horse and Griffin,** Church Street (© **01947/604857**). While surrounded by the character of the 18th-century structure, you may enjoy curried fish or a carcasonne cassoulet. The White House and Griffin also rents out 10 comfortable bedrooms, each with a private bathroom, TV, and coffeemaker, costing £58 ($107) a night in a double, including breakfast.

8 Durham ✦✦✦

403km (250 miles) N of London; 24km (15 miles) S of Newcastle upon Tyne

This medieval city took root in 1090 after the Normans, under William the Conqueror, took over and began construction of Durham's world-renowned cathedral and castle on a peninsula surrounded by the River Wear. The cathedral, "Half Church of God, half Castle 'gainst the Scots," was built as a shrine to protect the remains of St. Cuthbert, while also providing a sturdy fortress against the warring Scots to the north.

The cathedral castle thrust Durham into its role as a protective border post for England. For centuries, Durham Castle was the seat of the prince bishops—kings of the wild northern territories in all but name—and a pilgrimage site for Christians coming to pay tribute to St. Cuthbert, a monk on Lindisfarne. His life of contemplation and prayer led to his consecration as a bishop in 685 and his sainthood after death.

Today, Durham boasts a university (built on the cornerstone of the castle) and is a good base for exploring this stretch of the North Sea coast, as well as the unspoiled rolling hills and waterfalls of the Durham Dales in the North Pennines.

ESSENTIALS

GETTING THERE Trains from London's King's Cross Station arrive hourly during the day, with the trip taking about 3 hours, and trains from York leave every 15 minutes, arriving approximately an hour later. Durham lies on the main London-Edinburgh rail line. For information, call © **0845/748-4950** or visit www.railtrack.co.uk.

National Express buses from London arrive twice daily, with the trip taking about 5 hours. For information, call **National Express** at © **0870/580-8080** or visit www.nationalexpress.com.

If you're driving from London, follow the A1(M) north to Durham.

VISITOR INFORMATION The **Durham Tourist Office** is at Millennium Place (© **01913/843720**), and is open year-round Monday through Saturday from 9:30am to 5:30pm, and Sunday from 11am to 5pm.

SPECIAL EVENTS At the **Durham Folk Festival,** held the last weekend in July, you can sing, clog, or just cavort to music; almost every event is free. The weekend also includes free camping along the River Wear, though you'd better arrive early on Friday if you want to get a choice spot. In early June, crowds swarm along the riverbank to cheer the crew racing the **Durham Regatta.**

SEEING THE SIGHTS

Durham Castle ✦ Facing the Durham Cathedral from the opposite side of the "Palace Green," this was the seat of the prince bishops of Durham for more than 800 years. In 1832, it became the first building of the fledgling local college, now Durham University; it still houses University College. During university breaks, it offers unique bed-and-breakfast accommodations to the public.

Palace Green. Ⓒ **01913/743800.** Admission £3.50 ($6.50) adults, £2.50 ($4.65) children, £8 ($15) family ticket. Guided tours Easter–Sept daily 10am–12.30pm and 2–4:30pm; other times of the year Mon, Wed, Sat–Sun 2–4:30pm. Closed during university Christmas breaks.

Durham Cathedral ★★★   Under construction for more than 40 years, the cathedral was completed in 1133, and today is Britain's largest, best-preserved Norman stronghold and one of its surviving Romanesque palaces. The structure is not only breathtaking to view, it is also architecturally innovative, the first English building with ribbed vault construction. It is also the first stone-roofed cathedral in Europe, an architectural necessity because of its role as a border fortress.

The treasury houses such relics as the original 12th-century doorknocker, St. Cuthbert's coffin, ancient illuminated manuscripts, and more. You can still attend daily services in the sanctuary.

Palace Green. Ⓒ **01913/864266.** www.durhamcathedral.co.uk. Free admission to cathedral (donation required); tower £2 ($3.70) adults, £1 ($1.85) children, £5 ($9.25) family ticket; treasury £2 ($3.70) adults, 50p (95¢) children, £5 ($9.25) family ticket; Monk's Dormitory 80p ($1.50) adults, 20p (35¢) children; £1.50 ($2.80) family ticket; audiovisual Visitors' Exhibition 80p ($1.50) adults, 20p (35¢) children, £1.50 ($2.80) family ticket. Cathedral: mid-June to Aug daily 9:30am–8pm; Sept–Apr Mon–Sat 9:30am–6:15pm, Sun 12:30–5pm. Guided tours July to mid-Sept Mon–Sat at 10:30am and 2pm (also 11:30am during Aug). Donations are required. Treasury: Mon–Sat 10am–4:30pm; Sun 2–4:30pm. Monk's Dormitory: Apr–Sept Mon–Sat 10am–3:30pm; Sun 12:30–3:15pm. Audiovisual Visitors' Exhibition: Mar–Oct Mon–Sat 10am–3pm.

Oriental Museum   This is the nation's only museum devoted entirely to Eastern culture and art. The display covers all major periods of art from ancient Egypt through India, as well as relics from Tibet, China, and Japan.

Elvet Hill off South Rd. Ⓒ **01913/747911.** Admission £1.50 ($2.80) adults, 75p ($1.40) children 5–16 and seniors, £3.50 ($6.50) family ticket. Mon–Fri 10am–5pm; Sat–Sun noon–5pm.

OUTDOOR PURSUITS

Fishing is a good sport all along the rivers Tees and Wear, and in the several reservoirs and ponds throughout the county. Boating is also available, and **Brown's Boat House,** Elvet Bridge (Ⓒ **01913/869525**), rents rowboats for pulls up or down the Wear, as well as offering short cruises April through October, at the price of £4.50 ($8.35) for adults and £2 ($3.70) for children.

Hikers can take the challenge provided by the 435km (270 miles) of trails (64km/40 miles of which are in the county) along the **Pennine Way,** the **Weardale Way's** 126km (78-mile) course along the River Wear from Monkwearmouth in Sunderland to Cowshill in County Durham, or the **Teesdale Way,** running 145km (90 miles) from Middleton in Teesdale to Teesmouth in Cleveland. Rambles along the public footpaths in town are supplemented by more than 80km (50 miles) of hiking trails, which follow the tracks of a former railroad outside of town. Seven such trails make use of interlinked routes and range from the 7.5km (4½-mile) **Auckland Walk** to the 17km (11-mile) **Derwent Walk.** If you don't feel like going it alone, there are also more than 200 guided walks throughout the county, providing background on the history, culture, and plant and animal life of the surrounding area; contact the tourist office (see "Visitor Information," above).

Cyclists can opt for road biking along quiet country lanes and converted railway routes, or mountain biking in **Hamsterley Forest.** The acclaimed **C2C national cycle route** passes through the Durham Dales and North Durham, on a 225km (140-mile) signposted route. Both road and mountain-bike rentals are available at several locations, including **Cycle Force 2000 Ltd.**, 87 Claypath St. (ⓒ **01913/840319**), open Monday through Friday from 9am to 5:30pm, Saturday from 9am to 5pm, and Sunday from 11am to 3pm. A bike rental costs £12 ($22) per day, with a £38 ($70) deposit.

WHERE TO STAY

Georgian Town House ⒱ᵃˡᵘᵉ   This is the most desirable B&B in Durham, an unusually decorated place lying on a steep cobbled Georgian terrace street, close to everything, including the cathedral. It is a wonder of decoration, especially the reception hallway with its stenciled pillars and leaf patterns. It's almost like entering an arbor in sunny Sicily. In the lounge, papier mâché "stars" and "moons" twinkle on the walls. Sofas are placed around the fireplace where guests can mingle. Rooms, except for a cramped single, are tastefully decorated and are light and airy. The small bathrooms include showers. The house has a panoramic view of the cathedral and castle. Children under 5 are not accepted at this establishment.

10 Crossgate, Durham DH1 4PS. ⓒ and fax **01913/868070**. 7 units. £60–£80 ($111–$148) double. Rates include breakfast. No credit cards. *In room:* TV, coffeemaker.

Royal County ⓐ   This is where we prefer to stay in Durham. Though some critics consider this an anonymous chain hotel (it's part of the Marriott chain), it has many winning features in its three Georgian buildings, plus a convenient location right in the heart of Durham. Skillfully converted from a row of riverside houses, it was once the family home of the Queen Mother before being turned into one of the region's premier hotels. Many of its original details have been retained, including an oak staircase that was transported here from Loch Leven, the Scottish castle where Mary Queen of Scots was held prisoner. The bedrooms all maintain a high standard of comfort and furnishings, though they vary in size. Most rooms are large enough to rent to families, and bathrooms, for the most part, come with tub-and-shower combinations.

Old Elvet, Durham DH1 3JN. ⓒ **800/228-9290** in U.S. and Canada, or 01913/866821. Fax 01913/860704. www.marriott.com. 150 units. £155–£170 ($287–$315) double, £150–£315 ($278–$583) suite. AE, DC, MC, V. **Amenities:** 2 restaurants; bar; heated indoor pool; health club; Jacuzzi; sauna; 24-hr. room service; babysitting; laundry service; dry cleaning; nonsmoking rooms. *In room:* TV, dataport, minibar, coffeemaker, hair dryer, iron/ironing board, trouser press.

Three Tuns Hotel   Still going strong after all these years, this hotel is the reincarnation of a 16th-century coaching inn that once housed travelers heading north into Scotland. Almost all traces of its former role are gone, and the property is run by the Swallow chain. Bedrooms have been completely modernized and furnished to a high, if not exciting, standard. The best and most spacious rooms are the executive units, but each room has a good comfort level. Two rooms are large enough for families. Bathrooms are roomy, and most are equipped with tub and shower. The public rooms have more character and are roomy and inviting.

New Elvet, Durham DH1 3AQ. ⓒ **01913/864326**. Fax 01913/861406. www.swallowhotels.com. 50 units. £110–£140 ($204–$259) double; £120–£230 ($222–$426) suite. Rates include breakfast. AE, DC, MC, V. **Amenities:** Restaurant; bar; 24-hr. room service; babysitting; laundry service; dry cleaning; nonsmoking rooms. *In room:* TV, coffeemaker, hair dryer, iron/ironing board, trouser press.

WHERE TO DINE

Bistro 21 ⓐ CONTINENTAL   A big hit locally, this is a bright, farm-themed bistro. Chef Mark Henderson's cuisine is precise and carefully prepared, with market-fresh ingredients that are allowed to keep their natural essence without being overly sauced or disguised. We especially recommend trying the blackboard specials, such as fish cakes with buttery spinach or pork chops with creamed cabbage and potatoes. The food is full of flavor and rather forceful, borrowing from all over Europe—certainly the Mediterranean—but also offering traditional British fare at times, such as deep-fried plaice and chips. You can finish with one of the rich desserts, including double chocolate truffle cake. But if you want to be terribly old-fashioned and very English, you'll ask for the toffee pudding with butterscotch sauce. It's prepared to perfection here.

Aykley Heads House, Aykley Heads. ℂ 01913/844354. Reservations recommended. Main courses £11–£20 ($20–$36); fixed-price lunch £13–£15 ($24–$28). AE, DC, MC, V. Mon–Fri noon–2pm and 7–10:30pm; Sat noon–2pm and 6–10:30pm.

DURHAM AFTER DARK

Much of Durham's nightlife revolves around its university students. When school is in session, **The Hogs Head,** 58 Saddler St. (ℂ 01913/869550), is a popular traditional English-style pub. It's open Monday through Saturday from 11am to midnight, and Sunday from noon until 10:30pm. **Coach and Eight,** Bridge House, Framwellgate Bridge (ℂ **01913/863284**), has disco Thursday through Sunday nights and is open Monday through Thursday from 11am to 11pm, Friday and Saturday from 11am to 1:30pm, and Sunday from 11am to 10:30pm.

SIDE TRIPS TO THE DURHAM DALES, BARNARD CASTLE & BEAMISH

This densely populated county of northeast England was once pictured as a dismal place, with coalfields, ironworks, mining towns, and shipyards. Yet the **Durham Dales,** occupying the western third of the county, is a popular panorama of rolling hills, valleys of quiet charm, and wild moors. **Teesdale** is particularly notable for its several waterfalls, including **High Force,** the largest waterfall in England, which drops a thundering 21m (70 ft.) to join the River Tees. It is equally known for the rare wildflowers that grow in the sugar limestone based soil of the region; they have helped it earn protection as a National Nature Reserve.

Also notable is **Weardale,** once the hunting ground of Durham's prince bishops, with its idyllic brown sandstone villages. For more information on the wide range of options the area has to offer, contact the **Durham Dales Centre,** Castle Garden, Stanhope, Bishop Auckland, County Durham DL13 2SJ (ℂ **01388/ 527650;** fax 01388/527461). Hours are November through March, Monday through Friday from 10am to 4pm and Saturday and Sunday from 11am to 4pm; and April through October daily from 10am to 5pm.

The 12th-century **Barnard Castle** 🐾 (ℂ 01833/690909; www.barnard-castle. co.uk) is an extensive Norman ruin overlooking the River Tees. It is open daily, April through October from 10am to 5:30pm, November through March Wednesday to Sunday from 10am to 1pm and 2 to 4pm. Admission is £2.60 ($4.80) for adults, and £1.30 ($2.40) for students and children under 16.

Barnard Castle is also home to the **Bowes Museum** 🐾 (ℂ **01833/690606;** www.bowesmuseum.org.uk), a sprawling French-style château housing one of Britain's most important collections of European art, including paintings from Goya to El Greco, plus tapestries, ceramics, costumes, musical instruments, and French and English furniture. There is also a children's gallery. The museum is open daily from 11am to 5pm. Admission is £6 ($11) for adults; £5 ($9.25) for children over 16, students, and seniors; and £15 ($28) for a family ticket. Children under 16 are free. Buses run from Durham several times daily.

North of England Open Air Museum West of Chester-le-Street, 13km (8 miles) southwest of Newcastle upon Tyne, and 19km (12 miles) northwest of

Durham City, this is a vivid re-creation of an early-19th-century village. A costumed staff goes through the motions of daily life in shops, houses, pubs, a newspaper office, and garage, as well as a Methodist chapel, village school, home farm, and railway station. An average summer visit takes around 4 hours, and a winter visit, including the town and railway only, takes about 2 hours.

Just off A693 in Beamish. ℃ 0191/370-4000. www.beamish.org.uk. Admission spring and summer £14 ($26) adults, £7 ($13) children; winter £5 ($9.25) for all. Free for children under 5. Spring and summer daily 10am–5pm; off season Sat–Sun and Tues–Thurs 10am–4pm. Closed Dec 13–Jan 3.

9 Hexham, Hadrian's Wall ★★ & the Pennine Way

489km (304 miles) N of London; 60km (37 miles) E of Carlisle; 34km (21 miles) W of Newcastle upon Tyne

Above the Tyne River, the historic old market town of Hexham has narrow streets, an old market square, a fine abbey church, and a moot hall. It makes a good base for exploring Hadrian's Wall and the Roman supply base of Corstopitum at Corbridge-on-Tyne, the ancient capital of Northumberland.

ESSENTIALS

GETTING THERE   Take one of the many daily trains from London's King's Cross Station to Newcastle upon Tyne. At Newcastle, change trains and take one in the direction of Carlisle. The fifth stop after Newcastle will be Hexham. For schedules and information, call ℃ **0845/748-4950** or visit www.railtrack.co.uk.

Hexham lies 23km (14 miles) southeast of Hadrian's Wall. If you are primarily interested in the wall (rather than in Hexham), get off the Carlisle-bound train at the third stop (Haltwhistle), which is 4km (2½ miles) from the wall. At either of these hamlets, you can take a taxi to whichever part of the wall you care to visit. Taxis line up readily at the railway station in Hexham but less often at the other villages. If you get off at one of the above-mentioned villages and don't see a taxi, call ℃ **01434/321064** and a local taxi will come to get you. Many visitors ask their taxi drivers to return at a prearranged time (which they gladly do) to pick them up after their excursion on the windy ridges near the wall.

National Express coaches to Newcastle and Carlisle connect with Northumbria bus no. 685. Trip time to Hexham from Carlisle is about 1½ hours and from Newcastle about 1 hour. For information, call ℃ **0870/580-8080** or visit www.nationalexpress.com. Local bus services connect Hexham with North Tynedale and the North Pennines.

If you're driving from Newcastle upon Tyne, head west on the A69 until you see the cutoff south to Hexham.

VISITOR INFORMATION   The **Tourist Information Centre** at Hexham is at the Wentworth Car Park (℃ **01434/652220**). It's open from Easter to October Monday through Saturday from 9am to 6pm (until 5pm in Oct), and Sunday from 10am to 5pm; November through March, Monday through Saturday from 9am to 5pm.

HADRIAN'S WALL & ITS FORTRESSES

Hadrian's Wall ★★, which extends for 118km (73 miles) across the north of England, from the North Sea to the Irish Sea, is particularly interesting for a stretch of 16km (10 miles) west of Housesteads, which lies 4km (2¾ miles) northeast of Bardon Mill on the B6318. Only the lower courses of the wall have been preserved intact; the rest were reconstructed in the 19th century using original stones. From the wall, there are incomparable views north to the Cheviot Hills along the Scottish border and south to the Durham moors.

The wall was built in A.D. 122 after the visit of the emperor Hadrian, who was inspecting far frontiers of the Roman Empire and wanted to construct a dramatic line between the empire and the barbarians. Legionnaires were ordered to build a wall across the width of the island of Britain, stretching 118km (73 miles), beginning at the North Sea and ending at the Irish Sea.

The wall is one of Europe's top Roman ruins. The western end is accessible from Carlisle, which also has an interesting museum of Roman artifacts; the eastern end can be reached from Newcastle upon Tyne (where you can see some remains on the city outskirts, as well as a nice museum at the university).

You can find more information about Hadrian's Wall at **www.hadrians-wall.org**.

From early May to late September, the Tynedale Council and the Northumberland National Park run a **bus service** that visits every important site along the wall, then turns around in the village of Haltwhistle and returns to Hexham. Buses depart from a point near the railway station in Hexham six times a day. Call ✆ **01434/652220** for more information. The cost is £6 ($11) for adults, £4 ($7.40) for children, and £12 ($22) for a family ticket. Many visitors take one bus out, then return on a subsequent bus 2, 4, or 6 hours later. Every Sunday, a national park warden leads a 2½-hour walking tour of the wall, in connection with the bus service. The Hexham tourist office (see "Visitor Information," above) provides further details.

Housesteads Fort and Museum ⭐⭐ Along the wall are several Roman forts, the largest and most well preserved of which was called *Vercovicium* by the Romans. This substantially excavated fort, on a dramatic site, contains the only visible example of a Roman hospital in Britain.

5km (3 miles) northeast of Bardon Mill on B6318. ✆ 01434/344363. Admission £3.50 ($6.50) adults, £2.60 ($4.80) students and seniors, £1.80 ($3.35) children 5–16. Apr–Sept daily 10am–6pm; Oct–Mar daily 10am–4pm. Closed Dec 25–26 and Jan 1.

Roman Army Museum ⭐ Close to the village of Greenhead, the Roman Army Museum traces the influence of Rome from its early beginnings to the expansion of the empire, with emphasis on the role of the Roman army and the garrisons of Hadrian's Wall. A barracks room depicts army living conditions. Realistic life-size figures make this a strikingly visual museum experience.

Within easy walking distance of the Roman Army Museum is one of the most imposing and high-standing sections of Hadrian's Wall, **Walltown Crags;** the height of the wall and magnificent views to the north and south are impressive.

At the junction of A69 and B6318, 29km (18 miles) west of Hexham. ✆ 01697/747485. www.vindolanda.com. Admission £3.50 ($6.50) adults, £3 ($5.55) students and seniors, £2.20 ($4.05) children, £20 ($37) family ticket. Feb–Mar and Oct–Nov 10am–5pm, Apr–Sept 10am–6pm. Closed late Nov to early Feb.

Vindolanda This is another well-preserved fort south of the wall, the last of eight successive forts to be built on this site. An excavated civilian settlement outside the fort has an interesting museum of artifacts of everyday Roman life.

Just west of Housesteads, on a minor road 2km (1¼ miles) southeast of Twice Brewed off B6318. ✆ 01434/344277. www.vindolanda.com. Admission £4.50 ($8.35) adults, £8.30 ($15) students and seniors, £2.90 ($5.35) children. Feb–Mar and Oct to mid-Nov 10am–5pm; Apr–Sept 10am–6pm; mid-Nov to late Jan Wed–Sun 10am–4pm. Closed late Jan to mid-Feb.

HIKING THE PENNINE WAY IN NORTHUMBERLAND NATIONAL PARK

Northumberland National Park, established in 1956, encompasses the borderlands that were a buffer zone between the warring English and Scots during the

13th and 14th centuries. Today, the park comprises almost 1,035 sq. km (400 sq. miles) of the least populated area in England and is noted for its rugged landscape and associations with the northern frontier of the ancient Roman Empire.

Touching the border with Scotland, the park covers some of the most tortuous geology in England, the Cheviot Hills, whose surfaces have been wrinkled by volcanic pressures, inundated with sea water, scoured by glaciers, silted over by rivers, and thrust upward in a complicated series of geological events. Much of the heather-sheathed terrain here is used for sheep grazing; woolly balls of fluff adorn hillsides ravaged by high winds and frequent rain.

Northumberland Park includes the remains of Hadrian's Wall, one of the most impressive classical ruins of northern Europe. Footpaths run alongside it and there are a variety of walks in the country to the north and south of the monument. One of the most challenging hiking paths in Britain, the **Pennine Way** 🌟🌟, snakes up the backbone of the park. The 129km (80 miles) of the 403km (250-mile) path that are in the park are clearly marked; one of the most worthwhile (and safest) hikes is between Bellingham and the Hamlet of Riding Wood.

You can purchase a map of the trails, priced at 50p (85¢), at almost any local tourist office in the district. There are **National Park Centres** at Once Brewed (✆ **01434/344396**), Rothbury (✆ **01669/620414**), and Ingram (✆ **01665/578248**). The Head Office is at Eastburn, South Park, Hexham, Northumberland NE46 1BS (✆ **01434/605555;** www.nnpa.org.uk).

NEARBY PLACES TO STAY & DINE

Anchor Hotel   This is the social center of the village. Ideally situated for visitors to the wall and its surroundings, between Haltwhistle (14km/9 miles away) and Hexham (11km/7 miles), this riverside village pub was once a coaching inn on the route from Newcastle to Carlisle. The building, which was constructed in 1700 near the edge of the North Tyne River (which still flows within a few feet of its foundations), sits in the heart of the tiny village of Haydon Bridge. The cozy bar is a local hangout. In the country dining room, wholesome evening meals are served. The bedrooms are comfortably furnished, albeit a bit small, and each comes with a cozy bed. Bathrooms are also small with shower stalls (some have tubs).

John Martin St. (on A69, 11km/7 miles west of Hexham), Haydon Bridge, Northumberland NE47 6AB. ✆ 01434/684227. Fax 01434/684586. 10 units. £55–£60 ($102–$111) double. Rates include English breakfast. AE, MC, V. **Amenities:** Restaurant; bar. *In room:* TV, coffeemaker, hair dryer, iron/ironing board.

George Hotel   Standing on the banks of the Tyne, this country hotel opens onto gardens leading to the riverbank. It's a convenient base for visiting Hadrian's Wall. The hotel dates from the 18th century, when the original structure was built of Roman stone. It has been extensively refurbished to a high standard, and all bedrooms are comfortably furnished and well equipped. Bathrooms are a bit cramped and are equipped with a shower and tub.

Chollerford, Humshaugh, near Hexham, Northumberland NE46 4EW. ✆ 01434/681611. Fax 01434/681727. www.georgehotel-chollerford.com. 47 units. £120 ($222) double. Rates include English breakfast. AE, DC, MC, V. Take A6079 8km (5 miles) north of Hexham. **Amenities:** Restaurant; bar; indoor heated pool; sauna; health club; 24-hr. room service; laundry service; dry cleaning; nonsmoking rooms. *In room:* TV, coffeemaker, hair dryer, iron/ironing board, trouser press.

Hadrian Hotel   Ideal for a stopover along Hadrian's Wall, the Hadrian lies on the only street of the hamlet of Wall, 5.5km (3½ miles) north of Hexham. It's an ivy-covered 18th-century building erected of stones gathered long ago from the site of the ancient wall. The owners have carefully refurbished the place. Each recently renovated bedroom is attractive, and all the rooms have been modernized and offer comfortable double or twin beds. Three rooms have a tub only. One room has a shower only, and two rooms have neither tub nor shower. All rooms are nonsmoking. The hotel has a private garden and a beer garden that serves as a warm-weather extension of its pub.

Wall, near Hexham, Northumberland NE46 4EE. © **01434/681232**. Fax 01434/681512. www.hadrianhotel. com. 6 units. £60 ($111) double. Rates include English breakfast. MC, V. **Amenities:** Restaurant; 2 bars. *In room:* TV, coffeemaker, hair dryer.

Langley Castle Hotel ★ *Finds*   To experience a stately home, we recommend this hotel located on 4 hectares (10 acres) of woodlands at the edge of Northumberland National Park, southwest of Haydon Bridge and about 11km (7 miles) west of Hexham. It's the only medieval fortified castle home in England that receives paying guests. The castle, built in 1350, was largely uninhabited after being damaged in 1400 during an English and Scottish war, until it was purchased in the late 19th century by Cadwallader Bates, a historian, who spent the rest of his life carefully restoring the property to its original beauty. Medieval features here include the 14th-century spiral staircase, stained-glass windows, huge open fireplaces, 2m (7-ft.) thick walls, and many turrets. The luxuriously appointed bedrooms vary in size; some have whirlpools or saunas in the well-maintained bathrooms. An adjacent building has extra accommodations, including four new suites, as well as a small conference room with a view of the castle. The hotel has an elegant drawing room, with an adjoining oak-paneled bar.

Langley-on-Tyne, Hexham, Northumberland NE47 5LU. © **01434/688888**. Fax 01434/684019. www. langleycastle.com. 18 units. £109–£199 ($202–$368) double; £219 ($405) suite. Rates include English breakfast. AE, DC, MC, V. From Hexham, go west on A69 to Haydon Bridge, then head south on A686 for 3km (2 miles). **Amenities:** Restaurant; bar; gift shop; limited room service; babysitting; laundry service; dry cleaning. *In room:* TV, dataport, coffeemaker, minibar, hair dryer, iron/ironing board, trouser press.

19

Cardiff & South Wales

No longer the dreary coal-exporting port as it was so often depicted in the 20th century, **Cardiff,** the capital of Wales, is hot and happening—one of the most attractive cities of Britain to visit. Cardiff (*Caerdydd* in Welsh) is a large seaport built on the tidal estuary of the Taff River.

Enriched by the Industrial Revolution, Cardiff declined after World War II with the closing of coal mines, railroads, and factories. The old industrial city is now a progressive, inviting modern port, as exemplified by the waterfront along Cardiff Bay. Here you'll find renewal at its best, with restaurants, hotels, and a hands-on exhibit, Techniquest.

Cardiff can be your launching pad for the treasures of South Wales, which has turned a bright, new face to the world and is no longer known for its depressing stories of slag heaps, dreary cottages, and denuded hillsides that were once proudly forested.

In fact, South Wales is imbued with some of the great beauty spots of Britain: **Brecon Beacons National Park,** 835 sq. km (519 sq. miles) of beauty and pleasure grounds with nature reserves; **Gower Peninsula,** an area of outstanding natural beauty stretching for 23km (14 miles) from the Mumbles to Worms Head in the West; and, finally, **Pembrokeshire Coast National Park,** one of the smallest national parks of Britain (only 362 sq. km/225 sq. miles) but an area acclaimed for its coastal scenery.

On the western side of Cardiff, the city of **Swansea** on Swansea Bay of the Bristol Channel, seems a natural starting place for a visit to Southwest Wales. After a sojourn in the vicinity of the port city, the beautiful **Gower Peninsula,** Swansea's neighbor, draws you westward. You can explore where Dylan Thomas, the country's outstanding 20th-century poet, was born, and then move on to the west to Laugharne, where the poet lived, wrote, and is buried.

Swansea is on the western edge of West Glamorgan County. When the counties of Wales were realigned and consolidated in 1973, Pembrokeshire and Carmarthenshire, familiar names in Welsh history, became part of Dyfed County, an even older designation for the area they occupy. In this southwestern corner of the country, you'll be introduced to the land of St. David and Celtic crosses, of craggy coastlines and the cromlechs marking the burial places of prehistoric humans.

In addition to Swansea, you'll find two more excellent bases outside Cardiff—**Tenby,** one of the most famous coastal resorts of Wales, its charm and character dating from the Middle Ages, plus **St. Davids,** a tiny cathedral city, birthplace of the patron saint of Wales.

Two major attractions that you may want to seek out even on a rushed visit are **Pembroke Castle,** oldest castle in West Wales, and seat of the earls of Pembroke, and **Tintern Abbey,** in the Wye Valley, founded in 1131, once one of the richest and most important monastic houses of Wales.

1 Cardiff ⁂

249km (155 miles) W of London; 177km (110 miles) SW of Birmingham; 64km (40 miles) SE of Swansea

If you remember Cardiff's dull, industrial reputation from yesteryear, you may not want to fit the capital of Wales into your already busy schedule. But to omit it would be a shame, because it has blossomed into one of the most inviting cities of Britain, and is an ideal base for exploring its own attractions, plus the major scenic beauty spots of South Wales.

You can visit it for its castles and museums. The National Museum of Wales is the treasure trove of the principality—from paintings to silver, from ceramics to dinosaur skeletons—and the Welsh Folk Museum, on 40 hectares (100 acres) of parkland, is one of Europe's leading open-air museums. A couple of castles is a worthy sightseeing goal, including Cardiff Castle, an extravaganza of whimsy, color, and rich architectural detail—built on the site of a Roman fort—and Caerphilly Castle, an imposing moated fortress whose massive water defenses form the second largest castle area in Britain. On the outskirts, Llandaff Cathedral is built on the site of a religious community from the 16th century.

ESSENTIALS

GETTING THERE   In recent years, Cardiff has greatly expanded its air facilities, and flights now wing in from across Europe. Airlines that service **Cardiff International Airport** (© 01446/711111; www.cial.co.uk) include **British Airways** (© 0870/850-9850; www.britishairways.com), which offers flights to Brussels, Paris, Belfast and points throughout southern Ireland, and Scotland; **KLM** (© 0870/507-4074; www.klm.com), which offers transfers, through Amsterdam, to points around the world. **Ryan Air** (© 0871/246-0000; www.ryan air.com) flies to Dublin and points throughout Britain that include Newcastle, Edinburgh, and Aberdeen.

The fastest way to get from London to Cardiff is aboard **Air Wales** (© 0870/777-3131; www.airwales.co.uk), which offers direct air service from London City Airport. Flights leave twice a day Monday to Friday. There is also 1 flight on Sunday. From Cardiff to London, there are two flights a day Monday to Friday; there is also a flight on Sunday. The flight takes only 1 hour.

The **Cardiff Bus Service** operates bus no. X91, which travels between the airport and the railway station at hourly intervals daily from 5:20am to 11:35pm, Monday to Friday. On Saturdays, the X91 and 95 operate from 7:10am to midnight and on Sundays services X5 and X91 operate between 8:15am and 10:15pm. The cost of a one-way trip is £3 ($5.55).

Trains arrive in Cardiff at the Central Station on Wood Street, in back of the bus station. Trains from London pull in at the rate of one every hour during the day; the trip takes 2 hours. Trains also arrive every hour from Glasgow and Edinburgh going via Crewe; trip time is 7 hours. For rail information and schedules, call © 0845/748-4950 or visit www.railtrack.co.uk. For bus and motor routes into Cardiff, call © 0870/580-8080 or visit www.nationalexpress.com. The trip is about 3½ hours from London.

VISITOR INFORMATION   For information about Cardiff and its environs, the **Cardiff Visitors Centre** is at 16 Wood St. (© 029/2022-7281), in the heart of the city. Between November and March, it's open daily from 10am to 5pm; and Sunday from 10am to 2pm. Between April and October, it is open daily 9am to 5pm. A branch office at Cardiff Bay, the Tube, Harbour Drive (© 029/2046-3833), lying 2.5km (1½ miles) to the south, is open daily from 10:30am to 5pm.

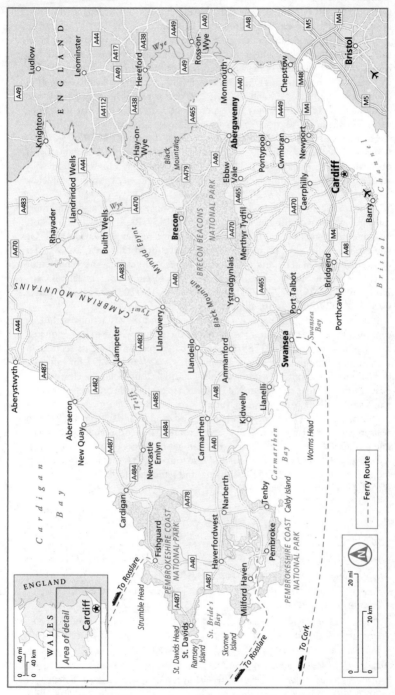

ENGLAND

Ludlow

Leominster

A44

A417

A49

A49

Hereford

A438

Ross-on-Wye

A40

A48

M5

M4

Wye

Knighton

A49

A112

A438

Hay-on-Wye

A465

Monmouth

A40

Chepstow

M48

Bristol

Llandrindod Wells

A44

Black Mountains

Abergavenny

A449

M4

Newport

M4

Cardiff

Rhayader

A470

A483

Builth Wells

A470

Wye

A479

Ebbw Vale

Pontypool

Cwmbran

Mynydd Epynt

Brecon

A465

Merthyr Tydfil

Caerphilly

A470

Barry

A483

BRECON BEACONS NATIONAL PARK

A40

A470

A48

Bristol Channel

CAMBRIAN MOUNTAINS

Tywi

Black Mountain

Ystradgynlais

A465

Bridgend

M4

A48

Aberystwyth

A487

Lampeter

A482

Llandovery

A40

Llandeilo

Ammanford

A48

Port Talbot

Swansea

Porthcawl

A44

A483

A482

A485

Swansea Bay

Aberaeron

Teifi

A487

New Quay

A484

Newcastle Emlyn

A484

Carmarthen

A40

Kidwelly

Llanelli

Cardigan Bay

Worms Head

Cardigan

A478

Narberth

Carmarthen Bay

Caldy Island

Cardigan

Fishguard

PEMBROKESHIRE COAST NATIONAL PARK

Haverfordwest

A40

Tenby

Pembroke

PEMBROKESHIRE COAST NATIONAL PARK

To Rosslare

Strumble Head

A487

St. Davids Head

St. Davids

Ramsey Island

A487

St. Bride's Bay

Skomer Island

A487

Milford Haven

A40

To Rosslare

To Cork

- - - Ferry Route

ENGLAND

WALES

Cardiff

Area of detail

40 mi

40 km

20 mi

20 km

0

GETTING AROUND   If you don't have a car, you must depend on taxis, buses, or your trusty feet to get around in Cardiff.

There's fairly good bus service, even to the sights in the environs. Your hotel staff will usually be able to help you plan a day's outing. Note that prices of bus routes vary with the time of day and according to the number of zones you want to travel in. One-way travel within zone 1 (the commercial heart of the city) costs between 75p ($1.40) and £1.25 ($2.30) per person. One-way travel across all four zones of the city (a very large metropolitan area, taking in far-flung suburbs) costs from £1.50 to £1.75 ($2.80–$3.25) per person.

For bus routes, go to **BWS Caerdydd,** Wood Street (© **0870/608-2608**), which is the office of Cardiff City Transport. Across from the bus station, it is open Monday to Friday from 8:30am to 5:30pm; Saturday 9am to 4:30pm. Bus service on Sunday morning tends to be infrequent, and service stops completely every night at 11pm.

Taxis are usually easy to find, especially in the busy shopping areas, and most cab fares within Cardiff range from £4 to £10 ($7.40–$19) each. The most prominent taxi ranks are at the rail and bus station and at St. David's Hall. Or you can have your hotel or the place where you've dined call you a taxi. Wonder of wonders, the meter starts ticking only when you get into the vehicle, not when it leaves the station, as is the case in most U.K. cities. For service, call **Capital Cabs** at © **029/2077-7777, Black Cabs** at © **029/2034-3343,** or **Premier Cabs** at © **029/2056-5656,** all operating 24 hours a day.

One of the most efficient ways to see Cardiff and the attractions within its central core involves joining up with one of the open-top bus tours conducted by **City Sightseeing** (© **01789/294466** for information about its services in Cardiff and throughout the United Kingdom, or **029/2038-4291** for information specifically about its services within Cardiff). Tours follow a clearly signposted itinerary that begins outside Cardiff Castle (at Castle St.), between April and October, daily from 10am to 4pm; November 8 to December 28 (excluding Christmas Day and Dec 26) only on Saturday and Sunday from 10:30am to 3:30pm (no tours Jan–Mar). Tours cover a route that incorporates the most visible monuments of Cardiff. Participants can get on or get off the bus at any of the designated stops, returning for the next bus to carry them on to the next monument. Adults pay £7 ($13), students and seniors £5 ($9.25), children 5-15 £2.50 ($4.65), family ticket £17 ($31).

FAST FACTS: Cardiff

American Express An office is at 3 Queen St. (© **029/2064-9305**).

Area Code The area code for Cardiff is **029.**

Dentist For dental emergencies, contact **James Hull Dental Care,** 23 The Parade (© **029/2048-1486**).

Doctor For medical emergencies, dial © **999** and ask for an ambulance. Doctors are on 24-hour call service. A full list of doctors is posted at all post offices, or else visitors can ask at their hotel desk.

Drugstores To get a prescription filled, go to **Boots the Chemist.** There are outlets all over town. The main dispensing service is at 5 Wood St. (© **029/2037-7043**), open Monday through Friday from 8:30am to 6pm, Saturday from 9am to 5:30pm, and Sunday from 11am to 5pm.

Emergencies To summon police or call firefighters, dial © **999,** the same number used to call an ambulance.

Hospitals The most visible and best-accessorized hospital in Cardiff is the **University Hospital of Wales** (also known as **The Heath Hospital**), Heath Park (© **029/2074-7747**).

Internet Access To stay in touch, you can go to the **Coffee Republic,** 83 St. Mary's St. (© **0161/888-2318**). It charges £3 ($5.55) per hour for use of its facilities. Open Monday to Friday from 7am to 7pm, Saturday and Sunday from 9am to 4pm.

Maps You can obtain detailed maps for free from the **Cardiff Visitors Centre** at 16 Wood St. (© **029/2022-7281**).

Police In an emergency, dial © **999.** Otherwise, contact the **Central Cardiff Police Station,** Cathays Parks (© **029/2022-2111**).

Post Office The main post office is at 2 Hill St. (© **0845-722-3344**), open Monday to Friday 9am to 5:30pm and Saturday from 9am to 1pm.

EXPLORING THE TOWN
The Welsh capital has many interesting things to see, from antiquities to something as modern as Epstein's controversial carving, *Christ in Majesty,* at Llandaff Cathedral. If you're in Cardiff for only a short time, try to see the major sights described below.

CARDIFF BAY'S INNER HARBOUR ✯
Allow 2 hours to visit this redeveloped area of the old dockland of Tiger Bay, lying about 2.5km (1½ miles) south of the town center. The salty old sea dogs of yesteryear who used to hang out here between sails wouldn't recognize the place today. No longer tawdry, it bustles with shops, restaurants, pubs, and attractions.

In the 19th century, when the area was called Tiger Bay, it became notorious among sailors around the world. The setting for many a novel, Tiger Bay meant poverty, crime, and violence. Today, the panoramic view of the harbor is worth the visit alone, as are the scenic promenades along the bay and even a science center.

Drop in at the **Cardiff Bay Visitor Centre,** The Tube, Harbour Dr. (© **029/ 2046-3833**), to pick up any information about the area. Admission is free, and it is open daily from 9:30am to 5pm, standing next to the Welsh Industrial and Maritime Museum.

Techniquest ✯ is the chief attraction here (Stuart St.; © **029/2047-5475;** www.techniquest.org), Britain's leading science discovery center. Here you can enjoy 160 hands-on exhibits, and you can visit both a Science Theatre and Planetarium. The attraction was founded in 1986 with the aim of developing people's understanding of science and technology. Some 100,000 people—both young and old—visit it annually. Admission is £6.75 ($12) for adults, £4.65 ($8.60) for children ages 4 to 16 (free for children ages 3 and under), or £19 ($34) for a family ticket. Open Monday through Friday from 9:30am to 4:30pm, Saturday and Sunday from 10:30am to 5pm. Last admission is 45 minutes before closing.

THE TOP ATTRACTIONS
Cardiff Castle ✯   Some 1,900 years of history are embodied in this castle located in the heart of the city. The Romans first built a forum on this site, and you can see the remains of massive 3m (10-ft.) thick stone walls. The Normans

constructed a castle on what was left of the Roman fort, and much of the Norman work still exists, added to by medieval lords. It came under assault in the Anglo-Welsh wars and was besieged during the English civil war. The third marquess of Bute, by then the owner, had it restored in the 19th century by Victorian architect William Burges, who transformed the interior into the extravaganza of whimsy, color, and rich architectural detail you see today. The Welsh Regimental Museum and the First Queen's Dragoon Guards Regimental Museum are also here. Admission includes the full conducted tour.

Castle St. ⓒ **029/2087-8100.** www.cardiffcastle.com. Admission £5.80 ($11) adults, £3.50 ($6.50) children, students, and seniors. Mar–Oct daily 9:30am–5pm; Nov–Feb daily 9:30am–4pm. Bus: 32 or 62.

National Museum of Wales ⋒   This imposing white, classic building with a columned entrance and a large cupola houses eclectic art and science collections. Along with City Hall, it stands at the Civic Centre. The diverse exhibits here focus on natural science, industry, archaeology, and geology, plus there are extensive collections of silver, china, and glass (some dating from 1250). The emphasis is on the story of Wales from earliest times. There are also modern and classic sculptures and works from old masters and modern artists from Rembrandt to Kokoschka.

Much of the museum's ambience comes from the openness and light that fills the main entrance and hall below the high ceiling. From the floor of the rotunda, you can look up to the mezzanine gallery that girdles the main hall. The exhibits are at the head of the impressive staircase from the main hall. Also on this level is the French Impressionist collection—our favorite part of the museum—which includes Monet's *Waterlilies,* Renoir's *Parisian Girl,* and Manet's haunting *The Rabbit.* Here you can also see Rodin's bronze couple *The Kiss,* and paintings by Rubens, Cézanne, Augustus John, and Brangwyn. A well-stocked bookstore is situated off the main hall.

Cathays Park in the Civic Centre. ⓒ **029/2039-7951.** www.nmgw.ac.uk. Free admission except for special exhibitions (prices vary). Tues–Sun 10am–5pm. Closed some public holidays. Bus: 32 or 62.

Llandaff Cathedral ⋒   This cathedral is in the tiny city of Llandaff, which stood just outside the western boundary of Cardiff until 1922 when it was made a part of the capital. It still retains its village atmosphere, with modern shops in old half-timbered buildings. The cathedral stands in a green hollow at a place where religious history goes back 1,400 years. It began as a religious community founded by St. Teilo in the 6th century, with many churches under its aegis scattered throughout South Wales. A 10th-century Celtic cross is all that's left of the pre-Norman church. Among relics of the Norman church erected on-site is a fine arch behind the high altar. The west front, built in the 13th century, is one of the best medieval works of art in Wales. Cromwell's army used the cathedral as a beer house and post office; then in 1941 a German bomb severely damaged the building. Postwar reconstruction gave the cathedral two fine new features: the Welsh Regiment Chapel and Sir Jacob Epstein's soaring sculpture *Christ in Majesty.* Epstein's striking work, which dominates the interior of the structure, has elicited mixed reactions from viewers. The ruin of the 800-year-old Bishop's Palace has been made into a peaceful public garden. Call for times of services.

Cathedral Rd. ⓒ **029/2056-4554.** Free admission (donations requested). Daily 7am–7pm. Bus: 24, 25, 60, 62, 122, or 123.

Caerphilly Castle ⋒⋒   About 13km (8 miles) north of Cardiff is this imposing moated fortress built partly on the site of a Roman fort. It was constructed by Earl Gilbert de Clare, Lord of Glamorgan, as protection against invasion by

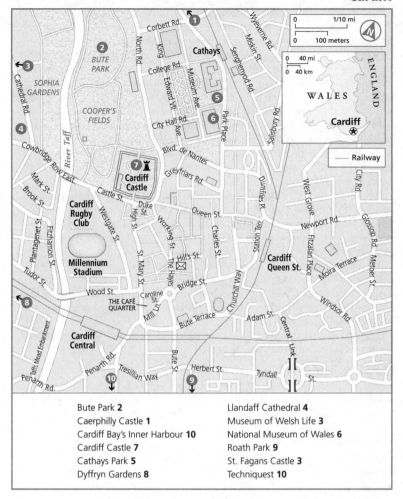

Bute Park **2**
Caerphilly Castle **1**
Cardiff Bay's Inner Harbour **10**
Cardiff Castle **7**
Cathays Park **5**
Dyffryn Gardens **8**

Llandaff Cathedral **4**
Museum of Welsh Life **3**
National Museum of Wales **6**
Roath Park **9**
St. Fagans Castle **3**
Techniquest **10**

the Welsh prince Llewelyn ap Gwynedd in the 13th century. The massive water defenses of the castle form the second-largest castle area in Britain. You will note the leaning tower as you approach the castle, a result of efforts by Cromwell to blow up the towers. Perhaps you'll see the castle ghost, the Green Lady. She is supposed to be the spirit of a French princess who loved a handsome Welsh prince. When her husband, the Norman lord of Caerphilly, learned of the matter, he sent her into exile, but her ghost is still supposed to be here, lamenting her lost love. You should come here mainly to see the impressive layout of the castle, with its defenses and great gatehouse, along with a fortified dam separating the outer moat from the inner moat. Wander also into the Great Hall. What you don't get is a luxurious interior filled with fascinating paintings or antiques.

On the A469 at Caerphilly. ℂ **029/2088-3143**. www.caerphillycastle.org. Admission £3 ($5.55) adults, £2.50 ($4.65) children ages 15 and under. Apr 1–June 1 daily 9:30am–5pm; June 2–Sept 28 daily 9:30am–6pm; Sept 29–Oct 26 daily 9:30am–5pm; Oct 27–Mar 31 9:30am–4.30pm; Mon–Sat 11am–4pm Sun. Bus: 26 from Cardiff leaves for Caerphilly every hour during the day (also buses 71 or 72). Caerphilly train with several departures daily from Central Station in Cardiff.

Museum of Welsh Life 𝒜𝒜   One of the most interesting places to visit in all of Wales is this museum, which provides a glimpse of Welsh life in centuries past. In the wooded parkland of an Elizabethan mansion, you can visit a treasury of ancient buildings that have been brought from their original sites all over the country and re-erected, in some cases even restored to their former use. In this superb collection of traditional buildings, widely distributed over the 40 hectares (100 acres) of parkland, you can see a 15th-century Tudor farmhouse furnished in the fashion of its day, cottages, a tollhouse, a schoolhouse, a chapel, and a cockpit. You'll also see a woolen mill and a flour mill from long ago put back into use so that people of the present can see how such work was done back in the days before electricity, steam power, or other modern conveniences. A wood turner and a cooper (barrel maker) are also at work, using the tools and materials of another age.

Besides the open-air museum, you can also visit the handsome headquarters building of the **Welsh Folk Museum** with its wealth including costumes, agricultural farm equipment used to till Welsh fields centuries ago, and articles of material culture, from Welsh dressers and cooking utensils to love spoons and early day toys.

Also on the grounds is **St. Fagans Castle,** the 16th-century mansion that was given to the National Museum of Wales by the earl of Plymouth as a center for the folk museum. The mansion house, built inside the curtain wall of a Norman castle, with its formal gardens, has been refurbished and restored to the way it was at the end of the 18th century.

St. Fagans. ✆ 029/2057-3500. www.nmgw.ac.uk/mwl. Free admission. Daily 10am–5pm. Bus: 32 leaving from the bus station in Cardiff every hour during the day.

PARKS & GARDENS

Cardiff has been called a city of parks, with some 1,092 hectares (2,700 acres) of well-designed parklands. **Bute Park,** in the heart of the city, spreads its green swath along the River Taff for the pleasure of residents and visitors.

Of special interest, **Roath Park,** Lake Road West (✆ **029/2075-5328**), is east of the city center, offering facilities for boating and fishing on its 13-hectare (32-acre) lake, as well as tennis courts and bowling greens. Rose and dahlia gardens, a subtropical greenhouse, a children's play area, and an island bird sanctuary add to the pleasures found here. The lighthouse clock tower in the lake is a memorial to Captain Scott. Admission is free, and it's open daily from 10:30am to 1pm and 2 to 4:30pm. Bus: 32 or 62.

Close to 5km (3 miles) from Cardiff, **Dyffryn Gardens,** St. Nicholas (✆ **029/2059-3328**), stands in a secluded valley in the Vale of Glamorgan. This park of 20 hectares (50 acres) contains a landscaped botanical garden. Herbaceous borders, a rose garden, a rock garden, and the largest heather garden in Wales are found here, along with an extensive arboretum. Grass walks invite you for long, leisurely strolls through the grounds. A palm house, orchid house, cactus, and succulent house along with seasonal display houses of potted plants are also on view. Admission is £3.05 ($5.65) for adults, £2.50 ($4.65) for students and children. A family ticket goes for £7 ($13). Open from April to September 10am to 6pm.

SHOPPING

Whether you're looking for gifts to take home, hunting for souvenirs, or just browsing, you'll like the shops of Cardiff. They are many and varied, ranging from a multiplicity of offerings in a modern shopping precinct, **St. David's Centre**—a stone's throw from the castle—to the stalls of a covered market. Bus: 2, 3,

7, 8, or 9. Shops are usually open Monday through Friday from 9am to 5pm, to 9pm on Thursday.

The **main shopping streets** are St. Mary, High, Castle, Duke, and Queen, plus the Hayes. Most of this area has been made into a pedestrian mall, with trees, shrubs, and gracious Edwardian arcades. These arcades, a dozen in all, are the most famous shopping precincts in all of Wales. The best known is the **Castle Arcade,** constructed in 1887. The interior has a fascinating first-floor wooden gallery with a wooden second floor overhanging it. Dating from 1858, the **Royal Arcade** is the oldest of the city's shopping arcades. Look for the original Victorian storefronts at nos. 29, 30, and 32. The **Morgan Arcade** from 1896 is the best preserved. Note the first-floor Venetian windows and the original slender wooden storefronts such as nos. 23 and 24. All in all, the arcades stretch to a length of 797m (2,655 ft.) in the city.

In the St. David's Shopping Centre is a branch of **Marks & Spencer,** 72 Queen St. (✆ **029/2037-8211**), one of the country's oldest branches of a major chain store, offering clothing with emphasis on British-made goods. A food section contains a range of high-quality specialty items. This is the anchor store in the enclosed center, which has shops opening off wide walkways.

David Morgan, 26 The Hayes (✆ **029/2022-1011**), is the largest independent department store in Wales, launched by the son of an impoverished tenant farmer in early Victorian times. The present store dates from 1879, offering a wide array of Welsh gifts and souvenirs for the visitors, along with such substantial merchandise as clothing for the locals. It offers restaurants, a coffee shop, a snack bar, and a salon. Bus: 1 or 2.

The best Welsh craft shop in the center is **Castle Welsh Crafts,** 1 Castle St. (✆ **029/2034-3038**), opposite the castle entrance. Mailing service is available, and VAT-refund forms are available for overseas visitors.

Markets are held at several sites. The **Central Indoor Market** on St. Mary Street is open Monday through Friday. The **Outdoor Fruit and Vegetable Market,** St. David Street and Mary Ann Street, is open Monday through Saturday. On Bessemer Road, an **open-air market** is held on Sunday morning.

For a novel shopping jaunt, visit **Jacob Antique Centre,** West Canal Wharf (✆ **029/2039-0939**), to see what's for sale from Grandmother Welsh's attic. Perhaps a Victorian fireplace, 19th-century jewelry, antique brass or hardware, pocket watches, and certainly furnishings mainly from Victoria's heyday. Bus: 2 or 3.

Close to St. David's Centre, the **Capitol Shopping Centre** along Queen Street is another place to shop for bargains or special gifts. In the complex is one of Britain's best men's stores, **Austin Reed,** 13–14 The Capitol (✆ **029/2022-8357**). Bus: 70, 78, 80, or 82.

At the **Martin Tinney Gallery,** 18 St. Andrews Crescent (✆ **029/2064-1411**), a short distance from the Cardiff rail station, you'll find the region's best commercial galleries. Finally, **Craft in the Bay,** The Flourish, Lloyd George Avenue (✆ **029/2048-4611**), features the largest selection of handmade quality crafts in Wales—baskets, pottery, jewelry, handcrafted furniture, ceramics, and the like.

WHERE TO STAY
EXPENSIVE

Angel Hotel ℛ   This elegant Victorian hotel across from Cardiff Castle was *the* place to stay in South Wales when it was first built. Over the years it has attracted everybody from Garbo to the Beatles to every prime minister of

Britain. There is no way it will ever regain its old supremacy, as greater hotels such as Cardiff Bay and St. David's Hotel & Spa have long surpassed it, but the Angel is still there and still good—it and has regained some of its old prestige following a restoration in 2000—a world of neo-Doric decor, *trompe-l'oeil* ceilings, Waterford crystal chandeliers, and hand-stippled faux-marble columns. As befits a hotel of this age, rooms come in a wide variety of styles and sizes ranging from standard (the smallest) to deluxe (spacious and superior in every way).

Castle St., Cardiff, CF10 1SZ. ℰ **029/2064-9200.** Fax 029/2039-6212. www.paramount-hotels.co.uk. 102 units. £88–£180 ($163–$333) double; £150–£240 ($278–$444) suite. AE, DC, MC, V. **Amenities:** Restaurant; bar and lounge; 24-hr. room service; babysitting; nonsmoking rooms. *In room:* A/C, TV, dataport, coffeemaker, hair dryer, iron/ironing board.

Egerton Grey Country House Hotel 𝒦 *(Kids)*

Sixteen kilometers (10 miles) west of the city, this elegant country-house hotel lies in a bucolic setting in the Vale of Glamorgan. The 17th-century house has been carefully restored, and is filled with antiques, paintings, and porcelain. In nippy weather you can warm yourself by the open fires. Standing amidst 2.8 hectares (7 acres) of gardens, it faces the sea in the hamlet of Porthkerry, within easy driving distance of the Brecon Beacons and Gower Peninsula. It was once a rectory and private residence but was opened as a small luxurious house in 1988. All the rooms are nonsmoking, spacious, and exceedingly comfortable; some have four-poster beds. The suites offer beautiful coastal views. Guests can enjoy the library or a magnificent Edwardian drawing room, and can dine in the first-class mahogany-paneled restaurant. ***Note:*** Children over 10 years are welcome; the hotel has plenty of grounds where kids can run and play.

Porthkerry, near Barry and Cardiff, Vale of Glamorgan, CF62 3BZ. ℰ **01446/711666.** Fax 01446/711690. www.egertongrey.co.uk. 10 units. £115 ($213) double; £130 ($241) suite. AE, MC. From junction 33 of M4 follow signs to the airport, bypassing Barry and turning left at the small roundabout, signposted Porthkerry. After about 457m (1,500 ft.), turn left again at the signpost to the hotel. **Amenities:** Restaurant; limited room service; babysitting; laundry service. *In room:* TV, coffeemaker, hair dryer, trouser press.

St. David's Hotel & Spa 𝒦𝒦𝒦 *(Finds)*

A strikingly contemporary structure, St. David's dwarfs the competition, rising above the new waterfront development. A seven-story atrium towers above the lobby, an unusual sight for a Welsh hotel. An immediate hit, it is the first five-star hotel to arrive in Wales and is the only one in South Wales that qualifies as one of the Leading Hotels of the World. You get the highest level of service in South Wales, the ultimate in comfort, and the best leisure facilities. St. David's is especially known for its extensive spa and beauty facilities. Roomy and beautifully furnished bedrooms offer floor-to-ceiling windows and open onto private balconies with panoramic sweeps of the bay. The marble bathrooms are state of the art and offer Italian toiletries and bathrobes. A superb modern European cuisine is presented nightly in the hotel's restaurant.

Havannah St., Cardiff Bay, Cardiff CF10 5SD. ℰ **029/2031-3018.** Fax 029/2048-7056. www.rfhotels.com. 136 units. £205 ($379) double; from £260 ($481) suite. AE, DC, MC, V. Parking £4.20 ($7.75). **Amenities:** Restaurant; bar; indoor heated pool; health club; spa; Jacuzzi; sauna; 24-hr. room service; babysitting; laundry service; dry cleaning; rooms for those with limited mobility; nonsmoking rooms. *In room:* A/C, TV, dataport, coffeemaker, hair dryer, safe, trouser press.

MODERATE

Hanover International Hotel & Club 𝒦𝒦

Not the equal of St. David's Hotel & Spa, which is in a class by itself, this is our runner-up in the area. It too lies in the heart of the waterfront development and has already become a new Cardiff landmark. It combines modern, ocean-liner-style architecture with a restored, part-Victorian warehouse, and it does so dramatically with a maritime theme. Appropriately, the color schemes are aquamarine. Adding yet another atrium to the city's hotels, it uses glass elevators in the style pioneered by the Hyatt chain. Bedrooms are spacious and beautifully furnished with comfort in mind. Some family rooms are available, and some accommodations are reserved for nonsmokers. Bathrooms are roomy and superbly equipped.

Schooner Way, Atlantic Wharf, Cardiff Bay, Cardiff CF10 4RT. ✆ **029/2047-5000.** Fax 029/2048-1491. www.hanover-international.com. 134 units. £85–£150 ($157–$278) double, from £155 ($287) suite. Rates include breakfast. AE, DC, MC, V. **Amenities:** 2 restaurants; 2 bars; indoor heated pool; health club; spa; Jacuzzi; sauna; rooms for those with limited mobility. *In room:* A/C, TV, dataport, coffeemaker, hair dryer.

Jurys Cardiff 🖍 *Kids*   Adjacent to the Cardiff International Arena, this refurbished hotel is stylish and classic, ideal for both business travelers and vacationers. There's a vibrant spirit about the place that attracts us. Spacious and well-furnished bedrooms are grouped around a central atrium, which gives access to the hotel's fashionable public rooms. The accommodations are among the city's finest, with some of the best amenities. Some units are suitable for both nonsmokers and persons with disabilities. A few family rooms are available, and children are given a very hospitable welcome.

Mary Ann St., Cardiff CF10 2JH. ✆ **029/2034-1441.** Fax 029/2022-3742. www.jurysdoyle.com. £59–£265 ($109–$490) double. Rates include breakfast. AE, DC, MC, V. **Amenities:** Restaurant; Irish-themed bar; 24-hr. room service; babysitting; laundry service; dry cleaning. *In room:* TV, dataport, coffeemaker, hair dryer, safe, trouser press.

New House Country 🖍   On the fringe of Cardiff this elegant Georgian mansion is our choice for a tranquil retreat from the city. Opening onto panoramic views—on a clear day you can see the North Devon Coast—the hotel is imbued with an inviting country-house flavor, as evoked by open fires, exquisite furnishings, and beautifully restored bedrooms. The individually designed bedrooms, many with four-poster beds, are spacious and comfortable. Although traditional, there is modern luxury here. Bathrooms are roomy and sumptuous, with deluxe toiletries. Most of the bedrooms are in a large annex, and rooms here are as good as those in the main building. Three are large enough for families, and three units are also set aside for nonsmokers.

Thornhill, Cardiff CF14 9UA. ✆ **029/2052-0280.** Fax 029/2052-0324. www.newhousehotel.com. 36 units. £120 ($222) double, £150 ($278) suite. AE, DC, MC, V. **Amenities:** Restaurant; bar; lounge; 24-hr. room service; rooms for those with limited mobility. *In room:* A/C (in some), TV, dataport, coffeemaker, hair dryer, iron/ironing board.

INEXPENSIVE

The Abbey Hotel   Built in 1898 as a home for a wealthy sea captain and his family, this house retains many of its original features and is one of the better and more reasonably priced B&Bs. Richard Burton once attended elocution lessons in the public lounge back when the hotel was a private school. Bedrooms are small but comfortably furnished, often in a "Great Aunt" style, and have shower-only bathrooms. A few have four-posters, and many have VCRs. Breakfast is the only meal served, but the staff can recommend one of the many restaurants nearby.

149–51 Cathedral Rd., Cardiff CF11 9PJ. ✆ **029/2039-0896.** Fax 029/2023-8311. 28 units (shower only). £60–£90 ($111–$167) double; £75–£100 ($139–$185) triple. Rates include continental breakfast. MC, V. **Amenities:** Nonsmoking rooms. *In room:* TV, VCR (some), coffeemaker, hair dryer (in some).

The Big Sleep Hotel 🖍 *Value*   What are pictures of the actor John Malkovich doing scattered throughout this hotel? The actor, who made a career out of playing "evil bastards," is one of the major shareholders. And his hotel has been named one of *Conde Nast Traveller*'s "coolest places to stay." A rather dull office tower built in the 1960s has been successfully transformed into a hotel with a certain chic minimalism but most affordable prices. Each of the midsize bedrooms is individually decorated with contemporary pieces. Family rooms and rooms for those with limited mobility are available. The best rooms are the "New on Ninth," though they cost more. All accommodations come with a new bathroom that's well maintained. If there's a downside, it's that some of the bedrooms overlook the rail tracks nearby, a rather noisy location.

Bute Terrace, Cardiff CF 2FE. ✆ 029/2063-6363. Fax 029/2063-6363. www.thebigsleephotel.com. 81 units. Mon–Thurs £58–£89 ($107–$165) double; Fri–Sat £55 ($102) double; Sun £45 ($83). Suite £99–£135 ($183–$250) all week. Rates include breakfast. AE, DC, MC, V. **Amenities:** Breakfast room; bar; laundry service; dry cleaning; nonsmoking rooms. *In room:* TV, dataport, coffeemaker, hair dryer, iron.

Lincoln Hotel 🄺🄸🄳🅂 This Victorian house provides a cozy and reasonably priced nest along popular Cathedral Road. The majestic home was created in 1900 by joining together two older residences, resulting in a superb and completely restored hotel. Surprisingly, the hotel is named for Abraham Lincoln, not the English cathedral city of Lincoln. The four-poster units exude romance, but there are also modern facilities. Rooms are spacious, with well-kept bathrooms, and furnishings offer both style and comfort. Several family rooms are available. Smoking is not permitted in the guest rooms. You can meet your fellow guests in the snug sitting room.

118 Cathedral Rd., Cardiff CF11 9LQ. ✆ 029/2039-5558. Fax 029/2023-0537. www.lincolnhotel.co.uk. 18 units. £75–£90 ($139–$167) double, £85–£120 ($157–$222) double with 4-poster. Rates include buffet breakfast. AE, DC, MC, V. **Amenities:** Bar; breakfast only room service; laundry service; dry cleaning. *In room:* TV, coffeemaker, hair dryer, iron/ironing board, trouser press.

Town House 🄰 *Value* The best B&B in Cardiff, preferable even to the neighboring Lincoln, this classic Victorian town house, it lies in the shadow of the great Norman castle and has been completely restored and tastefully decorated. Its original architectural details are still here, including the mosaic-tiled floors in the elegantly decorated hallway, the stained-glass windows so beloved of Victorians, and even the original fireplaces in the public lounge and dining area. The cosmopolitan guesthouse's roomy bedrooms are immaculately furnished and have excellent bathrooms. The location is a 10-minute walk from the city center. The entire property is nonsmoking.

70 Cathedral Rd., Cardiff CF11 9LL. ✆ 029/2023-9399. Fax 029/2022-3214. www.thetownhousecardiff. co.uk. 8 units. £53–£63 ($98–$117) double. Rates include breakfast. AE, MC, V. **Amenities:** Breakfast room. *In room:* TV, coffeemaker, hair dryer.

WHERE TO DINE
EXPENSIVE

Le Gallois 🄰 CONTINENTAL For the flavors of the Mediterranean, this restaurant is without peer in Cardiff. The chef and patron, Padrig Jones, served under the enfant terrible of English chefs, the famous Marco Pierre White, and Jones learned his lessons well, scoring some knockout dishes from his own culinary imagination as well. In a stylish, contemporary atmosphere, this family-run favorite is two-tiered with clean, bold lines. Fashion and technique are evident in the salt-marsh Welsh rump of lamb with fondant potatoes, marinated Provençale vegetables, and a tomato and fresh basil jus. The fish dishes are also a delight, especially the steamed sea bass with crab and a chile salsa.

6–10 Romilly Crescent, Canton. ✆ 029/2034-1264. Reservations required. Fixed-price lunch £13–£27 ($24–$50); fixed-price dinner £25–£35 ($46–$65). AE, MC, V. Tues–Sat noon–2:30pm and 6:30–10:30pm.

MODERATE

Gilby's Restaurant SEAFOOD/WELSH   Near the Culverhouse Cross roundabout, two old converted farm buildings are now the venue for some of the finest viands in and around Cardiff. It's a lively place, popular with punters, who come here mainly for the fresh seafood. A young team in the kitchen turns out one tempting dish after another. Our preferred selection is the grilled whole fish, although you can also take delight in the sticky glazed shank of lamb with a confit of garlic and a bean ragout. A traditional Welsh dish is a platter of fish-cakes with braised leeks. For dessert, who could say no to the lemon tart with a side dish of amaretto-spiked pistachio ice cream?

Old Port Rd., Culverhouse Cross. ℰ 029/2067-0800. Reservations recommended. Main courses £8.95–£25 ($17–$46); fixed-price lunch Tues–Sat £12 ($22), Sun £15 ($28); fixed-price dinner Tues–Fri £15 ($28). AE, MC, V. Tues–Sat noon–2:30pm (until 3:30pm Sun) and 6–10pm. From M4 133 follow signs for Airport/Cardiff West; take A4050 Barry/Bairport Rd., turning right at the first roundabout.

Woods Brasserie MODERN BRITISH/CONTINENTAL   In the old Pilotage Building down by the dock, this is a haven of modernity, serving not only the best of Britain, but also dishes inspired by the cuisines of the Pacific Rim and the Mediterranean. Martyn Peters is addicted to Asian flavorings, such as a sweet chile sauce used to perk up pork tenderloin (ginger and garlic help, too). Aberdeen Angus filet, tender and juicy, is marvelously combined with a Gorgonzola polenta. Wales temptingly turns up on the menu in a rump of Welsh salt-march lamb with a red onion tart.

Pilotage Building, Stuart S., Cardiff Bay. ℰ 029/2049-2400. Reservations required. Main courses £9.50–£22 ($18–$41). AE, DC, MC, V. Tues–Sat noon–2pm and 7–10pm; Sun 11:30am–2pm.

INEXPENSIVE

Armless Dragon WELSH   About 1.6km (1 mile) north of the center in a busy suburb, this popular restaurant occupies a 19th-century stone core and is known for its simple, unpretentious, and nutritious food. The kitchen hires skilled chefs whose suppliers offer the best in Welsh produce and meats. The cooks are strong on their "taste of Wales" dishes, as exemplified by such delights as deep-fried laverballs coated in sunflower and sesame seeds, Brecon lamb bro-chettes, and a delicious mussel quiche. The place attracts both students and the family trade. One of our favorite dishes is roast Monmouthshire pork with a cockle and coriander sauce. Save room for ginger cake with rhubarb compote.

97 Wyeverne Rd. ℰ 029/2038-2357. Reservations recommended. Main courses £10–£17 ($19–$31); fixed-price lunch £8–£10 ($15–$19). MC, V. Tues–Fri noon–2pm; Tues–Sat 7–9pm. Closed Dec 25–26.

Harry Ramsden's SEAFOOD   This member of a chain serves the best fish and chips in Wales, at least according to its devotees. Until we finish sampling hundreds of others, we'll have to let the claim remain. Under crystal chandeliers, with nostalgic pictures displayed, this is both a place for traditional British cui-sine, mainly seafood, as well as entertainment. Begin perhaps with a prawn cock-tail. You can opt for fish platters, such as a 14-ounce batter-fried haddock with chips. If you finish the whole thing, you can have any dessert you want for free. You can also try such other main dishes as chargrilled chicken with fresh veg-etables. At a table opening onto a view of Cardiff Bay, you can sample such tra-ditional favorite desserts as a bread-and-butter pudding. On certain nights, there is live entertainment such as jazz bands, making the whole night festive.

Landsea House, Stuart St. ℰ 029/2046-3334. Reservations recommended. Main courses £6.80–£13 ($12–$24). AE, DC, MC, V. Daily noon–9pm.

La Brasserie, Champers, Le Monde *Kids* CONTINENTAL   Benigno Martinez enjoys one of the best dining formulas in the city—a three-in-one winner—a wine bar, a brasserie, and a Spanish bodega. A bustling, informal atmosphere prevails, and much of young Cardiff turns up here nightly, beginning with the bar food in Champers, which in this case means the tastiest tapas in town. La Brasserie was originally built as a warehouse in the 19th century. You order your drinks from a wood-topped bar and food from an attendant, who waits behind a well-stocked display case. The establishment serves 50 kinds of wine. Opt for the spit-roasted suckling pig or a platter of fresh oysters. Game including grouse, woodcock, and partridge is featured in season. Le Monde concentrates on fresh fish, including a delectable Marseilles-style fish soup and sea bass baked in rock salt. Of course, the regulars always seem to gravitate to the whole lemon sole. Something new and novel? Opt for the ostrich kabobs. At Champers you get a lively Spanish atmosphere with a cuisine to match. If your family, including the kids, wants real food instead of a Big Mac, this is an appealing choice because of its variety, quality, and reasonable prices.

60 St. Mary St. ⓒ 029/2023-4134. www.le-monde.co.uk. Reservations not needed. Main courses £9.95–£24 ($19–$44); fixed-price lunch £6.95–£9.95 ($13–$19). MC, V. Mon–Sat noon–2:30pm and 7pm–2am; Sun noon–2:30pm. Closed Dec 15–26.

CARDIFF AFTER DARK

There's no Soho in Cardiff, but you can find many interesting places to go after dark.

   St. David's Hall (see below) is one of Britain's leading centers of music, offering an extensive program, including visits by international conductors, soloists, and orchestras. Top rock and pop artists also appear there. The most outstanding local troupe is the **Welsh National Opera,** which *Punch* magazine acclaimed as "the world's best opera company."

   For information about after-dark diversions, pick up a brochure from the Cardiff tourist office *(Cardiff 2005),* revised annually. In it you'll find a selective rundown of the city's most worthwhile entertainment.

THE PERFORMING ARTS

The most innovative space for musical presentations in Britain—outside London, that is—is **St. David's Hall** (or Neuadd Dewi Sant in Welsh), The Hayes (ⓒ 029/ 2087-8444; www.newtheatrecardiff.co.uk). Designed in an octagonal format of shimmering glass and roughly textured concrete, it is the most comprehensive forum for the arts in Wales. A number of world-class orchestras appear regularly, along with popular music stars—everybody from Tina Turner to Welsh-born Tom Jones. Dance, films, and classical ballet, among other events, are also presented.

   The hall maintains an information desk for the sale of tickets throughout the day. It also has dining facilities, plus a changing exhibition of art. Prince Charles laid the hall's cornerstone, and the Queen Mother officially opened the arts center in 1983. The top-notch acoustics are attributed to its interior arrangements of a series of interlinked sloping terraces, any of which can be opened or closed for seating depending on the size of the audience.

   Instant confirmed bookings for events are available by phone with a Visa or MasterCard daily from 10am to 6 or 8pm, depending on the concert schedule. The box office is open Monday through Saturday from 10am to 8pm (but only until 6pm on days when there's no performance). On Sunday, hours are from 10am to either 6pm or until 1 hour before the start of a scheduled performance. Ticket prices depend on the event. Bus: 1 or 2.

A charming Edwardian building from 1906, the **New Theatre,** Park Place (© **029/2087-8889;** www.newtheatrecardiff.co.uk), is the city's second cultural venue, seating 1,000 patrons for major productions of drama, ballet, contemporary dance, and pantomime. As of this writing, it is also the home of the Welsh National Opera, although this troupe is scheduled to move to the new Wales Millennium Centre in 2005. Many theatergoers often enjoy shows here before they head for London's West End. The box office is open Monday through Saturday from 10am to 8pm. If there's no performance scheduled, the ticket office closes at 6pm. Most tickets generally cost from £9 to £47 ($17–$87) . Bus: 70, 78, 80, or 82.

Cardiff's main repertory theater, **Sherman Theatre,** Senghennydd Road (© **029/2064-6900;** www.shermantheatre.co.uk), is on the campus of the University of Wales. It has two auditoriums—the Main Theatre and the more intimate Arena Theatre. More than 600 performances a year are staged here, including drama, dance, and Welsh folkloric performances. The box office is open Monday through Saturday from 10am to 8pm (until 6pm if no performance is scheduled). The cost for most tickets is £9 ($17) for adults or £6 ($11) for students and children. Bus: 70, 78, 80, or 82.

Finally, **Chapter,** Market Road, in Canton (© **029/2030-4400;** www.chapter. org), is an arts center complete with a theater; two movie facilities; three galleries and artists' studios; video, photography, and silk-screen workshops; a dance studio; a book shop; two bars; and a restaurant. Its box office is open Monday through Friday from 10am to 8:30pm, Saturday and Sunday from 1:30 to 8:30pm. Take bus no. 17, 18, or 31.

PUBS & BARS

A local favorite, **Angel Tavern,** in the Angel Hotel, Castle Street (© **029/2064-9200**), is still charming after all these years. Ales are drawn by hand pumps from the cellars of this traditional tavern, walled with red brick, its ceiling supported by heavy wooden beams. Facing Cardiff Castle, it is on the corner of Castle and Westgate streets. Bars meals are served at lunch—not in the actual tavern but in the street-level cocktail lounge of the hotel. Take bus no. 1 or 2.

Another traditional favorite is **The Park Vaults,** in The Thistle Hotel, Park Lane (© **029/2038-3471**), a cozy pub and bistro format. Stained-glass windows evoke Victorian nostalgia. You can also come here for a pub dinner. Bus: 8 or 9.

More modern and attracting a younger crowd, **Salt,** Stuart Street, Mermaid Quay (© **029/2049-4375**), is a two-story bar that serves some of the best mixed drinks in town—from champagne cocktails to red wine. Bus: 8.

A hangout for rugby fans, **City Arms,** 10 Quay St. (corner of Quay and Womanby sts.; © **029/2022-5258**), attracts sports enthusiasts, and is the most likely venue for any pop star or celebrity likely to be visiting Wales. Bus: 50, 51, 52, 70, 71, or 72.

GAY CLUBS

Exit Club, 48 Charles St. (© **029/2064-0101**), is a hot spot that is usually crowded and cruisy. Its precincts accommodate the Richard Burton or Dylan Thomas wannabes of the 21st century. Surveying the dance floor of heavy drinking hot guys, one patron claimed, "You want to get 'em before they're too pissed." There's no cover before 9:30pm; after that hour, you pay from £2 to £3 ($3.70–$5.55). Open Monday through Saturday from 6pm to 1am, Sunday from 6pm to 2am.

2 Abergavenny

262km (163 miles) W of London; 78km (49 miles) NE of Swansea; 49km (31 miles) NE of Cardiff

This flourishing market town of nearly 10,000 people is called "the Gateway to Wales," and it's certainly the gateway to the Brecon Beacons, which lie to the west. The Welsh word *aber* means the mouth of a river, and Abergavenny lies at the mouth of the River Gavenny, where it joins the River Usk. The town is in a valley with mountains and hills spread around it. Humankind has found this a good, sometimes safe place to live for some 5,000 years, as revealed by archaeological finds from the late Neolithic Age. The Romans established one of their forts here; centuries later a Norman castle was built nearby.

Try to be in Abergavenny on a market day. On Tuesday and Friday, you can shop among stalls carrying a wide selection of goods, ranging from antiques, food, and clothing to furniture and junk. On Tuesday, there is also a livestock market.

Abergavenny is renowned as a center for outdoor holiday activities, including pony trekking, hill walking and climbing, golfing, hang gliding, and fishing. A Leisure Centre provides for indoor sports. The tourist office (see below) keeps an up-to-date list of activities available at any season.

ESSENTIALS

GETTING THERE   The town is linked by rail to both Shrewsbury and Hereford (in England) and to Newport, a distance of 31km (19 miles) to the southwest, in Wales. From Newport, rail connections are made to Cardiff, Bristol, and London. The Abergavenny Rail Station is on Station Road, off Monmouth Road. It usually takes 2½ hours if you're arriving from London. For rail information and schedules, call © **0845/748-4950** or visit www.railtrack.co.uk.

The no. X3 or X4 Stagecoach Bus from Hereford arrives four times per day. Bus no. 21 arrives six times per day from Brecon, and bus nos. 20 and 21 arrive at the rate of twelve per day from Newport (from which connections are made to Cardiff). For information, call © **0870/608-2608,** or visit www.stagecoach bus.com.

If driving, from Hereford, take the A465 southwest; from Cardiff take the M4 motorway east toward London, but cut north along the A4042 toward Abergavenny.

VISITOR INFORMATION   The town's Civic Society has laid out a **Town Trail,** listing buildings and other points of interest.

From Easter to September, for information about Abergavenny and its environs, get in touch with the **tourist information center,** Swan Meadows, Monmouth Road (© **01873/857588**). Open April through October daily from 10am to 6pm; November through March daily from 10am to 1pm and 2 to 4pm.

SEEING THE SIGHTS

Only fragments of the 12th-century **Abergavenny Castle,** on Castle Street, remain, but a gruesome segment of its history is remembered. An early owner of the fortress, the Norman knight William de Braose, angered at the slaying of his brother-in-law by Welsh lords of Gwent, invited a group of them to dinner and had them murdered as they sat unarmed at his table. Visitors today fare better in visiting. Admission is free, and it's open daily from dawn to dusk.

The **Abergavenny Museum,** Castle Street (© **01873/854282**), is in a house attached to the 19th-century hunting lodge on the castle grounds. The museum contains archaeological artifacts, farming tools, and a fascinating collection of old prints and pictures. A Welsh farmhouse kitchen and the contents of an old saddler's shop are on display. Admission is free. Open March through October Monday through Saturday from 11am to 1pm and 2 to 5pm, Sunday from 2 to 5pm. November through February, Monday through Saturday from 11am to 1pm and 2 to 4pm.

St. Mary's Parish Church, Monk Street, is all that's left of a 12th-century Benedictine priory church. Little remains of the original Norman structure, as the building was redone from the 13th to the 15th century. It is believed that Cromwell's troops, which were billeted in Abergavenny for a while during the siege of Raglan Castle, did some damage to the church and its tombs. In the Herbert Chapel are a number of sarcophagi of lords of Abergavenny and family members, with requisite effigies on top. The oldest brass memorial in the church records a death in 1587. The 15th-century Jesse Tree in the Lewis Chapel is an unusual, 3.4m (10-ft.) long woodcarving portraying Christ's family tree growing out of the body of Jesse, father of David. There is also a Norman font, as well as some 14th-century oak choir stalls. In spite of vandalism that has been committed in the church throughout the centuries, the building is kept open most days for worship and inspection. The hours will be found in the porch or at the parking lot hut. For information, call the vicarage (© **01873/853168**).

WHERE TO STAY

Bear 🅐 (Value   This 15th-century coaching inn is hailed for its evocative atmosphere, bedrooms, and cuisine—a winning combination. About 8km (5 miles) northwest of Abergavenny in a charming little town, the hotel has been upgraded to keep up with modern times, but the old character has been respected—for example, some units with four-posters also have Jacuzzi tubs. In summer, a secluded outdoor garden is the place to sit and watch a Welsh twilight. A recent addition is a range of newly installed superior bedrooms bordering a courtyard; this annex was designed in the style of an old Tudor manse. Or you can opt for the individually furnished bedrooms in the main building, which come in a variety of styles. The standard rooms, the least desirable, are at the front of the hotel, and have showers, whereas the deluxe and executive rooms are larger and have shower-bath combos or Jacuzzis with separate shower stalls. The restaurant is always winning awards for best hotel pub grub in Great Britain or else AA rosettes for a "taste of Wales." Fresh local produce and homegrown herbs are used—try the Welsh lamb or salmon from the Usk and Wye rivers.

High Street, Crickhowell, Powys NP8 1BW. © 01873/810408. Fax 01873/811696. www.bearhotel.co.uk. 34 units. £79–£102 ($146–$189) double; £149 ($276) suite. Rates include breakfast. AE, MC, V. On A40 between Abergavenny and Brecon. **Amenities:** Restaurant; bar; rooms for those with limited mobility. *In room:* TV, dataport, coffeemaker, hair dryer.

Llansantffraed Court 🅐🅐   You'll have to drive 16km (10 miles) from Abergavenny to reach it, but this hotel is worth the journey. As you head up the drive, an impressive redbrick country house in William and Mary style comes into view. It's set on extensive and well-kept grounds with a small lake, everything opening onto distant views of the Brecon Beacons. The midsize bedrooms are comfortably furnished, each with en-suite bathrooms, and some offer panoramic views of the surrounding mountains. Some of the accommodations contain four-posters, and a number of units are set aside for nonsmokers. The dining room, serving Welsh and French cuisine, is decorated with oak beams and oil paintings and has an outdoor terrace.

Llanvihangel Gobion, Abergavenny NP7 9BA. © 01873/840678. Fax 01873/840674. www.llch.co.uk. 21 units. £92–£102 ($170–$189) double; £160 ($296) suite. Rates include breakfast. AE, DC, MC, V. At A465/A40

Abergavenny intersection take B4598 signposted to Usk. Continue toward Raglan until you see the hotel. **Amenities:** Restaurant; bar; room service (7am–11pm); laundry service; dry cleaning; rooms for those with limited mobility. *In room:* TV, dataport, minibar, coffeemaker, iron, trouser press.

WHERE TO DINE

Walnut Tree Inn ⊀ WELSH/ITALIAN   This popular restaurant wins praise all over the British Isles—and rightly so. Francesco Mattioli and Stephen Terry are the dynamic duo on the Welsh culinary landscape. Energetic and enthusiastic, they cultivate an inventive and fresh cuisine. Come here for full-flavored dishes that may include grilled breast of wood pigeon, tagliolini with lobster and fresh basil, or roast cod with sautéed pumpkin and Italian lentils. Many British dishes are classic and ever so appealing to the palate, including roast breast of Gressinham duck with braised red cabbage and blackberry sauce or roast woodcock with a red wine *jus* and bread sauce.

Llandewi Skirrid. ⓒ 01873/852797. Reservations recommended. Main courses £6.75–£22 ($12–$40). MC, V. Tues–Sun noon–2:30pm; Tues–Sat 7–10pm. Closed 2 weeks at Christmas. Take B4521 4.8km (3 miles) northeast of Abergavenny.

SIDE TRIPS FROM ABERGAVENNY
TINTERN ABBEY

The famous Wye Valley winds north from Chepstow, passing by the Lancaut Peninsula at the foot of the Windcliffe, a 243m (800-ft.) hill with striking views over the Severn estuary and the English border as far as the south part of the Cotswolds. About 1.6km (1 mile) or so farther north, you come to the little village of Tintern.

Now in magnificent ruins, **Tintern Abbey** ⊀⊀ (ⓒ **01291/689251**) is in the exact center of this riverside village and is the focal point of the town. The Cistercian abbey is one of the greatest monastic ruins of Wales, and it was only the second Cistercian foundation in Britain and the first in Wales. The abbey was founded in 1131 and was active until the dissolution of the monasteries by King Henry VIII. Most of the standing structure dates from the 13th century, when the abbey was almost entirely rebuilt. It became one of the richest and most important monastic houses in Wales. Wordsworth was one of the first to appreciate the serene beauty of the abbey remains, as his poetry attests. There is ample parking quite near the entrance, and refreshments are available nearby.

Admission is £3 ($5.55) for adults, and £2.80 ($5.20) for children; family ticket £8.50 ($16). Open April, May, and October daily from 9:30am to 5pm; June through September daily from 9:30am to 6pm; November through March Monday through Saturday from 9:30am to 4pm and Sunday from 11am to 4pm.

To get here from Abergavenny, take the A40 east to Monmouth, from which you can connect with the A466 south along the trail of Offa's Dyke to Tintern.

3 Brecon & Brecon Beacons National Park

275km (171 miles) W of London; 64km (40 miles) N of Cardiff

This busy little market town is the main base for touring Brecon Beacons National Park. Brecon, situated where the Usk and Honddu rivers meet, is the center of a farming section.

The Romans thought the area was a good place for a military encampment to discourage the Celts, and in A.D. 75 they built a fort, **Y Gaer,** about 4km (2½ miles) west of the present town. To get to Y Gaer, you walk across private farm fields. You can look around for no admission charge.

Brecon Castle, built in 1093, is practically nonexistent, but it was militarily important when Llewelyn the Great and later Owain Glyndwr were battling against outsiders who wanted sovereignty in Wales. However, at the close of the Civil War after Cromwell's visitations, the people of Brecon, tired of centuries of strife, pulled the castle down. All that's left is a section of wall joined to the Castle of Brecon Hotel and the Ely Tower, named for the bishop of Ely imprisoned there by Richard III. Access to the ruins is without charge, and there's no time limit on when it can be viewed. Oddly, it lies on the grounds of the Castle of Brecon Hotel and requires a transit through the hotel lobby to view it.

Of special interest is the fortified red sandstone priory church of St. John the Evangelist, with its massive tower, now the **Cathedral of Swansea and Brecon,** Priory Hill (© **01874/623857**). It stands high above the River Honddu. The oldest parts of the cathedral date from the 12th century. It's open daily from 8am to 6:30pm and admission is free.

ESSENTIALS

GETTING THERE   Go from Cardiff to Merthy Tydfil, then take one of the **Stagecoach Red and White Buses** (© **0870/608-2608;** www.stagecoachbus. com) on through the park to the town of Brecon, which is the last stop on the bus line. Monday through Saturday, five buses make the connection. Travel time is about 90 minutes. From Cardiff, motorists can head north along A470.

VISITOR INFORMATION   The **Brecon Tourist Information Office** is in the Cattle Market Car Park (© **01874/622485**). Open daily from 9:30am to 5:30pm in summer; Monday to Saturday 9:30am to 5pm and Sunday 10am to 4pm in winter.

SEEING THE SIGHTS

BRECON BEACONS NATIONAL PARK ✿✿✿

Brecon Beacons National Park comprises 835 sq. km (519 sq. miles) of land from the Black Mountains in the west. National parks in the British Isles are maintained differently from those in the United States. Here people own land, live, and work within the park boundaries, though the landscape is safeguarded, and access to the park area is provided.

The park takes its name from the mountain range in the center of the park area. Pen y Fan, the highest peak in the range, rises to nearly 914m (3,000 ft.). The park contains sandstone moors covered with bracken, and limestone crags with wooded gorges. Vast stretches of open common land lie in pastoral country. Farming is the main industry of the park. You can enjoy drives over the mountains, but walking or pony trekking are the best ways to explore the park.

There are nature reserves, a mountain center, and 51km (32 miles) of canal. The limestone area contains Britain's deepest cave system. A number of ancient monuments and historic buildings lie within the park boundaries.

For information regarding the park and its facilities, call one of the **National Park Information Centres,** the main one being at Wharton Mount, Glamorgan Street, in Brecon (© **01874/624437**). Other information numbers include © **01873/857588** in Abergavenny, and © **01550/720693** in Llandovery.

The park's southern boundary is only 40km (25 miles) from Cardiff, 23km (14 miles) from Swansea, and 16km (10 miles) from Newport. Abergavenny lies on the eastern boundary.

Run by the Brecon Beacons National Park Committee, the **Mountain Centre,** near Libanus (© **01874/623366;** www.brecon-beacons.com), 8km (5 miles) southwest of Brecon, offers a good point from which to begin your tour of the park. The center a spacious lounge, displays explaining the major points of interest, talks and films, an informative staff, a picnic area, a refreshments buffet, and toilets. Wheelchairs have access to all parts of the building.

The center is open daily, except Christmas Day, from 9:30am; the buffet is open from 10:30am (10am July–Aug). Closing times vary according to the time of year. The center shuts its doors at 5pm in March through June, September, and October; at 6pm in July and August; and at 4:30pm from November to February. Closing is a half hour later on Saturday, Sunday, and bank holidays from April to June and in September. The buffet closing time varies, so check when you go to the center.

Over the millennia, the force of flowing water has carved underground caverns through the extensive limestone regions in the southwestern portions of the Brecon Beacons National Park. Experienced cavers can explore many of these by making arrangements with one of the caving clubs, through the National Park Information Centres. However, only the **Dan-yr-Ogof Showcaves,** Abercraf (© **01639/730801;** www.dan-yr-ogof-showcaves.co.uk), are open to the general public, including children. Midway between Brecon and Swansea on the A4067, this is the largest showcave complex in western Europe. Visitors are able to follow dry, firm walkways to see stalagmite and stalactite formations under floodlights. Tours through Dan-yr-Ogof, Cathedral Cave, Bone Cave, and the Dinosaur Park last about 2½ hours. The complex is open from Easter to the end of October, daily from 10am to 3pm (it closes at 5pm in high season). The charge is £8.50 ($16) for adults and £5.50 ($10) for children (accompanied children under age 4 are admitted free). There is a restaurant, craft shop, museum, dry-ski slope, and information center at the caves.

WHERE TO STAY & DINE
EXPENSIVE

Llangoed Hall 🏵🏵🏵 Sir Bernard Ashley, widower of Laura Ashley, presides over one of the great country houses of Wales. In the Wye Valley, 18km (11 miles) northeast of Brecon, the house opens onto panoramic views of the Black Mountains. The Welsh Parliament, so it is said, stood on this site 1,400 years ago. A former Jacobean manor house, it was redesigned in 1912 by the celebrated architect Cloug Williams-Ellis, who had wanted to create the aura of a great Edwardian country house party. Sir Bernard has gone even beyond the Edwardians in this fantasy, creating grand luxury with the help of floor-to-ceiling Laura Ashley fabrics, of course—that and his own personal art collection. The individually decorated bedrooms and suites are spacious and elegant, as are the bathrooms. All offer extras such a fresh fruit, sherry, and a small selection of books. A library in the south wing is the only surviving part of the original Jacobean mansion that stood on this spot in 1632.

Llyswen, Brecons, Powys LD3 0YP. © **01874/754525.** Fax 01874/754545. www.llangoedhall.com. 23 units. £200 ($370) double; £360 ($666) suite. Rates include breakfast. AE, DC, MC, V. On A470, 3.2km (2 miles) northwest of Llyswen. **Amenities:** Restaurant; 2 outdoor tennis courts; 24-hr. room service; laundry service; dry cleaning; fishing; nonsmoking rooms. *In room:* TV, coffeemaker, hair dryer.

MODERATE

Felin Fach Griffin 🏵 *(Finds)* This is an exceptional discovery for Wales, much of it looking as if you'd wandered back through a time capsule. Old-fashioned though it may look, it is absolutely comfortable and up-to-date. Crisp white linen and soft goose-down pillows top ornate beds placed on stripped floorboards, and will make you want to linger in bed long into the morning.

Bedrooms are beautifully maintained, quietly elegant, and three have four-poster beds. Each comes with a small, immaculate bathroom.

Felin Facvh (A470, directly east of Brecon), Powys LD3 OUB. ℭ **01874/620111.** Fax 01874/620120. www.eatdrinksleep.ltd.uk. 7 units. £93–£115 ($172–$213). Rates include full breakfast. MC, V. **Amenities:** Restaurant; bar; breakfast-only room service. *In room:* Beverage maker, hair dryer, iron.

Nant Ddu Lodge ⟨Kids⟩   This is your best bet for staying in the heart of the Brecon Beacons National Park. Originally built as a shooting lodge during the 19th century for Lord Tredegar, its name translates as "Black Stream," but that is hardly meant to suggest pollution, as its situation is idyllic for walking, fishing, and escaping from urban pressures. Though unified with a common hunter's theme, each of the small to midsize bedrooms is different from its neighbor and equipped with tiny bathrooms. The superior rooms offer extras such as bathrobes and wide-screen TVs; a few have four-poster beds. There are panoramic views of the mountains from all the bedrooms. Family rooms with sofa beds are available. In 2003, the hotel opened a spa offering all of the latest treatments.

Cwm Taf, Brecon, CF Powys CF48 2HY. ℭ **01685/379111.** Fax 01685/377088. www.nant-ddu-lodge.co.uk. 28 units. £80–£100 ($148–$185) double. Rates include buffet breakfast. AE, MC, V. Beside the A470, 8km (5 miles) north of Merthyr Tydfil and 19km (12 miles) south of Brecon. **Amenities:** Bistro; bar; indoor heated pool; breakfast-only room service; health club; spa; sauna. *In room:* TV/VCR, coffeemaker, hair dryer, trouser press.

INEXPENSIVE

Canter Selyf ⟨Finds⟩   One of the historic properties of Brecon, this town house dates from the 17th century. Close to St. Mary's Church, this Georgian house is one of the most convenient locations in town. When viewed only from the front, the property looks rather small, but it's a nice spread, complete with a large walled garden enclosed by a Norman wall. Much of the 17th century architecture remains inside, although subsequent additions were made in the following century. The bedrooms still have their former beamed ceilings, cast-iron beds, and Georgian fireplaces, along with private bathrooms with showers. Guests meet fellow guests in the formal sitting room. Smoking is not permitted.

5 Lion St., Brecon, Powys LD3 7AU. ℭ **01874/622904.** Fax 01874/622315. www.cantreselyf.co.uk. 3 units. £55–£65 ($102–$120) double. Rates include full breakfast. No credit cards. Closed Dec. **Amenities:** Restaurant; bar; limited room service; laundry service. *In room:* TV, beverage maker, hair dryer, iron/ironing board.

Griffin Inn ⟨Value⟩   Though hardly in the league of Llangoed, this little oasis is infinitely more affordable. Outside Brecon, it was originally constructed in the 15th century as a cider house. Today it's an inn popular with fishermen who come hoping to get lucky while casting into the River Wye. Behind its ivy-covered facade, four generations of the Stockton family have received guests into their tidy bedrooms. The inn itself is one of the oldest in the Upper Wye Valley, and lake fishing, pony trekking, and hiking are part of the summer fun in the Brecon Beacons. A few years ago, the Griffin was voted "Britain's Pub of the Year," so drinking is still big here and the food is popular with locals. But we gravitate to the small to midsize bedrooms and their somewhat cramped baths, soaking up the atmosphere of old beams and exposed stonework.

Llyswen, near Brecon, Powys LD3 OUR. ℭ **01874/754241.** Fax 01874/754592. 7 units. £50 ($93) double. MC, V. Lies 16km (10 miles) northeast of Brecon at the junction of A4079 and A470. **Amenities:** Restaurant. *In room:* TV, coffeemaker.

Three Cocks Hotel ⟨Value⟩   This 15th-century inn, surrounded by the countryside of the Brecon Beacons, is one of the best-known little inns of Wales. It deserves its fame. As you pass through the tiny hamlet of Three Cocks, don't blink, or you might miss the inn—a stone building, which over the years has incorporated the trunk of a live tree into one of its walls. The inn and its elegant restaurant are operated by Mr. and Mrs. Michael Winstone, who extend very cordial hospitality to their guests. Downstairs is an elegant paneled drawing room, and upstairs are midsize bedrooms that have modern furnishings and well-kept bathrooms. Throughout the inn is richly furnished with antiques, Oriental rugs, and oil paintings, with log fires burning on chilly nights. There's no TV in the rooms, but you can find one in a separate sitting room.

Three Cocks, Brecon, Powys LD3 0SL. © **01497/847215.** Fax 01497/847339. www.threecockshotel.com. 7 units. £70 ($130) double. Rates include Welsh breakfast. MC, V. On A438, 18km (11 miles) northeast of Brecon and 6.4km (4 miles) southwest of Hay-on-Wye. **Amenities:** Restaurant. *In room:* No phone.

4 Swansea & Gower Peninsula ★

307km (191 miles) W of London; 64km (40 miles) W of Cardiff; 131km (82 miles) W of Bristol

Vikings, Normans, English, Welsh, industry, seaport activity, holiday magic, and cultural prominence—all have combined to make the Swansea of today. It's tough, bold, and fun. Parks abound, and the tender loving care bestowed on them has caused Swansea to be a winner of the "Wales in Bloom" award year after year.

Swansea entered recorded history some 800 years ago, bearing a Viking name believed derived from "Sweyn's ey," or Sweyn's island. The Sweyn in question may well have been Sweyn Forkbeard, king of Denmark (987–1014), known to have been active in the Bristol Channel. Normans founded the marcher lordship of Gower, with its capital at Swansea, and a small trading community grew up here, as sea-going business, including coal exportation, became important through the Middle Ages. In the early 18th century at the town at the mouth of the River Tawe (Swansea's Welsh name is Abertawe), copperworks began to be built, and soon it was the copper capital of the world, as well as a leading European center for zinc refining, tin plating, steel making, and many chemical activities.

This "ugly, lovely city," as native son Dylan Thomas described it, has today pretty well obliterated the ugliness. Devastation of the town center by German air raids during World War II led to complete rebuilding. Traditional industries in the Lower Swansea Valley have vanished, leaving economic woes and an industrial wasteland. Reclamation and redevelopment, however, have long been underway. The leveling of old mine tips and slag heaps and the planting of trees in their stead points to a more attractive Swansea for both today and tomorrow. Clean industries are coming in, but they are being placed out in wooded areas and suitable industrial parks, and they do not cast a pall over the city. Nonetheless, if your time clock allows for only one of the major cities of South Wales, make it Cardiff.

ESSENTIALS

GETTING THERE   Trains arrive from both Cardiff and from London every 60 minutes throughout the day. The trip takes about an hour from Cardiff, about 3 hours from London. The Swansea Railway Station is on High Street. For reservations and information, call © **0845/748-4950** or visit www.raitrack.co.uk.

   National Express Coaches (© **0870/580-8080;** www.nationalexpress.com) arrive in Swansea about once an hour from London, Manchester, Birmingham, and Cardiff. From Cardiff, motorists can continue west along the M4.

VISITOR INFORMATION   The **City of Swansea Information Centre,** Plymouth Street (© **01792/468321**), is open year-round, Monday through Saturday from 9:30am to 5:30pm. Between June and September, it's also open every Sunday from 9:30am to 5:30pm. Its services are duplicated within

Swansea

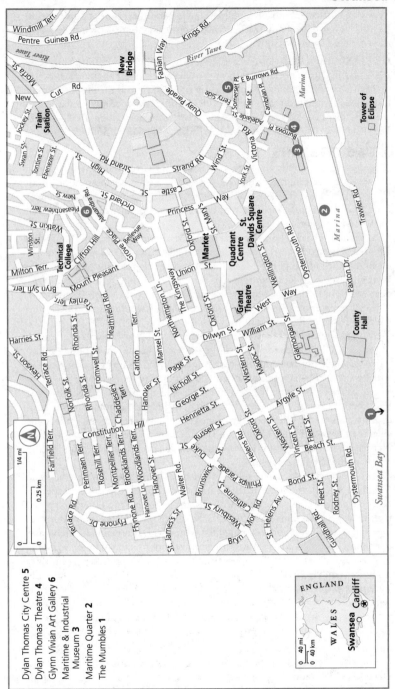

Dylan Thomas City Centre **5**
Dylan Thomas Theatre **4**
Glynn Vivian Art Gallery **6**
Maritime & Industrial Museum **3**
Maritime Quarter **2**
The Mumbles **1**

Swansea's historic suburb of Mumbles at the **Mumbles Tourist Information Centre,** Dunns Lake (© **01792/361302**), open only from March to October, daily from 9:30am to 5:30pm.

GETTING AROUND   Swansea is serviced by a good bus network, buses leaving from the Quadrant Bus Station, at the Quadrant Shopping Centre. Bus nos. 4, 4A, 110, or 120 link the train station at 35 High St. and the bus station. For bus schedules and information, call © **0870/608-2608** or visit www.stagecoach bus.com. Because distances are usually short, consider calling a taxi—either **Data Cabs** (© **01792/474747**) or **A.A. Taxis** at (© **01792/360600**).

SEEING THE SIGHTS

In a once-dirty waterfront area, a **Maritime Quarter** has emerged. Lying between the city center and the seafront, it is centered on the historic South Dock and its Half Tide Basin and is complete with urban villages and a modern marina on the Swansea Yacht Haven. Open spaces, a promenade, and a sea wall round out the scene.

A statue of Dylan Thomas stands in the Maritime Quarter, and the **Dylan Thomas Theatre** is nearby at 7 Gloucester Place (© **01792/473238;** www. dylanthomastheatre.org.uk). Many different types of plays are presented here (look for listings in local newspapers), not just works by Dylan Thomas. The poet was born in the Uplands, a residential area of Swansea, at 5 Cwmdonkin Dr., a steep street off Walter Road. You can walk in **Cwmdonkin Park** close by, which the poet made famous in his writings.

Swansea is one of the few Welsh cities to have a beach within walking distance of the center. A **promenade** leads all the way to Oystermouth, 6.4km (4 miles) away, although you can drive the route on the A4067. Along the way you pass a rugby and cricket ground and the entrance to the city's largest park, Singleton. About halfway down the bay is a nine-hole golf course and a well-equipped resort beach, in an area known as Blackpill. It includes the entrances to the city's country park, Clyne Valley, and the Clyne Gardens. Before long you come to the villages of Westcross and Norton, and then comes Oystermouth, which has a Norman castle renowned for its imposing position on a headland commanding a view of the bay and Swansea.

Eight kilometers (5 miles) south of Swansea, across Swansea Bay, lies **The Mumbles** ⊕. It has been compared to the Bay of Naples because of its shape and beauty, especially after dark. This former fishing village has two faces (both pleasing): By day it has a tranquil atmosphere, but when the sun goes down Mumbles bursts into action and becomes a nightlife center, with crowded pubs, clubs, and restaurants. Mumbles has been attracting tourists since Victorian times, when the handsome pier was built, as in most British sea towns. It protrudes 274m (900 ft.) from Mumbles Head into the bay and affords sweeping views. Away from the seafront, you can see tiny fishermen's cottages built into the limestone rock. Souvenirs and examples of local crafts are in shops that cling to the hillside. Yachting, swimming, fishing, beach games, and bowling are enjoyed here.

Glynn Vivian Art Gallery ⊕(Finds)   Founded in 1911, although little known, this gallery is one of the treasure troves of art in Wales. It was created by Richard Glynn Vivian, scion of a copper industrialist family. An inveterate traveler and art collector, he wanted to pass on his treasures to the world. The special reason to visit is to see the 20th-century collection of Welsh artists, including Ceri Richards, Josef Herman, and Evan Walters. We are especially fond of Alfred Janes's penetrating portrait of Dylan Thomas from 1964. There are also displays of elegant porcelain and pottery, both European and Asian. On-site is an unusual gift shop with a selection of original works by Welsh artists, including ceramics, glass, and jewelry.

Alexandra Rd. ⓒ **01792/516903.** Free admission. Tues–Sun 10am–5pm.

WHERE TO STAY

Beaumont   In its moderate-price bracket, this is the town's leading choice, lying only a short walk from the town center and a 10-minute taxi ride from the rail depot. A family run hotel, it looks like a large private village, and its public rooms are done with traditional styling and old-fashioned warmth, evoking the comforts of a middle-class Welsh home. The midsize bedrooms have been furnished with comfort and style in mind, and the bathrooms with tub or shower are well organized with tidy cubicles. The executive rooms are larger and have sunken tubs in the tiled bathrooms; some have four-poster beds. There is a conservatory-style restaurant for home-cooked Welsh, Italian, and French fare.

72–73 Walter Rd., Swansea SA1 4QA. ⓒ **01792/643956.** Fax 01792/643044. www.beaumonthotel.co.uk. 16 units. £70–£90 ($130–$167) double. AE, DC, MC, V. **Amenities:** Restaurant; bar; limited room service; non-smoking rooms. *In room:* TV, dataport, coffeemaker, trouser press.

Fairyhill 𝓡   Sometimes the most fun in Swansea is leaving it. If you want to escape from the world, head to this stone-built 18th-century manor set on 10 hectares (25 acres) of wooded grounds that also hold a lake and a fishing stream. It's an ideal base for exploring not only Swansea but also the little populated Gower Peninsula that juts out into the British Channel west of Swansea and offers a good deal of natural beauty. After passing through a sumptuously appointed lounge, you are directed to one of the individually styled bedrooms—most often medium-size with a snug but efficient bathroom. Crackling log fires and deep-cushioned sofas create the aura of a cozy, snug country house. A real "taste of Wales" emerges from the menu. *Note:* Children under 8 are not accepted as guests. Smoking is not allowed in the property.

Reynoldston SA3 1BS. ⓒ **01792/390139.** Fax 01792/391358. www.fairyhill.net. 8 units. £140–£245 ($259–$453). Rates include breakfast. MC, V. Outside Reynoldston off the A4118 from Swansea (18km/11 miles) away. **Amenities:** Restaurant; bar; massage; limited room service. *In room:* TV, coffeemaker, iron/ironing board.

Swansea Marriott 𝓡𝓡   This is the town's premier choice—the best amenities, the most dramatic location, and the most luxurious bedrooms. The four-story structure lies on the marina, opening onto panoramic views over the bay. By Swansea standards, it is large and bustling, attracting an equal mix of business clients and tourists. The hotel offers spacious bedrooms and roomy baths, each immaculate and comfortable.

Maritime Quarter, Swansea SA1 3SS. (℃) **800/228-9290** in the U.S. and Canada, or 01792/642020. Fax 01792/ 650345. www.marriott.com. 117 units. £100–£144 ($185–$266) double. Rates include breakfast. AE, DC, MC, V. **Amenities:** Restaurant; bar; indoor heated pool; health club; Jacuzzi; sauna; limited room service; laundry service; dry cleaning; rooms for those with limited mobility; nonsmoking rooms. *In room:* A/C, TV, dataport, minibar, coffeemaker, hair dryer, iron/ironing board, trouser press.

Windsor Lodge Hotel   Architecturally undistinguished, this is a nonetheless welcoming family-run hotel, close to the town center. It offers good value and cozy bedrooms with decent furnishings and tidy bathrooms for the night. The building itself is 2 centuries old and has been sheltering wayfarers to Swansea for decades. You never know who is likely to turn up. We once encountered former President Jimmy Carter and Rosalynn Carter leaving the inn after having enjoyed a lunch here. Your hosts, Pam and Ron Rumble, maintain medium-size bedrooms that are well cared for and provide a good night's sleep. The decoration is modern, and the location is about a 5-minute walk to the train station.

Mount Pleasant, Swansea SA1 6EG. (℃) **01792/642158.** Fax 01792/648996. www.windsor-lodge.co.uk. 19 units. £65–£75 ($120–$139) double. Rates include breakfast. AE, DC, MC, V. **Amenities:** Restaurant; bar; limited room service. *In room:* TV, coffeemaker.

WHERE TO DINE

La Braseria SPANISH   No, this is not Madrid, although this Spanish bodega (in Swansea, of all places) evokes sunny Spain, and is only a 5-minute walk from the train station. It's a marvelous change of pace when you've had too many leeks and too much Welsh lamb. The food, prepared daily from fresh ingredients, complements the list of Spanish wines and champagne; this is not the place for "lager louts." Come here for the town's best chargrilled meats. Tossed on that grill is everything from tender suckling pig to great chunks of beef to ostrich. Flavors are straightforward here, as the cooks don't like to mess up their grills with a lot of sauces. Likewise, they prepare the catch of the day in the same way, be it shark, bass, or snapper. Specific choices change according to the seasons, the availability of ingredients, and the inspirations of the chefs.

28 Wind St. (℃) **01792/469683.** Reservations recommended. Main courses £6–£19 ($11–$35); fixed-price 2-course lunch £8.50 ($16). AE, DC, MC, V. Mon–Sat noon–2:30pm and 7–11:30pm.

Didier & Stephanie (★ (Value CONTINENTAL/WELSH   This eatery despite is known for its good food and good value. The restaurant is about a 3-minute walk west of the center in a fully renovated Victorian house. The restaurant is to be lauded for its search for market-fresh ingredients and the deft preparation in the kitchen. Their inspiration is ever changing but reflected by such dishes as a velvet smooth and tasty pumpkin soup, an unusual dish for Wales. Some of their dishes, such as pigs' trotters, may sound inappropriate but are in fact amazing concoctions filled with delicacy and flavor. Equally good are such long-standing favorites as salmon in a creamy saffron sauce or boeuf bourguignon.

56 St. Helen's Rd. (℃) **01792/655603.** Reservations recommended. Main courses £11–£13 ($20–$24); 2- to 3-course fixed-price lunch £7.70–£13 ($14–$23). AE, MC, V. Tues–Sat noon–2pm and 7–9pm.

SWANSEA AFTER DARK

Long gone are the days when Swansea's nocturnal entertainment consisted of a handful of battered pubs with a jukebox blaring out pre-Beatles tunes. Since the 1990s gentrification of many areas of Swansea's central core, there has been an explosion of nightlife options, many of them focusing on the city's nightlife-related pride and joy—Wind (it rhymes with "wined and dined") Street. The best way to explore the place involves popping in and out of any of the pubs, bars, and shops that appeal to you along this cobble-covered thoroughfare, especially on evenings when the City Council has blocked off traffic, transforming it into a pedestrian-only walkway that—on weekend evenings—becomes very crowded.

Some of our favorites include **The Bank Statement,** 57–58 Wind St. (© **01792/455477**), a pub and restaurant contained within the grandly ornate premises of what was built as a bank during the Victorian age. Nearby is the **Bar SA1,** 2 Wind St. (© **01792/630941**), where a 19th-century storefront serves up copious portions of pub grub, platters, and foaming mugfuls of local ale. More self-consciously trendy, evoking a hip bar in faraway London, is the **No Sign Wine Bar,** 56 Wind St. (© **01792/465300**), where you're likely to see members of the local TV news team, off-duty, sampling whatever French, Chilean, or Californian vintage happens to be uncorked at the moment.

Other streets, each nearby, but none as densely packed as Wind Street with bars and restaurants, also have goodly numbers of nightlife offerings. **O'Brian's Exchange Bar,** 10 The Strand (© **01792/645345**), and **Fagin's,** 63 The Kings Way (© **01792/481951**), offer glimpses of Ireland, with live music and generous amounts of Celtic *joie de vivre.* **The Potters Wheel,** 86–88 The Kings Way (© **01792/465113**), a member of the same chain as the above-mentioned Bank Statement, offers food and drink in a setting that's nostalgically evocative of turn-of-the-20th-century Wales. Business deals by day, and the occasional romantic dialogue by night, tend to be consummated within. **The Hanbury,** 43 The Kings Way (© **01792/641824**), has food that is a cut above what you might expect within most workaday pubs.

In addition to the **Dylan Thomas Theatre** (see above), Swansea has a cultural side as well. **The Grand Theatre,** Singleton Street (© **01792/475715**), adjacent to the Quadrant Shopping Centre, is a Victorian theater that has been refurbished and redeveloped into a multimillion-pound theater complex. The venue hosts international opera, ballet, and theater companies, plus one-night-stands that often feature internationally known entertainers. It also has its own schools of song and dance.

SIDE TRIPS FROM SWANSEA
GOWER PENINSULA ✿

The first area in Britain designated "an area of outstanding natural beauty," Gower is a broad peninsula stretching about 22km (14 miles) from the Mumbles to Worms Head in the west. This attraction begins 6.4km (4 miles) west of Swansea on A4067. The coastline of Gower starts at Bracelet Bay, just around the corner from the Mumbles. You can drive—at least to some parts of the peninsula—but the best way to see its sometimes-rugged, sometimes-flat coast is to walk, even for short distances if you don't have time to make the complete circuit.

There are many and varied beaches on Gower: **Caswell Bay,** with its acres of smooth, golden sand and safe swimming; **Langland,** a family attraction with facilities for golf, swimming, tennis, and surfing; and **Rotherslade,** which at high tide features some of the largest waves around the peninsula crashing onto the shore. Secluded **Pwil-du** is a place to sunbathe in solitude, despite the crowds elsewhere along the coast, and there are numerous other small coves tucked away beneath the cliffs. **Oxwich Bay** is one of the largest on the peninsula, with 4.8km (3 miles) of uninterrupted sand, where you can enjoy beach games, picnics, water-skiing, and sailing. Windsurfing is popular at Oxwich too. Oxwich village, at one end of the bay, is a typical Gower hamlet of cottages and tree-lined lanes. There is a nature reserve here that is home to some rare orchid species.

After the commercial and often-crowded Oxwich beach, you may be happy to see **Slade,** which has to be approached on foot down a steep set of steps. The spotless beach is usually wind-free. Around the next corner, you'll find the villages of **Horton** and **Port Eynon,** with a long, curving beach backed by sand dunes. Refreshments are available on the beach, and the two villages offer nighttime entertainment.

From Port Eynon, a spectacular 7.2km (4½-mile) cliff walk, leads past Culver Hole, Paviland Cave, Mewslade, and Fall Bay to Worms Head and Rhossilli. The **Paviland Caves** can be explored. It was here that human remains have been found dating back 100,000 years. **Worms Head** is a twisted outcrop of rock shaped into the form that sometimes, depending on the tides, looks like a prehistoric worm sticking its head up out of the water. **Rhossilli** is a long, sweeping bay and a beach reached from the treeless village of Rhossilli, with a church and houses perched 61m (200 ft.) up on the cliff tops. This is an international center for hang gliding. Halfway along the beach at Llangennith is the most popular surfing site on the peninsula. Rolling dunes connect it with Broughton Bay and Whitford Sands, and eventually you come to **Penclawdd,** a little village where a centuries-old cockle industry still thrives. If the tide is right, you can see the pickers with their rakes and buckets gleaning the tiny crustaceans from the flats.

Although the coastal attractions are Gower's biggest lure, there are pleasant farms, attractive country roads, and places of interest inland. **Parc le Breos (Giant's Grave)** burial chamber, almost in the center of the peninsula, close to Parkmill on the A4118, is an ancient legacy from Stone Age people. The remains of at least four people were found there. A central passage and four chambers are in a cairn about 21m (70 ft.) long. **Pennard Castle** has suffered under ravages of weather and time, but from the north you can see the curtain wall almost intact. Admission is free.

Weobley Castle, Llawrhidian (© **01792/390012**), on North Gower, is actually a fortified house rather than a castle. There was no space for a garrison, and the rooms were for domestic purposes. On the northern edge of bare upland country, it overlooks the Llanrhidian marshes and the Loughor estuary. There are substantial remains of this 13th- and 14th-century stronghold, and the view is panoramic. Weobley is off the Llanrhidian-Cheriton road, 11km (7 miles) west of Gowerton. It is open daily 9:30am to 6pm. Entrance costs £2 ($3.70) for adults or £1.50 ($2.80) for children ages 16 and under and students.

Even though it is protected from development, Gower has been invaded by caravans (mobile homes), recreational vehicles, beach huts, retirement homes, and bungalows. Nevertheless, you can still find solitude in secluded bays and especially in the center of the peninsula, along the Cefn Bryn ridge or on Rhossilli Down. From the top of **Cefn Bryn,** 185m (609 ft.) above sea level, you can see the entire peninsula and far beyond on clear days. By taking the Green Road, which runs the length of the ridge from Penmaen, you'll find a path about 1km (½ mile) east of Reynoldston which leads to **Arthur's Stone,** a circular burial chamber. The mound of earth that once covered it has been weathered away, but you can see the huge capstone that protected the burial place. From Rhossilli Down, at 192m (632 ft.), the English coast comes into view. Here also are megalithic tombs, cairns, and barrows.

LAUGHARNE: MEMORIES OF DYLAN THOMAS

Laugharne (pronounced *Larne*), 24km (15 miles) east of Tenby, is a hamlet looking out over broad waters. This ancient township on the estuary fed by the River Taf (not be confused with the River Taff in Cardiff) and the River Cywyn, was for centuries a bone of contention between Welsh, English, Cromwellians, and royal supporters. However, it did not come into the limelight of public attention until after the death of its adopted son, Swansea-born Dylan Thomas, and his acclaim as one of the great poets of the 20th century.

Head west from Swansea along the A4070, which becomes the A484 sign-posted north to Carmarthen. Once in Carmarthen, continue west along the A40 to St. Clears where you cut southeast along the A4066 to Laugharne.

Seeing the Sights

Dylan Thomas Boathouse (★), along a little path named Dylan's Walk, is the waterside house where the author lived with his wife, Caitlin, and their children until his death in 1953 during a visit to America. In the boathouse, a white-painted little three-story structure wedged between the hill and the estuary, you can see the family's rooms, photographs, interpretive panels on his life and works, an audio and audiovisual presentation that portrays him reading some of his work, a small art gallery, a book and record shop, and a little tearoom where you can have tea and Welsh cakes while you listen to the poet's voice and look out over the tranquil waters of the wide estuary.

On the way along the path, before you come to the boathouse, there's a little shack where this untidy wretch of a man wrote many of his minor masterpieces. You can't enter it, but you can look through an opening and see his built-in plank desk. Wadded-up scraps of paper on the floor give the feeling that he may have just stepped out to visit a favorite pub. The boathouse is open from April to the first week of October, daily from 10am to 5:30pm (last entrance at 5pm). Admission is £2.95 ($5.45) for adults, £1.25 ($2.30) for children. For more information, call © **01994/427420;** www.dylanthomasboathouse.com.

The poet is buried in the churchyard near the **Parish Church of St. Martin,** which you pass as you drive into town. A simple wooden cross marks his grave. A visit to the church is worthwhile. It dates from the 14th century and is entered through a lych-gate (iron gate), with the entrance to the church guarded by ancient yew trees. Memorial stones and carvings are among the interesting things to see.

Laugharne Castle, a handsome ruin called the home of the "Last Prince of Wales," sits on the estuary at the edge of the town. A castle here, Aber Corran, was first mentioned in 1113, believed to have been built by the great Welsh leader Rhys ap Gruffydd. The present romantic ruins date from Tudor times. Dylan Thomas described the then ivy-mantled castle as a "castle brown as owls."

Where to Dine

Stable Door Restaurant (★) INTERNATIONAL/BRITISH A stable block in days gone by, this is the finest dining choice in the area, serving meals with taste and flair. Recently restored by its owner, Wendy Joy, it operates behind walls that were originally built in the 14th century to house horses Edward I brought from England during the construction of a nearby castle. Later, Oliver Cromwell's forces shot cannon into it when the masters of the castle switched their loyalties back to the Royalist side. Today, it's the most likable and enjoy-able restaurant in the area, serving a menu of fresh ingredients that is varied and artfully prepared. On a windy day, we blew in here with the wind to sample the homemade soup of the day with freshly baked bread, although the Stilton, wal-nut, and port pâté looked equally tempting. The menu suggests that the chef gains inspiration from many countries. From Greece comes an authentic mous-saka, and from Hungary a savory paprika pork with baby mushrooms and sour cream. The Thai vegetable and creamed-coconut curry delighted our party, and was followed by a white- and dark-chocolate layered terrine.

Market Lane. ✆ **01994/427777**. Reservations recommended. Main courses £10–£15 ($19–$28). AE, MC, V. Wed–Sat 7–10pm; Sun 12:30–2pm.

A MUSEUM

National Botanic Museum ✿ Lying 32km (20 miles) northwest of Swansea, this mammoth project is the first modern botanic garden in Britain dedicated to science, education, and leisure. A project costing £45 million, this 229-hectare (568-acre) Regency estate was developed by financier William Paxton in the late 18th century, with walled gardens, lakes, and cascades. Its centerpiece is a magnificent Great Glasshouse, the largest single span greenhouse in the world, blending in naturally with the rolling and bucolic Tywi Valley. The greenhouse is dedicated to threatened Mediterranean climates of the world, and its interior includes a ravine, rock faces, bridges, and waterfalls. Laboratories on the property mean that this garden of Wales is fast becoming the European pacesetter in conservation and reproductive biology.

Middleton Hall, Llanarthne. ✆ **01558/668768**. Admission £6.95 ($13) adults, £3.50 ($6.50) children, £18 ($33) family ticket. Easter–Oct daily 10am–6pm (last admission at 5pm); Nov–Mar daily 10am–4.30pm (last admission at 3.30pm).

5 Pembrokeshire

This county boasts Britain's smallest national park, Pembrokeshire Coast National Park. It's unique in that it extends over cliff and beaches whereas most parks encompass mountains or hill country. The coastline takes in 290km (180 miles) of sheer rugged beauty, with towering cliffs and turbulent waters. **Tenby** is the chief resort for exploring the park, but **Pembroke** and **St. Davids** also make worthy stopovers.

TENBY ✿

The leading resort in Pembrokeshire, Tenby is packed with vacationers during the summer months, but it has a charm and character dating from medieval times, which makes it an interesting place to visit at any time of year. The location is 85km (53 miles) west of Swansea and 148km (92 miles) west of Cardiff.

The main southern rail line through Tenby is run by Wales on Wales of Borders Trains (✆ **0870/900-0773;** www.arrivatrainswales.co.uk). Trains run from Swansea seven times a day Monday through Friday and six times a day on Saturday and Sunday. For information, go to the **Tourist Information Office** at the Croft (✆ **01834/842402**). It is open November through March Monday through Saturday from 10am to 4pm; April and May daily from 10am to 5pm; June through September daily from 10am to 5:30pm (until 9pm July–Aug); and in October Monday through Saturday from 10am to 5pm.

SEEING THE SIGHTS

There was already a Welsh village here when the Normans built **Tenby Castle,** now in ruins. Today the castle attracts interest because of its location on the headland overlooking the town and harbor. The town walls had four gates, one of which, the West Gate, known as Five Arches, remains. The west wall is in good condition. Tenby was also a target during the Civil War.

Tenby Museum and Art Gallery, Castle Hill (✆ **01834/842800**), is housed near the ruins of Tenby Castle. Exhibits cover the geology, archaeology, and natural history of the district, as well as the history of Tenby from the 12th century.

In the art gallery you'll see works by Augustus and Gwen John, and Charles Norris, a local artist of the early 19th century. Open April through October daily from 10am to 5pm; November through March Monday through Friday from 10am to 5pm. Admission costs £2 ($3.70) for adults or £1 ($1.85) for children.

Tudor Merchant's House, Quay Hill (© **01834/842279**), is a beautifully furnished medieval dwelling of the 15th century with a fine Flemish chimney. On three interior walls, paintings with designs similar to Flemish weaving patterns were discovered under years of whitewash. Open April through September Monday, Tuesday, and Thursday to Saturday from 10am to 5pm, and Sunday 1 to 5pm; Monday, Tuesday, Thursday, and Friday 10am to 3pm; noon to 3pm Sunday. Admission costs £2 ($3.70) for adults or £1 ($1.85) for children under age 16.

Tenby's parish church, **St. Mary's,** dates from the 13th century and is the largest parish church in Wales. Giraldus Cambrensis (Gerald the Welshman), a great religious leader of the 13th century, was the first rector. Charging no admission, it is open daily from 8am to 6pm.

In the bay just 3.2km (2 miles) south of Tenby, little **Caldy Island** has long been a Roman Catholic venue. A Celtic monastic cell is believed to have been here, and today it is farmed by Cistercian monks, whose abbey is the island's outstanding attraction. From the 12th century until the dissolution of the monasteries by Henry VIII, a Benedictine priory was here. For the next few centuries, lay people living on the island farmed and quarried limestone until, in 1906, English Benedictines established a community here.

The Benedictines left solid evidence of their occupation: the refectory, gatehouse, and the priory's lodging, which is now used as a guesthouse. In 1929, the Cistercian order took over the island, and today they produce perfume, chocolate, and dairy products, all sold locally. Only male visitors are allowed to enter the monastery, but anyone can visit St. David's Church, the Old Priory, and St. Illtud's Church, with a leaning stone spire. Inside St. Illtud's is a 6th-century Ogham stone, a relic of the time when monks from Ireland came here to establish their religious house. The writing on the Ogham stones was Celtic, which was then translated into Latin by the monks.

Allow about 2 hours for a visit. Access to the island is via a boat that runs only between Easter and late September Monday through Friday from 10am to 4pm. In July and August boats run on Saturday. The vessels depart every 20 minutes; the crossing also takes 20 minutes. A round-trip passage costs £8 ($15) per person, regardless of age. For information about all aspects of the island, including boat access, call © **01834/844453.**

WHERE TO STAY & DINE

Fourcroft Hotel　This is our favorite hotel within the town itself, though we prefer the greater elegance and secluded location of Penally Abbey (see below). On the cliffs above Tenby's sheltered North Beach, the hotel lies a 5-minute walk from the medieval walled town center. Fourcroft forms part of a landmarked Georgian terrace, built more than 150 years ago as summer homes for Londoners. The front bedrooms are generally more spacious and open onto a view of the sea. All the rooms, however, have modern comfort, ranging from midsize to spacious, with roomy, well-kept bathrooms. Guests can use a private garden walk leading to the beach. Other amenities include a human-size chess set, a snooker table, a children's playground, and a restaurant and lounge offering views of the sea.

North Beach, Tenby, Pembrokeshire SA70 8AP. © **01834/842886.** Fax 01834/842888. www.fourcroft-hotel. co.uk. 48 units. £78–£118 ($144–$218) double. AE, DC, MC, V. Limited free parking for 6 cars. **Amenities:** Restaurant; bar; outdoor heated pool; fitness center; Jacuzzi; sauna; limited room service; nonsmoking rooms. *In room:* TV, dataport (in some), coffeemaker, hair dryer.

Penally Abbey ⚑   This country-house hotel—the finest lodging in the area— opens onto a gracious, timeless world. The house is 2 centuries old, but parts of its foundation date from the 6th century, and a flowering garden partially conceals the ruins of St. Deniol's Chapel and a Flemish chimney of a long-ago homestead. The wide-open sea and the still-functioning Cistercian monastery on Caldey Island contribute to the panoramic sweep from the terraces. The house is built of Pembrokeshire stone, containing ogee-headed doors, large square windows, and Gothic-inspired architectural details. The spacious bedrooms are full of character, often enhanced by a four-poster bed. Superior period furnishings are used, and the medium-size bathrooms are immaculately kept. We prefer the rooms in the family house to the newer ones in the annex. There's a dining room of candlelit elegance, serving Welsh and continental cuisine.

Penally, Tenby, Pembrokeshire SA70 7PY. © **01834/843033.** Fax 01834/844714. www.penally-abbey.com. 12 units. £128–£154 ($237–$285) double. Rates include breakfast. Discounts for children sharing parent's room. AE, MC, V. 3.2km (2 miles) southwest of town by A4139. **Amenities:** Restaurant; heated indoor pool; rooms for those with limited mobility; nonsmoking rooms. *In room:* TV, dataport, coffeemaker, minibar, hair dryer.

PEMBROKE

At a point 92km (57 miles) west of Swansea and 156km (97 miles) west of Cardiff, the ancient borough of Pembroke is the most English town in South Wales. It was never really a typical Welsh town, because the Normans and the English had such a strong hold on it. It was settled by English and Flemish people, and its first language was always English. It is visited for two reasons today—to see Pembroke Castle, one of the most impressive in South Wales, and to use it as a base for exploring the national park.

Pembroke received its charter about 1090 from King Henry I and was built around Pembroke Castle, a great fortress set on a rocky spur above the town. The town walls formed the castle's outer ward, and the entire complex, a 22km (14-mile) wide medieval defense system, can still be viewed as a fortified town, with the castle as its hub.

Most trains coming to Pembroke require transfers in Swansea, an hour's travel away. From Swansea, there are six trains per day, and from Swansea, trains fan out to many other points within Britain. For railway information, call © **0870/ 900-0773** or visit www.arrivatrainswales.co.uk.

There are bus connections into Pembroke from Tenby about every hour throughout the day Monday through Saturday, with limited service on Sunday. For bus information about service from Wales into Pembroke, call © **0870/ 608-2608** or visit www.stagecoachbus.com. For information about long-distance bus transit from London or big cities of the English Midlands, call **National Express** at © **0870/580-8080** or visit www.nationalexpress.com.

Pembroke maintains a tourist information office—Pembroke Visitor Centre, Commons Road (© **01646/622388**)—that's open between Easter and October only, daily from 10am to 5:30pm. The rest of the year, people should contact the year-round tourist office in Haverfordwest: The **Tourist Information Centre,** 19 Old Bridge, Haverfordwest (© **01437/763110**). Between November and Easter, it's open Monday through Saturday from 10am to 4pm. From Easter to October, it's open daily from 10am to 5:30pm.

VISITING THE CASTLE

Pembroke Castle 🅐🅐   With its massive keep and walls, the castle still looks formidable, although little inside it remains. It is the oldest castle in West Wales, and for more than 300 years it was the seat of the earls of Pembroke. It was founded by the Montgomerys in 1093, and work began on the fine masonry a century later with the circular great tower, or keep. Dominating the castle, the tower stands 22m (75 ft.) high and is the finest of its type in Britain. Home to such great leaders as Earl William Marshal, regent to Henry III, and to the early Tudors, the castle was also the birthplace of Henry VII ("Harri Tewdwr"). During the Civil War, the castle was held in turn for both Parliament and the king. Cromwell arrived in person to start the siege that led to its final surrender. A vast cavern underneath the castle, called the Wogan, is where food and water were stored. The water defenses of the fortress can still be traced in a millpond on the north and in marshes on the south, outside the walls, as well as in the River Pembroke over which it looms.

Main St. 🅒 **01646/681510.** www.pembrokecastle.co.uk. Admission £3 ($5.55) for adults, £2 ($3.70) students and children. Apr–Sept daily 9:30am–6pm; Mar and Oct daily 10am–5pm; Nov–Feb daily 10am–4pm.

WHERE TO STAY

Coach House Hotel   Built along traditional lines after World War II (though the facade dates back to medieval times), this family room hotel is the best place for lodgings within the town itself, although the Court (see below) at Lamphey is far more elegant. Bedrooms are small to midsize, each comfortably furnished with a little shower-only bathroom. Set on the main thoroughfare of Pembroke, the hotel has a classic facade of black and white. View it mainly as an overnight stopover and don't expect a lot of style.

116 Main St., Pembroke, Pembrokeshire SA71 4HN. 🅒 **01646/684602.** Fax 01646/687456. 14 units. £50–£70 ($93–$130) double. Rates include breakfast. AE, MC, V. **Amenities:** Restaurant; bar; laundry service; dry cleaning nearby (2-min. walk). *In room:* TV, dataport, coffeemaker, hair dryer (available at reception).

Lamphey Court Hotel 🅐   This impressive Georgian mansion set on several acres of landscaped gardens adds a touch of class to the area. This Best Western affiliate is by far the finest place for lodging and dining in the area. Both the public rooms and the bedrooms have a certain grandeur. Many units are spacious enough for family suites. You can stay in the house where the units are more traditional or in an 11-room annex where accommodations may not have tradition but are quite luxurious as well. Local produce is cooked to perfection in the formal restaurant. Bar food is also available.

Lamphey, Pembrokeshire SA71 5NT. 🅒 **800/528-1234** in the U.S., or 01646/672273. Fax 01646/672480. www.lampheycourt.co.uk. 37 units. £105–£145 ($194–$268) double. Rates include breakfast. AE, DC, MC, V. Take A477 to Pembroke, turning left at Village Milton (Lamphey is signposted from there). **Amenities:** Restaurant; bar; heated indoor pool; night-lit tennis court; health club; Jacuzzi; sauna; solarium; limited room service; babysitting; rooms for those with limited mobility; nonsmoking rooms. *In room:* TV, dataport, coffeemaker, hair dryer, trouser press.

WHERE TO DINE

Left Bank CLASSICAL FRENCH   Other than the hotels, this is the only truly good independent restaurant in the area. Right in the heart of town, it was converted from an old bank that went belly up. Invitingly informal with a sympathetic staff, it has a limited menu but one with a fine selection of temptations. Seasonal produce from the Welsh countryside is emphasized. The restaurant offers dishes for vegetarians and a separate area for nonsmokers. The restaurant sits on the left bank of the Cleddau River. Peruse the menu while relaxing in a brasserie-like decor. Tired of the Welsh lamb we saw passing by, we opted for a splendid filet of perfectly cooked Welsh Black beef, which was made all the more inviting with parsnip "crisps" and a well-flavored sauce. Save room for the velvety chocolate mousse with a raspberry sorbet—it's perfect.

63 Main St. ℂ **01646/622333**. Reservations recommended. Fixed-price dinners £24–£28 ($44–$52); lunch main courses around £8 ($15). AE, DC, MC, V. Tues–Sat noon–2:30pm and 7–9:30pm. Closed Dec 24–26 and 2 weeks in Jan.

ST. DAVIDS ✿✿

St. Davids and its environs are in a part of the Pembrokeshire Coast National Park that had inhabitants far back in Paleolithic and Mesolithic times. About 5,000 years ago, New Stone Age (Neolithic) farmers arrived and made their homes here. They didn't leave many traces, but their tombs, or cromlechs, have survived. Many lie on or near St. Davids Head, on Newport Bay, and in the Preseli foothills. Many people believe that the massive blue or foreign stones at Stonehenge came from the Preseli hills more 4,000 years ago. Bronze Age cairns have also been found in the Preseli region.

Iron Age Celts came here, bringing with them from Gaul the beginnings of the Welsh and Gaelic languages. Near St. Davids, walls built during that era are still in use around fields. The Romans ignored this part of Wales, and contacts with Ireland, where fellow Celts lived, were strong. Irish tribes settled in Dyfed in the 3rd and 4th centuries, and then the monastic movement in the early Christian church was brought by Irish and spread by Welsh missionaries, when a vigorous Christian community was established on the St. Davids Peninsula.

The coming of the Normans did not really affect this section of Wales, and Welsh is still widely spoken here. In Tudor times and later, village seafaring came in, taking the mining output of coal, silver, and lead out of small village ports. All this has changed of course, and today the coastal area is a popular holiday territory, with beaches, boating, fishing, and other leisure pursuits taking over.

There's a tremendous allure to one of Britain's most visited surf beaches, **Whitesands** ✿, which is located 3.2km (2 miles) northwest of St. Davids. From June to early September, lifeguards are on duty. Access to this windswept beach is free, but there's a £1.50 ($2.80) charge for parking. Whitesands is noted for some of the consistently best surf waves in Britain. As such, it's the site of surfing exhibitions, where participants arrive from as far away as Huntington Beach, California.

The tiny cathedral city of St. Davids is the birthplace of the patron saint of Wales. The countryside around it is centuries away from the hurry of modern times. The cathedral lies in a grassy hollow of the River Alun, chosen by St. David for its small monastic community because the site was hidden from approach by attackers from land and from sea, yet it was conveniently only a mile from the waters of St. Bride's Bay.

Dewi Sant (later St. David), son of a Welsh chieftain and a Welsh woman named Non, was a Celtic religious leader in the 6th century. The little church he and his monks built where the present cathedral stands was burned down in 645, rebuilt, sacked and burned by the Danes in 1078, and then burned again in 1088. After that, a Norman cathedral was built, its organization changing from the Celtic monastic to diocesan type. The stone village of St. Davids grew up on the hill around the secluded church.

St. Davids lies 117km (73 miles) west of Swansea and 180km (112 miles) west of Cardiff. Motorists take the A487 to reach St. Davids from Haverfordwest, 24km (15 miles) away. **Richard Brothers** (ℂ **01239/613756**) runs buses from Haverfordwest to St. Davids every hour; a one-way ticket costs only £3 or £4 ($5.55–$7.40) round-trip. Haverfordwest is the nearest rail station.

For information, the tourist office is at **The Grove** (© **01437/720392**), open from Easter to October from 9:30am to 5:30pm daily. From November to Easter, open Monday through Saturday from 10am to 4pm.

SEEING THE SIGHTS

With its ornately carved roof and a Norman nave, **St. Davids Cathedral** 🎯🎯, Cathedral Close (© **01437/721885;** www.stdavidscathedral.org.uk), is a magnificent example of medieval religious architecture. Its reliquary contains what are supposed to be the bones of St. David. The nave, a product of 3 centuries of craftsmanship, is a place of medieval beauty. The choir stalls, from the late 15th century, have witty, even lighthearted misericord carvings (those on the hinged seats in the stalls). Visitors are welcome at the cathedral, open Monday, Tuesday, Thursday, and Friday from 8:30am to 6pm, Wednesday and Saturday 8:30am to 4:30pm. Donations are accepted to help with the upkeep of the building.

Associated with the cathedral, the ruins of **Bishop's Palace,** Cathedral Close (© **01437/720517**), stands across the meadow and river, with the gatehouse, battlements, and curtain walls showing how even such a place needed fortification in medieval days. An outstanding sight is the elegant arcaded parapet that runs along both main walls. You can visit the palace ruins; note especially the fine piscina at the east end of the chapel's south wall. The site is open April daily from 9:30am to 5pm; May through September daily from 9:30am to 5pm (until 6pm in June); October daily 9:30am to 5pm; November through March Monday through Saturday from 9:30am to 4pm and Sunday from noon to 2pm. Admission is £2.50 ($4.65) for adults or £2 ($3.70) for children.

The cathedral is no longer Roman Catholic, nor is it Church of England. It is a member of the Church of Wales. When St. David was canonized in the 12th century, the pope declared that two pilgrimages to St. Davids were worth one to Rome, and three pilgrimages equaled one to Jerusalem. You can make such a pilgrimage today; although the pope's promise may not have been honored since the days of Henry VIII, we can promise you an interesting and educational tour of St. Davids peninsula.

Porth Clais, at the mouth of the River Alun about 1.6km (1 mile) south from St. Davids, was the seaport used by travelers to Ireland and elsewhere for centuries before and after the birth of Christ, and then by pilgrims making their way to St. Davids. In medieval days it became a coal port, and lime kilns were used to reduce limestone to slaked lime for use on fields, in building, and for household purposes. The restored lime kilns can be seen.

A little eastward around the bay on a headland is **St. Non's Chapel,** now in ruins, supposedly built on the spot where St. David was born. It is dedicated to his mother. St. Non's Well is there also, reportedly in full flow. Its waters were said to have healing properties in the past. The site can be viewed 24 hours a day without charge.

WHERE TO STAY

Ramsey House *Value*   The town's best bargain lies 1km (½ mile) from the cathedral on the road to Porthclais. An adults-only establishment, it stands amid manicured gardens and looks very much like the private house it is. Just 1km (½ mile) from the house, you can reach the Pembrokeshire Coast Path that takes you along some of the most panoramic coastal scenery in Wales. Mac and Sandra Thompson are on hand to escort you to one of their immaculately kept midsize bedrooms, each with a cozy and efficient private bathroom. We prefer the second-floor rooms because of their views, either of the sea, cathedral, or open country. For those who don't like stairs, there are ground-floor rooms. The entirely non-smoking hotel serves the best Welsh breakfast in town.

Lower Moor, St. Davids, Pembrokeshire SA62 6RP. © **01437/720321.** Fax 01437/720025. www.ramsey house.co.uk. 6 units. £85–£89 ($157–$165) double. Rates include breakfast and dinner. MC, V. **Amenities:** Restaurant. *In room:* TV, coffeemaker, hair dryer.

Warpool Court Hotel ⑥   This hotel, a 5-minute walk from the heart of the city, is the town's premier address, far outdistancing all competitors. A country house overlooking the sea, it is privately owned and set amid secluded gardens of great natural beauty. The vine-covered structure overlooks one of the most beautiful coastal stretches in Wales. Originally the cathedral choir school, it has been successfully transformed into a hotel with a courteous staff. Most of the rooms are midsize to spacious, and some are large enough for families. The more expensive rooms offer sea views. Asa Williams, who lived here early in the 20th century, decorated some 3,000 tiles, which are positioned throughout the house—some are embellished with Celtic illuminations. The hotel's restaurant offers exceptional cuisine and a varied menu, though seafood is the specialty.

Southwest 1km (½ mile) by Port Clais Rd., St. Davids, Dyfed SA62 6BN. © **01437/720300.** Fax 01437/ 720676. www.warpoolcourthotel.com. 25 units. £65–£100 ($120–$185) per person. Rates include breakfast. AE, DC, MC, V. **Amenities:** Restaurant; bar; covered heated swimming pool (Easter–Oct only); outdoor tennis court; health club; sauna; game room; babysitting; rooms for those with limited mobility. *In room:* TV, coffeemaker, hair dryer.

WHERE TO DINE

Morgan's Brasserie ⑥ WELSH/CONTINENTAL   Unless you dine at one of the inns, this is by far the best independent restaurant in town, and has been since it opened back in 1993. Peruse the menu while admiring the art collection on the walls. The chef is known for making use of local produce and market-fresh ingredients. The fresh fish is rushed here from the Pembrokeshire coast after it lands at the nearby port of Milford Haven. Blackboard menus display the catch of the day. Meat-eaters will also find the most reliable Welsh spring lamb or "black steaks" from the countryside, even game in season. Our party found the roast Gressingham duck supreme worth the trip here. All dishes are cooked to order and specially prepared to bring out the best flavor.

20 Nun St. © **01437/720508.** Reservations required. Main courses £11–£17 ($20–$31). MC, V. Mon–Sat 7–9pm. Closed Jan–Feb.

20

North Wales

North Wales is a rewarding target for those willing to seek it out. Distinctly different from England, it is linguistically and culturally different from most of Britain and is known for its beauty spots, a land of mountains and lakes interspersed with castles. The most powerful of the Welsh princes held sway here, and the residents remain staunchly nationalistic. British families flock to the coastal resorts on holidays, especially in July and August, whereas others prefer to seek out the footpaths of Snowdonia National Park.

Mountain peaks and steep wooded slopes, spectacular estuaries and rugged cliffs brooding over secluded coves, lakes, little rivers, and valleys with tiny towns looking as if they were carved out of granite—all these join to make up **Snowdonia National Park.** The park, with slate mines, moors, heavy forests, mountain lakes, grain fields, and pastures, swift-moving rivers, and sandy beaches, takes its name from Snowdon, at 1,085m (3,560 ft.) the highest peak in Wales and England. Most of the Snowdonia area is in the County of Gwynedd, once the ancient Welsh kingdom of that name. Its prince, Owen ap Gwynedd, never agreed to let himself be reduced to the status of baron under the English kings. Because his terrain was mountainous and wild, it

helped him stave off an invasion by forces accustomed to fighting on flat land.

The rocky, majestic crags of Snowdonia National Park are rivaled by the mighty walls and soaring towers of **Caernarfon Castle,** the best example of castle-building in medieval Wales. Caernarfon (formerly spelled Caernarvon) and its neighbors, Anglesey and the Lleyn Peninsula, reaching out from its northwest and west, are all part of the County of Gwynedd. Legends of holy islands and druidical mysteries flourished among the Celtic peoples who lived in this area in long-ago centuries.

Many of the native-born people of this region are of blood stock little changed over the centuries. Most are bilingual, with English as their second tongue, and signs are usually in both languages.

The County of Clwyd, in northeastern Wales, has miles of sandy beaches along its north coast; highland ranges, peat bogs, and deep valleys lush with greenery in the center; coal country to the southeast; and industry, agriculture, and sheep farming in the section nearest the estuary of the River Dee and the English border. What is now Clwyd (by order of Parliament since 1973) was before that time Denbighshire and Flintshire.

1 Llanberis

376km (234 miles) W of London; 11 km (7 miles) SE of Caernarfon

The starting point for going up Snowdon by mountain railway, Llanberis nestles between Lake Padarn and Lake Peris. Views of outstanding beauty greet your eyes, both man-made sights and natural wonders.

The **Snowdon Mountain Railway** ★ runs from Llanberis to within a few yards of the top of the Snowdon peak at about 1,085m (3,560 ft.). The only rack-and-pinion train in Britain, it is also the steepest train ride, and the view from the top platform, where the train stops, is one of the most panoramic in the country. It's possible to see some 160km (100 miles) away into Ireland, especially the peaks of the Wicklow Mountain chain, on the clearest and brightest of days. Another "great little train" in the region is the Llanberis Lake Railway, which takes you along Lake Padarn. The purpose of the trains in this area and in the Vale of Ffestiniog to the south was to bring the "gray gold" from slate caverns for shipping all over the world. For information and schedules, call © **0870/ 458-0033** or visit www.snowdonrailway.co.uk. Trains run between May and October, costing £20 ($37) for adults round-trip and £14 ($26) for children under age 15.

Padarn Country Park (© **01286/870892**), open daily until dusk, has marked footpaths that will take you past the Vivian Quarry, with its dramatic slate cliffs and deep pools, through galleries where slate was worked, and to lookouts from which the Snowdon range and the lakes can be viewed. The entrance to these 283 hectares (700 acres) of countryside are signposted from High Street and begin .8km (½ mile) north of the town center.

Craft workshops and a woodcraft center are open at the park, where you can watch artisans work in clay, copper, slate, and wood. One workman specializes in Celtic folk harps, including miniature models and do-it-yourself kits.

Dolbadarn Castle ruins overlook Lake (Llyn) Padarn in the Llanberis pass, .8km (½ mile) east of Llanberis, a relic of the time when the pass was used by the conquering armies. It is notable for its location and a mortared masonry tower that still stands. You can take a look around the meager ruins for free.

ESSENTIALS

GETTING THERE   The nearest rail station is at Bangor, 14km (9 miles) north of Llanberis. From Bangor, four buses run Monday to Saturday in the evening only, 6:30, 7, 8, and 10:40pm; buses depart in front of Bangor's railway station. Contact the **Arriva Bus Company** (© **0870/608-2608;** www.arriva.co.uk). Because of the many stops en route, buses take about 40 minutes each way.

Two buses per hour make the run between Llanberis and Caernarfon, Monday through Saturday only. Bus timetables are available from the Llanberis Tourist Information Office (see below) and the Caernarfon Tourist Information Office (see section 4 on "Caernarfon," later in this chapter).

Motorists from Caernarfon head southeast along the A4086.

VISITOR INFORMATION   The **Llanberis Tourist Information Office,** 41B High St. (© **01286/870765**) is open from Easter to the end of October daily from 9:30am to 5:30pm. The rest of the year, it's open Wednesday, Friday, Saturday, and Sunday from 11am to 4pm.

SEEING THE SIGHTS

Nearly a kilometer (½ mile) north of the center of Llanberis in Padarn Country Park (see above), the **Welsh State Museum** (© **01286/870630**) is a minor museum in the workshops of Dinorwic slate quarry, one of the largest in Britain until it closed in 1969. Slate-mining communities were intensely Welsh, nonconformist in religion, and radical in politics, as films shown here reveal. The exhibitions, which should take no more than 30 minutes of your time, are mainly of interest to those who have a particular interest in this aspect of Welsh life of long ago. Admission is free. It's open from Easter to October daily from

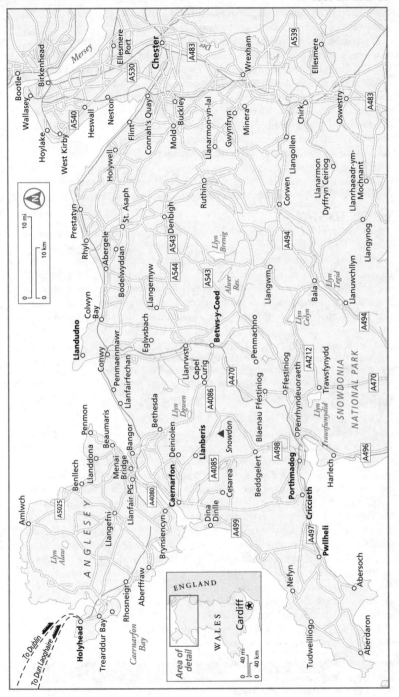

North Wales

10am to 5pm; off season Sunday to Friday from 10am to 4pm. Take the A4086 at the start of the lake railway and Padarn Country Park.

Electric Mountain Visitor Centre, along the A4086 (© **01286/870636**), is a scientific-looking observation center, functioning as the meeting point between the public and one of the most technologically advanced power stations in Wales. Set about .4km (¼ mile) north of Llanberis, it incorporates a hydro-electric system harnessing the waters of a pair of nearby lakes, whose turbines and channels are concealed deep within the mountains so as not to spoil the natural beauty of the nationally protected site. Entrance to the visitor center is free. Hours of visitation in April, May, September, and October are daily from 10:30am to 4:30pm, June to August daily 9:30am to 5:30pm, and November to March Wednesday to Sunday 10:30am to 4:30pm. Once you get here, if a staff member isn't busy with other tasks, you can take a tour of the turbines for a fee of £6 ($11) for adults, £3 ($5.55) for children under age 15.

WHERE TO STAY

Royal Victoria Hotel   Although it's a venue for local weddings and social functions and is a bit stuffy, this is nonetheless the most prestigious address in town. Royal Victoria is long established at the foothills of Snowdon, between Padarn and Peris lakes, a bucolic setting. The bedrooms in general are spacious and recently modernized, with comfortable and endurable furniture and well-maintained private baths. Four rooms are set aside for families. The place bustles with activity, often providing live entertainment at night or arranging mountain treks during the day.

Llanberis, Gwynedd, LL55 4TY. © **01286/870253.** Fax 01286/870149. www.royal-victoria-hotel.co.uk. 111 units. £60 ($111) double. Rates include breakfast. Discounts available for children under 15 staying in parent's room. AE, DC, MC, V. **Amenities:** Restaurant; large dining room with a conservatory opening onto the lakes; bar; limited room service; nonsmoking rooms. *In room:* TV, coffeemaker, hair dryer.

WHERE TO DINE

Y Bistro ⟨⋆⟩ TRADITIONAL WELSH   When it comes to food, this is the only hot ticket in town. Nothing else matters—there's not even a good inn here. For more than 2 decades, we've been popping in here to see what the Robertses (Nerys and Danny) are offering on their "taste of Wales" menu, and we've never been disappointed. Nerys has appeared on numerous British TV shows about cuisine and has won many deserved accolades for her cooking skills. The place is so Welsh that it even offers wines from Wales, although you should stick to the French and Spanish vintages. Excellent use is made of local produce. Here's a chance to learn some Welsh when ordering. *Eog peris* is a delectable locally smoked salmon in a creamy sauce; *ffryth* is a chilled melon flavored with orange zest and Cointreau, a delightful way to launch yourself in such game dishes as a perfectly roasted and herb-seasoned pheasant or succulent pigeon breasts. Try the tasty appetizer, lamb ribs flavored with honey, mint, and rosemary. The Welsh wine tastes better when cooked with grapes to make a sauce to flavor the melt-in-your-mouth pork tenderloins.

43–45 High St. © **01286/871278.** Reservations required. Main courses £14–£16 ($26–$30). MC, V. Mon–Sat 7:30–10pm. Closed Mon–Tues in winter.

2 Betws-y-Coed ⟨⋆⟩

363km (226 miles) W of London; 70km (44 miles) SE of Holyhead

This idyllic Snowdonia village, with tumbling rivers, waterfalls, and mountains, is nestled in the tree-lined valley of the River Conwy. It has an antique church with a Norman font; old bridges, stone houses, and hotels on rocky outcrops; and woodland paths.

Although crowded in summer, this town is one of the best centers for exploring North Wales. It's mainly a one-street town, but you get the feel that you're in the great outdoors far removed from England's polluted cities of the Midlands. There's an alpine feeling about the place.

The town is known for its eight bridges, of which our favorite is the Waterloo Bridge at the village's southern end, the construction of Telford in 1815 in cast iron. There's also a suspension bridge near St. Michael's Church. If you walk upon it, it sways in the wind but seems perfectly safe. The most regal bridge is Pont-y-Pair, "the bridge of the cauldron," bounding the Llugwy River to the north. In fact, walking across the bridges of Betws-y-Coed and taking in the views is one of the main reasons to come here.

ESSENTIALS

GETTING THERE   The **Conwy Valley** line between Llandudno and Blaenau Ffestiniog passes through Betws-y-Coed with six trains daily Monday through Saturday (only two trains on Sun). For rail information and schedules, call ✆ **0845/748-4950** or visit www.railtrack.co.uk.

The **Arriva** bus company services Betws-y-Coed from both Llandudno and Porthmadog. For schedules, call ✆ **0870/608-2608** or visit www.arriva.co.uk.

Motorists from Llandudno can take A470 south.

VISITOR INFORMATION   For information about the town and Snowdonia National Park, head for the **local tourist office** at Holyhead Road in the town center (✆ **01690/710426**). It's open from Easter to October daily from 10am to 6pm; off season daily from 9:30am to 4:30pm.

SEEING THE SIGHTS

If time is short, we'd skip the minor sights of town—that is, after you've walked over those bridges—and head instead for one of the beauty spots of Wales, the **Swallow Falls** 🎇 and **Miners Bridge.** Take the A5 for 3.2km (2 miles) to the west of Betws-y-Coed. The Swallow Falls is one of the most mystical and evocative—also one of the most powerful—in Wales. It's composed of a series of waterfalls strung together, creating a mist. Miners Bridge is a wooden footbridge impregnated with pitch for preservation and dating from the late 18th century. It's not a conventional flat bridge, but rather it's a steeply inclined "staircase"-style bridge, with elevation much higher on one end than on the other. The Miners Bridge doesn't charge anything to visit—and, as such, many walkers opt for a brisk half-hour riverfront walk from the center of Betws-y-Coed, with the bridge as their final destination. You'll pay £1 ($1.85) to see the falls, however. There's no guardian—just drop a coin into a tollbooth, and visit anytime you want, night or day.

Again, and only if you have time, there are two more evocative places to visit in the area. One is **Dolwyddelan Castle** at the hamlet of Dolwyddelan (✆ **01690/750366**).

Standing lonely on a ridge, this castle was the birthplace of Llewlyn the Great, according to tradition. It was certainly his royal residence. Restored to its present condition in the 19th century, the castle's remains look out on the rugged grandeur of Moel Siabod peak. A medieval road from the Vale of Conwy ran just below the west tower, which made this a strategic site for a castle to control passage. About 1.6km (1 mile) from Dolwyddelan, the castle is accessible by a rough track off the A470 to the southwest of Betws-y-Coed, on the road to Blaenau

Ffestiniog. To enter, adults pay £2 ($3.70); children under age 16 £1.50 ($2.80) (free for those age 4 and under). Open April through September daily from 9:30am to 6:30pm; off season Monday to Saturday from 9:30am to 4pm, Sunday from 11am to 4pm.

One of the premier literary sights of Wales, **Ty Mawr,** Wybrnant, Penmachno (© **01690/760213**), lies 11km (7 miles) southeast of Betws-y-Coed. From the town, head southwest for 5.6km (3½ miles), going west of Penmachno along B4406 the rest of the way. At the head of the little valley of Gwybernant, this cottage is where Bishop William Morgan was born in the 16th century. He was the first person to translate the Bible into Welsh, and his translation is viewed even today as a masterpiece and the foundation of modern Welsh literature. It's an isolated stone-walled cottage with a slate roof that you might pass by unless you knew its pedigree. Between April and September, it's open Thursday through Sunday from noon to 5pm. In October, it is open only Thursday, Friday, and Sunday from noon to 4pm. Admission is £2.20 ($4.05) for adults and £1.10 ($2.05) for children.

WHERE TO STAY & DINE
EXPENSIVE
Tan-y-Foel Country House Hotel ★★★ *Finds* A 16th-century manor house, this gem is the best hotel in the area, opening onto a panoramic sweep of Conwy Valley, with Snowdonia looming in the background. Stay here if you can, forsaking all other places. Vibrant fabrics and modern paintings bring you into the 21st century, but the atmosphere is still yesterday. It is set on 3.2 hectares (8 acres) of woodlands and pastures 3.2km (2 miles) north of town. Charm and grace prevail in the public and private rooms. The latter are moderate to spacious, each individually furnished with immaculate little bathrooms. Two rooms are in an annex and have less charm. All units are nonsmoking. We prefer one of the four bedrooms opening onto the front of the hotel, as they offer the best views.

The hotel's cuisine is better than all its competitors. Owner/chef Janet Pitman has even gone on the BBC to tell Britain the secret of making her Celtic pancakes with Carmarthen ham, pork, and apple purée.

Capel Garmon, near Betws-y-Coed, LL26 0RE. © **01690/710507.** Fax 01690/710681. www.tyfhotel.co.uk. 7 units. £182–£232 ($337–$429) double. Rates include breakfast. MC, V. No children age 7 and under accepted. From Betws-y-Coed, take A5 onto A470, heading north to Llanrwst, turning at the signpost for Capel Garmon. **Amenities:** Restaurant; limited room service. *In room:* TV, hair dryer, iron/ironing board.

MODERATE
Henllys Hotel (The Old Courthouse) ★★ This is a good, centrally located best bet for those who like B&B style luxury but want the amenities of a small inn as well. Once a Victorian magistrates' court, the hotel has been successfully converted and set in lovely gardens along the river, just a 3-minute walk from the city center. You can dine in the antique courtroom where prisoners were sentenced long ago, have a lager in the police station bar, and sleep either in the judge's chambers or the "handcuff room." Bedrooms range from small to spacious, and each has been cleverly converted, offering much comfort from the new mattresses to the nicely appointed bathrooms, with a choice of tub or shower. At this nonsmoking establishment, some rooms are suitable for persons with disabilities. Try to avoid the smallest room in the house, originally a single cell reserved "for a ruffian." It still has bars on the door.

In the cozy, galleried dining room, Barbara Valadini is known in town for her fine and imaginative Welsh fare.

Old Church Rd., Betws-y-Coed, LL24 0AL. ℭ 01690/710534. Fax 01690/710884. www.guesthouse-snowdonia.co.uk. 8 units. £63–£70 ($117–$130) double. Rates include breakfast. MC, V. *In room:* TV, cof-feemaker, hair dryer (on request), iron (on request).

The Park Hill Hotel ⭐   About a 5-minute walk west of town, this small Vic-torian hotel is surrounded by secluded gardens and opens onto panoramic views of the Conwy and Llugwy valleys. For such a small hotel, it offers some excep-tional recreational facilities and is also known for its justly praised cuisine. Your hosts, Jaap and Ghislaine Buis, run a good little inn, with moderately sized bed-rooms and small but well-kept bathrooms. Front rooms are preferable to those on the side. Furnishings are traditional, and one room is graced with a four-poster.

Llanwst Rd., Betws-y-Coed, Gwynedd LL24 0HD. ℭ 01690/710540. Fax 01690/710540. 9 units. £56–£80 ($104–$148) double. Rates include breakfast. MC, V. No children under age 6. **Amenities:** Bar; indoor heated pool; whirlpool; sauna. *In room:* TV, coffeemaker, no phone.

Ty Gwyn ⭐   This is one of the most charming hotels and pubs in town. You could ask Teddy Roosevelt, if he were still around. Much has changed since the American president stayed here in the late 1800s, but much is still the same as well. Laden with carved beams and local artifacts, Ty Gwyn is low slung, sitting on the opposite side of Waterloo Bridge from the rest of town. Inside it's a world of old prints and chintz, time-darkened beams, and copper pans. Originally it was a coaching inn from the 16th century, drawing horsemen traveling between London and the ferryboats to Ireland. The rooms, often small, are still comfort-ably furnished, often with a four-poster or a half-tester bed (ca. 1800). Most rooms have a shower only, though two have a tub-shower combo. The best unit has a "health spa" tub, small lounge, and private balcony. The four rooms with-out private bathrooms share two small bathrooms equipped with a shower only; the rooms themselves have wash basins with hot and cold running water.

Along the A5, Betws-y-Coed, Gwynedd LL24 0PSG. ℭ 01690/710383. 13 units, 9 with bathroom. £36 ($67) double without bathroom; £60 ($111) double with bathroom; £80 ($148) four-poster room. Rates include breakfast. Children under 12 stay free in same room with 2 paying adults. AE, MC, V. **Amenities:** Restaurant; pub. *In room:* TV, coffeemaker, no phone.

3 The Lleyn Peninsula ⭐⭐

Separating Cardigan Bay and its northern arm, Tremadog Bay, from Caernarfon Bay, the gentle western Lleyn Peninsula thrusts out alone into the Irish Sea. It's bounded by the mountains of Snowdonia on the east and by the sea. Having lit-tle communication with the outside world before the coming of railroads and highways, the peninsula has a large Welsh-speaking population, although most people also have English as a second language, made necessary by the influx of people coming here to retire, to do business, or just to take holidays.

The peninsula takes its name from an Irish tribe, the Celtic Legine or Laigin, who didn't have very far to go from home to invade the country of fellow Celts. They were followed by missionaries and pilgrims in the Christian era. The dis-tance from Ireland is so short that when you stand on National Trust property high on a cliff above St. Mary's Well you can often see the Wicklow Mountains of Ireland with the naked eye.

The Lleyn Peninsula has beaches, hills, farmland, moorland, villages nestled in the hollows, trees, heather, gorse, and country lanes. There are traces of hill forts here, and you can find standing stones, monastery ruins, pilgrim trails, holy wells (four of them), and nonconformist chapels. Sporting enthusiasts find fishing, golf, watersports, and rough shooting.

For information on the peninsula, get in touch with the **Tourist Information Centre, Min Y Don, Station Square,** Pwllheli (© **01758/613000**). The two best towns on the peninsula are Porthmadog and Criccieth (see below).

Pwllheli, lying 13km (8 miles) to the west of Criccieth, is the principal transportation hub of the peninsula, with daily buses arriving from London. Buses also pull in here every hour from Bangor. You may not want to linger in Pwllheli, but take a connecting bus to either Porthmadog or Criccieth, which make better centers.

BritRail's Cambrian Coast line, which begins at Aberystwth, with a change of trains at Machynlleth, takes you to both Porthmadog and Criccieth. Call © **0845/748-4950** or visit www.railtrack.co.uk for more information.

PORTHMADOG

The estuary of the River Glaslyn has long been the scene of shipping and fishing activity, emptying as it does into Tremadoc Bay and thence into Cardigan Bay.

This is the main town east of the Lleyn Peninsula. It grew up as a slate-shipping port on the coast near the mouth of the River Glaslyn. T. E. Lawrence (Lawrence of Arabia) was born in Tremadog, close by.

The town was named after a "Celtification" of the English name of its builder, William Madocks, a mining mogul who built the town from scratch between 1808 and 1811. The harbor that later figured so prominently in the town's history was custom-built between 1821 and 1825. In the 1870s, as many as 1,000 vessels a year pulled into harbor here to haul away slate. At its peak in 1873, 116,000 tons of Blaenau slate were shipped from this harbor to points throughout the empire and the world.

The location is 428km (266 miles) west of London and 32km (20 miles) south of Caernarfon. The **Wales Information Centre,** High Street (© **01766/512981**), is open Thursday through Tuesday from Easter to October from 10am to 6pm. Off-season hours are Thursday through Tuesday from 10am to 5pm.

SEEING THE SIGHTS

The view of the mountains of Snowdonia from Porthmadog Cob, the embankment, is panoramic. Porthmadog is the coastal terminal of the Ffestiniog Railway, and a small museum may be visited at the station. The town has access to beaches at Borth-y-Gest and Black Rock Sands, where cars may be driven onto the beach. Other than the scenery, attractions are not exceptional.

The production of traditional tapestries and tweeds can be observed at the small **Brynkir Woollen Mill,** Golan, Garndolbenmaen (© **01766/530236**), in a beautiful rural setting. The products are available for sale at this mill shop. Admission is free; it is open Monday through Friday from 10am to 4pm. Head out the A487 for 5.6km (3½ miles) from Porthmadog.

WHERE TO STAY & DINE

Hotel Portmeirion ★★★ *Finds*   There's nothing like it in Wales. Sir Clough Williams-Ellis set out to build an idyllic village on a romantic coast, and he succeeded. Standing amid one of the finest scenic settings in Wales, this hotel existed as an early Victorian villa before it was converted into an evocative hotel in 1926. The hotel was partially reconstructed after its destruction by fire in 1981.

Writers such as H. G. Wells and George Bernard Shaw became habitués, Noël Coward wrote *Blithe Spirit* here in 1941, and the cult TV classic, *The Prisoner,* was filmed here in the late '60s. The hotel overlooks Cardigan Bay from its own private peninsula. The decor inside is exotic: fabrics from Kashmir, paintings from Rajasthan, tiles from Delft, and wallpaper from New York. Many of the rooms have half-tester or four-poster beds. About a dozen units are in the main house, the rest in a cluster of "village houses." In the main house, some rooms are cramped, whereas accommodations in the cluster of houses outside are often more spacious. Four accommodations are designated for families or small groups traveling together. The best sea views are from the rooms in the main house, however. Bathrooms are sumptuous.

At the highly praised restaurant, chefs use local produce as a foundation of daily changing menus. The modern Welsh cuisine has many Mediterranean influences. Call for a dinner reservation even if you're not a guest—the experience is worth it.

Portmeirion, Gwynedd, LL48 6ET (off A487, signposted from Minffordd, 3.2km (2 miles) west of Portmeirion). 𝒞 01766/770000. Fax 01766/771331. www.portmeirion-village.com. 37 units. £135–£175 ($250–$324) double, from £240 ($444) suite. AE, DC, MC, V. **Amenities:** 2 restaurants; outdoor pool (heated May–Sept only); outdoor tennis court; limited room service; babysitting. *In room:* TV, coffeemaker, hair dryer.

CRICCIETH

Now in ruins, **Criccieth Castle** (𝒞 01766/522227), built as a native Welsh stronghold, is on a grassy headland and offers a commanding view of Tremadoc Bay. During its years as an active fortress, it changed hands—Welsh to English and back and forth—until it was finally sacked and burned in 1404 by Owain Glyndwr, never to rise again as a fortification. The castle houses an interesting exhibition on the theme of the native castles of Welsh princes. On a fine day, from its heights you can see westward to the tip of the peninsula, north and east to Snowdonia, and far down the bay to the south. Admission costs £2.80 ($5.20) for adults or £2 ($3.70) for students and children ages 5 to 16 (children ages 4 and under free). A family ticket goes for £7 ($13). Open April and May daily from 10am to 5pm, June through September daily from 10am to 6pm, October daily 10am to 5pm. The castle's exhibition center is closed the rest of the year, but you can still enjoy the panoramic view.

About 3km (2 miles) west of Criccieth in Llanystumdwy, you can visit **Highgate,** the boyhood home of David Lloyd George, prime minister of Britain in the 1914–18 war years, and also the **Lloyd George Memorial Museum** (𝒞 01766/522071), designed by Sir Clough Williams-Ellis of Portmeirion fame (see above). The museum outlines the statesman's life, and the main displays illustrate his political career and include a collection of "freedom" caskets, a "talking head" portrayed by Philip Madoc, the actor, with excerpts of three of Lloyd George's famous speeches, and an audiovisual display. Admission is £4 ($7.40) for adults, £3 ($5.55) for children, or £8.50 ($16) for a family ticket. From April to June, it is open Monday through Saturday from 10:30am to 5pm (open Mon–Fri in May); July through September daily from 10:30am to 5pm; and October Monday through Friday from 11am to 4pm. Lloyd George's grave is nearby on the banks of the swift-running River Dwyfor, shaded by large oak trees. The name of the hamlet, Llanystumdwy, means "the church at the bend of the River Dwyfor."

St. Cybi's Well, Llangybi, is 6.4km (4 miles) northwest of Criccieth on a minor road. Of 6th-century origin, only two chambers remain of the holy well, although in the mid–18th century a bathhouse was built to surround the font. You can visit it free.

North of the well is the site of a small Iron Age hill fort. **Tourist information** about the Criccieth area is available from Porthmadog (see above).

WHERE TO STAY & DINE

Bron Eifion Country House Hotel ★★   On 2 hectares (5 acres) of well-manicured gardens, this baronial mansion is the finest and most elegant place to stay in the area. This tranquil Welsh country estate lies close to the Snowdonia National Park and makes a good base for exploring the area. The interior looks like it would make a good place to stage an Agatha Christie murder mystery. Alan and Carole Thompson are warm and gracious hosts. You'll surely be impressed by their grand stairway and the minstrels' gallery, with its lofty timbered roof. Rooms are spacious and traditionally furnished; some have four-poster beds. Bathrooms are good-size and well kept. You can wander the lovingly tended gardens evoking the south of France. There's a candlelit restaurant in old conservatory overlooking the floodlit gardens. A special flambé menu is a highlight.

Criccieth, Gwynedd, LL52 OSA. ℂ **800/528-1234** in the U.S., or 01766/522385. Fax 01766/522003. www. broneifion.co.uk. 19 units. £106–£120 ($196–$222) double. Rates include breakfast. MC, V. Lies .8km (½ mile) outside Criccieth on A497 signposted Pwllheli. **Amenities:** Restaurant; breakfast-only room service; babysitting; laundry service; 1 room for those with limited mobility; nonsmoking rooms. *In room:* TV, dataport, coffeemaker, hair dryer, trouser press.

The Lion Hotel *Kids*   This former private home from the 19th century lies in the town's most enviable spot: beside the village green behind a painted stone facade. The lager-drinking pubbers of town head here at sundown, and it's a lively, cozy nest for an overnight stop and some good Welsh cookery. Rooms are homelike and often small but comfortably furnished with tidy housekeeping and somewhat cramped bathrooms, most often with shower. There are a few rooms designed to accommodate guests with limited mobility. Families are especially welcome here, as the hotel sets aside separate bedrooms for them, and offers early dinners for children. The inn also has such devices as "baby-listening" facilities along with cots and high chairs that are provided, and all rooms are nonsmoking.

In addition to staying in the main building, you can also find lodgings in the Castle Cottage, offering a dozen well-furnished bedrooms. Half of these accommodations open onto panoramic views of the castle.

Y Maes, Criccieth, Gwynedd LA52 LL52. ℂ **01766/522460.** Fax 01766/523075. www.lionhotelcriccieth. co.uk. 46 units. £60–£68 ($111–$125) double. Rates include breakfast. AE, MC, V. **Amenities:** Restaurant; pub; breakfast-only room service. *In room:* TV, coffeemaker, hair dryer.

4 Caernarfon ★★

400km (249 miles) W of London; 100km (68 miles) W of Chester; 48km (30 miles) SE of Holyhead; 14km (9 miles) SW of Bangor

In the 13th century, when King Edward I of England had defeated the Welsh after long and bitter fighting, he felt the need for a castle in this area as part of his network of fortresses in the still-rebellious country. He ordered the construction of one on the site of an old Norman castle at the western end of the Menai Strait, where the River Seiont flows into the sea, a place from which his sentinels could command a view of the land around all the way to the mountains and far out across the bay to the Irish Sea. Based either on his firsthand observations (historians believed he might have visited Constantinople during his involvement in the Crusades) or based on ancient drawings of Constantinople procured by his architect, the Savoy-born James St. George, the walls were patterned after the fortifications surrounding ancient Byzantium. Most of the walls of the 13th-century town still stand, although growth outside the walls has been inevitable.

The main reason to flock here today is to see the castle. After that, you will have seen the best of Caernarfon and can press on to another town for the night, or else stay at one of the local inns. The downside? Tourist buses overrun the place in summer. Other than the castle, there is nothing in the town that needs to take up too much of your time.

ESSENTIALS

GETTING THERE   There's no railway station in Caernarfon; the nearest connection is through Bangor to which Caernarfon is linked by bus.

Buses run between Caernarfon and Bangor, a 25-minute ride, every 20 minutes throughout the day. Bus timetables are available either by calling the tourist office (see below), or by dialing ✆ **0870/608-2608** or visit www.arriva.co.uk.

If driving from Bangor, head southwest along the A487; from Porthmadog (see above) head north along the A487.

VISITOR INFORMATION   The **Caernarfon Tourist Information Centre** is at Oriel Pendeitsh, 1 Castle St. (✆ **01286/672232**). From November to April, it's open Monday through Saturday from 10am to 4:30pm; the rest of the year, it's open daily from 9:30am to 5:30pm.

SEEING THE SIGHTS

Every Saturday, a market is held in **Castle Square,** where there's a statue of David Lloyd George, prime minister of Great Britain between 1916 and 1922, who is generally credited, along with King George V, for leading the United Kingdom through the rigors of World War I. He's also credited with introducing what's defined today as Britain's national health care system. Born in Manchester, he was reared on the nearby Lleyn Peninsula, and was later instrumental in preserving the remnants of the town's famous castle (see below).

The nearest thing Wales ever had to a royal palace is **Caernarfon Castle** ★★★, described by Dr. Samuel Johnson after a visit in 1774 as "an edifice of stupendous majesty and strength." Legend has it that after the birth, in 1301, of the son of Edward I in this castle, he showed the infant boy to the Welsh, calling him "the native-born prince who can speak no English." Since that time the title "Prince of Wales" has belonged to every male heir-apparent to the English throne. The eyes of the world were on Caernarfon in 1969 when it was the scene of the investiture of Charles as Prince of Wales.

The castle is open to visitors. Although in some places only the shell of the wall remains, some rooms and stone and wooden steps remain so that you can climb up into it. Eagle Tower has an exhibition on the ground floor showing the history of the fortress and of the town around it. In the northeast are exhibits on the princes of Wales. You can also visit the **Regimental Museum of the Royal Welch Fusiliers** (the regiment retains the Old English spelling of the word *Welsh*), which occupies all three floors of Queen's Tower and contains many items of interest relating to the regiment and its military history. In 2000, millions of pounds were spent on the renovation and enlargement of this historic castle, with additional exhibition space for the museum set up within the Chamberlain Tower. It is the castle as a whole that's of interest—not one special exhibition or hall. Allow 1½ hours.

Between late May and the end of September, the castle is open daily from 9:30am to 6pm. From Easter to late May, and during all of October, it's open daily from 9:30am to 5pm. From November to Easter, it's open Monday through Saturday from 9:30am to 4pm and Sunday from 11am to 4pm. Admission costs

£4.50 ($8.35) for adults, and £3.50 ($6.50) for students and children under age 16. For more information, call © **01286/677617.**

Today the town's quays are less animated than they were during the heyday of the region's slate mining, when boats lined up to haul roofing tiles off to points as far away as London, the United States, the mainland of Europe, and India. In the mid-1990s, a full-service marina, with about 60 slips, was built to accommodate the increasing numbers of yachts and pleasure craft that moor here when not in use. The year-round population of the town today is between 10,000 and 11,000.

The Romans recognized the strategic importance of northwest Wales and maintained a fort at **Segontium** for some 3 centuries. Excavations on the outskirts of Caernarfon on the A4085 have disclosed foundations of barracks, bathhouses, and other structural remains. Finds from the excavations are displayed in the **museum** (© **01286/675625**) on the site. Open from Easter to late September, Monday through Saturday from 10am to 5pm, Sunday from 2 to 5pm; from October to Easter, it's open Monday through Saturday from 10am to 4pm, Sunday from 2 to 4pm. Admission is free. Some archaeologists and historians think that native Britons may have been displaced from the site, which was one of their strongholds at the time of the Roman invasion. There are no outstanding relics here; allow about 30 minutes to walk about.

WHERE TO STAY

Celtic Royal Hotel ✯　Carved out of a 19th-century grand hotel shell, and massively enlarged, this is the blockbuster and leading choice in town. Its uniformed, well-trained staff grew accustomed long ago to groups of visitors pulling in by motor coach to see the famous castle, just a 3-minute walk away. The hotel's current look derives from a 1996 face-lift and radical enlargement of what had become a dowdy and outmoded "grand hotel" built in 1843. Today, most of the antique original vestiges lie within the hotel's lobby, with bedrooms and dining facilities placed within modern, three-story wings that contain all of the conveniences you'd expect from a first-class property. The midsize bedrooms are blandly uncontroversial, outfitted in pastels with comfortable furnishings and small bathrooms with shower units. Several rooms have been outfitted for those with limited mobility.

The restaurant is for formal dining, but the Irish Pub, site of nightly live music and a convivial hub, is more fun.

Bangor St., Caernarfon, Gwynedd LL55 1AY. © **01286/674477.** Fax 01286/674139. www.celtic-royal.co.uk. 110 units. £100 ($185) double. Rates include breakfast. AE, MC, V. **Amenities:** Restaurant; bar; leisure center with indoor heated pool; gym; steam room; vertical sun shower; sauna; 24-hr. room service; nonsmoking rooms. *In room:* TV w/pay movies, coffeemaker, hair dryer.

Gwesty Seiont Manor ✯✯ (Kids)　In the tranquil Welsh countryside, this is one of the best bases for exploring Snowdonia National Park. It can also be an excellent base for visiting the Isle of Anglesey. With a slight exaggeration, the owners proclaim, "We're a Pandora's box of wondrous treasures." Constructed from the original farmstead of a Georgian manor house, the hotel has been tastefully converted into a honeycomb of spacious rooms, each with good-size bathrooms and all with views over 60 hectares (150 acres) of parkland. Eight bedrooms are set aside for nonsmokers. Come here for seclusion, a sense of style, and some of the best leisure facilities in the area. It's also a great family favorite. Several bedrooms are set aside for families and offer VCRs and a selection of children's videos. All rooms have either a small balcony or a terrace.

The hotel restaurant's award-winning chefs concentrate on local produce when available. We still remember that fresh sea bass with spinach and red pesto sauce.

Llanrug, Caernarfon LL55 2AQ. © **01286/673366.** Fax 01286/672840. www.handpicked.co.uk. 28 units. £165 ($305) double. Rates include breakfast. AE, MC, V. From Caernarfon, head east on A4086 for 3.2km (2 miles). **Amenities:** Restaurant; indoor heated pool; gym; sauna; solarium; 24-hr. room service; babysitting; laundry service; rooms for those with limited mobility. *In room:* TV, dataport, coffeemaker, hair dryer.

Stables (*Kids* Those who don't like living in a stable should rethink their prejudice. This unusual hotel was constructed around stone stables that were famous locally many years ago for horse breeding. Some of the trained horses here eventually ended up helping fight South Africa's Boer War. Today those stables have been considerably enlarged with modern wings and slate roofs whose materials and angles match those of the original core. Most of the good-size and comfortably furnished accommodations with commodious private baths are in an L-shaped annex whose innermost corner shelters a swimming pool. Several of the bedrooms have four-poster beds, which we find more desirable; a trio of rooms are rented to families. Just in case you're interested, guests may bring their own horses to the stables here.

Atmospheric dining and drinking facilities have been installed in the oldest part of the original stables. A few of the stall doors have been retained, along with the exposed beams and trusses of the roofline.

Llanwnda, near Caernarfon. Gwynedd LL55 2UF. © **01286/830711.** Fax 01286/830413. www.caernarfon. com/stables.html. 23 units. £64 ($118) double. Rates include breakfast. MC, V. From Caernarfon, follow the B4366 9.6km (6 miles) east, and follow signs to Bethel. **Amenities:** Restaurant; pub; limited room service; babysitting; nonsmoking rooms. *In room:* TV, coffeemaker, hair dryer (in some), iron/ironing board.

Ty'n Rhos Country House Hotel & Restaurant (★★ This is the most charming, best furnished, and most appealing country-house hotel in the neighborhood of Caernarfon. It's the centerpiece of 29 hectares (72 acres) of land, some of which is devoted to well-maintained forests and gardens, the remainder of which is leased out to tenant farmers for grazing of sheep and cattle. Maintained as a perky family-owned business by several generations of the Kettle family, it originated in the 19th century as a farmhouse, although the antiques-laden, chintz-draped version you'll see today is a far cry from its original humble origins. Log fires blaze in the rustic-looking lounge, a dining room (see below) attracts nonguests from the region, and couples looking for a romantic interlude in the Merry Old Wales of long ago have been known to disappear into the bedrooms for weekends. Guests enjoy bird-watching walks around the private lake, and strolls on the footpaths that meander across the sprawling property. The midsize and nonsmoking bedrooms are attractively furnished with tidily kept bathrooms adjoining. All units have a complete bathroom, except two, which have showers instead of tubs. One room is equipped for guests in wheelchairs. The lounge with its slate inglenook fireplace offers an impressive collection of whiskies.

Llanddeiniolen LL55 3AE. © **01248/670489.** Fax 01248/670079. www.tynrhos.co.uk. 14 units. £80–£120 ($148–$222) double. Rates include breakfast. AE, MC, V. From Caernarfon, take the B4366 for 9.6km (6 miles) east, following the signs to Bethel. **Amenities:** Restaurant; bar; limited room service; croquet. *In room:* TV, dataport, coffeemaker, hair dryer.

WHERE TO DINE

Ty'n Rhos Country Hotel & Restaurant CONTINENTAL The most endearing restaurant in the vicinity of Caernarfon occupies the elegant premises of what was originally built in the 1800s as a simple farmhouse, and which was intensely gentrified by the resident owners. Meals are served with views out toward manicured gardens and inward to the sight and scents of at least one blazing log fireplace. This is good country cooking without pretensions. Fresh produce is served, and the cuisine is strong on flavors but not overpoweringly so. The menu changes, but we've particularly enjoyed such dishes as Welsh lamb sausage with creamy potatoes served with a sweet-onion sauce, just like your Welsh grandmother used to make. Rack of lamb also appears in a more modern version infused with a fresh rosemary sauce with a lemon-flavored couscous serving as an added delight. The creamy leeks with saffron sauce overpower the grilled sea bass, however. Save room for that glazed lemon tart with nutmeg custard and homegrown rhubarb as an accompaniment.

Llanddeiniolen (for directions, see above). © 01248/670489. Reservations recommended. Fixed-price 2-course menu £19 ($34), 3 course £22 ($40). AE, MC, V. Daily 6:30–8:15pm.

5 The Isle of Anglesey ⊛⊛

The Welsh name of this island is Mon (the Romans called it Mona), and it is called Mon, Mam Cymru, or Anglesey, Mother of Wales. If this is true, we must say that the child doesn't much resemble the mother. The scenery differs totally from that of the mainland, with low-lying farmland interrupted here and there by rocky outcrops. The landscape is dotted with single-story whitewashed cottages, and the rolling green fields stretch down to the sea—all against a backdrop of the mountains of Snowdonia across the Menai Strait, which divides this island from the rest of Wales.

Visitors cross the strait by one of the two bridges built by celebrated engineers of the 19th century: the **Menai Suspension Bridge,** designed by Thomas Telford and completed in 1826; and the **Britannia Bridge,** originally a railroad bridge, which was the work of Robert Stephenson. The Britannia, a neighbor of the suspension bridge, had to be rebuilt after a devastating fire that destroyed its pitch and timberwork; it now carries both trains and cars on two different levels. The bridges are about 1.6km (1 mile) west of Bangor on the mainland.

Many people have passed through Anglesey on the train that operates between London and Holyhead, for a ferry journey to Ireland. A stopover for a day in Anglesey is recommended. Neolithic tombs of Stone Age settlers have been found on the island, as have Iron Age artifacts. The Romans left artifacts behind, as did the early Christians who settled here.

The coming of steamers and then of the railroad brought Victorian-era visitors. However, if you're not really sold on antiquity, there's a lot to do on Anglesey that is totally in tune with today. Yachting, sea fishing, and leisure centers that offer swimming, squash, and other activities are within easy reach wherever you stay. Golf, tennis, nature walks, pony trekking, canoeing—whatever—are offered in the daytime, and in the evening you can wine, dine, even dance to the latest music.

ESSENTIALS

GETTING THERE   The island has good bus service. For information about bus service on the island, call **Arriva Cymru** at © 0870/608-2608 or visit www. arriva.co.uk. The major route (bus no. 4) runs between Bangor and Holyhead via Llangefni. Buses operate at the rate of two per hour during the day Monday through Saturday, but on Sunday service is curtailed to six buses (between 10am and 8:40pm). Bus no. 53 goes from Bangor to Beaumaris every 30 minutes during the day Monday through Saturday. All buses cross the Menai Bridge at the town of Menai Bridge (see below).

VISITOR INFORMATION   To find out about activities on the island, call or write for a brochure from the **Wales Tourist Board Information Centre,** Railway Station Site, Llanfairpwllgwyngyllgogerychwyrndrobwllllantysiliogogogoch, Isle of Anglesey (✆ **01248/713177**). Open April through October Monday through Saturday from 9:30am to 5:pm and Sunday from 10am to 5pm; November through March, Monday through Friday from 9:30am to 1pm and 1:30 to 5pm, and Sunday from 10am to 5pm.

MENAI BRIDGE

The small town of Menai Bridge, 4km (2½ miles) west of Bangor, has several points of interest. Take a stroll westward along the Belgian Promenade, a walk constructed along the strait during World War II by Belgian refugees. You can go under the bridge, past some standing stones, which were recently erected, and Coed Cyrnol, a pinewood, to **Church Island.** The island's 14th-century **Church of St. Tysilio** was originally founded in the 7th century by St. Tysilio, son of the royal house of Powys and grandson of St. Pabo. St. Pabo is believed to have been a northern British chief who sought asylum on Anglesey. There is no phone to call for information, and hours are erratic.

Menai Bridge is the site every October 24 of the **Ffair-y-Borth fair,** which has been held here since the 16th century. Today, it's really a flea market, not worth a trip unless you're in the area.

This is an excellent place from which to view the Menai Strait sailing regatta in August each year.

For information, the little **tourist office** (✆ **01248/713177**) lies on High Street in the Pringle Sweater Shop. Its hours are irregular, depending on volunteers.

WHERE TO STAY & DINE

Gazelle   This former posting inn beside the Menai Straits is your top choice for a combined hotel, restaurant, and pub in the area. If you're arriving late in the day, it can be your overnight stopover and gateway to Anglesey, which you can explore the next day. Nearly 5km (3 miles) from the center of Menai Bridge, beside the road signposted to Beaumaris, the hotel's quay-side pub has panoramic views of both the waterfront and the mountains. It's the best place to meet locals and visitors, the latter of whom often have yachts moored nearby. The inn is attractively decorated; old Welsh dressers and time-blackened settles give the place character. Bedrooms are small to moderate in size, each simply decorated but comfortable. Bathrooms are just adequate for the function—nothing more. Some guests have to use the bathrooms in the hallways.

Substantial bar meals are served as well as full dinners in the restaurant. Solid Welsh fare includes fresh fish and local lamb. The Gazelle has the best food in the area, so try to dine here even if you're not staying as a guest.

Glyn Garth, Menai Bridge, Isle of Anglesey LL59 5PD. ✆ **01248/713364.** Fax 01248/713167. www.gazelle hotel.com. 8 units, 5 with bathroom. £35–£60 ($65–$111) double. MC, V. 3.2km (2 miles) northeast of Menai Bridge along A545. **Amenities:** Restaurant; limited room service; babysitting. *In room:* TV, coffeemaker.

LLANFAIR PG (LLANFAIRPWLLGWYNGYLLGOGERYCHWYRN-DROBWLLLLANTYSILIOGOGOGOCH)

Practically a suburb of Menai Bridge is a village to the west that has been heard of all over the world. Its fame is its name: Llanfairpwllgwyngyllgogerychwyrndrobwllllantysiliogogogoch, or something like that. It means "St. Mary's Church in the Hollow of the White Hazel near a Rapid Whirlpool and the Church of St. Tysilio near the Red Cave." The thought has been voiced that perhaps the name was invented as a tourist attraction. You can get the longest train platform ticket in the world from the station here, giving the full name. On maps and most references it is usually called "Llanfair PG" to differentiate it from several other Llanfairs in Wales. The first Women's Institute in Britain was founded here in 1915.

You're sure to see the **Marquess of Anglesey's column,** standing 27m (90 ft.) high on a mount 76m (250 ft.) above sea level. It has a statue of the marquess on top, to which visitors can climb (115 steps up a spiral staircase). The marquess lost a leg while he was second in command to the duke of Wellington at Waterloo and was thereafter called "One Leg" ("Ty Coch" in Welsh).

SEEING THE SIGHTS
Plas Newydd
About 1.6km (1 mile) southwest of the village with the long name, on the A4080, from a turn off the A5 almost opposite the Marquess of Anglesey Column, is **Plas Newydd, Llanfair PG** ★★ (© **01248/714795;** www.nationaltrust. org.uk), standing on the shores of the Menai Straits. It was the home of the seventh marquess of Anglesey, but is now owned by the National Trust. An ancient manor house, it was converted between 1783 and 1809 into a splendid mansion in the Gothic and neoclassical styles. Its Gothic Hall features a gallery and elaborate fan vaulting. In the long dining room, see the magnificent *trompe-l'oeil* mural by Rex Whistler. A military museum houses relics and uniforms of the Battle of Waterloo where the first marquess of Anglesey lost his leg. The beautiful woodland garden and lawns are worth visiting. The mansion is open to visitors. The gardens are open Saturday to Wednesday from 11am to 5:30pm from April to November 2, whereas the home can be visited only Saturday through Wednesday from noon to 5pm, also from April to November 2. A combined ticket for both the house and garden costs £8 ($15) for adults and £3 ($5.55) for children under age 16.

WHERE TO STAY
Carreg Bran Country Hotel   Set at the edge of the village, within a 10-minute walk from the center, this hotel dates from the late 1800s, when it was a privately owned manor house. Today, much altered and enlarged from its original design, it sports a white-painted brick facade and a modern wing that contains the simple but efficient and well-scrubbed small to midsize bedrooms, with little bathrooms containing shower stalls. Seven units are rented to nonsmokers. This is the only conventional hotel in town, providing more rooms than any of its smaller and less accessorized competitors. Since the building's transformation into a hotel occurred during the mid-1970s, some of the infrastructure might seem a bit dated, but overall, it provides comfortable and safe lodgings.

Church Lane. Llanfair PG, Anglesey LL61 5YH. © **800/528-1234** in the U.S., or 01248/714224. Fax 01248/ 715983 www.carregbran.uk.com. 29 units. £69 ($128) double. Rates include breakfast. AE, DC, MC, V. **Amenities:** Restaurant; pub; cocktail lounge; limited room service. *In room:* TV, dataport, coffeemaker, hair dryer, trouser press.

WHERE TO DINE
Penrohos Arms BRITISH/WELSH   In the town with the long name, this is your best bet for pub grub for the night. It's especially inviting after you've climbed the Anglesey monument and are ready for a cold beer. You can't miss it, as it lies in the center of the village opposite the famous rail station of the village

with the impossible name. The food is typical and standard, but it's made from fresh ingredients. If you like steak with mushrooms, fried seafood, or sausage and mashed potatoes, this is for you.

The pub also lets four bedrooms, each comfortable and costing £35 ($65) double, with breakfast included. Expect a TV and a small cubicle with a shower and toilet. Rooms have a chintz-filled decor inspired by Laura Ashley, but no phones. Views from the bedroom windows overlook the peaks of Snowdonia.

Holyhead Rd. Llanfair PG, Anglesey, LL61 5YQ. ℂ **01248/714620.** Reservations not needed. Main courses £4.50–£12 ($8.35–$22); lunch platters £2.50–£4.50 ($4.65–$8.35). DC, MC, V. Mon–Sat 11am–11pm; Sun noon–11pm.

6 Holyhead & Holy Island

550km (342 miles) NW of London; 346km (215 miles) NW of Cardiff; 305km (190 miles) N of Swansea

The largest town on Anglesey, Holyhead (it's pronounced Holly-head—don't ask us why) is not actually on Anglesey at all but on Holy Island. However, the two islands have long been linked. Packet boats between Holyhead and Ireland were recorded as far back at 1573.

The harbor of Holyhead was reconstructed in 1880 and now serves as a terminal for container-bearing ships.

People have come to this far point of northern Wales for a long, long time by water. Celtic invaders, early Christian missionaries, Romans, Vikings—whoever— have made their way here and in many cases stayed on for centuries.

ESSENTIALS

GETTING THERE   Holyhead is the terminus of the **North Wales Coast** rail line. Trains arrive hourly during the day from Cardiff, Bangor, Llandudno, Chester, Birmingham, and London. For information and schedules, call ℂ **0845/748-4950** or visit www.railtrack.co.uk. **Arriva** buses pull into Holyhead from Bangor every 30 minutes during the day. There is no station here, buses arriving along both London Road and Market Street. For information and schedules, call ℂ **0870/608-2608** or visit www.arriva.co.uk.

A causeway carries motorists across on the A5, which comes all the way from London, and a Four Mile Bridge on B4545 also links Holy Island to Anglesey.

Two unrelated ferryboat companies operate service between Holyhead and the Irish port of Dun Laoghaire, a railway and highway junction close to Dublin. (Some of them continue on even into Dublin harbor.) Both companies run conventional ferryboat service (transit time 3½ hours each way, with two departures daily). Both types of conveyance are suitable for both passengers and cars, although the catamarans cannot carry freight. Transit costs £20 ($37) round-trip on the conventional ferryboats; £30 ($56) round-trip on the catamarans for passengers traveling and returning on the same days. For more information, contact either the **Stena Line** (ℂ **0870/570-7070;** www.stenaline.co.uk) or **Irish Ferries** (ℂ **0870/532-9129;** www.irishferries.ie). Irish Ferries operates only between Holyhead and Dublin; it does not operate between Holyhead and Dun Laoghaire.

VISITOR INFORMATION   Information is available at the **Kiosk,** Stena Line, Terminal 1 (ℂ **01407/762622**), open daily in summer from 8:30am to 6pm. Open year-round, hours are from 8:30am to 6pm daily.

SEEING THE SIGHTS

Holyhead Mountain ⚐ is the highest point in Anglesey, at 216m (710 ft.). From the rocky height, you can see the Isle of Man, the Mourne Mountains in Ireland,

Snowdonia, and Cumbria on a clear day. The summit is the site of an ancient hill fort and the ruins of an Irish settlement from the 2nd to the 4th century A.D. The towering cliffs of North and South Stack are home to thousands of sea birds, and gray seals breed in the caves below. At the southern point of the mountain, **South Stack** is an automatic lighthouse built in 1808. It's 27m (91 ft.) high (60m/197 ft. above mean high water) and can be seen for 32km (20 miles). It's noted for its antique walls, its strategic position, and a state-of-the-art light beam. Open March through September daily from 8am to 6pm, charging £4 ($7.40) for adults or £3 ($5.55) for children under age 16. For information, contact the **Royal Society for the Protection of Birds** at 𝒞 **01407/763043.**

On Friday and Saturday, **general markets** are held in Holyhead.

St. Cybi's Church, Market Street (no phone), near the town center, is on the site of a 6th-century church; a Roman fort from the 3rd century also stood here. The site is open daily from 8am to 6pm; admission is free. For information, contact the tourist office (see above).

WHERE TO STAY & DINE

Boathouse Hotel   If you decide to overnight before taking a ferry in the morning, this hotel is just a few minutes' walk away from the terminal. The town's finest inn, it lies in a stellar position looking out over the water and the Holyhead Mountains, which can be seen through the bedroom windows. The midsize bedrooms are pleasantly and comfortably furnished, and the bathrooms, though small, are spic-and-span, with shower units. Most of the accommodations are nonsmoking, and one unit is large enough for families.

Newry Promenade, Newry Beach, Holyhead LL65 1YF. 𝒞 **01407/762094.** Fax 01407/764898. www. boathouse-hotel.co.uk. 17 units. £70 ($130) double. Rates include breakfast. AE, MC, V. **Amenities:** Bar lounge with food service; 24-hr. room service; rooms for those with limited mobility; nonsmoking rooms. *In room:* TV, coffeemaker.

Bull Hotel *(Kids)*   A bustling hotel, the long-popular Bull stands right at the approach to Holyhead. We'd give its competitor, the Boathouse, a slight edge, but the Bull is almost as good. We prefer the more comfortable midsize rooms in the main building, as opposed to the newer and more sterile ones in the annex, but both are comfortable, containing tidy bathrooms with showers. Four rooms are large enough for families. Because of its popular bars, the Bull is heavily patronized by the locals.

London Rd. Valley, Holyhead LL65 3DP. 𝒞 **01407/740351.** Fax 01407/742328. 14 units. £55 ($102) double. Rates include breakfast. AE, DC, MC, V. **Amenities:** 2 bars serving food. *In room:* TV, coffeemaker.

7 Conwy ⟨★⟩

387km (241 miles) NW of London; 59km (37 miles) E of Holyhead; 35km (22 miles) NE of Caernarfon

Unlike Llandudno, its 19th-century neighbor, Conwy is an ancient town. With its mighty medieval castle and complete town walls, this is a richly historic place.

The Conwy estuary is crossed by three **bridges** that lead to Conwy. The handsome suspension bridge was built in 1826 by Thomas Telford, bridge-builder extraordinaire. It looks as if it runs right into the castle, but it doesn't. It's closed to vehicular traffic now, but you can walk across it for free and marvel at how it served as the main entrance to the town for so long, with its narrow lanes and the sure bottleneck at the castle end. It replaced the ferry that was previously the only means of crossing the river. An exhibit of Telford's work is in the tollhouse. You can also see Robert Stephenson's tubular railroad bridge built in 1848, and the modern arched road bridge, completed in 1958.

St. Mary's, the parish church, stands inside the town walls on the site of 12th-century Cistercian abbey. In it are a Byzantine processional cross, a beautiful Tudor cross, and a 15th-century screen of fine workmanship. The churchyard contains a grave associated with William Wordsworth's poem *We Are Seven.*

ESSENTIALS

GETTING THERE   Trains run between Conwy and Llandudno, Bangor, and Holyhead, with easy connections to the rest of Wales. Llandudno is only a 4-minute ride away. For schedules and information, call ✆ **0845/604-0500.**

Arriva buses from Bangor heading for Llandudno pass through Conwy every 20 minutes during the day. Call ✆ **0870/608-2608** or visit www.arriva.co.uk for schedules and more information. Motorists from England head west along the North Wales coastline on A548.

VISITOR INFORMATION   The local tourist board at the **Conwy Castle Visitor Centre,** Castle Street (✆ **01492/592248**), dispenses information from Easter to May daily from 9:30am to 5pm; June to September daily 9:30am to 6pm; October 9:30am to 5pm; November to Easter Monday to Saturday 9:30am to 4pm and Sunday 11am to 4pm.

SEEING THE SIGHTS

Aberconwy House   This is the only remaining medieval merchant's house in Conwy, a town that used to have hundreds of them. Dating from the 14th century, this structure is owned by the National Trust, and houses an exhibition depicting the life of Conwy from Roman times. It includes a re-created 18th-century kitchen and a mussel-fishing corner, with the traditional instruments still used by the industry.

Castle St. and High St. ✆ 01492/592246. Admission £2.20 ($4.05) adults, £1.10 ($2.05) children under age 16, £5.50 ($10) family ticket. Mar 29–Nov 2 Wed–Mon 11am–5pm.

Conwy Castle ✹✹   The town centers around Conwy Castle. Edward I had this masterpiece of medieval architecture built after he conquered the last native prince of Wales, Llewelyn. The English king put up massive castles to convince the Welsh that he was the supreme authority. The castle follows the contours of a narrow strip of rock, the eight towers commanding the estuary of the River Conwy. The town wall that protected the borough, chartered by Edward in 1284, is almost intact, with 21 flanking towers and three twin-towered gateways. Visitors to the town can walk the walls. This is one castle you can't possibly miss seeing, as the road runs almost close enough for you to touch the walls in place. Allow an hour to visit.

Castle St. ✆ 01492/592358. www.castlewales.com/conwy.html. Admission £3.50 ($6.50) adults, £3 ($5.55) children under 16. Apr–May and Oct daily 9:30am–5pm; June–Sept daily 9:30am–6pm; Nov–Mar Mon–Sat 9:30am–4pm, Sun 11am–4pm. Closed Dec 24–26, Jan 1.

WHERE TO STAY & DINE

Groes Inn ✹✹   Oozing with four centuries of atmosphere and old-fashioned charm, this dates from 1573 and was the first licensed house in Wales. Although it has expanded over the years, the original core is still here, evoked by log fires, antiques, and open-beamed, time-blackened ceilings. For history buffs, it's the finest choice in the area. The accommodations are in a separate house away from the pub noise, and each midsize unit is comfortably furnished and equipped with a modernized bathroom. Rooms open onto bucolic views of sheep grazing in the fields and of rolling hills. The best units have balconies or private terraces.

One room has a four-poster bed; another is set up for guests in wheelchairs. Stop in for a lager or a hearty, home-cooked pub dinner.

Tyn-y-Groes, Conwy. LL32 8TN. ℂ 01492/650545. Fax 01492/650855. www.groesinn.com. 14 units. £95–£146 ($176–$270) double. AE, DC, MC, V. Lies 4.8km (3 miles) south of Conwy on B5106. **Amenities:** Restaurant; pub; breakfast-only room service; 1 room for those with limited mobility; nonsmoking rooms. *In room:* TV, coffeemaker, hair dryer.

The Old Rectory ⭑   The Welsh motto for the house, *Hardd Hafan Hedd*, means a beautiful haven of peace—and so it is. From its hillside perch, with terraced gardens, the inn sweeps across the Conwy Estuary for a view of Conwy Castle and the Snowdonia mountain range. Once the Tudor home of the rectors of the parish for centuries, it is furnished with paintings and antiques. A night here is like entering a bygone era. Each good-size bedroom has its own charm and style; a few have four-poster or half-tester beds. Comfort is foremost, from the sleep-inducing bed to the well-maintained private bathroom.

Wendy Vaughan is a grand chef, producing high-quality and creative dishes that have a light touch and artistic presentation. The Conwy salmon is a winner, and hormone-free meats are served, including succulent mountain Welsh lamb.

Llansanffraid, Glan Conwy, Conwy LL28 5LF. ℂ 01492/580611. Fax 01492/584555. www.oldrectorycountry house.co.uk. 6 units. £99–£169 ($183–$313) double. Rates include breakfast. Take the A470 4.8km (3 miles) from Conwy; Old Rectory is .8km (½ mile) south from A55/A470 junction on the left. No children under age 5. **Amenities:** Restaurant; bar; breakfast only room service; nonsmoking rooms. *In room:* TV, dataport, coffeemaker.

8 Llandudno ⭑

391km (243 miles) NW of London; 69km (43 miles) E of Holyhead

This Victorian seaside resort—the largest in Wales—nestles in a crescent between the giant headlands of the **Great Orme** and the **Little Orme,** which received their names from early Vikings who thought they resembled sea serpents when their bases were shrouded in mist. This premier resort of Wales has two beaches, one on the northern edge of town, flanking a boardwalk and the Irish Sea, and the other on the west side of town, opening onto the mountains of Snowdonia and the Conwy Estuary.

Llandudno was built beginning around 1850 by the Mostyn family, after whom many local roads, avenues, and sites are named. It was conceived as a means to cash in on the already-proven proclivity of the British of Queen Victoria's day—particularly the great middle classes—to go to the seashore in summer. It is built in a typically Victorian way with a promenade along the beach. The Victorian elegance and tradition of Llandudno has been maintained in the architecture of its buildings, but there the days-gone-by atmosphere stops.

ESSENTIALS

GETTING THERE   **BritRail** operates about six trains a day from London's Euston Station, many of which require changes of equipment in either Crewe or Chester, and in some cases, both. Overall, with waiting time included, it takes about 2½ hours to reach Llandudno from London by train. For information about this or any other railway schedule in Wales, call ℂ **0845/604-0500.**

During the day, the **Arriva Bus Company** (ℂ **0870/608-2608** for information about any bus timetable in Wales; www.arriva.co.uk) maintains buses to and from Bangor. They depart every 60 minutes.

If driving from England, take the M6 to the M56, then head across North Wales along the A55.

VISITORS INFORMATION The **Llandudno Tourist Information Centre,** 1–2 Chapel St. (© **01492/876413**) is open between April and October every day from 10am to 6pm. From November to March, it's open Monday to Wednesday, Friday, and Saturday from 9:30am to 4:30pm.

SEEING THE SIGHTS

From the summit of the **Great Orme** (206m/679 ft.), you get a panoramic view of the North Wales coast. You can walk up to the top if you're really energetic, but we advise other means. At Happy Valley, exotic sheltered gardens lie at the foot of the Great Orme, near the pier at the west end of the Llandudno Bay promenade. Take the **Great Orme Tramway** (© **01492/575275**) to reach the top. The tramway has been carrying passengers to the summit since 1902. It operates only between mid-March and October, daily from 10am to 6pm. It costs £4 ($7.40) round-trip for adults, £2.80 ($5.20) for children under age 14. It is closed in winter, during which period you can drive along a spectacular cliff-edge road, the Marine Drive, which winds uphill in a circular route that reaches a point near the summit of the Great Orme. Cars pay a toll of £1 ($1.85) each.

Just above the Marine Drive is the ancient **Church of St. Tudno,** from which the town derives its name. The present stone building dates from the 12th century, but the church was founded 600 years earlier. Between April and October, it's open 24 hours a day, and between June and September, there are open-air worship services every Sunday at 11am. For more information about the church and its services, or to gain entrance during other times of the year, contact the Reverend P. Cousins at © **01492/876624.**

At the end of the north-shore promenade, one of Britain's finest Victorian piers was built jutting 699m (2,295 ft.) out into the bay at the base of the Great Orme, with an ornate covered pavilion at the end. You can find entertainment, food, fishing, or just relaxation on the pier. The north-shore beach is busy in summer, with traditional British seaside activities, including donkey rides, Punch and Judy shows, boat trips, and a children's fun land across the promenade.

The seafront's most visible public monument is the **North Wales Theatre,** The Promenade (© **01492/872000;** www.nwtheatre.co.uk). Built in the early 1990s, it had what amounted to the longest stage in Britain, until the more recent construction of a theater in Bournemouth surpassed it by a mere 15cm (6 in.). Throughout the year, it's the venue for a changing roster of entertainment that includes everything from opera to rock 'n' roll concerts. Recent performances have included *Phantom of the Opera on Ice.* Most shows begin at 7:30pm. Tickets cost £7 to £28 ($13–$51).

Amgueddfa Llandudno Museum, 17–19 Gloddaeth St. (© **01492/876517**), displays development of Llandudno as a seaside resort. Period rooms are open to viewers. It is open Easter through October Tuesday through Saturday 10:30am to 1pm and 2 to 5pm, Sunday 2:15 to 5pm; Tuesday to Saturday 1:30 to 4:30pm the rest of the year. Admission is £1.50 ($2.80) for adults, 75p ($1.40) for children, £3.50 ($6.50) family ticket.

WHERE TO STAY
VERY EXPENSIVE

Bodysgallen Hall *(Finds* This is the finest address in the north of Wales, a dramatic 17th-century country house set in 80 hectares (200 acres) of parkland and manicured gardens. It would be the only suitable address for the novelist Henry James, were he alive today. Skillfully restored, it offers architectural merit combined with 21st-century comfort. The hall has a 13th-century tower that was a lookout post for Conwy Castle, 2.5km (1½ miles) away. You can still climb the tower for a panoramic view. Each of the spacious and elegant bedrooms evokes a certain period in their styles and colors; some have four-poster beds. Bathrooms are large and state of the art. Some of the units, as good as those in the main house, are in converted cottages. Wherever you wander, the past is evoked with wood-paneled walls, oil paintings, and open fires.

One snippy British food critic felt that after 2 days the menu in the restaurant becomes monotonous. We once based here for a week, however, and found infinite variety in game, including pigeon and venison, and local fare such as smoked salmon and Welsh rabbit, even Welsh veal in an old-fashioned honey and mead sauce. Call for a reservation if staying elsewhere; it's a memorable culinary experience, in cuisine, atmosphere, and service.

3.2km (2 miles) southeast along A470 from Llandudno, Llandudno LL30 IRS. ℂ **01492/584466.** Fax 01492/ 582519. www.bodysgallen.com. 35 units. £165–£290 ($305–$537) double. MC, V. No children under age 8. **Amenities:** Restaurant; bar; indoor heated pool; outdoor tennis court; health club; spa; laundry service; dry cleaning; 1 room for those with limited mobility; nonsmoking rooms. *In room:* TV, dataport, fridge, hair dryer.

EXPENSIVE

Empire Hotel ★★★   In an ocean of tacky hotels, this one is a winner, the best within the town itself. It is, in fact, one of the best hotels in North Wales. Off the Promenade, near the Great Orme cable car, it looks down on the pier and Happy Valley, about 274m (900 ft.) away. Family managed, it is furnished with antiques and fine paintings in the Victorian tradition. Bedrooms are medium-size to spacious—luxuriously furnished with excellent marble bathrooms, which are impeccably kept. A Victorian annex, known as "Number 72," contains eight of the establishment's finest rooms, filled with Victorian antiques, French linen, touches of silk, and a bathtub-cum-Jacuzzi. We prefer these to the accommodations in the main building. You get luxury and style throughout, and not a lot of attitude. The public areas carry out the Victorian theme, and are known for their collection of Russell Flint prints.

The award-winning Watkins restaurant presents an excellent fixed-price menu changed daily and based whenever possible on local produce.

Church Walks, Llandudno, Conwy LL30 2HE. ℂ **01492/860555.** Fax 01492/860791. www.empirehotel. co.uk. 58 units. £70–£110 ($130–$204) double; £120 ($222) suite. AE, DC, MC, V. **Amenities:** Restaurant; bar; 2 pools (1 indoor, 1 outdoor); solarium; sauna; limited room service; laundry service; beauty treatments; live entertainment. *In room:* TV, coffeemaker, hair dryer.

St. Tudno Hotel ★★   For fans of *Alice in Wonderland,* this is the only place to stay in town. Alice Liddell, immortalized by Lewis Carroll in *Alice in Wonderland,* checked in here at the age of 8 on her first visit to Llandudno in 1861. It's a charming Victorian terraced seafront hotel that escapes the tacky curse of many of its neighbors. The hotel has kept abreast of the times—you won't fall down the rabbit hole if checking in here—and is one of the top seafront hotels in North Wales. Richly decorated inside, it is opulent and luxurious, with first-class service. Martin and Janette Bland offer a beautiful product with individually designed bedrooms that come in a variety of sizes. Rooms in the rear have slightly less glamour but are more tranquil and a lot cheaper. Traditionalists prefer to check into the Alice Suite. Public rooms evoke the Victorian era.

If you're not a guest, call for a dinner reservation; St. Tudno offers some of the area's finest dining. Local seafood is prominently featured (try the Conwy mussel risotto with saffron). Welsh specials have flair—not the usual drab British resort food. Chefs aren't afraid to toss alcohol into the skillets to enhance flavor.

Llandudno

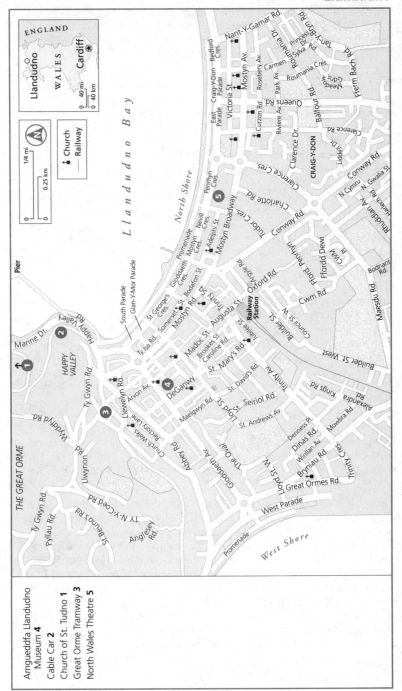

Amgueddfa Llandudno
    Museum **4**
Cable Car **2**
Church of St. Tudno **1**
Great Orme Tramway **3**
North Wales Theatre **5**

North Promenade, Llandudno, Gwynedd LL30 2LP. ✆ **01492/874411.** Fax 01492/860407. www.st-tudno. co.uk. 18 units. £104–£205 ($192–$379) double; £166–£280 ($307–$518) Alice Suite. Rates include breakfast. AE, MC, V. **Amenities:** Restaurant; bar; heated indoor pool; limited room service; babysitting; rooms for those with limited mobility; nonsmoking rooms. *In room:* TV, dataport, minibar, coffeemaker, hair dryer.

INEXPENSIVE

Tan Lan Hotel ★ *Value*   This is your best bet for the night if you're seeking good value accommodations on the tranquil west shore of Llandudno. It lies under the Great Orme, and its owners offer cozy lodgings and a warm welcome. The rooms upstairs are a bit quieter, but all are medium-size, brightly decorated, and well-furnished, with firm mattresses and small but adequate bathrooms that are kept immaculately clean. A trio of units are big enough for families and children get a warm welcome. All bedrooms are nonsmoking. Owners Kerry and Peter Saunders are a font of information about touring in the area.

The dining room, decorated in the best tradition of the English play *Separate Tables,* is known for a varied menu—nothing too experimental, however.

Great Orme's Rd., West Shore, Llandudno, Conwy LL30 2AR. ✆ **01492/860221.** Fax 01492/870219. www. tanlanhotel.co.uk. 17 units. £46–£58 ($85–$107) double. Rates include breakfast. MC, V. **Amenities:** Restaurant; bar; 2 lounges; garden for drinks. *In room:* TV, dataport, coffeemaker, hair dryer.

WHERE TO DINE

Kings Head ★ BRITISH/INTERNATIONAL   This is the oldest and most evocative pub in town, with a 300-year-old pedigree, a prominent logo that features every Brit's favorite royal, Henry VIII, and bottle-glass windows. This place used to welcome scores of miners, and in their memory, instead of a ploughman's lunch of bread and cheese, it offers a miner's platter (essentially the same, we find). All arriving patrons enter the establishment by passing through the pub, then remain for either a pint or two, or settle down for a meal that's available within the pub or within a separate dining room. Lunches are simpler than dinners and feature standard but not exceptional dishes, such an excellent—and always popular—version of steak and ale pie. Dinners are more elaborate, with fresh fish, such as sea bass enlivened by a lemon-flavored butter sauce; and hearty meat dishes, such a tender and flavor-filled filet steak with pepper sauce.

Old Rd. ✆ **01492/877993.** Reservations not necessary. Lunch platters £5–£8 ($9.25–$15); dinner main courses £6.25–£15 ($12–$28). DC, MC, V. Food service daily noon–2:30pm; Mon–Sat 6–11pm; Sun 2:30–11pm. Bar Mon–Sat 11am–11pm; Sun noon–11pm.

Richard's Bistro ★ WELSH/CONTINENTAL   Richard Hendey's cuisine and friendly service have brought him a faithful list of habitués nightly. In his basement bistro, a short walk from the pier, he spins his own culinary magic in the kitchen, turning out satisfying meals that are full of flavor. From the carnivore to the vegetarian, he aims to please, and does so admirably well. Not for the faint of heart, his perfectly roasted Welsh lamb comes with its own sautéed kidneys, everything bound together in a red-wine and grainy mustard sauce. A blackboard announces the seafood specials of the day, and generally these dishes are your best bet. His chargrilled filet of gray mullet with a white-wine sauce properly showcases this chef's talents. Everything is handled with admirable ease. Once you see the toffee apple cheesecake with caramel sauce float by, you'll somehow manage to make room for it.

7 Church Walks. ✆ **01492/877924.** Reservations required. Fixed-price menu £24 ($44). AE, MC, V. Tues–Sat 5:30–11pm.

Appendix:
England in Depth

1 History 101

FROM MURKY BEGINNINGS TO ROMAN OCCUPATION Britain was probably split off from the continent of Europe some 8 millennia ago by the continental drift and other natural forces. The early inhabitants, the Iberians, were later to be identified with stories of fairies, brownies, and "little people." These are the enterprising people who are believed to have created Stonehenge, but despite that great and mysterious monument, little is known about them.

They were replaced by the iron-wielding Celts, whose massive invasions around 500 B.C. drove the Iberians back to the Scottish Highlands and Welsh mountains, where some of their descendants still live today.

In 54 B.C., Julius Caesar invaded England, but the Romans did not become established there until A.D. 43. They went as far as Caledonia (now Scotland), where they gave up, leaving that land to "the painted ones," or the warring Picts. The wall built by Emperor Hadrian across the north of England marked the northernmost reaches of the Roman Empire. During almost 4 centuries of occupation, the Romans built roads, villas, towns, walls, and fortresses; they farmed the land and introduced first their pagan religions, then Christianity. Agriculture and trade flourished.

FROM ANGLO-SAXON RULE TO THE NORMAN CONQUEST When the Roman legions withdrew, around A.D. 410, they left the country open to waves of invasions by Jutes, Angles, and Saxons, who established themselves in small kingdoms throughout the former Roman colony. From the 8th through the 11th century, the Anglo-Saxons contended with Danish raiders for control of the land.

By the time of the Norman conquest, the Saxon kingdoms were united under an elected king, Edward the Confessor. His successor was to rule less than a year before the Norman invasion. The date 1066 is familiar to every English schoolchild. It marked an epic event, the only successful military invasion of Britain in history, and one of England's great turning points: King Harold, the last Anglo-Saxon king, was defeated at the Battle of Hastings, and William of Normandy was crowned William I.

One of William's first acts was to order a survey of the land he had conquered, assessing all property in the nation for tax purposes. This survey was called the *Domesday Book,* or "Book of Doom," as some pegged it. The resulting document was completed around 1086 and has been a fertile sourcebook for British historians ever since.

Norman rule had an enormous impact on English society. All high offices were held by Normans, and the Norman barons were given great grants of lands; they built Norman-style castles and strongholds throughout the country. French was the language of the court for centuries—few people realize that heroes such as Richard the Lionheart probably spoke little or no English.

FROM THE RULE OF HENRY II TO THE MAGNA CARTA   In 1154, Henry II, the first of the Plantagenets, was crowned (reigned 1154–89). This remarkable character in English history ruled a vast empire—not only most of Britain but Normandy, Anjou, Brittany, and Aquitaine in France.

Henry was a man of powerful physique, both charming and terrifying. He reformed the courts and introduced the system of common law, which still operates in moderated form in England today and also influenced the American legal system. But Henry is best remembered for ordering the infamous murder of Thomas à Becket, Archbishop of Canterbury. Henry, at odds with his archbishop, exclaimed, "Who will rid me of this turbulent priest?" His knights, overhearing and taking him at his word, murdered Thomas in front of the high altar in Canterbury Cathedral.

Henry's wife, Eleanor of Aquitaine, the most famous woman of her time, was no less of a colorful character. She accompanied her first husband, Louis VII of France, on the Second Crusade, and it was rumored that she had a romantic affair at that time with the Saracen leader, Saladin. Domestic and political life did not run smoothly, however, and Henry and Eleanor and their sons were often at odds. The pair has been the subject of many plays and films, including *The Lion in Winter, Becket,* and T. S. Eliot's *Murder in the Cathedral.*

Two of their sons were crowned kings of England. Richard the Lionheart actually spent most of his life outside England, on crusades, or in France. John was forced by his nobles to sign the Magna Carta at Runnymede, in 1215—another date well known to English schoolchildren.

The Magna Carta guaranteed that the king was subject to the rule of law and gave certain rights to the king's subjects, beginning a process that eventually led to the development of parliamentary democracy as it is known in Britain today. This process would have enormous influence on the American colonies many years later. The Magna Carta became known as the cornerstone of English liberties, though it only granted liberties to the barons. It took the rebellion of Simon de Montfort half a century later to introduce the notion that the boroughs and burghers should also have a voice and representation.

THE BLACK DEATH & THE WARS OF THE ROSES   In 1348, half the population died as the Black Death ravaged England. By the end of the century, the population of Britain had fallen from four million to two million.

England also suffered in the Hundred Years' War, which went on intermittently for more than a century. By 1371, England had lost much of its land on French soil. Henry V, immortalized by Shakespeare, revived England's claims to France, and his victory at Agincourt was notable for making obsolete the forms of medieval chivalry and warfare.

After Henry's death in 1422, disputes arose among successors to the crown that resulted in a long period of civil strife, the Wars of the Roses, between the Yorkists, who used a white rose as their symbol, and the Lancastrians with their red rose. The last Yorkist king was Richard III, who got bad press from Shakespeare, but who is defended to this day as a hero by the people of the city of York. Richard was defeated at Bosworth Field, and the victory introduced England to the first Tudor, the shrewd and wily Henry VII.

THE TUDORS TAKE THE THRONE   The Tudors were unlike the kings who had ruled before them. They introduced into England a strong central monarchy with far-reaching powers. The system worked well under the first three strong and capable Tudor monarchs, but it began to break down later when the Stuarts came to the throne.

Henry VIII is surely the most notorious Tudor. Imperious and flamboyant, a colossus among English royalty, he slammed shut the door on the Middle Ages and introduced the Renaissance to England. He is best known, of course, for his treatment of his six wives and the unfortunate fates that befell five of them.

When his first wife, Catherine of Aragon, failed to produce an heir, and his ambitious mistress, Anne Boleyn, became pregnant, he tried to annul his marriage, but the pope refused, and Catherine contested the action. Defying the power of Rome, Henry had his marriage with Catherine declared invalid and secretly married Anne Boleyn in 1533.

The events that followed had profound consequences and introduced the religious controversy that was to dominate English politics for the next 4 centuries. Henry's break with the Roman Catholic Church and the formation of the Church of England, with himself as supreme head, was a turning point in English history. It led eventually to the Dissolution of the Monasteries, civil unrest, and much social dislocation. The confiscation of the church's land and possessions brought untold wealth into the king's coffers, wealth that was distributed to a new aristocracy that supported the monarch. In one sweeping gesture, Henry destroyed the ecclesiastical culture of the Middle Ages. Among those executed for refusing to cooperate with Henry's changes was Sir Thomas More, humanist, international man of letters, and author of *Utopia*.

Anne Boleyn bore Henry a daughter, the future Elizabeth I, but failed to produce a male heir. She was brought to trial on a trumped-up charge of adultery and beheaded; in 1536, Henry married Jane Seymour, who died giving birth to Edward VI. For his next wife, he looked farther afield and chose Anne of Cleves from a flattering portrait, but she proved disappointing—he called her "The Great Flanders Mare." He divorced her the same year and next picked a pretty young woman from his court, Catherine Howard. She was also beheaded on a charge of adultery but, unlike Anne Boleyn, was probably guilty. Finally, he married an older woman, Catherine Parr, in 1543. She survived him.

Henry's heir, sickly Edward VI (reigned 1547–53), did not live long. He died of consumption—or, as rumor has it, overmedication. He was succeeded by his sister, Mary I (reigned 1553–58), and the trouble Henry had stirred up with the break with Rome came home to roost for the first time. Mary restored the Roman Catholic faith, and her persecution of the adherents of the Church of England earned her the name of "Bloody Mary." Some 300 Protestants were executed, many burned alive at the stake. She made an unpopular and unhappy marriage to Philip of Spain; despite her bloody reputation, her life was a sad one.

Elizabeth I (reigned 1558–1603) came next to the throne, ushering in an era of peace and prosperity, exploration, and a renaissance in science and learning. An entire age was named after her: the Elizabethan age. She was the last great and grand monarch to rule England, and her passion and magnetism were said to match her father's. Through her era marched Drake, Raleigh, Frobisher, Grenville, Shakespeare, Spenser, Byrd, and Hilliard. During her reign, she had to face the appalling precedent of ordering the execution of a fellow sovereign, Mary, Queen of Scots. Her diplomatic skills kept war at bay until 1588, when at the apogee of her reign, the Spanish Armada was defeated. She will be forever remembered as "Good Queen Bess."

FROM THE RESTORATION TO THE NAPOLEONIC WARS   The reign of Charles II was the beginning of a dreadful decade that saw London decimated by the Great Plague and destroyed by the Great Fire.

His successor, James II, attempted to return the country to Catholicism, an attempt that so frightened the powers that be that Catholics were for a long time deprived of their civil rights. James was deposed in the "Glorious Revolution" of 1688 and succeeded by his daughter Mary (1662–94) and William of Orange (1650–1702). (William of Orange was the grandson of Charles I, the tyrannical king whom Cromwell helped to depose.) This secured a Protestant succession that has continued to this day. These tolerant and levelheaded monarchs signed a bill of rights, establishing the principle that the monarch reigns not by divine right but by the will of Parliament. William outlived his wife, reigning until 1702.

Queen Anne then came to the throne ruling from 1702 until her own death in 1714. She was the sister of Mary of Orange and was another daughter of James II. The last of the Stuarts, Anne marked her reign with the most significant event, the 1707 Act of Union with Scotland. She outlived all her children, leaving her throne without an heir.

Upon the death of Anne, England looked for a Protestant prince to succeed her and chose George of Hanover who reigned from 1714–27. Though he spoke only German and spent as little time in England as possible, he was chosen because he was the great-grandson of James I. Beginning with this "distant cousin" to the throne, the reign of George I marked the beginning of the 174-year rule of the Hanoverians who preceded Victoria.

George I left the running of the government to politicians and created the office of prime minister. Under the Hanoverians, the powers of Parliament were extended, and the constitutional monarchy developed into what it is today.

The American colonies were lost under the Hanoverian George III, but other British possessions were expanded: Canada was won from the French in the Seven Years' War (1756–63), British control over India was affirmed, and Captain Cook claimed Australia and New Zealand for England. The British became embroiled in the Napoleonic Wars (1795–1815), achieving two of their greatest victories and acquiring two of their greatest heroes: Nelson at Trafalgar and Wellington at Waterloo.

THE INDUSTRIAL REVOLUTION & THE REIGN OF VICTORIA

The mid- to late 18th century saw the beginnings of the Industrial Revolution. This event changed the lives of the laboring class, created a wealthy middle class, and transformed England from a rural, agricultural society into an urban, industrial economy. England was now a world-class financial and military power. Male suffrage was extended, though women were to continue under a series of civil disabilities for the rest of the century.

Queen Victoria's reign (1837–1901) coincided with the height of the Industrial Revolution. When she ascended the throne, the monarchy as an institution was in considerable doubt, but her 64-year reign, the longest tenure in English history, was an incomparable success.

The Victorian era was shaped by the growing power of the bourgeoisie, the queen and her consort's personal moral stance, and the perceived moral responsibilities of managing a vast empire. During this time, the first trade unions were formed, a public school system was developed, and railroads were built.

Victoria never recovered from the death of her German husband, Albert. He died from typhoid fever in 1861, and the queen never remarried. Though she had many children, she found them tiresome but was a pillar of family values nonetheless. One historian said her greatest asset was her relative ordinariness.

Middle-class values ruled Victorian England and were embodied by the queen. The racy England of the past went underground. Our present-day view of England is still influenced by the attitudes of the Victorian era, and we tend to forget that English society in earlier centuries was famous for its rowdiness, sexual license, and spicy scandal.

Victoria's son Edward VII (reigned 1901–10) was a playboy who had waited too long in the wings. He is famous for mistresses, especially Lillie Langtry, and his love of elaborate dinners. During his brief reign, he, too, had an era named after him: the Edwardian age. Under Edward, England entered the 20th century at the height of its imperial power. At home, the motorcar and the telephone radically changed social life, and the women's suffrage movement began.

World War I marked the end of an era. It had been assumed that peace, progress, prosperity, empire, and even social improvement would continue indefinitely. World War I and the troubled decades of social unrest, political uncertainty, and the rise of Nazism and fascism put an end to these expectations.

THE WINDS OF WAR   World War II began in 1939, and soon thereafter Britain found a new and inspiring leader, Winston Churchill. Churchill led the nation during its "finest hour." From the time the Germans took France, Britain stood alone against Hitler. The evacuation of Dunkirk in 1940, the blitz of London, and the Battle of Britain were dark hours for the British people, and Churchill is remembered for urging them to hold onto their courage. Once the British forces were joined by their American allies, the tide finally turned, culminating in the D-day invasion of German-occupied Normandy. These bloody events are still remembered by many with pride, and with nostalgia for the era when Britain was still a great world power.

The years following World War II brought many changes to England. Britain began to lose its grip on an empire (India became independent in 1947), and the Labour government, which came into power in 1945, established the welfare state and brought profound social change to Britain.

QUEEN ELIZABETH RULES TO THE PRESENT DAY   Upon the death of the "wartime king," George VI, Elizabeth II ascended the throne in 1953. Her reign has seen the erosion of Britain's once-mighty industrial power, and, in recent years, a severe recession.

Political power has seesawed back and forth between the Conservative and Labour parties. Margaret Thatcher, who became prime minister in 1979, seriously eroded the welfare state and was ambivalent toward the European Union. Her popularity soared during the successful Falklands War, when Britain seemed to recover some of its military glory for a brief time.

Though the queen has remained steadfast and punctiliously has performed her ceremonial duties, rumors about the royal family abounded, and in the year 1992, which Queen Elizabeth labeled an *annus horribilis,* a devastating fire swept through Windsor Castle, the marriages of several of her children crumbled, and the queen agreed to pay taxes for the first time. Prince Charles and Princess Diana agreed to a separation, and there were ominous rumblings about the future of the House of Windsor. By 1994 and 1995, Britain's economy was improving after several glum years, but Conservative prime minister John Major, heir to Margaret Thatcher's legacy, was coming under increasing criticism.

The IRA, reputedly enraged at the slow pace of peace talks, relaunched its reign of terror across London in February 1996, planting a massive bomb that ripped through a building in London's Docklands, injuring more than 100 people and killing two. Shattered, too, was the 17-month cease-fire by the IRA, which brought hope that peace was at least possible. Another bomb went off in Manchester in June.

Headlines about the IRA bombing gave way to another big bomb: the end of the marriage of Princess Diana and Prince Charles. The Wedding of the Century had become the Divorce of the Century. But details of the $26 million divorce settlement didn't satisfy the curious: Scrutiny of Prince Charles's relationship with Camilla Parker-Bowles, as well as gossip about Princess Diana's love life, continued in the press.

In 1997, the political limelight now rested on the young Labour leader Tony Blair. From his rock-star acquaintances to his "New Labour" rhetoric, which is chock-full of pop-culture buzzwords, he is a stark contrast to the more staid Major. His media-savvy personality obviously registered with the British electorate. On May 1, 1997, the Labour Party ended 18 years of Conservative rule with a landslide election victory. At age 44, Blair became Britain's youngest prime minister in 185 years, following in the wake of the largest Labour triumph since Winston Churchill was swept out of office at the end of World War II.

Blair's election—which came just at the moment when London was being touted by the international press for its renaissance in art, music, fashion, and dining—had many British entrepreneurs poised and ready to take advantage of what they perceived as enthusiasm for new ideas and ventures. Comparisons to Harold Macmillan and his reign over the Swinging Sixties were inevitable, and insiders agreed that something was in the air.

However, events took a shocking turn in August 1997 when Princess Diana was killed—along with her companion, Harrods heir Dodi al-Fayed—in a high-speed car crash in Paris.

"The People's Princess" still continued to dominate many headlines in 1998 with bizarre conspiracy theories about her death. But the royal family isn't the real force in Britain today. The spotlight remains on Tony Blair, who is moving ahead in streamlining the government.

Blair continues to lead Britain on a program of constitutional reform without parallel in the last century. Critics fear that Blair will one day preside over a "disunited" Britain, with Scotland breaking away and Northern Ireland forming a self-government.

Of course, the future of the monarchy still remains a hot topic of discussion in Britain. There is little support for doing away with the monarchy in Britain today in spite of wide criticism of the royal family's behavior in the wake of Diana's death. Apparently, if polls are to be believed, some three-quarters of the British populace want the monarchy to continue. Prince Charles is even making a comeback with the British public and has appeared in public—to the delight of the paparazzi—with his longtime mistress, Camilla Parker-Bowles. At the very least, the monarchy is good for the tourist trade, on which Britain is increasingly dependent. And what would the tabloids do without it?

The big news among royal watchers in Britain early in 2002 was the death of Princess Margaret at age 71, followed 7 weeks later by the death of Queen Mother Elizabeth at the age of 101. The most popular royal, the Queen "Mum" was a symbol of courage and dignity, especially during the tumultuous World War II years when London was under bombardment from Nazi Germany. The remains of the Queen Mother were laid to rest alongside her husband in the George VI Memorial Chapel at St. George's at Windsor Castle. The ashes of Princess Margaret were also interred with her parents in the same chapel.

At the dawn of the millennium, major social changes occurred in Britain. No sooner had the year 2000 begun than Britain announced a change of its code of conduct for the military, allowing openly gay men and women to serve in the armed forces. The action followed a European court ruling in the fall of 1999 that forbade Britain to discriminate against homosexuals. This change brings Britain in line with almost all other NATO countries, including France, Canada, and Germany. The United States remains at variance with the trend.

After promising beginnings, the 21st century got off to a bad start in Britain. In the wake of mad-cow disease flare-ups, the country was swept by a foot-and-mouth-disease epidemic that disrupted the country's agriculture and threatened one of the major sources of British livelihoods, its burgeoning tourist industry. After billions of pounds in tourism were lost the panic has now subsided. The government has intervened to take whatever preventive measure it can.

Following the September 11, 2001, terrorist attacks, Tony Blair and his government joined in a show of support for the United States, condemning the aerial bombardments and loss of life. Not only that, British joined in the war in Afghanistan against the dreaded Taliban. However, by 2003, Blair's backing of George Bush's stance against President Saddam Hussein of Iraq had brought his popularity to an all-time low.

Britain's involvement in Iraq remains an unpopular cause. In February 2003, an estimated million protesters, the largest demonstration in the history of London, gathered to oppose military intervention in Iraq.

On an economic front, Britain still shies away from joining the so-called euro umbrella. In June 2003, Tony Blair and Chancellor Gordon Brown declared that abandoning British pound sterling in favor of the euro, prevailing on the Continent, was not right for the country at this time.

2 Pies, Pudding & Pints: The Lowdown on British Cuisine

The late British humorist George Mikes wrote that "the Continentals have good food; the English have good table manners." But the British no longer deserve their reputation for soggy cabbage and tasteless dishes. Contemporary London—and the country as a whole—boasts fine restaurants and sophisticated cuisine.

If you want to see what Britain is eating today, just drop in at Harvey Nichol's Fifth Floor in London's Knightsbridge for its dazzling display of produce from all over the globe.

The new buzzword for British cuisine is *magpie,* meaning borrowing ideas from global travels, taking them home, and improving on the original.

Be aware that many of the trendiest, most innovative restaurants are mind-blowingly expensive, especially in London. We've pointed out some innovative but affordable choices in this book, but if you're really trying to save on dining costs, you'll no doubt find yourself falling back on the traditional pub favorites (or better still, turning to an increasingly good selection of ethnic restaurants).

WHAT YOU'LL FIND ON THE MENU IN ENGLAND   On any pub menu, you're likely to encounter such dishes as the **Cornish pasty** and **shepherd's pie.** The first, traditionally made from Sunday-meal leftovers and taken by West Country fishers for Monday lunch, consists of chopped potatoes, carrots, and onions mixed together with seasoning and put into a pastry envelope. The second is a deep dish of chopped cooked beef mixed with onions and seasoning, covered with a layer of mashed potatoes, and served hot. Another version is **cottage pie,** which is minced beef covered with potatoes and also served hot. Of course, these beef dishes are subject to availability. In addition to a pasty, Cornwall also gives us **Stargazy Pie**—a deep-dish fish pie with a crisp crust covering a creamy concoction of freshly caught herring and vegetables.

The most common pub meal, though, is the **ploughman's lunch,** traditional farm-worker's fare, consisting of a good chunk of local cheese, a hunk of home-made crusty white or brown bread, some butter, and a pickled onion or two, washed down with ale. You'll now find such variations as pâté and chutney occasionally replacing the onions and cheese. Or you might find **Lancashire hot pot,** a stew of mutton, potatoes, kidneys, and onions (sometimes carrots). This concoction was originally put into a deep dish and set on the edge of the stove to cook slowly while the workers spent the day at the local mill.

Among appetizers, called **starters** in England, the most typical are potted shrimp (small buttered shrimp preserved in a jar), prawn cocktail, and smoked salmon. You might also be served fish pie, which is very light fish pâté. Most menus will feature a variety of soups, including cock-a-leekie (chicken soup flavored with leeks), perhaps a game soup that has been doused with sherry, and many others.

Among the best-known traditional English meals is **roast beef** and **Yorkshire pudding** (the pudding is made with a flour base and cooked under the roast, allowing the fat from the meat to drop onto it). The beef could easily be a large sirloin (rolled loin), which, so the story goes, was named by James I when he was a guest at Houghton Tower, Lancashire. "Arise, Sir Loin," he cried, as he knighted the leg of beef before him with his dagger. (Again, because of the mad-cow crisis, beef dishes may not be available or advisable.) Another dish that makes use of a flour base is toad-in-the-hole, in which sausages are cooked in batter. Game, especially pheasant and grouse, is also a staple on British tables.

On any menu, you'll find **fresh seafood:** cod, haddock, herring, plaice, and Dover sole, the aristocrat of flatfish. Cod and haddock are used in making British **fish and chips** (chips are fried potatoes or thick french fries), which the true Briton covers with salt and vinegar. If you like **oysters,** try some of the famous Colchester variety. On the west coast, you'll find a not-to-be-missed delicacy: **Morecambe Bay shrimp.** Every region of England has its seafood specialties. In Ely, lying in the marshy fen district of East Anglia, it might be fenland eel pie with a twiggy seaweed as your green vegetable. Amphire also grows here in the salt marshes and along the Norfolk Coast. It's pickled in May and June and appears as a delicacy on many summer menus.

The **East End of London** has quite a few interesting old dishes, among them tripe and onions. In winter, Dr. Johnson's favorite tavern, the Cheshire Cheese on Fleet Street, offers a beefsteak-kidney-mushroom-and-game pudding in a suet case; in summer, there's a pastry case. East Enders can still be seen on Sunday at the Jellied Eel stall by Petticoat Lane, eating eel, cockles (small clams), mussels, whelks, and winkles—all with a touch of vinegar.

The British call desserts **sweets,** though some people still refer to any dessert as **pudding. Trifle** is the most famous English dessert, consisting of sponge cake soaked in brandy or sherry, coated with fruit or jam, and topped with cream custard. A **fool,** such as gooseberry fool, is a light cream dessert whipped up from seasonal fruits. Regional sweets include the **northern flitting dumpling** (dates, walnuts, and syrup mixed with other ingredients and made into a pudding that is easily sliced and carried along when you're "flitting" from place to place). Similarly, **hasty pudding,** a Newcastle dish, is supposed to have been invented by people in a hurry to avoid the bailiff. It consists of stale bread, to which some dried fruit and milk are added before it is put into the oven.

Cheese is traditionally served after dessert as a savory. There are many regional cheeses, the best known being cheddar, a good, solid, mature cheese.

Others are the semi-smooth Caerphilly, from a beautiful part of Wales, and Stilton, a blue-veined crumbly cheese that's often enjoyed with a glass of port.

A TASTE OF WALES   The food served in Wales is often indistinguishable from that in England, but there are a number of specialties you should try that you won't find elsewhere.

The **leek** is one of the national emblems of Wales, and is used in a number of dishes. The selection of the leek for this national honor is lost in the dim past, although associated with St. David, patron saint of Wales. Today the leek is worn on St. David's Day, March 1, a national holiday.

Among dishes in which the leek is used is **cawl mamgu,** a rich soup or stew. The most commonly used recipe calls for lamb or mutton, turnips (the Welsh call them Swedes), carrots, potatoes, parsnips, onions, and leeks. At home the broth is often served first with bread, the meat and vegetables being used as a main course. In some sections of the country, home-cured bacon is the meat used, brewed up with finely chopped vegetables. The **leek pastie,** usually made in the shape of a little leek, is a popular appetizer or side dish.

The potato became a dietary staple of Wales in the 18th century. **Anglesey** eggs feature potatoes and leeks as well as cheese. **Punchnep** is a combination of potatoes and turnips served with heavy cream. **Teisen nionod,** or onion cake, is a tasty, slow-baked potato-and-onion dish.

Most people are familiar with **Welsh rarebit** (or rabbit, if you prefer), but another cheese dish you should try that is not found elsewhere is **Glamorgan sausage,** a meatless concoction of onion, cheese, breadcrumbs, and seasonings, shaped like sausages, dipped in breadcrumbs, and fried. Another good dish, **skirettes,** is sort of mashed-potato pancake with a difference. The difference is supplied by grated walnuts, prawns, hard-boiled eggs, onion, cheddar cheese, and spices. It's all given a breadcrumb coating and baked or deep-fried.

Faggots used to be made of meat fragments left over after pig slaughter, wrapped in membrane that covers the pig's abdominal organs, and shaped like sausages. Today it's all a little more palatable sounding, being made of liver, bacon, onions, breadcrumbs, and sage, cooked and served cold.

Rabbit, chicken, turkey, duckling, game, even pheasant appear on the menus, and a rabbit casserole is offered in some restaurants as a Taste of Wales, so popular is the meat. Special dishes include a **poacher's pie** (containing beef, rabbit, chicken, and game) and **Welsh salt duck,** which rivals any offered on Asian menus. Predominant on the list of what to eat while in Wales are freshwater fish and seafood. **Trout and salmon** prevail among the products of rivers and lakes, tumbling practically from the fisherman's creel to your plate, with a little detour through the kitchen. Perhaps you'll get to taste a rare salmon, **gwyniad,** which is found only in Bala Lake. Baked trout with bacon is a favorite.

From the ocean and coastal waters come crabs, lobsters, sewin (sea trout), crayfish, mackerel, herring, Pollack, bass, hake, ling, whiting, and flat fish, as well as cockles, limpets, scallops, and mussels. The Romans were great cockle eaters, as revealed by huge mounds of the shells found in excavating the sites occupied by the long-ago conquerors. You may enjoy the **cockle-and-bacon pie** offered on some menus, or Gower scallops and bacon. Mussel stew and mussel and queenie (scallop) cawl, which is like a bouillabaisse, are popular dishes.

The Welsh word for bread is *bara*. At least once, you should try **laverbread (bara lawr),** which has probably been part of the Welsh diet since prehistoric times. It's made of laver weed, a parchmentlike seaweed, which is boiled and mixed with oatmeal, shaped into laverbread cakes, and fried like pancakes. It's full of vitamins and minerals. You'll find it on all Taste of Wales menus, so take a nibble at least. **Bara ceirch,** a flat oatcake, is rolled very thin and cooked on a griddle. A rich, currant bread, **bara brith,** is found all over the country, although the ingredients may vary. It's baked in a loaf, and some cooks use raisins and candied citrus peel along with the currants.

Perhaps you'll get a chance to sample **Welsh cakes** made with currants. You may want to buy some at Dylan Thomas's boathouse at Laugharne and munch them with your tea as you look across the wide estuary where the poet had much the same view as his Iron Age predecessors. **Oat biscuits** are another treat, much like the oatmeal cookies you may have had back home. Desserts (*puddings* they're called here, whatever their form) seem to be mainly **fruit crumbles**—blackberry, apple, what have you—topped with custard and/or thick cream.

AFTERNOON TEA   Many Brits still enjoy afternoon tea, which may consist of a simple cup of tea or a formal tea that starts with tiny crustless sandwiches filled with cucumber or watercress and proceeds through scones, crumpets with jam or clotted cream, followed by cakes and tarts—all accompanied by a proper pot of tea. The tea at Brown's, in London, is quintessentially English, whereas the Ritz's tea is an elaborate affair, complete with orchestra and dancing.

In the country, tea shops abound, and in Devon, Cornwall, and the West Country you'll find the best cream teas; they consist of scones spread with jam and thick, clotted Devonshire cream. It's a delicious treat, indeed. People in Britain drink an average of four cups of tea a day, though many younger people prefer coffee.

WHAT TO WASH IT ALL DOWN WITH   English pubs serve a variety of cocktails, but their stock-in-trade is beer: brown beer, or bitter; blond beer, or lager; and very dark beer, or stout. The standard English draft beer is much stronger than American beer and is served "with the chill off," because it doesn't taste good cold. Lager is always chilled, whereas stout can be served either way. Beer is always served straight from the tap, in two sizes: half pint (8 oz.) and pint (16 oz.).

One of the most significant changes in English drinking habits has been the popularity of wine bars, and you will find many to try, including some that turn into discos late at night. Britain isn't known for its wine, though it does produce some medium-sweet fruity whites. Its cider, though, is famous—and mighty potent in contrast to the American variety.

Whisky (spelled without the *e*) refers to scotch. Canadian and Irish whiskey (spelled with the *e*) are also available, but only the very best stocked bars have American bourbon and rye.

While you're in England, you may want to try the very English drink called **Pimm's,** a mixture developed by James Pimm, owner of a popular London oyster house in the 1840s. Though it can be consumed on the rocks, it's usually served as a Pimm's Cup—a drink that will have any number and variety of ingredients, depending on which part of the world (or empire) you're in. Here, just for fun, is a typical recipe: Take a very tall glass and fill it with ice. Add a thin slice of lemon (or orange), a cucumber spike (or a curl of cucumber rind), and 2 ounces of Pimm's liquor. Then finish with a splash of either lemon or club soda, 7-Up, or Tom Collins mix.

The English tend to drink everything at a warmer temperature than Americans are used to. So if you like ice in your soda, be sure to ask for lots of it, or you're likely to end up with a measly, quickly melting cube or two.

Index

Great Trips Like Great Days Begin with a Plan

FranklinCovey and Frommer's Bring You *Frommer's Favorite Places*® Planner

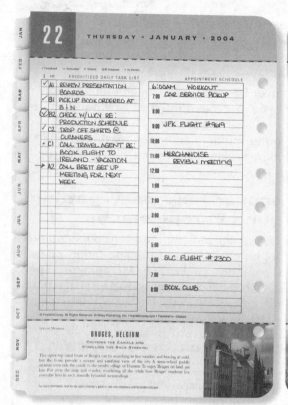

Classic Size Planning Pages $39.9

The planning experts at FranklinCovey have teamed up with the travel experts at Frommer's. The result is a full-year travel-themed planner filled with rich images and travel tips covering fifty-two of Frommer's Favorite Places.

- Each week will make you an expert about an intriguing corner of the world
- New facts and tips every day
- Beautiful, full-color photos of some of the most beautiful places on earth
- Proven planning tools from FranklinCovey for keeping track of tasks, appointments, notes, address/phone numbers, and more

Save 15%

when you purchase Frommer's Favori Places travel-themed planner and a binder.

Order today before you next big trip.

www.franklincovey.com/frommers
Enter promo code 12252 at checkout for discount. Offer expires June 1, 2005.

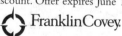

Frommer's is a trademark of Arthur Frommer.

Travel Tip: He who finds the best hotel deal has more to spend on facials involving knobbly vegetables.

Hello, the Roaming Gnome here. I've been nabbed from the garden and taken round the world. The people who took me are so terribly clever. They find the best offerings on Travelocity. For very little cha-ching. And that means I get to be pampered and exfoliated till I'm pink as a bunny's doodah.

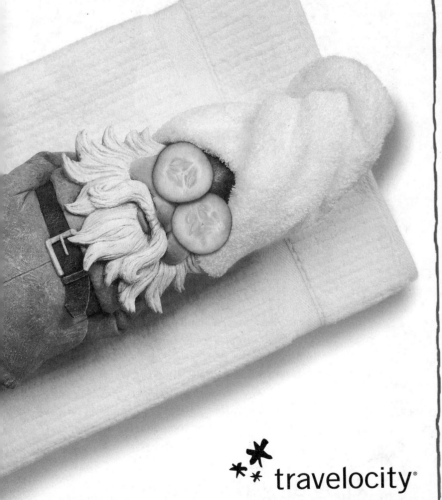

travelocity®

1-888-TRAVELOCITY / travelocity.com / America Online Keyword: Travel

Travel Tip: Make sure there's customer service for any change of plans — involving friendly natives, for example.

One can plan and plan, but if you don't book with the right people you can't seize le moment and canoodle with the poodle named Pansy. I, for one, am all for fraternizing with the locals. Better yet, if I need to extend my stay and my gnome nappers are willing, it can all be arranged through the 800 number at, oh look, how convenient, the lovely company coat of arms.

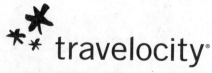